BUSINESS REORGANIZATIONS
Third Edition

BUSINESS REORGANIZATIONS

Third Edition

Michael A. Gerber
Professor of Law
Brooklyn Law School

George W. Kuney
Lindsay Young Distinguished Professor of Law and
Director of the Clayton Center for Entrepreneurial Law
The University of Tennessee College of Law

ISBN: 978-1-4224-7729-8
Looseleaf ISBN: 978-1-4224-8165-3
eBook ISBN: 978-1-5791-1670-5

Library of Congress Cataloging-in-Publication Data

Gerber, Michael A., author.
Business reorganizations / Michael A. Gerber, Professor of Law, Brooklyn Law School; George W. Kuney, Lindsay Young Distinguished Professor of Law, The University of Tennessee College of Law. -- Third edition.
pages cm.
Includes index.
ISBN 978-1-4224-7729-8
1. Corporate reorganizations--United States. 2. Bankruptcy--United States. 3. United States. Bankruptcy. Chapter 11, Reorganization. I. Kuney, George W., author. II. Title.
KF1544.G369 2013
346.73'06626--dc23

2013035289

NOTE TO USERS
To ensure that you are using the latest materials available in this area, please be sure to periodically check the LexisNexis Law School web site for downloadable updates and supplements at www.lexisnexis.com/lawschool.

Editorial Offices
121 Chanlon Rd., New Providence, NJ 07974 (908) 464-6800
201 Mission St., San Francisco, CA 94105-1831 (415) 908-3200
www.lexisnexis.com

MATTHEW◆BENDER

About the Authors

Michael Gerber is a Professor Law, former Interim Dean, and Director of the Business Boot Camp program at Brooklyn Law School. For many years he also served as the Associate Dean for Development. He writes and lectures on corporate governance in bankruptcy, bankruptcy ethics, the treatment of intellectual property interests in bankruptcy, dot-com bankruptcies, international and comparative insolvency law, and other business bankruptcy and reorganization topics. He is a contributing author of Collier on Bankruptcy, the leading treatise on bankruptcy law. At Brooklyn Law School, he helps lead the annual Barry Zaretsky Roundtable, which focuses on cutting-edge bankruptcy issues, and he is the director of the law school's foreign summer study programs in Beijing and Bologna. He is a member of the School's Dennis J. Block Center for the Study of International Business Law and the School's Center for the Study of Business Law and Regulation. Prior to joining the faculty, Professor Gerber practiced law at Proskauer Rose. He has twice served on the Merit Selection Panel for a Bankruptcy Judge in the Eastern District of New York and on the Committee on Bankruptcy and Corporate Reorganization of the New York City Bar. He is a member of the Federal Bar Council, the New York City Bar Association, and the American Bar Association.

George W. Kuney is the Lindsay Young Distinguished Professor of Law and Director of the Clayton Center for Entrepreneurial Law at The University of Tennessee College of Law in Knoxville, Tennessee. He holds a J.D. from the University of California, Hastings College of the Law, an M.B.A. from The University of San Diego, and a B.A. in economics from the University of California, Santa Cruz. Before joining the UT faculty in 2000, he was a partner in the Allen Matkins firm's San Diego office. Previously, he practiced with the Howard Rice and Morrison & Foerster firms in his hometown of San Francisco, doing litigation and transactional work largely in the context of business restructuring and insolvency. He teaches business law courses, including: Business Associations, Contracts, Contract Drafting, Commercial Law, Consumer Bankruptcy, Debtor-Creditor, Mergers and Acquisitions, Representing Enterprises, and Workouts and Reorganizations. Kuney writes books and articles about business, contracts, commercial law, and insolvency-related topics; advises clients nationwide regarding bankruptcy, restructuring, reorganization, and related subjects; and conducts training seminars for law firm associates and summer associates regarding business law and transactional drafting.

Acknowledgements

The authors thank Wendy G. Patrick, University of Tennessee College of Law Class of 2013, for her extensive and detail-oriented assistance with the preparation of this book.

TABLE OF CONTENTS

TABLE OF CONTENTS

TABLE OF CONTENTS

TABLE OF CONTENTS

TABLE OF CONTENTS

TABLE OF CONTENTS

TABLE OF CONTENTS

TABLE OF CONTENTS

TABLE OF CONTENTS

TABLE OF CONTENTS

TABLE OF CONTENTS

TABLE OF CONTENTS

TABLE OF CONTENTS

Chapter 1

INTRODUCTION: AN OVERVIEW OF CHAPTER 11

§ 1.01 MEET YOUR CLIENT: THE GREAT AMPHYDYNAMICS BUSINESS DISASTER

The following article appeared in yesterday's edition of *Mismanagement Week*. Please read it.

Amphydynamics Skips Debt Payment

Does Chapter 11 Loom For Star-Crossed Parent & Progeny?

Deteriorating Economy, High Labor & Interest Costs, Liquidity Drought Blamed for Severe Cash Flow Problems

Unions Disagree: Cite Bad Management

(New York —) The New York City-based Amphydynamics Corporation, long a shining star of the American electronics industry, looked more like a black hole last Monday, when its chairman, Headley Charisma, announced that the company would miss an interest payment to BigBank when it comes due next week. The company and its subsidiaries lost millions last year and continue to report operating losses. Analysts have suggested that the company is on the verge of seeking relief under Chapter 11 of the Bankruptcy Code.

Amphydynamics Corporation is the hub of the Amphydynamics empire. It assembles and manufactures business and consumer electronic equipment such as computers, calculators, toys, and home entertainment products. It employs more than 500 workers at its factories in St. Louis and San Diego. Once a model of profitability, Amphydynamics Corporation is publicly held, but still dominated by CEO Headley Charisma and Vice President and General Counsel Carol Charisma, the children of the company's founder.

Subsidiaries Hurt Too

Amphydynamics Corporation owns Kid-Vid, Inc. which manufactures a popular line of video game consoles that communicate wirelessly with the Internet and HDTVs. It also operates Comp-U-All, a nationwide chain of retail outlets that sells its own and other name-brand computer products. If the somber mood of the employees at the Newport Beach branch of Comp-U-All is any indication, there are unspoken fears that some, if not all of these stores, which last year produced an unimpressive pre-tax margin of 2% on sales, may close soon.

"I expect they will have to close at least half their stores," said Harriet Mehlman, a retail consultant. "Some are in bad locations, some haven't been updated in years, some will never make money," she added.

Many Strikes, Few Hits, Some Serious Errors

Analysts familiar with the company attribute its current difficulties to several problems.

A long strike by factory workers last year disrupted deliveries, resulting in delayed collection of accounts receivable, and cancellation of orders. The strike ended when management and the unions signed on to a five-year collective bargaining agreement with terms that analysts think may have been too generous and that the company now finds onerous.

The problems of the electronics divisions also have been blamed on unexpectedly slow sales as consumers feel the pinch of a recession that is likely to be longer and deeper than experts originally predicted. The company is also being squeezed by stiff foreign and domestic competition in the personal computer and gaming console markets. Ironically, the failure of weaker competitors has been draining business away from Amphydynamics, as these companies conduct their own going out of business sales.

Lack of liquidity in the credit markets is also taking its toll. Like many manufacturers, Amphydynamics borrows money early in the year to produce goods to be sold later in retail stores. Two weak holiday seasons have left the company heavy on inventory and short on cash.

Charisma Optimistic, Creditors Balk

Yesterday, speaking from a prepared text, Headley Charisma expressed optimism that the company will be able to reverse its recent trend of losses by taking several significant steps:

- The company plans to shut down unprofitable retail outlets and auction valuable leaseholds.

- The company reportedly can achieve substantial savings by shuttering its St. Louis manufacturing plant and consolidating all manufacturing operations in San Diego.

- The company is hoping to gain a strong foothold in domestic and international markets with a new generation smartphone that provides enhanced data security, doesn't drop calls, and has a keyboard that is big enough for even the largest thumbs.

"We are fundamentally a very strong, very sound company," Charisma said. "Our earnings from operations are positive, before giving effect to debt service. If we can cut expenses, bring our new products to market, and work things out with our creditors, we will emerge from this process stronger than ever."

The challenge management faces is that a number of creditors may not be willing to ride out the storm. Amphydynamics is heavily indebted to several banks. For weeks, Amphydynamics officials have sought to negotiate a waiver of defaults and a deferral of payments, but those talks are reported to be deadlocked. "We were hoping for time and enough cash to get us through the first quarter of the New Year, but the banks are playing hard ball," Carol Charisma said. "We're running out of cash."

"We're out of patience with the Charismas," said Joshua Colman, head of the workout unit of BigBank, agent for the syndicate. "Our thinking is that now is the time to bring in a crisis manager who will either turn the company around or sell it or shut it down."

Headley Charisma, however, has stated repeatedly that the company is not for sale. "My family has been in this business for more than two decades. We're not going to walk away from it now. We are not going to abandon our employees, who have helped us get to where we are today, nor will we desert our loyal customers and suppliers. We're in it to win it."

But trade creditors are also becoming balky. In recent weeks, the company failed to make payments to many of its major suppliers. This has led many to demand cash before delivery and others to halt shipments altogether. "It's no secret anymore that they're cash tight," the vendor said. "The banks could set-off at any moment. No one wants to get caught. Can you blame us?"

Meanwhile, so-called vulture investors have begun to demonstrate an appetite for the company. Insurance companies and others that hold significant positions in Amphydynamics bonds reportedly have been approached by at least one private equity fund that has offered to purchase the distressed debt securities for 25 cents on the dollar.

"The vultures should stop circling, and bondholders that sell their bonds are short-sighted," Headley Charisma scoffed. "We're not dead yet."

§ 1.02   COUNSELING YOUR CLIENT: ALTERNATIVES FOR FINANCIALLY BELEAGUERED DEBTORS

[A]   Liquidation

Headley and Carol Charisma have just arrived at your law office. Headley hands you a copy of the *Mismanagement Week* article and asks you to read it. You do. Carol asks, "What would you advise?"

"Well," you begin, "truth is an absolute defense to libel. Are these things true?"

"We're not here to talk about libel," Headley sighs. "We're here to talk about Chapter 11. The article says we're thinking about filing. Should we?"

"Well," you begin, "we need to explore the options carefully. No matter what you read in the papers, Chapter 11 is not the only, nor necessarily the best, resort for financially plagued debtors."

"You mean we could file straight bankruptcy," Carol jumps in. You remember that she went to law school and practiced briefly before going to work in the family business.

"Correct," you say. "For reasons that I am sure you readily can imagine [and that are explored more fully in § 1.08 of this chapter] some businesses cannot be rehabilitated and should be liquidated. In a Chapter 7 liquidation case, a trustee marshals the assets of the debtor, sells them, and distributes the proceeds among the debtor's creditors. In furtherance of the Bankruptcy Code's 'fresh start' policy, a worthy individual debtor is discharged of liability on most prepetition debts. Corporations and partnerships also may liquidate in Chapter 7, but, unlike individual debtors, corporations and partnerships do not receive a discharge. They don't need a fresh start, because, after their business is wound up and their assets are liquidated, they cease to exist."

"But we don't want to *liquidate* the business," Headley says. "We want to save it. All we need is some time. I know that if we can bring our new smartphone to market in time for the holidays, and if we trim some operations and get some help from the unions, we can make it. Dad would have wanted us to try."

"I understand," you say. "But Chapter 11 isn't the only way to save a business, and it may not be the best way to save this business. Have you thought about a workout?"

Headley rolls his eyes in Carol's direction. "I'm trying to save my business and he wants me to go the gym?"

[B]   Out-of-Court Restructurings

"No, Headley," Carol explains, "Sometimes it's possible for a financially troubled business to obtain the relief it needs by negotiating a private, out-of-court debt restructuring agreement with its creditors. When creditors agree to be paid less than the full amount of their claims, the agreement is known as a 'composition.' When creditors agree to be paid in full, but over a longer period of time, the agreement is known as an 'extension.' Sometimes these agreements involve both composition and extension, but, in any case, today these contractual restructurings are more commonly known as 'workouts.' "

One of the advantages of a workout is that it's accomplished outside of court. "The company negotiates an agreement or series of agreements with creditors that adjust the company's obligations. For a workout to work, you are going to have to reach an agreement with the company's lenders, its suppliers, and other creditors. Also, if creditors are going to exchange part of their claims for stock, you will have to reach an agreement with stockholders as well, because their position will be diluted.

The agreement would provide how much each creditor will be paid, whether payments will be in a lump sum or in installments, and what happens in the event of a default. For example, will the original terms be reinstated or is only the modified amount due? The workout agreement would also provide that the creditors agree to 'stand still,' and not undertake individual collection efforts, so long as the debtor is performing in accordance with the terms of the agreement. Of course, whether or not you can get creditors to sign on to a workout agreement will depend on a number of factors. One is your credibility. Do they have any faith in you as managers and in your business plan and cash flow projections? They will want assurances that the company is paying withholding and other taxes and maintaining insurance. They will want to know what kind of cash and credit the company needs to operate and where the company will get it. They will want to know about your employee and labor relations situations. They may want you to maintain a certain ratio of assets to liabilities. The bottom line is that they will want to have some comfort that they will fare better in a workout than if they act immediately to enforce their claims or force a liquidation."

"But," Carol says, "if we can achieve a consensual, out-of-court restructuring, we avoid the stigma and cost of bankruptcy. We avoid having to deal with bankruptcy lawyers and committees of creditors. We don't have to deal with a judge. We don't have to blab about our business strategy and plans to the whole wide world. We don't have to deal with customers that are afraid to buy our products or with suppliers that are afraid to ship just because we're in bankruptcy and think we won't be around to honor our warranties or pay our bills. Do you think we can get the creditors to go along, Headley?"

"I'm sure I can work something out with most of my suppliers, if the alternative is for the company to go out of business and for them to lose a valued customer. As for BigBank, we've had a relationship for years, and I get along very well with Andy Nicoll, our loan officer," Headley says.

"Well, most banks and institutional lenders have a special department, sometimes known as a 'workout group,' to deal with problem loans. Chances are you won't be dealing with Mr. Nicoll, but with a new banker who may be more interested in recovering what the company owes the bank than in maintaining a long-term banking relationship with Amphydynamics. Or, you might find yourself dealing with a third party, a so-called, vulture investor, who has purchased the claim from your original creditor."

"Hmm, that would explain why Andy hasn't been returning my calls," Headley sighs. "And while we're on the subject, I should tell you that although we have a pretty good relationship with most of our suppliers, there are a few that have it in for us. They'd just as soon see the company go out of business as survive. Then there are those folks who are suing us — the whackos who claim that playing our video games caused them to develop — what do they call it — 'Hystereo.' "

"Hystereo?"

This time it's Carol's turn to roll her eyes. "It's a newly identified condition — characterized by a sensitivity to noise, blurred vision, and an inability to cope with three dimensions. Some people call it a 'virtual illness.' "

"It sounds like a products liability lawyer's fantasy."

"And a manufacturer's nightmare. I can tell you that no matter what kind of truce we reach with our other creditors, the chances of getting these plaintiffs and their lawyers to stand still are nil."

"That," you explain, "is one of the problems with out-of-court workouts. They have their advantages, but they're not always workable. If you can get all your creditors to agree to stand still, fine, but collection efforts by even one recalcitrant creditor can interfere with a debtor's ability to do business, if the problem claim is large enough. You say that some of your creditors 'have it in for you.' That's also important for another reason. In my experience, the willingness of creditors to submit to a stand-still agreement and work things out sometimes — not always — depends on the willingness of management to step down. Finally, you need to bear in mind that out-of-court arrangements provide only limited relief. A workout isn't going to be much help to a debtor who has no free assets and needs a large cash infusion to keep operating. A workout may not alleviate suppliers' fears about shipping on a credit basis. It won't help a debtor that needs relief from burdensome leases and contracts. Frequently, a business in trouble falls into all these categories. If so, it is a likely candidate for relief under Chapter 11 of the Bankruptcy Code, provided that it has a viable business that is worth saving."

§ 1.03   BUSINESS REORGANIZATIONS: THE CONTOURS OF CHAPTER 11 AND ITS PURPOSE AND PLACE IN THE BANKRUPTCY CODE

[A]   The Theory of Chapter 11

"Somehow I had a feeling this little *kabuki* dance would lead us back to Chapter 11. What's the magic of Chapter 11?"

"A good question. Chapter 11 provides for what is, in essence, a judicially-supervised composition and extension of a debtor's debt burden. But Chapter 11 provides more than judicial supervision. The magic, as you put it, of Chapter 11 is that, at least in theory, it facilitates the revitalization of a failing business by allowing it to accomplish things that might be much more difficult or virtually impossible to achieve outside of Chapter 11. For example:

- Chapter 11 enables a debtor to do business free of harassment by creditors.

- Chapter 11 enables a debtor to continue to do business while it trims fat, shuts down unprofitable operations, rejects or renegotiates burdensome contracts, including leases and collective bargaining agreements, and develops a viable business plan.

- Chapter 11 enables a debtor to borrow new funds, and, in some cases, even subordinate pre-existing mortgages and security interests.

- Chapter 11 enables a debtor to develop a debt restructuring plan that may bind even creditors who do not accept it."

Headley shakes his head. "Look, I don't want you to think I fail to understand my self-interest, but I can't help but wonder why my company, or any company, should be entitled to the benefits of Chapter 11. Why shouldn't a company that can't make it just be shut down or, if it has some value, be auctioned off?"

"Chapter 11 is indeed, controversial,[1] but the theory behind Chapter 11 is that society as a whole benefits, and the risk of loss to all parties is reduced, when a

---

[1] The debate over the utility of Chapter 11 is discussed in more detail in chapter 9.

salvageable business is rescued rather than liquidated and sold piecemeal. Therefore, assets of a going business should not be disposed of until a prognosis as to salvageability is made. As the drafters of Chapter 11 put it:

> The purpose of a reorganization case, unlike a liquidation case, is to restructure a business's finances so that it may continue to operate, provide its employees with jobs, pay its creditors, and produce a return for its stockholders. The premise of a business reorganization is that assets that are used for production in the industry for which they were designed are more valuable than those same assets sold for scrap. Often, the return on assets that a business can produce is inadequate to compensate those who have invested in the business. Cash flow problems may develop and require creditors of the business, both trade creditors and long-term lenders, to wait for payment of their claims. If the business can extend or reduce its debts, it often can be returned to a viable state. It is more economically efficient to reorganize than to liquidate, because it preserves jobs and assets.[2]

"The drafters were also guided by two other beliefs that are fundamental to the structure and content of Chapter 11. The first is the belief that the prospects for rehabilitating an ailing business are greatly improved if the debtor seeks treatment in Chapter 11 when the business is still viable. The second is the belief that the most expeditious, fairest, and most economical route to reorganizing and rehabilitating a debtor is through a process of negotiation and consensus. However, having said that, I have to add that many large Chapter 11 cases of recent vintage have involved sales of major assets and operations.

"Let me walk you through the Chapter 11 process from beginning to end so that you will see how this ethos plays out and get a sense of what, at least in theory, can — and cannot — be achieved through a Chapter 11 filing for a company such as Amphydynamics. Then we can make an informed choice about what route to pursue."

"I'm all ears," Headley says.

[B] Statutory Road Map

Business reorganization cases, like other kinds of bankruptcies, are governed primarily by the United States Bankruptcy Code, which is contained in Title 11 of the United States Code. The Bankruptcy Code was adopted as part of the Bankruptcy Reform Act of 1978, which became effective on October 1, 1979.[3] Cases commenced prior to that date were governed by The Bankruptcy Act of 1898 as amended from time to time over the course of its eighty year existence. When lawyers refer to the old law (an increasingly rare occurrence) they sometimes call it "the Bankruptcy Act," and sometimes just "the Act." We will use the terms "Bankruptcy Code" or "Code" when referring to the bankruptcy law currently in force, and we will use the terms "Former Bankruptcy Act" or "Act" when referring

---

[2] H.R. Rep. No. 95-595, 95th Cong., 1st Sess. 220 (1977).

[3] Pub. L. 95-598, 95th Cong., 2d Sess, 92 Stat. 2551, *et seq.* (1978).

to the now repealed 1898 Bankruptcy Act.

The 1978 legislation had two main parts. Title I contained the substantive law of Bankruptcy. Title II contained important amendments to the Judicial Code, including Title 28 of the United States Code, governing the structure, jurisdiction, and staffing of bankruptcy courts and other administrative matters. Title II also established the United States Trustee System, which began as an experimental pilot program, but was made permanent in 1986.[4] From time to time since 1978, most notably in 1984, 1986, 1994, and 2005, the Bankruptcy Code and these other related statutes have undergone amendment. In connection with the 1994 round of amendments, Congress took the additional step of creating a National Bankruptcy Review Commission. The Commission was directed to investigate and study issues and problems relating to the Bankruptcy Code and the bankruptcy system and to make recommendations for "improving and updating" the Code without disturbing the "fundamental tenets" of existing law.[5] On October 20, 1997, the Commission issued a report containing some 170 individual recommendations, a number of which would have affected Chapter 11 cases, but which for the most part were ignored.[6]

Instead, in 1998, both the Senate and the House of Representatives passed the Bankruptcy Abuse Prevention and Consumer Protection Act of 1998. However, the two houses passed different versions, and Congress became distracted by a White House scandal and adjourned before the differences could be resolved. Over the course of the next seven years, versions of this Bill were reintroduced but were derailed for one reason or another. Like Rasputin, however, the Bill would not die:

- In 2000, the House and Senate resolved their differences and adopted a conference report but President Clinton pocket vetoed the bill.

- In 2001, two different versions were again passed by the House and the Senate. After a considerable delay in forming a conference committee to resolve the differences in the two bills, a committee finally was named. Then the September 11th terrorist attacks and a recession intervened. The legislation was put on hold.

- In summer of 2002, a conference report was approved by the House-Senate conferees. On what to many appeared to be the eve of enactment, the conference report was abruptly pulled from the House calendar, mainly because of controversy surrounding a provision that would prevent anti-abortion protestors from using bankruptcy to avoid liability incurred as a result of protesting outside abortion clinics, but also because of labor opposition based on concern that the "clinic access" provisions might be applied to peaceful labor picketing.

Although, as students of Russian history know, Rasputin finally did die, the bankruptcy reform legislation did not. In 2005, legislation substantially similar to the 2002 Conference Report, minus the "abortion clinic" provision, was adopted by

---

[4] *See* discussion in § 1.05[C], below.

[5] H.R. Rep. No. 183-835, at 59.

[6] National Bankruptcy Review Commission, Bankruptcy: The Next Twenty Years (1997).

both houses. On April 20, 2005, President Bush signed the Bankruptcy Abuse Prevention and Consumer Protection Act of 2005 into law. A few of the amendments went into effect immediately, but most became effective with respect to bankruptcy cases commenced on and after October 17, 2005. Although the 2005 amendments are most well known for the changes they wrought in the law governing consumer bankruptcy cases, the amendments also produced some important changes in the law governing Chapter 11 business reorganization cases.

The Bankruptcy Code is organized in nine chapters. The seven original chapters (1, 3, 5, 7, 9, 11 and 13) are odd-numbered.[7] The drafters reserved the even numbers for future additions to the Code. One of those even numbers was put into use in 1986, when Chapter 12 was enacted. A new Chapter 15 was added in 2005.

Chapters 7, 9, 11, 12, 13 and 15 respectively provide the basic framework for the five species of bankruptcy cases. Chapter 7 governs liquidation or so-called "straight bankruptcy" cases. Chapter 9 governs the restructuring of debts by municipalities. Chapter 12, which was added to the Code in 1986, permits family farmers to restructure their debts and retain ownership of their farms. Chapter 13, entitled "Adjustment of Debts of an Individual with Regular Income," allows individual wage earners to avoid liquidation and hold on to their property while they make payments to creditors out of their future income. Chapter 15, entitled "Ancillary and Cross-Border Cases," is based on the Model Law on Bankruptcy adopted by the United Nations Commission on International Trade Law. It provides guidelines for access to U.S. courts by representatives of foreign debtors, recognition of foreign proceedings and foreign relief, and encourages cooperation and direct communication among domestic and foreign courts.

Chapter 11, which is entitled "Business Reorganizations," contains much of the procedural and substantive framework for business rescue cases, but it is not free standing. Although the central focus of a business reorganizations case is Chapter 11 itself, many provisions of other chapters of the Code are applicable in Chapter 11 cases. Chapter 1 of the Code contains "general provisions," such as definitions, rules of construction, and statutes of limitations. These are applicable in all bankruptcy cases, including Chapter 11 cases. Chapter 3 of the Code relates to case administration. Its provisions govern such matters as commencement of cases, meetings of creditors, the automatic stay, sale and use of property, and the treatment of unperformed contracts. These are also generally applicable in all types of bankruptcy cases, including Chapter 11 cases. Chapter 5 of the Code governs property of the estate, the trustee's avoiding powers, and the proof, allowance, and priority of claims. Its provisions are also generally applicable in Chapter 11. Even certain sections of Chapter 7, the liquidation chapter, are incorporated by reference into Chapter 11. *See, e.g.*, Code § 1106.

Procedure in bankruptcy cases is governed by the Federal Rules of Bankruptcy Procedure. These rules were drafted (and have been revised from time to time) by

---

[7] There also was a temporary Chapter 15 that contained the provisions governing the powers and duties of U.S. Trustees in Chapter 11 cases when the U.S. Trustee system was in its test phase. Chapter 15 was deleted when the pilot U.S. Trustee system was adopted nationwide and its provisions were integrated into other sections of the Code. In 2005, current Chapter 15, which governs cross-border bankruptcy cases, was added to the Code.

an Advisory Committee of judges, scholars, and practitioners. The rules are promulgated by the Supreme Court pursuant to the authority of 28 U.S.C. § 2075. In many judicial districts, local bankruptcy rules also apply.

Finally, Title 18 of the U.S. Code provides in §§ 151–157 and in §§ 1519–1520 that certain acts committed in connection with a bankruptcy case are crimes. These bad acts include concealing estate property, presenting false claims, and destruction of documents.

§ 1.04   COMMENCEMENT OF A CHAPTER 11 CASE: PRE-FILING CONSIDERATIONS

[A]   Form and Content of the Petition

Headley is growing impatient. "All this is very interesting, but how exactly do we get into Chapter 11?"

You explain that a Chapter 11 case is commenced by the filing of a petition by or against a debtor.[8]

"*Against a* debtor? You mean a debtor can be put into Chapter 11 involuntarily, as well as voluntarily?" Carol asks.

Carol is correct. Code § 303(a) authorizes the commencement of an involuntary Chapter 11 case. However, involuntary Chapter 11 cases are even less common than involuntary Chapter 7 cases. One may wonder why, if creditors were going to bother with bankruptcy at all, they would ever be inclined to force a debtor into Chapter 11 rather than 7. One possibility is that creditors believe that it suits their interests to keep a debtor operating, albeit under supervision. This might be the case when the debtor is an important customer or supplier or when the debtor is perceived to be worth more as a going concern than if its component parts were broken up and sold piecemeal. Another reason that creditors may resort to an involuntary Chapter 11 filing is to invoke the trustee's avoiding powers without forcing the debtor into liquidation. For example, creditors who believe that a debtor's property is being fraudulently or preferentially transferred may force the debtor into Chapter 11 in order to undo such transfers and prevent future ones. The filing against Baldwin-United Corporation is a case in point. Baldwin-United was unable to pay certain creditors' claims as they came due, and in order to induce those creditors to forebear, it gave them security interests in some valuable and previously unencumbered assets. Other creditors, who did not want to see those free assets become encumbered, filed an involuntary Chapter 11 petition against Baldwin in order to have the transfers of the security interests avoided as preferences. The petition was filed just as the 90-day preference window was about to close.[9]

---

[8] Code §§ 301, 303.

[9] The genesis of the filing is recounted in *In re Baldwin-United Corp*, 79 B.R. 321, 324-27 (Bankr. S.D. Ohio 1987).

You then direct their attention to Official Forms Nos. 1–7, which appear following the Rules of Bankruptcy Procedure. "The petition itself is pretty simple and straightforward. It requires that you provide certain identifying information — the debtor's name and address, whether the debtor is an individual or corporation or some other kind of entity, what chapter the debtor is filing in, and a declaration that the filing is authorized. In addition, the petition must contain an estimate of the debtor's assets and liabilities, as well as an estimate of the number of creditors, employees, and equity security holders. When the debtor is a corporation, as is Amphy, its board of directors must authorize the filing of the petition."[10]

Next, you walk Headley and Carol through certain other documents that, pursuant to Bankruptcy Code § 521 and Federal Rule of Bankruptcy Procedure 1007, are to be filed simultaneously with, or soon after, the filing of the petition. They include:

- A list of the debtor's creditors and equity security holders. This list will enable the clerk of the court to send notices to these parties.

- A list of the debtor's 20 largest unsecured creditors. The purpose of this list is to aid the United States Trustee in organizing a creditors' committee.

- A schedule of assets and liabilities.

- A schedule of current income and expenditures.

- A statement of financial affairs.

- A schedule of executory contracts and unexpired leases.

In addition, some judicial districts have adopted local rules imposing their own additional filing requirements. For example, the Southern District of New York requires, among other things, that a petition be accompanied by: a brief description of the history of the debtor's business and the factors precipitating the Chapter 11 filing; a statement of the location of the debtor's substantial assets, books and records; a statement of weekly payroll; and a statement of amounts to be paid to officers, directors, and consultants of the debtor.[11]

Carol studies the petition and schedules and looks up, slightly perplexed. "I notice that the petition doesn't say that the company is insolvent."

"That's right. Remember, I said that the Code's drafters wanted to encourage debtors to file early, when there is still a viable business left to reorganize. By eliminating the requirement that a debtor be insolvent, they sought to do just that."[12]

---

[10] In *Price v. Gurney*, 324 U.S. 100 (1945), the Court found that authority to file on behalf of a corporation is vested in "those who have the power of management" pursuant to state law and the certificate of incorporation — typically the board of directors. The Court rejected the argument that the filing of a petition by a stockholder on the corporation's behalf was in the nature of a derivative action. 314 U.S. at 105–07.

[11] S.D.N.Y. Local Bankruptcy Rules 1007-1, 1007-2, which supplement Fed. R. Bankr. P. 1007.

[12] Under the former Bankruptcy Act, a debtor had to be insolvent in the balance sheet or cash flow

Nevertheless, the overwhelming majority of debtors entering Chapter 11 are either insolvent in the "balance sheet sense" — their liabilities exceed their assets — or insolvent in the "cash flow" or "equitable sense" — unable to pay their debts as they come due.[13]

[B]   Where to File: Venue of Chapter 11 Cases

Amphydynamics is a Delaware corporation, with corporate offices located in New York City. Kid Vid is a New Jersey corporation also headquartered in New York. Comp-U-All is incorporated in New York but has stores located all over the country. Where these companies should file is an issue that has to be resolved at the outset. The rules governing venue of Chapter 11 cases are contained in 28 U.S.C. §§ 1408–1410. Generally, bankruptcy cases are to be commenced in the district in which the debtor had its domicile, residence, principal place of business, or principal assets for the 180 days immediately preceding the filing date. Code § 1408(1). Alternatively, a debtor may file in a district in which a bankruptcy case involving its affiliate, general partner, or partnership is pending. 28 U.S.C. § 1408(2). For a large corporation such as Amphydynamics, which is incorporated in one state and headquartered in another, and which has assets and affiliates located all over the country, these rules provide a number of venue options that can be exercised strategically.

Should a debtor file in the district in which most of its creditors are headquartered, or in a locale that will make it more costly and difficult for creditors to monitor the case? Should a debtor file in the district in which its bankruptcy attorneys are most well known? Should a debtor seek a district whose judges have a reputation (deserved or not) for being sympathetic to debtors? If the case is going to involve difficult issues of downsizing, plant closings, and layoffs, should a debtor try to minimize bad publicity and political pressure by filing in a district in which it has no factories and few employees?

To appreciate how these venue rules can be strategically invoked, consider the case of Eastern Airlines. Eastern was headquartered in Miami and most of its operations were concentrated there, but Eastern's management wanted to file in the Southern District of New York. Eastern had a small, New York-based subsidiary, Ionosphere Clubs, Inc., that operated frequent flyer lounges at airports. Ionosphere was only a tiny part of the Eastern empire, and it also happened to be solvent; but it proved to be Eastern's ticket to New York. Ionosphere filed a Chapter 11 petition in New York, and a few minutes later so did Eastern, flying in on its subsidiary's coattails. More recently, Enron Corporation, incorporated in Oregon and headquartered in Houston, did the same thing. After a small affiliate filed in the Southern District of New York, Enron did too. Professor Lynn LoPucki believes that these flexible affiliate venue rules, which permit a debtor to file outside its "natural habitat," have had a the effect of forcing bankruptcy judges to compete for big cases by adopting policies and procedures

---

sense in order to be eligible to file a voluntary petition. *See, e.g.*, § 130 of former Chapter X and § 323 of former Chapter XI. The problem with that requirement was that for many debtors it meant that filing came too late — when the situation was hopeless.

[13] See the cases and discussion in § 1.08.

that debtors, their attorneys, and postpetition lenders find attractive, but which may subvert the bankruptcy process. According to Professor LoPucki, the competition for cases has led judges to be overly generous with professional fees and executive compensation, overly tolerant of conflicts of interest, and overly reluctant to replace corrupt managers, even in extreme cases. He also believes that competition for cases has led courts to be inordinately liberal in authorizing sales of major assets and allowing debtors to selectively pay prepetition claims while the case is pending.[14] Not everyone agrees.[15] Each of these topics is considered in subsequent sections of the text.

[C] When to File; What to Pack

"We've talked about whether and where to file, but what about *when* to file?" Carol asks. "Isn't timing important, too?"

You mentioned earlier that a debtor need not and should not wait until its situation is hopeless to file. Now you explain that there are also other timing considerations to weigh. Of course, not every debtor has the luxury of choosing when to file a Chapter 11 petition. Sometimes, events that a debtor cannot control — such as an imminent foreclosure sale or a sudden interruption in cash flow — make immediate filing a necessity. In other cases, though, debtors can try to time filing to minimize disruption and maximize their prospects for survival. For example, conventional wisdom is that a debtor should try to file at a point in its business cycle when it has enough cash on hand to pay salaries and meet other operating expenses, at least for a while.

"Bankruptcy experts are fond of saying that 'in Chapter 11, cash is king.' When you're getting ready to go into Chapter 11, you should try to pack as much money as you can. A major practical concern for a Chapter 11 debtor, especially in the early days of a case, is the source of funding for its ongoing operations. A debtor that can't meet operating expenses during the pendency of the case is not a good candidate for rehabilitation. What is the source of this funding? There are a few possibilities. If a debtor is fortunate, it will file at a time when it has a substantial amount of cash or cash equivalents on hand. Since, thanks to the automatic stay, prepetition creditors are held at bay, this 'cash on hand' doesn't have to be used to pay them. It can be used to meet current expenses. Similarly, if ongoing operations are generating cash, that, too, can be used to fund operations."

"Let me make sure I understand this," Headley says. "After the petition is filed, I stop paying creditors?"

"You stop paying holders of *prepetition* claims. Think of it this way: at the moment of filing, the company, in a sense, writes itself a new 'interim' balance sheet

---

[14] *See* Statement of Professor Lynn M. LoPucki before the Subcommittee on Commercial and Administrative Law, Committee on the Judiciary, United States House of Representatives, Oversight Hearing on the Administration of Large Business Bankruptcy Reorganizations: Has Competition for Big Cases Corrupted the Bankruptcy System? July 21, 2004; L. LoPucki, *Courting Failure: How Competition for Big Cases is Corrupting the Bankruptcy Courts* (University of Michigan Press 2005).

[15] *See, e.g.,* R. Rasmussen, *Empirically Bankrupt,* 2007 Colum. Bus. L. Rev. 179; H. Miller, *Chapter 11 Reorganization and the Delaware Myth,* 55 Vand. L. Rev.1987 (2002).

that shows no current liabilities, but does show all the assets that the debtor owned at the time it filed. I emphasize 'interim' and 'in a sense,' because those prepetition obligations don't really go away; they will be dealt with down the reorganization road in the reorganization plan. But, in the meantime, they are held in abeyance."

"Like I said, we stop paying creditors."

"Like *I* said, you stop paying holders of debts that you incurred *prepetition*. You will, however, keep paying debts as they are incurred during the pendency of the case, including, for example, utility bills, employee salaries, and the cost of materials. These are administrative expenses and may be paid currently."

"What if we are cash-short and can't fund operating expenses out of current income?"

"Then we will need to cut expenses, increase revenues, borrow money, or do all three. The Code authorizes debtors to borrow money and incur indebtedness in order to stay in business [as we will see in chapter 5], and it offers a number of inducements to lenders and suppliers to encourage them to do business with debtors. Even before a company files, management should be thinking about how it will fund operations and be trying to line up post-petition financing, known as debtor in possession or DIP financing. I also want you to consider the possibility that a debtor that is unable to generate income sufficient to met even current expenses and is unlikely ever to do so is a debtor that does not belong in Chapter 11. Ironically, the same liquidity crisis that drives debtors in the direction of bankruptcy may also make the prospects of a successful reorganization elusive, because debtors will have difficulty obtaining DIP financing. Moreover, [as we will see in chapter 5] some DIP lenders will only provide financing for a short period of time, just long enough to permit the debtor to conduct an orderly liquidation of the business. Some lenders use DIP financing as a 'loan to own' technique. Their goal is to convert their DIP loan into an equity stake in the company that emerges from bankruptcy. Of course, even if DIP lenders don't demand it, cutting losses may require you to consider trimming operations and selling off assets."

"Are there any other decisions to make before we file?" Headley asks.

"You will also need to select attorneys and perhaps other professional consultants, such as accountants, who will represent the debtor in connection with the case. This, conveniently, brings us to the next topic we need to discuss, and that is what will happen once we get into Chapter 11."

§ 1.05 THE EARLY DAYS OF A CHAPTER 11 CASE

[A] Property of the Estate

Carol remembers from her basic bankruptcy course that upon the filing of a bankruptcy petition something called the "estate" is created, and that this estate comprises virtually all property of the debtor as of the commencement of the case. Code § 541. Thus, Amphy's estate includes all the company's real property and personal property, such as inventory and equipment, accounts receivable, trademarks, patents, and contract rights. It includes the stock that Amphy owns in its subsidiaries, but it does not include the subsidiaries' assets themselves.[16] Property of the estate includes property that is subject to a mortgage or a security interest, even if the property is in the possession of a secured creditor. The significance of this last point is that the debtor may be able to get the property back to use in the in the operation of the business.[17]

[B]   The Automatic Stay

"As I mentioned earlier, at the moment the petition is filed, the automatic stay goes into effect, bringing virtually all efforts to enforce claims against the debtor and the estate to an abrupt halt." Code § 362. Carol is well acquainted with the automatic stay, not only from the basic bankruptcy course she took when she was a law student, but also as a result of having confronted it from time to time in her dealings with customers of Amphydynamics. "I can't tell you how many times I've received calls or notices telling me that I have to stop trying to collect because some deadbeat . . . I mean, um, some customer of ours has filed Chapter 11. I guess the shoe is on the other foot now." You tactfully agree and remind Carol that the automatic stay, at least in theory, serves the interests of creditors as well as debtors by preventing the debtor from being dismembered while it attempts to rationalize its business plan and restructure its finances.

Headley is clearly intrigued. "This means that our suppliers and the banks have to stop trying to collect from us, right?" Headley asks.

"Right, unless they get relief from the stay."

Headley looks thoughtful. "What about the Hystereo plaintiffs?"

"They're stayed too."

"Some of the loans made to Amphy were guaranteed by our subsidiaries. Can a creditor that is stayed from suing Amphy bring an action against a subsidiary to enforce one of those upstream guarantees?"

You warn that the act of putting Amphydynamics into Chapter 11 does not have the automatic effect of putting its subsidiaries in. Since, generally speaking, the stay only protects entities that have filed bankruptcy petitions, there may be a need to file petitions on behalf of those subsidiaries as well. Although each filing will create a separate Chapter 11 debtor and a separate estate, you explain that it is usually possible to arrange for "administrative consolidation" and "joint administration" of related cases, and that at some later point the doctrine known as "substantive consolidation" might be invoked to consolidate, or merge, the separate estates into a single pool of assets and liabilities.[18]

---

[16] *In re Beck Industries, Inc.*, 479 F.2d 410 (2d Cir. 1973).

[17] *U.S. v. Whiting Pools, Inc.*, 462 U.S. 198 (1993).

[18] *See* chapter 8 of the text.

[C]   The Bankruptcy Court and the United States Trustee System

Earlier, you told Headley and Carol that a Chapter 11 case is commenced by the filing of a petition. Now you expand. A Chapter 11 petition, like other kinds of bankruptcy petitions, is filed with the bankruptcy court. Bankruptcy courts have their own presiding judges, clerks, and administrative staffs, but technically they are organized as units of the federal district courts,[19] and their jurisdiction over bankruptcy cases and proceedings is referred to them by the district courts.[20] Bankruptcy judges are appointed for a 14-year term by the judges of the Court of Appeals presiding over the district in which the bankruptcy judges sit.[21] At this juncture you *could* rhapsodize on the problematic nature of bankruptcy court jurisdiction and the continuing controversy over whether bankruptcy judges ought to be given Article III status, including life tenure, guaranteed salary, and correspondingly broad jurisdiction, but, recognizing that Carol has already studied these matters in her basic bankruptcy course and that Headley would find the topic of bankruptcy jurisdiction Byzantine, if not downright bizarre, you refrain.[22]

Yet, you can't stop there, because to say that a bankruptcy judge "presides over" a Chapter 11 case is to say very little about what a bankruptcy judge actually does. If, however, you even skim through the Code, you will see the judge's role begin to take shape. First, you will see that a number of Code sections require court approval of certain actions before they may be undertaken. Court authorization is required, for example:

- to retain attorneys and other professionals (§ 327);
- to borrow money and incur indebtedness (§ 364);
- to reject or assume executory contracts (§ 365);
- to sell property outside the ordinary course of business (§ 363); and
- to use cash collateral if the creditor whose claim is secured by it will not consent to the use (§ 363).

Next, one will see that bankruptcy judges may also be called on to resolve disputes as a case unfolds. For example parties may ask a judge to:

- order the turnover of estate property (§ 542);
- determine the validity of a lien (§ 506);
- grant relief from the automatic stay (§ 362);
- determine the amount and validity ("allowability") of a claim (§ 502);
- subordinate a claim (§ 510);

---

[19] 28 U.S.C. § 151.

[20] 28 U.S.C. § 1334.

[21] 28 U.S.C. § 152.

[22] The problem of bankruptcy jurisdiction has been the topic of much commentary. *See, e.g.,* Erwin Chemerinsky, *Ending the Marathon, It is Time to Overrule Northern Pipeline,* 65 Am. Bankr. L. J. 311 (1991); Daniel J. Meltzer, *Legislative Courts, Legislative Power and the Constitution,* 65 Ind. L. Rev. 291 (1990).

- dismiss a case improvidently brought or to convert it to another chapter (§ 1112);

- replace management with a trustee (§ 1104); and

- determine whether a reorganization plan should become effective (§ 1129).

This is just a partial list of powers and duties, and it might be hard to believe that the statutory role of the bankruptcy judge in a business rescue case is now more limited than it was during the days in which the former Act was in force. The expansive role that bankruptcy judges then played was considered problematic for several reasons.[23]

Under the Act, when trustees were appointed in reorganization cases, the presiding bankruptcy judge appointed them, worked closely with them in the conduct of the business, and also resolved disputes that arose between them and other parties. By determining who was chosen to serve as trustee, the judge also indirectly influenced the identity of the professionals chosen to represent them. This close relationship compromised the appearance of bankruptcy judges as impartial arbiters of disputes. Many observers believed that even in cases in which no trustee was appointed and the debtor remained in possession, judges had a tendency to become overly involved with management in the conduct of the business.

Under the former Act, bankruptcy judges presided at meetings of creditors, where the debtor might be examined about its business and affairs and testimony that would not be admissible in a trial might be elicited. Later, in the course of resolving disputes, judges frequently found that they were unable to recall whether the information on which they were basing their holdings was something they had heard at a meeting of creditors, something that was told to them in an *ex parte* meeting with the trustee, or evidence that was actually adduced at trial. In addition, because they presided at creditors' meetings at which creditors' committees were organized, bankruptcy judges could influence the composition of creditors' committees and thus, indirectly, influence the identity of the lawyers and other professionals the committees retained.

There were other problems. As the person who was responsible for the selection of the trustee and the supervision of the trustee or debtor in possession, judges often felt personally responsible for the success or failure of "their" debtors and "their" cases. This close identification of some judges with their cases led one bankruptcy practitioner to tell the drafters of the new Code that "the bankruptcy court is the only court I appear in, in which the judge is an interested party."[24]

These factors were believed to have led to an unusually close relationship between bankruptcy judges and the bankruptcy bar, especially the lawyers who represented trustees and debtors, and gave rise to a perception among nonbankruptcy practitioners that there was a "bankruptcy ring" of lawyers who

---

[23] The reasons this expansive judicial role was regarded as so problematic are discussed in the Report of the Committee on the Judiciary, House of Representatives, to Accompany H.R. 8200 H.R. Rep. No. 95-595, 95th Cong., 1st Sess., pp. 88-110 (1977).

[24] *Id.*

were the beneficiaries of judicial favoritism.

Whether these abuses were real or merely perceived remains a topic of disagreement; however, the drafters of the 1978 Bankruptcy Reform Act were determined to eliminate the clubbish quality that at least seemed to permeate the system. The solution was to divest the judges of many of the appointive, supervisory, and administrative duties they had been performing and transfer these functions to a new entity, the Office of the United States Trustee. The United States Trustee Program, which is administered by the Justice Department, was initially established on an experimental pilot basis in 18 judicial districts but was implemented nationwide in 1986.[25] The Attorney General appoints a U.S. Trustee to serve in each district for a five year term[26] and assistant U.S. Trustees to serve in districts with busy dockets. The U.S. Trustee program is now responsible for the administration of bankruptcy cases in 48 states, Puerto Rico, and Guam. The judicial districts in North Carolina and Alabama do not have U.S. Trustees but do have Bankruptcy Administrators performing similar functions.

Now, bankruptcy judges no longer appoint Chapter 11 trustees. Under Code § 1104, a bankruptcy judge determines whether there are grounds for appointing a trustee, but, if the court finds that a trustee should be appointed, the U.S. Trustee makes the actual appointment. (Alternatively, creditors may choose to elect a trustee. Code § 1104(b).) Similarly, bankruptcy judges no longer appoint creditors to serve on creditors' committees. That job, too, has been given to U.S. Trustees. Code § 1103.

The United States Trustee has standing to raise, appear, and be heard on any issue in a case, although the United States Trustee may not, itself, propose a Chapter 11 reorganization plan.[27] The United States Trustee also has the authority to supervise the administration of cases and trustees.[28] In cases in which United States Trustees "consider it appropriate," they may review and comment on reorganization plans and disclosure statements; insure that operating reports and schedules are filed and that fees are paid; monitor the work of creditors' committees; review professional fee applications; and monitor the progress of cases.[29]

An interesting policy statement issued by the Executive Office for United States Trustees suggests that the extent of their involvement in a given case may depend on the extent of creditor involvement, and it provides an overview of the role that the U.S. trustee may play:

> In a Chapter 11 case with significant creditor interest, the United States Trustee's role should be one of facilitating creditor involvement and ensuring the integrity of the process. . . . It is imperative that creditor committees be promptly formed. A date and site for holding the initial

---

[25] 28 U.S.C. § 581.

[26] 28 U.S.C. § 581(b).

[27] 11 U.S.C. § 307.

[28] 28 U.S.C. § 586(a)(3).

[29] 28 U.S.C. § 586.

creditors meeting must be determined and coordinated with the Clerk of the Court in order that notice of the filing can be mailed out. The initial debtor interview or other procedure advising the debtor of the law's various responsibilities must be held within days of the filing as it plays a significant role in ensuring that case administration proceeds efficiently and effectively. *All these efforts should be directed toward fostering creditor participation in a case. Beyond these initial stages of the case, substantial work will remain in fulfillment of the United States Trustee's monitoring responsibility.* . . . [T]he United States Trustee should remain familiar with the course and progress of a case in order that he may provide the court with an informed and reasoned evaluation of any proposed disclosure statement and application for compensation that may be filed. We must monitor a case to provide an intelligent response based upon an overall evaluation of the results obtained in a case.

Efforts should not be directed towards actively litigating specific issues.

We have the duty to supervise cases in general and to seek for individual cases the presence of adverse interests that will ensure that the significant issues in the case are confronted by the parties and, if necessary, resolved by the court. We are not to substitute our business judgment for that of creditors and other parties-in-interest with a financial stake in the outcome of a bankruptcy case. Undoubtedly, there will be circumstances where the United States Trustee believes it appropriate to assert positions in a chapter 11 case, and if necessary, have it resolved by the court. In these circumstances, the necessary adverse interests are perhaps not present, or, over the course of a case, cease to exist. These circumstances are left to your sound discretion (emphasis added).[30]

You have piqued Carol's interest. "Has the establishment of the U.S. Trustee Program had the desired effect?" she asks. The authors of the Report of the National Bankruptcy Review Commission believe that if judicial and appointive/administrative roles had not been separated, "it is virtually certain that during the remarkably tumultuous 1980's the old bankruptcy system would have been considered a national scandal and the reforms enacted in response would have been draconian. Cronyism, *per se*, is no longer a systemic problem in bankruptcy." [31] On the one hand, as we will see, in recent years there has been a fair amount of questioning about the efficacy of Chapter 11, and some have suggested that an unintended consequence of limiting the role of bankruptcy judges has been to make the process more costly and less efficient. Interestingly, in 1994, § 105 of the Bankruptcy Code was amended to make clear that the bankruptcy courts have the power to hold status conferences and to issue orders "to ensure that the case is handled expeditiously and economically." To some, this amendment constituted an acknowledgment that the attempt to get the judges out of the board room and confine them to the courtroom may have gone too far. On the other hand, as noted

---

[30] Policy Statement issued by the Executive Office for United States Trustees, March 8, 1990, reprinted in 1 *Collier on Bankruptcy* ¶ 6.17[1] n. 6 (15th edition 2004).

[31] Report of the National Bankruptcy Review Commission at 847 (Volume I 1997).

before, others have argued that other aspects of the bankruptcy system, such as competition among judges for large cases, has influenced where cases are filed.[32]

[D]   Operation and Control of the Business in Chapter 11: Trustees and Debtors in Possession

You go on. In a Chapter 7 liquidation case, a trustee will be elected or appointed to take charge of the estate. Code §§ 701,702, 704. That doesn't happen in a Chapter 11 case. When a Chapter 11 case is commenced, the debtor automatically becomes a "debtor in possession." Code § 1101(1). The implications of this are numerous, but what is important to understand at this juncture is that it means that in many cases, those who managed the debtor prior to filing will continue to manage it after the filing. Sometimes, when they are referring to a debtor in possession, bankruptcy *cognoscenti* use the shorthand, "DIP."

Headley looks surprised. "In other words, I continue to serve as Chairman and CEO? And Carol stays on as Vice President for Legal Affairs? Yow! Much as I admire my own integrity and business acumen, isn't this a little like leaving a fox in charge of the chicken coop?" Headley asks.

"Be careful," you warn. "You may be insulting foxes all over the country by comparing them to debtors in possession."

"Alright," Headley says, "but isn't it a little counter-intuitive to leave the folks who presided over the failure of the business in charge?" You explain that Congress had its reasons.[33] When Chapter 11 was being developed, one of the most controversial issues was who should manage the business while a case is pending. The controversy arose out of the wreckage of prior business reorganizations law, primarily former Chapters X and XI of the Bankruptcy Act. Both former chapters were vehicles for rescuing distressed businesses, but Chapter X was conceived with larger, public companies in mind, whereas Chapter XI was designed for smaller, mom-and-pop businesses. One of the major differences between the two chapters was that Chapter X, but not Chapter XI, mandated appointment of a trustee.[34] The job of the trustee was to take charge of the business, report on any acts of misconduct, fraud, or mismanagement by the prior managers, prepare a report on the condition of the business, and formulate a plan of reorganization.[35] Chapter XI, in contrast, contained no provision for the appointment of a trustee.[36] This important difference between former Chapters X and XI reflected the belief that although an independent trustee was necessary to protect the interests of creditors and public security holders in large cases, it might be counterproductive in cases involving smaller companies, whose owners and managers were one and the same

---

[32] L. LoPucki, *Courting Failure: How Competition for Big Cases is Corrupting the Bankruptcy Courts* (University of Michigan Press 2005).

[33] These reasons are more fully explored in chapter 3, *below*.

[34] Appointment of a trustee was required in any case in which claims against the debtor exceeded $250,000, which as a practical matter meant virtually every case. Former Bankruptcy Act § 156.

[35] Former Bankruptcy Act § 167; former Bankruptcy Rules §§ 10-208, 10-202.

[36] Former Bankruptcy Act § 332 gave courts discretion to appoint a receiver, but as a practical matter receivers rarely were appointed.

and whose creditors — as the saying goes — would often be happier dealing with a "devil that they know" rather than with an unfamiliar trustee.[37] Problems arose, however, because although Chapter XI was developed with small, closely held companies in mind, its doors were open to corporate debtors of any size.[38] As a result, Chapter XI, rather than Chapter X, became the reorganization-chapter-of-choice for managers of very large companies who did not wish to relinquish control to a trustee. Sometimes a debtor's choice of chapter was extensively litigated. The consequence, observers noted, was that in many cases the debtor would die while the litigants were fighting over what operating table it should be on.[39]

When Congress considered overhauling the Bankruptcy Act, there was much debate over whether this kind of litigation could and should be eliminated by merging the two reorganization chapters into one. The compromise that emerged is embodied in Code § 1104(a), which provides, in part, that the debtor will be continued in possession unless, on motion of a party in interest or the United States Trustee, the court shall order the appointment of a trustee "for cause, including fraud, dishonesty, incompetence, or gross mismanagement of the affairs of the debtor by current management," or "if such appointment is in the interests of creditors, any equity security holders, and other interests of the estate." This presumption that management will remain at the helm is philosophically related to the elimination of the requirement that a debtor be insolvent in order to be eligible for Chapter 11 relief. By leaving managers presumptively in charge of the business, the drafters sought to eliminate one powerful disincentive to timely filing: fear of being ousted in favor of a trustee. By eliminating the insolvency requirement, the drafters sought to make timely filing possible. The drafters sought to create an environment in which managers would neither be required, nor have an incentive, to postpone filing until the business was beyond repair. By leaving them in control of both the business and the plan process, the drafters sought to encourage them to file when there was still a viable business to reorganize.

A debtor in possession has virtually all the powers of a Chapter 11 trustee. In fact, one should keep in mind when reading the Code, that in many contexts, a reference to "trustee" should be read as a reference to a "trustee/DIP." Code § 1107(a) provides that subject to certain limitations, "a debtor in possession shall have all the rights . . . powers . . . and duties of a trustee." The purpose of casting the rights and duties of a debtor in possession in terms of the rights and duties of trustees was to eliminate the need to refer specifically to the debtor in possession in the many sections of the Code that confer rights or impose duties on trustees and that are applicable in other chapters in addition to Chapter 11. As we will see in more detail in chapter 4, these powers include the authority to operate the business, Code §§ 1108, 1107; the power to use, sell, and lease property, including property that is encumbered by liens, Code § 363; and the power — for a limited

---

[37] *See* Coogan, Broude & Glatt, *Comments on Some Reorganization Provisions of the Pending Bankruptcy Bills*, 30 Bus. Law. 1149, 1150 (1975).

[38] Chapter X was open only to corporate debtors (former Bankruptcy Act § 106(5)), but Chapter XI was open to corporations, individuals, and partnerships (former Bankruptcy Act § 4, 306(3)).

[39] *S.E.C. v. Canandaigua Enterprises Corp.*, 339 F.2d 14, 19 (2d Cir. 1964).

time, the *exclusive power* — to propose a reorganization plan. Code § 1121.

"The good news," you tell Headley, "is that, in the vast majority of cases, the debtor remains in possession. But, having said that, I don't want you to think of Chapter 11 as a sinecure for management.

"One reason is that we know from experience that even when creditors don't seek appointment of a trustee, they sometimes utilize the leverage that they have as suppliers and future lenders to force a change in management. We also know that sometimes stockholders will attempt to force management changes through their power to elect directors. Whether or not that will happen in this or any case really depends on how much faith creditors and perhaps stockholders have in management's honesty and ability to turn things around and maximize their recovery.

"Another reason that you should not think of Chapter 11 as a sinecure is that although a debtor in possession has virtually all the rights and powers of a trustee, it also has many of the duties including the fiduciary duties of a Chapter 11 trustee. As you will see, your fiduciary duties arguably run to creditors, stockholders, and other parties to the case, and [as we will see in chapter 4] serving their sometimes conflicting interests can be a real challenge.

"Interestingly, there is one duty that a trustee has that a debtor in possession does not."

"What's that?" Headley asks.

"A trustee is required to investigate the 'acts, conduct, assets, liabilities, and financial condition of the debtor' and report on any 'fraud, dishonesty, incompetence, misconduct, mismanagement, or irregularity in the management of the affairs of the debtor.' But a debtor in possession is not required to do the same." Code §§ 1106(a)(3), (4); 1107(a).

"I guess I can see why," Headley says.

[E]   Examiners

You mention that if appointment of a trustee is not warranted, but there is a need for a disinterested person to investigate certain transactions or perform some other function that the debtor in possession is not inclined or qualified to perform, there is an in-between step that the court can take: appointment of an examiner pursuant to Code § 1104(c). In such a case, the United States Trustee will make the actual appointment. § 1104(d). If the examiner does find evidence of the kind of misconduct described in § 1104(a) — fraud, dishonesty, incompetence, or gross mismanagement — then the court may at that point order appointment of a trustee.

[F]   Meetings of Creditors

"Just in case it isn't already clear, you need to know that once you commence a Chapter 11 case, you can't just slink away and hide. What you have started is a judicial proceeding, and the schedules of assets and liabilities and the operating reports that you file with the court become part of the public record. Moreover, although a Chapter 11 case is commenced by the filing of papers with a court, it is more than just a judicial proceeding; it is a *process* — of investigation, examination, negotiation, valuation, and business prognostication — that in theory is supposed to lead to a negotiated, consensual plan for restructuring the company's debt and rehabilitating the company's business. In other words, the Code requires that you meet with creditors and other parties in interest as the case — no, make that *so the case* — progresses to a satisfactory conclusion."[40]

"How do we actually do this?" Headley asks.

"There are several ways, but to begin, let me tell you about the '341 meeting.' "

"Wow, I guess we'll need to hurry. It's already 2:45."

Carol winces. "No, Headley, not '3:41.' It's called a '341 meeting' because it's mandated by § 341 of the Code. I've actually attended a few of these meetings myself."

You explain that Bankruptcy Code § 341(a) provides that "[w]ithin a reasonable time after the order for relief there shall be a meeting of creditors." Bankruptcy Rule 2003(a) provides that the meeting is to be held between 20 and 40 days after the order for relief.[41]

Consistent with the aim of separating the judicial and investigatory functions, the Code also makes it clear that the judge is neither to preside at nor even attend these meetings. Code § 341(c). The U.S. Trustee calls and presides at the meeting. Bankruptcy Rule 2003(a), (b).

One purpose of the 341 meeting is organizational. The U.S. Trustee may use it as an opportunity to confer with creditors and appoint a creditors' committee. In some districts, and especially in larger cases, the U.S. Trustee may even follow the custom, not mandated by statute, of convening an organizational meeting prior to the formal 341 meeting for the purpose of forming a creditors' committee. Representatives of the debtor generally attend this meeting and may use it as a forum for soliciting creditor support for the reorganization effort and for calming (or at least trying to calm) creditor anxiety.

The other purpose of the § 341 meeting is to give creditors and their representatives the opportunity to examine the debtor about its financial condition, its plans for continued operations, its sources of operating revenue, and other information that creditors will need to evaluate their position in the case. Code § 343 requires the debtor to appear at the meeting and submit to this examination.

"Wait a second," Headley interrupts. "They're supposed to do this in one meeting? At the beginning of the case? How long does this meeting go on?"

You acknowledge that a thorough investigation of the debtor and its affairs is unlikely to be accomplished within the compass of a single § 341 meeting, and

---

[40] *See* Code §§ 1103(d), 1107(a).

[41] The petition is the "order for relief" in a voluntary case. Code § 301. (Code § 341(b) authorizes, but does not require, the United States Trustee to order a meeting of equity security holders.)

explain that commonly the meeting will be adjourned and reconvened from time to time as the case progresses. You also point out that apart from the 341 meeting, parties may compel the debtor and other entities to appear and be examined on matters relating to the case by asking the court to order what is known as a Rule 2004 examination. Bankruptcy Rule 2004(b) provides that the examination "may relate only to the acts, conduct, or property or to the liabilities and financial condition of the debtor, or to any matter which may affect the administration of the debtor's estate, or to the debtor's right to a discharge. ... In a ... reorganization case under Chapter 11 ... the examination may also relate to the operation of any business and the desirability of its continuance, the source of any money or property acquired or to be acquired by the debtor for purposes of consummating a plan ... and any matter relevant to the case or to the formulation of a plan."

Finally, you explain that although the § 341 meeting provides a formal mechanism for debtor-creditor interaction, it is by no means the only, or most productive, setting for talks between the debtor and the creditors' committee. Conferences and negotiations regarding the operation of the business, the elements of a plan of reorganization, and other important issues are typically conducted at informal, off-the-record, meetings of the creditors' committee and large creditors to which other creditors may or may not be invited.

"That's the second or third time you've referred to creditors' committees," Headley says. "Care to clue me in?"

[G]   Appointment & Role of Committees in Chapter 11 Cases

As we've seen, in most Chapter 11 cases, the debtor remains in possession. Those who managed the business in happier times continue to manage it when it is in the throes of Chapter 11. In addition, as we will see, those who manage the debtor in possession also control, at least for a limited time, the plan formulation process. Who, then, speaks for creditors and stockholders in a Chapter 11 case? Who *watches, listens, and negotiates* on their behalf?

Without limiting the right of any individual creditor to act on its own behalf, or the ability of groups of creditors to act collectively,[42] the Code assigns this important role to entities known as official creditors' committees and equity security holders' committees. According to the Code drafters, committees are to serve as "the primary negotiating bodies for the formulation of a plan of reorganization. They will represent the various classes of creditors and equity security holders from which they are selected. They will also provide supervision of the debtor in possession and of the trustee, and will protect their constituents' interests."[43]

Committee powers and duties are set forth in somewhat more detail in Code § 1103. As soon as possible after a committee is organized, the debtor in possession

---

[42] See Code § 1109(b), which provides that, "A party in interest, including the debtor, the trustee, a creditors' committee, an equity security holders' committee, a creditor, an equity security holder, or any indenture trustee, may raise and may appear and be heard on any issue in a case under this chapter."

[43] House Report at 401.

or trustee is required to meet with it "to transact such business as may be necessary and proper." Code § 1103(d). According to § 1103(c), the business of a committee includes investigating the "acts, conduct, assets, liabilities, and financial condition of the debtor," evaluating the "operation of the debtor's business and the desirability of continuing it," participating in "the formulation of a plan," requesting the appointment of a trustee or examiner in an appropriate case, and "performing such other services as are in the interests of those represented."

Again, Headley looks shocked. "Did I hear you say that this committee would be second-guessing me about *the desirability of continuing the business*?"

"Well, yes. The committee will be trying to figure out how to maximize the amount that creditors recover, and that could involve determining whether the company is worth more if it is kept intact as a going concern or if it is liquidated in whole or part. The committee might urge, for example, that some operations be discontinued to stem losses or sold to raise cash to pay their claims."

"It sounds like these people are all over the place," Headley moans. "Who's running the business, these committees or me?"

You agree that the boundaries of committee power can sometimes be a source of tension in a case and observe that the level of committee activity is going to vary from case to case. You explain that although a committee is authorized to "consult with" the debtor, it is not supposed to manage the business.[44] Nevertheless, in order for the committee to perform its functions, it will need access to information that Headley might regard as confidential. You warn Headley that the committee will be monitoring and influencing, if not actually making, decisions about such matters as executive compensation, expansion or contraction of the business, asset sales, and incurring debt. This means the committee will be orbiting, if not actually occupying, the executive suite and that the court may give weight to the committee's position on these and other matters.

The Code also provides that the U.S. Tustee *may* appoint committees to represent equity holders. Even if the U.S. Trustee does not of its own volition appoint an equity committee, the court may order the U.S. Trustee to do so. Code § 1102(a)(2). Equity committees ordinarily will consist of the persons holding the seven largest amounts of securities. Code § 1102(a)(1), (b)(2).

[H] Role of the Securities and Exchange Commission

Headley says, "Hmm . . . We're a public company. Outside of Bankruptcy we have to pay a lot of attention to the securities laws or we'll find ourselves under investigation by the SEC. Does filing for bankruptcy free us from SEC scrutiny?"

You explain that under the former Bankruptcy Act, Chapter XI conferred no special standing on the SEC. In Chapter X cases, however, the SEC performed an important statutory role as an advocate for public security holders and as an advisor to the court on many matters, including the fairness of plans, professional

---

[44] *See, e.g., In re Structurlite Plastics Corp.*, 91 B.R. 813 (Bankr. S.D. Ohio 1988); *In re UNR Industries, Inc.*, 30 B.R. 609 (Bankr. N.D. Ill. 1982); and chapter 4, *below*.

fee applications, and managerial misconduct.[45] Moreover, a Chapter X reorganization plan could not be submitted to creditors until the SEC rendered its advisory report on it, a requirement that some critics regarded as time consuming and therefore costly.

At the same time that it merged Chapters X and XI into Chapter 11, Congress also scrapped much of the role of the SEC. The reasoning was that under the Code, the interests of public security holders are, in theory, protected by committees and by the Code's provisions regarding the formulation and content of reorganization plans and the process for voting plans up or down. As is explained in § 1.07, and explored more fully in chapter 9 of the text a plan may not be voted on unless creditors and equity holders receive a court-approved disclosure statement containing "adequate information." Code § 1125(b). These changes, Congress believed, rendered the SEC's role in Chapter 11 cases somewhat redundant:

> The premise underlying the consolidated chapter 11 of this bill is the same as the premise of the securities law. If adequate disclosure is provided to all creditors and stockholders whose rights are to be affected, then they should be able to make an informed judgment on their own, rather than having the court or the Securities and Exchange Commission inform them in advance of whether the proposed plan is a good plan. Therefore, the key to the consolidated chapter is the disclosure section.[46]

The Bankruptcy Code does not eliminate the SEC's role in Chapter 11 cases altogether. Although it does not confide any special advisory role or standing as a party in interest to the SEC, the Code, in § 1109(a), provides that the SEC "may raise and may appear and be heard on any issue in a case under this Chapter, but may not appeal from any judgment, order, or decree entered in the case."[47] If the SEC so requests, notices that are sent to creditors must also be sent to it. Bankruptcy Rule 2002(j).

Several years after Chapter 11 went into effect, the SEC voted unanimously to scale back its involvement in bankruptcy cases. The Commission decided that instead of intervening as a matter of course in all cases, it would appear more selectively and offer opinions only in cases where important legal precedents and policy issues, with impact beyond the confines of any particular case, are at stake.[48]

---

[45] *See* Bankruptcy Act §§ 172, 173, 175, and Bankruptcy Rule 10-303, now repealed.

[46] H.R. Rep. No. 595, 95th Cong., 1st. Sess. 226 (1977).

[47] The limitation on the SEC's right of appeal is not a creature of the Code. The same limitation was contained in former Bankruptcy Rule 10-210(c), and, apparently, reflected the notion that if the parties themselves were not inclined to take an appeal, the government should not be allowed to stall proceedings with its own appeal. The SEC may participate in appeals brought by others.

[48] *SEC to Reduce Its Involvement in Bankruptcies*, Wall St. J., Dec. 23, 1983, p. 4, col. 1; King, *Collier on Bankruptcy 15th Edition Revised* ¶ 1109.03[3].

§ 1.06 THE MIDDLE PHASE OF A CHAPTER 11 CASE

You explain to Headley and Carol that the early days of a Chapter 11 case can be extremely hectic, but that once they are past, and the transition into Chapter 11 is complete, things may calm down a bit. This does not mean that the pressure is off; merely that it subsides. During this phase of the case, the focus of management will generally be on management, *i.e.*, operating the business as it attempts to rationalize it and formulate a viable business plan. This will require evaluating operations, markets, and competition. It often involves determining which operations should be continued and which should be sold or shut down. It may require major sales or purchases of assets. If assets or operations are sold, the proceeds may be used to fund operations or payments to creditors, or both. The debtor's managers will retain business professionals, as well as lawyers, to assist in this diagnostic and planning process, and, as discussed previously, the creditors' committee and individual large creditors will be consulted on these issues too. During this period, the debtor may be returning to court to ask for permission to incur indebtedness or to sell estate property outside the ordinary course. Code §§ 363, 364. The debtor may also be considering what executory contracts and leases to assume or reject and asking for court permission to do so. Code § 365. During this phase, the debtor may also begin the process of examining claims and objecting to improper ones. Not least of all, management may begin discussing and negotiating the terms of a reorganization plan with the creditors' committee, important creditors, and other constituencies.

§ 1.07 THE PLAN PHASE OF A CHAPTER 11 CASE

The culmination of an ideal Chapter 11 case is the court's confirmation of a reorganization plan that is the product of negotiation among the debtor and its various constituencies and that has been approved by these constituencies — a so-called "consensual plan." The process of negotiating a reorganization plan may begin shortly after a petition is filed or not until many months later. (In a so-called pre-negotiated case, the terms of the plan may be worked out prior to the Chapter 11 filing.) Generalizing is difficult, because each case seems to have a dynamic and a timetable of its own. Such variations are possible because, even though the Code gives the debtor the exclusive right to file a reorganization plan during the first 120 days of a case, and an additional 60 days to solicit and get votes in favor of the plan, these periods may be, and frequently are, extended by the court at the debtor's request. Code § 1121. Size and complexity — the need for more time to develop a viable business plan — are the usual grounds for extending the exclusive period, but, as we will see, some critics of Chapter 11 believed that judges granted extensions too routinely in plain vanilla cases, and the critics pressed for legislation that would curb that practice. As a result of the 2005 amendments, bankruptcy judges are now constrained from extending this exclusive period beyond a date that is 20 months after the date of the Chapter 11 order for relief. Code § 1121(d)(2)(B). Once the exclusive period expires, any party in interest may file a plan. Thus, competing plans are possible.

Furthermore, as we will see in later chapters, many Chapter 11 cases of recent and current vintage have resulted in a sale of the debtor's business rather than a traditional reorganization in which the interests of prepetition creditors and stockholders are in some form preserved.

Generally, a reorganization plan will serve two functions. One is to describe what is going to happen to the debtor and its assets. If the debtor is going to continue to operate, the plan will contain a description of the debtor's business plan. If the debtor is going to be sold to or merged with another entity, the plan will describe the terms. The second function of a plan is to provide for the treatment of claims and equity interests. In this sense, a plan is basically an agreement between a debtor and its creditors and equity holders that says how and how much the debtor will pay them in satisfaction of their claims and interests. A plan might provide for stretching out the maturity of claims or for a reduction in interest charges. A plan might reduce claims by some amount (hence the cliché, "ten cents on the dollar"), or eliminate some claims and interests altogether. Code § 1123. A plan might provide for the exchange of debt for equity in a reorganized company. As we will see, investors may acquire debt of a troubled company for the purpose of acquiring ownership and control of the firm that emerges from Chapter 11 by converting that debt into equity.

Before a reorganization plan can be confirmed by the court, it has to be accepted by a majority of creditors and interest holders. Code §§ 1129(a), 1126. Before votes on a plan can be solicited from creditors and interest holders, they must receive a court-approved disclosure statement that provides "adequate information" about the plan so that they can make an informed judgment about it. Code § 1125. The process works essentially like this: The terms of plan are developed, and the plan and a disclosure statement are filed with the court. The court will then hold a hearing on the adequacy of the disclosure statement. If the court approves the disclosure statement, the plan proponent will mail the disclosure statement, the plan (or a summary of the plan), ballots, and other materials to creditors and interest holders who may then vote for or against the plan. If the plan is accepted by the required majorities, the proponent of the plan will ask the court to confirm it, which the court may or may not do after holding a hearing on confirmation and objections to it. Code § 1129(a) contains a list of requirements that a plan must satisfy in order to be confirmed by the court.

The effect of confirmation of a plan is to discharge the debtor of liability on all claims that arose prior to confirmation, except to the extent that they are provided for in the plan. Code § 1141(d).

Headley, who has been uncharacteristically quiet for a while as you have been summarizing these rules interrupts. "So let's say I have a $100 claim. The plan could provide that I will be paid a total of $30 in three annual installments of $10 each?"

"That's right. In such a case the plan is scaling down the claim and stretching out payment. This is a composition and extension."

"And if the plan is confirmed, what happens to the other $70 of my claim?"

"It's discharged. The claim holder is forever enjoined from trying to collect it."

"Wow! If I were a creditor, why would I ever want to vote in favor of a plan that did that?"

"Perhaps it's the best you can do. Perhaps the debtor is a customer that you want to keep in business. There may be other good reasons, but the best is that you might otherwise be compelled to accept less. Even if a plan is not accepted by the required majorities of each class, it can still be confirmed by the court if it satisfies certain economic standards. Code § 1129(b). When a plan is confirmed by this route, it is said to be 'crammed down' the throats of those non-accepting parties."

"Lovely," Headley says. "Thanks for sharing that with me."

"Is that it? Does confirmation end the case?" Carol asks.

You explain that the case does not quite end with confirmation. The case is closed only when a final decree is entered. Code § 350; Bankruptcy Rule 3022. You also point out that although some plans provide for payments to be made over a period of many years, the case is likely to be closed long before the final plan payment is made.

§ 1.08   ELIGIBILITY TO SEEK RELIEF IN CHAPTER 11

Thus far, our discussion has focused on what Amphydynamics, its managers, and other parties can expect if Amphy seeks relief in Chapter 11. All of this begs the question of whether Amphy is entitled to seek relief in Chapter 11, and this raises several other interrelated questions: (1) Is Amphy the *kind of debtor* that is entitled to file a Chapter 11 petition? (2) Is the purpose of Amphy's filing consistent with the goals of Chapter 11? (3) Are those goals achievable in Amphy's case?

Our analysis begins with Code § 109, although it will not end there. Read that section now, along with the definitions of "person" and "corporation," in Code § 101, and then consider which of the following entities is eligible to file a Chapter 11 petition:

(1) Amphydynamics, Inc., a corporation;

(2) Amphy Ventures, Ltd., a limited partnership in which Amphydynamics Inc. is the general partner;

(3) Amphy Development, LLC, a limited liability company;

(4) Orange County, California;

(5) Leyback & Reade, a law partnership;

(6) National Commercial Bank;

(7) Southern & Atlantic Railroad;

(8) Lehman Brothers Holding, Inc., a holding company;

(9) Lehman Brothers Financial Services Inc., a stock brokerage firm; or

(10) Headley Charisma, CEO of Amphydynamics?

In thinking about whether Headley is or should be eligible to file a Chapter 11 petition, you may find the following Supreme Court opinion helpful.

TOIBB v. RADLOFF
United States Supreme Court
501 U.S. 157 (1991)

JUSTICE BLACKMUN delivered the opinion of the Court.

In this case we must decide whether an individual debtor not engaged in business is eligible to reorganize under Chapter 11 of the Bankruptcy Code, 11 U.S.C. § 1101 et seq.

I

From March 1983 until April 1985, petitioner Sheldon Baruch Toibb, a former staff attorney with the Federal Energy Regulatory Commission, was employed as a consultant by Independence Electric Corporation (IEC), a company he and two others organized to produce and market electric power. Petitioner owns 24 percent of the company's shares. After IEC terminated his employment, petitioner was unable to find work as a consultant in the energy field; he has been largely supported by his family and friends since that time.

On November 18, 1986, petitioner filed in the United States Bankruptcy Court for the Eastern District of Missouri a voluntary petition for relief under Chapter 7 of the Code, 11 U.S.C. § 701 et seq. The Schedule of Assets and Liabilities accompanying petitioner's filing disclosed no secured debts, a disputed federal tax priority claim of $11,000, and unsecured debts of $170,605.[1] Petitioner listed as nonexempt assets his IEC shares and a possible claim against his former business associates. He stated that the market value of each of these assets was unknown.

On August 6, 1987, the Chapter 7 trustee appointed to administer petitioner's estate notified the creditors that the Board of Directors of IEC had offered to purchase petitioner's IEC shares for $25,000. When petitioner became aware that this stock had such value, he decided to avoid its liquidation by moving to convert his Chapter 7 case to one under the reorganization provisions of Chapter 11.

The Bankruptcy Court granted petitioner's conversion motion, and on February 1, 1988, petitioner filed a plan of reorganization. Under the plan, petitioner proposed to pay his unsecured creditors $25,000 less administrative expenses and priority tax claims, a proposal that would result in a payment of approximately 11 cents on the dollar. He further proposed to pay the unsecured creditors, for a period of six years, 50 percent of any dividends from IEC or of any proceeds from the sale of the IEC stock, up to full payment of the debts.

On March 8, 1988, the Bankruptcy Court on its own motion ordered petitioner to show cause why his petition should not be dismissed because petitioner was not

---

[1] Because petitioner's unsecured debts exceeded $100,000 and he had no regular income, he was ineligible to proceed under Chapter 13 of the Code, 11 U.S.C. § 1301 et seq. *See* § 109(e). [Beginning in 1994, § 109(e) has been amended at three-year intervals to establish a higher debt ceiling for Chapter 13 eligibility. However, even if Toibb filed his petition today and did not bump into the debt ceiling, he still apparently could not satisfy § 109(e)'s "regular income" requirement. — Eds.]

engaged in business and, therefore, did not qualify as a Chapter 11 debtor. At the ensuing hearing, petitioner unsuccessfully attempted to demonstrate that he had a business to reorganize.[2] Petitioner also argued that Chapter 11 should be available to an individual debtor not engaged in an ongoing business. On August 1, the Bankruptcy Court ruled that, under the authority of *Wamsganz v. Boatmen's Bank of De Soto*, 804 F.2d 503 (CA8 1986), petitioner failed to qualify for relief under Chapter 11.

The United States District Court for the Eastern District of Missouri, also relying on *Wamsganz*, upheld the Bankruptcy Court's dismissal of petitioner's Chapter 11 case. The United States Court of Appeals for the Eighth Circuit affirmed, holding that the Bankruptcy Court had the authority to dismiss the proceeding sua sponte, and that the Circuit's earlier *Wamsganz* decision was controlling. *In re Toibb*, 902 F.2d 14 (1990).[3] Because the Court of Appeals' ruling that an individual nonbusiness debtor may not reorganize under Chapter 11 clearly conflicted with the holding of the Court of Appeals for the Eleventh Circuit in *In re Moog*, 774 F.2d 1073 (1985), we granted certiorari to resolve the conflict.[4] 498 U.S. 1060 (1991).

II

A

In our view, the plain language of the Bankruptcy Code disposes of the question before us. Section 109, 11 U.S.C. § 109, defines who may be a debtor under the various chapters of the Code. Section 109(d) provides: "Only a person that may be a debtor under chapter 7 of this title, except a stockbroker or a commodity broker, and a railroad may be a debtor under chapter 11 of this title." Section 109(b) states: "A person may be a debtor under chapter 7 of this title only if such person is not — (1) a railroad; (2) a domestic insurance company, bank, . . . or (3) a foreign insurance company, bank, . . . engaged in such business in the United States." The Code defines "person" as used in Title 11 to "include [an] individual." § 101(35). Under the express terms of the Code, therefore, petitioner is "a person who may be

---

[2] Petitioner does not seek further review of the question whether he is engaged in an ongoing business.

[3] The Eighth Circuit also agreed with what it regarded as the supporting precedent of *In re Little Creek Development Co.*, 779 F.2d 1068 (CA5 1986), and *In re Winshall Settlor's Trust*, 758 F.2d 1136 (CA6 1985).

[4] The named respondent, Stuart J. Radloff, was dismissed as Chapter 7 trustee when the Bankruptcy Court converted petitioner's case to one under Chapter 11. Mr. Radloff did not participate in the proceedings before the Court of Appeals and refrained from responding to Mr. Toibb's petition for certiorari filed with this Court. We therefore specifically requested the United States Trustee, *see* 28 U.S.C. § 581(a)(13), to respond. In doing so, the United States Trustee indicated his agreement with petitioner's position and suggested that, if this Court decided to review the case, it might wish to appoint counsel to defend the Eighth Circuit's judgment. We then invited James Hamilton, Esq., of Washington, D.C., a member of the Bar of this Court, to serve as amicus curiae in support of the judgment of the Court of Appeals. 498 U.S. 1065 (1991). Mr. Hamilton accepted this appointment and has well fulfilled this assigned responsibility.

a debtor under chapter 7" and satisfies the statutory requirements for a Chapter 11 debtor.

The Code contains no ongoing business requirement for reorganization under Chapter 11, and we are loath to infer the exclusion of certain classes of debtors from the protections of Chapter 11, because Congress took care in § 109 to specify who qualifies — and who does not qualify — as a debtor under the various chapters of the Code. Section 109(b) expressly excludes from the coverage of Chapter 7 railroads and various financial and insurance institutions. Only municipalities are eligible for the protection of Chapter 9. § 109(c). Most significantly, § 109(d) makes stockbrokers and commodities brokers ineligible for Chapter 11 relief, but otherwise leaves that Chapter available to any other entity eligible for the protection of Chapter 7. Congress knew how to restrict recourse to the avenues of bankruptcy relief; it did not place Chapter 11 reorganization beyond the reach of a nonbusiness individual debtor.

B

The amicus curiae in support of the Court of Appeals' judgment acknowledges that Chapter 11 does not expressly exclude an individual nonbusiness debtor from its reach. He echoes the reasoning of those courts that have engrafted an ongoing-business requirement onto the plain language of § 109(d) and argues that the statute's legislative history and structure make clear that Chapter 11 was intended for business debtors alone. *See, e. g., Wamsganz v. Boatmen's Bank of De Soto*, 804 F.2d at 505 ("The legislative history of the Bankruptcy Code, taken as a whole, shows that Congress meant for chapter 11 to be available to businesses and persons engaged in business, and not to consumer debtors"). We find these arguments unpersuasive for several reasons.

First, this Court has repeated with some frequency: "Where, as here, the resolution of a question of federal law turns on a statute and the intention of Congress, we look first to the statutory language and then to the legislative history if the statutory language is unclear." *Blum v. Stenson*, 465 U.S. 886, 896, 104 S. Ct. 1541, 79 L. Ed. 2d 891 (1984). The language of § 109 is not unclear. Thus, although a court appropriately may refer to a statute's legislative history to resolve statutory ambiguity, there is no need to do so here.

Second, even were we to consider the sundry legislative comments urged in support of a congressional intent to exclude a nonbusiness debtor from Chapter 11, the scant history on this precise issue does not suggest a "clearly expressed legislative intent. . . contrary . . ." to the plain language of § 109(d). *See Consumer Product Safety Comm'n v. GTE Sylvania, Inc.*, 447 U.S. 102, 108, 100 S. Ct. 2051, 64 L. Ed. 2d 766 (1980). The amicus does point to the following statement in a House Report:

> "Some consumer debtors are unable to avail themselves of the relief provided under chapter 13. For these debtors, straight bankruptcy is the only remedy that will enable them to get out from under the debilitating effects of too much debt." H. R. Rep. No. 95-595, p. 125 (1977).

Petitioner responds with the following excerpt from a later Senate Report:

"Chapter 11, Reorganization, is primarily designed for businesses, although individuals are eligible for relief under the chapter. The procedures of chapter 11, however, are sufficiently complex that they will be used only in a business case and not in the consumer context." S. Rep. No. 95-989, p. 3 (1978).

These apparently conflicting views tend to negate the suggestion that the Congress enacting the current Code operated with a clear intent to deny Chapter 11 relief to an individual nonbusiness debtor.

Finally, we are not persuaded by the contention that Chapter 11 is unavailable to a debtor without an ongoing business because many of the Chapter's provisions do not apply to a nonbusiness debtor. There is no doubt that Congress intended that a business debtor be among those who might use Chapter 11. Code provisions like the ones authorizing the appointment of an equity security holders' committee, § 1102, and the appointment of a trustee "for cause, including fraud, dishonesty, incompetence, or gross mismanagement of the affairs of the debtor by current management ... ," § 1104(a)(1), certainly are designed to aid in the rehabilitation of a business. It does not follow, however, that a debtor whose affairs do not warrant recourse to these provisions is ineligible for Chapter 11 relief. Instead, these provisions — like the references to debtor businesses in the Chapter's legislative history — reflect an understandable expectation that Chapter 11 would be used primarily by debtors with ongoing businesses; they do not constitute an additional prerequisite for Chapter 11 eligibility beyond those established in § 109(d).

III

Although the foregoing analysis is dispositive of the question presented, we deal briefly with amicus' contention that policy considerations underlying the Code support inferring a congressional intent to preclude a nonbusiness debtor from reorganizing under Chapter 11. First, it is said that bringing a consumer debtor within the scope of Chapter 11 does not serve Congress' purpose of permitting business debtors to reorganize and restructure their debts in order to revive the debtors' businesses and thereby preserve jobs and protect investors. This argument assumes that Congress had a single purpose in enacting Chapter 11. Petitioner suggests, however, and we agree, that Chapter 11 also embodies the general Code policy of maximizing the value of the bankruptcy estate. *See Commodity Futures Trading Comm'n v. Weintraub*, 471 U.S. 343 (1985). Under certain circumstances a consumer debtor's estate will be worth more if reorganized under Chapter 11 than if liquidated under Chapter 7. Allowing such a debtor to proceed under Chapter 11 serves the congressional purpose of deriving as much value as possible from the debtor's estate.

Second, amicus notes that allowing a consumer debtor to proceed under Chapter 11 would permit the debtor to shield both disposable income and nonexempt personal property. He argues that the legislative history of Chapter 11 does not reflect an intent to offer a consumer debtor more expansive protection than he would find under Chapter 13, which does not protect disposable income, or Chapter 7, which does not protect nonexempt personal assets. As an initial matter, it makes no difference whether the legislative history affirmatively reflects such an intent, because the plain language of the statute allows a consumer debtor to proceed under Chapter 11. Moreover, differences in the requirements and protections of each chapter reflect Congress' appreciation that various approaches are necessary to address effectively the disparate situations of debtors seeking protection under the Code.

Amicus does not contend that allowing a consumer debtor to reorganize under Chapter 11 will leave the debtor's creditors in a worse position than if the debtor were required to liquidate. Nor could he. Section 1129(a)(7) provides that a reorganization plan may not be confirmed unless all the debtor's creditors accept the plan or will receive not less than they would receive under a Chapter 7 liquidation. Because creditors cannot be expected to approve a plan in which they would receive less than they would from an immediate liquidation of the debtor's assets, it follows that a Chapter 11 reorganization plan usually will be confirmed only when creditors will receive at least as much as if the debtor were to file under Chapter 7. Absent some showing of harm to the creditors of a nonbusiness debtor allowed to reorganize under Chapter 11, we see nothing in the allocation of "burdens" and "benefits" of Chapter 11 that warrants an inference that Congress intended to exclude a consumer debtor from its coverage. *See* Herbert, *Consumer Chapter 11 Proceedings: Abuse or Alternative?*, 91 Com. L. J. 234, 245–248 (1986).

Amicus also warns that allowing consumer debtors to proceed under Chapter 11 will flood the bankruptcy courts with plans of reorganization that ultimately will prove unworkable. We think this fear is unfounded for two reasons. First, the greater expense and complexity of filing under Chapter 11 likely will dissuade most consumer debtors from seeking relief under this Chapter. *See* S. Rep. No. 95-989, at 3; *see also* Herbert, *supra*, at 242–243. Second, the Code gives bankruptcy courts substantial discretion to dismiss a Chapter 11 case in which the debtor files an untenable plan of reorganization. *See* §§ 1112(b) and 1129(a).

Finally, amicus asserts that extending Chapter 11 to consumer debtors creates the risk that these debtors will be forced into Chapter 11 by their creditors under § 303(a), a result contrary to the intent reflected in Congress' decision to prevent involuntary bankruptcy proceedings under Chapter 13. In particular, he suggests that it would be unwise to force a debtor into a Chapter 11 reorganization, because an involuntary debtor would be unlikely to cooperate in the plan of reorganization — a point that Congress noted in refusing to allow involuntary Chapter 13 proceedings. *See* H. R. Rep. No. 95-595, at 120.

We find these concerns overstated in light of the Code's provisions for dealing with recalcitrant Chapter 11 debtors. If an involuntary Chapter 11 debtor fails to cooperate, this likely will provide the requisite "cause" for the bankruptcy court to convert the Chapter 11 case to one under Chapter 7. *See* § 1112(b). In any event, the argument overlooks Congress' primary concern about a debtor's being forced into bankruptcy under Chapter 13: that such a debtor, whose future wages are not exempt from the bankruptcy estate, § 1322(a)(1), would be compelled to toil for the benefit of creditors in violation of the Thirteenth Amendment's involuntary servitude prohibition. *See* H. R. Rep. No. 95-595, at 120. Because there is no comparable provision in Chapter 11 requiring a debtor to pay future wages to a creditor, Congress' concern about imposing involuntary servitude on a Chapter 13 debtor is not relevant to a Chapter 11 reorganization.

IV

The plain language of the Bankruptcy Code permits individual debtors not engaged in business to file for relief under Chapter 11. Although the structure and legislative history of Chapter 11 indicate that this Chapter was intended primarily for the use of business debtors, the Code contains no "ongoing business" require- ment for Chapter 11 reorganization, and we find no basis for imposing one. Accordingly, the judgment of the Court of Appeals is reversed.

It is so ordered.

Dissenting opinion of JUSTICE STEVENS omitted.

NOTES AND QUESTIONS

(1)   Why did Sheldon Toibb initially file a Chapter 7 petition, rather than a Chapter 11 petition? Why did the board's offer to buy the stock from the trustee induce Toibb to convert the case to Chapter 11? What would Toibb have received from the sale of the stock had the case remained in Chapter 7?

(2)   Toibb's plan provided that creditors would receive a cash payment of their pro rata share of $25,000 (less administrative and priority tax claims) plus 50% of any dividends or proceeds generated by the sale of the stock. Why did Toibb propose this treatment for creditors? *See* Code § 1129(a)(7). If you were one of Toibb's unsecured creditors, would you support conversion of the case from Chapter 7 to Chapter 11?

(3)   In *Toibb v. Radloff*, the Supreme Court put to rest the question of whether individual debtors are eligible for admission to Chapter 11. They are. It also settled the question of whether all debtors must be engaged in an "ongoing business" to be eligible for Chapter 11 relief. They do not. However, the Court did not rule out the possibility that some filings might be judged improper — and therefore subject to dismissal or conversion — for other reasons. The opinion also left unanswered the question of how long, and under what circumstances, a debtor should be entitled to *remain* in Chapter 11.

Whether a debtor should be allowed to linger in Chapter 11 — let alone enter it in the first place — is an important consideration, because Chapter 11 cases take time, and some cases take too much time, in the view of critics of the system. According to a study cited in the 1997 Report of the National Bankruptcy Review Commission, the average time from filing of a petition to the confirmation of a reorganization plan was more than two years. In nearly two-thirds of the studied cases, plans were confirmed in the second or third year after filing, with some cases taking more than five years. This does not mean that two-thirds of petitions are confirmed. In point of fact, the majority of cases do not result in confirmed reorganization plans. As one court observed, "It is our empirical observation that many more plans of reorganization are contemplated than are proposed; fewer still are confirmed; and even fewer are consummated." *Rosenberg Real Estate Equity*

Fund III v. Air Beds, Inc. (In re Air Beds, Inc.), 92 B.R. 419, 424 (B.A.P. 9th Cir. 1988). After lingering for a while — sometimes for a very long while — cases are either converted to Chapter 7 or dismissed. While cases are lingering, administrative expenses accumulate, asset values erode, and creditors' recoveries are diminished."[1]

Why do cases founder this way? One reason is that too many debtors that seek refuge in Chapter 11 have no business being there, not merely because (like Sheldon Toibb) they have no business to reorganize, but because the businesses they do have are beyond resuscitation and because (unlike Sheldon Toibb's filing) their filings are not calculated to achieve even the broader Chapter 11 goal of maximizing the value of estate property and enhancing the return for creditors. One court has diagnosed the problem in such cases as the "terminal euphoria" of doomed debtors. *Little Creek Development Co. v. Commonwealth Mortgage Corp. (In re Little Creek Development Co.)*, 779 F.2d 1068, 1073 (5th Cir. 1986). The next opinion presents an early example of the syndrome. It is followed by a more recent example.

IN RE VICTORY CONSTRUCTION CO., INC.
United States Bankruptcy Court for the Central District of California
9 B.R. 549, *modified*, 9 B.R. 570 (1981)

ROBERT L. ORDIN, BANKRUPTCY JUDGE

MEMORANDUM OPINION ON COMPLAINT TO VACATE STAY FOR CAUSE (LACK OF GOOD FAITH OF THE DEBTOR IN FILING ITS PETITION UNDER CHAPTER 11)

I. Introduction

On August 11, 1980, Victory Construction Co., Inc., a California corporation (hereinafter "Victory") filed a petition under Chapter 11. The debtor's sole asset is a parcel of improved real property known as 8511 Beverly Place, Los Angeles, California (hereinafter called the "real property"). [The court then explained that the property was subject to several liens securing obligations totaling $2,889,278.71. Nine days after the petition was filed, several of the secured creditors filed a complaint seeking relief from the automatic stay so that they could enforce their liens against the real property, or, in the alternative, dismissal of the debtor's petition on the grounds that it was not filed "in good faith." Ed.]

---

[1] Lynn M. LoPucki, *The Debtor in Full Control — Systems Failure Under Chapter 11 of the Bankruptcy Code?*, 57 Am. Bankr. L.J. 99, 100 (1983). On the other hand, observers of the current generation of cases believe that many cases are completed too quickly, with the debtors' income-producing assets sold prematurely, at the earliest stages of a case, well before the debtor's prospects can be evaluated and a reorganization plan can be negotiated.

1. Issues To Be Determined

Plaintiffs seek an order vacating the automatic stay and permitting foreclosure of their defaulted liens, for cause. They assert as "cause": (a) that Victory did not file its Chapter 11 petition in "good faith"; (b) that plaintiffs have neither received nor been offered "adequate protection" of their interest in the property and (c) that Victory has no equity in the real property, and the property is not necessary to an effective reorganization. In addition, plaintiffs assert that the debtor's lack of good faith in filing the petition requires the court to dismiss the Chapter 11 case in its entirety.

2. The "Good Faith" Issue

The "good faith" issue may be analyzed as follows:

(1)   Does a debtor's lack of "good faith" in filing a Chapter 11 case constitute "cause" to vacate the automatic stay under § 362(d)(1)?

(2)   Does the law impose a "good faith" condition on debtor's right to file or maintain a proceeding under Chapter 11?

If the answer to these questions is negative, plaintiff's right to relief in this case is limited to a consideration of the issues of adequate protection, the existence of equity, and whether the property is necessary to an effective reorganization.

(3)   Was the debtor's petition in this case filed in "good faith"?

"Good faith" as a standard of confirmation in debtor rehabilitation or reorganization proceedings, or as a condition to the debtor's right to file and maintain proceedings aimed at rehabilitation or reorganization, has appeared in many provisions of the Bankruptcy Act of 1898; and the courts have explored the meaning of the term in a wide variety of fact situations and circumstances. While many of the cases merely use the term or refer to "good faith" provisions of the statutes without contributing to an understanding of its meaning, a large number of cases attempt and make a meaningful analysis and contribute to an understanding of the concept. . . .

As the cases disclose, however, judicial analysis of the meaning, scope, and dimension of "good faith" in rehabilitation or reorganization cases has not differentiated between the "good faith" required to confirm a plan of arrangement, and the "good faith" required at the outset as a condition of the right to file and maintain the proceeding. Moreover, an understanding of the cases requires some knowledge of the provisions of the statutes to which they refer and an appreciation of the purposes and philosophies embodied in these laws.

Accordingly, a cursory examination of the provisions and purposes of these statutes will be useful.

. . . .

[The court then reviewed the various precursors to the current Bankruptcy Code and found that "good faith" was either an express or implied requirement for filing under all of them.]

(xi) Title 11

While "good faith" is made a condition to the confirmation of a plan under Chapter 11 and Chapter 13, Title 11 does not contain a provision expressly conditioning the right to file or maintain a proceeding on the "good faith" of the debtor at the time the proceeding is initiated.

The "good faith" confirmation standard is expressed as follows:

> The plan has been proposed in good faith and not by any means forbidden by law. [Sections 1129(a)(3) and 1325(a)(3)].

Review of these statutory provisions discloses that: (i) Sections 74, 77, 77B, Chapter IX, and Chapter X each contained an express "good faith" filing requirement, Section 75, Chapters XI, XII, XIII of the Act, and Chapters 11 and 13 of the Code do not; and (ii) prior to Chapters XI, XII, and XIII, and the Code, Section 75 was the only reorganization or rehabilitation section which did not contain a "good faith" filing requirement.[5]

As the term "good faith" continued to appear in these rehabilitation and reorganization statutes, the case law was developing and imparting dimension and scope to the term. The issue was often raised early in the proceeding by secured creditors who asserted (i) that the filing was an attempt to delay foreclosure despite the lack of any rational basis to believe that a composition or extension was possible, and (ii) that the proceeding was a sham, or device to deprive the secured creditor of rightful recourse to its collateral.

. . . .

When Chapter X was adopted, the concepts and principles derived from these cases were codified in the statutory definition of "good faith." The statutory examples in which "good faith" was excluded were in large measure restatements or elaborations of the principles or language derived from the cases decided under prior law. The development of "good faith" continued, as did the recognition of its "generality" as a term with well recognized meaning, emphasized by the language of Chapter X.

As we have seen, Chapters XI, XII and XIII contained no "good faith" filing requirement. This "gap" was filled by the courts!

. . . .

[M]ost of the judicial current flows in the same direction: to require "good faith" as a condition of the right to file and process the proceeding. . . .

---

[5] The Supreme Court explained this omission in *Wright v. Vinton Branch*, 300 U.S. 440, 57 S. Ct. 556, 81 L. Ed. 736 (1937). Section 75 was emergency legislation enacted to deal with the plight of the farmer as a result of the Great Depression. The farmer's situation could not be measured by standards applicable to other debtors. Generally, there was no reasonable potential for rehabilitation in the accepted sense. The moratorium was to give the farmer time to recover and was not dependent on whether or not he could propose a plan which was economically feasible at the outset. "Good faith" as a condition to the right to file would require that rehabilitation be within the farmer's grasp. The imposition of such a condition would have nullified the purpose of the legislation.

Lack of Good Faith as Grounds to Dismiss a Chapter 11 Case

The provisions of the Code dealing with rehabilitation and reorganization must be viewed as direct lineal descendants of a legal philosophy solidly embedded in American bankruptcy law. Review and analysis of Sections 74, 75, 77, 77B, Chapters IX, X, XI, XII and XIII, and cases decided under these sections, disclose a common theme and objective: avoidance of the consequences of economic dismemberment and liquidation, and the preservation of ongoing values in a manner which does equity and is fair to rights and interests of the parties affected. But the perimeters of this potential mark the borderline between fulfillment and perversion; between accomplishing the objectives of rehabilitation and reorganization, and the use of these statutory provisions to destroy and undermine the legitimate rights and interests of those intended to benefit by this statutory policy. That borderline is patrolled by courts of equity, armed with the doctrine of "good faith": the requirement that those who invoke the reorganization or rehabilitation provisions of the bankruptcy law must do so in a manner consistent with the aims and objectives of bankruptcy philosophy and policy — must, in short, do so in "good faith."

. . . .

"Good faith" must therefore be viewed as an implicit prerequisite to the filing or continuation of a proceeding under Chapter 11 of the Code.

Lack of Good Faith as "Cause" for Relief from Stay

Historically, the issue of the debtor's "good faith" in filing was often raised at the outset of the proceeding by entities whose financial interests were threatened by the delay and expense associated with processing a case through the bankruptcy court: senior and junior lienholders, bondholders, indentured trustees; in short, all whose financial stake in the debtor would be dissipated or destroyed by continued operation of the debtor's business, or by any procedure except immediate liquidation. Courts soon learned to expect the plea of the party seeking dismissal that its economic interests can be salvaged by immediate liquidation, but will be destroyed by the continuation of a proceeding which is doomed at the outset by the economics of the case.

The authors of the Code well understood the impact of the filing of the case, and the potential for loss to those financially involved with the debtor. . . . [T]he Code structured an arena in which to litigate these matters expeditiously and efficiently at the outset of the case. Sections 362(d) and (e) and 28 U.S.C. § 1471(a) through (e) were designed to accommodate the needs of the litigants for immediate resolution of these disputes. Had such provisions been included in prior rehabilitation and reorganization sections of the law, the debtor's "good faith" in seeking relief in the bankruptcy court might not have been so painstakingly explored.

These provisions of the Code may be said to provide a remedy for the evil that the traditional motion to dismiss for "lack of good faith" was intended to eliminate. That remedy takes the form of the provisions of the Code (i) defining the basis upon which affected interests may be relieved from the impact of the Chapter 11, *i.e.*, the stay; and (ii) conferring jurisdiction on the Chapter 11 court to hear and determine such disputes at the outset of the case. [Section 362(d) and (e); 28 U.S.C. § 1471(a)-(e)].

Those who seek such relief need only show "cause" [§ 362(d)(1)]. The Code expresses the matter as follows:

> On request of a party in interest and after and a hearing, the court shall grant relief from the stay.
>
>   . . . .
>
> (1) for cause, including the lack of adequate protection.
>
>   . . . .

The most traditional challenge to the "good faith" of the debtor was mounted by secured creditors who sought to avoid the threat of serious and irreversible harm to their economic interests while the debtor plodded forward in search of a means of financial rehabilitation. The right to "adequate protection" as a condition to further restraint against lien enforcement and continued use or exploitation of the collateral is a statutory recognition of the seriousness of that threat and the legitimacy of the plea for relief. The echo of this plea, sounding through the cases under Sections 74, 75, 77B, and Chapters X, XI, and XII, is heard repeatedly in the courts now administering the new **Chapter 11**.

The Code has isolated and identified this type of litigation over the debtor's "good faith" in the provisions of Section 362(d)(1), which address the lack of "adequate protection" to a party seeking relief.

    . . . .

Accordingly, and for the foregoing reasons, the debtor's lack of "good faith" in filing a case under Chapter 11 is "cause," independent of the existence or lack of adequate protection, to vacate the automatic stay under § 362(d)(1).

    . . . .

3. Did the Debtor Act in "Good Faith"?

The conduct of the debtor may be summarized as follows:

Prior to the acquisition of the real property in issue on March 24, 1980, the debtor was a dormant corporation, substantially without assets or income, and engaged in no business activities.

On that date, it acquired a quitclaim deed to the real property valued at between $2,760,000 and $3,300,000, (i) subject to seven liens securing an aggregate indebtedness of approximately $2,900,000; (ii) which had a rental income of approximately $2,000 per month; (iii) and required an expenditure of $15,000 per month to service payments of interest only on the existing liens (without payment of principal); (iv) all of which liens were then in default and foreclosure, stayed only by the automatic stay resulting from bankruptcy proceedings of the former owner; (v) for a purchase price of $107,500, all of which was borrowed from its president and sole shareholder.

The debtor purchased the property (i) fully aware that all stays against lien enforcement resulting from the seller's bankruptcy would terminate on passage of title to the debtor, and (ii) without having concluded any enforceable agreements with the lienholders whereby terms of payment were extended or foreclosure efforts were stayed, or deferred.

The purchase was concluded at a time when the debtor had no financial assets, net worth, or enforceable commitments which would enable it to make the payments required to existing lienholders.

The purchase was made with knowledge that the interest rates on the existing liens were far below current interest rates in the real estate market, and with the intent to finance the acquisition of the property by keeping these liens in place with a minimum amount of front money cash.

At the time of the purchase, the debtor knew and intended that litigation would be instituted to prevent foreclosure of the property in the event the negotiations with the lienholders failed.

When negotiations failed, the debtor filed suit (in July 1980) in the state court to enjoin foreclosure. When that litigation proved unsuccessful, and a foreclosure sale was fixed (August 12, 1980), the debtor filed this petition under Chapter 11 of the Code (August 11, 1980).

At no time since acquiring title to the property has the debtor made any payments to the lienholders-plaintiffs in this adversary proceeding.

These facts and circumstances support the following conclusions:

The debtor is attempting to use the provisions of Chapter 11 to create and organize a new business, not to reorganize or rehabilitate an existing enterprise, or to preserve going concern values of a viable or existing business.

The debtor knowingly and with full awareness of the economic risks embarked on a speculative real estate promotion, the keystone of which was the ability to retain existing low interest liens in place.

This course of conduct was pursued with knowledge that the failure of negotiations with lienholders would leave litigation as the only means available to delay foreclosure (except for payment of the amounts in default).

The debtor was operated and guided by persons with shrewd and sophisticated appreciation of (i) the financial realities of the real estate market and real estate finance, (ii) the types of legal recourse available to forestall or delay foreclosure, and (iii) the loss, expense, delay and attrition to secured creditors associated with litigation of the sort contemplated by debtor if negotiations with the lienholders failed.

This Chapter 11 proceeding is primarily motivated by the desire to protect and preserve the existing low-interest liens on the property as a means of financing the acquisition with a minimum of front money cash.

Accordingly:

1. This is not a proceeding within the contemplation, intent, or purpose of Chapter 11 of the Code.

2. The debtor has acted with the intent to take advantage of the secured creditors' exposure to delay, loss, expense and attrition incident to further prolonged litigation to enforce their rights against the collateral, and has not acted with that candor, frankness, sincerity and willingness to do equity which are the indicia of "good faith".

3. The purpose of a quitclaim to fully encumbered property on the eve of foreclosure, with intent to use Chapter 11 to delay the secured creditors in enforcement of their rights, is inconsistent with the purpose, spirit, and intent of the statute, under the facts and circumstances here presented.

4. The analysis and principles expressed by the courts called upon to deal with the good faith issue in cases relating to the "new debtor syndrome" fully support the determination that the debtor did not act in good faith in filing this Chapter 11 petition.

5. There is neither a going business nor going concern value to preserve or protect in this case, and the preservation of this speculative venture should not be undertaken at the expense of secured creditors.

6. The debtor has purchased its way into court. Justice, equity and public policy prohibit this.

7. The petition was not filed with a genuine intent and desire to use the provisions of Chapter 11 for its intended purpose, but solely to prevent foreclosure while the debtor created a vehicle for profit through use of the secured creditors' collateral at low interest not currently available in the real estate market. That is a misuse of the reorganization process. The Code is not to be abused by the extension of its rights and privileges to those not within its contemplation.

6. Conclusion

Plaintiffs are entitled to immediate relief from all stays against enforcing their respective rights against the collateral. This relief being granted, dismissal of the debtor's petition, under the circumstances here present, will serve no constructive purpose.

SO ORDERED.

NESTER v. GATEWAY ACCESS SOLUTIONS, INC. (IN RE GATEWAY ACCESS SOLUTIONS)

United States Bankruptcy Court, Middle District of Pennsylvania

374 B.R. 556 (2007)

ROBERT N. OPEL, II, BANKRUPTCY JUDGE

OPINION[1]

. . . .

I. Jurisdiction

The Court has jurisdiction of this "core" proceeding by virtue of 28 U.S.C. §§ 1334 and 157(b)(2)(A).

II. Background

This Chapter 11 case was filed on January 9, 2007. The Debtor qualifies as a small business as that term is defined in § 101(51D)[3] and all the accelerated deadlines and duties attendant to being a small business debtor apply herein. *See generally* 11 U.S.C. §§ 308, 1116 & 1121(e). To date, no disclosure statement or plan of reorganization has been filed despite the exclusivity time period during which only the Debtor could file a plan having lapsed with no motion to extend it. The final deadline for filing a plan of reorganization expires on November 5, 2007.

The Movants in this case include: Andrew C. Nester, former President and Director of the Debtor who resigned on June 23, 2006; Benjamin C. Steele, former Chief Financial Officer of the Debtor who resigned on June 23, 2006; and, David F. Wiesner, former Director of the Debtor who resigned on June 23, 2006. Both Nester and Wiesner have filed Proofs of Claim in this case seeking a total of over $196,000.00. The other two Movants are Steele & Associates LLC and Anchor Bay

---

[1] Drafted with the assistance of law clerk, Kathryn F. Evans, Esquire.

[3] The term "small business debtor" —

(A) subject to subparagraph (B), means a person engaged in commercial or business activities (including any affiliate of such person that is also a debtor under this title and excluding a person whose primary activity is the business of owning or operating real property or activities incidental thereto) that has aggregate noncontingent liquidated secured and unsecured debts as of the date of the petition or the date of the order for relief in an amount not more than $2,190,000 (excluding debts owed to 1 or more affiliates or insiders) for a case in which the United States trustee has not appointed under section 1102(a)(1) a committee of unsecured creditors or where the court has determined that the committee of unsecured creditors is not sufficiently active and representative to provide effective oversight of the debtor; and

(B) does not include any member of a group of affiliated debtors that has aggregate noncontingent liquidated secured and unsecured debts in an amount greater than $2,190,000 (excluding debt owed to 1 or more affiliates or insiders).

Corporation who have both filed substantial Proofs of Claim in the case seeking over $426,000.00 (collectively "Movants").

The Debtor's primary assets consist of FCC licenses and leases to operate wireless broadband services. The Debtor's Schedules value the lease rights at $1,097,206.00. Schedule D lists secured claims of $282,288.19; Schedule E lists priority claims of $121,336.48; and, Schedule F lists unsecured claims of $1,499,179.87. Thus, the total scheduled liabilities are less than the $2,000,000.00 debt ceiling for a small business debtor. 11 U.S.C. § 101(51D).

The Debtor, Gateway Access Solutions, Inc. ("Debtor"), was incorporated under the laws of Nevada and currently has only one member on its Board of Directors, Dr. S. Mark Poler ("Dr. Poler"). Dr. Poler testified that he appointed himself to the position of corporate secretary. Dr. Poler has been a full time anesthesiologist for Geisinger Health System, a health care provider, for the past seventeen years. When discussing his work habits, Dr. Poler testified he works six to seven days a week at the hospital and feels guilty if he puts in less than eight hours each day. Dr. Poler testified that, in addition to his hospital work, he devotes an additional forty hours a week to duties for the Debtor working from home.

The Debtor also has an "acting president," Gary Semans ("Semans"), who was originally employed as a consultant through his company, Popnet. Although it is not completely clear from the record what the role of "acting president" entails, the record reflects that Semans is in charge of negotiating contracts on behalf of the Debtor, has limited authority to sign those contracts, and has no authority to sign checks. Semans has had varying health problems during this case. Despite the state of Semans' health, Dr. Poler maintains that Semans has had an active email and telephonic presence concerning the Debtor's affairs and is still devoting many hours a week to the Debtor. In addition to a corporate secretary and acting president, the Debtor employs one other full time employee and one other part time employee. The Debtor has no present intention to hire any additional management or sales representatives.

III. Discussion

(A) 11 U.S.C. § 1112(b)

The Movants are seeking to convert this case to a Chapter 7 case pursuant to § 1112(b)(1) which was recently redrafted by Congress as part of the Bankruptcy Abuse Prevention and Consumer Protection Act of 2005, Pub. L. No. 109-8, 119 Stat. 23 (2005) ("BAPCPA"). Section 1112(b)(1) now provides:

> (b)(1) Except as provided in paragraph (2) of this subsection, subsection (c) of this section, and section 1104(a)(3), on request of a party in interest, and after notice and a hearing, absent unusual circumstances specifically identified by the court that establish that the requested conversion or dismissal is not in the best interests of creditors and the estate, the court shall convert a case under this chapter to a case under chapter 7 or dismiss a case under this chapter, whichever is in the best interests of creditors and the estate, if the movant establishes cause.

Prior to the 2005 BAPCPA amendments, this Subsection of the Bankruptcy Code provided, in part, that:

> . . . the court may convert a case under this chapter to a case under chapter 7 of this title or may dismiss a case under this chapter, whichever is in the best interest of creditors and the estate for cause, including . . . 11 U.S.C. § 1112(b) (prior to 2005 amendments).

Thus, the statutory language has been changed from permissive to mandatory. The amendments to § 1112 limit the Court's discretion to refuse to dismiss or convert a Chapter 11 case upon a finding of cause.

. . . .

Still, as quoted above, conversion or dismissal may be disallowed if the Debtor specifically identifies "unusual circumstances" which establish conversion is not in the best interest of creditors. Such circumstances are not defined in the statute. *See* 11 U.S.C. § 1112(b).

Pre-BAPCPA, § 1112(b) listed ten illustrative examples of "cause" for a Chapter 11 case to either be dismissed or converted to a Chapter 7 liquidation. 11 U.S.C. § 1112(b)(1)-(10) (prior to 2005 amendments).

Under BAPCPA, sixteen illustrative examples of "cause" are listed. Section 1112(b)(4) provides:

(4) For purposes of this subsection, the term "cause" includes —

(A) substantial or continuing loss to or diminution of the estate and the absence of a reasonable likelihood of rehabilitation;

(B) gross mismanagement of the estate;

(C) failure to maintain appropriate insurance that poses a risk to the estate or to the public;

(D) unauthorized use of cash collateral substantially harmful to 1 or more creditors;

(E) failure to comply with an order of the court;

(F) unexcused failure to satisfy timely any filing or reporting requirement established by this title or by any rule applicable to a case under this chapter;

(G) failure to attend the meeting of creditors convened under section 341 (a) or an examination ordered under rule 2004 of the Federal Rules of Bankruptcy Procedure without good cause shown by the debtor;

(H) failure timely to provide information or attend meetings reasonably requested by the United States trustee (or the bankruptcy administrator, if any);

(I) failure timely to pay taxes owed after the date of the order for relief or to file tax returns due after the date of the order for relief;

(J) failure to file a disclosure statement, or to file or confirm a plan, within the time fixed by this title or by order of the court;

(K) failure to pay any fees or charges required under chapter 123 of title 28;

(L) revocation of an order of confirmation under section 1144;

(M) inability to effectuate substantial consummation of a confirmed plan;

(N) material default by the debtor with respect to a confirmed plan;

(O) termination of a confirmed plan by reason of the occurrence of a condition specified in the plan; and

(P) failure of the debtor to pay any domestic support obligation that first becomes payable after the date of the filing of the petition.

We must now apply these new standards to the facts presented.

(B) 11 U.S.C. § 1112(b)'s Burden Shifting

Pursuant to § 1112(b)(1), the initial burden lies with the Movants to establish "cause" for conversion. As noted above, a list of what constitutes "cause" is found in § 1112(b)(4). Generally, such lists are viewed as illustrative rather than exhaustive, and the Court should "consider other factors as they arise." (Citations omitted).

If the Movants establish "cause", then the burden shifts to the Debtor to prove it falls within the § 1112(b)(2) "unusual circumstances" exception to § 1112(b)(1)'s mandatory conversion. Congress explained the exception, stating it only applies if: "(1) the debtor or a party in interest objects and establishes that there is a reasonable likelihood that a plan will be confirmed within the time periods set forth in section 1121(e) and 1129(e), or if these provisions are inapplicable, within a reasonable period of time; (2) the grounds for granting such relief include an act or omission of the debtor for which there exists a reasonable justification for such act or omission; and (3) such act or omission will be cured within a reasonable period of time." H.R. Rep. No. 109-31(1) at 94 (April 8, 2005), *reprinted in* 2005 U.S.C.C.A.N. 88.

(C) Movants Have Established Cause Under 11 U.S.C. § 1112(b)(4)

As noted above, "cause" is defined by a non-exhaustive list of sixteen factors enumerated in § 1112(b)(4). The applicability of the factors is partly dependent on where in the bankruptcy reorganization process we find the debtor. For example, how old is the case? Has exclusivity expired? Has a disclosure statement or, in a small business case, a plan containing adequate information, been approved?

Here, the Debtor allowed exclusivity to expire on July 9, 2007 and has not filed a plan or disclosure statement. The Movants' conversion Motion largely focuses upon:

(A) substantial or continuing loss to or diminution of the estate and the absence of a reasonable likelihood of rehabilitation;

(B) gross mismanagement of the estate;

. . . .

(D) unauthorized use of cash collateral substantially harmful to 1 or more creditors;

. . . .

(I) failure timely to pay taxes owed after the date of the order for relief or to file tax returns due after the date of the order for relief;

(J) failure to file a disclosure statement, or to file or confirm a plan, within the time fixed by this title or by order of the court;

. . . .

There are no outstanding allegations that the Debtor has failed to timely file reports or attend court mandated hearings such as the 341 hearing, nor [are] there any allegations that the Debtor is uninsured. Dr. Poler testified the Debtor was current in its tax payments and the deadlines to file and confirm a plan have not yet expired making Subsections (I) and (J) inapplicable grounds for cause in this instance. Lastly, there have been no allegations of misuse of cash collateral in a manner that would substantially harm any of the creditors. Therefore, the Court's inquiry will focus on whether the Movants have established cause under Subsections (A) or (B) of § 1112(b)(4).

(D) 11 U.S.C. § 1112(b)(4)(A) Substantial or Continuing Loss or Diminution of the Estate and Absence of a Reasonable Likelihood of Rehabilitation

The language in new § 1112(b)(4)(A), "substantial or continuing loss to or diminution of the estate and the absence of a reasonable likelihood of rehabilitation" is almost identical to the pre-BAPCPA amendment § 1112(b)(1)'s provision of "continuing loss to or diminution of the estate and absence of reasonable likelihood of rehabilitation." Therefore, the Court finds that the former case law expounding on former § 1112(b)(1) is equally applicable to new § 1112(b)(4)(A). In a 1991 decision, the Third Circuit summarized the precedent on this factor:

> The Supreme Court has said that "[h]owever honest in its efforts the debtor may be, and however sincere its motives, the District Court is not bound to clog its docket with visionary or impracticable schemes for resuscitation." *Tennessee Publishing Co. v. American Nat'l Bank*, 299 U.S. 18, 22, 57 S.Ct. 85, 87, 81 L.Ed. 13 (1936). "[T]here must be 'a reasonable possibility of a successful reorganization within a reasonable time.' " *United Sav. Ass'n v. Timbers of Inwood Forest Assocs.*, 484 U.S. 365, 376, 108 S.Ct. 626, 632, 98 L.Ed.2d 740 (1988). "Courts usually require the debtor do more than manifest unsubstantiated hopes for a successful reorganization." *In re Canal Place Ltd. Partnership*, 921 F.2d 569, 577 (5th Cir. 1991); *In re Brown*, 951 Fed.2d 564, 572 (3d Cir. 1991).

Thus, the inquiry here is twofold. First, the Court must look at the track record of the Debtor to determine if it is suffering losses or making gains. Second, the Court must determine whether rehabilitation is likely given the evidence presented at hearing.

The Debtor admits its monthly operating reports reflect a downward trend, but urge the Court not to look at the current operating income but rather at the value of the Debtor's assets which it hopes to sell. While the record is replete with Dr. Poler's references to negotiations for asset sales and potential new customers, very few details were elicited at the conversion hearing. The Court notes that only one potential buyer was referred to by name despite the record in the case being sealed.[5] Further, the Debtor did not offer any documentary evidence at the hearing; no draft plan, no financial projections nor any purchase offers. The Court recognizes the genuine desire Dr. Poler has for the company to succeed, and the Court does not question his intentions. However, a majority of his answers were based on optimistic hypothetical projections of undocumented future deals and unnamed future customers. For example, when asked on direct examination what the Debtor would require to reorganize and come out of bankruptcy, Dr. Poler replied that if one made optimistic projections it would take three to four months after a cash infusion to buy new equipment and serve additional customers; however, if one made less optimistic projections, it would take nine to twelve months to become cash-flow positive on a regular basis.

When asked on cross-examination if his projections could be substantiated by anything in writing, Dr. Poler admitted they could not, pointing out that the Debtor has not recently focused on projections stating it was "[a] very small company. We have only so much time and energy, and we have not spent time in recent months on making projections. We focused on the business of keeping the operations going and addressing the issues of the Court." (Audio Record of 9/13/07 at 4:07 p.m.). When pressed further as to the existence of any business model, Dr. Poler stated that the business model could not be discussed at the hearing because "we don't have any of those models here . . . we can't even begin to discuss them. That sort of cash flow and business model is a very complicated thing. It's very difficult to discuss when you are actually working in the spreadsheet much less in very round ambiguous terms in conversation." When asked on cross examination why those models were not produced even though they were explicitly asked for in discovery, Dr. Poler had no explanation.

When asked about future business plans of the Debtor, Dr. Poler discussed selling certain leases for capital and possibly expanding their business dealings with Geisinger Health System, a health care provider to whom the Debtor provides internet service. He also mentioned possibly acquiring a cash-flow positive business with one thousand customers from another corporation who no longer wanted to participate in the wireless internet market. Ultimately, Dr. Poler admitted that many of the "potential customers" the Debtor had contacted or been contacted by would not even commence negotiations until after it had emerged from bankruptcy. No documentation was produced by the Debtor — no commitment letters, no contracts, no emails. Neither were any other witnesses produced to substantiate any of the claims made by Dr. Poler regarding the negotiations with other companies or potential customers. An exhibit introduced at hearing listed a total of

---

[5] All other potential buyers and customers were referred to in very generalized terms such as "a nationally known company" or customers in rural communities or large companies who were said to have contacted the Debtor.

twenty-two customers. Dr. Poler testified that new customer charges range from $39.99 to $119.00 per month.

The Debtor asks the Court to rely solely on Dr. Poler's testimony as grounds for not converting the case. In construing Dr. Poler's credibility, the Court notes that Dr. Poler's records show, post-petition, he has loaned the Debtor in excess of $119,000.00. Further, Geisinger Health System, Dr. Poler's primary employer, is using the Debtor for some of its internet service. Dr. Poler is also scheduled as a pre-petition creditor with claims totaling over $475,000.00. He also acknowledged that interruption of internet services from the Debtor to his primary employer, Geisinger Health System, would be "awkward." The Court cannot ascribe the same weight to his testimony that it would give to that of a disinterested accountant or even a salaried, non-creditor officer or director.

Based upon the above, the Court finds that there is an absence of a reasonable likelihood of rehabilitation of the Debtor in Chapter 11.

With regard to the other prong of § 1112(b)(4)(A), whether the Debtor has suffered continuing losses or diminution of the estate, the Court looks to both the financial prospects of the Debtor and the financial records filed with the Court. The track record of the Debtor suggests a pattern of declining assets and substantial continuing losses. Negative cash flow and an inability to pay current expenses as they come due can satisfy the continuing loss or diminution of the estate standard for purposes of § 1112(b). . . .

At the conversion hearing, the Debtor's October 31, 2006 Financial Statement was admitted into evidence. The Financial Statement shows cash of $384,427.00 on October 31, 2006. The Debtor's schedules show a combined checking account balance of $272,649.06, presumably as of the January 9, 2007 petition date. At the time of the conversion hearing, the Debtor had filed a total of seven monthly operating reports. The reports, most of which were amended, were introduced into evidence. They show a sharp decline in Debtor's cash position. The amended January report shows cash beginning of month of $125,739.00. The amended June report shows cash beginning of month of $11,870.00. No accountant or other expert supplied testimony concerning the Debtor's financial condition.

From January 1, 2007 to July 31, 2007, the Debtor's earnings from accounts receivable and sales totaled $30,671.00. The Debtor's disbursements during this period totaled $335,800.00. Over the same time period, the Debtors amended monthly reports show post-petition loans totaling $172,230.00. Further, a ledger prepared by Dr. Poler was admitted into evidence and shows post-petition borrowings of $233,000.00. (Movants' Exhibit No. 13).

The above facts and figures clearly indicate that the estate is diminishing rapidly at the expense of the creditors. Further troubling is the extensive administrative costs from professional fees that are accumulating as the case lingers in Chapter 11. The Court notes fee applications have been filed by the Debtor's professionals, as of the hearing date, totaling approximately $115,000.00. The applications have not been approved and the figures are net of retainers. The Court is troubled that the accruing post-petition professional claims are not accounted for in Debtor's monthly reports. The post-petition loans detailed above could also subject the Debtor to further administrative claims. The Court finds there is a substantial and continuing diminution of the estate.

(E) Gross Mismanagement of the Estate

Another major impediment the Court sees to the Debtor's rehabilitation is the lack of a focused reorganization management team. Failure to maintain an effective corporate management team has been held to constitute gross mismanagement. . . . The Debtor's sole director works no less than six or seven days a week putting in more than eight hours on each of those days as an anesthesiologist, and then comes home and works another forty plus hours on rehabilitating the Debtor. The only other management is the "acting president" who is ill and was unable to appear at the conversion hearing, either in person or telephonically. The Debtor's time management issues were evidenced when Dr. Poler was asked if he had any business models or projections to present to the Court to establish the likelihood of reorganization. He replied he has not had time recently to work on projections given that he barely had time to keep the business going from day to day and prepare Court documents. The Court recognizes that Semans' health concerns are beyond his control. The time constraints imposed on Dr. Poler by the nature of the anesthesiology profession are likewise unavoidable. However, the Court believes that successful restructuring of a business of this size and complexity requires more time and experience than present management can marshal.

It was also fairly evident from Dr. Poler's testimony that he was not closely monitoring the monthly operating reports filed in this case. Illustratively, the monthly operating reports listed the post-petition loans made to the Debtor as coming from Dr. Poler and one other person. He testified at the hearing that the loans really came from over eighteen different people; eleven of whom are his colleagues at his primary employer, Geisinger Health System. Dr. Poler testified that he does not personally review nor sign the monthly operating reports before they are filed. He testified he knows that the accountants prepare them but beyond that he had no knowledge of what process they went through before they were filed. The Debtor's accountants did not testify at the conversion hearing. Dr. Poler later testified that he does not review the monthly operating reports because he relies on Semans to interpret the Debtor's financial information. Only the original January monthly operating report was signed on behalf of the Debtor; the remainder are unsigned. These reports are required by § 308 and should at the very least have been signed by Debtor's counsel.[7]

That being said, of the seven monthly operating reports filed, five had to be amended because of errors. . . .

A debtor-in-possession is vested with significant powers under the provision of the Bankruptcy Code. As is often the case, those powers come with certain responsibilities. Significantly, a debtor-in-possession owes a fiduciary duty to its creditors. A debtor-in-possession has a duty to keep the Court and its creditors informed about the status and condition of its business. The Court has serious

---

[7] Fed. R. Bankr. P. 9011(a) "every petition pleading, written motion, and other paper . . . shall be signed by at least one attorney of record."

questions as to whether the Debtor's monthly reports, and some of the aspects of Dr. Poler's testimony discussed herein, meet the required standards.

Perhaps the greatest indicia of mismanagement is Dr. Poler's practice of making and accepting loans on an oral basis on behalf of the Debtor. Dr. Poler testified that the Debtor was currently being funded by loans from individuals which were made orally and on terms agreed to by him. As of the conversion hearing, the Debtor had received at least $233,000.00 in loans pursuant to these verbal agreements negotiated by Dr. Poler. He testified that the interest rate was 12% per annum. No notes or other loan documents were executed. Apparently, the loans have no agreed to payback date and they will be repaid "when the company is able to repay it." Dr. Poler testified that repayment terms had not been explicitly discussed and stated "these individuals made these contributions to maintaining the solvency of the company voluntarily, understanding that it was uncertain we would be able to repay them but with the expectation that we would." Further, the Court has never been asked to approve the numerous post-petition loans the corporate Debtor has obtained. There is no evidence that these corporate borrowings were authorized by resolution or other corporate action.

Some background on the Debtor's efforts concerning post-petition financing is in order. In April 2007, the Debtor filed a Motion seeking Court approval for the Debtor to obtain a post-petition secured credit line of $250,000.00 from Dr. Poler. The financing would have borne interest at 10% per annum. The Motion identified Dr. Poler as the lender. Limited objections were filed and, after hearing, Court approval of the proposed secured loan was denied. As part of his testimony at the conversion hearing, Dr. Poler testified that in actuality, the line of credit funds would have been obtained from a number of "participants" whose funds would be funneled through Dr. Poler to the Debtor. This was not disclosed in seeking Court approval of the credit line.

The Court finds that entering into unapproved, unauthorized corporate borrowings on "oral terms" is evidence of gross mismanagement of the estate. These informal borrowings could leave the estate subject to claims by lenders for inflated or fraudulent sums. How would the estate defend against such claims without any loan documentation? Also, one who makes loans to a Chapter 11 debtor without Court approval does so at his peril. *In re Lehigh Valley Professional Sports Club, Inc.*, 260 B.R. 745, 750 (Bankr. E.D.Pa. 2001). There is nothing in the record to show that the Debtor disclosed this risk to the many post-petition lenders.

It is not in the best interests of creditors to allow these practices to continue. Gross mismanagement alone is sufficient grounds for conversion from Chapter 11 to Chapter 7.

. . . .

(F) 11 U.S.C. § 1112(b)(2) Debtor's Burden to Specifically Identify "Unusual Circumstances" Such That it Would Be in the Best Interest of Creditors to Stay in Chapter 11

In order for the Court to deny conversion under § 1112(b)(1), the Court must be able to "specifically identify" factors to establish conversion is not in the best interest of the creditors and the estate. 11 U.S.C. § 1112(b)(2). *See also*, H.R. Rep. No. 109-31(1) at 94 (2005), *reprinted in* 2005 U.S.C.C.A.N. 88, 2005 WL 832198 (Congressional Record stating that § 1112(b) was amended "to mandate that the court convert or dismiss a chapter 11 case . . . the court must specify the circumstances that support the court's finding that conversion or dismissal is not in the best interests of the estate."). The Debtor filed a post-conversion hearing brief which essentially asserts three sets of special circumstances: (1) problems caused by the Debtor's former directors, who are the Movants; (2) reorganizational difficulties caused by the Movants' multiple objections herein; and, (3) the Debtor's post-conversion Brief also argues that conversion is not in the best interests of creditors.

The Court is inclined to believe that "unusual circumstances" under § 1112(b)(2) should be presently existing conditions or facts, rather than perceived past mistakes or events.

. . . .

The Court . . . believes that the likelihood of rehabilitation in this case would have been enhanced if Dr. Poler had spent less time looking in the rearview mirror and more time in piloting the Debtor toward a prompt reorganization.

. . . .

The Debtor's Brief suggests that it is in the best interests of creditors for the Debtor to remain in Chapter 11 and sell its lease rights. The record suggests otherwise. There was no testimony that any purchaser was interested in buying the Debtor as a going concern. The Court finds that a liquidation by a Chapter 7 trustee will be more likely to yield a greater distribution to creditors than for the Debtor to remain in Chapter 11. The Court believes that the value of the Debtor's assets can be more effectively realized by a Chapter 7 trustee than by the Debtor. Chapter 7 cases generally have lower administrative expenses and bankruptcy trustees are accustomed to consummating the sale of a variety of assets, tangible and intangible. Therefore, conversion is in the best interest of creditors.

IV. Conclusion

Under BAPCPA, the Court must make a decision which fosters the best interests of creditors. This is not a change from prior law.

It is significant to the Court that four of the five Movants filed Proofs of Claim which total approximately $628,897.00. This sum represents nearly one-third of the scheduled pre-petition debt. The fact that these creditors support conversion is not determinative of the outcome, but it must be given serious consideration.

Ultimately, the Debtor has left the Court to wonder about elements which were its burden to establish. Is there a reasonable likelihood of rehabilitation? Does the Debtor, in fact, have a plan to reorganize? If so, why keep it secret from the Court and its creditors? Has the Debtor made any financial projections to establish some feasibility to even a skeletal plan? Again, if so, why keep it a secret?

. . . .

It is in the best interests of creditors to grant the conversion to Chapter 7 thereby stemming the operating losses and allowing for a prompt and orderly liquidation. This should provide a distribution to creditors in accordance with the Bankruptcy Code's priorities.

NOTES AND QUESTIONS

(1) *Was Sheldon Toibb a Model Debtor?* Can you reconcile the *Toibb, Victory,* and *Gateway* holdings? Consider this: If the primary purpose of Chapter 11 is to maximize the value of the estate in order, among other things, to enhance the recovery for creditors, isn't Sheldon Toibb's case a paradigm Chapter 11 case? After all, what would Toibb's creditors have recovered in a Chapter 7 liquidation? What did they stand to recover under Toibb's Chapter 11 plan? How would Victory's or Gateway's creditors have fared if their Chapter 11 cases were allowed to continue, compared to if they were dismissed? Did Victory even have any creditors other than the secured creditors who opposed the filing?

Sheldon Toibb was not, strictly speaking, a going business, but he did own an interest in a troubled business, and his purpose in filing was to preserve the value of that interest for himself and, perhaps secondarily, his creditors. As the Supreme Court pointed out, the preservation of asset values and the maximization of creditor recovery are among the vaunted goals of reorganization policy. Isn't Toibb's situation easily distinguished from that of a moribund debtor who invokes Chapter 11 in order to postpone the inevitable while it holds estate property hostage and speculates with it at the expense of creditors?

Is "bad faith" still a basis for dismissing a case or granting stay relief in light of the Supreme Court's holding that a debtor may seek relief in Chapter 11 even if it is not engaged in a going business? As the *Gateway* opinion demonstrates, even in the post-*Toibb* era, courts have continued to show an unwillingness to let debtors linger or languish in Chapter 11 when their prospects for recovery are bleak, or when their purpose in filing is merely delay, when that delay does nothing to benefit creditors, and when continuation of the case serves no discernable legitimate purpose.

(2) *SARE Scare.* The *Victory Construction* opinion is a bit long in the tooth, having been decided in 1982 and subsequently vacated as moot. It nevertheless is included here, because it provides an "excellent" exegesis on the development of the good faith doctrine,[1] and because it also provides an early example of a particular species of Chapter 11 case that has become the bane of creditors and courts: the Single Asset Real Estate ("SARE") case.

SARE cases follow a common scenario. The debtor is a corporation or partnership whose sole asset is an apartment or office building. The property is subject to a mortgage. A downturn in the real estate market produces a decline in rental

---

[1] Not everyone agrees. *Compare Little Creek Development Co. v. Commonwealth Mortgage Co. (In re Little Creek Development Co.),* 779 F.2d 1068, 1971 (5th Cir. 1986), *with* Janet A. Flaccus, *Have Eight Circuits Shorted? Good Faith and Chapter 11 Bankruptcy Petitions,* 67 Am. Bankr. L.J. 401, 412 (1993).

income, making it impossible for the debtor to service its mortgage debt. The downturn in the market also means depressed real estate values, and, as a result, the amount of the debt often exceeds the value of the property. The mortgagee is the debtor's largest creditor, and often its only significant creditor. The debtor has few if any employees. The debtor defaults. The debtor and the mortgagee are unable to work things out, and the mortgagee takes steps to foreclose. In order to stave off foreclosure — indeed often on the very eve of foreclosure — the debtor files a Chapter 11 petition, invoking the automatic stay and stopping the foreclosing creditor in its tracks.[2] In many cases, the debtor's owners are less concerned about losing their investment than they are about the dire tax consequences of foreclosure.[3] After the petition is filed, the mortgagee responds by seeking relief from the automatic stay or dismissal or conversion of the case on the grounds that the petition was filed "in bad faith."

To many, SARE cases have long been the *bete noire* of Chapter 11. Secured creditors hate them, because they tie up their collateral for the duration of the case, unless they manage to get relief from the stay or the case dismissed. If the real estate is worth less than the amount of the claim it secures, the claim is not accruing interest, because, as you may recall from the basic bankruptcy course, interest does not accrue on un- or undersecured claims. Code § 502(b)(2). Meanwhile, financially strapped debtors may not be paying real estate taxes and performing maintenance. As a result, collateral values and the position of the secured creditor are eroding. Thus, the risks and costs of SARE cases fall mainly on secured creditors. Bankruptcy judges don't particularly crave SARE cases either, because they clog their dockets with cases that are not especially interesting and that often are doomed. Commentators criticize SARE cases as inconsistent with the Chapter 11 policy of maximizing capital and going concern values for the benefit of the entire creditor body, because in most cases, the objecting secured creditor *is* the creditor body (unsecured creditors being few or non-existent), and the asset is worth what it's worth, irrespective of who owns it. Thus, SARE cases are usually two-party disputes involving a debtor and a mortgagee; unsecured creditors rarely have more than a *de minimus* stake in the outcome. Nevertheless, debtors continue to file SARE cases because they believe they have everything to gain and little to lose by so doing. This, however, is not always the case. From time to time, courts have

---

[2] In some, but not all cases, in an attempt to isolate the sick property from well performing assets, the debtor will first convey the distressed property to a new entity, which in turn files the Chapter 11 petition. When the property is transferred to a new or different entity on the eve of commencing a Chapter 11 case, the case bears the additional taint of the "new debtor syndrome."

[3] Professors Carlson and Williams explain why: "A foreclosure constitutes a taxable event for these investors — an event that could trigger bad tax developments for high income investors. A quick example will serve to illustrate the matter. Suppose a real estate partnership buys a building for $150 based on nonrecourse secured financing of $100. Recession hits, and the building declines to a value of $80 — common enough numbers in the early 1990s. Suppose further that the basis of the property has been adjusted from $150 to $70 because of depreciation deductions enjoyed by [the investors] in prior years. If the lender forecloses on the property, the partners would have to report $30 in gain (i.e., $100 (debt) – 70 (adjusted basis) = 30). The tax liability is particularly galling in that the gain is entirely a phantom. The partners have not actually received the $30. Rather this phantom gain is merely attributed to them. Yet the partners must pay their tax in *real* dollars, not phantom ones, and in the year in which the foreclosure sale takes place." David Gray Carlson & Jack F. Williams, *The Truth About the New Value Exception to Bankruptcy's Absolute Priority Rule*, 21 Cardozo L. Rev. 1303, 1311–12 (2000)

sanctioned attorneys and debtors for commencing a case in bad faith. *See* R. Bankr. P. 9011; *In re Marsch*, 36 F.3d 825 (9th Cir. 1994); *In re Y.J. Sons & Co., Inc.*, 212 B.R. 793 (Bankr. D.N.J. 1997).

Although the clearest case of bad faith may be where the debtor files knowing the situation is hopeless, it is, as courts have pointed out, "unlikely that a debtor will ever acknowledge its own bad faith; therefore one will reach conclusions about [a debtor's] intent from the totality of the circumstances surrounding the filing of the case." *In re Roxy Real Estate Co., Inc.*, 170 B.R. 571, 573 (Bankr. E.D. Pa. 1993). Thus, "determining whether the debtor's filing for relief is in good faith depends largely upon the bankruptcy court's on-the-spot evaluation of the debtor's financial condition, motives, and the local financial realities. Findings of lack of good faith in proceedings based on §§ 362(d) or 1112(b) have been predicated on certain recurring but non-exclusive patterns, and they are based on a conglomerate of factors rather than on any single datum." *In re Little Creek Development Co.*, 779 F.2d 1068, 1072 (5th Cir. 1986). In a cyclical real estate market, courts have been faced time and time again with SARE cases, and they have developed a list of "circumstantial factors," generally regarded as indicative of a bad faith filing:

1. The debtor has few or no unsecured creditors;

2. There has been a previous bankruptcy petition by the debtor or a related entity;

3. The pre-petition conduct of the debtor has been improper;

4. The petition effectively allows the debtor to evade court orders;

5. There are few debts to non-moving creditors;

6. The petition was filed on the eve of foreclosure;

7. The foreclosed property is the sole or major asset of the debtor;

8. The debtor has no ongoing business or employees;

9. There is no possibility of reorganization;

10. The debtor's income is not sufficient to operate;

11. There was no pressure from non-moving creditors;

12. Reorganization essentially involves the resolution of a two-party dispute;

13. A corporate debtor was formed and received title to its major assets immediately before the petition; or

14. The debtor filed solely to create the automatic stay.

See, e.g., In re Wentworth, 83 B.R. 705, 707 (Bankr. D.N.D. 1988). One court has suggested that the label "bad faith" is something of a misnomer, at least when applied to debtors that are gripped by terminal euphoria rather than a more evil intent to delay and harass creditors. *In re McCormick Road Associates*, 127 B.R. 410 (N.D. Ill. 1991). Another has suggested that a debtor's subjective intent is not determinative. Rather, the issue is whether the goal of the filing is to "achieve objectives outside the legitimate scope of the bankruptcy laws." *Marsch v. Marsch (In re Marsch)*, 36 F.3d 825, 828 (9th Cir. 1994).

In 1994, in order to curb perceived abuses in single asset cases, Code § 362(d) was amended by the addition of a new subsection (3). New subsection (d)(3) was itself amended in 2005. Section 362(d)(3) now provides that in a single asset real estate case, if a creditor whose claim is secured by a mortgage on the real estate requests relief from the stay, the court must grant relief unless, within the later of 90 days after the commencement of the case or 30 days after the court determines that § 362(d)(3) applies, a single asset real estate debtor files a plan that has a reasonable possibility of being confirmed within a reasonable time or begins making interest payments to the secured creditor at the applicable nondefault contract rate of interest. In order to determine whether § 362(d)(3) applies, the court must determine that the case is a single asset real estate case. Code § 101(51B) defines "single asset real estate" as "real property constituting a single property or project, other than residential real property with fewer than 4 residential units, which generates substantially all of the gross income of a debtor who is not a family farmer and on which no substantial business is being conducted by the debtor other than the business of operating real property. . . . " Interestingly, in *In re Webb Mountain LLC*, 2008 U.S. Dist. LEXIS 10030 (E.D. Tenn. Feb. 8, 2008), the court held that the existence of § 362(d)(3) signals that the Code expressly permits single asset real estate bankruptcies and that the single asset nature of a case is not necessarily evidence of bad faith. The court also rejected the notion that "[b]leak financial health cannot be considered 'atypical' or 'extraordinary' in the bankruptcy setting" and thus indicative of bad faith." *Id.* at *12.

Yet another weapon in the mortgagee's arsenal is Code § 362(d)(4), which was added by the 2005 amendments. It gives bankruptcy courts authority to enter orders granting relief from the stay "in rem." Such a stay "runs with the land" so to speak. It addresses a problem similar to the one depicted in the *Victory* case. Suppose that Devonshire Company, which owns an office building, files a Chapter 11 petition. The bank that holds a mortgage on the property moves for relief from the stay in order to commence or continue a foreclosure action. The bankruptcy court grants relief, but before the bank can get a judgment of foreclosure and sell the property, Devonshire transfers the office building to Victory Construction Company, which, in turn, files a Chapter 11 petition. Code § 362(d)(4) provides that if a court finds that the bankruptcy filing by Victory was part of a scheme to delay, hinder and defraud creditors, then an order granting relief from the stay, if properly recorded under applicable state law, would continue to apply to the subject property (as opposed to the debtor) in bankruptcy cases filed within two years of recording. Thus, serial filings to prevent foreclosure on a piece of property would be thwarted. Section 362(d)(4) provides an exception to the in rem stay for subsequent filings necessitated by changed circumstances or other good cause. We will examine § 362(d)(4) more closely in chapter 3 of the text.

Another weapon in the secured creditor's arsenal is Code § 362(d)(2), which provides for relief from the automatic stay with respect to an act against property when the debtor lacks equity in the property and the property is not necessary to an effective reorganization. If there is no hope of reorganizing the debtor's business, one can argue that the property cannot be said to be "necessary" within the meaning of this section. As a practical matter, at least from a SARE debtor's perspective, stay relief, dismissal, and even conversion to Chapter 7 produce the same devastating result: foreclosure and liquidation.

Although SARE cases do account for a large share of "bad faith" cases, SARE cases are not always found to be commenced in bad faith. For example, in cases where a debtor does have substantial equity in the real property, courts have reasoned, with justification, that the petition should not be dismissed, at least not before the debtor has had time to propose a reorganization plan, even though some other indicia of bad faith may be present. *See, e.g., In re Can-Alta Properties, Ltd.*, 87 B.R. 89 (B.A.P. 9th Cir. 1988). Conversely, in a case where the debtor displayed what might be regarded as very bad faith by threatening to tie up a foreclosure action "for years," and by filing its Chapter 11 petition in a district located 700 miles from its creditors and assets, the court found that the debtor was so tainted by "an intent to abuse the judicial process and the purposes of the reorganization provisions," that the case should be dismissed even though the debtor had equity in the property and a successful reorganization was possible. *Phoenix Piccadilly, Ltd. v. Life Insurance Co. of Va. (In re Phoenix Piccadilly, Ltd.)*, 849 F.2d 1393 (11th Cir. 1988).

Where a debtor lacks equity in the property, but proffers some reasonable hope for developing a successful reorganization plan within a reasonable time, is dismissal appropriate? *See In re I-95 Technology-Industrial Park, L.P.*, 126 B.R. 11 (Bankr. D.R.I. 1991), and *In re Alyucan Interstate Corp.*, reproduced in chapter 3 of the text , wherein the courts, in the absence of any other signs of bad faith, favored giving the debtor time and a chance to reorganize.

(3) *Dismissal or Conversion under § 1112(b).* Although bad faith has been found to be "cause" for converting or dismissing a case under Code § 1112(b), that section also provides several specific examples of cause that may be independent of a debtor's subjective intent. They also contemplate problems that may be identified at later stages of the case, not necessarily at the outset. For example, Code § 1112(b)(4)(A) authorizes conversion or dismissal when the value of the estate is eroding and there is no reasonable likelihood of rehabilitating the debtor, Code §§ 1112(b)(4)(J) and (M) are aimed at cases in which there is a failure to propose and confirm a plan in a timely fashion.

Of course, when, as in *Gateway*, enough time has passed, only hindsight is required to see that the goals of Chapter 11 can't be met within a reasonable time, at a reasonable cost, or at all. When the likelihood of a successful rehabilitation is demonstrably slim, prompt conversion of a case from Chapter 11 to Chapter 7 or dismissal makes good economic sense — judicial and otherwise. When motions are made early on in a case, the decision is apt to be harder. If you were the judge, what information would you want in order to fairly evaluate a debtor's prospects? Would you want to know if anyone in the debtor's business is making money? Does what the debtor sells work? Are there non-revenue generating expenses that can be eliminated? If the debtor's assets are decreasing in value, is there any way to reverse that trend? Does the debtor have unprofitable operations that it can shed and profitable divisions that it can retain? Would a change in management turn the business around? Note that Code § 1112(b)(1) contemplates the appointment of a trustee or examiner as an alternative to conversion or dismissal. The role of trustees and examiners is discussed in chapter 4 of the text.

Notably, the viability of a debtor is an issue that surfaces from time to time, in various contexts, at various stages of a Chapter 11 case. The debtor's ability to rehabilitate or reorganize may be determinative of such critical questions as whether the debtor should be permitted to incur post-petition indebtedness, whether it should be permitted to assume executory contracts, and whether it should be allowed to spend cash collateral and consume other property of the estate in the operation of the business. Thus, even if no party moves for conversion or dismissal, the viability of the debtor is an issue that is likely to surface even before a court is asked to rule on the feasibility of a debtor's reorganization plan.

The term "rehabilitation" as employed in Code § 1112(b)(4)(A) means "to reestablish a business," not to liquidate it. Resnick & Sommer, *Collier on Bankruptcy* ¶ 1112.04[6][a] (16th Edition 2012). What about a debtor who files for the stated purpose of conducting an orderly liquidation of its assets pursuant to Code § 1123(a)(5)(D), which provides that a Chapter 11 plan may provide for "the sale of all or part of the estate"? What about a case in which, soon after a petition is filed, the practical necessity of selling its most valuable assets becomes apparent? According to Professors Baird and Rasmussen, "Many [firms] use Chapter 11 merely to sell their assets and divide up the proceeds. TWA filed only to consummate the sale of its planes and landing gates to American Airlines. Enron's principal assets, including its trading operation and its most valuable pipelines, were sold within a few months of its bankruptcy petition. Within weeks of filing for Chapter 11, Budget sold most of its assets to the parent company of Avis. Similarly, Polaroid entered Chapter 11 and sold most of its assets to the private equity group at BankOne." D. Baird & R. Rasmussen, *The End of Bankruptcy*, 55 Stan. L. Rev. 751, 751–52 (2002). More recently, companies such as Lehman Brothers, and Linens & Things, and, of course, General Motors and Chrysler, have filed Chapter 11 petitions and proceeded to market and sell key assets and divisions. Were such cases commenced in bad faith? If losses are continuing, must the case be converted or dismissed? If Chapter 11 provides a more efficient mechanism for wringing value out of a firm's assets than does a Chapter 7 liquidation, isn't it the preferable route? Was Sheldon Toibb seeking to reorganize his "business" or to liquidate it?

(4) *Victory Part Deux*. This brings us back to the *Victory Construction* case. One might reasonably expect that promptly after Judge Ordin entered his unflinching order granting relief from the stay, the property at 8511 Beverly Place would have gone on the auction block. This is not what happened. Victory appealed from Judge Ordin's order and sought a stay pending the outcome of the appeal. Judge Ordin agreed to stay his order, but only on the condition that Victory pay to Hadley, the secured creditor owed $1.3 million, monthly interest at the then prevailing market rate of 18%. In addition, Judge Ordin demanded that Victory keep up with taxes, fire insurance premiums, and payments on liens senior to Hadley's. What happened next has been chronicled as follows:

> One might have thought that the focus would have shifted to the appellate panel at this point, but it was not to be so. Instead on May 19, 1981, Victory, enjoying the protection of its appeal stay, made the logical next move of a Chapter 11 debtor — it proposed a plan. The plan undertook, among other things, to reinstate Hadley at his original contract rate. The debtor later abandoned that first plan, evidently anticipating that

Judge Ordin would deny confirmation. Instead, the debtor on December 10, 1981 offered an amended plan. The most noteworthy distinctions of the amended plan were, first, a 50 percent increase in the interest rate proposed for Hadley (from eight to 12 percent), and, second, the inclusion of a personal guarantee from Severyn Ashkenazy and his brother, Arnold Ashkenazy.

Over the next year and a half, that amended plan subsided into a farrago of conflict where it very nearly disappeared. There were a succession of objections, hearings on objections, findings, objections to findings and the like, all of which seemed to accomplish little on either side, except to generate attorneys' fees. Hadley was the principal opponent but along about the end of 1982 he picked up an ally — Cal Fed, previously quiescent but henceforth energetically active in opposition.

In re Victory Construction Co., 42 B.R. 145, 146–148 (Bankr. C.D. Cal. 1984).

On February 15, 1984, three years after Judge Ordin ordered relief from the stay and several months after Judge Ordin retired from the bench, the Bankruptcy Appellate Panel for the Ninth Circuit rendered its decision on Victory's appeal. *In re Victory Construction Co.*, 37 B.R. 222 (B.A.P. 9th Cir. 1984). The Appellate Panel reviewed Victory's post-appeal conduct, noting the propriety of such an approach:

> Ordinarily an appellate court should base its decision on the facts as they existed at the time the trial court made its decision. However, the on-going nature of bankruptcy proceedings, on occasion, creates situations where the reviewing court may take notice of fundamental events occurring after the entry of the judgment from which appeal was taken.

37 B.R. at 227 (citation omitted). In so doing, the court found that in the time which had elapsed, the debtor's principals had contributed sufficient funds to pay off several claims and bring all secured claims current. In addition, the debtor had managed to propose a second amended reorganization plan that provided that Victory would pay interest to the remaining secured creditors at the market rate, rather than the contract rates, which were lower. The appellate panel further noted that Judge Ordin, himself, in the course of one of several hearings on the debtor's proposed reorganization plan, had suggested the possibility that Victory had, by its conduct, "purged" itself of bad faith:

> THE COURT: Now, wait a second. When Victory picked this parcel out of the Leslie Linder bankruptcy, you had a six year note at 8% totally defaulted as to interest.
>
> MR. MORITZ [the secured creditor's attorney]: And a right to foreclose.
>
> THE COURT: Right. Okay. Victory bought it and went into a Chapter 11 with it and is now in cash going to bring you to the same position you had been — as you had been getting interest payments currently through the Leslie Linder bankruptcy to the current time. Now, that means that Victory is going to give Hadley and Ashkenazy and his brother is going to stand behind Victory, close behind them. Now, to assure Hadley the benefit of the bargain that Hadley made before Mr. Roven came in the picture. Now, Mr.

Moritz, fair is fair. You have always maintained the position of injured innocence, and the Court has sustained it because I think the facts warrant it, but now we have a cash current position where Hadley is in the position he bargained for plus four percent and a guarantor. It is very difficult for me to understand what you are arguing for unless you are arguing that everything has been tainted with speculator's blood when they walked in. I think, Mr. Moritz, that deceleration is a right of a debtor. And in this case with a new solvent guarantor and a raising of the interest rate by 50%, that it is hard not to believe you are taking two positions.

One, punitive where you are the bad guy and therefore you just perish. And number two, there has been an increase in the market and we want our cut. . . . Victory bought a transaction that your people voluntarily entered into and because they filed the bankruptcy in bad faith . . . but now what they have done, they have purged the bad faith . . . . they have proposed a plan which in and of itself is not bad faith. They are no longer seeking to secure the benefit of what they did.

MR. MORITZ: They are benefitting by cheap financing.

THE COURT: Sir, your clients are being brought current. You have a 50% increase in the interest rate and you have a solvent guarantor.

37 B.R. at 227–28. In light of the debtor's changed position, the appellate panel concluded that the appeal had been rendered moot and vacated Judge Ordin's order:

As a result of the trial court's de facto reversal of its own order, substantial payments have been made by the debtor, the purpose and application of which remain undefined but require consideration in the light of the changed relationship which now obtains between appellees and the debtor. There is little question but that events subsequent to appeal have outrun the original issues, thereby rendering them moot.

37 B.R. at 228–29.

But wait. There's more. About six months after the appellate panel vacated Judge Ordin's order, Judge Ayer, who succeeded Judge Ordin, confirmed Victory's reorganization plan. *In re Victory Construction Co.*, 42 B.R. 145 (Bankr. C.D. Cal. 1984). At the same time, and with deference in every direction, he set forth his view of how the good faith of a Chapter 11 debtor ought to be measured:

I am of course not free to excise the concept of good faith from the law of bankruptcy, even if I chose. *See e.g.*, 11 U.S.C. 1129(a)(3) (1982) ("good faith" as a statutory confirmation standard); *In re Thirtieth Place, Inc.*, 30 B.R. 503 (B.A.P. 9th Cir. 1983). But the cases make it clear that this provision is to be read restrictively. It is on this basis that I review the issue of good faith one more time.

Victory is a one-asset, secured-credit real estate case, after the manner of an old Chapter XII. Whatever may have been the rule four years ago, it now seems clear that a one-asset, secured-credit real estate case is properly within the jurisdiction of the bankruptcy court. Indeed, cases of this sort account for perhaps as much as half of our Chapter 11 docket.

Victory was a moribund corporation, revivified to take title to the asset in question, just shortly before filing. In *Thirtieth Place, supra,* the appellate panel ordered relief on facts that bear a superficial similarity to these — a shell corporation, created to take title to the subject property. But the differences seem to me to be crucial. First, it appears that the corporation in *Thirtieth Place* took title solely for the purpose of filling the proceeding. The record here supports a different inference. It seems almost certain that Roven considered bankruptcy as a possibility before taking title in Victory. But it seems equally likely that he also wanted to continue negotiating with his creditors, and he wanted to avoid bankruptcy if possible. Second, *Thirtieth Place* is a case of pure self-dealing. The transferor and transferee were in essence the same enterprise. The transaction was a peel-off, presumably to protect the transferor's balance sheet. Here, the transferor was a third party — the trustee of the London Club. He could have refused to sell to Victory if he wished. He could have insisted on a guarantee from Roven. And Roven could have walked away. Evidently the trustee, in a position to appraise the risks, thought this was the best deal he could get.

. . . .

What seems to bother Hadley and Cal Fed most in this case is that Roven appears to be a man unterrified by the idea of bankruptcy. He creates corporations to insulate his personal assets. If their future is promising, he sees to it that they get money — very carefully, like water in a drip irrigation system. If not, he seeks the protection of the court. He clearly takes the possibility of bankruptcy into account. Indeed, perhaps the most remarkable thing about this record is that the man who as trustee sold the London Club to Victory is the same man who as attorney represented Devonshire in its Chapter XI case (he also now represents Ashkenazy in this case). There has never been any secret of this, and so far as I can tell, none of the creditors asserts that there is any specific impropriety here. But it does suggest a certain inbred, neurasthenic quality that is bound to aggravate the frustration of anyone who thinks a debtor ought to pay his bills.

All of this might suggest "bad faith" to the person on the street. But ironically, as I tried to suggest above, a too free use of the concept in the bankruptcy court may increase, rather than reduce, the confusion in a case like this, and correspondingly increase the capacity of debtors to keep creditors at bay. I do not think that Congress, glossed by the appellate panel, intended me to use the concept in that way. For these reasons, I think the general issue of "good faith" must be resolved in favor of the debtor, and I so hold.

I do not for a moment suggest that a case should proceed as this one has proceeded.

42 B.R. at 149–50.

(5) *Postpetition Behavior Warranting Dismissal.* "Cause" for dismissal has also been found where debtors have abused the court's jurisdiction and their creditors' patience by their post-petition behavior. Thus, in *In re Kerr*, 908 F.2d 400, 404 (8th Cir. 1990), the Court of Appeals upheld the bankruptcy court's dismissal of a case, explaining that the debtors had violated court orders by failing to provide monthly financial reports, by transferring estate property without court approval and, by commingling the debtor's assets with assets of related entities. Similarly, and not surprisingly, in *In re Rognstad*, 121 B.R. 45 (Bankr. D. Hawaii 1990), the court dismissed a petition filed two years earlier, because the debtors had failed to file financial statements and pay quarterly fees, had transferred assets without the court's knowledge or permission, had filed a false statement of affairs, and had disobeyed various court orders. This is the kind of problematic behavior that is covered by Code §§ 1112(b)(4)(E)–(K).

(6) *Appeal Bond Cases.* A number of Chapter 11 cases have been commenced by debtors who were unable to post supersedeas bonds to stay enforcement of judgments pending appeal. The most famous of these involved Texaco, the oil company. Its competitor, Pennzoil Company, obtained a $10.53 billion judgment against Texaco for tortious interference with a merger agreement between Pennzoil and Getty Oil Company. To avoid execution on its assets, Texaco was required to post a bond at least equal to the total amount of the judgment plus interest, which amounted to about $13 billion. This sum was far more, all agreed, than the world's entire surety bond capacity at the time and arguably more than Texaco's net worth. Six days after Texaco failed to obtain relief from the Supreme Court, Texaco filed a Chapter 11 petition, stating that the filing was the only way to pursue its appeal. Interestingly, the Texaco filing was not contested on the grounds that it was a bad faith attempt to avoid the bonding requirement. Other cases, however, have been challenged as bad faith filings, and courts have disagreed about whether such filings are in bad faith. In *In re Alton Telegraph Printing Co.*, 14 B.R. 238 (Bankr. S.D. Ill. 1981), the debtor-newspaper sought Chapter 11 protection after a large libel judgment was entered against it. The bankruptcy court refused to dismiss the petition, explaining,

> [T]he debtor, the Alton Telegraph, is an ongoing and viable business that would not be involved in a Chapter 11 bankruptcy if it were not for the libel judgment . . . pending against it. . . . The Telegraph employs a substantial number of people and is a viable business. The debtor has filed a plan of reorganization, and the case is progressing through the court in an orderly and expeditious manner. . . . It is clear, however, that in light of the judgment . . . the Alton Telegraph is not in sound financial shape at the present time, and is eligible for relief under the Code.
>
> The debtor alleges that it has been forced into bankruptcy in order to avoid the forced sale and liquidation of its business to satisfy the libel judgment. . . . It admits that it was not able to obtain a supersedeas bond to forestall execution because of the amount of the judgment in relation to the Telegraph's net worth.

14 B.R. at 241. But, in *In re Marsch*, 36 F.3d 825 (9th Cir. 1994), the court reached the opposite conclusion, holding that the debtor could not use Chapter 11 to avoid

posting an appeal bond where she had the clear ability to satisfy the judgment:

> The bankruptcy court found that the debtor's Chapter 11 petition was filed solely to delay collection of the restitution judgment and to avoid posting an appeal bond. Even assuming a Chapter 11 petition may be used for this purpose when enforcement of a judgment would cause severe business disruption, a question we leave open, this would not help the debtor here. ... [T]he debtor had the financial means to pay the judgment. Moreover, because she wasn't involved in a business venture, the judgment didn't pose any danger of disrupting business interests . . . [T]he debtor's petition was filed in bad faith. Dismissal of the petition for cause pursuant to section 1112(b) was proper.

36 F.3d at 829. Are the two cases distinguishable? If so, how would these courts have come out in *Texaco/Pennzoil*?

(7) *Is Insolvency a Requirement for "Good Faith?"* Many cases dismissed on bad faith grounds involve debtors that are perceived to be too sick to be rehabilitated. Might a debtor be too healthy to qualify for Chapter 11 relief? To be eligible for relief under Chapters X or XI of the former Bankruptcy Act, a debtor had to be insolvent or unable to pay its debts as they matured. Chapter 11 contains no insolvency requirement. Cases, such as the historic one filed by Johns-Manville Corp., have tested the implications of that change.

When Manville, the world's largest manufacturer of asbestos containing products, filed a Chapter 11 petition, it stated that the sole reason for filing was its inability to defend the many thousands of product liability lawsuits then and soon to be pending against it all over the country. The actions had been brought by plaintiffs who claimed that they had developed asbestos-related diseases as a result of coming into contact with products manufactured by Manville.

Some 16 months after the case was filed, four separate motions to dismiss the Manville petition pursuant to section 1112(b) were filed by various parties in interest. Three of the movants were asbestos manufacturers that were co-defendants with Manville in many of the pending state court actions. The essence of their argument was that since the Bankruptcy Code contained no provisions for dealing with asbestos claims that arose in the future (so-called "future claims"), the case was doomed from the outset and therefore commenced in bad faith.

The bankruptcy court disagreed. The court concluded that such claims could be dealt with in Chapter 11, and indeed, on the same day that it decided the dismissal motions, the court issued a separate opinion holding that future asbestos claimants were entitled to representation in the *Manville* case. *In re Johns Manville Corp.*, 36 B.R. 743 (Bankr. S.D.N.Y. 1984). The fourth motion to dismiss was made by the "Committee of Asbestos-Related Litigants and/or Creditors," also known as the Asbestos Committee, which had been organized early in the case to represent the products liability plaintiffs. It was composed mainly of the plaintiffs' attorneys. The Committee alleged that Manville had exaggerated "the profundity of its economic distress" and had "concocted evidence to meet the requirements for filing a Chapter 11 petition."

The court denied the motion, finding that insolvency was not the admission ticket to Chapter 11, and that in any case, "Manville is a real company with a substantial amount of real debt and real creditors clamoring to enforce this real debt." The court explained that Manville's filing was not tainted by any of the factors associated with bad faith filings; that Manville's directors had decided to file only after careful analysis had indicated that the company faced a minimum of $1.9 billion in projected liability to asbestos disease victims; that the company's auditors had directed it to book a reserve for contingent liability in this amount; that Manville was also faced with a huge contingent liability for asbestos related property damage; and that its insurance carriers were disclaiming coverage. Finally, the court reasoned that "upon dismissal, Manville would become a target for economic dismemberment, liquidation, and chaos, which would benefit no one except the few winners of the race to the courthouse. The economic reality of Manville's highly precarious financial position due to massive debt sustains its eligibility to and candidacy for reorganization." *In re Johns-Manville Corp.*, 36 B.R. 727 (Bankr. S.D.N.Y. 1984).

The opposite conclusion was reached in the opinion that follows.

OFFICIAL COMM. OF UNSECURED CREDITORS v. NUCOR CORP. (IN RE SGL CARBON CORP.)
United States Court of Appeals, Third Circuit
200 F.3d 154 (1999)

SCIRICA, CIRCUIT JUDGE.

[The debtor, SGL Carbon, a wholly-owned, U.S. subsidiary of a large German corporation, manufactured graphite electrodes used in the steel industry. In 1997, the United States government began investigating SGL and other graphite electrode makers for alleged price fixing. At about the same time, various steel manufacturers filed antitrust class actions against SGL. Six other customers filed individual actions against SGL in the U.S. and Canada. In December of 1998, SGL filed a Chapter 11 petition. Accompanying the petition was a proposed reorganization plan that provided that all creditors would be paid in full, except for the antitrust plaintiffs, who would receive credits — good for a limited time — against future purchases of SGL products. The day after the petition was filed the debtor issued a press release announcing that it had filed solely "to protect itself against excessive demands made by plaintiffs in civil antitrust litigation and in order to achieve an expeditious resolution of the claims against it." 200 F.3d at 157. The press release also stated:

> SGL CARBON Corporation believes that in its case Chapter 11 protection provides the most effective and efficient means for resolving the civil antitrust claims.

. . . .

> "SGL CARBON Corporation is financially healthy," said Wayne T. Burgess, SGL CARBON Corporation's president. "If we did not face [antitrust] claims for such excessive amounts, we would not have had to file for Chapter 11. We expect to continue our normal business operations."

. . . .

However, because certain plaintiffs continue to make excessive and unreasonable demands, SGL CARBON Corporation believes the prospects of ever reaching a commercially practicable settlement with them are remote. After much consideration, SGL CARBON Corporation determined that the most appropriate course of action to address the situation without harming its business was to voluntarily file for chapter 11 protection.

. . . .

At the same time, the chairman of the debtor's parent company told securities analysts that the debtor was "financially healthier" than before. He denied that the antitrust litigation was "starting to have a material impact on the debtor's ongoing operations," and he explained that the debtor's use of Chapter 11 was "fairly innovative [and] creative" because "usually Chapter 11 is used as protection against serious insolvency or credit problems, which is not the case [with SGL Carbon's petition]."

The United States Trustee formed a nine-member Official Committee of Unsecured Creditors, including eight antitrust plaintiffs and one trade creditor. The committee promptly filed a motion to dismiss SGL Carbon's bankruptcy petition on the grounds that it was a "litigation tactic designed to frustrate the prosecution of the civil antitrust claims pending against [SGL Carbon] and preserve [SGL Carbon's] equity from these claims." The district court refused to dismiss the case and the committee appealed. The Third Circuit framed the issue as "whether, on the facts of this case, a Chapter 11 petition filed by a financially healthy company in the face of potentially significant antitrust liabilities complies with the requirements of the Bankruptcy Code." The court held that it did not. After concluding that § 1112(b) imposes a good faith requirement, the court turned to the question of whether that requirement had been satisfied:]

The requisite fact intensive inquiry requires determining where SGL Carbon's petition falls along the spectrum ranging from the clearly acceptable to the patently abusive.

[T]he District Court found SGL Carbon's Chapter 11 petition was filed in good faith for two reasons: first, because the distractions caused by the antitrust litigation "posed a serious threat to [SGL Carbon's] continued successful operations," and second, because the litigation might result in a judgment that could cause the company "financial and operational ruin," SGL was required to file when it did. Although mindful of the careful consideration given by the able District Court, we believe each of these findings of fact was clearly erroneous.[11]

Although there is some evidence that defending against the antitrust litigation occupied some officers' time, there is no evidence this "distraction" posed a "serious threat" to the company's operational well being. At his deposition, Theodore Breyer [the Vice President in charge of SGL Carbon's North American Carbon/Graphite

---

[11] Although we conclude these findings were clearly erroneous, we do not hold that under the proper circumstances managerial distraction and other litigation harms may not constitute factors contributing to good faith.

Business Unit] testified the antitrust litigation consumed a significant portion of his time. But Breyer also noted the Carbon/Graphite Business Unit had met all of its financial targets during the nine months preceding filing. Additionally, Breyer testified that only his business unit was heavily involved in the antitrust litigation, recognizing that any management distraction affecting the rest of SGL Carbon resulted from the bankruptcy filing and not the antitrust litigation. As noted, SGL AG [the debtor's parent company] and SGL Carbon officers insisted the company was financially healthy despite the litigation. In addition, SGL AG's Chairman denied that the litigation was having a "material negative impact on [the debtor's] operations." In light of all the evidence, we believe the District Court's finding to the contrary is mistaken.

We also find clearly erroneous that SGL Carbon's Chapter 11 petition was filed at the appropriate time to avoid the possibility of a significant judgment that "could very well force [SGL Carbon] out of business." There is no evidence that the possible antitrust judgments might force SGL Carbon out of business. To the contrary, the record is replete with evidence of SGL Carbon's economic strength. At the time of filing, SGL Carbon's assets had a stipulated book value of $400 million, only $100,000 of which was encumbered. On the date of the petition, SGL Carbon had $276 million in fixed and non-disputed liabilities. Of those liabilities, only $26 million were held by outsiders as the remaining liabilities were either owed to or guaranteed by SGL AG. Although SGL Carbon's parent, SGL AG, recorded a $240 million charge on its books as "its best estimate of the potential liability and expenses of the SGL Carbon Group in connection with all civil and criminal antitrust matters," SGL Carbon is only one part of the SGL Carbon Group covered by the reserve.

Whether or not SGL Carbon faces a potentially crippling antitrust judgment, it is incorrect to conclude it had to file when it did. As noted, SGL Carbon faces no immediate financial difficulty. All the evidence shows that management repeatedly asserted the company was financially healthy at the time of the filing. Although the District Court believed the litigation might result in a judgment causing "financial and operational ruin" we believe that on the facts here, that assessment was premature. A Chapter 11 petition would impose an automatic stay on all efforts to collect the judgment and would allow the company the exclusive right to formulate a reorganization plan under which the amount of the judgment could be adjusted to allow the company to reorganize. SGL Carbon has offered no evidence it could not effectively use those protections as the prospect of such a judgment became imminent.[13]

The District Court's finding that the petition had to be filed at that particular time to avoid financial ruin and therefore was made in good faith is clearly contradicted by the evidence.

The District Court was correct in noting that the Bankruptcy Code encourages early filing. It is well established that a debtor need not be insolvent before filing for

---

[13] The Texaco Corporation's use of the bankruptcy protections is instructive. See *In re Texaco*, Inc., 84 B.R. 893 (Bankr. S.D.N.Y. 1988). Texaco resorted to bankruptcy only after suffering an $11 billion judgment. Even saddled with such a large judgment, bankruptcy provided Texaco a means of reorganizing and continuing as a going concern.

bankruptcy protection. It also is clear that the drafters of the Bankruptcy Code understood the need for early access to bankruptcy relief to allow a debtor to rehabilitate its business before it is faced with a hopeless situation.[14] Such encouragement, however, does not open the door to premature filing, nor does it allow for the filing of a bankruptcy petition that lacks a valid reorganizational purpose.

SGL Carbon, therefore, is correct that the Bankruptcy Code does not require specific evidence of insolvency for a voluntary Chapter 11 filing. But SGL Carbon cites no case holding that petitions filed by financially healthy companies cannot be subject to dismissal for cause. At any rate, as we explain more fully, SGL Carbon's ability to meet its debts is but one of many factors compelling the conclusion it did not enter Chapter 11 with a valid reorganizational purpose.

We do not hold that a company cannot file a valid Chapter 11 petition until after a massive judgment has been entered against it. Courts have allowed companies to seek the protections of bankruptcy when faced with pending litigation that posed a serious threat to the companies' long term viability. *See, e.g., Baker v. Latham Sparrowbush Assocs. (In re Cohoes Indus. Terminal Inc.)*, 931 F.2d 222 (2d Cir. 1991); *In re The Bible Speaks*, 65 B.R. 415 (Bankr. D. Mass. 1986); *In re Johns-Manville*, 36 B.R. 727 (Bankr. S.D.N.Y. 1984). In those cases, however, debtors experienced serious financial and/or managerial difficulties at the time of filing. In *Cohoes*, the Court of Appeals for the Second Circuit found a good faith filing, in part, because "it [was] clear that Cohoes [the debtor] was encountering financial stress at the time it filed its petition. . . . " 931 F.2d at 228. In *Bible Speaks*, pending litigation had already had an adverse effect on the debtor's financial well being as it was experiencing "a cash flow problem which prevents it from meeting its current obligations," compounded by an inability to obtain financing. 65 B.R. at 426. In *Johns-Manville*, the debtor was facing significant financial difficulties. A growing wave of asbestos-related claims forced the debtor to either book a $1.9 billion reserve thereby triggering potential default on a $450 million debt which, in turn, could have forced partial liquidation, or file a Chapter 11 petition. Large judgments had already been entered against Johns-Manville and the prospect loomed of tens of thousands of asbestos health-related suits over the course of 20–30 years.[15] For these reasons, SGL Carbon's reliance on those cases is misplaced. The mere possibility of a future need to file, without more, does not establish that a petition was filed in "good faith." *See, e.g., In re Cohoes Indus. Terminal Inc.*, 931 F.2d at 228 ("Although a debtor need not be in extremis in order to file [a Chapter 11] petition, it must, at least, face such financial difficulty that, if

---

[14] *See, e.g.*, Alan N. Resnick, *Bankruptcy As A Vehicle for Resolving Enterprise-Threatening Mass Tort Liability*, 148 U. Pa. L. Rev. (forthcoming 2000) M12.

[15] A large number of pending or potential claims also contributed to two other mass tort related bankruptcy petitions. The 1985 bankruptcy petition of the A.H. Robins Company came only after "the Company had settled 9,238 claims for approximately $530,000,000" and "still faced over five thousand pending cases in state and federal court." *In re A.H. Robins*, 89 B.R. 555, 557 (Bankr. E.D. Va. 1988). Similarly, at the time it filed for bankruptcy Dow Corning Corporation faced 440,000 potential claimants which had resulted in the filing of more than "19,000 individual silicone-gel breast implant lawsuits and at least 45 putative silicone-gel breast implant class actions." *In re Dow Corning Corp.*, 211 B.R. 545, 553 (Bankr. E.D. Mich. 1997).

it did not file at that time, it could anticipate the need to file in the future."). SGL Carbon, by its own account, and by all objective indicia, experienced no financial difficulty at the time of filing nor any significant managerial distraction. Although SGL Carbon may have to file for bankruptcy in the future, such an attenuated possibility standing alone is not sufficient to establish the good faith of its present petition.

[S]everal cases hold that a Chapter 11 petition is not filed in good faith unless it serves a valid reorganizational purpose. Similarly, because filing a Chapter 11 petition merely to obtain tactical litigation advantages is not within "the legitimate scope of the bankruptcy laws," courts have typically dismissed Chapter 11 petitions under these circumstances as well. *See id.*

. . . .

[W]here, as here, the timing of the filing of a Chapter 11 petition is such that there can be no doubt that the primary, if not sole, purpose of the filing was a litigation tactic, the petition may be dismissed as not being filed in good faith.

. . . .

It is easy to see why courts have required Chapter 11 petitioners to act within the scope of the bankruptcy laws to further a valid reorganizational purpose. Chapter 11 vests petitioners with considerable powers — the automatic stay, the exclusive right to propose a reorganization plan, the discharge of debts, etc. — that can impose significant hardship on particular creditors. When financially troubled petitioners seek a chance to remain in business, the exercise of those powers is justified. But this is not so when a petitioner's aims lie outside those of the Bankruptcy Code.

. . . .

An examination of the reorganization plan SGL Carbon filed simultaneously with its Chapter 11 petition also suggests the petition was not motivated by a desire to reorganize or rehabilitate SGL Carbon's business. Under the proposed plan, all creditors — including SGL Carbon's parent SGL AG — other than civil antitrust judgment creditors are to be paid in full in cash. Antitrust judgment creditors, by contrast, would be required to accept limited-time credits to purchase SGL Carbon's products. The plan's differing treatment of creditors suggests SGL Carbon's petition was not filed to reorganize the company but rather to put pressure on antitrust plaintiffs to accept the company's settlement terms.

. . . .

SGL Carbon places great emphasis on *In re The Bible Speaks*, 65 B.R. 415 (Bankr. D. Mass. 1986), and *In re Johns-Manville*, 36 B.R. 727 (Bankr. S.D.N.Y. 1984), two bankruptcy court cases relied on by the District Court. After considering those cases, we conclude they are not dispositive.

. . . .

In *Bible Speaks*, the bankruptcy court found the litigation had "already produced a significant effect" on the debtor; because of the uncertainty surrounding the litigation, the debtor was "unable to obtain financing." Carbon has not alleged the antitrust litigation has had a similar effect and such evidence is absent from the record. In addition, the court in *Bible Speaks* found that a significant judgment in the litigation would "probably terminate [the debtor's] existence." There is no evidence SGL Carbon could not effectively use Chapter 11 following a judgment in the antitrust litigation. Also, the court found the litigation prevented the debtor in *Bible Speaks* from making "financing [arrangements] or any type of long range plans." SGL Carbon has not alleged the antitrust litigation has impeded its financing or planning activities; instead, the petitioner has repeatedly insisted the litigation has had no material effect on its operations. Finally, the court in *Bible Speaks* found that dismissal was not warranted because Chapter 11 was in the best interests of the debtor and its creditor. *See id.* at 429. There is no such finding in this case.

We also believe reliance on *In re Johns-Manville* is misplaced.

. . . .

In *Johns-Manville*, the bankruptcy court found the company had a "compelling" and "pressing" need to reorganize. *Id* at 730. As we have explained, SGL Carbon has no such need.[22] Prior to the Chapter 11 filing, the Johns Manville plaintiffs had recovered nearly $4 million in punitive damages against the company. The litigation affected by SGL's Chapter 11 petition, in contrast, is in its nascent stages. Johns-Manville faced "approximately 16,000 lawsuits pending as of the filing date" with the prospect of the "filing of an even more staggering number of suits" over the course of 20–30 years. *Johns-Manville*, 36 B.R. at 729. By contrast, SGL Carbon faces a known and finite number of suits. In addition, the *Johns-Manville* Court made clear that its decision was based on factors other than the debtor's financial health. Unlike this case, the Johns-Manville creditors pursued their motion only after sixteen months of bargaining over an acceptable reorganization plan resulted in a deadlock. In denying the creditors' motion to dismiss, the court stated it would "bear in mind the strategical motivations underlying [creditors'] pursuit of these motions at this time" and would recognize "the progress toward a successful, perhaps consensual, reorganization that has already taken place." The Official Committee of Unsecured Creditors here did not delay in filing the motion to dismiss SGL Carbon's Chapter 11 petition; nor does SGL Carbon allege the creditors' motion was spurred by an intent to extract concessions in stalled negotiations. This case, therefore, involves neither the creditors' "strategical motivations" nor the "progress towards a successful . . . reorganization" that colored the *Johns-Manville* Court's opinion. *Id.*

Based on the facts and circumstances of this case, we conclude SGL Carbon's Chapter 11 petition lacks a valid reorganizational purpose and consequently lacks good faith making it subject to dismissal "for cause" under 11 U.S.C. § 1112(b).

In reaching our conclusion, we are cognizant that it is growing increasingly difficult to settle large scale litigation. We recognize that companies that face

---

[22] For example, the *Johns-Manville* Court noted that the company would have had to book a $1.9 billion tort liability reserve had it not filed for Chapter 11. This booking would in turn have accelerated $450 million in outstanding debt and could have forced liquidation. SGL Carbon has not shown the failure to file for Chapter 11 would cause it such harm.

massive potential liability and litigation costs continue to seek ways to rapidly conclude litigation to enable a continuation of their business and to maintain access to the capital markets. As evidenced by SGL Carbon's actions in this case, the Bankruptcy Code presents an inviting safe harbor for such companies. But this lure creates the possibility of abuse which must be guarded against to protect the integrity of the bankruptcy system and the rights of all involved in such proceedings. Allowing SGL Carbon's bankruptcy under these circumstances seems to us a significant departure from the use of Chapter 11 to validly reorganize financially troubled businesses.

NOTES AND QUESTIONS

(1) The Third Circuit identified the issue as whether "a financially healthy company" could file a Chapter 11 petition. What is "a financially healthy company"? Would the Third Circuit have allowed the *Johns-Manville* case to continue? If you were representing a company that was involved in litigation and contemplating Chapter 11, would you be able to identify the point at which filing would serve a proper "reorganizational purpose"? What advice would you give to your client about how to run its public relations campaign?

(2) One response of lenders to the problem of single asset real estate cases has been to try to construct real estate entities in a way that makes filing difficult from the get-go and, if the debtor does manage to file, makes dismissal on good faith grounds likely. These entities are structured so that the only asset is the real estate project; the only creditors are the mortgagees. The directors of the entities are often employees of the lenders, who have pledged not to put the entity into bankruptcy. Real estate entities that are structured in this way are referred to as "bankruptcy remote." The next case tests the vitality of this approach.

IN RE GENERAL GROWTH PROPERTIES, INC.
United States Bankruptcy Court Southern District of New York
409 B.R. 43 (2009)

MEMORANDUM OF OPINION

ALLAN L. GROPPER, UNITED STATES BANKRUPTCY JUDGE

Before the Court are five motions (the "Motions") to dismiss certain of the Chapter 11 cases filed by one or more debtors (the "Subject Debtors") that are owned directly or indirectly by General Growth Properties, Inc. ("GGP"). One of the Motions was filed by ING Clarion Capital Loan Services LLC ("ING Clarion"), as special servicer to certain secured lenders; one of the Motions was filed by Helios AMC, LLC ("Helios"), as special servicer to other secured lenders; and three of the Motions were filed by Metropolitan Life Insurance Company and KBC Bank N.V. (together, "Metlife", and together with ING Clarion and Helios, the "Movants"). Each of the Movants is a secured lender with a loan to one of the Subject Debtors. The primary ground on which dismissal is sought is that the Subject Debtors' cases were filed in bad faith. It is also contended that one of the Subject Debtors was

ineligible to file. The above-captioned debtors (the "Debtors") and the Official
Committee of Unsecured Creditors appointed in these cases (the "Committee")
object to the Motions. Based on the following findings of fact and conclusions of law,
the Motions are denied.

BACKGROUND

GGP, one of the Debtors, is a publicly-traded real estate investment trust
("REIT") and the ultimate parent of approximately 750 wholly-owned Debtor and
non-Debtor subsidiaries, joint venture subsidiaries and affiliates (collectively, the
"GGP Group" or the "Company").[6] The GGP Group's primary business is shopping
center ownership and management; the Company owns or manages over 200
shopping centers in 44 states across the country. These include joint venture
interests in approximately 50 properties, along with non-controlling interests in
several international joint ventures. The GGP Group also owns several commercial
office buildings and five master-planned communities,[7] although these businesses
account for a smaller share of its operations. The Company reported consolidated
revenue of $ 3.4 billion in 2008. The GGP Group's properties are managed from its
Chicago, Illinois headquarters, and the Company directly employs approximately
3,700 people, exclusive of those employed at the various property sites.

I. Corporate Structure

The corporate structure of the GGP Group is extraordinarily complex, and it is
necessary to provide only a broad outline for purposes of this opinion. GGP is the
general partner of GGP Limited Partnership ("GGP LP"), the company through
which the Group's business is primarily conducted.[9] GGP LP in turn controls,
directly or indirectly, GGPLP, L.L.C., The Rouse Company LP ("TRCLP"), and
General Growth Management, Inc. ("GGMI").[10] GGPLP L.L.C., TRCLP and GGMI
in turn directly or indirectly control hundreds of individual project-level subsidiary
entities, which directly or indirectly own the individual properties. The Company
takes a nationwide, integrated approach to the development, operation and
management of its properties, offering centralized leasing, marketing, management, cash management, property maintenance and construction management.[11]

---

[6] As further discussed below, 388 of the entities in the GGP Group have filed for Chapter 11
protection: 360 filed on April 16, 2009 and an additional 28 filed on April 22, 2009. For purposes of
convenience, April 16th is used as the "Petition Date" herein.

[7] The GGP Group's principal master planned communities, which are large-scale, long-term community development projects, are located in Columbia, Maryland; Summerlin, Nevada; and Houston, Texas.
Revenue is generated from these properties through the sale of improved land to homebuilders and
commercial developers.

. . . .

[9] GGP owns 96% of GGP LP, with outside parties holding the remaining 4%.

[10] GGP LP, GGPLP, L.L.C., and TRCLP are each Debtors, while GGMI is a non-Debtor affiliate that
provides management services to the GGP Group, the joint ventures and other unrelated third parties.

[11] "Through this centralized management process, GGP LP provides national support with respect to
substantially all aspects of business operations. Accounting, business development, construction,
contracting, design, finance, forecasting, human resources and employee benefits, insurance and risk

II. Capital Structure

As of December 31, 2008, the GGP Group reported $29.6 billion in assets and $27.3 billion in liabilities. At that time, approximately $24.85 billion of its liabilities accounted for the aggregate consolidated outstanding indebtedness of the GGP Group. Of this, approximately $18.27 billion constituted debt of the project-level Debtors secured by the respective properties, $1.83 billion of which was secured by the properties of the Subject Debtors. The remaining $6.58 billion of unsecured debt is discussed below.

A. Secured Debt

The GGP Group's secured debt consists primarily of mortgage and so-called mezzanine debt. The mortgage debt is secured by mortgages on over 100 properties, each of which is typically owned by a separate corporate entity. The mortgage debt can in turn be categorized as conventional or as debt further securitized in the commercial mortgage-backed securities market.

(i) Conventional Mortgage Debt

The conventional mortgage debt is illustrated, on this record, by three of the mortgages held by Metlife. Each of the three mortgages was an obligation of a separate GGP subsidiary. There is no dispute that some of the Subject Debtors that issued the Metlife mortgages were intended to function as special purpose entities ("SPE"). SPE's typically contain restrictions in their loan documentation and operating agreements that require them to maintain their separate existence and to limit their debt to the mortgages and any incidental debts, such as trade payables or the costs of operation Metlife asserts, without substantial contradiction from the Debtors, that SPE's are structured in this manner to protect the interests of their secured creditors by ensuring that "the operations of the borrower [are] isolated from business affairs of the borrower's affiliates and parent so that the financing of each loan stands alone on its own merits, creditworthiness and value. . . . "[15] In addition to limitations on indebtedness, the SPE's organizational documents usually contain prohibitions on consolidation and liquidation, restrictions on mergers and asset sales, prohibitions on amendments to the organizational and transaction documents, and separateness covenants. Standard and Poor's, Legal Criteria for Structured Finance Transactions (April 2002).

---

management, property services, marketing, leasing, legal, tax, treasury, cash management and other services are provided or administered centrally for all properties under the GGP Group's ownership and management. Only the most basic building operational needs are addressed at the individual property level." (Mesterharm Decl., April 16, 2009, P 17.)

[15] Sometimes referred to as a "single-purpose entity" or "bankruptcy remote entity," an SPE has been described by one commentator as "an entity, formed concurrently with, or immediately prior to, the closing of a financing transaction, one purpose of which is to isolate the financial assets from the potential bankruptcy estate of the original entity, the borrower or originator." David B. Stratton, *Special-Purpose Entities and Authority to File Bankruptcy*, 23-2 Am. Bankr. Inst. J. 36 (March 2004). "Bankruptcy-remote structures are devices that reduce the risk that a borrower will file bankruptcy or, if bankruptcy is filed, ensure the creditor procedural advantages in the proceedings." Michael T. Madison, *et. al.*, *The Law of Real Estate Financing*, § 13:38 (2008).

The typical SPE documentation also often contains an obligation to retain one or more independent directors (for a corporation) or managers (for an LLC). . . . The Company's view of the independent directors and managers is that they were meant to be unaffiliated with the Group and its management. It appears that some of the secured lenders believed they were meant to be devoted to the interests of the secured creditors, as asserted by a representative of Helios. In any event, this aspect of the loan documentation is discussed further below.

Although each of the mortgage loans was typically secured by a separate property owned by an individual debtor, many of the loans were guaranteed by other GGP entities.

. . . .

The typical mortgage loan for the GGP Group members had a three to seven-year term, with low amortization and a large balloon payment at the end. Some of the mortgage loans had a much longer nominal maturity date, but these also had an anticipated repayment date ("ARD"), at which point the loan became "hyper-amortized," even if the maturity date itself was as much as thirty years in the future. Consequences of failure to repay or refinance the loan at the ARD typically include a steep increase in interest rate, a requirement that cash be kept at the project-level, with excess cash flow being applied to principal, and a requirement that certain expenditures be submitted to the lender for its approval.[18] The Debtors viewed the ARD as equivalent to maturity and the consequences of a loan becoming hyper-amortized as equivalent to default, and historically sought to refinance such loans so as to avoid hyper-amortization.

(ii) Commercial Mortgage-Backed Securities

Many of the GGP Group's mortgage loans were financed in the commercial mortgage-backed securities ("CMBS") market, represented on these Motions by each of the loans serviced by ING Clarion and Helios, as special servicers. In a typical CMBS transaction, multiple mortgages are sold to a trust qualified as a real estate mortgage conduit ("REMIC") for tax purposes. The REMIC in turn sells certificates entitling the holders to payments from principal and interest on this large pool of mortgages. The holders of the CMBS securities typically have different rights to the income stream and bear different interest rates; they may or may not have different control rights. The REMIC is managed by a master servicer that handles day-to-day loan administration functions and services the loans when

---

[18] Examples of the consequences of an ARD can be seen with respect to three of the ING Clarion loans. The ING Clarion loan on the GGP-Tucson Mall L.L.C. reached its ARD on October 13, 2008. The Debtors were unable to refinance or repay the loan and as a result a cash trap was triggered and the interest rate increased from 5% to 9.26%. While the lender agreed to defer collecting additional interest in cash and to add the obligation to the current principal balance of $118,000,000, the cash trap required application of any excess cash to the outstanding principal and interest until the loan was paid in full. For the Valley Plaza Mall, if the loan goes into hyper-amortization, the regular interest rate of 3.9% is increased to the greater of the regular interest rate plus 5% or the Treasury Rate plus 5%. The outstanding principal balance of the loan is currently $96,000,000. The same increase is true of the Visalia Mall, with an ARD of January 11, 2010 and a regular interest rate of 3.77%. The outstanding principal balance of the loan is currently $42,000,000.

they are not in default. A special servicer takes over management of the REMIC upon a transfer of authority. Such transfers take place under certain limited circumstances, including: (i) a borrower's failure to make a scheduled principal and interest payment, unless cured within 60 days, (ii) a borrower's bankruptcy or insolvency, (iii) a borrower's failure to make a balloon payment upon maturity, or (iv) a determination by the master servicer that a material and adverse default under the loan is imminent and unlikely to be cured within 60 days. While a master servicer is able to grant routine waivers and consents, it cannot agree to an alteration of the material terms of a loan or mortgage. A special servicer has the ability to agree to modify the loan once authority has been transferred, but often only with the consent of the holders of the CMBS securities, or in some cases the holders of certain levels of the debt.

(iii) Mezzanine Debt

The Debtors are also obligors on so-called mezzanine loans from at least four lenders, of which one, Metlife, is a Movant on these motions to dismiss. In these transactions generally, and in the Metlife mezzanine loan in particular, the lender is the holder of a mortgage on the property held by one of the Subject Debtors. The lender makes a further loan, ordinarily at a higher interest rate, to a single-purpose entity formed to hold the equity interest in the mortgage-level borrower. The loan to the single-purpose entity is secured only by the stock or other equity interest of the mortgage level borrower. The single-purpose entity typically has no other debt and its business is limited to its equity interest in the property-owning subsidiary.

B. Unsecured Debt

In addition to secured debt, members of the GGP Group were obligated on approximately $6.58 billion of unsecured debt as of the Petition Date. Other than trade debt incurred by some of the project-level Debtors, most of this debt was an obligation of one or more of the holding companies, generally at the top levels of the corporate chart.

. . . .

C. Other Debt

The GGP Group had entered into five interest-rate swap agreements as of December 31, 2008. The total notional amount of the agreements was $1.08 billion, with an average fixed pay rate of 3.38% and an average variable receive rate of LIBOR. The Company made April 2009 payments to only one of the counterparties, and two of the swaps have been terminated. Additionally, as of December 31, 2008, the Company also had outstanding letters of credit and surety bonds in the amount of $286.2 million.

With respect to the Company's joint venture interests, GGP LP is the promissor on a note in the principal amount of $245 million, payable to the Comptroller of the State of New York, as trustee for the New York State Common Retirement Fund, and due on February 28, 2013. It is secured by a pledge of GGP LP's member interest in the GGP/Homart II L.L.C. joint venture. Additionally GGP LP is the promissor on a note in the amount of $93,712,500, due on December 1, 2012, payable to Ivanhoe Capital, LP, and secured by a pledge of GGP LP's shares in the GGP Ivanhoe, Inc. joint venture.

D. Equity

GGP had 312,352,392 shares of common stock outstanding as of March 17, 2009. GGP is required, as a REIT, to distribute at least 90% of its taxable income and to distribute, or pay tax on, certain of its capital gains. During the first three quarters of 2008, GGP distributed $476.6 million, or $1.50 per share, to its stockholders and GGP LP unitholders, but it suspended its quarterly dividends as of the last quarter of 2008.

III. The Events of 2008–2009

Historically, the capital needs of the GGP Group were satisfied through mortgage loans obtained from banks, insurance companies and, increasingly, the CMBS market. As noted above, these loans were generally secured by the shopping center properties and structured with three to seven-year maturities, low amortization rates and balloon payments due at maturity. (Nolan Decl., June 16, 2009, P 9.) There is no dispute that the Company's business plan was based on the premise that it would be able to refinance the debt. The testimony of Thomas Nolan, the President and Chief Operating Officer of GGP, is that "[t]his approach was standard in the industry, so for many years, it has been rare to see commercial real estate financed with longer-term mortgages that would fully amortize."

However, in the latter half of 2008, the crisis in the credit markets spread to commercial real estate finance, most notably the CMBS market. This in turn affected the ability of the GGP Group to refinance its maturing debt on commercially acceptable terms. The GGP Group attempted to refinance its maturing project-level debt or obtain new financing, contacting dozens of banks, insurance companies and pension funds. It also contacted national and regional brokers and retained the investment banking firms of Goldman Sachs and Morgan Stanley to attempt to securitize and syndicate the loans.

. . . .

Unable to refinance, the Company began to tap more heavily into its operating cash flow to pay both its regular expenses and financial obligations. This in turn left the Company short of cash to meet prior commitments towards development and redevelopment costs. As additional mortgage loans began to mature, the Company's liquidity problems grew worse. . . . Based on the state of the markets, the GGP Group began to contemplate the necessity of a Chapter 11 restructuring. Several of the loans went into default and one of the lenders, Citibank, commenced foreclosure proceedings on a defaulted loan on March 19, 2009. On April 16, 2009, 360 of the Debtors filed voluntary petitions under Chapter 11 of the Bankruptcy Code. An additional 28 of the Debtors filed for protection on April 22, 2009, for a total of 388 Debtors in the above-captioned Chapter 11 cases.

Upon filing, the Debtors did not dispute that the GGP Group's shopping center business had a stable and generally positive cash flow and that it had continued to perform well, despite the current financial crisis. Specifically, they stated "[t]he Company's net operating income ('NOI'), a standard metric of financial performance in the real estate and shopping center industries, has been increasing over time, and in fact increased in 2008 over the prior year despite the challenges of the general economy." Despite this, faced with approximately $18.4 billion in outstanding debt that matured or would be maturing by the end of 2012, the Company believed its capital structure had become unmanageable due to the collapse of the credit markets.

. . . .

At an early stage in the cases it became clear that several lenders intended to move to dismiss, and the Court urged all parties who intended to move to dismiss any of the cases to coordinate their motions. Six motions were filed (three by Metlife), with one party subsequently withdrawing its motion. ING Clarion and Helios, which hold CMBS debt, argued that their cases should be dismissed because they were filed in bad faith in that there was no imminent threat to the financial viability of the Subject Debtors. ING Clarion also contended that Lancaster Trust, one of the Subject Debtors, was ineligible to be a debtor under the Bankruptcy Code. Metlife, which holds conventional mortgage debt, similarly argued that the Subject Debtors were not in financial distress, that the cases were filed prematurely and that there was no chance of reorganization as there was no possibility of confirming a plan over its objection.

DISCUSSION

I. Bad Faith Dismissal

The principle that a Chapter 11 reorganization case can be dismissed as a bad faith filing is a judge-made doctrine. In the Second Circuit, the leading case on dismissal for the filing of a petition in bad faith is *C-TC 9th Ave. P'ship v. Norton Co. (In re C-TC 9th Ave. P'ship)*, 113 F.3d 1304 (2d Cir. 1997), which in turn relied on *Baker v. Latham Sparrowbush Assocs. (In re Cohoes Indus. Terminal, Inc.)*, 931 F.2d 222 (2d Cir. 1991). Under these decisions, grounds for dismissal exist if it is clear on the filing date that "there was no reasonable likelihood that the debtor intended to reorganize and no reasonable probability that it would eventually emerge from bankruptcy proceedings." *In re C-TC 9th Ave. P'ship*, 113 F.3d at 1309–10, quoting *In re Cohoes*, 931 F.2d at 227 (internal citations omitted). One frequently-cited decision by Chief Judge Brozman of this Court has restated the principle as follows: "[T]he standard in this Circuit is that a bankruptcy petition will be dismissed if both objective futility of the reorganization process and subjective bad faith in filing the petition are found." *In re Kingston Square Assocs.*, 214 B.R. 713, 725 (Bankr. S.D.N.Y. 1997) (emphasis in original); *see also In re RCM Global Long Term Capital Appreciation Fund, Ltd.*, 200 B.R. 514, 520 (Bankr. S.D.N.Y. 1996).

[The court pointed out that no one factor is determinative of good faith, and that the factors usually associated with bad faith filings by single asset real estate debtors were not present here.]

These Movants instead argue that the filings, when examined from the perspective of the individual Debtors, were premature. The third Movant, Metlife, did not expressly disavow reliance on the *C-TC* formulation. However, its contentions were not based on the argument that the debtors did not intend to reorganize. Metlife argued that the Debtors could never confirm a plan over its objection, implying that Metlife would never agree to a plan proposed by the Debtors. Then, having staked out a position that the Debtors might characterize as evidence of bad faith, Metlife contended that the Subject Debtors' subjective bad faith was evidenced by the prematurity of the filing and various actions taken by the Debtors that are further analyzed below.

A. Objective Bad Faith: Prematurity

All three Movants support their contention that the Chapter 11 filings of these Debtors were, in effect, premature by reliance on the few cases that have dismissed Chapter 11 petitions where the debtor was not in financial distress at the time of filing, where the prospect of liability was speculative, and where there was evidence that the filing was designed to obtain a litigation advantage. The leading decision is *In re SGL Carbon Corp.*, 200 F.3d 154 (3d Cir. 1999), in which the debtors filed Chapter 11 petitions for the express purpose of protecting themselves from antitrust litigation. At the same time they published a press release touting their financial health, as well as their denial of any antitrust liability. The Third Circuit held that "the mere possibility of a future need to file, without more, does not establish that a petition was filed in 'good faith.' " *Id.* at 164. The principle of *SGL Carbon* was followed by this Court in *In re Schur Mgmt. Co.*, 323 B.R. 123 (Bankr. S.D.N.Y. 2005), where two debtors filed for bankruptcy to avoid a possible judgment from a personal injury suit in which they denied all liability and which had yet to go to trial. In *Schur Mgmt.*, this Court noted that "[i]t would be sheer speculation to guess as to the amount of a judgment, whether it would be imposed on one or both debtors and whether it would impair healthy companies with only $14,075 in aggregate liabilities and a net positive cash flow." 323 B.R. at 127.

In *SGL Carbon and Schur Mgmt.*, the prospect of any liability from pending litigation was wholly speculative. By contrast, the Subject Debtors here carry an enormous amount of fixed debt that is not contingent. Movants argue nevertheless that none of the Subject Debtors had a mortgage with a maturity date earlier than March 2010, and that the Subject Debtors should have waited until much closer to the respective maturity dates on their loans to file for bankruptcy. Movants contend in effect that the prospect of liability was too remote on the Petition Date for the Subject Debtors, and that the issue of financial distress and prematurity of filing cannot be examined from the perspective of the group but only on an individual-entity basis. Accepting for the moment this latter proposition, the question is whether the Subject Debtors were in actual financial distress on the Petition Date and whether the prospect of liability was too remote to justify a Chapter 11 filing.

(i) The Financial Distress of the Individual Project Debtors

The record on these Motions demonstrates that the individual debtors that are the subject of these Motions were in varying degrees of financial distress in April 2009. Loans to four of the Subject Debtors had cross-defaulted to the defaults of affiliates or would have been in default as a result of other bankruptcy petitions.[24] Of the loans to the remaining sixteen Subject Debtors, one had gone into hyper-amortization in 2008. Interest had increased by 4.26%. Five of the Subject Debtors had mortgage debt maturing or hyper-amortizing in 2010, two in 2011, and one in 2012. The remaining seven Subject Debtors were either guarantors on maturing loans of other entities or their property was collateral for a loan that was maturing, or there existed other considerations that in the Debtors' view placed the loan in distress, such as a high loan-to-value ratio.

The Debtors' determination that the Subject Debtors were in financial distress was made in a series of Board meetings following substantial financial analysis. The Debtors established that in late 2008 they hired a team of advisors to assist in the evaluation of either an in-court or an out-of-court restructuring. The team included Miller Buckfire as restructuring advisor, Alix Partners LLP as financial advisor, and both Weil Gotshal & Manges and Kirkland & Ellis as legal advisors. The process of evaluating the Company's restructuring options took approximately six weeks and encompassed a total of seven Board meetings and three informational sessions. During these meetings, the Boards discussed general considerations applicable to the project-level companies, as well as specific facts relating to the individual properties, with both GGP personnel and the financial, restructuring and legal advisors available. The Boards specifically focused on: "the collapse of the commercial real estate financing market; the challenges facing the CMBS market and the practical difficulties of negotiating with CMBS servicers to meaningfully modify loan terms; integration of the project entities with GGP Group and requirements for securing DIP financing; and the consequences of filing an entity for bankruptcy individually, outside a coordinated restructuring with other GGP entities." The Boards also concentrated on three of the above-referenced filing factors: "(i) defaults or cross-defaults with other loans; (ii) loans that were maturing in the next three to four years; and (iii) other financial considerations indicating that restructuring would be necessary, including a loan-to-value ratio above 70 percent."

In addition to these general considerations, the Boards discussed each project-level entity individually. For each entity, Robert Michaels, the Vice Chairman of GGP, "provided an overview of its financial and operational considerations, including the property's performance, outlook, and projected capital needs. In addition, for each entity, the Boards received written materials consisting of a fact sheet on the property, an income statement, and a draft board resolution." In these meetings, the Debtors divided the various property-level entities into separate groups to evaluate whether to file each individual entity.[26] On April 15, 2009 the Boards separately

---

[24] There was some dispute at the time of trial as to whether certain of the loans were actually in default. (*See* Hr'g. Tr. 203:17-205:17, June 17, 2009.) The fact that the parties still could not, as of June 2009, agree whether there was a default establishes that on the Petition Date the Debtors could not have been confident that the loans would not be accelerated and foreclosure proceedings commenced.

[26] The entities were separated into Groups A through G. Ten factors were used to consider whether

voted to put most of the project-level Debtors into bankruptcy. Certain Subject Debtors acted by written consent of the directors or managers. Fourteen entities were left out of the filing, as none of the ten filing factors was applicable. Movants contend that, in the name of the "doctrine" of "prematurity," the Debtors had a good faith obligation to delay a Chapter 11 filing until they were temporally closer to an actual default. For the following reasons, these Debtors were justified in filing Chapter 11 petitions when they did.

We start with the statute. Chapter X of the former Bankruptcy Act expressly required that a petition be filed in good faith, providing that "[u]pon the filing of a petition by a debtor, the judge shall enter an order approving the petition, if satisfied that it complies with the requirements of this chapter and has been filed in good faith, or dismissing it if not so satisfied." Bankruptcy Act of 1898 § 141, 11 U.S.C. § 541 (1976) (repealed 1978). Neither Chapter XI nor XII contained a similar good faith requirement, and the good faith provisions were one of the many parts of Chapter X that debtors avoided by filing under Chapter XI and that Congress rejected when it structured Chapter 11 of the Bankruptcy Reform Act of 1978.

Indeed, when Congress adopted the Bankruptcy Abuse Prevention and Consumer Protection Act of 2005 ("BAPCPA"), it significantly strengthened the provisions of § 1112, requiring the Court to dismiss or convert an abusive Chapter 11 case.[29] BAPCPA added several factors to the prior list of grounds for dismissal. Significantly, it did not provide expressly that a Chapter 11 case should be

---

to file an entity for bankruptcy, although other considerations were applied depending on the facts and circumstances related to the entity. The ten factors included:

(1) The Company is a borrower or guarantor under a credit facility that is currently in default and for which no forbearance has been obtained.

(2) The Company is a borrower or guarantor under a credit facility that is currently in a forbearance period that can be terminated at the Lender's discretion.

(3) The default of General Growth Properties, Inc. or another entity within the General Growth Properties structure and/or a bankruptcy filing by an entity guaranteeing the Company's debt triggers an Event of Default under the Company's existing loan.

(4) The Company owns a property which is subject to an existing cash trap that has been implemented.

(5) The Company is a borrower or guarantor under a loan that matures within the next three to four years.

(6) The Company is part of a project in which one or more subsidiaries or affiliates are under consideration for filing to facilitate a restructuring.

(7) The Company is the general partner of a partnership that is under consideration for filing.

(8) The Company is subject to multiple other filing considerations, including a loan which has a loan-to-value ratio in excess of 70%.

(9) The Company holds unencumbered assets and is filing to facilitate the inclusion of such assets as part of an overall corporate restructuring.

(10) The Company may be part of a non-core asset disposition process that could be facilitated by a section 363 sale in bankruptcy.

(Helios Trial Ex. 16.)

[29] For example, § 1112 now provides that if there is "cause" for dismissal or conversion, the Court *must* act, within a brief period and after a hearing, "absent unusual circumstances specifically identified by the court that establish that the requested conversion or dismissal is not in the best interest of creditors and the estate." 11 U.S.C. § 1112(b)(1).

dismissed for bad faith in filing, and all of the listed grounds for dismissal relate to a debtor's conduct *after* the filing, not before. Similarly, in 2005 Congress added several provisions designed to shorten Chapter 11 cases,[30] but it omitted any requirement that the Court hold an initial hearing on a Chapter 11 debtor's *bona fides* or good faith.

The Code's omission of any such hearing, which would doubtless invite significant litigation at the start of every Chapter 11 case, is nevertheless consistent with another of the Code's innovations, ordinarily leaving the debtor in possession and not appointing a trustee. These provisions carry out the goal of the 1978 Bankruptcy Code to incentivize a debtor to file earlier rather than later, so as to preserve the value of the estate.

In light of the statute, this Court declines the invitation to establish an arbitrary rule, of the type desired by Movants, that a debtor is not in financial distress and cannot file a Chapter 11 petition if its principal debt is not due within one, two or three years. The Movants did not establish that the Debtors' procedures for determining whether to file the individual Subject Debtors were unreasonable or that the Debtors were unreasonable in concluding that the disarray in the financial market made it uncertain whether they would be able to refinance debt years in the future. There was no evidence to counter the Debtors' demonstration that the CMBS market, in which they historically had financed and refinanced most of their properties, was "dead" as of the Petition Date, and that no one knows when or if that market will revive. Indeed, at the time of the hearings on these Motions, it was anticipated that the market would worsen, and there is no evident means of refinancing billions of dollars of real estate debt coming due in the next several years. The following testimony of Allen Hanson, an officer of Helios, is telling: "Q. Helios is aware that there are debt maturities that will occur in 2009, 2010, 2011 and 2012 that the CMBS market will not be able to handle through new CMBS issuances, correct? A. Based on the circumstances we see today, yes." (*See* Hanson Dep. Tr. 155: 25-156:6, June 5, 2009; Hanson Dep. Tr. 144:14-145:10.)

It is well established that the Bankruptcy Code does not require that a debtor be insolvent prior to filing.

. . . .

"The Bankruptcy Act does not require any particular degree of financial distress as a condition precedent to a petition seeking relief." Many other cases have denied motions to dismiss, despite the fact that the subject debtors were able to meet current expenses. In *In re Century/ML Cable Venture*, 294 B.R. 9 (Bankr. S.D.N.Y. 2003), for example, the Court denied a motion to dismiss because, despite being able to meet current expenses, the debtor had "a huge financial liability which it does not have the ability to pay out of current cash flow, and without a substantial liquidation of its assets." 294 B.R. at 35–36.

. . . .

The foregoing is not to assert that every stand-alone company with ample cash flow would necessarily act in good faith by filing a Chapter 11 petition three years

---

[30] *See, e.g.*, the amendment to § 1112(d) putting a limit on extensions of exclusivity.

before its only debt came due. However, contrary to Movants' contentions, the Court is not required in these cases to examine the issue of good faith as if each Debtor were wholly independent. We turn to the interests of the Group as a whole.

(ii) The Interests of the Group

Movants argue that the SPE or bankruptcy-remote structure of the project-level Debtors requires that each Debtor's financial distress be analyzed exclusively from its perspective, that the Court should consider only the financial circumstances of the individual Debtors, and that consideration of the financial problems of the Group in judging the good faith of an individual filing would violate the purpose of the SPE structure. There is no question that the SPE structure was intended to insulate the financial position of each of the Subject Debtors from the problems of its affiliates, and to make the prospect of a default less likely. There is also no question that this structure was designed to make each Subject Debtor "bankruptcy remote." Nevertheless, the record also establishes that the Movants each extended a loan to the respective Subject Debtor with a balloon payment that would require refinancing in a period of years and that would default if financing could not be obtained by the SPE or by the SPE's parent coming to its rescue. Movants do not contend that they were unaware that they were extending credit to a company that was part of a much larger group, and that there were benefits as well as possible detriments from this structure. If the ability of the Group to obtain refinancing became impaired, the financial situation of the subsidiary would inevitably be impaired.

The few cases on point support the Debtors' position that the interests of the group can and should be considered. In *In re U.I.P. Engineered Products Corp.*, 831 F.2d 54 (4th Cir. 1987), the Court addressed the propriety of Chapter 11 filings by solvent subsidiaries of a parent corporation that had filed its own Chapter 11 case shortly before the subsidiaries filed. Creditors sought to dismiss the subsidiaries' cases, arguing that the timing of the filings and the subsidiaries' admitted solvency evidenced an abuse of the bankruptcy process. *See id.* at 56. The Court found otherwise, stating that is was irrelevant whether the subsidiaries could independently demonstrate good faith for their filings. Rather, the question was whether the wholly-owned subsidiaries "should have been included in their parent company's bankruptcy estate, when the parent company had filed in good faith for Chapter 11 reorganization." *Id.* The Court found that it was "clearly sound business practice for [the parent] to seek Chapter 11 protection for its wholly-owned subsidiaries when those subsidiaries were crucial to its own reorganization plan." *Id.* The Court explained that the nature of a corporate family created an " 'identity of interest'. . . that justifies the protection of the subsidiaries as well as the parent corporation." *Id.* The Fourth Circuit also relied on the pre-Code case of *Duggan v. Sansberry*, 327 U.S. 499, 66 S. Ct. 657, 90 L. Ed. 809 (1946), which stated that it was Congress' intent "ordinarily to allow parent and subsidiary to be reorganized in a single proceeding, thereby effectuating its general policy that the entire administration of an estate should be centralized in a single reorganization court." *Id.* at 510–11.

. . . .

Movants do not contend that the parent companies acted in bad faith in filing their own Chapter 11 petitions. The parent companies depended on the cash flow from the subsidiaries, but much of the project-level debt was in default: from January 1, 2009 through the second week of April 2009, $1.1 billion of the GGP Group project-level debt had matured, none of which the Company had been able to refinance. As of the Petition Date, billions of dollars of project-level debt had also reached hyper-amortization, with several secured lenders having imposed cash traps. In March 2009, Citibank, a lender on one of the defaulted loans, had begun foreclosure proceedings against one property. In addition to the project-level debt, the Group had debt of more than $8.4 billion at the parent level. Much of this debt was in default and it, too, could not be refinanced. Beyond the unsecured debt of the parent companies were thousands of equityholders who depended, in large part, on the net cash flow of and the equity in the project-level Debtors as a principal source of protection for their investment.

Faced with the unprecedented collapse of the real estate markets, and serious uncertainty as to when or if they would be able to the refinance the project-level debt, the Debtors' management had to reorganize the Group's capital structure. Movants do not explain how the billions of dollars of unsecured debt at the parent levels could be restructured responsibly if the cash flow of the parent companies continued to be based on the earnings of subsidiaries that had debt coming due in a period of years without any known means of providing for repayment or refinance. That is not to conclude, as Movants imply, that the interests of the subsidiaries or their creditors should be sacrificed to the interests of the parents and their creditors. As further discussed below, there need be no sacrifice of fundamental rights. The point is that a judgment on an issue as sensitive and fact-specific as whether to file a Chapter 11 petition can be based in good faith on consideration of the interests of the group as well as the interests of the individual debtor.

Indeed, there is authority that under the circumstances at bar, the interests of the parent companies *must* be taken into account. The Operating Agreements of many of the project-level Debtors contained provisions that required the appointment of two "Independent Managers." The Operating Agreements do not enumerate the duties of the Independent Managers except in the following instance, which is obviously highly relevant to the instant Motions: "To the extent permitted by law ... the Independent Managers shall consider only the interests of the Company, *including its respective creditors*, in acting or otherwise voting on the matters referred to in Article XIII(p)." Article XIII(p) requires the "unanimous written consent of the Managers of the Company, including both of the Independent Managers" before the SPE can take any action to file or consent to the filing, as debtor, of any bankruptcy proceeding. (*Id.*) The Operating Agreements further provide that, "in exercising their rights and performing their duties under this Agreement, any Independent Manager shall have a fiduciary duty of loyalty and care similar to that of a director of a business Corporation organized under the General Corporation Law of the State of Delaware." (*Id.*)

The drafters of these documents may have attempted to create impediments to a bankruptcy filing; in considering a filing, the Independent Managers are directed to consider only the interests of the Company, including its "creditors" — meaning the lender as the only substantial creditor of the entity. However, it is also provided, appropriately, that the Independent Managers can act only to the extent permitted by applicable law, which is deemed to be the corporate law of Delaware. Delaware law in turn provides that the directors of a solvent corporation are authorized — indeed, required — to consider the interests of the shareholders in exercising their fiduciary duties. In *North American Catholic Educational Programming Foundation, Inc. v. Gheewalla*, 930 A.2d 92 (Del. 2007), the Delaware Supreme Court held for the first time that the directors of an insolvent corporation have duties to creditors that may be enforceable in a derivative action on behalf of the corporation. But it rejected the proposition of several earlier Chancery cases that directors of a Delaware corporation have duties to creditors when operating in the "zone of insolvency," stating

> [w]hen a solvent corporation is navigating in the zone of insolvency, the focus for Delaware directors does not change: directors must continue to discharge their fiduciary duties to the corporation and its shareholders by exercising their business judgment *in the best interests of the corporation for the benefit of its shareholder owners.*

930 A.2d at 101 (emphasis supplied). This statement is a general formulation that leaves open many issues for later determination — for example, when and how a corporation should be determined to be insolvent. But there is no contention in these cases that the Subject Debtors were insolvent at any time — indeed, Movants' contention is that they were and are solvent. Movants therefore get no assistance from Delaware law in the contention that the Independent Managers should have considered only the interests of the secured creditor when they made their decisions to file Chapter 11 petitions, or that there was a breach of fiduciary duty on the part of any of the managers by voting to file based on the interests of the Group.

The record at bar does not explain exactly what the Independent Managers were supposed to do. It appears that the Movants may have thought the Independent Managers were obligated to protect only their interests. For example, an officer of ING Clarion testified that "the real reason" he was disturbed by the Chapter 11 filings was the inability of the Independent Managers to prevent one:

> Well, my understanding of the bankruptcy as it pertains to these borrowers is that there was an independent board member who was meant to, at least from the lender's point of view, meant to prevent a bankruptcy filing to make them a bankruptcy-remote, and that such filings were not anticipated to happen.

However, if Movants believed that an "independent" manager can serve on a board solely for the purpose of voting "no" to a bankruptcy filing because of the desires of a secured creditor, they were mistaken. As the Delaware cases stress, directors and managers owe their duties to the corporation and, ordinarily, to the shareholders. Seen from the perspective of the Group, the filings were unquestionably not premature.

B. Inability to Confirm a Plan

In addition to prematurity, Metlife contends that objective futility has been established and its cases should be dismissed because the Subject Debtors will never be able to confirm a plan over its opposition.[35] In making this argument, it is Metlife that is acting prematurely. There is no requirement in the Bankruptcy Code that a debtor must prove that a plan is confirmable in order to file a petition. . . . Courts have consistently refused to dismiss on this ground before a plan has been proposed. These cases reflect the reality that parties often find it in their best interests to agree on the terms of a plan, despite their litigating posture, as well as the fact that debt can always be left unimpaired.

. . . .

Metlife's argument that a plan cannot be confirmed over its objection reflects its view of the leverage it has in the subject cases. Its invocation of its asserted leverage is ironic, in view of the fact that Metlife also asserts that the Subject Debtors' filings were taken in subjective bad faith. In any event, we turn to the requirement that a Chapter 11 filing be made in subjective good faith.

C. Subjective Faith

The second element in analyzing whether a Chapter 11 petition has been filed in good faith is whether the debtor has exercised subjective good faith. The test in *C-TC 9th Ave. P'ship* is a two-fold test, requiring proof of subjective bad faith as well as objective futility. 113 F.3d at 1309–10. . . .

Movants do not contend that the Boards of the respective debtors did not act deliberately, or that they did not have an intent to reorganize the companies. In addition to their contentions relating to prematurity and lack of financial distress, they assert that the Subject Debtors acted in subjective bad faith because (i) they failed to negotiate prior to filing, and (ii) the initial "Independent Managers" of several of the SPE's were fired and replaced shortly before the Petition Date.

(i) Failure to Negotiate

The Bankruptcy Code does not require that a borrower negotiate with its lender before filing a Chapter 11 petition. BAPCPA contains a requirement that a consumer debtor obtain credit counseling before filing, 11 U.S.C. § 109(h), and an obscure provision of BAPCPA provides that an unsecured claim on a consumer debt can be reduced by up to 20% if the lender "unreasonably refused to negotiate a reasonable alternative repayment schedule," as defined. 11 U.S.C. § 502(k). Neither of these provisions has any relevance here, except to demonstrate that Congress knows how to impose a filing requirement when it wants to do so. There are often good reasons for a commercial borrower and its lender to talk before a bankruptcy case is filed. But that does not mean that a Chapter 11 case should be deemed filed in bad faith if there is no prepetition negotiation.

On this record, there is no evidence that pre-filing talks would have been adequate to deal with the extent of the problem. Indeed, there is no evidence

---

[35] Metlife's argument is that the Metlife Debtors have no other creditors, that it holds the only impaired claim and that the Debtors will never be able to satisfy the condition of § 1129(a)(10) of the Bankruptcy Code that the plan be accepted by one class of impaired creditors.

Movants would have been willing to work with the Subject Debtors. None of the Movants adduced testimony from witnesses with final decision-making authority who said that they would have been willing to refinance or modify the terms of the respective Subject Debtors' loans. There is much evidence in the record that the Debtors could not even get the CMBS lenders to talk to them. . . .

Metlife was not encumbered with the master servicer/special servicer structure, but there is no indication that it would have readily agreed to a refinancing of any of its loans. Internal documents from Metlife's files show that its investment analysts had concluded that the loan-to-value ratios on several of its properties were too high and that millions of dollars of debt had to be repaid before refinancing would be considered. In December 2008, the head of real estate investments at Metlife identified its debt exposure to GGP (as a group) as a "lessons learned opportunity." A director and member of the research group responded, "We wouldn't do a loan with GGP now, given their problems." Metlife followed up in March 2009, by identifying GGP's "deteriorating financial capacity" as a reason to downgrade the Providence Place loan below investment grade, and it decided that Metlife should "take a pass" on the loan at maturity, rather than refinance or extend the loan. Obviously, none of this proves what Metlife would have done if the Debtors had opened negotiations before filing under Chapter 11, but it does support the conclusion that the Debtors' decision not to negotiate before filing was reasonable and made in good faith.[37]

(ii) The Discharge of the Independent Managers

The second principal bad faith charge against the Debtors is that they engineered the discharge of the original Independent Managers of some of the Subject Debtors and replaced them with other Independent Managers. The basic facts are not in dispute. As discussed above, the Operating Agreements of some of the SPE's required that there be two independent managers or directors. The organizational documents permitted these independent managers to be supplied by a "nationally recognized company that provides professional independent directors, managers and trustees." In the cases at bar, Corporation Service Company ("CSC") supplied at least two "independent managers" who served on the Boards of over 150 project-level debtors.[38] It does not appear that these managers had any expertise in the real estate business and as mentioned above, some of the lenders thought the independent managers were obligated to protect their interests alone. As articulated by Debtors' counsel, "the assumption by the lenders was that the independent director was not really independent."

In any event, it is not disputed that the CSC-appointed independent managers

---

[37] On the subject of good faith, it is also suggestive that Metlife now states that it categorically refuses to agree to a plan that impairs its claim. (Metlife Reply, P 22.) Such inflexibility and unwillingness to negotiate undermines Metlife's contention that it would have been willing to work with the Debtors prepetition to refinance its loans.

[38] Although the record is not altogether clear, it appears that CSC supplies these directors in the same fashion as it provides filing and other ministerial services for corporations. Nolan testified that "My understanding is that they serve on multiple boards. I do not know how they source their directors." (Hr'g Tr. 218: 12-17, June 17, 2009).

were, prior to the Petition Date, terminated from the Boards of those of the Subject Debtors that maintained the independent-manager requirement. The terminations "came as a surprise" to the independent managers because there was "no prior indication such termination was being contemplated." Moreover, the managers did not learn of their termination until after the bankruptcy filings. It is also undisputed that the Debtors selected two "seasoned individuals," Charles Cremens and John Howard, to serve as successor independent managers or directors on the Boards. Cremens and Howard served on the Boards during the spring of 2009 when the Debtors reviewed their restructuring prospects and ultimately voted to file under Chapter 11. Nolan explained the decision to replace the independent managers as follows:

> Given the significance, complexity, and time-consuming nature of assessing potential bankruptcy filings involving numerous entities, the project enti- ties' stockholders and members desired independent managers with known experience in restructuring environments and complex business decisions, who understood the capital markets, who could commit significant time to learning about the projects, and who would bring critical, independent thinking to the restructuring challenges these project entities were facing.

Nolan also asserted that the terminations were not disclosed to CSC or to the original managers themselves until after the bankruptcy filings due to concern that such information "could subject the company to publicity about potential restruc- turing strategies ... " and because the Debtors had no contractual obligation to inform the managers.

On this record it cannot be said that the admittedly surreptitious firing of the two "Independent Managers" constituted subjective bad faith on the part of the Debtors sufficient to require dismissal of these cases. The corporate documents did not prohibit this action or purport to interfere with the rights of a shareholder to appoint independent directors to the Board. The new Independent Managers satisfied the requirements of that position. As discussed above, the Independent Managers did *not* have a duty to keep any of the Debtors from filing a bankruptcy case. As managers of solvent companies charged to act in the same fashion as directors of a Delaware corporation, they had a *prima facie* fiduciary duty to act in the interests of "the corporation and its shareholders." *Gheewalla*, 930 A.2d at 101. It may be for that reason that the two CSC-nominated Independent Managers voted in favor of the Chapter 11 filings of those debtors on whose boards they still served.

In *In re Kingston Square Assoc.*, the Court declined to grant motions to dismiss on bad faith grounds where the debtors' management, precluded from filing voluntary cases, colluded with creditors to engineer involuntary filings. The Court found that this far more egregious action was "suggestive of bad faith," but that the cases should not be dismissed as the collusion was not rooted in a "fraudulent or deceitful purpose" but designed "to preserve value for the Debtors' estates and creditors." 214 B.R. at 734, 736.

The Debtors here have established that the filings were designed "to preserve value for the Debtors' estates and creditors," including the Movants. Movants are wrong in the implicit assumption of the Motions that their rights were materially impaired by the Debtors' Chapter 11 filings. Obviously, a principal purpose of bankruptcy law is to *protect* creditors' rights. *See Young v. Higbee Co.*, 324 U.S. 204, 210, 65 S. Ct. 594, 89 L. Ed. 890 (1945). Secured creditors' access to their collateral may be delayed by a filing, but secured creditors have a panoply of rights, including adequate protection and the right to post-petition interest and fees if they are oversecured. 11 U.S.C. §§ 361, 506(b). Movants complain that as a consequence of the filings they are receiving only interest on their loans and have been deprived of current amortization payments, and Metlife complains that it is not even receiving interest on its mezzanine loan, which is secured only by a stock interest in its borrower's subsidiary. However, Movants have not sought additional adequate protection, and they have not waived any of their rights to recover full principal and interest and post-petition interest on confirmation of a plan. Movants complain that Chapter 11 gives the Debtors excessive leverage, but Metlife asserts it has all the leverage it needs to make sure that its rights will be respected.

It is clear, on this record, that Movants have been inconvenienced by the Chapter 11 filings. For example, the cash flows of the Debtors have been partially interrupted and special servicers have had to be appointed for the CMBS obligations. However, inconvenience to a secured creditor is not a reason to dismiss a Chapter 11 case. The salient point for purposes of these Motions is that the fundamental protections that the Movants negotiated and that the SPE structure represents are still in place and will remain in place during the Chapter 11 cases. This includes protection against the substantive consolidation of the project-level Debtors with any other entities. There is no question that a principal goal of the SPE structure is to guard against substantive consolidation, but the question of substantive consolidation is entirely different from the issue whether the Board of a debtor that is part of a corporate group can consider the interests of the group along with the interests of the individual debtor when making a decision to file a bankruptcy case. Nothing in this Opinion implies that the assets and liabilities of any of the Subject Debtors could properly be substantively consolidated with those of any other entity.

These Motions are a diversion from the parties' real task, which is to get each of the Subject Debtors out of bankruptcy as soon as feasible. The Movants assert talks with them should have begun earlier. It is time that negotiations commence in earnest.

. . . .

CONCLUSION

For the reasons set forth above, the motions to dismiss are denied. The Debtors are directed to settle an order on five days' notice.

§ 1.09   WHAT PRICE GLORY: DETERMINING THE VALUE OF THE ENTERPRISE[*]

Valuation is the *leitmotif* of a Chapter 11 case. As we will see as the course and the Amphydynamics case unfolds:

- The fundamental theory of Chapter 11 is that a business is more valuable — to creditors, employees, owners, and society at large — if it is maintained as a going concern rather than liquidated, because assets that are used for production are more valuable than those same assets sold for scrap.

- The value of the debtor is what is supposed to be preserved in a Chapter 11 case and also what is supposed to be distributed. What creditors will receive in compensation of their claims largely depends on the value of the debtor; so does the ability of equity holders to retain an interest in the reorganized debtor.

- If a reorganization plan proposes that creditors will receive shares of stock in exchange for debt, the value of the reorganized debtor must be determined in order to know what those shares are worth and how they should be distributed. If a reorganization plan proposes that creditors will receive deferred **cash** payments over a period of time, the present value of that stream of payments must be determined in order to know the actual value of what creditors will receive.

- The fairness of a reorganization plan is ultimately judged by how the plan distributes the value of the reorganized business.

- When creditors seek dismissal or conversion of a Chapter 11 case, they may be saying that the debtor's liquidation value exceeds its going concern value.

- When a secured creditor seeks relief from the automatic stay on the grounds that its interest in collateral is not adequately protected, the value of the collateral must be determined.

[A]   Determining the Present Value of a Stream of Payments

The concept of "present value" is important in several contexts in a Chapter 11 case:

1. Generally speaking, in order for a reorganization plan to become effective, it must be accepted by creditors and confirmed by the court. A plan can be confirmed even if it is not unanimously accepted by creditors. The code protects creditors who vote against a plan by assuring them that a court will not confirm a plan unless creditors will receive under the plan "property of a value, *as of the effective date of the plan*," that is not less than what they would receive in the event the debtor were liquidated under Chapter 7. Code § 1129(a)(7).

---

[*] This discussion is in part adapted from Arthur R. Pinto & Douglas M. Branson, *Understanding Corporate Law.* Copyright 1999 by Matthew Bender & Co., Inc. with permission of the publisher.

2. In some instances a reorganization plan can be confirmed even over the objection of even a majority claim or interest holders. In order for a plan to be confirmed in this situation, members of the class must receive "property of a value, *as of the effective date of the plan*" equal to the allowed amount of their claims or the value of their interests. Code § 1129(b)(2)(B), (C).

3. In order for a reorganization plan to be confirmed, holders of certain kinds of priority claims must receive "deferred cash payments of a value, *as of the effective date of the plan*," equal to the allowed amount of their claims. Code § 1129 (a)(9). The House Report explained, "This contemplates a present value analysis that will discount value to be received in the future. . . . "[1]

If a plan provides for a lump sum payment today of, say, $1,000, determining the present value of that payment is easy. The value of the payment is equivalent to the amount of the payment, because $1,000 received today is worth $1,000. But suppose a plan proposes to pay creditors $1,000 in ten annual installments of $100. The first payment will be made today, on what we may call the effective date of the plan. The nine remaining installments will be paid on the first through ninth anniversaries of the effective date. In this case, the *value* of only the first payment is equivalent to the *amount* of the payment. The *value* of the sum of the nine remaining payments is less than the *amount* of the sum of the payments. Although you undoubtedly realize this intuitively, it's useful to think about why this is the case.

Think about it this way. A creditor who receives $1,000 today could invest that cash in any number of ways, including, for example, in her own business, or in stocks, in bonds, or even in risk-free U.S. Treasury obligations. If she does this, she will probably have more than $1,000 a year from today. If she invests this $1,000 in risk-free Treasury bills that are paying 10% annual, non-compounded interest, at the end of a year she would have $1,100. This effect can also be viewed and understood from the opposite perspective. The creditor might ask, "Assuming that I can earn 10% on my investment, how much do I have to invest today in order to have $1,000 a year from today?" The answer is: a little more than $900.

These observations about the time value of money are reflected in the concept of "present value." They tell us that the present value of $1,000 received a year from now is worth about $900 today, assuming two things: (1) that we would earn 10% on our investment; and (2) that the $1,000 is actually paid as promised. As we will see, these are important and tricky assumptions.

Determining the present value of future payments is accomplished in two steps. The first step is to calculate the amount to be paid in the future. If a plan promises to pay $1,100 a year from today, the calculation is simple. The amount to be paid in the future is $1,100. If the plan promises to pay $1,000 plus 10% interest a year from now, the amount to be paid is $1,100.

The next step is to reduce the amount to be paid in the future to its current dollar value. As the first example demonstrates, this can be done by selecting a rate

---

[1] *See, e.g.*, H.R. Rep. 95-595, 1st Sess. at 414.

of return at which an amount today could be invested to yield the promised amount on the date it is promised to be paid. This interest rate is used to discount, or reduce, the future payment to its current dollar value. Sometimes this is also referred to as the "discount rate." Thus, in a world where the creditor could earn 10% on the money if she had it to invest today, a promise to pay $1,100 a year from now (whether $1,100 in principal or $1,000 in principal plus $100 in interest) has a present value of $1,000. To think of it yet another way, if the creditor were to sell this promise to the bank that factors her accounts receivable, the bank would pay her no more than $1,000 (and probably a little less in order to insure a profit). If the interest rate that the debtor promises to pay is equivalent to the discount rate, the present value and face value of the amount to be paid are equivalent. If the interest rate is less than the discount rate, then the debtor must increase the interest rate, or the principal amount, or the number of payments in order for the present value and face value to be equivalent.

Assume that you represent a creditor who is owed $4,500. The debtor's plan proposes to pay your client $1,100 on the effective date of the plan and $1,100 in cash on each of the first, second, third, and fourth anniversaries of the effective date. Certainly, the amount of the sum of the payments-$5,500-exceeds the amount of the claim. However, in order to determine whether the present value of the sum of the payments equals the amount of the claim, the present value of the stream of payments must be determined.

Thanks to calculators and present value tables, even law students who (like one of the authors) were English majors can determine the present value of future payments with relative ease. Look at the present value table below. You will see that, assuming a discount rate of 10 percent, the present value of $1,100 received one year from now is $1,100 x .909 or $999.99. The present value of $1,100 received two years from now is $1,100 x .826 or $908.60. The present value of $1,100 received three years from now is $1,100 x .751 or $826.10. The present value of $1,100 received four years from now is $1,100 x .683 = $751.30. Thus, the present value of the future payments is 990.00 + 908.60 + 826.10 + 751.30 = $3,476.00. To this must be added the initial payment of $1,100 made today. Thus, the present value of the promised payments ($4,585.90) not only equals, but slightly exceeds the $4,500 claim.

Present Value of $1: What a Dollar at End of Specified Future Year is Worth Today

Year	3%	4%	5%	6%	7%	8%	10%	12%	15%	20%
1	0.971	0.962	0.952	0.943	0.935	0.926	0.909	0.893	0.870	0.833
2	0.943	0.925	0.907	0.890	0.873	0.857	0.826	0.797	0.756	0.694
3	0.915	0.889	0.864	0.840	0.816	0.794	0.751	0.712	0.658	0.579
4	0.888	0.855	0.823	0.792	0.763	0.735	0.683	0.636	0.572	0.482
5	0.863	0.822	0.784	0.747	0.713	0.681	0.621	0.567	0.497	0.402
6	0.837	0.790	0.746	0.705	0.666	0.630	0.564	0.507	0.432	0.335
7	0.813	0.760	0.711	0.665	0.623	0.583	0.513	0.452	0.376	0.279
8	0.789	0.731	0.677	0.627	0.582	0.540	0.467	0.404	0.327	0.233
9	0.766	0.703	0.645	0.592	0.544	0.500	0.424	0.361	0.284	0.194
10	0.744	0.676	0.614	0.558	0.508	0.463	0.386	0.322	0.247	0.162

Year	3%	4%	5%	6%	7%	8%	10%	12%	15%	20%
11	0.722	0.650	0.585	0.527	0.475	0.429	0.350	0.287	0.215	0.135
12	0.701	0.625	0.557	0.497	0.444	0.397	0.319	0.257	0.187	0.112
13	0.681	0.601	0.530	0.469	0.415	0.368	0.290	0.229	0.163	0.093
14	0.661	0.577	0.505	0.442	0.388	0.340	0.263	0.205	0.141	0.078
15	0.642	0.555	0.481	0.417	0.362	0.315	0.239	0.183	0.123	0.065
16	0.623	0.534	0.458	0.394	0.339	0.292	0.218	0.163	0.107	0.054
17	0.605	0.513	0.436	0.371	0.317	0.270	0.198	0.146	0.093	0.045
18	0.587	0.494	0.416	0.350	0.296	0.250	0.180	0.130	0.081	0.038
19	0.570	0.475	0.396	0.331	0.277	0.232	0.164	0.116	0.070	0.031
20	0.554	0.456	0.377	0.312	0.258	0.215	0.149	0.104	0.061	0.026
25	0.478	0.375	0.295	0.233	0.184	0.146	0.092	0.059	0.030	0.010
30	0.412	0.308	0.231	0.174	0.131	0.099	0.057	0.033	0.015	0.004
35	0.355	0.253	0.181	0.130	0.094	0.068	0.036	0.019	0.008	0.002
40	0.307	0.208	0.142	0.097	0.067	0.046	0.022	0.011	0.004	0.001
50	0.228	0.141	0.087	0.054	0.034	0.021	0.009	0.003	0.001	0.000

The hard part about calculating the present value of stream of payments is determining what discount rate to apply. This is not a trivial issue. If you study the present value tables, you will see that a slight difference produces a significant impact on the value as well as the amount of the payments. The rate should include compensation for the time value of money, or "pure" interest. This is the amount that would be paid on a risk-free obligation, such as a Treasury bill. The rate should also include compensation for the risk that the debtor will default.

Although the concept of present value is of considerable importance in Chapter 11 cases, the Bankruptcy Code offers no guidance about how to select an appropriate discount rate, leaving bankruptcy courts to adopt differing approaches. We will revisit this problem in chapter 9.

PROBLEM: HOW MUCH IS AMPHYDYNAMICS WORTH?

Assume that the assets of Amphydynamics include a manufacturing plant and warehouse that it purchased ten years ago and that are subject to a mortgage. The assets also include manufacturing equipment, inventory, contract rights, accounts receivable, copyrights and trademarks. Amphydynamics has liabilities as well, including obligations to the bank that holds a mortgage on the factory, other bank lenders, and suppliers. (Amphydynamics may also be contingently liable to those individuals who claim to have developed Hystereo as a result of playing the company's video games, but for the sake of simplicity we will disregard those claims for purposes of this exercise.)

[B]   Determining Book Value

One way to analyze the value of a business such as Amphydynamics is to examine the financial statements prepared by the company's accountants. One of those statements is called the balance sheet. The balance sheet lists the assets of the business on the left side and the liabilities and equity on the right side. The balance sheet is like a snapshot. It captures the financial position of Amphydynamics on one day, usually the last day of the company's fiscal year. For example, distilled to its essentials, the balance sheet of Amphydynamics might look like this:

Assets		**Liabilities**	
Cash	$300,000	Mortgage	$1,000,000
Accounts Receivable	200,000	Accounts Payable	1,100,000
Equipment	400,000		$2,100,000
Inventory	500,000		
Land	100,000		
Building	600,000		
Depreciation	(300,000)		
	$1,800,000		
		Net Worth	($300,000)
		Total Liabilities & Net Worth	$1,800,000

If one subtracts the liabilities ($2,100,000) from the assets ($1,800,000), what remains is the equity (–$300,000). In this example, Amphydynamics is insolvent in the balance sheet sense, as its liabilities exceed its assets. The company appears to have a negative net worth of $300,000. Although the balance sheet is useful in understanding the financial condition of a business, it has shortcomings for valuation purposes. These are the result of the use of cost-based accounting methods, the depreciation of certain fixed assets, and the exclusion of certain intangible assets from the calculation.

Under generally accepted accounting principles,[2] assets are listed on the balance sheet at their cost or at a lower amount if the market value of the asset has fallen to below cost. If an asset was purchased many years ago and has appreciated in value, the appreciation would not be reflected on the balance sheet. Thus, this balance sheet tells us that Amphydynamics paid $600,000 for the factory. It does not tell us what is worth today, even though the value might be twice the purchase price. If, however, the market is lower and the value of the factory has declined, the balance sheet would have to report the lower figure. This cost based accounting method is conservative. It is intended to prevent businesses from overvaluing assets in the course of adjusting them to market value, behavior that, if unchecked, could defraud creditors and investors.

The second shortcoming of the balance sheet involves depreciation. Assume that the factory was purchased for $600,000. According to the balance sheet, the net value of the factory is $300,000. The reason is depreciation.

---

[2] Financial statements are prepared in accordance with "Generally Accepted Accounting Principles" often abbreviated as "GAAP." The Financial Accounting Standards Board ("FASB") is the primary source of these accounting principles. The SEC requires the use of GAAP by publicly traded corporations.

When the building was purchased, it was listed on the balance sheet at $600,000. However, even though Amphydynamics may have paid $600,000 in one lump sum to buy the building, accounting principles do not permit the entire cost to be treated as an expense in the year of purchase. Instead, because the building is expected to have an extended useful life, accounting principles require that the useful life be estimated and that the expense of buying the building be spread out over that period. There is a corresponding entry on the balance sheet. The balance sheet value of the asset is reduced — "depreciated" — by the same amount each year. If we estimate that the building has a useful life of 20 years, the balance sheet value of the building must be reduced by $30,000 annually, even if the market value of the factory is actually rising. This accounting approach is used for all capital assets other than land. Thus, depreciation is another reason that balance sheet figures for capital assets often do not reflect their actual market value.

Yet another problem with using the balance sheet to value a business relates to the treatment of intangible assets such as trade names, copyrights, patents, and trademarks. These assets may be very valuable, and they may have cost millions to develop, but their true market value is not usually reflected on the balance sheet. Similarly, the "goodwill," that a company develops in the course of doing business including customer, employee, and supplier relationships, and brand recognition — reputation in the marketplace — is not recorded on the balance sheet, even though it, too, may be very valuable.[3]

[C]   Liquidation Value

Although the purpose of Chapter 11 is to resuscitate a failing business, liquidation value is an important benchmark in a Chapter 11 case, because not all reorganizations succeed. As discussed above, a business that is worth more if it is liquidated than if it is reorganized has no business lingering in Chapter 11. A Chapter 11 plan that does not provide for creditors as much as they would receive in a Chapter 7 liquidation cannot be confirmed over creditor opposition. § 1129(a)(7).

Liquidation value focuses on the amount for which assets could be sold. If a balance sheet accurately depicted the market value of assets, the sum of those assets (minus the sum of actual liabilities) would tell us the liquidation value of a business. Since the balance sheet does not usually reflect market value, it must be determined. Of course, the best way to determine the market value of an asset is to sell it, but that approach is not practical. As a result, liquidation value is likely to be established though the testimony of investment bankers, appraisers, auctioneers and other experts, and the conditions under which assets are presumed to be sold will greatly affect their estimated liquidation value.

---

[3] The value of intangible assets and goodwill is recorded on the balance sheet only when they are purchased outright in connection with the acquisition of a business.

[D]   Going Concern Valuation: Determining Reorganization Value by Predicting the Future

Book value and liquidation value focus on the value of a firm's individual assets. However, when investors think about how much they are willing to pay to acquire a business, they are usually focusing on how much money a group of assets, functioning as a unit, will generate. Thus, it is not the sum of the market value of individual assets that determines the value of a business; rather it is the amount of income that those assets can generate in the future that is determinative.[4]

In a well known case, *Consolidated Rock Products Co. v. DuBois*, 312 U.S. 510 (1941), the Supreme Court held that in determining the value of a debtor that is undergoing reorganization, the focus must be on future earnings, not the book or appraised value of assets. The Court explained:

> [T]he commercial value of property consists in the expectation of income from it. Such criterion is the appropriate one here, since we are dealing with the issue of solvency arising in connection with reorganization plans involving productive properties. It is plain that valuations for other purposes are not relevant to or helpful in a determination of that issue, except as they may indirectly bear on earning capacity. The criterion of earning capacity is the essential one if the enterprise is to be freed from the heavy hand of past errors, miscalculations or disaster, and if the allocation of securities among the various claimants is to be fair and equitable. Since its application requires a prediction as to what will occur in the future, an estimate, as distinguished from mathematical certitude, is all that can be made. But that estimate must be based on an informed judgment which embraces all facts relevant to future earning capacity and hence to present worth, including, of course, the nature and condition of the properties, the past earnings record, and all circumstances which indicate whether or not that record is a reliable criterion of future performance.

Id. at 526 (citations and quotations omitted). The going concern value of a reorganized company is sometimes referred to as "reorganization value." Determining the "going concern value" or "reorganization value" of a business requires valuing "the whole enterprise by a capitalization of prospective earnings." *Id.* at 525.

[1]   Capitalization of Future Earnings

Valuing a business based on future returns involves calculating the present value of future returns by predicting how much one expects to earn from the business in the future, how long into the future those earnings will continue, and determining the present value of that future return. The last step is necessary because the earnings are not received all at once, but rather are received in a stream of earnings over time. As explained above ("Determining the Present Value of a Stream of Payments"), present valuing this stream of earnings requires taking inflation, lost opportunities, and risk into account to determine an appropriate discount rate.

---

[4] In a case in which the liquidation value exceeds going concern value, or in which an investor plans to break up the assets and sell them, this general statement will not apply.

How would one calculate the value of Amphydynamics if income were predicted to be $1,000,000 a year in perpetuity, and inflation, lost opportunities, and risk were to result in a discount rate of 20%? In other words, how much would one have to invest today at a rate of return of 20% in order to earn $1,000,000 a year? The answer is $5,000,000. The formula is: PV = A/R where PV means present value, A means the annual return in the future and R means the rate of return or discount rate.

Assuming $1,000,000 a year forever at a 20% rate of return, the value of this investment is calculated by dividing $1,000,000 by 20%. Thus, the amount one needs to invest now to earn $1,000,000 a year forever at 20% is $5,000,000. If the rate of return was 25%, the present value would be $4,000,000. In the first example the investor would be willing to pay five times earnings; in the second only four. The higher the risk of inflation, the risk of default, and the cost of opportunities forgone, the higher the rate. The higher the rate, the lower the present value.

[2] Discounted Cash Flow

Many analysts (and, as we will see, many courts) take what is generally regarded as a more sophisticated approach and look not at earnings, but at the cash the business will receive in order to estimate its going concern value. For example, the income statement of Amphydynamics may look something like the following:

Income	$2,500,000
Expenses	– 1,130,000
Depreciation	– 30,000
Profit	1,340,000
Taxes	– 340,000
Net Profit	1,000,000

When a corporation prepares its income statement, it reports gross income minus expenses, including depreciation. The remainder is profit, on which taxes are paid. After taxes, net profit, or earnings, is what remains. As we have seen, some of the expense items that reduce profits (and taxes), such as depreciation, do not involve actual cash expenditures. Consequently, many investors believe that a business's "cash flow" (*i.e.*, the amount of cash actually generated) provides a more accurate indication of value than do earnings. *See, e.g.*, Bradford Cornell, *Corporate Valuation* 102-03 (1993). For valuation purposes, "cash flow" means income minus earnings before interest, taxes, depreciation, and amortization ("EBITDA") *less* capital expenditures, cash taxes, and net changes in working capital accounts. For example, in the case of Amphydynamics, the reported profits were $1,000,000, but the cash actually flowing in the business was $1,030,000.

In the opinion that follows, the bankruptcy court employs the discounted cash flow method to value a relatively small cellular telephone system. First, cash flows for a period of five years are estimated. Then the terminal value of the business at the end of the forecast period is determined. Then the projected cash flows and terminal value are discounted to present value.

In addition to providing a useful example of how courts apply the discounted cash flow method of valuing a business, the opinion may help readers plumb the mysteries of their cellular phone bills.

IN RE CELLULAR INFORMATION SYSTEMS, INC.
United States Bankruptcy Court Southern District of New York
171 B.R. 926 (1994)

BURTON R. LIFLAND, BANKRUPTCY JUDGE

Memorandum Decision and Order on Competing Plans of Reorganization

[The Debtors, which owned controlling interests in several cellular telephone systems, filed a reorganization plan, and their Bank creditors filed a competing plan. The bankruptcy court found that before it could judge whether the plans fairly and equitably distributed the value of the business to creditors and equity holders, it first had to determine the Debtor's going concern value. In the following portion of the opinion, the court, after a week-long trial, undertakes the valuation exercise.]

I. The Debtors' Going Concern Value

The Debtors assert that their going concern value lies between $134 and $159 million. The Banks argue that this value is $101.4 million. The parties do agree, however, that it is appropriate to determine the Debtors' going concern value through application of the discounted cash flow methodology ("DCF"). Although the parties' respective expert witnesses also testified as to the merits of other valuation methodologies, including the comparable sales and company approaches, these techniques were primarily used to measure the reliability and credibility of their respective DCF analyses.

A. DCF Analysis

A DCF analysis, in general terms, depends on the following three criteria:
1. The size of the expected future cash streams to be generated by the business;
2. The discount rate employed in determining the present value of these income streams;
3. The terminal multiplier used to capture any residual value remaining in the business at the end of the projection period.

Not surprisingly, the Debtors' and Banks' respective expert witnesses disagree with respect to each of these criteria.

The Debtors' expert witness, Mr. Harvey Tepner, is a senior vice president at Dillon, Reed & Co., Inc., an investment banking house. Mr. Tepner has advised debtors, creditors and equity security holders in the chapter 11 cases of, among others, American Health Care Management, The LTV Corporation, Resorts

International, Texaco and U.S. Home. Mr. Tepner was qualified "as an expert in valuations and review of feasibility of financial projections in reorganization cases." Prior to this engagement, however, Mr. Tepner had only minimal experience in valuing cellular telephone companies,[11] and had never advised a purchaser of a cellular telephone system. Mr. Tepner's valuation of the Debtors was based, in part, upon a modification of a cash flow projection which had initially been generated by the Debtors' management.

The Banks' expert witnesses, Mr. John Sanders and Mr. John Kane, have considerable experience in valuing and analyzing the operations of cellular telephone companies. Mr. Sanders is a principal at Harrison, Bond & Pecaro, a consulting firm which provides valuation appraisals to communications industry clients. Mr. Sanders has valued approximately twenty-five cellular companies over the last two years and was qualified as "an expert in the valuation of cellular companies." Mr. Sanders assigned a separate going concern value to each of the Debtors' systems after he and members of his firm visited the Debtors' markets, inspected technical facilities, interviewed employees, and compiled data on competitors and economic conditions in those markets.

Mr. Kane is president of Kane, Reese Associates, which provides valuation, management, and technical consulting to the communications and media industries. Mr. Kane was qualified as "an expert in the operations of cellular companies[,]" and as "an expert in valuing cellular systems."[12]

Mr. Kane and members of his firm inspected the Debtors' systems, interviewed the Debtors' management and reviewed the Debtors' operating reports, roaming agreements, billing records and financial statements.

1. Cash Flow Projections

The Banks' expert witnesses testified that the Debtors' cash flow projections[13] are not realistic.[14] This difference in opinion does not arise from dry technical considerations, but from fundamentally different views of the merits of the Debtors' business strategy. While the parties' experts' opinions diverged on a number of fronts, the Debtors' ability to generate substantial roamer revenue (as hereinafter described) lies at the core of the dispute over the Debtors' cash flow projections.

The Debtors project future cash flow, as measured in terms of EBITDA, as follows: $6.3 million in 1994; $10.3 million in 1995; $15.3 million in 1996; $20.9 million

---

[11] Mr. Tepner last valued a cellular company over a decade ago.

[12] The Banks, however, relied primarily on the report Mr. Sanders prepared with respect to the Debtors' going concern value. *See* Harrison, Bond & Pecaro Appraisal of Fair Market Value of Certain Operating Assets of C.I.S. Operating Co.-1, Inc., as of August 30, 1993, admitted into evidence as Banks' Exhibit 55 ("Sanders Valuation Report").

[13] For the purpose of a DCF analysis, the proper measure of cash flow is Earnings Before Interest, Taxes, Depreciation, and Amortization ("EBITDA"), less capital expenditures, net changes in working capital accounts, and cash taxes. However, as the parties referred to EBITDA during the trial, I will also use this as a measure of cash flow.

[14] As Mr. Kane stated, "I think the [Debtors'] projections don't pass the straight face test and I don't mean this as cruelly as it sounds, but they don't work."

in 1997; $28 million in 1998. The Debtors project that annual EBITDA will remain at $28 million between 1999 and 2003.

a. Debtors' Projections of Roamer Revenue

[The FCC has divided the nation into 734 areas; 306 are designated as Metropolitan Statistical Areas ("MSAs") and 428 are designated as Rural Statistical Areas ("RSAs"). Debtors operate cellular telephone systems in nine MSAs and five RSAs]. Those persons who have contracted with the Debtors for cellular telephone service within one of these MSAs or RSAs are referred to as home subscribers. When a cellular telephone user who is not a home subscriber travels through one of these MSAs or RSAs, she is said to "roam" into these service areas. When she uses her cellular phone while in one of the Debtors' MSAs or RSAs, her telephone call is processed by the Debtors' cellular system and the Debtors charge a fee for the use of their system. Rates for roamer calls are set under certain bilateral agreements which the Debtors have entered into with various other cellular telephone companies.[15]

Several of the Debtors' cellular systems serve sparsely populated areas which are adjacent to better populated regions. The Debtors compare their roamer business to a telecommunications toll road, assessing fees from travelers who make telephone calls while traversing through one of their systems. While approximately 10% of the average cellular company's revenue is derived from roamers, over 45% of the Debtors' current cash flow is attributable to roamer revenue.[16]

---

[15] The cellular telephone business is organized as a duopoly within each market. The FCC has granted two licenses to operate a cellular system in each service area, one to the local telephone company and the second, by lottery, to another entity. The former are referred to in industry parlance as "wireline carriers," the later as "non-wireline carriers." The Debtors operate wireline and non-wireline carriers in different markets. The roamer customer is not billed directly by the Debtors for roaming calls, but by her home cellular company. As the rates for roaming calls can exceed fees for calls made within one's home cellular system, cellular companies often subsidize their users' roaming charges and do not bill their customers the full rate charged under the applicable bilateral agreement.

If a customer's home service provider is a wireline carrier, her roamer call is serviced by the wireline carrier in the service area she roams into. Although the parties' respective expert witnesses testified as to the possibility that a wireline customer could access the non-wireline carrier while roaming, current technology does not presently allow the customer such freedom of choice. Therefore, where the Debtors operate a wireline carrier, they enter into roaming agreements with other wireline carriers, and vice-versa.

[16] A system-by-system analysis of the Debtors' roamer revenues for the twelve month period ending December 31, 1992 yields the following approximate results:

System	Percentage of Revenue Attributable to Roamers
Pine Bluff	54%
Florence	51%
Laredo	38%
Lubbock	35%
Wisconsin Cluster	89%

See Sanders Valuation Report at 24. In addition, Mr. Sanders' uncontroverted testimony was that $2.1 million of the $2.9 million increase in revenue for the ten months ending 1992 was attributable to roamer

The Banks' expert witnesses credibly demonstrated that Mr. Tepner had failed to account for a variety of competitive pressures, thus rendering his roamer cash flow projections unrealistic.[17] The Debtors' current bilateral roaming agreements generally provide for a $3 per day access fee and a 99 cent per minute telephone usage charge. Mr. Tepner assumed that this rate would remain steady for the first five years after confirmation.

Messrs. Sanders and Kane testified that competitive pressures would either result in decreased roamer usage at the present rates or a decrease in such rates, including the elimination of the $3 per day access charge. They testified that the trend in the cellular industry is to create integrated, seamless webs of regional and even national cellular coverage. Such webs are part of a strategy to stimulate usage of cellular phones among all strata of society by reducing the cost of cellular phone calls.[18]

The Banks' expert witnesses provided examples of downward roamer pricing pressure, describing several cellular networks which presently charge substantially less than $3 per day and 99 cents per minute in roaming fees. . . . [T]his comparison provides a striking example of the competitive pressures the Debtors currently face and foreshadows future challenges. In view of Messrs. Sanders and Kane respective credible testimony, I conclude that the Debtors' aggressive projections of roamer revenue are not convincing.

b. Debtors' Projections of Home Subscriber Revenue

Messrs. Kane and Sanders also testified that the Debtors' projections of home subscriber revenue were not realistic. Although the Debtors primarily depend upon roamer revenues, home subscriber revenues account for a significant portion of projected future cash flows. The Debtors forecast that home subscriber revenue will increase in excess of 20% annually during the first five years post-confirmation. Mr. Tepner asserted that such growth is in accord with projected industry growth rates. Messrs. Sanders and Kane testified, however, that the Debtors' systems, both in terms of their demographics and geographic synergies, are below industry norms.

Mr. Sanders analyzed the demographics of each service area in which the Debtors operate a cellular system.[21] Although the demographic data is rather dry, the following brief recapitulation underscores the difficulties the Debtors will

---

revenue. The Debtors project the following compound growth in roamer revenue: 32% in 1994, 41% in 1995, 40% in 1996, 35% in 1997 and 30% in 1998.

[17] Mr. Kane opined that the Debtors' reliance on roamer revenue "just defies gravity, defies what is going on in the industry."

[18] Mr. Sanders noted that this strategy is in accord with the application of classic diffusion theory to an industry which relies on a new or emerging technology. According to Mr. Sanders, classic diffusion theory holds that the first purchasers of a new product or service are those who value it the most and will therefore pay more for it. As the product becomes more widely disseminated within society, consumers who are more cost-conscious begin to use, or buy into, the new technology. Per unit profit margins are decreased, resulting in economic pressure on marginal producers or service providers. While Mr. Tepner also testified that prices would decrease as more people use cellular phones, he did not conclude that the Debtors' roamer charges would be affected in this fashion.

[21] The Debtors did not challenge any of the facts or demographic projections reported in the

encounter in attempting to realize increases in the number of subscribers and in overall cellular telephone usage on a par with national industry norms.

In the Pine Bluff, Arkansas system, population is projected to grow by 0.1% annually until 1996, compared to projected annual growth of 1.0% for the nation as a whole. Effective Buying Income ("EBI") growth is expected to lag behind the national average, and EBI per household in 1991 was only 76% of the national average. EBI is an important measurement because persons with significant disposable incomes are more likely to use cellular telephones. The system area's unemployment rate was 12.1% in 1992, comparing unfavorably with the 7.6% national rate. In the Florence, Alabama system, population is expected to grow by 0.1%, and while household EBI growth should be consistent with national averages, 1991 household EBI was only 71% of the national average. Furthermore, 42% of the area's households earn less than $20,000 annually.

The Laredo, Texas system presents a slightly different picture. Here, population growth is strong, 2.5% annually until 1996, but the economic picture remains grim. Income growth is expected to lag behind national averages, and per household EBI in 1991 was only 73% of the national average. The system area's 1992 unemployment rate was 9.4%. The Lubbock, Texas system's population is projected to grow less swiftly than the nation's. Overall EBI growth is expected to lag behind the national average and household EBI is only 86% of the national average. The unemployment rate, however, is approximately 1% below the national average.

As the foregoing demographic data indicate, it appears unlikely that the Debtors' markets will provide fertile ground for the revenue growth called for under their projections.[22] The Debtors' markets have the capability of producing such revenue, the Debtors will have to compete in each market against those cellular companies which Mr. Kane referred to as the industry's "big boys" during the trial.

While there was some dispute as to the number of subscribers which certain of the Debtors' competitors had in certain markets, there is no question that the Debtors compete against larger, better financed companies . . . [that] are concentrating on developing regional webs or clusters of cellular coverage, [and that] enjoy economies of scale which are not available to the Debtors, who have small, geographically dispersed markets.[24] This disadvantage, combined with the Debtors' lackluster marketing efforts[25] and their markets' poor demographics, leads to the

---

Sanders Valuation Report, and did not dispute Mr. Sanders' conclusion that "the economic potential for many of the subject markets is not impressive."

[22] The Debtors asserted that the lower cost of living in these service areas means that below average EBI would not preclude persons from using cellular telephones. The Debtors, however, did not adduce any credible testimony in support of this argument.

[24] As Mr. Sanders noted, in CIS "we have a very, very small system down near the Mexican border in Laredo, we have a very, very small system up near the Canadian border in northern Wisconsin, we have another small system that's located in the isolated part of the northern Texas panhandle, we have another system that's located in a rural and relatively low income area of Arkansas."

[25] Mr. Sanders also testified that the Debtors have a relatively high churn rate. A churn rate is the percentage of a system's customers who cancel service subscriptions during a particular time period. A system with a high churn rate must generate a substantial amount of new customers in order to simply keep its subscriber base from shrinking.

conclusion that the Debtors will encounter significant difficulty in meeting their home subscriber projections.[26]

In view of the foregoing, I do not find that the Debtors' cash flow projections provide a credible foundation from which to confidently determine the Debtors' going concern value.

c. Banks' Cash Flow Projections

Mr. Sanders projected the Debtors' future cash flows on a system-by-system basis. The Debtors did not challenge Mr. Sanders' more conservative projections, and I need not summarize those figures here. I find, because the Debtors do not operate geographically contiguous cellular clusters, that it is appropriate to value each of the Debtors' systems separately. I further find, in light of the Debtors' business plan, competitive pressures, industry trends and Mr. Sanders' experience in and knowledge of the cellular industry, that Mr. Sanders' projections of revenue from cellular operations are credible.

However, just as Mr. Tepner underestimated certain competitive challenges, Mr. Sanders did not account for the Debtors' net operating losses ("NOLs"). As previously noted, taxes are subtracted, along with capital expenditures and the net change in working capital accounts, from EBITDA to yield the income stream valued in a DCF analysis. A corporation, generally speaking, may use its NOLs to shelter future income from taxation. Mr. Sanders' explanation that he did not consider the Debtors' NOLs because he was valuing certain assets, as opposed to the Debtors' stock is not persuasive in the context of a DCF analysis. As consideration of the NOLs would increase the Debtors' cash flows for the purpose of a DCF valuation, Mr. Sanders' valuation must be adjusted accordingly.

2. Discount Rate

The next issue is application of the appropriate discount rate. Mr. Tepner employed a range of between 12.5% and 17.5%, and Mr. Sanders used 14%.

Mr. Tepner employed a Weighted Average Cost of Capital ("WACC") analysis to determine the discount rate. The WACC approach involves selecting companies which are similar in size, business mix, and profitability to the company which is to be valued. Mr. Tepner calculated that these companies' average after tax cost of debt and equity ranged from 11% to 11.5%. Mr. Tepner adjusted these figures to reflect that the Debtors are much smaller and face significantly greater risks than the cellular companies used in his WACC analysis. This adjustment yielded a discount rate in the 12.5% to 17.5% range.

Mr. Sanders testified that he generally uses a 12% discount rate when valuing a cellular company, and he used this rate in a valuation of the Debtors' assets

---

[26] In addition, I note that the Debtors may not have appropriately accounted for a decline in rates charged to home subscribers. The Debtors projected that such rates would decline by 3% per year while Mr. Kane reported that the leading investment bank in the cellular industry, Donaldson, Lufkin & Jenrette, has projected annual declines of 6% in such charges. In adjusting the Debtors' cash flow projections, Mr. Kane assumed that the Debtors' home subscriber rates would decline by 4% annually.

conducted in April 1992. In valuing the Debtors as of August 30, 1993, however, Mr. Sanders used a 14% discount rate. Mr. Sanders testified that he increased the discount rate because of the level of risk associated with his projections. The Debtors asserted that Mr. Sanders improperly double-counted risk, as he used more conservative cash flow projections and then additionally used a discount rate increased by 2% to account for risk. Accounting for risk in more than one element of a financial valuation model, however, is not improper per se. If circumstances warrant, the risk component in a valuation analysis may be allocated between the cash flow projections and discount rate.

The cellular telephone industry faces substantial systematic, industry-wide risk due to the possibility of technological obsolescence. As Mr. Sanders noted in his report, "in recent years, the FCC has issued many additional licenses for other mobile communications technologies, such as Specialized Mobile Radio ('SMR'), paging, Personal Communications Networks ('PCN'), and conventional mobile telephones. Cellular telephone operators face increasing competitive pressure from these and other emerging technologies." Mr. Tepner also stated that competing technologies pose a substantial business risk to the cellular industry, but he considered that such technologies would not affect the Debtors' relatively remote markets for some time. In view of the fact that certain of these technologies are, in part, designed to foster wireless communication across the entire nation, I do not share Mr. Tepner's optimism.

Therefore, given the level of risk associated with the Debtors' operations, both in terms of competitors within their industry and competing technologies, I conclude that Mr. Sanders has not, through application of a 14% discount rate, overstated the level of business risk in his projections. I note that Mr. Sanders' customary 12% rate practically mirrors Mr. Tepner's pre-adjustment 11%-11.5% range, and Mr. Sanders' 14% rate lies below the median point of the range of discount rates Mr. Tepner applied.

3. Terminal Multiple

The third element of the analysis involves the calculation of a terminal value, the residual value remaining in the business at the end of the projection period. Mr. Tepner used a range of terminal multiples between 6 and 8, implying a discount rate of between 12.5% and 16.7%. Despite Mr. Tepner's claims that his terminal multipliers "reflect a conservative base for valuation," they actually rely on a lower range of discount rates than he used in his DCF analysis. As previously noted, the upper limit of that range was 17.5%. Thus, Mr. Tepner asserted, through the choice of his terminal multiples, that despite the increased risks from emerging new technologies and larger, more efficient competitors, the Debtors' enterprise will actually be less risky after five years. This does not appear to be an especially conservative analysis.

Mr. Sanders also appears to have strayed in his terminal calculations. Mr. Sanders adjusted his terminal value downward to reflect a capital gains charge after a sale of the Debtors' systems in the year 2003. This treatment was erroneous. A terminal value is a short-cut for determining the Debtors' ability to generate cash flow between the end of the projection period and perpetuity. It does not represent a sale of the company per se.[62] And since it summarizes future cash flows after, inter alia, taxes, it already takes ordinary income taxation into account. By making a downwards adjustment to his sales value to account for a supposed capital gains charge, he improperly lowers the Debtors' going concern value. This error, however, is tempered by the fact that it occurs in the later years of the analysis, where the accumulated discount rate serves to minimize the present value of such error.

In view of the foregoing discussion, and after considering all of the credible evidence and testimony adduced during the trial, I conclude that the Debtors' going concern value is $110 million.

B. Alternative Valuation Methodologies

Both parties employed alternative valuation methodologies, the comparable sales and comparable company approaches, to bolster their primary DCF analyses. As I have arrived at the Debtors' going concern value through application of a DCF analysis which was predicated upon Mr. Sanders' analysis, I will very briefly address why I do not find Mr. Tepner's comparable sales and company valuation techniques apt under the circumstances.

As their names imply, these valuation methodologies require the identification of sales and companies, respectively, which are comparable to these Debtors. I do not find that these methodologies are of any assistance in this matter due to the absence of comparable sales and companies, respectively. A comparable company analysis purports to impute a value for the Debtors based on the market capitalization of similar companies. *See* "Summary of Financial Information for Selected Cellular Companies," admitted into evidence as Debtors' Exhibit 73. However, the companies which Mr. Tepner identified for comparison are not only much larger than these Debtors, but as Mr. Tepner recognized, are more mature because they have track records of generating positive EBITDA. I conclude that because of the lack of comparable companies this methodology is of limited assistance to the Court.

NOTES AND QUESTIONS

(1)   In their article, *Reorganization Value*, 51 Bus. Law. 419, 440 (1996), Peter Pantaleo and Barry Ridings observe that courts "have not had an easy time properly applying the discounted cash flow analysis in reorganization cases." Although they regard *Cellular Information Systems* as one of the better valuation cases, they detected some flaws in the court's analysis:

> [T]he debtors' expert used a WACC in the range of 12.5% to 17.5% to discount the cash flows during the projection period and "terminal multiples between six and eight" to calculate terminal value. The multiples implied a capitalization rate of between twelve and one-half percent and sixteen and seven-tenths percent (1/6 = .167%; 1/8 = .125%). This range, the court noted, was lower than the 12.5% to 17.5% range of discount rates

---

[62] Although, at least in theory, cash flow times a properly determined terminal multiple should represent the price a buyer would be willing to pay for a business.

used to discount the projected cash flows. The court interpreted this to mean that, according to the debtors, "despite the increased risks from emerging new technologies and larger, more efficient competitors, the Debtors' enterprise will actually be less risky after five years." The court thought that this was unrealistic and rejected the terminal value that the debtors proposed.

> The court's mistake was to equate a capitalization rate to a discount rate. The WACC, in that case, was used to discount a stream of future cash flows during the projection period that assumed a certain rate of growth. The growth rate was not reflected in the WACC, but in the cash flows during the projection period. At the end of the projection period, a multiple was used that presumably reflected both the cost of capital (which was implied in the WACC) and future growth expectations (which, during the projection period, were reflected in the cash flows, but not in the WACC). Therefore, unless zero future growth had been anticipated at the end of the projection period there should have been no reason to assume that the capitalization rate would equal or approximate the WACC.

Id. (footnotes omitted).

(2)   In his classic article, *The Law and Language of Corporate Reorganization*, 17 U. Chi. L. Rev. 565 (1950), Professor Walter Blum observed that the difference between market value and reorganization value was that the former was "real" and that the latter was the product of three guesses:

> The first is an estimate of the annual income which the business hereafter most probably will earn. . . . The second guess pertains to the probable life of the business as a going concern after reorganization. . . . The third guess, which generally is most consequential consists of picking a proper rate at which to capitalize the projected earnings.

Id. at 573–74. Thus, Professor Blum observed:

> The difference between market value and reorganization value is a touchstone for analyzing the reorganization system. Market value is a real value in that it not only is expressible in dollar terms but is realizable in dollars. Property can always be exchanged for cash at market price because that price is made by those who are ready and willing to back up their own estimates of value with money. For the same reason market value can always be ascertained objectively by noting the highest bid. In marked contrast, reorganization value has the opposite characteristics. It is a fictional value which cannot command real money dollar for dollar. It is not set by the estimates of persons who are standing in back of them with a willingness to invest their own funds. Accordingly, it can never be objectively ascertained or verified, but always remains in the realm of opinion or belief.

Id. at 572.

The court in *In re Mirant Corp.*, 334 B.R. 800 (Bankr. N.D. Tex. 2005) made a similar observation.

At best, the valuation of an enterprise like Mirant Group is an exercise in educated guesswork. At worst it is not much more than crystal ball gazing. There are too many variables, too many moving pieces in the calculation of value of Mirant Group for the court to have great confidence that the result of the process will prove accurate in the future. Moreover, the court is constrained by the need to defer to experts and, in proper circumstances, to Debtors' management. The law governing the court, from *Till* to *Protective Comm.* was developed in cases far different from that at bar.

It may be that there are better ways to determine value than through courtroom dialectic. That said, the court must work within the system created by Congress — and , in valuing a company in chapter 11, that system contemplates an adversary contest among parties before a neutral judge. The court believes all participants in the Valuation Hearing performed their duties to their constituencies, Debtors' estates, the public and the court, for which it expresses its appreciation.

Do you agree? We will revisit this topic in chapter 9, § 9.10[C][1].

Chapter 2

FIRST THINGS FIRST: A LOOK AT CHAPTER 11 "FIRST-DAY ORDERS"

§ 2.01 INTRODUCTION

Immediately after a Chapter 11 petition is filed, the debtor's attorneys may ask the court to approve what are commonly known as "first-day orders." Although Code §§ 1108 and 1107 provide that, unless the court orders otherwise, Chapter 11 trustees and debtors in possession have the authority to operate the business, and although Code § 363(c)(1) provides that they may use, sell, or lease property in the ordinary course of business without notice and a hearing, these first-day orders are necessary because a number of things that debtors commonly need or want to do at the outset of a case do not fit the definition of ordinary and cannot be done without court approval. These things may include retaining attorneys and other professional assistants, continuing to use pre-petition bank accounts and allowing banks to pay checks issued pre-petition, implementing key employee retention plans (commonly known as "KERPS"), using cash collateral despite the objection of the creditor whose claim is secured by that collateral, and obtaining credit in order to keep the business going. In some instances, debtors may seek permission to do things that the Code does not expressly authorize a debtor to do even with court approval. For example, at the outset of cases, debtors seek permission to honor frequent flyer miles or gift certificates or to pay prepetition claims of selected trade creditors in order to secure their continued cooperation during the reorganization. There is no statutory authority for such "critical vendor" payments, and as we will see, they are controversial.

Although courts and practitioners continue to use the term "first-day order," it is now a bit of a misnomer. The drafters of the recently revised Rules of Bankruptcy Procedure were concerned about the "flurry of activity that takes place during the first days of a bankruptcy case," because "[t]his activity frequently takes place prior to the formation of a creditors' committee, and it also can involve substantial amounts of material for the court and parties in interest to review and evaluate." Advisory Committee Notes, Bankruptcy Rule 6003. To slow things down, they adopted new Rule 6003, which you should read now. It provides, "Except to the extent that relief is necessary to avoid immediate and irreparable harm, the court shall not, within 21 days after the filing of the petition," grant certain categories of relief that historically have been available in the opening days of a case. These categories of relief include authorization to employ professionals, authorization to sell assets outside of the ordinary course of business, authorization to pay prepetition claims, and authorization to assume or assign executory contracts. The waiting period does not apply to authorization to obtain debtor in possession financing. As you will see in the materials that follow, some courts have applied the irreparable harm escape hatch generously.

In this chapter, we consider several common types of first-day orders, including orders authorizing a debtor to retain professionals (such as attorneys and accountants); to pay critical vendors; to implement key employee retention plans; and to use cash collateral. There is another type of order, often requested on the first day of a case, which we do not consider in this chapter. It is an order that authorizes a debtor in possession to obtain financing. This type of order, sometimes referred to as a "DIP financing order," is considered in depth in chapter 4.

§ 2.02 AUTHORIZATION TO RETAIN PROFESSIONALS

[A] Section 327(A): Professionals Must Be "Disinterested"

PROBLEM 2.1

You have represented Amphydynamics Corp. for several years, and Headley and Carol Charisma have great confidence in your judgment and your lawyering skills. They want to retain you to prepare and file a Chapter 11 petition on Amphy's behalf and to represent the company as debtor in possession. You are gratified by their faith in you, but you are wondering whether you are eligible to serve in this capacity. Code § 327(a) provides that a trustee "with the court's approval, may employ one or more attorneys, accountants, appraisers, auctioneers, or other professional persons, that *do not hold or represent an interest adverse to the estate, and that are disinterested* persons, to represent or assist the trustee in carrying out the trustee's duties." (Emphasis added.) Code § 327(a) makes § 327(a) applicable to debtors in possession, as well. Code § 101(14) provides a definition of "disinterested person." Code § 1107(b) and Code § 327(e) provide limited exceptions to the disinterested person rule. Please read those sections of the Code and the following materials. As you do, consider the following questions:

1. Does the fact that Amphydynamics Corp. owes you $100,000 for services rendered over the past year in connection with matters not related to the Chapter 11 filing disqualify you from representing the debtor in possession?

2. If that outstanding bill is a problem, would payment in full prior to the Chapter 11 filing solve it?

3. Last year, you prepared Headley's will and health proxy. Does this affect your eligibility to represent Amphydynamics Corp., the debtor in possession?

4. Last year, you represented BigBank by negotiating and drafting an agreement relating to software development for the bank's on-line banking system. BigBank is one of Amphy's prepetition creditors. Does this affect your ability to represent the debtor in possession?

5. Suppose that ten weeks into the case, on motion of the creditors' committee, the court orders appointment of a trustee. Are you eligible to represent the trustee?

IN RE THE LESLIE FAY COMPANIES
United States Bankruptcy Court, Southern District of New York
175 B.R. 525 (1994)

Tina L. Brozman, United States Bankruptcy Judge

Rarely am I faced with a motion as troubling as this one, the United States Trustee's motion to disqualify Weil, Gotshal & Manges ("Weil Gotshal"), the debtors' counsel, from further representation of its clients and to deny the firm fees because of its failure to disclose what the United States Trustee ("U.S. Trustee") dubs disabling conflicts. The motion is predicated upon the report of an examiner who had concluded that Weil Gotshal was not disinterested when retained and had failed to reveal to the court the connections which led to his conclusion. I am in accord with the examiner's assessment, although I do not share his view that the appropriate sanction is limited to imposition on Weil Gotshal of a portion of the costs which he incurred investigating Weil Gotshal's status. Indeed, it is the nature of the sanction which is the troubling element here for, as the examiner found, Weil Gotshal has rendered services competently and loyally to the debtors, notwithstanding its derelictions in the area of disclosure, and the debtors undoubtedly will be harmed by Weil Gotshal's complete removal from the case some twenty months into the reorganization effort. This fear of harm to the debtors is shared by both official committees as well as the examiner.

I.

A. Background[1]

The Leslie Fay Companies, Inc. ("Leslie Fay") is a large, publicly-owned corporation primarily engaged in designing, manufacturing, and selling women's dresses, suits, and sportswear. It is one of the few large American clothing manufacturers which still manufactures in the United States.

On January 29, 1993, Leslie Fay's controller, Donald Kenia, disclosed to senior management that he had been making unsupported entries into Leslie Fay's general ledger, resulting in a significant misstatement of its financial standing. Two days later, senior management informed Leslie Fay's board of directors (the "Board" or "Board of Directors") which in turn disclosed the existence of the false entries to the general public.

The Board directed its audit committee (the "Audit Committee") to conduct an investigation into the facts and circumstances surrounding the accounting irregularities. At the time, the Audit Committee was composed of three independent, non-management directors: Ira J. Hechler, a private investor; Ralph Destino, Chairman of Cartier, Inc.; and Michael L. Tarnopol, a senior officer at Bear Stearns & Co. ("Bear Stearns"). The Board then appointed Steven Friedman, the only other

---

[1] The parties do not dispute the facts, most of which are drawn from the examiner's report or the court's own file.

outside director of Leslie Fay, to join Hechler, Destino, and Tarnopol on the Audit Committee and in their investigation of the accounting irregularities. Friedman is a senior manager of Odyssey Partners L.P. ("Odyssey"), a large partnership that acts principally as a merchant bank.

Included in the Audit Committee's charter were the identification of all parties who may have been involved in the accounting irregularities and the consideration of possible legal claims that could be asserted on behalf of Leslie Fay. Toward those ends, the Audit Committee retained the accounting firm of Arthur Anderson & Co. and Weil Gotshal. Prior to its retention by the Audit Committee, Weil Gotshal had not done any work for Leslie Fay, whose general outside counsel was the law firm of Parker, Chapin, Flattau & Klimpl ("Parker Chapin").

In late February, 1993, the Audit Committee issued preliminary results of its work, announcing that Leslie Fay's 1991 profits had been overstated by over $12 million. Accordingly, the accounting firm of BDO Seidman ("Seidman"), Leslie Fay's independent auditors, officially withdrew its signature from Leslie Fay's 1991 financial statements. The Audit Committee had also learned by this point that Kenia's initial representation that he alone was responsible for the false entries was not true. As was later confirmed, the fraud reached to Leslie Fay's chief financial officer, Paul Polishan.

B. Weil Gotshal's Court-Approved Retention and the Subsequent Questions

The consequences of this burgeoning scandal were calamitous to Leslie Fay. Lenders and suppliers froze its credit lines, and Leslie Fay was unable to secure the financing necessary for the continued operation of its business. This led to an expansion of Weil Gotshal's role to include advice on financial restructuring. On April 5, 1993, nine weeks into the Audit Committee's investigation, Weil Gotshal filed chapter 11 petitions on behalf of Leslie Fay and its affiliates (the group referred to for convenience as "Leslie Fay"). The same day, Weil Gotshal submitted an application for retention as counsel for the debtors in possession, which was approved by the Hon. Cornelius Blackshear of this court. The order contemplated that Weil Gotshal would continue in its work for the Audit Committee as part and parcel of its representation of the debtors. The U.S. Trustee, the only party in interest to receive notice, had indicated that he did not object to the retention.

By late September, the Audit Committee completed its investigation, and on September 27, 1993, it disclosed its findings to the Board of Directors. The Audit Committee concluded that there was no evidence that any member of the debtors' current[2] senior management or the Board of Directors knew of or participated in the fraudulent entries, which it estimated totaled some $160 million. The Audit Committee also discovered, contrary to what was originally believed, that the accounting irregularities dated back to at least 1990. These findings were made public on September 29, 1993.

At just about this time, questions regarding Weil Gotshal's disinterestedness were raised by the official committee of unsecured creditors (the "Creditors'

---

[2] By this time, Polishan was no longer Leslie Fay's chief financial officer.

Committee"). A hearing on first interim fee applications had been set for November 4, 1993. Both the Creditors' Committee and the U.S. Trustee filed objections to Weil Gotshal's request for fees on the grounds that Weil Gotshal was not disinterested as required by § 327(a),[3] and had failed to file a full and complete disclosure as required by Fed. R. Bankr. P. 2014.[4]

Weil Gotshal responded to the objections by asserting that it had met the Code's disinterestedness requirement and had fully satisfied its disclosure obligations in its retention affidavit. In addition, Weil Gotshal submitted a supplemental affidavit containing information regarding certain of its previously-undisclosed relationships that had been questioned by the Creditors' Committee.

C. Appointment of the Examiner

On December 2, 1993, in response to the cloud hovering over Weil Gotshal's representation of the debtors, Leslie Fay moved for the appointment of an examiner to look into Weil Gotshal's disclosure and disinterestedness and the veracity of the Audit Committee's report in light of those issues. The Creditors' Committee agreed that I should appoint an examiner, but asked that the scope of the examiner's retention be expanded beyond that proposed by Leslie Fay. On December 16, 1993, I ordered the appointment of an examiner who would be charged with two tasks, the first of which was

> undertaking such investigation and analyses as are necessary to formulate a recommendation to the Court as to whether the law firm of Weil, Gotshal & Manges, in its capacity as attorneys for the Debtors in Possession herein, under the circumstances of these chapter 11 cases and in accordance with section 327 of the Bankruptcy Code and Rule 2014 of the Federal Rules of Bankruptcy Procedure, is disinterested or holds or represents an interest adverse to the Debtors' estates or made adequate disclosure.

The second task assigned to the examiner was to evaluate whether (i) there were any viable claims that could be asserted against any other parties in connection with the accounting irregularities that could increase the size of the chapter 11 estate and; (ii) whether the Audit Committee's work in that regard had been acceptable or if further investigating was necessary. I approved the appointment of Charles A. Stillman as examiner on January 18, 1994. Over the next six months, the examiner conducted a thorough investigation into Weil Gotshal's alleged conflicts and into the

---

[3] Section 327(a) provides:

> Except as otherwise provided in this section, the trustee, with the court's approval, may employ one or more attorneys . . . that do not hold or represent an interest adverse to the estate, and that are disinterested persons, to represent or assist the trustee in carrying out the trustee's duties under this title.

The requirements of the section apply equally to a debtor in possession by virtue of section 1107 of the Code. *See* 2 L. King, *Collier on Bankruptcy*, P 327.01 at n.1a (15th ed. 1994).

[4] Rule 2014 deals with applications for professional employment in bankruptcy cases and requires "a verified statement of the person to be employed setting forth the person's connections with the debtor, creditors or any other party in interest, their respective attorneys and accountants, the United States trustee, or any person employed in the office of the United States trustee."

Audit Committee's investigation of the accounting irregularities.

D. What the Examiner Found

1. The Audit Committee Membership

The disclosure of the accounting irregularities in early 1993 prompted a flurry of litigation. Weil Gotshal represented the Audit Committee members with respect to some of these matters. Class actions were filed charging certain officers and directors, including members of the Audit Committee, with securities fraud (the "Securities Fraud Litigation"), on the grounds that, as members of the Audit Committee, they knew or should have known of the irregularities, and that the irregularities caused a precipitous drop in the price of Leslie Fay stock. Weil Gotshal represented the Audit Committee in these actions, negotiating an agreement to drop the members' names from the litigation, subject to certain conditions. In addition, a shareholder's derivative suit was commenced in state court (the "Derivative Suit"), charging the Audit Committee with essentially the same impropriety that the Securities Fraud Litigation alleged. Weil Gotshal accepted service of process on behalf of the Audit Committee members, but had done nothing more with regard to this lawsuit prior to Weil Gotshal's retention in the chapter 11 cases.[5]

2. Weil Gotshal's Relationships with the Potential Targets of Its Investigation

Whereas prior to Weil Gotshal's retention by the Audit Committee it had never represented Leslie Fay, it did maintain professional and personal relationships with parties that had an interest in the outcome of the Audit Committee investigation. Yet none of these relationships was disclosed to the court.

(a) Tarnopol/Bear Stearns

Michael L. Tarnopol is a director of Leslie Fay and was a member of the Audit Committee throughout the period when the accounting irregularities were taking place. He is also a senior officer at Bear Stearns. Bear Stearns, a large investment bank, is a valuable client of Weil Gotshal, and was so at the time of Weil Gotshal's retention by Leslie Fay. Weil Gotshal admitted to the examiner that it would not initiate a lawsuit against Bear Stearns on behalf of another client without Bear Stearns' consent.

Bear Stearns was the lead underwriter in a secondary public offering of 2.1 million shares of Leslie Fay stock, then valued at approximately $40 million (the "Stock Sale") in June, 1991, well after the accounting irregularities began.

---

[5] The Justice Department got into the act as well, commencing an investigation into the accounting fraud at Leslie Fay. The Audit Committee assured the United States Attorney of its intent to fully cooperate with the investigation. Typically, Weil Gotshal was responsible for responding to information requests by the U.S. Attorney on behalf of the Audit Committee.

The examiner concluded that Tarnopol was a potential target of the Audit Committee's investigation.

(b) Friedman/Odyssey

Steven Friedman is a director of Leslie Fay who was appointed to the Audit Committee when the accounting irregularities came to light. At the time of Weil Gotshal's retention, he was also a general partner of Odyssey. Odyssey is another longstanding client of Weil Gotshal, one against whom Weil Gotshal also would not initiate suit absent the client's consent. Additionally, Odyssey and Friedman were the owners of the 2.1 million shares that were the subject of the Stock Sale.

Weil Gotshal also represented Friedman personally, providing him with estate planning services in 1988 and 1989. It has done the same for other Odyssey partners. Moreover, two other Odyssey partners had served on Leslie Fay's Board of Directors during the period of the accounting irregularities.

The examiner found that Friedman, like Tarnopol, was a potential target of the Audit Committee's investigation.

(c) BDO Seidman

Seidman was Leslie Fay's independent auditor during the period of the accounting irregularities. It was Seidman that had certified Leslie Fay's false financial statements. That Seidman was a natural target of the Audit Committee's investigation is obvious. Not surprisingly, Seidman was a party to both the Securities Fraud Litigation and the Derivative Suit. Seidman is also a Weil Gotshal client, albeit on a much smaller scale than Bear Stearns or Odyssey. Weil Gotshal has represented Seidman in two matters. One matter involved the nonpublic investigation of a former Seidman client by a federal regulatory agency. Weil Gotshal assisted Seidman in furnishing documents requested by that agency. That matter was inactive at the time of Weil Gotshal's retention by Leslie Fay. Weil Gotshal also represented Seidman in a malpractice lawsuit commenced against Seidman in June, 1992. As of the date of Weil Gotshal's retention by court order, the case was still active, although the amount of fees involved in that case was relatively small.

3. Weil Gotshal's Undisclosed Representation of Leslie Fay's Seventh Largest Creditor

At the time of Weil Gotshal's retention, Forstmann & Co. ("Forstmann") was Leslie Fay's seventh largest creditor, with a claim of approximately $700,000. It subsequently sold its claim and resigned from the Creditors' Committee. Weil Gotshal was general outside counsel to Forstmann through 1991 and since then has served Forstmann in a more limited role, nonetheless continuing to represent Forstmann on a variety of matters.

E. The Extent of Weil Gotshal's Disclosure

In connection with Weil Gotshal's retention application of April 5, 1993, Alan B. Miller, a partner of the firm, submitted an affidavit of retention to the court in which he professed that, to the best of his knowledge, Weil Gotshal did not "hold[] or represent[] any interest adverse to the debtors or their estates in the matters upon which [Weil Gotshal] was to be employed." The affidavit disclosed that Weil Gotshal had been working for the Audit Committee, had counseled Leslie Fay with regard to its efforts to restructure its debt, and had assisted it in the filing of the chapter 11 petitions. The affidavit also disclosed generally that Weil Gotshal represented entities that were "claimants of the Debtors in matters totally unrelated to the Debtors' cases." Some examples of those claimants were listed, although Forstmann was not one of them. (Even after the Creditors' Committee was formed and Forstmann was made a member, Weil Gotshal did not disclose its representation of Forstmann.) In addition, the affidavit contained the boilerplate statement that Weil Gotshal was involved in numerous unrelated matters with attorneys and accountants that represented parties-in-interest in the chapter 11 cases, but that none of those relationships was adverse to Leslie Fay.

Weil Gotshal did not disclose, however, that it had professional relationships with individual Audit Committee members. It did not disclose that it represented Bear Stearns and Odyssey, and that those companies were connected to Friedman and Tarnopol, respectively. It did not disclose Bear Stearns' and Odyssey's relationship to the Stock Sale. Similarly, Weil Gotshal did not disclose its relationship with Seidman, despite the fact that, even at the time, Weil Gotshal recognized that Leslie Fay might have claims against Seidman.

F. The Examiner's Conclusions

The examiner concluded that "Weil Gotshal was not disinterested in the matter, and did not make proper disclosure, as mandated by the Bankruptcy Code and related provisions." Specifically, he found that Weil Gotshal had failed to disclose its relationship to two of the members of the Audit Committee and the firms of which they were partners, to Seidman and to one of the debtors' largest unsecured creditors. And he concluded that these undisclosed relationships, if known, would have cast substantial doubt on whether Weil Gotshal could conduct a fair and impartial investigation for the Audit Committee.[6] However, he also found that "the conflict presented [was] principally one of perception: under all the circumstances, there [was] a fair perception that because of multiple representations and client relationships, Weil Gotshal would be unable to act solely in the debtors' best interests." According to the examiner, Weil Gotshal caused the debtors no actual injury, and represented them in an exemplary fashion. Thus, he concluded, the appropriate sanction would be the disallowance out of future fees of some of the cost of his investigation into Weil Gotshal's disinterestedness and disclosure, but he recommended that "disqualifying Weil Gotshal, or imposing a sanction beyond such limited allowance of fees, [was] not warranted."

---

[6] However, he did not believe that the Forstmann connection presented a conflict. I concur in that view, but believe that it should have been disclosed nonetheless pursuant to Rule 2014.

II.

The U.S. Trustee took a different view of things and on October 19, 1994, moved to disqualify Weil Gotshal from serving as counsel to the debtor in possession and for the imposition of economic sanctions. The U.S. Tsrustee bases his motion upon the findings of the examiner, disagreeing, however, with his conclusion that no actual harm accrued to Leslie Fay. Although the U.S. Trustee does not question the examiner's opinion that Weil Gotshal vigorously represented Leslie Fay, he believes that Weil Gotshal's asserted lack of disinterestedness called the integrity of the Audit Committee's investigation into question, regardless of how thoroughly the investigation was actually performed. According to the U.S. Trustee, "when the credibility of an action by the Debtors' counsel is an integral element of the very task to be performed — as it was in this case — any 'conflict' which exists in performing that function causes actual harm."

In response to the U.S. Trustee's motion, Weil Gotshal vigorously denies that it ever had any conflict of interest or that it did not meet its disclosure obligations. In Weil Gotshal's view, "the U.S. Trustee's allegations are simply wrong as a matter of fact and law." (Weil Gotshal Memorandum of Law at 2). Trying to turn the defense of its actions into an attack on the motives of those who have raised any question, Well Gotshal has labeled the initial Creditors' Committee challenge as a pressure tactic and the U.S. Trustee's motion as a vindictive action prompted by certain newspaper articles which must have been unsettling to the Trustee. This is somewhat startling given the existence of a report by an independent examiner which concluded that there was substance to the concerns first voiced by the Creditors' Committee.

Perhaps ironically, the Creditors' Committee now opposes the U.S. Trustee's motion, at least to the extent that it seeks to disqualify Weil Gotshal.[7] As mentioned earlier, the Creditors' Committee fears grave harm to Leslie Fay, and, by extension, its creditors, stockholders and employees, should Weil Gotshal be disqualified. The Committee's preferred remedy is an economic sanction. The Official Committee of Equity Security Holders (the "Equity Committee") essentially concurs with the Creditors' Committee, admitting that disclosure was not complete but recommending that disqualification is unwarranted.

III.

There are two grounds upon which the U.S. Trustee bases his motion, first, that Weil Gotshal did not make the complete disclosure mandated by Fed. R. Bankr. P. 2014 and second, that Weil Gotshal was in fact not disinterested at the time of its retention in the chapter 11 cases, in violation of section 327(a) of the Code. The legal standards governing each theory are distinct and deserve separate attention. The facts to which the law must be applied will follow the discussion of the legal standards.

---

[7] Since the time that the Creditors' Committee first challenged Weil Gotshal's entitlement to fees, the membership of that committee has almost completely changed. Also changed is the identity of its counsel.

A. Legal Standards Governing Retention

Section 327(a) of the Code, quoted earlier in this decision, seemingly imposes two requirements on a trustee or debtor in possession seeking to employ counsel: (i) that the attorney does not hold or represent an interest adverse to the estate and (ii) that the attorney is disinterested. The word "disinterested" is a term of art, defined in section 101(14) of the Code as, among other things, not having "an interest *materially adverse* to the interest of the estate . . . ." (emphasis added). It is from this immediately apparent that the statutory definition of "disinterested" includes the first prong of the requirements for retention under section 327(a) (although the definition of "disinterested" includes the concept of materiality which is not mentioned in section 327). Thus, the First Circuit has noted that "the twin requirements of disinterestedness and lack of adversity telescope into . . . a single hallmark." *In re Martin*, 817 F.2d 175, 180 (1st Cir. 1987).

The requirements of section 327 cannot be taken lightly, for they "serve the important policy of ensuring that all professionals appointed pursuant to [the section] tender undivided loyalty and provide untainted advice and assistance in furtherance of their fiduciary responsibilities." *Rome v. Braunstein*, 19 F.3d 54, 58 (1st Cir. 1994). "Once counsel is employed, 'a lawyer owes his allegiance to the entity and not to the stockholder, director, officer, employee, representative or other person connected with the entity.' " Concern with the proper attention to fiduciary obligation has prompted a major treatise on bankruptcy to observe that section 327's standards "are to be rigidly applied." 2 L. King, Collier on Bankruptcy, ¶ 327.03 (15th ed. 1994).

The Code does not attempt to define what constitutes an adverse interest. However, interests are not considered "adverse" merely because it is possible to conceive a set of circumstances under which they might clash. *See TWI International, Inc. v. Vanguard Oil and Service Co.*, 162 Bankr. 672, 675 (S.D.N.Y. 1994) (conflicts that are "hypothetical or theoretical" not a basis for disqualification). The more difficult area is when a live conflict of interest has not quite emerged, yet the factual scenario is sufficiently susceptible to that possibility so as to make the conflict more than merely "hypothetical or theoretical." The courts have been far from uniform in the way they have formulated tests for dealing with this type of situation.

A handful of courts has held or implied that only "actual," and not "potential," conflicts of interest are disabling. A greater number of courts, including some in this district, have concluded that even "potential" conflicts of interest are disabling. Yet other courts have been critical of the very distinction between actual and potential conflicts. Recently, in *TWI International*, decided in the Southern District of New York, 162 Bankr. at 675, the district court stated that " 'disqualification should be mandated when an actual, as opposed to hypothetical or theoretical, conflict is present. This in no way precludes disqualification for a potential conflict. The test is merely one of a potential actual conflict.' " *Id.*

The debate over this issue may be more semantic than substantive, for a close review of the cited cases indicates that the results were largely driven by the facts of each case. And indeed, in the context of section 327, that is precisely the way it should be. Potential conflicts, no less than actual ones, can provide motives for attorneys to act in ways contrary to the best interests of their clients. Rather than worry about the potential/actual dichotomy it is more productive to ask whether a professional has "either a meaningful incentive to act contrary to the best interests of the estate and its sundry creditors — an incentive sufficient to place those parties at more than acceptable risk — or the reasonable perception of one." *In re Martin*, 817 F.2d at 180–81. In other words, if it is plausible that the representation of another interest may cause the debtor's attorneys to act any differently than they would without that other representation, then they have a conflict and an interest adverse to the estate.

B. Legal Standards Governing Disclosure

Fed. R. Bankr. P. 2014 requires that a professional seeking employment in a bankruptcy case submit a "verified statement . . . setting forth the person's connections" to the debtor, creditors and any other party in interest. The purpose of Rule 2014, as expressed by the Collier treatise,

> is to provide the court (and the United States Trustee) with information necessary to determine whether the professional's employment meets the broad test of being in the best interest of the estate. To that end, a failure to disclose any fact which may influence the court's decision may result in a later determination that disclosure was inadequate and sanctions should be imposed on the professional. The fact that disclosure was made elsewhere (*e.g.*, in the debtor's schedules) is not likely to ameliorate a court's reaction to incomplete disclosure.

8 L. King, Collier on Bankruptcy, ¶ 2014.03 (15th ed. 1994). Rule 2014 disclosure requirements are to be strictly construed. All facts that may have any bearing on the disinterestedness of a professional must be disclosed.

Consistent with the duty placed on the professional, it is the responsibility of the professional, not of the court, to make sure that all relevant connections have been brought to light. So important is the duty of disclosure that the failure to disclose relevant connections is an independent basis for the disallowance of fees or even disqualification.

C. The Application of the Law to the Facts

1. Weil Gotshal Represented Interests that were Materially Adverse to the Debtors at the Time of its Retention.

Leslie Fay's bankruptcy, while certainly not unique, was at least unusual in that it was a direct consequence of fraud that had been perpetrated against the company, its shareholders, and its creditors. When the petitions were filed on April 5, 1993, the Audit Committee was far from completing the investigation it had undertaken; thus there was no way to be sure of the extent of the irregularities, or whether others besides Kenia and Polishan may have been involved. The Justice Department had already begun a criminal investigation into the fraud, and private party civil suits had also been commenced naming, among others, Leslie Fay's directors and its accountants. Because Weil Gotshal was requesting retention not only as Leslie Fay's general bankruptcy counsel but also to complete an investigation into a fraud which may have reached into senior management or even the board of directors, it was especially important that the court ensure that counsel was completely disinterested. Thus, it was incumbent upon Weil Gotshal to be particularly thorough in its retention affidavit. Unfortunately, Weil Gotshal failed to give the court the ability to consider whether the firm had disabling conflicts. At the time of its retention, Weil Gotshal had significant ties to three potential targets of investigation, and yet told neither the court nor the U.S. Trustee.

Weil Gotshal's connections to Tarnopol and Friedman were not insignificant, as Weil Gotshal would have this court find. Both held positions in the highest tiers of Bear Stearns and Odyssey, respectively, which were large and valuable clients of Weil Gotshal. Thus, Weil Gotshal had a perceptible economic incentive not to pursue the possibility of claims against Tarnopol and Friedman with the same vigor and intensity it might have otherwise applied.

Weil Gotshal does not deny that it would not have been disinterested had there been viable claims against Tarnopol and Friedman, but rather contends that by the time it had been retained on April 5, it was clear that no such claims existed. This is said to be so for a number of reasons. First, the Audit Committee was already nine weeks into its investigation, and no evidence had turned up to implicate the Audit Committee or the Board of Directors. Second, according to Weil Gotshal, the scope of liability for outside directors under Delaware law is so narrow that any claims against them were "speculative and hypothetical." I disagree on both counts.

Weil Gotshal relies heavily on the fact that, during the interviews conducted prior to the commencement of chapter 11 proceedings, Mr. Kenia admitted that the adjustments to Leslie Fay's financial records were made at his direction. He also stated that the adjustments were made without the knowledge or participation of the independent auditors or the Board of Directors. It is amazing that Weil Gotshal would give so much weight to the "admission" of a man who had committed wholesale fraud upon the company whose finances it was his job to protect, and who had already lied at least once by denying Polishan's involvement in the fraud. As it so happens, it was later discovered "that the adjustments had taken place over a longer time than previously asserted by Mr. Kenia," further confirmation that Kenia was not to be taken at his word.[8] Moreover, I am unpersuaded that Weil Gotshal could have been certain of the outcome of the Audit Committee's investigation in April, when that investigation would not be completed until September. By its own admission, Weil Gotshal did not realize the full scope of the accounting irregularities until the middle of May. In light of all this, Weil Gotshal's claim that it knew at the time of its court-approved retention that the outside directors could not have been liable rings hollow.

It is true that the outside directors had significant protections under Delaware law, but that is a far cry from saying that they could under no circumstances have

---

[8] This means, too, that Weil Gotshal could not and did not know when it was retained by court order whether Leslie Fay might have any claims against Bear Stearns, Odyssey and Friedman arising out of the Stock Sale, another area in which Weil Gotshal had entanglements.

been found liable. For example, because the investigation was not nearly completed as of the petition date, it is was impossible to say for certain that the directors had not been "reckless," which, as the examiner pointed out and Weil Gotshal did not deny, might provide a basis of liability under Delaware law. Apparently, the outside directors thought enough of their potential liability to file indemnification claims against Leslie Fay in this court. At any rate, I do not deny that Weil Gotshal may have had an honest belief in the likely immunity of Leslie Fay's outside directors. "The point, however, is that such a determination must be made by the counsel who is in a position to make an independent judgment." *[In re] Bohack*, 607 F.2d at 263. And here, the attorneys with the entanglements were the ones who were determining whether Leslie Fay would have claims against the outside directors. Vis-a-vis two of those directors, Weil Gotshal had an adverse interest because it had an incentive to discount any possible liability so as to preserve its substantial client relationships with the firms of which the directors were principals. And with respect to Friedman, Weil Gotshal had represented him personally, wholly separate and apart from his affiliation with Leslie Fay.

I also find that Weil Gotshal was not disinterested relative to Seidman. Seidman was Leslie Fay's independent auditor throughout the period of the irregularities, and was therefore a very obvious target of potential plaintiffs. Indeed, Seidman was named in both the Derivative Suit and the Securities Fraud Litigation. Weil Gotshal does not deny this, nor does it deny that Leslie Fay may still have claims against Seidman.[9] Rather, it defends its disinterestedness by pointing to the relative insignificance of Seidman as a client to Weil Gotshal. (At the time of Leslie Fay's chapter 11 filing, Weil Gotshal was representing Seidman with regard to two matters, one of which was already inactive and one which subsequently became so, and the total fees in those cases approximated $40,000.) The short answer to this is that Weil Gotshal should be presumed to be loyal to its client. That the client may not be a major client is no reason to think that Weil Gotshal would ignore the relationship.

In any event, the size of the billing is irrelevant for another reason as well. Dennis J. Block, a Weil Gotshal partner, admitted in a deposition conducted by the examiner that Weil Gotshal would not have sued Seidman even if the facts warranted it. This, stated Block, was because Weil Gotshal represented accountants and "as a matter of Weil Gotshal policy," would therefore "not sue an accounting firm, period." Block testified that Weil Gotshal "told the audit committee and the board" of this policy, and had further told them:

> If in fact it turned out that there would be a reason to take action against Seidman we would look at the facts, we'd tell them what the facts are but that would be something, ultimately, one, [sic] we'd be unwilling to handle because we don't sue accounting firms and that would be something that the company would have to deal with other counsel on.

Although Weil Gotshal told the Audit Committee about its policy, it elected not to

---

[9] These potential claims are currently being evaluated by counsel to the Creditors' Committee, which took responsibility for these claims after Weil Gotshal's possible conflicts with regard to them came to light.

impart this important information to either myself or the U.S. Trustee, an omission that is simply inexcusable. There are two problems with Weil Gotshal's nondisclosure. Certainly that information was relevant to whether Weil Gotshal's retention was in the best interest of the estate given that it would not sue Seidman and retention of special counsel might have entailed additional cost to the estate. But in addition, this undisclosed condition of employment particularly when coupled with a client relationship with Seidman cast doubt on whether Weil Gotshal was the proper independent counsel to conduct the investigation into Seidman's conduct and possible liability. An unbiased investigation of the facts is no less crucial than an unbiased evaluation of the law in assessing potential claims. By unilaterally reserving the role of investigating Seidman to itself, Weil Gotshal created the "opportunity for the exercise of [its] conflicting interests," by projecting the facts in a light more favorable to Seidman than it should have. *In re Codesco*, 18 Bankr. at 999. I do not say that Weil Gotshal actually did that, nor do I mean to disparage Weil Gotshal's integrity by suggesting that it probably would have. But when evaluating conflicts of interest, I must do so objectively, "irrespective of the integrity of the person under consideration." *In re Martin*, 817 F.2d at 181.

As Judge Friendly noted in *In re Ira Haupt & Co.*, 361 F.2d 164, 168 (2d Cir. 1966), quoted with approval in *Bohack*, 607 F.2d at 263, "the conduct of bankruptcy proceedings not only should be right but must seem right." And here, Weil Gotshal's conduct of an investigation where it had undisclosed ties to three of the targets just does not seem right. The better solution, as I will expand upon shortly, would have been for Weil Gotshal to decline the Audit Committee's representation. But in any case, once Leslie Fay filed for chapter 11 relief, it was no longer Weil Gotshal's decision to make. It was for the court, and not Weil Gotshal, to determine whether in fact a conflict existed and, if so, what the remedy should be. The "decision should not be left to counsel, whose judgment may be clouded by the benefits of potential employment." *Rome v. Braunstein*, 19 F.3d at 59 (citation omitted).

Weil Gotshal was also connected with Forstmann, Leslie Fay's seventh largest creditor, but I do not believe that those connections are sufficient to render Weil Gotshal interested with regard to Forstmann.

Section 327(c) of the Code provides that

> . . . a person is not disqualified for employment under this section solely because of such person's employment by or representation of a creditor, unless there is objection by another creditor or the United States trustee, in which case the court shall disapprove such employment if there is an actual conflict of interest.

Based upon the U.S. Trustee's submissions on his disqualification motion, it is not clear to me that the U.S. Trustee actually objects to Weil Gotshal's retention on the grounds of its Forstmann connection. However, I do not believe that Weil Gotshal's representation of Forstmann on unrelated matters constituted an actual conflict of interest in any case. At the time of its retention, Weil Gotshal was no longer Forstmann's regular counsel and there has been no showing that Forstmann was adverse to Leslie Fay. Had there been a problem with Forstmann's claim or had Forstmann been the recipient of an alleged voidable transfer, other counsel, such as Parker Chapin (the debtors' general counsel), could have handled the matter. In other words, any possible problem with Forstmann did not go to the heart of what Weil Gotshal was retained to do. This is not to say, however, that Weil Gotshal was free to keep secret its connection with Forstmann, a subject about which I will say more later.

2. Weil Gotshal did not Make a Complete and Candid Disclosure as Required by Rule 2014, Thereby Causing Actual Injury to Leslie Fay

As I have explained, the requirements of Fed. R. Bankr. P. 2014 are more encompassing than those governing the disinterestedness inquiry under section 327. For while retention under section 327 is only limited by interests that are "materially adverse," under Rule 2014, "all connections" that are not so remote as to be de minimus must be disclosed. Consequently, there is "no merit to the . . . argument that [a party] did not have to disclose its connections . . . because its attorneys did not feel that a conflict existed." Weil Gotshal had no right to "make a unilateral determination regarding the relevance of a connection."

Weil Gotshal urges that it is not necessary to disclose connections to companies with which the members of the debtor's board of directors are affiliated. As a general statement, that may have some validity. But where counsel is being retained to conduct an investigation into the actions of, among others, senior management and the members of the board of directors, most assuredly connections with entities affiliated with board members that could cause pressure on investigating counsel must be disclosed. It is by the same rationale that the connection with Seidman had to be disclosed.

Not only did Weil Gotshal violate Rule 2014 by not disclosing its connections to Friedman, Tarnopol and Seidman, it also violated the rule by not disclosing its connection to Forstmann, one of the largest creditors which served for a short while on the Creditors' Committee. Forstmann had employed Weil Gotshal as its regular counsel through 1991 and was still using Weil Gotshal on a more limited scale at the time of the April 5 filing. This was not merely a de minimus connection. The boilerplate language to the effect that Weil Gotshal may have in the past represented, currently represents, and may in the future represent entities which are claimants of the debtors was insufficient to alert the court to Weil Gotshal's representation of a creditor which was high on the list of the debtors' twenty largest creditors (from which list a creditors' committee is normally selected). The boilerplate is reasonable to cover inadvertent failures to disclose insignificant connections; it is not an adequate substitute for disclosure of representation of known and significant creditors. To rule any other way would be to eviscerate the disclosure requirements of Rule 2014(a). At a minimum, the order retaining Weil Gotshal should have carved out from the firm's role the responsibility for considering the bona fides of the Forstmann claim and Forstmann's prepetition course of dealing with Leslie Fay. By not disclosing its connection with Forstmann, Weil Gotshal caused the court to skip over an area which deserved some attention.

Weil Gotshal's nondisclosure caused Leslie Fay very real harm. The Creditors' Committee spent time and energy examining Weil Gotshal's relationships to determine if it should request some form of relief. Leslie Fay itself felt compelled to ask for the appointment of an examiner to inquire into Weil Gotshal's compliance with the law. Not only was this examination necessary, but because of Weil Gotshal's undisclosed relationships it was necessary as well for the examiner to insure that Weil Gotshal's work for the Audit Committee was free from reproach. In other words, the examiner had to investigate the investigation. This entailed duplication of much of what Weil Gotshal had already done, at considerable expense to the estate.[10] Weil Gotshal suggests that the Audit Committee's retention of Arthur Andersen was sufficient to "sanitize" the investigation without the necessity of the examiner reviewing the work product. I cannot agree. Whereas the accountants are competent and diligent, their role was to uncover what was wrong with the debtors' books and records, not to determine liability therefore. It was simply beyond their expertise to render any opinion on what claims Leslie Fay might possess arising out of the fraud, and whether it was worthwhile to pursue such claims. At further expense to the estate, the Equity Committee was required to respond to the motion for sanctions so as to protect its constituency. These are tangible costs which Weil Gotshal foisted upon the estate by virtue of its nondisclosure. Thus, we are not faced solely with upholding the integrity of the bankruptcy process, although, of course, that is an important concern as well.

The shame in all of this is that the heavy financial and emotional toll in this matter could have been avoided completely. For had Weil Gotshal revealed its connections at the time it requested court approval of its retention, an examiner could have been appointed early on to review and then complete the Audit Committee's investigation, and, if warranted, special counsel could have been thereafter appointed to institute suit. This arrangement might even have permitted Weil Gotshal's retention, albeit in a narrower role. Unfortunately, Weil Gotshal's silence prevented that from happening. I do not mean to suggest that I believe Weil Gotshal to have been venal. The examiner's report shows that not to have been so. Harvey Miller, the partner from Weil Gotshal who argued this motion, reminded me that he had spent the last 30 years upholding the integrity of this court. I believe him to have been truthful in that statement. But that does not excuse the firm's arrogating to itself the decision as to whether it had a conflict of interest with the case in general or with the Audit Committee investigation in particular. Weil Gotshal was mandated to reveal any connections which might cast any doubt on the wisdom of its retention and leave for the court the determination of whether a conflict existed. It did not comply with that obligation.

D. The Sanctions to be Granted

The foregoing discussion brings us right back to where I began, with the troubling aspects of this motion. I have wide discretion in my selection of an appropriate remedy. I could embrace the approach preferred by the Committees and the examiner, imposition of a monetary sanction which could be as large as the disgorgement of all fees or as small as a portion of the fees charged to the estate by the examiner and his professionals. I could also grant the motion to disqualify Weil

---

[10] It is true that the examiner found no problems with the Audit Committee's investigation and characterized Weil Gotshal's work on its behalf as "thorough, diligent, and professional." Nonetheless, because of Weil Gotshal's conflicts of interest, this could not be assumed but had to be confirmed by the examiner's lengthy investigation.

Gotshal from further representation of the debtors and either provide or not provide for a disgorgement of fees already awarded.

As the Second Circuit noted in *Bohack*, the Circuit has been loathe in the nonbankruptcy context to separate a client from his or her chosen attorney where the alleged misconduct does not prejudice the opposing party and taint the litigation in which the attorney is appearing. Yet, the Circuit Court took pains to point out, where the choice of counsel must be approved by the court as appropriate, such that the integrity of the judicial process is implicated, the cost and delay of replacing counsel with a conflict of interest may be outweighed. Moreover, in the bankruptcy context we are not constrained simply by the Code of Professional Responsibility but by the Bankruptcy Code itself.

There is no question but that here the facts, if disclosed, would have led to a legitimate worry that Weil Gotshal could not impartially represent the debtors in their investigation of the financial irregularities and the decisions whether and whom to sue. Because the court was not armed with the facts, there was no meaningful opportunity provided for the court to determine whether to approve or disapprove Weil Gotshal's retention. Plainly, this implicates the integrity of the judicial process by which disinterested counsel is selected. On the other hand, by virtue of the reports prepared by the examiner, we know that Weil Gotshal actually performed the investigation competently and consistent with its fiduciary obligations to the estates. This suggests that the harm to Leslie Fay, which has been a victim first of an accounting scandal and then of a legal one, should assume some importance in the equation by which an appropriate sanction is selected.

The cases have been here some 20 months. During that time Leslie Fay has endured the forced departure of its financial staff, which is a blow no debtor in possession would willingly suffer; a crippling strike this past summer; and now, financial results which are far from those targeted, necessitating an expensive reevaluation of its business strategy. The financial burdens to Leslie Fay of remaining in chapter 11 are enormous. It may not be able to withstand the great delay and cost occasioned by the departure of the counsel with whom it has worked so long. It must begin the process of emerging from this court.

In an effort to reconcile the twin concerns of preserving the integrity of the bankruptcy process and the viability of the reorganization case, I have determined that I will permit Weil Gotshal to remain in the case to complete what it has begun. That is, Weil Gotshal may see the case through to reorganization and may finish those contested matters and adversary proceedings in which it is presently engaged. New counsel is to be brought in, however, to handle new matters such as litigation regarding claims, any avoidance actions and suits for relief arising out of the accounting irregularities. (To the extent that some of these matters could be handled more efficiently by counsel to one or the other of the committees, rather than special counsel to the debtors, I would consider that as well.) I reach this decision to retain Weil Gotshal for existing matters cognizant that the examiner found that: (i) nondisclosure aside, Weil Gotshal had performed the investigation properly and (ii) after exhaustive review, there were no viable claims to be asserted against senior management or Friedman and Tarnopol such that Weil Gotshal's conflict has now been eliminated. To the extent that Weil Gotshal may be called upon in a limited fashion to provide background to new counsel, I trust that it will not seek to charge this expense to its client, an expense caused solely by Weil Gotshal's conduct.

With respect to the economic sanction which is sought by the U.S. Trustee, relief is plainly warranted there, too, both for nondisclosure and pursuant to section 328 of the Code, which permits the court to deny compensation for services and reimbursement of expenses of a professional person retained pursuant to section 327 if, at any time during that employment, the professional person is not disinterested or holds an adverse interest to the interest of the estate with respect to the matter on which the professional person is employed. Given that I am disqualifying Weil Gotshal from handling new matters, I am limiting the economic sanction to disgorgement of the costs, direct and indirect, of both of the examiner's investigations and of the failure to disclose. This should relieve Leslie Fay of the burden imposed by its counsel. I have insufficient information to fix that number now. The costs are to include, however, not only the approximately $800,000 in fees and expenses incurred by the examiner and his professionals, but also those incurred by the Committees in dealing with Weil Gotshal's relationships and its disqualification or retention, because Leslie Fay would not otherwise have had to bear that expense. I decline to require Weil Gotshal to disgorge the fees paid it in connection with the Audit Committee investigation because that would foist upon Weil Gotshal the cost of not one, but two, investigations. One investigation would have been necessary in any event and was therefore an expense that is not related to Weil Gotshal's nondisclosure. In the event that Weil Gotshal, the Committees and the U.S. Trustee are unable to agree on the sum to be disgorged, they may schedule a further hearing to fix that number.

The motion of the U.S. Trustee is granted in part and denied in part. SETTLE ORDER consistent with this decision.

IN RE MARVEL ENTERTAINMENT GROUP, INC.
United States Court of Appeals, Third Circuit
140 F.3d 463 (1998)

[All of the stock of Marvel Entertainment Group was owned by several holding companies, which, in turn were controlled by financier Ronald Perelman. The holding companies issued bonds that were secured by the Marvel shares. Marvel, which was in trouble as a result of flagging comic book, sticker, and trading card sales, filed a Chapter 11 petition. Marvel's prepetition lenders, including Chase Bank, held over $600 million in claims against Marvel, and, led by Chase, they were active participants in the case. Also active in the case was a group of distressed debt traders, led by financier Carl Icahn. Both before and after the Chapter 11 filing, the Icahn interests had purchased — at a steep discount — a significant number bonds and other debt claims by Marvel's holding companies. With the bonds in default, the Icahn interests attempted to vote the Marvel shares and replace the Perelman board, but the Perelman directors refused to step down. A bitter fight over the method used to reconstitute the board ensued — the by-laws authorized more than one method — and the bankruptcy court issued a restraining order preventing Icahn from voting his stock. After about six months of litigation, the district court allowed the Icahn interests to vote their shares and take control of Marvel.

Over the next several months, the Icahn interests and the Lenders dickered over the terms of a plan. The plans proposed by the Icahn interests provided in essence that the Icahn interests would purchase the lenders' claims at a substantial discount and take control of the reorganized company. The talks went nowhere. In the fall, the Icahn-controlled DIP brought an action in district court against Perelman and the Lenders alleging that they had breached their fiduciary duties to the debtor, that they had made or received fraudulent and preferential transfers, and other claims. The complaint also alleged that lenders had conspired with Perelman to sabotage reorganization efforts. At the same time, the Icahn interests asked the district court to remove the Chapter 11 case and all related matters to the district court. The lenders initially opposed this request and moved for the appointment of a trustee. Subsequently, all parties agreed to withdrawal of the Marvel cases from the bankruptcy court and their transfer to the district court. The district court granted the lender's motion to appoint a trustee. The debtor appealed.

The Third Circuit affirmed. It held that appointment of a trustee was warranted where the debtor in possession and creditors were so sharply divided on critical issues that they were incapable of resolving them or making any real progress toward the formulation of a reorganization plan. The court cautioned that it was not creating a per se rule requiring the appointment of a trustee in every acrimonious case, noting that some acrimony is inevitable in a Chapter 11 case. However, the court said, where hostilities are so severe that they jeopardize the reorganization effort, appointment of a trustee is appropriate . . . and necessary. The U.S. Trustee appointed former Third Circuit Judge John J. Gibbons to serve as trustee. Gibbons then moved for authorization to appoint his law firm, Gibbons, Del Deo, Dolan, Griffinger & Vecchione, P.C., as counsel to the trustee. The bond indenture trustee, LaSalle National Bank, acting on behalf of the Icahn interests, objected to retention of the firm. The district court held that because the firm had represented one of the creditors, Chase Bank, in matters unrelated to the Chapter 11 case, the firm was disqualified from representing the trustee. The Court of Appeals reversed. Excerpts from the opinion follow.]

ALDISERT, CIRCUIT JUDGE.

The U.S. Trustee recommended Gibbons to serve as trustee. Pursuant to this recommendation, Gibbons disclosed that the Firm was representing Chase in an unrelated matter. The representation did not involve litigation, but only construction financing for the New Jersey Performing Arts Center, a community organization. The Firm's representation of Chase generated a total of $48,000 in fees in 1997, about 0.1% of the Firm's revenue that year. Its representation was virtually complete at the time Gibbons was selected as trustee. In addition, Gibbons disclosed that Chase had granted the Firm an unconditional waiver of any conflicts which might arise from Gibbons's service as trustee. The waiver included an authorization permitting the Firm to represent Gibbons in any matter adverse to Chase. The district court appointed Gibbons as trustee on December 22, 1997 after considering the U.S. Trustee's recommendation and reviewing Gibbons's disclosure form.

Gibbons subsequently moved for an order authorizing employment of the Firm as trustee's counsel. In conjunction with this motion, Gibbons submitted an affidavit from the Firm which was materially identical to Gibbons's prior disclosures in its description of the Firm's representation of Chase; it stated that the Firm had represented Chase "from time to time," and that it currently was representing Chase in the Arts Center financing.

In light of the Firm's relationship with Chase, the Icahn interests filed an objection to the Firm's employment as counsel, and LaSalle filed a preliminary statement with the district court questioning whether the Firm was "disinterested," as required by the Bankruptcy Code. § 327(a). The Firm responded to this statement with a letter indicating that it could properly serve as trustee's counsel, documenting this claim with Chase's waiver of conflicts and a letter mutually terminating all attorney-client relations between Chase and the Firm.

The district court held a hearing on January 15, 1998 to consider the Firm's employment. At that time, the Firm's representation of Chase had already been terminated. LaSalle argued that it wanted to reserve its rights to object to the Firm's employment if a conflict involving Chase later appeared, and stated that "the appearance of a conflict of interest . . . creates some discomfort." Similarly, the Icahn interests said that "the termination of the [Firm's and Chase's attorney-client] relationship does go a long ways toward the legal issues that were presented," but that "we still have an appearance issue . . . that could impact on subsequent determinations by the trustee." Thus, it is clear that LaSalle and the Icahn interests were concerned not with an actual conflict of interest, but with the "appearance" that the Firm would not act impartially.

On January 27, 1998, the district court denied Gibbons's motion for an order authorizing employment of the Firm as trustee's counsel, reasoning that the Firm's "representation of Chase taints the image of objectivity that the trustee and his counsel should possess." Gibbons immediately filed both this appeal challenging the district court's decision and a petition for a writ of mandamus. On February 12, 1998, we granted Gibbons's motion to expedite the appeal and petition and consolidated these cases with the Icahn interests' prior appeal from the appointment of a trustee.

. . . .

The district court's disqualification of the Firm is reviewed for an abuse of discretion. *See In re B H & P, Inc.*, 949 F.2d 1300, 1317 (3d Cir. 1991). "An abuse of discretion exists where the district court's decision rests upon a clearly erroneous finding of fact, an errant conclusion of law, or an improper application of law to fact."

. . . .

IV.

Having concluded that the district court was within its discretion in ordering the appointment of a trustee, we turn now to Gibbons's appeal. Gibbons argues that the district court erred when it disapproved the employment of the Firm as trustee's counsel.

The Bankruptcy Code allows the trustee of a bankruptcy estate to employ attorneys to assist him in his duties. § 327(a). In determining the standards under which an attorney may serve in this capacity, we must, of course, begin with the language of the statute. Section 327(a) first provides that the trustee may employ attorneys "that do not hold or represent an interest adverse to the estate." *See also* § 327(c) (district court shall disapprove trustee's employment of an attorney who has represented a creditor "if there is an actual conflict of interest"). Section 327(a) also requires that the attorney be a "disinterested person[]." A "disinterested person" is defined, in relevant part, as a person who:

> does not have an interest materially adverse to the interest of the estate or of any class of creditors or equity security holders, by reason of any direct or indirect relationship to, connection with, or interest in, the debtor or an investment banker specified in subparagraph (B) or (C) of this paragraph, or for any other reason.

11 U.S.C. § 101(14)(E). A plain reading of this section suggests that one is a "disinterested person" only if he has an interest that is materially adverse to a party in interest in the bankruptcy. The interest in question may be materially adverse either for one of the specific reasons delineated in the statute or "for any other reason."

We conclude that in considering Gibbons's motion for an order authorizing employment of the Firm as trustee's counsel, the district court applied an incorrect legal standard under §§ 327(a) and 101(14)(E), and even under the proper standard its denial of the motion was not a permissible exercise of discretion.

A.

We previously interpreted the standards applicable to employment of trustee's counsel under §§ 327(a) and 101(14)(E) in *B H & P*, 949 F.2d 1300. Insofar as both parties have somewhat misread *B H & P*, and urge upon us such conflicting interpretations of it, we have studied our previous decision in great detail and today expressly reiterate its holding: (1) Section 327(a), as well as § 327(c), imposes a per se disqualification as trustee's counsel of any attorney who has an actual conflict of interest; (2) the district court may within its discretion — pursuant to § 327(a) and consistent with § 327(c) — disqualify an attorney who has a potential conflict of interest and (3) the district court may not disqualify an attorney on the appearance of conflict alone.

In *B H & P*, an S corporation, and both of its principal shareholders each filed for bankruptcy. The cases were consolidated and a single trustee and law firm were appointed to represent all three estates. After the corporation filed a fraud and breach of fiduciary duty suit against the shareholders, the corporation's primary secured lender alleged that the trustee and the law firm had a conflict of interest. The district court disqualified the trustee and the law firm from serving the shareholders' estates, and we affirmed.

In reiterating *B H & P*'s precise rule on attorney disqualification under § 327(a), we focus only on that section of *B H & P* which discussed the standards for attorney disqualification. In Part IV of the opinion, we said:

While the bankruptcy court recognized that by the terms of section 327(c) "disapproval of employment is mandatory where there is an actual conflict," it does not follow "that there is no discretion [under section 327(a)] to disapprove employment when the conflict is "potential."

The court then held that the court should generally disapprove employment of a professional with a potential conflict, with certain possible exceptions. First of all, . . . there may occasionally be large cases where every competent professional in a particular field is already employed by a creditor or a party in interest . . . .

The other exception is where the possibility that the potential conflict will become actual is remote, and the reasons for employing the professional in question are particularly compelling. This court will not attempt here to define the parameters of this exception, which necessarily will depend upon the facts of a particular case. I will, however, note that even in such situations, employment of a professional with a potential conflict is disfavored.

We do not find error in the bankruptcy court's articulation of the standard governing conflict of interest applicable to professionals . . . . As we have said, denomination of a conflict as "potential" or "actual" and the decision concerning whether to disqualify a professional based upon that determination in situations not yet rising to the level of an actual conflict are matters committed to the bankruptcy court's sound exercise of discretion.

Id., 949 F.2d at 1316–1317 (citations omitted).

This passage clearly indicates that § 327(a) allows disqualification of attorneys only if they have an actual or a potential conflict of interest. In addition, the first sentence of the passage cuts against the trustee's contention, in light of § 327(c), that the Firm may only be disqualified based on an actual conflict.

We reiterate the teachings of *B H & P*: Section 327(a) presents a per se bar to the appointment of a law firm with an actual conflict, and gives the district court wide discretion in deciding whether to approve the appointment of a law firm with a potential conflict. Therefore, the district court erred when it held that it could disqualify as disinterested any person who "in the slightest degree might have some interest or relationship that would even faintly color the independence and impartial attitude required by the Code and the Bankruptcy Rules." App. at 39 (quoting *B H & P*, 949 F.2d at 1308, in turn quoting isolated language from the district court opinion in that case, not our discussion of the standards for attorney disqualification). Following this faulty reasoning, LaSalle contends that section 327(a), as interpreted in *B H & P*, allows disqualification of a law firm for a mere "appearance of impropriety." We disagree with this contention.

To be sure, *B H & P*, 949 F.2d at 1313, does contain a reference to the "appearance of conflict." For several reasons, however, we find this reference to be "a marginal comment [which] will not bear the heavy weight [LaSalle has] placed on it." *See Rivet v. Regions Bank*, 118 S. Ct. 921, 139 L. Ed. 2d 912 (U.S. 1998) (declining to credit a previous footnote that was not essential to the decision in the previous case). First, part IV of *B H & P*, which interprets section 327(a) and from which we quoted extensively above, makes no mention whatsoever of appearances of conflict. Part IV mentions only actual and potential conflicts. Second, we do not believe that *B H & P*'s discussion of § 101(14)(E)'s disinterest requirement, as applied to the disqualification of a trustee, mandates a conclusion that apparent conflicts alone allow a finding of disinterestedness. In this context, we said in *B H & P* that "in some circumstances, the potential for conflict and the appearance of conflict may, without more, justify removing a trustee from service." 949 F.2d at 1313. At the risk of parsing language too finely, the conjunctive reference to potential conflict and appearance of conflict indicates that the two together, but not appearance alone, can justify disqualification. This conclusion is supported by the next passage of our opinion, where we note that "it must be made clear that 'horrible imaginings alone cannot be allowed to carry the day. Not every conceivable conflict must result in sending [the trustee] away to lick his wounds.' " *Id.* (quoting *In re Martin*, 817 F.2d 175, 183 (1st Cir. 1987)). To allow disqualification merely on the "appearance of impropriety" indeed would allow "horrible imaginings alone" to carry the day. Finally, in *B H & P* we affirmed the district court's determination that the attorneys in that case had an "actual conflict of interest." In light of this determination, we do not find *B H & P*'s transitory reference to the appearance of conflict to be controlling. We therefore reject LaSalle's invitation to read an appearance of conflict disqualification into § 327(a). Section 327(a) permitted the district court to disqualify the Firm only if it had an actual or potential conflict of interest.

B.

Even applying the proper standard, the district court's disqualification of the Firm would amount to an abuse of discretion. The Firm's conflict here is not potential or actual. LaSalle acknowledges as much when it states that its concern is "the ability of [the Firm] to act with total objectivity and avoid even the appearance of 'possible unfairness and partiality.' " The Firm has never represented Chase on a matter related to this bankruptcy and severed all attorney-client relations with Chase in anticipation of its selection as trustee's counsel. If we were to uphold the district court's order under these circumstances, it is with the utmost difficulty that we could imagine how a law firm with any prior relationship to a secured creditor could ever serve as trustee's counsel. Such a result would be tantamount to a per se rule, which we refused to adopt in *B H & P*.

The district court's exercise of its discretion is further called into question by the anomalous situation in which it approved Gibbons's appointment as the trustee in this case, and then disapproved the employment of the Firm, in which he is the first named partner, as trustee's counsel. Sauce for the goose, then, is not sauce for the gander. The disclosures in reference to both Gibbons's appointment and the Firm's employment are the same. They revealed the Firm's representation of Chase and that Chase had granted the Firm an unconditional waiver of conflicts. Also, unlike when the court approved Gibbons's appointment as trustee, while the motion for approval of the Firm's employment as counsel was pending, Chase and the Firm terminated their attorney-client relationship. Given these facts, a logical basis for this inconsistency is evanescent, if not infinitesimal. There is an irreconcilable conflict with dictates of good reason in the notion that Gibbons, as the head of the

Firm, is eligible to serve as trustee, but the Firm is ineligible to serve as his counsel.

This anomaly is particularly troubling and augments the primary reason why we reverse the district court's denial of the trustee's motion. We reverse the district court because it utilized a faulty premise in reaching its conclusion. It applied the incorrect legal standard and thus strayed beyond an appropriate exercise of discretion by disqualifying the Firm under § 327(a) based solely on the appearance of conflict. The trustee was within his rights and prerogative to select the Firm as his counsel. To deny the trustee's choice was to commit reversible error.

NOTES AND QUESTIONS

(1) Are the *Leslie Fay* and *Marvel* cases distinguishable? Are the opinions based on the nature and materiality of the conflicting interests or on the adequacy of disclosure? According to the *Marvel* opinion, Code §§ 327(a) and (c) impose a per se rule of disqualification where there is an actual conflict; give the court discretion to disqualify or not to disqualify where there is a potential conflict; and do not permit the court to disqualify a professional where there is merely an appearance of a conflict. Were the conflicts alleged in *Leslie Fay* actual, potential, or merely apparent? Does the *Marvel* opinion explain how to gauge the threat of a potential conflict becoming an actual one? Does it explain how to balance that threat against the benefit to the estate of retaining a particular professional?

(2) The *Marvel* court did not consider whether, even in the absence of a disinterestedness problem, the trustee should have been allowed to retain his own law firm to represent him. The district court thought this might be a problem, and, indeed some courts have suggested that a trustee should not be permitted to employ his or her own firm, absent a showing of good cause for doing so. One concern is that a trustee will not be as objective about reviewing the fees of a firm with which he has a relationship. Another is that the firm will wind up doing trustee's work. *See, e.g., In re Showcase Jewelry Design, Ltd.*, 166 B.R. 205 (Bankr. E.D.N.Y. 1994). Other courts have allowed trustees to retain their own firms as counsel. *See, e.g., In re Gem Tire & Service*, 117 B.R. 874 (Bankr. S.D. Tex. 1990); *In re Butler Industries, Inc.*, 101 B.R. 194 (C.D. Cal. 1989), *aff'd*, 114 B.R. 695 (C.D. Cal. 1990). As a practical matter, when trustees are not allowed to retain their own firms as counsel, they may hire another trustee's firm to perform the work with the express or implied reciprocal arrangement that the other trustee will hire their firm to perform his or her work. Does this practice make a prohibition on trustees hiring their own firm illusory or ineffective?

(3) Whether a lawyer (or other professional) may represent a debtor in possession if the lawyer is owed fees for services rendered prior to the commencement of the bankruptcy case is a question that has long divided courts. As we have seen, Code § 327(a) provides that the bankruptcy court may authorize a trustee or debtor in possession to retain a professional only if that professional is a "disinterested person," as defined in Code § 101(14)(A) and does not hold or represent an interest "adverse to the estate." A professional to whom fees are owed for pre-petition services is a "creditor" within the meaning of Code § 101(10) of the Code and therefore does not qualify as a "disinterested person." Thus, § 327(a), on its face, would appear to answer the question, and the answer would be "No. A

professional who holds a claim for prepetition services is not disinterested and may not be retained by a trustee or debtor in possession." However, Code § 1107(b) carves out an exception of sorts for debtors in possession, as distinct from trustees. Section 1107(b) provides that, notwithstanding § 327(a), a person is not disqualified from employment by a debtor in possession *solely* because the person previously represented the debtor. Still, § 1107(b) does not conclusively answer the question either, because this section is silent on the issue of *professionals who are owed fees* on account of their prior representation of the debtor.

The majority of the circuit courts that have attempted to harmonize these two sections have held that § 1107(b) is to be narrowly construed. Thus, although the mere fact of prior employment by the debtor is not, in and of itself, grounds for disqualification, other factors arising from that prior employment may be. Thus, the rule has developed that lawyers and other professionals who are creditors *may not* be retained to serve as bankruptcy counsel to a debtor in possession. For example, in *In re Siliconix, Inc.*, 135 B.R. 378 (N.D. Cal. 1991), *U.S. Trustee v. Price Waterhouse*, 19 F.3d 138 (3d Cir. 1994), and *U.S. Trustee v. Andover Togs, Inc.*, 2001 U.S. Dist. LEXIS 2690 (S.D.N.Y. Mar. 13, 2001), the courts refused to permit the debtor in possession to employ accounting firms that held claims for services performed for the debtor prepetition. *In Pierce v. Aetna Life Insurance Co. (In re Pierce)*, 809 F.2d 1356 (8th Cir. 1987), the court reached the same conclusion with respect to an attorney who held a claim for prepetition legal services. In addition, the court found that the attorney was disqualified because he had secured his fee by taking a mortgage on the debtor's property. The court found that, as the holder of a mortgage on estate property (and one that was probably avoidable at that!), the attorney held an interest that was adverse to the estate. Moreover, the court ruled that by failing to disclose the existence of the mortgage, the attorney had committed "a classic violation" of the disclosure requirements embodied in Code § 328(a) and Bankruptcy Rule 2014(b). The court ordered the attorney to disgorge the fee he had been paid.

A minority of courts have taken a more flexible approach. For example, the First Circuit has rejected a per se bar on employment of professionals who are also creditors, explaining, "At first blush, [§ 327(a)] would seem to foreclose the employment of an attorney who is in any respect a 'creditor.' But, such a literalistic reading defies common sense and must be discarded as grossly overbroad. After all, any attorney who may be retained or appointed to render professional services to a debtor in possession becomes a creditor of the estate just as soon as any compensable time is spent on account. Thus, to interpret the law in such an inelastic way would virtually eliminate any possibility of legal assistance for a debtor in possession, except under a cash-and-carry arrangement or on a *pro bono* basis." *In re Martin*, 817 F.2d 175, 180 (1st Cir. 1987). Instead, the court suggested the employment of a balancing test that weighs such factors as the lawyer's familiarity with the debtor, the cost of replacing the attorney, the potential time delay necessary to obtain a replacement, the amount of unpaid fees, and the possibility for "actual conflict."

Interestingly, an attorney who has a claim based on routine services rendered in connection with the bankruptcy filing itself is also a creditor and technically not "disinterested." However, even courts that interpret § 1107(b) narrowly, as a matter of practice and practicality routinely permit such attorneys to be retained by the debtor in possession. *See, e.g., In re Roberts*, 46 B.R. 815, 849 (Bankr. D. Utah 1985), *affirmed in part, reversed in part en banc* 75 B.R. 402 (D. Utah 1987). Some courts have permitted professionals who are owed fees to waive their claims to avoid being disqualified. *See, e.g., In re Watervliet Paper Co.*, 96 B.R. 768, 774 (Bankr. W.D. Mich. 1989). The common practice, when funds are available, is for the debtor's counsel to take a retainer and bill prepetition work against the retainer, transferring and applying the retainer against outstanding fees on a current basis just before the petition is filed so that, as of the date and time of the filing, the firm is owed nothing.

The National Bankruptcy Review Commission recommended that § 1107(b) be amended by the addition of the following italicized language:

> (b) Notwithstanding § 327(a) of this title, a person is not disqualified for employment under § 327 of this title by a debtor in possession solely because of such person's employment by or representation of the debtor before the commencement of the case, *or solely because of such person's being the holder of an insubstantial unsecured claim against or equity interest in the debtor.*

(4)   Suppose the debtor paid the professional fee prior to the commencement of the bankruptcy case? Would that solve the disinterestedness problem? In cases where the professional fees had been outstanding and were not being paid currently on ordinary business terms, it may not, and it may in fact create an additional problem, if the payment constitutes an avoidable preference. *See, e.g., In re Pillowtex, Inc.*, 304 F.3d 246 (3d Cir. 2002). Debtor's counsel may avoid this problem by having the debtor remain current on its legal bills.

(5)   Section 327(e) provides that a trustee or debtor in possession may employ an *attorney* who is not " 'disinterested' " by reason of prior representation of the debtor " 'for a specified special purpose, other than to represent the trustee in conducting the case,' " provided that the attorney neither holds nor represents any interest adverse to the debtor or to the estate with respect to the matter on which the attorney is to be employed. This exception applies only to the retention of an attorney, and not to the retention of other kinds of professionals, such as accountants. *U.S. Trustee v. Andover Togs, Inc.*, 2001 U.S. Dist. LEXIS 2690 (S.D.N.Y. Mar. 13, 2001). Such an attorney, who could not be retained as general bankruptcy counsel, could be retained to represent the debtor in connection with other kinds of matters. Explaining the purpose of section 327(e), the court observed:

> [I]t is very common for a debtor-in-possession to require numerous non-bankruptcy lawyers to deal with specific state law choses-in-action that were commenced pre-petition, or to handle other ongoing legal matters only indirectly related to the debtor's bankruptcy and that require the expertise of an attorney in a specialized field of law other than bankruptcy.

U.S. Trustee v. Andover Togs, Inc., 199 B.R. 4, 7 (Bankr. S.D.N.Y. 1996). So, for example, such an attorney might be retained under § 327(e) to represent the debtor in connection with labor negotiations, or securities litigation, or tax matters.

(6) Bankruptcy is a place where the Code's own ethical rules and other standards of ethical conduct — such as the Code of Professional Responsibility — may not only intersect but sometimes collide. For example, Code § 327(c), which permits an attorney to represent a trustee and a creditor, might conflict with Canon 9 of the Model Code of Professional Responsibility in jurisdictions where both apply. Canon 9 directs lawyers to avoid even the appearance of professional impropriety. Interestingly, in a case decided outside of the bankruptcy context, *Grievance Committee for the Southern District of New York v. Simels*, 48 F.3d 640 (2d Cir. 1995), the court held that federal courts, when interpreting disciplinary rules, are not bound by interpretations of state courts or the opinions of bar committees and are free to interpret or apply an ethical rule differently in order to give effect to federal law or policy. While not bound, however, it is an open question whether a bankruptcy court's retention order would necessarily insulate the lawyer's conduct from challenge under state law. Indeed, in at least one case a Chapter 7 Trustee has sued the debtor's accountants in the preceding Chapter 11 for malpractice.

[B]   The Rule 6003 21-Day Cooling-Off Period

IN RE FIRST NLC FINANCIAL SERVICES, LLC
United States Bankruptcy Court Southern District of Florida
2008 Bankr. LEXIS 1466 (2008)

PAUL G. HYMAN, CHIEF JUDGE

The Debtors' Application requested the entry of an order at the first-day hearings in these cases, prior to the 20th day post-petition,[1] approving *on an interim basis until a final hearing could be convened after more fulsome notice to parties-in-interest and the United States Trustee*, the employment of counsel for the Debtors-in-Possession. The Debtors and Berger Singerman, P.A. agreed that all objections to the retention of Berger Singerman, P.A. would be preserved to the final hearing and that the *de novo* standard of review would govern.

In its Objection, the United States Trustee took the position that Rule 6003 of the Federal Rules of Bankruptcy Procedure, effective December 1, 2007, makes no provision for interim relief, and that, unless immediate and irreparable harm can be shown, no relief of any sort may be obtained short of the 20 days stated in the Rule. The Court disagrees.

Because of the recent effective date of Rule 6003 — December 1, 2007 — the Court has not before had occasion to consider this issue. In this Court's opinion, Rule 6003 permits interim relief of this nature. The Advisory Committee commentary plainly suggests that courts rely on the procedures and advanced case law under Rule 4001(b)(2) and (c)(2) for implementation of new Rule 6003. And the Rules referred to as models provide for bifurcation of relief into interim and final

---

[1] [Rule 6003, as originally enacted in 2007, provided for a 20-day cooling-off period. In 2009, the rule was amended to provide for a 21-day period so that the period would be a multiple of seven days. — Eds.]

components. As Collier on Bankruptcy notes, "The first clause of Rule 6003 provides that the prohibitions in the rule apply '[e]xcept to the extent that relief is necessary to avoid immediate and irreparable harm'. The Committee Note indicates that this language was taken from Rules 4001(b)(2) and (c)(2) on use of cash collateral and financing orders and that decisions under those rules would provide guidance for how a court should interpret this provision." Collier on Bankruptcy, P 6003.03 (15th Edition Rev. 2007). Moreover, nothing in the text of Rule 6003 precludes entry of an interim order. *See id.* (noting that there are many situations where "the interim and final relief division would work well"). The Application is a perfectly appropriate one for this form of procedural relief, and the terms of the interim relief proposed by the Debtors and Berger Singerman, P.A. are sufficient to address the legitimate concerns of the drafters of Rule 6003.

Mr. Allison testified that in his many years of experience as financial consultant and as chief restructuring officer in literally hundreds of business bankruptcy reorganization cases, he has never seen a debtor-in-possession without counsel in the first 20 days of the case. Moreover, it was his well-formed opinion that unless counsel was immediately available, the effects on these estates could be devastating. The Court finds Mr. Allison and his testimony to be entirely credible and agrees that without counsel for 20 days, these cases would be immediately and irreparably harmed.

The United States Trustee conceded, as it had to do, that limited liability companies and corporations are prohibited from appearing in court *pro se*, and therefore, they require the services of a licensed attorney to appear on their behalf. In conjunction with section 327(a)'s requirement that the bankruptcy court must approve the debtor-in-possession's employment of counsel, the Debtors are correct that they would not be capable of pressing their requests for first-day relief if this Court did not first grant this Application's request for interim relief approval.

Because of the lack of precedent on this issue, the Court turned to Collier on Bankruptcy for guidance. The treatise instructs that

> So long as the court allows full compensation from day one of the case to the professionals who are not officially retained by court order for a short period and also allows fair compensation to a professional who is unexpectedly not retained, there will be no prejudice to anyone by the 20-day wait and thus no reason to use the special provision of Rule 6003 allowing earlier consideration of matters if necessary to avoid immediate and irreparable harm.

Collier on Bankruptcy,. P 6003.02[2] What Collier seemingly overlooks in this comment, however, is that counsel may not be paid if its employment is not first approved by the court. So, to accomplish Collier's goal of compensating a professional who labors during the first 20 days of a case only to learn at the final hearing that its employment is not approved, the court would have to first enter an order *approving* the professional's employment back to the petition date, then *allow the compensation* for the work performed, and then *deny approval* of further employment. This is a most unwieldy and peculiar procedural two-step, which is ill advised and is unnecessary as this Court reads the Rule. Accordingly, it is hereby

ORDERED that:

1. The Application is GRANTED on an interim basis.

2. The Objection is OVERRULED for the reasons stated on the record, all of which are incorporated herein.

3. The employment by the Debtors, as debtors-in-possession, of Berger Singerman, P.A., as general counsel in these Chapter 11 cases is AP-PROVED pursuant to 11 U.S.C. § 327(a), on an interim basis, pending the final hearing as set forth below.

4. The employment of Berger Singerman, P.A. by the Debtors shall be *nunc pro tunc* to the Petition Date.

5. Berger Singerman, P.A. shall apply for compensation and reimbursement of costs, pursuant to 11 U.S.C §§ 330 and 331, at its ordinary rates, as they may be adjusted from time to time, for services rendered and costs incurred on behalf of the Debtors. Berger Singerman, P.A. will apply for compensation and reimbursement of costs.

6. The Court shall conduct a final hearing (the "Final Hearing") on the Application on February 12, 2008 at 1:00 p.m. at the United States Bankruptcy Court, Flagler Waterview Building, 1515 N. Flagler Drive, West Palm Beach, Florida.

7. Entry of this Interim Order is without prejudice to the rights of any party-in-interest to interpose an objection to the Application, and any such objection will be considered on a *de novo* standard at the Final Hearing.

8. This Court shall retain jurisdiction to hear and determine all matters arising from or related to the implementation of this Order.

NOTES AND QUESTIONS

(1)   Does Rule 6003 present particular problems for attorneys in jurisdictions in which courts adhere to the principle that provides that retention orders should not be entered *nunc pro tunc* absent a showing of extraordinary circumstances? *See, e.g., In re Milwaukee Engraving Co.*, 219 F.3d 635 (7th Cir. 2000), *cert. denied*, 531 U.S. 1112 (2001). Members of the Bankruptcy Judges Advisory Group to the Bankruptcy Rules Advisory Committee have expressed that concern, among others. Memorandum from Bankruptcy Judges Advisory Group to Advisory Committee on Bankruptcy Rules (April 24, 2008), *available at* http://www.uscourts.gov/uscourts/ RulesAndPolicies/rules/BK%20Suggestions%202008/08-BK-D-Suggestion-Bankruptcy%20Rules%20Advisory%20Committee.pdf.

(2)   Note that Rule 6003 does not prohibit courts from hearing motions on certain first-day orders during the first 21 days after the filing. It simply prohibits courts from granting relief before the expiration of the waiting period.

(3)   Although Rule 6003 was intended, in part, to encourage uniform practice with respect to first-day orders, it may not have achieved that goal. At around the same time as the *First Financial* opinion was rendered in Florida, a judge in the Southern District of New York declined to authorize the interim retention of

debtor's counsel before the expiration of the waiting period. Although it found that a delay in retention might be a source of "heartburn" and "consternation" to debtor's proposed counsel, the court found no evidence that the delay would "be a source of immediate and irreparable harm to the debtor or to the debtors' estate or to the interest of creditors." Notably, the court did authorize the immediate retention of a claims handling agent. The court explained, "I think that claims agents, if not retained in a mega case, at the very beginning of the case, could be a source of immediate and irreparable harm. . . . [T]here's a need for clarity in the market right away as to what claimants should do with their claims." Transcript of First-day Hearing Before the Honorable James M. Peck United States Bankruptcy Judge at 120–23, *In re Quebecor World (USA) Inc.*, Case No. 08-1-152-JMP (Bankr. S.D.N.Y. Jan. 23, 2008). The same judge, in one of the largest bankruptcy cases in history, entered an order four days after the petition was filed authorizing Lehman Brothers to sell its investment banking and capital markets operations (including its Manhattan headquarters building) to Barclay's capital. Bankruptcy Judge Peck found that time was of the essence and that the divisions were wasting assets. The District Court agreed. *Bay Harbour Management, LLC v. Lehman Bros. Holdings, Inc. (In re Lehman Bros. Holding, Inc.)*, 415 B.R. 77 (S.D.N.Y. 2009).

§ 2.03 AUTHORIZATION TO PAY "CRITICAL VENDORS"

PROBLEM 2.2

Amphy has always done business with CitiCircuits on an open account. Citi supplies the circuit boards and many of the components that Amphy uses to build its products. On the petition date, Amphy's account with Citi had an outstanding balance of over $125,000. There are only two suppliers in the area that can supply the full range of components that Amphy needs. Since the petition, Citi has refused to do business with Amphy. Headley Charisma has offered to pay C.O.D., but Citi's president, Sam Stubborn, has refused, saying he won't do business with Amphy unless it brings its account current by paying the prepetition debt. Headley wants to preserve this important supplier relationship. He asks: "Can't we just pay them?" You refer him to Code § 549. Frustrated with your answer, Headley asks, "Can't we explain to the court that in order to reorganize we need to protect our relationship with important trade creditors like Citi? Won't the court understand that?" Before you respond, consider the opinions that follow:

SPORTFAME OF OHIO, INC. v. WILSON SPORTING GOODS, CO. (IN RE SPORTFAME OF OHIO, INC.)
United States Bankruptcy Court, N.D. Ohio
40 B.R. 47 (1984)

OPINION AND ORDER

Walter J. Krasniewski, Bankruptcy Judge.

This matter came on for trial on November 17, 1983 upon plaintiff's complaint for an injunction to require defendant to sell inventory to it on a cash basis, for attorney's fees and costs for an alleged violation of the automatic stay of 11 U.S.C. § 362(a), and to set aside an alleged preferential transfer under 11 U.S.C. § 547(b). While finding a violation of stay and granting injunctive relief, the Court declines to award attorney's fees. The transfers in question should be avoided as preferential.

INJUNCTION AND AUTOMATIC STAY

Plaintiff, Sportfame of Ohio, Inc. (Sportfame), runs four retail sporting goods stores in Ohio, three of which are located in Toledo, one in Findlay. Plaintiff carries a wide variety of goods and, in addition to supplying customers at its stores, employs salespeople to call on schools and institutions with sports programs directly.

Defendant, Wilson Sporting Goods Company (Wilson), has sold its line of sporting goods to plaintiff at wholesale for almost 10 years until recently when it refused to ship any further goods to plaintiff. Defendant had supplied plaintiff with a wide variety of its name brand products which are widely advertised and promoted.

On February 14, 1983 plaintiff filed a voluntary petition under Chapter 11 of the Bankruptcy Code. In the twelve month period prior to the filing of the petition, plaintiff had purchased some $45,000 worth of goods from defendant at wholesale and sold them at retail to its customers for approximately $70,000. Sometime prior to the filing of the petition, plaintiff became in arrears with defendant for shipments of goods in the amount of approximately $18,000. Due to the arrearage, defendant ceased shipping goods to plaintiff prior to the filing of the petition.

In March and April of 1983 Sam R. Shible, president of Sportfame, contacted defendant's credit manager by telephone in an attempt to have shipments of inventory resumed. On these occasions, Mr. Shible attempted to buy goods from defendant for cash. Defendant, while aware of the Chapter 11 proceeding, refused to resume shipments of goods unless plaintiff brought its account current or made arrangements to pay 100% of the arrearage.

As a result of defendant's refusal to fill plaintiff's orders, plaintiff can no longer supply its customers with the Wilson line of sporting goods. According to the evidence adduced at trial, many of plaintiff's individual and institutional customers have asked for certain Wilson goods by name. These same customers many times either refuse or are reluctant to accept as replacements other lines of goods carried by plaintiff. Plaintiff's president testified that its inability to fill orders for Wilson goods will result in customer dissatisfaction and loss of profits.

Plaintiff asserts that defendant's refusal to resume shipments of goods absent full payment of its debt contravenes 11 U.S.C. § 362(a)(6) which stays "any act to collect, assess, or recover a claim against the debtor that arose before the commencement of the case . . . ." Plaintiff seeks an injunction that would require defendant to resume supplying it with inventory on a cash basis and attorney's fees and costs for the present action. Defendant asserts that the complaint fails to state a claim upon which relief can be granted.

. . . .

Plaintiff first contends that defendant's refusal to ship goods to it is in violation of § 362(a)(6) of the Code which provides that a petition in bankruptcy operates as a stay of "any act to collect, assess, or recover a claim against the debtor that arose before the commencement of the case under this title . . . ." Defendant denies this contention, instead asserting that it cut off shipment of goods prior to the filing of the petition in this case and that, instead of asking for repayment of its debt, it only sought to encourage debtor to submit a plan calling for 100% repayment of its debts. Upon the evidence adduced at trial in this case, the Court concludes that defendant's actions contravene § 362 of the Code.

The only witness produced at trial to testify as to defendant's reasons for refusal to ship goods to the debtor was Sam R. Shible, president of debtor. Mr. Shible contacted defendant Wilson's credit manager by telephone on three separate occasions shortly after the filing of the petition in this case. On each occasion Mr. Shible, as debtor's representative, offered to pay cash on delivery or cash in advance to Wilson in exchange for their resumption of supply of the Wilson line of sporting goods. On the first two of these occasions, near the first of March and first of April of 1983 respectively, Wilson's representative refused to ship goods to debtor absent payment or arrangements to pay the full amount of the prepetition debt owed to them. On the last of these contacts, prompted in part by an attempt to fill an order for a golf club ordered for one of plaintiff's customers, Wilson also suggested that it might consider filling orders if and when debtor submitted a plan calling for repayment of 100% payment to debtor's creditors. In addition, Wilson's representative suggested that debtor advise its customer to obtain his order from another retailer.

On the basis of this testimony the Court finds that defendant's sole animus in refusing to ship goods to debtor for cash was its desire to coerce debtor's repayment of its prepetition indebtedness and that this act, albeit a passive one, was an "act to collect, assess, or recover a claim against the debtor" in contravention of 11 U.S.C. § 362(a)(6).

As one commentator has remarked, "[t]he stay of section 362 is extremely broad in scope and . . . should apply to almost any type of formal or informal action against the debtor or property of the estate." 2 *Collier on Bankruptcy*, ¶ 362.04 at 362–27 (15th ed. 1979). Section 362(a)(6), in particular, was intended to prevent any kind of attempt to collect prepetition debts:

Paragraph (6) prevents creditors from attempting in any way to collect a prepetition debt. Creditors in consumer cases occasionally telephone debtors to encourage repayment in spite of bankruptcy. Inexperienced, frightened, or ill-counseled debtors may succumb to suggestions to repay notwithstanding their bankruptcy. This provision prevents evasion of the purpose of the bankruptcy laws by sophisticated creditors.

House Report No. 95-595, 95th Cong., 1st Sess. 342 (1977); Senate Report No. 95-989, 95th Cong., 2d Sess. 50-51 (1978), U.S. Code Cong. & Admin. News 1978, pp. 5787, 5836–5837, 6298. In the present case, although it was the debtor and not the creditor who initiated the contact and despite the fact that this is not a consumer bankruptcy, under the circumstances of this case, Wilson's act was inherently coercive and against the spirit of the bankruptcy laws.

Debtor's sole business is the sale of sporting goods to its consumer and institutional customers. The evidence was uncontradicted that the Wilson line of goods, due to advertising and name brand identification, were both in demand and often irreplaceable in the minds of debtor's customers. In addition, debtor sold nearly $70,000 worth of Wilson goods at retail in the year prior to the filing of the petition.

In early 1983 when debtor was suffering from cash flow problems and being subjected to legal action by certain of its creditors, it filed a petition for reorganization under Chapter 11 of the Bankruptcy Code in an effort to reorganize itself. At this time, while struggling to maintain its competitive status in the sporting goods market and keep its business alive, it contacted Wilson, a major supplier with whom debtor had transacted business for nearly 10 years. In an effort to fill both existing and projected future orders of Wilson goods, debtor offered to pay cash to Wilson for any shipments of postpetition goods. Despite Wilson's awareness of debtor's financial difficulties and in apparent indifference to the opportunity presented for itself to make a profit, in "carrot on a stick" fashion, Wilson refused to supply goods to debtor unless it made payment or arrangements to pay all existing indebtedness to it.

While perhaps unremarkable otherwise, Wilson's actions take on an added significance upon the filing of a petition in bankruptcy. Wilson could have simply refused, for any reason, to sell goods to debtor or offered no explanation for its refusal to do business. Instead, its sole reason for refusing to sell goods to debtor was its desire to collect its prepetition debt. The act in this context had the effect of interfering with the reorganization effort, a result at odds with the purpose of the bankruptcy laws.

As plaintiff points out, an analogy can be drawn from those cases that have found that a state university's refusal to issue a transcript to a debtor absent payment of prepetition debt, in addition to constituting a type of discriminatory treatment by a governmental unit proscribed by 11 U.S.C. § 525, when motivated by the sole purpose of attempting to collect a prepetition debt, violated § 362(a)(6). *Board of Trustees v. Howren (In re Howren)*, 10 B.R. 303, 7 BCD 43 (Bkrtcy.D.Kan.1980).

. . . .

More directly on point is *In re Haffner*, 25 B.R. 882, 9 BCD 1293

(Bkrtcy.N.D.Ind.1982). In *Haffner*, the debtors were farmers operating as debtor-in-possession under Chapter 11 of the Bankruptcy Code. Debtors sought to store grain with the Commodity Credit Corporation (CCC) and receive cash advances in a transaction which, while technically a loan, in actuality is a sale with the option to repurchase and sell on the open market if and when prices increase over the subsidized level assured by CCC. When debtor sought to complete such a transaction they were told the transaction could be made only if CCC retained, or setoff from the amount that otherwise would be paid to the debtors, amounts which were due or allegedly due from a prepetition transaction of a similar nature in accordance with federal regulations. The Court found that the regulations, to the extent that they require the retention of money to recover prepetition debts in a postpetition transaction, violated the automatic stay of § 362(a)(6). 25 B.R. at 886, 9 BCD at 1295. The court further remarked:

> The automatic stay set out in Bankruptcy Code Section 362 is very broad in scope. The language of the statute and the legislative history make Congress' intent clear. "The automatic stay is one of the fundamental debtor protections provided by the bankruptcy laws. It gives the debtor a breathing spell from his creditors. It stops *all collection efforts . . .* , all harassment and all foreclosure actions." [Emphasis Added.] H.R. Rep. No. 595, 95 Cong. 1st Sess. 340 (1977). U.S. Code Cong. & Admin. News 1978, pp. 5787, 6296. "Paragraph (6) prevents creditors from attempting *in any way* (emphasis added) to collect a pre-petition debt." *Id.* at 342, U.S. Code Cong. & Admin. News 1978, p. 6298.

> . . . Furthermore, refusal to enter into the transaction except for payment of prepetition debts is itself a type of action taken against the debtor.

25 B.R. at 886–887, 9 BCD at 1295. The court went on in *Haffner* to order the CCC to enter into the transaction with debtor and to pay over the usual amount to debtor without any setoff.

It seems clear from the foregoing discussion that ample authority exists for the finding that Wilson violated the automatic stay by refusing to enter into cash transactions with debtor absent payment of its prepetition debt where its sole motivation was to collect its prepetition debt. While clear, in retrospect, that the stay was violated, due to the relatively obscure nature of the violation in this case, the Court is inclined to deny debtor's prayer for costs and attorney's fees in this case. Debtor's prayer for an injunction requiring Wilson to fill postpetition orders for goods, however, should be granted.

The courts in *In re Parkman, supra*, 27 B.R. at 460, and *In re Haffner, supra*, 25 B.R. at 882, 9 BCD at 1293, were apparently compelled to remedy the violation of stay found in those cases by ordering the creditor to permit the debtor to attend classes, in the former case, and to transact business with the debtor without exercising a right to setoff, in the latter. Due to the extraordinary nature of the injunctive remedy, however, the Court is disinclined to grant debtor's application for a permanent injunction enjoining Wilson to supply it with inventory absent a more thorough analysis under traditional standards for the grant of injunctive relief.

. . . .

The fundamental requirements for issuance of an injunction in the federal courts are a showing that one party will suffer irreparable harm unless the other party is restrained from taking a threatened action and that there is no adequate remedy of law. *See, e.g., Beacon Theatres v. Westover*, 359 U.S. 500, 506–07, 79 S.Ct. 948, 954, 3 L.Ed.2d 988 (1959); *Gilley v. United States*, 649 F.2d 449, 454 (6th Cir.1981). In the present case, plaintiff has met its burden of showing a serious threat of irreparable injury to its business and the lack of an adequate remedy at law. Furthermore, balancing the equities between the parties and considering the public interest, the Court holds that sound discretion favors the issuance of an injunction.

Plaintiff has no adequate remedy at law. "An 'adequate remedy at law' is a remedy that is plain and complete and as practical and efficient to the ends of justice as the remedy in equity by injunction." *Usaco Coal Co. v. Carbomin Energy, Inc.*, 689 F.2d 94, 99 (6th Cir. 1982). In the present case, it would be difficult, if not impossible, to ascertain the damages resulting to plaintiff resulting from defendant's failure to ship Wilson sporting goods. It seems clear, however, that, given the prominence of Wilson goods and debtor's past sales of Wilson products, debtor has and will suffer direct loss of profits if an injunction did not issue.

Even so, the more critical remedy that equity alone would provide in this case is to promote the success of this reorganization effort and to help prevent the extinction of debtor's business. "The fundamental purpose of reorganization is to prevent a debtor from going into liquidation, with an attendant loss of jobs and possible misuse of economic resources." *NLRB v. Bildisco & Bildisco*, 465 U.S. 513, 104 S.Ct. 1188, 1197, 79 L.Ed.2d 482, 497 (1984). Although debtor failed to show that the present reorganization effort would fail absent issuance of the injunction, given the above policy and the inherent difficulty in making such a showing in the early stages of a reorganization effort, the better policy would be that, given a showing of significant injury to debtor's business, the court could presume that it would render the reorganization difficult or impossible. Clearly, assessment of damages would not compensate for the possible permanent damage to or loss of debtor's sole business resulting from defendant's action in this case. "An injunction is proper to prevent the threatened extinction of a business." *Engine Specialties, Inc. v. Bombardier Ltd.*, 454 F.2d 527 (1st Cir. 1972).

The circumstances leading to the finding of a lack of an adequate remedy of law in this case also demonstrate the fact that the threatened injury would be irreparable.

> If an injury cannot be adequately remedied at law, because damages would be either inadequate or unascertainable, the injury is generally held irreparable. . . . Thus, the requirements of irreparable injury and lack of adequate legal remedy merge.

International Ass'n of Firefighters, Local 2069 v. City of Sylacauga, 436 F.Supp. 482, 492 (N.D. Ala. 1977). Here the possible loss of profits and resulting damage to or failure of this reorganization effort, in addition to requiring an equitable remedy, constitute a threat of irreparable harm.

Having once met the prerequisites for issuance of an injunction, the more significant factor in the Court's grant of equitable relief in this case is the Court's consideration of the equities involved. "As a general matter it may be said that '[s]ince all or almost all equitable remedies are discretionary, the balancing of equities and hardships is appropriate in almost any case as a guide to the [court's] discretion.'" *Tennessee Valley Author. v. Hill*, 437 U.S. 153, 194, 98 S.Ct. 2279, 2301, 57 L.Ed.2d 117, 146 (1978). The possible harm to debtor and its reorganization effort in this case, detailed above, has already been discussed. Defendant, by contrast, has made no showing and made no arguments that it would suffer any harm by being required to accept cash for selling goods to plaintiff and turning a profit. Furthermore, to the extent that an injunction would promote the success of the reorganization effort in this case, it will increase the possibility of defendant and all of the creditors in this case being paid the money owed to them.

Finally public policy favors issuance of an injunction in this case. Defendant's action, in violation of the automatic stay, should be remedied by way of injunction. Also, ignoring the coercive effect of defendant's refusal to do business with debtor, its motive can only be explained by spite or ill-will towards the debtor and its effort to emerge as a successfully reorganized entity. An injunction in this case pursuant to § 105(a) of the Code is thus "necessary or appropriate" to carry out the provisions of Title 11.

There remains the question of the terms and duration of the order. The debtor shall be required to pay cash either in advance of or upon receipt of goods. Upon receipt of debtor's order, Wilson should ship goods without undue delay and shall not unreasonably discriminate against debtor's orders. As far as possible, the parties shall operate on a normal business relationship consistent with their previous course of dealing over the past ten years. Although debtor has requested an order of unlimited duration, the spirit of this order, to remedy the violation of stay and promote the rehabilitation effort, can only justify its continuance through the course of this reorganization proceeding.

. . . .

For the foregoing reasons, it is hereby,

ORDERED that the Wilson Sporting Goods Company, its officers, agents, servants, employees, and attorneys, and those persons in active concert or participation with them who receive actual notice of this order by personal service or otherwise be, and hereby are, enjoined and restrained as follows: Wilson shall ship goods to Sportfame of Ohio, Inc. on its order upon receipt of cash in advance or upon arrangement for cash on delivery; Wilson shall ship goods without undue delay and shall not unreasonably discriminate against Sportfame's orders; as far as possible, Wilson and Sportfame shall transact business on a normal basis consistent with their dealings for the past 10 years. It is further,

ORDERED that this injunction be effective until the later of the time this case is dismissed or converted or all payments under a confirmed plan of reorganization have been completed.

NOTES AND QUESTIONS

(1)   Would your answer be different if Adam Adamant had simply refused to do business with Amphy but had not insisted on repayment of pre-petition debt?

(2)   Would your answer be different if instead of only two suppliers, there were many suppliers of the circuit boards used by Amphy?

(3)   Headley is concerned that if the court compels CitiCircuits to do business with Amphy, the relationship will be difficult and uncooperative. He asks: "Can't we just pay them?" *See* 11 U.S.C. § 549.

(4)   Frustrated with your answer, Headley asks, "Can't we explain to the court that in order to reorganize we need to protect our relationship with important trade creditors like Citi? Can't we get permission from the court to pay Citi's prepetition debt in the interest of a successful reorganization?" Consider the opinion that follows.

IN RE KMART CORPORATION
United States Court of Appeals for the Seventh Circuit
359 F.3d 866 (2004)

EASTERBROOK, CIRCUIT JUDGE.

On the first day of its bankruptcy, Kmart sought permission to pay immediately, and in full, the prepetition claims of all "critical vendors." (Technically there are 38 debtors: Kmart Corporation plus 37 of its affiliates and subsidiaries. We call them all Kmart.) The theory behind the request is that some suppliers may be unwilling to do business with a customer that is behind in payment, and, if it cannot obtain the merchandise that its own customers have come to expect, a firm such as Kmart may be unable to carry on, injuring all of its creditors. Full payment to critical-vendors thus could in principle make even the disfavored creditors better off: they may not be paid in full, but they will receive a greater portion of their claims than they would if the critical-vendors cut off supplies and the business shut down. Putting the proposition in this way implies, however, that the debtor must *prove*, and not just allege, two things: that, but for immediate full payment, vendors *would* cease dealing; and that the business will gain enough from continued transactions with the favored vendors to provide some residual benefit to the remaining, disfavored creditors, or at least leave them no worse off.

Bankruptcy Judge Sonderby entered a critical-vendors order just as Kmart proposed it, without notifying any disfavored creditors, without receiving any pertinent evidence (the record contains only some sketchy representations by counsel plus unhelpful testimony by Kmart's CEO, who could not speak for the vendors), and without making any finding of fact that the disfavored creditors would gain or come out even. The bankruptcy court's order declared that the relief Kmart requested — open-ended permission to pay any debt to any vendor it deemed "critical" in the exercise of unilateral discretion, provided that the vendor agreed to furnish goods on "customary trade terms" for the next two years — was "in the best interests of the Debtors, their estates and their creditors". The order did not explain why, nor did it contain any legal analysis, though it did cite 11 U.S.C. § 105(a).

. . . .

Kmart used its authority to pay in full the pre-petition debts to 2,330 suppliers, which collectively received about $300 million. This came from the $2 billion in new credit (debtor-in-possession or DIP financing) that the bankruptcy judge authorized, granting the lenders super-priority in post-petition assets and revenues.[1] . . . Another 2,000 or so vendors were not deemed "critical" and were not paid. They and 43,000 additional unsecured creditors eventually received about 10 [cents] on the dollar, mostly in stock of the reorganized Kmart. Capital Factors, Inc., appealed the critical-vendors order immediately after its entry on January 25, 2002. A little more than 14 months later, after all of the critical-vendors had been paid and as Kmart's plan of reorganization was on the verge of approval, District Judge Grady reversed the order authorizing payment. 291 B.R. 818 (N.D. Ill. 2003). He concluded that neither § 105(a) nor a "doctrine of necessity" supports the orders.

Appellants insist that, by the time Judge Grady acted, it was too late. Money had changed hands and, we are told, cannot be refunded. But why not? Reversing preferential transfers is an ordinary feature of bankruptcy practice, often continuing under a confirmed plan of reorganization. . . . If the orders in question are invalid, then the critical-vendors have received preferences that Kmart is entitled to recoup for the benefit of all creditors. Confirmation of a plan does not stop the administration of the estate, except to the extent that the plan itself so provides. . . . Several provisions of the Code do forbid revision of transactions completed under judicial auspices. For example, the DIP financing order, issued contemporaneously with the critical-vendors order, is sheltered by 11 U.S.C. § 364(e): "The reversal or modification on appeal of an authorization under this section to obtain credit or incur debt, or of a grant under this section of a priority or a lien, does not affect the validity of any debt so incurred, or any priority or lien so granted, to an entity that extended such credit in good faith, whether or not such entity knew of the pendency of the appeal, unless such authorization and the incurring of such debt, or the granting of such priority or lien, were stayed pending appeal." Nothing comparable anywhere in the Code covers payments made to pre-existing, unsecured creditors, whether or not the debtor calls them "critical." Judges do not invent missing language.

Now it is true that we have recognized the existence of a long-standing doctrine . . . that detrimental reliance comparable to the extension of new credit against a promise of security, or the purchase of assets in a foreclosure sale, may make it appropriate for judges to exercise such equitable discretion as they possess in order to protect those reliance interests. . . . Appellants say that we should recognize their reliance interests: after the order, they continued selling goods and services to Kmart (doing this was a condition of payment for pre-petition debts). Continued business relations may or may not be a form of reliance (that depends on whether the vendors otherwise would have stopped selling), but they are not *detrimental*

---

[1] [A debtor's ability to obtain postpetition financing is examined in detail in chapter 5 of the text. — Eds.]

reliance. The vendors have been paid in full for post-petition goods and services. If Kmart had become administratively insolvent, and unable to compensate the vendors for post-petition transactions, then it might make sense to permit vendors to retain payments under the critical vendors order, at least to the extent of the post-petition deficiency. Because Kmart emerged as an operating business, however, no such question arises. The vendors have not established that any reliance interest — let alone any language in the Code — blocks future attempts to recover preferential transfers on account of prepetition debts.

. . . .

Thus we arrive at the merits. Section 105(a) allows a bankruptcy court to "issue any order, process, or judgment that is necessary or appropriate to carry out the provisions of" the Code. This does not create discretion to set aside the Code's rules about priority and distribution; the power conferred by § 105(a) is one to implement rather than override. . . . Every circuit that has considered the question has held that this statute does not allow a bankruptcy judge to authorize full payment of any unsecured debt, unless all unsecured creditors in the class are paid in full. . . . We agree with this view of § 105. "The fact that a [bankruptcy] proceeding is equitable does not give the judge a free-floating discretion to redistribute rights in accordance with his personal views of justice and fairness, however enlightened those views may be." *In re Chicago, Milwaukee, St. Paul & Pacific R.R.*, 791 F.2d 524, 528 (7th Cir. 1986).

A "doctrine of necessity" is just a fancy name for a power to depart from the Code. Although courts in the days before bankruptcy law was codified wielded power to reorder priorities and pay particular creditors in the name of "necessity" — *see Miltenberger v. Logansport Ry.*, 106 U.S. 286, 1 S. Ct. 140, 27 L. Ed. 117 (1882); *Fosdick v. Schall*, 99 U.S. 235, 25 L. Ed. 339 (1878) — today it is the Code rather than the norms of nineteenth century railroad reorganizations that must prevail. *Miltenberger* and *Fosdick* predate the first general effort at codification, the Bankruptcy Act of 1898. Today the Bankruptcy Code of 1978 supplies the rules. Congress did not in terms scuttle old common-law doctrines, because it did not need to; the Act curtailed, and then the Code replaced, the entire apparatus. Answers to contemporary issues must be found within the Code (or legislative halls). Older doctrines may survive as glosses on ambiguous language enacted in 1978 or later, but not as freestanding entitlements to trump the text.

. . . .

So does the Code contain any grant of authority for debtors to prefer some vendors over others? Many sections require equal treatment or specify the details of priority when assets are insufficient to satisfy all claims. *E.g.*, 11 U.S.C. §§ 507, 1122(a), 1123(a)(4). Appellants rely on 11 U.S.C. §§ 363(b), 364(b), and 503 as sources of authority for unequal treatment. Section 364(b) reads: "The court, after notice and a hearing, may authorize the trustee to obtain unsecured credit or to incur unsecured debt other than under subsection (a) of this section, allowable under section 503(b)(1) of this title as an administrative expense." This authorizes the debtor to obtain credit (as Kmart did) but has nothing to say about how the money will be disbursed or about priorities among creditors. . . . Section 503, which deals with administrative expenses, likewise is irrelevant. Pre-filing debts are not administrative expenses; they are the antithesis of administrative expenses. Filing a petition for bankruptcy effectively creates two firms: the debts of the pre-filing entity may be written down so that the post-filing entity may reorganize and continue in business if it has a positive cash flow. . . . Treating pre-filing debts as "administrative" claims against the post-filing entity would impair the ability of bankruptcy law to prevent old debts from sinking a viable firm.

That leaves § 363(b)(1): "The trustee [or debtor in possession], after notice and a hearing, may use, sell, or lease, other than in the ordinary course of business, property of the estate." This is more promising, for satisfaction of a pre-petition debt in order to keep "critical" supplies flowing is a use of property other than in the ordinary course of administering an estate in bankruptcy. Capital Factors insists that § 363(b)(1) should be limited to the commencement of capital projects, such as building a new plant, rather than payment of old debts — as paying vendors would be "in the ordinary course" but for the intervening bankruptcy petition. To read § 363(b)(1) broadly, Capital Factors observes, would be to allow a judge to rearrange priorities among creditors (which is what a critical-vendors order effectively does), even though the Supreme Court has cautioned against such a step. *See United States v. Reorganized CF&I Fabricators of Utah, Inc.*, 518 U.S. 213, 116 S. Ct. 2106, 135 L. Ed. 2d 506 (1996). . . . Yet what these decisions principally say is that priorities do not change unless a statute supports that step; and if § 363(b)(1) is such a statute, then there is no insuperable problem. If the language is too open-ended, that is a problem for the legislature. Nonetheless, it is prudent to read, and use, § 363(b)(1) to do the least damage possible to priorities established by contract and by other parts of the Bankruptcy Code. We need not decide whether § 363(b)(1) could support payment of some pre-petition debts, because this order was unsound no matter how one reads § 363(b)(1).

The foundation of a critical-vendors order is the belief that vendors not paid for prior deliveries will refuse to make new ones. Without merchandise to sell, a retailer such as Kmart will fold. If paying the critical vendors would enable a successful reorganization and make even the disfavored creditors better off, then all creditors favor payment whether or not they are designated as "critical." This suggests a use of § 363(b)(1) similar to the theory underlying a plan crammed down the throats of an impaired class of creditors: if the impaired class does at least as well as it would have under a Chapter 7 liquidation, then it has no legitimate objection and cannot block the reorganization.[2] For the premise to hold true, however, it is necessary to show not only that the disfavored creditors *will* be as well off with reorganization as with liquidation — a demonstration never attempted in this proceeding — but also that the supposedly critical vendors would have ceased deliveries if old debts were left unpaid while the litigation continued. If vendors will deliver against a promise of current payment, then a reorganization can be achieved, and all unsecured creditors will obtain its benefit, without preferring any of the unsecured creditors.

Some supposedly critical vendors will continue to do business with the debtor because they must. They may, for example, have long term contracts, and the automatic stay prevents these vendors from walking away as long as the debtor

---

[2] [The ability of a debtor to confirm a plan of reorganization over creditor opposition is examined in detail in chapter 9 of the text. — Eds.]

pays for new deliveries. *See* 11 U.S.C. § 362. Fleming Companies, which received the largest critical-vendors payment because it sold Kmart between $70 million and $100 million of groceries and related goods weekly, was one of these. No matter how much Fleming would have liked to dump Kmart, it had no right to do so. It was unnecessary to compensate Fleming for continuing to make deliveries that it was legally required to make. Nor was Fleming likely to walk away even if it had a legal right to do so. Each new delivery produced a profit; as long as Kmart continued to pay for new product, why would any vendor drop the account? That would be a self-inflicted wound. To abjure new profits because of old debts would be to commit the sunk-cost fallacy; well-managed businesses are unlikely to do this. Firms that disdain current profits because of old losses are unlikely to stay in business. They might as well burn money or drop it into the ocean. Again Fleming illustrates the point. When Kmart stopped buying its products after the contract expired, Fleming collapsed (Kmart had accounted for more than 50% of its business) and filed its own bankruptcy petition. Fleming was hardly likely to have quit selling of its own volition, only to expire the sooner.

Doubtless many suppliers fear the prospect of throwing good money after bad. It therefore may be vital to assure them that a debtor will pay for new deliveries on a current basis. Providing that assurance need not, however, entail payment for pre-petition transactions. Kmart could have paid cash or its equivalent. (Kmart's CEO told the bankruptcy judge that COD arrangements were not part of Kmart's business plan, as if a litigant's druthers could override the rights of third parties.) Cash on the barrelhead was not the most convenient way, however. Kmart secured a $2 billion line of credit when it entered bankruptcy. Some of that credit could have been used to assure vendors that payment would be forthcoming for all post-petition transactions. The easiest way to do that would have been to put some of the $2 billion behind a standby letter of credit on which the bankruptcy judge could authorize unpaid vendors to draw. That would not have changed the terms on which Kmart and any of its vendors did business; it just would have demonstrated the certainty of payment. If lenders are unwilling to issue such a letter of credit (or if they insist on a letter's short duration), that would be a compelling market signal that reorganization is a poor prospect and that the debtor should be liquidated post haste.

Yet the bankruptcy court did not explore the possibility of using a letter of credit to assure vendors of payment. The court did not find that any firm would have ceased doing business with Kmart if not paid for pre-petition deliveries, and the scant record would not have supported such a finding had one been made. The court did not find that discrimination among unsecured creditors was the only way to facilitate a reorganization. It did not find that the disfavored creditors were at least as well off as they would have been had the critical-vendors order not been entered. For all the millions at stake, this proceeding looks much like the Chapter 13 reorganization that produced *In re Crawford*, 324 F.3d 539 (7th Cir. 2003). Crawford had wanted to classify his creditors in a way that would enable him to pay off those debts that would not be discharged, while stiffing the creditors whose debts were dischargeable. We replied that even though classification (and thus unequal treatment) is possible for Chapter 13 proceedings, see 11 U.S.C. § 1322(b), the step would be proper only when the record shows that the classification would produce some benefit for the disfavored creditors. Just so here. Even if § 362(b)(1) allows critical-vendors orders in principle, preferential payments to a class of creditors are proper only if the record shows the prospect of benefit to the other creditors. This record does not, so the critical-vendors order cannot stand.

AFFIRMED

NOTES AND QUESTIONS

(1)   According to the *Kmart* opinion, a court may approve payments to critical vendors if: (1) the debtor is able to show that the vendors will cease doing business with the debtor if their prepetition claims are not paid, and (2) non-preferred creditors would in some way benefit from the payments or at least not be harmed by them. If a creditor threatens to withhold shipments until a prepetition obligation is paid, does that threat violate the stay? How as a practical matter, can a debtor show on the first day of a case that the cost of paying prepetition creditors at the outset of a case will be offset by savings and benefits realized over the course of a case?

(2)   What if Adam Adamant approaches Headley, suggesting that he has a way of solving the problem without compromising his principles? Amphydynamics, he suggests, can just pay CitiCircuits 150% of list price for its products, and Adam will keep track of the overpayments and return to charging list price when Amphy has overpaid by the same amount as the prepetition debt. "It's a free country, Headley," Adam says. "I can charge my customers whatever price I want to. They can always go elsewhere." Headley asks you about this idea, which sounds expedient to him. What course of action do you advise him to take in response?

(3)   Which approach, *Sportfame, Kmart*, or the doctrine of necessity, places the debtor in the strongest bargaining position with its creditors? Which approach is likely to minimize the amount of cash required to continue the debtor's operations? Which is most likely to allow the debtor to retain congenial relations with its suppliers?

(4)   Although a number of courts, like the Seventh Circuit, have rejected the necessity of payment doctrine, others are more comfortable with it. *Compare, e.g., Chiasson v. J. Louis Matherne & Associates (In re Oxford Management, Inc.)*, 4 F.3d 1329 (5th Cir. 1993); *In re B&W Enterprises, Inc.*, 713 F.2d 534 (9th Cir. 1983), *with In re Lehigh & New England Railway Co.*, 657 F.2d 570 (3d Cir. 1981); *In re Penn Central Transportation Co.*, 467 F.2d 100 (3d Cir. 1972); *In re Just For Feet, Inc.*, 242 B.R. 821 (D. Del. 1999); *In re Eagle Pitcher Industries, Inc.*, 124 B.R. 1021 (Bankr. S.D. Ohio 1991). In a post-*Kmart* decision involving a large auto parts and systems manufacturer, the bankruptcy judge authorized more than $50 million in payments to critical vendors, but only if they agreed to supply goods on normal credit terms to the debtor in possession. The court's order provided that any vendor that accepted a payment and then refused to ship on normal credit terms would be forced to disgorge the payment received. *In re Dana Corp.*, No. 06-10354 (Bankr. S.D.N.Y. March 29, 2006) (Amended Final Order Pursuant to Sections 105(a), 363(b), (364)(b) and 503(b)(9) of the Bankruptcy Code Authorizing the Debtors to Pay Prepetition Claims of Certain Essential Suppliers and Administrative Claim-

holders and Granting Certain Relief.) If you were an attorney representing a debtor, would this be a factor to consider when deciding in what venue to file? If you were a supplier who hoped to achieve critical-vendor treatment, would you urge the debtor to take that into account? If you were a judge who wanted to attract "interesting" cases to your jurisdiction, would you be inclined to demonstrate some flexibility on this issue? At least one commentator thinks so. *See* L. LoPucki, *Courting Failure: How Competition for Big Cases is Corrupting the Bankruptcy Courts* (University of Michigan Press 2005). *See also* Michael St. James, *Why Bad Things Happen in Large Chapter 11 Cases: Some Thoughts about Courting Failure*, 7 Transactions 169 (2005) (reviewing *Courting Failure* and other related works); Lynn LoPucki, *Courting Failure? The Effects of Venue Choice on Big Bankruptcies: Response: Where Do You Get Off? A Reply to Courting Failure's Critics*, 54 Buffalo L. Rev. 511 (2006).

(5)   If a debtor and its critical vendor are parties to an executory contract, and the debtor assumes the contract pursuant to Code § 365, the debtor would be required to cure defaults by, among other things, paying the vendor's prepetition claim. § 365(b)(1)(A). As you will see in chapter 7 of the text, a debtor may have many reasons for wanting to postpone until the last possible moment a decision whether to assume or reject a contract. Might the *Kmart* decision force debtors to confront the issue earlier than they would like?

(6)   By contrast, if a debtor is a party to a requirements contract with a supplier, and they decide to "assume" the contract under Code § 365, they will be required to cure any prepetition defaults. Is this result any different from the behavior that is prohibited in *K-Mart*?

(7)   The necessity of payment doctrine has been invoked outside the critical vendor context. For example, in *In re Ionosphere Clubs, Inc.*, 98 B.R. 174, 175 (Bankr. S.D.N.Y. 1989), the court authorized the debtor, Eastern Airlines, to pay prepetition wages, medical benefit, and business expense claims of some of its employees. The court found that payment of the claims was "critical . . . in order to preserve and protect [the] business and ultimately reorganize, retain its currently working employees and maintain positive employee morale." Striking workers did not receive such payments.

(8)   The necessity of payment doctrine originated in an old railroad receivership case. In *Miltenberger v. Logansport, Crawfordsville & Southwestern Ry.*, 106 U.S. 286, 311, 1 S. Ct. 140, 163, 27 L. Ed. 117, 121 (1882), the Supreme Court found that "many circumstances may exist which may make it necessary and indispensable to the business of the road and the preservation of the property, for the receiver to pay preexisting debts . . . . Yet the discretion to do so should be exercised with very great care." The Seventh Circuit reasoned that such "older doctrines" were useful as "glosses on ambiguous language" but powerless to "trump the text" of the Code. In subsequent chapters of this casebook, you will encounter opinions in which courts provide relief by invoking long-established equitable doctrines that never made it into the Bankruptcy Code. When you do encounter those "old doctrines" consider whether the adoption of the Code "curtailed" them and whether that is a good thing.

(9)   Bankruptcy Rule 6003 provides that "a motion to pay all or part of a claim that arose before the filing of the petition" may not be granted during the first 20

days of a case, except to the extent that relief is necessary to avoid immediate and irreparable harm. Does this new rule implicitly authorize critical vendor payments? Can such authorization be given through a rule of procedure?

(10) Bankruptcy Code § 503(b)(9), which was enacted as part of the 2005 Amendments, presents another device for paying what might be critical vendor claims. It provides that "After notice and a hearing, there shall be allowed administrative expenses . . . including . . . the value of any goods received by the debtor within 20 days before the commencement of a case . . . which . . . have been sold to the debtor in the ordinary course of such debtor's business." Although § 503(b)(9) speaks only in terms of allowance, and does not specify when such claims are to be paid, in some instances, courts have authorized actual payment of such claims early in cases not only to critical vendors but to noncritical vendors, as well. Does this harm the other unsecured creditors, given that these claims will be entitled to priority anyway?

§ 2.04 AUTHORIZATION TO USE CASH COLLATERAL

INTRODUCTION & PROBLEM

Suppose that Amphydynamics borrowed $10,000,000 from Bank and granted Bank a security interest in its inventory and the proceeds of the sale of that inventory. Suppose that on the day that Amphy filed its Chapter 11 petition, it owned inventory valued at $4,000,000 and had $3,000,000 in cash proceeds on hand. A day after the petition was filed, Amphy sold $100,000 worth of inventory and generated additional proceeds. Under Code § 552(b)(1), Bank's security interest would extend to the proceeds that are generated by the sale of that inventory, even though the sale took place and the proceeds were generated after the petition was filed. Is a Chapter 11 debtor free to deploy that cash in the operation of the business?

As we will see in Chapter 6, use of property by a trustee or debtor is generally governed by Code § 363(c)(1), which provides that a trustee or debtor in possession may use, sell, or lease estate property in the ordinary course of business without notice and a hearing. Thus, Amphy is presumptively allowed to sell its inventory in the ordinary course of operating the business. A different rule applies to the debtor's use of property that is "cash collateral" (as defined in § 363(a)). If you compare Code §§ 361(1) and (2), you will see that the Code treats the use of collateral and cash collateral very differently. Under § 363(c)(1), a trustee or debtor is presumptively entitled to sell, use, or lease property in the ordinary course of business, even if that property collateralizes a debt. The burden is on the secured creditor to convince the court to stop the debtor from using the collateral or to convince the court to condition the debtor's continued use of the collateral on its ability to adequately protect the secured creditor's interest in the collateral by, *e.g.*, making economic depreciation payments or providing a replacement lien. *See* Code §§ 362(d)(2), 363(e), 361. In contrast, under § 363(c)(1), a debtor or trustee is not presumptively entitled to use cash collateral. Before a debtor or trustee may use cash collateral, they must obtain the secured creditor's consent or the court's authorization. Moreover, under § 363(c)(4), the trustee or debtor must segregate and account for any cash collateral in its possession.

Recognizing that the debtor's need to use cash collateral may be urgent, and that an application to use cash collateral over a secured creditor's objection may be brought to the court at a very early stage of the case, § 363(c)(3) provides for an expedited hearing, "scheduled in accordance with the needs of the debtor," and directs the court to "act promptly on any request for authorization" to use cash collateral. Bankruptcy Rule 4001(b) provides that a final hearing on a cash collateral motion may be held on no less than 15 days notice, but that a preliminary hearing may be held earlier. However, prior to a final hearing, the court may authorize the use of only so much cash collateral as is necessary to avoid immediate and irreparable harm to the estate. Notably, hearings on motions to use cash collateral are not subject to the let's-put-the-brakes-on-for-20-days provisions of Rule 6003. In fact, Rule 4001 motions are expressly excluded from the coverage of Rule 6003.

So, when should a court permit the use of cash collateral over a creditor's objection? That question is explored in the materials that follow.

IN RE DYNACO CORP.
United States Bankruptcy Court, District of New Hampshire
162 B.R. 389 (1993)

James E. Yacos, Bankruptcy Judge

These jointly administered chapter 11 cases came before the Court for hearing on October 5, 1993 and October 14, 1993 upon debtors' Motion for Continued Use of Cash Collateral, filed on October 1, 1993, and an Objection thereto filed by State Street Bank & Trust Company, the secured creditor having a claim upon the cash collateral involved. The Official Committee of Unsecured Creditors supports debtors' requested use of cash collateral.

. . . .

The issue presented by debtors' cash collateral request is whether a court can grant debtors' requested use of cash collateral when the record indicates that debtors' collateral base will suffer a decline of approximately $540,000 in the third and fourth months of post-petition operation, but when further documentation shows that debtors will reverse that decline and restore the original level over a more extended operational period.

. . . .

After a review of the entire record in this matter, including considerable testimony and documentary evidence, extensive oral arguments of counsel, memoranda and supplemental memoranda, the Court determines that it is appropriate to consider the long-term picture of debtors' business projections rather than a short-term snapshot, and that in this instance the debtors have established grounds warranting their use of their cash collateral, such grounds consisting of a showing of adequate protection to the objecting creditor and realistic projections of equity over an extended operational period. The bases for these determinations are discussed below.

Facts

These debtors operated plants in New Hampshire (Dynaco Corporation) and in Arizona (Dynaco West Corporation) on an affiliated basis producing circuit boards for the use of various large manufacturing concerns in this country. Their customer base was made up of prime corporations that were well satisfied by the work produced by the debtors. The debtors' receivables show a historical collection rate of 98 percent, which corroborates this satisfaction. The debtors' financial problems stem from the declining defense spending by the federal government in recent years, debtors' need to shift more of their work into civilian contracts, and debtors' accompanying need to reduce their costs during the transitional period.

The debtors had determined in 1992 that due to the decline in defense spending and contracting, which was a large part of their business, they would have to shift more of their work into civilian contracts. They also recognized that they would no longer be able to cover the overhead in the two plants. Accordingly, in the Spring of 1993 they determined, with the concurrence of State Street Bank & Trust Company, that the operations should be consolidated into the Arizona facility. Under federal law they were required to give a 60-day notice to their employees about the termination of the New Hampshire operations. This notice was given on May 18, 1993. Surprisingly, many of the employees left earlier than expected and the debtors were presented with a situation in which they had to cover a reduced operation with high overhead expenses in New Hampshire. It was important for debtors to maintain their operations since preservation of the customer base was a primary goal.

State Street Bank & Trust Company, the objecting creditor here, agreed to the consolidation of operations into Arizona, and the costs involved, as being appropriate to preserve the customer base of these debtors and to reduce overhead costs. However one "cost" which evidently was not fully evaluated by either the debtors or the Bank prior to debtors' consolidation was the danger that the disruption of customer orders even before the actual period of the move might interrupt the acceptance of customer orders and in effect cause an additional decline in cash flow for that reason. The debtors had assumed that their [New Hampshire] employees would stay for the two months prior to the chapter 11 filing to accept and service orders in a more or less normal fashion before the move but as indicated above many of the employees left early. The "two-month glitch" caused by this development is at the heart of the financial problem which has led to the present dispute between the debtors and State Street Bank & Trust Company.

On July 23, 1993, debtors' filed for relief under Chapter 11 of the Bankruptcy Code. On July 27, 1993, debtors filed an Emergency Motion for Authority to Use Cash Collateral, which the Court granted that date with the limitation that such usage extended only until a hearing could be held on the accompanying financing agreement. Thereafter the Court entered a series of orders continuing and extending debtors' authority to use cash collateral. All but the initial limited order were consented to by State Street Bank & Trust Company. By orders entered in

August 1993, the Court authorized debtors to continue and complete their planned movement of the Derry, New Hampshire plant and equipment to the Tempe, Arizona facility.

Cash Collateral Adequate Protection

Debtors seeking to reorganize under Chapter 11 of the Bankruptcy Code frequently need to use their cash and proceeds therefrom in order to continue with their business operations. However said cash and proceeds are often subject to security interests of pre-petition lenders and debtors must obtain court authorization to use this "cash collateral." § 363(b). The Court must ensure that, to the extent the debtor is entitled to use cash collateral, there is adequate protection of the creditor's security interest so as to maintain the "benefit of the bargain that the secured creditor originally made with the debtors. §§ 361, 363(e). This requires a showing that the value of the creditor's security interest is protected and the debtor's use of cash collateral will not threaten that interest. As one court explained:

> In reviewing an application under 11 U.S.C. § 363 which provides for the use of cash collateral, the Court must balance two irreconcilable and conflicting interests. The holder of a lien on cash collateral must not be left unprotected by unrestricted use of the collateral by the debtor. However, the purpose of Chapter 11 is to rehabilitate debtors and generally access to cash collateral is necessary in order to operate a business.

In re Stein, 19 Bankr. 458, 459 (Bankr. E.D. Pa. 1982). Another court observed that, in view of the broad powers given a trustee (or debtor-in-possession under § 1107), "it is apparent that the Congress intended business under reorganization to proceed in as normal a fashion as possible." *In re Prime, Inc.*, 15 Bankr. 216, 219 (Bankr. W.D. Mo. 1981).

The pertinent inquiry to ascertain whether the Bank's security interest is adequately protected requires a determination of the value of the Bank's interest and whether the debtors' proposed use of their cash collateral would impair that interest. Adequate protection will take many forms, only some of which are set forth in section 361 of the Bankruptcy Code, and must be determined based upon equitable considerations arising from the particular facts of each proceeding.

With regard to a lien of this nature, i.e., a "floating lien" of a blanket nature on changing and cycling soft collateral,[3] the appropriate adequate protection, and the concomitant valuation of collateral appropriate for a determination of adequate protection, is a showing that the level of such a fluctuating base of items of collateral that are constantly cycling through different shapes and forms, as the business operation continues, will in fact remain at the same magnitude (in terms of ongoing operational values) during the relevant period of debtor-in-possession business operation in the chapter 11 reorganization proceedings.

The appropriate view of a relevant period for this purpose is not a "snapshot" showing a fluctuation downward, during one selected short period of the business

---

[3] From raw materials into work-in-process, into inventory, into receivables, into cash, into purchase of new raw materials.

operation, but rather a "motion picture" showing the cycling of soft collateral during a period long enough to evaluate the question of whether the secured creditor is or is not being exposed to a substantial danger of a permanent decline in the level of the soft collateral supporting its floating lien. If the debtors make a solid showing that their continued operation of their business during the relevant period will pose no serious danger of such a decline, there is no need for any additional adequate protection in terms of "new money" to be infused into the enterprise by the equity holders or junior creditors to protect the secured creditor's present position in the collateral. On the other hand, if the evidence before the Court establishes that a permanent decline in the soft collateral level is likely, the Court generally will require infusion of cash by the investors in the enterprise to assure adequate protection of the security interest involved, under the rubric that the Court will not allow the debtors to "risk other people's money" to salvage their own position.

The rationale for this approach stems from the underlying rationale of chapter 11 itself, i.e., a rehabilitative proceeding in which the goal is to restructure the debtors' finances and operations in such manner as will extract the maximum intrinsic value of the enterprise. Since the equity holders and the general unsecured creditors are at the bottom of the "totem pole" of priority of claims against the assets of the enterprise, it is often tempting for those junior interests to don rose-colored glasses in evaluating the prospects for future operations and reorganization. It is the Court's task to scrutinize the data and projections supplied by the debtors with this danger in mind. When the issue is raised early in the reorganization proceeding, the Court will generally permit the business operation to continue, at least to the point of plan formulation, if the debtors make a solid evidentiary showing to support their projections that survive the appropriate scrutiny. It is always a difficult judgment call early in the case but I believe these debtors have met that standard.

In *In re T.H.B. Corp.*, 85 Bankr. 192 (Bankr. D. Mass. 1988), the bankruptcy court was presented with a cash collateral request and held that, because the senior lienholder's security interest was adequately protected, the debtor could use its cash collateral. In making its adequate protection determination, the court noted as an alternative basis for decision that under one theory of adequate protection "the concept consists of stability in collateral value rather than any particular level of value." *Id.* at 194, citing *Bankers Life Insurance Co. v. Alyucan Interstate Corp.*, 12 Bankr. 803 (Bankr. D. Utah 1981), and *United Savings Association of Texas Timbers of Inwood Forest Associates, Ltd.*, 484 U.S. 365, 108 S. Ct. 626, 629, 98 L. Ed. 2d 740 (1988). The court further observed that part of the Bank's adequate protection was the "fact that the proceeds of accounts receivables are being used by the Debtor to generate new inventory and accounts" and that "the use of the Bank's cash collateral . . . is an element of the Bank's adequate protection," *Id.* at 195, similar to my findings in this case. *See also Federal Nat. Mort. v. Dacon Bolingbrook Assoc.*, 153 Bankr. 204, 214 (N.D. Ill. 1993) (security interest adequately protected to extent debtor reinvested rents in operation and maintenance of the property); *In re Stein*, 19 Bankr. 458, 460 (1982) (cash collateral usage allowed where such use is essential "in order to meet operational costs" . . . and where the "secured position can only be enhanced by the continued [business] operation . . .").

In the present case the debtors have made an effective showing that, notwithstanding a drop in the third and fourth months of operation in the level of the soft collateral involved, up to a maximum of $540,000 of value on a going concern basis, the business operation will in fact result in the original level of that soft collateral being restored by June of 1994, such original level being $5,400,000 as of September 26, 1993.[6]

The primary cause of the current decline in the level of soft collateral was the fact that the move of the New Hampshire plant and equipment to the Arizona plant not only took somewhat longer than planned but also, as noted above, caused an unplanned early interruption in their ability to take new orders and to perform the same. This temporary interruption and decline, in my judgment, is an aberration and does not take away from the debtors' demonstrated ability to generate new business in the civilian marketplace, to collect an extraordinarily high percentage of their receivables from their customers, and to manage their affairs more efficiently and more effectively with the changes that have been incorporated into the Arizona operation with the aid of the professional management group authorized by prior Court order.

. . . .

The Court specifically finds on the evidence presented that the debtors will be able to reach their $15 million projected level of sales during their 1994 fiscal year ending September 30, 1994, and that their effective cost-cutting, quality control, and increased efficiency measures already adopted will support the net results included within its projections for its 1994 fiscal year. The debtors have made a very strong showing in that regard. The objecting creditor called no witnesses to the contrary and relied only on cross-examination to make its rebuttal case. That rebuttal effort in my judgment did not shake the otherwise convincing testimony put forward by the debtors.[7]

The alternative is to force the debtors to close down their operations and thus doom any effort at reorganization which will hopefully extract the maximum value of the assets involved to the benefit of all classes of creditors and other constituencies involved in this case.

The objection by the secured creditor, to the extent that it relies on the decision in *In re Tenney Village Co., Inc.*, 104 Bankr. 562 (Bankr. D.N.H. 1989), is misplaced. That decision, by visiting Judge Queenan, involved a determination under section 364 of the Bankruptcy Code as to whether a new financing party would be given a super-priority lien that would prime existing liens upon the property in question.

---

[6] The date of September 26, 1993 is relevant in that it was at that point that the State Street Bank & Trust Company indicated that it would not consent to any further use of cash collateral and stated it would oppose the debtors' request for further cash collateral usage. The argument by the Bank that the original filing date of July 23, 1993 should be employed as a baseline level for adequate protection purposes is not sustained in my view by either the logic and purpose of the inquiry being made or under the applicable case law.

[7] The Bank called no witnesses to refute the uncontroverted testimony and analysis put forward by the debtors that regardless of any other issues there was no question that the debtors could operate on a break-even basis for at least six months and that there was no danger that there might be a termination in operations during that period. Therefore I accept the debtors' contention that there is no reason to focus on liquidation scenarios at this time.

The Court there ruled that a § 364 priming order displacing existing liens must clearly show that after the super-priority lien is placed upon the property the existing lien holders' security interests, valued in terms of what they could obtain from a commercially reasonable disposition of the property in question, would leave them unimpaired notwithstanding the priming lien. . . . In my view it makes a big difference whether we are talking about a § 364 priming lien situation, in which the total encumbrances against the property of the estate are being increased compared to a § 363 proposal for the use of cash collateral in which the pertinent inquiry is whether the level of the fluctuating collateral involved will be maintained.

If the objecting creditor's reading of the *Tenney Village* opinion were to be carried over to the § 363 cash collateral usage context, it would effectively destroy the prospects for reorganization of most chapter 11 debtors.[10] If a company had sufficient value in its soft collateral, at foreclosure sale valuation levels, or even orderly liquidation levels, it would be very unlikely to need chapter 11 relief in the first place. Moreover, a secured creditor who takes a blanket lien on soft collateral has to know that the collateral will fluctuate in its level. As indicated above, it is the level of value that is crucial for adequate protection purposes in this specific context.

The crucial inquiry in the § 363 context, and the purpose for which the valuation and adequate protection determinations are being made, is whether the debtors' ongoing operation [will] in fact keep the level of soft collateral essentially the same during the period prior to plan confirmation, or denial of confirmation, or whether some additional cash infusion of "new money" should be required to assure the secured creditor that the level of soft collateral will be maintained in the ongoing business operation. In the present case, I believe the debtors have made the requisite showing in that regard and there is no need or justification for the requiring at this time any additional cash infusions to provide adequate protection.

The "Equity Cushion" Argument

The foregoing formulation of the appropriate test and standard for determining adequate protection of cycling soft collateral, pursuant to sections 361 and 363 of the Bankruptcy Code, does not require that the secured claimant be protected by an "equity cushion" on an overall basis with regard to all collateral securing its loans. This is not a motion for stay relief under section 362 of the Bankruptcy Code in which such an inquiry would be appropriate. As stated above, the question of adequate protection of cycling, soft collateral presents unique considerations in the cash collateral usage context which do not necessarily raise the same concerns

---

[10] Cash collateral usage in the early stages of a chapter 11 reorganization proceeding is simply unique in that if the debtor were to be required to provide dollar-for-dollar new money replacement to cover a temporary decline in the cash collateral level few debtors coming into the bankruptcy court for reorganization would be able to comply. The secured creditor could arguably force a termination of the debtor's business operations without having to grapple with the questions of its overall equity position, and the need for an effective reorganization, which are presented under § 362(d) of the Bankruptcy Code when a secured creditor seeks relief from the automatic stay to foreclose. Here, State Street Bank & Trust Company has not filed a motion for relief from the automatic stay but has only sought to prohibit the debtors' further use of cash collateral.

relevant to static assets that are not being "used" in the business operation.[11]

The test with regard to usage of soft collateral is not whether the secured party took enough collateral of all kinds to protect itself prior to the bankruptcy, or more particularly whether it monitored carefully enough the level of its floating lien on soft collateral to protect itself, but rather whether what it actually had in terms of the level of its floating lien on its fluctuating collateral base will be preserved until a plan of reorganization is determined.

To the extent however that the secured creditor here argues, and certain case decisions may well suggest, that an absence of an equity cushion on an overall basis is pertinent to adequate protection of soft collateral under section 363 of the Bankruptcy Code, I do find upon the record before me that the debtors have established that on an overall basis, including all collateral available to the secured creditor, whether in these estates or as provided by the secured personal guarantees of the equity holders, that there is an equity cushion at fair market and going concern values of approximately 17 percent over the secured debt involved.[12] It was stipulated at the hearing that the total secured debt of State Street Bank & Trust Company was in the amount of $4,049,000. The evidence presented establishes fair market and going concern values of the total collateral involved of $4,859,000 as of the end of November 1993.

When there is a showing of an overall oversecured position of a secured creditor in the cash collateral usage context, this Court has previously ruled that the "as is necessary" language of section 363(e) of the Bankruptcy Code may justify denial of any further adequate protection in the unique situation of cash collateral (there involving rents as cash collateral) if on an overall basis the secured creditor is oversecured and protected by a clear equity cushion.

Conclusion

On the showing made by the debtors, the Court finds and concludes that the debtors have established that there is no significant danger to the secured creditor that the level of the soft collateral supporting the creditor's floating lien will not be restored within the projected period of operations of the debtors' business. Notwithstanding the conceded decline in cash flow, the debtors have established that State Street Bank & Trust Company will have the appropriate adequate protection, as is necessary for the lien involved, during the further course of the debtors' operations while a plan of reorganization is being formulated and filed on

---

[11] In this context "static" refers to assets that do not regenerate in the ordinary course and cycle of the business operation, such as realty, equipment, machinery and the like.

[12] When considering an "equity cushion" contention, this Court will look at a continuum of values, from fair market values down to forced sale values, depending on how substantial the prospects for successful reorganization are in the particular case; the time elapsed from the filing of the case and the degree of progress toward a reorganization during that elapsed time; and various other pertinent factors. In the present case, as indicated above, I believe the present financial downturn is an aberration due to the agreed-upon move to the Arizona facility and that these debtors have substantial prospects for a successful reorganization.

or before March 1, 1994.[14]

NOTES AND QUESTIONS

(1) *Modes of Protecting Cash Collateral.* Determining the extent to which a debtor should be allowed to use cash collateral requires a bankruptcy judge to perform a delicate balancing act. As the court observed *In re Prime, Inc.*, 15 B.R. 216, 216–17 (Bankr. W.D. Mo. 1981), "the challenge is to determine that funding arrangement which will keep debtor operating while maintaining adequate protection for the creditor."

For example, in an early case in which the debtor-manufacturer was operating at a loss, but "there was a substantial backlog of orders and [the] debtor had reduced costs by trimming its work force without . . . reducing capacity," the court allowed the debtor to use cash collateral, subject to stringent conditions:

> In an ongoing business, where the creditor's security is in accounts receivable and inventory, the value of the security will diminish through use, although it should be replenished as the business continues. The Court is not obligated to protect the creditor better than it did itself when making the loan and obtaining security. At the same time, the Court cannot allow the security to be diminished. The policy of the Code, as was that of the predecessor statutes, is to encourage reorganization if there is a reasonable possibility of success. At the beginning of the reorganization process, the Court must work with less evidence than might be desirable and should resolve issues in favor of the reorganization, where the evidence is conflicting.

> Here, while there are disputes as to the value of the security, even conservative appraisals reveal values in excess of the debt, although not what could be considered a comfortable amount. It is incumbent upon the Court, therefore, to make specific requirements upon debtor to insure that the creditors will receive adequate protection.

> ORDERED that debtor be, and it is hereby authorized to use cash collateral in the conduct of its business, subject to the following conditions:

> 1. The preparation of monthly financial reports, including profit and loss and balance sheets, such preparation to be preceded by a physical inventory, all consistent with the design provided by [the debtor's new auditors] Ernst & Whinney.

> 2. The preparation, on a weekly basis, of a report indicating new accounts and accounts collected and the amounts of each.

> 3. The preparation of a report on a monthly basis showing inventory replaced, by item and amount, the value of replacement to be in the rate of 25% of the value of goods manufactured.

---

[14] If debtors fail to file a plan by this deadline, the Court would reconsider debtors' use of its cash collateral upon request of a creditor and possibly require cash payments to said creditor so as to maintain the secured creditor's position.

4. A report, on a monthly basis, of any equipment purchased or sold.

5. The payment to Capital for Business of the sum of $300.00 per week on the principal amount of its loan.

6. The payment to Commerce Bank of the sum of $200.00 per week on the principal amount of its loan.

7. Arrangements for the payment of taxes due, to be made within one month of this order.

8. Payment of interest due to be made in a timely fashion.

9. Previous orders as to salaries of officers and for payment of rent shall remain in effect.

ORDERED further that all acts required herein shall be reported to the Court, in writing, and a copy served upon counsel for Commerce Bank and Capital for Business and all reports required shall be filed with the Court and served upon counsel.

ORDERED further that Commerce Bank shall apply the funds presently in its possession to interest due in September on all loans due it and Capital for Business and the balance applied to the principal on loans made by Commerce Bank.

In re Heatron, Inc., 6 B.R. 493, 496–97 (Bankr. W.D. Mo. 1980). As that multi-faceted adequate protection package suggests, courts have adopted a cafeteria approach in fashioning adequate protection, the range of which is exemplified by the following cases:

- Where creditors hold a mortgage on the debtor's real property, and an assignment of rents, a number of courts have authorized debtors to use the rents but only for the purpose of operating and maintaining the real property. *See, e.g., Federal Nat'l Mortgage Assn. v. Dacon Bolingbrok Assoc. Ltd. Partnership*, 153 B.R. 204 (N.D. Ill. 1993); *In re Constable Plaza Assoc.*, 125 B.R. 98 (Bankr. S.D.N.Y. 1991); *In re McCombs Properties VI, Ltd.*, 88 B.R. 261 (Bankr. C.D. Cal. 1988). In *In re Marion Street Partnership*, 108 B.R. 218 (Bankr. D. Minn. 1989), the court also ordered the debtor to provide monthly operating statements and open its books to the creditor, and imposed a deadline for the filing of a plan. The court cautioned that if rents proved insufficient to pay current operating expenses, or if the debtor failed to meet the deadline for filing a plan, the court would entertain a motion to convert or dismiss the case.

- Where the creditor had a security interest in a car dealer's inventory and proceeds, the court found that the interest entitled to adequate protection was the wholesale value of the cars. The auto dealer was permitted to use gross profits provided it remitted the wholesale value of each car to the creditor. *In re George Ruggiere Chrysler-Plymouth, Inc.*, 727 F.2d 1017 (11th Cir. 1984).

- Where a creditor with security interest in inventory, accounts, and real property was undersecured, the court nevertheless permitted the debtor to use the cash proceeds of its accounts provided that $1.00 worth of new receivables was substituted for each 85 cents of cash released to the debtor. In addition, the court ordered the debtor to: (1) make monthly interest payments to the creditor; (2) file periodic inventory reports with the creditor; (3) furnish revised profit and cash flow projections; (4) use cash collateral solely to meet payroll, utility, insurance and direct production costs; (5) maintain insurance on all non-cash collateral; and (6) pursue efforts to refinance its indebtedness and sell the business as a going concern. *In re C.F. Simonin's Sons, Inc.*, 28 B.R. 707 (Bankr. E.D.N.C. 1983).

• Where expert testimony indicated that the creditor, which also had a security interest in inventory and all other personal property of the debtor, was oversecured, the court allowed the debtor, a lumber company, to use cash collateral for a period not to exceed 60 days. As further conditions, the court ordered the debtor to (1) retain a marketing consultant; (2) maintain sales and inventory at specific levels; (3) reduce the company president's salary; (4) take steps to reduce operating expenses; and (5) file bi-weekly reports to the bank. The court also ordered the debtor *not* to (6) sell any fixed assets without the consent of the bank; (7) increase payroll expenses; or (8) pay any prepetition obligations. *In re Potvin Lumber Co.*, 24 B.R. 54 (Bankr. D. Vt. 1982).

• Where the debtor was a construction company, use of cash collateral was premised on the grant to creditors of a blanket lien on all the debtor's property, periodic payments, improvements in operations, cuts in operating expenses, and creditor access to books and records. *In re Markim, Inc.*, 15 B.R. 56 (Bankr. E.D. Pa. 1981).

• Where the liquidation value of accounts, machinery, fixtures, and equipment securing a loan was 2.3 times the secured indebtedness, the court found that "it borders on the frivolous for [the creditor] to argue that it is not adequately protected." *In re Anderson-Walker Industries, Inc.*, 3 B.R. 551, 552 (Bankr. C.D. Cal. 1980).

(2) *Setoff and Cash Collateral.* Typically, a creditor's security interest in "cash collateral" is the product of a security agreement with the debtor. However, cash also becomes cash collateral when it is subject to a creditor's right of setoff. Assume that on the day before the filing, Amphydynamics owed Bank $100,000, and Bank had on deposit in a regular checking account $60,000 of Amphydynamics' funds. Code § 553 allows a creditor to offset against a prepetition debt it owes the debtor. Hence, assuming no improprieties or irregularities, on the day before the filing, the Bank could have "zeroed down" the Amphydynamics account and applied the $60,000 deposit to reduce the $100,000 claim. Although § 553 validates the right of setoff, Code § 362(a)(7) automatically stays exercise of the right after a bankruptcy petition is filed. Thus, if the Bank failed to set off prior to the filing, although its right to setoff is preserved, it would not be able to exercise the right, absent relief from the stay. Code § 506(a) provides that a creditor whose right of setoff is stayed has a secured claim to the extent that it could have set off. Thus, in this example, the bank would have an allowed secured claim of $60,000 and an allowed unsecured claim of $40,000. The bank account is deemed to be "cash collateral" as defined in § 363(a). What, as a practical matter, can a bank do to prevent a debtor from using

this cash collateral without the bank's consent or court permission? *See* the Supreme Court's opinion in *Citizens Bank of Maryland v. Strumpf* reprinted in chapter 3.

(3) *For Every Good Deed There's a Punishment.* Suppose you represent a golf club maker, such as Wilson Sporting Goods, in *the Sport Fame* case. Suppose that the debtor orders a shipment of golf clubs and volunteers to pay for them in cash, in full, upon delivery. The debtor has the cash flow to do this, because, fortunately, the debtor has cash on hand. Your client ships the golf clubs; the debtor pays in full on delivery as promised; and the debtor resells the golf clubs to customers. Suppose that a few months later, the case is converted from Chapter 11 to Chapter 7, and a trustee is appointed. The trustee commences an adversary proceeding against your client to recover the cash payment made for the golf clubs sold and delivered. The trustee does not claim that the cash payment was preference or a fraudulent transfer, because it wasn't. What the trustee claims is that the debtor used cash collateral to make the payment, without consent of the secured creditor or the permission of the court. Thus, the trustee says, the unauthorized use of cash collateral is avoidable pursuant to Code §§ 363(c)(2) and 549(a). Should the bankruptcy judge order your client to disgorge the cash payment? *Compare Marathon Petroleum Co., LLC v. Cohen (In re Delco Oil, Inc.)*, 599 F.3d 1255 (11th Cir. 2010), *with Dill v. Brad Hall & Assoc. (In re Indian Capitol Distributing, Inc.)*, 2011 Bankr. LEXIS 3892 (Bankr. D.N.M. Oct. 5, 2011).

§ 2.05   COMMITTEES IN CHAPTER 11 CASES

Who speaks for creditors and stockholders in a Chapter 11 case? Who watches, listens, and negotiates on their behalf? Without limiting the right of any individual party in interest to act on its own behalf, the Code assigns this watchdog role to creditors' committees and, in some cases, equity security holders' committees. The formation and function of committees is governed by Code §§ 1102 and 1103. Please read those sections now.

PROBLEM 2.3

Shortly after Amphy and its affiliated companies filed their bankruptcy petitions, the U.S. Trustee convened an organizational meeting for the purpose of appointing an Official Committee of Unsecured Creditors. The U.S. Trustee is thinking about forming one 12-member committee to serve in all of the related cases, with the expectation that committee members may decide to form subcommittees to deal with issues pertaining to particular debtors. The following creditors have expressed interest in serving on the committee:

- MacroBank, which holds a mortgage of Amphy's manufacturing plant. The plant is believed to be worth $9,000,000, which is less than the $10,000,000 debt it secures. Hence, MacroBank holds a deficiency claim. MacroBank has said that it intends to seek relief from the automatic stay so that it may commence a foreclosure action.

- BigBank, which holds a claim of $12,000,000 that is secured by an interest in Amphy's equipment, inventory, and receivables, valued at a total of approximately $8 million. Headley has approached Josh Colman, BigBank's workout officer, to determine whether BigBank would be interested in providing postpetition debtor in possession financing, and, if so, on what terms.

- MiniBank and MetroBank, the two largest unsecured bank creditors of Comp-U-All, Inc. You will recall that Comp-U-All is Amphy's retail affiliate that sells Amphy and other name-brand computer and electronic products. The banks' claims are based on unsecured lines of credit.

- Lewis Lessor, a real estate developer, who has leased several stores to Comp-U-All. Management of Comp-U-All is in the process of deciding which locations to close and which to continue. Lessor would like to recover the premises and re-lease them at a higher rent.

- Two trade creditors that are suppliers of inventory to Comp-U-All. These suppliers would like to see the debtors reorganize and are interested in doing business with Comp-U-All while it is operating in Chapter 11. A third trade creditor that has sought appointment to the committee is CitiCircuits, which has long been a thorn in management's side. CitiCircuits balked at signing on to an out-of-court workout agreement, and later, after the Chapter 11 filing, refused to ship component parts to Amphy unless Amphy agreed to pay what it owed CitiCircuits.

- Loach Group, a private equity fund that purchased several million dollars in publicly traded unsecured bonds of Amphydynamics a few weeks before the Chapter 11 filings. Loach CEO Beth Algae has hinted that her firm does not rule out selling the bonds. Nor, she said, does her firm rule out purchasing additional bonds, or claims, or stock with an eye toward converting the claims into a controlling interest in the reorganized company. Loach Group, she says, is not entirely happy with the debtor in possession financing package offered by BigBank and may offer to provide financing.

- Hector Medina, an officer of the union that represents the workers employed at Amphy's manufacturing plants.

- Sylvia Plinth, an attorney who represents a number of the people who claim to have developed the illness known as "hystereo" as a result of exposure to Amphydynamics video games.

Are these creditors eligible to serve on the Committee? Should there be more than one committee? If certain creditors hold claims against more than one related debtor, whether by virtue of guarantees or separate transactions, should that be taken into account in the committee formation process? How aligned are the interests and incentives of these creditors? Would a Committee with an odd number of members function more efficiently? Read Code §§ 1102 and 1103 and the materials that follow.

IN RE AMERICA WEST AIRLINES

United States Bankruptcy Court for the District of Arizona
142 B.R. 901 (1992)

ROBERT G. MOOREMAN, CHIEF JUDGE

This matter is before the Court pursuant to the Motion of Kawasaki Leasing International, Ltd. ("Kawasaki") for an Order Reappointing them to the Unsecured Creditors' Committee ("Committee").

. . . .

On June 26, 1991 America West Airlines, Inc. ("Debtor") filed its Chapter 11 petition. On July 10, 1991, the United States Trustee appointed the original Committee comprising eight (8) members including four large unsecured general or trade creditors, three bond or debenture holders and one non-voting member. Kawasaki was included in the Committee as one of the general or trade unsecured creditors.

Thereafter and on or about December 12, 1991, the Court approved Kawasaki's Debtor-In-Possession financing Order wherein Kawasaki loaned $23,000,000 to Debtor. In the DIP loan, Kawasaki received a claim secured by substantially all of Debtor's assets and constituting an allowed priority claim over the Sec. 503(b) and Sec. 507(b) administrative claimants except for certain claims. Additionally, as part of the DIP loan package, Debtor assumed an Aircraft Finance Agreement with Kawasaki which converted approximately $54,000,000 of unsecured claims into allowed administrative claims under Section 503(b). Pursuant to the DIP loan package, upon confirmation of the plan of reorganization, 85% of Kawasaki's outstanding pre-petition claim based on the Aircraft Finance Agreement is secured by the collateral securing the DIP loan and the remaining 15% of the outstanding balance is to be treated as a general unsecured claim.

The U.S. Trustee received a letter dated January 23, 1992 from the Committee's counsel indicating the Committee's request to remove Kawasaki from the Committee. After discussions between the counsel for the Committee and for Kawasaki, the U.S. Trustee in a detailed and comprehensive letter dated February 25, 1992, attached and incorporated herein by reference, notified Kawasaki of the U.S. Trustee's decision to remove Kawasaki from the official Committee. Further discussions and correspondence ensued but the U.S. Trustee did not change its initial decision and as a result of the U.S. Trustee decision, Kawasaki filed the instant motion.

The Court finds and concludes on this record that the U.S. Trustee has the authority to appoint as well as remove members of official committees. The standard in determining whether the U.S. Trustee has abused authority is whether the U.S. Trustee acted arbitrarily and capriciously. The Court finds and concludes that the U.S. Trustee conducted a thorough and complete analysis of the entire matter presented. In making this decision to remove Kawasaki, the U.S. Trustee deliberated with the Committee for over 4 weeks and then even reconsidered its decision to remove Kawasaki. The U.S. Trustee thereafter determined that

Kawasaki did not currently hold a claim for purposes of Committee representation and that Kawasaki is not representative of claims comprising the committee. The U.S. Trustee did not argue that Kawasaki has an impermissible potential or actual conflict of interest, the U.S. Trustee deferred to the Committee to make such an argument as may be appropriate.

The Court will first review the issue of whether the U.S. Trustee abused its discretion in determining that Kawasaki was not a proper representative of the unsecured creditor's interests. A member's ability to represent the unsecured creditor's committee is an important factor in determining whether the member should serve on the committee. The Court finds and concludes that Kawasaki's interests have changed dramatically since it became a post-petition financier with priority status. Kawasaki obtained liens upon virtually all of Debtor's collateral due to the DIP loan package. Additionally, Kawasaki restricted the use of certain accounts and obtained power to sell Debtor's collateral with minimum notice in exercise of its remedies. Consequently, Kawasaki has an entirely different perspective than any other member on the official unsecured creditor committee as well as unsecured creditors.

A Bankruptcy Court has ruled that an undersecured creditor may sit on a committee but warned of situation like the case at bar. *In re Walat Farms, Inc.*, 64 Bankr. 65 (Bankr. E.D. Mich. 1986). The Court in *Walat Farms* cautioned that in some circumstances an undersecured creditor could be required to wear two hats that were diametrically opposed. For example, an undersecured creditor's interests would be served if the estate's primary collateral were liquidated rather than face the delay of a plan of reorganization which benefits the unsecured creditors. The undersecured creditor with its collateral comprising a majority of an estate may also seek the lifting of the automatic stay which could lead to a liquidation of the entire estate and providing for only a nominal amount for the unsecured creditors. Even in the event the estate would not be liquidated, the undersecured creditor would be in a position to exert its power in the negotiation stages of a plan of reorganization with the potential of receiving favorable treatment at the expense of the unsecured creditors. It appears to the Court that there are other situations where Kawasaki's best interests would be in direct contravention of the unsecured creditors' interests in the proposed scenario. In the event Kawasaki would be required to make a choice between its self-interest versus the interests of the unsecured creditors the choice would be difficult.

Another factor in determining whether the interests of unsecured creditors [are] being adequately represented is whether the members on the official unsecured creditors committee consider the creditor capable of representing [their] interests. In the instant case, the members of the Committee agree that Kawasaki would be unable to properly represent the interests of the unsecured creditors and unanimously voted to require Kawasaki to resign or be removed.

Finally, it occurs to the Court that no harm will occur if Kawasaki is not reappointed. Kawasaki has not shown any benefits that the Official Unsecured Creditors' Committee would receive if Kawasaki remained on the Committee. Based on the record, it appears that the Committee can properly serve its function without Kawasaki's presence. Therefore, on this record the Court finds and concludes that the U.S. Trustee did not abuse its discretion when it removed Kawasaki.

APPENDIX

U.S. Department of Justice
United States Trustee
District of Arizona
320 North Central Avenue, Suite 100
Phoenix, Arizona 85004
(602) 379-3092

February 25, 1992
Penn A. Butler
Henry C. Kevane
Murphy, Weir & Butler
101 California Street, 39th Floor
San Francisco, CA 94111
David C.L. Frauman
Milbank, Tweed, Hadley & McCloy
601 South Figueroa Street, 13th Floor
Los Angeles, CA 90017

In re: America West Airlines

No. 91-07505-PHX-RGM

Dear Gentlemen:

As you know, counsel for the Official Creditors' Committee ("Committee") has requested the United States Trustee to remove Kawasaki Leasing International, Ltd. ("Kawasaki") as a member of the Committee. The United States Trustee has carefully reviewed the Committee's request, and for the following reasons, has reconstituted this Committee resulting in the removal of Kawasaki as a Committee Member.

The United States Trustee ("Trustee") has clear authority to reconstitute a creditors' committee. *See, In re First RepublicBank Corp.*, 95 Bankr. 58, 60 (Bankr. N.D. Tex. 1988) ("The United States trustee has administrative authority over committee membership.") and *In re Texaco Inc.*, 79 Bankr. 560, 565 (Bankr. S.D.N.Y. 1987) ("Any requests for changes in the membership or size of previously appointed committees may now be addressed to the United States Trustee. . . . ").

Based upon this authority, the Trustee reviewed correspondence from both the Committee and Kawasaki as well as the Court's December 12, 1991, Final Order Authorizing Debtor to (i) Obtain Additional post-petition financing pursuant to 11 U.S.C. § 364(C); (ii) Assume Modified Aircraft Finance Agreement; and (iii) Enter Into Amended Credit Agreement ("Order") to determine whether the current nature of Kawasaki's claim was "of the kinds represented" on the committee. 11 U.S.C. § 1102(b)(1). Originally, Kawasaki was appointed to the Committee based upon their pre-petition unsecured claim exceeding $43 million. This claim, according to the Order, was converted to a post-petition administrative priority claim under 11 U.S.C. § 503(b) in December, 1991. At the present time, it appears that Kawasaki does not hold an unsecured claim, but only a future contingent unsecured claim, assuming debtor confirms a plan of reorganization. Due to the changed nature of Kawasaki's claim, the Trustee is justified in reconstituting the Committee. *See generally In re Texaco Inc.*, 79 Bankr. at 566–561.

Counsel for the Committee raises other reasons for removing Kawasaki including a conflict of interest due to Kawasaki's providing the debtor with post-petition financing. These additional reasons alone might not justify reconstituting the Committee, but the changed nature of Kawasaki's claim as well as the cumulative effect of the Committee's additional reasons further justifies the Trustee's action.

Please find enclosed a copy of the Notice of Appointment of the Reconstituted Official Creditors' Committee that the Trustee lodged with the Court today. It also reflects the recent resignation of Froley, Revy Investment Company. Their name has been removed from the Committee. The Trustee does not intend, at this time, to appoint any replacement.

Thank you for your cooperation during the deliberative process and for providing us with helpful information.

Sincerely yours,
ADRIANNE KALYNA
Acting United States Trustee
District of Arizona
DON C. FLETCHER
Attorney Advisor

NOTES AND QUESTIONS

(1) *Appointment Mandatory.* Code § 1102(a)(1) provides that the United States Trustee "*shall* appoint a committee of creditors holding unsecured claims." Thus, assuming that there are creditors willing to serve, appointment of an unsecured creditors' committee is compulsory.

If, however, a debtor qualifies as a "small business" as defined in Code § 101(51C), on request of a party in interest, and for cause, the court may dispense with a committee. Code § 1102(3). At least one court has held that "something more than a general assertion" by the debtor that "a creditors' committee . . . may translate into additional costs to the Debtor's estate" is required to justify dispensing with a committee in a small business case. *In re Haskell-Dawes, Inc.*, 188 B.R. 515, 520 (Bankr. E.D. Pa. 1995). The court pointed out that one of the roles of a committee would be to negotiate better treatment for creditors, and that if it succeeded, "there would be no disadvantage posed to the unsecured creditors." *Id.* at 521. Interestingly, as the leading treatise points out, the smaller a case is, the more important the role of a committee is likely to be, because "no individual unsecured creditor has enough of an economic stake in the process to justify the cost of monitoring the proceedings" on its own. King, 7 *Collier on Bankruptcy*, ¶ 1102.04[2] (Matthew Bender 15th Ed. Revised 2000).

(2) *Size and Composition of Committees*. Code § 1102(b)(1) provides that an unsecured creditors' committee shall ordinarily consist of the creditors, willing to serve, that hold the seven largest claims against the debtor. You will recall that a debtor is required to file with its petition a list of its 20 largest unsecured creditors. This list assists the U.S. Trustee in identifying prospective committee members. Of course, "ordinarily" does not mean "necessarily." For example, in a multi-billion-dollar case involving a huge retailer, the U.S. Trustee appointed a 15-member committee. *In re Hills Stores Co.*, 137 B.R. 4 (Bankr. S.D.N.Y. 1992). In a small case, the committee may consist of fewer than seven creditors. *In re M.H. Corp.*, 30 B.R. 266 (Bankr. S.D. Ohio 1983). U.S. Trustees have flexibility to depart from the seven-largest-creditors model in order to form a committee that represents diverse creditor interests. For example, a case involving a debtor that has only bank and trade creditors may require a smaller and less diverse committee than a debtor whose creditor constituency includes banks, suppliers, landlords, employees, customers, and products liability claimants.

(3) *Eligibility of Representatives of Creditors to Serve on Committees*. According to Bankruptcy Code § 1102, a creditors' committee normally is to consist of persons holding claims against the debtor. Whether *representatives* of claim holders are entitled to seats on committees is not as clear. In *In re American Federation of Television and Radio Artists*, 30 B.R. 772 (Bankr. S.D.N.Y. 1983), a law firm claimed that it was entitled to membership on the creditors' committee by virtue of the fact that a court had ordered the debtor to pay more than $1 million in attorney's fees to a client of the firm. The court disagreed, reasoning that since the fees had been awarded to the client, not the law firm, the firm was not a creditor of the debtor and not entitled to a seat on the committee. On the other hand, in the *Johns-Manville* Chapter 11 case, the U.S. Trustee for the Southern District of New York appointed a "Committee of Asbestos Related Litigants and/or Creditors," to represent the interests of individuals with asbestos-related health claims. That committee consisted of one victim of asbestos-related disease and several attorneys for other claimants.

Despite — or perhaps because of — the fact that Chapter 11 cases and the reorganization of troubled businesses can have a substantial impact on employees, jobs, and the status of collective bargaining agreements, the qualification of employees and union or pension plan representatives to serve on creditors' committees has been a source of some controversy. For example, the author of the law review article that introduced this section suggested:

A . . . fundamental conflict arises when the person seeking membership on a committee is already duty bound to represent a particular sub-class within the larger class to be represented by the committee. Such a situation would arise where a labor union seeks membership on a committee of unsecured creditors in a chapter 11 case. By virtue of the duty which the union owes its members, the debtor's employees, it will have an obligation to try to keep the debtor's business going and, therefore, its members employed. This duty creates a clear conflict with respect to the determination of whether the continued operation of the debtor is in the best interests of the general unsecured creditors at large and may disqualify the labor union from active membership on the committee.

Andrew DeNatale, *The Creditors' Committee Under The Bankruptcy Code — A Primer*, 55 Am. Bankr. L.J. 56 (1981). However, a number of courts have held that employees and their representatives are no more conflicted than other creditors and that they should not be excluded. For example, in *In re Altair Airlines, Inc.*, 727 F.2d 88 (3d Cir. 1984), the court held that the Airline Pilots Association was not too conflicted to serve on a creditors' committee:

> Undoubtedly ALPA's members may be interested in a plan of reorganization which preserves both their jobs and their collective bargaining agreement, while other creditors may be interested in liquidation, or a reorganization involving a merger with a non-union airline. Such conflicts of interest are not unusual in reorganizations. Materialman creditors, for example, may sometimes prefer to forego full payment for past sales in hopes of preserving a customer, while lenders may prefer liquidation and prompt payment. Section 1103(c)(2) contemplates that the Creditors' Committee may "investigate the acts, conduct, assets, liabilities, and financial condition of the debtor, the operation of the debtor's business, *and the desirability of the continuance of such business.*" (Emphasis supplied). There is no reason why the voice of the collective bargaining representative should be the one claimant voice excluded from the performance of that statutory role. The Bankruptcy Code [by virtue of its provisions allowing rejection of collective bargaining agreements] has been said to be "in tension with our national labor policy, as expressed in the National Labor Relations Act." But that tension does not suggest that collective bargaining representatives should have no role in the reorganization process. Quite the contrary: resolution of the tension suggests that those representatives should be heard in appropriate cases. Clearly a case in which unpaid sums due under a collective bargaining agreement amount to the second largest unsecured claim against the debtor's estate is an appropriate case.

727 F.2d at 90. *See also In re Barney's Inc.*, 197 B.R. 431, 442–44 (Bankr. S.D.N.Y. 1996).

In *In re Schatz Federal Bearings Co.*, 5 B.R. 543 (Bankr. S.D.N.Y. 1980), a union sought membership on a creditors' committee, asserting that its $462,000 claim for unpaid pension obligations made it one of the debtor's largest creditors. The court concluded that the union was entitled to a committee seat because the debtor's pension obligations had been incorporated into the collective bargaining agreement between the debtor and the union, and the obligation, therefore, flowed to the union. In *In re Altair Airlines, Inc.*, 727 F.2d 88 (3d Cir. 1984), the Third Circuit reversed a bankruptcy court's ruling that a union could not serve on a creditors' committee on behalf of member-pilots who were owed back wages. The Court of Appeals declined to distinguish between obligations owed directly to the union and those owed "through" the union to employees. "That distinction is entirely too metaphysical to serve as a guide for construction of the Bankruptcy Code," the court explained. *Id.* at 90.

The Bankruptcy Review Commission recommended that unions be eligible for appointment to committees and that in appropriate cases separate employee creditors' committees be appointed. National Bankruptcy Review Commission,

Bankruptcy: The Next Twenty Years, Final Report (1997) pp. 502–05.

(4) *Fiduciary Duties of Committee Members.* A creditor or stockholder who serves on a creditors' or equity security holders' committee "undertakes to act in a fiduciary capacity on behalf of the members of the class he represents." *In re Johns-Manville Corp.*, 53. B.R. 879, 886 (Bankr. S.D.N.Y. 1985); *In re ABC Automotive Products Corp.*, 210 B.R. 437, 441 (Bankr. E.D. Pa. 1997). A committee and its members are "charged with pursuing whatever lawful course best serves the interests of the class. . . . represented." *Official Unsecured Creditors' Committee v. Stern (In re SPM Manufacturing Corp.)*, 984 F.2d 1305, 1315 (1st Cir. 1993). Committee members who perform their duties in good faith and who do not engage in willful misconduct or activity that is beyond the scope of their authority enjoy immunity from legal action arising out of their service on the committee. *Central Transport, Inc. v. Roberto (In re Tucker Freight Lines, Inc.)*, 62 B.R. 213 (Bankr. W.D. Mich. 1986).

As the *America West* case suggests, although some conflicts of interest are intolerable, some are unavoidable, because "each unsecured creditor has a conflict with every other unsecured creditor in the sense that absent a 100% distribution, the elimination or reduction of any such claim will benefit all others." *In re Microboard Processing, Inc.*, 95 B.R. 283, 285 (Bankr. D. Conn. 1989). Some conflicts may be apparent at the outset of a Chapter 11 case; others will surface as the case unfolds. Consider whether, and with what precautions, if any, you would allow the following creditors to take a seat on (or remain on) the creditors' committee in the Amphydynamics case.

- A bank that loaned money to Amphy and that operates in an area of the city where Amphy has marginal operations that it is considering shutting down.

- A bank that may have received a preferential payment or taken an improper setoff. *See In re White Motor Credit Corp.*, 18 B.R. 720 (Bankr. N.D. Ohio 1980).

- A creditor that holds a disputed claim. *See In re Microboard Processing, Inc.*, 95 B.R. 283, 285 (Bankr. D. Conn. 1989); *In re Grynberg*, 10 B.R. 256 (Bankr. D. Colo. 1981).

- A creditor that holds a disputed claim and commences a state court action against the debtor in violation of the automatic stay. *See In re Johns-Manville Corp.*, 26 B.R. 919, 926 (Bankr. S.D.N.Y. 1981).

- A trade creditor that expects "a piece of the action" if the company gets back on its feet and emerges from Chapter 11.

- A competitor of the debtor that also happens to be a creditor by virtue of a judgment on an antitrust claim. *See In re Wilson Foods Corp.*, 31 B.R. 272 (Bankr. W.D. Okla. 1983).

- A creditor that has been purchasing claims from other creditors or attempting to sell its claim. *See In re Federated Dep't Stores*, 1991 Bankr. LEXIS 288 (Bankr. S.D. Ohio 1991); *In re Spiegel*, 292 B.R. 748 (Bankr. S.D.N.Y. 2003); *In re Kuhns*, 101 B.R. 243 (Bankr. D. Mont. 1989).

(5) *Communicating with Constituents.* Code § 1102(b)(3), which was added by the 2005 amendments, imposed additional duties on members of official creditors' committees. Section 1102(b)(3)(A) requires the committee to provide "access to information for creditors who hold claims of the kind represented by the committee and who are not members of the committee." In a high-profile case involving financial services company Refco, Inc., members of the official creditors' committee asked the bankruptcy judge to clarify their duties under this Code section. Here are excerpts from the court's opinion:

> An official committee of creditors plays pivotal role in the bankruptcy process. The function of an official creditors committee is to aid, assist and monitor the debtor to ensure that the unsecured creditors' views are heard and their interests promoted and protected. . . . Official committees have diverse duties: they are the primary negotiating bodies for a chapter 11 plan; they also provide supervision of the debtor and execute an oversight function; they may investigate the debtor's assets and affairs; and they may perform such other services as are in the interest of the unsecured creditor body.

> Broadly speaking,

> The creditors' committee is not merely a conduit through whom the debtor speaks to and negotiates with creditors generally. On the contrary, it is purposely intended to represent the necessarily different interests and concerns of the creditors it represents. It must necessarily be adversarial in a sense, though its relation with the debtor may be supportive and friendly. There is simply no other entity established by the Code to guard those interests. The committee as the sum of its members is not intended to be merely an arbiter but a partisan which will aid, assist, and monitor the debtor pursuant to its own self-interest.

> *In re Daig Corp.*, 17 B.R. 41, 43 (Bankr. D. Minn. 1981).

> It is well recognized that, to fulfill these roles, the members of an official committee owe a fiduciary duty to their constituents — in the case of an official creditors committee, to all of the debtor's unsecured creditors.

> It is important to keep these functions in mind when sorting out the circumstances under which a creditors committee should not be required to make information available to its constituents. For example, in performing its oversight and negotiation function, a committee acts as the voice of all of the unsecured creditors, many of whom lack the resources to speak for themselves and all of whom benefit from the representative role played by the committee. . . . This means that committee members should and will receive commercially sensitive or proprietary information from the debtor and other parties (including each other, because plan negotiations are as often conducted between unsecured creditor groups as between the unsecured creditors and the debtor), often in the context of settlement discussions. It has frequently been held that committee members' fiduciary duties of loyalty and care to the unsecured creditor body require such

information to be held in confidence. Otherwise, communications between the committee and third parties and among committee members themselves would be improperly curtailed, or the debtor might be harmed with a resulting decline in the creditors' recovery.

When the debtor has public stock or debt, moreover, the securities laws may preclude the debtor from disclosing material non-public information on a selective basis to committee members absent a binding confidentiality agreement. In addition, a committee's selective disclosure of material non-public information that it has developed on its own (including the results of inter-creditor negotiations and its own investigations) may raise similar issues, although the underlying concern would not be a breach of the securities laws as much as a breach of members' fiduciary duties of loyalty and care to all unsecured creditors by profiting from, or enabling selected creditors to profit from, non-public information obtained as a result of committee membership.

Maintaining the parties' reasonable expectations of confidentiality, therefore, is often critical to a committee's performance of its oversight and negotiation functions, compliance with applicable securities laws, and the proper exercise of committee members' fiduciary duties.

Maintaining confidentiality against unsecured creditors generally also may be necessary to preserve a committee's attorney-client privilege. That privilege clearly can be enforced against those who are not represented by the committee or who are standing in an adversarial relationship to the unsecured creditors as a group.

On the other hand, although a committee's assent to a plan or a transaction does not bind its members, let alone its constituents, the importance of a committee's recommendations should require a committee to remain in touch with its constituents to determine their reasonable views.

How should a committee balance the foregoing tension, however — that is, the committee's need to preserve access to sensitive information (which usually is the only information of any value to unsecured creditors, whether for legitimate or illegitimate purposes), to protect the attorney-client privilege, and to comply with the securities laws, on the one hand, against the right of unsecured creditors to be informed of material developments in the case before they are presented with what in practical terms may be a *fait accompli*, on the other?

In Refco's case . . . the balance has been achieved by not requiring in the first instance — that is, without further court order — the Committee's disclosure of information (a) that could reasonably be determined to be confidential and non-public or proprietary, (b) the disclosure of which could reasonably be determined to result in a general waiver of the attorney-client or other applicable privilege, or (c) whose disclosure could reasonably be determined to violate an agreement, order or law, including applicable securities laws. Because many, if not all, of the adverse consequences of releasing certain information discussed above may be acceptably reduced or eliminated by the requesting party's agreement to be bound by confidentiality and/or trading constraints; however, the order further provides that the Committee shall take into account the requesting party's willingness to agree to such constraints when the Committee determines whether to release otherwise protected information. Consistent with Code section 1102(b)(3)(C), the order also contemplates that the Court will promptly decide disputes over the provision of such information if they are not resolved by the parties.

In re Refco, Inc., 336 B.R. 187, 195–199 (Bankr. S.D.N.Y. 2006).

(6) *Appointment of Additional Committees.* The drafters of the Code recognized that a single committee might not be sufficient to accommodate all competing interests. Accordingly, Code § 1102(a)(1) provides that the U.S. Trustee may appoint, in addition to the mandatory unsecured creditors' committee, such "additional committees of creditors or of equity security holders that the United States Trustee deems appropriate." In addition, Code § 1102(a)(2) provides that the court may order the U.S. Trustee to appoint additional committees "if necessary to insure the adequate representation of creditors or of equity security holders." Parties seeking the appointment of additional committees need not bring the matter to the United States Trustee before raising it with the court, *In re Dow Corning Corp.*, 194 B.R. 121, 129 (E.D. Mich. 1996), although at least one commentator suggests that the request be brought first to the U.S. Trustee and to the court only if the U.S. Trustee denies it. *Collier on Bankruptcy*, ¶ 1102.07[1] (Matthew Bender, 15th Ed. Revised 2000).

"Additional committees" have been appointed to represent, for example, secured creditors, *In re Diversified Capital Corp.*, 89 B.R. 826 (Bankr. C.D. Cal. 1988); creditors who were also competitors of the debtor, *In re Texaco, Inc.*, 73 B.R. 960 (Bankr. S.D.N.Y. 1987); subordinated creditors, *In re Nova Real Estate Inv. Trust*, 10 B.R. 90 (Bankr. S.D. Fla. 1981); and products liability claimants, *In re Johns-Manville Corp.*, 60 B.R. 842 (S.D.N.Y. 1986); *In re Dow Corning Corp.*, 194 B.R. 121 (Bankr. E.D. Mich. 1996).

The National Bankruptcy Review Commission has cautioned that "because expenses of a creditors' committee are borne by the bankruptcy estate, additional committees are the exception and not the rule. For example, cases with mass tort liabilities might have a tort claimants' committee and another unsecured creditors' committee representing trade and other conventional unsecured creditors. A solvent debtor with a large number of equity holders might need an equity committee, while a case with a highly complex debt structure might warrant additional creditors' committees to represent different priority creditor interests. Absent these circumstances, the Chapter 11 system contemplates that one committee accommodate the differences between the members of [the] unsecured creditors community and the size of their debts." National Bankruptcy Review Commission, *Bankruptcy: The Next Twenty Years, Final Report* (1997) p. 494. The court in *In re Sharon Steel Corp.*, 100 B.R. 767, 778 (Bankr. W.D. Pa. 1989), was more blunt. It explained, "reconciliation of differing interests of creditors within a single committee is the norm. . . . [S]eparate committees . . . and . . . separate teams of professionals rarely contribute to the spirit of compromise that is intended as the guiding star of chapter 11." *Id.*

Another factor militating against appointment of separate committees is gridlock. A proliferation of committees may complicate negotiations and obstruct the road to consensus. Nevertheless, fear of added cost and gridlock alone does not justify the failure to appoint an additional committee where one is required to insure adequate representation. *In re Hills Stores Co.*, 137 B.R. 4 (Bankr. S.D.N.Y. 1992). The difficulty is in determining when that situation exists. Since each case has its own facts and politics, the analysis is necessarily case specific, and because there are no bright lines to assist the court in measuring the adequacy of representation, that analysis sometimes seems tortured. *See, e.g., In re Dow Corning Corp.*, 194 B.R. 121 (E.D. Mich. 1996).

(7)　*Multiple Committees for Multiple Debtors.* Amphydynamics files a Chapter 11 petition. So do two of its wholly owned subsidiaries. How many unsecured creditors' committees should there be?

In cases involving multiple, related debtors, separate committees for each debtor might be required. Some courts have found that Code § 1102(a)(1) on its face, as well as sound policy, require the appointment of a separate committee for each debtor. As one court reasoned, "[C]reditors of one debtor cannot be presumed to have a material or other qualifying interest in the assets or future of an affiliated debtor." *In re White Motor Credit Corp.*, 18 B.R. 720 (Bankr. N.D. Ohio 1980). *See also In re Parkway Calabasas, Ltd.*, 89 B.R. 832, 835 n. 3 (Bankr. C.D. Cal. 1988). That per se approach was rejected in *In re McLean Industries, Inc.*, 70 B.R. 852 (Bankr. S.D.N.Y. 1987). In that case, the court found "no indication that Congress gave any thought to jointly administered cases," nor that Congress "intended to require a committee for each case." *Id.* at 862. Concerned that the cost of appointing multiple committees in cases involving related debtors "could be extreme," the court concluded that it should only be incurred when necessary to insure adequate representation. The court did, however, caution against overloading a committee with creditors of only one debtor to the disadvantage of creditors of related debtors. Where related debtors share many of the same creditors, is the case easier? What about a case in which there were transfers of funds or assets between affiliated debtors that may be subject to avoidance as preferences or fraudulent transfers? In such a case does a single committee provide adequate representation?

(8)　*Role of Court in Committee Formation.* There is no doubt that under Code § 1102(a)(2) a bankruptcy court has power to order the United States Trustee to appoint "additional committees." Does a bankruptcy court also have power to alter the composition of existing committees by adding or subtracting members? Does it have power to order the United States Trustee to appoint a more representative committee? To disband committees? The problem arises because, until 1986, § 1102(c) expressly authorized the court to "change the membership or the size of a committee . . . if the membership of such committee is not representative of the different kinds of claims or interests to be represented." However, in 1986, when the U.S. Trustee system was adopted nationwide, and the power to appoint committees was transferred to U.S. Trustees, subsection (c) was deleted in its entirety and without explanation.

The case law considering whether the court has power to reconstitute a committee has been described as "in . . . disarray . . . a disjointed patchwork of decisions that cannot be reconciled easily." *In re Dow Corning Corp.*, 194 B.R. 121, 130 (Bankr. E.D. Mich. 1996). At one end of the spectrum is the view that the court has no power to add or subtract committee members. *See, e.g., In re New Life Fellowship, Inc.*, 202 B.R. 994, 997 (Bankr. W.D. Okla. 1996); *In re Drexel Burnham Lambert Group, Inc.*, 118 B.R. 209, 210 (Bankr. S.D.N.Y. 1990). At the other end of the spectrum is the view that adequacy of representation is a legal issue and that the court has broad authority to alter the composition of a committee to achieve adequate representation. *See, e.g., In re Sharon Steel*, 100 B.R. 767, 785–86 (Bankr. W.D. Pa. 1989). The middle ground is the view that the court can order the United States Trustee to alter committee membership upon a finding that the United States Trustee's original appointment was either arbitrary or capricious or an abuse of discretion. *In re Columbia Gas Systems, Inc.*, 133 B.R. 174, 176 (Bankr. D. Del. 1991).

Interestingly, as the court in *Dow Corning* pointed out, nothing in the Code gives U.S. Trustees the power to alter the makeup of committees, yet U.S. Trustees routinely do just that when the need arises. From this the court concluded that since there is no statutory authority for changing the composition of a committee once it has been appointed, "there is also no reason to believe that the court, pursuant to its powers under § 105(a), should not fill that statutory void when alteration becomes necessary." 194 B.R. at 131. The National Bankruptcy Review Commission recommends that "section 1102(a) be amended to authorize courts to review creditor committee composition and the qualifications of the members for purposes of ensuring that the committees are adequately representative." National Bankruptcy Review Commission, *Bankruptcy: The Next Twenty Years, Final Report* (1997) p. 499.

(9) *Appointment and Role of Committee Counsel and other Professionals.* Code § 1103(a) authorizes a committee, with the court's approval, to employ one or more attorneys, accountants, or other agents to represent the committee or perform services for the committee. The role of an attorney who is retained to represent a committee has been described as that of "an educator and advisor regarding fiduciary duties and the reorganization process in general, a mediator of intra-committee and inter-creditor disputes, a consensus builder when no clear majority exists, a facilitator for those members lacking in representation and resources when the best interests of creditors are at issue, and a representative and advocate in court for the entire creditor class." Carl A. Elkund & Lynn W. Roberts, *The Problem with Creditors' Committees in Chapter 11: How to Manage the Inherent Conflicts Without Loss of Function*, 5 Am. Bankr. Inst. L. Rev. 129, 144 (1997) (footnotes omitted).

Some courts have held that an attorney retained to represent a committee has a fiduciary duty to committee constituents, as well as to the committee itself. *United Steel Workers of America v. Lampl (In re Mesta Machine Co.)*, 67 B.R. 151, 157 (Bankr. W.D. Pa. 1986); *Pan Am Corp. v. Delta Airlines, Inc.*, 175 B.R. 438, 514 (S.D.N.Y. 1994). That view has been criticized. "The professionals represent the committee itself and not the entire class represented by the committee. . . . The committee itself represents the members of the class and the professionals follow the instructions of the committee. The professionals should not be placed in a position [where] they are expected or encouraged to second guess the committee as to how best further the interests of the committee's constituency." King, 7 *Collier on Bankruptcy* ¶ 1103.03[7] (Matthew Bender 15th Ed. Revised 2000).

You may recall that under Code § 327, a professional retained by a trustee or debtor in possession must be "disinterested" and must not hold or represent an interest adverse to the estate. Code § 1103(b), which governs attorneys and accountants retained by a committee, is more liberal. It provides that they may not, while employed by the committee, "represent any other entity having an adverse interest in connection with the case," but further provides that "[r]epresentation of one or more creditors of the same class as represented by the committee shall not per se constitute the representation of an adverse interest." May a lawyer simultaneously represent, in a matter unrelated to the case, a committee and a creditor that is also an insider of the debtor? A creditor that may have received a voidable preference or fraudulent transfer? A creditor that holds a disputed claim? May a lawyer who is not disinterested represent a committee? What about a lawyer who *holds* an interest adverse to the estate? Section 1103(b) does not prohibit it. Nevertheless, since Code § 328(c) gives the court discretion to deny compensation to any professional who is not disinterested or who holds an adverse interest, a professional is well advised to disclose those conditions in its application for retention. *See* discussion in chapter 1.

(10) *Reimbursement of Committee Members' Expenses.* Although the Bankruptcy Code has always authorized official committees to retain professionals at the estate's expense, until 1994, the Code did not authorize individual committee members to obtain reimbursement of expenses they incurred in the performance of their duties as committee members. For example, the Code did not authorize reimbursement for travel or lodging expenses incurred in connection with committee meetings. However, in 1994, subsection (F) was added to Code § 503(b)(3). It grants administrative expense priority to actual, necessary expenses incurred by a member of a committee appointed under Code § 1102 in the performance of committee duties. This provision will, for example, permit committee members to obtain reimbursement for the cost of traveling to meetings, but it does not entitle a member to be paid for serving on the committee.

In *First Merchants Acceptance Corp. v. J.C. Bradford & Co. (In re First Merchants Acceptance Corp.)*, 198 F.3d 394 (3d Cir. 1999), the Court of Appeals, in a case of first impression, held that § 503(b)(3)(F) permitted a committee member to obtain reimbursement for legal fees paid to its (not the committee's) attorney for services that the attorney rendered with the knowledge of, and at the request of, committee members and committee counsel. Does the Third Circuit's holding conflict with the requirement that a committee obtain court approval before retaining an attorney? *See* Code § 1103(a).

(11) *Creditors' Committee "Derivative Actions."* Assume that you have been retained to represent the Amphydynamics creditors' committee. In the course of examining the company's books and records, the committee discovers that a few weeks prior to filing its petition, the company made a large payment — probably preferential — to Bank. Lawyers for Amphydynamics say that their client is not

inclined to bring a preference action against the Bank, ostensibly because the likelihood of success on the merits does not justify the cost. Committee members believe that Amphydynamics is not inclined to sue to recover the preference, because Headley Charisma personally guaranteed the loan. Does the committee have standing to pursue an action on behalf of a debtor in possession?

Borrowing from corporate law principles governing derivative actions — which makes sense, given that creditors are the residual owners of an insolvent debtor — some courts have allowed committees to bring actions on behalf of the estate. However, before asking the court for authority to sue, the committee must first demand that the debtor (or trustee) bring the action, unless such a demand would be clearly futile. *See Official Committee of Unsecured Creditors ex rel. Cybergenics Corp. v. Chinery*, 330 F.3d 548 (3d Cir) *(en banc), cert dismissed*, 540 U.S. 1002 (2003); *Canadian Pacific Forest Products v. J.D. Irving, Ltd. (In re Gibson Group, Inc.)*, 66 F.3d 1436 (6th Cir. 1995). In addition, the committee must show the existence of a colorable claim that, based on a cost-benefit analysis, would benefit the estate if the action were successful. *Commodore Electronics Ltd. v. Gould (In re Commodore Int'l Ltd.)*, 262 F.3d 96 (2d Cir. 2001); *In re Valley Park, Inc.*, 217 B.R. 864 (Bankr. D. Mont. 1998); *In re America's Hobby Center, Inc.*, 223 B.R. 275 (Bankr. S.D.N.Y. 1998). Authorizing a committee to bring a suit that the debtor in possession is reluctant to bring may be a less drastic alternative to appointing a trustee or examiner in a case where the debtor has a conflict of interest. *In re Monsour Medical Center*, 5 B.R. 715 (Bankr. W.D. Pa. 1980); *Liberal Market v. Malone & Hyde, Inc.*, 14 B.R. 685 (Bankr. S.D. Ohio 1981).

(12) *Equity Committees: The Poverty of Their Position.* Among the kinds of "additional committees" contemplated by Code § 1102(a) are committees to represent the interests of equity security holders. Should shareholders of an *insolvent* corporation be entitled to the benefits of an equity holders' committee? In *In re Emons Industries, Inc.*, 50 B.R. 692, 694 (Bankr. S.D.N.Y. 1985), the court held that "generally no equity committee should be appointed" to negotiate the terms of a reorganization plan on behalf of stockholders "when it appears that a debtor is insolvent because neither the debtor nor the creditors should have to bear the expense of negotiating over the terms of what is in essence a gift." On the other hand, in *Bank Creditors Group v. Hamill (In re White Motor Credit Corp.)*, 27 B.R. 554 (Bankr. N.D. Ohio 1982), the district court affirmed the bankruptcy court's refusal to admit evidence regarding the solvency of the company, calling such evidence "irrelevant in light of the fact that an equity security holders' committee is specifically authorized by § 1102(a)(2) and inasmuch as the interests of the security holders cannot be determined until a reorganization plan is formulated." 27 B.R. at 558. More recently, in a case in which the solvency of the debtor could not be easily determined, the court held that the debtor was not *hopelessly* insolvent, and that appointment of an equity committee was appropriate. *In re Wang Laboratories, Inc.*, 149 B.R. 1 (Bankr. D. Mass. 1992).

PROBLEM 2.4

Suppose that on further reflection, and after the U.S. Trustee described the fiduciary duties of official committee members, Beth Verdant decided that the Loach Group should not pursue a seat on the committee. She does not want to put

Loach Group in the position of being bound by the fiduciary duties imposed on official committee members. She recognizes that the interests of Loach and other unsecured claimholders may be very different. Loach acquired its claims in anticipation of either selling them at a profit or retaining them (and accumulating more) if, as its analysts believe, creditors will emerge as the new owners of the reorganized company. Yesterday she received a call from the manager of another investment fund inviting her to join what he referred to as an "ad hoc" or unofficial committee of similarly situated claimholders. What are the benefits of joining an ad hoc committee? What are the burdens? Consider the following two opinions rendered in the Northwest Airlines case.

IN RE NORTHWEST AIRLINES CORPORATION (NORTHWEST I)

United States Bankruptcy Court Southern District Of New York
363 B.R. 701 (2007)

Allan L. Gropper, United States Bankruptcy Judge

Debtors Northwest Airlines Corporation *et al.* ("Debtors") have moved to require an *ad hoc* committee of equity security holders (the "Committee") to supplement a statement pursuant to Bankruptcy Rule 2019 filed by counsel for the Committee. Debtors argue that the current 2019 statement is inadequate in that it fails to disclose "the amounts of claims or interests owned by the members of the committee, the times when acquired, the amounts paid therefore, and any sales or other disposition thereof," as required by Rule 2019. For the reasons set forth hereafter, Debtors' motion is granted.

The Committee

The Committee first appeared in the above-captioned proceedings by a notice of appearance dated January 11, 2007. The notice of appearance was filed by the law firm of Kasowitz, Benson, Torres & Friedman LLP ("KBT&F") on behalf of "the Ad Hoc Committee of Equity Security Holders," comprised of "certain institutions holding common stock issued by Northwest Airlines Corp . . . ." In a pleading dated January 16, 2007, KBT&F filed the "Verified Statement of Kasowitz, Benson, Torres & Friedman LLP Pursuant to Bankruptcy Rule 2019(a)." The statement contains the following information: KBT&F appears "on behalf of the Ad Hoc Committee of Equity Security Holders . . . ;" it identifies the 11 members of the Committee; discloses that, "[t]he members of the Ad Hoc Equity Committee own, in the aggregate, 16,195,200 shares of common stock of Northwest and claims against the Debtors in the aggregate amount of $164.7 million" and that, "[s]ome of the shares of common stock and some of the claims were acquired by the members of the Ad Hoc Equity Committee after the commencement of the Cases;" states that KBT&F has been retained as "counsel to the Ad Hoc Equity Committee in the Cases pursuant to an engagement letter in the form annexed as Exhibit B hereto;" and states that KBT&F does not own any claims against or interests in the Debtors and that the members of the Committee are responsible for the firm's fees "subject to their right to have the Debtors reimburse KBT&F's fees and disbursements and other expenses by order of the Court."

The engagement letter attached to the 2019 Statement confirms the agreement of the signatory "to become a member of the Ad-hoc Committee of Equity Holders in connection with the Northwest bankruptcy cases." It further states that in consideration of the firm's "provision of services to the Committee," the members of the Committee agree to pay the Firm, on a *pro rata* basis, for its services and that in addition thereto, "the Committee may, at the culmination of the matters for which the Firm has been engaged, pay to the Firm, at the Committee's sole discretion, a performance fee . . . ." The *pro rata* obligation of each member of the Committee to pay fees is based on its individual holdings of Northwest common stock as of December 26, 2006, divided by the total holdings of the Committee, subject to periodic revision. By an amendment to the Rule 2019 statement, dated January 19, 2007, KBT&F disclosed that there were now 13 Committee members with an aggregate of "19,065,644 shares of common stock of Northwest and claims against the debtors in the aggregate amount of $264,287,500."

Bankruptcy Rule 2019

Rule 2019(a) provides, in relevant part:

> In a chapter 9 municipality or chapter 11 reorganization case, except with respect to a committee appointed pursuant to § 1102 or 1114 of the Code [an official committee], every entity or committee representing more than one creditor or equity security holder . . . shall file a verified statement setting forth
>
> > (1) the name and address of the creditor or equity security holder;
> >
> > (2) the nature and amount of the claim or interest and the time of acquisition thereof unless it is alleged to have been acquired more than one year prior to the filing of the petition;
> >
> > (3) . . . in the case of a committee, the name or names of the entity or entities at whose instance, directly or indirectly, the employment was arranged or the committee was organized or agreed to act; and
> >
> > (4) with reference to the time of . . . the organization or formation of the committee . . . the amounts of claims or interests owned by . . . the members of the committee . . . the times when acquired, the amounts paid therefore, and any sales or other disposition thereof.

By its plain terms, the Rule requires disclosure of "the amounts of claims or interests owned by the members of the committee, the times when acquired, the amounts paid therefore, and any sales or other disposition thereof." The statement filed by KBT&F on behalf of the Committee fails to disclose this information and is insufficient on its face.

The Committee's only substantive argument in response is that Bankruptcy Rule 2019 applies, by virtue of its lead-in clause, only to "every entity or committee representing more than one creditor or equity security holder." KBT&F contends that no member of the Committee represents any party other than itself, that only KBT&F as counsel represents "more than one creditor or equity security holder," and that KBT&F does not have any claims or interests in the Debtors or anything to disclose. However, the Rule cannot be so blithely avoided. KBT&F's clients appeared in these Chapter 11 cases as a "Committee." Their notice of appearance was as a committee, and it is the "Ad Hoc Committee" that has moved for the appointment of an official shareholders' committee and has been actively litigating discovery issues in numerous hearings and conferences before the Court. Counsel was retained by the "Committee" and is compensated by the "Committee" on the basis of work performed for the Committee (and not each individual member). The law firm does not purport to represent the separate interests of any Committee member; it takes its instructions from the Committee as a whole and represents one entity for purposes of the Rule.

There may be cases where a law firm represents several individual clients and is the only entity required to file a Rule 2019 statement, on its own behalf. That appears to have been the case in *In re CF Holding Corp.*, 145 B.R. 124 (Bankr. D. Conn. 1992), relied on by the Committee. There, a firm represented multiple creditors, and the Court distinguished the case before it from the situation where a group had been formed. It quoted from *Wilson v. Valley Electric Membership Corp.*, 141 B.R., 309, 314 (E.D. La. 1992), where Judge Sear, chairman of the Advisory Committee at the time the Bankruptcy Rules were amended in 1986, commented in dicta, "Rule 2019 more appropriately seems to apply to the formal organization of a group of creditors holding similar claims, who have elected to consolidate their collection efforts . . . ." That is exactly the situation in this case, except that here there are shareholders rather than creditors. Where an *ad hoc* committee has appeared as such, the committee is required to provide the information plainly required by Rule 2019 on behalf of each of its members.

Ad hoc or unofficial committees play an important role in reorganization cases. By appearing as a "committee" of shareholders, the members purport to speak for a group and implicitly ask the court and other parties to give their positions a degree of credibility appropriate to a unified group with large holdings. Moreover, the Bankruptcy Code specifically provides for the possibility of the grant of compensation to "a committee representing creditors or equity security holders other than a committee appointed under section 1102 of this title [an official committee], in making a substantial contribution in a case under chapter 9 or 11 of this title." 11 U.S.C. § 503(b)(3)(D). A committee purporting to speak for a group obviously has a better chance of meeting the "substantial contribution" test than an individual, as a single creditor or shareholder is often met with the argument that it was merely acting in its own self-interest and was not making a "substantial contribution" for purposes of § 503(b)(3). *See In re Richton Int'l Corp.*, 15 B.R. 854, 855-56 (Bankr. S.D.N.Y. 1981) ("Those services which are provided solely for the client-as-creditor . . . are not compensable.").[1]

Unofficial committees have long been active in reorganization cases, and the

---

[1] Counsel for an unofficial committee is also entitled to seek reimbursement. 11 U.S.C. § 503(b)(4). It is this section on which KBT&F was presumably relying when it reserved its rights, in its retention letter, to have the Debtors reimburse its fees.

influential study in the 1930's by Professor (later Justice) William O. Douglas for the Securities and Exchange Commission centered on perceived abuses by unofficial committees in equity receiverships and other corporate reorganizations. *See* Report on the Study and Investigation of the Work, Activities, Personnel and Functions of Protective and Reorganization Committees (1937). The four-volume SEC report led directly to the adoption of Chapter X and Rule 10-211 thereunder, which provided for disclosure of the "personnel and activities of those acting in a representative capacity" in order to help foster fair and equitable plans free from deception and overreaching. 13A King *et al.*, Collier on Bankruptcy, ¶ 10-211.04 (14th ed. 1976). Although they made many other changes to the law and rules relating to reorganizations, the drafters of the 1978 Bankruptcy Code and the rules thereunder retained the substance of former Rule 10-211 in Bankruptcy Rule 2019 as "a comprehensive regulation of representation in chapter 9 and chapter 11 reorganization cases." Advisory Committee Note to Bankruptcy Rule 2019; see also Report of the Commission on Bankruptcy Laws of the United States, H.R.Doc. No. 137, 93d Cong., 1st Sess. 242-43 (1973). The Rule is long-standing, and there is no basis for failure to apply it as written. Although the Committee argues that the Rule has been frequently ignored or watered down, there is no shortage of cases applying it. *See In re Okla. P.A.C. First Ltd. P'ship*, 122 B.R. 387, 391 (Bankr. D. Ariz. 1990), quoting Collier on Bankruptcy: "The Code contemplates that there will be unofficial committees. Any such unofficial committee must comply with Rule 2019 by its terms . . . ."; *see also Baron & Budd P.C. v. Unsecured Asbestos Claimants Comm.*, 321 B.R. 147, 166 (D. N.J. 2005); *In re Ionosphere Clubs, Inc.*, 101 B.R. 844, 852 (Bankr. S.D.N.Y. 1989); *In re Keene*, 205 B.R. 690 (Bankr. S.D.N.Y. 1997); *In re Kaiser Aluminum Corp.*, 327 B.R. 554, 558 (D. Del. 2005).

Based on the issue before the Court, the Debtors' motion is granted. The Committee is required to comply with Bankruptcy Rule 2019 and file an amended statement within three business days.

IT IS SO ORDERED.

IN RE NORTHWEST AIRLINES CORP. (NORTHWEST II)
United States Bankruptcy Court Southern District Of New York
363 B.R. 704 (2007)

ALLAN L. GROPPER, UNITED STATES BANKRUPTCY JUDGE

By order entered February 26, 2007, the Court, on motion of debtors Northwest Airlines Corporation *et al.* (the "Debtors"), required an *ad hoc* committee of equity security holders that had appeared in these chapter 11 cases (the "Committee") to comply with the plain requirements of Bankruptcy Rule 2019 and file an amended Rule 2019 statement. The Committee has moved for an order that would permit the amended statement to be filed under seal, to be available only to the Court and the U.S. Trustee. The Committee proposes to seal that part of the information required by Rule 2019 that discloses the specifics of the purchases and sales of the Debtors' securities made by Committee members. The motion is opposed by the Debtors, by the official creditors' committee, and by Bloomberg News ("Bloomberg"), which moved to intervene.[1] In *In re Orion Pictures Corp.*, 21 F.3d 24, 27 (2d Cir. 1994), the debtor sought to seal confidential commercial information consisting of the terms of a promotional agreement between the debtor and a major customer that the Court found would give competitors, who sought to make the information public, a direct competitive advantage. The Second Circuit held that under § 107(b) protection is available if an interested party could show "that the information it sought to seal was 'confidential' and 'commercial' in nature." *Id.*[2]

The Second Circuit nevertheless recognized in *Orion* that § 107(b) creates an exception to the general principle that "[i]n most cases, a judge must carefully and skeptically review sealing requests to insure that there really is an extraordinary circumstance or compelling need." *Id.* Moreover, as provided in § 107(a) of the Bankruptcy Code, it is a basic tenet of our jurisprudence that court records are public and "open to examination by an entity at reasonable times without charge." 11 U.S.C. § 107(a); *see, e.g., Lugosch v. Pyramid Co. of Onondaga*, 435 F.3d 110 (2d Cir. 2006) (discussing Constitutional and common law rights of access to documents filed in court.)[3] Moreover, the Circuit Court in *Orion* narrowly defined the term "commercial" as used in § 107(b) as "information which would cause 'an unfair advantage to competitors by providing them information as to the commercial operations of the debtor.' " 21 F.3d at 27, quoting *Ad Hoc Protective Comm. for 10-1/2% Debenture Holders v. Itel Corp. (In re Itel Corp.)*, 17 B.R. 942, 944 (B.A.P. 9th Cir. 1982).[4]

In its initial papers, the Committee tried to bring itself within the construction

---

[1] Bloomberg states that its motion is "an effort to ensure that the public has a full and accurate understanding of the events occurring in this Chapter 11 proceeding, including the motivations and interests of the players who seek to control an important public company." (Memorandum of Law, p. 1) The parties have consented to the intervention. The Committee's motion is based on § 107(b) of the Bankruptcy Code, which provides:

> On request of a party in interest, the bankruptcy court shall, and on the bankruptcy court's own motion, the bankruptcy court may —
>
> > (1) protect an entity with respect to a trade secret or confidential research, development, or commercial information . . . .

[2] Bankruptcy Rule 9018 similarly provides that "the court may make an order which justice requires (1) to protect the estate or any entity in respect of a trade secret or other confidential research, development, or commercial information. . . . "

[3] Indeed, it has been held that the policy interest in favor of public access "is at its zenith where issues concerning the integrity and transparency of bankruptcy proceedings are involved." *In re Food Mgmt. Group, LLC*, 359 B.R. 543 (Bankr. S.D.N.Y. 2007); *see also Gitto v. Worcester Telegram & Gazette Corp. (In re Gitto Global Corp.)*, 422 F.3d 1, 7 (1st Cir. 2005), quoting *Ferm v. United States Trustee (In re Crawford)*, 194 F.3d 954, 960 (9th Cir. 1999) (unrestricted access to bankruptcy records "fosters confidence among creditors regarding the fairness of the bankruptcy system.").

[4] In *Itel*, the Court rejected the proposition that information was "commercial" within the meaning of § 107(b) merely because it related to business affairs. This is consistent with the holdings of other courts in bankruptcy and non-bankruptcy contexts. *See, e.g., In re Handy Andy Home Improvement Centers, Inc.*, 199 B.R. 376, 382 (Bankr. N.D. Ill. 1996) ("A document does not contain commercial information merely because it is used in a commercial industry. Commercial information is information which would give a competitor an unfair advantage."); *Diamond State Ins. Co. v. Rebel Oil Co., Inc.*, 157 F.R.D. 691, 697 (D. Nev. 1994) (motion to quash a subpoena under F.R.C.P. 45(c)(3)(B)(i)) ("Confidential commercial information is information which, if disclosed, would cause substantial economic harm to the competitive position of the entity from whom the information was obtained.")

of "commercial" in *Orion* by contending that the information it seeks to seal would allow competitors of the funds that make up the Committee to discern the members' "investment strategies." This improbable contention was unsupported by the affidavits filed on behalf of the Committee by three of its members, and counsel at oral argument conceded that the "trading strategies" of his clients are not at issue. There is thus no basis for the contention that § 107(b), as construed in *Orion*, mandates that the information required by Rule 2019 be sealed on request. The issue is not, as the Committee would have it, that § 107(b) as a statute trumps the requirements of Bankruptcy Rule 2019. The Court's duty instead is to enforce Bankruptcy Rule 2019 in a manner consistent with protecting the legitimate rights of the parties and the public interest, keeping in mind that § 107(b) provides a broader mandate in favor of sealing documents than applies in non-bankruptcy cases.[5]

In deciding the instant motion with due concern for the above interests, we start with the fact that Bankruptcy Rule 2019 is a disclosure rule. As discussed in the Court's memorandum of February 26, 2007, it requires unofficial committees that play a significant public role in reorganization proceedings and enjoy a level of credibility and influence consonant with group status to file a statement containing certain information. The direct antecedent of Rule 2019 was Rule 10-211 under former Chapter X of the Bankruptcy Act, which was adopted following an exhaustive SEC Report on the Study and Investigation of the Work, Activities, Personnel and Functions of Protective and Reorganization Committees (1937) (hereafter, the "SEC Report"). Among other things, the SEC Report warned of possible conflicts of interest by outside as well as inside financial interests, finding that "these conflicts permeate the entire protective committee system. Their elimination is as essential towards making the outside groups effective and responsible as it is towards eliminating the abuses of the insiders." *SEC Report*, Part I at 880.[6] As one step toward this end the Commission recommended that persons who represent more than 12 creditors or stockholders (including committees) be required to file with the court a sworn statement containing the information now required by Rule 2019.[7] The Report also recommended that "[a]ttorneys who appear in the proceedings should be required to furnish similar information respecting their clients." The SEC specifically found that the foregoing information "will provide a routine method of advising the court *and all parties in interest* of the actual economic interest of all persons participating in the proceed-ings." Recommendation 9, *SEC Report*, Part I at 902 (emphasis added.) The SEC

---

[5] Even if there were a conflict between § 107(b) and Rule 2019, the Court's duty would be to reconcile them, if possible. *See In re Henderson*, 197 B.R. 147, 155 (Bankr. N.D. Ala. 1996) ("Rules and statutes, however, should be interpreted, if possible, to be in harmony.") (internal citations omitted); *see also Pittsburgh & Lake Erie R.R. Co. v. Ry. Labor Executives' Ass'n*, 491 U.S. 490, 510, 109 S. Ct. 2584, 105 L. Ed. 2d 415 (1989).

[6] The Report further found that "the conflicts which do exist" in the outside groups "are in fact made the more obnoxious if these groups operate under the guise of independent committees, for security holders are induced more readily to believe that in the hands of these self-styled independents their cause will be honestly and rigorously served." *SEC Report* at 880. For a thorough discussion of the SEC study, as well as the view that conditions might not have been as bad as the SEC Report suggested, *see* David A. Skeel, Jr., *Debt's Dominion: A History of Bankruptcy Law in America*, ch. 4 (2001).

[7] The Rule as actually adopted and as now formulated is not limited to groups of 12 or more.

Report thus contemplated public dissemination of the information, and there is no reason to assume that the drafters believed that the goals of the Rule could be achieved if the required information were filed secretly.

Much has changed in reorganization practice since the 1930's, but the disclosure required by what is now Bankruptcy Rule 2019 is substantially the same. The facts of this case illustrate why public disclosure is still needed.

As noted above, there is no support in the record for the Committee's initial contention that it has sought to protect its members' "investment strategies." The affidavits filed on this motion by representatives of three of the Committee members disclose why they want to keep the data confidential. There, the Committee representatives identify the damage that would allegedly result from public disclosure of the information required by Bankruptcy Rule 2019 as follows:

> Obviously the circumstances could and do vary greatly, but it clearly would damage our bargaining position and give our counterparties an unfair advantage if they were to know our basis or acquisition cost of the assets we were trying to sell. Just as car dealers do not disclose to customers their actual acquisition cost of their cars, and builders do not disclose to potential home buyers their actual cost to build homes, we do not disclose to potential counterparties our basis in our investments . . . *See. e.g.*, Decl. of Daniel Krueger, p. 3.

The Committee members do not advance their position when they compare themselves to car or real estate salesmen. It bears recalling that this Committee purports to control 27 percent of the outstanding stock of the Debtors and that it has repeatedly asked the Court to give credibility to its claims that the Debtors' equity has substantial value, that the Debtors' management has wrongfully undervalued the equity, and that it intends to mount a contest as to the valuation of these Debtors. By acting as a group, the members of this shareholders' Committee subordinated to the requirements of Rule 2019 their interest in keeping private the prices at which they individually purchased or sold the Debtors' securities. This is not unfair because their negotiating decisions as a Committee should be based on the interests of the entire shareholders' group, not their individual financial advantage. Their counsel admitted at oral argument of this motion that in negotiations between a committee and other parties in interest, the question is whether a tranche is being treated fairly, not the price at which individual members might be induced to sell. If that is so, and it should be, it cannot harm the legitimate interests of members of an *ad hoc* committee to put pricing information on the table.[8]

In any event, any interest that individual Committee members may have in

---

[8] It has also been held (in a different context) that preserving leverage is not usually an interest that would justify sealing court records. *See Geltzer v. Andersen Worldwide, S.C.*, 2007 U.S. Dist. LEXIS 6794 (S.D.N.Y. Jan. 30, 2007) ("There is no discernable public interest, or interest of the bankruptcy estates, in preserving [the defendant's] 'leverage' as against other parties . . . ."); *In re Alterra Healthcare Corp.*, 353 B.R. 66, 76 (Bankr. D. Del. 2006) (an order that sealed certain information was vacated; the Court, in response to the contention that disclosure would help litigants against the debtor said, "[a]n unfair advantage to a tort claimant of a debtor, however, does not create an unfair advantage to its market competitors.")

keeping this information confidential is overridden by the interests that Rule 2019 seeks to protect. Rule 2019 protects other members of the group — here, the shareholders — and informs them where a committee is coming from by requiring full disclosure of the securities held by members of the committee and the respective purchases and sales. This Committee contends that it did not take on any fiduciary responsibility to the shareholders as a group when it appeared in these cases. Assuming, *arguendo*, for purposes of this motion that the Committee does not act as a fiduciary, Rule 2019 is based on the premise that the other shareholders have a right to information as to Committee member purchases and sales so that they make an informed decision whether this Committee will represent their interests or whether they should consider forming a more broadly-based committee of their own. It also gives all parties a better ability to gauge the credibility of an important group that has chosen to appear in a bankruptcy case and play a major role.

The utility to other shareholders of information as to the purchases and sales made by members of this Committee is underscored by two facts of record. First, it has been disclosed that Committee members own a very significant amount of debt, as well as stock. Rule 2019 is based on the premise that other shareholders have a right to know whether the debt purchases were made at the same time as the purchases of stock, a fact that might raise questions as to divided loyalties. Second, each of the three representative Committee members admits in his declaration that he might decide to sell out at any time. *See, e.g.*, the declaration of Daniel Krueger, where it is stated, "[a]lso, we or other members of the Ad Hoc Equity Committee may desire to sell our respective claims to third parties at some point, or make some other similar deal with someone who currently is not an interest holder in this case. Disclosure of our acquisition cost likewise will prejudice our ability to sell or negotiate such a deal with third parties." (P 7) The possibility that members of an *ad hoc* committee will sell and leave a group without a representative is exactly why there are disclosures required under Rule 2019. Rule 2019 gives other members of the class the right to know where their champions are coming from. Granting the motion to seal would scuttle the Rule.

The motion to seal is denied. An amended Rule 2019 Statement as required by this Court's order of February 26, 2007, should be filed on the Court's docket as soon as feasible and in any event within three business days from the date of this order.

IT IS SO ORDERED.

NOTE ON RULE 2019 AND THE AFTERMATH OF *NORTHWEST*

At about the same time that Judge Gropper ruled in *Northwest Airlines*, another court held that an ad hoc "group" of note holders *was not* a "committee" for purposes of Rule 2019. *In re Scotia Development LLC*, 2007 Bankr. LEXIS 4731 (Bankr. S.D. Tex. Apr. 18, 2007). In *In re Washington Mutual, Inc.*, 419 B.R. 271 (Bankr. D. Del. 2009), the court held that a note holders "group" *was* a "committee."

Opinions such as *Northwest Airlines* did not sit well with distressed security investors, who lobbied The Advisory Committee on Bankruptcy Rules to repeal Rule 2019.[23] They were particularly concerned with the requirement that they disclose the purchase date and price of their holdings. They argued that such information "is proprietary information confidential to the purchaser" and that "requiring the disclosure of the purchase price and trade date will have a chilling effect on the willingness of distressed security investors to (a) trade in such distressed securities in the future, and (b) participate in the bankruptcy process."[24] They also argued that "the chilling effect on distressed security investors will result in more expense and time for Bankruptcy Courts because, without ad hoc committees, the Courts will be clogged with duplicative psleadings filed by similarly situated claim holders."[25]

Bankruptcy Judge Robert E. Gerber, a Southern District of New York colleague of Judge Gropper (the author of the *Northwest* opinions), urged the Advisory Committee to revise, rather than repeal, Rule 2019.[26] He observed that in recent years, the dynamics of Chapter 11 cases — particularly large cases — has changed, and that "[i]n many, if not most of the largest cases, the traditional creditors in chapter 11 cases — those left holding the bag when business fail — have in large part been replaced as players in the chapter 11 process by investors in distressed debt who become stakeholders in the reorganization process by choice."[27] He pointed out that their presence "by itself is not necessarily bad, and is sometimes good thing." They provide a way out for prepetition claim holders and "in some cases . . . provide other valuable services, such as needed financing or bidding for assets before the end of the . . . case."[28] On the other hand, distressed debt investors, Judge Gerber wrote, "have their own agendas . . . without a broader regard for spending the time and effort necessary to stabilize the business, and/or maximize its value for the good of all."[29] Although he expressed doubt that the disclosure of price paid for holdings served an important purpose, he did recommend disclosure of other facts that would help the court and other parties understand the motivation of distressed debt investors when they took a position on important issues in a Chapter 11 case. He urged the amendment of Rule 2019 to "make clear that it requires disclosure of short positions, or derivatives with the same economic substance,"[30] so that parties would know whether the investors were "betting on the failure of the chapter 11 case, on delay in creditors' receiving

---

[23] Report of the ABA Section of Business Law Business Bankruptcy Committee Special Task Force on Bankruptcy Rule 2019 at p. 3 (December 12, 2008), available at http://www.uscourts.gov/uscourts/RulesAndPolicies/rules/BK%20Suggestions%202008/08-BK-P-Suggestion-ABA%20Section%20of%20Business%20Law%20%28Baxter%29.pdf.

[24] *Id.*

[25] *Id.*

[26] Letter from Hon. Robert E. Gerber, United States Bankruptcy Judge, Southern District of New York, to Advisory Committee on Bankruptcy Rules (January 9, 2009), *available at* http://html.documation.com/cds/NCBJ2010/PDFs/017_6.pdf.

[27] *Id.* at 2.

[28] *Id.*

[29] *Id.* at 2–3.

[30] *Id.* at 10.

payment, or on decreased recoveries by another creditor constituency."[31] He urged the addition of a requirement of disclosure of interests in credit default swaps so that the court and other parties in interest will know which entities do or do not have "skin in the game."[32] He urged that Rule 2019 be clarified to make clear that it covers multiple creditors acting in concert and represented by the same counsel, whether or not they acknowledge that they are members of a "committee."[33]

The Advisory Committee on Bankruptcy Rules proposed amendments to Rule 2019, which were approved by the Supreme Court in April, 2011. Amended Rule 2019 took effect on December 1, 2011. Please read it now.

The distinction (if there ever was one) between "committees," "groups," or just a bunch of folks working together has been eliminated. Disclosure, in the form of a verified statement, must be provided by "every group or committee that consists of or represents, and every entity that represents, multiple creditors or equity security holders that are (A) acting in concert to advance their common interests, and (B) not composed entirely of affiliates or insiders of one another." Rule 2019(b). The verified statement must list each member of the committee and list each "disclosable economic interest" held by each member that was acquired within a year of the petition date. Rule 2019(c). A "disclosable economic interest" is "any claim, interest, pledge, lien, option, participation, derivative instrument, or any other right or derivative right granting the holder an economic interest that is affected by the value, acquisition, or disposition of a claim or interest." Rule 2019(a)(1). The date — by quarter and year — on which the interest was acquired must be disclosed, unless the interest was acquired more than one year before the bankruptcy petition was filed. Rule 2019(c)(2). Amended Rule 2019 does not require the disclosure of the consideration paid for that economic interest, but the Advisory Committee Notes make clear that a court may order "the discovery of that information or its disclosure . . . pursuant to authority outside this rule." That presumably might include the examination of an entity pursuant to Bankruptcy Rule 2004.

---

[31] *Id.* at 8.

[32] *Id.*

[33] *Id.* at 10.

Chapter 3

THE AUTOMATIC STAY

§ 3.01 INTRODUCTION; BASIC FEATURES OF THE AUTOMATIC STAY

After hearing your description of Chapter 11, Headley says, "Chapter 11 certainly sounds like an option for us. I'd like you to start preparing the documents necessary for us to file a petition. In the meantime, however, I'd like to see if I can negotiate an agreement among the creditors that will allow Amphy to get back on its feet." You tell him that you can have the petition and supporting documents ready in a few days, and that you will await his instructions.

PROBLEM 3.1

Headley decided the best thing to do was to call a meeting of his major creditors. He was able to convince Josh Colman and Andy Nicoll of BigBank and the attorney representing three of Amphy's four largest suppliers to attend. Also present were the attorneys representing the "Hystereo Plaintiffs," the former fans of Amphydynamics video games who claim to have developed a strange illness, called Hystereo, as a result of exposure to the games. At the meeting, Headley laid out his plan for turning the company around. He explained that while the company was currently short of cash, all it needed was 90 days until it could bring its new low-cost, flat-screen web appliances to market. In order to accomplish this, all of the creditors at the meeting would need to agree to a moratorium on payments of all existing debts. BigBank would need to loan an additional $500,000, which would be secured by a pledge of Charisma's stock in Gene Expressions, Inc. The suppliers would continue to do business with Amphy on a cash basis, and the Hystereo plaintiffs would agree to stay their lawsuit for 90 days so that Charisma can focus on getting the company back on its feet. He further explained that if no agreement could be reached, Amphy would file for bankruptcy the next day.

A. Assume you are the lawyer for BigBank. Further assume that BigBank's loan is secured by Amphy's inventory, receivables, and equipment and the value of that collateral is 90% of the debt owed to BigBank. In other words, BigBank's claim is undersecured. Assume that Colman and Nicoll have told you that the Gene Expressions stock is worth about $600,000. What risks does BigBank face if it agrees to stand still?

B. Assume you are the lawyer for one of the three suppliers at the meeting. Would you prefer to accept the standstill agreement or allow Amphy to file?

C. Assume you are the lawyer for the Hystereo plaintiffs. Would you prefer to accept the standstill agreement or allow Amphy to file?

The meeting turned out to be a relative success. While initially suspicious, BigBank agreed to loan $400,000 in return for a pledge of the Gene Expressions stock, as well as personal guaranties from Headley and Carol. BigBank also agreed to forego any debt repayments and to refrain from pursuing its remedies so long as Amphy refrained from paying any past-due trade debt, no judgments were entered against Amphy, and no other creditor began to seize assets. The three trade creditors also agreed to stand still, so long as Amphy made no payments to the fourth trade creditor.

Pleased with himself, Headley calls you into his office and says: "Stop working on the bankruptcy petition, and write up a workout agreement for everyone to sign. When you're done, I'll take you out for a nice dinner as thanks for all your good work." You retire to your office to prepare the documents, concerned that Headley's euphoria might be short-lived.

Unfortunately, your pessimism turns out to be well-founded. Before you could print out the final draft of the agreement, CitiCircuits, the supplier that boycotted the meeting, filed suit against Amphy and, by alleging that Amphy was conveying away assets, managed to convince a state court judge to order a prejudgment attachment of Amphy's inventory. Upon learning of this, BigBank took steps to repossess its collateral and exercised its right to set off cash that Amphy had on deposit at the bank against the debt that Amphy owes it. Some other suppliers filed their own suits. Still others called Headley and told him if he didn't file a bankruptcy petition on behalf of Amphy, they would file an involuntary petition themselves.

Headley calls you in a state of despair and confusion. "I guess time has run out. We're going to have to file the petition after all. But I have one question. Why is it that my suppliers are threatening to put the company into bankruptcy themselves. What's in it for them?"

You remind Headley that bankruptcy is not just a debtor's remedy and that it serves the collective interests of creditors, as well, by avoiding the piecemeal dismantling of a debtor by the most aggressive creditors and by providing for a fair and equitable distribution of the debtor's assets. You also remind Headley that in a Chapter 11 case, the goal is not to merely liquidate the debtor but to give it a chance to reorganize its business and financial affairs and to continue to operate and provide a better return for creditors. To achieve this goal, a debtor needs breathing room — an opportunity to recoup its strength, evaluate is position, rationalize its business plan, restructure its finances, and reach an accord with creditors. These efforts would be thwarted if a debtor could be dismembered — or distracted — by its creditors after the filing. Therefore, Code § 362 imposes, upon the filing of a bankruptcy petition, an automatic stay of most types of proceedings against the debtor or its property. The Code's legislative history describes the purpose and operation of the automatic stay:

> The automatic stay is one of the fundamental debtor protections provided by the bankruptcy laws. It gives the debtor a breathing spell from his creditors. It stops all collection efforts, all harassment, and all foreclosure actions. It permits the debtor to attempt a repayment or reorganization plan, or simply be relieved of the financial pressures that drove him into bankruptcy.

The automatic stay also provides creditor protection. Without it, certain creditors would be able to pursue their own remedies against the debtor's property. Those who acted first would obtain payment of the claims in preference to and to the detriment of other creditors.

H.R. Rep. No. 95-595, at 340 (1977).

Code § 362(a) describes the scope of the automatic stay. Under § 362(a), the filing of a petition operates as an injunction against:

- the commencement or continuation of any action or proceeding against the debtor that was or could have been commenced prior to the filing. § 362(a)(1).

- the enforcement against either the debtor or against property of the estate a judgment obtained prior to the commencement of the case. § 362(a)(2).

- any act to obtain property of the estate or property from the estate. § 362(a)(3).

- all efforts to collect from the debtor a debt that arose prior to the commencement of the case. § 362(a)(6).

- all efforts to obtain or enforce a lien on property of the estate. § 362(a)(4).

- all efforts to enforce a lien on property of the debtor to the extent the lien secures a prepetition claim. § 362(a)(5).

PROBLEM 3.2

As you know, about a year ago, several ardent fans of video games manufactured by Amphydynamics developed a strange illness called Hystereo. A couple of months ago, they commenced a lawsuit against Amphy. At the time of Amphy's bankruptcy filing, the suit had not progressed very far. Amphy had moved to dismiss the suit, and that motion was denied. The plaintiffs had served a notice of deposition on Amphy's head of research and development.

1.   That deposition is scheduled for tomorrow. Will it take place?

2.   Suppose the plaintiffs only want to ask one question, "Do you have product liability insurance?"

3.   Assume, under governing state law, the statute of limitations on their claims expires on March 1. On Feb. 26, Amphy filed a Chapter 11 petition. What will happen to their claims? *See* Code § 108(c).

Before you answer those questions, read the *Floyd Weed* opinion that follows.

FLOYD WEED v. FLEET TIRE MART
United States District Court, Southern District of Iowa
1980 U.S. Dist. LEXIS 16924 (Bankr. S.D. Iowa Apr. 15,1980)

[Plaintiff Floyd Weed commenced a products liability suit against the two defendants in district court in Iowa. Subsequently, defendant Mansfield Tire & Rubber Co. filed a Chapter 11 petition in the Bankruptcy Court for the Northern District of Ohio. Mansfield informed the Iowa court that the company was in

Chapter 11 and that the lawsuit was stayed. Excerpts from the court's opinion follow.]

O'Brien, District Judge.

ORDER

This matter is before the Court on defendants' motions to dismiss and defendants' suggestion of stay. Upon due consideration, the Court is of the opinion that the motions to dismiss should be denied, but that the action as against Defendant Mansfield Tire and Rubber Company should be stayed pending further action by the Bankruptcy Court. However, this action should continue as between plaintiff and Defendant Fleet Tire Mart. The Court will take up these matters separately.

By pleading filed November 14, 1979 Defendant Mansfield Tire notified the Court that it had, on October 1, 1979, filed a voluntary petition for relief under Chapter 11 of the Bankruptcy Act, Title 11 of the United States Code, in the United States Bankruptcy Court for the Northern District of Ohio, Eastern Division. 11 U.S.C. § 362(a) provides that the filing of such a petition:

> [operates as a stay, applicable to all entities, of (1) the commencement or continuation, including the issuance or employment of process, of a judicial, administrative, or other action or proceeding against the debtor that was or could have been commenced before the commencement of the case under this title, or to recover a claim against the debtor that arose before the commencement of the case under this title. . . .]

Section 362(b) lists several circumstances in which the stay does not apply, none of which are appropriate in the instant case. Accordingly, this Court must stay this action as against Defendant Mansfield Tire.

Plaintiff has alleged that Defendant Mansfield may have a policy of products liability insurance and that if there is such a policy the present action will not affect the assets in the bankrupt's estate. Plaintiff argues that if there is such an insurance policy, the reasons for the stay would not exist and the stay should not apply. Plaintiffs' argument is initially quite appealing. Nevertheless Defendant Mansfield has submitted an affidavit, filed March 21, 1980, that it has no such policy of liability insurance and plaintiff admits that he is unsure whether such a policy in fact exists. Plaintiff requests that any stay not be imposed until he has had an opportunity to conduct discovery to determine if there is such an insurance policy. However, plaintiff has cited no authority which would allow the postponement of the stay pending such discovery, nor has the Court's research revealed any such authority. The terms of the statute are quite clear. The stay is automatic upon the filing of the petition in bankruptcy; there is no provision for additional discovery in this action before the stay becomes effective.

Plaintiff may seek relief from the operation of this stay from the Bankruptcy Court. Section 362(d) provides that:

> On request of a party in interest and after notice and a hearing, the court shall grant relief from the stay provided under subsection (a) of this

section, such as by terminating, annulling, modifying, or conditioning such stay —

(1)   for cause . . . or

(2)   with respect to a stay of an act against property, if (A) the debtor does not have an equity in such property; and (B) such property is not necessary to an effective reorganization.

See also Section 362(e)–(g). Any discovery concerning the existence of a policy of products liability insurance may be conducted by leave of the Bankruptcy Court. If such a policy is found to exist, or if there is other sufficient reason to lift the stay as against the plaintiff herein, application may be made to the Bankruptcy Court for relief from the stay. The operation of § 362 merely stays the proceedings against the debtor before this Court and does not divest this Court of jurisdiction or terminate this action. *Donald F. Duncan, Inc. v. Royal Tops Mfg. Co.*, 381 F.2d 879 (7th Cir. 1967), cert. den. 390 U.S. 905; *In re Gerstenzang*, 52 F.2d 863 (S.D.N.Y. 1931). Therefore, if plaintiff is granted relief from the stay by the Bankruptcy Court, he may immediately resume his action against Defendant Mansfield in this Court.

To aid this Court in the ultimate resolution of this action as against Defendant Mansfield Tire, Mansfield shall file a brief report to this Court concerning the current status of the bankruptcy proceeding, said report to be filed sixty days from the date of this order. Plaintiff is also directed to file a brief report to this Court sixty days from the date of this order concerning the efforts made in the Bankruptcy Court, if any, to obtain relief from the stay.

Defendant Fleet Tire has not separately requested a stay as against it in this Court. Furthermore, § 362 operates as a stay only against the debtor, in this case, Mansfield Tire. There is nothing in the statute that requires this Court to stay the action as against Defendant Fleet Tire. The Court notes that five of the eight counts alleged in plaintiff's complaint state separate causes of action against Defendant Fleet Tire. Upon the present state of the record, there is no reason to stay the action as against Defendant Fleet Tire. Therefore, the action shall proceed as between plaintiff and Fleet Tire.

NOTES AND QUESTIONS

(1)   The district court in *Floyd Weed* said that any discovery of the debtor could only be conducted "with leave of the Bankruptcy Court." Which bankruptcy court? Could plaintiff petition an Iowa bankruptcy court for relief from the stay, or would plaintiff have to seek relief in the bankruptcy court in which the debtor's Chapter 11 case was pending? *Compare In re Coleman Am. Co.*, 6 B.R. 251 (Bankr. D. Colo. 1980) (Bankruptcy Court for the District of Colorado held that it had jurisdiction to hear complaint for relief from automatic stay despite fact that debtor's case was pending in Bankruptcy Court for the District of Kansas), *with In re Coleman American Companies*, 8 B.R. 384 (Bankr. D. Kan. 1981) (creditor held to have violated automatic stay by petitioning for relief from stay in Bankruptcy Court for the District of Colorado, rather than the District of Kansas, where the debtor's case was pending).

(2)   Plaintiffs, who had commenced an antitrust class action against a steel company which later filed a Chapter 11 petition, moved for relief from the stay to let discovery go forward in *In re Penn-Dixie Industries, Inc.*, 6 B.R. 832 (Bankr. S.D.N.Y. 1980). Specifically, plaintiffs requested that the debtor respond to interrogatories asking for names of customers who purchased steel during the period when the alleged violations occurred. Whether the other case should be allowed to proceed, the court said, depended on whether the proceeding "is not connected with, or will not interfere with, the pending bankruptcy case, so as to not violate the purpose and policy of the automatic stay." 6 B.R. at 836. The court found that allowing discovery to proceed would disrupt the reorganization effort:

> Plaintiffs' requested relief from the automatic stay does not ask for permission to proceed in full with their antitrust suit. What they seek is specific production of lists to aid discovery in litigation outside this Court that is already stayed. Nowhere does the Bankruptcy Code or Rules of Bankruptcy Procedure provide for this, and to require the Debtor to comply with the request will necessitate a deviation from the Debtor's duties and responsibilities in this reorganization (not to mention the costs of compliance). That consideration cannot be shrugged off as de minimis. Interference by creditors in the administration of the estate, no matter how small, through the continuance of a preliminary skirmish in a suit outside the Bankruptcy Court is prohibited. In short, the Debtor should not be required to devote energy to this collateral matter at this juncture.
>
> Plaintiffs' instant thrust is but a preludial tussle between the parties that is impermissible. This Court will not allow Plaintiffs to chip away piecemeal at the Debtor's automatic stay protection.

6 B.R. at 836–837. Do you think the application of this standard in the *Floyd Weed* case would produce the same result? In *Teledyne Indus. v. Eon Corp.*, 373 F. Supp. 191 (S.D.N.Y. 1974), the court concluded that the stay did not bar discovery of a debtor as a non-party witness. The same court, though a different judge, later found that examination of a debtor even as a non-party witness should be permitted only if it would not interfere with pending bankruptcy proceedings. *In re Johns-Manville, Inc.*, 40 B.R. 219 (S.D.N.Y. 1984).

(3)   Suppose that prior to the commencement of Amphy's Chapter 11 case, the Hystereo plaintiffs had moved for summary judgment against Amphy, and their motion had been granted. May Amphy now appeal from the summary judgment order? Notwithstanding that section 362, by its terms, stays only proceedings against a debtor, the courts are in agreement that applicability of the stay depends not on whether the appeal is taken by or against the debtor but on whether the underlying case was brought by or against the debtor. The Third Circuit has explained what initially might seem to be a pretty strained interpretation as follows:

> In our view, § 362 should be read to stay all appeals in proceedings that were originally brought against the debtor, regardless of whether the debtor is the appellant or appellee. Thus, whether a case is subject to the automatic stay must be determined at its inception. That determination should not change depending on the particular stage of the litigation at which the filing of the petition occurs. . . .

We can hypothesize an appeal by a debtor from an adverse judgment rendered in an action brought against it by one of its creditors. If the appeal is permitted because it is an appeal "by" the debtor, and the debtor prevails on the appeal, we question the effect of such an interpretation if the creditor decides to bring the case to a higher court. Is this second level of appeal then stayed because the appeal is not one "against" the debtor? The unfairness of such an approach is obvious.

Assoc. of St. Croix Condo. Owners v. St. Croix Hotel, 682 F.2d 446, 449 (3d Cir. 1982). *See also Raymark Indus., Inc. v. Lai*, 973 F.2d 1125, 1126 (3d Cir. 1992) ("The automatic stay . . . applies to a pre-petition state court action against a debtor who has posted a cash deposit to stay execution on a judgment pending appeal."); *Cathey v. Johns-Manville Sales Corp.*, 711 F.2d 60 (6th Cir. 1983) (where debtor was defendant in initial proceeding, appeals filed by debtor prior to filing petition in bankruptcy were stayed).

(4)   Suppose that after the commencement of Amphy's Chapter 11 case, Amphy moves for summary judgment against the Hystereo plaintiffs. What is the effect of Amphy's motion? As with appeals, a postpetition motion for summary judgment by a debtor in a suit originally filed against such debtor violates the automatic stay. But what if the debtor moves for summary judgment prepetition, and the court rules postpetition? In *Ellis v. Consol. Diesel Elec. Corp.*, 894 F.2d 371 (10th Cir. 1990), the lower court, after the commencement of the debtor's bankruptcy case, decided a summary judgment motion in favor of the defendant-debtor. The plaintiffs sought to appeal from the summary judgment decision. The Tenth Circuit found that the summary judgment had been granted in violation of the automatic stay, and, therefore, there was no ruling from which the plaintiffs could appeal.

(5)   If the statute of limitations on a prepetition claim against the debtor expires while the automatic stay is in effect, is the claim holder time-barred from asserting the claim? The world — even the world of insolvency — is not so cruel. Code § 108(c) provides that if applicable, non-bankruptcy law fixes a limitations period and if that period had not expired before the date of the bankruptcy petition, the limitations period does not expire until the later of: (a) the end of the period fixed by non-bankruptcy law, or (b) 30 days after the termination or expiration of the automatic stay.

§ 3.02   ACTS AGAINST PROPERTY OF THE ESTATE

Headley is beginning to look overwhelmed and a little bit disoriented. "Back when we first met, you told me that we could use Chapter 11 to keep the business going. I'm beginning to wonder whether I should have trusted you. Even assuming that we can figure out a way to purchase circuit boards from CitiCircuits, we still have a whole bunch of problems. Citi has obtained a pre-judgment attachment of our inventory. How are we supposed to do business without inventory? Can they sell our inventory out from under us?"

"Don't panic," you say. Subsections (2) through (4) of § 362(a) stay actions against — or to obtain possession of, create, perfect, or enforce a lien against — "property of the estate." If you have taken an introductory bankruptcy course, you are familiar with the concept of "property of the estate." For readers who have not taken the introductory course, or who could use a refresher, an overview of the concept follows.

Code § 541(a) broadly defines property of the estate as including "all legal or equitable interests of the debtor in property as of the commencement of the case." According to the legislative history, the definition is broad enough to include tangible and intangible property, contracts, patents, copyrights, trademarks, causes of action, and other forms of property. H.R. Rep. No. 95-595, at 367 (1977). Indeed, even the right to take a tax loss may be considered property of the estate. *Official Comm. of Unsecured Creditors v. PSS Steamship Co., Inc. (In re Prudential Lines, Inc.)*, 928 F.2d 565 (2d Cir. 1991) ("The fact that the right to a NOL carryforward is intangible and has not yet been reduced to a tax refund also does not exclude it from the definition of property of the estate.").

Section 541(a) further provides that such property is property of the estate "wherever located and by whomever held." Thus, property which belongs to the debtor but which is in the possession of a third party is property of the estate. How does a trustee or debtor recover property from the hands of a third party? Code § 542(a), entitled "Turnover of property to the estate," generally requires an entity in possession of property of the estate[1] to deliver such property to the trustee or debtor. If the entity fails to do so, the debtor or trustee may seek an order of the court requiring the entity to "turnover" the property.

The leading case construing the turnover section is *United States v. Whiting Pools, Inc.*, 462 U.S. 198 (1983), which, although law of the land, appears to be based upon the possible misconception of the Court that § 541 refers to property as things rather than *interests* in property, of which the debtor had only a right of redemption. Whiting was in the swimming pool sales and service business. It owed $92,000 in back taxes to the federal government. The Internal Revenue Service obtained a tax lien on, and then seized, Whiting's equipment, vehicles, inventory, and office supplies. The very next day, Whiting filed a Chapter 11 petition and was continued as debtor in possession. Intending to proceed with a tax sale of the seized property, the IRS moved for a declaration that the automatic stay did not apply to the IRS or, alternatively, for relief from the stay. Whiting counterclaimed for an order compelling the IRS to turn the property over pursuant to § 542(a). The bankruptcy court found that the IRS was bound by the automatic stay and ordered it to turn the seized property over to the debtor. The district court reversed, and the Second Circuit reversed the district court. The Supreme Court affirmed, holding that "the reorganization estate includes property of the debtor that has been seized by a creditor prior to the filing of a petition for reorganization." 462 U.S. at 209. The Court explained:

> In proceedings under the reorganization provisions of the Bankruptcy Code, a troubled enterprise may be restructured to enable it to operate successfully in the future. Until the business can be reorganized pursuant to a plan . . . the trustee or debtor-in-possession is authorized to manage

---

[1] Actually, § 542(a) refers to the turnover of "property that the trustee may use, sell, or lease under § 363." Section 363 states that the trustee may use, sell, or lease "property of the estate." — Eds.

the property of the estate and to continue the operation of the business.
. . .

The reorganization effort would have small chance of success, however,
if property essential to running the business were excluded from the estate.
. . . Thus, to facilitate the rehabilitation of the debtor's business, all the
debtor's property must be included in the reorganization estate.

This authorization extends even to property of the estate in which a
creditor has a secured interest. . . .

Both the congressional goal of encouraging reorganizations and Congress' choice of methods to protect secured creditors suggest that Congress
intended a broad range of property to be included in the estate. . . .

The statutory language reflects this view of the scope of the estate. As
noted above, § 541(a) provides that the "estate is comprised of all the
following property, wherever located: . . . all legal or equitable interests of
the debtor in property as of the commencement of the case." 11 U.S.C.
§ 541(a)(1).

Most important, in the context of this case, § 541(a)(1) is intended to
include in the estate any property made available to the estate by other
provisions of the Bankruptcy Code. Several of these provisions bring into
the estate property in which the debtor did not have a possessory interest
at the time the bankruptcy proceedings commenced.

Section 542(a) is such a provision. It requires an entity (other than a
custodian) holding any property of the debtor that the trustee can use
under § 363 to turn that property over to the trustee. . . . While there are
explicit limitations on the reach of § 542(a), none requires that the debtor
hold a possessory interest in the property at the commencement of the
reorganization proceedings.

As does all bankruptcy law, § 542(a) modifies the procedural rights
available to creditors to protect and satisfy their liens.

. . . .

In effect, § 542(a) grants to the estate a possessory interest in certain
property of the debtor that was not held by the debtor at the commencement of reorganization proceedings. The Bankruptcy Code provides secured creditors various rights, including the right to adequate protection,
and these rights replace the protection afforded by possession.

This interpretation of § 542(a) is supported by the section's legislative
history. Although the legislative reports are silent on the precise issue
before us, the House and Senate hearings from which § 542(a) emerged
provide guidance. Several witnesses at those hearings noted, without
contradiction, the need for a provision authorizing the turnover of property
of the debtor in the possession of secured creditors . . .

Any other interpretation of § 542(a) would deprive the bankruptcy estate
of the assets and property essential to its rehabilitation effort and thereby

would frustrate the congressional purpose behind the reorganization provisions.

. . . .

When property seized prior to the filing of a petition is drawn into the Chapter 11 reorganization estate, the Service's tax lien is not dissolved; nor is its status as a secured creditor destroyed. The IRS, under § 363(e), remains entitled to adequate protection for its interests, to other rights enjoyed by secured creditors, and to the specific privileges accorded tax collectors. Section 542(a) simply requires the Service to seek protection of its interest according to the congressionally established bankruptcy procedures, rather than by withholding the seized property from the debtor's efforts to reorganize.

462 U.S. at 203–212.

"Okay, I get it," says Headley, "the inventory is property of the estate, even though the Sheriff has seized it, and the Sheriff has to turn it over under § 542. But does that solve the problem? What effect does the bankruptcy have on the attachment? Even if we get the inventory back, can we sell it, and if we sell it, can we use the proceeds?"

Carol helps you out here asking, "Wouldn't the attachment be a preference?" "Exactly," you say. "En route to its holding, the Supreme Court observed that § 541(a) sweeps into the estate any property made available to the estate by other provisions of the Bankruptcy Code. These are the 'trustee's avoidance power' provisions with which you probably are familiar from your basic bankruptcy course. A trustee or debtor in possession in a Chapter 11 case possesses the same avoiding powers as a trustee in a liquidation case. Thus, § 541(a)(3) draws into the reorganization estate property recoverable by means of the avoidance of a lien, a preferential transfer, a fraudulent conveyance, or an improper setoff."

PROBLEM 3.3

Speaking of setoff, Headley says, "I've just heard from one of our banks that it is 'freezing' our account. How are we supposed to do business if we can't use the cash in our bank account. Isn't money in the bank property of the estate?" Can the bank do that?

CITIZENS BANK OF MARYLAND v. STRUMPF
Supreme Court of the United States
516 U.S. 16 (1995)

Justice Scalia delivered the opinion of the Court.

We must decide whether the creditor of a debtor in bankruptcy may, in order to protect its setoff rights, temporarily withhold payment of a debt that it owes to the debtor in bankruptcy without violating the automatic stay imposed by 11 U.S.C. § 362(a).

I

On January 25, 1991, when respondent filed for relief under Chapter 13 of the Bankruptcy Code, he had a checking account with petitioner, a bank conducting business in the State of Maryland. He also was in default on the remaining balance of a loan of $5,068.75 from the bank. Under 11 U.S.C. § 362(a), respondent's bankruptcy filing gave rise to an automatic stay of various types of activity by his creditors, including "the setoff of any debt owing to the debtor that arose before the commencement of the [bankruptcy case] against any claim against the debtor." § 362(a)(7).

On October 2, 1991, petitioner placed what it termed an "administrative hold" on so much of respondent's account as it claimed was subject to setoff — that is, the bank refused to pay withdrawals from the account that would reduce the balance below the sum that it claimed was due on respondent's loan. Five days later, petitioner filed in the Bankruptcy Court, under § 362(d), a "Motion for Relief from Automatic Stay and for Setoff." Respondent then filed a motion to hold petitioner in contempt, claiming that petitioner's administrative hold violated the automatic stay established by § 362(a).

The Bankruptcy Court ruled on respondent's contempt motion first. It concluded that petitioner's "administrative hold" constituted a "setoff" in violation of § 362(a)(7) and sanctioned petitioner. Several weeks later, the Bankruptcy Court granted petitioner's motion for relief from the stay and authorized petitioner to set off respondent's remaining checking account balance against the unpaid loan. By that time, however, respondent had reduced the checking account balance to zero, so there was nothing to set off.

The District Court reversed the judgment that petitioner had violated the automatic stay, concluding that the administrative hold was not a violation of § 362(a). The Court of Appeals reversed. "[A]n administrative hold," it said, "is tantamount to the exercise of a right of setoff and thus violates the automatic stay of § 362(a)(7)." 37 F.3d 155, 158 (C.A. 4 1994). We granted certiorari. 514 U.S. 1035, 115 S.Ct. 1398, 131 L.Ed.2d 286 (1995).

II

The right of setoff (also called "offset") allows entities that owe each other money to apply their mutual debts against each other, thereby avoiding "the absurdity of making A pay B when B owes A." *Studley v. Boylston Nat. Bank*, 229 U.S. 523, 528, 33 S.Ct. 806, 808, 57 L.Ed. 1313 (1913). Although no federal right of setoff is created by the Bankruptcy Code, 11 U.S.C. § 553(a) provides that, with certain exceptions, whatever right of setoff otherwise exists is preserved in bankruptcy. Here it is undisputed that, prior to the bankruptcy filing, petitioner had the right under Maryland law to set off the defaulted loan against the balance in the checking account. It is also undisputed that under § 362(a) respondent's bankruptcy filing stayed any exercise of that right by petitioner. The principal question for decision is whether petitioner's refusal to pay its debt to respondent upon the latter's demand constituted an exercise of the setoff right and hence violated the stay.

In our view, petitioner's action was not a setoff within the meaning of § 362(a)(7).

Petitioner refused to pay its debt, not permanently and absolutely, but only while it sought relief under § 362(d) from the automatic stay. Whether that temporary refusal was otherwise wrongful is a separate matter — we do not consider, for example, respondent's contention that the portion of the account subjected to the "administrative hold" exceeded the amount properly subject to setoff. All that concerns us here is whether the refusal was a setoff. We think it was not, because — as evidenced by petitioner's "Motion for Relief from Automatic Stay and for Setoff" — petitioner did not purport permanently to reduce respondent's account balance by the amount of the defaulted loan. A requirement of such an intent is implicit in the rule followed by a majority of jurisdictions addressing the question, that a setoff has not occurred until three steps have been taken: (i) a decision to effectuate a setoff, (ii) some action accomplishing the setoff, and (iii) a recording of the setoff. *See, e.g., Baker v. National City Bank of Cleveland*, 511 F.2d 1016, 1018 (C.A. 6 1975) (Ohio law); *Normand Josef Enterprises, Inc. v. Connecticut Nat. Bank*, 230 Conn. 486, 504-505, 646 A.2d 1289, 1299 (1994). But even if state law were different, the question whether a setoff under § 362(a)(7) has occurred is a matter of federal law, and other provisions of the Bankruptcy Code would lead us to embrace the same requirement of an intent permanently to settle accounts.

Section 542(b) of the Code, which concerns turnover of property to the estate, requires a bankrupt's debtors to "pay" to the trustee (or on his order) any "debt that is property of the estate and that is matured, payable on demand, or payable on order . . . except to the extent that such debt may be offset under section 553 of this title against a claim against the debtor." 11 U.S.C. § 542(b).

. . . .

Section 553(a), in turn, sets forth a general rule, with certain exceptions, that any right of setoff that a creditor possessed prior to the debtor's filing for bankruptcy is not affected by the Bankruptcy Code. It would be an odd construction of § 362(a)(7) that required a creditor with a right of setoff to do immediately that which § 542(b) specifically excuses it from doing as a general matter: pay a claim to which a defense of setoff applies.

Nor is our assessment of these provisions changed by the fact that § 553(a), in generally providing that nothing in the Bankruptcy Code affects creditors' prebankruptcy setoff rights, qualifies this rule with the phrase "[e]xcept as otherwise provided in this section and in sections 362 and 363." This undoubtedly refers to § 362(a)(7), but we think it is most naturally read as merely recognizing that provision's restriction upon when an actual setoff may be effected — which is to say, not during the automatic stay. When this perfectly reasonable reading is available, it would be foolish to take the § 553(a) "except" clause as indicating that § 362(a)(7) requires immediate payment of a debt subject to setoff. That would render § 553(a)'s general rule that the Bankruptcy Code does not affect the right of setoff meaningless, for by forcing the creditor to pay its debt immediately, it would divest the creditor of the very thing that supports the right of setoff. Furthermore, it would, as we have stated, eviscerate § 542(b)'s exception to the duty to pay debts. It is an elementary rule of construction that "the act cannot be held to destroy itself." *Texas & Pacific R. Co. v. Abilene Cotton Oil Co.*, 204 U.S. 426, 446, 27 S.Ct. 350, 358, 51 L.Ed. 553 (1907).

Finally, we are unpersuaded by respondent's additional contentions that the administrative hold violated §§ 362(a)(3) and 362(a)(6). Under these sections, a bankruptcy filing automatically stays "any act to obtain possession of property of the estate or of property from the estate or to exercise control over property of the estate," 11 U.S.C. § 362(a)(3), and "any act to collect, assess, or recover a claim against the debtor that arose before the commencement of the case under this title," § 362(a)(6). Respondent's reliance on these provisions rests on the false premise that petitioner's administrative hold took something from respondent, or exercised dominion over property that belonged to respondent. That view of things might be arguable if a bank account consisted of money belonging to the depositor and held by the bank. In fact, however, it consists of nothing more or less than a promise to pay, from the bank to the depositor, *see Bank of Marin v. England*, 385 U.S. 99, 101, 87 S.Ct. 274, 276, 17 L.Ed.2d 197 (1966); *Keller v. Frederickstown Sav. Institution*, 193 Md. 292, 296, 66 A.2d 924, 925 (1949); and petitioner's temporary refusal to pay was neither a taking of possession of respondent's property nor an exercising of control over it, but merely a refusal to perform its promise. In any event, we will not give § 362(a)(3) or § 362(a)(6) an interpretation that would proscribe what § 542(b)'s "except[ion]" and § 553(a)'s general rule were plainly intended to permit: the temporary refusal of a creditor to pay a debt that is subject to setoff against a debt owed by the bankrupt.

The judgment of the Court of Appeals for the Fourth Circuit is reversed. It is so ordered.

NOTES AND QUESTIONS

(1) What, according to Justice Scalia, is the difference between a "setoff" prohibited by 362(a)(7) and the "administrative freeze" permitted in *Strumpf*? Is there a practical difference, as far as the debtor is concerned?

(2) "Okay," says Headley, "I understand the distinction between a setoff and a freeze, but didn't you tell me that 362(a)(3) prohibits any act to take control of 'property of the estate'? Hasn't the bank taken control of my property?" Is a bank balance "property of the estate"? How does Justice Scalia answer this objection?

(3) "By the way," Headley says, "I've heard rumors that one of our competitors is buying up stock of Amphy and may be considering a tender offer. Isn't that a violation of the automatic stay?" "No," you tell him. "As a general rule, the shares of stock in a corporation are property of the individual stockholders and not the property of the corporation. As one court has said, 'A corporation has no property interest in the shares of its stock owned by its stockholders." ' *In re Calamity Jane's Inc., 22 B.R. 5 (Bankr. D.N.J. 1982); see also Official Bondholders Comm. v. Chase Manhattan Bank (In re Marvel Entm't Group)*, 209 B.R. 832, 839 (D. Del. 1997) ("Although the Debtors argue that the objective of the bondholders and the Indenture Trustee is to 'seize control of the assets and properties of Marvel to effect a recovery of the loans advanced.' . . . Marvel is apparently not a party to the indentures and is thus not contractually obligated to repay the bondholders").

However, where a creditor appears to be using its power over stock to control the debtor in order to enhance its recovery as a creditor, rather than as a shareholder, courts have found that the creditor's action violates 362(a)(3). *In re Fairmont Comm. Corp.*, 1993 Bankr. LEXIS 2326 (Bankr. S.D.N.Y. Mar. 3, 1993) ("We are not faced — I should say confronted — with the conventional case of a shareholder seeking to invoke its corporate governance rights because the power to appoint a director which Price [the noteholder/stockholder] now wishes to exercise stems from its status as Fairmont's largest unsecured creditor and is implicated only because Price has not been paid."); *In re Bioastal Corp.*, 1989 Bankr. LEXIS 2046 (Bankr. M.D. Fla. Nov. 21, 1989) ("It is without dispute that Mesa is a creditor of Bicoastal. It is equally without dispute [that] if Mesa is permitted to control the Board, it will, in fact obtain, possess and exercise control over the operation of the Board only subject to the jurisdiction of this Court. This court is disinclined to interpret [362(a)(3)] narrowly . . . "). *Cf. 48th St. Steakhouse, Inc. v. Rockefeller Group, Inc. (In re 48th St. Steakhouse)*, 835 F.2d 427, 431 (2d Cir. 1987), *cert. denied*, 485 U.S. 1035 (1988) ("[W]here a non-debtor's interest is intertwined . . . with that of a debtor . . . [and an] action taken against the non-bankrupt party would inevitably have an adverse impact on property of the bankrupt estate, then such action should be barred by the automatic stay.").

§ 3.03 STAYS OF ACTIONS AGAINST NON-DEBTORS

[A] Direct Actions Against Insurers

PROBLEM 3.4

Suppose the Hystereo plaintiffs decide to bring an action against Imprudential Insurance, Amphy's products liability insurance company. Should the suit against the insurer be allowed to proceed?

(a) Would your answer change if the limits of the insurance policy clearly exceeded any possible liability to the Hystereo plaintiffs?

(b) Is the suit barred by the automatic stay?

(c) If not, is there any other basis for stopping the suit against the insurance company?

A.H. ROBINS CO. v. PICCININ
United States Court of Appeals, Fourth Circuit
788 F.2d 994 (4th Cir. 1986)

DONALD RUSSELL, CIRCUIT JUDGE:

Confronted, if not overwhelmed, with an avalanche of actions filed in various state and federal courts throughout the United States by citizens of this country as well as of foreign countries seeking damages for injuries allegedly sustained by the use of an intrauterine contraceptive device known as a Dalkon Shield, the manufacturer of the device, A.H. Robins Company, Incorporated (Robins) filed its petition under Chapter 11 of the Bankruptcy Code, 11 U.S.C. §§ 101 et seq., in August, 1985.

Background

The device, which is the subject of these suits, had been developed in the 1960s by Dr. Hugh Davis at the Johns Hopkins Hospital in Baltimore, Maryland.[2] In mid-1970 Robins acquired all patent and marketing rights to the Dalkon Shield and engaged in the manufacture and marketing of the device from early 1971 until 1974, when it discontinued manufacture and sale of the device because of complaints and suits charging injuries arising allegedly out of the use of the device. The institution of Dalkon Shield suits did not, however, moderate with the discontinuance of manufacture of the device, since Robins did not actually recall the device until 1984.[3] By the middle of 1985, when the Chapter 11 petition was filed the number of such suits arising out of the continued sale and use of the Dalkon Shield device earlier put into the stream of commerce by Robins had grown to 5,000. More than half of these pending cases named Robins as the sole defendant; a co-defendant or co-defendants were named in the others. Prior to the filing, a number of suits had been tried and, while Robins had prevailed in some of the actions, judgments in large and burdensome amounts had been recovered in others. Many more had been settled.[4] Moreover, the costs of defending these suits both to Robins and to its insurance carrier had risen into the millions. A large amount of the time and energies of Robins' officers and executives was also being absorbed in preparing material for trial and in attending and testifying at depositions and trials. The problems arising out of this mounting tide of claims and suits precipitated this Chapter 11 proceeding.

The filing of the Chapter 11 petition automatically stayed all suits against Robins itself under section 362(a) of the Bankruptcy Code, even though no formal order of stay was immediately entered. *See In re Larmar Estates*, 5 B.R. 328, 330 (Bankr. E.D.N.Y. 1980). But a number of plaintiffs in suits where there were defendants other than Robins, sought to sever their actions against Robins and to proceed with their claims against the co-defendant or co-defendants. Robins responded to the move by filing an adversary proceeding in which it named as defendants the plaintiffs in eight such suits pending in various state and federal courts. In that proceeding, the debtor sought (1) declaratory relief adjudging that the debtor's products liability policy with Aetna Casualty and Insurance Company (Aetna) was an asset of the estate in which all the Dalkon Shield plaintiffs and claimants had an interest and (2) injunctive relief restraining the prosecution of the actions against its co-defendants.

. . . .

The debtor's application for a temporary restraining order and for the setting of

---

[2] Book Note, 99 Harv.L.Rev. 875 (1986) (reviewing Engelmayer and Wagman, Lord's Justice: One Judge's Battle to Expose the Deadly Dalkon Shield I.U.D. (1985)).

[3] In response to that recall, Engelmayer & Wagman, supra, note 2, at 878, n. 8, state that 4,500 women had removed the shield as of August, 1985, at a cost of $1,600,000.

[4] Engelmayer & Wagman, *supra*, note 2, at 876, n. 6, state that of the approximately 7,500 Dalkon Shield cases settled from 1972 to February 1985, fewer than 40 went to a jury. A recent article in the Nat.L.J., p. 10, (March 17, 1986), states that by mid 1985, Robins, along with its insurer, Aetna Casualty & Surety Company, "had paid roughly $517 million for 25 trial judgments and 9,300 settlements since the first verdict in 1975."

a date for a hearing on the request for preliminary injunction in the adversary proceeding was heard ex parte by the district judge who had jurisdiction over the proceedings.[5] The district judge granted at the time a temporary restraining order in the proceedings and set a hearing on the debtor's application for a preliminary injunction. On that same day, Robins mailed by first-class mail and by Federal Express to all the defendants and their attorneys at their addresses "Notice of Hearing on Plaintiff's Motion for Preliminary Injunction."

. . . .

After receiving certain testimony, admitting various records, and hearing arguments of parties, the district court granted Robins' request for a preliminary injunction.

In his order granting the preliminary injunction, the district judge found (1) that continuation of litigation in the civil actions threatened property of Robins' estate, burdened and impeded Robins' reorganization effort, contravened the public interest, and rendered any plan of reorganization futile; (2) that this burden on Robins' estate outweighed any burden on the Dalkon claimants caused by enjoining their civil actions; and (3) that all remaining insurance coverage in favor of the debtor under its liability policy issued by Aetna was property of the Robins' Chapter 11 estate. The district judge then held that all actions for damages that might be satisfied from proceeds of the Aetna insurance policy were subject to the stay pursuant to 11 U.S.C. § 362(a)(3) and enjoined further litigation in the eight civil actions, pursuant to 11 U.S.C. § 362(a)(1), (3) as supplemented by 11 U.S.C. § 105.

Only the defendants Piccinin, the Mosas, and Conrad filed timely notices of appeal from the grant of the preliminary injunction. Their appeals, questioning the propriety of that preliminary injunction as against suits by Robins' co-defendants is the first of the issues now before this Court.

. . . .

I

The initial question in the appeal of the first issue relates to the court's jurisdiction to grant a stay or injunction of suits in other courts against co-defendants of the debtor or of third parties; none of the parties herein contest the jurisdiction of the bankruptcy court to stay actions against the debtor itself in any court. Jurisdiction over suits involving co-defendants or third-parties may be bottomed on two statutory provisions of the Bankruptcy Act itself as well as on the general equitable powers of the court. The first of these statutory grants of jurisdiction is found in section 362, 11 U.S.C. The purpose of this section by its various subsections is to protect the debtor from an uncontrollable scramble for its assets in a number of uncoordinated proceedings in different courts, to preclude one

---

[5] Section 104 of the 1984 Amendments to the Bankruptcy Code provides that "[i]n each judicial district, the bankruptcy judges in regular active service shall constitute a unit of the district court to be known as the bankruptcy court for the district. Each bankruptcy judge . . . may exercise the authority conferred under this chapter . . . except as otherwise provided by law or by rule or order of the district court."

creditor from pursuing a remedy to the disadvantage of other creditors, and to provide the debtor and its executives with a reasonable respite from protracted litigation, during which they may have an opportunity to formulate a plan of reorganization for the debtor. *Matter of Holtkamp*, 669 F.2d 505, 508 (7th Cir. 1982). As the Court in *Fidelity Mortg. Investors v. Camelia Builders, Inc.*, 550 F.2d 47, 55 (2d Cir. 1976), cert. denied, 429 U.S. 1093, 97 S.Ct. 1107, 51 L.Ed.2d 540, put it, "[t]he stay insures that the debtor's affairs will be centralized, initially, in a single forum in order to prevent conflicting judgments from different courts and in order to harmonize all of the creditors' interests with one another."

Section 362 is broken down into several subsections, only two of which are relevant on this appeal. The first of such subsections is (a)(1), which imposes an automatic stay of any proceeding "commenced or [that] could have been commenced against the debtor" at the time of the filing of the Chapter 11 proceeding; the second is (a)(3), which provides similar relief against suits involving the possession or custody of property of the debtor, irrespective of whether the suits are against the debtor alone or others. We shall discuss the extent of jurisdiction given the bankruptcy court under these two subsections, beginning with (a)(1).

(a)

Subsection (a)(1) is generally said to be available only to the debtor, not third party defendants or co-defendants. The rationale for this narrow construction of the statute has been stated in *Lynch v. Johns-Manville Sales Corp.*, 710 F.2d 1194, 1196-1197 (6th Cir. 1983), and in our own case of *Williford v. Armstrong World Industries, Inc.*, 715 F.2d 124, 126–27 (4th Cir. 1983), and it need not be repeated here. However, as the Court in *Johns-Manville Sales Corp.*, 26 B.R. 405, 410 (S.D.N.Y. 1983) remarked, in discussing the oft-cited case, *Royal Trucks & Trailer v. Armadors Meritina Salvadoreana*, 10 B.R. 488, 491,[9] "there are cases [under 362(a)(1)] where a bankruptcy court may properly stay the proceedings against non-bankrupt co-defendants" but, it adds, that in order for relief for such non-bankrupt defendants to be available under (a)(1), there must be "unusual circumstances" and certainly " '[s]omething more than the mere fact that one of the parties to the lawsuit has filed a Chapter 11 bankruptcy must be shown in order that proceedings be stayed against non-bankrupt parties." ' This "unusual situation," it would seem, arises when there is such identity between the debtor and the third-party defendant that the debtor may be said to be the real party defendant and that a judgment against the third-party defendant will in effect be a judgment or finding against the debtor. An illustration of such a situation would be a suit against a third-party who is entitled to absolute indemnity by the debtor on account of any judgment that might result against them in the case. To refuse application of the statutory stay in that case would defeat the very purpose and intent of the statute. This fact was recognized by the court in *In re Metal Center*, 31 B.R. 458 (D. Conn. 1983).

In *Metal Center* the third-party plaintiff had been sued, along with the debtor, on his guaranty of the debtor's obligation. The third-party was entitled to be

---

[9] This case is generally cited on the strict construction of this subsection.

indemnified by the debtor on account of any judgment rendered against him because of his guaranty. While the action against both the debtor and the guarantor was pending, the debtor filed its Chapter 11 petition. The action was stayed against the debtor but the plaintiff sought to continue his suit against the guarantor. The guarantor at this point moved to stay the action as against him. The bankruptcy court reviewed the motion because of the possible "effect upon the debtor of a state court judgment against Gardner [the guarantor]." In discussing the issue, the court first dismissed as inapplicable to the facts of this case the situation where the third-party defendant was "independently liable as, for example, where the debtor and another are joint tortfeasors or where the nondebtor's liability rests upon his own breach of duty." It noted that in such a case "the automatic stay would clearly not extend to such non debtor." But, in contrast to those situations, it declared that "where, however, a debtor and nondebtor are so bound by statute or contract that the liability of the nondebtor is imputed to the debtor by operation of law, then the Congressional intent to provide relief to debtors would be frustrated by permitting indirectly what is expressly prohibited in the Code." It concluded with the statement: "Clearly the debtor's protection must be extended to enjoin litigation against others if the result would be binding upon the debtor's estate," and this is so, whether the debtor is a party or not. 31 B.R. at 462.

It is true that, although the third-party defendant in *Metal Center* was found to be entitled to indemnity from the debtor, the court held that the situation was not such as to qualify for a stay under section 362(a)(1). The court reached this conclusion because in its opinion the judgment in the suit against the third-party would not be binding on the bankruptcy court. Of course, if the indemnitee, who has suffered a judgment for which he is entitled to be absolutely indemnified by the debtor, cannot file and have allowed as an adjudicated claim the actual amount of the judgment he has secured but must submit his claim for allowance in the bankruptcy proceeding with the prospect that his claim may not be allowed in the full amount of the judgment awarded in favor of him, the indemnitee will be unfairly mulcted by inconsistent judgments and his contract of indemnity in effect nullified. We do not accept such reasoning with its shocking result and would find a stay under (a)(1) acceptable. Apparently the court in *Metal Center* recognized the inconsistency and the injustice resulting from its refusal to sustain a stay under (a)(1) for it did grant a stay of the action against the third-party but on equitable grounds, finding in justification that "severing and remanding [the plaintiff's action against the indemnitee to the state court for trial and judgment would] . . . potentially expose[] Gardner [the indemnitee] to inconsistent judgments." 31 B.R. at 463. While, as we have said, it seems that a ruling sustaining the stay in that case under section 362(a)(1) would have been more logical and appropriate, it is unimportant whether the stay is granted under section 362(a)(1) or on equitable grounds: the result is the same; a stay is proper in such a situation.

In *Seybolt v. Bio-Energy of Lincoln, Inc.*, 38 B.R. 123 (D. Mass. 1984), the issue was similar to that in *Metal Center*, i.e., whether a guarantor entitled to indemnity by the debtor would be entitled to seek a stay under section 362(a)(1). In granting the stay in that case, the Court, after quoting the language of *Metal Center* with respect to the case in which "the liability of the non-debtor is imputed to the debtor by operation of law," said:

The concept that notice and an opportunity to defend binds the principal on a judgment against a guarantor (in a case in which the principal did not participate) springs from notions of res judicata. If George Seybolt recovers a judgment against the guarantors in the state court, Bio-Energy Associates' assertion that the $100,000 was not a loan but a contribution to capital may well be rendered moot when the guarantor subsequently asserts a claim against it for indemnity. At the very least, the dual litigation of these issues in the state court and the bankruptcy court is not judicially economic and potentially exposes Bio-Energy, Inc. and Bio-Energy Associates to inconsistent judgments. *See In re Metal Center, Inc., supra,* at 463.

Accordingly, I find that George Seybolt's claims against the individual guarantors are within this Court's jurisdiction and should be stayed until an appropriate motion for relief from stay is filed and granted by the bankruptcy court. 38 B.R. at 127–28.

In re Brentano's, 27 B.R. 90 (S.D.N.Y. 1983), also involved the situation of a guarantor of a debtor in a Chapter 11 proceeding who was entitled under contract to indemnity by the debtor against any judgment against him. While the case did not directly concern section 362 but the question of bankruptcy jurisdiction, the language of the court appears relevant on the issue under review here. It said that the action against the guarantor-indemnitee "could and would affect the estate in bankruptcy," since, under the indemnity agreement, "a judgment in favor of the [plaintiff] in the guaranty action would automatically result in indemnification liability against Brentano's" [i.e., the indemnitor]. Accepting this language one would have difficulty in not concluding that the action was in effect one against the debtor and as such would qualify for relief under (a)(1). *Brentano's* is cited and discussed in *Pacor, Inc. v. Higgins,* 743 F.2d 984, 995 (3d Cir. 1984), which was an asbestos case. The issue in *Pacor,* as in *Brentano's,* was one of bankruptcy jurisdiction. The court described the facts in *Brentano's* and stated the resulting legal situation as follows:

> In *Brentano's,* however, it is clear that the action between the landlord and MacMillan could and would affect the estate in bankruptcy. By virtue of the indemnification agreement between Brentano's and MacMillan, a judgment in favor of the landlord on the guarantee action would automatically result in indemnification liability against Brentano's. *See also In re Johnie T. Patton, Inc.,* 12 B.R. 470 (Bankr. D. Nev. 1981); *In re Lucasa International, Ltd.,* 6 B.R. 717 (Bankr. S.D.N.Y. 1980); *In re Brothers Coal Co.,* 6 B.R. 567 (Bankr. W.D. Va. 1980) (all involving guarantors of debtor's obligations). Moreover, even in the absence of an explicit indemnification agreement, an action by a creditor against a guarantor of a debtor's obligations will necessarily affect [that] creditor's status vis a vis other creditors, and administration of the estate therefore depends upon the outcome of that litigation. 743 F.2d at 995.

Pacor, however, found *Brentano's* inapplicable in its case because:

> In this case, however, there would be no automatic creation of liability against Manville on account of a judgment against Pacor. Pacor is not a contractual guarantor of Manville, nor has Manville agreed to indemnify

Pacor, and thus a judgment in the Higgins-Pacor action could not give rise to any automatic liability on the part of the estate. 743 F.2d at 995.

The clear implication of the decision is that, if there had been a contract to indemnify, a contrary result would have been in order.

(b)

But (a)(1), which stays actions against the debtor and arguably against those whose interests are so intimately intertwined with those of the debtor that the latter may be said to be the real party in interest, is not the only part of section 362 providing for an automatic stay of proceedings. Subsection (a)(3) directs stays of any action, whether against the debtor or third- parties, to obtain possession or to exercise control over property of the debtor. A key phrase in the construction and application of this section is, of course, "property" as that term is used in the Act. Section 541(a)(1) of the Bankruptcy Act defines "property" in the bankruptcy context. It provides that the "estate is comprised of all the following property, wherever located . . . all legal or equitable interests of the debtor in property as of the commencement of the case." The Supreme Court in construing this language in *United States v. Whiting Pools, Inc.*, 462 U.S. 198, 205, n. 9, 103 S. Ct. 2309, 2313, n. 9, 76 L. Ed. 2d 515, quoted this language in the legislative history of the Section:

> The scope of this paragraph [541(a)(1)] is broad. It included all kinds of property including tangible or intangible property, causes of action (*see* Bankruptcy Act § 70a(6)), and all other forms of property currently specified in section 70a of the Bankruptcy Act.

Under the weight of authority, insurance contracts have been said to be embraced in this statutory definition of "property." *In re Davis*, 730 F.2d 176, 184 (5th Cir. 1984). For example, even the right to cancel an insurance policy issued to the debtor has uniformly been held to be stayed under section 362(a)(3). Lam, *Cancellation of Insurance: Bankruptcy Automatic Stay Implications*, 59 Am-.Bank.L.J., 267 (1985), (extensively reviewing the cases to this effect). A products liability policy of the debtor is similarly within the principle: it is a valuable property of a debtor, particularly if the debtor is confronted with substantial liability claims within the coverage of the policy in which case the policy may well be, as one court has remarked in a case like the one under review, "the most important asset of [i.e., the debtor's] estate," *In re Johns Manville Corp.*, 40 B.R. 219, 229 (S.D.N.Y. 1984). Any action in which the judgment may diminish this "important asset" is unquestionably subject to a stay under this subsection. *In re Johns Manville Corp.*, 33 B.R. 254, 261 (Bankr. S.D.N.Y. 1983). Accordingly actions "related to" the bankruptcy proceedings against the insurer or against officers or employees of the debtor who may be entitled to indemnification under such policy or who qualify as additional insureds under the policy are to be stayed under section 362(a)(3).[10]

---

[10] There is nothing in *In Re White Motor Credit*, 761 F.2d 270, 274 (6th Cir.1985), in any way contrary to this conclusion; in fact, it sustains the construction of the statute adopted by us. In *White*, the parties were in agreement that the products liability insurance was adequate to cover all claims filed but the court cautioned that had this not been so, the result in that case would have been different:

> Were it not for the fact that all parties are in agreement that the insurance coverage is

(c)

The statutory power of the bankruptcy court to stay actions involving the debtor or its property is not, however, limited to section 362(a)(1) and (a)(3). It has been repeatedly held that 11 U.S.C. § 105 which provides that the bankruptcy court "may issue any order, process, or judgment that is necessary or appropriate to carry out the provisions of this title," "empowers the bankruptcy court to enjoin parties other than the bankrupt" from commencing or continuing litigation. *In re Otero Mills, Inc.*, 25 B.R. 1018, 1020 (D. N.M. 1982).[11]

In that case, the Court said:

Appellant cites only one case decided under the 1978 Bankruptcy Code which found that the bankruptcy court lacked [under § 105] the power to enjoin parties from pursuing actions against non-bankrupts in state court. *In re Aboussie Brothers Construction Co.*, 8 B.R. 302 (D.C.E.D. Mo. 1981). In *Aboussie*, the court did not address § 105(a), but relied on cases decided under the old Bankruptcy Act to hold that there was no jurisdiction to enjoin parties from pursuing actions which did not involve the bankrupt directly. The pre-1978 Act confined jurisdiction to "the debtor and his property, wherever located." Act of June 22, 1938, ch. 575, § 1, 52 Stat. 906 (1938). Under the new Bankruptcy Code, the jurisdictional statute provides that the bankruptcy court shall have jurisdiction "of all civil proceedings

---

adequate to cover all filed claims, it would be necessary to liquidate all claims before any insurance was paid out; otherwise, some claimants would receive an unequal portion of the insurance assets of the debtor.

It is obvious from that statement of the court that *White* actually sustains the result reached by us that, if the liability insurance is inadequate to satisfy in full all claims under the insurance, the actions by claimants should be stayed and the claims should be "liquidated" in the bankruptcy court.

[11] There can be no dispute that the Bankruptcy Reform Act of 1978 and like language later in section 1334(b) of the Bankruptcy Amendments of 1984 greatly enlarged the jurisdiction of the bankruptcy courts and were, as stated in the legislative history, intended to "leave no doubt as to the scope of the bankruptcy court's jurisdiction over disputes." H.Rep. No. 95-595, 95th Cong.2d Sess. 445, reprinted in 1978 U.S., Code Cong. & Adm.News, 5963, 6401. Those sections provide jurisdiction in the bankruptcy case over any proceedings arising in or related to a title 11 case. The accepted definition of the "related to" in these statutes is that declared in *Pacor, Inc. v. Higgins*, 743 F.2d 984, 994 (3d Cir. 1984):

An action is related to bankruptcy if the outcome could alter the debtor's rights, liabilities, options or freedom of action (either positively or negatively) and which in any way impacts upon the handling and administration of the bankrupt estate.

See also Note, *Selective Exercise of Jurisdiction in Bankruptcy-Related Civil Proceedings*, 59 Tex. L. Rev. 325, 330–31 (1981):

One can imagine controversies over which the new bankruptcy courts [under 1471(b)] would have jurisdiction even if neither the debtor nor a representative of the estate were a party, and it is difficult to imagine any instance in which a bankruptcy court would not have jurisdiction if the debtor were a party.

It is true that both *Pacor* and the Texas Note were referring to section 1471(b) of the 1978 Act. That section, however, was re-enacted in the exact words of the repealed 1471(b) in section 1334(a) and (b) of the 1984 Act. Therefore, "[t]he jurisdiction conferred on the district court [under the 1984 Act's section 1334(a) and (b)] is exactly the same jurisdiction that was conferred on the district courts under the Bankruptcy Reform Act [of 1978]." Taggart, *The New Bankruptcy Court Systems*, 59 Am.Bank.L.J. 231, 239 (1985). To the same effect, King, *Jurisdiction and Procedure Under the Bankruptcy Amendments of 1984*, 38 Vand.L.Rev. 675, 677 (1985).

arising under title 11 or arising in or related to cases under title 11." 28
U.S.C.A. § 1471 (Supp.1982). This broader jurisdictional statute, combined
with § 105(a), grants the bankruptcy court power to enjoin parties from
proceeding in state court against non-bankrupts where the state proceeding is related to a case arising under Title 11. 25 B.R. at 1020.

In stating the same scope for section 105, the Court in *Johns-Manville Corp.*, 26
B.R. 420, 425 (S.D.N.Y. 1983), quoting from 2 Collier on Bankruptcy §§ 362.02 and
362.05 (15th ed. 1982), put the matter thus:

> [Section 362 of the Code] does not attempt to state the jurisdiction of the
> bankruptcy court with respect to stays and injunctive relief or to determine
> the boundaries of the exercise of the court's injunctive power.

> Section 105 which is the successor to Section 2A(15), gives the court the
> power to issue any order, process or judgment that is necessary or
> appropriate to carry out the provisions of this title.

> [T]he exceptions to the automatic stay of § 362(a) which are set forth in
> § 362(b) are simply exceptions to the stay which protect the estate
> automatically at the commencement of the case and are not limitations
> upon the jurisdiction of the bankruptcy court or upon its power to enjoin.
> That power is generally based upon § 105 of the Code. The court will have
> ample power to enjoin actions excepted from the automatic stay which
> might interfere in the rehabilitative process whether in a liquidation or in
> a reorganization case.

See to the same effect, In re Landmark, 19 B.R. 556, 559 (N.D. Ohio 1982); *In re
Larmar Estates, Inc.*, 5 B.R. 328, 330-31 (S.D.N.Y. 1980).

Accepting that section 105 confers on the bankruptcy court power under its
expanded jurisdiction as expressed in section 1471(b) [28 U.S.C.] of the Bankruptcy
Reform Act of 1978 and now section 1334(b), 28 U.S.C. of the 1984 Bankruptcy
Amendments to enjoin suits against parties in other courts, whether state or
federal, it is necessary to mark out the circumstances under which the power or
jurisdiction may be exercised. In *Otero Mills*, supra, the Court approved a ruling
that "[t]o so enjoin a creditor's action against a third party, the court must find that
failure to enjoin would effect [sic] the bankruptcy estate and would adversely or
detrimentally influence and pressure the debtor through the third party." 25 B.R. at
1020. In *Johns-Manville*, the Court phrased somewhat fuller the circumstances
when section 105 may support a stay:

> In the exercise of its authority under § 105, the Bankruptcy Court may use
> its injunctive authority to "protect the integrity of a bankrupt's estate and
> the Bankruptcy Court's custody thereof and to preserve to that Court the
> ability to exercise the authority delegated to it by Congress." Pursuant to
> the exercise of that authority the Court may issue or extend stays to enjoin
> a variety of proceedings [including discovery against the debtor or its
> officers and employees] which will have an adverse impact on the Debtor's
> ability to formulate a Chapter 11 plan. 40 B.R. at 226.

(d)

Beyond these statutory powers under section 362 and section 105 to enjoin other actions whether against the debtor or third-parties and in whatsoever court, the bankruptcy court under its comprehensive jurisdiction as conferred by section 1334, 28 U.S.C., has the "inherent power of courts under their general equity powers and in the efficient management of the dockets to grant relief" to grant a stay. *Williford v. Armstrong World Industries, Inc., supra,* 715 F.2d at 127, *Austin v. Unarco Industries, Inc.,* 705 F.2d 1, 5 (1st Cir. 1983). In exercising such power the court, however, must "weigh competing interests and maintain an even balance" and must justify the stay "by clear and convincing circumstances outweighing potential harm to the party against whom it is operative." *Williford, supra, Metal Center* and *Seybolt,* discussed *supra,* are illustrative of situations in which courts have found sufficient grounds to grant a stay under this power.

(e)

There are thus four grounds on which the bankruptcy court may enjoin suits against the bankrupt or its assets and property. In some instances only one of these grounds may be relevant; in an involved and complex case, several or even all of the grounds may require consideration. The present case is such an involved and complex case. It has a striking similarity to a Chapter 11 proceedings initially begun in the bankruptcy court of the Southern District of New York, concerning the reorganization of the Johns-Manville Corporation. In that proceeding, which was litigated both in the New York and Louisiana courts, many of the issues posed on this aspect of the case were raised and analyzed by the courts of the two circuits and the decisions resolving such issues present in a practical form the application of the power of a bankruptcy court to stay actions relating to the bankruptcy proceeding against the debtor, its property and their operations.

. . . .

II.

The district court in this case applied the test for a grant of preliminary injunctive relief as stated by us in *Blackwelder Furniture,* 550 F.2d 189, 195 (4th Cir. 1977), and *Televest v. Bradshaw,* 618 F.2d 1029, 1032 (4th Cir. 1980). It found, as had the Johns-Manville courts, that irreparable harm would be suffered by the debtor and by the defendants since any of these suits against these co-defendants, if successful, would reduce and diminish the insurance fund or pool represented in Aetna's policy in favor of Robins and thereby affect the property of the debtor to the detriment of the debtor's creditors as a whole. The likelihood of success by the debtor under these circumstances appeared indisputable. The hardships which would be suffered irreparably by the debtor and by its creditors generally in permitting these plaintiffs to secure as it were a preference in the distribution of the insurance pool herein to which all creditors were entitled, together with the unquestioned public interest in promoting a viable reorganization of the debtor can be said to outweigh any contrary hardship to the plaintiffs. Such was the finding in the *Manville* cases and that finding does not appear unreasonable here.

The appellants, however, suggest that the record is insufficient to support such findings by the district judge. We disagree. The record is not extensive but it includes every fact considered by the courts in the *Manville* cases to be necessary for their decision. The rights of Dr. Davis, Dr. Clark and the two Robins to indemnity and their status as additional insureds under Robins' insurance policy are undisputed on the record. That there are thousands of Dalkon Shield actions and claims pending is a fact established in the record and the limited fund available under Robins' insurance policy is recognized in the record. It seems incontestable that, if the suits are permitted to continue and discovery allowed, any effort at reorganization of the debtor will be frustrated, if not permanently thwarted. It is obvious from the record that if suits are permitted to proceed against indemnitees on claims on which the indemnitees are entitled to indemnity by Robins, either a binding judgment against the debtor will result or, as the court in *Metal Center* said, inconsistent judgments will result, calling for the exercise of the court's equitable powers. In our opinion, the record was thus more than adequate to support the district court's grant of injunctive relief. Certainly, the district court did not commit an abuse of discretion in granting the injunction herein.

The appellants add a final complaining note that the district judge stated in his decision that the "Conclusions of Law" made by him should apply "with equal force to all defendants similarly situated who are brought to the attention of the court." This is little different, however, from the language of the court in the *Manville* cases in which there was a broad, general injunction against all present or future suits.

In summary, we have no difficulty in sustaining the grant of a preliminary injunction herein. We are sustained in this conclusion by the fact, recognized by the district judge on the record, that any Dalkon Shield plaintiff may at any time petition for the vacation of the stay as it affects his or her suit and he or she is entitled to a hearing on such petition. Actually, there is one such petition pending and the district judge has agreed to set a hearing on that petition.

In summary, we affirm the district court's order staying the suits of the plaintiffs against the debtor and all co-defendants.

[B] Suits Against Co-Debtors

PROBLEM 3.5

a.   In addition to suing Amphy's product liability insurer, the Hystereo plaintiffs sued Headley Charisma personally, alleging that he was aware of the risks associated with playing video games. Yesterday Headley received voluminous discovery requests, and he has received a notice of deposition for a week from next Friday. Headley storms into your office, slams the papers down on your desk, and says, "How can I deal with this garbage and run the company at the same time?" Can you do anything for him?

b.   Assume for the purpose of this problem that Headley Charisma personally guaranteed the loan that BigBank made to Amphy. Just after the petition was filed, BigBank sued Headley on the guaranty. Headley tells you that he has about $500,000 of equity in his house and $100,000 in the bank. He had planned to contribute a significant part of those assets to Amphy to help fund the reorganization, if necessary. He also tells you he can't figure out why the bank is pursuing him. After all, Amphy owes BigBank millions. "What difference does a few hundred thousand dollars make?" he asks. Can you answer his question? Can you stop the guaranty suit?

F.T.L., INC. v. CRESTAR BANK (IN RE F.T.L., INC.)
United States Bankruptcy Court, Eastern District of Virginia
152 B.R. 61 (1993)

MEMORANDUM OPINION

Douglas O. Tice, Jr., Bankruptcy Judge.

This adversary proceeding[1] comes before the court on a complaint for injunctive relief filed by debtor and the principals of the debtor. Plaintiffs seek to temporarily enjoin Crestar Bank from foreclosing on the personal residence of Frank Lash, Jr., and Robyn Lash. Crestar Bank is the primary creditor of the debtor, and its lien on the residence arises from the Lashes' personal guarantee of the debtor's obligation to Crestar. A foreclosure sale had been scheduled for January 28, 1993. The court heard evidence on January 21, 1993, and ruled from the bench that unusual circumstances in this case justified an injunction for a period of 90 days. This memorandum opinion supplements the court's bench ruling.

Findings of Fact

Debtor ("FTL") operates a car wash under the trade name Car-Robics Brushless Auto Wash in Newport News, Virginia. On July 31, 1991, debtor filed a voluntary bankruptcy petition under chapter 11. Frank Lash, Jr., and Robyn Lash ("Lashes") are officers and directors of FTL, and together they hold 60 percent of the stock in FTL. Although Frank Lash, Jr., is the president of FTL, his sons Frank Lash, III, and Tom Lash oversee the day to day operations of the business. Frank Lash, Jr., is a pharmacist, and his primary occupation is operating a small pharmacy. However, the Lashes' pharmacy is of inconsequential value, and the Lashes' primary assets are their ownership interest in FTL and their personal residence in which they have substantial equity.

Crestar Bank is the primary secured creditor of FTL, holding secured debt of approximately $785,000.00. Frank Lash, Jr., and Robyn Lash personally guaranteed this debt. In January 1992 Crestar secured a judgment lien against the Lashes and subsequently perfected its lien against the Lashes' personal residence. A foreclosure sale on the residence was scheduled for January 28, 1993. Crestar also issued suggestions in garnishment on the Lashes' personal bank accounts.

---

[1] Although movants filed this adversary proceeding for injunctive relief, this matter initially came before the court on plaintiff's motion for preliminary injunction. This memorandum opinion is being written in the adversary proceeding because in my view this is a more appropriate procedure for seeking injunctive relief of this nature.

Since the commencement of this case [FTL] has made monthly adequate protection payments to Crestar in the approximate amount of $11,000.00. This amount represents the monthly payments of principal and interest due prepetition. The evidence indicates that FTL is currently operating at a profit and that these adequate protection payments will likely continue throughout the bankruptcy case. All the assets of FTL are fully insured as is the Lashes' residence.

FTL filed its amended plan of reorganization in December 1992. The plan calls for the Lashes to contribute all the equity in their home to the reorganization. The Lashes are prepared to accomplish this through a home equity loan, and they have already obtained a $115,000.00 written loan commitment from First Fidelity Mortgage to be secured by a second deed of trust on their residence. In addition, FTL is conceivably 30–45 days away from a commitment on a SBA loan through NationsBank. However, this loan is conditioned upon the continued ownership and management of FTL by the Lash family and the personal guarantee of the Lashes. Frank Lash, III, and Tom Lash have been able to secure new financing commitments of approximately $41,000.00, and a personal friend of the Lashes, Don Sweeney, has expressed interest in investing up to $30,000.00 in FTL if a plan is eventually confirmed.

Discussion and Conclusions of Law

The plain language of 11 U.S.C. § 362 provides only for the automatic stay of judicial proceedings and enforcement of judgments against the debtor or the property of the estate. *Credit Alliance Corp. v. Williams*, 851 F.2d 119, 121 (4th Cir. 1988). This court has previously held that in the absence of compelling unusual circumstances, guarantors of a debtor must file their own bankruptcy petition to receive the benefits of bankruptcy law. *See Crumpler v. Wetsel Seed Company (In re Southside Lawn & Garden)*, 115 B.R. 79, 81 (Bankr. E.D. Va. 1990). Nothing in § 362 suggests Congress intended to strip from creditors of a bankrupt debtor the protection they sought and received when they required a third party to guaranty the debt.[2] *Credit Alliance Corp. v. Williams*, 851 F.2d at 121. The very purpose of a guarantee is to assure a creditor that in the event the debtor defaults, the creditor will have someone to look to for reimbursement. *Credit Alliance Corp. v. Williams*, 851 F.2d at 122 (citing *Rojas v. First Bank National Ass'n*, 613 F. Supp. 968, 971 (E.D.N.Y. 1985)).

While the automatic stay provisions are generally said to be available only to the debtor and not to third party guarantors, the Fourth Circuit has held that in unusual circumstances the bankruptcy court can enjoin proceedings against non-debtor third parties pursuant to 11 U.S.C. § 105(a). *A.H. Robins Co. v. Piccinin*, 788 F.2d 994, 1002–04 (4th Cir. 1986); *accord Willis v. Celotex Corp.*, 978 F.2d 146, 149–50 (4th Cir. 1992); *Dalkon Shield Claimants Trust v. Reiser (In re A.H. Robins Co., Inc.)*, 972 F.2d 77, 82 (4th Cir. 1992). Where the identity of the

---

[2] Congress knew how to extend the automatic stay to nonbankrupt parties when it intended to do so. Chapter 13, for example, contains a narrowly drawn provision to stay proceedings against a limited category of individual cosigners of consumer debts. *See* 11 U.S.C. § 1301(a); *Credit Alliance Corp. v. Williams*, 851 F.2d at 121.

debtor and the third party are inexorably interwoven so that the debtor may be said to be the real party against whom the creditor is proceeding a bankruptcy court may exercise equitable jurisdiction to enjoin proceedings against non-debtor third parties. 11 U.S.C. § 105(a); *A.H. Robins Co. v. Piccinin*, 788 F.2d at 1004 (citations omitted). For example, a situation may exist where proceeding against the third party would actually reduce or diminish property the debtor could otherwise make available to the creditors as a whole. *A.H. Robins Co. v. Piccinin*, 788 F.2d at 1008. Allowing such action would undermine two basic principles of chapter 11: to provide creditors with a compulsory and collective forum to sort out their relative entitlement to a debtor's assets and to provide the debtor with a realistic opportunity to formulate a plan of reorganization. *See A.H. Robins Co. v. Piccinin*, 788 F.2d at 998; *see also* Thomas H. Jackson, *The Logic and Limits of Bankruptcy* 4 (1986).

However, before the court can grant injunctive relief the court must find:

1. The plaintiff is likely to succeed on the merits;

2. The plaintiff has shown that irreparable injury will result without such relief;

3. Issuing the injunction would not substantially harm other interested parties; and

4. The public interest is best served by preserving the status quo until the merits of the controversy can be fully considered.

See Blackwelder Furniture Co. v. Seilig Manufacturing Co., 550 F.2d 189, 193 (4th Cir. 1977).

I believe this four-part test is satisfied and that this case presents the kind of "unusual circumstances" set forth in *Robins* that warrant a temporary injunction against Crestar to cease collection activities against the Lashes. *A.H. Robins Co. v. Piccinin*, 788 F.2d at 999.

First, the evidence establishes that the collection activities against the Lashes arise from FTL debt to Crestar, not direct personal obligations of the Lashes to Crestar. The evidence also establishes that FTL is currently operating at a profit with several promising avenues of new financing on the horizon. With a brief "respite from protracted litigation" the Lash family may be able to successfully reorganize this debtor. *A.H. Robins Co. v. Piccinin*, 788 F.2d at 998. Accordingly, the court believes the debtor is "likely to succeed on the merits" by proposing a confirmable chapter 11 plan.

Second, the facts establish that proposing a confirmable plan will be virtually impossible without the active involvement of Frank Lash, Jr., in pursuing new financing arrangements. If Frank Lash, Jr., filed his own bankruptcy petition he probably would not be able to contribute the equity in his residence to the debtor's plan of reorganization as proposed, and his ability to secure new financing for the debtor would be foiled. Accordingly, the court must conclude that "irreparable harm will occur" to the debtor's realistic opportunity to reorganize if collection activities against the Lashes are allowed to continue.

Third, the evidence establishes that little or no harm will be caused to Crestar if it is temporarily enjoined from collection activities against the Lashes.[3] What Crestar seeks through foreclosure on the Lashes' residence is effectively being proposed under the plan of reorganization by the Lashes contributing all the equity in their home to the plan; as the primary secured creditor Crestar will be the beneficiary of these funds. The Lashes are not holding back any substantial asset that would otherwise be available to Crestar via the Lashes' guarantor liability. Moreover, since the commencement of this case Crestar has received and will continue to receive monthly adequate protection payments equivalent to the monthly payments of principal and interest due prepetition. Given its predominant secured creditor position it is unlikely that a plan can be confirmed over Crestar's objection. Accordingly, the court must find that issuing a temporary injunction "will not substantially harm" Crestar or any other interested party.

Fourth, the court believes the creditors as a whole are best served by giving this debtor an opportunity to propose a plan of reorganization. By seeking to foreclose on the Lashes' residence Crestar is attempting to opt-out of chapter 11's compulsory and collective forum of sorting out the creditors' relative entitlement to the debtor's assets. The creditors as a whole deserve the opportunity to evaluate and vote on a plan of reorganization in this case. Accordingly, the court concludes that the "public interest is best served by maintaining the status quo" and enjoining Crestar's collection activities against the Lashes for a period of 90 days or until the merits of the debtor's plan can be promptly and fully considered at a confirmation hearing.

Accordingly, the court will enjoin Crestar's collection activities against the Lashes for a period of 90 days.

NOTES AND QUESTIONS

(1)   After the Fourth Circuit decided the *A.H. Robins* case, it clarified its views in *Credit Alliance Corp. v. Williams*, 851 F.2d 119, 121 (4th Cir. 1988), which allowed a suit to go forward against a guarantor. *See also In re Chugach Forest Prods., Inc.*, 23 F.3d 241 (9th Cir. 1994) (foreclosure by a stevedore of a maritime lien which arose against a boat, not owned by the debtor, for work performed on the debtor's behalf did not violate the automatic stay, even though the boat contained lumber owned by the debtor); *Variable-Parameter Fixture Dev. Corp. v. Morpheus Lights, Inc.*, 945 F. Supp. 603 (S.D.N.Y. 1996) (suit against principal of the debtor on an alter ego theory not stayed). How does Judge Tice distinguish the *Credit Alliance* case and cases like it?

(2)   Judge Tice said that before issuing an injunction under § 105, the court must

---

[3] This injunction is temporary only, and issued to assist the debtor through a crucial point in the reorganization proceedings; the injunction will expire in 90 days or upon confirmation of a plan. The need for permanent injunctive relief in this case is remote because any confirmed plan would likely render unavailable the Lashes' main asset, the equity in their home. Moreover, this court is disinclined to permanently enjoin collection activities against a non-debtor because 11 U.S.C. § 524(e) arguably prevents what would in effect be granting a discharge to a non-debtor. *See* Peter M. Boyle, *Non-Debtor Liability in Chapter 11: Validity of Third-Party Discharge in Bankruptcy*, 61 Fordham L. Review 421, 447 (1992). This type of extraordinary relief may be appropriate in rare circumstances like *A.H. Robins* but should not be liberally granted.

conclude that the traditional test for a preliminary injunction has been met:

1. The plaintiff is likely to succeed on the merits;

2. The plaintiff has shown that irreparable injury will result without such relief;

3. Issuing the injunction would not substantially harm other interested parties; and

4. The public interest is best served by preserving the status quo until the merits of the controversy can be fully considered.

What is the irreparable harm that will be suffered? Are we concerned about harm to Charisma, to the creditors, or to somebody or something else? Why is the estate harmed if Charisma pays the company's debts? When the court finds that there is a "likelihood of success on the merits," is it concluding that Charisma has a meritorious defense against liability and is likely to prevail in the guaranty suit? The *F.T.L.* court said, "the evidence establishes that little or no harm will be caused to Crestar if it is temporarily enjoined from collection activities against the Lashes. What Crestar seeks through foreclosure on the Lashes' residence is effectively being proposed under the plan of reorganization." Is the court right that Crestar is getting precisely what it would get if it foreclosed on the residence? If you seek to have the lawsuit against Charisma stayed, whom do you represent?

[C] Suits Against Key Employees of the Debtor

PROBLEM 3.6

What if the Hystereo plaintiffs sued Chloe Charisma, Amphy's head of research and development, seeking to hold her personally liable for their injuries? Should such a suit be stayed?

While the automatic stay does not extend to employees of the debtor, *Sav-A-Trip, Inc. v. Belfort*, 164 F.3d 1137 (8th Cir. 1999), in *Wickes v. Groebner (In re Wickes)*, No. LA-82-6107 (Bankr. C.D. Cal. Aug. 14, 1982), the court temporarily enjoined various class actions against present and former officers of the debtor because the court believed that a judgment against the officers might have some res judicata effect adverse to the company, that the debtor could be exposed to claims for contribution and indemnification, and that the depositions of the officers might be used against the debtor. The court reasoned:

> Wickes may be constrained to participate in the Class Actions in order to attempt to minimize the risks it otherwise runs. In that event, Wickes will have to devote a significant portion of its limited manpower and financial resources to adequately satisfy the duplicative discovery requirements of the Class Actions. Such participation will irreparably harm Wickes in that it will interfere with the administration of the estates and impede the rehabilitation efforts of the debtor in possession.

Similarly, in *In re Johns-Manville, Inc.*, 26 B.R. 420 (Bankr. S.D.N.Y. 1983), *aff'd sub nom., Johns-Manville Corp. v. Asbestos Litigation Group*, 40 B.R. 219, (S.D.N.Y. 1984), the bankruptcy court stayed a class action against the directors of

Manville because "its true object [was] the debtor itself." The bankruptcy court explained:

> By means of an as yet uncertified class action brought two weeks after the bankruptcy petitions were filed and the stay became effective, Jeffrey Herrman and Linda J. Herrman instituted a lawsuit against certain officers and directors of Manville. In this purported class action, too, the plaintiffs allege that Manville's public disclosures misstated its potential litigation costs in violation of the federal securities laws.
>
> . . . .
>
> Manville has demonstrated that the requirements for applying Section 105 of the Code to extend the parameters of the Section 362 stay have been fulfilled here. This is because a stay of the Herrman litigation is both "necessary and appropriate" in order to carry out the purpose of Section 362, debtor protection. *See* discussion of authorities regarding Section 105 supra at pp. 13–18. This Court finds that the Herrman suit is nothing more than an effort to circumvent Section 362 by suing Manville's officers and directors when the real party in interest is Manville. In all but formal detail, the Herrman litigation is against the debtor within the meaning of Section 362. *See* the Herrman Complaint ¶ 7, 32 and 45 . . . which demonstrates that the relief sought is directed against the debtor itself. In these complaint paragraphs it is alleged that Manville, not the individual defendants, benefitted from alleged misstatements causing the company's stock to sell at inflated prices.
>
> An adverse judgment in the Herrman case would have serious consequences for the debtors' estate. Manville's By-Laws require it to indemnify its officers and directors for their litigation expenses, including any amounts paid to satisfy a judgment of liability, so long as the conduct at issue was intended to benefit the company. *See* Von Wald Affidavit ¶ 9. Although Manville believes that the insurance policies which it has in force cover these expenses, the insurance company has reserved its right to contest coverage and to terminate on 30 days notice the payment of defense costs.
>
> . . . .
>
> Moreover, there is a risk that Manville would be found to be a controlling nonparty in the Herrman action. It thus could be collaterally estopped in subsequent suits from relitigating issues determined against its officers and directors. Even if it is not so bound, Manville may be disadvantaged in subsequent suits. The deposition or trial testimony of its senior executives may be used against the Company in such actions. Yet Manville will not have the benefit of the most fundamental protections available to a party defendant, such as the right of cross-examination.
>
> Manville faces more immediate burdens as well. On November 17, 1982, the plaintiffs in the Herrman action served interrogatories and document requests. Although ostensibly addressed to the individual defendants, the interrogatories seek to impute to the officers and directors any knowledge

or conduct of companies by which they are employed, i.e., Manville.

. . . .

Further, the interrogatories and document requests seek information and internal documents of Manville which relate solely to the Company's affairs. For example, the Herrmans demand all documents and information regarding Manville's organizational structure, and its relationship with its auditors.

. . . .

They also seek Manville's internal financial reports, insurance policies, legal files, and research reports.

If the individual defendants were required to respond fully to these discovery demands, Manville would have to divert personnel from its financial, legal, and insurance departments, as well as secretaries, paralegals, clerks, and others.

. . . .

Moreover, all of the directors, including the Chairman of Manville's Board, would have to invest substantial time in fashioning their responses, particularly to those interrogatories dealing with their background and knowledge and to those document requests seeking information from their files. Manville expects that the plaintiffs will seek further discovery, including depositions of the individual defendants and other Manville personnel. Indeed, apparently as a prelude to additional discovery, the interrogatories require the defendants to identify the managing agents, officers, and directors of all Manville subsidiaries, divisions or affiliates, all outside auditors, all Manville personnel who participated in audits or other internal accounting activities, and all persons present at discussions concerning litigation costs.

. . . .

These burdens are compounded many fold by the hundreds of other litigations pending against Manville's officers, directors, employees, insurers, and other agents. In these litigations, too — in many of which Manville's Chairman is a named defendant — the Company confronts extensive and burdensome discovery demands.

. . . .

Manville faces more pressing obligations in the bankruptcy proceedings which have commanded and will continue to command the attention of its officers, directors, counsel, financial analysts, and administrative personnel. A number of Manville personnel, mostly members of management, have been summoned for examination pursuant to Bankruptcy Rule 205, and the Company has received a number of document requests from official creditor's committees. Further, to fulfill its responsibilities in this proceeding, Manville must conduct financial analyses, prepare numerous schedules, and generate many other filings. Manville's Chairman, in particular, has found it necessary to devote substantial time to the reorganization. Responding to discovery and mounting a defense in the Herrman suit will draw him and other Manville personnel away from these responsibilities, as well as from the important and time-consuming tasks involved in running a multibillion dollar, diversified corporate enterprise.

. . . .

Furthermore, because much of the discovery the Herrmans seek is in essence directed against Manville, the privileges which apply to any of the materials requested are Manville's. Thus, Manville may be forced to intercede in pretrial discovery to protect its interests. Also, as in *Wickes, supra*, the statements of the employees the Herrmans seek to depose may be taken as corporate policy and the company could possibly be collaterally estopped in subsequent suits from relitigating the issues determined in the Herrman litigation.

The facts set forth above establish that the continuation of the Herrman litigation threatens adversely to impact on property of the debtor's estate as well as disrupt the reorganization proceedings and frustrate Manville's efforts to achieve financial rehabilitation. This Court will therefore exercise its power pursuant to Sections 362 and 105 to thwart that threat.

. . . .

The Herrmans, on the other hand, have made no showing that they would be prejudiced by a stay pending the completion of these proceedings. The delay Manville seeks will not diminish the potential liability at issue or in any way complicate the Herrman's evidentiary burdens. Indeed, the Abrams suit, which predates the Herrman action and covers for the most part an earlier period, was stayed automatically by the filing of the bankruptcy petition. Yet the plaintiff class in that litigation, of which the Herrmans purport to be members, have not requested relief from the stay or made any claim of undue prejudice. Indeed prejudice to the Herrmans, if any, is sharply diminished by the parallel Rule 205 discovery ongoing and available to the Herrmans.

26 B.R. at 428–31.

[D] Suits Against Partners of the Debtor

The courts are divided on the question of whether suits against individual partners of debtor partnerships should ever be stayed. On the face of it, it would appear that enjoining such suits would contradict Code § 723. Code § 723 — which codified what was known as the "jingle rule" — requires a partnership trustee in a liquidation case to seek recovery of any deficiency of partnership assets to satisfy partnership liabilities by pursuing the assets of general partners who have filed bankruptcy petitions. Under § 723, the partnership trustee shares equally with the individual creditors of individual partners. The predecessor of Code § 723, former Act § 5g (11 U.S.C. § 23g), also authorized a partnership trustee to pursue assets of general partners, but only after claims of individual creditors of the partners were satisfied. In reality, the policy underlying both these provisions would seem to militate in favor of staying suits against non-debtor partners. The reason is explained in *Elemar Assocs. v. Goldsmith*, 14 CBC 574 (Bankr. S.D.N.Y. 1977).

In that case, a creditor holding a judgment against a debtor partnership sought to enforce it against a general partner of the debtor. On motion of the debtor, the bankruptcy court enjoined the creditor from pursuing any post-judgment remedies against any of the debtor's general partners. The court reasoned:

> To allow defendant here to take those assets for himself on his debt would not only have adverse impact on the partnership's other creditors, but would, in all likelihood, frustrate the debtor's efforts in Chapter XI.

> Moreover, to permit the defendant to levy on assets which the debtor could employ to deal with its other creditors cuts against the grain of that equality of treatment which lies at the heart of Congress's grand scheme in dealing with insolvent entities. The Act denounces rewards to the creditors reaching the courthouse steps on the eve of bankruptcy in advance of other less diligent creditors.

> . . . .

> In striving to protect the integrity of the Chapter XI process as it unfolds, the court is, under [the predecessor of § 105], acting within its grant of power when it enjoins actions which might affect that process.

> . . . .

> The source of funds upon which a debtor could draw to give life to its plan must be preserved. This is not a situation where the debtor's property "is in some way" affected.

> . . . .

> It is a case where adverse effect on the partner's assets might terminate the Chapter XI prematurely.

14 C.B.C. at 580–582. *Accord, In re Old Orchard Inv. Co.*, 31 B.R. 599 (W.D. Mich. 1983). In *Old Orchard*, the court took great pains to distinguish between actions against partners and actions against guarantors or sureties of the debtor. The court explained that actions against the latter do not deplete a debtor's asset pool and have no effect on the ability of a debtor to reorganize. The court also distinguished between claims against partners that could be filed against the partnership and those that could only be brought against partners in their individual capacities. The former might be stayed, the court said, but the latter ought not.

The opposite result was reached by the court in *In re Aboussie Bros. Constr. Co.*, 8 B.R. 302 (E.D. Mo. 1981). There, the district court affirmed the bankruptcy court's refusal to enjoin a creditor of the debtor partnership from pursuing a state court action against the individual partners. The court was unimpressed by the argument that allowing the suit to continue would impair the individual partners' ability to contribute fresh funds to the reorganization effort. The district court reasoned, "[A]dverse effect upon the Debtor, alone, however, is not sufficient justification for the exercise of jurisdiction over the property of the partners." 8 B.R. at 303. The court said only that it "disagreed" with the result reached in *Elemar*. Do you?

More recent cases suggest that while the automatic stay does not extend to partners of the debtor, a supplemental stay might be granted under § 105, but only upon a showing of extraordinary circumstances. *See Patton v. Bearden*, 8 F.3d 343, 349 (6th Cir. 1993) ("In the present case, the defendants do not even allege that the judgments here will render them insolvent or impair their ability to help with reorganizational efforts. Rather, the Beardens merely rely on their status as general partners to urge extension of the automatic stay for their benefit. Thus, even if a debtor-partnership may under unusual circumstances seek an injunction prohibiting action against its partners, requests for such relief can only be presented to the bankruptcy court"); *Teachers Ins. and Annuity Ass'n of Am. v. Butler*, 803 F.2d 61, 65–66 (2d Cir. 1986) ("While we decline to define under what circumstances, if any, a bankruptcy court may properly exercise § 105 jurisdiction to issue a stay with respect to non-bankrupt [partner] co-defendants, it is clear that any such jurisdiction cannot extend to efforts made in bad faith by non-bankrupt [partner] co-defendants in order to escape from the liability imposed by an adverse . . . court judgment.").

§ 3.04   EXCEPTIONS TO THE AUTOMATIC STAY

[A]   The Governmental, Police, and Regulatory Power Exception

[1]   In General

PROBLEM 3.7

You may recall that Amphy's subsidiary, Metal Case, Inc., is in the business of reclaiming precious metals from discarded electronic products. Suppose that a month before Amphy filed a bankruptcy petition, the state environmental protection agency commenced an investigation of claims that toxic wastes discharged from its processing plant were contaminating a nearby waterway. A week after the bankruptcy case was commenced, the agency commenced a civil action under applicable environmental law to compel the company to cease discharging the toxic effluent and to clean up the damage it has already caused. The agency said it will seek to impose civil monetary penalties if the violations continue. What is the effect of the automatic stay on the agency's actions? Read *NLRB v. Evans*, Code § 362(b)(4), and the materials that follow.

NLRB v. EVANS PLUMBING CO.
United States Court of Appeals, Fifth Circuit
F.2d 291 (1981)

Before HILL, FAY AND ANDERSON, CIRCUIT JUDGES

PER CURIAM

This case involves a petition by the National Labor Relations Board ("NLRB") for summary entry of judgment to enforce the Board's decision ordering the respondent Evans Plumbing Company ("Evans") to reinstate with back pay two employees whom it discriminatorily discharged. Evans, who filed a voluntary petition in bankruptcy, opposes entry of judgment on the ground that the proceedings before the NLRB should have been stayed by the automatic stay provision of the Bankruptcy Act of 1978, 11 U.S.C.A. § 362(a)(1) (1979). We hold that this NLRB proceeding falls within a statutory exemption to the automatic stay provision and grant the Board's petition for summary entry of judgment.

I.

On or about February 15, 1980, Evans discharged Jack T. Lee and F. J. Meeks for complaining to their union about alleged mismanagement of their vacation funds by Evans. A charge of unfair labor practices was filed and the matter set down for a hearing. On August 8, 1980, the day before the commencement of the hearing, Evans filed a voluntary petition in bankruptcy in the Northern District of Alabama. On the day of the hearing, Evans' counsel appeared and moved to continue the Board proceedings in order that the bankruptcy court might determine whether the proceeding fell within the automatic stay provision of the Bankruptcy Act. Evans' motion was apparently overruled and the hearing was held. On September 30, 1980, the administrative law judge ("ALJ") found that Evans had committed an unfair labor practice by discharging Lee and Meeks and ordered them reinstated with back pay. The order was promptly transmitted to the Board to await the filing of exception by Evans. Evans failed to file any exception within the time provided by the Board's rules and regulations and the Board adopted the ALJ's decision. This petition followed.

II.

We are faced with a threshold question of first impression under the new Bankruptcy Act: whether the automatic stay provision applies to an enforcement proceeding by the NLRB. We conclude that this action falls within an exception to the automatic stay provision.

The automatic stay provision, 11 U.S.C.A. § 362 (1979), provides in part:

(a) Except as provided in subsection (b) of this section, a petition filed under section 301, 302, or 303 of this title operates as a stay, applicable to all entities, of —

(1) the commencement or continuation, including the issuance or employment of process, of a judicial, administrative, or other proceeding against the debtor that was or could have been commenced before the commencement of the case under this title, or to recover a claim against the debtor that arose before the commencement of the case under this title;

. . . .

(b) The filing of a petition under section 301, 302, or 303 of this title does not operate as a stay —

. . . .

(4) under subsection (a)(1) of this section, of the commencement or continuation of an action or proceeding by a governmental unit to enforce such governmental unit's police or regulatory power;

(5) under subsection (a)(2) of this section, of the enforcement of a judgment, other than a money judgment, obtained in an action or proceeding by a governmental unit to enforce such governmental unit's police or regulatory power;[1]

As explained in the legislative history of the Bankruptcy Act of 1978:

Paragraph (4) excepts commencement or continuation of actions and proceedings by governmental units to enforce police or regulatory powers. Thus, where a governmental unit is suing a debtor to prevent or stop violation of fraud, environmental protection, consumer protection, safety, or similar police or regulatory laws, or attempting to fix damages for violation of such a law, the action or proceeding is not stayed under the automatic stay. Paragraph (5) makes clear that the exception extends to permit an injunction and enforcement of an injunction, and to permit the entry of a money judgment, but does not extend to permit enforcement of a money judgment. Since the assets of the debtor are in the possession and control of the bankruptcy court, and since they constitute a fund out of which all creditors are entitled to share, enforcement by a governmental unit of money judgment would give it preferential treatment to the detriment of all other creditors.

House Report No. 95-595, 95th Cong., 2d Sess. at 343, reprinted in 1978 U.S. Code Cong. and Adm. News, 5787, 6299. *See also* Senate Report No. 95-989, 95th Cong., 2d Sess. p. 52, reprinted in 1978 U.S. Code Cong. and Adm. News, 5787, 5838. The crucial issue is whether the NLRB is a governmental unit and whether this action is one to enforce police or regulatory powers. It is clear that the NLRB is a governmental unit. This action was undertaken to enforce the federal law regulating the relationship between employer and employee. We can safely conclude therefore that this is an exercise of police or regulatory powers which places it within the § 362(b)(4) exemption to the automatic stay. [2]

---

[1] [In 1998, subsections (4) and (5) were merged into a single subsection (4). — Eds.]

[2] Our conclusion finds some support, albeit in dicta, in two recent decisions of the Seventh and Ninth

We note that our decision today would permit the entry of judgment for injunctive relief and for back pay; however, should it be necessary to enforce the judgment for back pay, a different question would be presented. We express no opinion as to whether an action to execute or enforce a money judgment would be exempt from the automatic stay.[3]

The Board's petition for summary entry of judgment is hereby Granted.

[2]   What Is an Action to Enforce a Money Judgment?

(1) In *Penn Terra Ltd. v. Dept. of Envt. Res.*, 24 B.R. 427, (Bankr. W.D. Pa. 1982), the debtor asserted that the automatic stay barred a state agency from taking steps to enforce a consent decree executed by the debtor prior to its Chapter 7 filing. The decree required the debtor, a coal strip mining company, to undertake costly land reclamation measures. The bankruptcy court found that requiring the debtor to expend funds for cleanup was essentially an action to enforce a money judgment and therefore subject to the stay. The district court affirmed the bankruptcy court's ruling, but the Court of Appeals for the Third Circuit reversed, reasoning as follows:

> This case demonstrates the difficulty encountered when two governmental policies — one federal and one state — come into arguable conflict. On the one hand, the federally created bankruptcy policy requires that the assets of a debtor be preserved and protected, so that in time they may be equitably distributed to all creditors without unfair preference. On the other hand, the environmental policies of the Commonwealth of Pennsylvania require those within its jurisdiction to preserve and protect natural resources and to rectify damage to the environment which they have caused. The potential conflict between these two policies is presented in this case, in which the Commonwealth has attempted to force a company which has petitioned in bankruptcy to correct violations of state antipollution laws, even though this action would have the effect of depleting assets which would otherwise be available to repay debts owed to general creditors.
>
> . . . .

Circuits. *In re Bel Air Chateau Hospital, Inc.*, 611 F.2d 1248 (9th Cir. 1979), and *In the Matter of Shippers Interstate Service, Inc.*, 618 F.2d 9 (7th Cir. 1980), held that the automatic stay provisions of the old Bankruptcy Act did not operate to stay unfair labor practice proceedings before the NLRB. In *In re Bel Air*, the court stated:

> This result appears harmonious with the new bankruptcy law. . . . Under 11 U.S.C. § 362(a)(1) the filing of a petition will normally operate as a stay of judicial or administrative proceedings. Section 362(b)(4), however, provides that the filing of a petition does not automatically stay an action by a governmental unit to enforce the government's police or regulatory power.

611 F.2d at 1251.

[3] Similarly, we express no opinion as to whether the bankruptcy court has power under 11 U.S.C.A. § 105(a) (1979) to issue a discretionary stay notwithstanding the exemption of the Board's action from the automatic stay. *See In re King Memorial Hospital, Inc.*, 4 B.R. 704 (Bkrtcy.S.D.Fla. 1980), and *In re Bel Air Chateau Hospital, Inc.*, 611 F.2d at 1251.

At its core, interpretation of section 362 involves questions of federal supremacy and preemption. It is undisputable that the Commonwealth is normally empowered to regulate the environment, in its role as protector of the public health and welfare, and thus may rightfully compel adherence to environmental standards. Penn Terra claims, however, that in this instance, the federal government has pre-empted that power through the Bankruptcy Code.

While Congress, under its Bankruptcy power, certainly has the constitutional prerogative to pre-empt the States, even in their exercise of police power, the usual rule is that congressional intent to pre-empt will not be inferred lightly. Pre-emption must either be explicit, or compelled due to an unavoidable conflict between the state law and the federal law.

. . . .

Given the general rule that preemption is not favored, and the fact that, in restoring power to the States, Congress intentionally used such a broad term as "police and regulatory powers," we find that the exception to the automatic stay provision contained in subsections 362(b)(4)–(5) should itself be construed broadly, and no unnatural efforts be made to limit its scope. The police power of the several States embodies the main bulwark of protection by which they carry out their responsibilities to the People; its abrogation is therefore a serious matter. Congress should not be assumed, therefore, to have been miserly in its refund of that power to the States. Where important state law or general equitable principles protect some public interest, they should not be overridden by federal legislation unless they are inconsistent with explicit congressional intent such that the supremacy clause mandates their supersession. For the same policy reasons, the "exception to the exception" created by subsection 362(b)(5), rendering "enforcement of a money judgment" by a government unit susceptible to the automatic stay, should be construed narrowly so as to leave to the States as much of their police power as a fair reading of the statute allows.

. . . .

In using the words "enforcement of a money judgment," Congress did not provide any definition for that term. Its meaning must therefore be gleaned from the commonly accepted usage and from whatever indications of congressional intent we find persuasive.

. . . .

In common understanding, a money judgment is an order entered by the court or by the clerk, after a verdict has been rendered for plaintiff, which adjudges that the defendant shall pay a sum of money to the plaintiff. Essentially, it need consist of only two elements: (1) an identification of the parties for and against whom judgment is being entered, and (2) a definite and certain designation of the amount which plaintiff is owed by defendant. It need not, and generally does not, contain provisions for its enforcement. *See generally* 49 C.J.S. Judgments, §§ 71–82 (describing proper form of money judgment). As the legislative history explicitly notes the mere entry of a money judgment by a governmental unit is not affected by the automatic stay, provided of course that such proceedings are related to that government's police or regulatory powers.

Quite separate from the entry of a money judgment, however, is a proceeding to enforce that money judgment. The paradigm for such a proceeding is when, having obtained a judgment for a sum certain, a plaintiff attempts to seize property of the defendant in order to satisfy that judgment. It is this seizure of a defendant-debtor's property, to satisfy the judgment obtained by a plaintiff-creditor, which is proscribed by subsection 362(b)(5).

At least as a matter of form, it is clear to us that the proceeding initiated by DER in Commonwealth Court was not to enforce a money judgment. Indeed, it could not have resulted even in the mere entry of a money judgment. DER brought its action in equity to compel the performance of certain remedial acts by Penn Terra. It did not seek the payment of compensation to the Commonwealth's coffers, and the injunction actually issued by the Commonwealth Court did not direct such payment. This proceeding, therefore, could never have resulted in the adjudication of liability for a sum certain, an essential element of a money judgment. Since this action was in form and substance . . . not one to obtain a money judgment, it follows that it could not be one to enforce the payment of such a judgment.

   . . . .

[A]n important factor in identifying a proceeding as one to enforce a money judgment is whether the remedy would compensate for past wrongful acts resulting in injuries already suffered, or project against potential future harm. Thus, it is unlikely that any action which seeks to prevent culpable conduct in futuro will, in normal course, manifest itself as an action for a money judgment, or one to enforce a money judgment. This is consistent with our earlier observations, since a traditional money judgment requires liquidated damages, i.e. a sum certain, and one cannot liquidate damages which have not been suffered due to conduct not yet committed. Nor can one calculate such a sum with any certainty. Indeed, the very nature of injunctive relief is that it addresses injuries which may not be compensated by money.

   . . . .

Were we to find that any order which requires the expenditure of money is a "money judgment," then the exception to section 362 for government police action, which should be construed broadly, would instead be narrowed into virtual nonexistence. Yet we cannot ignore the fundamental fact that, in contemporary times, almost everything costs something. An injunction which does not compel some expenditure or loss of monies may often be an effective nullity.

It appears that, in defining the scope of the exception to the automatic stay, the Bankruptcy Court in this case placed too much weight on the value of preserving the corpus of the debtor's funds and estate under its own exclusive control. Admittedly, that goal is normally central to the statutory scheme of the Bankruptcy Code. As noted at the beginning of this opinion, however, in some instances this policy is in inexorable conflict with other, no less salutary, governmental goals. We believe that the resolution of this conflict is contained in the statute itself. In enacting the exceptions to section 362, Congress recognized that in some circumstances, bankruptcy policy must yield to higher priorities. Indeed, if the policy of preservation of the estate is to be invariably paramount, then one could not have exceptions to the rule. Congress did provide for exceptions, however, we may assume that the goal of preserving the debtor's estate is not always the dominant goal.

We believe that the inquiry is more properly focused on the nature of the injuries which the challenged remedy is intended to redress — including whether plaintiff seeks compensation for past damages or prevention of future harm — in order to reach the ultimate conclusion as to whether these injuries are traditionally rectified by a money judgment and its enforcement. Here, the Commonwealth Court injunction was, neither in form nor substance, the type of remedy traditionally associated with the conventional money judgment. It was not intended to provide compensation for past injuries. It was not reducible to a sum certain. No monies were sought by the Commonwealth as a creditor or obligee. The Commonwealth was not seeking a traditional form of damages in tort or contract, and the mere payment of money, without more, even if it could be estimated, could not satisfy the Commonwealth Court's direction to complete the backfilling, to update erosion plans, to seal mine openings, to spread topsoil, and to implement plans for erosion and sedimentation control. Rather, the Commonwealth Court's injunction was meant to prevent future harm to, and to restore the environment.

Penn Terra Ltd. v. Dept. of Envtl. Res., 733 F.2d 267 at 269–78, (3d Cir. 1984). In a footnote, however, the court did suggest that some suits ought not be allowed to proceed:

We also acknowledge that exercise of a State's police powers may, depending on the circumstances, take the form of an execution on a money judgment. For example, if a coal mining company conducted operations in violation of applicable surface reclamation laws, then the assessment and collection of a civil penalty to serve as a punishment and deterrence against future violations would be no less an exercise of the police power than if the State had ordered the company to cease operations entirely. *See* Surface Mining Control and Reclamation Act of 1977, 30 U.S.C. §§ 1201-1328 (Supp. II 1978) (imposing civil penalties against mine operators who violate provisions of Act). It is important to remember that § 362(b)(5), which prohibits governmental units from enforcing money judgments while the automatic stay is in effect, does not exclude such enforcement by definition from the meaning of "police power," or imply that when a state seeks to execute a money judgment it is not acting for the public health, safety, or welfare. Section 362(b)(5) is merely an exception to the rule that the exercise of police power by a State is not affected by the automatic stay.

733 F.2d at 274, n. 7.

Do you agree with the opinion of the Court of Appeals or the bankruptcy court? Can you explain the Court of Appeals' distinction between a suit to collect a penalty and a suit to compel a debtor to repair prior damage? Is cleanup necessarily dependent on obtaining relief from the stay? Does the state have any alternative means of repairing environmental damage?

In subsequent cases, courts answered the question that the *Evans* court left open. Although the § 362(b)(4) exception permits the *entry* of a money judgment, the collection of that money judgment falls within the exception to the exception, and thus is stayed. *See, e.g., NLRB v. 15th Avenue Iron Works, Inc.*, 964 F.2d 1336 (2d Cir. 1992); *NLRB v. Continental Hagen Corp.*, 932 F.2d 828 (9th Cir. 1991).

(2) In determining whether an action by a governmental unit falls within the police and regulatory power exception to the stay, courts have sometimes applied "the pecuniary purpose" and "public policy" tests. In *In re Commerce Oil Co.*, 847 F.2d 291, 295 (6th Cir. 1988), the court explained, "Under the pecuniary purpose test, reviewing courts focus on whether the governmental proceeding relates primarily to the protection of the government's pecuniary interest in the debtor's property, and not to matters of public safety. Those proceedings which relate primarily to matters of public safety are excepted from the stay. Under the public policy test, reviewing courts must distinguish between proceedings that adjudicate private rights and those that effectuate public policy. Those proceedings that effectuate a public policy are excepted from the stay." So, for example, an NLRB action based on an unfair labor practice complaint satisfies both tests, because it is not an action to protect the government's own financial stake, and it is an action to effectuate a public policy — compliance with federal labor laws. *Commerce Oil*, 847 F.2d at 295. On the other hand, an attempt by the FCC to cancel a debtor's telecommunications services licenses because the debtor failed to pay a prepetition debt owed to the government failed both tests. *In re Nextwave Pers. Commc'ns Inc.*, 244 B.R. 253 (Bankr. S.D.N.Y. 2000). Similarly, an action to preclude the debtor, a mental health center, from participating in the Medicaid reimbursement program was stayed because the court found that it was animated by the government's "pecuniary purpose." *In re Psychotherapy and Counseling Center, Inc.*, 195 B.R. 522 (Bankr. D.D.C. 1996)

(3) What is the difference between a "money judgment" and a "claim"? In *Ohio v. Kovacs*, 469 U.S. 274 (1985), the Supreme Court held that an obligation of a Chapter 7 debtor to clean up a hazardous waste site was a "claim" that was dischargeable under the Code. Can these two cases be reconciled?

(4) What if Metal Case had not been sued by a governmental agency, but by Concerned Citizens for the Environment, a nonprofit public organization concerned with environmental protection and preservation, acting as a "private attorney general"? Would the action be stayed, or would it fall within the exception? In *In re Revere Copper and Brass, Inc.*, 32 B.R. 725, 727 (S.D.N.Y. 1983), the court

construed the term "governmental unit" narrowly and held that it "refers exclusively to actual governmental groups and not to organizations acting in a governmental capacity." Other courts have been more liberal. In *United States ex rel. Doe v. X, Inc.*, 246 B.R. 817 (Bankr. E.D. Va. 2000), the court held that a *qui tam* action brought under the False Claims Act fell within the § 362(b)(4) exception. In *Alpern v. Lieb*, 11 F.3d 689 (7th Cir. 1993), the court held that a proceeding to impose sanctions under Federal Rule of Civil Procedure 11 was exempt from the stay. The court reasoned, "Rule 11 is not a simple fee-shifting provision, designed to reduce the net cost of litigation to the prevailing party. It directs the imposition of sanctions for unprofessional conduct in litigation, and while the form of sanction is often and was here an order to pay attorney's fees to the opponent in the litigation, it is still a sanction, just as an order of restitution in a criminal case is a sanction even when it directs that payment be made to a private person rather than to the government. The Rule 11 sanction is meted out by a governmental unit, the court, though typically sought by a private individual or organization — a nongovernmental litigant, the opponent of the litigant to be sanctioned. There is no anomaly, given the long history of private enforcement of penal and regulatory law. The private enforcer, sometimes called a 'private attorney general,' can be viewed as an agent of the 'governmental unit,' the federal judiciary, that promulgated Rule 11 in order to punish unprofessional behavior." 11 F.3d at 690. Do you agree?

[B]   Actions Brought in Bankruptcy Court

An action brought in bankruptcy court to liquidate a claim — even a pre-petition claim — does not violate the stay. *See In re Atreus Enterprises, Ltd.*, 120 B.R. 341 (Bankr. S.D.N.Y. 1990), where a creditor brought an action in bankruptcy court against the debtor, asking the court to determine their respective rights under a joint venture agreement entered into prepetition. Judge Schwartzberg said:

> This adversary proceeding illustrates an important and fundamental exception to the automatic stay which is not listed among the specific exceptions delineated under 11 U.S.C. § 362(b). Any action to recover property, to collect money, to enforce a lien, or to assert a prepetition claim against the debtor which would otherwise be enjoined by § 362(a) if initiated in any other context, is not subject to the automatic stay if commenced in the bankruptcy court where the debtor's bankruptcy case is pending.

> The automatic stay is intended as an umbrella to protect a debtor temporarily from the shower of law suits and collection efforts by creditors outside the bankruptcy court administering the debtor's case in order to afford the debtor a breathing spell for the purpose of concentrating on the financial, rehabilitative and distributive procedures applicable in the bankruptcy court where the debtor's case is pending. The automatic stay was never intended to bar the bankruptcy court from exercising its statutory mandate to determine and allow claims and interests pursuant to §§ 501 and 502; to determine the value of liens and other secured interests in property in accordance with § 506; or to decide dischargeability suits against the debtor and to enter judgments for amounts found to be

nondischargeable under § 523. Indeed, in addition to its authority to hear and determine any and all core proceedings described in 28 U.S.C. § 157(b)(1), the bankruptcy court is expressly authorized to determine actions against the debtor and others which might be otherwise related to a case under title 11, as provided under 28 U.S.C. § 157(c)(1).

[C]   Effect of the Automatic Stay on States

One question that remains unsettled is the effect of the automatic stay on states that take actions to collect on prepetition debts. There is no doubt that Congress intended the automatic stay to apply to states. Section 106(a) of the Bankruptcy Code provides: "Notwithstanding an assertion of sovereign immunity, sovereign immunity is abrogated as to a governmental unit to the extent set forth in this section with respect to [among others] Sections 105 . . . 362, . . . 547, 548, 549, 550 . . ." This language was added in 1994 when the Supreme Court's decisions in *Hoffman v. Conn. Dept. of Income Maint.*, 492 U.S. 96 (1989), and *U.S. v. Nordic Village, Inc.*, 503 U.S. 30 (1992), held that the prior version of § 106 did not operate to abrogate state sovereign immunity or waive federal sovereign immunity.

The Supreme Court's holdings in *Seminole Tribe v. Florida*, 517 U.S. 44 (1996) and *Alden v. Maine*, 527 U.S. 706 (1999), that private citizens may not sue states in federal court to enforce federally created rights appear to overrule amended § 106, at least in part. *Seminole Tribe* and its progeny affect bankruptcy law in two important ways. First, it affects the Court's power to enjoin state collection efforts pursuant to the automatic stay and to discharge injunctions, and, second, it alters the bankruptcy trustee's power to recover money from states pursuant to its various avoidance powers. To understand these two contexts, it might be useful to keep two stories in mind: the "injunction story" and the "avoidance story."

First, the injunction story: Frank Ponzi runs an investment company called Ponzi Investments in the state of Virginia. The company owes $1,000,000 in back taxes to the state. As it turns out, Frank is neither a very smart stock picker nor very honest, and he loses all of his investors' money and then some. The company files for bankruptcy. At the moment of the filing, the automatic stay goes into effect and prohibits individual creditors, including states, from seeking to collect their debts by unilateral action.

Second, the avoidance story: As it turns out, Ponzi also had a $200,000 personal state tax liability. Shortly before Ponzi Investments filed for bankruptcy, Ponzi raided the corporate bank account and used the money to pay his personal state income taxes.[1] Here, the Federal Bankruptcy Code creates a number of federal rights of action and vests enforcement power in the bankruptcy trustee. These causes of action include actions to avoid preferences and fraudulent conveyances, each of which would, pre-*Seminole Tribe*, give the bankruptcy trustee the power to recover the $200,000 from the state.

---

[1] These facts are loosely modeled on *I.R.S. v. Nordic Village*, except that the tax liability in *Nordic Village* was to the federal rather than state government, and the transfer occurred post-petition.

Seminole Tribe would at first appear to have little effect on the injunction story. Even after *Seminole Tribe*, the automatic stay will prevent state officials from seizing the assets of Ponzi Investments. While states themselves are immune from suit under *Seminole Tribe*, bankruptcy court injunctions bind state officials acting in their official capacity. Under *Ex parte Young*, 209 U.S. 123 (1908), such officials are not immune, and state officials who violate the automatic stay can be held in contempt. While, in *Seminole Tribe*, the Court declared that no "*Ex parte Young*" type injunction was available under the Indian Gaming Act, this was a holding based on statutory interpretation, rather than constitutional limitation. In the Court's view, Congress enacted a detailed remedial scheme when it enacted the Indian Gaming Act, and this remedial scheme did not include the power to enjoin state officials. However, the Court expressly stated, albeit in a footnote, that such an action would have been available if Congress had intended to create it:

> Contrary to the claims of the dissent, we do not hold that Congress cannot authorize federal jurisdiction under *Ex parte Young* over a cause of action with a limited remedial scheme. We find only that Congress did not intend that result in the Indian Gaming Regulatory Act.

517 U.S. at 75, n.17 (1996). However, even once one accepts that the automatic stay binds state officials, if not states themselves, this leaves open the question of what happens once a state has violated the automatic stay and now possesses property of the debtor. Would a turnover action under Code § 542 be barred by *Seminole Tribe*?

The courts' treatment of the "avoidance story" does not offer much hope. Most courts have agreed that *Seminole Tribe* precludes avoidance actions against states.[2] After *Seminole Tribe*, the trustee of Ponzi Investments will not be able to recover the money Frank Ponzi stole from the company and handed over to the to the state to pay his personal taxes. While the Bankruptcy Court can prevent state action in the future, here an *Ex parte Young* type injunction will do no good. The state has the money, or the asset, and the trustee wants to sue to get it back. Prior to *Seminole Tribe*, this transfer would have been avoidable as either a preference or as a fraudulent conveyance. However, if the trustee is viewed as a private citizen suing a state, then under *Seminole Tribe* the Eleventh Amendment would appear to bar the suit. Indeed, the Supreme Court seems to take this view as well. The majority opinion in *Seminole Tribe* expressly criticizes the Seventh Circuit's decision in In re *Merch. Grain, Inc.*, 59 F.3d 630 (7th Cir. 1995), a bankruptcy case involving a preference action under 11 U.S.C. § 547, and, in a companion case, summarily vacated that decision and remanded. 517 U.S. 1130 (1996).

---

[2] *Sacred Heart Hosp. v. Pennsylvania Dep't of Welfare*, 204 B.R. 132 (Bankr. E.D. Pa. 1997); *In re Martinez*, 196 B.R. 225 (Bankr. D.P.R. 1996); *Sparkman v. Fla. Dep't of Revenue (In re York-Hannover Devs., Inc.)*, 201 B.R. 137 (Bankr. E.D.N.C. 1996) (fraudulent conveyance action brought by the bankruptcy trustee against Florida Department of Revenue barred by the Eleventh Amendment). One court has suggested that an action for money damages might be available under the Fourteenth Amendment for violations of the automatic stay. *Headrick v. Georgia*, 200 B.R. 963, 967 (Bankr. S.D. Ga. 1996) ("Article I empowers Congress to grant debtors the privileges and immunities of the Bankruptcy Code, and the Fourteenth Amendment gives Congress the right to enforce those privileges and immunities by creating private rights of action against the States.").

In a Ninth Circuit case, California forced a debtor to pay outstanding prepetition taxes in violation of the automatic stay. The bankruptcy court ordered the state to refund the money as a sanction but stated that it had the power to do so only because the state had waived its sovereign immunity by filing a proof of claim in the bankruptcy. *Cal. Employment Dev. Dep. v. Taxel*, 98 F.3d 1147, 1152 (9th Cir. 1996). Another bankruptcy court has held that the state does not waive its sovereign immunity simply by taking possession of property of the estate postpetition. *In re Pinnacle Health Enters.*, 1999 U.S. Dist. LEXIS 8400 (D. Del. May 7, 1999).

§ 3.05   WHEN IS A CLAIM A CLAIM?

PROBLEM 3.8

Headley is concerned. The number of Hystereo plaintiffs seems to be increasing by the day. He wants to know how those claims will be dealt with in bankruptcy, so he asks you to analyze the following hypotheticals:

a. Assume that a law professor, Leonard Slippenfall, purchased an Amphyvideo game prepetition, and then developed a bad case of Hystereo and sued, also prepetition. What is the status of his claim? Is his suit stopped by the automatic stay?

b. Now assume that the Amphy video game is still being sold in retail outlets. Further assume Prof. Slippenfall purchased a Amphy video game after the petition date, and then came down with a bad case of Hystereo. Would his lawsuit be barred by the automatic stay?

c. What if Prof. Slippenfall purchased the video game prepetition, but did not use the game or develop Hystereo until after the petition was filed?

d. What if Prof. Slippenfall never purchased the video game, but nevertheless developed Hystereo after visiting his friend Web Walker, postpetition, and playing the game at his house?

Consider the following case:

GRADY v. A.H. ROBINS CO.
United States Court of Appeals for the Fourth Circuit
839 F.2d 198 (1988)

WIDENER, CIRCUIT JUDGE:

Rebecca Grady and the Legal Representative of the Future Claimants appeal an order of the district court deciding that Mrs. Grady's claim against A. H. Robins Co., Inc. (Robins) arose prior to the date Robins sought protection under the Bankruptcy Code and therefore was subject to the automatic stay provision of 11 U.S.C. § 362(a)(i). We affirm.[1]

---

[1] We use the terms district court and bankruptcy court interchangeably in our opinion. The district court did not refer this proceeding to a bankruptcy judge under 28 U.S.C. § 157.

Robins, a pharmaceutical company, was the manufacturer and marketer of the Dalkon Shield, an interuterine contraceptive device, from 1971 to 1974. Production was discontinued in 1974 because of mounting concerns about the device's safety. Because of the overwhelming number of claims filed against it because of the Dalkon Shield, Robins filed a petition for reorganization under Chapter 11. . . . On August 21, 1985, Mrs. Grady had inserted a Dalkon Shield some years before but thought that the device had fallen out. On August 21, 1985, she was admitted to Salinas Valley Memorial Hospital, Salinas, California, complaining of abdominal pain, fever and chills. X-rays and sonograms revealed the presence of the Dalkon Shield. On August 28, 1985, the Dalkon Shield was surgically removed. Mrs. Grady was discharged from the hospital but not long after returned to her physician, complaining of persistent pain, fever and chills. She was again admitted to the hospital on November 14, 1985, on which admission she was diagnosed as having pelvic inflammatory disease, and underwent a hysterectomy. She blames the Dalkon Shield for those injuries.

On October 15, 1985 (almost two months after Robins filed its petition for reorganization), Mrs. Grady filed a civil action against Robins in the United States District Court for the Northern District of California. The case was subsequently transferred to the Eastern District of Virginia.

Mrs. Grady then filed a motion in the bankruptcy court, seeking a decision that her claim did not arise before the filing of the petition so that it would not be stayed by the automatic stay provision of the Code. If the claim arose when the Dalkon Shield was inserted into her, the district court reasoned, then it would be considered a claim under the Bankruptcy Code and its prosecution would be stayed by the provisions of 11 U.S.C. § 362(a)(i). If, however, the claim was found to arise when the injuries became apparent, then it might not be a claim for bankruptcy purposes and the automatic stay provision would be inapplicable.

The bankruptcy court determined that Mrs. Grady's claim against Robins arose when the acts giving rise to Robins' liability were performed, not when the harm caused by those acts was manifested. The court rejected Mrs. Grady's contention that the court must look to state law to determine when her cause of action accrued and equate that with a right to payment. It concluded that the court must follow federal law in determining when the claim arose. It held that the right to payment under 11 U.S.C. § 101(4)(A) of Mrs. Grady's claim arose when the acts giving rise to the liability were performed and thus the claim was pre-petition under 11 U.S.C. § 362(a)(1).

We emphasize the narrowness of the district court's holding. It held only that the automatic stay provision of 11 U.S.C. § 362 applied, and we have recited its reasoning to arrive at that conclusion. It did not decide whether or not Mrs. Grady's claim would constitute an administrative expense under 11 U.S.C. § 503(b)(1)(A), and it also did not decide whether or not the Future Tort Claimants would have a dischargeable claim within the reorganization case. We affirm, although our reasoning may vary somewhat from that of the district court.

. . . .

The district court correctly noted that the automatic stay is particularly critical to a debtor seeking to reorganize under Chapter 11 because he needs breathing room to restructure his affairs. While the importance of § 362 cannot be over-emphasized, its coverage extends only to claims against the debtor that arose prior to the filing of its petition.

11 U.S.C. § 101(4), as pertinent, defines a claim to be a

> (A) right to a payment, whether or not such right is reduced to judgment, liquidated, unliquidated, fixed, contingent, matured, unmatured, disputed, undisputed, legal, equitable, secured or unsecured;

Congress intended that the definition of claim in the Code be as broad as possible, noting that "the bill contemplates that all legal obligations of the debtor, no matter how remote or contingent, will be able to be dealt with in the bankruptcy. It permits the broadest possible relief in the bankruptcy court," H. R. Rep. No, 595, 95th Cong., 1st Sess, 309 (1977), S. Rep. No, 989, 95th Cong., 2d Sess, 21–22 (1978), reprinted in 1978 U.S. S. Code Cong. & Adm., News, 5787 at 5807-8 and 6266. The courts have consistently recognized the very broad definition to be given to claims.

While the parties agree that the term claim is broadly defined under the Bankruptcy Code, they disagree over whether Mrs. Grady's suit falls within that definition. Mrs. Grady primarily relies upon *Matter of M. Frenville Co.* . . . to support her contention that her claim falls outside the protection of the automatic stay.

Prior to filing its petition, Frenville, an independent auditing firm, had employed Avellina and Bienes (A & B), an accounting firm, to prepare its financial statement. After the bankruptcy petition was filed, several banks which had received the financial statement sued A & B, claiming that the statement was negligently prepared. A & B moved for relief from the automatic stay in order that it could bring Frenville into those lawsuits as a third-party defendant for their indemnification.

The court concluded that a pre-petition act by a debtor giving rise to later liability is not enough to bring an action within the definition of a claim. It held that the right to payment must exist pre-petition before a claim can exist. Because the Bankruptcy Code does not provide when a right to payment arises, the court turned to state law for its answer. Because A & B had had no right under state law to seek indemnification from Frenville before the banks filed their suit, the claim was held to arise post-petition and therefore was not barred by the automatic stay provision of 362(a)(1).

Mrs. Grady argues that her cause of action against Robins did not accrue until after Robins had filed its reorganization petition and therefore the stay provision is inapplicable. Under California law, she argues that she could not have sued Robins until she knew the nature of her injuries.[4] The argument goes that because she had

---

[4] Mrs. Grady takes the position that, under California law, a cause of action does not accrue until the injured person knows or by the exercise of reasonable diligence should have discovered the cause of the injury when that injury results without perceptible trauma. *Warrington v. Charles Pfizer & Co.*, 274 Cal. App. 2d 564, 567, 80 Cal. Rptr. 130, 132 (1969).

Since Mrs. Grady's injuries manifested themselves the same day as the filing of Robins' petition, we

no right to payment from Robins under state law until she was injured, and since that injury occurred after the reorganization petition was filed, the stay provision of § 362 should not bar her case from its prosecution. While not agreeing that state law necessarily controls, the Future Tort Claimants agree that Mrs. Grady had no pre-petition right of payment from Robins and therefore no claim under the Bankruptcy Code.

Robins argues that the district court was correct in declining to apply the reasoning of *Frenville* and in its conclusion that Mrs. Grady's claim falls within the definition set out in § 101(4)(A) because the tortious conduct occurred prior to the filing of the petition. Robins relies primarily upon [several cases that] decline to apply the reasoning in *Frenville* and conclude that claim accrual for bankruptcy purposes must be determined in light of bankruptcy law and not state law.

We have found no court outside the Third Circuit which has followed the reasoning and holding of *Frenville*. All of the cases coming to our attention which have considered the issue have declined to follow *Frenville's* limiting definition of claim. We likewise decline to follow *Frenville*, and our reasoning follows.

We commence with the proposition that " . . . except where federal law, fully apart from bankruptcy, has created obligations by the exercise of power granted to the federal government, a claim implies the existence of an obligation created by State law." *Vanston Committee v. Green*, 329 U.S. 156, 167, 170 (1946) (Justice Frankfurter concurring), and further, from that concurring opinion, that "[b]ankruptcy legislation is superimposed upon rights and obligations created by the laws of the States." 329 U.S. at 171. The opinion of the court in *Vanston* further stands for the proposition that "In determining what claims are allowable and how a debtor's assets are to be distributed, a bankruptcy court does not apply the law of the State where it sits." 329 U.S. at 162. So, the bankruptcy Code is superimposed upon the law of the State which has created the obligation. Congress has the undoubted power under the bankruptcy article, U.S. Const. Art. I, § 8 cl. 4, to define and classify claims against the estate of a bankrupt. In the case of a claim as noted above, the legislative history shows that Congress intended that all legal obligations of the debtor, no matter how remote or contingent, will be able to be dealt with in bankruptcy. The Code contemplates the broadest possible relief in the bankruptcy court. Also, that history tells us that the automatic stay is one of the fundamental debtor protections provided by the bankruptcy laws. It provides a breathing spell to the debtor to restructure his affairs, which could hardly be done with hundreds or thousands of creditors persevering in different courts all over the country for a first share of a debtor's assets. Absent a stay of litigation against the debtor, dismemberment rather than reorganization would, in many or even most cases, be the inevitable result.

With those thoughts in mind, we turn to the pertinent parts of the statutes at hand. Section 362(a)(1) provides for an automatic stay of, among other things, judicial action against the debtor " . . . to recover a claim against the debtor that arose before the commencement of the case under this title." Section 101(3)(A)

---

are far from certain that her claim should not be treated as pre-petition in all events. We will assume, however, for the purposes of this case that they manifested themselves under California law a few days later when her Dalkon Shield was discovered to be in place.

defines a claim to be a "right to payment whether or not such right is reduced to judgment, liquidated, unliquidated, fixed, contingent, matured, unmatured, disputed, undisputed, legal, equitable, secured or unsecured."

The *Frenville* case, in construing these two sections, identified the crucial issue as "when did [the] right to payment arise." It found that a right to payment must exist prior to the filing of the petition, and by that the court obviously meant the right to the payment of money immediately, for it distinguished cases involving sureties which it reasoned involved a right to payment immediately upon the signing of a contract of suretyship, but contingent upon the occurrence of a future event. The court obviously was of the view, which is that espoused by Mrs. Grady and the Future Tort Claimants, that, so far as § 362 is concerned, there is no such thing as a contingent tort claim.

While we do not dispute that the result obtained in *Frenville* is not irrational, with respect, we decline to follow it, and while the numerous cases which have declined to follow *Frenville*, many of which we have referred to above, have done so for a variety of reasons, we draw our conclusion largely from the words of the statute.

Shortly after the commencement of this case, the bankruptcy court created a class of claimants called "Future Tort Claimants." While we have been unable to find an order precisely describing the class created, the notices which have been sent out by the multiplied thousands by the bankruptcy court and which were approved by order of the bankruptcy court, to which exception has not been taken, describe this class as follows:

> "Though not aware of any injury, I may have been injured by my use or another's use of the Dalkon Shield."

Code § 101(3)(A) provides for a "right to payment" whether or not "such right" is "contingent." Black's Law Dictionary 5th Ed., 1979, defines "contingent" as follows, and we adopt this definition, there being no indication that Congress meant to use the word in any other sense:

> **Contingent**. Possible, but not assured; doubtful or uncertain; conditioned upon the occurrence of some future event which is itself uncertain, or questionable. Synonymous with provisional. This term, when applied to a use, remainder, devise, bequest, or other legal right or interest, implies that no present interest exists, and that whether such interest or right ever will exist depends upon a future uncertain event.

Mrs. Grady's claim, as well as whatever rights the other Future Tort Claimants have, is undoubtedly "contingent." It depends upon a future uncertain event, that event being the manifestation of injury from use of the Dalkon Shield. We do not believe that there must be a right to the immediate payment of money in the case of a tort or allied breach of warranty or like claim, as present here, when the acts constituting the tort or breach of warranty have occurred prior to the filing of the petition, to constitute a claim under § 362(a)(1). It is at once apparent that there can be no right to the immediate payment of money on account of a claim, the existence of which depends upon a future uncertain event. But it is also apparent that Congress has created a contingent right to payment as it has the power to create a contingent tort or like claim within the protection of § 362(a)(1). We are of opinion that it has done so.

Not only do we think that a literal heading of the statute requires the result we have reached, our reading is fortified by other considerations. The broad reading of the word "claim" required by the legislative history and the cases, *see, e.g., Ohio v. Kovacs*, is considerable support. That the legislative history contemplates "the broadest possible relief in the bankruptcy court" also enters our reasoning. If Mrs. Grady and the Future Tort Claimants, who had no right to the immediate payment of money at the time of the filing of the petition, were participants in a Chapter 7 proceeding, the chances are that they would receive nothing, for no compensable result had manifested itself prior to the filing of the petition.

We also find persuasive the fact that the district court probably had authority to achieve the same result by staying Mrs. Grady's suit under 11 U.S.C. § 105(a) in the use of its equitable powers to assure the orderly conduct of reorganization proceedings.

We emphasize, as did the district court, that we do not decide whether or not Mrs. Grady's claim or those of the Future Tort Claimants are dischargeable in this case. Neither do we decide whether or not post-petition claims constitute an administrative expense. We hold only that the Dalkon Shield claim in the case before us, when the Dalkon Shield was inserted in the claimant prior to the time of filing of the petition, constitutes a "claim" "that arose before the commencement of the case" within the meaning of 11 U.S.C. § 362(a)(1).

The order appealed from is AFFIRMED.

NOTES AND COMMENTS

(1)   The court in *Grady* stated that a claim arises for bankruptcy purposes when the "conduct" that results in the claim occurs. Since the decision in *Grady*, two circuits have revisited the issue of when products liability claims arise and reached somewhat different conclusion. The debtor in *In re Piper Aircraft Corporation*, 162 B.R. 619 (Bankr. S.D. Fla.), *aff'd*, 168 B.R. 434 (Bankr. S.D. Fla. 1994), *aff'd*, 58 F.3d 1573 (11th Cir. 1995), was a manufacturer of general aviation aircraft. The burden of product-liability suits relating to accidents involving Piper aircraft forced the company into bankruptcy. A purchaser, Pilatus Aircraft Limited, wished to purchase the assets of Piper out of the bankruptcy but only if it could purchase those assets free of the product-liability claims. The problem was that between 50,000 and 60,000 Piper aircraft were still in operation as of the petition date. The court noted:

> [A]ccidents involving these aircraft undoubtedly will occur. Thus, additional though presently unidentifiable individuals will have similar product liability, property damage or other claims as a result of incidents occurring after confirmation of the Debtor's Chapter 11 plan of reorganization, but arising out of or relating to aircraft or parts manufactured, sold, designed, or distributed by the Debtor prior to confirmation.

Id. at 621. The court noted "that the Conduct Test may define a § 101(5) claim too broadly in some situations," *id.* at 625, and articulated a "relationship" test, saying:

We know that some planes in the existing fleet of Piper aircraft will crash, and we know that there may be injuries, deaths and property damage as a result. We also know that under theories of negligence and products liability, Piper, if it remains in existence, would be liable for some of these damages. Even so, there is no way to identify who the victims will be or to identify any particular prepetition contact, exposure, impact, privity or other relationship between Piper and these potential claimants that will give rise to these future damages.

. . . .

The Conduct Test and the Relationship Test are not mutually exclusive theories. Requiring that there be some prepetition relationship between the Debtor and claimant would not change the analysis or results of the Conduct Test cases. In fact, such a requirement appears to be implicit in those decisions. In the asbestos cases, the future claimants were individuals who were known to have had prepetition exposure to the dangerous product. *See, e.g., Waterman*, 141 B.R. at 556 (claims arose "at the moment the asbestos claimants came into contact with the asbestos"). Likewise, in *A.H. Robins*, the court determined that the claim arose when the claimant was inserted with a Dalkon Shield. *Grady v. A.H. Robins Co.*, 839 F.2d at 203. And in *Edge*, the court noted that the Bankruptcy Code recognizes a claim for the victim of prepetition misconduct "at the earliest point in the relationship between victim and wrongdoer." *Edge*, 60 B.R. at 699. Thus, the Conduct Test cases presume not only that there was prepetition conduct, but also that there was some prepetition relationship between the debtor's conduct and the claimant.

The theories advanced by prior cases exploring the outer limits of the concept of claim, when thus reconciled, lead to the conclusion that in order for a future claimant to have a "claim" under § 101(5), there must be some prepetition relationship, such as contact, exposure, impact, or privity, between the debtor's prepetition conduct and the claimant. This is not to suggest that any and every prepetition relationship will give rise to a claim. Rather, a prepetition relationship connecting the conduct to the claimant is a threshold requirement.

. . . .

Pilatus and the Legal Representative also argue that all individuals injured from Piper aircraft manufactured before confirmation should be treated equally, regardless of whether their injuries occur pre-confirmation or post-confirmation. Determining that the Future Claimants do not hold "claims," they argue, would cause disparate treatment based solely on the fortuity of when a crash occurs. This argument is framed by a hypothetical: Should crash victim Jones be able to share in plan distributions if his plane crashes pre-confirmation, while crash victim Smith receives nothing under the plan if his plane crashes post-confirmation?

The Court concludes that the answer is yes, their treatment can and should be different. In bankruptcy, as in life, timing matters. There is a major distinction between Jones and Smith. Jones can be identified presently; Smith cannot. Jones knows that he has a claim against Piper; Smith does not.

Id. at 625–29. The Eleventh Circuit affirmed the bankruptcy court decision in *Piper*, but refined the "relationship" test slightly, stating that the events which create the relationship can occur any time before the *confirmation* of the plan.

The Fifth Circuit Court of Appeals purported to adopt the "relationship" test in *Lemelle v. Universal Mfg. Co.*, 18 F.3d 1268 (5th Cir. 1994), a case involving a mobile home fire. There the court said:

> The injury suffered, i.e., the death of the decedents, occurred simultaneously with the manifestation of that injury in December 1985, years after Winston's reorganization plan had been confirmed. The design and manufacture of the mobile home in question thus resulted in no tortious consequence until a fire started in that mobile home in December 1985. Further, there is no evidence in the record to indicate when Forbes and her family acquired this mobile home or from whom they acquired it. There is no evidence to establish that Winston, as the manufacturer of the mobile home in question, should have even known of Forbes' and her family's existence.
>
> Where, as here, the injury and the manifestation of that injury occurred simultaneously — more than three years after Winston filed its petition and more than two years after the plan was confirmed, we think that, at a minimum, there must be evidence that would permit the debtor to identify, during the course of the bankruptcy proceedings, potential victims and thereby permit notice to these potential victims of the pendency of the proceedings. *See Chateaugay*, 944 F.2d at 1003; *Piper*, 162 B.R. at 628. This record is devoid of any evidence of any pre-petition contact, privity, or other relationship between Winston, on the one hand, and Forbes or the decedents, on the other. We think the absence of this evidence precludes a finding by the district court that the claims asserted by Forbes were discharged in Winston's bankruptcy proceedings. *See Chateaugay*, 944 F.2d at 1005; *Piper*, 162 B.R. at 627; *Gypsum*, 139 B.R. at 409.

Id. at 1277. Is the Eleventh Circuit test consistent with the Fifth Circuit test?

Which approach is more likely to facilitate the reorganization of Amphy? Which approach makes better sense from a policy standpoint?

§ 3.06   RELIEF FROM THE AUTOMATIC STAY: INTRODUCTION

"So," Headley, says to you, "the automatic stay prevents creditors from seizing Amphy's assets, but what good does that do us? What can we do with them?" "Good question," you say. "The benefits of the automatic stay would be illusory if, in a Chapter 11 case, a trustee or debtor in possession were unable to use such property to advance the rehabilitation of the business. For example, assume that BigBank, which loaned money to Amphy, has a security interest in Amphy's inventory and the proceeds thereof. Staying the bank from enforcing its security interest in the inventory would be meaningless if Amphy were not allowed to sell the inventory to its customers. Moreover, enjoining the bank from enforcing its security interest in the proceeds generated by the sale of the inventory would also be futile if Amphy could not deploy the proceeds in the ongoing business."

"Boy, if I were a creditor I'd be hopping mad," says Headley. "Can we use bankruptcy to keep the creditors at bay indefinitely?" "No," you say. "Generally, the automatic stay continues in effect until a case is closed, dismissed, or a discharge is granted or denied.[1] The automatic stay of actions against property of the estate continues in effect until the property ceases being property of the estate."[2]

"Gee," says Headley, "that could be a long time. Does this mean that secured creditors or other third parties having interests in property of the estate must wait and pray while the debtor has its way with the property?"

"Not quite," you say. "As one judge laconically observed, 'even secured parties have rights'[3] and these rights are safeguarded by three sections of the Code that operate in unison."

1. One is Code § 363, which governs what the debtor or trustee may do with property while the automatic stay is in effect. It also gives the court the power to condition the debtor's continued use of property on the debtor's ability to adequately protect the interest of another entity in the property.

2. The second is Code § 361, which sets forth a non-exclusive list of ways in which "adequate protection" may be provided.

3. Finally, in the event the debtor or trustee is unable to provide the necessary "adequate protection," Code § 362(d)(1) authorizes the court to lift the stay and allow the creditor to enforce its interest in the property. Section 362(d)(2) also authorizes relief from the stay of actions against property when (a) the debtor has no equity in the property; and (b) the property is not necessary to the debtor's reorganization.

The operation of these sections is examined in the materials that follow.

§ 3.07 THE CONCEPT OF ADEQUATE PROTECTION

[A] Periodic Payments

PROBLEM 3.9

You will recall that Amphy's subsidiary Metal Case, Inc. is in the business of reclaiming precious metals — such as gold, silver, platinum, palladium, and copper — from discarded computers and electronic equipment. The recycled metals are

---

[1] *See* Code § 362(c)(2).

[2] *See* Code § 362(c)(1).

[3] *In re Groundhog Mountain Corp.*, 1975 U.S. Dist. LEXIS 16792, at *14 (Bankr. S.D.N.Y. May 6, 1975).

then resold. Metal Case's business planners have always viewed Japan as the primary market for their recycled metal products, but trade talks between Japan and the United States have not progressed as quickly as the company's business planners had hoped.

Metal Case financed its production equipment purchases through a loan from MegaBank to Metal Case and Amphy as co-borrowers. The bank holds a security interest in the equipment. The loan agreement, which the parties made a few years ago, provides for fluctuating interest payments at a rate two points above prime. When Amphy entered into this agreement, it was able to handle the debt service. However, at current rates, which are unexpectedly higher, Amphy finds it impossible to make payments, and the loan is in default.

Soon after Amphy filed its Chapter 11 petition, Mega Bank moved, pursuant to Code § 362(d)(1) and Bankruptcy Rule 9014, for relief from the automatic stay in order to enforce its security interest. In support of its motion, it alleged the following:

1. The debtor owes MegaBank $15,000,000.

2. The equipment securing the debt has a "liquidation value" of $13,000,000, and the value appears to be stable.

3. During the period following the commencement of the Chapter 11 case, Metal Case has made no payments to MegaBank.

4. MegaBank's interest is not "adequately protected."

5. Therefore, MegaBank should be granted relief from the stay so that it may foreclose its lien on the property.

Assume that the debtor cannot make payments at the contracted rate. Is MegaBank entitled to relief from the stay? Is the Bank's interest "adequately protected"? What if the value of the equipment appears to be declining at a rate of 10% a year? Short of ordering the debtor to make payments in accordance with the loan agreement, what relief can the court order to provide that the bank is adequately protected?

Read on.

IN RE BERMEC CORP.
United States Court of Appeals, Second Circuit
445 F.2d 367 (1971)

Before MANSFIELD, CIRCUIT JUDGE, MACMAHON AND GURFEIN, DISTRICT JUDGES

PER CURIAM

On March 29, 1971 Bermec Corporation ("Bermec") filed a petition under Chapter XI of the Bankruptcy Act, and by order of the District Court was permitted to remain as debtor-in-possession. On April 16, 1971, Bermec, with the permission of the District Court, filed an amended petition under Chapter X of the Bankruptcy Act. Secured creditors of Bermec, including appellants Pacar Financial Corp.

("Pacar"), White Motor Corp. ("White"), International Harvester Credit Corp. ("Harvester"), and Ford Motor Credit Corp. ("Ford"), opposed the Chapter X petition on the ground that it was not "filed in good faith" because "it is unreasonable to expect that a plan of reorganization can be effected."

Judge Metzner appointed Referee in Bankruptcy Herzog as a Special Master to hear and report on the approval of the petition, pursuant to the statutory requirement that "the District Court shall enter an order approving the petition if satisfied that it complies with the requirements of this chapter and has been filed in good faith and the material allegations are sustained by the proofs, or dismissing it if not so satisfied" (11 U.S.C. Section 544). The Special Master held a hearing upon notice at which two witnesses testified — Herbert Degnan, the President of the Debtor, on behalf of the petitioner, and Robert W. Anderson, a consultant of Ryder Systems, an expert in the lease trucking industry, on behalf of the objecting secured creditors. The Special Master filed a report in which he reviewed the evidence and found that it is not unreasonable to expect that a plan of reorganization can be effected and that the petition was filed in good faith. He recommended that an order be entered, approving the petition. On motion by the Debtor to confirm the Special Master's Report, Judge Metzner made the recommended order approving the petition. Pacar, Harvester, Ford and White, secured creditors, appealed from the order. We affirm.

Bermec is engaged in the business of leasing trucks and tractor-trailers throughout the United States and Canada. It operates 65 maintenance terminals. It has 600 employees with a monthly payroll of $500,000. There are approximately 15,000 shareholders. During the last four years it has sustained substantial operating losses and is presently unable to meet its obligations. The Special Master also found that Bermec is insolvent.

The Special Master noted that the manufacturing group of secured creditors which includes appellants are opposed to any reorganization that would not provide complete and immediate payment of the secured indebtedness and contend that their collateral is depreciating rapidly and quick enforcement of their liens is essential for their protection. He found, however, that despite present losses of $500,000 each month, certain affirmative steps can be taken which could result in a profitable or at least a break-even operation. Among the steps that can be taken by the Trustees according to Degnan's testimony were the following: (1) the favorable renegotiation of certain unprofitable rental-of-equipment contracts under the threat of rejection by the Trustees; (2) revenue improvement by a substantial seasonal increase in revenues in the ensuing Summer months; (3) the sale of excess equipment which could result in substantial operating savings; (4) savings on revenues arising from escalation clauses; (5) more effective fuel control; and (6) anticipated new business which would produce a large percentage of profit because fixed costs would already have been met. The Special Master accepted these estimates as reasonable after reviewing the testimony of Mr. Anderson as well. The District Court confirmed the findings.

. . . .

Appellants argue that the petitioner has failed to show that it is reasonable to expect that a plan of reorganization can be effected in this case. Upon a review of the evidence we do not agree. A specific plan of reorganization need not be contained in the petition. "The petitioner need only demonstrate that there exists a reasonable possibility of successful reorganization." *See Grubbs v. Pettit*, [282 F.2d 557 (2 Cir. 1960)]; *Matter of Castle Beach Apartments, Inc.*, 113 F.2d 762 (2 Cir. 1940).

We are conscious of the deep concern of the manufacturing secured creditors lest their security depreciate beyond adequate salvage, but we must balance that with the Congressional mandate to encourage attempts at corporate reorganization where there is a reasonable possibility of success. Nor can we find clearly erroneous the finding that the Trustees will be able to pay the "economic depreciation" on the secured creditors' equipment so as approximately to preserve their status quo. In sum, we cannot find the prospect so hopeless as to require setting aside the order below as might have been required in a case where there was, indeed, no reasonable possibility of a successful reorganization.

While the expressed intention of certain secured creditors to reject any plan that does not provide full payment must be weighed, the intention is not enough to defeat the petition. Creditors have been known to change their minds when a plan is actually put on the table. Furthermore, means might in any event be found to pay off such creditors as remain adamant. (*Wachovia Bank & Trust Co. v. Dameron*, 406 F.2d 803 (4 Cir. 1969); *Corr v. Flora Sun Corp.*, 317 F.2d 708 (5 Cir. 1963).)

The order is affirmed.

NOTES AND QUESTIONS

(1) *Legislative History.* The *Bermec* opinion is the inspiration for the method of adequate protection outlined in Code § 361(1). According to the Code's legislative history:

> The first method of adequate protection outlined is the making of cash payments to compensate for the expected decrease in value of the opposing entity's interest. This provision is derived from *In re Bermec Corporation*, 445 F.2d 367 (2d Cir. 1971), though in that case it is not clear whether the payments offered were adequate to compensate the secured creditors for their loss. The use of periodic payments may be appropriate where, for example, the property in question is depreciating at a relatively fixed rate. The periodic payments would be to compensate for the depreciation and might, but need not necessarily, be in the same amount as payments due on the secured obligation.

S. Rep. No. 95-989, at 54 (1978).

(2) *Calculating Payments.* Although the Second Circuit opinion does not mention it, the Bermec trustee proposed to make monthly payments to secured creditors of 12 percent per annum of the original cost of trucks and 10 percent per annum of the original cost of trailers. Bankruptcy "referee" Asa Herzog (as he was then known) described the process by which the payment scheme was formulated this way:

The trustee recognizes the propriety of adopting some measure of protection for the secured creditors during the period of reorganization. There is merit to the contention that use of the trucks and trailers by the debtor's lessees, as well as the mere passage of time, will depreciate their value.

. . . .

The trustee's proposal is that the value of the security be maintained by payment of a sum equivalent to actual current depreciation of the value of the rolling stock. The testimony of the debtor's president . . . was to the effect that the present estimated rate of economic depreciation spread levelly against the remaining useful life of the vehicles is 12 percent per annum for the power equipment, and 10 percent for the trailers of the original cost of the vehicles. This testimony was not contradicted by any evidence adduced by the secured creditors. In his brief, the trustee projects a monthly cash flow of $675,000 which he estimates will be sufficient to permit payment to the secured creditors of the amount of the economic depreciation of the equipment securing their claims. He also sets forth a program whereby current monthly payments will be made and whereby [certain missed] payments will be made up. This, I am satisfied, is a fair and equitable method of protecting the interests of the secured creditors.

In re Bermec Corp., No. 71-B-0291 (Bankr. S.D.N.Y. July 15, 1971). Observe that although the trustee used the actual cost of the equipment as the basis for calculating monthly depreciation, it is not clear from the opinion whether the standard against which any decline in value was to be measured was: (1) the actual cost of the equipment, (2) the value of the equipment at the time the reorganization petition was filed, or (3) the value of the equipment at the time relief from the stay was sought. Which standard do you think is appropriate? The Code's legislative history states that adequate protection "is intended to protect a creditor's allowed secured claim," 124 Cong. Rec. 32,395 (1978) (remarks of Rep. Edwards), and Code § 506(a) provides that:

An allowed claim of a creditor secured by a lien on property in which the estate has an interest . . . is a secured claim to the extent of the value of such creditor's interest in the estate's interest in such property . . . and is an unsecured claim to the extent that the value of such creditor's interest . . . is less than the amount of such allowed claim.

Does this suggest an answer? In *In re Wolsky*, 46 B.R. 262 (Bankr. D.N.D. 1984), the debtors proposed to compensate a secured creditor for any depreciation in the value of equipment which occurred during the interim between the creditor's motion for relief from the stay and the confirmation of a reorganization plan. The court found such compensation inadequate. It held that in order to provide adequate protection, the debtors had to provide compensation for decreases that occurred after the commencement of the Chapter 11 case. This is consistent with the approach taken in *In re Alyucan Interstate Props., Inc.*, reprinted below.

[B] Replacement Liens

PROBLEM 3.10

The adequate protection approach prescribed in Code § 361(1) and the *Bermec* case will not work in every context. For one thing, a debtor whose cash flow is insufficient to service regular installment payments may not be in a position to meet regular "economic depreciation" payments either. Moreover, although depreciation payments seem appropriate where fixed, regularly depreciating assets (such as land, buildings, machinery, and equipment) are involved, depreciation payments are not practical where rapidly depreciating or perishable current assets (such as inventory or accounts receivable) are at risk. Inventory is subject to use and sale as well as to deterioration, obsolescence, and decline in price due to market changes. With the passage of time, receivables also may become partly or totally worthless and have to be written off.

Assume that in order to raise cash to meet operating expenses, Amphy borrowed $10,000,000 from BigBank and granted the bank a security interest in existing and after-acquired inventory and proceeds. When an unanticipated shutdown of foreign markets slowed sales, Amphy found it impossible to make any payments whatsoever to BigBank out of operating income. However, inasmuch as Amphy owned its manufacturing plant outright, it decided to attempt to sell the building and lease it back in order to raise cash. Although Amphy failed to find a buyer in time to avoid Chapter 11, appraisers say the fair market value of the plant is about $7,000,000. They also say the property would bring in considerably less if sold at a bankruptcy auction.

BigBank, too, has moved for relief from the stay so that it may sell the inventory and begin collecting Amphy's accounts receivable. In support of its motion, it alleges the following:

1. Amphy owes the bank $10,000,000.

2. The inventory securing the debt has a liquidation value of $5,000,000, and the accounts receivable have a value of $2,000,000. The manufacturing equipment is worth an estimated $1,000,000.

3. Amphy is three months in arrears on installment payments and has made no payments since the Chapter 11 case was commenced.

4. The bank's interest is not adequately protected.

5. Therefore, the automatic stay should be lifted in order to permit the bank to enforce its security interest.

Given Amphy's inability to make payments on the BigBank loan out of operating revenue and its inability (to date) to generate any revenue by selling the warehouse, is relief from the stay to permit BigBank to enforce its security interest in Amphy's inventory and accounts inevitable?

Read Code § 361(2), the *In re American Kitchen Foods* opinion, which follows, and the notes following the opinion.

IN RE AMERICAN KITCHEN FOODS, INC.
United States Bankruptcy Court, District of Maine
1976 Bankr. LEXIS 6 (1976)

CYR, BANKRUPTCY JUDGE

American Kitchen Foods, Inc. (Delaware), hereinafter referred to as American Kitchen Foods [AKF], a holding company, filed its original Chapter XI petition with this court, along with eight of its first and second tier subsidiaries, on October 17, 1975. The defendants were principally engaged in raising, purchasing and processing potatoes and other vegetables for the retail and institutional markets. The schedules reflect assets with a book value of $46,000,000 and liabilities approximating $44,000,000 on a consolidated basis.

American Kitchen Foods is a publicly held corporation whose stock, until immediately prior to the inception of these proceedings, was traded on the American Stock Exchange. The defendants own and operate potato and vegetable processing facilities in Caribou and Presque Isle, Maine, as well as in Grand Forks, North Dakota. The defendants have employed upward of 5,000 employees, in Maine, Minnesota and North Dakota, and are of considerable local importance, particularly in Maine. The evidence adduced to date indicates that the Maine processing operations have been generally profitable, whereas expansion into the midwest resulted in a disastrous capital drain, perhaps amounting to as much as $25,000,000 over the past several years. Except for the Maine processing and refrigeration facilities, which have already achieved profitability on a fiscal year basis, the defendants plan to pare all remaining properties and business interests.

The claims of Chemical Bank and First Pennsylvania Bank, N.A. aggregated about $11,400,000 on October 17, 1975 . . . . The loans were allegedly cross-collateralized and secured by first liens on accounts receivable, proceeds, contract rights and other intangible personal property of the defendants, including pledges of the stock of AFK subsidiaries; all raw and processed inventory and proceeds; the processing plant, equipment and fixtures located in Grand Forks; and a second and third real estate mortgage on the Grand Forks refrigeration plant.

Immediately before the filing of the original petitions, the plaintiffs implemented default procedures interdicting the defendants' cash flow from accounts receivable, inventory and proceeds. There was no cash to defray the cost of essential services like labor, electricity and fuel, without which business operations could not continue and substantial losses would surely ensue as a result of the inevitable deterioration of perishable inventories. A $170,000 payroll was past due, exclusive of tax withholdings. Defendants were in arrears for vital utility services as well. Upon filing their petitions, the defendants represented to the court that operations could not continue unless cash flow was resumed immediately.

Counsel for American Kitchen Foods appeared before the court (along with plaintiff's counsel) at the time the original petitions were filed and requested . . . permission to retain and use the collateral claimed by the plaintiffs in order to generate urgently needed operating funds. The defendants further demanded immediate revocation of the lien enforcement notification given to account debtors and inventory warehousemen, by the plaintiffs, as well as the release of a much smaller sum recovered by the plaintiffs before the commencement of the proceedings. The court entered the operating order, including provision for the requested relief, over the objection of the plaintiffs, after hearing the arguments and representations of all counsel at considerable length.[4]

Defendants argued that the collateral was worth far more than the amount of the plaintiffs' secured claims. They basically contended for a going-concern collateral valuation standard. Accounts receivable were valued by the defendants at $3,500,000; inventory at cost was represented at $7,200,000[5] and the Grand Forks real and personal property was valued at $9,400,000. Defendants represented that fresh potato inventory and new packaging materials were worth $400,000 and $1,500,000, respectively. The plaintiffs, on the other hand, employing a liquidation valuation standard, were not prepared to concede that the collateral was worth anything approaching the amount of their claims.

The court determined that the valuations ascribed by the debtors far more nearly approached the aggregate true conversion value of the collateral. The debtors tendered and the court authorized certain additional collateral to indemnify

---

[4] "The debtors in possession be and they hereby are authorized in the operation of their businesses, and until further order of this court (a) to sell inventories, merchandise and products of every kind and description now held by the debtors and hereafter produced or acquired in the ordinary course of business and collect and use the proceeds thereof, in whatever form, and (b) to collect and realize upon all accounts, proceeds, contract rights and chattel paper, now and hereafter owned by the debtors, and to use the proceeds thereof (including any proceeds constituting collateral for any secured creditor at the time of such filing) in whatever form; provided however that the debtors in possession shall report in writing to any creditor claiming a lien or other security interest in or to any inventory, accounts, contract rights, chattel paper or proceeds, as to the creation, collection and disposition of any and all inventory, on a weekly basis, and, mailed on a daily basis, with respect to accounts receivables, including credits, freights and discounts with respect thereto.

"That to the extent use is made of such assets and proceeds, the claim of any creditor holding or entitled to the benefit of a valid security interest therein shall constitute a valid and enforceable secured claim against the assets of the debtors in possession whether now existing or hereafter acquired, and shall be entitled to priority in payment as an expense of administration, secured (subject to valid liens existing at the time of filing of the petitions herein as to which the lien herein granted has not been substituted) by all property of the debtors in possession, including but not limited to inventories, merchandise, accounts, contract rights, chattel paper, instruments, securities, general intangibles, equipment and fixtures, and real property and the proceeds thereof of the debtors in possession (whether received by it from the debtors or acquired on or after the date of filing of the petitions herein).

"That until further order of this court the debtors in possession shall be entitled to sell, collect and use such inventory, merchandise products, accounts and proceeds in the operations of their businesses, and it is further provided that any creditor claiming to be the holder of a security interest affected hereby may commence proceedings in this court on notice to the debtors in possession and such other persons as the court may designate for a termination of the authorization herein made for the continued use of all of such assets by the debtors in possession and for such protective provisions with respect thereto as the court may deem appropriate."

¶¶ 15, 16 & 17, "Order Authorizing Debtors to Remain in Possession and to Operate Business," entered October 17, 1975.

[5] Cost approximated $.17 per pound, market value about $.25 per pound.

the plaintiffs against any diminution of their collateral as a result of its continuing retention and use by the defendants. Most important among the additional assets subjected to the plaintiffs' liens as a safeguard against diminution are the huge, fully equipped and operating processing plants at Presque Isle and Caribou, Maine. The unencumbered Presque Isle facilities alone have a value of between $6,000,000 and $15,000,000. There were other unencumbered assets, including thousands of acres of valuable farm lands, as well as more than $1,000,000 worth of farm machinery.

A Collateral Valuation Standard

At this stage in the discussion it becomes apparent that the principal judgmental problems involved in lien impairment litigation in Chapter XI proceedings ultimately relate to the valuation of the collateral as at the date of the original petition, as of the time of trial on the complaint for relief from stay and, finally, at whatever point in time the collateral is recovered by the secured party for application to the debt. The former task involves judicial hindsight and is therefore easier, as a rule, then where neither the amount nor the condition of the collateral can be confidently forecast due to the not inconsiderable uncertainty surrounding rehabilitation efforts and, even more important, the precise point in time when the collateral is to be converted into cash or its equivalent.

It is a rare Chapter XI proceeding in which the rub does not come over exactly such valuation issues. The debtor is on the brink of a shutdown in operations, which can only be averted by permitting it to continue to utilize the collateral, including, in many instances, proceeds from inventory and accounts receivable, to defray the costs of the continued operations, whether overhead, operating or both. The difficulty is increased by the fact that it sometimes serves the interests of secured creditors to attempt to whipsaw the debtor by insisting upon a going-concern or fair-market valuation at the commencement of the proceedings, but a forced-sale valuation later on, in order to demonstrate more extensive collateral depletion or diminution following the petition. A secured creditor is then better positioned to assert that retention and use of the collateral by the debtor has rendered the secured creditor an involuntary lender entitled to priority payment from the estate for the impairment of its lien.

Without question judicial assessment of the elusive intangibles invariably involved in projecting possible future collateral impairment risk is an inescapably crude and uncertain process. It is also undeniable that debtor rehabilitation often would be foreclosed entirely were there an absolute bar to venturing any collateral erosion whatever. Often, recourse to a realistic and consistent valuation standard would demonstrate that the debtor is merely making use of the collateral margin, viz., the amount by which the value of the collateral exceeds the debt it secures; in other words, the equity.

"Liquidation" Value

The court must consider whether liquidation or some other valuation standard is more appropriate for measuring collateral margin and diminution in Chapter XI arrangement proceedings. . . . While a forced-sale standard for appraising collateral may comport with the economic realities in ordinary bankruptcy [liquidation] proceedings, it may be altogether unsuitable in circumstances where the collateral consists of inventory and accounts, and the debtor continues to operate, and where reasonable prospects persist that it can continue to generate and collect accounts receivable and sell and replace inventories in the ordinary course.

A Standard Based On Commercial Reasonableness

In the event of default and subject to the provisions of its contract, a secured creditor is entitled to convert [liquidate] its collateral into cash for application to its debt pursuant to local law. Where the collateral consists of personal property, its conversion value is the net amount recoverable from a sale or other disposition conducted in a commercially reasonable manner pursuant to [a state's enacted version of UCC Article 9, part 6 (UCC § 9-601 *et. seq.*) — Eds.]; in the case of real estate collateral, it is the net amount recoverable in a mortgage foreclosure sale.

It is misleading to describe the disposition of collateral as a "liquidation," except in the sense that it may accomplish a conversion of the collateral from an illiquid to a liquid state. "Liquidation" value in a collateral conversion context is not necessarily a with "forced sale" value; particularly is that so since the universal adoption of the Uniform Commercial Code, which provides significant safeguards for ensuring improved recoveries from collateral dispositions conducted by secured parties. The more noteworthy Uniform Commercial Code safeguards are the important notice and redemption rights accorded the debtor and other secured parties, which mandate that every disposition be conducted in a commercially reasonable manner. While the Uniform Commercial Code expressly rejects the notion that a sale be deemed not to have been made in a commercially reasonable manner solely because a better price could have been obtained, it is very evident purpose was to curb the cozy practice accounting for the dismal recoveries commonly achieved in the past through public or private sales at which the secured party often obtained the collateral "for a song" because its voice alone was raised in the bidding.

The commercial reasonableness requirement currently imposed on virtually all collateral dispositions involving personal property is no less appropriate for Chapter XI collateral impairment valuation purposes.

. . . .

The customary practice in bankruptcy courts has been to use forced sale valuations for all appraisals, without sufficient regard to the nature of the proceedings. But the bankruptcy court is neither constitutionally nor otherwise required to reject more commercially reasonable collateral conversion methods in preference for forced sales at levels which substantially worsen the losses of all parties to the proceedings, including the secured party.

The competitive chill generated by forced sales is notorious and relentless. Forced-sale valuations should be confined to use in cases where the circumstances of the debtor and the nature and condition of the collateral and its marketplace leave no commercially reasonable alternative. Where there is no practicable alternative except to submit to the influence of bargain basement buyers sanguine in the knowledge that salvage recoveries will reward their wait, "judicial sales" may be appropriately associated with forced-sale or liquidation recoveries, which is commonly the case in ordinary bankruptcy proceedings where collateral must be disposed of almost immediately, "as is" and at minimal expense.

But where circumstances are such, as they assuredly are in this case, that the debtor continues to operate as a going concern, that the collateral is being preserved in excellent condition, and where active retail and institutional markets continue to support an average markup for the debtors' products approximating one-third over cost, valuation at forced sale levels would constitute a clear repudiation of the commercial realities. There can be no question but that the debtors' inventory, accounts receivable, equipment and other chattel collateral can be converted into cash in the orderly course of its business at prices ranging from 30% to 80% above forced sale recovery levels.

A forced sale in these circumstances could not be considered commercially reasonable. Even outside the rehabilitative framework of Chapter XI, it would seem that a secured party attempting it could be restrained under the Uniform Commercial Code. Arbitrary indulgence of the forced sale fiction is neither necessary nor warranted merely because the debtor's business continues under the auspices of Chapter XI. Where collateral is used or produced under Chapter XI by a going business which offers reasonable prospects that it can continue, the value of the collateral is equitable with the net recovery realizable from its disposition as near as may be in the ordinary course of the business.

It is little more than the articulation of an unexceptional business judgment to hold that, wherever practicable, conversion in the ordinary course of business should be considered the most commercially reasonable collateral disposition, simply because and to the extent that it is more productive. Where collateral includes inventory and receivables the distinction can be of enormous significance. While its business is operating, a Chapter XI debtor can continue to convert receivables at face value and sell inventory at market. Once business operations cease, receivables and inventory will return only a disappointing fraction of their value, particularly if they have to be liquidated in ordinary bankruptcy proceedings. It would be inept to ignore and prodigal to decline that collateral margin in the rehabilitation process.

A Uniform Collateral Valuation Standard

Whatever merit commends selection of the most economically realistic collateral valuation standard available in the circumstances of a given arrangement proceeding militates just as persuasively in favor of its consistent enforcement in respect to the same collateral throughout the proceedings. Consistency in collateral valuation obviously does not mean that collateral will be assigned the same value throughout the proceedings as at their commencement, but merely that the most commercially reasonable disposition practicable in the circumstances should be the standard universally applicable in all cases and at every phase of each case.

Debtors in possession, receivers or trustees should not be facilitated in their efforts to foist upon the secured party the risk of collateral depletion or diminution, including the risk of diminution due to declines in market value, where the collateral was retained at the instance and for the benefit of the debtor, rather than the secured party. The controlling concept is one of fundamental fair play. The risk of loss should pass from the party in jeopardy to the one who placed him there. A secured party isolated from its collateral is entitled to recoup losses occasioned by the depletion and diminution of its collateral from the inception of the arrangement proceedings to the abandonment or reclamation of the collateral or to the adjudication or dismissal of the arrangement proceedings.

The measurement of collateral margin and diminution in Chapter XI arrangement proceedings should consist of an informed projection as to the net amounts recoverable upon conversion of the collateral into cash in a commercially reasonable manner, under whatever legal and economic conditions are then known or may reasonably be presumed to exist. In measuring collateral diminution, actual conversion should be conducted subject to the direction of the court, with a view to maximizing recoveries. The diminution (appreciation) should approximate the difference between the net collateral value assigned as at the initiation of the proceedings and the actual or projected net recoveries from a commercially reasonable disposition under court direction. Conversely, collateral margin or equity at the commencement of the proceedings consists of the amount by which projected net recoveries from a commercially reasonable disposition exceed the debt secured.

NOTES AND QUESTIONS

(1) *Replacement Liens.* The *American Kitchen Foods* case arose under the former Bankruptcy Act, but it demonstrates the method of adequate protection authorized by Code § 361(2). That section provides that adequate protection may be provided by the granting of "an additional or replacement lien" to the extent that the debtor's use, sale, or lease of property results in a decrease in the value of the property. As the legislative history explains, "The purpose of this method is to provide the protected entity with a means of realizing the value of the original property, if it should decline during the case, by granting an interest in additional property from whose value the entity may realize its loss." H.R. Rep. No. 95-595, at 339-340 (1977). The "additional property" in which a security interest was granted in *American Kitchen Foods* included two "huge, fully equipped and operating processing plants," "thousands of acres of valuable farm lands," and "more than $1,000,000 worth of farm machinery."

(2) *Security Interests in After-Acquired Property and Proceeds.* In *American Kitchen Foods*, the debtors, prior to filing their Chapter XI petitions, had granted the banks a security interest in, inter alia, inventory, equipment, receivables, and the proceeds thereof. It also appears that the security agreement between the debtors and the banks gave the banks a security interest in after-acquired property. The effect of bankruptcy on such after-acquired property clauses is governed by Code § 552.

Section 552(a), which codifies prior case law, generally provides that property acquired after the commencement of the case is not subject to any lien resulting from a security agreement entered into by the debtor before the commencement of the case. For example, assume that on January 1, Amphy granted the bank a security interest in "all inventory now owned and hereafter acquired." Assume further that on June 1, Amphy filed its Chapter 11 petition and that one week later it received and took title to a shipment of inventory. Even though Uniform Commercial Code § 9-204 authorizes the granting of security interests in after-acquired property, Bankruptcy Code § 552(a) nullifies the security interest with respect to property acquired after a bankruptcy filing. Thus, no security interest would attach to the inventory Amphy acquired a week after the filing.

Suppose however, that Amphy had granted the bank a security interest in "inventory and the proceeds thereof." U.C.C. § 9-306(1) defines "proceeds" as "whatever is received upon the sale, collection or other disposition of collateral or proceeds. Insurance payable by reason of loss or damage to the collateral is proceeds, except to the extent that it is payable to a person other than a party to the security agreement. Money, checks, deposit accounts, and the like are 'cash proceeds.' All other proceeds are 'non-cash proceeds.' " U.C.C. § 9-306(4) sets forth rules for identifying proceeds in the event of a debtor's insolvency.

Would a security interest in proceeds coming into existence after the commencement of the case also be nullified? The answer is no, because § 552(b) provides an exception to the general rule expressed in § 552(a). Section 552(b) provides that if a security agreement extends to proceeds, product, offspring, rents, or profits of property that the debtor had before the commencement of the case, then such proceeds, product, offspring, rents, or profits are subject to the security interest. For example, assume that on May 30, Amphy owned $1,000,000 worth of inventory. On June 1 Amphy filed its Chapter 11 petition. On June 3, it sold $500,000 worth of that inventory to a customer on credit, creating an account receivable. Because the bank had a security interest in prepetition inventory and its proceeds, and because the account receivable represents proceeds of the inventory, the bank has a valid and enforceable security interest in the account receivable. On the other hand, had Amphy filed its Chapter 11 petition on June 1, taken title to inventory on June 2, and sold the inventory on June 3, the bank would not have a security interest in the proceeds of the June 3 sale.

Of course, even though § 552(b) validates security interests in postpetition proceeds of prepetition collateral, such interests may not be enforced absent relief from the automatic stay. As you can readily imagine, most debtors will want to redeploy proceeds in the business — to purchase new inventory, to pay salaries, and to meet other operating expenses.

(3) *Valuation of Property.* As the *American Kitchen Foods* opinion makes clear, the determination of whether a secured creditor is adequately protected will routinely require a valuation of the property securing the claim, but the valuation process is anything but routine. Neither Code § 361, governing adequate protection, nor Code § 362, governing the automatic stay, prescribe a method for valuing property. The omission is described in the legislative history this way:

> The section specifies four means of providing adequate protection. They are neither exclusive nor exhaustive. They all rely, however, on the value of the protected entity's interest in the property involved. The section does not specify how value is to be determined, nor does it specify when it is to be

determined. These matters are left to case-by-case interpretation and development. It is expected that the courts will apply the concept in light of facts of each case and general equitable principles. It is not intended that the courts will develop a hard and fast rule that will apply in every case. The time and method of valuation is not specified precisely, in order to avoid that result. There are an infinite number of variations possible in dealings between debtors and creditors, the law is continually developing, and new ideas are continually being implemented in this field. The flexibility is important to permit the courts to adapt to varying circumstances and changing modes of financing.

Neither is it expected that the courts will construe the term value to mean, in every case, forced liquidation value or full going concern value. There is wide latitude between those two extremes. In any particular case, especially a reorganization case, the determination of which entity should be entitled to the difference between the going concern value and the liquidation value must be based on equitable considerations based on the facts of the case. It will frequently be based on negotiation between the parties. Only if they cannot agree will the court become involved.

H.R. Rep. No. 95-595, at 339 (1977) at 339. Thus, the standard of "commercial reasonableness" propounded by Judge Cyr in *American Kitchen Foods* seems to have been endorsed by the drafters of the Code. *See also Assocs. Commercial Corp. v. Rash*, 520 U.S. 953 (1997), reprinted in Chapter 8, § 8.04[B].

(4)   *The Whipsaw.* Judge Cyr observed that one difficulty in valuing property in reorganization cases arises from the fact that it sometimes serves the interests of secured creditors to attempt to whipsaw the debtor by insisting on a going concern or fair market valuation at the commencement of the proceedings, but a forced sale valuation later on, in order to demonstrate more extensive collateral depletion or diminution following the petition. The purpose of taking such inconsistent positions, Judge Cyr observed, is that "a secured creditor is then better positioned to assert that retention and use of the collateral by the debtor has rendered the secured creditor an involuntary lender entitled to priority payment from the estate for the impairment of its lien."

Judge Cyr's observation is best understood in light of the treatment accorded a secured creditor in *In re Yale Express System, Inc.*, 384 F.2d 990 (2d Cir. 1977). Judge Cyr did not cite *Yale Express*, but it seems likely that he had the facts of that case in mind when he referred to "priority payment." The debtor, Yale, a trucking company, purchased trucks and trailers from Fruehauf Corporation. To secure the purchase price, Freuhauf was granted a security interest in the trucks and trailers. Shortly after the purchase, Yale filed a Chapter X petition and halted installment payments to Fruehauf. Fruehauf sought permission of the court to foreclose on the trucks and trailers. The trustee opposed the request but offered to fix the value of Fruehauf's security interest and promised that the reorganization plan would treat as an administrative expense any decline in value occasioned by delay of foreclosure. (Administrative expenses, then, as now, were entitled to priority in distribution. *See* Code § 507(a)(1) and former Act § 64a(1).) Finding that a successful reorganization was possible and that the trustee's offer assured that "Fruehauf's position in any reorganization will be unaffected by possible depreciation," 384 F.2d . at 992, the court denied relief from the stay.

The point Judge Cyr was making in *American Kitchen Foods* was that such a promise of administration expense treatment gave secured creditors an incentive to overvalue property early in the case and undervalue it later, when a plan is proposed or the reorganization effort is abandoned.

A couple of observations are in order.

First, note that the form of adequate protection contrived by the Yale trustee is expressly disapproved in Code § 361(3). The Code drafters rejected administrative expense treatment "because such protection is too uncertain to be meaningful." S. Rep. No. 95-589, at (1978). This is because the need for adequate protection is greatest in precisely the situation in which the promise of administrative expense treatment is likely to do the least good: in the event a reorganization fails and liquidation ensues. When a case is converted from Chapter 11 to Chapter 7, the administrative expenses of the superseding liquidation have priority over the administration expenses of the aborted Chapter 11 case. In such a case, assets are likely to be inadequate to protect secured creditors from any decline in value of their security. Note that in *American Kitchen Foods*, the debtor proposed to protect the banks by promising that any loss would give rise to an administrative claim secured by a lien on property. Presumably, adequate protection in the form of a secured administrative claim would not be prohibited by § 361(3).

Second, the whipsaw is not as invidiously pro-creditor as Judge Cyr's observation might suggest. It cuts many different ways, and it is wielded by debtors as well as creditors. As you will see in the cases that immediately follow, a debtor's purpose is usually served by maximizing the value of security when relief from the stay is sought. The more equity a debtor has in property securing a debt, the easier it is for the debtor to fashion adequate protection and the less likely it is that relief from the stay will be forthcoming. Conversely, it may serve a debtor's purpose to minimize the value of collateral at a later stage of a case in order to avoid having to treat claims as secured. It may serve a secured creditor's purpose to show low or rapidly declining value in secured property in order to support a request for relief from the stay. But later in the case, the same creditor may be inclined to overstate the value of the security in order to assert a larger secured claim. Such inconsistent positions are possible — if not always plausible — because the valuation of property for purposes of determining whether relief from the stay is "binding only for the purposes of the specific hearing and is not to have a res judicata effect." S. Rep. No. 95-989, at 54 (1978).

[C] Other Methods of Providing Adequate Protection: The Equity Cushion/ Opportunity Costs/Indubitable Equivalent Concepts

PROBLEM 3.11

Assume the Amphydynamics manufacturing plant building referred to in Problem 3.11 is not owned by Amphy free and clear but is subject to a $10,000,000, 12 percent mortgage held by MacroBank. Assume further that no matter what approach is used to appraise the property, all appraisers agree that it has a value of $11,000,000. The appraisers also agree that the value of the property is stable and that costs of sale will be around $600,000. Amphy's cash flow is so tight that it cannot manage to make any kind of payments to the bank, and interest is accruing on the note at a rate of $100,000 per month.

Should the bank be granted relief from the stay for the purpose of foreclosing its mortgage on the factory building? Under what circumstances, if any, would you continue the stay in effect?

IN RE ALYUCAN INTERSTATE CORP.
United States Bankruptcy Court, District of Utah
12 B.R. 803 (1981)

RALPH R. MABEY, BANKRUPTCY JUDGE

INTRODUCTION AND BACKGROUND

This case raises the question whether an "equity cushion" is necessary to provide adequate protection under 11 U.S.C. Section 362(d)(1). This Court concludes that it is not.

On January 14, 1981, Alyucan Interstate Corporation (debtor), a construction and real estate development firm, filed a petition under Chapter 11 of the Code. On May 4, Bankers Life Insurance Company of Nebraska (Bankers Life), holder of a trust deed on realty owned by debtor, brought this action for relief from the automatic stay under Section 362(d). The complaint alleges that the realty secures a debt in the principal amount of $1,220,000 and that Bankers Life is not adequately protected. On May 20, the preliminary hearing contemplated by Section 362(e) was held. After receiving evidence, the Court fixed the value of the realty on the date of the petition at $1,425,000 and found that there had been no erosion in that value as of the hearing. The debt owing was $1,297,226 as of the petition, and with interest accruing at roughly $8,000 per month, had increased to $1,330,761 as of the hearing. Thus, there was an "equity cushion" of $127,774 or approximately nine percent of the value of the collateral, as of the petition, which had decreased to $94,239, or approximately six and one half percent of the value of the collateral, as of the hearing. As interest accumulates, and if no payments are made, this cushion will dissipate within a year.

THE MEANING OF ADEQUATE PROTECTION

Section 362(d)(1) mandates relief, in some form, from the stay "for cause, including the lack of adequate protection of an interest in property." The only cause asserted in this proceeding is a lack of adequate protection.

Adequate protection is not defined in the Code. This omission was probably deliberate. Congress was aware of the turbulent rivalry of interests in reorganization. It needed a concept which would mediate polarities. But a carefully calibrated concept, subject to a brittle construction, could not accommodate the "infinite number of variations possible in dealings between debtors and creditors." H.R. Rep. No. 95-595, 95th Cong., 1st Sess. 339 (1977). This problem required, not a formula, but a calculus, open-textured, pliant, and versatile, adaptable to "new ideas" which are "continually being implemented in this field" and to "varying circumstances and changing modes of financing." *Id*. Adequate protection was requisitioned to meet these needs. Its meaning, therefore, is born afresh out of the "reflective equilibrium" of each decision,[3] understood through analysis of the reorganization context and the language of Section 362(d).

A. The Reorganization Context

Relief from the stay cannot be viewed in isolation from the reorganization process. Bankruptcy in general and Chapter 11 in particular are "procedural devices" for the rehabilitation of financially embarrassed enterprises. H.R. Rep. No. 95-595, 95th Cong., 1st Sess. 10 (1977). The process presupposes dynamic rather than static uses of property and denouement in a plan which accommodates the many, not just the few.

The automatic stay, within this framework, is designed "to prevent a chaotic and uncontrolled scramble for the debtor's assets in a variety of uncoordinated proceedings in different courts." *Fidelity Mortgage Investors v. Camelia Builders, Inc.*, 550 F.2d 47, 55 (2d Cir. 1976). It grants a "breathing spell" for debtors to regroup. It shields creditors from one another by replacing "race" and other preferential systems of debt collection with a more equitable and orderly distribution of assets. It encourages rehabilitation: debtors may seek its asylum while recovery is possible rather than coasting to the point of no return; creditors, realizing that foreclosure is useless, may rechannel energies toward more therapeutic ends. *See, e.g.*, Hearings on H.R. 31 and H.R. 32 Before The Subcomm. on Civil and Constitutional Rights of the House Comm. on the Judiciary, 94th Cong., 1st Sess., Ser. 27, Pt. 1, at 321–322, 490–491 (1975).

Although self-help and other unilateral recourse against debtors are forbidden, creditors are not left remediless. They may act through committees with professional assistance, often at the expense of the estate, or by seeking appointment of a trustee or examiner. Conversion to Chapter 7 and dismissal are options. Within

---

[3] Not only is the concept kaleidoscopic, but also the circumstances to which it applies will change from creditor to creditor, and from hearing to hearing, or even as to the same creditor in different hearings. It follows, and Congress intended, that the outcome of a relief from stay hearing is not res judicata for any subsequent hearing. *See, e.g.*, Sen. Rep. No.95-989, 95th Cong., 1st Sess. 54 (1978).

certain time constraints, they may file a plan.

In short, the adequate protection vouchsafed creditors in Chapter 11 is interim protection, designed not as a purgative of all creditor ailments, but as a palliative of the worst: re-organization, dismissal, or liquidation will provide the final relief. During this interim, the policies favoring rehabilitation and the benefits derived from the stay should not be lightly discarded. Alternative remedies are available to creditors. Indeed, even relief from the stay need not mean termination of the stay. Section 362(d) provides for relief, such as "terminating, annulling, modifying, or conditioning" the stay. Thus, relief may be fashioned to suit the exigencies of the case.

B. The Language of Section 362(d)

Turning from Chapter 11 at large to Section 362(d) in specific, several issues must be addressed. First, what is the "interest in property" being protected? Second, what aspects of the "interest in property" require protection? Third, from what is the "interest in property" being protected? Fourth, what is the method of protection?

(1) *What is the "interest in property" being protected?* The legislative history mentions only "the interest of a secured creditor or co-owner of property with the debtor" in connection with adequate protection. H.R. Rep. No. 95-595, 95th Cong., 1st Sess. 338 (1977). Within these classes of creditors, however, "the interests of which the court may provide protection . . . include equitable as well as legal interests. For example, a right to redeem under a pledge or a right to recover property under a consignment are both interests that are entitled to protection." *Id.* This classification is important because adequate protection depends upon the interest and property involved. Protection afforded a lessor, for example, may be different from that afforded a secured creditor. Treatment of a secured creditor who faces turnover may be different from treatment of a secured creditor who has not repossessed. Treatment of a senior lienholder may be different from treatment of a junior lienholder. Similarly, protection may vary if the property is real or personal, tangible or intangible, perdurable or perishable, or if its value is constant, depreciating, or subject to sudden or extreme fluctuations. Also relevant is the proposed use or idleness of the property.

(2) *What aspects of the "interest in property" require protection?* Adequate protection is concerned with the value of the interest in property. The legislative commentary to Section 361 underscores this point: "Though the creditor might not receive his bargain in kind, the purpose of the section is to insure that the secured creditor receives *in value* essentially what he bargained for." *Id.* at 339. (Emphasis supplied.) The legislative history reemphasizes this point by noting that adequate protection is "derived from the fifth amendment protection of property interests," id., citing *Wright v. Union Central Insurance Co.*, 311 U.S. 273, 61 S. Ct. 196, 85 L. Ed. 184 (1940), and *Louisville Bank v. Radford*, 295 U.S. 555, 55 S. Ct. 854, 79 L. Ed. 1593 (1935). In *Wright*, Justice Douglas held that the bank received "the value of the [interest in] property" and that "there is no constitutional claim of a creditor to more than that." *Id.* 311 U.S. at 278, 61 S. Ct. at 199. Debtors were allowed to redeem the property at its appraised price, despite an obligation which exceeded

the value of the collateral by $10,000. Thus, the "interest in property" entitled to protection is not measured by the amount of the debt but by the value of the lien.[10] A mushrooming debt, through accrual of interest or otherwise, may be immaterial, if the amount of the lien is not thereby increased, while vicissitudes in the market, loss of insurance or other factors affecting the value of the lien are relevant to adequate protection. The purpose of adequate protection is to assure the recoverability of this value during the hiatus between petition and plan, or in the event the reorganization is stillborn, between petition and dismissal.[11]

(3) *From what is the "interest in property" being protected?* The short answer is from any impairment in value attributable to the stay. (In hearings pursuant to 11 U.S.C. Sections 363 and 364 the answer would be from any impairment in value attributable to the use, sale, or lease or grant of a lien on the interest in property. *See* 11 U.S.C. Section 361.) The stay does not cause, but it may forestall a creditor from preventing or mitigating, a decline in value. Some harm to collateral, however, may be unavoidable with or without the stay. Likewise, creditors may acquiesce in some harm to collateral for business or other reasons notwithstanding the stay. In these situations, and others which may arise, any impairment in value may not be attributable to the stay. Hence, not every decline in value must be recompensed, only those which, but for the stay, could be and probably would be prevented or mitigated.

(4) *What is the method of protection?* The method of affording adequate

---

[10] Lien is used herein as a shorthand expression for allowed secured claim under 11 U.S.C. Section 506(a). Where a creditor is undersecured, this is the value of the collateral. Where he is oversecured, it is the amount of the debt plus interest and other expenses if they accrue. Compare 11 U.S.C. Section 502(b)(2) with 11 U.S.C. Section 506(b). . . .

[11] Some cases have interpreted adequate protection more in terms of contractual benefits than economic values. They have focused on language in the legislative history suggesting that secured creditors must receive the "benefit of their bargain." H.R. Rep. No.95-595, 95th Cong., 1st Sess. 339 (1977). Congress, however, was not referring to the contractual bargain between creditors and debtors because the next portion of the House Report acknowledges "there may be situations in bankruptcy where giving a secured creditor an absolute right to his bargain may be impossible or seriously detrimental to the bankruptcy laws. Thus, this section [Section 361] recognizes the availability of alternate means of protecting a secured creditor's interest. Though the creditor might not receive his bargain in kind, the purpose of the section is to insure that the secured creditor receives in value essentially what he bargained for." *Id.* Whether and to what extent noncontractual or business elements of a bargain may be factored into the adequate protection equation is problematical. Some courts, employing an equity cushion analysis (discussed below), insist that a ratio of debt to collateral is "bargained for" between debtor and creditor and must be considered in determining adequate protection. *See, e. g., In re Pitts,* 2 B.R. 476, 478 (C.D. Cal. 1979) ("No secured creditor structures a transaction in such fashion that the value of the property equals the amount of his claim. The existence of an equity, in terms of collateral value in excess of the secured creditor's claim, is an elementary and fundamental part of the transaction"). The stream of inquiry along this path, however, may be difficult to contain. Many business motives, which may or may not be expressed in the documents memorializing a transaction, could then become relevant to adequate protection. As a practical matter, for example, foreclosure may not be an attractive prospect for some lenders who are, after all, in the business of loaning money not managing properties. Hence, their bargain is primarily for payment with interest and, as a last resort, for liquidation with its burdens of custodial care and costs. Foreclosure may likewise pose regulatory complications. Banks and insurance companies are traditionally limited in the amount of illiquid assets, such as realty, which they can carry at any given time in their portfolio. *See, e.g.,* 1B Utah Code Ann., Section 7-3-30 (1971) and 4A Utah Code Ann., Section 31-13-17 and 31-13-18 (1974).

protection, as noted above, will vary with the interest in property to be protected. In some cases,[12] the debtor need do nothing, either because the value of the interest in property is not declining or because the decline in value is not attributable to the stay. If the stay is responsible for a decline in value, Section 361 states three illustrative methods for providing adequate protection. Some courts, however, have not looked beyond its trilogy of alternatives. Others have insisted on a showing of indubitable equivalence. These approaches miss the mark: they violate the non-prescriptive character of Section 361, and may simply exchange one imponderable for another. Indubitable equivalence is not a method; nor does it have substantive content. Indeed, something "indubitable" is more than "adequate;" "equivalent" is more than "protection;" hence, the illustration may eclipse the concept. At best, it is a semantic substitute for adequate protection and one with dubious, not indubitable, application to the question of relief from the stay. *See, e.g.*, 2 Collier on Bankruptcy ¶ 361.01(1) at 361-4 -361-5 (15th ed. 1980).

C. Application to This Proceeding

In this proceeding, the "interest in property" is the lien of Bankers Life on the realty of debtor. It is a trust deed and therefore may be peremptorily foreclosed. *See* 6A Utah Code Ann., Sections 57-1-19 *et seq.* (1974). It is a first lien with ample collateral to protect Bankers Life. The collateral and therefore the lien are not declining or subject to sudden depreciation in value. Bankers Life is suffering no pain cognizable under Section 362 as a result of the stay, and relief from the stay is therefore, at this juncture, unnecessary.

Moreover, this property is essential to the reorganization of the debtor. Foreclosure and liquidation of the property would run counter to this need and would deprive debtor and other creditors of its going concern value. If liquidation is allowed, it should occur under the aegis of the Court and in the interests of all. Bankers Life is no better qualified to handle this liquidation than the debtor or the trustee. Indeed, Bankers Life may be ill-equipped to undertake this task, both because its interests are parochial and because, for regulatory or other reasons, it may be a reluctant caretaker. *See* discussion *supra* note 11.

. . . .

In any event, Bankers Life has other remedies under the Code. A trustee has been appointed. It may work with him or with creditor committees to negotiate a sale of the property. It can seek dismissal or conversion to Chapter 7. It can propose a plan of liquidation. In short, the application of adequate protection to the facts of

---

[12] The legislative history notes that the debtor-in-possession or trustee, not the court, must provide adequate protection. Otherwise, the court is forced into an administrative role at odds with the spirit of the Code. "If the party that is affected by the proposed action objects, the court will determine whether the protection provided is adequate." H. Rep. No.95-595, 95th Cong., 1st Sess. 338, 6295 (1977). Courts, however, have gone beyond this adjudicative function, and in some instances, have actively fashioned protection for creditors. *See, e. g., In the Matter of Pleasant Valley, Inc.*, 6 B.R. 13, 17-18 (D. Nev. 1980) (debtor ordered to pay taxes, assessments, and interest on specified terms and conditions and to provide insurance of specified kinds and amounts and deed of trust on additional property). This result may be inevitable given the exigencies and informalities of relief from stay proceedings. Indeed, it grows out of the language of Section 362(d) which mandates relief such as "modifying" or "conditioning" the stay.

this case avoids the trauma of relief from the stay and maintains the equilibrium of interests in this reorganization.

THE EQUITY CUSHION ANALYSIS

In contrast to these principles, there is a trend toward defining adequate protection in terms of an "equity cushion": the difference between outstanding debt and the value of the property against which the creditor desires to act. Where the difference is substantial, a cushion is said to exist, adequately protecting the creditor. As interest accrues, or depreciation advances, and the margin declines, the cushion weakens and the stay may be lifted.[13] Naturally, courts disagree on what is an acceptable margin.[14] The emerging view, however, may be that the stay should be terminated when the cushion will be absorbed through interest, commissions, and other costs of resale. The cushion analysis enjoys practical appeal and ease of application.

------

[13] This, according to one commentator, is "perhaps the most important [line of] cases dealing with adequate protection." Schimberg, "Uniform Commercial Code Annual Survey: Secured Transactions," 36 Bus. Law. 1347, 1396 (1981).

[14] The cushion analysis was first articulated in *In re Pitts*, 2 B.R. 476. The collateral, a home, was valued at $125,000, while the debt and costs of foreclosure and resale were fixed at $105,875, leaving a cushion of $19,125 or 15 percent. This was deemed "minimal," "fragile," and "precarious," but enough. The court emphasized the need for regular, periodic review in order "to avoid dissipation of whatever protection the cushion affords." *Id.* at 478 and 479. The fact that plaintiff was a junior lienholder and therefore would be "squeezed" as the senior lien accrued interest was not stressed, nor have later opinions discussed the significance of this point in terms of the cushion analysis or adequate protection. In *In re Hutton-Johnson Co., Inc.*, 6 B.R. 855 (S.D.N.Y. 1980), a first lienholder on realty was undersecured at the date of the petition. The property was not depreciating in value. The court alluded to a bargained for debt-collateral ratio but noted "it does not follow that the concept of adequate protection is designed to put the secured creditor in the same position it was in when it initially negotiated the transaction." *Id.* at 860. This statement runs counter to language in *Pitts. See* discussion *supra* note 11. . . . Nevertheless, the creditor's undersecured status, *ipso facto*, was deemed conclusive on the issue of adequate protection. In *In the Matter of Pleasant Valley, Inc.*, 6 B.R. 13 (D. Nev.1980), there was a 2.6 percent cushion. The court found that the land was not depreciating in value, but ruled that "nothing should be permitted which *reduces* plaintiffs' protection." *Id.* at 17 (emphasis in original). The court also ruled that a first lienholder on land would not be adequately protected unless debtor paid taxes, insurance, monthly interest, and gave added security. In *In re Tucker*, 5 B.R. 180 (S.D.N.Y. 1980), a cushion of 7.4 percent was believed inadequate protection for a junior lienholder on realty, although other circumstances weighted the decision against debtor. In *In re Castle Ranch of Ramona, Inc.*, 3 B.R. 45 (S.D. Cal. 1980), a cushion of 8.6 percent was held inadequate to protect a first lienholder on realty, although the opinion elsewhere suggests the absence of equity and is not straightforward in its application of a cushion analysis. In *In the Matter of Lake Tahoe Land Company, Inc.*, 5 B.R. 34 (D. Nev. 1980), the court found that termination of the stay was appropriate for "cause" independent of the adequate protection issue. Although the lender was undersecured the court noted in dictum that a 40 to 50 percent cushion for lenders on raw ground would be necessary to afford adequate protection. In *In re Rogers Development Corp.*, 2 B.R. 679 (E.D. Va. 1980), the court held a 17 percent cushion for a first lienholder on land to be adequate protection. In *In re San Clemente Estates*, 5 B.R. 605 (S.D. Cal.1980), the court held a 65 percent cushion for a first lienholder on land to be adequate protection. The court noted that this "quantitative approach may have the salutary effect of giving precise guidance as to the standard to be used, but it does seem to be inconsistent with the Congressional intent that each case is to be judged on its facts." *Id.* at 610. The court further noted that if development projections were not met and the land had to be marketed in its present condition, this would require a new valuation of the property resulting in a 17 percent cushion which would be "precariously close to being inadequate." *Id.* at 611.

This Court rejects a cushion analysis upon four grounds: (1) It is inconsistent with the purpose of adequate protection. (2) It is inconsistent with the illustrations of adequate protection found in Section 361. (3) It is inconsistent with the statutory scheme of Section 362(d). (4) It has no basis in the historical development of relief from stay proceedings.

(1) The cushion analysis, by focusing on the ratio of debt to collateral, obscures the purpose of adequate protection, viz., to guard against impairment of a lien. This blurring of objectives may produce improper results. If Bankers Life had been undersecured at the petition, for example, the absence of cushion would have dictated relief from the stay, even though the stay did not impair its lien and notwithstanding the usual appreciation in the value of realty.

(2) Since the thrust of adequate protection is to assure maintenance of the value of the lien, it is largely compensatory. Sections 361(1) and (2) therefore speak not in terms of preserving equity but in terms of compensating for any "decrease in the value of [an] interest in property."[15] Moreover, the cushion analysis, because it is confined to the relationship between debt and collateral in a specific property, ignores the recoverability of value, not only from the property at stake but also from other sources. Sections 361(1) and (2), which provide for interim payments and replacement liens, contemplate that value from other assets held by debtors may be appropriated to supply any needed protection. Indeed, the legislative history to Section 361 suggests the use of sureties or guarantors for this purpose. *See* H.R. Rep. No. 95-595, 95th Cong., 1st Sess. 340 (1977). *But see In re Kenny Kar Leasing, Inc.*, 5 B.R. 304 (C.D. Cal. 1980). Even if the debtor has no other assets, it is nevertheless conceivable that an enterprise valuation, which approaches value in terms of capitalized earnings, could show an income potential sufficient to meet the adequate protection standard.

(3) Under Section 362(d)(2) a lack of equity, absent a further showing that the property is unnecessary to an effective reorganization, does not warrant relief from the stay. This statutory provision expresses a legislative judgment, first, that it is the *absence* of equity rather than any particular cushion which is the criterion for relief from stay, and second, that the absence of equity is not alone dispositive — the court must still weigh the necessity of the property to an effective reorganization. The cushion analysis is inconsistent with this judgment. It makes surplusage out of Section 362(d)(2) which speaks in terms of equity and reorganization. Indeed, this dual requirement emphasizes the role of equity, when present, not as a cushion, but to underwrite, through sale or credit, the rehabilitation of debtors.[17]

---

[15] Even Section 361(3), the indubitable equivalent standard, had its genesis in *In re Murel Holding Co.*, 75 F.2d 941 (2d Cir. 1935), where Judge Hand opined: "It is plain that "adequate protection' must be completely compensatory." *Id.* at 942.

[17] Sections 362(d)(1) and (d)(2) are separated by the disjunctive "or," which is defined in 11 U.S.C. Section 102(5) to mean "not exclusive." This suggests, as a number of cases have held, that (d)(1) and (d)(2) provide alternate criteria for relief from the stay. This conclusion, however, may be questioned on two grounds. First, the preface to (d)(2) speaks of stays of "an act against property." This suggests that (d)(2) may be the exclusive standard for relief from the stay where property is involved. This suggestion is reinforced by legislative history which earmarks (d)(2) "to solve the problem of real property mortgage foreclosures of property where the bankruptcy petition is filed on the eve of foreclosure." 124 Cong. Rec. H 11,092-11,093 (September 28, 1978). Section 362(e) speaks even more specifically of "the stay of any act

(4) The cushion analysis is alien to the development of stay litigation. The stay provisions in Chapter proceedings in the Act, former 11 U.S.C. Sections 714, 814, and 828, as implemented through Bankruptcy Rules 10-601, 11-44, and 12-43, allowed relief "for cause shown." This was interpreted to require consideration of a number of factors, including the presence of equity, the likelihood of harm to the creditor, prospects for reorganization, and essentiality of the property in the operation of the estate. *See, e.g.*, Peitzman and Smith, "The Secured Creditor's Complaint: Relief from the Automatic Stays in Bankruptcy Proceedings," 65 Cal. L. Rev. 1216, 1226 (1977).

Although the "idea of equity" became "something of a totem for courts," *id.* at 1227, it was equity in the sense contemplated under Section 362(d)(2), not an equity cushion. Thus, it was acknowledged that "deciding whether to continue or vacate the stay solely on the ground of the debtor's equity in the property may produce an unjust result," for example where "the encumbered property is so vital to the operation of debtor's business that foreclosure will simply not be allowed." *Id.*

Similarly, another commentator describes the "operative equities" which are weighed in relief from stay actions, to include the debtor's need for the property, harm to the creditor, stage of the proceedings, and "how persuasive the indications are that the debtor can fabricate a plan susceptible of confirmation," but warns against "red herrings." "One of these is the oft mentioned concern as to how much equity the debtor has in property sought by a secured creditor. If the equity is large, that is the reason for granting relief [to the debtor] which might be denied if it were not. Yet, that judgment ought to be largely immaterial, since the equity can presumably be salvaged for the debtor in liquidation of the property as part of the administration of the estate or upon its surrender to the secured creditor, particularly where the court exercises its discretion to control the time and manner of liquidation. It is submitted that the real determinants should be and probably are the factors just suggested. For example, if a debtor badly needs the property and its vital signs are strong, the size of its equity shouldn't have much bearing on the situation, although a large equity does make a decision favorable to the debtor more palatable for all concerned." Festersen, "Equitable Powers in Bankruptcy Rehabilitation: Protection of the Debtor and the Doomsday Principle," 46 Am.Bank.L.J. 311, 332-333 (1972).

Professor Kennedy, the leading commentator on stays under the Act, concurs with these views: "The existence of an equity is not . . . and should not be, indispensable to the continuation of a stay. Congress explicitly authorized the bankruptcy court to enjoin lien enforcement when appropriate in the pursuit of the

---

against property of the estate." Such particularized draftsmanship may connote a special distinction and purpose. The courts, however, have shown indifference on this score, and have applied (d)(1), which refers to adequate protection of an "interest in property," to relief from stay actions concerning property. Second, the legislative backdrop to "or" is illuminating: "Or" means "not exclusive," which in turn means "if a party 'may do (a) or (b),' then the party may do either or both." Sen. Rep. No.95-989, 95th Cong., 2d Sess. 83 (1978) as discussed in Klee, "Legislative History of the New Bankruptcy Law," 28 DePaul L. Rev. 941, 959 (1979). Does the court, then, have discretion to apply either (d)(1) or (d)(2) alone or both (d)(1) and (d)(2) together in determining whether relief from the stay is appropriate? And given the legislative history noted above, in the case of a foreclosure on realty, should the court ordinarily defer to (d)(2)?

objective of rehabilitation under Chapter XI. If the secured creditor is adequately protected from injury resulting from the stay, the collateral is essential to the reorganization, and a reorganization in the interest of unsecured creditors is a realistic possibility, the absence of an equity should be immaterial. The presence or absence of an equity does not have comparable importance in Chapter X or a Chapter XII case, because it is at least theoretically possible for a plan confirmed under either of these chapters to reduce or otherwise alter the rights of secured creditors in the property subject to their liens." Kennedy, "The Automatic Stay in Bankruptcy," 11 U. Mich. J. Law. Ref. 175, 247–248 (1978).[18]

CONCLUSION

Adequate protection is a concept designed to balance the rights of creditors and debtors in the preliminary stages of reorganization. It is, in each case, ad hoc. For this reason the cushion analysis, which may be helpful in general, falls short in the particular. It is not fully alert to the legislative directive that "the facts," in each hearing under Section 362(d), "will determine whether relief is appropriate under the circumstances." H.R. Rep. No. 95-595, 95th Cong., 1st Sess. 344 (1977). The facts of each case, thoughtfully weighed, not formularized, define adequate protection.

PROBLEM 3.12

Assume that the value of the Amphydynamics manufacturing plant is $9,000,000, and the debt secured by the plant is $10,000,000. Assume further that the mortgagee, MacroBank, demands adequate protection in the form of monthly payments in an amount equal to the amount of income the bank would earn if it were able to enforce its mortgage, sell the assembly plant at a foreclosure sale, and invest the sales proceeds. Should the bankruptcy court order Amphy to make such payments or dismiss the case if Amphy can't?

---

[18] A further reason for rejecting the cushion analysis is tactical in nature. If the value of the interest in property at the date of the petition is the benchmark from which adequate protection is measured, see In re Curlew Valley Associates . . . creditors, logically, should argue for a high value which accentuates any decline in worth. The Commission Report, in contrast, noted that "a benchmark in determining the adequacy of protection is the liquidation value of the collateral at the date of the petition." Report of the Commission on the Bankruptcy Laws of the United States, H. Doc. No. 93-137, Part II, at 237 (1973). Creditor groups which testified at hearings on the bills incorporating the Commission proposals were unanimous in their criticism of this provision. See, e. g., statement of John J. Creedon, Chairman, Subcommittee on Federal Bankruptcy Legislation, American Life Insurance Association, and statement of Robert J. Grimmig on behalf of the American Bankers Association, Hearings Before the Subcomm. on Civil and Constitutional Rights of the House Comm. on the Judiciary, 94th Cong., 1st Sess., Ser. 27, Pt. 1, at 1607 and 1754 (1976) ("The measure of protection in the case of a secured creditor should be the 'fair value' rather than the "liquidation value' of his security"); ("The test should be the going-concern value of [the] security . . . the value should be determined [as of] the time of the filing of the petition"). Using a going-concern value, however, would be at cross-purposes with the cushion analysis which argues for a value low enough to be swallowed by the debt.

UNITED SAVINGS ASS'N v. TIMBERS OF INWOOD FOREST ASSOCIATIONS, LTD.

Supreme Court of the United States

484 U.S. 365 (1988)

JUSTICE SCALIA delivered the opinion of the Court.

Petitioner United Savings Association of Texas seeks review of an en banc decision of the United States Court of Appeals for the Fifth Circuit, holding that petitioner was not entitled to receive from respondent debtor, which is undergoing reorganization in bankruptcy, monthly payments for the use value of the loan collateral which the bankruptcy stay prevented it from possessing. *In re Timbers of Inwood Forest Associates, Ltd.*, 808 F.2d 363 (1987). We granted certiorari, 481 U.S. 1068 (1987), to resolve a conflict in the Courts of Appeals regarding application of §§ 361 and 362(d)(1) of the Bankruptcy Code, 11 U.S.C. §§ 361 and 362(d)(1) (1982 ed. and Supp. IV). Compare *Grundy Nat. Bank v. Tandem Mining Corp.*, 754 F. 2d 1436, 1440–1441 (CA4 1985); *In re American Mariner Industries, Inc.*, 734 F. 2d 426, 432–435 (CA9 1984); *see also In re Briggs Transp. Co.*, 780 F. 2d 1339, 1348–1351 (CA8 1985).

I

On June 29, 1982, respondent Timbers of Inwood Forest Associates, Ltd., executed a note in the principal amount of $4,100,000. Petitioner is the holder of the note as well as of a security interest created the same day in an apartment project owned by respondent in Houston, Texas. The security interest included an assignment of rents from the project. On March 4, 1985, respondent filed a voluntary petition under Chapter 11 of the Bankruptcy Code, 11 U.S.C. § 101 et seq. (1982 ed. and Supp. IV), in the United States Bankruptcy Court for the Southern District of Texas.

On March 18, 1985, petitioner moved for relief from the automatic stay of enforcement of liens triggered by the petition, *see* 11 U.S.C. § 362(a), on the ground that there was lack of "adequate protection" of its interest within the meaning of 11 U.S.C. § 362(d)(1). At a hearing before the Bankruptcy Court, it was established that respondent owed petitioner $4,366,388.77, and evidence was presented that the value of the collateral was somewhere between $2,650,000 and $4,250,000. The collateral was appreciating in value, but only very slightly. It was therefore undisputed that petitioner was an undersecured creditor. Respondent had agreed to pay petitioner the postpetition rents from the apartment project (covered by the after-acquired property clause in the security agreement), minus operating expenses. Petitioner contended, however, that it was entitled to additional compensation. The Bankruptcy Court agreed and on April 19, 1985, it conditioned continuance of the stay on monthly payments by respondent, at the market rate of 12% per annum, on the estimated amount realizable on foreclosure, $4,250,000 — commencing six months after the filing of the bankruptcy petition, to reflect the normal foreclosure delays.

. . . .

The court held that the postpetition rents could be applied to these payments. *See id.*, at 460. Respondent appealed to the District Court and petitioner cross-appealed on the amount of the adequate protection payments. The District Court affirmed but the Fifth Circuit en banc reversed.

We granted certiorari to determine whether undersecured creditors are entitled to compensation under 11 U.S.C. § 362(d)(1) for the delay caused by the automatic stay in foreclosing on their collateral.

II

When a bankruptcy petition is filed, § 362(a) of the Bankruptcy Code provides an automatic stay of, among other things, actions taken to realize the value of collateral given by the debtor. The provision of the Code central to the decision of this case is § 362(d), which reads as follows:

> "On request of a party in interest and after notice and a hearing, the court shall grant relief from the stay provided under subsection (a) of this section, such as by terminating, annulling, modifying, or conditioning such stay —
>
> "(1) for cause, including the lack of adequate protection of an interest in property of such party in interest; or
>
> "(2) with respect to a stay of an act against property under subsection (a) of this section, if —
>
> "(A) the debtor does not have an equity in such property; and
>
> "(B) such property is not necessary to an effective reorganization."

The phrase "adequate protection" in paragraph (1) of the foregoing provision is given further content by § 361 of the Code, which reads in relevant part as follows:

> "When adequate protection is required under section 362 . . . of this title of an interest of an entity in property, such adequate protection may be provided by —
>
> "(1) requiring the trustee to make a cash payment or periodic cash payments to such entity, to the extent that the stay under section 362 of title . . . results in a decrease in the value of such entity's interest in such property;
>
> "(2) providing to such entity an additional or replacement lien to the extent that such stay ... results in a decrease in the value of such entity's interest in such property; or
>
> "(3) granting such other relief . . . as will result in the realization by such entity of the indubitable equivalent of such entity's interest in such property."

It is common ground that the "interest in property" referred to by § 362(d)(1) includes the right of a secured creditor to have the security applied in payment of the debt upon completion of the reorganization; and that that interest is not adequately protected if the security is depreciating during the term of the stay. Thus, it is agreed that if the apartment project in this case had been declining in value petitioner would have been entitled, under § 362(d)(1), to cash payments or additional security in the amount of the decline, as § 361 describes. The crux of the present dispute is that petitioner asserts, and respondent denies, that the phrase "interest in property" also includes the secured party's right (suspended by the stay) to take immediate possession of the defaulted security, and apply it in payment of the debt. If that right is embraced by the term, it is obviously not adequately protected unless the secured party is reimbursed for the use of the proceeds he is deprived of during the term of the stay.

The term "interest in property" certainly summons up such concepts as "fee ownership," "life estate," "co-ownership," and "security interest" more readily than it does the notion of "right to immediate foreclosure." Nonetheless, viewed in the isolated context of § 362(d)(1), the phrase could reasonably be given the meaning petitioner asserts. Statutory construction, however, is a holistic endeavor. A provision that may seem ambiguous in isolation is often clarified by the remainder of the statutory scheme — because the same terminology is used elsewhere in a context that makes its meaning clear . . . or because only one of the permissible meanings produces a substantive effect that is compatible with the rest of the law. . . . That is the case here. Section 362(d)(1) is only one of a series of provisions in the Bankruptcy Code dealing with the rights of secured creditors. The language in those other provisions, and the substantive dispositions that they effect, persuade us that the "interest in property" protected by § 362(d)(1) does not include a secured party's right to immediate foreclosure.

Section 506 of the Code defines the amount of the secured creditor's allowed secured claim and the conditions of his receiving postpetition interest. In relevant part it reads as follows:

"(a) An allowed claim of a creditor secured by a lien on property in which the estate has an interest . . . is a secured claim to the extent of the value of such creditor's interest in the estate's interest in such property . . . and is an unsecured claim to the extent that the value of such creditor's interest . . . is less than the amount of such allowed claim . . .

"(b) To the extent that an allowed secured claim is secured by property the value of which . . . is greater than the amount of such claim, there shall be allowed to the holder of such claim, interest on such claim, and any reasonable fees, costs, or charges provided for under the agreement under which such claim arose."

In subsection (a) of this provision the creditor's "interest in property" obviously means his security interest without taking account of his right to immediate possession of the collateral on default. If the latter were included, the "value of such creditor's interest" would increase, and the proportions of the claim that are secured and unsecured would alter, as the stay continues — since the value of the entitlement to use the collateral from the date of bankruptcy would rise with the passage of time. No one suggests this was intended. The phrase "value of such creditor's interest" in § 506(a) means "the value of the collateral." H.R. Rep. No.

95-595, pp. 181, 356 (1977); *see also* S. Rep. No. 95-989, p. 68 (1978). We think the phrase "value of such entity's interest" in § 361(1) and (2), when applied to secured creditors, means the same.

Even more important for our purposes than § 506's use of terminology is its substantive effect of denying undersecured creditors postpetition interest on their claims — just as it denies *over* secured creditors postpetition interest to the extent that such interest, when added to the principal amount of the claim, will exceed the value of the collateral. Section 506(b) provides that *"[t]o the extent* that an allowed secured claim is secured by property the value of which . . . is greater than the amount of such claim, there shall be allowed to the holder of such claim, interest on such claim." (Emphasis added.) Since this provision permits postpetition interest to be paid only out of the "security cushion," the undersecured creditor, who has no such cushion, falls within the general rule disallowing postpetition interest. *See* 11 U.S.C. § 502(b)(2). If the Code had meant to give the undersecured creditor, who is thus denied interest on his *claim*, interest on the value of his *collateral*, surely this is where that disposition would have been set forth, and not obscured within the "adequate protection" provision of § 362(d)(1). Instead of the intricate phraseology set forth above, § 506(b) would simply have said that the secured creditor is entitled to interest "on his allowed claim, or on the value of the property securing his allowed claim, whichever is lesser." Petitioner's interpretation of § 362(d)(1) must be regarded as contradicting the carefully drawn disposition of § 506(b).

Petitioner seeks to avoid this conclusion by characterizing § 506(b) as merely an alternative method for compensating oversecured creditors, which does not imply that no compensation is available to undersecured creditors. This theory of duplicate protection for oversecured creditors is implausible even in the abstract, but even more so in light of the historical principles of bankruptcy law. Section 506(b)'s denial of postpetition interest to undersecured creditors merely codified pre-Code bankruptcy law, in which that denial was part of the conscious allocation of reorganization benefits and losses between undersecured and unsecured creditors. "To allow a secured creditor interest where his security was worth less than the value of his debt was thought to be inequitable to unsecured creditors." *Vanston Bondholders Protective Committee v. Green*, 329 U.S. 156, 164 (1946). It was considered unfair to allow an undersecured creditor to recover interest from the estate's unencumbered assets before unsecured creditors had recovered any principal. *See id.*, at 164, 166; *Ticonic Nat. Bank v. Sprague*, 303 U.S. 406, 412 (1938). We think it unlikely that § 506(b) codified the pre-Code rule with the intent, not of achieving the principal purpose and function of that rule, but of providing oversecured creditors an alternative method of compensation. Moreover, it is incomprehensible why Congress would want to favor undersecured creditors with interest if they move for it under § 362(d)(1) at the inception of the reorganization process — thereby probably pushing the estate into liquidation — but not if they forbear and seek it only at the completion of the reorganization.

Second, petitioner's interpretation of § 362(d)(1) is structurally inconsistent with 11 U.S.C. § 552. Section 552(a) states the general rule that a prepetition security interest does not reach property acquired by the estate or debtor postpetition. Section 552(b) sets forth an exception, allowing postpetition "proceeds, product, offspring, rents, or profits" of the collateral to be covered only if the security agreement expressly provides for an interest in such property, and the interest has been perfected under "applicable nonbankruptcy law." . . . Section 552(b) therefore makes possession of a perfected security interest in postpetition rents or profits from collateral a condition of having them applied to satisfying the claim of the secured creditor ahead of the claims of unsecured creditors. Under petitioner's interpretation, however, the undersecured creditor who lacks such a perfected security interest in effect achieves the same result by demanding the "use value" of his collateral under § 362. It is true that § 506(b) gives the oversecured creditor, despite lack of compliance with the conditions of § 552, a similar priority over unsecured creditors; but that does not compromise the principle of § 552, since the interest payments come only out of the "cushion" in which the oversecured creditor *does have* a perfected security interest.

Third, petitioner's interpretation of § 362(d)(1) makes nonsense of § 362(d)(2). On petitioner's theory, the undersecured creditor's inability to take immediate possession of his collateral is always "cause" for conditioning the stay (upon the payment of market rate interest) under § 362(d)(1), since there is, within the meaning of that paragraph, "lack of adequate protection of an interest in property." But § 362(d)(2) expressly provides a different standard for relief from a stay "of an act against property," which of course includes taking possession of collateral. It provides that the court shall grant relief "if . . . (A) the debtor does not have an equity in such property [*i.e.*, the creditor is undersecured]; *and* (B) such property is not necessary to an effective reorganization." (Emphasis added.) By applying the "adequate protection of an interest in property" provision of § 362(d)(1) to the alleged "interest" in the earning power of collateral, petitioner creates the strange consequence that § 362 entitles the secured creditor to relief from the stay (1) if he is undersecured (and thus not eligible for interest under § 506(b)), *or* (2) if he is undersecured *and* his collateral "is not necessary to an effective reorganization." This renders § 362(d)(2) a practical nullity and a theoretical absurdity. If § 362(d)(1) is interpreted in this fashion, an undersecured creditor would seek relief under § 362(d)(2) only if his collateral was not depreciating (or it was being compensated for depreciation) and he was receiving market rate interest on his collateral, but nonetheless wanted to foreclose. Petitioner offers no reason why Congress would want to provide relief for such an obstreperous and thoroughly unharmed creditor.

Section 362(d)(2) also belies petitioner's contention that undersecured creditors will face inordinate and extortionate delay if they are denied compensation for interest lost during the stay as part of "adequate protection" under § 362(d)(1). Once the movant under § 362(d)(2) establishes that he is an undersecured creditor, it is the burden of the *debtor* to establish that the collateral at issue is "necessary to an effective reorganization." *See* § 362(g). What this requires is not merely a showing that if there is conceivably to be an effective reorganization, this property will be needed for it; but that the property is essential for an effective reorganization *that is in prospect*. This means, as many lower courts, including the en banc court in this case, have properly said, that there must be "a reasonable possibility of a successful reorganization within a reasonable time." 808 F. 2d, at 370–371, and nn. 12–13, and cases cited therein. The cases are numerous in which § 362(d)(2) relief has been provided within less than a year from the filing of the bankruptcy petition.[1] And while the bankruptcy courts demand less detailed showings during the four months in which the debtor is given the exclusive right to put together a plan, *see* 11 U.S.C. §§ 1121(b), (c)(2), even within that period lack of any realistic prospect of effective reorganization will require § 362(d)(2) relief.[2]

III

A

Petitioner contends that denying it compensation under § 362(d)(1) is inconsistent with sections of the Code other than those just discussed. Petitioner principally relies on the phrase "indubitable equivalent" in § 361(3), which also appears in 11 U.S.C. § 1129(b)(2)(A)(iii). Petitioner contends that in the latter context, which sets forth the standards for confirming a reorganization plan, the phrase has developed a well-settled meaning connoting the right of a secured creditor to receive present value of his security-thus requiring interest if the claim is to be paid over time. It is true that under § 1129(b) a secured claimant has a right to receive under a plan the present value of his collateral. This entitlement arises, however, not from the phrase "indubitable equivalent" in § 1129(b)(2)(A)(iii), but from the provision of § 1129(b)(2)(A)(i)(II) that guarantees the secured creditor "deferred cash payments . . . of a value, *as of the effective date of the plan*, of at least the value of such [secured claimant's] interest in the estate's interest in such property." (Emphasis added.) Under this formulation, even though the undersecured creditor's "interest" is regarded (properly) as solely the value of the collateral, he must be rendered payments that assure him that value *as of the effective date* of the plan. In § 361(3), by contrast, the relief pending the stay need only be such "*as will result in the realization* . . . of the indubitable equivalent" of the collateral. (Emphasis added.) It is obvious (since §§ 361 and 362(d)(1) do not entitle the secured creditor to immediate payment of the principal of his collateral) that this "realization" is to "result" not at once, but only upon completion of the reorganization. It is *then* that he must be assured "realization . . . of the indubitable equivalent" of his collateral. To put the point differently: similarity of outcome between § 361(3) and § 1129

---

[1] See, *e. g., In re Findley*, 76 B.R. 547, 555 (Bkrtcy. Ct. ND Miss. 1987) (6 months); *In re Efcor, Inc.*, 74 B.R. 837, 843–845 (Bkrtcy. Ct. MD Pa. 1987) (4 months); *In re Belton Inns, Inc.*, 71 B.R. 811, 818 (Bkrtcy. Ct. SD Iowa 1987) (1 year); *In re Louden*, 69 B.R. 723, 725–726 (Bkrtcy. Ct. ED Mo. 1987) (10 months); *In re Playa Development Corp.*, 68 B.R. 549, 556 (Bkrtcy. Ct. WD Tex. 1986) (7 months); *In re Cablehouse, Ltd.*, 68 B.R. 309, 313 (Bkrtcy. Ct. SD Ohio 1986) (11 months); *In re Pacific Tuna Corp.*, 48 B.R. 74, 78 (Bkrtcy. Ct. WD Tex. 1985) (9 months); *In re Development, Inc.*, 36 B.R. 998, 1005–1006 (Bkrtcy. Ct. Haw. 1984) (6 months); *In re Boca Development Associates*, 21 B.R. 624, 630 (Bkrtcy. Ct. SDNY 1982) (7 months); *In re Sundale Associates, Ltd.*, 11 B.R. 978, 980–981 (Bkrtcy. Ct. SD Fla. 1981) (5 months); *In re Clark Technical Associates, Ltd.*, 9 B.R. 738, 740–741 (Bkrtcy. Ct. Conn. 1981) (9 months).

[2] *See, e.g., In re Anderson Oaks (Phase I) Limited Partnership*, 77 B.R. 108, 109, 110–113 (Bkrtcy. Ct. WD Tex. 1987) ("immediately after the bankruptcy filings"); *In re New American Food Concepts, Inc.*, 70 B.R. 254, 262 (Bkrtcy. Ct. ND Ohio 1987) (3 months); *In re 6200 Ridge, Inc.*, 69 B.R. 837, 843–844 (Bkrtcy. Ct. ED Pa. 1987) (3 months); *In re Park Timbers, Inc.*, 58 B.R. 647, 651 (Bkrtcy. Ct. Del. 1985) (2 months); *In re Bellina's Restaurants II, Inc.*, 52 B.R. 509, 512 (Bkrtcy. Ct. SD Fla. 1985) (1 month); *In re Anchorage Boat Sales, Inc.*, 4 B.R. 635, 641 (Bkrtcy. Ct. EDNY 1980) (4 months); *In re Terra Mar Associates*, 3 B.R. 462, 466 (Bkrtcy. Ct. Conn. 1980) (2 months).

would be demanded only if the former read "such other relief . . . as will give such entity, *as of the date* of the relief, the indubitable equivalent of such entity's interest in such property."

Nor is there merit in petitioner's suggestion that "indubitable equivalent" in § 361(3) connotes reimbursement for the use value of collateral because the phrase is derived from *In re Murel Holding Corp.*, 75 F.2d 941 (CA2 1935), where it bore that meaning. *Murel* involved a proposed reorganization plan that gave the secured creditor interest on his collateral for 10 years, with full payment of the secured principal due at the end of that term; the plan made no provision, however, for amortization of principal or maintenance of the collateral's value during the term. In rejecting the plan, *Murel* used the words "indubitable equivalence" with specific reference not to interest (which was assured), but to the jeopardized principal of the loan:

> "Interest is indeed the common measure of the difference [between payment now and payment 10 years hence], but a creditor who fears the safety of his principal will scarcely be content with that; he wishes to get his money or at least the property. We see no reason to suppose that the statute was intended to deprive him of that in the interest of junior holders, unless by a substitute of the most indubitable equivalence." *Id.*, at 942.

Of course *Murel*, like § 1129, proceeds from the premise that in the confirmation context the secured creditor is entitled to present value. But no more from *Murel* than from § 1129 can it be inferred that a similar requirement exists as of the time of the bankruptcy stay. The reorganized debtor is supposed to stand on his own two feet. The debtor in process of reorganization, by contrast, is given many temporary protections against the normal operation of the law.

Petitioner also contends that the Code embodies a principle that secured creditors do not bear the costs of reorganization. It derives this from the rule that general administrative expenses do not have priority over secured claims. *See* §§ 506(c); 507(a). But the general principle does not follow from the particular rule. That secured creditors do not bear one kind of reorganization cost hardly means that they bear none of them. The Code rule on administrative expenses merely continues pre-Code law. But it was also pre-Code law that undersecured creditors were not entitled to postpetition interest as compensation for the delay of reorganization. *See supra*, at 373; *see also infra*, at 381. Congress could hardly have understood that the readoption of the rule on administrative expenses would work a change in the rule on postpetition interest, which it also readopted.

Finally, petitioner contends that failure to interpret § 362(d)(1) to require compensation of undersecured creditors for delay will create an inconsistency in the Code in the (admittedly rare) case when the debtor proves solvent. When that occurs, 11 U.S.C. § 726(a)(5) provides that postpetition interest is allowed on unsecured claims. Petitioner contends it would be absurd to allow postpetition interest on unsecured claims but not on the secured portion of undersecured creditors' claims. It would be disingenuous to deny that this is an apparent anomaly, but it will occur so rarely that it is more likely the product of inadvertence than are the blatant inconsistencies petitioner's interpretation would produce. Its inequitable effects, moreover, are entirely avoidable, since an undersecured creditor is entitled to "surrender or waive his security and prove his entire claim as an unsecured one." *United States Nat. Bank v. Chase Nat. Bank,* 331 U.S. 28, 34 (1947). Section 726(a)(5) therefore requires no more than that undersecured creditors receive postpetition interest from a solvent debtor on equal terms with unsecured creditors rather than ahead of them — which, where the debtor is solvent, involves no hardship.

B

Petitioner contends that its interpretation is supported by the legislative history of §§ 361 and 362(d)(1), relying almost entirely on statements that "[s]ecured creditors should not be deprived of the benefit of their bargain." H.R. Rep. No. 95-595, at 339; S. Rep. No. 95-989, at 53. Such generalizations are inadequate to overcome the plain textual indication in §§ 506 and 362(d)(2) of the Code that Congress did not wish the undersecured creditor to receive interest on his collateral during the term of the stay. If it is at all relevant, the legislative history tends to subvert rather than support petitioner's thesis, since it contains not a hint that § 362(d)(1) entitles the undersecured creditor to postpetition interest. Such a major change in the existing rules would not likely have been made without specific provision in the text of the statute . . . it is most improbable that it would have been made without even any mention in the legislative history.

Petitioner makes another argument based upon what the legislative history does *not* contain. It contends that the pre-Code law gave the undersecured creditor relief from the automatic stay by permitting him to foreclose; and that Congress would not have withdrawn this entitlement to relief without any indication of intent to do so in the legislative history, unless it was providing an adequate substitute, to wit, interest on the collateral during the stay.

The premise of this argument is flawed. As petitioner itself concedes . . . the undersecured creditor had no absolute entitlement to foreclosure in a Chapter X or XII case; he could not foreclose if there was a reasonable prospect for a successful rehabilitation within a reasonable time. *See, e.g., In re Yale Express System, Inc.,* 384 F. 2d 990, 991–992 (CA2 1967) (Chapter X); *In re Nevada Towers Assocs.,* 14 Collier Bankr. Cas. (MB) 146, 151–156 (Bkrtcy. Ct. SDNY 1977) (Chapter XII); *In re Consolidated Motor Inns,* 6 Collier Bankr. Cas. (MB) 18, 31–32 (Bkrtcy. Ct. ND Ga. 1975) (same). Thus, even assuming petitioner is correct that the undersecured creditor had an absolute entitlement to relief under Chapter XI, Congress would have been faced with the choice between adopting the rule from Chapters X and XII or the asserted alternative rule from Chapter XI, because Chapter 11 of the current Code "replaces chapters X, XI and XII of the Bankruptcy Act" with a "single chapter for all business reorganizations." S. Rep. No. 95-989, at 9; *see also* H.R. Rep. No. 95-595, at 223–224. We think § 362(d)(2) indicates that Congress adopted the approach of Chapters X and XII. In any event, as far as the silence of the legislative history on the point is concerned, that would be no more strange with respect to alteration of the asserted Chapter XI rule than it would be with respect to alteration of the Chapters X and XII rule.

Petitioner's argument is further weakened by the fact that it is far from clear that there was a distinctive Chapter XI rule of absolute entitlement to foreclosure.

At least one leading commentator concluded that "a Chapter XI court's power to stay lien enforcement is as broad as that of a Chapter X or XII court and that the automatic stay rules properly make no distinctions between the Chapters." Countryman, Real Estate Liens in Business Rehabilitation Cases, 50 Am. Bankr. L.J. 303, 315 (1976). Petitioner cites dicta in some Chapter XI cases suggesting that the undersecured creditor was automatically entitled to relief from the stay, but the courts in those cases uniformly found in addition that reorganization was not sufficiently likely or was being unduly delayed. . . . Moreover, other Chapter XI cases held undersecured creditors not entitled to foreclosure under reasoning very similar to that used in Chapters X and XII cases. . . . The at best divided authority under Chapter XI removes all cause for wonder that the alleged departure from it should not have been commented upon in the legislative history.

The Fifth Circuit correctly held that the undersecured petitioner is not entitled to interest on its collateral during the stay to assure adequate protection under 11 U.S.C. § 362(d)(1). Petitioner has never sought relief from the stay under § 362(d)(2) or on any ground other than lack of adequate protection. Accordingly, the judgment of the Fifth Circuit is

Affirmed.

[D]   Periodic Payments

NOTES AND QUESTIONS

(1)   *Vitality of the Equity Cushion Doctrine.* Although in *Alyucan* Judge Mabey rejected the equity cushion doctrine as simplistic, to many other courts it remains "the classic form of protection for a secured debt justifying the restraint of lien enforcement." *In re Mellor*, 734 F.2d 1396, 1400 (B.A.P. 9th Cir. 1984). *See also In re Hagendorfer*, 42 B.R. 17 (S.D. Ala. 1984); *In re Winslow Center Assocs.*, 32 B.R. 685 (Bankr. E.D. Pa. 1983); *In re Wilhoit*, 34 B.R. 14, 16 (Bankr. M.D. Fla. 1983). Indeed, some courts have held that the secured creditor may insist on payments of postpetition interest, in addition to depreciation, in order to protect the equity cushion. *Ingersoll-Rand Fin. Corp. v. 5-Leaf Clover Corp. (In re 5-Leaf Clover Corp.)*, 6 B.R. 463 (Bankr. S.D. W. Va. 1980) ("The debtor may postpone and continuously advance the impairment date by regular payments which at least equal the combined depreciation and interest on the debt. In this manner the equity ratio will be maintained at the appropriate level."). More recently, in *Orix Credit Alliance v. Delta Res., Inc. (In re Delta Res.)*, 54 F.3d 722 (11th Cir. 1995), the Eleventh Circuit cast into doubt whether cases like *5-Leaf Clover* survive *Timbers*:

> Ordinarily, creditors are not allowed a claim for interest accruing on their debts during bankruptcy proceedings. *Timbers*, 793 F.2d at 1385. Yet, as an exception to that rule, an oversecured creditor, but not an undersecured creditor having the same risk (indeed, it is possible for the undersecured creditor's risks to be much larger quantitatively), is entitled to receive postpetition interest as part of its claim at the time of confirmation of a plan or reorganization, that is, at or near the conclusion of the bankruptcy case.

11 U.S.C. § 506(b). Judge Randall of the Fifth Circuit explained the rationale for this exception.

> [T]he interest provisions of the Code and its predecessors, as interpreted by the Supreme Court for almost a century, are premised on the equitable principle that the unencumbered assets of a debtor's estate will not be used to benefit one class of creditors at the expense of another. . . [Thus,] [a]llowing a claim for postpetition interest by an oversecured creditor, . . . is not inconsistent with that equitable principle, *because only assets encumbered by the creditor's lien will be used to fund the payment of postpetition accrued interest.*

Timbers, 793 F.2d at 1387 (emphasis added).

Nevertheless, the Supreme Court has indicated that an oversecured creditor's allowed secured claim for postpetition interest, which is determined near the conclusion of the bankruptcy case, must be denied to the extent that, together with the principal amount of the claim, it exceeds the value of the collateral. Or put another way, the oversecured creditor's allowed secured claim for postpetition interest is limited to the amount that a creditor was oversecured at the time of filing.

> Even more important for our purposes than § 506's use of terminology is its substantive effect of denying undersecured creditors postpetition interest on their claims — just as it denies oversecured creditors postpetition interest to the extent that such interest, when added to the principal amount of the claim, will exceed the value of the collateral. Section 506(b) provides that *[t]o the extent that* an allowed secured claim is secured by property the value of which . . . is greater than the amount of such claim, there shall be allowed to the holder of such claim, interest on such claim." (Emphasis added.) Since this provision permits postpetition interest to be paid only out of the "security cushion," the undersecured creditor, who has no such cushion, falls within the general rule disallowing postpetition interest. *See* 11 U.S.C. § 502(b)(2). If the Code had meant to give the undersecured creditor, who is thus denied interest on his claim, interest on the value of his *collateral,* surely this is where that disposition would have been set forth, and not obscured within the "adequate protection" provision of § 362(d)(1). Instead of the intricate phraseology set forth above, § 506(b) would simply have said that the secured creditor is entitled to interest "on his allowed claim, or on the value of the property securing his allowed claim, whichever is lesser.

Timbers, 484 U.S. at 372–73.

The Supreme Court has recognized that an undersecured creditor may be entitled to adequate protection to ensure against the decline in the value of its collateral. However, an undersecured creditor is not entitled to receive postpetition "interest on its collateral *during the stay* to assure adequate protection under 11 U.S.C. § 362(d)(1)." *Timbers,* 484 U.S. at 382 (emphasis added).

Ordinarily, the matter of adequate protection is determined at or near the inception of a bankruptcy case. By contrast, the determination of a creditor's secured status, pursuant to 11 U.S.C. § 506, comes at or near the conclusion of a bankruptcy case.

> Under [11 U.S.C.] § 506(c), the debtor may recover from property securing a creditor's allowed secured claim the reasonable and necessary costs and expenses of preserving or disposing of the property, to the extent of any benefit to the creditor. If, after reducing the amount of the allowed secured claim by the amount of that recovery, the creditor is oversecured, it is entitled to interest at the contract rate on its net allowed secured claim. § 506(b). *The timing of the payment of accrued interest to an oversecured creditor (at the conclusion of the proceeding) is doubtless based on the fact that it is not possible to compute the amount of the § 506(c) recovery (and, accordingly, the amount of the net allowed secured claim on which interest is computed) until the termination of the proceeding.*

Timbers, 793 F.2d at 1407

Similarly, we conclude that 11 U.S.C. § 506(b), providing for postpetition interest on oversecured claims, read *in pari materia* with 11 U.S.C. § 362(d)(1), concerning conditioning the automatic stay on adequate protection, and 11 U.S.C. § 502, regarding the allowance of claims, requires that the payment of accrued postpetition interest to an oversecured creditor await the completion of reorganization or confirmation of the bankruptcy case. The *ratio decidendi* enunciated by the Supreme Court in Timbers that an undersecured creditor is not entitled to receive postpetition interest on its collateral during the stay to assure adequate protection under 11 U.S.C. § 362(d)(1) applies equally well to an oversecured creditor. Such an interpretation of the Bankruptcy Code is consistent whether the *secured creditor* is undersecured or oversecured, otherwise "§ 506(b) would simply have said that the secured creditor [whether oversecured or undersecured] is entitled to interest on his allowed claim, or on the value of the property securing his allowed claim, whichever is lesser." *Timbers*, 484 U.S. at 372–73 (emphasis added). Accordingly, viewing the allowance of postpetition interest to oversecured creditors as a limited exception only,[8] we hold that an oversecured creditor's interest in property which must be adequately protected encompasses the decline in the value of the collateral only, rather than perpetuating the ratio of the collateral to the debt. The bankruptcy court accomplished that by allowing adequate protection in the amount of accruing depreciation. *See In re Westchase I Assoc.*, 126 B.R. 692 (W.D.N.C. 1991); David G. Epstein et al., Bankruptcy § 3–27, at 142–43 (1993).

We think this rule results in the appropriate balance between the conflicting interests of the oversecured creditor on the one hand and the

---

[8] *See,* Niall L. O'Toole, Adequate Protection and Postpetition Interest in Chapter 11 Proceedings, 56 Am.Bank.L.J. 251 (1982).

estate, as well as other creditors, secured and unsecured, on the other hand. As one commentator points out:

> [t]here is certainly no reason intrinsic to the phenomenon of credit that entitles over-secured creditors to interest out of their collateral before junior creditors, whether secured [perhaps by the identical collateral] or unsecured, receive any of their principal.

Niall L. O'Toole, *Adequate Protection and Postpetition Interest in Chapter 11 Proceedings*, 56 Am.Bank.L.J. 251, 253 (1982).

Orix Credit Alliance, Inc. v. Delta Res., Inc. (In re Delta Res.), 54 F.3d 722, 729–30 (11th Cir. 1995).

Some courts have articulated a sort of corollary to Judge Mabey's approach that might be summed up this way: If the absence of an equity cushion is not dispositive of the existence of adequate protection, then the presence of an equity cushion should not be wholly dispositive of the question either. Not content to rely on equity alone, they have required even debtors in strong equity positions to take additional steps to provide adequate protection to secured creditors. *See In re Mr. D. Realty Co.*, 27 B.R. 359, 365 (Bankr. S.D. Ohio 1983) (net equity cushion of $630,000 on debt of $3.3 million held sufficient protection if debtor continued to make periodic payments to creditor); *In re Trident Corp.*, 19 B.R. 956, 958 (Bankr. E.D. Pa. 1982) (a $30,000 equity cushion held insufficient where debtor was neither maintaining insurance on the property nor making mortgage, tax, or interest payments).

(2)   If the value of the property is stable, and the debtor is maintaining insurance, is the creditor entitled to adequate protection payments?

(3)   Bear in mind that the methods of providing adequate protection described in Code § 361 are not mutually exclusive. On the contrary, a debtor or trustee might fashion an adequate protection package that incorporates more than one device, such as payments of economic depreciation combined with a replacement lien.

(4)   *Fabric of the Cushion.* Suppose that MegaBank holds a $1,000,000 claim against Metal Case secured by a lien on equipment valued at $1,300,000. Is it adequately protected by an equity cushion? Suppose the claim is secured by a lien on $1,300,000 worth of inventory. Is your conclusion the same? The vast majority of cases in which debtors have been allowed to rest on their equity without taking other steps to provide adequate protection have involved debts secured by real property. Compare the cases cited above and in Note 14 of the *Alyucan* opinion with *In re Llewellyn*, 27 B.R. 481 (Bankr. M.D. Pa. 1983) (cushion of 59 % in machinery and inventory collateral held adequate protection for lender). Do you think the equity cushion analysis has any more validity in the context of a debt secured by real estate than it does in a case involving collateral such as equipment or inventory? Why or why not?

(5)   *Equity vs. Equity Cushion.* Whereas "equity" has been defined as "the value, above all secured claims against the property, that can be realized from the sale of the property for the benefit of the unsecured creditors," *La Jolla Mortgage Fund v. Rancho El Cajon Assoc.*, 18 B.R. 283, 287 (Bankr. S.D. Cal. 1982), "equity cushion" has been defined as "the value in the property, above the amount owed to

the creditor with a secured claim, that will shield that interest from loss due to any decrease in value of the property during the time the automatic stay remains in effect." *In re Mellor*, 734 F.2d 1396, 1400 n.2 (9th Cir. 1984). Thus, a determination whether a debtor has "equity" in property requires a comparison of all debts secured by property with the value of the property. A determination whether a secured creditor is adequately protected by an equity cushion requires a comparison of that creditor's claim with the value of the property less the amount of any senior secured claims against the property.

For example, assume that Amphy's assembly plant is subject to a first mortgage of $10,000,000 and a second mortgage of $7,000,000. The plant has a fair market value of $15,000,000. Does the debtor have any "equity" in the property? Is the first mortgagee protected by an "equity cushion"? Is the second mortgagee protected by an "equity cushion"? What will happen to the value of the second lienholder's secured claim as interest accrues on the first lienholder's mortgage? How can that interest be adequately protected? Is the second lienholder entitled to adequate protection payments when the first lienholder is not?

(6) *Burden of Proof.* Under Code § 362(g), the party requesting relief from the stay has the burden of proof on the issue of the debtor's equity in the property. However, the debtor bears the burden of proving that an equity cushion exists and that it provides adequate protection. *See In re Annex Camera*, 26 B.R. 587 (Bankr. S.D.N.Y. 1983).

(7) *Relationship of Sections 362(d) and 363(e).* According to Judge Mabey, in a hearing on a request for relief from the automatic stay under § 362(d) the court should determine whether the interest in property is being protected from any "impairment in value attributable to the stay." He also said in a hearing on a motion under Code § 363(e), the court should determine whether the interest in property is being protected from impairment in value "attributable to the use, sale, or lease . . . " of the property. *In re Callister*, 15 B.R. 521 (Bankr. D. Utah 1981). Can you think of many situations in which property protected by the stay is not being used, sold, or leased by the debtor? Are §§ 362(d) and 363(e) at least partly redundant?

[E]   When Adequate Protection Turns Out to Be Inadequate

IN RE CALLISTER
United States Bankruptcy Court, District of Utah
15 B.R. 521 (1981)

RALPH R. MABEY, BANKRUPTCY JUDGE

FACTUAL AND PROCEDURAL BACKGROUND

This case raises issues concerning the superpriority provision of 11 U.S.C. Section 507(b).

Debtor, the sole proprietor of a trucking business, filed a petition under Chapter 11 on December 12, 1980. Ingersoll-Rand Financial Corporation (Rand), which holds a security interest in three tractors and two trailers, filed a complaint seeking relief from the automatic stay on January 2, 1981. A hearing was held January 23. At that time, the parties stipulated that the collateral was worth $129,000, that the debt owing was $106,248, and that debtor would pay $1,232 per month beginning February 1 to Rand. Debtor also agreed to insure the equipment as required in the security agreements. A procedure was established for lifting the stay in the event of default. The court ruled that Rand was adequately protected under this arrangement. Two payments were made, but debtor defaulted May 1, and the stay was lifted June 5. The case was converted to Chapter 7 on August 5.

Meanwhile, counsel for debtor filed an application for allowance and payment of fees in the amount of $9,052 under 11 U.S.C. Section 331. Counsel for the unsecured creditors committee likewise requested fees in the amount of $2,994. Rand objected, claiming that the fees might be allowed but not paid because it was entitled to a superpriority under 507(b).[8]

Hearings were held August 18 and 19. The evidence showed that two of the three tractors underwent repair from January to June and therefore conferred no benefit on the estate. The third tractor was used for approximately three weeks but it caught fire and was destroyed. Through inadvertence, no insurance was in force to indemnify this casualty. The trailers were used without mishap.

The court values the collateral as of June 5 at $68,900. Subtracting costs of repair in the amount of $7,097 leaves $61,803. Hence, the collateral has dwindled in worth by $67,197. At least four factors account for this decrease. The uninsured loss equals $19,411. Error in the stipulation is responsible for $33,447.[15] Market forces caused a loss of $7,993.[16] Use caused a loss of $6,346.[17] No share of the loss through market

---

[8] Counsel for debtor filed their application for fees on May 15 and it was heard on June 18. Counsel for the unsecured creditors committee filed their application for fees on August 11 and it was heard on September 29. In both instances the fees were allowed but payment was suspended because of the claim for a superpriority.

[15] The security agreements, executed in June, 1980, show that the equipment was financed for $110,450. It is unclear whether this was the price or whether, and in what amount, a down payment may have been made. Hughes testified that the 1978 tractor was sold for $44,850, the 1977 tractors for $28,750 each, and the trailers for $10,450 each, for a total of $123,250. The equipment was valued by stipulation in January, 1981, after approximately eight months of use, at $129,000. Thus, there was a difference between the Hughes price and the stipulated value of $5,750. Since there was no evidence that this type of equipment appreciates in value, and since an escalation in value is improbable, this amount represents a mistake in the stipulation. But even this amount is understated since it does not account for depreciation through use between June and January. Monthly payments under the security agreements, which are ordinarily keyed to depreciation, were $3,866. This amount, however, includes interest which was per diem $51.38 (this was as of June 17, 1981 and therefore may require adjustment) or for thirty days $1,541. This would make monthly principal payments of $2,325 or for eight months $18,600. (In contrast, the stipulated figure of $1,232 for eight months yields $9,856.) Thus, the mistake in price of $5,750 and depreciation of $18,600 equals $24,350. The stipulated value of $129,000 contained two additional errors. First, it did not account for the cost of repairs at $7,097. Second, it did not account for the value of siding which debtor placed on but later removed from one trailer at $2,000. Cumulative error equals $33,447.

[16] This figure is deduced by elimination. It is the difference between the decline in worth of the collateral and all other items of loss.

[17] The trailers were the only equipment which depreciated through use. They had a stipulated worth of $22,000 on January 23 and were valued at $11,400 on June 5 for a difference of $10,600. The entire

forces is allocated to the trailers. Because of the error in the stipulation, the allowed secured claim on January 23 was $95,553, not $106,248. The allowed secured claim on June 5 was $61,803, for a reduction of $33,750.

These facts raise several issues which may be classified under the headings of statutory construction, allowance, and rank. Under statutory construction: May a creditor ineligible for an administrative claim under 11 U.S.C. Section 503(b) qualify for superpriority status under 507(b)? Under allowance: Are losses caused by failure to obtain insurance, an error in the stipulation, market forces, and depreciation recompensable under 507(b)? Under rank: Does the superpriority take precedence over interim fees under 331? Under what, if any, circumstances may fees be paid notwithstanding the existence of or potential for a superpriority? These questions are discussed below.

Is The Superpriority an Administrative Expense or Something More?

The superpriority provision is found in 507(b) which states:

> If the trustee, under Section 362, 363, or 364 of this title, provides adequate protection of the interest of a holder of a claim secured by a lien on property of the debtor and if, notwithstanding such protection, such creditor has a claim allowable under subsection (a)(1) of this section arising from the stay of action against such property under Section 362 of this title, from the use, sale, or lease of such property under Section 363 of this title, or from the granting of a lien under Section 364(d) of this title, then such creditor's claim under such subsection shall have priority over every other claim under such subsection.

11 U.S.C. Section 507(a)(1) gives priority to "expenses allowed under Section 503(b)" which include, in part, "the actual, necessary costs . . . of preserving the estate."[19]

Debtor maintains that only creditors who have claims under 503(b) and who lose adequate protection may enjoy the benefit of 507(b). This view draws support from the face of 507(b) which speaks of "a claim allowable under subsection (a)(1) of this section" which in turn refers to 503(b).[20] But 507(b), on closer analysis, is the proverbial prism in the fog. A review of its language, history, and relation to adequate protection, however, may elucidate its meaning.

---

difference, however, is not attributable to depreciation through use. A portion, $4,254, is due to error in the stipulation. *See supra* note 15.

[19] Rand has both filed a claim and made a motion for superpriority under 507(b). Filing a claim may be inappropriate. In contrast to 11 U.S.C. Section 502(a) which provides that claims, once filed and absent objection, are deemed allowed, 503(a) and (b), and by analogy 507(b), contemplate the filing of "a request for payment of an administrative expense," which "after notice and a hearing," on certain conditions, may be allowed. *But cf.* 3 Collier on Bankruptcy ¶ 503.02 (15th ed. 1980).

[20] Rand argues that whether it qualifies for an administrative claim under 503(b) is irrelevant. The use of the trailers, in any event, was probably an actual, necessary cost of preserving the estate. The uninsured loss may likewise fit this category. *Cf. Reading Co. v. Brown*, 391 U.S. 471, 88 S.Ct. 1759, 20 L.Ed.2d 751 (1968).

The Language of 507(b)

The use of property for the estate creates an administrative claim under 503(b). Curbing repossession of property through the stay, without more, may not lead to the same result. Section 507(b), however, treats property used and property subject to the stay, implying that both, so long as they lose adequate protection, meet the standards of 503(b). Indeed, commentators appear to equate inadequate protection with allowability under 503(b). *See, e.g.,* 3 Collier on Bankruptcy 507.05 at 507-46 (15th ed. 1980) ("In essence, [507(b)] affords a superpriority to post-petition creditors in whose case the protection given by the trustee is inadequate to protect the creditor's interest *thereby resulting in an administrative expense claim under Section 503(b)(1)(A)*.") (Emphasis supplied.) The facts, however, may belie this assumption. Here, for example, debtor needed the equipment, but circumstance, for the most part, kept it idle. If the equipment has not been an "actual, necessary cost . . . of preserving the estate," does it nevertheless qualify as a superpriority because its use is implicit in 507(b)?

History of the Superpriority

The superpriority may be difficult to articulate by statute, because it is equitable in origin and genealogy. The Commission would have permitted the trustee to use collateral subject to a request "to modify the stay by imposing such conditions on the use of the property or the proceeds thereof as will adequately protect the secured party." Report of the Commission on the Bankruptcy Laws of the United States, H.Doc. No. 93-137, pt. II, Section 7-203(b)(2) (1973). Granting administrative priority was an appropriate conditi[o]n "if it is clear that the proceeds of the liquidation of property of the estate available to pay the claim will be sufficient." *Id.* at Note 3.

The authority for this proposal was *In re Yale Express System, Inc.*, 384 F.2d 990 (2d Cir. 1967).

      . . . .

Yale Express alarmed lenders and they mounted an attack on its codification. One observer wrote that "granting a priority just postpones the day of reckoning until the date of confirmation of the debtor's plan and, in turn, presupposes that a plan will be confirmed." It is, "granting an ephemeral future priority as a device for avoiding present reality." Murphy, "Use of Collateral in Business Rehabilitation: A Suggested Redrafting of Section 7-203 of the Bankruptcy Reform Act," 63 Cal. L. Rev. 1483, 1505 (1975).

Notwithstanding this critique, the concept of an administrative priority as a means of providing adequate protection was written into Section 361(3) of H.R. 8200. *See* H.R. 8200, 95th Cong., 1st Sess. (1977). The House Report cautioned that "this method, more than the others, requires a prediction as to whether the unencumbered assets that will remain if the case is converted from reorganization to liquidation will be sufficient to pay the protected entity in full. It is clearly the most risky, from the entity's perspective, and should be used only when there is relative certainty that administrative expenses will be able to be paid in full in the event of liquidation." H.R. Rep. No. 95-595, 95th Cong., 1st Sess. 340 (1977), U.S.

Code Cong. & Admin. News 1978, pp. 5787, 6296. The Senate disagreed and omitted the concept of an administrative priority as a means of providing adequate protection "because such protection is too uncertain to be meaningful." Sen. Rep. No. 95-989, 95th Cong., 1st Sess. 54 (1978), U.S. Code Cong. & Admin. News 1978, p. 5840.

As enacted, Section 361 dropped subsection (3) of H.R. 8200 because "in every case there is the uncertainty that the estate will have sufficient property to pay administrative expenses in full." 124 Cong. Rec. H11, 092 (daily ed., September 28, 1978). Language forbidding use of administrative priorities in fashioning adequate protection took its place. The concept, however, was not entirely abandoned. It was grafted on to 507 so that "to the extent the protection [under Section 361] proves to be inadequate after the fact, the creditor is entitled to a first priority administrative expense." *Id.* Floor leaders commented further that "Section 507(b) . . . is new and is derived from the compromise contained in the House with respect to adequate protection under Section 361. Subsection (b) provides that to the extent adequate protection of the interest of a holder of a claim proves to be inadequate, then the creditor's claim is given priority over every other allowable claim entitled to distribution under Section 507(a)." *Id.* at 11,095.

The Superpriority and Adequate Protection

The superpriority is the stepchild of adequate protection and they enjoy a symbiotic relationship. Adequate protection was designed to "mediate polarities" in Chapter 11 and is therefore "not a formula, but a calculus, open-textured, pliant, and versatile, adaptable to 'new ideas' which are 'continually being implemented in this field' and to 'varying circumstances and changing modes of financing;'" its meaning "is born afresh out of the 'reflective equilibrium' of each decision." *In re Alyucan Interstate Corp.*, 12 B.R. 803, 7 B.C.D. 1123, 1124 (Bkrtcy. D. Utah 1981). It was intended as "interim protection, designed not as a purgative of all creditor ailments, but as a palliative of the worst: reorganization, dismissal, or liquidation will provide the final relief." *Id.*

The superpriority, because of its equitable underpinnings, is also, in large measure, fact-specific. But unlike adequate protection, it is not a fulcrum for balancing interests; it is an interest to be weighed in the balance. Moreover, it will emerge, most often, not during the interim between petition and plan, but when debtors are in the throes of liquidation and during the final, most uncertain stage of bankruptcy. Thus, whereas adequate protection shields the creditor in the first instance from impairment in the value of his "interest in property," the superpriority was intended to recapture value unexpectedly lost during the course of a case: "It establishes a statutory fail-safe system in recognition of the ultimate reality that protection previously determined the 'indubitable equivalent' . . . may later prove inadequate." *In re Marine Optical, Inc.*, 10 B.R. 893, CCH Bankr .L. Rep. ¶ 67,991 at 78,993 (Bkrtcy. App. D. Mass. 1981).

Guidelines for Allowance of a Superpriority

Guidelines for allowing a superpriority may be distilled from 507(b), its language, history, and relation to adequate protection. The language of 507(b), especially in relation to 503(b), is difficult to plumb. Indeed, 503(b) and 507(b) may be at odds. One is keyed to preserving the estate, the other is designed to protect secured creditors. Coincidentally, they reflect the tension of interests in this case between counsel who request fees and Rand which demands superpriority. If 507(b) is faithful to one of these purposes, it may be untrue to the other.

The history of the superpriority and its relation to adequate protection share this ambivalence. If the Commission proposal, *Yale Express*, and H.R. 8200 are the antecedents of 507(b), then 503(b) with its criteria of need and usefulness to the estate has relevance. But Congress may have discounted these views, establishing a "statutory failsafe" to reimburse creditors where there is a shortfall in adequate protection. *See* 124 Cong. Rec. H11, 092 (daily ed., September 28, 1978). This reimbursement may not be reducible to the ambit of 503(b). Indeed, if only administrative expenses qualify under 507(b), the measure of allowance may be fair rental value, or some other indicia of use. A different yardstick, however, may gauge the miscarriage of adequate protection.

The parties seek a **ruling that** the superpriority must be allowed either as an administrative expense **or as a** guarantee of adequate protection. But neither approach is satisfactory. The statute is a confederation of principles; it cannot be "construed" to favor one at the expense of another; it should be interpreted to account for the merits of all. Hence, equitable considerations, arising from the facts of each case, should be examined. The rights and importance of other interests must be weighed. The manner in which adequate protection was provided and the role of the superpriority as a "backstop" should be considered.

Problems of Allowance

The Uninsured Loss

Rand argues that adequate protection in the form of a stipulation to procure insurance was afforded; noncompliance resulted in the uninsured destruction of the tractor; therefore adequate protection failed and 507(b) comes into play.

True, the superpriority is born when adequate protection fails. But whether adequate protection has failed depends upon whether and how it has been provided. In this regard, Rand may misconceive the purpose of adequate protection which shelters creditors "from any impairment in value attributable to the stay. . . . "

The uninsured loss may not have been attributable to the stay for at least two reasons. First, the risk occasioned by the stay, and for which protection in the form of insurance was afforded, was that the tractor, before repossession, would be damaged. There was, however, another risk at work, viz., the risk of inadvertently failing to obtain insurance. Protection against this risk was not and indeed could not have been afforded.

If this risk were allocated between debtor and Rand outside bankruptcy, naturally, it would be borne by debtor, who, as between the two innocent parties, was in a better position to prevent the inadvertence. But the risk must be allocated not only between debtor and Rand, but also between Rand and other administrative claimants. As between these parties, Rand was in a better position to prevent the mistake and therefore arguably it should suffer the loss.

Second, the loss which flowed, not from the accident, but from the oversight, while unprotectible under 361, was preventable by Rand. The security agreements permit Rand, when the debtor does not obtain insurance, to pay the premium and charge the account. Under 11 U.S.C. Section 506(b), when the creditor is oversecured, this supplements the allowed secured claim, increasing the lien entitled to protection. Although the fact of reorganization invites more than ordinary diligence by creditors, Rand did not ascertain whether insurance was bought, nor did it exercise its right to default under the stipulation. Indeed, Rand, from one view, may have "acquiesced" in the harm to its collateral.

Nevertheless, deciding whether loss is attributable to the stay, using the abstraction of "cause," in this case, is speculative. The conflict between debtor, Rand, and administrative claimants may be overdrawn. The debtor is a debtor in possession, the fiduciary representative of the estate. The interest of administrative claimants is his stewardship. Even absent court order, this includes the procurement of insurance. A rule which might relax this duty, where possible, should be avoided. *Cf. Reading Co. v. Brown*, 391 U.S. 471, 483, 88 S.Ct. 1759, 1765, 20 L.Ed.2d 751 (1968). The assertion that the failure to insure was preventable, while compelling under other circumstances, is not convincing on these facts. A degree of reliance upon stipulations is warranted, and Rand, with less than a month to act, did not sleep on its rights. These considerations mandate allowance of the uninsured loss as a superpriority.

Error in the Stipulation

Stipulations raise another complex of problems. On one hand, they show cooperation between creditors and the estate which should be required. They reduce costs otherwise incurred in litigation and permit a constructive allocation of resources. They lessen the judicial burden of administering the estate, an important principle of the Reform Act.

. . . .

On balance, Rand is not entitled to a superpriority for the loss attributable to the error in the stipulation. Disallowance under these circumstances will not discourage stipulations. Rather, it will further care in their formulation. Rand was less the cooperative creditor than reluctant caretaker of its collateral. Hence, its motive in stipulating is not an equitable consideration in its favor. Given the incalculability of values, some misapprehension is expected; but this error was not the product of excusable neglect. It was a gross miscalculation which could have been easily detected. Indeed, the disparity between the price and stipulation should have warned Rand that something was amiss, prompting investigation, and discovery of the trailer siding and unpaid repair bills. Rand is experienced with this type of collateral, familiar with values and industry trends. Given its sophistication and leverage under the Code, it enjoys substantial bargaining power with debtor. Thus, its claim that it relied upon the representations of debtor in arriving at the stipulated value is unpersuasive. Under these circumstances, equity will look past the form of the stipulation to the substance of the value. The value of $129,000 was a fiction. The loss of $33,447 was no loss. This amount should not be credited toward a superpriority.

Market Forces

Both sides acknowledge the interposition of the market: several carriers have folded and are liquidating their equipment; newer models are more attractive to entrepreneurs. This combination of circumstances has lowered prices.

The property at stake and its susceptibility to market forces are factors to be considered in determining adequate protection. . . . Arguably, Rand should have accounted for these forces in negotiating the stipulated interim payments. But the collapse of freighters and the inauguration of products are not readily foreseeable. In this regard, Rand, like debtor, is at the mercy of events beyond its control. Rand did not speculate on the market at the expense of the estate; it was reasonably prompt in obtaining relief from the stay and mitigating damage. The loss resulting from market forces therefore "ought not equitably to be saddled on [Rand] but on [the estate] for whose supposed benefit the restraint was imposed." . . .

Depreciation Through Use

Since the trailers were used and useful to the estate, debtor, in principle, should not object to loss through depreciation as a superpriority. The question is how much loss. The stipulation provided for interim payments, which if paid, from February to May, would have totaled $4,928. Actual depreciation equaled $6,346. *See supra* note 17. Should Rand receive the amount it bargained for in the stipulation or the amount of real loss? Equity recommends the former. Rand was not bereft in bankruptcy. It had the background and tools to insure that payments were commensurate with depreciation. Indeed, if it had calculated depreciation based upon the security agreements, *see supra* note 15, the amount would have been $9,300. This figure, unlike the stipulated payments, approximates the real loss. The court is reluctant to penalize the estate for an error which could have been remedied by Rand. The depreciation allocable to superpriority is therefore $4,928, minus payments received in the amount of $2,464 . . . .

Calculating the Superpriority

In principle, calculation of the superpriority is straightforward; the error in the stipulation, however, complicates the figures in this case. Ordinarily, the loss eligible for superpriority status should be deducted from the value of the collateral at the adequate protection hearing. The extent to which this erodes the allowed secured claim on that date constitutes the allowed superpriority. Here, eligible loss equaled $19,411 for the burned tractor, $7,993 for market decline, and $2,464 for depreciation, for a total of $29,868. The value of the collateral and the allowed secured claim on January 23, making adjustments for the error in the stipulation, was $95,553; the value of the collateral and the allowed secured claim on June 5 was $61,803, for a reduction of $33,750. The allowed secured claim is diminished by more than the eligible loss. The difference of $3,882 is the ineligible loss attributable to depreciation through use. Hence, the eligible loss is the allowed superpriority.

If adjustments were not made for the error in the stipulation, the result would be different. The loss of $29,868 would be subtracted from $129,000, i.e., it would be charged against the "equity cushion" which existed on that date. The brunt of the loss would be borne by the estate, and would erode the allowed secured claim ($106,248) by only $7,116. This would be the allowed superpriority.

Since the stipulated value was not credited for purposes of determining loss, however, it should not be a factor in calculating the superpriority. The adjusted figures are therefore used, yielding a superpriority of $29,868.

Problems of Rank

Rand argues that the superpriority has precedence over claims allowed under 503(b). Attorneys fees may be allowed under 503(b)(2). Thus no fees may be paid until the superpriority is satisfied. This argument is flawed, however, for several reasons.

Fees are allowed under 11 U.S.C. Section 330 and classified as administrative expenses under 503(b)(2). But while other administrative expenses must wait until confirmation, 11 U.S.C. Section 1129(a)(9), or liquidation, 11 U.S.C. Section 726, for reimbursement,[38] fees are payable on an interim and therefore a preeminent basis under 331. Not only the statutory scheme but also reasons of policy support this preeminence of fees under 331.[38a]

Lenders like Rand may be involuntarily harnessed to the ordeal of reorganization, but fee claimants voluntarily contribute to the ideal of rehabilitation. Section 331 encourages this volunteerism and, as an inducement to work for the estate, is a vital provision of the Reform Act which places the burden of administration upon trustees, creditor committees, and their professional representatives. . . . Absent this incentive, it would be difficult to assure continued efficient management. *See, e.g.,* 2 Collier on Bankruptcy, *supra* ¶ 331.02 at 331-5 . Requests for adequate protection in Chapter 11 are ubiquitous; each raises the spectre of a superpriority. If the superpriority, in turn, might preempt interim fees, it would jeopardize the further provision of services. The result would not be attractive. The administrators might mutiny: but the case, whether in Chapter 11 or in a superseding Chapter 7, would not care for itself. They might cut corners: but this would cause delay, which

---

[38] With the exception of 331, the Code is silent as to when administrative claims are payable. As a practical matter, and under the auspices of prior case law, the court may permit the payment of operating expenses as they are incurred in a reorganization. *Cf. In re Standard Furniture Company*, 3 B.R. 527, 6 B.C.D. 270, 273 (Bkrtcy. S.D.Cal.1980).

[38a] Section 507(b) gives the superpriority precedence over claims allowed under 507(a), or in other words, over claims allowed under 503(b). Fees, however, may be allowed under 330 and 331. When allowed under these provisions, instead of 503(b)(2), they are not subject to the regimen of 507. Moreover, as indicated in the text, fees are not only allowed but also payable under 331. Section 507(b), in contrast, is silent respecting payment. This gives a de facto preeminence to fees.

is anathema to creditors, especially those holding a superpriority who are waiting for confirmation or liquidation. They might demand exorbitant retainers at the beginning of each case: but for most debtors this either would be impossible or would decrease their chances for rehabilitation.[40]

These dangers do not dictate that in every instance fees must be paid ahead of the superpriority. Section 331 says that fees "may" be paid on an interim basis. There is a presumption, for the reasons outlined above, that they will be paid notwithstanding the existence of a superpriority. This presumption may be strengthened, for example, where a trustee or his representative who is requesting fees was installed at the behest of a creditor entitled to a superpriority. *Cf. In re Hotel Associates, Inc.*, 6 B.R. 108, 114 (Bkrtcy. E.D. Pa. 1980). But it is rebuttable under appropriate equitable circumstances. *Cf.* 2 Collier on Bankruptcy, *supra* 331.01 at 331-3 ("The genesis of interim compensation is rooted in the equity powers of the bankruptcy court"). These circumstances, however, are not present in this case.

IT IS THEREFORE ORDERED:

1. Rand is allowed a superpriority in the amount of $29,868.

2. Fees of counsel for debtor and the unsecured creditors committee which have been previously allowed shall be paid forthwith.

NOTES AND QUESTIONS

(1) If Rand had been granted a superpriority of $29,868, Rand's claim would have ranked ahead of the fees of creditors' committee counsel. Why then were the attorney's fees paid immediately, while Rand was required to wait until the conclusion of the case? This question was addressed in *In re Wise Transp., Inc.*, 148 B.R. 52, 54–55 (Bankr. N.D. Okla. 1992):

> The case now before this Court is a classic example of "inadequate adequate protection." In such circumstances, the remedy is clear on the face of the statute. The Bank is entitled to be repaid from estate funds, to the extent that "adequate protection" for use of its cash collateral has proved inadequate, ahead of all other Ch. 11 priority claims and administrative expenses including H & W's fee as attorney for Wise Inc.

> H & W argues that, notwithstanding all this, it should be paid its fees ahead of any payments to the Bank. As authority, H & W offers the case of *In re Callister*, 15 B.R. 521 (B.C., D. Utah 1981). The Bank offers in turn the case of *In re Colter*, 53 B.R. 958 (B.C., D. Col. 1985), which "expressly rejects the *Callister* decision," Bank's response p. 5.

> In *In re Callister, supra*, the Bankruptcy Court for the District of Utah, Mabey, J., awarded interim fees under § 331 to attorneys for debtor and an unsecured creditors' committee, and ordered them paid notwithstanding pendency of a secured creditor's claim for reimbursement for "inadequate

---

[40] It is likewise unfair, if not unrealistic, to expect counsel to underwrite the reorganization. This would drive experienced and expert counsel to more reliably lucrative fields of practice.

adequate protection." The Bankruptcy Court ruled that "[t]here is a presumption that [interim fee awards] will be paid notwithstanding the existence of a superpriority," although such presumption "is rebuttable under appropriate equitable circumstances." *Id.*

In *In re American Resources Management Corp.*, 51 B.R. 713 (B.C., D. Utah 1985), Clark, J., the Bankruptcy Court for the District of Utah revisited its previous decision in *In re Callister.* Judge Clark noted that Judge Mabey's decision was properly read in light of the fact that "the debtor [estate] had $323,122 in unencumbered assets," 51 B.R. at pp. 718 n. 14, 720, and *see* 15 B.R. at p. 523 n. 7, which said funds were sufficient to pay all professional fees and superpriority claims in full. The only question was whether, under such circumstances, interim fees might be paid off now, without waiting to pay off the superpriority first. That is, *Callister* concerned mere timing of distribution; Judge Mabey properly held that he had some discretion in the timing of payments, even if it meant paying an "inferior" professional fee earlier than a "superior" superpriority claim; and in this ruling he was properly affirmed on appeal. But where there was not enough money to eventually satisfy all administrative-type claims in full, the "circumstances" which might justify judicial use of discretion were missing; and the Court was required by statute to satisfy superpriority-type administrative claims in preference to, and if necessary at the expense of, other types of administrative claims.

The Bankruptcy Court's opinion in *In re Callister* has been much criticized and often rejected, *see e.g. In re Flagstaff Foodservice Corp.*, 739 F.2d 73 (2nd Circ. 1984), *In re KNM Roswell Ltd. Partnership*, 126 B.R. 548 (B.C., N.D. Ill. 1991), *In re California Devices, Inc.*, 126 B.R. 82 (B.C., N.D. Cal. 1991), *In re Tri-County Water Ass'n*, 91 B.R. 547 (B.C., D.S.D. 1988), *In re Colter, Inc., supra, In re Mobile Air Drilling Co., Inc.*, 53 B.R. 605 (B.C., N.D. Ohio 1985), *In re Becker*, 51 B.R. 975 (B.C., D. Minn. 1985). According to *In re American Resources Management Corp.*, these cases have properly refused to follow an improper reading of *Callister. Callister's* real message is consistent with statute; and when *Callister* is so read, it need not be rejected.

This Court agrees, and adopts *In re American Resources Management Corp.*'s interpretation of *In re Callister.*

In the present case, interim fees have already been awarded but have never been paid; and the question is not interim disposition of sufficient funds but final distribution of insufficient funds. These circumstances do not support any exercise of judicial discretion. In this case, 11 U.S.C. § 507(b) and related statutes plainly require that, after payment of Ch. 7 administrative expenses, what little money is left in this estate must go to satisfy the Bank's superpriority claim for "inadequate adequate protection," at the expense of H & W's claim for attorney fees for representing the former debtor-in-possession.

Id.

(2)   After *Orix*, must the creditor show that the debtor benefitted from the use of the collateral in order to be entitled to an inadequate protection claim?

[F]   Review: Fun With Adequate Protection

Debtor, who owns and operates an apartment building, files a Chapter 11 petition on January 1. On January 15, the bank that holds a mortgage on the building moves for relief from the automatic stay on the grounds that its interest in the property is not adequately protected. On that date, the property is worth $200,000 and the Bank's claim is $200,000. One expert testifies that the value of the property is stable; another expert testifies that the value of the property is declining. The court decides that it will not grant relief from the stay, provided that the debtor provides adequate protection in the form of monthly payments of $1,000 to protect the bank from any decline in the value of the collateral.

Example I

Ten months later, when it appears that the debtor is incapable of being resuscitated, the court converts the case to Chapter 7. At that point the property is worth $250,000.

In this case, the $10,000 in adequate protection payments that the bank received should be applied to its secured claim. What is the amount of its allowed secured claim? Because, under Code § 506(b), postpetition interest accrues on oversecured claims such as the bank's, the bank will hold an allowed secured claim of $200,000 plus interest of, say, $200 a month or $2,000 over the course of 10 months. If the adequate protection payments are applied to the bank's secured claim, when all is said and done, the bank's recovery will look like this:

Allowed Secured Claim:	$202,000	
Distribution to Secured Creditor:	$192,000	Proceeds of sale of property
		Adequate protection payments
	10,000	received
Total Recovery	$202,000	

Example II

Ten months later, when it appears that the debtor is incapable of being resuscitated, the court converts the case to Chapter 7. At that point the property is worth $190,000.

In this case, the $10,000 in adequate protection payments that the bank received should be applied to its unsecured claim. What is the amount of its unsecured claim? Because the bank holds a claim of $200,000 collateralized by property worth $190,000, under Code § 506(a), the bank holds a secured claim of $190,000 and an unsecured claim of $10,000. What happened to postpetition interest? Since the bank is undersecured, it does not hold an allowable claim for postpetition interest according to Code § 502(b)(2). If the adequate protection payments are applied to the bank's unsecured claim, when all is said and done, the bank's recovery will look like this:

Allowed Secured Claim: $190,000
Allowed Unsecured Claim: 10,000
Total $200,000
Distribution to Secured Creditor: $190,000 Proceeds of sale of property
                                             Adequate protection payments
                                    10,000 received
Total Recovery $200,000

Example III

Assume that the value of the property does, in fact, remain stable during the 10-month life of the Chapter 11 case, so that when the court converts the case to Chapter 7 the property is worth $200,000. At that point the bank will hold an allowed secured claim of $200,000. Because no interest accrued postpetition, in the absence of an agreement in an adequate protection order or stipulation to the contrary, the adequate protection payments cannot be treated as payments on account of interest (i.e., an "add on"). The estimate will retain $10,000 of the sale proceeds. Thus, the bank's recovery will look like this:

Allowed Secured Claim: $200,000
Distribution to Secured Creditor: $190,000 Proceeds of sale of property
                                    10,000 Adequate protection payments
                                             received
Total Recovery $200,000

Example IV

Assume that the value of the property declines twice as fast as anticipated, so that when the court converts the case to Chapter 7, the value of the property is $180,000. The $10,000 in adequate protection payments will be applied in partial satisfaction of the bank's $20,000 unsecured claim. Because adequate protection turned out to be inadequate, the bank will have a $10,000 "inadequate protection claim" under Code § 507(b). Such a claim is entitled to priority over administrative expense claims and unsecured claims.

Allowed Secured Claim: $190,000
Allowed Unsecured Claim: 10,000
Total $200,000
Distribution to Secured Creditor: $180,000 Proceeds of sale of property
                                             Adequate protection payments
                                    10,000 received
                                             § 507(b) "inadequate protection"
                                    10,000 payment
Total Recovery $200,000

§ 3.08 RELIEF FROM THE STAY: DEBTOR'S LACK OF EQUITY IN, AND NEED FOR, THE PROPERTY

PROBLEM 3.13

In *Timbers*, Justice Scalia rejected the lender's contention that undersecured creditors would suffer "inordinate and extortionate delay" if they were denied adequate protection in the form of lost opportunity payments, explaining that such creditors could always seek relief from the stay by invoking Code § 362(d)(2). Please read that section now. The following opinion depicts it in action.

IN RE ANCHORAGE BOAT SALES, INC.

United States Bankruptcy Court, Eastern District of New York

4 B.R. 635 (1980)

BORIS RADOYEVICH, BANKRUPTCY JUDGE.

[In 1977, the debtor and Midlantic Bank executed a security agreement under which Midlantic agreed to provide floor plan financing in exchange for a security interest in the debtor's inventory, accounts receivable, and certain contract rights. In 1978 and 1979, the debtor's bookkeeping system "misfunctioned," with the result that Midlantic was not repaid, as it should have been, as boats were sold. In exchange for not immediately enforcing its claim and security interest, Midlantic was granted a security interest in additional property of the debtor. By the time the debtor filed its Chapter 11 petition in February, 1980, the debtor held property valued at $1,194,000, all of it subject to Midlantic's lien. Midlantic's claim exceeded $1,316,000. Business forecasts (prepared by Midlantic) indicated that the debtor would suffer a net loss of $106,000 in the next 12 months. The court found that the debtor's own predictions of a small profit during this period were "unrealistic," and concluded that "the prospects for reorganizing this debtor are not good." Midlantic commenced an adversary proceeding seeking, among other things, relief from the stay in order to enforce its security interest. — Eds.]

. . . .

CONCLUSIONS OF LAW — RELIEF FROM STAY

The plaintiff's complaint asserts claims for relief based on section 362(d) of the Code, 11 U.S.C. § 362(d). This section provides:

> (d) On request of a party in interest and after notice and a hearing, the court shall grant relief from the stay provided under subsection (a) of this section, such as by terminating, annulling, modifying, or conditioning such stay
>
> > (1) for cause, including the lack of adequate protection of an interest in property of such party in interest; or
> >
> > (2) with respect to a stay of an act against property, if

(A) the debtor does not have an equity in such property; and

(B) such property is not necessary to an effective reorganization.

Under subdivision (d)(2), which is primarily relied upon in the plaintiff's post-trial memorandum, the creditor has a right to relief from the automatic stay if the debtor has no equity in the property which is subject to the creditor's lien, and such property is not necessary to an effective reorganization. Section 362(g) places the burden of proof on the issue of "no equity" upon the party requesting relief from stay, and the burden of proof on all other issues is upon the party opposing such relief. 11 U.S.C. § 362(g).

Subdivision (d)(2) was added to section 362 of the proposed Bankruptcy Reform Act by House and Senate conferees to enable mortgagees to proceed against non-essential real property in reorganization cases in which the debtor has no equity in the real property. . . . 124 Cong. Rec. H11, 092 (daily ed. Oct. 6, 1978). According to the legislative history, subdivision (d)(2) is "intended to solve the problem of real property mortgage foreclosures of property where the bankruptcy petition is filed on the eve of foreclosure," *Id.* at H11, 092-93, but is "not intended to apply if the business of the debtor is managing or leasing real property, such as a hotel operation, even though the debtor has no equity if the property is necessary to an effective reorganization." *Id.* at H11, 093. Thus, subsection (d)(2) represents the view of Congress that a creditor is entitled to relief from stay in every case in which the two-pronged test of this subsection is met: relief from stay should be granted if there is no equity in the collateral, and the collateral is not essential to an effective reorganization. Congress has thereby taken away a certain amount of the discretion which formerly rested with Bankruptcy Judges under Bankruptcy Rule 11-44, and replaced it with its own value judgment that such facts warrant relief from stay in every instance.

This is not to say, however, that Congress envisioned the application of subsection (d)(2) only to provide relief from the stay of acts against realty. It is true that the legislative history uses real property as an example to show when relief from stay might be warranted. However, the language of the statute is not so limited, and should be read as applying to all property which is encumbered by a creditor's interest, including inventory and accounts receivable.

As noted above, the debtor does not have an equity in the property which is subject to the plaintiff's interests. Rather, the debt exceeds the value of the collateral by $121,575.72. The plaintiff contends that it has met its burden of proof under subsection (d)(2) because the debtor has no equity in its collateral and, in addition, the property is not necessary to an effective reorganization because there is no possibility of an effective reorganization.

It is undoubtedly true that property is not necessary to an effective reorganization if there is no possibility of an effective reorganization. This point is well taken and supported by ample authority. *E.g., In re Terra Mar Assocs.,* 3 B.R. 462, 6 B.C.D. 150 (D. Conn. 1980); *In re Paradise Boat Leasing Corp.,* 2 B.R. 482, 5 B.C.D. 1122 (Bankr. D.V.I. 1979) The Court has found that there is a gap of more than $100,000.00 between the value of the collateral and the amount of the plaintiff's claim. It also is clear that the debtor's operations are not likely to be profitable in the course of the next several months. Nothing in the record would indicate that the debtor has an outside source of funds which would enable the debtor to finance a plan of arrangement. All but two floor plan lenders have stopped making loans, Transcript of April 9, 1980, at 17, and only a few boat manufacturers have agreed to supply the debtor with inventory on a consignment basis. Nothing in the record would indicate that the debtor is able to generate sufficient revenues to meet its other obligations. There is nothing before the Court which would indicate that this debtor has any hope of confirming a plan of reorganization. As noted above, the party opposing relief from stay has the burden of proof on all issues other than lack of equity. Accordingly, the Court concludes that the debtor's encumbered property is non-essential property because there is no possibility that the debtor can reorganize itself. The stay should be lifted to allow the plaintiff to proceed, in a court of competent jurisdiction, to foreclose on its security interests.

NOTES AND QUESTIONS

(1) Judge Radoyevich observed, "It is undoubtedly true that property is not necessary to an effective reorganization if there is no possibility of an effective reorganization." The Supreme Court agreed with him in *United Savings Assoc. v. Timbers of Inwood Forest Assocs., Ltd.*, 484 U.S. 365, 375–76 (1987), saying that for property to be necessary for an effective reorganization, there "must be a reasonable possibility of a successful reorganization within a reasonable time." *See also, In re Pegasus Agency*, 101 F.3d 882, 887 (2d Cir. 1996) ("To demonstrate necessity, Pegasus had to show that the property is essential for an effective reorganization that is in prospect . . . [T]he bankruptcy judge concluded it could not succeed within a reasonable time. The court reached this conclusion for three reasons: (i) Pegasus's proposal relied on unsubstantiated assumptions and fanciful calculations, rather than verifiable research and financial analysis; (ii) by its own calculations, the plan's projected revenues fell short of paying the full indebtedness owed Grammas; and (iii) Hochman's commitment to fund the reorganization was not credible, given his testimony that he would invest in the development only if he could reap a million dollars profit or more, while the plan itself showed no promise of any such return." [Internal quotations omitted]).

(2) As counsel for Amphydynamics, what facts would you want to present to the judge to demonstrate that a successful reorganization was likely within a reasonable time?

Chapter 4

MANAGEMENT OF THE BUSINESS

§ 4.01 INTRODUCTION AND HISTORICAL NOTE

After a company files a Chapter 11 petition, *who* manages its affairs, and *for whom* are its affairs managed?

You undoubtedly will recall from your basic bankruptcy course that in every Chapter 7 liquidation case, a trustee administers the estate for the benefit of creditors. As the focus of a Chapter 7 case is on distributing property of the estate to creditors holding prepetition claims, the principal duties of a Chapter 7 trustee are to marshal assets, liquidate the assets, and distribute the proceeds to creditors. Although, under Code § 721, a trustee may, with the court's permission, operate the debtor's business for a limited time — for example, a trustee might complete the manufacture of goods for resale — a Chapter 7 case is fundamentally about winding things up.

A Chapter 11 business reorganization case, as we know, is different. It contemplates the continuation of the enterprise while efforts are made to rehabilitate or sell it and to formulate a plan for paying creditors. If the business is going to continue to operate, it has to be managed, but this raises some important questions that have been hotly debated over the years, including: Who should manage the business? For whose benefit should the business be managed?

Today, the presumption is that those who managed a business outside of Chapter 11 will continue to manage it in Chapter 11, and that management will be replaced only if there is a good reason to do so. This, however, is a relatively new approach, and to understand how and why it evolved, a brief excursion into bankruptcy history is necessary.

BACK TO THE FUTURE: THE EVOLUTION OF TRUSTEES AND DEBTORS IN POSSESSION PRACTICE UNDER THE FORMER BANKRUPTCY ACT, 1938 TO 1979

Up to this point you've been asked to think like an attorney. Now it's time to think like Headley Charisma, the CEO of the troubled Amphydynamics Corp. Assume that the year is 1970. (This will explain why all the characters around you look as if they just arrived from central casting to test for bit parts in *Austin Powers*.) Assume that your suppliers won't ship, that your banks won't extend more credit, and that your payroll is about to come due. Amphy is a public company, and you own a significant but not controlling interest in it. You consult with the company's attorney, who tells you that if you are going to attempt to reorganize the business in bankruptcy, you have to decide whether to file a Chapter X or Chapter XI petition on behalf of the company. Remember, this is the year 1970, so we are governed by the 1898 Bankruptcy Act[1] as amended from time to time by, among other things, the Chandler Act of 1938.[2] That is why, in the preceding sentence, we are speaking in Roman, not Arabic, numerals and why we are speaking about two business rehabilitation chapters, not one.[3] You ask your attorney to explain the differences between Chapter X and Chapter XI. She tells you that both are vehicles for restructuring debts, but that Chapter X was designed with larger, public companies in mind, whereas Chapter XI was designed for smaller, mom-and-pop businesses. You say, "Then by all means, let's go first class. Let's take the Chapter X route."

"Whoa," she says. "I'm afraid there's more to it than that." She explains that Chapter X was designed for the reorganization of corporations having multiple strata of debt and that it contains provisions for restructuring both secured claims and unsecured claims. "A Chapter X plan can scale them down, or stretch them out, and modify interest rates," she explains.

"That's good," you say. "We have several strata of debt. We have secured creditors, unsecured creditors, subordinated debenture holders. I would be happy to restructure some or all of that debt."

"Yes, but you need to bear in mind that a Chapter X plan can also modify the rights of stockholders, with or without their consent," she says. "As a Chapter X plan might very well provide that stock will be given to creditors in satisfaction of at least a portion of their claims, your creditors could very well wind up owning some or all of the stock in the company."

"Ouch," you say, "But I would never propose a plan that did that, unless *I* — I mean *we* stockholders — were getting something in return from creditors."

"Well, that's another interesting thing," she says. "In a Chapter X case, it may not be you who formulates the plan. In Chapter X, any party in interest can propose a reorganization plan, including a creditor, or a stockholder, but most likely the plan will be formulated not by you, but by *the trustee*."

You're a little bewildered. "What's a *trustee*?" you ask.

"I was afraid you would ask that, because this may hurt. Chapter X requires that in any case involving a debtor owing $250,000 or more — and that means virtually every case — a trustee has to be appointed. The trustee not only takes over running the business and developing a reorganization plan, but is also obligated to investigate the behavior of prior managers for evidence of mismanagement, misconduct, or fraud."

---

[1] Ch. 541, 30 Stat. 544 (1898) (repealed 1978).

[2] Ch. 575, 52 Stat. 480 (1938) (repealed 1978).

[3] If the primary focus of your case were the restructuring of debts secured by real property, you would have yet a third choice: Chapter XII. This chapter was "designed to accommodate a unique method of real estate financing [employed] in the Chicago area" and was similar in many respects to Chapter XI. H.R. Rep. No. 595, 95th Cong., 1st Sess. 224 (1977). Today, there is not a separate chapter for real estate debtors.

"You're right. That does hurt. Whose bright idea is this trustee business, anyway?"

"The idea of installing a receiver to take charge of a failing business is not new, but the presence of a trustee in Chapter X is attributable in no small part to recommendations made by a study group headed by William O. Douglas. I guess you've heard of him."

"I assume you are referring to the Supreme Court Justice, appointed by President Roosevelt in 1939, who retired from the Court in 1975. Interestingly, like FDR, he too was stricken with polio, but he recovered and became quite a sportsman. I believe he taught law school for a time and was fairly young when he was appointed to the Supreme Court."

"I'm impressed. However, you left out the fact that before Douglas became Justice Douglas he was Chairman of the SEC. This is important, because in that capacity, during the Great Depression, he headed a study of how corporate reorganization cases of that era were handled. The study resulted in a report that was very critical of the reorganization process.[4] Douglas was especially appalled by the behavior of insiders — or as he called them, 'reorganizers' — who manipulated the reorganization process in order to preserve their ownership and control of troubled businesses. I have brought a copy of the report with me so that you can see for yourself what Chairman Douglas's study group said on the subject:

> [R]eorganizers and investors will at times have different objectives in reorganizations. Investors will be interested in an expeditious, economical, fair, an honest readjustment of their company's affairs. They will be concerned with having the business restored to an efficient and trustworthy management as quickly as possible . . . . They will want fair treatment accorded them by those whose claims are senior or junior to their own. They will be desirous of keeping reorganization costs at a minimum.
>
> . . . .
>
> They will be desirous of having the company which emerges from the reorganization adequately financed. They will want that company to have a sound financial structure, so that there will be no immediate necessity for another receivership or bankruptcy.
>
> . . . .
>
> If their company has been a preserve for exploitation, they will want to be rid of the despoilers. They will want an extravagant, wasteful, inefficient, or faithless management ousted from control and a new one installed.
>
> . . . .

---

[4] The report, "Securities and Exchange Commission Report on the Study and Investigation of the Work, Activities, Personnel and Functions of Protective and Reorganization Committees," was published over the period 1937 to 1940 in eight parts. An analysis of Justice Douglas's work on the report is contained in Hopkirk, *William O. Douglas — His Work in Policing Bankruptcy Proceedings*, 18 Vand. L. Rev. 663 (1965).

Reorganizers have at times had objectives not only different from but incompatible with those of investors. Reorganizers have frequently been interested in expeditious reorganizations not primarily to avoid expense, not necessarily because of the desire to have dividend and interest payments quickly resumed, but largely because of their desire to consummate a reorganization of their own liking. Reorganizers frequently have not been concerned, in the manner of investors, with economy in reorganization, as economy would interfere with their profits. Reorganizers at times have not been interested in fair reorganizations, since fairness might seriously intrude into their own plans and affairs. Reorganizers at times have not desired honest reorganizations, in the investors' sense of the word, because such reorganizations would be costly to them. They have been motivated by other factors. And they have endeavored — in large measure with success — to mould the reorganization processes so as to serve their own objectives.[5]

"Douglas believed that one important way to curb insider abuse and protect public debt and equity holders was to replace management with an independent trustee in every case. As a practical matter, the Douglas recommendations were incorporated into Chapter X."

"So, what you're telling me is that if I put the company into Chapter X, I basically put myself out of a job."

"It's a possibility. If you do continue to work for the company, you do so at the pleasure and under the direction of the Chapter X trustee."

"Is there anything *else* you think I need to know about Chapter X?"

"A couple of things at least. Remember, Chapter X was designed for public companies and the SEC Commissioner was one of its architects, so you may not be surprised to know that Chapter X gives the SEC special standing to advocate on behalf of public debt and equity holders and to serve as an advisor to the court on many matters, including whether reorganization plans conform to the absolute priority rule."

"The *absolute priority rule*? That sounds strict," you say.

"Oh, it is. Distilled to its bitter essence, the rule means that under a reorganization plan, each class of claims or interest holders has to have its claims satisfied in full — but no more than in full — before the next lower class can receive anything. So, for example, in the case of a company such as yours, that has senior creditors (your bank and other working capital lenders), subordinated creditors (your subordinated debenture holders), and stockholders, the absolute priority rule requires that the senior creditors have their claims satisfied in full before more junior creditors can receive anything under a plan, and that all creditors have their claims satisfied in full before stockholders can receive or retain an interest under the plan."

---

[5] SEC Report on the Study and Investigation of the Work, Activities, Personnel and Functions of Protective and Reorganization Committees: Part I, Strategy and Techniques of Protective and Reorganization Committees (May 10, 1937) 2–5.

"What?" you ask. "Could you please run that by me again?"

"Let me give you a simple example. Suppose Amphydynamics Corp. has assets worth $10,000."

"Okay."

"Suppose Amphy owes creditors $20,000."

"It's insolvent."

"Correct. Now suppose that you propose a reorganization plan that provides that creditors will be paid 50 cents on the dollar, that subordinated debenture holders will get nothing, and that you and your fellow stockholders will retain your equity interest in the company."

"Sounds reasonable to me."

"But it violates the absolute priority rule, because you stockholders are retaining your ownership interest even though the claims of senior and subordinated creditors, who obviously occupy higher rungs on the priority ladder, aren't being satisfied in full."

"Yikes," you say. "Since the entire company isn't worth as much as what it owes, and since there isn't enough cash to go around, it sounds as if some or all of the stock will have to go to the creditors. That means that the creditors could wind up owning the company while we stockholders are shut out."

"That's right. That's absolute priority."

"That really does hurt. Is there any chance that you are going to tell me that the absolute priority rule is also the product of reforms urged by Douglas and others to curb abuses committed by insiders in the reorganization cases of yore?"

"You are a very intuitive, as well as erudite, client. You see, what would happen in too many of those 'cases of yore,' which, by the way, were called equity receiverships, is that senior creditors and stockholders would collaborate to retain control of the businesses at the expense of non-insider creditors."

"How did they do that?"

"The scheme is a little complicated [and we will look at it again more closely when we consider reorganization plans], but basically it worked something like this: When a company fell on hard times, a bondholder[6] friendly with the debtor's owner-managers would petition the court to appoint a receiver to take charge of the company's property. Then, with the consent of the bondholders, the receiver would sell the assets, often at what was believed to be a bargain price, to a new entity. Interestingly, the owners of this new entity were often identical to the owners of the old entity. The proceeds of sale would go to the bondholders. If, as was usually the case, the sale did not produce enough cash to pay their claims in full, the bondholders would retain a lien on the company's assets after they were sold to this new entity. When the dust settled, there would be a new entity that owned the

---

[6] "Bond" refers to a long-term debt instrument. The debt is typically secured by a lien on property of the issuer.

assets of the former entity. The owners of the new entity were the same insiders that were owners of the former entity. The secured creditors were identical to the secured creditors of the former entity."

"Whoa! There's something or someone missing here."

"You're right. The general unsecured creditors and the debenture holders are missing. These intermediate creditors would get little or nothing under these schemes."

"They've been frozen out! That doesn't seem fair and equitable."

"Once again you're right. Sometimes, when these transactions were challenged, they were denounced by the courts. The courts held that a plan that leapfrogged over the rights of intermediate creditors by allowing stockholders to retain an interest was neither fair nor equitable."

"What did they do about it?"

"The judicially prescribed antidote was the absolute priority rule, which, as you now can see, prevents stockholders, who occupy the bottom rung of the priority ladder, and senior creditors, who occupy the top rung, from conspiring to squeeze out the creditors and interest holders who occupy the in-between rungs. P.S., according to an important opinion written by *Justice* Douglas not long after he left the SEC for the Supreme Court,[7] the principle of absolute priority was incorporated into the predecessor of Chapter X of the Bankruptcy Act and in later opinions, courts held that the rule operated in Chapter X cases, too."[8]

"Why are you telling me all this, just now? I thought we were talking about *who* manages the business, and about Chapter 11 of the 1978 Bankruptcy Code, not about old Chapter X."

"Correct. But as you will see, when we start thinking about whose interests the managers of a Chapter 11 entity represent and to whom their fiduciary duties run, a basic understanding of the absolute priority concept will be very helpful."

"Okay," you say, "let me see if I understand this. The year is 1970. My trousers flare from the knee. If I file a Chapter X petition, I get fired, a trustee examines how I ran the business, the SEC gets involved, and unless there's a lot more value in the company than I can imagine, I can probably kiss my stock goodbye."

"Yes."

"Alright then. You said that as the CEO of a troubled company in 1970, I had a couple of options. Now might be a good time for you to tell me about the other one."

"Since this is 1970, your other choice is Chapter XI. As I've said before, Chapter XI was written with smaller, closely-held, so-called 'mom-and-pop' businesses in mind. Accordingly, it doesn't provide for as comprehensive a debt restructuring as Chapter X. For example, although Chapter XI provides for the restructuring of unsecured claims, there is no provision in Chapter XI for modifying secured claims.

---

[7] *Case v. Los Angeles Lumber Products Co.*, 308 U.S. 106 (1939).

[8] *Consolidated Rock Prods. Co. v. Du Bois*, 312 U.S. 510 (1941).

But, on the other hand, Chapter XI does not provide for the appointment of a trustee. If you were to put the company into Chapter XI, you would continue to manage the business as what we call a 'debtor in possession.' You'll also be happy to learn that, unlike Chapter X, Chapter XI does not provide for the alteration of stockholders' interests without stockholders' consent."

"Why are Chapters X and XI so different?"

"The differences are consistent with the Douglas Commission's view that in cases involving small, closely held businesses, the owners — 'mom and pop' — *are* the business and that in such cases the appointment of a trustee may be unnecessary and counterproductive. The fear was that by the time a trustee conquered the learning curve, got a handle on the business, and formed relationships with customers and suppliers, the business would be kaput. Some longtime observers of the bankruptcy scene concluded that creditors are sometimes happier dealing with the proverbial 'devil that they know' than with an independent trustee whom they don't know.[9] This is not because they are foolhardy, but because they understand the benefits of the personal leverage that is the basis and byproduct of long-term business relationships. Old management is more likely to continue to do business with old lenders and suppliers, whereas there is always a risk that trustees have or will form other associations. There was also a sense that in these smaller cases, investors did not need the protection of a trustee because the investors and managers are one and the same. The Douglas report compared cases involving closely and publicly held companies this way:

> [W]here the bankrupt is a small corporation with stock closely held by those who have managed the enterprise, the interposition of a corporate entity does not obscure the realities; there is a practical identity between the bankrupt corporation and its stockholders. Management and ownership are substantially one.
>
> . . . .
>
> The large corporate debtor is far removed from such a state of facts. With stock widely scattered in a multitude of small holdings, and management and stockholders distinct groups, little identity may remain between ownership and control. When such a corporation is in bankruptcy . . . it is irrelevant and confusing to speak of it as the debtor or bankrupt in the same way that these terms are applied to [closely held companies].[10]

"There are other differences, too. Chapter XI confers no special standing on the SEC to evaluate the fairness of restructuring plans, and, consistent with the theory that without mom and pop there can be no business, Chapter XI gives the debtor in possession the exclusive right to propose a reorganization plan."

---

[9] Coogan, Broude & Glatt, *Comments on Some Reorganization Provisions of the Pending Bankruptcy Bills*, 30 Bus. Law. 1149, 1150 (1975).

[10] "Securities and Exchange Commission Report on the Study and Investigation of the Work, Activities, Personnel, and Functions of Protective and Reorganization Committees," Part VIII, "A Summary of the Law Pertaining to Equity and Bankruptcy Reorganizations, and of the Commission's Conclusions and Recommendations," at 98 (Sept. 30, 1940).

"And what about the absolute priority rule?"

"I'm glad you asked, because it completes the analytical circle. There is no absolute priority rule in Chapter XI. If stockholders can convince a majority of creditors or more senior interest holders to take less under a plan so that stockholders can retain an interest in the business, Chapter XI says more power to them."

"Chapter XI sounds great, but why are you telling me about it? Amphydynamics isn't a mom-and-pop business. It's a large, public company."

"Yes, but listen to this. Even though Chapter XI was designed for smaller businesses, its doors were never closed to big ones, even large, publicly held companies such as Amphy. Amphy is at least facially eligible to seek relief in Chapter XI."

"On second thought, I think we should file a Chapter XI petition."

"I thought you would. Indeed, in light of what you now know about old Chapters X and XI of the former Act, you will not be surprised to learn that Chapter XI became the rehabilitation vehicle-of-choice not only of the managers of the small companies for which it was conceived, but also of the managers of large, publicly-held companies. Managers of even very large troubled companies found the Chapter XI climate irresistibly congenial."

"Can you blame them?"

"No. As Chapter XI contemplated the continuation of the debtor in possession, it minimized the risk that management would be ousted from control. As Chapter XI gave the debtor the exclusive right to propose a plan, it maximized management's leverage not merely in terms of negotiating a plan, but in terms of negotiating a plan that would preserve owners' (including management-owners') interests. Perhaps Chapter XI also appealed to some managers who wanted to avoid having their prior actions scrutinized by independent trustees. In any case, thanks to this preference for Chapter XI, by the 1970s, fewer than 10% of all business reorganization cases were commenced under Chapter X."[11]

"I'm not surprised."

"But the story doesn't end there."

"For some reason, that doesn't surprise me either."

"Often, when a large public company sought refuge in Chapter XI, a creditor or a creditors' committee would seek to have the case converted to Chapter X. Typically, they would contend that the company could not be rehabilitated in the absence of a Chapter X scale restructuring or the replacement of management by a trustee. But in many cases, the threat of conversion was applied merely to exact some concession from management. Sometimes the SEC would move for conversion, arguing that Chapter X was the only appropriate venue for debtors whose securities were publicly held. This argument was rejected by the Supreme Court. Do you want to guess who wrote the opinion?"

---

[11] H.R. Rep. No. 595, 95th Cong., 1st Sess. 222 (1977).

"Not Justice Douglas?"

"You guessed it. In *General Stores Corp. v. Shlensky*,[12] the Court held that neither the character of the debtor, nor the nature of its capital structure, should determine whether Chapter X or XI was the proper vehicle. Rather, Justice Douglas said, the character and qualifications of the management, the need for a trustee, and the extent of the needed restructuring should control. The problem was that these choice-of-chapter squabbles were not good for business and they often generated extensive (and expensive) litigation. As one court noted, in far too many cases the sickly debtors were dying while the litigants were fighting over what operating table they should be on."[13]

THE BANKRUPTCY REFORM ACT OF 1978

"That's terrible. What a waste."

"Congress agreed. And so, in the early 1970s, when Congress began to think about overhauling the Bankruptcy laws, there was much debate over whether a trustee was necessary in every case. Part and parcel of this debate was the question of whether choice-of-chapter litigation could and should be eliminated altogether by the creation of a single business rehabilitation chapter. The Commission on the Bankruptcy Laws of the United States, which had been established by Congress to study and recommend changes in the bankruptcy laws, recommended that Chapters X and XI be merged into a single rehabilitation chapter,[14] and that a trustee be appointed in any case involving a corporate debtor having debts of $1,000,000 or more and 300 security holders or more, unless a trustee was found to be unnecessary or too costly.[15] The SEC disagreed, taking the position that the need for a trustee in every public company case was as great in 1976 as it was in 1936, that a trustee would serve as the 'focal point' for investors, and that only a trustee could insure a fair 'allocation of assets, earnings, and

---

[12] *General Stores Corp. v. Shlensky*, 350 U.S. 462, 466–68 (1956). *See also Securities and Exchange Commission v. American Trailer Rentals*, 379 U.S. 594 (1965).

[13] *S.E.C. v. Canandaigua Enter. Corp.*, 339 F.2d 14, 19 (2d Cir. 1964).

[14] The Commission found:

> An independent trustee is often desirable, especially in a case involving the reorganization of a corporate debtor having substantial indebtedness and publicly held securities. At the other end of the spectrum is the closely held corporate debtor whose existing management is essential to the continued operation; in such a case an independent trustee is not always needed and is often counterproductive. An arbitrary dividing line, such as the dollar formula of Chapter X of the present act, is undesirable. Indebtedness alone is an adequate criterion. It does not take into consideration the nature of the ownership of the debtor or a need to continue existing management. This arbitrary approach has been a strong motive behind the expanded utilization of Chapter XI. It also has probably been a factor in delaying the commencement of reorganizations, to the ultimate detriment of security holders. . . .

> The Commission therefore recommends that the appointment of an independent trustee be discretionary, but that need for such an appointment be presumptive where indebtedness exceeds $1,000,000 and there are 300 or more security holders.

Report of the Commission on the Bankruptcy Laws of the United States, H.R. Doc. No. 93-137, 93d Cong., 1st Sess. Part I at 252–253 (1973).

[15] *Id.* at 221 (1973).

control.'[16] The Senate version of the bankruptcy bill followed the SEC's recommendation. It provided for mandatory appointment of a trustee in every public company case.[17] The Committee Report accompanying the bill explained:

> In a large public company, whose interests are diverse and complex, the most vulnerable today are public investors who own subordinated debt or equity securities. The bill, like chapter X, is designed to counteract the natural tendency of a debtor in distress to pacify large creditors, with whom the debtor would expect to do business, at the expense of small and scattered public investors. . . .
>
> [I]nvestor protection is most critical when the company in which the public invested is in financial difficulties and is forced to seek relief under the bankruptcy laws . . . As public investors are likely to be junior or subordinated creditors or stockholders, it is essential for them to have legislative insurance that their interests will be protected. Such assurance should not be left to a plan negotiated by a debtor in distress and senior or institutional creditors who will have their own best interest to look after.[18]

"The House version took a more flexible approach. Its drafters believed that the successful rehabilitation of many large, public companies in Chapter XI demonstrated that, in most cases at least, neither the public nor creditors would necessarily be harmed by the continuation of debtors in possession. On the contrary, the House view was that investors and creditors might actually benefit from the retention of experienced management, 'because the expense of a trustee is not required and the debtor, who is familiar with his business will be better able to operate it.'[19] Nevertheless, the House Committee acknowledged that there would be 'cases where a trustee is needed, because cases of fraud or gross mismanagement do arise.' Accordingly, the House bill authorized the appointment of a trustee, but only upon the showing that the protection of a trustee was needed, and that the costs and expenses of appointing a trustee would not be disproportionately higher than the value of the protection afforded."[20]

BACK TO THE PRESENT: A SINGLE REORGANIZATION CHAPTER AND TRUSTEES ONLY ON DEMAND

In the end, Congress did enact a single reorganization chapter, Chapter 11, which is a hybrid of Chapters X and XI. (By the time this course is over, you probably will form opinions as to whether this one-chapter-fits-all approach actually works.)

---

[16] Hearings Before the Subcommittee on Civil and Constitutional Rights of the House Committee on the Judiciary on H.R. 31 and H.R. 32, 94th Cong., 2d Sess., Part 4, 2177–79 (1976).

[17] The Senate version provided that "In the case of a public company, the court, within ten days after the entry of an order for relief under this chapter, shall appoint a disinterested trustee." S. 2266, 95th Cong. 2d Sess. (1978).

[18] Report of the Committee on the Judiciary, United States Senate, to Accompany S. 2266, S. Rep. No. 989, 95th Cong., 2d Sess. 9-10 (1978).

[19] H.R. Rep. No. 595, 95th Cong., 1st Sess. 232 (1977).

[20] *Id.*

The trustee controversy was resolved by the enactment of Code § 1104(a), which provides that the debtor will be continued in possession unless, on motion of a party in interest or the United States Trustee, the court orders the appointment of a trustee "for cause, including fraud, dishonesty, incompetence, or gross mismanagement of the affairs of the debtor by current management," or "if such appointment is in the interests of creditors, any equity security holders, and other interests of the estate." A third basis for appointing a trustee is found in Code § 1104(a)(3), which provides that even if grounds for conversion or dismissal exist, the court may order the appointment of a trustee if that would better serve the interests of the creditors and the estate. Code § 1112(b)(1) contains a parallel provision.

And what is the current status of the absolute priority rule? We will see that Chapter 11 does contain, in § 1129(b), a version of the rule, but it is not quite as absolute as its predecessor. Under Chapter 11's relaxed version of the rule, if members of a senior class accept a plan that permits members of lower classes to receive an interest at the seniors' expense, the court may confirm the plan. This important change altered the dynamics of reorganization cases and added a new layer of complexity to the question of whose interests are represented by management of a debtor in possession. However, in an era in which many debtors enter Chapter 11 heavily laden with secured debt and unable to obtain the financing they need to continue to operate, the only strategy is a quick sale of a debtor's most valuable assets, which means that the benefit of the relaxed absolute priority rule to unsecured creditors and stockholders is in some cases more theoretical than real.

There is one other thing that you should know as background to the cases and materials that follow. You'll recall that under Chapter X, any party could propose a plan, but typically the trustee did. You'll recall that under Chapter XI, only a debtor in possession could propose a plan. When the two chapters were merged into Chapter 11, a mixed approach was adopted. Today, Code § 1121 gives a debtor in possession the exclusive right, but only for a limited time, to propose a reorganization plan. When exclusivity expires or is terminated (and it terminates automatically upon the appointment of a trustee), any party in interest may propose a plan. § 1121(c)(1). In theory, this approach gives debtors leverage and an opportunity to negotiate the terms of a plan while preventing debtors from holding creditors and others hostage indefinitely.

Against this backdrop, we now turn to more current developments. As you read the materials that follow, keep in mind that when a trustee is not appointed or elected, the debtor is said to function as a "debtor in possession." Code § 1101(1) defines "debtor in possession" as synonymous with "debtor," except where a trustee is serving in the case. "Debtor" is defined in § 101 as "the person concerning which a case under this title has been commenced." "Person," according to § 101, includes an "individual, partnership, and corporation." Hence, a "debtor in possession" appears to be a Chapter 11 entity, the management of which has not been replaced by a trustee. Courts have held that in a case in which no trustee has been appointed, "there is no distinction between the 'debtor' and the 'debtor in possession,'" *Matter of Triangle Chemicals, Inc.*, 697 F.2d 1280, 1290 (5th Cir. 1983), and "there is no debtor entity separate and apart from the debtor in possession." *In re Chapel Gate Apartments, Ltd.*, 64 B.R. 569, 576 (Bankr. N.D. Tex. 1986). How to separate a "debtor in possession" from those who manage it, however, is a question that we will find ourselves pondering from time to time as this chapter and the Amphydynamics case progress.

If you haven't already done so, read Code § 1104 now, and then turn to the cases and materials that follow.

§ 4.02 GROUNDS FOR APPOINTMENT AND ELECTION OF TRUSTEES

TRADEX CORPORATION v. MORSE
United States District Court, District of Massachusetts
339 B.R. 823 (2006)

MEMORANDUM AND ORDER

The president and sole shareholder of the debtor in possession seeks reversal, on behalf of the debtor, of the bankruptcy court's appointment of a trustee to take possession of Tradex Corporation ("Tradex" or "the debtor") as part of voluntary Chapter 11 bankruptcy proceedings. For the reasons stated below, I affirm the bankruptcy court's decision.

I. Standard of Review

When a District Court reviews a decision of the bankruptcy court, findings of fact are upset only if clearly erroneous, but questions of law are subject to de novo evaluation. *See* Fed. R. Bankr. P. 8013. A discretionary decision of the bankruptcy court is overturned only when there has been abuse of that discretion.

In order to give effect to those precepts in this case, however, I must determine the standards, as matters of law and fact, for the appointment of a bankruptcy trustee, as well as what, if any, discretion is afforded to a bankruptcy judge in making such a determination.

II. Background

Tradex is a company that manages and leases a plastics manufacturing facility in Lunenberg, Massachusetts. Charles Gitto, Jr. is the president and sole shareholder of Tradex. On February 16, 2005, he signed a voluntary petition for relief under Chapter 11 of the bankruptcy code and became a debtor-in-possession. That petition did not conform with 11 U.S.C. § 521, which requires inclusion of a list of creditors, schedules of assets and liabilities, or a statement of financial affairs.[1] The day it was filed, the bankruptcy court ordered Tradex to file the required

---

[1] 11 U.S.C. § 521(1):

The debtor shall —

  (1) file a list of creditors, and unless the court orders otherwise, a schedule of assets and

information. Tradex filed a motion a week later requesting extension of the deadline to file the financial information, a motion the court denied. On March 3, Tradex filed a § 521 statement.

On March 15, 2005, a meeting of creditors was held pursuant to § 341 of the bankruptcy code at the Worcester, Massachusetts office of the United States Trustee. Mr. Gitto, asserting his Fifth Amendment privilege, did not attend. Instead, his wife, Krista Gitto, the office manager of the debtor, appeared on Tradex's behalf. Aspects of her testimony, along with certain pre-petition transactions of Tradex and an ongoing grand jury investigation into fraud allegations relating, *inter alia*, to Mr. Gitto and Tradex, caused concern on the part of the United States Trustee, who on April 1, 2005, filed a motion with the bankruptcy court to appoint a Chapter 11 trustee to replace Mr. Gitto. Before the hearing on the motion, the United States Trustee received a copy of the debtor's 2003 tax return, which heightened the Trustee's concerns. The debtor objected to the motion to appoint a trustee on April 6, 2005, arguing that the Trustee had not met her burden of establishing the need for such an appointment under § 1104(a)(1) or (2).

On April 7, 2005, the bankruptcy court held a hearing on the motion and relying upon both § 1104(a)(1) and (2) with a brief order granted it from the bench. Five days later, the Trustee requested that Attorney Ellen Carpenter be appointed as trustee, a request the court granted on April 13, 2005. On April 18, 2005, the debtor sought reconsideration of the court's decision to appoint a trustee. The court denied the debtor's request the following day, finding that the motion failed to meet the requirements of Rule 59(e) and that the "new information" regarding a loan was "insufficient to alter the previous decision of the Court" which "was based on several factors, including the principal's past dealings with the debtor."

Three days later Tradex appealed that decision to this court and filed a motion with the bankruptcy court requesting that appointment of the trustee be stayed pending appeal.[2] The bankruptcy court denied that request on April 25, 2005. On April 28, 2005, Tradex requested that I issue a stay pending appeal. I denied that request on May 2, 2005, and put the appeal on an expedited briefing and hearing schedule.

While I was satisfied by the conclusion of the hearing that the Bankruptcy Court's decision to appoint the Trustee was plainly well founded, I found the case law unhelpful in explaining the relevant standards. Consequently, I have taken some time to attempt to draft in this opinion a satisfactory basis for my decision to affirm the Bankruptcy Court.

---

liabilities, a schedule of current income and current expenditures, and a statement of the debtor's financial affairs . . . .

[2] The United States Trustee moves [Doc. 5] to dismiss the appeal and to strike the brief of Mr. Gitto on grounds he is not a proper appellant. In response, Mr. Gitto on behalf of the debtor moves [Doc. 7] to correct the brief by renaming the appellant as "Tradex corporation." In order to regularize the appellate record in this expedited appeal, I will allow recaptioning and consequently decline to dismiss the appeal.

III. Discussion

A. Section 1104(a)

The bankruptcy code empowers a bankruptcy court to appoint a trustee in a Chapter 11 proceeding under certain circumstances. Section 1104 of the Code provides:

> (a) At any time after the commencement of the case but before confirmation of a plan, on request of a party in interest or the United States trustee, and after notice and a hearing, the court shall order the appointment of a trustee —

> > (1) for cause, including fraud, dishonesty, incompetence, or gross mismanagement of the affairs of the debtor by current management, either before or after the commencement of the case, or similar cause, but not including the number of holders of securities of the debtor or the amount of assets or liabilities of the debtor; or

> > (2) if such appointment is in the interests of creditors, any equity security holders, and other interests of the estate, without regard to the number of holders of securities of the debtor or the amount of assets or liabilities of the debtor. 11 U.S.C. § 1104(a).

The appointment of a Chapter 11 trustee has been described as an " 'extraordinary' act." *Petit v. New England Mort. Servs., Inc.*, 182 B.R. 64, 68 (D. Me. 1995) (quoting *In re Ionosphere Clubs, Inc.*, 113 B.R. 164, 167 (Bankr. S.D.N.Y. 1990)) . . . . The default position is that current management will retain control of the company, *see In re Garland Corp.*, 6 B.R. 456, 460 (B.A.P. 1st Cir. 1980) . . . consistent with the "belief that current management is generally best suited to orchestrate the process of rehabilitation for the benefit of creditors and other interests of the estate." *In re Savino Oil & Heating Co.*, 99 B.R. 518, 524 (Bankr. E.D.N.Y. 1989). Courts consistently refer to this default position as a "presumption." *See, e.g.,* . . . *In re St. Louis Globe-Democrat*, 63 B.R. 131, 138 (Bankr. E.D. Mo. 1985) ("It is well-established that there is a strong presumption that a debtor in possession in a reorganization case should be permitted to continue to control and manage its estate."); *Ford*, 36 B.R. at 504 (same); *see also In re Sharon Steel Corp.*, 871 F.2d 1217, 1225 (3d Cir. 1989) (appointment of a trustee "should be the exception, rather than the rule"); *Deena Packaging*, 29 B.R. 706–07. But, it has also been said that § 1104 "represents a potentially important protection that courts should not lightly disregard or encumber with overly protective attitudes towards debtors-in possession." *Savino*, 99 B.R. at 525.

. . . .

Once the party seeking a trustee meets its burden, the court is seemingly required to — in the words of the statute, it "shall", 11 U.S.C. § 1104(a) — appoint a trustee. *Official Comm. of Asbestos Claimants v. G-I Holdings, Inc. (In re G-I Holdings, Inc.)*, 385 F.3d 313, 318 (3d Cir. 2004); *see In re Oklahoma Refining Co.*, 838 F.2d 1133, 1136 (10th Cir. 1988) ("Once the court has found that cause exists under § 1104, it has no discretion but must appoint a trustee.").

. . . .

B. Standard of Proof

Although it is undisputed that the party seeking appointment of a trustee bears the burden of persuasion, a question remains regarding the standard of proof necessary to meet the burden.

The First Circuit has not addressed the approach a court should take in determining whether to appoint a trustee. The First Circuit Bankruptcy Appellate Panel in *Garland* did comment in an opinion by now Circuit Judge Cyr that the

> appropriateness of the decision to appoint a reorganization trustee under Bankruptcy Code §§ 1104 . . . turns upon whether there was a sufficient showing of cause, including incompetence or gross mismanagement of the affairs of the debtor by current management, either before or after the commencement of the case, or, in the alternative, a showing that the appointment would be in the best interests of the creditors and the estate.

Garland, 6 B.R. at 460.

Just a few weeks prior to the *Garland* decision, Judge Gabriel described § 1104 as "a compromise providing for a flexible standard for the appointment of a trustee." *In re Eichorn*, 5 B.R. 755, 757 (Bankr. D. Mass. 1980). Although there is a presumption that a debtor will remain in possession, subsection (a)(1) "reflects criteria which mandate the appointment of a trustee for cause." *Id.* "Under this subsection the court's discretionary powers are circumscribed and are limited to a judicial determination of whether 'cause,' as defined, exists." *Id.* But as with the BAP in *Garland*, Judge Gabriel did not delineate the standard of proof that must be applied when taking up subsection (a)(1). Turning to subsection (a)(2), he seemed to find the discretion of the bankruptcy court not nearly so circumscribed as with subsection (a)(1). *Id.* at 758 ("Congress . . . has given the Bankruptcy Court the flexibility under Section 1104, subsection (a)(2), to allow the court to utilize its broad equity powers in determining whether the appointment of a trustee would be in the best interests of creditors, equity security holders and other interests of the estate.").

. . . .

It appears courts in the First Circuit courts have not directly determined what evidentiary standard to apply when determining whether a "sufficient showing" has been made for purposes of § 1104. However, as Judge Carter in *Petit* observed: "although the First Circuit has never held so directly, many courts require a showing of clear and convincing evidence supporting the motion prior to" appointment of a trustee. *Petit*, 182 B.R. at 69.

For example, the Third Circuit requires that the "party moving for appointment of a trustee . . . must prove the need for a trustee under either subsection [of § 1104(a)] by clear and convincing evidence." *In re Marvel Entertainment Group, Inc.*, 140 F.3d 463, 471 (3d Cir. 1998); *see G-I Holdings*, 385 F.3d 313; *Sharon Steel*, 871 F.2d 1217. The Fifth Circuit has also held that the moving party must meet its burden by "clear and convincing evidence." *In re Cajun Elec. Power Coop., Inc.*, 69 F.3d 746, 749 (5th Cir. 1995).

A number of bankruptcy courts have joined the Third and Fifth Circuits in applying a "clear and convincing" evidentiary standard. *See*, *e.g.*, *Sanders*, 2000 Bankr. LEXIS 263, at *8, (March 2, 2000) ("The appointment of a trustee is an extraordinary remedy that requires proof by clear and convincing evidence.").

Despite the fact that various courts have pronounced the appointment of a Trustee to be "extraordinary" and available only if the factual predicate is established by "clear and convincing" evidence, as a practical matter, whether the party has met its burden has consistently been left within the discretion of the bankruptcy court. The nature of that deference has been described in differing ways that further muddle the standards to be applied in reviewing a Trustee appointment decision.

Some courts, including the First Circuit Bankruptcy Appellate Panel, have said they must "accept the findings of the bankruptcy judge unless clearly erroneous." *Garland*, 6 B.R. at 460. In *Garland*, this led the BAP to conclude that the "findings of fact are amply supported by the record, and the conclusions of law, freely reviewable on appeal, comport with the legislative prescriptions of section 1104(a) . . . ." *Id.* at 461 (citation omitted). *Cf. In re Paolino*, 60 B.R. 828, 829 (E.D. Pa. 1986) ("The factual determinations made by the bankruptcy judge must be accepted by this court, unless I am convinced that they are clearly erroneous. While I freely concede that reasonable minds might differ as to the extent and seriousness of the debtor's derelictions, by no stretch of the imagination can the bankruptcy's judge's findings be deemed clearly erroneous.").

By contrast, the Fifth Circuit, in *Cajun Electric*, has said that the "district court's appointment of a trustee is reviewable only for abuse of discretion." *Cajun Electric*, 69 F.3d at 749 (citing *Sharon Steel*, 871 F.3d at 1225–26; *In re Dalkon Shield Claimants*, 828 F.2d 239, 242 (4th Cir. 1987)); . . . . And, in *Sharon Steel*, the Third Circuit rejected a clearly erroneous standard, as embraced by the First Circuit Bankruptcy Appellate Panel in *Garland*, and adopted "an abuse of discretion standard." *Sharon Steel*, 871 F.3d at 1225.

Despite the differing language used, there is widespread and consistent deference afforded to the bankruptcy court. *See*, *e.g.*, *Sharon Steel*, 871 F.2d at 1226 ("While § 1104(a) mandates appointment of a trustee when the bankruptcy court finds cause — seemingly requiring plenary review, a determination of cause . . . is within the discretion of the court.' ") (quoting *Dalkon Shield Claimants*, 828 F.2d at 242); *Dalkon Shield Claimants*, 828 F.2d at 241 ("The concepts of incompetence and dishonesty cover a wide spectrum of conduct and . . . the court has broad discretion in applying such concepts to show cause.").

The bankruptcy court appears to enjoy even more sweeping discretion under subsection (a)(2). *See In re Clinton Centrifuge, Inc.*, 85 B.R. 980, 983 (Bankr. E.D. Pa. 1988) ("Pursuant to § 1104(a)(1), a court must appoint a trustee once 'cause' is found; while section 1104 (a)(2) leaves the court with broad discretion to determine whether the interests of all constituencies would benefit from the appointment of a disinterested trustee.") . . . . In applying that discretion, some courts have supplied a list of factors to consider. For example, the *Colorado-Ute* court advised that,

> as to whether the appointment of a trustee is in the best interest of creditors pursuant to Section 1104(a)(2), the court should eschew rigid absolutes and look to the practical realities and necessities.

The court should also consider the following four factors:

> (i) the trustworthiness of the debtor;
>
> (ii) the debtor in possession's past and present performance and prospects for the debtor's rehabilitation;
>
> (iii) the confidence — or lack thereof — of the business community and of creditors in present management;
>
> (iv) the benefits derived by the appointment of a trustee, balanced against the costs of appointment.

Colorado-Ute, 120 B.R. at 176 (citations omitted).

Having canvassed this case law, I have come to conclude that an appointment court need find the factual predicates — "cause" or the best interests of relevant parties — by only a preponderance of the evidence. Clear and convincing evidence is not required. Recognizing that this is contrary to the explicit statements of most other courts that have directly addressed the subject, I nevertheless believe it is consistent with the reasoning and approach undergirding the case law in this area. Indeed, after describing the burden as "clear and convincing" and citing the extraordinariness of appointing a trustee, courts generally take up the question as one falling with the discretion of the bankruptcy courts, to which they defer, and do so in a way that directly or indirectly hollows out the "clear and convincing" standard cited.

. . . .

C. Bankruptcy Court's Decision

Turning to the case at hand, the parties offer no reason to question that the judge was persuaded, at least by a preponderance of the evidence, that both (a)(1) and (a)(2) were satisfied. The bankruptcy court did not explain its expedited decision in great detail. I will, therefore, review the arguments and information it was provided to determine whether a sufficient factual basis exists for the court, within its discretion, to conclude that the requirements of § 1104(a) had been met.

The Trustee summarized the bases upon which its request for a trustee appointment rest:

> Verified documents and testimony proffered by the Debtor revealed that Tradex through its principal, Gitto, failed to make straightforward and accurate disclosures to the court when the Debtor's schedules did not include all the Debtor's assets, liabilities, and payments made to insiders. The documents and testimony also revealed that Gitto improperly engaged in questionable inter-company transactions and commingled the affairs of

Tradex with those of Gitto Global by causing Tradex to grant a mortgage on its assets to collaterize [sic] a sale for the benefit of Gitto Global. Moreover, Tradex and Gitto were unable to substantiate Tradex's undocumented acquisition of the Vitrolite inventory. In addition, a grand jury investigation into allegations of fraud on the part of Tradex and Gitto was underway, which militated in favor of a trustee because this meant the debtor's management would be devoting significant attention to that matter — time that necessarily would come at the expense of the debtor's critical efforts to simultaneous reorganize and thereby enhance creditor recoveries. Further Gitto's decision to not make himself available to answer questions regarding the business and financial affairs of the Debtor meant the Debtor could not explain the serious inconsistencies between the debtor's tax returns and the statements the debtor made under penalty of perjury in it s bankruptcy filing.

. . . .

Furthermore the Debtor's creditors have levied substantial allegations, through related litigation and through Clinton's relief from stay motion, of bad faith, fraud and serious law enforcement violations. Finally, the bankruptcy court had previously found that Gitto had been siphoning excessive management fees from the Debtor's cash flow.

. . . .

Although certain of these allegations are disputed — in particular those surrounding the Vitrolite inventory and the implication of the court's finding regarding the "management fees" — the bankruptcy court appears to have credited a critical mass of the foregoing.

I begin by noting that the evidence before the bankruptcy court, compared to that relied upon by other courts, would appear sufficient to satisfy even a "clear and convincing" standard. The bankruptcy court did not expressly apply such a heightened standard, however, and nor, for the reasons set forth above, do I.

First, and perhaps most importantly, the inconsistencies and inaccuracies arising in the § 341 process raise serious concerns. "One of the most fundamental and crucial duties of a debtor-in-possession upon the filing of a Chapter 11 petition is to keep the Court and creditors informed about the nature, status and condition of the business undergoing reorganization." *Savino*, 99 B.R. at 526. Consequently, "where, as here, the Debtor fails to disclose material and relevant information to the Court and creditors, a Chapter 11 trustee is required." *Id.*; *see In re Oklahoma Refining Co.*, 838 F.2d 1133, 1136 (10th Cir. 1988) ("It is also established that failure to keep adequate records and make prompt and complete reports justifies the appointment of a trustee."); *Ford*, 36 B.R. at 504 ("Inherent in debtor's fiduciary obligations under the Code is the duty to file accurate financial reports disclosing all transactions involving estate assets . . . Any failure to file accurate financial statements is an omission contributing to cause for appointment of a trustee."); *see also Sanders*, 2000 Bankr. 263, at *11 ("Where a debtor fails to disclose material information to the Court and to the creditors, the appointment of a Chapter 11 trustee is appropriate. Misrepresenting the facts of a debtor's financial situation constitutes grounds for the appointment of a trustee.").

More particularly, a failure to provide accurate schedules to the court has been deemed sufficient "cause" under § 1104(a)(1). *See Sanders*, 2000 Bankr. 263; *see also Deena Packaging*, 29 B.R. at 707 ("Section 1104 . . . specifically proscribes certain conduct by debtors in possession; dishonesty is one such enumerated, prohibited act . . . . The trial record reveals that Deena's failure to include relevant financial data on their original and amended schedules raises questions of dishonest conduct."). The debtor first failed to submit schedules and later, after a denial of a request for an extension of time, submitted schedules contradicted by the testimony of Mrs. Gitto and tax returns not filed until the eve of the hearing held by the bankruptcy judge. Such facts call into question Mr. Gitto's assertion that these were simply oversights. And, even if they were, they are sufficient to raise questions about the ability of the bankruptcy court and creditors to rely upon Mr. Gitto's statements. Moreover, to the extent Mr. Gitto attempts to justify inaccurate statements by contending that Mrs. Gitto did not have a thorough understanding of the issues, that circumstance is his own doing. His unwillingness to testify prevents the bankruptcy court and creditors from receiving direct information regarding the ongoing management of the company from the person entrusted to act as a fiduciary.

The management of the company, Mr. Gitto contends, is so simple that there is no need for a trustee appointment. In this regard, Mr. Gitto would have it both ways. He talks about how simple the business of the company is, yet cites the cost of a trustee. He emphasizes how he only needs to receive checks and issue bills, but there were a series of unexplained "oversights" regarding this "simple" business and, in seeking an extension of time for filing its § 521 statement, the debtor referred to "the extremely complicated nature of the case, including difficulties accurately ascertaining and scheduling the Debtor's various assets and liabilities." To the extent the business is simple, the cost of the trustee is minimized. Moreover, the simplicity of the business weakens any "presumption" that might exist regarding a debtor remaining in possession. The presumption after all is based on the idea that a debtor is in the best position to understand the intricacies of the industry. As the court in *Petit* noted,

> the rationale for the presumption of a debtor remaining in possession of the estate has limited applicability here. In a typical Chapter 11 proceeding, the "Debtor" will be a business run by individuals with experience in that business. As long as there are no findings of fraud or other mismanagement by the current management, it can be assumed that the business would fare better being run by experienced management during the reorganization process. Here the Debtor is an individual who owns only one remaining asset, the cause of action. Thus, there is no "business" that requires day-to-day operation to generate profits. Accordingly, there is less of a need to have the Debtor continue in the management of her affairs.

Petit, 182 B.R. at 69 n. 7. So too here, where the debtor contends that all that needs to be done is the collection of rent and the arrangement of a sale of Tradex. There is no reason to question that a trustee can adequately perform these functions; and, there is substantial evidence calling into question the faith the court and debtors can have in the transparency and reliability of any statements made by Mr. Gitto, assuming that he is even willing to make statements on relevant matters.

The existence of a grand jury investigation and civil suits pursuing allegations relating to Mr. Gitto's business actions in regard to Tradex and other companies is also relevant to a determination regarding trustee appointment. *Cf. Oklahoma Refining*, 838 F.2d at 1136 n.2 ("Case law also supports lenders' claims that debtor's effort to manage the company was impeded by the existence of at least four criminal cases pending against either the debtor's president . . . or some of the affiliated companies."). Here, the bankruptcy judge was aware of such allegations not only through the trustee appointment process but also by virtue of overseeing a related bankruptcy proceeding. It would be inconsistent with the discretion and equitable powers afforded a bankruptcy court judge not to permit him to add such knowledge and experience to the balance.

Finally, questionable business transactions with related companies may also serve as grounds for appointment of a trustee. *See Oklahoma Refining*, 838 F.2d at 1136 ("There are many cases holding that a history of transactions with companies affiliated with the debtor company is sufficient cause for the appointment of a trustee where the best interests of the creditors require."). Such transactions appear in the record of the Bankruptcy Court regarding the debtor and affiliated entities here.

The bankruptcy court also referenced (a)(2) when appointing the trustee. One of the major debtors, LaSalle, voiced support for appointment and another, Clinton, was silent as to appointment at the hearing before the bankruptcy court. LaSalle is a plaintiff in a major lawsuit before me in the district court against Mr. Gitto and other principals of related organizations. Those proceedings and any resulting tensions between the parties were considered sufficiently factual by the court when evaluating the appropriateness of appointing a trustee. *7 Collier on Bankruptcy* § 1104.02[3][d][ii] (15th ed. rev.). The balance of interests here were sufficient to support the factual predicate under § 1104(a)(2).[8]

In sum, it is clear from the record placed before the bankruptcy court that inaccuracies and inconsistencies existed in the statements made by the debtor and its principals. There is no basis to question this factual predicate, and I find that it would not have been an abuse of discretion for the court to determine that such

---

[8] *Cf. St. Louis Globe-Democrat*, 63 B.R. at 138 n.9 (citation to Collier omitted):

> Veritas has also urged that the Court appoint a trustee under § 1104(a)(2). It should be noted that (a)(2) is written in the conjunctive and thus requires a finding that the appointment is in the interests of creditors, any equity security holders, and other interests of the estate. The Court is firmly convinced that the appointment is in the best interest of the creditors and other interests of the estate. However, upon the consideration of the evidence that was adduced, it is impossible to find that the appointment of a trustee is in the best interest of any equity security holders since, as sole shareholders, it appears that Mr. and Mrs. Gluck are the only equity security holders in the Globe. Since they are opposed to the appointment of a trustee, it is unreasonable under these circumstances to appoint a trustee pursuant to § 1104(a)(2).

This does not appear to be the common understanding of (a)(2)'s reach. It is unlikely that Congress intended to provide sole shareholders with what would in effect be veto power of § 1104(a)(2) trustee appointment regardless of how clearly appointment was, on balance, in the interest of other relevant parties.

evidence established "cause" under § 1104(a)(1). There was also more information before the court from this case which, evaluated in light of his experience with this and related cases, supplied sufficient grounds to find "cause" existed for purposes of § 1104(a)(1) and that appointment was warranted under § 1104(a)(2).

In short, even if there was insufficient evidence "that fraud or some other section 1104(a)(1) ground actually existed, the testimony was more than adequate to demonstrate to the bankruptcy court the extent to which the Debtor's creditors cannot place confidence in her to carry out her fiduciary obligations in their interest." *Petit*, 182 B.R. at 70. *Cf. Oklahoma Refining*, 838 F.2d at 1136 ("It is clear, both from the language of the statute and established case law, that the court need not find any of the enumerated wrongs in order to find cause for appointing a trustee. It is sufficient that the appointment be in the interest of creditors.").

IV. Conclusion

For the foregoing reasons, the decision of the bankruptcy court to appoint a Chapter 11 trustee for TRADEX is AFFIRMED.

IN RE IONOSPHERE CLUBS, INC.
United States Bankruptcy Court, Southern District of New York
113 B.R. 164 (1990)

Burton R. Lifland, Chief United States Bankruptcy Judge.

RULING ON MOTION BY CREDITORS' COMMITTEE FOR THE APPOINTMENT OF A CHAPTER 11 TRUSTEE

BACKGROUND

On March 9, 1989 (the "Filing Date") Eastern Airline, Inc. and its affiliate Ionosphere Clubs, Inc. (the "Debtors" or "Eastern") each filed a voluntary petition for relief under chapter 11, title 11, United States Code (the "Code"). Since the Filing Date, the Debtors have continued to operate their businesses as debtors-in-possession pursuant to Code §§ 1107 and 1108.

Approximately 13 months after the Filing Date, the Official Committee of Unsecured Creditors of Eastern (the "Committee"), pursuant to Code § 1104, has moved this Court to appoint a Chapter 11 trustee to replace the debtor-in-possession, in order "to enhance the value of the estate" and proceed toward a "viable reorganization." Prior to this time, the Committee has had a very cooperative relationship with the Debtors. For example, on at least two separate occasions, in July 1989 and February 1990, the Committee authorized the issuance of press releases in support of the Debtors' management. In addition, the Debtors have obtained the use of $320 million of escrowed unencumbered cash since the Filing Date without objection from the Committee. Moreover, since the Filing Date, the Committee has also supported the Debtors' asset disposition program, proceeds of which have been used to fund Eastern's massive losses totaling over $1.2 billion.

At the end of March, the Committee lost all confidence in Eastern's management when Eastern announced to the Committee that it once again would have to renege on its previous agreement entered into six weeks earlier, and embodied in what has been referred to as the "Fifty-Cent" plan. Eastern reported to the Committee that its previous forecast had to be modified and that its losses in 1990 were now being estimated at $329.7 million, which is $184.4 million more than the $145.3 million that had been forecast in January. The Committee responded to Eastern's new assessment by demanding that Texas Air Corp. ("Texas Air"), as Eastern's parent, indemnify on a subordinated basis the continuing staggering losses of Eastern. It was only after Texas Air failed to guarantee such an indemnification that the Committee filed its motion to appoint a trustee.

The Committee asserts in its motion that a trustee is warranted in this instance because, inter alia, (1) Eastern's devastating, constantly expanding and unending losses are extremely damaging to unsecured creditors and therefore to the interests of the estate; (2) Texas Air and Eastern have demonstrated their inability to project the results of operations to the extent that the Committee has lost confidence in their stewardship of the business; and (3) Eastern and Texas Air have repeatedly reneged on their plan of reorganization agreements with the Committee, such that the Committee has no confidence in the ability or willingness of the Debtors and its common equity holder to adhere to basic understandings.

DISCUSSION

Chapter 11 of the Code is designed to allow the debtor-in-possession to retain management and control of the debtor's business operations unless a party in interest can prove that the appointment of a trustee is warranted. The appointment of a trustee in a chapter 11 case is an extraordinary remedy. There is a strong presumption that the debtor should be permitted to remain in possession absent a showing of need for the appointment of a trustee.

. . . .

Although in this case a full four day evidentiary hearing was conducted, in considering a motion for the appointment of a trustee, a bankruptcy court is not required to conduct a full evidentiary hearing. The party requesting the appointment of a trustee has the burden of proof in showing "cause." The evidence supporting the motion for the appointment of a trustee must be clear and convincing.

The language of § 1104(a)(1) of the Code represents Congressional recognition that some degree of mismanagement exists in virtually every insolvency case. The philosophy of chapter 11 is to give the debtor a "second chance" and, consistent with such philosophy, current management should be permitted to identify and correct its past mistakes. H.R. Rep. No. 595, 95th Cong., 1st Sess. 220 (1977). While a certain amount of mismanagement of the debtor's affairs prior to the filing date may not be sufficient grounds for the appointment of a trustee, continuing mismanagement of the affairs of a debtor after the filing date is evidence of the need for the appointment of a trustee.

Code § 1104(a)(2) creates a flexible standard and allows the appointment of a trustee even when no "cause" exists. The House Report summarizes the reasons for Congress' adoption of a flexible standard for the appointment of trustees. The House Report, in part, reads as follows:

> The twin goals of the standard for the appointment of a trustee should be protection of the *public interest* and the interests of creditors, as contemplated in current chapter X and facilitation of a reorganization that will benefit both the creditors and the debtors, as contemplated in current chapter XI. Balancing the goals is a difficult process, and requires consideration of many factors.

H.R. Rep. No. 595, 95th Cong., 1st Sess. 232 (1977) (emphasis added). Where the debtor's business affects such a large segment of the general public, consideration of the "public interest" becomes a greater factor in deciding whether to order the appointment of a trustee. In this case, as has clearly been articulated by this Court time and time again, the flying public's interest must at all times be taken into account.

With respect to whether a trustee should be appointed under Code § 1104(a)(2), courts "eschew rigid absolutes and look to the practical realities and necessities," *In re Hotel Associates, Inc.*, 3 Bankr. 343, 345 (Bankr. E.D. Pa. 1980). Among the factors considered are: (i) the trustworthiness of the debtor; (ii) the debtor in possession's past and present performance and prospects for the debtor's rehabilitation; (iii) the confidence — or lack thereof — of the business community and of creditors in present management; and (iv) the benefits derived by the appointment of a trustee, balanced against the cost of the appointment.

Throughout this case, Eastern has continually made operating projections which it has failed to achieve with the resultant losses being borne by the unsecured creditors. For instance, in Eastern's April 1989 Business Plan it was projected that Eastern would suffer operating losses of approximately $636.4 million for the period from April through December, 1989, but concluded that Eastern would become marginally profitable in 1990, and have substantial net income in 1991 and thereafter. The actual results and current projections are as follows:

> (i) Losses from April 1989 through year end exceeded $865 million, more than 136% of the April Business Plan projections;

> (ii) Losses from September 1989 through year end exceeded $400 million, more than 170% of the August Business Plan projections of $235.5 million;

> (iii) Losses for 1990 are now projected to be $329.7 million, $184.4 million greater than the $145.3 million projected in the January Business Plan;

> (iv) Losses for 1991 are projected to be not less than another $120 million; and

> (v) Since the filing date, operating losses have amounted to more than $1.2 billion.

By admission of the Chairman of the Board, Frank Lorenzo, these losses have wiped out the parent Texas Air's equity.

Eastern has also come to a number of agreements with the Committee concerning potential plans of reorganization, but Eastern has been unable to meet the terms of such agreements. From the July 1989 plan which provided for the unsecured creditors to receive 100% of their claims plus post-petition interest, Eastern's most recent proposal now provides that unsecured creditors will receive only approximately 25% of their claims with most of the payments being spread over a number of years. An interim "Fifty-Cent" plan was considered. Thus each succeeding offer was one-half of the previous one.

A debtor-in-possession must act as a "fiduciary of his creditors" to "protect and to conserve property in his possession for the benefit of creditors," and to "refrain from acting in a manner which could damage the estate, or hinder a successful reorganization of the business." *In re Sharon Steel Corp.*, 86 Bankr. 455, 457 (Bankr. W.D. Pa. 1988). As the court in *Sharon Steel* observed, "the most common basis for appointing a trustee under§ 1104(a)(1) is for gross mismanagement and incompetence." *Id.* at 458.

A debtor-in-possession has all the duties of a trustee in a Chapter 11 case, including the duty to protect and conserve property in its possession for the benefit of creditors. "The job of a debtor-in-possession remains under the Code as that described by Judge Friendly — to get the creditors paid." *In re Pied Piper Casuals, Inc.*, 40 Bankr. 723, 727 (Bankr. S.D.N.Y. 1984); (citing *In re Grayson Robinson Stores, Inc.*, 320 F.2d 940 (2d Cir. 1963)). A debtor-in-possession's fiduciary obligation to its creditors includes refraining from acting in a manner which could damage the estate, or hinder a successful reorganization of the business. When a debtor-in-possession is incapable of performing these duties, a Chapter 11 trustee may be appointed.

. . . .

In *In re Cardinal Industries Inc.*, 109 Bankr. 755 (Bankr. S.D. Ohio 1990), the creditors committee, in moving for the appointment of a trustee, cited the debtor's inaccurate financial forecasts, failure to stem cash losses of $1.6 million since the bankruptcy filing, conflicts of interest and improper prepetition transfers. Noting that "unsecured creditors are being asked to wait five to ten years" for the debtors to generate income for distribution, and that creditors had "lost faith in the Debtors' intentions and abilities to reorganize their affairs," the court held that the failure to appoint a trustee would "jeopardize whatever chance exists to realize the potential value of these estates." The court went on to hold that "since the [unsecured creditors] are willing to risk the costs, uncertainties and dislocations, occasioned by the appointment of a trustee, the Court will exercise its equitable powers to order that appointment." *In re Cardinal Industries Inc.*, 109 Bankr. at 767.

Similarly in this case, this Court finds by clear and convincing evidence that the appointment of an operating trustee is warranted under these circumstances pursuant to both § 1104(a)(1) and especially (a)(2) of the Code. The Debtors' inability to formulate a business plan and make operating projections which have a longevity of more than several months, along with the continuing enormous operating losses being sustained by the estate, mandate that this Court order the appointment of a trustee "for cause, including . . . incompetence" under Code § 1104(a)(1). Moreover, pursuant to § 1104(a)(2) of the Code, the appointment of a trustee "is in the interest of creditors, . . . [and] other interests of the estate." It is undisputed that Texas Air no longer has any equity interest in Eastern. Consequently, the airline, in a sense, is now owned by its creditors who cannot be forced to subsidize a debtor-in-possession forever. In this instance, with Mr. Lorenzo at the throttle, . . . Eastern has used $1.2 billion to "fuel" this reorganization trip. The time has come to replace the pilot to captain Eastern's crew.

In opposition to the Committee's motion to appoint a trustee, the Debtors argue that the huge losses and missed projections were caused not by management errors, but because of unexpected cost increases and a general downturn in the airline industry. The Debtors also assert that even experts in the airline industry missed their projections during this time period. The Debtors' contentions, however, are unpersuasive. Irrespective of fault, the magnitude of the Debtors' losses together with the Debtors' inability to make reliable forecasts, even over a short period of time, supports a finding that Eastern's owner manager, as personified by the Chairman of the Board of both the parent and the Debtor, is not competent to reorganize this estate.

In addition, a substantial part of the Debtors' defense has revolved around its assertions that this is an extraordinary bankruptcy case and that Eastern's management has had to rebuild operations in the most adverse of circumstances in the context of an intense labor conflict. Indeed, this has been an extraordinary bankruptcy case in that the Committee has supported these Debtors for 13 months in hopes that they would be able to turn things around. However, $1.2 billion later, this has not occurred. Although it is undisputed that Texas Air's interest as equity holder has been wiped out, Texas Air as Eastern's parent has been unwilling or perhaps unable to adequately support these struggling Debtors through their stormy course in chapter 11. This is suggestive of parental neglect. Texas Air is now risking unsecured creditors' funds. If Texas Air is no longer willing or cannot put up adequate risk money to support Eastern, it cannot expect the unsecured creditors to continually fund and endure the perpetually mounting losses.

Another basis for change at this time can be found the DOT's finding in a 1988 report that the labor management discord, if not abated, could ultimately affect safety. [I]t would be inappropriate not to allow another manager to responsively address this problem.

If this Court were to deny the Committee's motion, the Committee has filed papers indicating that it will not support further use of escrowed unencumbered cash. Moreover, no other interest group will support the continued use of escrowed unencumbered cash without the appointment of a trustee. It is undisputed that without the further use of escrowed unencumbered cash, the estate will run short of operating funds. For this need alone, the interests of creditors, preferred shareholders, employees, and the flying public are better served by an order appointing an operating trustee.

CONCLUSION

This Court finds that clear and convincing evidence has been presented which mandates ordering the appointment of a trustee under both Code §§ 1104(a)(1) and 1104(a)(2). Therefore it is

ORDERED that The United States Trustee is directed to appoint an eminently qualified person, with the ability to continue to operate the airline, as quickly as is practical and such person is charged with operating Eastern Airlines as a going concern and exploring a viable business plan; and it is further

ORDERED that to minimize disruption, dislocation, and an irreversible dip into chaos, all professionals previously retained pursuant to Code § 327(a)–(d) shall remain retained by the estate subject to further order of this Court, and to the extent special authorization is required, it is accomplished pursuant to Code § 327(e), with the mandate to such professionals to continue providing all services including legal services as such are necessary and essential to the estate; and it is further

ORDERED that the trustee is hereby authorized to use up to $80 million of the escrowed unencumbered cash.

NOTES ON THE APPOINTMENT OF CHAPTER 11 TRUSTEES

(1) As you might expect, the settings in which courts have ordered the appointment of trustees depict a panorama of business and managerial ills. For example, courts have ordered the appointment of trustees in the following circumstances:

- The court found that management of a coal mining operation lacked marketing ability, was not maintaining equipment properly, was not supervising operations effectively, was shifting assets among the debtor and the owner's other related businesses, and had lost the confidence of creditors. *In re Concord Coal Corp.*, 11 B.R. 552 (Bankr. S.D. W. Va. 1981).

- A manufacturer and distributor of plastic greeting cards filed a Chapter 11 petition. A week later, a creditor moved for the appointment of a trustee. At a hearing on the motion, the court made the following findings of fact, among others: (1) The president of the debtor had been involved in three other failed businesses before he organized La Sherene. (2) Because the debtor was engaged in the same line of business as one of these failed companies, the debtor was forced to deal with the same suppliers, many of whom refused to do business with La Sherene unless it paid a 10 percent premium. (3) The debtor had been undercapitalized from its inception. (4) Even while the debtor's president was trying to convince creditors to extend new credit in order to keep the business afloat, he was arranging for the debtor to buy a pleasure boat on credit "for entertainment." (5) The debtor was suffering such severe cash flow problems that it sold invoices to its factor even before the goods related to the invoices were shipped to customers. (6) The debtor had written checks on insufficient funds. (7) The debtor had withheld $20,000 in taxes from employees' wages, but failed to remit the money to the taxing authority. (8) Despite the inadequate capitalization, tight cash flow, and generally shaky financial condition of the company, the management team was paying itself what the court considered "under the circumstances to be excessive compensation." (9) The managers of the company were good at marketing, creative, and artistic, but they were not good financial analysts, business planners, or managers. (10) The debtor's officers had a serious disagreement about how to run the business and one had been discharged shortly before the Chapter 11 filing. (11) Several key officers were also creditors of the debtor. (12) On the eve of filing, the debtor made payments to its attorney that may have been avoidable preferences. *In re La Sherene, Inc.*, 3 B.R. 169 (Bankr. N.D. Ga. 1980).

- On the eve of filing, management appeared "to have engaged . . . in a systematic siphoning of . . . assets to other companies under common control." *In re Sharon Steel Corp.*, 871 F.2d 1217, 1228 (3d Cir. 1989).

- The court lost confidence in management's candor and its ability to formulate a confirmable reorganization plan. *Hansen, Jones & Leta, P.C.*, 220 B.R. 434, 443 (D. Utah 1998).

- The relationship of management and creditors had become so acrimonious that there appeared to be no reasonable likelihood of any cooperation among the parties and the appointment of a trustee was necessary to resolve competing interests and move the case toward a confirmable plan. *In re Marvel Entertainment Group, Inc.*, 140 F.3d 463 (3d Cir. 1998). *See also In re Cajun Electric Power Corp.*, 74 F.3d 599 (5th Cir. 1996); and *In re Colorado-Ute Electric Assn.*, 120 B.R. 164 (Bankr. D. Colo. 1990).

- Debtor's management "padded" its list of unsecured creditors in order to oppose an involuntary Chapter 11 petition, failed to file tax returns, and lost the confidence of creditors. *In re Euro-American Lodging Corp.*, 365 B.R. 421 (Bankr. S.D.N.Y. 2007).

- A management agreement between the debtor and the manager of a hotel owned by the debtor so severely restricted the debtor's ability to make independent business decisions that the debtor could not discharge its fiduciary duties as debtor in possession. The court found that appointment was necessary to avoid "paralytic conflict." *In re Bellevue Place Assocs.*, 171 B.R. 615 (Bankr. N.D. Ill. 1994).

- The debtor's board of directors was hopelessly deadlocked and only an impartial trustee could work with the warring factions and facilitate the decision making process. *In re Advanced Electronics, Inc.*, 99 B.R. 249 (Bankr. M.D. Pa. 1989).

- The debtor was not guilty of "gross mismanagement," but was guilty of a "failure to manage." An auditor retained by the largest creditor testified that the debtor's books and records were in such disarray that they were incapable of being audited, that the debtor had no internal accounting controls, and that the debtor's financial personnel could not decipher their own bookkeeping entries. In addition, the debtor had been charged with deceptive trade practices. *In re U.S. Communications of Westchester, Inc.*, 123 B.R. 491 (Bankr. S.D.N.Y. 1991).

- The debtor failed to maintain adequate books and records, and paid operating expenses with funds withheld for taxes and union dues from employee payroll checks. *In re St. Louis Globe-Democrat, Inc.*, 63 B.R. 131 (Bankr. E.D. Mo. 1985).

- The debtor failed to pay property, sales, and other taxes. *In re Euro-American Lodging*, 365 B.R. 421 (Bankr. S.D.N.Y. 2007).

- The debtor failed to insure and maintain estate property. *Matter of Plantation Inn Partners*, 142 B.R. 561 (Bankr. S.D. Ga. 1992). *See also In re Hotel Assocs., Inc.*, 3 B.R. 343 (E.D. Pa. 1980).

- The debtor made preferential transfers to creditors whose loans had been guaranteed by the debtor's principal shareholder. *In re Tel-Net Hawaii, Inc.*, 105 B.R. 594 (Bankr. N.D. Hawaii 1989).

- The debtor's CEO was attempting to sell the debtor's most valuable assets to a purchaser with whom he had a "consulting" relationship. *Matter of Embrace Sys. Corp.*, 178 B.R. 112 (Bankr. W.D. Mich. 1995).

- The debtor concealed assets. *Petit v. New England Mortgage Services, Inc.*, 182 B.R. 64 (D. Me. 1995); *In re Giguere*, 165 B.R. 531 (Bankr. D.R.I. 1994); *In re Deena Packaging Industries, Inc.*, 29 B.R. 705 (Bankr. S.D.N.Y. 1983).

- Management had allegedly caused the debtor to engage in fraudulent transfers on the eve of filing. *In re Russell*, 60 B.R. 42 (Bankr. W.D. Ark. 1985).

- The debtor failed to produce financial records and file operating reports. *In re Sullivan*, 108 B.R. 555 (Bankr. E.D. Pa. 1989); *In re Cohoes Industrial Terminal, Inc.*, 65 B.R. 918 (Bankr. S.D.N.Y. 1986); *In re Paolino*, 53 B.R. 399 (Bankr. E.D. Pa. 1985).

(2) *Are Trustees Appointed or Anointed?* If a bankruptcy court orders the appointment of a trustee, then the United States Trustee, after consulting with parties in interest, makes the actual appointment. Code § 1104(d). The drafters' purpose in assigning the appointment power to United States Trustees, rather than to bankruptcy judges, was to allay fears that judges tended to show favoritism to trustees whom they had selected, H.R. Rep. No. 595, 95th Cong., 1st Sess. 88–90, 108 (1977), and that trustees tended to show too much deference to the judges who had selected them. The House Report accompanying a 1986 amendment to Code § 1104 observed:

> In many cases these trustees appeared in bankruptcy court before the very judges who appointed them to make recommendations regarding matters of the estate. In such circumstances, a trustee would often be reluctant to take positions contrary to the judges who appointed the trustee, even though a trustee was supposed to be an impartial administrator of the estate. This awkward relationship between trustees and judges created an improper appearance of favoritism, cronyism, and bias and generated great disrespect for the bankruptcy system.

H.R. Rep. No. 764, 99th Cong., 2nd Sess. 17–18 (1986).

The purpose of requiring the U.S. Trustee to consult with parties in interest is to facilitate the selection of qualified, competent trustees who inspire the parties' confidence. What happens if the court or parties in interest are dissatisfied with the U.S. Trustee's choice? Code § 1104(d) provides that the U.S. Trustee makes the appointment "subject to the court's approval." At the time that the U.S. Trustee seeks approval of the appointment, a party may lodge an objection. Bankruptcy Rule 2007.1. Code § 1104(d) does not give the court the power to appoint, nor the power to order the U.S. Trustee to appoint, a more suitable candidate. It does give the court a veto power, which is supposed to be used sparingly. *In re Plaza de Diego Shopping Center, Inc.*, 911 F.2d 820 (1st Cir. 1990). Courts have exercised this veto power when asked to approve candidates that they regarded as unqualified to operate the debtors' businesses. In *In re Ruffin, Inc.*, 10 B.R. 862 (Bankr. D.R.I. 1981), a case involving a troubled restaurant and tavern, the court chided the U.S. Trustee for appointing an attorney rather than an experienced accountant or restaurant manager. Similarly, in *In re Cardinal Indus., Inc.*, 113 B.R. 378, 379 (Bankr. S.D. Ohio 1990), the court vetoed the appointment of a distinguished attorney as trustee and insisted on an appointee with "specialized experience . . . with either the operation of real estate properties or manufacturing facilities." In both cases, the courts took the U.S. Trustees to task for failing to consult in good faith with parties in interest before asking the court to approve their appointments.

In 1994, the Code was amended by the adoption of a new § 1104(b), which now provides an alternative method for selecting a trustee. If, within 30 days after the court orders the appointment of a trustee, a party in interest requests it, the court shall convene a meeting of creditors for the purpose of electing a trustee. In a case in which a trustee has been appointed before the request for an election, the elected trustee supplants the appointed trustee. The elected trustee cannot, however, take office until the court gives its approval. During the limbo period, the appointed trustee continues to serve. Bankruptcy Rule 2007.1(b)(1).

(3)   *The Cost Factor.* One reason *not* to appoint a trustee in every case is that trustees can be costly. One cost to be considered is that of the delay associated with educating the trustee about the affairs of the debtor in order to get the trustee to that point on the learning curve where he or she can deal effectively with important issues facing the debtor. *See, e.g., Hansen, Jones & Leta, P.C. v. Segal*, 220 B.R. 434, 443 (D. Utah 1998). Another cost is that of compensation. Trustees, and their professional consultants, are entitled to be paid, and although trustees typically assume managerial control of the debtor, in many cases they require the aid of experienced business personnel to keep the business going. As the court observed in a case of a debtor that operated a coal mine, "The trustee will likely continue . . . employment of the operational personnel who apparently are experienced and competent at the mining of coal. The role for [top management] will be at the discretion of the trustee." *In re Concord Coal Corp.*, 11 B.R. 552, 555 (Bankr. S.D. W. Va. 1981).

Of course, appointment of a trustee does not necessarily result in just another layer of administrative expense. In some situations, the cost of a trustee may actually be offset by reductions in other personnel and by other benefits the trustee may bring. For example, in *In re Microwave Prods. of America, Inc.*, 102 B.R. 666 (Bankr. W.D. Tenn. 1989), the court found that appointment of a trustee was a net plus, because the trustee would replace costly outside business consultants and prosecute fraudulent transfer and conflict of interest claims that management was not inclined to pursue.

Interestingly, in a case in which the court found that management's behavior warranted the appointment of a trustee, but the court also found that management was operating the business profitably and more effectively than a trustee ever could, the court ordered the appointment of a trustee to serve a "watchdog" role only. Business decisions were left to management. *In re Bonded Mailings, Inc.*, 20 B.R. 781 (Bankr. E.D.N.Y. 1982). Similarly, in a case in which "serious accounting deficiencies, communication breakdowns, and record keeping problems" had caused creditors to lose confidence in management's ability to develop a business plan or propose a restructuring scheme, the court ordered the appointment of a trustee but strongly recommended that the trustee retain top management. The court advised, "It is clear to the Court that [the managers] have exceptional skills and knowledge related to [the debtor's] operations. Both men are also persons of integrity who have worked hard. Their talents should be retained and utilized by any appointed trustee. The Court further hopes that both men will remain with the companies and will support the trustee in developing a plan of reorganization which is in the best interests of all constituencies." *In re Cardinal Indus., Inc.*, 109 B.R. 755, 767 (Bankr. S.D. Ohio 1990).

When cause for appointing a trustee is found under § 1104(a)(1), appointment of a trustee appears to be mandatory and a cost-benefit analysis is inappropriate. *In re V. Savino Oil & Heating Co.*, 99 B.R. 518 (Bankr. E.D.N.Y. 1989). In contrast, when the court is acting pursuant to § 1104(a)(2), it is compelled to consider whether appointment is in the best interests of the estate, and cost is a factor that may be taken into account. *In re Cardinal Indus.*, 109 B.R. 755 (Bankr. S.D. Ohio 1990).

(4) *Exclusivity.* Code § 1121(b) provides that only the debtor may file a reorganization plan for the first 120 days of a Chapter 11 case. If, however, a trustee is appointed, this exclusive period terminates, and any party in interest can file a plan. Code § 1121(c)(1). Is termination of the debtor's exclusive right to file a reorganization plan a factor that should be taken into account in considering whether to order the appointment of a trustee? If so, is it because, in some sense the debtor's exclusive period belongs to management? Is management synonymous with the debtor? Is management synonymous with the debtor in possession? Or, is management just the group of individuals who operate the debtor in possession? Can you imagine how blurring the line between management and the debtor in possession might lead to problems? In *In re Colorado-Ute Electric Assn.*, 120 B.R. 164 (Bankr. D. Colo. 1990), the court held that where there is "cause" for appointing a trustee under § 1104(a)(1), delaying appointment of a trustee until after the expiration of the exclusive period is inappropriate. Should the approach be different when the question is whether appointment of a trustee is in the best interests of the estate under Code § 1104(a)(2)? It is interesting to note that in a number of cases, courts have ordered the appointment of a trustee because management appeared to be incapable of negotiating a reorganization plan. *See, e.g., In re Marvel Entertainment Group, Inc.*, 140 F.3d 463 (3d Cir. 1998); *In re Cardinal Industries, Inc.*, 109 B.R. 755, 767 (Bankr. S.D. Ohio 1990).

(5) *Trustee Alternative to Conversion or Dismissal.* When there is a possibility that a debtor can be salvaged, a court may prefer to appoint a trustee rather than convert or dismiss a case prematurely. For example, in a case involving the collapse of a suburban restaurant owned by the operators of New York City's famed disco, "Studio 54," the bankruptcy court adopted this approach. The landlord had moved for dismissal or conversion on the grounds, among others, that the debtor lacked the equipment necessary to continue in business and that the debtor had lost its liquor license and other operating permits. The debtor claimed it had access to new equipment and that its licenses would be restored. Rather than dismiss, the court appointed a trustee to investigate the feasibility of rehabilitating the business and to "assume control to the extent necessary to facilitate reorganization." *In re Steakloft of Oakdale*, 10 B.R. 182, 186 (Bankr. E.D.N.Y. 1981).

(6) *Sua Sponte Appointments.* You will recall that one of the reasons that the Code's drafters separated the power to order the appointment of a trustee from the power to do the actual appointing was to avoid the appearance of impropriety that arose from having a trustee appear before the same judge that appointed him or her. Does a court have the power to order the appointment of a trustee on the court's own motion? Code § 1104(a) provides that any "party in interest" may move for the appointment of a trustee. According to Code § 1109(2), the term "party in interest" includes "the debtor, the trustee, a creditors' committee, an equity security holders' committee, a creditor, an equity security holder, or any indenture trustee." There is some authority for the proposition that a court may not, on its own motion, order appointment of a trustee, because a court is not a "party in interest." *In re Mandalay Shores Coop. Housing Ass'n*, 22 B.R. 202 (Bankr. M.D. Fla. 1982). However, subsequent to holdings such as *Mandalay*, Code § 105(a) was amended to provide that "[N]o provision . . . for the raising of an issue by a party in interest shall be construed to preclude the court from, sua sponte, taking any action or making any determination necessary or appropriate to enforce or implement court orders or rules, or to prevent an abuse of process." In the wake of this amendment, several courts have concluded that courts may raise the issue of appointing a trustee on their own motion. *In re Bibo, Inc.*, 76 F.3d 256 (9th Cir. 1996), *cert denied sub nom, Fukutomi v. U.S. Trustee*, 519 U.S. 817 (1996); *Matter of Mother Hubbard, Inc.*, 152 B.R. 189 (Bankr. W.D. Mich. 1993). In *Mother Hubbard*, the court cautioned that courts should exercise this power sparingly and only if "persuasive evidence comes to the court's attention on the record which may lead to a conclusion that cause exists . . . . The court should not rely upon any extrajudicial knowledge that may be received, e.g., a letter to the court clerk, and should not launch an investigation or become involved in administrative matters." 152 B.R. at 197.

(7) *Operation of New Section 1104(e).* In 2005, in the wake of the infamous corporate scandals involving companies such as Enron, Congress added § 1104(e) to the Code. It provides that the United States Trustee must move for the appointment of a trustee "if there are reasonable grounds to suspect that current members of the governing body of the debtor, the debtor's chief executive or chief financial officer, or members of the governing body who selected the debtor's chief executive or chief financial officer, participated in actual fraud, dishonesty, or criminal conduct in the management of the debtor or the debtor's public financial reporting."

In *In re The 1031 Tax Group*, 374 B.R. 78 (Bankr. S.D.N.Y. 2007), the court denied the U.S. Trustee's motion for the appointment of a trustee pursuant to Code § 1104(e). The bankruptcy judge pointed out that although § 1104(e) compels the U.S. Trustee to move for the appointment of a trustee when fraud is shown or suspected, it does not compel the bankruptcy court to grant the motion. Whether the appointment of a trustee should be ordered, the court explained, continues to be governed by § 1104(a) and whether appointment of a trustee is justified by "cause," or by "the interests of creditors, any equity security holders, and other interests of the estate." Although the court found that the U.S. Trustee had established a *prima facie* case of fraud by prior management, it declined to order the appointment of a trustee, because, a few days before the filing of the Chapter 11 petition, and "[p]resumably, at least in part, to avoid the appointment of a . . . trustee," new management had been appointed. The court noted that the U.S. Trustee had acted prudently in questioning whether new management was tainted by an association with old management, but the court concluded that management authority had been completely and irrevocably transferred, obviating the need for a trustee. Moreover, the court found that appointing a trustee might derail progress in the case, given the existence of an "active creditors committee functioning effectively and working well with the debtors," and the fact that a plan had been filed. 374 B.R. at 91.

En route to its holding, the court noted that, as a number of commentators have pointed out, § 1104(e) is unclear in a number of respects. What constitutes "reasonable grounds to suspect" that fraud has occurred? Suppose that a director (as opposed to the debtor's CFO or CEO) engaged in fraud. In such a case, is the U.S. Trustee required to move for appointment of a trustee? *See 7 Collier on Bankruptcy* ¶ 1104.02[4][a] (16th ed. 2012).

Interestingly, about two months later, the bankruptcy court reversed course and ordered that a trustee be appointed. The court found that appointment was in the best interests of creditors because any hope of a quick administration of the case had evaporated, former management had not made good on its promises to fund payments to creditors, and the level of distrust among the debtors and creditors had grown more pronounced. *In re The 1031 Tax Group, LLC*, 374 B.R. 78 (Bankr. S.D.N.Y. 2007).

§ 4.03 APPOINTMENT OF EXAMINERS

There is a less drastic form of third-party intervention that falls short of the appointment of a trustee and the displacement of management: the appointment of an examiner. Code § 1104(c) authorizes the court to appoint an examiner on request of a party in interest in two situations. The first, which mirrors the grounds for the appointment of a trustee, is "if such appointment is in the interest of creditors, equity security holders, and other interests of the estate." § 1104(c)(1). The second ground for appointing an examiner is "if . . . the debtor's fixed, liquidated unsecured debts, other than debts for goods, services, or taxes, or owing to an insider, exceed $5,000,000." § 1104(c)(2).

The function of an examiner is primarily investigative. In fact, an examiner is directed to conduct the same kind of investigation that a trustee is required to perform. *See* Code §§ 1104(d)(3), (4) and 1106(b). For example, in *In re 1243 20th St.*,

Inc., 6 B.R. 683 (Bankr. D.D.C. 1980), the court ordered the appointment of an examiner to scrutinize the "complex interrelationship," of the debtor and related companies to determine whether any property of the debtor had been fraudulently transferred to them.

The appointment of an examiner may be the prelude to the appointment of a trustee, if the examiner's investigation does flush out evidence of managerial misconduct or other grounds. For example, in *In re Cumberland Investment Corp.*, 118 B.R. 3 (Bankr. D.R.I. 1990), the examiner reported that the debtor had allowed its inventory to fall into disarray, that it was not maintaining adequate security, that its accounting systems were muddled, that it was engaging in false advertising, and that it was ignoring the U.S. Trustee's reporting requirements. The court ordered the appointment of a trustee. Notably, to ensure the impartiality of examiners, the Code prohibits the examiner from going on to serve in the same case as the trustee or as a professional assistant to the trustee. Code §§ 321(b), 327(f).

Although examiners typically are appointed to investigate the operation of the debtor and allegations of fraud or mismanagement, Code § 1106(b) also permits the court to direct an examiner to perform the "duties of the trustee that the court orders the debtor in possession not to perform." Invoking this language, some courts have authorized appointment of examiners with "expanded powers" to do more than investigate and report. For example, examiners have been appointed:

- to sue to recover preferences and fraudulent conveyances, *Williamson v. Roppollo*, 114 B.R. 127 (W.D. La. 1990);

- to resolve a deadlock by mediating efforts to achieve a consensual plan of reorganization, *In re Public Service Co. of New Hampshire*, 99 B.R. 177 (Bankr. D.N.H. 1989); *In re UNR Industries, Inc.*, 72 B.R. 789 (Bankr. N.D. Ill. 1987);

- to assist the court in coping with a complex public utility regulatory structure, *In re Public Service Co. of New Hampshire*, 99 B.R. 177 (Bankr. D.N.H. 1989);

- to determine whether a law firm representing the debtor and a creditor-stockholder should be disqualified from representing the debtor and to advise the court on the status of negotiations to develop a consensual plan, *In re Jartran, Inc.*, 78 B.R. 524 (Bankr. N.D. Ill. 1987);

- to stabilize the relationship between a debtor and its bank lenders by monitoring budgets and operating reports, expediting approval of government contracts, and monitoring the retention and compensation of professionals, *In re Apex Oil Co.*, 111 B.R. 235 (Bankr. E.D. Mo. 1990);

- to investigate the leveraged buyout of the debtor in order to determine whether viable fraudulent transfer and other claims arose as a result of the transaction. The examiner filed reports describing in detail the transaction and analyzing potential causes of action. *In re Revco D.S., Inc.*, 1990 Bankr. LEXIS 2966 (Bankr. N.D. Ohio Dec. 17, 1990).

Some courts have held that these "expanded powers" may include the power to operate the debtor's business, *In re Boileau*, 736 F.2d 503 (9th Cir. 1984); *In re Liberal Market, Inc.*, 11 B.R. 742 (Bankr. S.D. Ohio 1981), but this appears to stretch the language of the Code and the intent of the drafters too far. Although § 1106(d) does authorize the court to direct an examiner to perform the trustee's *duties*, a trustee's duties do not include operation of the business. Code § 1108 says that a trustee *may* operate the business; it does not *require* the trustee to do so. Commentators fear that if the powers of examiners are routinely expanded to include operation of the business, Congress's preference for debtors in possession will be undermined, and the rigid standards for appointment of a trustee under § 1104(a)(1) will be undercut. *See, e.g.,* Barry L. Zaretsky, *Trustees and Examiners in Chapter 11,* 44 S.C. L. Rev. 907, 944 (1993). If management of the debtor is to be displaced, the better approach would be to accomplish it as Congress intended, by the appointment of a trustee pursuant to § 1104(a).

The § 1104(c)(2) requirement that an examiner be appointed where a debtor's unsecured debt exceeds $5,000,000 is said to be the last surviving remnant of the "public company exception" contained in the Senate version of the Code, which would have required the appointment of a trustee and an examiner in every case involving a public company. *See* S. Rep. No. 95-989, 95th Cong., 2d Sess., 114–15 (1978), U.S. Code Cong. & Admin. News 1978, p. 5787. Although § 1104(c)(2) is mandatory, some courts have refused to appoint an examiner on the grounds that an examiner's services were not required or that the cost was too great. *See, e.g., In re GHR Cos.,* 43 B.R. 165 (Bankr. D. Mass. 1984); *In re Shelter Resources Corp.,* 35 B.R. 304 (Bankr. N.D. Ohio 1983). Such rulings are plainly at odds with the statute. In *In re Revco, D.S. Inc.,* 898 F.2d 498 (6th Cir. 1990), the court held that the language of § 1104(c) really is as mandatory as it sounds. The bankruptcy court had found that the United States trustee's request for appointment of an examiner was "premature and unnecessary." The Court of Appeals reversed, holding that since the debtor's fixed, liquidated, unsecured debts exceeded $5,000,000, the court had no discretion and was required to appoint an examiner on motion of the United States Trustee. The Court of Appeals did, however, point out that under § 1104(c), the bankruptcy court had broad discretion to define and direct the examiner's investigation. Thus, the court could limit the scope of the examiner's work as well as the compensation the examiner is entitled to receive, thereby giving effect to the command of the statute while taking into account the practicalities of the case.

§ 4.04 OTHER APPROACHES TO CHANGING AND STRENGTHENING MANAGEMENT

Installing a trustee is not the only way to depose management. In a number of Chapter 11 cases, creditors, acting individually or collectively, have employed the leverage they possess as suppliers, lenders, and voters on forthcoming reorganization plans to pressure management into resigning in favor of a more amenable team. In cases involving larger companies particularly, management is prone to change on the eve of bankruptcy or soon afterwards. Professors LoPucki and Whitford demonstrated this in a study that they conducted of 43 large, publicly held companies that had sought relief in Chapter 11. They found that in the period beginning 18 months before filing and ending six months after confirmation of a reorganization plan, 91% of the companies experienced a change in CEO. The annualized turnover rate for CEO's was 167% for the period beginning three months before filing and ending two months after filing. The annualized turnover rate for the one-month period following confirmation was 307%. LoPucki & Whitford, *Corporate Governance in the Bankruptcy Reorganizations of Large Publicly Held Companies*, 141 U. Pa. L. Rev. 669 (1993). *See also* Gilson, *Bankruptcy Boards, Banks, & Blockholders*, 27 J. Fin. Econ. 355 (1990).

An early but interesting example of this phenomenon is a case involving the famous model train company Lionel, about which we will learn more in chapter 6, § 6.01. After Lionel filed a Chapter 11 petition, its two top officers resigned, reportedly under pressure from disgruntled creditors. According to an article that appeared in the Wall Street Journal, "The top-level management shakeup was linked to Lionel's creditors committee, made up of toy makers, commercial banks, and other companies that extended credit to Lionel." Hertzberg, *Lionel Corp. Replaces Saypol and Schilling, Its Two Top Officers*, Wall Street Journal, July 9, 1982, at 29, col. 1. The new management team would later cave in to pressure from the same creditors and acquiesce in the sale of Lionel's most valuable asset. Stockholders protested the proposed sale, and the Second Circuit Court of Appeals blocked it. *See In re The Lionel Corp.*, reprinted in chapter 6, § 6.01 of the casebook.

What if, prior to or shortly after a Chapter 11 filing, management is replaced by a new, apparently competent, team of managers, who are untainted by their predecessors' incompetence or malfeasance? A number of courts have held that in such cases, appointment of a trustee may not be justified. *See, e.g., In re The 1031 Tax Group, LLC*, 374 B.R. 78 (Bankr. S.D.N.Y. 2007); *In re Sletteland*, 260 B.R. 657, 672 (Bankr. S.D.N.Y. 2001). Recent empirical studies suggest that this may now be the norm, rather than the exception. Kenneth Ayotte & Edward R. Morrison, *Creditor Control and Conflict in Chapter 11*, J. Legal Analysis 511 (Summer 2009).

APPOINTMENT OF "RESPONSIBLE PERSONS" AND "CHIEF RESTRUCTURING OFFICERS"

Despite the fact that Code § 1104(a) appears to give a court only two choices ("debtor in possession" or "trustee"), some courts have found that they have the power to displace management without actually appointing a trustee. *In re Gaslight Inc.*, 782 F.2d 767 (7th Cir. 1986), is an early and well-known case in point. Seven months after Gaslight filed a Chapter 11 petition, the creditors' committee, frustrated by continuing operating losses and disenchanted with the efforts of the debtor's president and majority stockholder, persuaded the bankruptcy court to appoint a new manager to exercise the powers of the debtor in possession. Brandt, the new manager, was an experienced "turnaround" manager, *i.e.*, a management consultant experienced in advising troubled companies. The debtor's president consented to the appointment of this "responsible person" and agreed to remain as president under his supervision. A month later, the responsible person fired the president, asserting that he was performing no useful function, was subversive, and had been secretly paying himself interest on a prepetition loan that he had made to the debtor. At this point, the president argued that the bankruptcy court had no authority to appoint a responsible person. The Seventh Circuit disagreed:

Sections 105(a) and 1107(a) of the Bankruptcy Code provide adequate authority for the bankruptcy court to approve the replacement of the person designated to perform the duties and exercise the rights of the debtor in possession if the creditors' committee, the person presently in control and the majority and controlling shareholder of the debtor agree to this course of action. Of course such consent may be conditioned upon the inclusion of whatever provisions in the court's order the various parties may demand. Had Fredricks [the president and majority stockholder] resigned his position, he almost certainly could have exercised his prerogatives as majority and controlling shareholder to replace himself as a corporate officer with a nominee of his own choice and the bankruptcy court could then have designated Fredericks' replacement as the person entitled to exercise the rights and obligations of the debtor in possession. Fredricks could also have named someone as a chief executive officer exercising ultimate control while leaving himself as president. *See* Bankruptcy Rule 9001(5)(A). The bankruptcy court's order here achieved the same result more directly. Because of Fredricks' consent to the designation of Brandt as the person in ultimate control, there was no need in this case to appoint a trustee.

782 F.2d at 771. Do you think the court would have reached a different conclusion had all of the interested parties, including the former president, not agreed to the appointment of a responsible person in the first place? Why would the former president have consented to the appointment of a "responsible person"? Is the appointment of a responsible person consistent with the approach of § 1104, which contemplates the appointment of a trustee in just the sort of circumstances that the *Gaslight* case presented? If you were the United States Trustee, how would you view the selection of a responsible person by a court? If the issue is allowing creditors to have the trustee of their choice, doesn't § 1104(b), which authorizes creditors to elect a trustee, provide the mechanism for doing that?

The *Gaslight* approach was questioned and rejected by another court, which expressed its "considerable doubt that section 1107(a) can be used to appoint a trustee equivalent." *In re Adelphia Communications Corp.*, 336 B.R. 610, 620 (Bankr. S.D.N.Y. 2006). Notwithstanding allegations that the family that had controlled the debtors had engaged in egregious fraud and fiscal mismanagement, the court declined to appoint a trustee, because the debtor's board of directors had already been reconstituted, and new chief executive, chief operating, and chief financial officers had been appointed. The court also declined to appoint a responsible person, explaining:

Section 105(a), which provides in relevant part, that "the court may issue any order, process, or judgment that is necessary or appropriate to carry out the provisions of this title," is plainly an inappropriate basis upon which such relief can be based. This Court has already considered the propriety of a trustee under section 1104(a) of the Code — considering whether the appointment of such might be required by law or might be appropriate as a matter of discretion — and has rejected both. The Second Circuit has repeatedly held that the lower courts cannot use section 105(a) to circumvent the Code. Using section 105(a) to appoint a fiduciary to act as a trustee shorn of the name, but with few other substantive differences, would be the exact kind of wrongful judicial action that the Second Circuit has forbidden. Section 1104 already provides for two kinds of fiduciaries, trustees and examiners. The . . . Committee has not shown an entitlement to the first, and has not asked for the second. Appointing a trustee equivalent, under these circumstances, would be doing exactly what the Second Circuit told the lower courts *not* to do: using section 105(a) "to create substantive rights that are otherwise unavailable under applicable law," and to "invent remedies that overstep statutory limitations."

Id. at 664 (citations omitted).

Although the appointment of a trustee is to be ordered sparingly, and the continuation of the debtor in possession is to be the norm, and although the *Gaslight* approach is questionable, the replacement of problematic management — often at the behest of creditors — with new managers that are experienced in turning distressed companies around, has become has become increasingly routine, particularly in large cases. The status and role of such "Chief Restructuring Officers," as they are commonly known, is discussed in the article, The Role and Retention of the Chief Restructuring Officer, which can be found at http://www.americasrestructuring.com/08_SF/p200-205%20The%20role%20and%20retention.pdf

§ 4.05   RIGHT OF STOCKHOLDERS TO MEET AND ELECT DIRECTORS WHEN DEBTOR REMAINS IN POSSESSION

PROBLEM 4.1

Carol is curious. "Thus far, we've been considering the ability and leverage that creditors have to force changes in management of a debtor in possession. What about stockholders? Suppose that they are unhappy with the way management is running the business. Are stockholders able to replace us by calling a meeting and electing directors even while a Chapter 11 case is in progress?"

Before you respond to her question, consider the following opinions.

IN RE JOHNS MANVILLE CORP.
United States Court of Appeals for the Second Circuit
801 F.2d 60, 15 C.B.C.2d 646, 15 B.C.D. 319 (1986)

MAHONEY, CIRCUIT JUDGE:

This action, one segment in a long-running Chapter 11 reorganization proceeding, arose in consequence of the competing interests of creditors, stockholders, and the board of directors in the development of rehabilitation plans for appellee, the Manville Corporation ("Manville"), formerly Johns-Manville Corporation. Appellants are the Equity Security Holders Committee and individual members of that committee (collectively the "Equity Committee"), appointed by the bankruptcy court to represent the interests of stockholders in Manville's reorganization.

Section 1102(a)(2) of the Bankruptcy Code provides: "On request of a party in interest, the court may order the appointment of additional committees of creditors or of equity security holders if necessary to assure adequate representation of creditors or of equity security holders if necessary to assure adequate representation of creditors or of equity security holders. The court shall appoint any such committee." 11 U.S.C. § 1102(a)(2) (1982).

The Securities and Exchange Commission, although technically an appellee, shares the interests of the Equity Committee in the matter at hand.

Although it has standing to be heard in the first instance, the Securities and Exchange Commission does not have standing to appeal. 11 U.S.C. § 1109(a) (1982). It may, however, participate in an appeal taken by a party in interest. H.R. , 95th Cong., 1st Sess. 404, reprinted in 1978 U.S. Code Cong. & Ad. News 5963, 6360.

Manville is aligned for purposes of this appeal with the Committee of Asbestos Health Related Claimants and/or Creditors (the "Asbestos Health Committee"), which represents the interests of the victims of diseases resulting from exposure to asbestos who have presently existing claims in tort against Manville, and with the Legal Representative, who represents the interests of future claimants who have not yet manifested such diseases.

The instant conflict arises in part because each of the committees representing the various interests in Manville must depend upon the Manville board of directors to advance those interests in the bankruptcy court at this stage of the rehabilitation proceedings. As debtor, Manville had the exclusive right under the Bankruptcy Code to file rehabilitation plans for the first 120 days of reorganization, and the bankruptcy court in these proceedings has granted Manville several extensions prolonging its exclusive filing period. *See* 11 U.S.C. § 1121(b), (d) (1982 & Supp. III 1986). Therefore, although in theory each of the committees may one day have the opportunity to submit a rehabilitation plan to the bankruptcy court if Manville's own proposals are rejected or if a trustee is appointed to replace the Manville board, *see id.* § 1121(c), Manville has for three or four years enjoyed the exclusive right, after negotiating with the committees, to file proposed plans. And although any of the committees may decline to accept a plan submitted to the bankruptcy court for confirmation, the power to formulate such plans in the first instance or at least to exercise a voice in their formulation is clearly a desideratum under the program laid down by the Bankruptcy Code, because the bankruptcy court may confirm a plan with or without the acquiescence of all classes of claims . . . so long as at least one impaired class has accepted the plan and so long as the court determines that the plan "does not discriminate unfairly" and is "fair and equitable" to each impaired class that has not accepted it. 11 U.S.C. § 1129(b)(1) (1982 & Supp. III 1986).

In order to channel negotiations toward acceptable plans, the various factions interested in Manville's rehabilitation have formed ad hoc alliances when the occasion has called for them. The challenge all the committees have faced is to fashion a plan that will preserve Manville's capacity to generate enough revenue to pay existing creditors, to cover its liabilities to present and future tort claimants where liability is certain though its precise extent is unknown, and to satisfy

Manville's shareholders. The seemingly strange bedfellows in the instant litigation, Manville and the committees representing present and future tort claimants, have long struggled to devise a reorganization plan acceptable to each. Along the way they have at times been antagonists rather than allies. For example, the Asbestos Health Committee opposed Manville's first proposed plan, sanctioned by the Equity Committee and filed on November 21, 1983. Other disputes, such as the Asbestos Health Committee's initial refusal to represent future tort claimants, which led to litigation over the appointment of the Legal Representative and the Asbestos Health Committee's motion to dismiss Manville's Chapter 11 petition, which the Equity Committee opposed, also diverted the energies of all parties from negotiations that might earlier have led to an acceptable plan.

To their credit, Manville and the Legal Representative finally came to terms in August of 1985, formulating a plan that would earmark billions of dollars for payment to present and future asbestosis victims as well as to others damaged by the asbestos products that Manville once manufactured and sold. They have now received the blessing of the Asbestos Health Committee and apparently of the other creditor committees. Having reconciled their differences, however, they encountered opposition from the Equity Committee immediately following their breakthrough, on the eve of their submission of the plan to the bankruptcy court for confirmation. Under protest, the Equity Committee had been cut out of the negotiations that led to their plan, and if the product of Manville's new understanding with the tort claimants and other creditors is confirmed, equity may be diluted by 90% or more. *In re Johns-Manville Corp.*, 60 Bankr. 842, 846 (S.D.N.Y. 1986). Displeased with that prospect, which the Equity Committee views as evidence of the Manville board's abdication of its responsibilities to the shareholders, the Equity Committee brought an action in Delaware state court seeking to compel Manville to hold a shareholders' meeting, pursuant to section 211(c) of Delaware's General Corporation Law.

Del. Code Ann. tit. 8, § 211(c) (1983) provides that upon "a failure to hold the annual meeting . . . for a period of 13 months . . . after its last annual meeting, the Court of Chancery may summarily order a meeting to be held upon the application of any stockholder or director."

The Equity Committee's avowed purpose was to replace Manville directors, so that new directors might reconsider submitting the proposed plan. 60 Bankr. at 852 n. 20.

Manville countered with the instant action. At Manville's behest, the bankruptcy court issued an injunction prohibiting the Equity Committee from pursuing the Delaware action on the ground that the holding of a shareholders' meeting would obstruct Manville's reorganization. Denying the Equity Committee's motion for summary judgment, the bankruptcy court granted summary judgment to Manville sua sponte. *In re Johns-Manville Corp.*, 52 Bankr. 879, 891 (Bankr. S.D.N.Y. 1985). The district court affirmed. *In re Johns-Manville Corp.*, 60 Bankr. 842 (S.D.N.Y. 1986). On appeal, the Equity Committee argues that the district court erred in affirming the decision to enjoin, in affirming the grant of summary judgment to Manville, and in finding that the bankruptcy court had jurisdiction to issue the injunction.

[The court's discussion of the jurisdictional issue is omitted.]

The Injunction and the Grant of Summary Judgment

Turning, then, to the decision to enjoin, we first encounter the well-settled rule that the right to compel a shareholders' meeting for the purpose of electing a new board subsists during reorganization proceedings. *See In re Bush Terminal Co.*, 78 F.2d 662, 664 (2d Cir. 1935); *In re Saxon Industries*, 488 A.2d 1298 (1985); *In re Lionel Corp.*, 30 Bankr. 327, 330 (Bankr. S.D.N.Y. 1983). As a consequence of the shareholders' right to govern their corporation, a prerogative ordinarily uncompromised by reorganization, "a bankruptcy court should not lightly employ its equitable power to block an election of a new board of directors." *In re Potter Instrument Co.*, 593 F.2d 470, 475 (2d Cir. 1979). In accordance with this rule, the parties and the lower courts agree that the Equity Committee's right to call a meeting may be impaired only if the Equity Committee is guilty of "clear abuse" in attempting to call one. *See In re J.P. Linahan, Inc.*, 111 F.2d 590, 592 (2d Cir. 1940). The Equity Committee's principal argument is that the "clear abuse" standard was not satisfied. In addition, however, the Equity Committee seems to argue that the district court's analysis was incomplete; i.e., the Equity Committee contends that in reviewing the bankruptcy court's decision to issue the injunction, the district court should have required, in addition to a showing of clear abuse, the usual showing of irreparable injury.

An examination of both lower court decisions will clarify the analysis that follows. The bankruptcy court found that "any shareholder meeting and ensuing proxy fight has the potential to derail the entire Manville reorganization with devastating consequences or at least to delay or halt plan negotiations." *In re Johns-Manville Corp.*, 52 Bankr. at 888. Reviewing the bankruptcy court's findings, the district court concluded that the Equity Committee intended either to "torpedo" the reorganization or to acquire a bargaining chip in aid of its negotiation power. *In re Johns-Manville Corp.*, 60 Bankr. at 852. In either case, the district court reasoned, the bankruptcy court did not err in concluding that the Equity Committee was guilty of clear abuse. *Id.* at 852–53.

Taking the district court's latter point first, we cannot agree that the Equity Committee's professed desire to arrogate more bargaining power in the negotiation of a plan — in contrast to some secret desire to destroy all prospects for reorganization — may in itself constitute clear abuse. The law of this circuit directs that the shareholders' natural wish to participate in this matter of corporate governance be respected. In *In re Bush Terminal Co.*, 78 F.2d 662 (2d Cir. 1935), for example, this court reversed an order enjoining a shareholders' meeting to be called for the purpose of advancing a rehabilitation plan more favorable to equity. Expressly upholding the right of a majority shareholder to try to replace board members for that purpose, the court reasoned:

> The debtor is given the right to be heard on all questions. Obviously, the stockholders should have the right to be adequately represented in the conduct of the debtor's affairs, especially in such an important matter as the reorganization of the debtor. Such representation can be obtained only by having as directors persons of their choice . . . . The debtor is given the

power to propose a plan of reorganization. No reason is advanced why stockholders, if they feel that the present board of directors is not acting in their interest, or has caused an unsatisfactory plan to be filed on behalf of the debtor, should not cause a new board to be elected which will act in conformance with the stockholders' wishes.

Id. at 664.

The court in *In re Bush Terminal Co.* thus clearly intended to protect the right of stockholders to be heard in negotiations leading to a rehabilitation plan. As the court concluded, "If the right of stockholders to elect a board of directors should not be carefully guarded and protected, the statute giving the debtor a right to be heard or to propose a plan of reorganization could not truly be exercised, for the board of directors is the representative of the stockholders." *Id.* at 665. Under this analysis, the shareholders' mere intention to exercise bargaining power — whether by actually replacing the directors or by "bargaining away" their chip without replacing the board, as the district court suggests they may have wished to do — cannot without more constitute clear abuse. Unless the Equity Committee were to bargain in bad faith — e.g., to demonstrate a willingness to risk rehabilitation altogether in order to win a larger share for equity — its desire to negotiate for a larger share is protected. Moreover, if rehabilitation is placed at risk as a result of the other committees' intransigent unwillingness to negotiate with the Equity Committee, as opposed to their real inability, within some reasonable amount of time, to formulate any confirmable plan more satisfactory to equity, the Equity Committee should not alone bear the consequences of a stalemate by being deemed guilty of clear abuse.

We note that if Manville were determined to be insolvent, so that the shareholders lacked equity in the corporation, denial of the right to call a meeting would likely be proper, because the stockholders would no longer be real parties in interest. Although the bankruptcy court discussed the possibility of Manville's insolvency in connection with its treatment of the Equity Committee's request for retention of special counsel and reimbursement of expenses, *see In re Johns-Manville Corp.*, 52 Bankr. at 885, an issue that is not a subject of this appeal, the district court did not uphold the determination of clear abuse on that basis, and the parties have not briefed that issue.

In re Lionel Corp., 30 Bankr. 327 (Bankr. S.D.N.Y. 1983), buttresses our conclusion that shareholders' desire for leverage is not a basis for denying them an election, so long as leverage means only the improvement of their bargaining position or the assurance of their participation in negotiations. In *In re Lionel Corp.* the bankruptcy court held that the record failed to demonstrate how reorganization would be impeded merely because the shareholders might be successful in their quest to cause the reorganization to "take an entirely different turn." *Id.* at 330. Surely if the Equity Committee is permitted to elect new directors in order to redirect or alter the course of a reorganization — and the district court here explicitly recognized that the committee is permitted to do that, *see In re Johns-Manville Corp.*, 60 Bankr. at 850 — the Equity Committee should be permitted, in the district court's words of disapproval, to "use the threat of a new board as a lever vis-a-vis other interested constituencies and vis-a-vis the current

Manville board." *Id.* at 852. The Equity Committee denies that there is evidence tending to show that it meant to use any "threat" as a "lever," but if there is any such evidence, it would suggest only that the Equity Committee might be willing to back away from replacing the directors if it were to find the board more responsive to its interests. For related reasons, we are not persuaded that the Equity Committee's failure to call for a meeting at an earlier stage in the negotiations places its desire for leverage in a different light. If dissatisfaction with the board's representation of shareholders is a legitimate ground for calling a meeting, the Equity Committee did not waive the right to call a meeting by waiting until it became dissatisfied.

We do not suggest, of course, that an equity committees' delay in calling a shareholders' meeting may never contribute to a finding of clear abuse. As the Securities and Exchange Committee pointed out in its brief, an attempt to call a shareholders' meeting after a plan has been submitted to the bankruptcy court and after confirmation hearings have begun would usually be more disruptive to the proceedings than an earlier attempt would be. Such an attempt might also indicate bad faith and a willingness to risk jeopardy to rehabilitation. On the other hand, a rule that required a call before dissatisfaction had crystallized would only encourage preemptive efforts that might otherwise be avoided by negotiation. In this case, the Equity Committee apparently acted promptly upon learning of Manville's proposed plan and is certainly not accountable for any movement toward confirmation that may have occurred thereafter over its objections.

Finally, we reject appellees' suggestion that the availability to the Equity Committee of other means with which to oppose Manville's plan robs the Equity Committee of its chosen means. It is true that the Equity Committee could have sought the appointment of a trustee to displace Manville as the sole author of proposed plans and that it may later object to the confirmation of any plan Manville submits to the bankruptcy court. But those correctives provide only imperfect substitutes for a voice in the original formulation of a plan. More to the present point, perhaps, those avenues to shareholder satisfaction cannot be said to be exclusive in light of this circuit's legitimation of the shareholders' right to elect new directors for the frank purpose of advancing a plan they prefer.

In this connection, we must reject Manville's argument that a full inquiry into "clear abuse" would duplicate the confirmation proceedings that will follow submission of its present plan or any other. Unlike the analysis to determine clear abuse, the object of the confirmation proceedings will be to weigh Manville's proposed plan against other possible plans, taking into account the interests of impaired classes that object to Manville's proposals. In contrast, the determination whether the Equity Committee is guilty of clear abuse turns on whether rehabilitation will be seriously threatened, rather than merely delayed, if Manville's present plan is not submitted for confirmation now. *See In re Bush Terminal Co.*, 78 F.2d 662 (2d Cir. 1935); *In re J.P. Linahan, Inc.*, 111 F.2d 590 (2d Cir. 1940); *In re Lionel Corp.*, 30 Bankr. 327 (Bankr. S.D.N.Y. 1983). Quite apart from its right to contest confirmation, the Equity Committee has the right to a fair hearing on the latter question and to a decision that recognizes its right to influence its own board.

We now reach the district court's alternative ground for affirming the grant of summary judgment. The bankruptcy court's finding that the proposed stockholders' meeting might jeopardize the reorganization process, "or at least . . . delay or halt plan negotiations," 52 Bankr. at 888, a finding reflected in the district court's view that the Equity Committee might have intended to "torpedo" the reorganization, poses an issue more difficult than the question of the stockholders' desire for a voice in negotiations. While delay to rehabilitation would not by itself provide a ground for overriding the shareholders' right to govern Manville — delay being a concomitant of the right to change boards — real jeopardy to reorganization prospects would provide such a ground.

In *In re Potter Instrument Co.*, 593 F.2d 470 (2d Cir. 1979), this court upheld the bankruptcy court's refusal, upon a finding of clear abuse, to order a shareholders' meeting to be called for the purpose of electing new directors. We reasoned that "such an election might result in unsatisfactory management and would probably jeopardize both [the debtor's] rehabilitation and the rights of creditors and stockholders — sounding the 'death knell' to the debtor as well as to appellant himself." *Id.* at 475. In *In re Potter Instrument Co.*, however, the facts were distinct from those considered here, at least on the record before us. Potter, the appellant, had agreed in a consent decree with the Securities and Exchange Commission to limit his management in the debtor and not to vote against any action recommended by a majority of the board of directors. *Id.* at 474. Attempting to circumvent the agreement, Potter sought to elect new directors who would vote against a proposed plan that would cause the debtor to issue new stock to unsecured creditors and thereby dilute Potter's holdings. The bankruptcy court had found that approval of a plan could probably never be accomplished without issuance of the stock. In addition, the bankruptcy court had noted that it would not be likely to approve control of the debtor by Potter in light of the record before it. *Id.*

It thus appears that the Equity Committee might distinguish itself from the shareholder in *In re Potter Instrument Co.*, given the opportunity for an evidentiary hearing. The Equity Committee persuasively calls into question whether the bankruptcy court had any basis for concluding here that an election would jeopardize the reorganization process, particularly since the bankruptcy court's articulated basis appears to have been colored by an unsubstantiated suspicion that the Equity Committee affirmatively wished to jeopardize reorganization.

In reviewing the bankruptcy court's decision, the district court characterized its findings as follows:

> The dim prospects for a successful reorganization following the election of a new board led the bankruptcy court to question the Equity Committee's motivation in seeking a new election. By its own admission, the Equity Committee brought the Delaware action in order to derail the proposed plan. Either the appellants seek to destroy any prospect for a successful reorganization, or they wish to use the threat of a new board as a lever vis-a-vis other interested constituencies and vis-a-vis the current Manville board. Neither the interest in torpedoing the reorganization nor in acquiring a chip to be bargained away are legitimate. Judge Lifland, who was well aware of the dynamics of the Manville bankruptcy, had ample evidence from which to conclude that by either attempting to destroy the prospects for a successful reorganization or by merely attempting to

> strengthen its bargaining position without changing the current board, the Equity Committee was acting in a clearly abusive manner.

60 Bankr. at 852 (footnotes omitted). The bankruptcy court decision itself did not define the Equity Committee's supposed ill motives quite so clearly. At one point, however, the bankruptcy court observed that "section 105(a) contemplates the court's use of injunctive relief in precisely those instances where parties are attempting to obstruct the reorganization." 52 Bankr. at 889. The bankruptcy court then concluded that "the *carefully timed* Delaware action will have an adverse impact on the Debtor's ability to coalesce with others to formulate an acceptable Chapter 11 plan, resulting in irreparable harm and the impeding of the negotiation process." *Id.* at 890 (emphasis added). Perhaps Potter was willing to embark on a suicide mission, "sounding the 'death knell' to . . . himself" along with the debtor. But as the Equity Committee argues, the lower courts in this case pointed to no evidence to support any finding that it wished to "torpedo" the reorganization, which the Equity Committee contends would be an irrational goal from its perspective.

The bankruptcy court stated that it relied on "the cumulative record in this case" to distinguish it from *In re Lionel Corp.*, 30 Bankr. 327 (Bankr. S.D.N.Y. 1983), and *In re Saxon Industries*, 39 Bankr. 49 (Bankr. S.D.N.Y. 1984), and to justify application of the *In re Potter Instrument Co.* rationale. *See In re Johns-Manville*, 52 Bankr. at 888. The only evidence the bankruptcy court cited, however, apart from evidence that the Equity Committee meant to influence negotiations in its favor, was the affidavit of G. Earl Parker, a Manville director who might have been replaced if an election had been held. Parroting *In re Potter Instrument Co.*, Parker's affidavit merely concluded that "the consequences flowing from yet another stalemate would place in jeopardy the ability of the Debtors ever to confirm a plan of reorganization or to pay its just debts." 52 Bankr. at 888. The district court affirmed on the basis of the Parker affidavit, coupled with the bankruptcy court's "accumulated knowledge" about the case.

The evidence contained in the Parker affidavit, consisting principally in the conclusion quoted above, is insufficient to support the determination of clear abuse underlying the grant of summary judgment. *See* Fed. R. Civ. P. 56(e). While we agree with the district court that it was proper for the bankruptcy court to consider the record as a whole in determining whether summary judgment was appropriate, *see* Fed. R. Civ. P. 56(c) without being told which portions of the bankruptcy court's accumulated knowledge it relied on for decision, we cannot agree that no material issues of fact remain to be determined.

In Manville's view, the bankruptcy court did review the facts that led it to find "clear abuse," adverting in its opinion to the facts that Manville had been in bankruptcy for three years without any resolution, 52 Bankr. at 881; that Manville and committee representatives had engaged in extensive but fruitless negotiations, *id*; that Manville did not reach agreement with any other constituency until August 1985, *id.* at 882; that "within two weeks of the announcement of the Principal Elements Agreement, the Equity Committee filed its motion . . . for the purpose of instituting the Delaware Action," *id.*; and that "no shareholder or director has at any time sought to compel the calling of a shareholder's meeting for the years 1983, 1984 and 1985," *id*. We do not think that this bare recitation of the events culminating in Manville's plan and the Equity Committee's discontent, when added to the bankruptcy court's stated basis for decision, constitutes a showing that the Equity Committee committed clear abuse.

Moreover, as the Equity Committee argues, a finding of clear abuse must be supplemented by a finding of irreparable injury before an injunction may issue. The bankruptcy court seemed to assume that the two injuries coalesce; after finding clear abuse, it concluded without further analysis that an injunction was necessary to prevent irreparable harm to the reorganization. *In re Johns-Manville Corp.*, 52 Bankr. at 891. *Cf. In re Lionel Corp.*, 30 Bankr. at 329 (Although the shareholders wished to alter the course of reorganization, "Lionel has failed to demonstrate any irreparable harm, which factor alone requires a denial of an injunction."). In affirming the bankruptcy court, the district court did not discuss the irreparable injury prerequisite for relief.

Although the inquiries into clear abuse and irreparable injury will likely yield the same result in most if not all cases, an articulated analysis of irreparable injury would achieve a better focus and assist the reviewing court. In this connection, it is worth noting that *In re Potter Instrument Co.*, the only authority for a finding of clear abuse in circumstances resembling Manville's, did not deal with injunctive relief at all. There the court merely declined to direct a shareholders' meeting. In any event, on this record any harm to the reorganization was speculative enough that the irreparable injury requirement was not satisfied.

On the record before us we cannot say that either side is entitled to summary judgment in its favor. There may be evidence known to the bankruptcy court but unarticulated in its opinion to support the result it reached. Manville's burden on remand, however, will be altered in accordance with this opinion.

Conclusion

Whether the Equity Committee's call for a shareholder's meeting constitutes clear abuse and whether such a meeting would cause irreparable harm to Manville's reorganization are triable issues of fact. The summary judgment award to Manville is therefore reversed. On remand, the court should undertake a more elaborate inquiry into clear abuse and irreparable harm. Rather than focusing on the Equity Committee's conceded desire to enhance its bargaining position, the court should analyze the real risks to rehabilitation posed by permitting the Equity Committee to call a meeting of shareholders for the purpose of compelling reconsideration of Manville's presently proposed plan. We emphasize, however, that given its greater knowledge about this complex and perhaps fragile reorganization, the bankruptcy court may exercise its legitimate injunctive powers to control the future course of rehabilitation pursuant to appropriate legal standards and evidentiary showings.

[The dissenting opinion of Circuit Judge OAKES is omitted.]

NOTES AND QUESTIONS

(1) *Manville on Remand.* After conducting what it characterized as "an extensive trial," Bankruptcy Judge Lifland issued an 80-page opinion, *Manville Corporation v. Equity Security Holders Committee*, 66 B.R. 517 (Bankr. S.D.N.Y. 1986), presenting in toxic detail the history of the case and at least some facts supporting his belief that the meeting was being sought by rogue stockholders who would — and, what is more could — scuttle the reorganization effort if they did not have their way. Whether Judge Lifland strictly adhered to the Second Circuit's direction to shift its focus from the motivation of the committee to the risks inherent in calling an election is questionable. A substantial portion of the opinion on remand is devoted to a rehash of the obvious fact that the stockholders' objective was the withdrawal of the plan and to discrediting the committee's contention that it had been shut out of negotiations. Possibly this is because a finding of bad faith on the part of stockholders seems to presuppose a finding of good faith on the part of creditors and the debtor. Perhaps the Bankruptcy Judge believed this finding was necessary to lay to rest the Second Circuit's warning that "if rehabilitation is placed at risk as a result of the other committee's intransigent unwillingness to negotiate with the Equity Committee, as opposed to their real inability, within some reasonable amount of time, to formulate any confirmable plan more satisfactory to equity, the Equity Committee should not alone bear the consequences of a stalemate by being deemed guilty of clear abuse." Judge Lifland also took pains to point out, both in his opinion on the motion for summary judgment and in his opinion on remand, that among the stockholders who were pressing for a meeting were many who had purchased their shares *after* Manville had filed for Chapter 11 relief. Thus, he observed, "a major distinction between the equity and other committees should be noted. This committee's representation uniquely embraces individuals or shareholders who may have voluntarily acquired their interests after the filing of the petition." 66 B.R. at 522–33. The idea that the quality of the interests of those "equity players" who took a gamble on Manville stock is somehow less than the quality of the interests of creditors may be facially appealing. However, would not disenfranchising stockholders on that ground alone only have a depressing effect on the value of the stock of a Chapter 11 company and deprive prepetition stockholders of a very important escape hatch?

The opinion on remand does, however, marshal some evidence — primarily testimony by Manville officers, the Legal Representative, and counsel to various creditors' committees — in support of the bankruptcy court's stay of the stockholders' meeting. Based on such testimony, the court found that the consensus of the parties in support of the existing plan was so fragile and the possibility of developing another acceptable plan was so slight, that pulling the plan would destroy the prospects for reorganizing Manville. The result, he predicted, would be a motion to liquidate Manville, which he believed "would put everybody in a worse position, including the common shareholders." 66 B.R. at 538. The attorney appointed to represent the future asbestos claimants, testified:

> I do not think that Manville in its present guise can put forward a plan that will muster the support of any of the constituencies. And I know that to be an extravagant statement. But I have now been engaged in this process for two years. In the course of it, from having been told that a

resolution was impossible by every constituency now involved, we have come to a point where each of the constituencies has given up and accommodated itself so that we have in a sense a mosaic or a jigsaw puzzle which at its best is fragile.

For that to now be tampered with by the withdrawal of a plan so that major negotiations to realign positions can be undertaken, is to put us back for two years, with not only no promise of success but with a virtual promise of lack of success.

Id.

On the basis of the testimony of Manville's president and chief executive officer, Judge Lifland found that prolonging the reorganization would have "a negative impact on employee morale and the business opportunities available to the corporation," *Id.* at 539, which, in turn, would make it more difficult for the company to formulate an acceptable plan. The court found evidence of the stockholders' willingness to jeopardize the reorganization in the fact that "the consequence of the failure of this consensus are obvious to all," including, presumably, stockholders and also in a newsletter circulated among certain Manville shareholders. The newsletter contained a report by a litigation analyst for that group. The report read as follows:

[I]t appears questionable whether a litigation strategy will be effective in improving the position of shareholders to any great extent . . . Current shareholders might do well by simply torpedoing the agreement altogether, if possible, and then by paying off all existing claimants who have valid claims.

. . . .

[S]hareholders have little to lose and lots to gain by settling in for a long but well-orchestrated campaign to annihilate the current plan.

Id. at 534. Finding that the equity committee had introduced no evidence to rebut Manville's showing of irreparable harm, the court found that Manville had met its burden of proof and again enjoined the Committee from prosecuting an action to compel a meeting and election.

(2) *Lionel.* When the question of a stockholders' meeting arose in the *Lionel* case, the bankruptcy judge — who apparently was not as worried about the fragility of the case as was the *Manville* judge — agreed to let the state court decide whether to allow stockholders to meet. The judge in *Lionel* even seemed to welcome the possibility that a change in management might advance the progress of the case, observing, "if the defendants are able to elect a new board it may be that the reorganization here will take an entirely different turn." *In re Lionel Corp.*, 30 B.R. 327, 330 (Bankr. S.D.N.Y. 1983). The state court did order the Lionel board to call a meeting, observing:

[During bankruptcy] it is more important than in less turbulent and more normal times that the shareholders have a voice in the crucial decisions affecting their company's destiny. A period of crisis does not justify officeholders retaining their positions indefinitely. Democracy, whether political or industrial, is capable of dealing with difficulty and crisis, and is not to be suspended on the pretext of exigency.

Committee of Equity Security Holders of the Lionel Corp. v. Lionel Corp., N.Y.L.J., June 29, 1983, at 6. col. 4.

(3) *Is solvency relevant?* The Second Circuit's opinion in *Manville* left open the question of whether the right of stockholders to call an annual meeting subsists when the debtor is insolvent, although in dicta, the court noted, "[I]f Manville were determined to be insolvent, so that the shareholders lacked equity in the corporation, denial of the right to call a meeting would likely be proper, because the shareholders would no longer be real parties in interest." In *Saxon Industries, Inc. v. NKFW Partners*, 488 A.2d 1298 (Del. 1984), the court held that under Delaware law, the right to call a meeting was "clear" and "virtually absolute," and that the debtor's $200 million net worth deficit was not dispositive. The court explained that since, as a debtor in possession, "Saxon remained in control of its affairs, insolvency did not divest the stockholders of their right to elect directors. Normal corporate governance therefore continues." 488 A.2d at 1302. In another *Lionel* opinion, which is reprinted in chapter 6, § 6.01 of the text, the Second Circuit held that stockholders' views regarding the sale of a key subsidiary were entitled to weight and that the directors should take stockholder's interests, as well as the interests of creditors into account. The court reached this conclusion even though *Lionel* appeared to have a negative net worth of nearly $23 million.

Interestingly, nothing in the Bankruptcy Code itself suggests that corporate governance should be suspended because a debtor in possession is insolvent, and indeed the implication of some Code provisions is to the contrary. Stockholders of even an insolvent debtor are entitled to vote to accept or reject a plan. Code § 1126(a). Interestingly, under former Chapter X, stockholders of an insolvent debtor had no right to vote on a plan, and their acceptance of the plan was not a prerequisite to confirmation. A showing of solvency is not a statutory prerequisite to the appointment of an equity security holders' committee to negotiate on the stockholders' behalf, Code § 1102(a)(2), although the appointment of shareholder's committee may be inappropriate if the debtor is so "hopelessly insolvent" that stockholders have no equity and no prospect of ever having any. *See, e.g., In re Wang Laboratories, Inc.*, 149 B.R. 1, 3 (Bankr. E.D. Mass. 1992); *In re Emons Industries, Inc.*, 50 B.R. 692, 694 (Bankr. S.D.N.Y. 1985). Moreover, under the regime of Chapter 11, the absolute priority rule, which under the former Act required that all creditors' claims be satisfied in full before equity holders would be permitted to receive or retain any property under a reorganization plan, has been relaxed. Under the Code, if all impaired classes of claims vote by the requisite majorities to accept a plan that permits stockholders to receive or retain an interest, the court may confirm the plan. Code § 1129(a)(8). Thus, the absolute priority rule comes into play only when a class of claims or interests votes against the plan, and insolvency does not bar stockholders from voting on a plan or from receiving or retaining an interest in a reorganized entity if creditors agree to relinquish it. *See* Bankruptcy Code § 1129(b). The intent of Congress in relaxing the absolute priority rule in Chapter 11 also militates against using solvency as a litmus test for the right of stockholders to call a meeting. One reason for easing the absolute priority rule was to eliminate the need for costly, time consuming, and highly conjectural going concern valuations in every case. H.R. Rep. 95-595, 95th Cong., 1st Sess. 224 (1977). Another was to foster negotiated, consensual plans. H.R. Rep. 95-595, 95th Cong., 1st Sess. 225 (1977). These goals would be undercut by making a showing of solvency a prerequisite to the right to call a meeting and by denying stockholders the negotiating leverage they derive by exercising — or threatening to exercise — their corporate governance prerogatives.

In the opinion that follows, the court jumps in where the *Manville* court declined to tread and interferes with the corporate governance process. Why? Were the actions of the debtor's officers and directors consistent with their fiduciary duties?

IN RE LIFEGUARD INDUSTRIES, INC.
United States Bankruptcy Court, Northern District of Ohio
37 B.R. 3 (1983)

Randall J. Newsome, Bankruptcy Judge.

This Chapter 11 case is before the Court pursuant to an Application for Approval of New Management, a Motion to Confirm Appointment of New Directors, and a Motion for Appointment of Committee of Equity Security Holders. A hearing on said motions was commenced on August 16, 1983, and completed on August 23, 1983.

. . . .

The controversy underlying these motions contains all of the essential elements for a Greek drama, and accordingly a Prologue is in order.

Lifeguard Industries is a closely-held Ohio corporation primarily engaged in the manufacture of aluminum siding. Its principal place of business is located in Cincinnati, Ohio. It was launched in 1956 by Louis and Joseph Guttman. Louis Guttman was president of the corporation for its first year; Joseph succeeded him in that office in 1957, after Louis' death, and remained its president and chief executive officer until 1974. He was also the majority shareholder until his death on March 18, 1980. Marion Guttman, Joseph's wife, was a vice-president, but never played an active role in the business. Shirley Onie, Joseph's daughter, never had more than a passing acquaintance with the business of the corporation. Fred C. Guttman, one of Joseph's sons, became the president, secretary and chief operating officer in 1974, having started with the company in 1958. Joseph, however, continued to exert influence on the affairs of the corporation until his death.

Prior to Joseph's death, the corporate board of directors consisted of Joseph, Marion, and Fred Guttman. After Joseph's death, Marion Guttman and Fred Guttman were the only two members of the corporation's board of directors, notwithstanding the fact that the articles of incorporation called for a three-member board. However, as is true of many family-run corporations, corporate formalities were never strictly observed. Neither Shirley (who lives in Arlington, Virginia) nor Marion (who lives in Florida) took an active interest in Lifeguard's affairs after Joseph's death.

Beginning in mid-1980 and continuing through 1981, Lifeguard experienced operating losses and a severe cash flow problem. In December of 1981 BancOhio

National Bank, the company's primary lender, cut Lifeguard's line of credit in half. On June 10, 1982 Lifeguard filed its petition under Chapter 11.

The Chapter 11 case proceeded along uneventfully until June 30, 1983, when Fred Guttman submitted a disclosure statement and plan of reorganization on behalf of the debtor. Among other things, the plan of reorganization proposed to cancel all of the existing common stock in the corporation, and to reissue new common stock to certain key employees over a five year period. If the plan is confirmed, Fred Guttman will end up with 76% of the new common stock, with the remaining 24% being divided equally between the vice-presidents of manufacturing and marketing. The other shareholders (Shirley Onie, Marion Guttman, and the Estate of Joseph Guttman) will neither retain nor receive anything under the plan.

Apparently viewing the proposed plan as a virtual declaration of war, Shirley and Marion immediately launched a campaign to protect their ownership interest in the corporation and to oust Fred from control over the business. This campaign reached a crescendo during three heated shareholders meetings held on August 8, 1983. Both sides claim that they hold a majority of the voting rights in the stock of the corporation; both sides claim entitlement to elect their respective slates of directors and officers; both sides claim the right to control and operate the business. Both sides concede that there may not be a viable corporation left to control after the dust settles. The debtor is presently in desperate need of cash, and its cash collateral agreement with BancOhio expires on August 31, 1983. The bank noted on the record its reluctance to renew this agreement voluntarily. Virtually all of the debtor's assets are subject to a security agreement held by BancOhio.

The committee of unsecured creditors, which was allowed to intervene as a party in this dispute, takes no position on the issues regarding ownership of shares or the composition of the board of directors. However, the creditor's committee strongly objects to any change in management and to the appointment of an equity security holder's committee.

Having set the stage and introduced the dramatis personae, the Court hereby submits its findings of fact, opinion, and conclusions of law.

FINDINGS OF FACT

The Stock Ownership Issue

[The court, after analyzing various corporate records and voting agreements in light of governing state law, concluded that even though Fred Guttman owned 51% of Lifeguard's stock, a proxy that he had given to his father reduced his voting rights to less than a majority. Marion Guttman, Shirley Onie, and the Estate of Joseph Guttman (of which Onie was representative) were entitled to vote a majority of the shares. — Eds.]

The Management Issue

[A] Background

[The court then chronicled how, a few months before Lifeguard filed its Chapter 11 petition, Shirley Onie contacted a financial consultant (Gary Sycalik), who in turn contacted a management consultant (John Hevener) to locate a buyer or source of investment capital for the company. Fred met with Hevener, unaware that he had been retained by Shirley. Fred expressed interest in finding a buyer or new source of capital. He also told Hevener that he intended to eliminate the interests of the other stockholders and issue new stock to himself and key employees. Acting on the consultants' advice, Shirley resigned from Lifeguard's board of directors, triggering a by-law requiring that within 20 days after a vacancy occurs on the board, the president must call a shareholders' meeting. Counsel for the debtor sought guidance from the court as to whether the shareholders' meeting should be held. — Eds.]

[B] The Proposed Change In Management

. . . .

The newly-elected directors propose to change the management structure of the company by installing Gary Sycalik as president, Hevener as secretary, and Onie as treasurer, with Louis A. Epstein to continue as vice-president of marketing and James G. Wendell III to continue as vice-president of manufacturing. Fred Guttman would be employed as operations manager. It is unclear what (if any) his responsibilities would be, but it is clear that Fred Guttman would decline to accept the position regardless of what his responsibilities might be.

The new board of directors has also proposed the hiring of four consultants to act as a crisis management team. While the board agrees that Sycalik will act as coordinator of this team, they do not agree on who will run the day-to-day operations as chief executive officer. Hevener and Onie testified that Hevener will hold this position while Sycalik has testified that he intends to hold that position. Onie will play little, if any, role in the management of the company.

Both men have stated that they intend to move to Cincinnati and devote whatever time is necessary to perform their corporate duties at Lifeguard.

Hevener expects to be paid a salary of approximately $50,000 as chief executive officer. Sycalik was less specific as to his expected remuneration. However, he estimates that the services of the consultants which the board proposes to retain will cost the corporation approximately $40,000.00 over a two- to four-month period.

The Court notes in passing that neither Onie nor Sycalik nor Hevener intends to invest any of their own personal assets to financially resuscitate Lifeguard.

The new members of the board have proposed that Epstein and Wendell remain in their present positions. Neither Hevener nor Sycalik has ever met Epstein or Wendell, nor have they determined whether Wendell and Epstein are willing to remain employed for the corporation under the new management team. Both

Epstein and Wendell testified at the hearing, and both indicated a strong probability that they would leave if Fred Guttman were ousted from control. The parties generally concede, and the Court finds, that both Epstein and Wendell are exceptionally well-qualified for their positions.

Epstein has been employed with Lifeguard as the vice-president of sales and marketing since February of 1979. Prior to coming to Lifeguard, he was a sales manager for two other aluminum siding manufacturers over a fifteen-year period. In 1981 Lifeguard closed 12 of its 15 distribution centers in an effort to reduce its overhead and improve its cash flow. In turn, the prime customer base for its products changed from jobbers and contractors to independent wholesalers. Many of the wholesalers which Lifeguard now sells to were customers of the companies which Epstein previously worked for; it is reasonable to assume that many of these wholesalers would follow Epstein if he were to leave Lifeguard.

Wendell has been Lifeguard's vice-president of manufacturing since February of 1980. Prior to that he served as national sales manager for Mobil Oil's chemical division, which manufactures coatings for aluminum siding. He was also a plant manager for Crown Aluminum for four years.

From the evidence presented, the Court entertains serious misgivings as to whether Lifeguard could continue to operate if both Wendell and Epstein should abruptly resign from the company.

The qualifications of Sycalik, Hevener and Onie are not so apparent. According to his deposition, Sycalik has worked for at least seven entities since 1962. He was the founder of at least three of these entities. While the details of his responsibilities at these companies are sketchy, his business activities have included laser sales, land sales, satellite data-processing, holistic community development, estate planning, and management consulting.

He started Worldwide Capital Management Corporation approximately 2 years ago. The details of Worldwide's business activities and financial condition are equally sketchy. Sycalik was elusive as to the amount of his salary from the company. Because of a loss of records, the company has not yet filed its 1982 tax returns.

It is apparent that Sycalik knows little, if anything, about operating a manufacturing facility. His experience in manufacturing consists of eight months as a production planner in the 1960's.

Hevener's work history was better defined. He is certified under Pennsylvania law as a public accountant. During the 1960's he was the chief executive officer of an electrical construction firm, and later served as chief executive officer of a company which provided accounting and data processing services to the electrical construction industry. For the last three years he has been the chief financial officer and personnel director of Peneast Corporation, a stainless steel foundry and nickel recycling operation with yearly gross sales of three to six million dollars. His management consulting company, Hevener Associates, Inc., has not been very active over the past twelve months. Hevener concedes that it has not shown a profit for at least ten years. His experience in operating a manufacturing facility appears to be limited.

Mrs. Onie is the president and majority shareholder of Embassies International, a corporation engaged in the sale of military spare parts and equipment. While Embassies International has gross sales of approximately one million dollars per year, it has not filed a tax return since it was incorporated in 1980. Mrs. Onie offered no satisfactory explanation for this failure to file tax returns. She concedes that she has no knowledge of manufacturing, finance, or accounting.

She also freely admits that she knows virtually nothing about the business or personal backgrounds of Sycalik, Hevener, or the consultants whom they propose to retain. Notwithstanding this lack of knowledge, on August 3, 1983, Onie and Marion Guttman both executed agreements with Worldwide Capital Management Corporation whereby Worldwide would receive hourly fees, out-of-pocket expenses, and 50% of any equity which it succeeded in salvaging for Onie, Marion Guttman, and the Estate of Joseph Guttman in exchange for Worldwide's best efforts to protect their shareholder rights. To date, Onie has paid Worldwide in excess of $20,000, $7,500 of which was paid from the Estate of Joseph Guttman. (Sycalik depo. pgs. 104-105.) Part of this money has been distributed to Hevener and the attorneys representing Onie, Marion Guttman, and the Estate of Joseph Guttman.

Onie, Sycalik and Hevener share certain characteristics in terms of their qualifications to operate Lifeguard. None of the three has any knowledge of the aluminum siding industry; nor do they have a source of financing to solve Lifeguard's pressing financial problems; nor do they have a working knowledge of the business; nor do they have a clear plan of action for operating the business and solving the problems which they believe exist; nor do they have a clear idea of how they will utilize the services of the consultants which will compose their crisis management team.

. . . .

Onie, Sycalik and Hevener argue that Lifeguard is no longer a viable corporation, and that mismanagement by Fred Guttman is almost exclusively to blame for its demise. Among other things, they cite poor accounting procedures, inadequate financial controls, and unwise business decisions as justifications for immediately ousting Fred Guttman from control.

Based upon the evidence presented, the Court agrees with their contention that neither Fred Guttman nor Anita Gabor, company accounting manager, has an adequate grasp of the details of Lifeguard's financial condition, either past or present.

. . . .

Notwithstanding his lack of knowledge regarding the company's finances and the confused state of Lifeguard's financial picture, the evidence establishes that Fred Guttman has made a concerted effort to turn the business around, and that these efforts have met with some success.

As of 1980 the company operated fifteen regional warehouses, had 25 to 30 salesmen, 3 regional managers, and $11 million in yearly sales. The increased debt burden and decrease in sales caused by the rise in interest rates required that Guttman make some difficult decisions in 1980 and 1981. To cut down overhead and improve cash flow, the sales force was reduced dramatically, and 12 of the 15 warehouses were closed. However, the benefits from these actions were not quickly realized due to the expenses inherent in closing the warehouses. Other cost-saving measures were instituted, including the termination of the company's vice-president of finance, material specialist, and certain office personnel. Guttman cut his own salary from $115,000 per year to $85,000 per year.

The company incurred additional financial setbacks in the form of continuing theft losses (which are still being investigated) and the reduction of their line of credit by BancOhio. Because the company was forced to do business with their suppliers on a cash basis, and because the economy failed to improve, sales continued to decrease.

Primarily due to Guttman's efforts, however, the company has increased its highly profitable tolling operations, which consists of custom painting for other manufacturers. It has sought and obtained distributorship rights for vinyl siding, and has established new outlets for the sale of its aluminum siding. It is undisputed that the company will probably show a profit this year although the amount is subject to question due to the unreliability of its financial statements.

35. Based upon his testimony, as well as that of Wendell and Epstein, the Court finds that Fred Guttman has a good working knowledge of the aluminum siding industry, has performed capably as a manager of Lifeguard's business activities, and has made a significant personal and financial commitment to turning the company around. Based upon the above findings and all of the evidence presented in this case, the Court further finds that the best interests of creditors would not be served by allowing the new slate of officers to take over the day-to-day operations of the business, at least not at this critical time.

OPINION AND CONCLUSIONS OF LAW

The issues raised by the parties in this dispute are as difficult as they are unique. Counsel for Onie has argued that the ownership rights held by the shareholders include the right of the majority to change management and that such rights may not be abridged under the laws of Ohio. Counsel for the debtor has invited the Court to ignore the state law rights of the shareholders and simply abstain from deciding the issues presented.

The Court cannot accept either argument. Unfortunately, neither the Bankruptcy Code nor the case law provides extensive guidance for balancing the parties' competing interests. Indeed, neither the Court nor the parties have found any reported cases which bear any resemblance to the situation at hand.

However, the case law does provide certain basic principles which are applicable in this proceeding. There is little question that shareholders of a corporate debtor-in-possession retain their state law rights to control a corporation, and that such rights cannot be lightly cast aside by this Court.

. . . .

However, it is equally apparent that the shareholders' right to control a Chapter 11 debtor-in-possession is not without limitations under the Bankruptcy Code.

Section 1107(a) specifically provides that a debtor-in-possession shall have all (or almost all) of the rights, powers and duties of a trustee subject *"to such limitations or conditions as the court prescribes . . . "* Section 1108 states that "unless the Court orders otherwise, the trustee may operate the debtor's business." At least two courts have interpreted the language of § 1108 as prohibiting a court from interfering with a trustee's business judgments in operating a debtor's business. *In re Curlew Valley Associates*, 14 B.R. 506, 8 B.C.D. 495 (Bkrtcy. D. Utah 1981); *In re Airlift International, Inc.*, 18 B.R. 787, 8 B.C.D. 1196 (Bkrtcy. S.D. Fla. 1982). Those same two courts also noted *in dicta* that no similar restriction can be gleaned from the language and legislative history of § 1107(a).

This same conclusion was reached in *In re Lyon & Reboli, Inc.*, 24 B.R. 152, 9 B.C.D. 916 (Bkrtcy. E.D.N.Y. 1982), wherein it was held that § 105 and § 1107(a) of the Code vest the Court with the authority to review the propriety of salaries paid to the debtor-in-possession's officers. Judge Parente's reasoning is worth repeating here:

> At issue is not the wisdom or efficacy of a business decision, but the propriety of insiders bestowing upon themselves compensation which may be excessive and detrimental to the creditors. The corporations in question are closely held, and the actions of the officers are subject to little, if any, internal review. Prior to the confirmation of a negotiated plan which might fix the compensation of the officers, the court has an obligation, when application is made by a party in interest, to pass upon the propriety of the salaries of insiders where there is the potential for, and the prima facie appearance of, abuse.

24 B.R. 152, 9 B.C.D. at 917.

While the propriety of salaries is not at issue here, there have been allegations of, and certainly potential for, abuse of the corporation by insiders to the detriment of both the creditors and the equity security holders. Thus, the Court has an obligation to scrutinize the actions of the corporation when asked by a party in interest to do so.

We heartily concur in the view expressed in the above-cited decisions that business judgments should be left to the board room and not to this Court. It is not this Court's responsibility to determine whether Lifeguard should increase its tolling operations, change its product lines, increase its distributing activities, cut back its sales force, or manufacture vinyl siding. It *is* this Court's responsibility to protect creditors' interests from the actions of inexperienced, incapable, or foolhardy management, whether old or new.

It may well be that Shirley Onie's management team might ultimately usher in a new era of unprecedented prosperity at Lifeguard. But no concrete means or plan have been suggested for achieving this promised result. Indeed, the new management slate has demonstrated no real understanding of the immediate problems facing the business, or for that matter, the business itself. If they fail in their efforts, only the creditors lose. We do not believe that such unwilling gamblers should be required to take that risk.

Accordingly, the motion to confirm the appointment of new directors is

GRANTED; the application for approval of new management is DENIED. Since Shirley Onie is now effectively in control of the board of directors of the corporation, the Court views an equity security holders committee as unnecessary, and accordingly her motion to appoint such a committee is DENIED.

The Court further ORDERS as follows:

1. Fred Guttman, James Wendell, III, and Louis Epstein shall continue as President, Vice-President of Manufacturing, and Vice-President of Marketing and Sales at their present salary levels. They shall have sole and exclusive authority and responsibility for the day-to-day operation of Lifeguard Industries, Inc. Such authority and responsibility shall continue until the confirmation of a plan of reorganization or the expiration of four months, whichever occurs first. At such time the board of directors may install new officers of their choosing pursuant to the corporate code of regulations.

2. The newly-elected board of directors may propose a plan of reorganization on behalf of Lifeguard, such plan to be submitted within the next 60 days. The expense of preparing such plan shall be reimbursed by the corporation, subject to the approval of the Court. It may negotiate for the sale of the business, seek out sources of financing, engage in future planning for the business, and take any action pursuant to the terms of the Bankruptcy Code which it deems appropriate; the expenses for such activities and the retention of persons to engage in such activities shall be subject to the approval of the Court.

The members of the board of directors shall not direct, undertake, or in any way interfere with the day-to-day operations of Lifeguard until such time as a plan of reorganization is confirmed or the expiration of four months, whichever occurs first. Any inquiries, concerns, suggestions, or other communication of the members of the board of directors regarding the day-to-day operation of the corporation shall be set forth in writing and sent to Fred Guttman's attention. Fred Guttman shall respond in writing to such communications within 36 hours of their receipt. A copy of all such communications and replies thereto shall be served upon Mr. William H. Schorling, attorney for the creditors' committee.

3. Fred Guttman shall serve upon each member of the board of directors a copy of the debtor's regular monthly report filed with this Court. In addition, on October 1, November 1, and December 1, 1983, Fred Guttman shall serve the board of directors, Mr. William H. Schorling, and the Court with a written summary of significant sales, manufacturing and marketing activities of Lifeguard Industries which occurred during the previous month.

. . . .

It is so ordered.

§ 4.06 POWERS AND DUTIES OF TRUSTEES AND DEBTORS IN POSSESSION

[A] In General

[1] Duties of Trustees and Debtors in Possession

Several sections of the Code govern the duties of Chapter 11 trustees and debtors in possession. A good starting point is Code § 1106(a), which describes the duties of trustees. Section 1106(a) does not stand alone. In addition to listing seven specific duties, it provides that a Chapter 11 trustee is also required to perform the duties imposed on a Chapter 7 trustee by Code §§ 704(2), (5), (7), (8), and (9). Finally, Code § 1107(a) provides that subject to certain limitations, "a debtor in possession shall have all the rights . . . powers . . . and duties of a trustee . . . " Read those sections now. As you will see, the duties of trustees and debtors in possession are extensive. Among other things, they are required to:

1. *Account for all property received.* §§ 1106(a)(1) and 704(2). This provision makes a trustee or debtor in possession accountable for all property of the estate that they manage. This duty has been construed as encompassing a duty to appear on behalf of the estate to assert or defend claims by or against the estate. Resnick & Sommer, *7 Collier on Bankruptcy* ¶ 1106.03 (15th Ed. Revised 2009). Accordingly, it operates in conjunction with Code § 323, which provides that a trustee (or debtor in possession) is the "representative of the estate" having "the capacity to sue or be sued" on behalf of the estate.

2. *Examine proofs of claims and object to the allowance of improper claims.* §§ 1106(a)(1) and 704(5).

3. *Furnish such information concerning the estate and the estate's administration as is requested by a party in interest.* §§ 1106(a)(1) and 704(7).

4. *File periodic reports regarding the operation of the business to the court, the office of the United States Trustee, and tax authorities.* §§ 1106(a)(1) and 704(8). This section should be read in conjunction with Bankruptcy Rule 2015, which imposes additional reporting requirements.

5. *Make a final report and file a final account of the administration of the estate with the court and the United States Trustee.* §§ 1106(a)(1) and 704(9).

6. *File the list, schedules and statement required by Code § 521(1), if the debtor has not done so.* § 1106(a)(2). Section 521(1) provides that a debtor shall "file a list of creditors, and unless the court orders otherwise, a schedule of assets and liabilities, a schedule of current income and current expenditures, and a statement of the debtor's financial affairs." If the debtor fails to file these items, the trustee shall. Since § 1106(a)(2) requires the trustee to do what is normally required of the debtor, § 1106(a)(2) does not apply to debtors in possession. However, debtors in possession are not exempted from the underlying obligation to comply with the § 521 filing requirements.

7. *Investigate and report on the acts, conduct, assets, liabilities and financial condition of the debtor, the operation of the debtor's business and the desirability of the continuance of the business and any other matter relevant to the case or to the formulation of a plan.* The report, including any evidence of fraud, misconduct, or mismanagement and any cause of action available to the estate, is to be filed with the court and transmitted any creditors' committee, equity security holders' committee, or indenture trustee in the case, as well as to any other entity that the court designates. §§ 1106(a)(3), (4). A debtor in possession is exempt from investigating and reporting on its own conduct and affairs. § 1107(a). This does not mean that the conduct of management will not be scrutinized in any case in which the debtor remains in possession. An investigation may be undertaken by an examiner, § 1106(b), or by a creditors' or equity security holders' committee. § 1103(c)(2).

8. *File a plan of reorganization as soon as practicable, or recommend dismissal or conversion of the case.* § 1106(a)(5).

9. *Furnish tax information to taxing authorities for years in which the debtor filed no tax return.* § 1106(a)(6). The Supreme Court has held that a trustee must file federal tax returns for debtors and pay any taxes due, pursuant to 26 U.S.C. § 6012(b)(3), which provides that an assignee of "all or substantially all the property or business of a corporation" shall file tax returns for it. *Holywell Corp. v. Smith*, 503 U.S. 47 (1992). In addition, 26 U.S.C. § 6012(b)(4) provides that the returns of "an estate, a trust, or an estate of an individual under chapter 7 or 11" be made by the fiduciary thereof. Code § 346(c) requires a trustee to file state or local tax returns for corporate and partnership debtors.

Other sections of the Code impose additional duties on trustees and debtors in possession. For example:

1. A trustee or debtor in possession is required to meet and work with any creditors' or equity security holders' committee appointed under § 1102. Code § 1103(d).

2. A trustee or debtor in possession is required to collect and transmit withholding taxes. Code § 346(f).

3. A trustee is required to "make diligent inquiry" into facts that would require the court to deny an application for allowance of compensation to professional persons employed by the trustee, debtor, or a committee under § 327 or 1103. Code § 326(d).

4. Pursuant to Code § 343 and Bankruptcy Rule 4002, a debtor in possession is required to appear and submit to examination under oath at the meeting of creditors under Code § 341(a) of the Code. Creditors, an indenture trustee, or any trustee or examiner, or the United States Trustee may examine the debtor. Pursuant to Bankruptcy Rule 9001(5), a corporate debtor in possession will appear through its officers or directors; if the debtor is a partnership, it will appear through its general partners.

5. In addition to the duty to attend and submit to an examination when ordered to so do by the court, Bankruptcy Rule 4002 imposes additional duties on the debtor. They include the obligation to cooperate with the trustee, if one is appointed or elected, in the preparation of inventory, the examination of proofs of claim, and the administration of the estate.

[2] Rights and Powers of Trustees and Debtors in Possession

The rights and powers of a Chapter 11 trustee or debtor in possession are also expansive. As noted earlier, unless the court orders otherwise, a trustee is authorized to operate the debtor's business. Code § 1108. Since, pursuant to Code § 1107(a), a debtor in possession has virtually all the rights of a trustee, the debtor is also authorized to operate the business, subject to such limitations as the court prescribes.

Trustees and debtors in possession have other powers as well. For example, a trustee or debtor in possession may:

- Use, sell, or lease property of the estate. Code § 363.

- Borrow money an incur indebtedness. Code § 364.

- Reject, assume, or assign executory contracts. Code § 365.

- Retain attorneys, accountants, and other professional assistants. Code § 327(a), (b).

- Propose a reorganization plan. Code § 1121.

- Avoid prepetition transfers of the kind described in Code §§ 544, 547, and 548.

The operation of these sections and the interplay of trustees and debtors in possession with creditors, stockholders, and other parties in interest are examined in the cases and materials that follow.

[B] Authority to Operate and Manage the Business

COMMODITY FUTURES TRADING COMMISSION v. WEINTRAUB
Supreme Court of the United States
471 U.S. 343, 105 S. Ct. 1986, 85 L. Ed. 372 (1985)

[The Commodity Futures Trading Commission filed a complaint against Chicago Discount Commodity Brokers ("CDCB") alleging that it had violated the Commodity Exchange Act. On the same day that the complaint was filed, Frank McGhee, the sole director and officer of CDCB entered into a consent decree with the Commission. The consent decree provided for the appointment of a receiver. The receiver filed a voluntary bankruptcy petition on behalf of CDCB, seeking relief under Subchapter IV of Chapter 7 of the Bankruptcy Code, which provides for the liquidation of commodity brokers. (You may recall that commodity brokers and stockbrokers are not eligible for relief under Chapter 11. See Code § 109(d).) A trustee was appointed. The Commission served a subpoena on CDCB's former attorney, Gary Weintraub, seeking testimony about various matters, including misappropriation of customer funds by CDCB's officers and employees. Weintraub appeared, but refused to answer certain questions, asserting CDCB's attorney-client privilege. The Chapter 7 trustee agreed to waive the privilege on behalf of CDCB. McGhee argued that the trustee could not waive the privilege over his objection. Excerpts from the Court's opinion follow. Although the debtor was, as noted, liquidating under Chapter 7, the holding has important implications for Chapter 11 debtors as well.]

JUSTICE MARSHALL delivered the opinion of the Court.

The question here is whether the trustee of a corporation in bankruptcy has the power to waive the debtor corporation's attorney-client privilege with respect to communications that took place before the filing of the petition in bankruptcy.

. . . .

It is by now well established, and undisputed by the parties to this case, that the attorney-client privilege attaches to corporations as well as to individuals. *Upjohn Co. v. United States*, 449 U.S. 383 (1981).

. . . .

The administration of the attorney-client privilege in the case of corporations, however, presents special problems. As an inanimate entity, a corporation must act through agents. A corporation cannot speak directly to its lawyers. Similarly, it cannot directly waive the privilege when disclosure is in its best interest. Each of these actions must necessarily be undertaken by individuals empowered to act on behalf of the corporation.

. . . .

The parties in this case agree that, for solvent corporations, the power to waive the corporate attorney-client privilege rests with the corporation's management and is normally exercised by its officers and directors.

State corporation laws generally vest management authority in a corporation's board of directors. *See, e.g.,* Del. Code Ann., Tit. 8, § 141 (1983); N. Y. Bus. Corp. Law § 701 (McKinney Supp. 1983–1984); Model Bus. Corp. Act § 35 (1979). The authority of officers derives legally from that of the board of directors. *See generally* Eisenberg, Legal Models of Management Structure in the Modern Corporation: Officers, Directors, and Accountants, 63 Calif. L. Rev. 375 (1975). The distinctions between the powers of officers and directors are not relevant to this case.

The managers, of course, must exercise the privilege in a manner consistent with their fiduciary duty to act in the best interests of the corporation and not of themselves as individuals.

The parties also agree that when control of a corporation passes to new management, the authority to assert and waive the corporation's attorney-client privilege passes as well. New managers installed as a result of a takeover, merger, loss of confidence by shareholders, or simply normal succession, may waive the attorney-client privilege with respect to communications made by former officers and directors. Displaced managers may not assert the privilege over the wishes of current managers, even as to statements that the former might have made to counsel concerning matters within the scope of their corporate duties.

The dispute in this case centers on the control of the attorney-client privilege of a corporation in bankruptcy. The Government maintains that the power to exercise that privilege with respect to prebankruptcy communications passes to the bankruptcy trustee. In contrast, respondents maintain that this power remains with the debtor's directors.

As might be expected given the conflict among the Courts of Appeals, the Bankruptcy Code does not explicitly address the question before us.

. . . .

In light of the lack of direct guidance from the Code, we turn to consider the roles played by the various actors of a corporation in bankruptcy to determine which is most analogous to the role played by the management of a solvent corporation. *See Butner v. United States*, 440 U.S. 48, 55 (1979). Because the attorney-client privilege is controlled, outside of bankruptcy, by a corporation's management, the actor whose duties most closely resemble those of management should control the privilege in bankruptcy, unless such a result interferes with policies underlying the bankruptcy laws.

A.

The powers and duties of a bankruptcy trustee are extensive. Upon the commencement of a case in bankruptcy, all corporate property passes to an estate represented by the trustee. 11 U. S. C. §§ 323, 541. The trustee is "accountable for all property received," §§ 704(2), 1106(a)(1), and has the duty to maximize the value of the estate, *see* § 704(1). He is directed to investigate the debtor's financial affairs, §§ 704(4), 1106(a)(3), and is empowered to sue officers, directors, and other insiders to recover, on behalf of the estate, fraudulent or preferential transfers of the debtor's property, §§ 547(b)(4)(B), 548. Subject to court approval, he may use, sell, or lease property of the estate. § 363(b).

Moreover, in reorganization, the trustee has the power to "operate the debtor's business" unless the court orders otherwise. § 1108. Even in liquidation, the court "may authorize the trustee to operate the business" for a limited period of time. § 721. In the course of operating the debtor's business, the trustee "may enter into transactions, including the sale or lease of property of the estate" without court approval. § 363(c)(1).

As even this brief and incomplete list should indicate, the Bankruptcy Code gives the trustee wide-ranging management authority over the debtor. *See* 2 Collier on Bankruptcy para. 323.01 (15th ed. 1985). In contrast, the powers of the debtor's directors are severely limited. Their role is to turn over the corporation's property to the trustee and to provide certain information to the trustee and to the creditors. §§ 521, 343. Congress contemplated that when a trustee is appointed, he assumes control of the business, and the debtor's directors are "completely ousted." *See* H. R. Rep. No. 95-595, pp. 220–221 (1977).

While this reference is to the role of a trustee in reorganization, nothing in the Code or its legislative history suggests that the debtor's directors enjoy substantially greater powers in liquidation.

In light of the Code's allocation of responsibilities, it is clear that the trustee plays the role most closely analogous to that of a solvent corporation's management. Given that the debtor's directors retain virtually no management powers, they should not exercise the traditional management function of controlling the corporation's attorney-client privilege, *see supra*, at 348, unless a contrary arrangement would be inconsistent with policies of the bankruptcy laws.

B

We find no federal interests that would be impaired by the trustee's control of the corporation's attorney-client privilege with respect to prebankruptcy communications. On the other hand, the rule suggested by respondents — that the debtor's directors have this power — would frustrate an important goal of the bankruptcy laws. In seeking to maximize the value of the estate, the trustee must investigate the conduct of prior management to uncover and assert causes of action against the debtor's officers and directors. *See generally* 11 U. S. C. §§ 704(4), 547, 548. It would often be extremely difficult to conduct this inquiry if the former management were allowed to control the corporation's attorney-client privilege and therefore to control access to the corporation's legal files. To the extent that management had wrongfully diverted or appropriated corporate assets, it could use the privilege as a shield against the trustee's efforts to identify those assets. The Code's goal of uncovering insider fraud would be substantially defeated if the debtor's directors were to retain the one management power that might effectively thwart an investigation into their own conduct.

. . . .

V

Respondents do not seriously contest that the bankruptcy trustee exercises functions analogous to those exercised by management outside of bankruptcy, whereas the debtor's directors exercise virtually no management functions at all. Neither do respondents seriously dispute that vesting control over the attorney-client privilege in the trustee will facilitate the recovery of misappropriated corporate assets.

Respondents argue, however, that the trustee should not obtain control over the privilege because, unlike the management of a solvent corporation, the trustee's primary loyalty goes not to shareholders but to creditors, who elect him and who often will be the only beneficiaries of his efforts. *See* 11 U. S. C. §§ 702 (creditors elect trustee), 726(a) (shareholders are last to recover in bankruptcy). Thus, they contend, as a practical matter bankruptcy trustees represent only the creditors. We are unpersuaded by this argument. First, the fiduciary duty of the trustee runs to shareholders as well as to creditors. *See, e.g., In re Washington Group, Inc.*, 476 F.Supp. at 250; *In re Ducker*, 134 F. 43, 47 (CA6 1905). Second, respondents do not explain why, out of all management powers, control over the attorney-client privilege should remain with those elected by the corporation's shareholders. Perhaps most importantly, respondents' position ignores the fact that bankruptcy causes fundamental changes in the nature of corporate relationships. One of the painful facts of bankruptcy is that the interests of shareholders become subordinated to the interests of creditors. In cases in which it is clear that the estate is not large enough to cover any shareholder claims, the trustee's exercise of the corporation's attorney-client privilege will benefit only creditors, but there is nothing anomalous in this result; rather, it is in keeping with the hierarchy of interests created by the bankruptcy laws. *See generally* 11 U. S. C. § 726(a).

Respondents also ignore that if a debtor remains in possession — that is, if a trustee is not appointed — the debtor's directors bear essentially the same fiduciary obligation to creditors and shareholders as would the trustee for a debtor out of possession. *Wolf v. Weinstein*, 372 U.S. 633, 649–652 (1963). Indeed, the willingness of courts to leave debtors in possession "is premised upon an assurance that the officers and managing employees can be depended upon to carry out the fiduciary responsibilities of a trustee." *Id.*, at 651. Surely, then, the management of a debtor-in-possession would have to exercise control of the corporation's attorney-client privilege consistently with this obligation to treat all parties, not merely the shareholders, fairly. By the same token, when a trustee is appointed, the privilege must be exercised in accordance with the trustee's fiduciary duty to all interested parties.

To accept respondents' position would lead to one of two outcomes: (1) a rule under which the management of a debtor-in-possession exercises control of the attorney-client privilege for the benefit only of shareholders but exercises all of its other functions for the benefit of both shareholders and creditors, or (2) a rule under which the attorney-client privilege is exercised for the benefit of both creditors and shareholders when the debtor remains in possession, but is exercised for the benefit only of shareholders when a trustee is appointed. We find nothing in the bankruptcy laws that would suggest, much less compel, either of these implausible results.

VI

Respondents' other arguments are similarly unpersuasive. First, respondents maintain that the result we reach today would also apply to individuals in bankruptcy, a result that respondents find "unpalatable." Brief for Respondents 27. But our holding today has no bearing on the problem of individual bankruptcy, which we have no reason to address in this case. As we have stated, a corporation, as an inanimate entity, must act through agents. *See supra*, at 348. When the corporation is solvent, the agent that controls the corporate attorney-client privilege is the corporation's management. Under our holding today, this power passes to the trustee because the trustee's functions are more closely analogous to those of management outside of bankruptcy than are the functions of the debtor's directors. An individual, in contrast, can act for himself; there is no "management" that controls a solvent individual's attorney-client privilege. If control over that privilege passes to a trustee, it must be under some theory different from the one that we embrace in this case.

Second, respondents argue that giving the trustee control over the attorney-client privilege will have an undesirable chilling effect on attorney-client communications. According to respondents, corporate managers will be wary of speaking freely with corporate counsel if their communications might subsequently be disclosed due to bankruptcy. But the chilling effect is no greater here than in the case of a solvent corporation, where individual officers and directors always run the risk that successor management might waive the corporation's attorney-client privilege with respect to prior management's communications with counsel. Respondents also maintain that the result we reach discriminates against insolvent corporations. According to respondents, to prevent the debtor's directors from controlling the privilege amounts to "economic discrimination" given that directors, as representatives of the shareholders, control the privilege for solvent corporations. Respondents' argument misses the point that, by definition, corporations in bankruptcy are treated differently from solvent corporations. "Insolvency is a most important and material fact, not only with individuals but with corporations, and with the latter as with the former the mere fact of its existence may change radically and materially its rights and obligations." *McDonald v. Williams*, 174 U.S. 397, 404 (1899). Respondents do not explain why we should be particularly concerned about differential treatment in this context.

. . . .

VII

For the foregoing reasons, we hold that the trustee of a corporation in bankruptcy has the power to waive the corporation's attorney-client privilege with respect to prebankruptcy communications.

. . . .

It is so ordered.

JUSTICE POWELL took no part in the consideration or decision of this case.

[C]   Limitations on the Power to Manage the Business

The Supreme Court's opinion in *CFTC v. Weintraub* is notable not only for what it holds about the power to waive the attorney-client privilege but also for what it says more generally about who manages a corporation when it is in bankruptcy. As you know from your study of corporate law, a corporation is managed by its board of directors, who are elected by the corporation's owners, the stockholders. Although these directors are the ultimate managers of a corporation, the corporation's officers, who serve at the pleasure of the board, normally manage and operate the business on a day-to-day basis. As Justice Marshall pointed out, the appointment of a Chapter 11 trustee short-circuits the corporate chain of command. Management authority is transferred to the trustee, who, Justice Marshall observed, "plays the role most closely analogous to that of a solvent corporation's management." In contrast, when a debtor remains in possession, the debtor's directors retain their managerial role. Does management operate in the Chapter 11 environment with the same freedom and discretion that it does on the outside? That is the topic that we turn to here.

[1]   Ordinary Course of Business Transactions

IN RE CURLEW VALLEY ASSOCIATES
United States Bankruptcy Court, District of Utah
5 C.B.C.2d 255, 14 B.R. 506, 8 B.C.D. 495 (1981)

RALPH R. MABEY, BANKRUPTCY JUDGE.

MEMORANDUM DECISION ON JUDICIAL SUPERINTENDENCE,
TERMINATION, AND REPLACEMENT OF A TRUSTEE UNDER
CHAPTER 11

INTRODUCTION

This case raises the issues whether a mistake in business judgment by a trustee appointed under Section 1104(a)(1) justifies either judicial interference with his conduct under Section 1108 or his termination and replacement under Section 1105.

Debtor, an agribusiness, owns a 24,000 acre farm in northern Utah and southern Idaho. Its principal crops are alfalfa hay, alfalfa seed, barley, and wheat. It filed a petition under Chapter 11 in May, 1980, and worked the farm as a debtor in possession until a trustee was appointed in December, 1980. The case was dismissed pursuant to Section 1112(b) on April 3, 1981. The dismissal, however, was conditioned upon failure to obtain confirmation of a plan before July 4. This deadline was later extended to August 1.

The trustee discounted the prospects for rehabilitation, and commenced preparations for liquidation which would occur through either dismissal or implementation of a creditors' plan which had been recently filed. His program, in part, involved substitution of hay baling for hay cubing. This, in his view, among other things, allowed greater predictability of expenses, swifter disposition of hay, and more flexibility, since conversion to baling still permits cubing, but the reverse is not true.

. . . .

Debtor gainsayed the views of the trustee and requested an injunction against his program. Baling, it argues, is agronomically unsound, will result in a $500,000 loss of crop proceeds, and will defeat its opportunity to confirm a plan (which is predicated on cubing).

At a hearing held . . . on the eve of the hay harvest, the trustee asked for denial of the injunction on the ground that the decision to bale was made in good faith and for sound reasons and therefore could not be countermanded by the court. Debtor, on the other hand, because it feared substantial and irreversible economic consequences, asked the court to look behind the decision, to examine the expertise and data upon which it rested, and to weigh the best interests of the estate.

The position of debtor was underlined by this colloquy between counsel and court:

> Mr. Leta: If the evidence indicates that the decision is going to have substantial economic consequences, I don't believe the court can sit back and allow the trustee to make that mistake. How could the court justify the losses that would result from that if in fact the weight of the evidence indicates that it is going to cost more money and have greater economic consequences? It would in effect be condoning a bad decision. It would condone loss.

> The Court: [How can the court properly find that the trustee's expertise — a Ph.D. in agricultural economy — is inadequate when my expertise-an undergraduate degree in English literature-is non-existent?] Is there any deference to the trustee's expertise which the court is obligated to give his decision, or [should the court substitute itself for the trustee and itself weigh the agricultural and economic evidence presented?]

> Mr. Leta: In most judicial [forums], the trier of facts does not have the same expertise as the witnesses. I think in every judicial setting the court must look at the qualifications of the witnesses, but must look at the foundation for the testimony and must make a decision about what weight to give each witness based on that foundation. It would be no different if we were trying an antitrust lawsuit where there were complicated questions of marketing involved in that suit. That would perhaps be beyond the normal day-to-day range of experience, mine, the court's, but that's what the evidence is for, to test that evidence. Test that evidence and decide which evidence is most credible. The trustee may have his own evidence, his own basis. The court can look at that. The court can look at other evidence and decide for itself what would be in the best interest of creditors in this case. Therefore, I don't believe the debtor ought to be [obstructed or] restrained by some more heavier burden than the normal burden of [cause]. The trustee can be removed for cause under the statute. A trustee can be appointed for cause. A decision of the trustee in my view can be reversed for cause. That cause could include ineconomy or could include lack of information, include just a bad calculation. Perhaps the trustee made a mathematical error here, but whatever it is, if there is cause to reverse such a decision, then I think that is the standard that the court ought to apply. We believe in this case there is substantial cause. We believe the evidence will show that this estate will primarily suffer — first of all, the evidence will show that the decision to bale in the first instance has probably already cost the estate over $100,000. That is behind us now. We can't do anything about that decision. That was made by the trustee. The decision to bale the rest of the ranch will result in probably within our ability to reasonably calculate, losses . . . in excess of $500,000. Under the circumstances, it is proper for the court to hear the evidence and decide and obviously decide

for itself whether there is cause to reverse the trustee. (July 20 transcript of hearing, pages 15–19.)

The court, given the emergency status of the case, ruled from the bench. It concurred with the trustee and refused to hear the debtor's evidence. The debtor immediately moved to terminate the trustee and replace him with the debtor in possession. A hearing on this matter was scheduled for the next day. Renewed argument was held on the scope of the trustee's discretion and on his termination and replacement. The court ruled by telephone in the evening, reaffirming its refusal to interfere with the trustee and denying the motion to terminate and replace him. This memorandum decision elaborates the basis for these rulings.

JUDICIAL SUPERINTENDENCE OF THE TRUSTEE

The governing statute is Section 1108 which provides: "Unless the court orders otherwise, the trustee may operate the debtor's business." Debtor reads Section 1108 to mean that the court may limit, as well as bar, the trustee's operation of the estate. This reading, however, ignores the reason for its enactment, and its construction in light of other provisions and policies of the Bankruptcy Code.

The thrust of Section 1108 is that the trustee may operate the debtor's business. In other words, he may, but need not, manage the estate as a going concern, rather than in liquidation. Section 1108 thus reflects the policy of Chapter 11 to preserve, where possible, the going concern value of enterprises while recognizing that, in some instances, there will be no disparity between going concern and liquidation value, or that going concern may be less than liquidation value. *See, e.g.*, 5 Collier on Bankruptcy para. 1108.03 (15th ed. 1980). In these cases, the trustee should have far-reaching discretion to operate, intermit, or debar the debtor's business.

Since, however, operation of the debtor's business is the norm, *see, e.g.*, H.R. Rep. No. 95-595, 95th Cong., 1st Sess. 404 (1977), U.S. Code Cong. & Admin. News 1978, p. 5787, the "orders otherwise" language of Section 1108, at most, allows the court to direct the trustee, where he may not elect, to discontinue an enterprise. Hence, the "orders otherwise" language dovetails with Sections 305(a) and 1112(b) which authorize the suspension, dismissal, or conversion of a case. It does not express or imply a power in the court to condition the trustee's management of the estate.

This reasoning is consistent with the analysis in Collier, relied upon by debtor, which states: "Finally, section 1108 does not alter the court's authority to limit the discretion of the trustee with respect to operation of the debtor's business. Section 1108 does not limit the court to a black or white determination at the beginning of the case that the trustee shall, or in the alternative shall not, operate the debtor's business. On the contrary, the court can appropriately direct the trustee to cease operations of a certain designated portion of the debtor's business while permitting the trustee to continue operating the balance of such business." 5 Collier on Bankruptcy, *supra* para. 1108.03 at 1108-5. Collier speaks in terms of the cessation, in whole or part, of the business, not its revival or a change in operations.

The debtor, in contrast, reads Section 1108 as restricting the trustee who, from its standpoint, must operate the debtor's business "as he found it." This argument, however, overlooks the permissive "may:" the trustee may, but need not, run the business; if he has discretion to cease operations as a whole, he may modify them in part. . . . Moreover, a rule requiring the trustee to mimic the debtor may vitiate the basis for appointment of a trustee which in this case involved fraud and mismanagement, and the need for their correction. Surely debtor cannot mean that the trustee must seek court approval under Section 1108 to rectify abuses which were the reason for his appointment in the first instance.

Likewise, debtor's argument that baling complicates its effort to obtain confirmation of a plan assumes that the court must defer to debtors as proponents of plans. Appointment of a trustee, however, not only ousts the debtor as manager of the estate, but also, under Section 1121(c)(1), cuts off the period within which it has an exclusive right to file a plan. Indeed, creditors in this case have filed a plan which provides for liquidation of the estate. It is impractical for the trustee to coordinate his management of the estate with all plans; it is unfair for him to favor one plan at the expense of another. He must pursue an independent course. Debtor's assumption that it is entitled to preferment is therefore unwarranted.

This interpretation of Section 1108 is consistent with and complements other provisions in the Code. The relationship of Section 1108 with Sections 305(a) and 1112(b) has already been mentioned. A further example is Section 1107(a) which confers the powers of a trustee on a debtor in possession "subject to . . . such limitations or conditions as the court prescribes." Section 1107(a) thus permits judicial oversight where the debtor in possession acts as trustee. This permission does not appear in Section 1108. Such particularized draftsmanship suggests a desire to monitor debtors in possession but to allow fuller rein for trustees in the management of the estate.

The history of Section 1108 may further elucidate this point. Section 189 of the Act, former 11 U.S.C. Section 589, the predecessor to Section 1108, permitted a trustee or debtor in possession "upon authorization by the judge," to operate the business "during such period, limited or indefinite, as the judge may from time to time fix." Section 188 of the Act, former 11 U.S.C. Section 588, the predecessor to Section 1107(a), gave a debtor in possession the rights of a trustee "subject, however, at all times to the control of the judge and to such limitations, restrictions, terms, and conditions as the judge may from time to time prescribe." Despite the contrasting language of these sections, no distinction was drawn between the control exercised over trustees and debtors in possession. Collier, for example, notes that "the court may impose whatever conditions it deems necessary in the best interest of the estate," 6 Collier on Bankruptcy para. 8.12 at 1422 (14th ed. 1978) and elsewhere opines that "certainly the trustee was subject at all times to the judge's command." 13A Collier on Bankruptcy para. 10-207.04 at 10-207-3 (14th ed. 1977). These observations, however, may have been made in light of Rule 10-207, Fed. R. Bankr. P., which modified Section 189 by providing: "The court may authorize the trustee, receiver, or debtor in possession to conduct the business and manage the property of the debtor for such time and on such conditions as may be in the best interests of the estate." The Advisory Committee's Note perceived this change as a liberalization of the court's power vis a vis the trustee: "permitting the imposition of conditions is for the protection of public investors and creditors and goes beyond Section 189 of the Act in affording greater protection."

The Bankruptcy Commission proposal substituted an "administrator" for the court but otherwise followed Rule 10-207. Parties "aggrieved" by a decision to discontinue operations were permitted to commence a civil proceeding to obtain relief. Report of the Commission on the Bankruptcy Laws of the United States, H.R. Doc. No. 93-137, pt. II, Section 7-104 (1973). This meant that "the administrator . . . has the initial authority to determine whether or not the business should be operated. In making this decision, he should be influenced in large part by the opinion of the creditor's committee. If the administrator's decision with respect to the operation of the business is challenged by the debtor or any other interested party, resort may be had to the court and a prompt determination of that issue is contemplated." Trost, "Corporate Reorganizations Under Chapter VII of the 'Bankruptcy Act of 1973': Another View," 48 Am.Bank.L.J. 111, 128 (1974). This view was criticized by some who felt that "such a tremendous concentration of discretion in the Administrator conceivably may result in a liquidation upon the trustee's appointment as a consequence of the Administrator's refusal to permit the trustee or debtor to operate." Weintraub and Levin, "Chapter VII (Reorganizations) As Proposed By The Bankruptcy Commission: The Widening Gap Between Theory And Reality," 47 Am.Bank.L.J. 323, 326 (1973). The rejoinder, of course, was that "today the same broad discretion with respect to permitting the business to operate is vested in the judicial officer. Does the present concentration of discretion in the judicial officer lead any more to liquidation than tomorrow's concentration of discretion in the administrative officer? Is a judicial officer any more qualified to decide whether to close a business than an administrative officer?" Trost, "Corporate Reorganizations Under Chapter VII of the 'Bankruptcy Act of 1973': Another View," 48 Am.Bank.L.J. 111, 129 (1974). And in any event, closure of the business was ultimately left to the court. *Id.* at 114.

Others, sidestepping the administrator versus court controversy, nevertheless argued for a change of emphasis "in the area of closing and operating business." The Commission has the administrator deciding whether to close a business, and if anyone opposes that decision, he must go to court to get authority to operate the business. The National Bankruptcy Conference would reverse the procedure so that if the administrator wants to close a business, he had to go to court to get permission to do so. "Closing a business is almost a dispute by definition. Somebody is going to oppose that usually, so we feel that the business operation should not be discontinued without a court order in advance. Otherwise, it may be too late to reverse the decision as a practical matter." Testimony of George M. Treister, Vice-Chairman of the National Bankruptcy Conference, Hearings Before the Subcomm. on Civil and Constitutional Rights of the House Comm. on the Judiciary, 94th Cong., 1st Sess., Ser. 27, pt. 1, at 584 (1975).

Section 1108 emerged as a compromise of these disparate views, and altered prior law in at least three respects. First, instead of allowing the court to determine, in the first instance, whether a business may or may not operate, Section 1108 establishes a presumption of operation. Second, this presumption is rebuttable, and the enterprise may be discontinued, not necessarily by the court, but by the trustee. Third, Sections 1108 and 1107(a) bifurcate treatment of trustees and debtors in possession, remaining silent concerning judicial authority over the former, but allowing supervision over the latter. The implications are two-fold: reduced involvement by the court in the administration of estates, and a distinction between judicial surveillance of trustees and debtors in possession. *See, e.g.*, 5 Collier on Bankruptcy ¶ 1108.03 at 1108-4–1108-5 (15th ed. 1980).

Similar inferences may be drawn from 28 U.S.C. Section 959(a), Section 1104(c) and Section 1105 which allow suits against trustees, substitution of one trustee for another, and replacement of a trustee with the debtor in possession. Congress allowed and delimited these remedies for errant trustees, and thus sought to preclude the implication of others. In specific instances such as Section 1107(a), where it was willing to tolerate judicial surveillance, it knew how to say so.

Aside from these statutory bases, there are policy reasons for discouraging supervision of the trustee. First, as the court has noted elsewhere, reorganization involves the "turbulent rivalry" of many interests. *In re Alyucan Interstate Corp.*, 12 B.R. 803, 806 7 B.C.D. 1123, 1124 (D. Utah 1981). The trustee's business decisions will affect these interests. If parties, in their own right, or as putative representatives of the estate, question these decisions, the court may be deluged with motions. This would impede the expeditious administration of estates.

Second, "the reorganization process is not basically an adversary process. The reorganization process is one of controlled negotiation, much like labor negotiations are conducted between labor and management." Trost, "Corporate Reorganizations Under Chapter VII of the 'Bankruptcy Act of 1973': Another View," 48 Am.Bank.L.J. 111, 120 (1974). These negotiations are conducted by trustees, creditor committees, debtors, and their professional representatives. These parties are equipped, through experience, expertise, and powers under the Code to shepherd the estate toward reorganization. Judicial involvement blunts the give and take which is necessary to this process and ultimately derails the objective of private control in Chapter 11.

Third, disagreements over business policy are not amenable to judicial resolution. The courtroom is not a boardroom. The judge is not a business consultant. While a court may pass upon the legal effect of a business decision, (for example, whether it violates the antitrust laws), this involves a process and the application of criteria fundamentally different from those which produce the decision in the first instance. In short, the decision calls for business not legal judgment.

Fourth, and most important, a major goal of the bankruptcy reform movement was to divorce the court from ministerial duties and to confine it to adjudicative functions.

The separation of judicial and administrative functions was anticipated by commentators, *see, e.g.*, Gendel, "Summary Jurisdiction in Bankruptcy Related to Possible Referee Disqualification," 51 Cal. L. Rev. 755 (1963), and Triester, "Summary Judgment: Bankruptcy Jurisdiction: Is It Too Summary?" 39 So. Cal. L. Rev. 78 (1966), and was advocated by the Commission and Congress. *See* Report of the Commission on the Bankruptcy Laws of the United States, H.R. Doc. No. 93-137, pt. I, at 92–93, 248–249 (1973) ("Neither referees nor district judges can adequately police reorganizations. To the extent they attempt to do so, they create an appearance of bias . . . . The assurance of impartiality of the judge is also enhanced by having the administrator decide whether the business should be operated and the extent of any operation by the debtor"). H.R. Rep. No. 95-595, 95th Cong., 1st Sess. 89–91, 95–99, 107–109 (1977) (United States Trustee program and notice and hearing requirement will eliminate ministerial chores, the "bankruptcy ring," and "cronyism"). The idea was discussed and applauded in a score of articles. *See, e.g.*, Coogan, Broude, and Glatt, "Comments on Some Reorganization Provisions of the Pending Bankruptcy Bill," 30 Bus. Law. 398, 401 (1975); Hughes, "'Wavering Loss' Operating a Business During Reorganization Under Chapter 11 of the New Bankruptcy Code," 54 Am.Bank.L.J. 45, 59–61 (1980); King, "Chapter 11 of the 1978 Bankruptcy Code," 53 Am.Bank.L.J. 107, 112 (1979); Klee, "The New Bankruptcy Act," 64 A.B.A.J. 1865, 1967 (1978); Trost, "Business Reorganizations Under Chapter 11 of the New Bankruptcy Code," 34 Bus. Law. 1309, 1315–1316 (1979); Trost, "Corporate Reorganizations Under Chapter VII of the 'Bankruptcy Act of 1973': Another View," 48 Am.Bank.L.J. 111, 116–121 (1974); Trost and King, "Congress and Bankruptcy Reform Circa 1977," 33 Bus. Law. 489, 495–496, 531–532 (1978). There, of course, may be disagreement over what is a "judicial" and what is an "administrative" function. *See, e.g.*, Testimony of George M. Treister, Vice-Chairman of the National Bankruptcy Conference, Hearings Before the Subcomm. on Civil and Constitutional Rights of the House Comm. on the Judiciary, 94th Cong., 1st Sess., Ser. 27, pt. 1, at 583–598 (1975). Triester, for example, discounts the utility of this distinction, and instead draws the line between disputes and uncontested matters. In this regard, he notes that closure of a business "is almost a dispute by definition." *Id.* at 594.

Sound reasons underlie this goal. The quintessential predicate for administering justice is a neutral arbiter. A court which appoints a trustee and confers with him regularly and *ex parte* for the purpose of managing a business may find it difficult to rule impartially if those decisions in which it has participated are challenged. Impartiality is not improved by inviting input from others and transferring the decision making from a private to a public forum. The court is nevertheless cast as a "super-trustee" and overseer of the estate, asked now to determine company policy and later to reconcile the effects of that policy on competing interests. These problems were addressed by Congress:

> A bankruptcy judge may be required to grant a debtor in possession in a reorganization case authority to enter into a contract subject to certain terms and conditions. The judge may actually participate, through the debtor in possession, in negotiating the contract. He may work with the debtor in possession and a union to avert a strike that would ruin the business. He may advise the debtor in possession or the trustee in the management of the business, and issue frequent instructions for its conduct. Later in the case, that same judge may be faced with the responsibility for resolving a dispute that arises over the terms of the contract that he participated in negotiating or over the nature of the union's obligation to the debtor. An individual that is in effect a "party" to a contract simply cannot render a fair or impartial decision concerning its interpretation.

Here, for example, if the court determined that, as a matter of business policy, cubing was preferred, how could it rule if the lessor of the cubing equipment requested relief under either Section 362(d) or Section 365(b)(2)? Or how could it rule if debtor sought damages in a suit against the trustee?

. . . .

These factors add an additional dimension to the position of the bankruptcy judge. As the administrator of bankruptcy cases, and the individual responsible for the supervision of the trustee or debtor in possession, it is an easy matter for a bankruptcy judge to feel personally responsible for the success or failure of a case. Bankruptcy judges frequently view a case as "my case." The institutional bias thus generated magnifies the likelihood of unfair decisions in the bankruptcy court, and has caused at least one occasional bankruptcy practitioner to suggest that "the bankruptcy court is the only court I appear in which the judge is an interested party."

These problems are particularly acute in business rehabilitation cases. In Chapter X corporate reorganization cases, the judge must appoint the trustee, and then work with the trustee in the conduct of the business. The appearance of unfairness generated when the judge's appointee appears before the judge for a hearing is magnified because the judge must work so closely with the trustee in the management of the business undergoing reorganization. Though there is no trustee in a Chapter XI or Chapter XII arrangement case, the judge works closely with the debtor in possession in the management of the business. It is in these cases in which the judge's personal responsibility for the success or failure of a case is intense, with the consequent appearance of bias in the judge's consideration of disputes that arise in the case. H.R. Rep. No. 95-595, 95th Cong., 1st Sess. 90–91 (1977), U.S. Code Cong. & Admin. News 1978, pp. 6051, 6052.

Indeed, merger of the judicial and administrative roles may result in identification of the court with the estate, and the evils which flow in the wake of this alliance. As noted in the Commission Report:

> This problem is aggravated in metropolitan centers where there is sufficient concentration of bankruptcy business for a specialized bankruptcy bar to develop. Members of the specialized bar are a valuable source of knowledgeable and capable trustees on whom the [court] is able to draw when creditors do not elect a trustee. The involvement of the [court] in the administration of estates entails numerous conferences and communications that are informal and ex parte. The responsibility resting on a conscientious [court] under the present Act is thus conducive to the development of what appears to attorneys who are not included among the specialists, to their clients, and to the public generally, as an unseemly and continuing relationship between the referee and the members of the specialist bar. He is thus vulnerable to being linked by imputation to the so-called "bankruptcy ring" which is the opprobrious label frequently given to the specialized bankruptcy bar in a community. Report of the Commission on the Bankruptcy Laws of the United States, H.R. Doc. No. 93-127, pt. I, 93 (1973).

Thus, in Justice Douglas's words, bankruptcy judges may "flourish under Parkinson's Laws" and their power may increase "like that of a prince in a medieval kingdom." *Bankruptcy Rules and Official Bankruptcy Forms*, 411 U.S. 991, 993, 93

S. Ct. 3081, 3082, 37 L. Ed. 2d xxxi (1974). Those who abide their governance are rewarded with the largesse and patronage of the fiefdom. Those who do not are treated as serfs, saboteurs, and expatriates.

Compromises in the Reform Act prevent complete separation of administration and adjudication. But inroads were made. There should be no regression. Unless the Code directs otherwise, a wall of separation should be erected between the court and the estate.

As the court noted in its ruling from the bench: "The code provisions, in requiring court approval for certain actions of the trustee, carry with them the exclusion of the court's involvement in other unspecified actions of the trustee, unless the trustee has exceeded his statutory authority." (July 20 transcript, page 25.)

Whenever the court must define its role vis a vis the estate, it should draw the line in favor of judicial independence.

Commentators have echoed these views. Professor Trost, for example, has noted that, on motion, the court may invoke Section 1108 with Section 1112(b) to order a cessation of business but that otherwise it should avoid entanglement in the affairs of the estate:

> It is unclear from the statute [Section 1108] whether the court, on its own initiative, may terminate the business operation. Removing the bankruptcy court from its sometimes perceived present duty to monitor the operation and administration of business reorganization cases is an admirable goal, is essential to the separation of judicial and administrative functions and, hopefully, will be observed in spirit by the new and old members of the bankruptcy court alike. Until an appropriate pleading is filed the court's only function with respect to the operation of the business should be to change the composition of the creditors' committee if it is not representative. The bankruptcy judge should not worry about "how's the business doing?" The judge's job is to decide disputes. Although this may mean that assets will be dissipated in some operating cases because of the lack of interest or experience of the administrative personnel, the social costs of preventing such occurrences — the ex parte involvement of the bankruptcy judge in the administrative details of the case — is simply too great. If a party in interest requests the termination of the business the judge is to decide if the business should be terminated or converted to liquidation or the case dismissed.

Trost, "Business Reorganizations Under Chapter 11 of the New Bankruptcy Code," 34 Bus. Law. 1309, 1315–1316 (1979). *See also*, P. Murphy, Creditors' Rights in Bankruptcy, Section 15.06 at 15-8 (1980).

In short, the court will not entertain objections to a trustee's conduct of the estate where that conduct involves a business judgment made in good faith, upon a reasonable basis and within the scope of his authority under the Code.

In other words, so long as the trustee can articulate reasons for his conduct (as distinct from a decision made arbitrarily or capriciously), the court will not inquire into the basis for those reasons.

An analogy may be drawn to suits by shareholders against directors who, like trustees, in the exercise of business judgment, make decisions of policy for corporations: "Corporate management is vested in the board of directors. If in the course of management, directors arrive at a decision, within the corporation's powers (intra vires) and their authority, for which there is a reasonable basis, and they act in good faith, as the result of their independent discretion and judgment, and uninfluenced by any consideration other than what they honestly believe to be the best interests of the corporation, a court will not interfere with internal management and substitute its judgment for that of the directors to enjoin or set aside the transaction or to surcharge the directors for any resulting loss." H. Henn, Law of Corporations 482 (2d ed. 1970).

This rule is consistent with the "limited purpose" of Section 1108, *see* 5 Collier on Bankruptcy, *supra*, ¶ 1108.03 at 1108-9, and harmonizes that statute with other provisions in the law, such as Sections 305(a), 1104(c), 1105, 1107(a), 1112(b), and 28 U.S.C. Section 959(a). It reduces administrative burdens and furthers the goal of an independent court of bankruptcy. For these reasons, the motion under Section 1108 is denied.

TERMINATION AND REPLACEMENT OF THE TRUSTEE

Section 1105 provides: "At any time before confirmation of a plan, on request of a party in interest, and after notice and a hearing, the court may terminate the trustee's appointment and restore the debtor to possession and management of the property of the estate, and operation of the debtor's business."

Section 1105 "does not provide a fixed standard pursuant to which the court is to determine whether the trustee's appointment should be terminated." 5 Collier on Bankruptcy, *supra para.* 1105.01 at 1105-1. The legislative history notes that "this section would permit the court to reverse its decision to order the appointment of a trustee in light of new evidence." H.R. Rep. No. 95-595, 95th Cong., 1st Sess. 403 (1977), U.S. Code Cong. & Admin. News 1978, p. 6359. "Presumably," according to Collier, "the draftsmen intended that the trustee's appointment be rescinded if the court determines that, based upon facts which were not available at the time of the original hearing under Section 1104(a), the original order of appointment of a trustee was improvidently granted." 5 Collier on Bankruptcy, *supra* ¶ 1105.01 at 1105-1–1105-2.

Collier, however, expands upon this standard. The Code was designed to supply "maximum flexibility with respect to the management of the debtor's affairs during the pendency of the case." It follows that Section 1105 "permits the court to terminate the appointment of a trustee where conditions have changed subsequent to the court's order of appointment and the continued service by a trustee is not in the interests of creditors, equity security holders, and other interests of the estate." *Id.*

This "change in circumstance" test was employed by the court in *In re Eastern Consolidated Utilities, Inc.*, 1 C.B.C.2d 937, 3 B.R. 591 (Bankr. E.D. Pa. 1980). There a trustee was appointed because the debtor made post-petition preferential payments. Debtor, which had not opposed appointment of a trustee, later moved to terminate and replace him with the debtor in possession under Section 1105. Neither creditor who had requested appointment of a trustee resisted this motion. The court found that the post-petition payments were the result of "ill-advised legal counsel," and concluded that "the hiring of new counsel, combined with the stated intention of the principals of the debtor to comply with the requirements of the bankruptcy code, render the continued services of a trustee unnecessary." *Id.* at 593, 1 C.B.C.2d at 939. In short, "the circumstances which gave rise to the order appointing a trustee no longer exist." *Id.*

Assuming that either the "improvidence" or the "change in circumstances" rationale is correct, neither can be applied in this case. Debtor does not argue that appointment of the trustee was improvident in light of evidence which was earlier unavailable. Nor does it point to a change in those circumstances which called for his appointment, viz. fraud and mismanagement.

Moreover, debtor's position confuses the role of Sections 1104(a), 1104(c), and 1105. Section 1104(c) provides for removal of a trustee for cause (assuming an error in business judgment constitutes cause), in which case he is replaced by another trustee not the debtor. Thus, the focus of Section 1104(c), in part, is trustee misconduct. If Section 1105 is read to cover the same ground, it not only renders Section 1104(c) superfluous but also contravenes the legislative intent that, in such instances, the trustee is to be replaced with a "disinterested person." Likewise, the purpose for appointing a trustee under Section 1104(a) could be defeated, if a debtor may be put back in place on grounds unrelated to the reasons for his removal.

Indeed, the legislative history to Section 1104(a)(1) notes that "if the current management of the debtor gambled away rental income before the filing of the petition, a trustee should be appointed after the petition, whether or not post-petition mismanagement can be shown." 124 Cong. Rec. H11, 102 (daily ed. September 28, 1978). If pre-petition repentance of the debtor in possession does not obviate the need for a trustee, will a post-appointment change of heart make any greater difference?

For these reasons, the motion under Section 1105 is also denied.

IN RE UNR INDUSTRIES, INC.
United States Bankruptcy Court, Northern District of Illinois
30 B.R. 609 (1982)

Edward B. Toles, Bankruptcy Judge

. . . .

1. On July 29, 1982, the Debtors filed voluntary petitions for reorganization under Chapter 11 of the Bankruptcy Code, and on July 29, 1982, the Court entered an Order pursuant to Section 1108 of the Bankruptcy Code which continued the debtor in possession and recognized DAVID S. LEAVITT, Chairman of UNR Industries, Inc., as the designated party to act on behalf of the Debtors. Said Order provides in relevant part as follows:

3. In connection with the operation of the businesses of the Debtors, they shall have full power and authority:

(a) To employ, discharge and fix the compensation, salaries and wages for all managers, officers, directors, agents, employees and servants of the Debtors, as they may deem necessary and advisable for the proper operation of the Debtors' business and the management, preservation and protection of its property;

(b) To pay and satisfy out of any funds now or hereafter coming into the Debtors' possession all claims for wages, salaries and compensation of all managers, agents, employees and servants for services heretofore rendered wherein the same would be entitled to priority under the provisions of the Bankruptcy Code;

(c) To buy and sell merchandise, supplies and other property necessary and essential for the Debtors' operations, and to render services for cash or on credit;

(d) To purchase or otherwise acquire for cash or on credit such materials, equipment, machinery, supplies, services or other property as it may deem necessary and advisable in connection with the operation of the business and the management and preservation of the Debtors' property, and to pay for any such purchases made on credit when due;

(e) To enter into any contracts incidental to the normal and usual operation of the Debtors' businesses and the management and preservation of their property;

(f) To keep the property of the Debtors' estates insured in such manner and to such extent as it may deem necessary and advisable, and to pay such premiums as may be or become due thereon;

(g) To collect and receive all rents, issues, income and profits, and all outstanding accounts, things in action and credits due or to become due to the within estates, and to hold and retain all monies thus received to the end that the same may be applied under this or different or further orders of this Court;

(h) To pay and discharge out of any funds now or hereafter coming into the hands of the Debtors all taxes and similar charges lawfully incurred in the operation of said businesses and the preservation and maintenance of said property since the filing of said Chapter 11 petition.

On July 29, 1982, the U.S. Trustee was directed to appoint a committee of trade creditors, and on August 2, 1982 . . . said Committee was appointed. On August 9, 1982, said Committee was given leave to retain the law firm of Nachman, Munitz & Sweig.

2. On October 13, 1982, DAVID S. LEAVITT, as the designated officer to act on behalf of the Debtors, wrote a letter to Dennis Diczok, Vice President of Citibank

and a member of the Trade Creditors' Committee. Said letter modified the above-described operating order, as follows:

1. The Debtors in Possession will submit proposals for capital expenditures in excess of $50,000 to the Subcommittee for its review.

2. The Debtors in Possession will give the Subcommittee prior notice of any commitments to purchase raw steel inventory, if, as a result of such a commitment, the Debtors in Possession will exceed amounts budgeted for quarterly inventory purchases by 15% of the budgeted figures.

3. The Debtors in Possession will notify the Subcommittee prior to executing leases having a face value in excess of $50,000.

4. The Debtors in Possession will notify the Subcommittee prior to granting salary increases to all individuals currently earning in excess of $50,000 per year.

5. In the event he has not already done so, Bob Penn, will give Peat, Marwick & Mitchell, the Creditors' Committee's accountants, copies of (a) the 1982 Budget together with reports, if any, showing the variance, if any, between the budget figures and results of actual operations and (b) any quarterly budget revisions and forecasts with respect to the fiscal year ending December 31, 1982.

6. Bob Penn will meet with Peat, Marwick & Mitchell on a regular basis to discuss comparisons between budgeted expenditures and actual expenditures, preparation of future budgets, quarterly revisions of budgets, forecasts of future operations and such other matters as the Committee's accountants and the Debtors in Possession may agree upon.

7. Dennis Diczok will recommend to the full Creditor's Committee that the Committee form an Executive Committee with authority to approve transactions between the Debtors in Possession and third parties based upon offers with short time spans. . . .

8. The Debtors in Possession will notify the committee whenever its projected cash balance drops below $10.0 million.

9. Bob Penn will meet with a representative of Peat, Marwick, Mitchell & Co. on a weekly basis or as requested to review significant cash transactions.

10. The Debtors in Possession will not honor any warranty claim exceeding $50,000 without prior notification to the Subcommittee.

3. On December 17, 1982, the Trade Creditors filed the instant application to modify Paragraph 3 of the Operating Order and to add additional provisions, as follows:

A. Paragraph 3(a) of the Order shall be amended to add:

"; provided, however, that the debtors in possession shall give the Official Creditors' Committee (Committee) at least ten (10) days' prior written notice of any proposed salary increase to be given to any individual employee currently earning in excess of $50,000 per year."

B. Paragraph 3(c) of the Order shall be amended to add:

"; provided, however, the debtors in possession shall give to the Committee at least twenty (20) days' prior written notice of (i) any capital expenditures in excess of $50,000, which notice shall be given prior to the debtors in possession making any commitments for such expenditures; and, (ii) any commitment to purchase raw steel inventory, if, as a result of such commitment, the debtors in possession will exceed amounts budgeted for quarterly inventory purchases by 15% of the budgeted figures."

C. Paragraph 3(e) of the Order shall be amended to add:

"; provided, however, that the debtors in possession shall give the Committee at least twenty (20) days' prior written notice of the execution of any lease imposing upon the debtors in possession an aggregate obligation in excess of $50,000."

D. The following paragraphs shall be added to the Order:

15. "The debtors in possession shall furnish to Peat, Marwick & Mitchell (Peat Marwick), accountants for the Committee, copies of (i) the 1982 budget of the debtors, debtors in possession and their affiliates, together with reports, if any, showing the variance, if any, between the budget figures and the results of actual operations; and, (ii) any quarterly budget revisions and forecasts with respect to the fiscal year ending December 31, 1982."

16. "The debtors in possession shall meet with Peat Marwick on a regular basis to discuss comparisons between budgeted expenditures and actual expenditures, preparation of future budgets, quarterly revisions of budgets, forecasts of future operations and such other matters as Peat Marwick and the debtors in possession may agree upon."

17. "The debtors in possession shall notify the Committee immediately whenever its actual or projected aggregate cash balances drop below $10 million."

18. "The debtors in possession shall meet with representatives of Peat Marwick on a weekly basis or as requested to review significant cash transactions."

19. "The debtors in possession shall not honor any warranty claim exceeding $50,000 without giving the Committee at least twenty (20) days' prior written notice thereof."

4. On January 10, 1983, the Plaintiff's Committee filed a response to the application of the Trade Creditors, and requested that if the Operating Order is amended as requested by the Trade Creditors, that said amendments apply to the Plaintiff's Committee as well. On January 10, 1983, the Debtor filed its response to the Trade Creditors' application and argued that pursuant to Section 1103(c)(1) the

role of a creditors' committee, vis-a-vis a debtor's operation, is limited to consultation, and does not include involvement in day-to-day operations. The Debtor argues that in any event, the input and information requested by the Trade Creditors is already being provided, pursuant to the letter of agreement dated October 13, 1982, as set forth above.

The Court Concludes and Further Finds:

1. Under Section 1107 of the Bankruptcy Code, debtors in possession have all the rights, functions and duties of a Trustee appointed pursuant to Sections 1104 and 1106 of the Bankruptcy Code. Pursuant to Section 1108 of the Code, debtors in possession are automatically given leave, standing in the place of a Trustee pursuant to Section 1107, to operate their businesses after the filing of the Chapter 11 . . . . Chapter 11 debtors acting in the place of the Trustee act for the benefit of creditors, and it is the debtor's duty, not creditors, to protect and preserve assets . . . . [C]ourts have no authority to interfere with the day-to-day business decisions of Chapter 11 trustees . . . . *In re Curlew Valley Assocs.*, 14 B.R. 506, 512–513 (Bkrtcy. D. Utah 1981). The debtor in possession in a reorganization proceeding has all the powers of the trustee and all his liabilities.

The cases and statutory language evidence a clear intent on the part of Congress to allow debtors in possession, standing in the shoes of trustees, to conduct business as usual after the filing of Chapter 11, which does not encompass day-to-day input from creditors. In fact, the duties of creditors committees are finely delineated and include the following:

(1) consult with the trustee or debtor in possession concerning the administration of the case;

(2) investigate the acts, conduct, assets, liabilities, and financial condition of the debtor, the operation of the debtor's business and the desirability of the continuance of such business, and any other matter relevant to the case or to the formulation of a plan;

(3) participate in the formulation of a plan, advise those represented by such committee of such committee's recommendations as to any plan formulated, and collect and file with the court acceptances of a plan;

(4) request the appointment of a trustee or examiner under section 1104 of this title, if a trustee or examiner, as the case may be has not previously been appointed under this chapter in the case; and

(5) perform such other services as are in the interest of those represented.

If the Trade Creditors feel that the debtor is not capable of proper management then they may move for the appointment of a trustee or an examiner pursuant to Section 1104 of the Code . . . . As indicated in the letter dated October 13, 1982, the Debtors are providing much of the information requested by the Trade Creditors on an informal basis, and this Court has not been provided with any evidence that the Debtors have become uncooperative in the disclosure of relevant financial information. Under these circumstances, it would be unduly burdensome to the Debtors and of little benefit to the Trade Creditors to impose the obligations detailed in the instant application. Similarly, this Court can see no reasonable basis for granting the relief requested in the response of the Plaintiff's Committee.

NOTES AND QUESTIONS

Although Code §§ 1107 and 1108 vest broad operating authority in trustees and debtors in possession, and although the discretion to act with regard to "*ordinary* business matters without prior court approval" has been said to be "at the heart" of the powers of a trustee or debtor in possession, *In re DeLuca Distrib. Co.*, 38 B.R. 588, 591 (Bankr. N.D. Ohio 1984), this discretion is not unfettered. Indeed, despite the hands-off approach suggested by the courts in *Curlew* and *UNR*, the power of trustees and debtors in possession to operate the business and manage the case is subject to a number of practical and statutory constraints.

To begin with the practical, ask yourself this question: If, as the court observed in *UNR*, creditors are not entitled to any "input" in the day-to-day operation of the debtor's business, why did the debtor deign to consent to the conditions imposed by its creditors in the first place? Why was it providing the information requested by trade creditors "on an informal basis"?

What is going on here is an example of the operation in the bankruptcy setting of the psychoanalytic "reality principle," which describes the manner in which persons adjust to environmental demands in order to assure the ultimate satisfaction of their needs. Or, as the grandfather of one of the authors used to say, "If you want to get along, you have to go along." If a debtor is going to continue in business, it will usually need the support of lenders and suppliers. If a debtor is going to get its reorganization plan approved and confirmed, it will need the support of its creditor (and perhaps equity holder) constituencies. The price of garnering this support may be the adoption of operating procedures that enhance the debtor's credibility and give creditors a sense of security and a feeling that they are participating in the case. Recognizing this, even when they are under no statutory compulsion to do so, debtors may solicit the views of creditors on business decisions, and creditors may influence the conduct of a debtor's business affairs and the course of the case. *See generally* Lynn M. LoPucki & William C. Whitford, *Corporate Governance in the Bankruptcy Reorganization of Large, Publicly Held Companies*, 141 U. Pa. L. Rev. 669, 694–706 (1993). Bear in mind, though, that the foregoing observations about the influential role of creditors apply primarily to two types of cases. The first type is cases in which creditors actively participate. These tend to be larger cases. The reality is that, in many cases, creditors are not as involved or aggressive as were the creditors in the *UNR* case. The other type of case is the one in which the lenders that provide debtor in possession financing are also influencing — if not dictating — the manner in which the business is operated or liquidated. This is a topic that we considered in more detail in chapter 5, "Financing the Debtor's Operations," and chapter 6 "Preplan Sale of the Debtor's Business."

Sometimes trustees and debtors consult with creditors because they have to; the Bankruptcy Code itself prevents them from acting autonomously. Code § 1106(a), for example, requires a debtor in possession or a trustee to perform certain duties set forth in Code § 704(a). One of these duties is "unless the court orders otherwise, [to] furnish such information concerning the estate and the estate's administration as is requested by a party in interest." In a subsequent opinion in the *UNR* case, the same Judge Toles, who chided UNR's creditors for interfering with the debtor's ability to operate the business on a day-to-day basis, found that "[T]his statutory obligation to keep creditors and the Court informed regarding the status of its business undergoing reorganization, is perhaps one of the most important fiduciary obligations placed upon the debtor in possession." *In re UNR Indus., Inc.*, 42 B.R. 99, 101 (Bankr. N.D. Ill. 1984).

Moreover, there are some things that a trustee or debtor cannot do and some transactions that they cannot undertake without notice to interested parties and, in some cases, the court's advance approval. For example, as we saw in chapters 1 and 2, a trustee or debtor must obtain the court's permission before retaining professional assistants, Code § 327(a), and before incurring debt outside the ordinary course of business or on a secured or super-priority basis. Code § 364. As we will see in chapter 4, § 4.04, a trustee or debtor may not use "cash collateral" unless creditors who hold an interest in the collateral consent, or the court, after notice and a hearing, authorizes its use. Code § 363(c)(2). Similarly, a trustee or DIP must secure the court's approval before assuming or rejecting an executory contract. Code § 365. If, for example, a debtor operates a web site that collects customer's personally identifiable information, the debtor may not sell that information in violation of the debtor's privacy policy without court approval. Code § 363(b)(1). Certainly one incentive that debtors and trustees have for keeping creditors in the loop, and consulting with them on an informal basis even when consultation is not required, is to stockpile some credibility and goodwill to draw on when consultation is required.

[2]   Transactions Outside the Ordinary Course of Business

Another important Code provision that circumscribes the authority of debtors and trustees to operate the business is Code § 363(b)(1). Please read it and § 363(c)(1) now. As you will see § 363(c)(1) provides that if a trustee or DIP is authorized to operate the business, the trustee may enter into transactions, including the sale or lease of estate property, in the ordinary course of business. However, § 363(b)(1) provides that a trustee or DIP may use, sell, or lease property of the estate outside the ordinary course of business only after notice and a hearing. Thus, whether notice and a hearing are required depends on whether a transaction is "in the ordinary course of business." The distinction between transactions in the ordinary course of business and those outside the ordinary course of business, however, goes beyond the procedural requirements of notice and a hearing. The requirement of notice and a hearing means that creditors and other parties in interest, particularly the creditors' committee and other appointed committees, may have the opportunity to appear and question, oppose, or support these transactions and that courts will have an opportunity to scrutinize them. As one court has observed, "The framework of § 363 is designed to allow a trustee (or debtor in possession) the flexibility to engage in ordinary transactions without unnecessary creditor and bankruptcy court oversight, while protecting creditors by giving them an opportunity to be heard when transactions are not ordinary." *In re Roth American, Inc.*, 975 F.2d 949, 952 (3d Cir. 1992).

Although the determination of whether a transaction is in the ordinary course of business can have broad implications, "[n]either the Bankruptcy Code nor its legislative history provides a framework for analyzing whether particular transactions are in the ordinary course of a debtor's business." *Roth American*, 975 F.2d at 952. In order to determine whether or not a transaction is in the ordinary course of business, most courts have adopted a two-step inquiry. *Id.* This inquiry consists of looking at the transaction from "horizontal" and "vertical" dimensions. *Id.*

The horizontal dimension test asks "whether, from an industry-wide perspective, the transaction is of the sort commonly undertaken by companies in that industry." *Id.* at 953. It is fairly straightforward and easy to understand.

The vertical dimension test requires a bit more explanation. It is also known as the "creditor's expectation test," and it analyzes the transactions from the vantage point of a hypothetical creditor, asking whether the transaction poses that creditor with risks of a different nature from those that existed when he became a creditor. Under the vertical dimension test, "the touchstone of ordinariness is the interested parties' reasonable expectations of what transactions the debtor in possession is likely to enter in the course of business." *Id.* Thus, a debtor's pre-petition business practices and conduct are the primary focus of the vertical analysis. *Id.* The bankruptcy court must "also consider the changing circumstances inherent in the hypothetical creditor's expectations." *Id.* (citations omitted.) Here is a sampler of cases in which courts have applied the horizontal and vertical tests:

- *In re Catholic Bishop of Northern Alaska*, 414 B.R. 552 (Bankr. D. Alaska 2009): The court held that the construction and renovation of churches was in the ordinary course of business of the Fairbanks, Alaska Diocese. The court found that the horizontal test was satisfied, because these were the types of projects that other religious organizations might be expected to undertake. The court found that the vertical test was satisfied because the projects were similar to those that the Diocese, itself, had undertaken over the course of many years. Interestingly, although expenditures were in the ordinary course, the debtor requested the court's approval.

- *In re Nellson Nutraceutical, Inc.*, 369 B.R. 787 (Bankr. D. Del. 2007): The court found that modifications of the debtor's bonus compensation program satisfied both the horizontal and vertical dimension tests. The debtor's expert testified that such adjustments in bonus programs were common in the nutraceutical business, and the court found that this testimony was enough to satisfy the horizontal dimension test. The court also found that the adjustments were consistent with the debtor's own practices over the course of several years. Thus, the court found that the vertical dimension test was satisfied as well.

- *In re Circle K Corp.*, 141 B.R. 694 (Bankr. D. Ariz. 1992): The court held that the debtor's funding of day to day operating expenses with the proceeds of the sale and condemnation of real property was within the ordinary course of the debtor's business, because the debtor had made similar use of such proceeds in the past.

- *In re Miller Min., Inc.*, 219 B.R. 219 (Bankr. N.D. Ohio 1998): Post-petition payments on account of pre-petition secured claims were not in the ordinary course, because creditors would not expect any bankrupt company to make such payments without notice and a hearing involving all creditors.

- *In re Roth American, Inc.*, 975 F.2d 949 (3d Cir. 1992): Modification of a collective bargaining agreement was not an ordinary course of business transaction. Although the court found that the modification satisfied the horizontal dimension test, because manufacturing companies routinely enter into collective bargaining agreements, it did not satisfy the vertical dimension test, because creditors would expect notice and a hearing before a collective bargaining agreement was modified in a bankruptcy case.

The operation of § 363(b) is considered in the following opinion.

MEDICAL MALPRACTICE INSURANCE ASSOCIATION v. HIRSCH (IN RE LAVIGNE)
United States Bankruptcy Court, Southern District of New York
183 B.R. 65 (1995), *aff'd*, 199 B.R. 88 (1996),
aff'd, 114 F.3d 379 (2d Cir. 1997)

BURTON R. LIFLAND, CHIEF U.S. BANKRUPTCY JUDGE

. . . .

[Dr. Jeffery E. Lavigne], also known as Laser Medical Associates of New York, filed for bankruptcy under Chapter 11 . . . on October 8, 1992. No creditors' committee was appointed (section 1102) by the United States Trustee to exercise the powers and duties specified in section 1103.

Lavigne performed laser surgery in medical offices located throughout the New York metropolitan area. He advertised extensively as "MD-TUSH".[1] Lavigne was insured by Medical Liability Malpractice Insurance Company (MLM) until April 1992 when MLM cancelled the insurance. Thereafter, Lavigne obtained insurance from MMIA (Medical Malpractice Insurance Association). MMIA issued Lavigne a one-year claims-made professional liability insurance policy (the "Policy") effective April 1, 1992. The Policy covered liability for injury or damage arising out of the rendering of or failure to render professional services that occurred on or after [that date], as long as claims were first made during the policy period or any extended reporting period. Upon filing for Chapter 11 relief, Lavigne continued to do business and to manage his affairs as a debtor-in-possession. In this capacity, Lavigne renewed the Policy for a one-year period commencing April 1, 1993. However, by letter to MMIA dated September 24, 1993, Lavigne inexplicably cancelled the Policy. The record in this now converted Chapter 11 case reveals that, on or around [the time he cancelled the policy] disturbing events were taking place. Lavigne was faced with numerous tort claims at the time he filed for bankruptcy. Just prior to canceling the Policy, Lavigne decided to close his last remaining medical office in New York. Two days after canceling the Policy he attempted to commit suicide. Lavigne was hospitalized at St. Vincent's Hospital and put on

---

[1] A telephone number acronym describing his anatomical area of specialization.

suicide watch. Impaired, he was then transferred to a rehabilitative facility in New Hampshire and remained there through the end of November 1993 at which time he lost his license to practice medicine.

In response to Lavigne's cancellation letter, MMIA informed him by letter that the cancellation was effective as of September 28, 1993, and that his contractual option to purchase Tail Coverage would expire sixty days from termination; namely, on November 28, 1993. Lavigne did not purchase Tail Coverage within the prescribed period. The Court notes that Lavigne was incapacitated in the New Hampshire facility on the expiration date of the option.

Tail Coverage is insurance coverage which an insured may purchase upon cancellation or termination of a policy. Such coverage applies to claims which arise during the Policy period but which are first asserted after the Policy period. New York Insurance Law requires MMIA to provide this option. MMIA did so in the instant case in section IV of the Policy titled "Optional Extended Reporting Period".

On January 27, 1994, Lavigne's case was converted to one under Chapter 7 of the Code and Hal M. Hirsch was appointed Trustee of the estate. Because of the peculiar circumstances of the debtor's disability coupled with the unorthodox conduct of the debtor's operations by his attorney, a clear picture of the debtor's affairs was not readily obtainable by the Trustee. Upon being apprised of the facts, the Trustee sought to exercise the option to purchase Tail Coverage. In a letter to MMIA dated May 3, 1994, the Trustee requested MMIA to send all necessary documents to exercise the option. Instead of resolving the option issue, the parties entered into a Standstill and Tolling Agreement concerning the Policy which this court "so Ordered" on May 31, 1994. On September 29, 1994, MMIA terminated the Standstill and Tolling Agreement and advised the Trustee that it could not grant his request to purchase Tail Coverage for the Policy because, in its opinion, the option had already expired or, alternatively, was not available because the Policy had been rejected.

As an initial matter the Court must determine whether Lavigne's cancellation of the Policy was effective. Section 1107 of the Code provides a Chapter 11 debtor-in-possession, subject to limitations applicable to a trustee, all the rights, powers, and duties of such trustee, with few exceptions. Lavigne was a debtor-in-possession from the time he filed for bankruptcy on October 8, 1992, until conversion of the case on January 27, 1994. In that capacity, Lavigne was free to conduct his business, subject to, inter alia, limitations such as those imposed on debtors-in-possession by sections 363 and 365 of the Code.

Section 363 of the Bankruptcy Code — Ordinary Course of Business

Trustee asserts that Lavigne's cancellation of the policy was null and void because, inter alia, it was use of estate property outside the ordinary course of business for which notice, a hearing and court authorization was required pursuant to section 363 of the Code.

Lavigne's cancellation of the insurance policy was use of estate property. *See e.g.*, *In re Johns-Manville Corp.*, 26 Bankr. 420 (Bankr. S.D.N.Y. 1983), *aff'd*, 40 Bankr.

219 (S.D.N.Y. 1984), *aff'd sub nom.*, *MacArthur Co. v. Johns-Manville*, 837 F.2d 89 (2d Cir. 1988) (Insurance policies are property of the estate); *In re James A. Phillips, Inc.*, 29 Bankr. 391, 396, n. 3 (S.D.N.Y. 1983) ("The words 'use, sale or lease' seem intended to include the entire range of transactions the trustee or debtor might enter. . . . ").

Although section 363 is meant to facilitate a debtor's reorganization by allowing it to make decisions in the ordinary course of business, an extraordinary transaction undertaken by the debtor or trustee without notice and a hearing is unenforceable. *In re The Leslie Fay Companies, Inc.*, 168 Bankr. 294 (Bankr. S.D.N.Y. 1994). In *Leslie Fay* the court stated that:

> [t]he Code is not meant to straitjacket the debtor and prevent it from responding quickly to normal business demands; neither, however, is the Code meant to allow the debtor the same freedom it had when it got into financial trouble in the first place. For with bankruptcy come certain obligations to creditors, including affording creditors the right to be heard when the debtor proposes to do something beyond the ordinary.

Id. at 304; *see also In re Phillips*, 29 Bankr. 391, 394 (S.D.N.Y. 1983) (notice and a hearing are required "to assure interested persons of an opportunity to be heard concerning transactions different from those that might be expected to take place").

The legislative history of section 363 does not provide guidance as to the scope of the "ordinary course of business" standard, however, courts have adopted a "vertical" and "horizontal" analysis in determining whether a debtor's activity is within the ordinary course of business. *See In re Drexel Burnham Lambert*, 157 Bankr. 532 (S.D.N.Y. 1993); *In re Johns-Manville Corp.*, 60 Bankr. 612, 616 (Bankr. S.D.N.Y. 1986).

The vertical analysis is a creditor's expectation test which gauges the debtor's actions against the usual, internal modus operandi of the debtor's business and the interests of a hypothetical creditor. *In re Phillips*, 29 Bankr. at 394. This analysis requires the court to "examine the debtor's transaction from the vantage point of a hypothetical creditor and inquire whether the transaction subjects a creditor to economic risks of a nature different from those he accepted when he decided to extend credit." *In re Johns-Manville*, 60 Bankr. at 616. In fact, "the touchstone of ordinariness is the interested party's reasonable expectations of what transactions the debtor in possession is likely to enter in the course of its business". *Id.* at 616, (quoting *In re Phillips*, 29 Bankr. at 394). This analysis focuses on the debtor's pre and postpetition activities in an effort to discern any significant alterations in its activity.

The horizontal analysis considers the actions of the debtor in light of industry standards, comparing the debtor's business to other similar businesses to decide whether a type of transaction is in the course of that debtor's business or in the course of some other business. *See, e.g., In re Waterfront Companies, Inc.*, 56 Bankr. 31, 35 (Bankr. D. Minn. 1985).

MMIA argues that the above analyses are "fact-sensitive" and that because the Trustee failed to submit supporting evidence MMIA's summary judgment motion is not defeated. MMIA also asserts, without foundation, that it is usual and ordinary for a doctor who is discontinuing practice to cancel a claims-made policy and that, in the instant case, it was ordinary and customary for Lavigne to cancel because he did not need to cover any subsequent surgical occurrences.

. . . .

The Court disagrees. Lavigne's cancellation was an extraordinary transaction which required court authorization. As set forth previously, immediately following Lavigne's decision to cancel the Policy he closed his last office and attempted to commit suicide. Cancellation appeared to be part of an illogical and desperate course of action. The court finds that all of the circumstances extant at the time of Lavigne's cancellation make such act an extraordinary one.

Even if such action were not so obviously out of the ordinary course of business, the court finds it to be such under the vertical and horizontal analyses. Under the vertical analysis, a hypothetical malpractice claimant of Lavigne would not reasonably expect him to cancel his malpractice insurance in light of the bankruptcy proceeding, the cessation of his medical practice and the outstanding claims against him. Malpractice claimants and trade creditors would be looking to the proceeds of his practice for repayment and would expect him to retain coverage. The Policy provided the only form of protection for creditors' interests. A single, uninsured malpractice claim could **deplete all** of the assets of the debtor's practice. Under these circumstances, cancellation was not an ordinary transaction for Lavigne considering the risks he and his creditors were facing.

Under the horizontal test, a reasonable doctor in Lavigne's position, having ceased the conduct of his practice with the concomitant loss of the ability to raise revenue and facing a growing number of malpractice claims, would not have canceled his medical malpractice insurance policy or foregone the option to buy Tail Coverage. As stated in *Waterfront*, "some transactions either by their size, nature or both are not within the day-to-day operations of a business and are therefore extraordinary." *In re Waterfront*, 56 Bankr. at 35. *See also, In re Drexel*, 157 Bankr. at 537 (consent to modification of obligations of debtor fell outside scope of ordinary course of business transactions, and thus, notice and court approval required); *In re Anchorage Nautical Tours, Inc.*, 145 Bankr. 637, 642 (9th Cir. BAP 1992) (debtor's surrender of major asset intended to generate revenues to fund debtor's business operations not done in ordinary course of business, and thus, notice and hearing required); *In re Media Central, Inc.*, 115 Bankr. 119, 125 (Bankr. E.D. Tenn. 1990) (postpetition severance agreements whereby debtor gave its management team one year's salary upon termination of employment not executed in ordinary course of business, and thus, notice and hearing required); *In re McDonald Bros. Const., Inc.*, 114 Bankr. 989, 994 (Bankr. N.D. Ill. 1990) (debtor's transfer of estate funds to professional was outside ordinary course of business, and thus, court approval, after notice and hearing, required). Under the circumstances of a high risk medical surgical practice, as set forth above, the act of cancellation coupled with the failure to take up the tail policy is a form of professional suicide.

Lavigne's cancellation was not within the ordinary course of business and was ineffective, the Policy remained in effect as of the date of conversion to Chapter 7.

NOTES AND QUESTIONS

Now that you are familiar with § 363, do you think that in the *Curlew* case, the trustee's decision to bale, rather than cube, the hay could have been challenged on the grounds that it could only have been implemented after notice and a hearing? The court said no:

> Debtor argues, as an afternote to the controversy under Section 1108, that the baling program exceeds the trustee's authority under Section 363(b) . . . . Debtor avers that the trustee's actions constitute a use of property, extraordinary in light of debtor's previous business practice.
>
> . . . .
>
> Without addressing the issue whether baling is in the ordinary course of business, debtor's characterization of baling as a "use" of property seems inappropos. Indeed, the shift from cubing to baling results in less "use" of equipment. If, however, the hay is the property which, in debtor's view, is being "used," its "use" in baling is essentially the same as in cubing, viz., it is harvested, shipped, and sold. This points up the difficulty in conceptualizing debtor's argument under Section 363(b). The statute was intended to protect the collateral of secured creditors while debtor or a trustee continues to operate the business. It was not intended as a vehicle for challenging the trustee's management decisions.

14 B.R. at 514 n. 13. Do you agree with the court's analysis?

[D]   The Duty of Care and the Business Judgment Rule in Chapter 11

Outside of bankruptcy, the behavior of corporate officers and directors is governed by certain fiduciary obligations, one of which is the duty of care. The duty of care generally requires directors, in the performance of their duties, to exercise the care that an ordinarily prudent person would exercise under similar circumstances in a manner that person reasonably believed to be in the best interests of the corporation. *See, e.g.*, American Law Institute Principles of Corporate Governance § 4.01; Del. Code Ann. tit. 8 § 141(e) (1994); Model Business Corporation Act, § 8.30(a) (1996 supp.).

Outside of bankruptcy, a plaintiff seeking to prove that an officer or director breached the duty of care must overcome the so-called "business judgment rule." The business judgment rule is more concerned with the decision making process rather than with the decision itself, and it has been described as operating as both a presumption and as a substantive rule of law. Under the rule, a director or officer who acted diligently and on an informed basis, who had no self-interest in the subject matter of a particular decision, and who rationally believed that a decision was in the best interests of the corporation is presumed to have fulfilled his or her duty of care. *Aronson v. Lewis*, 473 A.2d 805, 812 (Del. 1984). A plaintiff may overcome the business judgment rule by showing, for example, that an action was tainted by a conflict of interest, or that a director acted without adequately informing himself or herself, or that a decision was so irrational that it had to have been made in bad faith. *See generally*, Dennis J. Block, et al., *The Business Judgment Rule: Fiduciary Duties of Corporate Directors* 20, 39 (4th ed. 1993). The business judgment rule has been rationalized on several grounds, including the recognition that even prudent and disinterested directors can make decisions that in hindsight seem improvident, *Washington Bancorporation v. Said*, 812 F. Supp. 1256, 1267 (D.D.C. 1993), and that directors are better equipped than judges to make business decisions, *see, e.g., International Insurance Co. v. Johns*, 874 F.2d 1447, 1458 n. 20 (11th Cir. 1989), and that stockholders can always "vote with their feet" by selling their shares, *Joy v. North*, 692 F.2d 880, 885 (2d Cir. 1985). The fact that a corporation is insolvent does not diminish the effectiveness of the business judgment rule. The rule protects "directors of solvent, barely solvent, and insolvent corporations." *Trenwick America Litigation Trust v. Ernst & Young LLP*, 906 A.2d 168 (Del. Ch. 2006), *aff'd mem. sub nom. Trenwick Litigation Trust v. Billet*, 931 A.2d 438 (Del. 2007).

In *Curlew*, the court likened the challenge to the trustee's decision to bail rather than cube the hay "to suits by shareholders against directors who, like trustees, in the exercise of business judgment, make decisions of policy for corporations." Although the business judgment rule has been said to have "vitality by analogy" in Chapter 11, *In re Integrated Resources, Inc.*, 147 B.R. 650, 656 (S.D.N.Y. 1992), the analogy is not perfect, and it seems to work best in cases involving challenges to ordinary course of business decisions after they have been made or implemented.

In the nonbankruptcy context, the business judgment rule is usually invoked *after*-the-fact i.e., after an allegedly improvident management decision has been made and executed — because that is when the critics learn of it. In these cases, the courts concern themselves with the process by which the decision was made, not the wisdom or consequences of a decision that in retrospect turned out to be wrong. In contrast, in Chapter 11, the issue of business judgment is often invoked *before*-the-fact, when a trustee or debtor in possession proposes to undertake a transaction that is, or is alleged to be, outside the ordinary course of business or one that by statute requires court authorization. In these cases, the courts are, understandably and avowedly, not only concerned with the process by which the decisions are made, but also with the effect the business decision will have on the estate and the Chapter 11 process. *In re Public Service Co. of New Hampshire*, 90 B.R. 575, 581 (Bankr. D.N.H. 1988). Given the opportunity to weigh the merits of a transaction, courts occasionally have, even as they professedly applied the business judgment rule. As a result, the standard that has evolved has permitted judges to go beyond the traditional corporate law scope of inquiry and superimpose their own business judgment upon that of trustees and debtors in possession. As the Court of Appeals for the Second Circuit observed in the context of a motion to assume an executory contract:

> "[A] bankruptcy court reviewing a trustee's or debtor-in-possession's decision to assume or reject an executory contract should examine a contract and the surrounding circumstances and apply *its* best 'business judgment' to determine if it would be beneficial or burdensome to the estate to assume it.
>
>   . . . .

> [T]he process of deciding a motion to assume is one of the bankruptcy court placing itself in the position of the trustee or debtor-in-possession and determining whether assuming the contract would be a good business decision or a bad one.
>
> . . . .
>
> [T]he bankruptcy court's 'business judgment' in deciding a motion to assume is just that — a judgment of the sort a businessman would make."

Orion Pictures Corp. v. Showtime Networks, Inc. (In re Orion Pictures Corp.), 4 F.3d 1095, 1098, (2d Cir. 1993) (emphasis supplied). It is difficult to read "business judgment" cases such as this one without concluding that the courts are not so much deferring, as they are concurring, in the business judgment of the trustees and debtors in possession. Other courts, however, have hewed to the traditional business judgment rule in evaluating such decisions. For example, in *In re Pomona Valley Medical Group*, 476 F.3d 665 (9th Cir. 2007), the court held that "the bankruptcy court should presume that the debtor in possession acted prudently, on an informed basis, in good faith, and in the honest belief that the action taken was in the best interests of the bankruptcy estate," and that a court should approve a decision "unless it finds that the debtor in possession's conclusion that rejection would be advantageous is so manifestly unreasonable that it could not be based on sound business judgment, but only on bad faith, or whim or caprice." *Id.* at 670.

A particularly searching standard of review undertaken in the name of business judgment has been applied in cases involving the sale, pursuant to § 363(b)(1), of all or substantially all of a debtor's assets outside the ordinary course of business and prior to acceptance and confirmation of a Chapter 11 reorganization plan. This topic is covered in chapter 6 of the text.

When courts have been called upon to review, *retrospectively*, actions taken by trustees and debtors in possession, courts have concluded that trustees and managers of debtors in possession, like officers and directors of corporations outside of bankruptcy, are bound by a duty of care. Although a mistake of judgment is not, itself, a basis for imposing liability, a mistake that results from a failure to live up to this standard of care is. This duty of care was not breached by trustee who:

- entered into a lease in the mistaken, but apparently reasonable belief that the business would continue to operate, *United States v. Sapp (In re Southern Foundation Corp.)*, 641 F.2d 182, 184 (4th Cir. 1981);

- made a carefully reasoned, but ultimately incorrect, decision not to pursue preference actions, *In re Haugen Construction Service, Inc.*, 104 B.R. 233 (Bankr. D.N.D. 1989).

In comparison, this duty of care was found to have been breached by a trustee who:

- failed to have snow removed from the roof of a grocery store with the result that the roof collapsed, destroying a valuable estate asset, *Reich v. Burke (In re Reich)*, 54 B.R. 995 (Bankr. E.D. Mich. 1985);

- failed to supervise a bookkeeper who embezzled funds, *Johnson v. Clark (In re Johnson)*, 518 F.2d 246, 251 (10th Cir. 1975), *cert. denied sub nom. Clark v. Johnson*, 423 U.S. 893 (1975);

- delegated "virtually all of his chief executive officer's duties" to employees, *In re Lowry Graphics, Inc.*, 86 B.R. 74 (Bankr. S.D. Tex. 1988).

Even outside of bankruptcy, the business judgment rule does not apply in certain contexts, including cases involving decisions that are tainted by self-interest, contests for control, and corporate mergers. *Smith v. Van Gorkom*, 488 A.2d 858 (Del. 1985). In cases where the business judgment rule does not protect a decision, the burden is on the officers and directors to demonstrate that challenged actions were reasonable and fair. *In re Croton River Club, Inc.*, 52 F.3d 41, 44 (2d Cir. 1995). In *In re Riodizio, Inc.*, 204 B.R. 417 (Bankr. S.D.N.Y. 1997), a debtor in possession moved to reject as an executory contract a warrant for the purchase of shares of stock in the debtor. The court noted that the debtor's managers had a personal interest in rejecting the warrant, because its exercise would dilute their holdings. As a result, the court concluded that they could not rely on the presumptions of the business judgment rule to support the application to reject the contract. The court therefore conducted an "independent review" of the rationale for rejection and identified several reasons that "confirm[ed] that rejection benefits the estate without any significant downside." *Id.* at 425. Did the court's approach differ materially from the approach taken by the court in *Orion Pictures*, where the decision to reject did not appear to be tainted by self-interest? Can it be argued that all Chapter 11 cases are fundamentally contests for control of the debtor and that therefore the business judgment rule should never apply to decisions made by managers of debtors in possession?

[E] The Duty of Loyalty in Chapter 11

[1] The Trustee's Duty of Loyalty

As readers know from their Corporations courses, the behavior of corporate management is not only governed by the duty of care discussed earlier in this chapter. Officers and directors are also bound by a duty of loyalty. This duty comprises an obligation to refrain from self dealing and to avoid conflicts of interests and even the appearance of impropriety. *See, e.g., Guth v. Loft, Inc.*, 5 A.2d 503 (Del. 1939). When an officer or director has a conflict of interest, the courts usually require that it be fully disclosed, and the officer or director bears the burden of proving the fairness of any decision or transaction that is tainted by a conflict. In other words, the business judgment rule does not apply. In contrast to the duty of care analysis that we talked about earlier, when the duty of loyalty is implicated, the judicial inquiry is concerned with both the decision making process and the substance of the decision. *Cinerama, Inc. v. Technicolor Inc.*, 663 A.2d 1156 (Del. 1986).

Over the years, courts have confirmed that bankruptcy trustees and debtors in possession are also bound by a duty of loyalty. One source of the *trustee's* duty of loyalty is the Bankruptcy Code itself, which, in Code § 1104(d), requires that a trustee be "disinterested," but this duty is also the product of a judicial determination that a bankruptcy trustee, like the trustee of a conventional personal trust, owes single-minded devotion to the interests of those on whose behalf he or she acts. According to the Restatement (Third) of Trusts § 78(1), "[A] trustee has the duty to administer the trust solely in the interest of the beneficiaries . . . ."

To understand the kind of behavior that constitutes a breach of this duty of loyalty, a good place to begin is the classic and often-cited case, *Bennett v. Gemmill (In re Combined Metals Reduction Co.)*, 557 F.2d 179 (9th Cir. 1977). In that case, the court held that a Chapter X trustee had violated his duty of loyalty by settling a claim against the estate held by his brother. The Ninth Circuit found a violation even though the judge presiding over the reorganization case approved the settlement with knowledge of the relationship:

> It is well established that a trustee in a reorganization is required to act in accordance with the highest standards. Almost fifty years ago Chief Judge Cardozo of the New York Court of Appeals expressed the rule thus:
>
> > Many forms of conduct permissible in a workaday world for those acting at arm's length, are forbidden to those bound by fiduciary ties. A trustee is held to something stricter than the morals of the market place. Not honesty alone, but the punctilio of an honor the most sensitive, is then the standard of behavior. As to this there has developed a tradition that is unbending and inveterate.
> >
> > Uncompromising rigidity has been the attitude of courts of equity when petitioned to undermine the rule of undivided loyalty by the "disintegrating erosion" of particular exceptions.
> >
> > . . . .
> >
> > Only thus has the level of conduct for fiduciaries been kept at a level higher than that trodden by the crowd. It will not consciously be lowered by any judgment of this court. Meinhard v. Salmon, 249 N.Y. 458, 463; 164 N.E. 545, 546 (1928).

557 F.2d at 196. The court explained that a trustee must not only avoid impropriety but also the appearance of impropriety, not merely to discourage disloyalty, but to fortify public confidence in the bankruptcy process.

Another celebrated case is *Mosser v. Darrow*, 341 U.S. 267, 271 (1951), in which the Supreme Court held that a trustee had breached this duty of loyalty by permitting two of his employees to trade in the securities issued by subsidiaries of the debtor. The transactions weren't secret. In fact, the employees were hired by the trustee with the express understanding that they would be allowed to continue to trade personally in these securities. The trustee testified that he had acceded to these terms because he believed that the two employees were indispensable. Justice Jackson held that the trustee, himself, could be surcharged for the profits made by his employees, even though he did not personally profit:

> A reorganization trustee is the representative of the court . . . . Equity tolerates in bankruptcy trustees no interest adverse to the trust. This is not because such interests are always corrupt but because they are always corrupting. By its exclusion of the trustee from any personal interest, it seeks to avoid such delicate inquiries as we have here into the conduct of its own appointees by exacting from them forbearance of all opportunities to

advance self-interest that might bring the disinterestedness of their administration into question.

341 U.S. at 271. Justice Jackson commented that if the trustee believed that the problematic arrangement with the employees was in the best interests of the reorganization effort, he could have protected himself from personal liability by following

> [t]he practice . . . well established by which trustees seek instructions from the court, given upon notice to creditors and interested parties, as to matters which involve difficult questions of judgment.
>
> . . . .
>
> It is hardly probable that a candid disclosure to creditors, to the court, and to interested parties would have resulted in instructions to have pursued this course; but, had it been authorized, at least the assenting creditors might have found themselves estopped to question the transaction.

Id.

These duty of loyalty cases have typically involved situations in which the trustees engaged in blatant self-dealing. For example, a Chapter 11 trustee who continued to operate a failing hotel as his personal fiefdom, concealing its hopeless prospects in order to prolong the case, inflate fees, and enjoy the hotel facilities was found to have breached this duty. *Lopez-Stubbe v. Rodriguez-Estrada (In re San Juan Hotel Corp.)*, 71 B.R. 413, 423 (D.P.R. 1987). The court found that the trustee's misappropriation of the hotel's facilities for personal use — including his daughter's wedding — "ooze[d] conflict of interest through every pore." 71 B.R. 413. The duty of loyalty was breached by a trustee who contracted with his own janitorial service company to provide cleaning services to the debtor, *York International Building Inc. v. Chaney (In re York International Building, Inc.)*, 527 F.2d 1061 (9th Cir. 1976), and by trustees who purchased property from the debtor, albeit at a fair price. *Donovan & Schuenke v. Sampsell*, 226 F.2d 804, 812 (9th Cir. 1955); *In re Lowry Graphics, Inc.*, 86 B.R. 74, 80 (Bankr. S.D. Tex. 1988); *In re Grodel Manufacturing, Inc.*, 33 B.R. 693, 694–95 (Bankr. D. Conn. 1983).

In *Mosser v. Darrow*, the *trustee* was surcharged for permitting his employees to trade in securities of the debtor's subsidiary. In *Butler's Shoe Corp. v. Kirschenbaum (In re Beck Industries, Inc.)*, 605 F.2d 624 (2d Cir. 1979), the court held that a *trustee's employees* are themselves fiduciaries bound by a duty of loyalty. Beck Industries was a large retailer of women's shoes and clothing. It had several operating divisions, one of which was headed by a fellow named Ross. A couple of years after Ross was hired, Beck filed a Chapter X petition and a trustee was appointed. The trustee wanted to retain Ross to run the company's retail shoe and ready-to-wear clothing division. An employment contract, approved by the court, provided that if Beck decided to sell the division, Ross would have a right of first refusal. In other words, he could buy the division by matching the highest offer. Later, when the division was put up for sale, Ross decided to exercise his option. The problem was that he kept secret the fact that he had entered into a joint venture with Butler's Shoe Corp., another potential bidder. This joint venture agreement provided that, after the sale, the division would be split up, with Ross taking the clothing units and Butler's taking the shoe units. Absent the joint venture agreement, Butler's would in theory have been bidding against Ross and other potential buyers, driving the price higher. After Ross won the right to exercise his option, another bidder, who discovered the scheme, argued that the sale should be set aside. The court agreed. The court rejected the notion that management should never be allowed to purchase estate assets — in fact it acknowledged that in some cases a management buyout might offer the best hope for a debtor's rehabilitation — but the court found that Ross's behavior was less than wholesome:

> Ross' status was hybrid. As a highly-positioned employee of Beck since 1969 and later of the . . . trustee, he had some "fiduciary" obligations. Clearly, for example, he was not at liberty to disclose to outsiders confidential information concerning the operations under his supervision. On the other hand, the first-refusal provision of the employment agreement created a built-in conflict of interest, but one which cannot be held against him since it was approved by the bankruptcy court on notice to all interested parties. *See Mosser v. Darrow*, 341 U.S. 267, 274, 71 S. Ct. 680, 95 L. Ed. 927(1951). He was not obliged, as the trustee was, to take affirmative action to obtain competing purchasers who would bid up the price to his disadvantage. He was free to sit things out but not to interfere.
>
> Anyone who has had the patience to read the [preceding description of Ross's conduct] will not require elucidation on how far Ross departed from this norm . . . . The genius of the [joint venture agreement] from the standpoint of Ross and Butler was to conceal that Butler was the real bidder and to use Ross' right of first refusal . . . not simply in his own interest but also in Butler's, and by both these tactics to keep the price down. Genius this may have been in Ross' and Butler's eyes, but it was an evil genius, and known to be, as shown by their concealment of it from the trustee and the court, with the result that the May 11 proceedings became a game of blind-man's buff. Bankruptcy courts do not tolerate such conduct even from those who are not fiduciaries . . . much less from one who is.

605 F.2d at 636.

Thus, the duty of loyalty encompasses an obligation to refrain from self-dealing and to avoid conflicts of interests and the appearance of impropriety and to treat all parties to the case fairly. *See, e.g., Sherr v. Winkler*, 552 F.2d 1367, 1374 (10th Cir. 1977); *In re Spielfogel*, 211 B.R. 133, 145–46 (Bankr. E.D.N.Y. 1997).

[2] The Debtor in Possession's Duty of Loyalty

If you re-read Code § 101(14), you will see that managers of a debtor in possession are by definition *not* disinterested. Nevertheless, courts hold that they, too, are governed by the duty of loyalty that binds trustees. For example, in *Wolf v. Weinstein*, 372 U.S. 633, 649–50 (1963), the Supreme Court held that the president and the general manager of a debtor in possession had breached their duty of loyalty to creditors and stockholders by trading in stock of the debtor:

The concept of leaving the Debtor in possession, as a "receivership without a receiver," was designed to obviate the need to appoint a trustee for the supervision of every small corporation undergoing reorganization, even though it appeared capable of carrying on the business during the proceeding.

. . . .

But so long as the Debtor remains in possession, it is clear that the corporation bears essentially the same fiduciary obligation to the creditors as does the trustee for the Debtor out of possession. Moreover, the duties which the corporate Debtor in possession must perform during the proceeding are substantially those imposed upon the trustee. It is equally apparent that in practice these fiduciary responsibilities fall not upon the inanimate corporation, but upon the officers and managing employees who must conduct the Debtor's affairs under the surveillance of the court. If, therefore — as seems beyond dispute from the very terms of the statute — the trustee is himself a fiduciary . . . logic and consistency would certainly suggest that those who perform similar tasks and incur like obligations to the creditors and shareholders should not be treated differently under the statute for this purpose.

The Supreme Court reaffirmed this principle in *Commodity Futures Trading Commission v. Weintraub*, which is reprinted earlier in this chapter. Not surprisingly, most of the reported cases involving breaches of the duty of loyalty by managers of debtors in possession have involved the same sort of self-dealing and misbehavior that would have gotten trustees in trouble, too. Here are a few examples:

- The CEO of the debtor in possession arranged for the sale of all the debtor's assets to an entity that he secretly owned. *Gumport v. China International Trust & Investment Corp. (In re Intermagnetics America, Inc.)*, 926 F.2d 912, 917 (9th Cir. 1991).

- The debtor's principals intentionally undervalued the estate's main asset, an apartment property, in order to induce creditors to settle for less than the fair value of their claims. *First Union National Bank v. Tenn-Fla Partners (In re Tenn-Fla Partners)*, 170 B.R. 946, 968–70 (Bankr. W.D. Tenn. 1994).

- The debtor failed to file the operating reports required by Code §§ 704 and 1106(a), failed to provide "voluntary and honest financial information" to creditors, and shifted assets between the debtor and non-debtor entities. *In re Sal Caruso Cheese, Inc.*, 107 B.R. 808, 817 (Bankr. N.D. N.Y. 1989).

- The debtor's officers usurped the debtor's business opportunities by diverting business to another company that they controlled. *Bernstein v. Donaldson (In re Insulfoams, Inc.)*, 184 B.R. 694 (Bankr. W.D. Pa. 1995).

- A director and former CEO of the debtor purchased claims against the debtor. *Cumberland Farms, Inc. v. Haseotes (In re Cumberland Farms, Inc.)*, 181 B.R. 678 (Bankr. D. Mass. 1995).

- The debtor failed to pursue a preference action because the debtor's parent company had guaranteed the underlying debt. *In re Tel-Net Hawaii, Inc.*, 105 B.R. 594 (Bankr. D. Haw. 1989).

Notably, these cases involved behavior that would warrant the appointment of a trustee under Code § 1104(a), which was the result in the *Gumport* and *Tel-Net* cases. The persistent misbehavior of management in the *Sal Caurso* and *First Union* cases led the court to convert them from Chapter 11 to Chapter 7.

[3]   Scope of Fiduciary Duties of Officers and Directors of Financially Troubled Companies

Carol has been thinking about the fiduciary duties of those who manage a debtor in possession, and she's troubled. She points out that, as Justice Frankfurter once observed, "[T]o say that a man is a fiduciary only begins [the] analysis. . . . To whom is he a fiduciary?" *SEC v. Chenery Corp.*, 318 U.S. 80, 85 (1943). "I bring this up," she explains, "because I couldn't help but notice that the Supreme Court, in that passage from *Wolf v. Weinstein* that you quoted, referred to obligations that are owed to creditors *and* shareholders. Does the Court really mean that? Do I, as a director of Amphydynamics, really owe fiduciary duties to both constituencies? Is that reasonable? Is it possible? I have to tell you that I have always thought my fiduciary duties as a director flowed to stockholders, not creditors, and the notion that I am expected to serve both constituencies makes me uneasy."

"I can understand why," you say, "but I do have to tell you that the scope of your fiduciary duties as an officer and director has broadened. You do correctly remember from your Corporations course that, generally speaking, so long as a corporation is solvent, the fiduciary obligations of its officers and directors run to stockholders, not to creditors. As one court commented, quite a long time ago:

> [I]t is difficult to perceive upon what principle a director of a corporation can be considered a trustee of its creditors. He is selected by the shareholders, not by creditors, he has no contractual relation with the latter; he represents a distinct entity, the corporation; and his relations to creditors [are] the same as the agent of an individual bears to creditors of such individual; and it is not pretended that in the latter case the agent would be the trustee of the creditors of his principal. And we think that by the great weight of authority such trust relation is distinctly repudiated *when the corporation is a going concern.*

"Webb v. Cash, 35 Wyo. 398 (Wyo. 1926) (emphasis supplied)."

"That works for me. A company's relationships with its creditors are governed for the most part by contract, aren't they? I remember from my contracts course that parties to a contract may have a duty to exercise good faith in performing the contract, *see, e.g.*, Restatement (Second) Contracts § 205; U.C.C. § 1-304, and I know that Amphy's creditors may have a claim against the company under bankruptcy or state law, if the company made any fraudulent transfers, *see, e.g.*, Bankruptcy Code § 548; Uniform Fraudulent Transfer Act §§ 1 *et seq*, but these principles don't seem to make a debtor the fiduciary of its creditors. On the other hand, your references to solvency and the financial health of the company haven't been lost on me. You're about to tell me that the fiduciary duty situation is murkier when the corporation is insolvent, aren't you?"

"I am," you say. You explain that courts do hold that when a corporation is insolvent, the scope of management's fiduciary duties does widen to include creditors as well as stockholders. Some courts reason that this change occurs because creditors are the residual owners of the assets of an insolvent corporation and that directors of an insolvent corporation therefore manage corporate properties for their benefit. *See, e.g., Davis v. Woolf*, 147 F.2d 629, 633 (4th Cir. 1945) ("The law by the great weight of authority seems to be settled that when a corporation becomes insolvent, or in a failing condition, the officers and directors no longer represent the stockholders, but by the fact of insolvency become trustees for the creditors."); *Automatic Canteen Co. v. Wharton (In re Continental Vending Machine Corp.)*, 358 F.2d 587, 590 (2d Cir. 1966) ("[D]irectors of an insolvent corporation occupy a fiduciary position toward the creditors, just as they do toward the corporation when it is solvent. We hold them trustees of the corporation's property on behalf of the creditors.").

[a]   *Credit Lyonnais Bank Nederland, N.V. v. Pathe Communications Corp.*: **The Discovery of the "Zone of Insolvency"**

You note, however, that in *Credit Lyonnais Bank Nederland, N.V. v. Pathe Communications Corp.*, 1991 Del. Ch. LEXIS 215 (Del. Ch. Dec. 30, 1991), the Delaware Chancery Court offered yet another rationale for treating officers and directors of an insolvent corporation as fiduciaries of creditors. The *Credit Lyonnais* case involved a failed leveraged buyout. Pathe Communications purchased most of the shares of MGM. Credit Lyonnais made loans to both Pathe and MGM to finance the LBO, and Pathe pledged its MGM shares to secure the loans. When Pathe defaulted, Credit Lyonnais exercised voting control of the MGM stock. The controlling stockholder of Pathe wanted to regain control of the shares. To raise enough cash to cure the loan defaults, he proposed the sale of some important MGM assets at what the MGM directors apparently regarded as "fire-sale" prices. The directors refused to authorize the sale, and the controlling stockholder sued, claiming that the directors had breached their fiduciary duties to stockholders. Chancellor Allen found that the board had neither acted improperly, nor breached any fiduciary duty by refusing to authorize the sale. The court held not that the fiduciary duties of directors abruptly shifted from stockholders to creditors upon the occurrence of insolvency, but, rather, that when a corporation is insolvent, or "in the vicinity of insolvency," the board had a duty to serve "the community of interests that sustained the corporation, to exercise judgment in an informed, good faith effort to maximize the corporation's long-term wealth creating capacity." 1991 Del. Ch. LEXIS 215, at *108–09. In what came to be a celebrated footnote, the Chancery Court pointed out that since a company that is insolvent or "in the vicinity of insolvency" is of little or no value to its stockholders, stockholders have an incentive to pursue high risk strategies to increase the value of their investment. If the strategy proves successful, the stockholders' position is improved. If the strategy fails, the entire cost is borne by the real risk bearers, the creditors. 1991 Del. Ch. LEXIS 215, at *108–09 n. 55.

"In other words, stockholders of an insolvent company have nothing to lose and everything to gain by betting the farm," Carol observes.

Yes, but if, as Chancellor Allen held, directors are deemed to be fiduciaries of the entire 'corporate enterprise,' including creditors as well as stockholders, directors would be prohibited from taking risky action that promotes the interests of stockholders only."

Carol is perplexed. "All this talk about the community of interests sounds very good, but how is it supposed to work? It seems to me that in the typical Chapter 11 case, the nice folks who make up that 'community of interests' have inherently conflicting and competing interests. What sense of community will they have? Earlier you asked me to read *In re Curlew Valley Associates*. Well, I read it and I haven't forgotten that, in that case, the bankruptcy court described a Chapter 11 case as a 'turbulent rivalry of interests.' That description is pretty apt. If you think back on it, we've seen in cases such as *Victory Construction Co.* [reprinted in chapter 1] that secured creditors may have an incentive to seek relief from the automatic stay in order to take possession of their collateral, no matter what the effect is on operations. Unsecured creditors and owners may have an incentive to put secured creditors' collateral at risk in order to keep even a moribund business going. In some cases [as we will see in chapter 6 of this book], creditors may press for the liquidation of important assets in order to speed up payment of their claims, while owners may have multiple incentives to oppose such sales. Employees may oppose the sale of a business if the buyer will not guarantee their jobs, while creditors may support the sale if it yields the highest price. We will see that creditors may favor substantive consolidation of a debtor with a financially healthier affiliated debtor [as we will see in chapter 7 of the book], while creditors of that affiliate may oppose it. Creditors may oppose a reorganization plan that permits equity holders to retain an interest in the reorganized entity [as we will see in chapter 9], whereas stockholders are likely to oppose any plan that distributes stock to creditors at their expense. So, counselor, how does a responsible board member discharge her duties to this so-called "community of interests"?

You suggest that Chancellor Allen's response would be that directors of troubled companies can deal with the problem of representing competing interests by "conceiving of the corporation as a legal and economic entity" and by recognizing that "circumstances may arise when the right (both the efficient and the fair) course to follow for the corporation may diverge from the choice that the stockholders (or the creditors, or the employees, or any single group interested in the corporation) would make if given the opportunity to act." 1991 Del. Ch. LEXIS at *108 n55.

Still, you have to concede that Carol has a point. The *Credit Lyonnais* opinion sparked nearly two decades of discussion and debate about the scope of the fiduciary duties of officers and directors of corporations that are insolvent or operating in the zone of insolvency.[1] The *Credit Lyonnais* opinion left many issues

---

[1] *See, e.g.*, E. Norman Veasey & Christine T. Di Guglielmo, *What Happened in Delaware Corporate Law and Governance from 1992–2004? A Retrospective on Some Key Developments*, 153 U. Pa. L. Rev. 1399 (2005); Steven L. Schwartz, *Rethinking a Corporation's Obligations to Creditors*, 17 Cardozo L.

unaddressed, including the contours of the zone of insolvency, whether the court had created a new cause of action for creditors of insolvent firms, whether directors' duties to creditors coexisted with their duties to shareholders or supplanted them, and how to avoid liability by properly discharging those duties. In a trilogy of subsequent decisions, the Delaware Supreme Court and Chancery Court revisited and clarified the reasoning and meaning of *Credit Lyonnais*.

[b]   *Production Resources Group L.L.C. v. NCT Group, Inc.: Credit Lyonnais* **Revisited and Restrained**

In *Production Resources Group L.L.C. v. NCT Group, Inc.*, 863 A.2d 772 (Del. Ch. 2004), the Chancery Court cautioned that the *Credit Lyonnais* opinion was never intended to establish a new cause of action for creditors of insolvent firms, but rather was intended to provide *a shield* to directors who, in good faith, rejected an improvident strategy urged upon them by stockholders. In *Production Resources*, a threshold issue was whether a creditor's direct action against directors and officers for breaches of their fiduciary duties was barred by a provision in the company's charter that exculpated the directors from liability for duty of care violations. The corporation had adopted the provision pursuant to the Delaware Code, which provides that a certificate of incorporation may eliminate or limit the personal liability of a director to the corporation or its stockholders for breach of the duty of care. The plaintiff asserted that, by virtue of its status as a creditor and the company's status as insolvent, the plaintiff was entitled to press its claims as direct claims, rather than as derivative claims, and that therefore the exculpatory provision did not apply. The defendants moved to dismiss, asserting that the claims were derivative claims belonging to the corporation, and thus within the scope of the charter's exculpatory provision.

The Chancery Court agreed with the defendant directors. The court acknowledged that when a firm has reached the point of insolvency, it is settled that under Delaware law, the firm's directors are said to owe fiduciary duties to the company's creditors, explaining that the fact of insolvency places the creditors in the shoes normally occupied by the shareholders: that of residual risk-bearers. The Chancery Court found, however, that to the extent that the complaint alleged that the directors and officers had mismanaged the firm, the creditor's claims were classically derivative in the sense that they involve injury to the corporation as an entity and any harm to the stockholders and creditors is purely derivative of the financial harm to the corporation itself. *Id.* at 790–91. Therefore, whether such claims are pressed by the stockholders of a solvent firm or by the creditors of an insolvent firm does not change the inherently derivative nature of the claims. The fact that the firm was insolvent, the court said, does not turn such claims into direct creditor claims, it simply provides creditors with standing to assert those claims. *Id.* at 776. The Court reasoned that to expose directors to liability to *creditors* for breach of duty of care claims, despite the existence of an exculpatory clause that

Rev. 647 (1996); Stephen R. McDonnell, *Geyer v. Ingersoll Publications Co.: Insolvency Shifts Directors' Burden from Shareholders to Creditors*, 19 Del. J. Corp. 177 (1994); Harvey R. Miller, *Corporate Governance in Chapter 11: The Fiduciary Relationship Between Directors and Stockholders of Solvent and Insolvent Corporations*, 23 Seton Hall L. Rev. 1467 (1993); Laura Lin, *Shift of Fiduciary Duty Upon Corporate Insolvency: Proper Scope of Directors' Duty to Creditors*, 47 Vand. L. Rev. 1485 (1993).

would bar *stockholders* from bringing such claims, would render such clauses useless precisely when directors need their protection the most, when, despite the directors good intentions, the business plan of the firm did not generate financial success and the firm has become insolvent. *Id.* at 777. The Court also balked at giving creditors more leeway than stockholders in pressing derivative claims given that "[c]reditors are typically better positioned than stockholders to protect themselves by the simple tool of contracting . . . and the law of fraudulent conveyance." *Id.* Thus, the Court held that the charter provision that insulated directors from liability for duty of care claims applied whether the claims were asserted by stockholders or creditors.

The Chancery Court took great pains to point out that directors, by engaging in robust negotiations with creditors, do not thereby breach their fiduciary duties to those creditors. The court rejected "the proposition that it is a breach of fiduciary duty for the board of an insolvent company to engage in vigorous, good-faith negotiations with a judgment creditor. That, in fact, might be the *duty* of a board, which necessarily has to balance the interests of all those with a claim to the firm's inadequate assets." *Id.*

The Chancery Court, in important *dicta*, revisited its opinion in *Credit Lyonnais*, and stated that despite what some courts and commentators had concluded, the Chancery Court had never intended in that opinion to establish a new cause of action for creditors of an insolvent firm. The Court explained:

> Somewhat oddly, a decision of this court that attempted to emphasize that directors have discretion to temper the risk that they take on behalf of the equity holders when the firm is in the "zone of insolvency" has been read by some as creating a new body of creditor's rights law. The *Credit Lyonnais* decision's holding and spirit clearly emphasized that directors would be protected by the business judgment rule if they, in good faith, pursued a less risky business strategy precisely because they feared that a more risky strategy might render the firm unable to meet its legal obligations to creditors and other constituencies.

> The obligation of directors in that context of high risk and uncertainty, said Chancellor Allen, was not "merely [to be] the agent of the residue risk bearers" but rather to remember their fiduciary duties to "the corporate enterprise" itself, in the sense that the directors have an obligation "to the community of interest that sustained the corporation . . . " and to preserve and, if prudently possible, to maximize the corporation's value to best satisfy the legitimate claims of all its constituents, and not simply to pursue the course of action that stockholders might favor as best for them. In other words, *Credit Lyonnais* provided a shield to directors from stockholders who claimed that the directors had a duty to undertake extreme risk so long as the company would not technically breach any legal obligations.

>   . . . .

> Creative language in a famous footnote in *Credit Lyonnais* was read more expansively by some, not to create a shield for directors from

stockholder claims, but to expose directors to a new set of fiduciary duty claims, this time by creditors. To the extent that a firm is in the zone of insolvency, some read *Credit Lyonnais* as authorizing creditors to challenge directors' business judgments as breaches of a fiduciary duty owed to them. Some cases in the courts of other jurisdictions have embraced this reading.

This view of the common law of corporations is not unproblematic. Arguably, it involves using the law of fiduciary duty to fill gaps that do not exist. Creditors are often protected by strong covenants, liens on assets, and other negotiated contractual protections. The implied covenant of good faith and fair dealing also protects creditors. So does the law of fraudulent conveyance. With these protections, when creditors are unable to prove that a corporation or its directors breached any of the specific legal duties owed to them, one would think that the conceptual room for concluding that the creditors were somehow, nevertheless, injured by inequitable conduct would be extremely small, if extant. Having complied with all legal obligations owed to the firm's creditors, the board would, in that scenario, ordinarily be free to take economic risk for the benefit of the firm's equity owners, so long as the directors comply with their fiduciary duties to the firm by selecting and pursuing with fidelity and prudence a plausible strategy to maximize the firm's value.

Id. at 788–89. The Chancery Court also rejected the notion that creditors of a firm that is not actually insolvent, but rather is occupying some murky zone of insolvency, have standing to assert derivative claims.

The "zone" issue is an admittedly confusing one. For example, once a firm becomes insolvent, there is little doubt that creditors can press derivative claims arguing that directors' pre-insolvency conduct injured the firm, which makes some of the Bankruptcy Court decisions discussing the zone interesting dictum. The more difficult issue is whether there is a zone in which the directors' duties to the firm fundamentally change and whether creditors can assert fiduciary duty claims (e.g., for injunctive relief) before the firm becomes insolvent. If creditors have standing to bring derivative claims in the "zone of insolvency," they will share that standing with stockholders, leading to the possibility of derivative suits by two sets of plaintiffs with starkly different conceptions of what is best for the firm.

Id at 790 n. 56

This, the court said, is why it would be "reluctant" to second-guess good-faith director conduct in the so-called zone, *id.*, and why, in the absence of self-dealing or other evidence of bad faith, it would be loathe to impose liability in situations when directors face a difficult choice between pursuit of a plausible, but risky, business strategy that might increase the firm's value to the level that equity holders will receive value and another course guaranteeing no return for equity but preservation of value for creditors. *Id.* n. 57.

The *Production Resources* opinion is important for several reasons. In it, the Chancery Court halted and reversed the ascent of the theory that directors of an insolvent firm are bound by a new set of fiduciary duties that are owed to creditors. At least under Delaware law, they are not. The *Credit Lyonnais* opinion did not create a new cause of action against directors of an insolvent corporation but, rather, established a protective shield for directors that declined to authorize risky transactions desired by stockholders. In addition, the Chancery Court held that although creditors of an insolvent corporation, as the firm's residual risk bearers, succeeded to the right of stockholders to assert breach of fiduciary duty claims, creditors, like stockholders, could only assert such claims derivatively, not directly. Last, the court suggested that the shift in scope of directors' fiduciary duties does not occur when a corporation is operating in the zone of insolvency, but only upon the occurrence of actual insolvency.

[c]   The Rise and Fall of the Deeping Insolvency Theory

Judicial efforts to contain and resolve the confusion generated by those who read creative language in *Credit Lyonnais* too expansively continued in two later opinions of the Chancery Court and the Supreme Court of Delaware. Both of these cases were decided against the backdrop of so-called Deepening Insolvency claims, and that makes a brief look at that now largely disapproved theory of recovery useful at this point.

"Deepening Insolvency" is a term that has been applied to describe another theory for holding managers, as well as professional consultants, and, in some cases, other creditors, liable for prolonging the existence of a financially troubled firm. The essence of the theory is that an insolvent firm "suffers a distinct and compensable injury when it continues to operate and incur more debt instead of promptly liquidating, and that a claim for this injury may be asserted by the firm's creditors." Some courts have recognized the existence of a distinct cause of action for deepening insolvency. The better and currently prevailing view is that merely extending the life of a troubled company, even at the cost of incurring additional debt, is not actionable and that some underlying misconduct is necessary to state a claim.

Over the years, some courts had suggested that conduct that prolongs the life of an insolvent firm gives rise to an independent cause of action. Thus, for example, in *Official Committee of Unsecured Creditors v. R. F. Lafferty & Co.* 267 F.3d 340 (3d Cir. 2001), the Creditors' Committee alleged that, in furtherance of a Ponzi scheme, the debtors' management, accountant, and underwriter misrepresented the financial condition of the debtors in order to "induce" the debtors to offer and sell debt securities. Increasing the debtor's debt burden, the complaint alleged, deepened the insolvency of the debtors and put them on the path to bankruptcy. *Id.* at 345. The Third Circuit Court of Appeals theorized that the Pennsylvania Supreme Court, applying state law, would conclude that where deepening insolvency causes damage to corporate property . . . the Pennsylvania Supreme Court would provide a remedy by recognizing a cause of action for that injury. *Id.* at 351. With respect to causation, the court reasoned that "the incurrence of debt can force an insolvent corporation into bankruptcy, thus inflicting legal and administrative costs on the corporation," that "bankruptcy creates operational limitations which hurt a corporation's ability to run its business in a profitable manner, that deepening insolvency, whether or not it results in bankruptcy can shake the confidence of parties dealing with the corporation . . . thereby damaging the corporation's assets," and that "prolonging an insolvent corporation's life through bad debt may simply cause the dissipation of corporate assets." *Id.* at 350. In contrast, the court said, [t]hese harms can be averted and the value of an insolvent corporation salvaged, if the corporation is dissolved in a timely manner, rather than kept afloat with spurious debt." *Id.*

Lafferty, however, was not a case in which the mere prolongation of the company's existence was alleged. Plaintiffs also claimed that defendants had conspired to produce fraudulent financial statements and to violate federal securities laws and that the auditors had aided and abetted management's breach of its fiduciary duties. *Id.* at 345–46. Thus, this was not a case in which a simple extension of credit that extended the life of the debtors caused injury but, rather, a case in which misconduct that was alleged to have occurred when the debtor was living on borrowed time did. Opinions such as *Lafferty* suggest that a breach of fiduciary duties may result in injury to a firm's value, which in the case of an insolvent company may render it *more* insolvent. However, misconduct (as opposed to a mistaken business judgment) that impairs the value of a firm would likely be actionable whether the firm was insolvent or not. The fact of insolvency may affect who may assert a breach of duty claim in these cases but not the basis of the claim.

In *Official Comm. of Unsecured Creditors v. Credit Suisse First Boston (In re Exide Techs., Inc.)*, 299 B.R. 732 (Bankr. D. Del. 2003), a creditors' committee sued a group of 81 banks and other lenders that had made a series of prepetition loans totaling some $900 million to the debtor. The committee alleged that the last of these loans was made by the banks to induce the debtor to acquire a competitor, apparently in the hope of staving off bankruptcy, while improving the position of the banks by giving them a lien on a larger pool of assets. The bankruptcy court expressly adopted the reasoning in *Lafferty* and concluded that the Delaware Supreme Court would recognize a claim for deepening insolvency when there has been damage to corporate property. Although the *Exide* opinion ostensibly supports the existence of an independent cause of action for deepening insolvency, the case was, like *Lafferty*, one in which the complaint was replete with allegations of fraud, mismanagement, and self-dealing. Thus, it, too, must be regarded as a case in which the acts that injured the corporation were not, *per se*, the extension of credit or the extension of the debtor's existence, but rather the misbehavior of the defendants that occurred when the debtor was living on borrowed time. Moreover, the bankruptcy court's prediction that the courts of Delaware would recognize a cause of action for deepening insolvency turned out to be wrong.

[d] *Trenwick America Litigation Trust v. Ernst & Young LLP*: Deepening Insolvency Meets the Business Judgment Rule

In *Trenwick America Litigation Trust v. Ernst & Young LLP*, 906 A.2d 168 (Del. Ch. 2006), *aff'd mem. sub nom. Trenwick Litigation Trust v. Billet*, 931 A.2d 438 (Del. 2007), a litigation trust, established pursuant to a Chapter 11 reorganization plan and vested with the right to bring claims owned by the debtor, sued former directors of the debtor and the debtor's parent company, asserting that the parent company had caused the debtor to take on more debt to support a business strategy that ultimately failed. The Chancery Court found that the complaint failed to plead any facts suggesting that the directors harbored a disloyal motive or acted on less than an informed basis. Moreover, the Chancery Court ruled that the claim against directors for deepening insolvency had to be dismissed:

> Delaware law does not recognize this catchy term as a cause of action, because catchy though the term may be, it does not express a coherent concept. Even when a firm is insolvent, its directors may, in the appropriate exercise of their business judgment, take action that might, if it does not pan out, result in the firm being painted in a deeper hue of red. The fact that the residual claimants of the firm at that time are creditors does not mean that the directors cannot choose to continue the firm's operations in the hope that they can expand the inadequate pie such that the firm's creditors get a greater recovery. By doing so, the directors do not become a guarantor of success. Put simply, under Delaware law, "deepening insolvency" is no more of a cause of action when a firm is insolvent than a cause of action for "shallowing profitability" would be when a firm is solvent. Existing equitable causes of action for breach of fiduciary duty, and existing legal causes of action for fraud, fraudulent conveyance, and breach of contract are the appropriate means by which to challenge the actions of boards of insolvent corporations.

Id. The Chancery Court again rejected the notion that the incantation of the word insolvency, or even more amorphously, the words zone of insolvency, should . . . declare open season on corporate fiduciaries, *id.* at 174, and force them into liquidation mode, simply because the creditors that had supplanted stockholders as the residual risk bearers of the enterprise might prefer (or in retrospect might have preferred) a liquidation strategy. The court held that there is no absolute fiduciary duty to liquidate a troubled company:

> Delaware law imposes no absolute obligation on the board of a company that is unable to pay its bills to cease operations and to liquidate. Even when the company is insolvent, the board may pursue, in good faith, strategies to maximize the value of the firm.

> Directors are expected to seek profit for stockholders, even at risk of failure. With the prospect of profit often comes the potential for defeat . . . . The general rule embraced by Delaware is the sound one. So long as directors are respectful of the corporation's obligation to honor the legal rights of its creditors, they should be free to pursue in good faith profit for the corporation's equityholders. Even when the firm is insolvent, directors are free to pursue value maximizing strategies, while recognizing that the firm's creditors have become its residual claimants and the advancement of their best interests has become the firm's principal objective.

> If the board of an insolvent corporation, acting with due diligence and good faith, pursues a business strategy that it believes will increase the corporation's value, but that also involves the incurrence of additional debt, it does not become a guarantor of that strategy's success. That the strategy

results in continued insolvency and an even more insolvent entity does not in itself give rise to a cause of action. Rather, in such a scenario the directors are protected by the business judgment rule. To conclude otherwise would fundamentally transform Delaware law.

Id.

The same result was reached by a bankruptcy court applying principles of New York corporate law. In *Kittay v. Atlantic Bank of New York (In re Global Service Group LLC)*, 316 B.R. 451 (Bankr. S.D.N.Y. 2004), the court flatly rejected the notion that, in the absence of other actionable misconduct, extending credit to an insolvent firm would, in and of itself, give rise to a cognizable claim. In that case, a Chapter 7 trustee alleged that the debtor's bank knew or should have known that the debtor would be unable to repay its loans due to its financial condition but loaned the debtor money anyway based upon its relationship with the company's principals and the strength of their personal assets. *Id.* at 455. The trustee alleged that as a result of the loan, the debtor was allowed to operate while insolvent and incurred additional debt that it could not repay, reducing any potential recovery for the creditors of the bankruptcy estate. *Id.* at 455–56. The court disagreed, explaining that merely prolonging a corporation's life should not result in liability:

> Instead, one seeking to recover for "deepening insolvency" must show that the defendant prolonged the company's life in breach of a separate duty, or committed an actionable tort that contributed to the continued operation of a corporation and its increased debt.

Id. at 459. Nor, the court held, should extending credit to an insolvent entity result in liability, even if the lender has doubts about the debtor's ability to repay:

> This may be bad banking, but it isn't a tort. A third party is not prohibited from extending credit to an insolvent entity; if it was, most companies in financial distress would be forced to liquidate. And while the Complaint alleges that Atlantic Bank made the loan on the strength of its relationship with the [principals] and their personal assets, this is neither surprising nor improper. Banks prefer to lend to those they know, and have the right to insist on guaranties and pledges of personal assets from the corporate principals. Notably, the Complaint does not allege or imply that Atlantic Bank extended the loans to enable the [principals] to siphon off the funds or commit some other wrong.

Id. at 459–60. The court reasoned that to impose on managers of an insolvent firm an absolute duty to liquidate would be inconsistent with the business judgment rule, which gives managers discretion to continue to operate a troubled business as they attempt to salvage its enterprise value, and contrary to the obligation of officers and directors of companies to serve the community of interest that sustained the corporation [and] to exercise judgment in an informed, good faith effort to maximize the corporation's long-term wealth creating capacity. *Id.* at 459–60. Therefore, a manager's incorrect but good faith decision to operate an insolvent business should not subject him to liability for deepening insolvency. The court also pointed out that imposing an absolute duty to liquidate would contravene the ethos underlying Chapter 11, which is to salvage, when possible, a troubled business in order to preserve jobs and asset values and provide a return to creditors and stockholders. *Id.* at 460. The court contrasted the U.S. approach to that of some foreign jurisdictions, such as the United Kingdom, where directors who continue to operate an insolvent business may be liable for wrongful trading.

[e]   *North American Catholic Educational Programming Foundation, Inc., v. Gheewalla*: A Derivative Claim is Still a Derivative Claim

Most of the reasoning of the Chancery Court in *Production Resources* and *Trenwick* was adopted by the Delaware Supreme Court in *North American Catholic Educational Programming Foundation, Inc., v. Gheewalla*, 930 A.2d 92 (Del. 2007). North American Catholic Educational Programming Foundation (NACEPF) was a creditor of Clearwire Holdings, Inc. Clearwire's business failed when the market for radio wave spectrum licenses collapsed in the wake of the bankruptcy of communications giant WorldCom. NACEPF sued the directors of Clearwire, alleging that, at a time when Clearwire was insolvent or in the zone of insolvency, the directors had breached their fiduciary duties by, among other things, failing to preserve the assets of Clearwire when it became apparent that Clearwire would not be able to continue as a going concern and would be liquidated.

The Delaware Supreme Court affirmed the Chancery Court's dismissal of the complaint, holding that the creditors of a Delaware corporation, even if it is insolvent or in the zone of insolvency have no right, as a matter of law, to assert direct claims for breach of fiduciary duty against the corporation's directors:

> It is well established that the directors owe their fiduciary obligations to the corporation and its shareholders. While shareholders rely on directors acting as fiduciaries to protect their interests, creditors are afforded protection through contractual agreements, fraud and fraudulent conveyance law, implied covenants of good faith and fair dealing, bankruptcy law, general commercial law, and other sources of creditor rights. Delaware courts have traditionally been reluctant to expand existing fiduciary duties.

> Accordingly, "the general rule is that directors do not owe creditors duties beyond the relevant contractual terms."

> In this case, [Plaintiff] argues that when a corporation is in the zone of insolvency, this Court should recognize a new direct right for creditors to challenge directors' exercise of business judgments as breaches of the fiduciary duties owed to them.

> Delaware corporate law provides for a separation of control and ownership. The directors of Delaware corporations have "the legal responsibility to manage the business of a corporation for the benefit of its shareholders owners." Accordingly, fiduciary duties are imposed upon the directors to regulate their conduct when they perform *that* function.

> In this case, the need for providing directors with definitive guidance compels us to hold that no direct claim for breach of fiduciary duties may

be asserted by the creditors of a solvent corporation that is operating in the zone of insolvency. When a solvent corporation is navigating in the zone of insolvency, the focus for Delaware directors does not change: directors must continue to discharge their fiduciary duties to the corporation and its shareholders by exercising their business judgment in the best interests of the corporation for the benefit of its shareholder owners.

Id. at 99–101.

Then the court turned to the question of whether creditors of corporations that are actually insolvent, as distinct from corporations that are merely in the vicinity of insolvency, may assert direct breach of fiduciary duty claims against directors. The court concluded that they may not:

It is well settled that directors owe fiduciary duties to the corporation. When a corporation is *solvent*, those duties may be enforced by its shareholders, who have standing to bring *derivative* actions on behalf of the corporation because they are the ultimate beneficiaries of the corporation's growth and increased value. When a corporation is *insolvent*, however, its creditors take the place of the shareholders as the residual beneficiaries of any increase in value.

Consequently, the creditors of an *insolvent* corporation have standing to maintain derivative claims against directors on behalf of the corporation for breaches of fiduciary duties. The corporation's insolvency "makes the creditors the principal constituency injured by any fiduciary breaches that diminish the firm's value." Therefore, equitable considerations give creditors standing to pursue derivative claims against the directors of an insolvent corporation. Individual creditors of an insolvent corporation have the same incentive to pursue valid derivative claims on its behalf that shareholders have when the corporation is solvent.

. . . .

Recognizing that directors of an insolvent corporation owe direct fiduciary duties to creditors would create uncertainty for directors who have a fiduciary duty to exercise their business judgment in the best interest of the insolvent corporation. To recognize a new right for creditors to bring direct fiduciary claims against those directors would create a conflict between those directors' duty to maximize the value of the insolvent corporation for the benefit of all those having an interest in it, and the newly recognized direct fiduciary duty to individual creditors. Directors of insolvent corporations must retain the freedom to engage in vigorous, good faith negotiations with individual creditors for the benefit of the corporation.

Accordingly, we hold that individual *creditors* of an *insolvent* corporation have *no right to assert direct* claims for breach of fiduciary duty against corporate directors. Creditors may nonetheless protect their interest by bringing derivative claims on behalf of the insolvent corporation or any *other* direct nonfiduciary claim . . . that may be available for individual creditors.

Id. at 101–103 (emphasis in original).

[F]   Reprise: Living with Competing Interests in Chapter 11

You explain to Carol that these opinions should provide a large measure of comfort to officers and directors of insolvent firms. They illustrate that their fiduciary duties are essentially the same as those of directors of a solvent corporation, even though the ultimate beneficiaries of those duties may change.

"So, what I gather is that directors and officers will properly discharge those duties by pursuing diligently, on an informed basis, and in good faith, strategies that they believe will increase or preserve the corporation's value. Even if, in retrospect, those strategies appear to have been misguided, they should not be held liable to the firm's residual owners, whether they are stockholders or creditors."

You agree, and to bring this chapter full circle, you point out that judging from both the Bankruptcy Code's legislative history and the structure of the Chapter 11 process itself, the Code drafters recognized that the interests of owners, creditors, and managers of troubled companies are potentially, if not inherently, divergent interests, and they favored, where possible, negotiated resolution of conflicts.

The Code's preference for debtors in possession is an example. As we saw at the beginning of this chapter, there were some people, including SEC officials, who urged that an independent trustee be appointed to serve in every Chapter 11 case in order to protect junior creditors and stockholders from managers "who might seek to pacify large creditors" or "have their own interests to look after." S. Rep. 95-989. 95th Cong., 2d Sess. 10 (1978). Nevertheless, Congress opted for a system that in the vast majority of cases would leave very much interested, and potentially conflicted, management in place and in control of the debtor in possession. As a counterbalance, § 1104(a) provides for appointment of a trustee for cause or if such appointment is in the interests of creditors. And as we saw earlier, courts have held that the inability of a debtor in possession to find a way to resolve competing interests is itself grounds for appointment of a trustee. *See, e.g., In re Marvel Entertainment Group, Inc.*, 140 F.3d 463 (3d Cir. 1998); *Wabash Valley Power Ass'n v. Rural Electrification Admin.*, 903 F.2d 445, 451 (7th Cir. 1990); *In re Cajun Electric Power Coop.*, 191 B.R. 659, 662–63 (M.D. La. 1995); *In re Colorado-Ute Electric Ass'n*, 120 B.R. 164, 176 (Bankr. D. Col. 1990); *In re Cardinal Industries, Inc.*, 109 B.R. 755, 767 (Bankr. S.D. Ohio 1990).

But the Code does more than provide for the appointment of a trustee in some cases. Even when there is no trustee, to give voice to these competing interests, Code § 1102 provides for the appointment of creditors' committees and, in appropriate cases, equity holders' committees, to "represent the various classes of creditors and equity security holders from which they are selected," and to "provide supervision of the debtor in possession and of the trustee," and "protect their constituents' interests." The committees also are to serve as "the primary negotiating bodies for the formulation of the plan of reorganization." H.R. Rep. 95-595, 95th Cong., 1st Sess. 401 (1977). *See* Code § 1103(c). Furthermore, Bankruptcy Code § 1109 gives any party in interest the right to appear and be heard on any issue.

In addition, as we saw in cases such as *Lavigne*, the Code provides for advance scrutiny by courts, creditors, stockholders, and other parties in interest of transactions that could materially affect their rights or the outcome of the Chapter 11 case. As the Amphydynamics case unfolds, we will see other transactions that are subjected to this same kind of scrutiny, such as DIP loans (chapter 5 of the text), sales of substantially all of the debtor's assets (chapter 6 of the text), and assumption and rejection of executory contracts (chapter 7 of the text). The point is that by subjecting such transactions to judicial scrutiny, the Code implicitly recognizes that trustees and managers of debtors in possession may be compelled to "choose sides." This process also gives management an opportunity to run difficult decisions through the court and secure the kind of "instructions," or judicial blessing, that Justice Jackson, in *Mosser v. Darrow*, suggested that the trustee should have sought before allowing his employees to trade in securities of the debtor. (Of course, Justice Jackson doubted that the court would have approved that arrangement.)

"Finally, Carol," you explain, "the process by which reorganization plans are to be negotiated, voted on, and judicially confirmed demonstrates that the Code drafters understood that these conflicts were inevitable and concluded that they should be resolved, if possible, by consensus achieved through negotiation among the interested parties, including the debtor in possession." As the drafters observed, "The purpose of the reorganization case is to formulate and have confirmed a plan of reorganization . . . The [voting] requirement necessitates negotiation among management, creditors and stockholders." H.R. Rep. 95-595, 95th Cong., 1st Sess. 221 (1977).

Code § 1121 gives the debtor in possession the exclusive right to propose a reorganization plan but does so only for a limited time. This section also provides for termination of the exclusive period in the event a trustee is appointed, and implicitly recognizes and approves of the possibility that holders of competing interests will propose competing plans. To the extent that it gives a debtor in possession the exclusive right to file a reorganization plan, the Code gives the debtor in possession leverage and gives creditors and equity holders an incentive to negotiate in good faith in order to reach a consensus as swiftly as possible. To the extent that the Code limits this period of exclusivity, it discourages debtors in possession from acting in bad faith and holding reorganization plans hostage to unreasonable demands.

As we will see in chapter 9 of the text, once a plan is proposed, it may not be voted on unless it is preceded or accompanied by a disclosure statement approved by the court as containing adequate information so that creditors and interest holders may make an informed judgment as to whether to accept or reject the plan. § 1125(b). Furthermore, a plan may not be confirmed by the court unless, among other things, it is accepted by a majority of each class of claims that is impaired by the plan or, failing that, the so called "cram down" standards are met. Code §§ 1129(a)(8), 1129(b). Finally, as we saw at the beginning of this chapter, and as we will see again in chapter 9, the Code also contains a relaxed version of the absolute priority rule. The rule formerly required that each class of claims or interests be satisfied in full before the next lower class could receive any property under a reorganization plan. Under the Code's relaxed version, senior classes have the option of relinquishing value to junior classes. By easing the rule, the drafters sought to make possible, and by making possible encourage, negotiated, consensual plans. The theory was that "negotiation among the parties after full disclosure will govern how the value of the reorganizing company will be distributed among creditors and stockholders." H.R. Rep. 95-595, 95th Cong., 1st Sess. 224 (1977).

Cumulatively, these provisions strongly suggest that the Code's drafters understood that, in the operation of the business as well as in the negotiation of reorganization plans, the interests of the debtor, creditors, and equity holders were essentially adverse and conflicting. Therefore, to conclude that a trustee or debtor in possession is duty bound to serve all interests all of the time, or even some interests all of the time, strains credulity, logic, and the provisions of the Code. What the realities of the Chapter 11 process do suggest is that a trustee or debtor in possession must exercise due care in making business decisions, refrain from self-dealing in the management of estate assets, make full disclosure of all dealings and their ramifications, and, when conflicts among constituencies do arise, negotiate honestly and in good faith in support of the particular position that they determine to be appropriate, based on the realities of the case. These realities include the prospects for successful reorganization, the need for creditor support of on-going operations, and the risks and feasibility of any proposed transaction or business plan.

Chapter 5

FINANCING THE DEBTOR'S OPERATIONS IN CHAPTER 11

§ 5.01 INTRODUCTION

PROBLEM 5.1

You will undoubtedly recall from the *Mismanagement Week* article reprinted in chapter 1 that Amphydynamics, following an extended series of losses, has been experiencing a serious cash squeeze. The company has been unable to make interest payments to its lenders. Several anxious banks have asserted their rights of setoff by applying funds that were on deposit in Amphydynamics' accounts to pay down claims that Amphydynamics owed the banks. Nervous suppliers have been demanding payment *before* delivery. Raw materials and inventory are consequently in short supply, and Amphy has been slow in filling customer orders. Unhappy customers are turning to other sources, and even Amphy's own retail outlets are running out of products to sell. As a result, operations are generating little cash, Amphy cannot pay salaries or other operating expenses, and Amphy is on the brink of shutting down. Amphy's cash flow problem has turned into a drought.

Assume that you are an attorney representing MicroMax, a longtime supplier of computer chips to Amphy. Max Matrix, the credit manager of MicroMax, has called you for advice, because *he* just got a call from Headley Charisma, who has asked him to ship a large order of chips on customary 30-day credit terms. Amphy needs those chips in order to manufacture flat screen monitors for sale to retailers. Of course, Max knows that Amphy is in Chapter 11, and he is trying to decide whether to ship. On the one hand, Amphy has always been a good customer, and he would like to oblige. Also, it's a sizable order, and he would be happy for the business. On the other hand, Max wants to know whether he is likely to be paid and wants to know what his status would be if he sells to Amphy on credit.

In thinking about how to answer Max's question, it may be useful to back up a couple of steps. As we have seen, Code §§ 1108 and 1107(a) authorize a trustee or debtor in possession to operate the debtor's business as they attempt to reorganize it. Code § 363(c)(1) authorizes the use, sale, or lease of estate property in the course of operating the business. In the meantime, by preventing creditors from enforcing their claims, the automatic stay of Code § 362 gives a debtor the breathing room it needs to recoup its strength, evaluate its position, rationalize its operations, and develop a plan of reorganization. Thus, Amphy is presumptively authorized to manufacture and sell those flat screen monitors without interference from creditors. However, as Amphy's plight suggests, debtors may need more than breathing room if they are to be resuscitated. They need oxygen.

In Chapter 11, that means cash, or at least credit. Read Code § 364. As the automatic stay provides a debtor breathing room, § 364 provides a delivery system for oxygen. It authorizes a trustee or debtor in possession to obtain credit and incur debt. It also establishes a hierarchy of incentives — "carrots" — that may be drawn on by debtors to induce lenders, suppliers, and others to extend credit. (As we will see, these "carrots" may also function as "sticks" to encourage those who extended credit to the debtor prepetition to extend additional credit postpetition.)

The approach is founded on several related principles. The first is the belief that keeping a viable debtor alive and operating as a going concern is desirable. The second is the recognition that extensions of credit may be necessary to do this. The third principle, which tempers the first two, is the sensibility that, because the cost of borrowing will be borne by the estate and its creditors, the debtor should borrow on the least onerous terms possible. The fourth principle, articulated in some cases, implicit in others, is that borrowing should only be permitted when it will enhance a viable debtor's prospects for recovery and not merely prolong the death throes of a moribund debtor. After all, if the debtor piles on postpetition debt only to fail, prepetition creditors, whose claims are subordinate to the claims of the new lenders, will pay the price.

§ 5.02   ADMINISTRATIVE PRIORITY TREATMENT — SECTIONS 364(A), (B); 503(B)

The first, cheapest, and thinnest "carrot" that the Code holds out to induce extensions of postpetition credit is an administrative expense priority. Code § 364(a) provides that if a trustee or debtor in possession is authorized to operate the business—and, as we've seen, in a Chapter 11 case the presumption under Code §§ 1108 and 1107 is that they are so authorized — they may obtain unsecured credit or incur unsecured debt *in the ordinary course of business*. In such a case, the party that extends credit will hold a first priority administrative expense claim allowable under Code § 503(b).

Section 503(b) allows as administrative expenses, "the actual, necessary costs and expenses of preserving the estate." Code § 507(a) provides that administrative expenses are entitled to priority in distribution ahead of the other kinds of priority unsecured claims described in that subsection. Note that § 364(a) governs *ordinary course* transactions. If an extension of credit is *outside the ordinary course of business*, § 364(b) controls. It provides that the transaction must be authorized by the court in order for the lender to enjoy administrative expense priority. As a practical matter, any lender of new funds with any degree of sophistication will want at least what is called a "comfort" order from the bankruptcy court finding that the proposed extension of credit is in the ordinary course of business and is an actual and necessary expense of preserving the estate, giving rise to an administrative priority claim under §§ 364(a), 503(b), and 507(a).

Section 364(a) is usually invoked by suppliers who ship on credit to the debtor while the case is pending, just as Headley has encouraged MicroMax to do. Suppose that MicroMax ships on the customary 30-day credit terms. Assuming, as it appears, that this extension of credit is in Amphy's ordinary course of business, Amphy can pay its debt to MicroMax as an expense of administration without the prior approval of the bankruptcy court. Although the obligation to MicroMax takes priority over the claims of prepetition creditors, those creditors in theory benefit from the arrangement because the sale of the completed monitors generates revenues that enlarge the estate. Had MicroMax declined to ship, the monitors could have been neither built nor sold. In a broader sense, by permitting Amphy to continue operations, the extension of credit also enhances the value of the company as a going concern. Accordingly, treating the amount owed MicroMax as an administrative expense and paying it ahead of other priority and general unsecured claims makes sense.

But, some caveats are in order.

If all goes well, a creditor such as MicroMax will ship and Amphy will pay in due course. But what if Amphy doesn't pay? What if the creditors' committee or some other party in interest objects to administrative expense treatment for such a debt? What if a Chapter 11 trustee is appointed under Code § 1104 and the trustee objects? What if the case is converted to Chapter 7 and the liquidating trustee objects?

If any of these things happen, the burden will be on the one who extends credit to show that the transaction was in the ordinary course of business. The Bankruptcy Code does not define the term "ordinary course of business." However, as we saw in chapter 4, the same phrase appears in a parallel provision, Code § 363(c)(1), which authorizes a trustee or debtor to use, sell, or lease estate property in the ordinary course of business, without notice and a hearing. In applying Code § 364(a), courts have generally employed the same analysis that they use in the § 363 context, the vertical and horizontal tests. First, they consider whether a loan or credit transaction is one that creditors could reasonably have expected the particular debtor in question to enter into in the normal course of its business (the "vertical" test). If the debtor has a history of entering into transactions of the same type, that will support a finding that the transaction is in the ordinary course. Then courts consider whether the transaction is of a type commonly undertaken by companies involved in the debtor's business (the "horizontal test"). If similar debtors routinely enter into similar transactions, that, too, will support a finding that the transaction is in the ordinary course.

Even if the transaction *is* within the debtor's ordinary course of business, a lender who claims to be entitled to administrative expense priority under § 364(a) must also show that the debt qualifies as an actual and necessary expense of preserving the estate under Code § 503(b)(1)(A). Consider this hypothetical: Bank makes a loan to debtor-corporation and takes a mortgage on the debtor's real estate. The CEO of the debtor guarantees the debtor's obligations to Bank. Later, the debtor is forced to seek relief in Chapter 11. The CEO advances funds to the debtor to enable it to make payments to Bank. Is that extension of credit an actual and necessary expense of preserving the estate? In *In re Massetti*, 95 B.R. 360 (Bankr. E.D. Pa. 1989), the court held it was not:

Section 503(b)(1) represents congressional recognition that, in chapter 11, the best opportunity for a business to reorganize occurs when postpetition suppliers of goods and services do not demand immediate payment. Such suppliers are highly unlikely to extend credit to an entity in bankruptcy unless they are granted priority of payment over prepetition unsecured creditors. Generally speaking, then, an administrative claim arises from a transaction with the debtor-in-possession which is beneficial to the continued operation of the debtor's business. Since the allowance of priority claims reduces the amount of the estate available to prepetition creditors, what constitutes an administrative expense is narrowly construed. Courts have allowed administrative claims only to those suppliers who were "induced" by the debtor-in-possession to provide goods and services . . . .
[I]t is difficult to envision that one who guarantees a loan made to the debtor is later induced by the debtor-in-possession, as opposed to acting voluntarily in his own self-interest, to provide postpetition funds to repay that loan when the debtor-in-possession fails to do so.

95 B.R. at 363. If the principal had simply made good on its guarantee and paid Bank directly, would the principal have had a claim against the estate? If so, what priority would the claim have enjoyed? *See* Code § 502(e). Unfortunately, this scenario of a debtor's principal "fronting" money for the debtor in order to keep it alive is all too frequent, especially in the case of smaller troubled businesses. Making matters worse, these principals often do not seek the advice of counsel before they front the money or cover the debtor's expenses, in part because they do not want to be told not to, do not want to be told that it would be prudent to bring a noticed motion to obtain a court order, and do not want to incur what they consider to be "unnecessary attorneys' fees" in connection with such a motion. In addition, like most entrepreneurs, they have a sometimes unfounded optimism that allows them to ignore the downside risk facing the debtor and the need to secure protections for themselves in advance of needing them.

If a postpetition lender fails to bring itself within the umbrella of §§ 364(a) and 503(b)(1)(A), it may be relegated to the status of a prepetition creditor holding an unsecured claim. Worse yet, it might find that its debt is not even allowable at all. This result, counterintuitive and harsh as it may seem, is possible because, according to Code § 501(a), only a "creditor" may file a proof of claim. According to Code § 101(10), *creditor* means an "entity that has a claim against the debtor that arose at the time of or before the order for relief." The obligation to Micromax is not one that arose at the time of or before the order for relief. Nor is it the kind of obligation that is deemed to have arisen before the order for relief. Code § 501(d). That is why in borderline cases, the best approach for those contemplating a postpetition extension of credit is to seek a comfort order from the bankruptcy court under § 364(a) or proceed under § 364(b) and secure court approval as an out-of-the-ordinary-course credit transaction. It is also why, as the following case demonstrates, those who extend credit without court approval may have to seek it retroactively.

IN RE OCKERLUND CONSTRUCTION CO.
United States District Court for the Northern District of Illinois
308 B.R. 325 (2004)

JACQUELINE P. COX, UNITED STATES BANKRUPTCY JUDGE.

The Chapter 11 debtor Ockerlund Construction Company ("Ockerlund") filed this case on November 5, 2003, after MB Financial Bank unexpectedly set off the funds in one of its bank accounts to satisfy an overdue loan obligation. On November 17, 2003, but before these parties reached a settlement whereby the bank returned seized funds to the debtor's account, the debtor's president Craig Ockerlund provided certain "emergency advances" so that the Oakton Community School construction project could proceed smoothly and so that the post-petition premiums due on the employees' health and dental insurance could be paid. Chapter 11 debtor Ockerlund subsequently filed the instant "Debtor's Motion to Repay Administrative Advances to Debtor's Principal Officer" to obtain Court approval for repaying Craig Ockerlund the $58,764.74 he advanced on November 17, 2003. The motion further alleges that no opportunity for a "Priority Administrative Order" existed before Mr. Ockerlund made these advances but does not detail why a court order was impossible to obtain. At the hearing on March 10, 2004, one of the two bonding companies involved, Atlantic Mutual, and one other creditor, Midwesco Services, Inc., objected to this motion, while the bank MB Financial supported it. With Court approval, Atlantic Mutual began providing post-petition financing to Ockerlund after November 2003 and obtained the priority protections available under 11 U.S.C. § 364(c).

. . . .

The question raised in this dispute, though, is not whether the proceeds from Mr. Ockerlund's "advance" were used in the ordinary course of business or were spent to cover probable administrative expenses; rather, as Midwesco correctly points out, the question is whether this advance qualifies as a valid post-petition extension of credit to the debtor in accordance with 11 U.S.C. § 364(a)–(b). *See In re Lite Coal Min. Co.*, 122 B.R. 692, 695–96 (Bankr. N.D. W. Va. 1990); *In re Massetti*, 95 B.R. 360, 363 (Bankr. E.D. Pa. 1989). This provision states as follows:

> (a) If the trustee is authorized to operate the business of the debtor under section 721, 1108, 1203, 1204, or 1304 of this title, unless the court orders otherwise, the trustee may obtain unsecured credit and incur unsecured debt in the ordinary course of business allowable under section 503(b)(1) of this title as an administrative expense.

> (b) The court, after notice and a hearing, may authorize the trustee to obtain unsecured credit or to incur unsecured debt other than under subsection (a) of this section, allowable under section 503(b)(1) of this title as an administrative expense.

11 U.S.C. § 364(a)–(b). If the $58,764.74 advance qualifies as a lawful extension of credit under § 364, the repayment thereof would receive administrative-expense priority in the bankruptcy case under § 503(b) and § 507(a). If the advance does not

qualify as such, legal authorities are split on the lender's eligibility for repayment from the bankruptcy estate, as discussed *infra*.

The first problem with approving this "advance" as a post-petition extension of credit is that it has only been asserted to be a post-petition extension of credit after the fact. No promissory note evidencing the debtor's intent to repay the sum is before the Court, as in other cases interpreting § 364, *see, e.g., In re Lodge America*, 259 B.R. 728, 731, 734 (D. Kan. 2001). Assuming, though, that the debtor construction company had an otherwise enforceable oral contract to borrow and repay money from its president without a negotiable instrument, the other dilemma presented by the motion is whether the debtor could have obtained the unsecured loan from its president without court approval after notice and hearing under § 364(a), or whether court approval after notice and hearing was required under § 364(b). The difference in this case will turn on whether the credit was obtained in the ordinary course of business, not on whether the credit funds were used or needed for § 503(b) administrative expenses, because the debtor did not secure prior court approval for the $58,764.74 advance. The so-called "emergency" need for funds to pay operating expenses nearly two weeks after the debtor filed this Chapter 11 case does not definitively answer the question of whether the $58,764.74 advance was an ordinary-course-of-business extension of credit. If anything, a true emergency would seem to indicate that a resort to out-of-the-ordinary-course means was necessary.

To prove that an unsecured post-petition loan was obtained in the ordinary course of the debtor's business, the debtor must pass the "vertical" dimensions test.[1] Under this test, the Court examines the reasonable expectations of creditors

---

[1] Other courts have additionally required the debtor to satisfy the "horizontal dimensions test" under which the debtor must show that the terms and circumstances of the extension of credit were consistent with the practices of the debtor's industry. *See In re Dant & Russell*, 853 F.2d 700, 704–05 (9th Cir. 1988); *In re Poff Constr.*, 141 B.R. 104, 106–07 (W. D. Va. 1991); *In re Lodge America*, 259 B.R. 728, 732 (D. Kan. 2001).

Judge Coar in *Martino v. First Nat'l Bank (In re Garofalo's Finer Foods)*, 186 B.R. 414, 428–30 (N. D. Ill. 1995), convincingly rejected this additional test as a matter of statutory construction. See also *In re Lodge America*, 239 B.R. 580, 583 (Bankr. D. Kan. 1999), *affirmed*, 259 B.R. 728 (D. Kan. 2001). *But cf. In re Husting Land & Development*, 255 B.R. 772, 779 (Bankr. D. Utah 2000), *affirmed*, 274 B.R. 906 (D. Utah 2002). To summarize, the ordinary-course-of-business defense to a preference action under § 547(c)(2) contains two so-called "subjective" elements requiring the creditor to show that (1) the antecedent credit extension at issue and (2) the debtor's preferential payment thereon both occurred in the ordinary course of business transactions that had developed between the debtor and the particular creditor-defendant at issue. *See id.* at 428. A third "objective" element requires the creditor to show that the payment terms under which the debtor made the preferential payment were consistent with industry-wide billing and payment practices. 11 U.S.C. § 547(c)(2)(C); *In re Tolona Pizza Products Corp.*, 3 F.3d 1029, 1031 (7th Cir. 1993).

By contrast, when a debtor-in-possession obtains unsecured post-petition credit without court approval under § 364(a), it does not need to establish the last two elements (including § 547(c)(2)(C)); rather, the statute only requires it to show that the debt has been incurred in a typical fashion when compared to the debtor-in-possession's own historical practice. *See Matter of Garofalo's Finer Foods*, 186 B.R. 414, 429 (N. D. Ill. 1995). In other words, only the overlapping language of § 364(a) and § 547(c)(2) requires a consistent interpretation, while the omission of language in § 364(a) that is present in § 547(c)(2) implies that Congress did not intend for bankruptcy courts to look at the business practices of other similar operations in the case at bar. Indeed, such a requirement creates a great hassle that is likely to produce redundant information. *See id.*

in light of their past relationship with the debtor and its incurrence of debt, including the amount, terms, frequency, sources, and timing of pre-petition extensions of credit from various sources. *See In re Poff Constr.*, 141 B.R. 104, 106 (W. D. Va. 1991); *In re Lodge America*, 259 B.R. 728, 732 (D. Kan. 2001); *Matter of Garofalo's Finer Foods*, 186 B.R. 414, 425–27 (N. D. Ill. 1995). "This showing is required merely to assure that neither the debtor nor the creditor did anything abnormal to gain an advantage over other creditors," *In re Lodge America*, 259 B.R. 728, 732 (D. Kan. 2001), and to ensure that creditors are not being subjected to different economic risks than those for which they bargained at the inception of the debtor-creditor relationship, *see Martino v. First Nat'l Bank (In re Garofalo's Finer Foods)*, 186 B.R. 414, 424–26 (N. D. Ill. 1995). In *Garofalo's*, for instance, the district court partially reversed the bankruptcy court's finding that all of the bank's post-petition extensions of overdraft credit were outside the ordinary course of business, remanding the case for the bankruptcy court to decide at what point in time the overdraft credits ceased being similar enough in both frequency and amount to the relevant pre-petition course of conduct to qualify for priority protection under § 364(a). *See id.* at 426–27.

The present motion, assuming all statements contained therein are true, does not satisfy the "vertical" dimension standard. It contains an argument concerning why the debtor needed an emergency advance of funds two weeks after it filed this case, but it does not argue that the debtor incurred the post-petition debt in the ordinary course of business, and, indeed, no evidentiary record exists to support this conclusion. *Cf. In re Lodge America*, 259 B.R. 728, 733 (D. Kan. 2001) (no evidence debtor had ever before obtained short-term financing to pay utility bills); *In re Lodge America*, 239 B.R. 580, 583–84 (Bankr. D. Kan. 1999), *affirmed*, 259 B.R. 728 (D. Kan. 2001).

If a debtor fails to establish that post-petition financing occurred in the ordinary course of business under § 364(a), some courts find that retroactive approval (a "nunc pro tunc" order) under § 364(b) and § 105(a) is possible but should be reserved for truly extraordinary and unusual circumstances, *cf. In re Massetti*, 95 B.R. 360, 364 (Bankr. E.D. Pa. 1989); *In re Lehigh Valley Professional Sports Clubs*, 260 B.R. 745, 750-51 & n. 13 (Bankr. E.D. Pa. 2001); *In re Blessing Industries*, 263 B.R. 268, 274 (Bankr. N.D. Iowa 2001),[2] although other courts go so far as to say

---

[2] The Blessing Industries court's commentary is instructive in the case at bar:

Despite the finding that no creditors were actually harmed by the unauthorized financing, Bolger has failed to demonstrate that extraordinary circumstances existed which prevented it from following the explicit mandates of the Bankruptcy Code.

Bolger claims that the funds were needed immediately and that it did not have time to seek court approval. However, the Court finds that this argument is not persuasive. Ten days passed from the initial discussions of the possible cash infusion until the funds were actually expended. The Bankruptcy Code provides for an expedited hearing in cases of emergency, and often a hearing can be scheduled as early as the next day. *See* Fed. R. Bankr. P. 4001(c).

Serious questions of due process exist in circumstances such as this. "Due process requires that interested parties have meaningful notice with adequate opportunity to object." *In re Commercial Millwright Service Corp.*, 1995 Bankr. LEXIS 2180, Bankr. No. 95-60007KW, slip op. at 2 (Bankr. N.D. Iowa Sept. 15, 1995). When parties attempt to keep a company afloat while disregarding procedural safeguards, the underlying purposes of the Code is frustrated.

that the case law under the 1898 Bankruptcy Act countenancing retroactive approval on equitable grounds has been eviscerated under the current Bankruptcy Code, *see In re Lodge America*, 259 B.R. 728, 734–35 (D. Kan. 2001); *Bezanson v. Indian Head National Bank (In re J.L. Graphics)*, 62 B.R. 750, 755 (Bankr. D.N.H. 1986), *aff'd, In re Cross Baking Co.*, 818 F.2d 1027 (1st Cir. 1987). The latter view is more in tune with controlling authority for this district. The Bankruptcy Court's equitable powers under 11 U.S.C. § 105(a) do not override specific Bankruptcy Code provisions; they supplement those provisions and fill in gaps and ambiguities, as the Seventh Circuit most recently noted in *In re Kmart Corp.*, 359 F.3d 866 (7th Cir. 2004) . . . . As to gaps and ambiguities in § 364 itself, the scheme Congress envisioned as a whole covers all post-petition financing situations (i.e., those in and out of the ordinary course of business) and would be incapacitated by retroactive approval of the ones demanding prior approval and notice to creditors; notice after a debtor has already taken action is generally not meaningful . . . . Bankruptcy Rule 4001(c) gives structure to this prior-notice requirement, contemplating prior court approval only after sending a required 15-day notice to the committee of unsecured creditors or to the 20 largest non-insider unsecured creditors. Interim approval on more limited notice under Bankruptcy Rule 4001(c)(2) is permitted pending a final hearing complying with this rule, but even this option requires prior court approval after the debtor either sends at least a two-day notice to parties in interest or presents a same-day affidavit showing cause for an emergency *ex parte* hearing. *See* Local Bankruptcy Rules 5096-1, 9013-3 to -4.

A final lingering question is whether the $58,764.74 advance, having not qualified for administrative-claim priority under § 364, is still eligible for treatment as a general unsecured claim or is not eligible for any distribution at all. Courts have come to different conclusions on this issue. Compare *In re Lodge America*, 239 B.R. 580, 585 (Bankr. D. Kan. 1999), *affirmed*, 259 B.R. 728 (D. Kan. 2001); *Martino v. First Nat'l Bank (In re Garofalo's Finer Foods)*, 186 B.R. 414, 423, 435 (N. D. Ill. 1995); *In re Massetti*, 95 B.R. 360, 366 n. 9 (Bankr. E.D. Pa. 1989); *In re Smith*, 72 B.R. 344, 351 (Bankr. S.D. Ohio 1987) (granting equitable lien in place of a valid § 364(c) lien), *affirmed*, 119 B.R. 558 (S. D. Ohio 1989); *In re John Deskins Pic Pac*, 59 B.R. 809, 812 (Bankr. W.D. Va. 1986) with *Matter of Alafia Land Development Corp.*, 40 B.R. 1, 5 (Bankr. M.D. Fla. 1984). None of these decisions contains a substantial discussion of the Bankruptcy Code's actual language concerning what constitutes a general unsecured claim. Most of them instead cite Collier on Bankruptcy, *see* 3 Lawrence P. King et al., *Collier on Bankruptcy* ¶ 364.03[2], at 364-8 (15th ed. rev. 2003), to support awarding the post-petition lender general-unsecured-claim status. Collier on Bankruptcy in actuality concedes the issue might be resolved both ways but declines to discuss the problem in detail, *see id.*, as no published decision apparently has done so.

This Court concludes that the *Alafia Land Development* case has the view that is more consistent with the statute. The definition of "claim" under the Bankruptcy Code is, to be sure, broad enough to encompass an unauthorized post-petition loan such as the one at issue. *See* 11 U.S.C. § 101(5). Nevertheless, the definition of who

---

At minimum, due process requires that other interested parties have notice of the transaction. *In re Blessing Industries*, 263 B.R. 268, 274 (Bankr. N.D. Iowa 2001).

is a "creditor" usually requires a right to payment from (or a "claim against") the debtor on or before the order for relief (the petition date in a voluntary case), *see* § 101(10), and only a "creditor" is entitled to file a "proof of claim" in a bankruptcy case, *see* § 501. Further, proofs of claims are "determined" and "allowed" in an "amount . . . as of the date of the filing of the petition," § 502(b), unless an explicit exception applies, *see* § 502(f)–(i).³ Thus, a holder of a post-petition "claim" that is not entitled to administrative-expense priority cannot be a creditor, cannot file a proof of claim, and, even if he could file one, cannot by definition have an "allowed" claim as of the petition date.

These basic limitations have ramifications in Chapter 11 cases. A holder of a post-petition "claim" that is not entitled to administrative-expense priority will not have class voting rights on account of an "allowed" general unsecured claim, *see* § 1123(a)(1), § 1126(a), (c), § 1129(a)(8), (10), and will also not be able to demand the following plan distributions from the bankruptcy estate by posing an objection to confirmation:

- a distribution equal to the present value of what it would have received for an "allowed unsecured claim" in a Chapter 7 liquidation case, *see* § 1129(a)(7)(A), § 726(a)(2), § 501,

- a cash distribution equal to what would have been an "allowed administrative expense" had it complied with § 364(b), *see* § 1129(a)(9)(A), § 503(b)(1), § 507(a)(1), and

- a distribution equal to the present value of the full "allowed amount of such claim," unless all junior claims and interests receive nothing in a cramdown scenario (the absolute-priority rule), *see* § 1129(b)(2)(B), § 502(b).

Ockerlund Construction Company could technically propose a Chapter 11 plan with a separate class of "claims" for unsecured post-petition debts that fail to qualify for administrative-expense priority, leaving this class "unimpaired" by providing for full and timely repayment of principal and interest. (A plan proponent can apparently create "unimpaired" classes of "claims" without regard for the claimant's qualification as a "creditor" or as an "allowed" claimant.⁴ *See* 11 U.S.C. § 1122(a), § 1123(a)(2), § 1124.) If such a plan proceeded to a cramdown confirmation hearing, though, a general unsecured creditor belonging to a class that receives less than full payment would have a sustainable objection due to the unfair discrimination in favor of an insider claim that otherwise holds equal priority under nonbankruptcy law. *See* 11 U.S.C. § 1129(b)(1); *In re Woodbrook Associates*, 19 F.3d 312, 321 (7th Cir. 1994); *In re Aztec Co.* 107 B.R. 585, 588–91 (Bankr. M.D. Tenn. 1989); 7 Lawrence P. King et al., *Collier On Bankruptcy* ¶ 1129.04[3][b][ii]–[v], [ix],

---

³ Technically speaking, a claim that has been filed is deemed "allowed" under § 502(a) until an interested party objects and the bankruptcy court sustains this objection under § 502(b). We have not yet reached a point at which the company president Mr. Ockerlund has filed a proof of claim subject to a creditor's objection. Nevertheless, if such a proof of claim were filed in this case, the Court assumes that Atlantic Mutual and Midwesco Services would lodge objections that are similar to their present objections to the allowance of Mr. Ockerlund's post-petition financing as an administrative expense.

⁴ These "unimpaired" classes do not vote for or against a plan because the law conclusively presumes that they accept it. 11 U.S.C. § 1126(f), § 1129(a)(8).

at 1129-74 to 1129-79 (15th ed. rev. 2003).[5] Other scenarios could evolve permitting some type of dividend for a post-petition general unsecured "claim" along with pre-petition general unsecured claimants, such as when all impaired classes "accept" a Chapter 11 plan and no individual creditor presents a valid objection to confirmation. 11 U.S.C. § 1126(c)–(d), § 1128(b), § 1129(a) (criteria for confirmation when every class of claims and interests has either accepted the plan or is unimpaired). Until that scenario presents itself, though, the Court has no apparent authority in light of the language and structure of the Bankruptcy Code to create some type of post-petition general unsecured claim for loans that fail to qualify for priority under § 503(b) and § 507(a)(1).

In the final scheme of things, the Court's conclusion on this last issue will not be as harsh as it first appears if this Chapter 11 case is administratively insolvent, leaving general unsecured claimants without a dividend anyway.

Conclusion

For the foregoing reasons, the objections of Atlantic Mutual and Midwesco Services are sustained, and the "Debtor's Motion to Repay Administrative Advances to Debtor's Principal Officer" is denied.

NOTES AND QUESTIONS

(1)   Although the focus of the analysis under Code § 364(a) is supposed to be on the nature of the credit transaction itself and not on how loan proceeds were spent, the reality is that in some cases, those elements are hard to separate, or, to put it another way, a transaction may fall outside the scope of ordinary for more than one reason. Thus, for example, in *In re C.E.N., Inc.*, 86 B.R. 303 (Bankr. D. Me. 1988), the debtor's president and sole shareholder made loans to enable the debtor to pay salaries and other operating expenses including utilities and insurance premiums. Those were routine expenses, and the court suggested that had they been incurred for the purpose of keeping the business going while it attempted to reorganize the loans might have qualified as ordinary course as well. However, the debtor was not seeking to reorganize but to liquidate. The court found that as liquidation was not in the debtor's ordinary course of business, expenses incurred in the process of liquidating were not in the ordinary course either.

(2)   As the *Ockerlund* court acknowledged, some courts will grant nunc pro tunc approval of non-ordinary course lending transactions. In *In re Lite Coal*, 122 B.R. 692 (Bankr. N.D. W. Va. 1990), the court held that nunc pro tunc approval is appropriate only if: (1) the court concludes that it would have approved the loan under § 364(b) if timely application had been made; (2) no creditor was injured by the continuation of the business made possible by the loan; and (3) the debtor and lender honestly believed they had the authority to enter into the transaction.

---

[5] "[A] plan proponent may pay classes of claims different amounts if there is a nonbankruptcy rationale for doing so, and if the discrimination is tailored to the nonbankruptcy rationale. . . . Unfair discrimination works . . . among claimants of equal nonbankruptcy priority." 7 Lawrence P. King et al., *Collier On Bankruptcy* ¶ 1129.04[3][b][v], [ix], at 1129-76, 1129-79 (15th ed. rev. 2003).

(3) In order for an obligation to receive administrative expense treatment under § 364(a) or (b), the obligation must qualify as an actual and necessary expense of preserving the estate as required by Code § 503(b)(1)(A). The *Ockerlund* court did not reach this issue because the transaction failed the ordinary course of business test and the court declined to consider granting nunc pro tunc approval. Some extensions of credit will not qualify for priority treatment because they actually work a disservice to the estate and creditors by prolonging the life of a moribund debtor while expenses accumulate and asset values erode. That does not mean that in order to qualify for priority treatment, an extension of credit must have enabled a debtor to reorganize. If the transaction enabled the debtor to continue to operate while it engaged in a good faith attempt to reorganize or conduct an orderly liquidation, that should be sufficient. Thus, for example, in *White Front Feed & Seed v. State Nat'l Bank of Platteville (In re Ramaker)*, 117 B.R. 959 (Bankr. N.D. Iowa 1990), the court held that a supplier that shipped grain, feed, and fertilizer to the debtor-farmer on credit was entitled to administrative priority even though the case subsequently was converted to Chapter 7.

§ 5.03 CREDIT WITH SUPERPRIORITY OR SECURED STATUS — CODE § 364(c), (d)

[A] Introduction

An administrative priority is nice, but it is no guarantee that a lender will be repaid. One reason is that, as the *Ockerland* case demonstrates, the debtor may turn out to be "administratively insolvent." This condition exists when assets are insufficient to cover even administrative expenses, let alone general unsecured claims. Liquidation is the usual result. The problem arises with enough frequency that, as we saw in chapter 3, the drafters of the Code took pains in Code § 361(3) to provide that a promise of administrative expense treatment to compensate a secured creditor for a decline in collateral value is *per se* not adequate protection. An administrative priority may also prove illusory if the debtor's assets are encumbered by liens because priorities only benefit creditors if there is unencumbered value to divide between them. If all of a debtor's assets are fully "liened up" (i.e., serving as collateral for debts in excess of their value), the debtor is administratively insolvent, and no amount of priority is going to help a creditor, absent avoidance of the liens as preferences, fraudulent conveyances, or the like, or as a surcharge of the collateral under Code § 506(c).

The kind of administrative priority available under Code § 364(a) and (b) may prove to be insufficient for other reasons as well. For example:

- Assume that a postpetition lender extends credit to Amphy pursuant to § 364(a) or (b) in the belief that the debtor has sufficient cash flow and other assets to cover the loan. Assume that the bank that holds a mortgage on Amphy's warehouse moves for relief from the stay. The court refuses to grant relief from the stay on the grounds that the bank is adequately protected by an equity cushion. Suppose that Amphy is later forced to sell the warehouse, and the warehouse turns out to be worth less than previously expected. To the extent that the bank's adequate protection turned out to be inadequate, it will have a superpriority claim under Code § 507(b). These "inadequate protection" claims take priority over administrative expenses.

- Assume that a postpetition lender extends credit to Amphy in the belief that Amphy's cash flow and other assets are sufficient to cover the loan. Amphy's attempt to rehabilitate fails and the case is converted to Chapter 7. The administrative expenses of the superceding Chapter 7 case will take priority over the administrative expenses of the superceded Chapter 11 case. Code § 727(b).

The Code's drafters anticipated that unattractive possibilities such as these might make lenders reluctant to extend credit on the terms described in §§ 364(a) and (b), and so they wrote § 364(c). That subsection provides that if a trustee or debtor is unable to arrange necessary financing on administrative expense terms, the court may, after notice and a hearing, authorize extension of credit on the following more onerous terms:

(1)   with priority over any or all administrative expenses;

(2)   secured by a lien on property of the estate that is not already subject to a lien; or

(3)   secured by a junior lien on property of the estate that is subject to a pre-existing lien.

[B]   Superpriorities and Non-Priming Liens — Code § 364(c)

The priority authorized by § 364(c)(1) is not the same as the administrative priority referred to in §§ 364(a)–(b) and 503(b). Indeed, the § 364(c)(1) priority is usually referred to as a "superpriority," because it takes precedence over other administrative expenses. It may also "prime" priority claims that arise when adequate protection turns out to be inadequate. *See* § 507(b).

The three options described in § 364(c) are not exclusive and may be employed separately or in combination. For example, in the *Ames* case that follows, the court authorized the debtor to borrow $250 million on an unsecured, superpriority basis. In the *Simasko* case, which is discussed in the *Ames* opinion, the lenders were granted superpriority claims secured by a lien on the debtor's assets. Securing the superpriority debt does not mean that the DIP lender's lien "primes" or has higher priority than already-existing liens on the property. Remember that there are two kinds of priority at issue in bankruptcy cases: (1) priority of secured creditors' liens in terms of entitlement to the value of particular pieces of collateral and (2) priority of entitlement to distribution of proceeds of unencumbered assets. The priorities and superpriorities we are discussing here fall in the second category. Remember, secured claims do not fall on the priority ladder; although unsecured deficiency claims (the balance due to a secured creditor after exhausting the value of the collateral) do.

To provide that a secured claim will also enjoy administrative superpriority may seem like a "belt *and* suspenders" approach, but it is not as redundant as it appears. Consider this hypothetical: a postpetition lender is induced to extend credit by the grant of a security interest in the debtor's inventory. If the case fails and the value of the inventory turns out to be less than the amount of the outstanding indebtedness, the lender will hold, to the extent of the deficiency, a plain vanilla administrative expense at best. But, if the lender is given *superpriority* secured status, the deficiency claim will take priority over those plain vanilla administrative expenses and any § 507(b) "inadequate protection" claims, as well as general unsecured claims.

Prudent lender's counsel, knowing that the protections of § 364(a), (b), and (c) are available, will seek to obtain the protections of these subsections, and most debtors in possession are willing to grant them rather than not obtain the credit they desire. This leaves the job of whittling down the protections to those that are absolutely necessary for the extension of credit to objecting creditors, the creditors' committee, or the court.

Finally, § 364(d) provides that if credit is not available on any other terms, the court may authorize the incurring of indebtedness "secured by a senior or equal lien on property of the estate that is [already] subject to a lien." In other words, the court may subordinate, or "prime," an existing lien if that is the price of financing the debtor and if the interest of the subordinated lienholder can be adequately protected. Less drastic is the granting of an "equal" — also known as "pari passu" — lien on the collateral at issue.

The operation of §§ 364(c) and (d) are considered in the materials that follow.

PROBLEM 5.2

Carol Charisma has approached Joshua Colman, a workout officer at BigBank, to discuss an extension of credit. Amphy, of course, is no stranger to BigBank. A few years ago, BigBank made a $2.1 million loan to Amphydynamics and took a security interest in the company's inventory and receivables. On the date Amphy filed its Chapter 11 petition, it owed BigBank $2 million in principal and accrued interest. On that date, Amphy's inventory and receivables, even valued on a going concern basis, were believed to be worth only a fraction of the amount of the outstanding debt. The company's liquidation value appeared to be even less. BigBank's credit analysts have done enough research to know that if Amphy is unable to obtain postpetition financing, liquidation will probably result and BigBank will recover at best a few cents on the dollar. BigBank is less than excited about extending new financing to Amphy, but, on the other hand, it might be worth its while to do so if it can enhance the recovery on its prepetition claim, minimize the risks of doing business with Amphy, and make an appropriate profit on the new loan. Josh's conversations with members of the creditors' committee and other knowledgeable sources lead him to believe that if BigBank does establish a credit facility for Amphy, suppliers will be encouraged to resume shipping on normal credit terms and Amphy will generate sufficient cash flow to service the loan. In addition, BigBank is concerned that if *it* does not extend postpetition credit to Amphy, some other lender will, creating indebtedness that ranks ahead of BigBank's prepetition claim. In fact, to minimize that threat, Josh has mentioned in passing to several members of the creditors' committee that if Amphy attempts to induce any competitor of BigBank to lend, BigBank will vigorously oppose the arrangement. The announcement has had the desired effect. BigBank's competitors are not interested in the expense and bother of lending their way into litigation — or more precisely litigating their way into lending — and Carol is having trouble identifying other willing lenders.

BigBank has indicated that it is willing to provide debtor in possession working capital financing in the form of a new revolving credit facility in an amount not to exceed $8 million. According to a memo drafted by Colman, the loan is to be made on the following terms and conditions, among others:

Amount. The outstanding principal amount loaned to Amphy is not to exceed 85% of Amphy's accounts receivable and 60% of inventory.

Security. The loan will be secured by a senior and exclusive lien on all of Amphy's inventory, accounts receivable, and all other unencumbered assets. In addition, the loan will be secured by a junior lien on all encumbered assets.

Priority. The loan will have superpriority status pursuant to Code § 364(c).

Interest and Maturity. The loan will bear interest at the prime rate plus 5%, payable monthly. The loan will mature 15 months from the date the bankruptcy court enters an order approving the financing arrangement.

Other Fees. A facility fee of $400,000 will be paid to BigBank upon entry of the court order approving the financing arrangement. Also, as a substitute for an origination fee, Amphy will apply $1 million of the new loan proceeds to paying off BigBank's prepetition claim. A commitment fee of .50% per annum on the average daily unused portion of the facility will be paid monthly in addition to interest.

Covenants. Amphy agrees not to sell its assets (other than inventory in the normal course of business), except pursuant to a court order that provides that the proceeds will be used to pay this loan. Amphy agrees not to incur any indebtedness senior to or pari passu with BigBank's unless BigBank consents. Amphy agrees not to make any capital improvement, incur any expense in excess of $100,000 (other than for the purchase of inventory and raw materials), or increase the compensation of any senior executive without the prior approval of BigBank.

Default. In the event of a default, the entire balance comes due. In addition to the failure to make timely payments or comply with the covenants discussed above, events of default include the appointment of a trustee, conversion of the case to Chapter 7, and dismissal of the case. Amphy agrees that, in the event of a default, it will consent to relief from the automatic stay to enable BigBank to enforce its claim and security interest.

Release. Amphy waives any objections and defenses it may have to BigBank's prepetition claim and releases BigBank from any and all liability related to the prepetition loan, including causes of action based on fraudulent transfer, preference, and lender liability theories.

Assume that you are the attorney representing the creditors' committee. In your discussions with the committee, you will be asked whether there are any viable grounds for objecting to the proposed financing agreement. Before you respond, read on.

IN RE AMES DEPARTMENT STORES, INC.
United States Bankruptcy Court for the Southern District of New York
115 B.R. 34 (1990)

HONORABLE HOWARD C. BUSCHMAN, III, UNITED STATES BANKRUPTCY JUDGE.

The instant motion by the debtors Ames Department Stores, Inc. ("Ames"), Eastern Retailers et al. and their fifty-one affiliated debtors (collectively "Debtors") for an order approving a $250 million post-petition financing agreement brings to the fore an examination of the considerations and circumstances under which such approval may be granted pursuant to 11 U.S.C. § 364(c) of the Bankruptcy Code.

. . . .

I

The Debtors are affiliated companies that own and operate nearly 700 department stores located in the Eastern and Middle Western United States and employing some 55,000 employees. They filed their petitions for reorganization under Chapter 11 of the Code on April 25, 1990.

In the three to four weeks prior to the filing of their petitions, the Debtors had discussions with and sought agreements for post-petition financing from four leading lending institutions. Two of these institutions could not, in Ames' judgment, meet the Debtors' timetables for providing funds. The Debtors entered into negotiations with Citibank N.A. and Chemical Bank. Ultimately, after numerous meetings and telephone conversations, the Citibank group offered $40 million of new financing on a secured and super-priority basis; that is, repayment of the loan would be secured by all of the assets of all of the debtors junior only to prior security interests and the obligation to repay be accorded a super-priority superior to all administrative expenses incurred and allowed in these cases. The financing would be subject to Ames not having cash losses exceeding $50 million. Further, interest would be paid on Citibank group's pre-petition loan of roughly $460 million and payment of that loan would be cross-collateralized and thus secured by the Debtors' post-petition assets except inventory.*

In addition, the Citibank group sought to recycle and elevate the pre-petition debt by providing for its payment from Ames' business and reloaned through a revolving credit facility as "new" money subject to a determination of their secured status.**

---

* [The issues raised by the financing technique known as "cross-collateralization" are discussed in more detail in Section 5.03[C], *below*. — Eds.]

** [In other words, under the financing arrangement proposed by Citibank, as Ames made payments on Citibank's prepetition claim, new funds would be made available to Ames via the Citibank postpetition revolving credit facility. As Ames borrowed new funds from the revolving credit facility and paid down

Chemical offered to provide $250 million in financing on an unsecured but super-priority basis. Further negotiations led to a definitive agreement accepted by the Debtors. The salient features of the financing agreement with Chemical are that Chemical and participating lenders would extend, on a super-priority basis, up to $250 million of cash and letter of credit financing until confirmation of a plan of reorganization or April 30, 1991, whichever is earlier. The amount of the loan within the $250 million cap is limited by a borrowing base equal to 30% of the book value of the Debtors' inventory substantially similar in salability and mix to that of recent operations. The Debtors would be jointly and generally liable for the full amount. Among the terms of default is the conversion of these cases to Chapter 7. Financial information is to be supplied to Chemical on a quarterly basis. The Debtors and Chemical are to negotiate, within the next 60 days, the question of whether the borrowing base can be increased to 40% of the retail value of inventory or 50% of the book value of inventory. The Debtors currently value their inventory at $1 billion to $1.1 billion — on a cost basis. Under the current 30% formula, it may be able to draw upon the entire commitment of $250 million.

By order to show cause dated April 27, 1990 and entered pursuant to Rule 4001(c) of the Bankruptcy Rules, this Court scheduled interim and final hearings with respect to the Debtors' motion for emergency relief and final approval of their agreement with Chemical. At the interim hearing, held on May 1, 1990, the Debtors sought $52 million of emergency financing. The Court, after several hours of testimony, authorized $25 million as the amount "necessary to avoid immediate and irreparable harm to the estate." Rule 4001(c)(2).[2] It was held that the standard was met with respect only to those amounts that were not for the purchase of inventory for some 74 stores that the Debtors had previously announced they would close . . . and not for those amounts covering . . . certain unidentified miscellaneous expenses or for continued construction of a new distribution center. To enable the Debtors to further identify miscellaneous expenses and to firm up their position regarding the 74 stores, a second interim hearing was scheduled for May 8, 1990. The Debtors, however, determined not to seek further emergency relief pending the final hearing.

The Debtors' need for financing is not disputed at the final hearing. During the month prior to filing their bankruptcy petitions, the Debtors lost trade credit that enabled the purchase of inventory for the stores. Since filing the petitions, they have enjoyed virtually no trade credit, a letter of credit bank has started to find discrepancies in documentation, and the Debtors have received few goods. Sales that aggregated $4.8 billion for the fiscal year ending January 1990 have fallen off by over 30% for the four week period ending May 12, 1990. Available cash now

---

the prepetition claim, Citibank's debt would be "recycled" from old into new debt and "elevated" from prepetition unsecured status to postpetition priority status. — Eds.]

[2] Rule 4001(c)(2) provides: "The Court may commence a final hearing on a motion for authority to obtain credit no earlier than 15 days after service of the motion. If the motion so requests, the Court may conduct a hearing before such 15-day period expires, but the Court may authorize the obtaining of credit only to the extent necessary to avoid immediate and irreparable harm to the estate pending a final hearing."

At the interim hearing, the Court held that the immediate and irreparable harm standard of Rule 4001(c)(2), insofar as applied to a business that hopes to reorganize as a going concern, is satisfied by the threatened loss of the business. . . .

exceeds $120 million principally because the Debtors continue to sell inventory without replacement.

Management forecasts that $150 million of the Chemical financing will be required. They seek authorization for $250 million of credit on the basis of their judgment that the additional availability will encourage suppliers gradually to extend credit. Their cash projections assume, *inter alia*, ability to attract 15-day trade credit for the next few months and 30-day trade credit thereafter. Trade credit is crucial. Because the Debtors logistically are unable to do business on a C.O.D. basis or provide letter of credit for domestic suppliers, the Creditors' Committee is not at all certain that trade credit will be forthcoming and suggest that inventory liens be offered to post-petition suppliers. To this the Debtors respond that they have discussions with some suppliers who have indicated that the current uncertainty lies in the need for approval of the Chemical financing. The Creditors' Committee does not oppose approval of the financing agreement with Chemical in its final form.

II

It is given that most successful reorganizations require the debtor-in-possession to obtain new financing simultaneously with or soon after the commencement of the Chapter 11 case. Section 364 establishes a series of possible post-petition transactions in which a debtor might obtain credit:

(i) unsecured credit with an administrative expense status, section 364(a) and (b);

(ii) unsecured credit with a priority over all administrative expenses (i.e. a super-priority), section 364(c)(1);

(iii) credit, or other indebtedness, secured by a lien on unencumbered property or with a junior lien on encumbered property, sections 364(c)(2) and (c)(3); and

(iv) credit, or other indebtedness, secured by a senior or equal lien on property of the estate that is already subject to a lien, if adequate protection is furnished to the holder of the lien, section 364(d).

For all of these different transactions, except the obtaining of unsecured credit in the ordinary course of business under section 364(a), court authorization after notice and an opportunity for a hearing is required.

In determining whether to approve such a transaction, the Court acts in its informed discretion. Section 364(c) and (d) both state that the court "*may* authorize . . . . (emphasis added). A court, however, may not approve any credit transaction under subsection (c) unless the debtor demonstrates that it has reasonably attempted, but failed, to obtain unsecured credit under sections 364(a) or (b). 11 U.S.C. 364(c) . . . [W]hile the trustee must make an effort to find alternative credit sources before section 364(d) becomes available, section 364 imposes no duty upon the trustee to seek credit from every possible lender . . . . Similarly, obtaining credit under section 364(d) may not be authorized if it appears that credit can be obtained under the other subsections of 364.

Once unavailability of less intrusive credit has been shown and adequate protection found if required, the bankruptcy courts, in applying discretion under section 364(b), (c), and (d) have recognized that their discretion is not unbridled. Acknowledging that Congress, in Chapter 11, delicately balanced the hope of debtors to reorganize and the expectations of creditors for payment, the courts have focused their attention on proposed terms that would tilt the conduct of the bankruptcy case; prejudice, at an early stage, the powers and rights that the Bankruptcy Code confers for the benefit of all creditors; or leverage the Chapter 11 process by preventing motions by parties-in-interest from being decided on their merits. *In re Tenney Village Co.*, 104 Bankr. 562, 567–70 (Bankr. D.N.H. 1989). They recognize that debtors-in-possession generally enjoy little negotiating power with a proposed lender, particularly where the lender has a pre-petition lien on cash collateral. At the same time, however, they permit debtors-in-possession to exercise their basic business judgment consistent with their fiduciary duties . . . .

From these two notions, it might appear that the cases are conflicted. The differences are, however, largely semantic. In *Tenney Village*, [the court found that the financing arrangement] violated the debtor's fiduciary duties to the estate and its creditors in that the "Financing Arrangement would pervert the reorganizational process from one designed to accommodate all classes of creditors and equity interests to one specially crafted for the benefit of the Bank and the Debtor's principals who guaranteed its debt." 104 Bankr. at 568. The bank was to effectively operate the debtor's business; its pre-petition liens would be immunized from attack by not only the debtor but by a creditors' committee even prior to the appointment of counsel; preference, fraudulent conveyance, lender liability and subordination claims of the estate would be waived; debtor's counsel would not be entitled to payment for any work in a dispute with the bank. Thus, the arrangement would skew the conduct of the bankruptcy case, destroy the adversary process that contemplates representation by counsel and deprive the estate of possible rights and powers before the creditors' committee counsel would have a reasonable time to examine whether the estate had viable claims.

No court of which we are aware has approved financing arrangements with such features. Indeed, it has been the uniform practice in this Court, particularly since the decisions in *General Electric Credit Corp. v. Peltz (In re Flagstaff Food Service Corp.)*, 762 F.2d 10 (2d Cir. 1985), and *General Electric Credit Corp. v. Levin & Weintraub (In re Flagstaff Food Service Corp.)*, 739 F.2d 73 (2d Cir. 1984),*** . . . to insist on a carve out from a super-priority status and post-petition lien in a reasonable amount designed to provide for payment of the fees of debtor's and the committees' counsel and possible trustee's counsel in order to preserve the adversary system. Absent such protection, the collective rights and expectations of all parties-in-interest are sorely prejudiced. It is similarly the practice of this Court not to approve financing arrangements containing clauses triggering default on the appointment of a trustee or examiner under section 1104. Such entrenchment of management may not be in the best interests of the estate and only precludes parties-in-interest from seeking to redress fraud or gross mismanagement through such an appointment. Nor are clauses requiring debtor retention of exclusivity

---

*** [*See* Note (3) following this opinion. — Eds.]

approved. Clauses providing for absolute control over fees and entrenchment of management clauses skew the carefully designed balance of debtor and creditor protections that Congress drew in crafting Chapter 11.[4]

Moreover, a proposed financing will not be approved where it is apparent that the purpose of the financing is to benefit a creditor rather than the estate. [*In re Crouse Group, Inc.*, 71 Bankr. 544, 550–51 (Bankr. E.D. Pa. 1987)] was such a case. There the debtor, a contractor, sought section 364(c) financing to meet job costs connected with certain construction projects. The proposed lender had bonded pre-petition the debtor's performance for those projects. At an interim hearing, the court approved emergency financing to fund pay roll for one week. In exchange for the loan, the lender received a "first position security interest" in the accounts receivable on the bonded projects. The debtor sought to extend the loan. The lender agreed because it needed more time to find a replacement contractor. The court refused to approve the arrangement. It found that, rather than benefit the estate by preserving its assets, the proposed agreement merely allotted more time for the lender to locate a replacement for the debtor while giving the lender priority status among creditors. Thus, the terms were not "fair, reasonable, and adequate under the circumstances."

Conversely, in [*In re Simasko Prod. Co.*, 47 Bankr. 444 (Bankr. D. Colo. 1985)], the court, where none of these factors were found, held that a debtor-in-possession's business judgment in seeking approval to enter into a super-priority loan secured by a senior lien in order to drill up to seven oil wells would not be disturbed on the basis of differing testimony regarding the providence of its decision. The court, in [*In re Federated Dep't. Stores, Inc.*, 1990 Bankr. LEXIS 472 (Bankr. S.D. Ohio 1990)], in authorizing a debtor-in-possession to enter into a credit agreement that, as it appears from the opinion, similarly did not skew the Chapter 11 case and was not principally for the benefit of a pre-petition creditor to the detriment of other parties in interest, found that the agreement was in the best interest of the estate and within the reasonable judgment of the debtor.

These cases consistently reflect that the court's discretion under section 364 is to be utilized on grounds that permit reasonable business judgment to be exercised so long as the financing agreement does not contain terms that leverage the bankruptcy process and powers or its purpose is not so much to benefit the estate as it is to benefit a party-in-interest.

---

[4] There are few reported decisions under section 364. The need for cash is usually immediate. If the court is inclined to grant an application for authority to obtain credit, the time necessary to write an opinion could effectively doom any chance of reorganization. Each judge in the Manhattan branch of this court is presented with at least two such applications each month. Such applications are regularly granted by bankruptcy courts, *see generally* R. Rosenberg, M. Lurey, M. Flics, L. King, *Collier Lending Institutions and the Bankruptcy Code* para. 4.04[3] (1989), provided the standards articulated in the text are not infringed. The standards noted above are usually orally articulated. Debtors' and lenders' counsel are usually aware of these standards and generally tailor their agreements to comply.

III

A.

Applying the standards of section 364(c) to the facts in this case, it is clear that the Debtors have met their burden of showing the unavailability of alternative unsecured financing. The cases clearly establish that although a debtor is not required to seek credit from every possible source, a debtor must show that it has made a reasonable effort to seek other sources of credit available under section 364(a) & (b) . . . . Here, the Debtors have approached four lending institutions with the capability of loaning the large sums necessary to maintain the Debtors' operations. Two of the lenders could not meet the Debtors' time demands and thereby enable the Debtors to order goods for the back to school season. The Debtors then initiated discussions with Citibank and Chemical and accepted Chemical's less onerous offer and rejected the offer by Citibank, the previous lender. The existence of additional lending institutions with the ability to loan $250 million to financially troubled companies is doubtful. Given that a quick cash infusion is necessary to preserve the Debtors' vulnerable seasonal enterprise and that the Debtors contacted four lenders with the ability to loan such large sums, including its former lenders, this Court is satisfied that the Debtors have demonstrated the unavailability of unsecured financing.

B.

As originally structured, the proposed agreement with Chemical gave rise to concerns for whether the Chapter 11 process was being leveraged. It provided for default on the appointment of a trustee or examiner with enlarged powers under Section 1104 of the Code. It contained no carve out for professional fees from the superpriority to be awarded to Chemical. It provided for default if the Court were to grant relief from the automatic stay at the request of any creditor owed in excess of $20 million.

These are the types of clauses that cause concern. They effectively preclude or limit the ability of parties in interest to seek appointment, pursuant to section 1104(a)(1) or (b), of a trustee or examiner with enlarged powers for fraud, dishonesty or incompetence of management . . . . A failure to provide a reasonable sum for professionals has, in other cases before this Court, left estates, creditors' committees and trustees without the assistance of counsel and the Court without the adversary system contemplated by Congress in 1978 when it, in enacting the Bankruptcy Code, recast the role of bankruptcy judges principally to one of resolving disputes. A provision providing for default or relief from the automatic stay, unless it is limited to the Debtor's principal asset, overreaches and can only be designed to skew the Court's disinterested decision of a motion for such relief with the knowledge that to grant the relief may affect hundreds of other creditors and thousands of employees.

At the final hearing, these clauses were modified. The order proposed excludes the appointment of a trustee or examiner with enlarged duties on grounds relating to fraud, dishonesty, incompetence, mismanagement and irregularities of current management. A reasonable carve out of $5,000,000 for fees of professionals is provided. Agreement has been reached with the Citibank group, the one group of creditors affected by the $20 million relief clause, that the clause is not effective as to them. The concerns noted above have thus been addressed. The financing agreement also provides for default if these cases are converted to Chapter 7. That clause does not raise the same concerns. On conversion, the reorganization will have ended and all the creditors will be left with the proceeds of liquidation.

. . . .

For the foregoing reasons, the motion is to be approved.

NOTES AND QUESTIONS

(1) *DIP Lending is Profitable and Low Risk.* As stated by one commentator:

> . . . DIP lending is a very safe and profitable type of corporate lending.

> At first blush, lending to a bankrupt company looks like a horrible idea — good money chasing bad. But it is actually one of the safest investments possible. A DIP financier typically has a court-approved, first priority, well-overcollateralized loan, and is guarded by a bevy of covenants that a lender could only dream of outside of bankruptcy, often including the right to appoint or approve of various officers of the debtor, dictation of a line-item budget for the debtor, asset sale timelines and requirements, the right to exercise self-help remedies upon default without court approval (what's that about an automatic stay?), and lots and lots of reporting requirements.

> While covenant defaults are common (and profitable for DIP lenders), payment defaults are virtually non-existent. There has only been a payment default in one major case. DIP lending is almost as safe as T-bills. What's more, it is (at least historically) very profitable. DIP loans are low risk, but bear much higher coupons than equivalent investment grade loans, and also include lots and lots of fees.

Adam Levitin, *DIP Lending Dries Up*, Credit Slips: A Discussion on Credit and Bankruptcy, http://www.creditslips.org/creditslips/2008/10/dip-lending-dri.html.

(2) *Slippery Slopes.* The *Tenney Village* opinion cited by Judge Buschman in *Ames* presents a model case of overreaching by a would-be DIP lender and is worth reviewing in a little more detail. The debtor, Tenney Village, owned and operated a ski area in New Hampshire and was developing condos on an adjoining tract of land. Tenney borrowed about $16 million from Savings Bank to construct the condos, giving the bank a mortgage on the condominium. The project got into trouble. Tenney filed for relief in Chapter 11 and then asked the court to approve — over the objection of other secured creditors and the creditors' committee — a financing agreement pursuant to which Savings Bank would advance another $1 million to be used for improving the ski area and the condominium tract. The protections sought by Savings Bank would never be sought by a lender outside of a bankruptcy case; general counsel for the lender would easily recognize that, with as much involvement and control as the Tenney proposal provided for, the bank would be vulnerable

to claims that it was a partner or joint venturer with the debtor and that its loan was really an equity interest, subject to subordination. The loan was to be secured by a mortgage on the ski area and the condominium tract. In the passage from the opinion that follows, the court discusses some of the loan agreement provisions that it found particularly troubling.

II. OVER-ALL EFFECT OF FINANCING AGREEMENT

The Financing Agreement, which runs to 47 pages, would give the Bank numerous rights concerning the Debtor's operations and the Chapter 11 reorganization. The Bank must first approve all specifications for the planned improvements, and the work is to be done under the direct supervision of the Bank's consultant who would have authority to stop the work at any time. The Debtor is required to hire a new chief executive officer who must be approved by the Bank; if the Debtor later fires him without the Bank's consent, the entire debt is subject to acceleration. The Debtor must obtain the Bank's prior approval of its plan to market condominium units; it also must hire a new marketing firm approved by the Bank. All sales of condominium units are to be at prices which meet specified minimum unit values, and all proceeds from unit sales, less only a broker's commission, must be remitted to the Bank. The Debtor would have to deposit other sales and rental proceeds in a collateral account at the Bank; the Bank could apply the balance in this account to its debt at any time.

The Bank's rights in the Chapter 11 reorganization are striking. The Bank is to hold $50,000 of the new loan in escrow for the fees and expenses of Debtor's counsel, who received a $25,000 retainer. Debtor's counsel is to be paid nothing from this account for any services devoted to claims or defenses against the Bank. Counsel agrees to give the Bank a monthly accounting of his services and expected fees, which cannot exceed $150 per hour and are subject to court approval. The entire amount of the Bank debt is given the highest administrative expense priority. The occurrence of any so-called "termination event" vacates the automatic stay to permit foreclosure, without further order of court. . . . Among the termination events are: (i) a plan of reorganization being confirmed over the Bank's objections, (ii) a third party obtaining relief from the automatic stay without the Bank's consent, and (iii) any creditor or other party in interest taking any action against the Bank. The Debtor, finally, waives all claims and defenses against the Bank, including the right to assert its preference, fraudulent transfer or other avoiding powers.

Under the guise of financing a reorganization, the Bank would disarm the Debtor of all weapons usable against it for the bankruptcy estate's benefit, place the Debtor in bondage working for the Bank, seize control of the reins of reorganization, and steal a march on other creditors in numerous ways. The Financing Agreement would pervert the reorganizational process from one designed to accommodate all classes of creditors and equity interests to one specially crafted for the benefit of the Bank and the Debtor's principals who guaranteed its debt. It runs roughshod over numerous sections of the Bankruptcy Code. Under its rights of approval and supervision, the Bank would in effect operate the Debtor's business. The Code permits this to be done only by a debtor or trustee. § 1108. All proceeds and rents would go to the Bank or to a collateral account it controls. The bankruptcy estate is supposed to receive all proceeds and rents from estate property, subject to cash collateral rights of secured parties. §§ 541(a)(6), 363. And the Bank would have the ultimate say over the very goal of this Chapter 11 case, a confirmed plan of reorganization. No longer could a plan be confirmed over the Bank's objection under the cram-down provisions of § 1129(b)(2)(A). Such a confirmation is a "termination event" which gives the Bank the right to foreclose upon all the Debtor's property without further order of court, assuming "no material change in circumstances," whatever that means. The automatic stay against foreclosure, and all questions concerning the Bank's adequate protection, become irrelevant despite the strictures of § 362.

Equally shocking is the Bank's attempt to disarm the representative of the bankruptcy estate. Its existing liens would become unassailable even before appointment of counsel to the creditors' committee, and it is given iron-clad defenses to all claims that might be asserted on the estate's behalf, whether they pertain to preference, fraudulent transfer, lender liability, subordination or any other matter. Surely no such right could be "burdensome" so as to qualify for abandonment under § 554. Nor has there been any attempt to demonstrate that these rights are of "inconsequential value," another ground for abandonment. If they have such little value, the Bank does not need the protection.

Not content with this, the Bank would close the purse strings to payment of Debtor's counsel for services devoted to any claim or defense against the Bank, except for the $25,000 retainer. Once this retainer is consumed, and retainers seem to go quickly these days, counsel could not expect to be paid in any contest with the Bank, whether it involves claims against the Bank for monetary recoveries or such matters as contesting the Bank's right to foreclose following a "termination event." There is no other source for payment of fees. Counsel therefore secured has an economic incentive to concentrate his efforts elsewhere, perhaps on matters less fruitful for the estate, even though his intentions may be pure. This temptation makes him doubly disqualified under § 327(a). He holds "an interest adverse to the estate" and he is not "disinterested." . . .

It is said that a Chapter 11 lender should not be required to finance the prosecution of claims and defenses against it. That is true. If the lender believes that this will occur, it can elect not to make the loan. It cannot expect, however, to change the rules of a Chapter 11 case. We have here much more than the common provision giving counsel to a creditors' committee a limited period to object to a lender's liens.

In re Tenney Village Co., 104 B.R. 562, 567–69 (Bankr. D. N.H. 1989).

(3)　*The Flagstaff Problem.* In *Ames*, Judge Buschman also noted that in the wake of two decisions in the Chapter 11 case of Flagstaff Food Corp., courts had adopted the practice of insisting on a "carve out" for professional fees in DIP financing orders. To understand the implications of that observation, it's helpful to know what happened in that case. Flagstaff was in the business of distributing foodstuffs, such as frozen french fries, to institutional customers. It filed a Chapter 11 petition. General Electric Credit Corp., its primary prepetition lender, agreed to advance additional operating funds to the debtor in possession. The financing order entered by the court provided that the GECC debt would have "priority in payment over any other debts . . . and over all administrative expenses of the kind specified in §§ 503(b) or 507(b) . . . secured by a lien on all property of whatever kind and nature of the borrowers and debtors in possession, and proceeds thereof." Notwithstanding the cash infusion, it became apparent that the reorganization effort would fail. Pursuant to Code § 331, the attorneys representing the debtor and the attorneys and accountants representing the unsecured creditors' committee requested $250,000 in interim fees. The bankruptcy court approved the fees. The lender appealed from the order on the grounds that the fees were being paid out of its collateral. The fee awards were affirmed by the district court, but the Second Circuit reversed, reasoning:

> The issue before us is whether, despite the super-priority lien given GECC in the Financing Order, the bankruptcy court subsequently might direct that interim fees and disbursements of attorneys and accountants be paid from the encumbered collateral . . . . These awards were affirmed by the district court. We hold this to be error.

> Attorneys may, as Levin & Weintraub did here, secure a portion of their fee in advance. If attorneys need more encouragement than this to participate in chapter 11 proceedings, Congress, not the courts, must provide it. Under the law as it presently exists, knowledgeable bankruptcy attorneys must be aware that the priority ordinarily given to administration expenses may "prove illusive in light of the various provisions in the Code for competing or super-priorities." *2 Collier on Bankruptcy* ¶ 364.02, at 364 n. 6 (15th ed. 1984). Section 364(c)(1) is such a provision.

> We conclude that the district court erred in holding that section 330 "empower[ed] the Bankruptcy Judge to make awards without reference to any schedule of priorities, without reference to any contractual agreement with respect to those priorities and on the basis of his assessment . . . that if actual and necessary services have been rendered, they should be compensated for." We hold, instead, that any fees payable from GECC's collateral must be for services which were for the benefit of GECC rather than the debtor or other creditors. Provision for such allowance is made in section 506(c) . . . . That is not the situation disclosed in appellees' affidavits.

> It is undisputed that the chapter 11 proceedings were initiated with the hope of effectuating Flagstaff's rehabilitation and with optimism that this could be accomplished. Such benefits as might be said to have accrued to GECC from the attempt to reorganize were incidental to the reorganization efforts and did not fall within the intended scope of section 506(c).

Gen. Elec. Credit Corp. v. Levin & Weintraub (In re Flagstaff Food Corp.), 739 F.2d 73, 75–77 (2d Cir. 1984). If you were considering making a loan to a debtor in possession, would you agree to a carve out for professional fees?

(4) *Another View.* Is Code § 364 just a goody bag of incentives to encourage lenders to extend credit to Chapter 11 debtors, or is it something more than that? Outside of bankruptcy, borrowers are commonly prohibited from incurring new debt that is senior to existing indebtedness. Loan agreements routinely restrict a borrower's ability to incur pari passu or junior priority debt. Enforcement of these covenants is suspended by the automatic stay. Is the judicial oversight imposed by § 364 a substitute for those contractual constraints? *See* George G. Triantis, *A Theory of the Regulation of Debtor-in-Possession Financing*, 46 Vand. L. Rev. 901 (1993).

(5) *It Couldn't Hurt.* You should not conclude on the basis of cases such as *Tenney* and *Roblin* that prepetition creditors habitually oppose DIP financing arrangements. In many cases, especially those involving debtors whose most valuable assets are encumbered by unavoidable liens, unsecured creditors will endorse the extension of credit, because they recognize that if the debtor does not solve its cash flow problems and is forced to liquidate, their recovery will be meager at best. *See, e.g., New York Life Ins. Co. v. Revco D.S., Inc. (In re Revco D.S., Inc.)*, 901 F.2d 1359, 1362 (6th Cir. 1990).

(6) *A Matter of Timing and Procedure.* Many debtors enter Chapter 11 in desperate need of cash. If they don't get it, they will die, and so debtors commonly seek permission to borrow within days and sometimes even hours of filing. However, allowing a debtor to pile on new debt before a realistic prognosis as to its viability can be made can be catastrophic to unsecured creditors if their prepetition claims are subordinated in what turns out to be a futile attempt to breathe life into a terminal debtor. Bankruptcy Rule 4001(c), which governs motions for obtaining court authorization to incur debt, attempts to mediate this conflict by placing a judicial hand on the money spigot. It enables a judge to hold an emergency hearing and authorize a debtor to incur a limited amount of debt right away, while requiring the debtor to return to court for a fuller hearing before it is authorized to borrow more.

According to Rule 4001(c)(1), the motion, accompanied by a copy of the proposed financing agreement, must be served on all official committees; if no creditors' committee has been appointed, it must be served on the debtor's 20 largest creditors. (You'll recall that a debtor must file a list of its 20 largest creditors with its petition. Bankruptcy Rule 1007(d).) The court may hold a *final* hearing on the motion no earlier than 15 days after the motion is served.

However, recognizing that a debtor may need faster action than that, the rule provides that the court may hold a preliminary hearing on very short notice, "but the court may authorize the obtaining of credit only to the extent necessary to avoid immediate and irreparable harm to the estate pending a final hearing." Rule 4001(c)(2). Note that in *Ames*, the court held that the irreparable harm standard can be satisfied by showing a "threatened loss of the business" if the credit is not authorized. Note also that the *Ames* court held an interim hearing about one week after the filing, on three day's notice, and authorized $25 million in emergency financing, not the entire $52 million in interim financing requested by the debtor. Two weeks later, it held a final hearing and authorized the debtor to borrow $250 million. Whether Rule 4001 solves the throwing-good-money-after-bad problem completely is arguable. As one court has noted, "With respect to the final element of [this] test, that financing be in the interest of creditors, the Court has never been sure that creditors ever have all the information necessary to determine with certainty where their best interest lies. *In re Roblin Indus., Inc.*, 52 B.R. 241, 245 (Bankr. W.D.N.Y. 1985).

(7) *Safe Harbor.* Bankruptcy Code § 364(e) provides that the reversal or modification on appeal of a financing order under § 364 will not affect the validity of any debt, priority, or lien authorized by the order to an entity that extended such credit in good faith. "In other words, a lender that extends credit in reliance on a financing order is entitled to the benefit of that order, even if it turns out to be legally or factually erroneous." *Kham & Nate's Shoes No. 2 v. First Bank of Whiting*, 908 F.2d 1351, 1355 (7th Cir. 1990). The lender is protected even if it knew an appeal was pending, unless a stay pending appeal was entered. The purpose of this provision has been described as "to overcome people's natural reluctance to deal with a bankrupt firm . . . as . . . lender by assuring them that so long as they are relying in good faith on a bankruptcy judge's approval of the transaction they need not worry about their priority merely because some creditor is objecting to the transaction and . . . trying to get the district court or the court of appeals to reverse the bankruptcy judge. The proper recourse for the objecting creditor is to get the transaction stayed pending appeal." *In re EDC Holding Co.*, 676 F.2d 945, 947 (7th Cir. 1982). Or, as the court in *Kham & Nate's* more succinctly put it, "If creditors fear that the rug will be pulled out from under them, they will hesitate to lend." 908 F.2d at 1355.

Bear in mind that a lender who does not act in good faith is not entitled to the protection of § 364(e). In *In re EDC Holding Co.*, 676 F.2d at 948, the court held that the lender failed the good faith test by knowingly advancing funds to enable a debtor to make improper payments to attorneys. The court explained that a lender is deemed not to have acted in good faith if "the transaction has an intended effect that is improper under the Bankruptcy Code . . . and it is irrelevant what the improper purpose is."

Also bear in mind that the safe harbor only extends to financing arrangements authorized "*under this section*" (emphasis added). What about arrangements that are not expressly authorized under § 364(e)? The reach of the safe harbor in such situations is considered in the section that follows.

[C]   Cross-Collateralization

PROBLEM 5.3

We saw in the preceding problem that a few years ago, BigBank made a $2.1 million loan to Amphydynamics and took a security interest in the company's inventory and receivables. On the date that Amphy filed its Chapter 11 petition, it owed BigBank $2 million and the inventory and receivables were believed to be worth considerably less than that. We also saw that BigBank is willing to make an additional loan to Amphy, provided the loan is secured by a senior lien on all of Amphy's unencumbered assets and a junior lien on all encumbered assets. Suppose BigBank demands that this new collateral secure not only its postpetition advances, but its prepetition claim as well. Is such a financing arrangement permissible? Suppose that over the objection of certain prepetition creditors, the bankruptcy court enters an order approving the arrangement and BigBank advances funds to Amphy. Suppose further that the objecting creditors appeal from the bankruptcy court order. In light of the § 364(e) safe harbor, should their appeal be dismissed as moot?

Reread Bankruptcy Code § 552 and Note 2 following the *American Kitchen Foods* case in § 3.07[B], *supra*. Then read the following case and notes.

SHAPIRO v. SAYBROOK MANUFACTURING CO. (IN RE SAYBROOK MANUFACTURING CO.)
United States Court of Appeals for the Eleventh Circuit
963 F.2d 1490 (1992)

Cox, Circuit Judge:

Seymour and Jeffrey Shapiro, unsecured creditors, objected to the bankruptcy court's authorization for the Chapter 11 debtors to "cross-collateralize" their prepetition debt with unencumbered property from the bankruptcy estate. The bankruptcy court overruled the objection and also refused to grant a stay of its order pending appeal. The Shapiros appealed to the district court, which dismissed the case as moot under section 364(e) of the Bankruptcy Code because the Shapiros had failed to obtain a stay. We conclude that this appeal is not moot and that cross-collateralization is not authorized under the Bankruptcy Code. Accordingly, we reverse and remand.

I. Facts and Procedural History

Saybrook Manufacturing Co., Inc., and related companies (the "debtors"), initiated proceedings seeking relief under Chapter 11 of the Bankruptcy Code on December 22, 1988. On December 23, 1988, the debtors filed a motion for the use of cash collateral and for authorization to incur secured debt. The bankruptcy court entered an emergency financing order that same day. At the time the bankruptcy petition was filed, the debtors owed Manufacturers Hanover approximately $34 million. The value of the collateral for this debt, however, was less than $10 million. Pursuant to the order, Manufacturers Hanover agreed to lend the debtors an additional $3 million to facilitate their reorganization. In exchange, Manufacturers Hanover received a security interest in all of the debtors' property — both property owned prior to filing the bankruptcy petition and that which was acquired subsequently. This security interest not only protected the $3 million of postpetition credit but also secured Manufacturers Hanover's $34 million prepetition debt.

This arrangement enhanced Manufacturers Hanover's position vis-a-vis other unsecured creditors, such as the Shapiros, in the event of liquidation. Because Manufacturers Hanover's prepetition debt was undersecured by approximately $24 million, it originally would have shared in a pro rata distribution of the debtors' unencumbered assets along with the other unsecured creditors. Under the financing order, however, Manufacturers Hanover's prepetition debt became fully secured by all of the debtors' assets. If the bankruptcy estate were liquidated, Manufacturers Hanover's entire debt — $34 million prepetition and $3 million postpetition — would have to be paid in full before any funds could be distributed to the remaining unsecured creditors.

Securing prepetition debt with pre- and postpetition collateral as part of a postpetition financing arrangement is known as cross-collateralization. The Second Circuit aptly defined cross-collateralization as follows:

> [I]n return for making new loans to a debtor in possession under Chapter XI, a financing institution obtains a security interest on all assets of the debtor, both those existing at the date of the order and those created in the course of the Chapter XI proceeding, not only for the new loans, the propriety of which is not contested, but [also] for existing indebtedness to it.

Otte v. Manufacturers Hanover Commercial Corp. (In re Texlon Corp.), 596 F.2d 1092, 1094 (2d Cir. 1979).

Because the Second Circuit was the first appellate court to describe this practice in *In re Texlon*, it is sometimes referred to as *Texlon*-type cross-collateralization. Another form of cross-collateralization involves securing postpetition debt with prepetition collateral. *See, e.g., In re Antico Manufacturing Co.*, 31 Bankr. 103, 105 (Bankr. E.D.N.Y. 1983). This form of non-*Texlon*-type cross-collateralization is not at issue in this appeal. *See* Appellant's Brief at 8-9. The Shapiros challenge only the cross-collateralization of the lenders' prepetition debt, not the propriety of collateralizing the postpetition debt. *Id.* at 10.

The Shapiros filed a number of objections to the bankruptcy court's order on January 13, 1989. After a hearing, the bankruptcy court overruled the objections. The Shapiros then filed a notice of appeal and a request for the bankruptcy court to stay its financing order pending appeal. The bankruptcy court denied the request for a stay on February 23, 1989.

The Shapiros subsequently moved the district court to stay the bankruptcy court's financing order pending appeal; the court denied the motion on March 7, 1989. On May 20, 1989, the district court dismissed the Shapiros' appeal as moot under 11 U.S.C. § 364(e) because the Shapiros had failed to obtain a stay of the financing order pending appeal, rejecting the argument that cross-collateralization is contrary to the Code. The Shapiros then appealed to this court.

II. Issues on Appeal

1. Whether the appeal to the district court and the appeal to this court are moot under section 364(e) of the Bankruptcy Code because the Shapiros failed to obtain a stay of the bankruptcy court's financing order.

2. Whether cross-collateralization is authorized under the Bankruptcy Code.

III. Contentions of the Parties

The lenders argue that this appeal is moot under section 364(e) of the Bankruptcy Code. That section provides that a lien or priority granted under section 364 may not be overturned unless it is stayed pending appeal. Even if this appeal were not moot, the Shapiros are not entitled to relief. Cross-collateralization is a legitimate means for debtors to obtain necessary financing and is not prohibited by the Bankruptcy Code.

The Shapiros contend that their appeal is not moot. Because cross-collateralization is not authorized under bankruptcy law, section 364(e) is inapplicable. Permitting cross-collateralization would undermine the entire structure of the Bankruptcy Code by allowing one unsecured creditor to gain priority over all other unsecured creditors simply by extending additional credit to a debtor.

. . . .

V. Discussion

A. Mootness

We begin by addressing the lenders' claim that this appeal is moot under section 364(e) of the Bankruptcy Code. Section 364(e) provides that:

> The reversal or modification on appeal of an authorization under this section to obtain credit or incur debt, or of a grant under this section of a priority or a lien, does not affect the validity of any debt so incurred, or any priority or lien so granted, to an entity that extended such credit in good faith, whether or not such entity knew of the pendency of the appeal, unless such authorization and the incurring of such debt, or the granting of such priority or lien, were stayed pending appeal.

11 U.S.C. § 364(e). The purpose of this provision is to encourage the extension of credit to debtors in bankruptcy by eliminating the risk that any lien securing the loan will be modified on appeal.

The lenders suggest that we assume cross-collateralization is authorized under section 364 and then conclude the Shapiros' appeal is moot under section 364(e). This is similar to the approach adopted by the Ninth Circuit in *Burchinal v. Central Washington Bank (In re Adams Apple, Inc.)*, 829 F.2d 1484 (9th Cir. 1987). That court held that cross-collateralization was "authorized" under section 364 for the purposes of section 364(e) mootness but declined to decide whether cross-collateralization was illegal per se under the Bankruptcy Code. Id. at 1488 n. 6. *See also Unsecured Creditors' Committee v. First National Bank & Trust Co. (In re Ellingsen MacLean Oil Co.)*, 834 F.2d 599 (6th Cir. 1987), cert. denied, 488 U.S. 817, 109 S. Ct. 55, 102 L. Ed. 2d 33 (1988).

We reject the reasoning of *In re Adams Apple* and *In re Ellingsen* because they "put the cart before the horse." By its own terms, section 364(e) is only applicable if the challenged lien or priority was authorized under section 364. *See* Charles J. Tabb, Lender Preference Clauses and the Destruction of Appealability and Finality:

Resolving a Chapter 11 Dilemma, 50 Ohio St. L.J. 109, 116–35 (1989) (criticizing *In re Adams Apple*, *In re Ellingsen*, and the practice of shielding cross-collateralization from appellate review via mootness under section 364(e)); *see also In re Ellingsen*, 834 F.2d at 607 (Merritt, dissenting) (arguing that section 364(e) was not designed to prohibit creditors from challenging prepetition matters and that "lenders should not be permitted to use their leverage in making emergency loans in order to insulate their prepetition claims from attack"). We cannot determine if this appeal is moot under section 364(e) until we decide the central issue in this appeal — whether cross-collateralization is authorized under section 364. Accordingly, we now turn to that question.

B. Cross-Collateralization and Section 364

Cross-collateralization is an extremely controversial form of Chapter 11 financing. Nevertheless, the practice has been approved by several bankruptcy courts . . . . Even the courts that have allowed cross-collateralization, however, were generally reluctant to do so . . . .

In [*In re Vanguard Diversified, Inc.*, 31 B.R. 364, 366 (Bankr. E.D.N.Y. 1983)] for example, the bankruptcy court noted that cross-collateralization is "a disfavored means of financing" that should only be used as a last resort. In order to obtain a financing order including cross-collateralization, the court required the debtor to demonstrate (1) that its business operations would fail absent the proposed financing, (2) that it is unable to obtain alternative financing on acceptable terms, (3) that the proposed lender will not accept less preferential terms, and (4) that the proposed financing is in the general creditor body's best interest. *Id.* This four-part test has since been adopted by other bankruptcy courts which permit cross-collateralization . . . .

The issue of whether the Bankruptcy Code authorizes cross-collateralization is a question of first impression in this court. Indeed, it is essentially a question of first impression before any court of appeals. Neither the lenders' brief nor our own research has produced a single appellate decision which either authorizes or prohibits the practice.

The lenders claim that the Sixth Circuit's decision in *In re Ellingsen* endorses cross- collateralization. Like *In re Adams Apple*, the issue in *In re Ellingsen* was whether section 364(e) rendered an appeal moot because the appellants failed to obtain a stay. Judge Wellford's opinion for the court notes that, while cross-collateralization is controversial, it appears to have been used and approved in the past. Therefore, "Congress would not have intended to exclude all cross-collateralization orders categorically from section 364(e)'s protection." *In re Ellingsen*, 834 F.2d at 602. The court concluded that the appeal was moot under section 364(e) because the bankruptcy court did not issue a stay of its cross-collateralization order. The court, however, did not hold that cross-collateralization itself was authorized under the Bankruptcy Code. In fact, Judge Nelson concurred separately to emphasize the limited scope of the court's decision, stating that he was uncertain as to whether section 364 permitted cross-collateralization. Id. at 606.

As noted above, the Ninth Circuit reached a similar conclusion in *In re Adams*

Apple.

. . . .

The Second Circuit expressed criticism of cross-collateralization in *In re Texlon.* The court, however, stopped short of prohibiting the practice altogether. At issue was the bankruptcy court's ex parte financing order granting the lender a security interest in the debtor's property to secure both prepetition and postpetition debt. The court, in an exercise of judicial restraint, concluded that:

> In order to decide this case we are not obliged, however, to say that under no conceivable circumstances could "cross-collateralization" be authorized. Here it suffices to hold that . . . a financing scheme so contrary to the spirit of the Bankruptcy Act should not have been granted by an ex parte order, where the bankruptcy court relies solely on representations by a debtor in possession that credit essential to the maintenance of operations is not otherwise obtainable.

In re Texlon, 596 F.2d at 1098. *See also In re Monach,* 41 B.R. at 862 (arguing that, if the *Texlon* court were faced with the merits of cross-collateralization, it would hold that the practice is forbidden). Although *In re Texlon* was decided under the earlier Bankruptcy Act, the court also considered whether cross-collateralization was authorized under the Bankruptcy Code. "To such limited extent as it is proper to consider the new Bankruptcy Act, which takes effect on October 1, 1979, in considering the validity of an order made in 1974, we see nothing in § 364(c) or in other provisions of that section that advances the case in favor of 'cross-collateralization.' " *In re Texlon,* 596 F.2d at 1098 (citations omitted).

Cross-collateralization is not specifically mentioned in the Bankruptcy Code . . . . We conclude that cross-collateralization is inconsistent with bankruptcy law for two reasons. First, cross-collateralization is not authorized as a method of post-petition financing under section 364. Second, cross-collateralization is beyond the scope of the bankruptcy court's inherent equitable power because it is directly contrary to the fundamental priority scheme of the Bankruptcy Code. See generally Charles J. Tabb, A Critical Reappraisal of Cross-Collateralization in Bankruptcy, 60 S. Cal. L. Rev. 109 (1986).

. . . .

By their express terms, sections 364(c) & (d) apply only to future — i.e., postpetition —extensions of credit. They do not authorize the granting of liens to secure prepetition loans.

. . . .

Given that cross-collateralization is not authorized by section 364, we now turn to the lenders' argument that bankruptcy courts may permit the practice under their general equitable power. Bankruptcy courts are indeed courts of equity, *see, e.g., Young v. Higbee Co.,* 324 U.S. 204, 65 S. Ct. 594, 89 L. Ed. 890 (1945); 11 U.S.C. § 105(a), and they have the power to adjust claims to avoid injustice or unfairness. *Pepper v. Litton,* 308 U.S. 295, 60 S. Ct. 238, 84 L. Ed. 281 (1939). This equitable power, however, is not unlimited.

[T]he bankruptcy court has the ability to deviate from the rules of priority and distribution set forth in the Code in the interest of justice and equity. The Court cannot use this flexibility, however, merely to establish a ranking of priorities within priorities. Furthermore, absent the existence of some type of inequitable conduct on the part of the claimant, which results in injury to the creditors of the bankrupt or an unfair advantage to the claimant, the court cannot subordinate a claim to claims within the same class.

In re FCX, Inc., 60 B.R. 405, 409 (E.D.N.C. 1986) (citations omitted).

Section 507 of the Bankruptcy Code fixes the priority order of claims and expenses against the bankruptcy estate. 11 U.S.C. § 507. Creditors within a given class are to be treated equally, and bankruptcy courts may not create their own rules of superpriority within a single class. *3 Collier on Bankruptcy* § 507.02[2] (15th ed. 1992). Cross-collateralization, however, does exactly that. As a result of this practice, postpetition lenders' unsecured prepetition claims are given priority over all other unsecured prepetition claims. The Ninth Circuit recognized that "[t]here is no . . . applicable provision in the Bankruptcy Code authorizing the debtor to pay certain prepetition unsecured claims in full while others remain unpaid. To do so would impermissibly violate the priority scheme of the Bankruptcy Code." *In re Sun Runner*, 945 F.2d at 1094 (citations omitted). *See also In re Tenney Village*, 104 B.R. at 570 (holding that § 364 does not authorize bankruptcy courts to change the priorities set forth in § 507.)

The Second Circuit has noted that, if cross-collateralization were initiated by the bankrupt while insolvent and shortly before filing a petition, the arrangement "would have constituted a voidable preference." *In re Texlon*, 596 F.2d at 1097. The fundamental nature of this practice is not changed by the fact that it is sanctioned by the bankruptcy court. We disagree with the district court's conclusion that, while cross-collateralization may violate some policies of bankruptcy law, it is consistent with the general purpose of Chapter 11 to help businesses reorganize and become profitable. Rehabilitation is certainly the primary purpose of Chapter 11. This end, however, does not justify the use of any means. Cross-collateralization is directly inconsistent with the priority scheme of the Bankruptcy Code. Accordingly, the practice may not be approved by the bankruptcy court under its equitable authority.

VI. Conclusion

Cross-collateralization is not authorized by section 364. Section 364(e), therefore, is not applicable and this appeal is not moot. Because Texlon-type cross-collateralization is not explicitly authorized by the Bankruptcy Code and is contrary to the basic priority structure of the Code, we hold that it is an impermissible means of obtaining postpetition financing. The judgment of the district court is REVERSED and the case is REMANDED for proceedings not inconsistent with this opinion.

NOTES AND QUESTIONS

(1) *Reverse Cross-Collateralization.* In *Shapiro v. Saybrook*, the court contrasted *"Texlon*-type cross-collateralization" with the type that occurs when *postpetition debt* is secured with collateral that the debtor owned prepetition. Doesn't Code § 364 expressly authorize this non-*Texlon* form?

(2) *Rules in Conflict.* In *Shapiro v. Saybrook*, the court denounced cross-collateralization as "contrary to the basic priority structure of the Code." Can you reconcile this view with the opinions that condone (if not endorse) the "doctrine of necessity," discussed in chapters 1 and 3, above, which allows a debtor to pay prepetition claims, such as employee wage claims, in order to facilitate the reorganization effort? In addition to subverting the Code's priority scheme, cross-collateralization also runs afoul of the spirit of Code § 552, which cuts off prepetition security interests in property acquired postpetition, and Code § 547, which makes preferential transfers voidable.

(3) *A More Direct Approach?* Suppose that the financing arrangement proposed by BigBank did not expressly provide that postpetition assets would be used to secure its prepetition claim. Suppose that instead it provided that in consideration of a further extension of credit, the bank would collect all of Amphy's receivables, remit 80% of them to Amphy and apply the remaining 20% to pay down the bank's prepetition claim. Would this arrangement be permissible? *See Official Comm. of Unsecured Creditors v. Gould Elecs. Corp.*, 1993 U.S. Dist. LEXIS 14318 (N.D. Ill. Sept. 20, 1993).

(4) Professor Charles J. Tabb, a longtime critic of cross-collateralization, has urged the adoption of a flat rule prohibiting it. In Tabb, *A Critical Reappraisal of Cross-Collateralization in Bankruptcy*, 60 So. Cal. L. Rev. 109 (1986), he pointed out that the *Texlon* DIP lender "advanced $667,000 over two months, and in return would have received from the cross-collateralization provision a return of $267,000 plus repayment of the principal . . . a return of forty percent in two months, or 240 percent per year." He suggested, among other things, that if the debtor and the DIP lender had stated the cost of the loan more concretely, the court and other creditors would have been in a position to evaluate it more realistically. He also expressed skepticism about the *Vanguard Diversified* court's view — widely adopted by most courts — that cross-collateralization is justified when the alternative is a liquidation scenario in which other creditors would receive little or nothing. DIP orders, he explained, are typically presented at such an early stage of a Chapter 11 case, that the prospects of a successful reorganization and the likely distribution in the event of a liquidation cannot be estimated in a meaningful way. Observe how the Bankruptcy Court for the Southern District of New York has dealt with requests for cross-collateralization in its "Guidelines for Financing Requests," which follows.

GUIDELINES FOR FINANCING REQUESTS
United States Bankruptcy Court, Souther District of New York
General Order No. M-274

The purpose of this document is to establish guidelines for cash collateral and financing requests under sections 363 and 364 of the Bankruptcy Code in the United States Bankruptcy Court for the Southern District of New York (the "Court"). Although it is recognized that each case is different, the Guidelines are designed to help practitioners identify common material issues that typically are of concern to the Court (at least on the first day of a case and/or where there is limited notice), and to highlight such matters so that, among other things, determinations can be made, if necessary, on an expedited basis.

Substantively, these Guidelines do not purport to establish rules that cannot be varied, but they do require disclosure of the "Extraordinary Provisions," discussed below, that ordinarily will not be approved in interim orders without substantial cause shown, compelling circumstances and reasonable notice.

It will be evident that many of the following guidelines are designed to deal with debtor in possession financing requests documented with a loan agreement and (for want of a better term) a long- form financing order. However, the Court would welcome the use of simplified orders, whenever possible, particularly in smaller cases and in connection with the debtor's use of cash collateral not involving the extension of new funds.

These guidelines are intended to supplement the requirements of sections 363 and 364 of the Bankruptcy Code and Bankruptcy Rules 4001(b) and (c).

I. MOTIONS

A. MOTION CONTENT

1. Single motion

(a) A single motion may be filed seeking entry of an interim order and a final order, which orders would be normally entered at the conclusion of the preliminary hearing and the final hearing, respectively, as those terms are used in Bankruptcy Rules 4001(b)(2) and (c)(2). In addition, where circumstances warrant, the debtor may seek emergency relief for financing limited to the amount necessary to avoid immediate and irreparable harm to the estate pending the preliminary hearing, but in the usual case, only a preliminary and a final hearing will be required.

(b) If the financing is to be extended pursuant to a loan agreement or similar agreement ("Agreement"), the Agreement should be attached to the motion.

(c) The motion should also include a copy of any proposed order for which entry is sought.

(d) Motions must be double-spaced and in form comply with all applicable rules of the Court.

2. Description of use of cash collateral or the material provisions of DIP financing.

The motion should ordinarily contain the following disclosure relative to the use of cash collateral or the financing, either in the text of the motion or in an attached term sheet:

(a) amount of cash to be used or borrowed, including (if applicable) committed amount, maximum borrowings (if less), any borrowing base formula, availability under the formula, and the purpose of the borrowing;

(b) material conditions to closing and borrowing, including any budget provisions;

(c) pricing and economic terms, including interest rates, letter of credit fees, commitment fees, any other fees, and the treatment of costs and expenses of the lender (and its professionals);

(d) collateral or adequate protection provided to the lender and any priority or superpriority provisions, including the effect thereof on existing liens, and any carve-outs from liens or superpriorities;

(e) maturity, termination and default provisions, including events of default, effect on the automatic stay and any cross-default provisions; and

(f) any other material provisions, including any Extraordinary Provisions, as defined in Section II(A), any provisions relating to change of control, and key covenants.

3. Adequacy of Budget.

Any motion for new financing or use of cash collateral must also include disclosure by the debtor as to whether it has reason to believe that any budget to which the debtor will be subject under the order will be adequate (in the context of all assets available to the debtor) to pay all administrative expenses due and payable during the period covered by the financing or the budget.

4. Extraordinary Provisions.

The motion must disclose prominently whether the financing includes any of the Extraordinary Provisions set forth in section II (A) of these Guidelines, and any accompanying order must also set forth these provisions prominently and conspicuously.

5. Efforts to Obtain Financing.

The motion should describe in general terms the debtor's efforts to obtain financing, the basis on which the debtor determined that the proposed financing was on the best terms available, and material facts bearing on the issue of whether the extension of credit is being extended in good faith.

6. Emergency Applications.

A motion that seeks entry of an Emergency Order or Interim Order should also describe the amount and purpose of funds sought to be borrowed on an emergency or interim basis and set forth facts to support a finding that immediate or irreparable harm will be caused to the estate if immediate financing is not obtained at a preliminary hearing or on an emergency basis.

B. <u>NOTICE.</u>

1. Notice of the hearing on (i) the Interim and (ii) the Final Order shall be given to the persons required by Rules 4001(b)(3) and 4001(c)(3), as the case may be, the United States Trustee and any other persons whose interests may be directly affected by the outcome of the motion or any provision of the proposed order. Notwithstanding the foregoing, emergency and interim relief may be entered after the best notice available under the circumstances; however, emergency and interim relief will ordinarily not be considered unless the United States Trustee and the Court have had a reasonable opportunity to review the motion, the financing agreement, and the proposed interim order, and the Court normally will not approve provisions that directly affect the interests of landlords, taxing and environmental authorities and other third-parties without notice to them.

2. Prospective debtors may provide substantially complete drafts of the motion, interim order, and related financing documents to the Office of the United States Trustee in advance of a filing, and the United States Trustee will hold such documents in confidence and without prejudice to the prospective debtor, and attempt to comment on such documents on or shortly after the filing. Debtors are strongly encouraged to provide drafts of financing requests, including proposed orders, to the United States Trustee as early as possible in advance of filing.

3. The hearing on a Final Order will not commence earlier than 15 days after service of the motion, in accordance with Bankruptcy Rules 4001(b)(2) and 4001(c)(2), and ordinarily will not commence until there has been a reasonable opportunity for the formation of a Creditors Committee under 11 U.S.C. § 1102 and either the Creditors Committee's appointment of counsel or reasonable opportunity to do so.

C. <u>PRESENCE AT HEARING.</u>

Except as otherwise ordered by the Court:

1. Counsel for the postpetition lender (or the entity whose cash collateral is to be consensually used) must be present at any hearing with respect to its financing or its collateral; and

2. A business representative of the debtor and lender and any party objecting to the financing, each with appropriate authority, must be reasonably available by telephone or present at the hearing for the purpose of making necessary decisions.

II. ORDERS

A. <u>EXTRAORDINARY PROVISIONS.</u>

The following provisions in a cash collateral or DIP financing order, or in a financing agreement to be approved under such an order, called "Extraordinary Provisions," must be disclosed conspicuously in the motion and order and justification therefor separately set forth:

1. <u>Cross-Collateralization.</u> Extraordinary Provisions include all provisions that elevate prepetition debt to administrative expense (or higher) status or secure prepetition debt with liens on postpetition assets that

such debt would not have by virtue of the prepetition security agreement or applicable law (for the purposes of these Guidelines, "Cross-Collateralization"), unless such status and liens are limited in extent to that necessary to accord the prepetition lender in a reorganization case adequate protection against a decline in the value of its collateral during the postpetition period. In connection with a request for Cross-Collateralization, the Court will consider, among other factors:

(i) the extent of the notice provided;[1]

(ii) the terms of the DIP financing and a comparison to the terms that would be available absent the Cross-Collateralization;

(iii) the degree of consensus among parties in interest supportive of Cross- Collateralization;

(iv) the extent and value of the prepetition liens held by the prepetition lender (and in particular the amount of any "equity cushion" that the prepetition lender may have), and

(v) whether Cross-Collateralization will give an undue advantage to prepetition lenders without a countervailing benefit to the estate.

An order approving Cross-Collateralization must ordinarily reserve the right of the Court to unwind the postpetition protection provided to the prepetition lender in the event that there is a timely and successful challenge to the validity, enforceability, extent, perfection, and (where appropriate) priority of the prepetition lender's claims or liens, or a determination that the prepetition debt was undersecured as of the petition date, and the Cross-Collateralization unduly advantaged the lender.

2. "Rollups." Rollups include the application of proceeds of postpetition financing to pay, in whole or in part, prepetition debt. Determination of the propriety of a rollup will normally take into account, to the extent applicable, the factors mentioned above in connection with Cross-Collateralization, and, in addition, the following:

(a) the nature and amount of new credit to be extended, beyond the application of proceeds of postpetition financing used to pay in whole or in part the prepetition debt;

(b) whether the advantages of the postpetition financing justify the loss to the estate of the opportunity to satisfy the prepetition secured debt otherwise in accordance with applicable provisions of the Bankruptcy Code, and the burdens on the estate of incurring an administrative claim;

(c) whether the rollup can be unwound (see below);

(d) availability under the terms of the DIP financing and a comparison to the terms that would be available in the absence of the rollup;

(e) the extent to which prepetition and postpetition collateral can, as a practical matter, be identified and/or segregated;

---

[1] *See Otte v. Manufacturers Hanover Commercial Corp. (In re Texlon Corp.)*, 596 F.2d 1092 (2d Cir. 1979).

(f) the extent to which difficult "priming" issues would have to be addressed in the absence of a rollup; and

(g) whether the postpetition advances are used to repay a pre-bankruptcy, "emergency" liquidity facility secured by first priority liens on the same collateral as the postpetition financing, where the prepetition facility was provided in anticipation of, or in an effort to avoid, a bankruptcy filing.

An order approving a rollup must ordinarily reserve the right of the Court to unwind the paydown of the prepetition debt in the event that there is a timely and successful challenge to the validity, enforceability, extent, perfection, and (where appropriate) priority of the prepetition lender's claims or liens, or a determination that the prepetition debt was undersecured as of the petition date.

3. Waivers and concessions as to validity of prepetition debt. The Court will not consider as extraordinary the debtor's stipulation as to validity, perfection, enforceability, priority and non-avoidability of a prepetition lender's claim and liens, and the lack of any defense thereto, provided that:

(a) the Official Committee of Unsecured Creditors (the "Committee"), appointed under section 1102 of the Bankruptcy Code, has a minimum of 60 days (or such longer period as the Committee may obtain for cause shown before the expiration of such period) from the date of the order approving the appointment of counsel for the Committee to investigate the facts and bring any appropriate proceedings as representative of the estate; or

(b) if no Committee is appointed, any party in interest has a minimum of 75 days (or a longer period for cause shown before the expiration of such period) from the entry of the final financing order to investigate the facts and file a motion seeking authority to bring any appropriate proceedings as representative of the estate; provided that

(c) the foregoing periods may be shortened in prepackaged or pre-arranged cases for cause shown.

4. Waivers. Extraordinary Provisions include those that divest the Court of its power or discretion in a material way, or interfere with the exercise of the fiduciary duties of the debtor or Creditors Committee in connection with the operation of the business, administration of the estate, or the formulation of a reorganization plan, such as provisions that deprive the debtor or the Creditors Committee of the ability to file a request for relief with the Court, to grant a junior postpetition lien, or to obtain future use of cash collateral. Notwithstanding the foregoing, and where duly disclosed, it will not be considered "extraordinary" for the debtor to agree to repay the postpetition financing in connection with any plan; for the debtor to waive any right to incur liens that prime or are pari passu with liens granted under section 364; for a financing order to contain reasonable limitations and conditions regarding future borrowings under section 364 or cash collateral usage under section 363 (including consent of the lender, subordination of future borrowings to

the priorities and liens given to the initial lender, and repayment of the initial loan with the proceeds of a subsequent borrowing); and for an order to provide that the lender has no obligation to fund certain activities of the debtor or the Committee, so long as the debtor or Committee is free to engage therein.

5. Section 506(c) waivers. Extraordinary Provisions include any waiver of the debtor's right to a surcharge against collateral under section 506(c); factors to be considered in connection with any order seeking such a waiver include whether the debtor's rights are (to the extent permitted by law) delegated to the Committee (or, if a Committee is not appointed, to any party in interest) and whether the carve-out includes expenses under section 726(b) (see below).

6. Liens on avoidance actions. Extraordinary Provisions include the granting of liens on the debtor's claims and causes of action arising under sections 544, 545, 547, 548 and 549 (but not liens on recoveries under section 549 on account of collateral as to which the lender has a postpetition lien), and the proceeds thereof, or a superpriority administrative claim payable from the proceeds of such claims and causes of action.

7. Carve-outs. Provisions relating to a carve-out that will be considered "extraordinary" include those that provide disparate treatment for the professionals retained by the Committee compared to professionals retained by the debtor or that do not include the fees of the U.S. Trustee, the reasonable expenses of Committee members, and reasonable fees and expenses of a trustee under section 726(b); however, reasonable allocations among such expenses can be proposed, and the lender may refuse to include in a carve-out the costs of litigation against it (but not the costs of investigating whether any claims or causes of action exist). Provisions relating to carve-outs should make clear when the carve-out takes effect (and, in this connection, whether it remains unaltered after payment of interim fees made before an event of default under the facility), and any effect of the carve-out on availability under the postpetition loan.

8. Termination; Default; Remedies. Extraordinary Provisions include terms that provide that the use of cash collateral will cease, or the financing agreement will default, on (i) the filing of a challenge to the lender's prepetition lien or to the lender's prepetition conduct; (ii) entry of an order granting relief from the automatic stay (except as to material assets); (iii) the grant of a change of venue with respect to the case or any adversary proceeding; (iv) the making of a motion by a party in interest seeking any relief (as distinct from an order granting such relief); and (v) management changes or the departure, from the debtor, of any identified employees. Clauses providing a reasonable maturity date for the post-petition debt and for termination of the loan or default of the postpetition debt (if not repaid) on dismissal of the case or on confirmation of a plan of reorganization, or on conversion to Chapter 7, or on the appoint ment of a trustee or an examiner with expanded powers, will not be considered to be extraordinary. Termination of the postpetition lender's commit-

ment to continue to advance funds after an event of default will not be considered extraordinary, but the following provisions will:

(a) failure to provide at least five business days' notice to the debtor and the Committee before the automatic stay terminates and the lender's remedies can be enforced; and

(b) failure to provide at least three business days' notice before use of cash collateral ceases, provided that the use of cash collateral conforms to any budget in effect.

B. INTERIM ORDERS.

An Interim Order will not ordinarily bind the Court with respect to the provisions of the Final Order provided that (i) the lender will be afforded all the benefits and protections of the Interim Order, including a DIP lender's section 364(e) and 363(m) protection with respect to funds advanced during the interim period, and (ii) the Interim Order will not bind the lender to advance funds pursuant to a Final Order that contains provisions contrary to or inconsistent with the Interim Order.

C. FORMAL PROVISIONS OF ORDERS.

An Interim Order will not ordinarily bind the Court with respect to the provisions of the Final Order provided that (i) the lender will be afforded all the benefits and protections of the Interim Order, including a DIP lender's section 364(e) and 363(m) protection with respect to funds advanced during the interim period, and (ii) the Interim Order will not bind the lender to advance funds pursuant to a Final Order that contains provisions contrary to or inconsistent with the Interim Order.

1. Findings of Fact. The order should limit recitation of findings to essential facts, including the facts required under section 364 regarding efforts to obtain financing on a less onerous basis and (where required) facts sufficient to support a finding of good faith under section 364(e). Non-essential facts regarding prepetition dealings and agreements may be included under the rubric of "stipulations" between the debtor and the lender or "background." Any emergency or interim order should include a finding that immediate and irreparable loss or damage will be caused to the estate if immediate DIP financing is not obtained and should state with respect to notice only that the hearing was held pursuant to Rule 4001(b)(2) or (c)(2), that notice was given to certain parties in the manner described, and that the notice was, in the debtor's belief, the best available under the circumstances. The Final Order may include factual findings as to notice. The Order should not incorporate by reference or refer to specific sections of a pre- or post-petition loan agreement or other document without a statement of the section's import. The Order should not contain any findings or provisions extraneous to the use of cash collateral or to the DIP financing.

2. Decretal Provisions. The Order should specify, in particular: any Extraordinary Provisions; any priorities or collateral granted; any effect of the borrowing on pre-existing liens; bankruptcy-specific events of default and the consequences thereof; any provisions relating to adequate protection; any acknowledgments or stipulations by the debtor as

to the prepetition debt; the purpose for which the loan is being made, and any restrictions on use of borrowings. The Order may permit the parties to enter into waivers or consents to the DIP loan agreement or amendments thereof provided that (i) the agreement as so modified is not materially different from that approved, (ii) notice of all amendments is filed with the Court, and (iii) notice of all amendments (other than those that are ministerial or technical and do not adversely affect the debtor) are provided in advance to counsel for any Committee, all parties requesting notice, and the U.S. Trustee.

3. _Conclusions of Law._ The interim order should not state that the Court has examined and approved the loan or other agreement; it may say, however, that the debtor is authorized to enter into it. Normally, the Interim and Final orders are sufficient if they state that the debtor is authorized to borrow on the terms and conditions of the loan or other agreement.

4. _Order to Control._ The order should ordinarily state that to the extent the loan or other agreement differs from the order, the order will control.

5. _Statutory Provisions Affected._ The order should specify those sections of the Bankruptcy Code that are being relied on, and identify those sectio ns that are, to the extent permitted by law, being limited or abridged.

6. _Conclusions re Notice._ The Final Order may contain conclusions of law with respect to the adequacy of notice under section 364 and Rule 4001.

[D]   Subordination of Existing Liens; Code § 364(d)

Amphy has been unable to find a lender who will advance funds on an unsecured basis, even if it receives a promise of superpriority treatment. BigBank will gladly lend Amphy the funds it needs to continue operating, provided that the bank receives a senior lien on all Amphy's real and personal property. However, much of this property is already subject to a mortgage or security interest. Can Amphy nevertheless give the bank what it demands in exchange for financing? Read § 364(d) and the materials that follow.

RESOLUTION TRUST CORP. v. SWEDELAND DEVELOPMENT GROUP, INC. (IN RE SWEDELAND DEVELOPMENT GROUP, INC.)
United States Court of Appeals for the Third Circuit
16 F.3d 552 (1994)

GREENBERG, CIRCUIT JUDGE.

. . . .

II. BACKGROUND

This case arises from Swedeland's development of a 508-acre golf course and residential project located in Hardystown Township, Sussex County, New Jersey, and known as Crystal Springs. Swedeland acquired the property in April 1989 and began construction later that year. The plans for the project included homes, a golf course, tennis courts, and an infrastructure such as roads and sewers. The golf course with its clubhouse opened on Memorial Day in 1991.

The project was very large and required substantial financing for acquisition of the property and construction of the improvements. Carteret supplied the financing through a series of loans totaling $37,000,000. For security, Carteret obtained a first mortgage on Swedeland's real estate in the Crystal Springs project, personal guarantees from Swedeland's principals, and a mortgage on real estate Swedeland owned which was . . . known as the Bowling Green Golf Course. The terms of the Carteret-Swedeland loan provided for the first $42,100 from the sale of each residential unit at Crystal Springs to be paid to Carteret, $12,100 to be applied to the loan for the Crystal Springs Golf Course and the balance to be applied to the other acquisition and construction loans.

Unfortunately, the project ran into financial difficulty which led Swedeland to seek additional financing from Carteret in April 1991. But Carteret was barred from granting that financing by restrictions in the Financial Institutions Reform, Recovery and Enforcement Act of 1989. Carteret, however, permitted Swedeland to use $2,250,000 from a collateral security escrow account established pursuant to the Swedeland-Carteret loan agreement to cure Swedeland's potential monetary defaults.

Apparently this additional financing was insufficient, for on August 2, 1991, Swedeland filed a petition under Chapter 11 in which it showed its debt to Carteret as being slightly in excess of $36,000,000. While Carteret contends that somewhat more was due, we are not concerned with the difference as it is undisputed that Carteret's security has been valued at all times since the filing of Swedeland's Chapter 11 petition at far less than Swedeland's debt to it. Indeed, the parties have accepted an appraisal obtained by Carteret, stating that the value of the Crystal Springs property is $18,495,000. When Swedeland filed the petition, 900 residential units remained to be built. Following the filing of the petition and a series of hearings, the bankruptcy court allowed Swedeland, over Carteret's objections, to use Carteret's cash collateral for operating expenses pursuant to 11 U.S.C. § 363. This cash collateral was derived from the proceeds of sales of units in the development.

Not surprisingly, in the fluid situation presented by the ongoing construction of a major real estate project, events moved rapidly in the bankruptcy court. Swedeland filed a motion pursuant to 11 U.S.C. § 364(d)(1) to obtain working capital and construction financing on a superpriority basis . . . . Section 364(d)(1) provides that the court, after notice and hearing "may authorize the obtaining of credit or the incurring of debt secured by a senior or equal lien on property of the estate that is subject to a lien only if": (1) the trustee is unable to obtain such credit otherwise, and (2) "there is adequate protection of the interest of the holder of the lien on the property of the estate on which such senior or equal lien is proposed to be granted."

Such financing would, of course, have subordinated Carteret's lien to a lien securing [the new] loan. Swedeland justified its motion by urging that the Crystal Springs Golf Course would generate a positive cash flow, the residential units could be completed and sold, and the completion of the project by the end of the century would result in Carteret being paid in full. Thus, Swedeland argued that Carteret was adequately protected.

While Carteret seems not to have contended that Swedeland could obtain the postpetition financing without the creation of a superpriority lien, it nevertheless opposed Swedeland's application.

. . . .

[The bankruptcy court authorized the debtor to borrow up to $3.9 million from two lenders, "Haylex" and "First Fidelity," secured by a superpriority lien on Carteret's collateral.]

The bankruptcy court concluded that Swedeland demonstrated that Carteret had adequate protection based upon four factors: (1) Swedeland would turn over to Carteret approximately $1,250,000 in the cash collateral account; (2) Swedeland would pay Carteret future release prices for every unit it sold; (3) the increased value of the Crystal Springs property due to the continued construction; and (4) the continued existence of Carteret's lien and security interest in the Bowling Green Golf Course and the personal guaranties given by Swedeland's principals.[16] The district court ruled that the bankruptcy court's findings were clearly erroneous because Swedeland offered no new consideration to Carteret to offset its diminution of interest as a result of the superpriority lien.

. . . .

Accordingly, none of the factors the bankruptcy court enumerated showed Carteret had adequate protection. We agree with the district court.

A. Cash Collateral

The April 10, 1992 order did not provide Carteret with increased protection when it required that the money in the cash collateral account be turned over to Carteret because Carteret was entitled to those monies even without the order. Prior to Swedeland's filing of the Chapter 11 petition, Carteret had a first mortgage on the Crystal Springs property and a lien on the proceeds from the sale of individual residential units. Under the Carteret-Swedeland agreement, Carteret agreed to release its lien on each unit upon the payment by Swedeland of a release price of $42,100 for the unit released. After filing for Chapter 11 protection, Swedeland requested permission to use the cash proceeds from the sale of the units to finance the continued construction of the project. It is these proceeds which we have been

---

[16] In addition, the bankruptcy court found that Swedeland's obligation to supply Carteret with regular reports and the court's intention to conduct a status conference in seven months contributed to Carteret's adequate protection. While we do not doubt that such procedural steps would be helpful to a pre-petition creditor, we do not regard them as substitutes for the more concrete items listed in section 361. To put it bluntly, Carteret could not convert them into cash.

terming "the cash collateral." Carteret objected to this application, but the bankruptcy court granted the request.

The bankruptcy court, however, recognized Carteret's liens and granted Carteret a continuing lien and security interest in and to all future sales proceeds and all other assets as adequate protection for allowing Swedeland to use the cash collateral to continue construction until December 31, 1991. Accordingly, Carteret previously had been granted a lien on these postpetition proceeds. Therefore, inasmuch as the bankruptcy court already had recognized and granted Carteret a continuing lien on the cash proceeds, it erred in considering those same proceeds to be additional protection permitting the section 364(d) authorization.

B. Release Prices

We reiterate that Carteret's mortgage entitled it to be paid the first $42,100 from the sale of each housing unit as a release price, with $30,000 to be applied to the balance due under the construction loan and $12,100 to be applied to the balance due under the golf course loan. In its postpetition proposal, Swedeland produced six scenarios providing for varying release prices, but only two contemplated Carteret being paid $42,100. Averaging the other four situations, Carteret was to be paid only $28,000 from the proceeds of the sale of each unit. Swedeland justified this reduction in the release price by contending that inasmuch as the Crystal Springs Golf Course was not to be sold and would be generating income, it did not have to be adequately protected . . . .

The bankruptcy court accepted this proposal to pay reduced release prices on a theory that Swedeland's projections showed that the residential debt could be satisfied . . . . We believe that Swedeland did not provide adequate protection to Carteret by proposing to reduce the payments which would be made to Carteret, particularly in the inherently risky circumstances of this Chapter 11 proceeding.

Furthermore, the reductions in the release price could not be justified on a theory that the Crystal Springs Golf Course was not to be sold. There was nothing new in Swedeland's undertaking to retain this asset as the original financing agreement between Swedeland and Carteret did not contemplate a sale of the golf course. Instead, it envisioned that Swedeland would own the course and Carteret's lien against it would be released on the sale of each residential unit. We are at a total loss to understand how a court can suggest that a prepetition creditor with a lien being subordinated to a superpriority lien can be thought to have adequate protection because an asset encumbered by its lien will remain so encumbered . . . . At bottom, the record does not support the bankruptcy court's view that the payment of the release price offered Carteret additional protection. Instead Swedeland's proposal placed Carteret in a worse situation than it was in before the Chapter 11 filing.

C. Increased Value of the Property

The bankruptcy court was also wrong in finding that Carteret derived adequate protection from the increased value of the Crystal Springs project through the contemplated continuing construction. As we have indicated, Carteret presented evidence, which Swedeland did not dispute, that the value of the Crystal Springs property was $18,495,000. Under the superpriority lien awarded to First Fidelity, it obtains $3,160,000 before Carteret receives anything. Thus, the only way to justify First Fidelity's superpriority lien based on the value of the property is to show that somehow Carteret's interest in the collateral ($18,495,000) has been increased by $3,160,000. The bankruptcy court apparently believed that the construction of the development and the potential sales increased the value of the property by this amount.

Yet, the evidence does not establish that the property has increased in value to compensate Carteret for the loss of its priority to First Fidelity. In the first place, continued construction based on projections and improvements to the property does not alone constitute adequate protection . . . . Those cases which have considered improvements to be adequate protection have done so only when the improvements were made in conjunction with the debtor's providing additional collateral beyond the contemplated improvements. *See, e.g., In re O'Connor*, 808 F.2d at 1396 (grant of additional, unencumbered collateral); *In re 495 Central Park Avenue Corp.*, 136 Bankr. 626 (Bankr. S.D.N.Y. 1992) (projected property improvements constituted adequate protection where annual rental income of $180,000 from an existing lease conditioned on improvements would increase value of real estate securing prepetition loan by at least $800,000, and superpriority postpetition loan financing the projected improvements amounted to only $650,000). We reject the notion that development property is increased in value simply because a debtor may continue with construction which might or might not prove to be profitable.

Neither does the possibility of selling the units show that the value of the property has increased to protect Carteret adequately.[17]

Indeed, as the district court pointed out, Swedeland's projections concerning how many units it will sell were belied by its historical performance. Swedeland already had defaulted on the loan to Carteret, the five-month sales projections for the period between August through December 1991 were below expectations, and the cash flow projections upon which the bankruptcy court relied were deficient as they did not provide for a reasonable developer's profit nor discount the projected eight-year cash flow to present value. In fact, the testimony showed that discounting would yield only a net present value of $14,340,303. The district court correctly found that this amount was insufficient to protect Carteret adequately. In this regard, we cannot resist pointing out that we do not doubt that Swedeland's original projections certainly could not have contemplated that within 28 months of acquiring the Crystal Springs property it would file a Chapter 11 petition.

---

[17] Swedeland relies on *In re Snowshoe Co.*, 789 F.2d 1085 (4th Cir. 1986), for the proposition that "operating projections may serve as a valid basis of adequate protection." But in that case the operating projections related to the debtor's ability to pay the superpriority loan which, as here, was much smaller than the subordinated debt. Furthermore, in Snowshoe the pre-petition creditor, unlike Carteret, had a secured loan for considerably less than the value of the property. We do not, however, imply by this observation that a creditor no matter how great its security can be adequately protected without receiving additional collateral or guarantees if the creation of a superpriority lien decreases its security. Of course, in this case unlike the debtor in Snowshoe, Swedeland is attempting to use operating projections to establish adequate protection of the pre-petition lien.

D. Personal Guarantees and Mortgage on Bowling Green

Finally, the bankruptcy court erred in concluding that the continued existence of the personal guarantees and the mortgage on the Bowling Green property constituted adequate protection. As with the cash collateral, Carteret was entitled to these anyway. Moreover, the lien on Bowling Green is worth only $6,715,000. Thus, even without the superpriority lien reducing Carteret's interest, this collateral undersecured Carteret.

In sum, even under the clearly erroneous standard, the district court correctly rejected the bankruptcy court's finding that there was adequate protection justifying the superpriority financing. It is clear that Swedeland failed to offer anything significant that would adequately protect Carteret. The law does not support the proposition that a creditor, particularly one like Carteret undersecured by many millions of dollars, may be adequately protected when a superpriority lien is created without the provision of additional collateral by the debtor. Based on all the above, the bankruptcy court erred in authorizing the postpetition financing on a superpriority basis.

We cannot close this portion of our opinion without pointing out that what happened here is quite disturbing. There, of course, is no doubt that the policy underlying Chapter 11 is quite important. Nevertheless, Congress did not contemplate that a creditor could find its priority position eroded and, as compensation for the erosion, be offered an opportunity to recoup dependent upon the success of a business with inherently risky prospects. We trust that in the future bankruptcy judges in this circuit will require that adequate protection be demonstrated more tangibly than was done in this case.

. . . .

NOTE ON PRIMING LIENS

Is the *Swedeland* court's insistence on some kind of "additional consideration" consistent with the Supreme Court's analysis of the nature of adequate protection in the *Timbers* case? (*Timbers* is reprinted in chapter 3, § 3.07[C].) Is it possible that adequate protection might mean something different in the automatic stay and priming lien contexts? Consider the following passage from another opinion:

> In this case, Acquvest [the prepetition lender] will bear the entire risk of loss on the [postpetition] financing and the debtors' scheme to develop and sell the . . . building lots. The risk in this speculative venture is obviously great. Acquvest is asked to underwrite this risk for the sole benefit of unsecured creditors and the debtors with no offsetting compensation or opportunity to benefit if the project is successful, and with no control whatever over the funding or the work. Not surprisingly, the courts have not endorsed similar requests. In *In re Chevy Devco*, 78 Bankr. 585 (Bankr. C.D. Calif. 1987), the Court stated:
>
> > Is a senior lienor being given less than full protections so that a junior creditor or interest can benefit from it? If so, this subordination should not be allowed. (78 Bankr. at 589).

. . . .

In this case the secured creditor is being made to subordinate so that those with lower priority can potentially make a profit. This is not to be allowed.

Further, under the facts of this case the secured creditor is being treated as if it were an investor. It is being asked to risk its money on the hope that there is a profit to be made. If there is failure, the creditor has no protection against loss. But unlike an investor, the creditor will not share in the gain if the project is successful. The debtor wants the best of all worlds — to use this creditor's money without risk and to keep the profits for itself. (78 Bankr. at 590.)

In re Mosello, 195 B.R. 277, 293 (Bankr. S.D.N.Y. 1996).

Despite such insistence that there be some "additional consideration," experience suggests that when a prepetition creditor is hugely oversecured, the courts have little reluctance about authorizing a priming lien. For example, in *In re Sky Valley, Inc.*, 100 B.R. 107 (Bankr. N.D. Ga. 1988), yet another case involving a troubled golf course developer, the prepetition lender's $2.8 million claim was secured by property that was worth at least $8.5 million, possibly "more if the debtor successfully reorganizes," the court observed. *Id.* at 114. Reassured that there was "no danger . . . that [the prepetition creditor's] loan will become unsecured to any degree," the court authorized the debtor to borrow $400,000 secured by a priming lien.

In contrast, in *Swedeland*, not only was the objecting creditor undersecured, but the court had grave doubts about the debtor's ability to reorganize. Indeed, in a portion of the opinion not reproduced here, the court granted the objecting creditor's motion for relief from the automatic stay on the grounds that the debtor had no equity in the property and that the property was not necessary to an effective reorganization because no reorganization was in prospect. *See* Code § 362(d)(2).

Interestingly, there is not a vast body of case law interpreting Code § 364(d). One reason may be that when prepetition lenders balk at being primed, the DIP lender walks away from the deal rather than lend its way into a litigation, which, in many cases, it will lose. Why will it lose? Because if a debtor has sufficient unencumbered collateral to provide the existing lender with adequate protection — either by a substantial equity cushion or by a new lien on new collateral — the debtor is likely to be able to find a new lender that will lend without a priming lien, taking instead the lien positions that would have to be offered to the old lender under 364(d). Another reason may be that when confronted with the threat of having their liens primed, some prepetition lenders agree to become the debtor's postpetition banker.

Chapter 6

PREPLAN SALE OF THE DEBTOR'S BUSINESS

§ 6.01 SALES OF SUBSTANTIALLY ALL OF THE DEBTOR'S ASSETS

As we saw in chapter 4 of the text, Code § 363 provides that a debtor in possession may enter into transactions, including the use, sale, or lease of estate property in the ordinary course of business, without notice and a hearing. In contrast, § 363(b)(1) provides that a debtor in possession, "*after* notice and a hearing, may use, sell, or lease other than in the ordinary course of business, property of the estate." (Emphasis added.) In this chapter, we consider a sale that unquestionably falls into the non-ordinary course category: the sale of all, or substantially all, of the debtor's assets. Chapter 11 was structured with the idea that a debtor would reorganize its business or, if reorganization proved to be impossible, liquidate pursuant to a plan of reorganization or liquidation that was approved by creditors and confirmed by a bankruptcy judge. That, however, has not prevented the occurrence — with notably increasing frequency — of sales, pursuant to § 363(b), of all or substantially all the assets of a debtor's business at a much earlier, preplan stage of the case.

Such sales typically unfold along the lines of the following scenario: The debtor lines up a proposed purchaser — often called a "stalking horse"[1] — and hammers out definitive transactional documents under which the purchaser will acquire any assets associated with the business (e.g., a division, a subsidiary, the entire business) that it desires. Often the agreement has been reached so quickly that the proposed purchaser's due diligence is not complete and the purchaser is not sure exactly what assets it wants to acquire. As a result, these transactional documents often give the purchaser the right to decline to purchase some of the assets, often with a corresponding reduction in the purchase price.

Once the stalking horse has been identified, in most cases a two-step court approval process is used. First, the sale proponents file a motion to approve the sale subject to the right of third party overbidders to outbid the stalking horse. At the hearing on this motion, the court will order that overbids must be in the same or substantially the same form as the proposed transaction with the stalking horse so

---

[1] The term "stalking horse" is either something of a misnomer or a cynical reference to what may be going on in the case. A "stalking horse" was, historically and literally, a horse-shaped screen behind which a hunter would hide while stalking game. Outside of bankruptcy, the term came to be used to describe a pretext or something used to conceal plans, often in the context of a person who tests a concept or proposal with some group on behalf of an undisclosed principal, and, if that person is successful, the principal can emerge to champion the concept or proposal with little risk of failure.

that the offers can be compared — apples to apples. The court will often also approve a break-up fee for the stalking horse to compensate it for its time and expense should it be outbid. At the same time, the court will set an overbid amount — the minimum bid increment over the initial proposed transaction that will be allowed. The overbid amount should be equal to or greater than the breakup fee so that the estate is not negatively affected by an overbid. The court will also order that notice of the potential auction and its terms be given in a manner that is appropriate under the circumstances. Typically, this means actual notice to all parties in interest and publication notice for the general public. The court will also set a date for the auction and the date on which a sale to the stalking horse or a higher bidder will be approved.

Interestingly, since the name of a business is often a valuable asset, the sale of assets may include the corporate name (as well as any trademarks and other forms of intellectual property). This may require a mid-case change of name for the debtor, which, by custom, is usually an abbreviation or reversal of the old name. Adoption of reverse spellings of the debtor's former name became something of a fad during the 1990s and 2000s. For example, FPA Medical Management, the debtor, sells its business and name to a newly formed purchaser and changes its name to "APF, Inc." The case will also be recaptioned to reflect the name change. Or CadKey, Inc. sells its business and name to a buyer and becomes "CK Liquidation Corp." Similarly, Chrysler LLC sold its name to the purchaser of its assets, a newly formed company to be named "Chrysler LLC," and changed its name to "Old Carco LLC." These name changes are not merely cosmetics. They have interesting implications. After the sale, the company that is currently doing business under the name that is stamped on the defective circular saw that causes your injury may not be the company that manufactured the saw at all. This raises the thorny issue of from whom so-called "future claimants" — those who are injured after the sale of the company by defective products manufactured before that sale — can recover. We consider that issue later in this chapter.

Sale of a business in Chapter 11 has many advantages over sales outside of the bankruptcy process. First, purchasers, as a rule, are not interested in buying their way into protracted negotiations and litigation with the debtor's creditors over which creditor is entitled to what share of the sales proceeds. Section 363(b) and (f) authorize the court to order a sale of assets free and clear of the liens, claims, and interests of others. This allows the assets to be put back into the stream of commerce, where they can, assumedly, remain productive, while the various lien-holders, claimants, and interest-holders sort out their competing claims to the proceeds. Postponing this time-consuming process means the sale can occur swiftly and without entanglement in the claims resolution process.

Second, sales under § 363 can produce bankruptcy court orders, findings of fact, and conclusions of law that provide protection from later lawsuits by the debtor's creditors and interest-holders against the purchaser and the debtor's insiders, such as officers and directors, and the attorneys involved. Outside of bankruptcy, the debtor's creditors and interest-holders can challenge an asset sale and seek to hold officers and directors liable for breach of their fiduciary duties in connection with their approval of the sale. Only in bankruptcy can the managers of a debtor obtain in advance of a sale what is essentially a declaratory judgment that these claims have no merit and that the sale represents a sound exercise of management's business judgment. The bankruptcy court may also enter an injunction prohibiting claimants from even asserting these claims.

Third, although Code § 1123(a)(5)(D) says a Chapter 11 reorganization plan may provide for the sale of all or substantially all of a debtor's assets, a sale pursuant to a plan requires going through the disclosure statement approval, balloting, and confirmation processes — all of which are costly and time consuming. Reorganizations under confirmed plans routinely take over a year — and many take much longer — to complete. By contrast, a § 363 sale can often be completed in as little as 60 to 90 days from the date that the Chapter 11 petition is filed. For example, the sales of Lehman Brothers, Chrysler, and General Motors during the Great Recession of 2009 set a speed record for mega-cases. The sales were accomplished in 5, 42, and 40 days, respectively.

These benefits of bankruptcy sales have made the bankruptcy courts into a forum of choice for those interested in acquiring the assets and businesses of financially distressed companies. This was not always the case. Under the old Bankruptcy Act and in the early days of the Code, preplan sales of businesses were disfavored and courts resisted them. In recent years, however, a lot of that judicial resistance has eroded, either because the benefits of this form of "reorganization" have became apparent or because, in an era of illiquidity, debtors cannot obtain the financing they need to continue operating and an early sale is the only way to wring maximum value out of the debtors' assets.

PROBLEM 6.1

While you have been attending to paper work, Headley and Carol Charisma have been negotiating the sale of Comp-U-All with what they regard as surprisingly positive results.

You will recall that Comp-U-All owns and operates retail stores in malls and shopping centers in several states. Comp-U-All's most valuable assets are its shopping center leases. They are of interest to other retailers, including Exerwise, LLC. Exerwise operates high-tech health clubs, and the premises currently occupied by the Comp-U-All stores would be excellent for its operations. Moreover, Exerwise can use some of Comp-U-All's inventory and wiring, because the Exerwise training program emphasizes something the company calls "Total Body & Mind Coordination," which is best developed through a combination of strenuous aerobic and video game exercises. Carol believes that the market value of the leases and inventory is about $35 million. Exerwise will pay $37 million if it can have access to the locations within 90 days. Exerwise says that it needs to close promptly so that it can have the spaces fitted out and operating in time for its "Special Two-For-One Spring Shape-Up Season." Exerwise says that if the deal cannot be closed within 90 days, Exerwise would have to pay considerably less or walk away from the deal.

Carol and Headley would like to sell Amphy's interest in Comp-U-All immediately and will be taking the matter up with the board of directors at the next meeting. They have asked you the following questions:

1. What factors should the board consider in weighing the merits of the sale?

2. Will court approval of the sale be required?

3. What if the creditors' committee or individual creditors oppose the sale? What if stockholders oppose it? What if they believe the leases should be auctioned off separately rather than as a block? What business is it of the creditors and shareholders, anyway, if the company can sell its interest in Comp-U-All for a decent price?

Before you respond, read the following opinions and the accompanying notes.

IN RE THE LIONEL CORP.
United States Court of Appeals, Second Circuit
722 F.2d 1063 (1983)

Before MANSFIELD, CARDAMONE and WINTER, CIRCUIT JUDGES

CARDAMONE, CIRCUIT JUDGE

This expedited appeal is from an order of United States District Judge Dudley B. Bonsal dated September 7, 1983, approving an order entered earlier that day by the United States Bankruptcy Court for the Southern District of New York (Ryan, J.). The order authorized the sale by Lionel Corporation, a Chapter 11 debtor in possession, of its 82% common stock holding in Dale Electronics, Inc. to Peabody International Corporation for $50 million.[1]

I — FACTS

On February 19, 1982, the Lionel Corporation — toy train manufacturer of childhood memory — and two of its subsidiaries, Lionel Leisure, Inc. and Consolidated Toy Company, filed joint petitions for reorganization under Chapter 11 of the Bankruptcy Code. Resort to Chapter 11 was precipitated by losses totaling $22.5 million that Lionel incurred in its toy retailing operation during the two-year period ending December 1982.

There are 7.1 million shares of common stock of Lionel held by 10,000 investors. Its consolidated assets and liabilities as of March 31, 1983 were $168.7 million and $191.5 million, respectively, reflecting a negative net worth of nearly $23 million. Total sales for 1981 and 1982 were $295.1 million and $338.6 million. Lionel's creditors hold approximately $135.6 million in pre-petition claims, and they are represented in the ongoing bankruptcy proceedings by an Official Creditors'

---

[1] The agreement between Lionel and Peabody provides that the parties will be relieved of their respective obligations to purchase and sell the Dale shares unless the closing takes place on or before November 30, 1983. In § 1.03 of the contract, the parties specifically contemplated the possibility of "a stay pending disposition of any appeal from the bankruptcy court's order." On November 22, 1983 Peabody made a motion under Fed. R. App. P. 27 requesting in part that this court extend the November 30 deadline. In view of the contract language, Peabody bargained for this provision. Accordingly, we deny its motion.

Committee whose 13 members hold $80 million of those claims. The remaining $55 million is scattered among thousands of small creditors.

Lionel continues to operate its businesses and manage its properties pursuant to 11 U.S.C. §§ 1107–1108, primarily through its wholly-owned subsidiary, Leisure. Leisure operates Lionel's presently owned 56 specialty retail stores, which include a number of stores formerly managed by Lionel's other subsidiary, Consolidated Toy. In addition to the stock of Leisure and Consolidated Toy, Lionel has other assets such as the right to receive royalty payments relating to the manufacture of toy trains.

Lionel's most important asset and the subject of this proceeding is its ownership of 82% of the common stock of Dale, a corporation engaged in the manufacture of electronic components. Dale is not a party to the Lionel bankruptcy proceeding. Public investors own the remaining 18 percent of Dale's common stock, which is listed on the American Stock Exchange. Its balance sheet reflects assets and liabilities as of March 31, 1983 of $57.8 million and $29.8 million, respectively, resulting in shareholders' equity of approximately $28.0 million. Lionel's stock investment in Dale represents approximately 34 percent of Lionel's consolidated assets, and its interest in Dale is Lionel's most valuable single asset. Unlike Lionel's toy retailing operation, Dale is profitable. For the same two-year period ending in December 1982 during which Lionel had incurred its substantial losses, Dale had an aggregate operating profit of $18.8 million.

On June 14, 1983 Lionel filed an application under § 363(b) seeking bankruptcy court authorization to sell its 82% interest in Dale to Acme-Cleveland Corporation for $43 million in cash. Four days later the debtor filed a plan of reorganization conditioned upon a sale of Dale with the proceeds to be distributed to creditors. Certain issues of the reorganization remain unresolved, and negotiations are continuing; however, a solicitation of votes on the plan has not yet begun. On September 7, 1983, following the Securities and Exchange Commission's July 15 filing of objections to the sale, Bankruptcy Judge Ryan held a hearing on Lionel's application. At the hearing, Peabody emerged as the successful of three bidders with an offer of $50 million for Lionel's interest in Dale.

The Chief Executive Officer of Lionel and a Vice-President of Salomon Brothers were the only witnesses produced and both testified in support of the application. Their testimony established that while the price paid for the stock was "fair," Dale is not an asset "that is wasting away in any sense." Lionel's Chief Executive Officer stated that there was no reason why the sale of Dale stock could not be accomplished as part of the reorganization plan, and that the sole reason for Lionel's application to sell was the Creditors' Committee's insistence upon it. The creditors wanted to turn this asset of Lionel into a "pot of cash," to provide the bulk of the $70 million required to repay creditors under the proposed plan of reorganization.

In confirming the sale, Judge Ryan made no formal findings of fact. He simply noted that cause to sell was sufficiently shown by the Creditors' Committee's insistence upon it. Judge Ryan further found cause — presumably from long experience — based upon his own opinion that a present failure to confirm would set the entire reorganization process back a year or longer while the parties attempted to restructure it.

The Committee of Equity Security Holders, statutory representatives of the 10,000 public shareholders of Lionel, appealed this order claiming that the sale, prior to approval of a reorganization plan, deprives the equity holders of the Bankruptcy Code's safeguards of disclosure, solicitation and acceptance and divests the debtor of a dominant and profitable asset which could serve as a cornerstone for a sound plan. The SEC also appeared and objected to the sale in the bankruptcy court and supports the Equity Committee's appeal, claiming that approval of the sale side-steps the Code's requirement for informed suffrage which is at the heart of Chapter 11.

The Creditors' Committee favors the sale because it believes it is in the best interests of Lionel and because the sale is expressly authorized by § 363(b) of the Code. Lionel tells us that its ownership of Dale, a non-operating asset, is held for investment purposes only and that its sale will provide the estate with the large block of the cash needed to fund its plan of reorganization.

From the oral arguments and briefs we gather that the Equity Committee believes that Chapter 11 has cleared the reorganization field of major pre-plan sales — somewhat like the way Minerva routed Mars — relegating § 363(b) to be used only in emergencies. The Creditors' Committee counters that a bankruptcy judge should have absolute freedom under § 363(b) to do as he thinks best. Neither of these arguments is wholly persuasive. Here, as in so many similar cases, we must avoid the extremes, for the policies underlying the Bankruptcy Reform Act of 1978 support a middle ground — one which gives the bankruptcy judge considerable discretion yet requires him to articulate sound business justifications for his decisions.

II — DISCUSSION

The issue now before this Court is to what extent Chapter 11 permits a bankruptcy judge to authorize the sale of an important asset of the bankrupt's estate, out of the ordinary course of business and prior to acceptance and outside of any plan of reorganization. § 363(b), the focal point of our analysis, provides that "[t]he trustee, after notice and a hearing, may use, sell, or lease, other than in the ordinary course of business, property of the estate." 11 U.S.C. § 363(b) (Supp. V 1981).

On its face, § 363(b) appears to permit disposition of any property of the estate of a corporate debtor without resort to the statutory safeguards embodied in Chapter 11 of the Bankruptcy Code, 11 U.S.C. § 1101 *et seq.* (Supp. V 1981). Yet, analysis of the statute's history and over seven decades of case law convinces us that such a literal reading of § 363(b) would unnecessarily violate the congressional scheme for corporate reorganizations.

A. Bankruptcy Act of 1867 — the "Perishable" Standard

An early statutory reference providing for the sale of a debtor's property prior to final liquidation of the estate in limited circumstances was § 25 of the Bankruptcy Act of 1867 (Act of March 2, 1867, 14 Stat. 517). Congress there stated:

> *And be it further enacted*, That when it appears to the satisfaction of the court that the estate of the debtor, or any part thereof, is of a *perishable nature*, or *liable to deteriorate in value*, the court may order the same to be sold, in such manner as may be deemed most expedient, under the direction of the messenger or assignee, as the case may be, who shall hold the funds received in place of the estate disposed of . . . . (emphasis added and in original).

The 1867 Act did not provide for reorganizations; nevertheless, the requirements that the property be of a perishable nature or liable to deteriorate in value and that there be loss if the same is not sold immediately were also found in General Bankruptcy Order No. XVIII(3), adopted by the Supreme Court in 1898. General Order in Bankruptcy No. XVIII, 89 F. viii (November 28, 1898).

From 1898 through 1937, the Bankruptcy Act did not contain a specific provision permitting pre-adjudication sales of a debtor's property. But, pursuant to General Order XVIII, this Circuit over fifty years ago upheld an order that approved a private, pre-adjudication sale of a bankrupt's stock of handkerchiefs. Not only was merchandise sold at a price above its appraised value, but Christmas sales had commenced and the sale of handkerchiefs would decline greatly after the holidays. Our court held that the concept of "perishable" was not limited to its physical meaning, but also included property liable to deteriorate in price and value. *In re Pedlow*, 209 F. 841, 842 (2d Cir. 1913). *See Hill v. Douglass*, 78 F.2d 851, 853–54 (9th Cir. 1935) (sale of road-making equipment of a contractor to prevent its repossession approved).

B. Chandler Act of 1938 — The "Upon Cause Shown" Standard

Section 116(3) of the 1938 Act, which was the immediate predecessor of § 363(b), was originally enacted as § 77B(c) in 1937. § 116(3) provided:

> Upon the approval of a petition, the judge may, in addition to the jurisdiction, powers and duties hereinabove and elsewhere in this chapter conferred and imposed upon him and the court (3) authorize a receiver or a trustee or a debtor in possession, upon such notice as the judge may prescribe and upon cause shown, to lease or sell any property of the debtor, whether real or personal, upon such terms and conditions as the judge may approve.

> This section applied in Chapter X proceedings, and a similar provision, § 313(2), pertained to Chapter XI cases . . . . These sections, as their predecessors, were designed to handle leases or sales required during the time lag between the filing of a petition for reorganization and the date when the plan was approved.

The Rules of Bankruptcy Procedure applicable in Chapters X and XI, the Act's reorganization procedures, provided for a sale of all or part of a bankrupt's property after application to the court and "upon cause shown." Rules 10-607(b), 11-54. Despite the provisions of this Rule, the "perishable" concept, expressed in the view that a pre-confirmation . . . sale was the exception and not the rule, persisted. As one commentator stated, "[o]rdinarily, in the absence of perishable goods, or depreciation of assets, or actual jeopardy of the estate, a sale will not be ordered" . . . *1 Collier on Bankruptcy* ¶ 2.28(3) (14th ed. 1978) (footnotes omitted).

Thirty years after *In re Pedlow, supra,* in *Frank v. Drinc-O-Matic, Inc.*, 136 F.2d 906 (2d Cir. 1943), we upheld the sale of a debtor's 19 vending machines that were subject to a vendor's lien and in the possession of their manufacturer. We noted that the trustee had no funds with which to redeem the machines and that six months had passed from the filing of the petition without proposal of a reorganization plan. Finally, we stated that appellate review of the power exercised by a lower court in directing a sale pursuant to § 116(3) was limited to whether the district court had abused its discretion. *Id.* at 906.

Citing § 116(3) of the Act, we next affirmed an order of a sale of vats, kettles and other brewing machinery which, with "the approach of warm weather . . . will, because of lack of use and refrigeration, deteriorate rapidly and lose substantially all their value." *In re V. Loewer's Gambrinus Brewery Co.*, 141 F.2d 747, 748 (2d Cir. 1944). While the court acknowledged the viability of the "perishable'" property concept, it upheld the sale even though virtually all of the income producing assets of the debtor were involved. The same proceeding, then entitled *Patent Cereals v. Flynn*, 149 F.2d 711 (2d Cir. 1945), came before us the following year. We said it made no difference whether sale of a debtor's property preceded or was made part of a plan of reorganization. *Id.* at 712. Nothing, we continued, in former § 216 (providing for the sale of a reorganizing debtor's property pursuant to a plan) precluded approval of a plan after a sale of all or a substantial part of the debtor's property. Section 216 merely permitted a plan providing for such sale and did not forbid a plan after such a sale has already taken place. *Id.* at 713.

Judge Ryan, in authorizing the sale of the Dale stock cited *Patent Cereals* as his authority. Appellees here cite *Patent Cereals* for the proposition that this court has abandoned the perishable property or emergency concept. We reject such a broad reading of *Patent Cereals* for several reasons. First, the decision involved an appeal from a denial of confirmation of a plan of reorganization, *i.e.*, the sale in that case was a *fait accompli*, it was not as here an appeal from an authorization of sale. Second, the earlier decision in *Loewer's Gambrinus Brewery, supra,* indicates that the court did view the original sale as involving perishable property. Third, subsequent cases in this Circuit confirm the misapprehension in appellees' and Judge Ryan's broad interpretation. *See In re Sire Plan, Inc.*, 332 F.2d 497 (2d Cir. 1964); *In re Pure Penn Petroleum Co., Inc.* 188 F.2d 851 (2d Cir. 1951).

The Third Circuit took an even stricter view in *In re Solar Mfg. Corp.*, 176 F.2d 493 (3d Cir. 1949). Acknowledging that a sale of corporate assets could occur outside and prior to a plan, yet expressing concern that sales of that nature do not adequately "protect the interests of those whose money is tied up in the tottering enterprise," the court concluded that pre-confirmation sales should be "confined to emergencies where there is imminent danger that the assets of the ailing business will be lost if prompt action is not taken." *Id.* at 494. This "emergency" approach was so appealing that our court cited *Solar Mfg. Corp.* with approval and held in *In re Pure Penn Petroleum Co.*, 188 F.2d 851 (2d Cir. 1951), that the debtor must plead and prove "the existence of an emergency involving imminent danger of loss of the assets if they were not promptly sold." *Id.* at 854.

Finally, in *In re Sire Plan, Inc.*, 332 F.2d 497 (2d Cir. 1964), corporate owners of a seven-story skeletal building then under construction filed for reorganization under Chapter X of the Act. Because of the site's close proximity to the impending 1964 World's Fair, Holiday Inns felt it was a favorable location for a hotel and accordingly offered to purchase it. The sale to Holiday Inns was affirmed under the *Patent Cereal* rationale. The Court stated that there is no requirement that the sale be in aid of a reorganization; but we further noted, as in *Pure Penn*, that the evidence demonstrated that in its exposed state a "partially constructed building is a 'wasting asset' [that] can only deteriorate in value the longer it remains uncompleted." *Id.* at 499.

More recently, other circuits have upheld sales prior to plan approval under the Bankruptcy Act where the bankruptcy court outlined the circumstances in its findings of fact indicating why the sale was in the best interest of the estate. *E.g.*, *In re Equity Funding Corporation of America*, 492 F.2d 793, 794 (9th Cir.), *cert. denied*, 419 U.S. 964 (1974) (finding of fact that because market value of asset was likely to deteriorate substantially in the near future, sale was in the estate's best interests); *In re Dania Corporation*, 400 F.2d 833, 835–37 (5th Cir. 1968), *cert. denied*, 393 U.S. 1118 (1969) (upholding sale of stock representing debtor's major asset where its value was rapidly deteriorating causing the reorganizing estate to diminish); *In re Marathon Foundry and Machine Co.*, 228 F.2d 594 (7th Cir. 1955) (heavy interest charges justified sale of stock which had been pledged to secure loan). In essence, these cases evidence the continuing vitality under the old law of an "emergency" or "perishability" standard. As we shall see, the new Bankruptcy Code no longer requires such strict limitations on a bankruptcy judge's authority to order disposition of the estate's property; nevertheless, it does not go so far as to eliminate all constraints on that judge's discretion.

C. The Bankruptcy Reform Act of 1978

Section 363(b) of the Code seems on its face to confer upon the bankruptcy judge virtually unfettered discretion to authorize the use, sale or lease, other than in the ordinary course of business, of property of the estate. Of course, the statute requires that notice be given and a hearing conducted, but [no] reference is made to an "emergency" or "perishability" requirement nor is there an indication that a debtor in possession or trustee contemplating sale must show "cause." Thus, the language of § 363(b) clearly is different from the terms of its statutory predecessors. And, while Congress never expressly stated why it abandoned the "upon cause shown" terminology of § 116(3), arguably that omission permits easier access to § 363(b). *See In re Brookfield Clothes, Inc.*, 31 B.R. 978, 984 (S.D.N.Y. 1983). Various policy considerations lend some support to this view.

First and foremost is the notion that a bankruptcy judge must not be shackled with unnecessarily rigid rules when exercising the undoubtedly broad administrative power granted him under the Code. As Justice Holmes once said in a different context, "[s]ome play must be allowed for the joints of the machine. . . ." *Missouri, Kansas & Texas Ry. Co. v. May*, 194 U.S. 267, 270 (1904). To further the purposes of Chapter 11 reorganization, a bankruptcy judge must have substantial freedom to tailor his orders to meet differing circumstances. This is exactly the result a liberal reading of § 363(b) will achieve.

Support for this policy is found in the rationale underlying a number of earlier cases that had applied § 116(3) of the Act. In particular, this Court's decision in *Sire Plan* was not hinged on an "emergency" or "perishability" concept. Lip service was paid to the argument that a partially constructed building is a "wasting asset;" but the real justification for authorizing the sale was the belief that the property's value depended on whether a hotel could be built in time for the World's Fair and that an advantageous sale after the opening of the World's Fair seemed unlikely. Thus, the reason was not solely that a steel skeleton was deteriorating, but rather that a good business opportunity was presently available, so long as the parties could act quickly. In such cases therefore the bankruptcy machinery should not straight-jacket the bankruptcy judge so as to prevent him from doing what is best for the estate.

Just as we reject the requirement that only an emergency permits the use of § 363(n), we also reject the view that § 363(b) grants the bankruptcy judge *carte blanche*. Several reasons lead us to this conclusion: the statute requires notice and a hearing, and these procedural safeguards would be meaningless absent a further requirement that reasons be given for whatever determination is made; similarly, appellate review would effectively be precluded by an irreversible order; and, finally, such construction of § 363(b) swallows up Chapter 11's safeguards. In fact, the legislative history surrounding the enactment of Chapter 11 makes evident Congress' concern with rights of equity interests as well as those of creditors.[3]

Chapter 5 of the House bill dealing with reorganizations states that the purpose of a business reorganization is to restructure a business' finances to enable it to operate productively, provide jobs for its employees, pay its creditors and produce a return for its stockholders. The automatic stay upon filing a petition prevents creditors from acting unilaterally or pressuring the debtor. *Report of the Committee on the Judiciary, House of Representatives, to accompany H.R. 8200*, H.R. Rep. No. 95-595, 95th Cong. 1st Sess. (1977) at 16, *reprinted in 2 Collier on Bankruptcy* (appendix) (15th ed. 1983) (hereinafter H.R. Rep. No. 95-595). The plan of reorganization determines how much and in what form creditors will be paid, whether stockholders will continue to retain any interests, and in what form the business will continue. Requiring acceptance by a percentage of creditors and stockholders for confirmation forces negotiation among the debtor, its creditors and its stockholders. *Id.* at 221. A fair analysis of the House bill reveals that

---

[3] The Commission on the Bankruptcy Laws of the United States submitted a draft provision that would have permitted resort to § 363(b) in the absence of an emergency, even in the case of "all or substantially all the property of the estate." *See* Report of the Commission on the Bankruptcy Laws of the United States, H.R. Doc. No. 93-137, 93rd Cong., 1st Sess. (1973) at 239 (proposed § 7-205 and accompanying explanatory note). Congress eventually deleted this provision without explanation, an action which we hardly consider dispositive of the issue before us here.

reorganization under the 1938 Chandler Act, though designed to protect creditors had, over the years, often worked to their detriment and to the detriment of shareholders as well. *Id.* at 221. The primary reason reorganization under the Act had not served well was that disclosure was minimal and reorganization under the Act was designed to deal with trade debt, not secured or public debt or equity. The present bill, it was believed, provides some form of investor protection to make it a "fairer reorganization vehicle." *Id.* at 226. The key to the reorganization Chapter, therefore, is disclosure. *Id.* To make disclosure effective, a provision was included that there be a disclosure statement and a hearing on the adequacy of the information it contains. *Id.* at 227. The essential purpose served by disclosure is to ensure that public investors are not left entirely at the mercy of the debtor and its creditors. For that reason the Securities and Exchange Commission, for example, has an absolute right to appear and be heard on behalf of the public interest in an orderly securities market. *Id.* at 228.

The Senate hearings similarly reflect a concern as to how losses are to be apportioned between creditors and stockholders in the reorganization of a public company. S. Rep. No. 95-989, 95th Cong. 2d Sess. 9 (1978), *reprinted in 3 Collier on Bankruptcy* (appendix) (15th ed. 1983) (hereinafter S. Rep. No. 95-989). Noting that "the most vulnerable today are public investors," the Senate Judiciary Committee Report states that the bill is designed to counteract "the natural tendency of a debtor in distress to pacify large creditors with whom the debtor would expect to do business, at the expense of small and scattered public investors." S. Rep. No. 95-989 at 10. The Committee believed that investor protection is most critical when the public company is in such financial distress as to cause it to seek aid under the bankruptcy laws. *Id.* The need for this protection was plain. Reorganization under the 1938 Act was often unfair to public investors who lacked bargaining power, and these conditions continued. Echoing the conclusion of the House Committee, the Senate Committee believed that the bill would promote fairer and more equitable reorganizations granting to public investors the last chance to conserve values that corporate insolvency has jeopardized. *Id.* at 10–11.

III — CONCLUSION

The history surrounding the enactment in 1978 of current Chapter 11 and the logic underlying it buttress our conclusion that there must be some articulated business justification, other than appeasement of major creditors, for using, selling or leasing property out of the ordinary course of business before the bankruptcy judge may order such disposition under § 363(b).

The case law under § 363's statutory predecessors used terms like "perishable," "deteriorating," and "emergency" as guides in deciding whether a debtor's property could be sold outside the ordinary course of business. The use of such words persisted long after their omission from newer statutes and rules. The administrative power to sell or lease property in a reorganization continued to be the exception, not the rule. *Collier on Bankruptcy* ¶ 2.28(b) (*supra*). In enacting the 1978 Code Congress was aware of existing case law and clearly indicated as one of its purposes that equity interests have a greater voice in reorganization plans —

hence, the safeguards of disclosure, voting, acceptance and confirmation in present Chapter 11.

Resolving the apparent conflict between Chapter 11 and § 363(b) does not require an all or nothing approach. Every sale under § 363(b) does not automatically short-circuit or side-step Chapter 11; nor are these two statutory provisions to be read as mutually exclusive. Instead, if a bankruptcy judge is to administer a business reorganization successfully under the Code, then — like the related yet independent tasks performed in modern production techniques to ensure good results — some play for the operation of both § 363(b) and Chapter 11 must be allowed for.

The rule we adopt requires that a judge determining a § 363(b) application expressly find from the evidence presented before him at the hearing a good business reason to grant such an application. In this case the only reason advanced for granting the request to sell Lionel's 82 percent stock interest in Dale was the Creditors' Committee's insistence on it. Such is insufficient as a matter of fact because it is not a sound business reason and insufficient as a matter of law because it ignores the equity interests required to be weighed and considered under Chapter 11. The court also expressed its concern that a present failure to approve the sale would result in a long delay. As the Supreme Court has noted, it is easy to sympathize with the desire of a bankruptcy court to expedite bankruptcy reorganization proceedings for they are frequently protracted. "The need for expedition, however, is not a justification for abandoning proper standards." *Protective Committee for Independent Stockholders of TMT Trailer Ferry, Inc. v. Anderson*, 390 U.S. 414, 450 (1968). Thus, the approval of the sale of Lionel's 82 percent interest in Dale was an abuse of the trial court's discretion.

In fashioning its findings, a bankruptcy judge must not blindly follow the hue and cry of the most vocal special interest groups; rather, he should consider all salient factors pertaining to the proceeding and, accordingly, act to further the diverse interests of the debtor, creditors and equity holders, alike. He might, for example, look to such relevant factors as the proportionate value of the asset to the estate as a whole, the amount of elapsed time since the filing, the likelihood that a plan of reorganization will be proposed and confirmed in the near future, the effect of the proposed disposition on future plans of reorganization, the proceeds to be obtained from the disposition vis-a-vis any appraisals of the property, which of the alternatives of use, sale or lease the proposal envisions and, most importantly perhaps, whether the asset is increasing or decreasing in value. This list is not intended to be exclusive, but merely to provide guidance to the bankruptcy judge.

Finally, we must consider whether appellants opposing the sale produced evidence before the bankruptcy court that such sale was not justified. While a debtor applying under § 363(b) carries the burden of demonstrating that a use, sale or lease out of the ordinary course of business will aid the debtor's reorganization, an objectant, such as the Equity Committee here, is required to produce some evidence respecting its objections. Appellants made three objections below: First, the sale was premature because Dale is not a wasting asset and there is no emergency; second, there was no justifiable cause present since Dale, if anything, is improving; and third, the price was inadequate. No proof was required as to the first objection because it was stipulated as conceded. The second and third objections are interrelated. Following Judge Ryan's suggestion that objections could as a practical matter be developed on cross-examination, Equity's counsel elicited testimony from the financial expert produced by Lionel that Dale is less subject than other companies to wide market fluctuations. The same witness also conceded that he knew of no reason why those interested in Dale's stock at the September 7, 1983 hearing would not be just as interested six months from then.[4]

The only other witness who testified was the Chief Executive Officer of Lionel, who stated that it was only at the insistence of the Creditors' Committee that Dale stock was being sold and that Lionel "would very much like to retain its interest in Dale." These uncontroverted statements of the two witnesses elicited by the Equity Committee on cross-examination were sufficient proof to support its objections to the present sale of Dale because this evidence demonstrated that there was no good business reason for the present sale. Hence, appellants satisfied their burden.

Accordingly, the order appealed from is reversed and the matter remanded to the district court with directions to remand to the bankruptcy court for further proceedings consistent with this opinion.

WINTER, CIRCUIT JUDGE, DISSENTING

In order to expedite the decision in this matter, I set forth my dissenting views in summary fashion.

The following facts are undisputed as the record presently stands: (i) Lionel sought a buyer for the Dale stock willing to condition its purchase upon confirmation of a reorganization plan. It was unsuccessful since, in the words of the bankruptcy judge, "the confirmation of any plan is usually somewhat iffy," and few purchasers are willing to commit upwards of $50 million for an extended period without a contract binding on the other party; (ii) every feasible reorganization plan contemplates the sale of the Dale stock for cash; (iii) a reorganization plan may be approved fairly soon if the Dale stock is sold now. If the sale is prohibited, renewed negotiations between the creditors and the equity holders will be necessary, and the submission of a plan, if any, will be put off well into the future; and (iv) the Dale stock can be sold now at or near the same price as it can be sold later.

The effect of the present decision is thus to leave the debtor in possession powerless as a legal matter to sell the Dale stock outside a reorganization plan and unable as an economic matter to sell it within one. This, of course, pleases the equity holders who, having introduced no evidence demonstrating a disadvantage to the bankrupt estate from the sale of the Dale stock, are now given a veto over it to be used as leverage in negotiating a better deal for themselves in a reorganization.

The likely results of today's decision are twofold: (i) The creditors will at some point during the renewed protracted negotiations refuse to extend more credit to Lionel, thus thwarting a reorganization entirely; and (ii) notwithstanding the majority decision, the Dale stock will be sold under § 363(b) for exactly the same

---

[4] As noted, the bidding for Dale started with a $43 million offer from Acme-Cleveland and has since jumped to $50 million. There is no indication that this trend will reverse itself.

reasons offered in support of the present proposed sale. However, the ultimate reorganization plan will be more favorable to the equity holders, and they will not veto the sale.

It seems reasonably obvious that result (i) is something that the statutory provisions governing reorganizations, including § 363(b), are designed to avoid. Result (ii) not only is contrary to the purpose of the reorganization provisions in causing delay and further economic risk but also suffers from the legal infirmity which led the majority to reject the proposed sale, the only difference between the two sales being the agreement of the equity holders.

The equity holders offered no evidence whatsoever that the sale of Dale now will harm Lionel or that Dale can in fact be sold at a reasonable price as part of a reorganization plan. The courts below were quite right in not treating their arguments seriously for they are the legal equivalent of the "Hail Mary pass" in football.[1]

The equity holders argue that Chapter 11's provisions for disclosure, hearing and a vote before confirmation of a reorganization plan stringently limit the authority of trustees under 11 U.S.C. § 363(b). However, a reorganization plan affects the rights of the parties as well as the disposition of assets, and there is no inconsistency in allowing the disposition of property outside the confirmation proceedings. Arguably, some transactions proposed under § 363(b) would, if carried out, eliminate a number of options available for reorganization plans and thereby pre-ordain a particular kind of plan or preclude a reorganization entirely. In such a case, a colorable claim can be made for a limitation on a trustee's power under § 363(b) narrowly tailored to prevent such a result in order to effectuate the core purposes of Chapter 11. However, it is not disputed that in the present case the final reorganization plan will include a sale of Dale stock. A sale now thus does not preclude any feasible reorganization plan.

NOTES AND QUESTIONS

(1) *Whose Business Judgment?* Did you catch the court's reference, early in the *Lionel* opinion, to *the judge's* business judgment? The court said that a bankruptcy judge, in deciding whether to authorize a § 363(b) sale, has "considerable discretion" but is required "to articulate sound business justifications for *his* decisions." Is it the judge's business judgment that should be determinative? In cases such as these, are we dealing with the same business judgment rule that applies when judging the conduct of directors and officers outside of bankruptcy? *Is this the same business judgment rule as the one found in nonbankruptcy corporate law?* The answer is "sort of." The corporate law business judgment rule is often applied retroactively, after a corporate decision has been made — for example, in a shareholder derivative action — and functions as presumption of correctness as

---

[1] With due respect to my colleagues, the problem of statutory interpretation is entirely straightforward and not deserving of a lengthy exigesis into legal history. The language of § 363(b) is about as plain as it could be and surely does not permit a judicial grafting of stringent conditions on the power of trustees. As for its legislative history, the words "upon cause shown" were dropped by the Congress from the predecessor to § 363(b) in 1978, a signal clearly dictating that Congress meant what it said . . . .

long as corporate directors have met their duties of care, loyalty, etc. In other words, as long as no breaches of duty are found, the corporate business judgment rule means that the directors' business judgment will be honored. The bankruptcy business judgment rule, on the other hand, is almost always used prospectively, when a decision has been proposed to the court for approval, and it is the court's business judgment that is being applied in making the decision. *See, e.g., Orion Pictures Corp. v. Showtime Networks, Inc. (In re Orion Pictures Corp.)*, 4 F.3d 1095, 1098 (2d Cir. 1993). Put another way, the corporate business judgment rule is one where the court defers to the directors, while the bankruptcy business judgment rule is one where the court must concur with the business judgment of the trustee or debtor in possession in order to approve the transaction.

(2)   *Extraordinary but Common.* Debtors who seek haven in Chapter 11 often know from the outset that their rehabilitation may require more than an infusion of cash and a restructuring of their debt burden. They recognize that rehabilitation may require the elimination of unprofitable operations and product lines and the sale of certain assets. For example, if you review the *Mismanagement Week* article about the impending Amphydynamics bankruptcy filing, reprinted in chapter 1, you will see that, at the time of the filing, Headley Charisma predicted that Amphydyamics would reverse its trend of losses not only by cutting costs and by expanding its market share, but also by shutting down unprofitable retail outlets, auctioning off valuable leaseholds, and selling its St. Louis assembly plant. Although such sales are certainly out of the ordinary course of business for debtors, the reality is that they often are the stuff of which business reorganizations are made. In some cases, these sales have the support of most parties, and they are accomplished before a plan is proposed. Consider the following description of events that occurred in a case involving a major retailer before the debtor's plan was submitted to creditors for their approval:

> [P]ursuant to a strategy of continuing to operate only in those areas, both business and geographic, where it has historically experienced profitability, the Company terminated its supermarket operations in the Pennsylvania, New Jersey, New York, Connecticut and Tampa, Florida areas, discontinued its J. M. Fields discount department store operations, and closed its meat processing and certain produce operations. The company is in the process of disposing of its interests in properties related to those operations and in any other properties and assets not essential to its on-going business. Proceeds from the dispositions will be primarily applied to the Company's obligations under the proposed Plan of Arrangement and used to fund a portion of the Company's capital improvements program and pay certain secured indebtedness . . . .

> These stores operated at a substantial loss during past years. Prior to the Court's authorization for discontinuation, the Company explored alternative means to accomplish this disposition including sale of the entire operation as a going business. Efforts to find a qualified buyer for the entire division as an operating unit were unsuccessful and, therefore, the Company, with Court approval, ceased operation of the stores and entered into arrangements for the liquidation of the store's inventory and sale of the related real estate interests and other assets.

> Net proceeds derived by the Company from sales or other dispositions
> of its assets or business, as described above, have been generally required
> by the Court and informal agreement with the Creditors' Committees to be
> segregated and set aside for ultimate payment to Creditors, rather than for
> use as working capital.

Sometimes, as in the *Lionel* case, such sales encounter opposition, the nature of
which typically depends on the terms of sale, the contemplated use of proceeds, and
the effect the sale will have on various interest groups.

For example, in *Lionel*, the unsecured creditors' committee pressed management to sell the Dale Electronics stock in order to produce a large "pot of cash" to
repay creditors under any forthcoming reorganization plan. The committee representing Lionel's equity holders opposed the sale. Why? One reason is that in a case
in which all assets are to be sold, the sale forecloses the continuation of the business
and the shareholders' participation in it. Another reason — one that will become
more apparent as you learn more about the negotiation and formulation of
reorganization plans — is that a sale for cash definitively fixes the value of the
assets, limiting the ability of equity holders to demand better treatment under a
plan on the theory that the going concern value of those assets is higher than the
value assigned to it by the plan proponent. Also, if the sale produces a "pot of cash"
that is less than the amount required to satisfy claims, the absolute priority rule
prevents equity holders from sharing in that pot, unless creditors allow value to
trickle down or equity purchases that opportunity with an infusion of acceptable
new value into the enterprise. But, if equity holders are able to block the sale, then,
as Judge Winter chided in his dissenting opinion in *Lionel*, equity holders
strengthen their "leverage in negotiating a better deal for themselves in a
reorganization." *See also, e.g., In re V. Loewer's Gambrinus Brewery Co.*, 141 F.2d
747 (2d Cir. 1944).

In *Lionel*, the unsecured creditors favored the sale because it would have
produced enough cash to repay a large part of their claims. Were that not the case
— for example, were the proceeds of the sale sufficient only to cover secured claims
and administrative expenses — the unsecured creditors would have been less
enthusiastic. *See, e.g., In re WHET, Inc.*, 12 B.R. 743 (Bankr. D. Mass. 1981). In such
a situation, the creditors would be in the position of the shareholders in Lionel —
they would be the first class on the priority ladder that is not covered by any value
if the sale goes through. That first "out of the money" class is always willing to
gamble on future appreciations in value, as it has, literally, nothing to lose.

Parties may also object to the manner in which proceeds of the sale are to be
deployed. In *Lionel*, the debtor proposed to use the "pot of cash" to pay creditors'
claims. The Charismas have not said what they intend to do with the proceeds of the
sale of Comp-U-All. What position do you think Amphydynamics' creditors and
shareholders, respectively, would take if management intended to use the proceeds
to pay day-to-day operating expenses? To pay legal and other administrative costs
associated with the Chapter 11 case? To invest in new business ventures?

(3) *The Current Form of the Business Justification Standard.* In *Lionel*, the
Second Circuit ruled that a preplan sale of substantial assets is permissible only if
"a sound business purpose dictates such action," and that the burden is on the

proponent of the sale to show that it does. Here are some examples of cases in which a sound business justification was found to exist:

- Even a trustee had been unable to operate the debtor, a radio station, profitably, and absent a sale, the debtor would have been forced to go off the air and forfeit its FCC license. *Stephens Indus., Inc. v. McClung*, 789 F.2d 386 (6th Cir. 1986);

- The debtor, a railroad, was operating at such substantial continuing losses that a prompt sale was the only alternative to shutting down. *In re Delaware & Hudson Ry.*, 124 B.R. 169 (D. Del. 1991);

- The debtor, a mining company, could no longer afford to maintain its mines and equipment, putting their value at serious risk. *In re Lady H. Coal Co.*, 193 B.R. 233 (Bankr. S.D. W. Va. 1996).

The legislative history is fairly clear that Chapter 11 cases were supposed to produce plans of reorganization for confirmation, not preplan liquidations. *See* H.R. Rep. No. 95-595, at 221 (1977) ("The purpose of the reorganization . . . case is to formulate and have confirmed a plan of reorganization. . . . "). Early cases, such as *Lionel*, focused on the overall (and possibly idealized) structure of the Chapter 11 process as one in which the debtor files its petition, the automatic stay is invoked, a creditors' committee is appointed, plan negotiations ensue, and, if those negotiations are successful, and the debtor and its supporters have "scaled the hurdles erected in Chapter 11," a plan is confirmed. *See, e.g., Institutional Creditors of Cont'l Air Lines, Inc. v. Cont'l Air Lines, Inc. (In re Cont'l Air Lines, Inc.)*, 780 F.2d 1223, 1226 (5th Cir. 1986.)

However, as more debtors and creditors found themselves in the swamp that a Chapter 11 case can become, insolvency professionals began to understand the usefulness of a quick sale of substantially all the assets of the bankruptcy estate followed by a simple plan (sometimes called a "pot plan") providing for distribution of proceeds by strict priority. In other cases, conversion to Chapter 7 is the exit strategy. Thus, debtors' and purchasers' counsel fastened upon *Lionel's* "articulated business justification" standard and promoted sales of substantial portions or substantially all of the estate's assets. In time, in reaction to these repeated requests for preplan sales, the judicial bias against preplan sales of substantially all of a debtor's assets eroded. Coupled with the acceptance of using Code § 363(f), discussed below, to erect a firewall to block successor liability claims against the purchaser, this evolution of judicial attitude has promoted the use of Chapter 11 as a liability-limiting "wrapper" for what would otherwise be rather a vanilla asset purchase and sale that could otherwise be negotiated, documented, and consummated in or out of bankruptcy. *See* George W. Kuney, *Hijacking Chapter 11*, 21 Emory Bankr. Dev. J. 19 (2004).

(4) *Why not Liquidate in Chapter 7?* In the current economic setting, where debtor in possession financing is not easily available, many Chapter 11 cases have been filed by debtors who understood that their prospects for reorganization were nil and that a sale of the debtor's assets was inevitable. Why did these debtors not file Chapter 7 petitions? One reason may be that the debtors did not wish to relinquish control of the sales process to a trustee or allow a trustee to conduct a review of prepetition transactions, including payments to creditors and transfers to

insiders. Even if prepetition conduct was entirely proper, nobody wants a third party appointee investigating their affairs. After all, even if you have paid all your income taxes, would you choose to undergo a full audit by the Internal Revenue Service if you could avoid it? Creditors may also have preferred to see the liquidation conducted by management that they know, rather than by a trustee. There is also a widely held belief that assets marketed by a going concern still operating in Chapter 11 are likely to fetch more than assets sold by a Chapter 7 trustee at "fire sale" prices. Finally, although Code § 721 contemplates the possibility of a Chapter 7 trustee operating the debtor's business "for a limited period" as it is being wound down and liquidated, this section is seldom used. Chapter 7 trustees are not in the business of running companies, and there is little upside potential for a Chapter 7 trustee and plenty of downside risk in terms of criticism and even liability.

(5) *Buyer Created Emergencies.* What if a buyer threatens to walk away from a deal if the sale is not consummated quickly? Is that a good business justification for a preplan sale? One court has warned that rationalizing a sale on such grounds would foster "the self-destructive proposition that an offer of purchase may itself beget the emergency and that an impatient purchaser may stampede a reorganization court." *In re Solar Mfg. Corp.*, 176 F.2d 493 (3d Cir. 1949).

(6) *Other Required Showings.* Courts also expect the proponent of a sale to show that reasonable notice of the sale has been given, that the purchase price is fair, and that the sale is proposed in good faith. *In re WBQ P'ship*, 189 B.R. 97 (Bankr. E.D. Va. 1995); *In re WHET, Inc.*, 12 B.R. 743, (Bankr. D. Mass. 1981). For an example of a case in which this standard was not met, see *In re Ancor Exploration Co.*, 30 B.R. 802 (N.D. Okla. 1983). In that case, the court was troubled by the fact that the sale was to an insider, that no attempt was made to shop the property, that there was no need for a quick sale, and that the sales price was suspicious.

Read the Second Circuit's opinion below with an eye towards whether or not the *Lionel* standard remains intact some 26 years later. Is *Lionel* still the gold standard by which proposed sales are to be judged?

INDIANA STATE POLICE PENSION TRUST v. CHRYSLER, LLC
United States Court of Appeals, Second Circuit
576 F.3d 108 (2009)

Dennis Jacobs, Chief Judge:

The Indiana State Police Pension Trust, the Indiana State Teachers Retirement Fund, and the Indiana Major Moves Construction Fund (collectively, the "Indiana Pensioners" or "Pensioners"), along with various tort claimants and others, appeal from an order entered in the United States Bankruptcy Court for the Southern District of New York, Arthur J. Gonzalez, Bankruptcy Judge, dated June 1, 2009 (the "Sale Order"), authorizing the sale of substantially all of the debtor's assets to New CarCo Acquisition LLC ("New Chrysler"). On June 2, 2009 we granted the

Indiana Pensioners' motion for a stay and for expedited appeal directly to this Court, pursuant to 28 U.S.C. § 158(d)(2). On June 5, 2009 we heard oral argument, and ruled from the bench and by written order, affirming the Sale Order "for the reasons stated in the opinions of Bankruptcy Judge Gonzalez," stating that an opinion or opinions would follow. This is the opinion.

In a nutshell, Chrysler LLC and its related companies (hereinafter "Chrysler" or "debtor" or "Old Chrysler") filed a pre-packaged bankruptcy petition under Chapter 11 on April 30, 2009. The filing followed months in which Chrysler experienced deepening losses, received billions in bailout funds from the Federal Government, searched for a merger partner, unsuccessfully sought additional government bailout funds for a stand-alone restructuring, and ultimately settled on an asset-sale transaction pursuant to 11 U.S.C. § 363 (the "Sale"), which was approved by the Sale Order. The key elements of the Sale were set forth in a Master Transaction Agreement dated as of April 30, 2009: substantially all of Chrysler's operating assets (including manufacturing plants, brand names, certain dealer and supplier relationships, and much else) would be transferred to New Chrysler in exchange for New Chrysler's assumption of certain liabilities and $2 billion in cash. Fiat S.p.A agreed to provide New Chrysler with certain fuel-efficient vehicle platforms, access to its worldwide distribution system, and new management that is experienced in turning around a failing auto company. Financing for the sale transaction — $6 billion in senior secured financing, and debtor-in-possession financing for 60 days in the amount of $4.96 billion — would come from the United States Treasury and from Export Development Canada. The agreement describing the United States Treasury's commitment does not specify the source of the funds, but it is undisputed that prior funding came from the Troubled Asset Relief Program ("TARP"), 12 U.S.C. § 5211(a)(1), and that the parties expected the Sale to be financed through the use of TARP funds. Ownership of New Chrysler was to be distributed by membership interests, 55% of which go to an employee benefit entity created by the United Auto Workers union, 8% to the United States Treasury and 2% to Export Development Canada. Fiat, for its contributions, would immediately own 20% of the equity with rights to acquire more (up to 51%), contingent on payment in full of the debts owed to the United States Treasury and Export Development Canada.

At a hearing on May 5, 2009, the bankruptcy court approved the debtor's proposed bidding procedures. No other bids were forthcoming. From May 27 to May 29, the bankruptcy court held hearings on whether to approve the Sale.[1] Upon extensive findings of fact and conclusions of law, the bankruptcy court approved the Sale by order dated June 1, 2009.

After briefing and oral argument, we affirmed the bankruptcy court's order on June 5, but we entered a short stay pending Supreme Court review. The Supreme Court, after an extension of the stay, declined a further extension.

The factual and procedural background is set out in useful detail in the opinions of Bankruptcy Judge Gonzalez. This opinion is confined to a discussion of the arguments made for vacatur or reversal. The Sale Order is challenged essentially on

---

[1] Twelve witnesses testified (either live or through depositions), and 48 exhibits were introduced.

four grounds. First, it is contended that the sale of Chrysler's auto-manufacturing assets, considered together with the associated intellectual property and (selected) dealership contractual rights, so closely approximates a final plan of reorganization that it constitutes an impermissible *"sub rosa* plan," and therefore cannot be accomplished under § 363(b). We consider this question first, because a determination adverse to Chrysler would have required reversal. Second, we consider the argument by the Indiana Pensioners that the Sale impermissibly subordinates their interests as secured lenders and allows assets on which they have a lien to pass free of liens to other creditors and parties, in violation of § 363(f). We reject this argument on the ground that the secured lenders have consented to the Sale, as per § 363(f)(2) . . . .

DISCUSSION

We review a bankruptcy court's conclusions of law *de novo*, and its findings of fact under the clearly erroneous standard. *See Babitt v. Vebeliunas (In re Vebeliunas)*, 332 F.3d 85, 90 (2d Cir. 2003).

The Indiana Pensioners characterize the Sale as an impermissible, *sub rosa* plan of reorganization. *See Pension Benefit Guar. Corp. v. Braniff Airways, Inc. (In re Braniff Airways, Inc.)*, 700 F.2d 935, 940 (5th Cir. 1983) (denying approval of an asset sale because the debtor "should not be able to short circuit the requirements of Chapter 11 for confirmation of a reorganization plan by establishing the terms of the plan *sub rosa* in connection with a sale of assets"). As the Indiana Pensioners characterize it, the Sale transaction "is a 'Sale' in name only; upon consummation, new Chrysler will be old Chrysler in essentially every respect. It will be called 'Chrysler'. . . . Its employees, including most management, will be retained . . . . It will manufacture and sell Chrysler and Dodge cars and minivans, Jeeps and Dodge Trucks . . . . The real substance of the transaction is the underlying reorganization it implements." Indiana Pensioners' Br. at 46 (citation omitted).

Section 363(b) of the Bankruptcy Code authorizes a Chapter 11 debtor-in-possession to use, sell, or lease estate property outside the ordinary course of business, requiring in most circumstances only that a movant provide notice and a hearing. 11 U.S.C. § 363(b).[2] We have identified an "apparent conflict" between the expedient of a § 363(b) sale and the otherwise applicable features and safeguards of Chapter 11.[3] *Comm. of Equity Sec. Holders v. Lionel Corp. (In re Lionel Corp.)*, 722 F.2d 1063, 1071 (2d Cir. 1983); *cf. Braniff*, 700 F.2d at 940.

In *Lionel*, we consulted the history and purpose of § 363(b) to situate § 363(b) transactions within the overall structure of Chapter 11. The origin of § 363(b) is the Bankruptcy Act of 1867, which permitted a sale of a debtor's assets when the estate or any part thereof was "of a perishable nature or liable to deteriorate in value." *Lionel*, 722 F.2d at 1066 (citing § 25 of the Bankruptcy Act of 1867, Act of March 2, 1867, 14 Stat. 517) (emphasis omitted). Typically, courts have approved § 363(b)

---

[2] Section 363(b)(1) provides: "The trustee, after notice and a hearing, may use, sell, or lease, other than in the ordinary course of business, property of the estate. . . ." 11 U.S.C. § 363(b)(1).

[3] § 363(b) may apply to cases arising under Chapters 7, 11, 12, and 13 of the Bankruptcy Code. In this, as in *Lionel*, we consider only its applicability in the context of Chapter 11 cases.

sales to preserve "wasting asset[s]." *Id.* at 1068 (quoting *Mintzer v. Joseph (In re Sire Plan, Inc.)*, 332 F.2d 497, 499 (2d Cir. 1964)). Most early transactions concerned perishable commodities; but the same practical necessity has been recognized in contexts other than fruits and vegetables. "[T]here are times when it is more advantageous for the debtor to begin to sell as many assets as quickly as possible in order to insure that the assets do not lose value." *Fla. Dep't of Revenue v. Piccadilly Cafeterias, Inc.*, 128 S. Ct. 2326, 2342, 171 L. Ed. 2d 203 (2008) (Breyer, J., dissenting) (internal quotation marks omitted); *see also In re Pedlow*, 209 F. 841, 842 (2d Cir. 1913) (upholding sale of a bankrupt's stock of handkerchiefs because the sale price was above the appraised value and "Christmas sales had commenced and . . . the sale of handkerchiefs depreciates greatly after the holidays"). Thus, an automobile manufacturing business can be within the ambit of the "melting ice cube" theory of § 363(b). As *Lionel* recognized, the text of § 363(b) requires no "emergency" to justify approval. *Lionel*, 722 F.2d at 1069. For example, if "a good business opportunity [is] presently available," *id.*, which might soon disappear, quick action may be justified in order to increase (or maintain) the value of an asset to the estate, by means of a lease or sale of the assets. Accordingly, *Lionel* "reject[ed] the requirement that only an emergency permits the use of § 363(b)." *Id.* "[I]f a bankruptcy judge is to administer a business reorganization successfully under the Code, then . . . some play for the operation of both § 363(b) and Chapter 11 must be allowed for." *Id.* at 1071.

At the same time, *Lionel* "reject[ed] the view that § 363(b) grants the bankruptcy judge *carte blanche*." *Id.* at 1069.[4] The concern was that a quick, plenary sale of assets outside the ordinary course of business risked circumventing key features of the Chapter 11 process, which afford debt and equity holders the opportunity to vote on a proposed plan of reorganization after receiving meaningful information. *See id.* at 1069–70. Pushed by a bullying creditor, a § 363(b) sale might evade such requirements as disclosure, solicitation, acceptance, and confirmation of a plan. *See* 11 U.S.C. §§ 1122–29. "[T]he natural tendency of a debtor in distress," as a Senate Judiciary Committee Report observed, is "to pacify large creditors with whom the debtor would expect to do business, at the expense of small and scattered public investors." *Lionel*, 722 F.2d at 1070 (quoting S. Rep. No. 95-989, 2d Sess., at 10 (1978), *as reprinted in* 1978 U.S.C.C.A.N. 5787, 5796 (internal quotation marks omitted)).

To balance the competing concerns of efficiency against the safeguards of the Chapter 11 process, Lionel required a "good business reason" for a § 363(b) transaction:[5]

> [A bankruptcy judge] should consider all salient factors pertaining to the proceeding and, accordingly, act to further the diverse interests of the debtor, creditors and equity holders, alike. [A bankruptcy judge] might, for example, look to such relevant factors as the proportionate value of the

---

[4] If unfettered use of § 363(b) had been intended, there would have been no need for the requirement of notice and hearing prior to approval.

[5] The *Lionel* standard has subsequently been adopted in sister Circuits. *See, e.g., Stephens Indus. v. McClung*, 789 F.2d 386, 389–90 (6th Cir. 1986); *Inst. Creditors of Continental Air Lines, Inc. v. Continental Air Lines, Inc. (In re Continental Air Lines, Inc.)*, 780 F.2d 1223, 1226 (5th Cir. 1986).

asset to the estate as a whole, the amount of elapsed time since the filing, the likelihood that a plan of reorganization will be proposed and confirmed in the near future, the effect of the proposed disposition on future plans of reorganization, the proceeds to be obtained from the disposition vis-a-vis any appraisals of the property, which of the alternatives of use, sale or lease the proposal envisions and, most importantly perhaps, whether the asset is increasing or decreasing in value. This list is not intended to be exclusive, but merely to provide guidance to the bankruptcy judge.

722 F.2d at 1071.

After weighing these considerations, the Court in *Lionel* reversed a bankruptcy court's approval of the sale of Lionel Corporation's equity stake in another corporation, Dale Electronics, Inc. ("Dale"). The Court relied heavily on testimony from Lionel's Chief Executive Officer, who conceded that it was "only at the insistence of the Creditors' Committee that Dale stock was being sold and that Lionel 'would very much like to retain its interest in Dale,'" *id.* at 1072, as well as on a financial expert's acknowledgment that the value of the Dale stock was not decreasing, *see id.* at 1071–72. Since the Dale stock was not a wasting asset, and the proffered justification for selling the stock was the desire of creditors, no sufficient business reasons existed for approving the sale.

In the twenty-five years since *Lionel*, § 363(b) asset sales have become common practice in large-scale corporate bankruptcies. *See, e.g.*, Robert E. Steinberg, *The Seven Deadly Sins in Section 363 Sales*, Am. Bankr. Inst. J., June 2005, at 22, 22 ("Asset sales under § 363 of the Bankruptcy Code have become the preferred method of monetizing the assets of a debtor company."); Harvey R. Miller & Shai Y. Waisman, *Does Chapter 11 Reorganization Remain A Viable Option for Distressed Businesses for the Twenty-First Century?*, 78 Am. Bankr. L.J. 153, 194–96 (2004). A law review article recounts the phenomenon:

> Corporate reorganizations have all but disappeared . . . . TWA filed only to consummate the sale of its planes and landing gates to American Airlines. Enron's principal assets, including its trading operation and its most valuable pipelines, were sold within a few months of its bankruptcy petition. Within weeks of filing for Chapter 11, Budget sold most of its assets to the parent company of Avis. Similarly, Polaroid entered Chapter 11 and sold most of its assets to the private equity group at BankOne. Even when a large firm uses Chapter 11 as something other than a convenient auction block, its principal lenders are usually already in control and Chapter 11 merely puts in place a preexisting deal.

Douglas G. Baird & Robert K. Rasmussen, *The End of Bankruptcy*, 55 Stan. L. Rev. 751, 751–52 (2002) (internal footnotes omitted). In the current economic crisis of 2008–09, § 363(b) sales have become even more useful and customary.[6] The "side

---

[6] For instance, Lehman Brothers sold substantially all its assets to Barclays Capital within five days of filing for bankruptcy. Lehman Brothers filed for bankruptcy in the early morning hours of September 15, 2008. On September 20, 2008, the bankruptcy court approved the sale to Barclays of Lehman's investment banking and capital markets operations, as well as supporting infrastructure including the Lehman headquarters in midtown Manhattan for $1.7 billion. *See Bay Harbour Mgmt., L.C. v. Lehman*

door" of § 363(b) may well "replace the main route of Chapter 11 reorganization plans." Jason Brege, Note, *An Efficiency Model of § 363(b) Sales*, 92 Va. L. Rev. 1639, 1640 (2006).

Resort to § 363(b) has been driven by efficiency, from the perspectives of sellers and buyers alike. The speed of the process can maximize asset value by sale of the debtor's business as a going concern. Moreover, the assets are typically burnished (or "cleansed") because (with certain limited exceptions) they are sold free and clear of liens, claims and liabilities. [The section of the court's opinion dealing with successor liability issues is reprinted in the next section of the casebook.] . . . A § 363 sale can often yield the highest price for the assets because the buyer can select the liabilities it will assume and purchase a business with cash flow (or the near prospect of it). Often, a secured creditor can "credit bid," or take an ownership interest in the company by bidding a reduction in the debt the company owes. *See* 11 U.S.C. § 363(k) (allowing a secured creditor to credit bid at a § 363(b) sale).

This tendency has its critics. *See, e.g.*, James H.M. Sprayregen et al., *Chapter 11: Not Perfect, but Better than the Alternative*, Am. Bankr. Inst. J., Oct. 2005, at 1, 60 (referencing those who "decr[y] the increasing frequency and rise in importance of § 363 sales"). The objections are not to the quantity or percentage of assets being sold: it has long been understood (by the drafters of the Code,[7] and the Supreme Court[8]) that § 363(b) sales may encompass all or substantially all of a debtor's assets. Rather, the thrust of criticism remains what it was in Lionel: fear that one class of creditors may strong-arm the debtor-in-possession, and bypass the requirements of Chapter 11 to cash out quickly at the expense of other stakeholders, in a proceeding that amounts to a reorganization in all but name, achieved by stealth and momentum. *See, e.g., Motorola, Inc. v. Official Comm. of Unsecured Creditors and J.P. Morgan Chase Bank, N.A. (In re Iridium Operating LLC)*, 478 F.3d 452, 466 (2d Cir. 2007) ("The reason *sub rosa* plans are prohibited is based on a fear that a debtor-in-possession will enter into transactions that will, in effect, short circuit the requirements of Chapter 11 for confirmation of a reorganization plan." (internal quotation marks and alteration omitted)); Brege, *An Efficiency Model of § 363(b) Sales*, 92 Va. L. Rev. at 1643 ("The cynical perspective is that

---

Bros. Holdings Inc. (In re Lehman Bros. Holdings Inc.), No. 08-cv-8869(DLC), 2009 U.S. Dist. LEXIS 20893, (S.D.N.Y. Mar. 13, 2009) (affirming the § 363(b) sale order).

[7] As stated in *Lionel*, "[t]he Commission on the Bankruptcy Laws of the United States submitted a draft provision that would have permitted resort to § 363(b) in the absence of an emergency, even in the case of 'all or substantially all the property of the estate.' *See* Report of the Commission on the Bankruptcy Laws of the United States, H.R. Doc. No. 93-137, 93rd Cong., 1st Sess. (1973) at 239 (proposed § 7-205 and accompanying explanatory note). Congress eventually deleted this provision without explanation . . . ." *Lionel*, 722 F.2d at 1069–70 n.3.

[8] The Supreme Court has noted that § 363(b) is sometimes used to sell all or substantially all of a debtor's assets. In a footnote in *Florida Department of Revenue v. Piccadilly Cafeterias*, the Court wrote:

> Chapter 11 bankruptcy proceedings ordinarily culminate in the confirmation of a reorganization plan. But in some cases, as here, a debtor sells all or substantially all its assets under § 363(b)(1) (2000 ed., Supp. V) before seeking or receiving plan confirmation. In this scenario, the debtor typically submits for confirmation a plan of liquidation (rather than a traditional plan of reorganization) providing for the distribution of the proceeds resulting from the sale.

128 S. Ct. at 2330 n.2.

[§ 363(b)] serves as a loophole to the otherwise tightly arranged and efficient Chapter 11, through which agents of the debtor-in-possession can shirk responsibility and improperly dispose of assets."); *see also* Steinberg, *The Seven Deadly Sins in § 363 Sales*, Am. Bankr. Inst. J., at 22 ("Frequently, . . . the § 363 sale process fails to maximize value . . . .").

As § 363(b) sales proliferate, the competing concerns identified in *Lionel* have become harder to manage. Debtors need flexibility and speed to preserve going concern value; yet one or more classes of creditors should not be able to nullify Chapter 11's requirements. A balance is not easy to achieve, and is not aided by rigid rules and prescriptions. *Lionel*'s multi-factor analysis remains the proper, most comprehensive framework for judging the validity of § 363(b) transactions.

Adopting the Fifth Circuit's wording in *Braniff*, 700 F.2d at 940, commentators and courts — including ours — have sometimes referred to improper § 363(b) transactions as "*sub rosa* plans of reorganization." *See, e.g., In re Iridium*, 478 F.3d at 466 ("The trustee is prohibited from such use, sale or lease if it would amount to a *sub rosa* plan of reorganization."). *Braniff* rejected a proposed transfer agreement in large part because the terms of the agreement specifically attempted to "dictat[e] some of the terms of any future reorganization plan. The [subsequent] reorganization plan would have to allocate the [proceeds of the sale] according to the terms of the [transfer] agreement **or forfeit** a valuable asset." 700 F.2d at 940. As the Fifth Circuit concluded, "[t]he debtor and the Bankruptcy Court should not be able to short circuit the requirements of Chapter 11 for confirmation of a reorganization plan by establishing the terms of the plan *sub rosa* in connection with a sale of assets." *Id.*

The term "*sub rosa*" is something of a misnomer. It bespeaks a covert or secret activity, whereas secrecy has nothing to do with a § 363 transaction. Transactions blessed by the bankruptcy courts are openly presented, considered, approved, and implemented. *Braniff* seems to have used "*sub rosa*" to describe transactions that treat the requirements of the Bankruptcy Code as something to be evaded or subverted. But even in that sense, the term is unhelpful. The sale of assets is permissible under § 363(b); and it is elementary that the more assets sold that way, the less will be left for a plan of reorganization, or for liquidation. But the size of the transaction, and the residuum of corporate assets, is, under our precedent, just one consideration for the exercise of discretion by the bankruptcy judge(s), along with an open-ended list of other salient factors. *See Lionel*, 722 F.2d at 1071 (a bankruptcy judge should consider "such relevant factors as the proportionate value of the asset to the estate as a whole").

Braniff's holding did not support the argument that a § 363(b) asset sale must be rejected simply because it is a sale of all or substantially all of a debtor's assets. Thus a § 363(b) sale may well be a reorganization in effect without being the kind of plan rejected in *Braniff*.[9] *See, e.g., Fla. Dep't of Revenue v. Piccadilly Cafeterias,*

---

[9] The transaction at hand is as good an illustration as any. "Old Chrysler" will simply transfer the $2 billion in proceeds to the first lien lenders, and then liquidate. The first lien lenders themselves will suffer a deficiency of some $4.9 billion, and everyone else will likely receive nothing from the liquidation. Thus the Sale has inevitable and enormous influence on any eventual plan of reorganization or liquidation. But it is not a "*sub rosa* plan" in the *Braniff* sense because it does not specifically "dictate," or "arrange" *ex*

Inc., 128 S. Ct. at 2330 n.2. Although *Lionel* did not involve a contention that the proposed sale was a *sub rosa* or *de facto* reorganization, a bankruptcy court confronted with that allegation may approve or disapprove a § 363(b) transfer that is a sale of all or substantially all of a debtor's assets, using the analysis set forth in *Lionel* in order to determine whether there was a good business reason for the sale. *See In re Iridium*, 478 F.3d at 466 & n. 21 ("The trustee is prohibited from such use, sale or lease if it would amount to a *sub rosa* plan of reorganization . . . . In this Circuit, the sale of an asset of the estate under § 363(b) is permissible if the 'judge determining [the] § 363(b) application expressly find[s] from the evidence presented before [him or her] at the hearing [that there is] a good business reason to grant such an application.' " (citing *Lionel*, 722 F.2d at 1071)).

The Indiana Pensioners argue that the Sale is a *sub rosa* plan chiefly because it gives value to unsecured creditors (*i.e.*, in the form of the ownership interest in New Chrysler provided to the union benefit funds) without paying off secured debt in full, and without complying with the procedural requirements of Chapter 11. However, Bankruptcy Judge Gonzalez demonstrated proper solicitude for the priority between creditors and deemed it essential that the Sale in no way upset that priority. The lien holders' security interests would attach to all proceeds of the Sale: "Not one penny of value of the Debtors' assets is going to anyone other than the First-Lien Lenders." Opinion Granting Debtor's Motion Seeking Authority to Sell, May 31, 2009, ("Sale Opinion") at 18. As Bankruptcy Judge Gonzalez found, all the equity stakes in New Chrysler were entirely attributable to *new* value — including governmental loans, new technology, and new management — which were not assets of the debtor's estate. *See, e.g., id.* at 22–23.

The Indiana Pensioners' arguments boil down to the complaint that the Sale does not pass the discretionary, multifarious *Lionel* test. The bankruptcy court's findings constitute an adequate rebuttal. Applying the *Lionel* factors, Bankruptcy Judge Gonzalez found good business reasons for the Sale. The linchpin of his analysis was that the only possible alternative to the Sale was an immediate liquidation that would yield far less for the estate — and for the objectors. The court found that, notwithstanding Chrysler's prolonged and well-publicized efforts to find a strategic partner or buyer, no other proposals were forthcoming. In the months leading up to Chrysler's bankruptcy filing, and during the bankruptcy process itself, Chrysler executives circled the globe in search of a deal. But the Fiat transaction was the *only* offer available. Sale Opinion at 6; *see id.* at 16-17 ("Notwithstanding the highly publicized and extensive efforts that have been expended in the last two years to seek various alliances for Chrysler, the Fiat Transaction is the only option that is currently viable. The only other alternative is the immediate liquidation of the company.").[10]

The Sale would yield $2 billion. According to expert testimony[11] — not refuted by

---

ante, by contract, the terms of any subsequent plan.

[10] The bankruptcy court noted that Chrysler had discussed potential alliances with General Motors, Fiat, Nissan, Hyundai-Kia, Toyota, Volkswagen, Tata Motors, GAZ Group, Magna International, Mitsubishi Motors, Honda, Beijing Automotive, Tempo International Group, Hawtai Automobiles, and Chery Automobile Co. Sale Opinion at 6.

[11] The Indiana Pensioners moved to strike the testimony of Chrysler's valuation witness because he

the objectors — an immediate liquidation of Chrysler as of May 20, 2009 would yield in the range of nothing to $800 million.[12] Id. at 19. Crucially, Fiat had conditioned its commitment on the Sale being completed by June 15, 2009. While this deadline was tight and seemingly arbitrary, there was little leverage to force an extension. To preserve resources, Chrysler factories had been shuttered, and the business was hemorrhaging cash. According to the bankruptcy court, Chrysler was losing going concern value of nearly $100 million each day. Sale Order at 7.

On this record, and in light of the arguments made by the parties, the bankruptcy court's approval of the Sale was no abuse of discretion. With its revenues sinking, its factories dark, and its massive debts growing, Chrysler fit the paradigm of the melting ice cube. Going concern value was being reduced each passing day that it produced no cars, yet was obliged to pay rents, overhead, and salaries. Consistent with an underlying purpose of the Bankruptcy Code — maximizing the value of the bankrupt estate — it was no abuse of discretion to determine that the Sale prevented further, unnecessary losses. *See Toibb v. Radloff*, 501 U.S. 157, 163, 111 S. Ct. 2197, 115 L. Ed. 2d 145 (1991) (Chapter 11 "embodies the general [Bankruptcy] Code policy of maximizing the value of the bankruptcy estate.").

The Indiana Pensioners exaggerate the extent to which New Chrysler will emerge from the Sale as the twin of Old Chrysler. New Chrysler may manufacture the same lines of cars but it will also make newer, smaller vehicles using Fiat technology that will become available as a result of the Sale — moreover, at the time of the proceedings, Old Chrysler was manufacturing no cars at all. New Chrysler will be run by a new Chief Executive Officer, who has experience in turning around failing auto companies. It may retain many of the same employees, but they will be working under new union contracts that contain a six-year no-strike provision. New Chrysler will still sell cars in some of its old dealerships in the United States, but it will also have new access to Fiat dealerships in the European market. Such transformative use of old and new assets is precisely what one would expect from the § 363(b) sale of a going concern.

[The balance of the court's opinion is reprinted in § 6.02, infra. — Eds.]

CONCLUSION

We have considered all of the objectors-appellants' contentions on these appeals and have found them to be without merit. For the foregoing reasons, we affirm the June 1, 2009 order of the bankruptcy court authorizing the Sale.

---

has a financial interest in the outcome of the case: his firm would receive a transaction fee when the Sale was consummated. The bankruptcy court denied the motion on the grounds that such arrangements are typical; that the Indiana Pensioners did not object to the retention of the witness's firm; and that the witness's interest goes to weight of the evidence, not admissibility. Sale Opinion at 19 n.17. The Indiana Pensioners have not persuaded us that the bankruptcy court abused its discretion. *See generally Gen. Elec. Co. v. Joiner*, 522 U.S. 136, 138–39, 141–43, 118 S. Ct. 512, 139 L. Ed. 2d 508 (1997); *Ball v. A.O. Smith Corp.*, 451 F.3d 66, 69 (2d Cir. 2006) ("We review the bankruptcy court's evidentiary decisions for abuse of discretion.").

[12] The expert's earlier estimates of liquidation value had been higher. For example, in early May 2009, the same expert opined that a liquidation might yield between nothing and $1.2 billion. But, from the beginning of May until the end, Chrysler expended $400 million in cash collateral. Sale Opinion at 19.

Not all courts, however, apply *Lionel* in as permissive a fashion as the *Chrysler* court. Consider the following opinion, in which the judge concluded that the sale proponents had "reached too far." What factors led the court to reach that conclusion? Are the operative facts substantially different from those of the *Chrysler* case?

IN RE ON-SITE SOURCING, INC.

United States Bankruptcy Court, Eastern District of Virginia
412 B.R. 817 (2009)

ROBERT G. MAYER, UNITED STATES BANKRUPTCY JUDGE

The issue before the court is the extent to which a chapter 11 debtor may substitute a § 363 sale for a chapter 11 plan. The debtor reached too far in this case. While the sale will be approved, those portions that are a substitute for a chapter 11 plan will be excised. This memorandum opinion supplements the oral ruling of the court disallowing the proposed unsecured creditors trust. In order to fully appreciate the § 363 sale proposal, it is necessary examine the debtor's pre-petition sales efforts, the debtor's pre-petition debt structure and the debtor-in-possession's post-petition financing.

Background

Pre-Petition Sales Efforts

On-Site Sourcing, Inc.[1] filed a voluntary petition in bankruptcy pursuant to chapter 11 of the United States Bankruptcy Code on February 4, 2009, at 8:53 p.m. Over the next five hours the debtor filed twelve additional pleadings. The one at issue, a motion to approve auction procedures and the sale of substantially all of the debtor's assets (Docket Entry 10), was filed just after midnight, at 12:47 a.m., on February 5, 2009.[2] That morning, the court granted the debtor's motion for an expedited hearing on its first day motions which included the motion to approve the auction procedures and the sale of substantially all of the debtor's assets. The hearing was set for the following day, February 6, 2009.

It was immediately obvious from the papers filed in the case and the statements of counsel in court that this case was filed to facilitate Integreon Discovery Solutions (DC), Inc.'s purchase of substantially all of the debtor's assets. It appears that

---

[1] Two related entities also filed petitions. All three debtors are being jointly administered.

[2] The breadth of the motion is captured, in part, by its title: "Motion of the Debtors for Entry of Orders (I)(A) Establishing Bid Procedures Related to the Sale of Substantially All of the Debtors' Assets, (B) Scheduling a Hearing to Consider the Sale, (C) Approving the Form and Manner of Notice of Sale by Auction, (D) Establishing Procedures for Noticing and Determining Cure Amounts and (E) Granting Related Relief; and (II)(1) Approving Asset Purchase Agreement and Authorizing the Sale Free and Clear of All Liens, Claims, Encumbrances and Interests, (2) Authorizing the Assumption and Assignment of Certain Executory Contracts and Unexpired Leases and (3) Granting Related Relief."

nothing would have prevented a non-bankruptcy UCC sale but the parties sought a § 363 sale instead. The essence of the case and the events leading to the filing of the petition are captured in the debtor's sale motion. The debtor stated:

> 8. By 2008, the Debtors could no longer service their secured debt and entered into several forbearance agreements and amended credit facilities to negotiate revised repayment terms. In late 2008, still significantly leveraged and facing continued revenue decreases, the Debtors were facing liquidation. As part of a final offer to their secured lenders, the Debtors, along with their advisors, solicited potential purchasers of the business. After speaking to a number of potential buyers, both strategic and financial, as well as investment bankers and business brokers, the Debtors engaged in further discussions with six interested parties (the "Other Interested Parties"). These marketing efforts resulted in a competitor, Integreon Managed Solutions, Inc., agreeing to assume the role of the Debtors' secured lenders and negotiate the possible sale of the business. The secured debt (in a principal amount of approximately $35,000,000) was assigned to Integreon by the Debtors' former secured lenders in early 2009. The bankruptcy case was filed in order to pursue the highest and best offer for the sale of the Debtors' business operations.

> 9. Ultimately, the Debtors' discussions and negotiations with Integreon prior to and after the assignment of the Debtors' secured debt to Integreon resulted in the proposed asset purchase agreement (the "APA") described herein. Based on the Debtors' consultations with its financial advisors and other relevant considerations, the Debtors believe that it is in the best interest of the Debtors, their estates, creditors and other stakeholders to enter into the APA. In particular, the APA or a similar transaction would allow a significant portion of the Debtors' business to continue operations as a going concern thereby maintaining the important services the Debtors provide to their customers and, most importantly, preserving many of the jobs of the employees of the Debtors.

[Citation omitted.] The debtor clarified and disclosed that the secured debt was originally assigned to Integreon Managed Solutions, Inc. which then assigned it to its wholly-owned subsidiary, Integreon Discovery Solutions (DC), Inc. The latter entity is referred to as Integreon in this opinion.

The debtor's debt structure was a bit more complicated. There was subordinated debt and intracreditor subordination agreements. Integreon resolved this complication by acquiring the subordinated debt as well as the bank loan . . . .

DIP Financing Motion

One of the first day motions was a debtor-in-possession financing motion. Not surprisingly, the proposed DIP lender was Integreon. Integreon was the sole pre-petition secured creditor. The debt, while secured by a lien on almost all of the debtor's assets, was significantly undersecured. The debt was about $35 million, but Integreon proposed to pay and the debtor proposed to accept $28 million for substantially all of the debtor's assets as a going concern. As the sole secured creditor with a lien on assets worth less than its debt, it controlled the debtor's ability to obtain financing from any other source, assuming that in the then challenged environment there was another source. As the prospective purchaser of the debtor's assets as a going concern, it was in Integreon's best interests to assure that the debtor continued in operation. And that required post-petition funding.

The proposed DIP loan contained many provisions generally frowned upon and frequently rejected by most bankruptcy courts. Integreon proposed to loan the debtor $40 million even though the debtor only needed about $1 million, less receipts, to operate during the pendency of the sale of substantially all of its assets to Integreon, a period that was intended to be 30 to 60 days. The proposed loan term capped this period at 90 days. The $40 million was to be used to pay-off Integreon's pre-petition secured debt and replace it with post-petition debt. The provision would have promoted Integreon's pre-petition $7 million unsecured portion of its debt to an administrative claim.[3] In addition, Integreon was to be paid a lending fee of 0.75%, or $300,000, on the $40 million loan. It was to have a lien on all assets of the debtor, including all recoveries under chapter 5 of the Bankruptcy Code. It was to have priority and super-priority liens on all collateral over all other liens and claims under § 364(d). All obligations under the DIP loan were to be allowed administrative expense claims with a priority under § 364(c)(1) over any and all other administrative expenses of the kind specified or ordered pursuant to any provision of the Bankruptcy Code, including, but not limited to, §§ 105, 326, 328, 503(b), 507(a), 507(b) and 726. The effect of the proposed DIP loan was to foreclose the possibility of any other creditor receiving any distribution from the debtor, including all administrative claimants.

Certain administrative claimants were protected by proposed carve-outs. Integreon agreed that court fees, the United States Trustee's fees, fees incurred by a chapter 7 trustee not to exceed $50,000, a premium on directors and officers tail insurance not to exceed $30,000, and certain professional fees not to exceed $50,000 after a carve-out trigger notice would be carved-out from its lien and administrative claim.

The remedy in the event of a default under the proposed DIP loan, including the maturity of the loan in 90 days, was immediate and assured. The automatic stay would immediately terminate without further order of the court and Integreon could immediately utilize its remedies under the DIP loan documents.

---

[3] Bankruptcy Code § 506(a)(1) provides that an allowed secured claim is a secured claim only to the extent of the value of collateral and is an unsecured claim as to the balance. The DIP Financing Motion requested, in addition to a blanket lien on all of the debtor's assets, Bankruptcy Code § 364(c) protection which would also make Integreon's DIP loan an administrative claim with priority over any and all administrative expenses provided in §§ 503(b) and 507(b). This protection is important only if a DIP loan is not fully covered by the proposed collateral. Here, the "new" post-petition loan is clearly as undersecured as the "old" pre-petition loan. The effect would be to convert the pre-petition unsecured loan into a post-petition superpriority administrative claim. If the other unsecured creditors had even a glimmer of hope of receiving any distribution before the proposed DIP loan, they certainly had none under the proposed DIP loan. Integreon's pre-petition unsecured claim would be paid ahead of them as a post-petition superpriority administrative claim. [Note to students: If this financing scheme sounds familiar, that is because it is an example of the kind of "rollover" discussed in chapter 5 of the text. — Eds.]

The Sale Motion

The Sale Motion was filed with the petition and the DIP Financing Motion. The debtor and Integreon sought a prompt sale which would have effectively prevented any individual creditor from undertaking any meaningful review and analysis of the proposed sale. The sale did not proceed as quickly as anticipated, however, and the Unsecured Creditors Committee was able to become involved.[4]

The terms of the proposed sale benefitted Integreon and could have, had there been any other realistic interest, chilled the bidding. The Sale Motion proposed a break-up fee to Integreon of $560,000 plus additional expenses not to exceed $250,000.[5] Integreon's initial bid was to be $28,000,000. The minimum bid for any qualified bidder was $28,810,000 so that the break-up fee and expenses would be covered if there were another successful bidder. Thereafter, the bidding increment was $500,000. The sale was to be free and clear of all interests and claims.

Modifications to the Proposed Sale Obtained by Unsecured Creditors Committee

The Unsecured Creditors Committee ultimately supported the sale on modified terms. The proposed modifications provided that Integreon would forgive its deficiency claim; that certain assets would be excluded from the sale, specifically, tax refunds and chapter 5 causes of action against officers and directors (except three key employees that Integreon intended to retain) and 35% of all other chapter 5 causes of action. The pre-sale budget line for the Committee's attorneys was increased from $115,000 to $225,000, which Integreon agreed to pay. In addition, a general unsecured creditors trust was to be established. Integreon agreed to fund the trust with a lump sum payment of $132,500, a one-half interest in all tax refunds and the immediate payment of the Committee's professional's carve-out.

The United States Trustee objected to some of the proposed modifications. The sale was approved without the general unsecured creditors trust and without the releases for the three key employees. The funds that Integreon was to have paid to the trust were paid to the debtor.

No plan of reorganization has been filed. It appears from the comments of counsel that a plan, if it is filed, will be a liquidating plan and that there are no significant assets remaining to be liquidated after the consummation of the sale to Integreon.

---

[4] The Unsecured Creditors Committee requested a Rule 2004 examination of Integreon which both Integreon and the debtor opposed. The examination was never authorized but the parties appear to have cooperated enough to satisfy the Unsecured Creditors Committee's informational requests.

[5] Break-up fees can serve a useful purpose in bankruptcy auctions. But merely reciting the theoretical benefits in a motion does not insure that they inure to the benefit of the estate. One frequently proffered benefit is that the break-up fee encourages a reluctant prospective bidder to perform its due diligence and make the first bid, thereby opening a vigorous auction. If it is not the successful bidder, it is compensated for its efforts and reimbursed for its expenses, the compensation being justified by opening the auction in circumstances where there may have been no other reasonable bid. This is not the situation in this case. Integreon made its decision to purchase On-Site's electronic discovery business when it purchased the bank's note and the subordinated debt. It committed to the acquisition at that moment. It needed no other incentive to open the bidding. Indeed, it appears to have actively cooperated with the debtor in filing the case and seeking a quick § 363 sale. The break-up fee purchased nothing in this case.

Discussion

The difficulty with this case is not the decision to sell the debtor's assets in bankruptcy rather than through a non-bankruptcy UCC sale or the skill of the attorneys in identifying their client's interests and endeavoring to maximize them, but in recognizing the proper line between sales under § 363 before the confirmation of a chapter 11 plan and sales under § 1123(a)(5)(D) after confirmation of a chapter 11 plan. There are substantial differences in the procedures between the two sale methods and the creditor protections available. They are concisely stated in *In re Gulf Coast Oil Corp.*:

> A § 363(b) sale is generally viewed as quicker. Only a motion and a hearing are required, and most courts apply a "business judgment test" to determine whether to approve the sale. By contrast, confirmation of a chapter 11 plan usually involves (i) preparation, court approval, and distribution of a disclosure statement, (ii) voting by creditors to accept or to reject the plan, and (iii) determination by the Court of whether the plan meets statutory confirmation standards.

In re Gulf Coast Oil Corp., 404 B.R. 407, 415 (Bankr. S.D. Tex. 2009) (footnotes omitted).

This issue is not new. An early and still important case under the Bankruptcy Code of 1978 is *Committee of Equity Security Holders v. The Lionel Corp. (In re Lionel Corp.)*, 722 F.2d 1063 (2nd Cir. 1983). There the Court of Appeals reversed an order authorizing a pre-confirmation § 363(b) sale while expressly recognizing the authority of the bankruptcy court to authorize pre-confirmation § 363(b) sales in proper circumstances.

[The bankruptcy court then quoted extensively from the *Lionel* decision. — Eds.]

Judge Steen explains the development of the jurisprudence of chapter 11 § 363(b) sales in the Fifth Circuit in *In re Gulf Coast Oil Corp.* The discussion generally reflects the development of the law throughout the United States. He concludes that under the existing jurisprudence in the Fifth Circuit:

> The debtor in possession or trustee in a chapter 11 case must consider its fiduciary duties to all creditors and interest holders before seeking approval of a transaction under § 363(b).

> The movant must establish a business justification for the transaction and the bankruptcy court must conclude, from the evidence, that the movant satisfied its fiduciary obligations and established a valid business justification.

> A sale, use, or lease of property under § 363(b) is not *per se* prohibited even though it purports to sell all, or virtually all, of the property of the estate, but such sales (or proposed sales of the crown jewel assets of the estate) are subject to special scrutiny.

> Parties that oppose § 363(b) transactions on the basis that they constitute a *sub rosa* chapter 11 plan must articulate the specific rights that they

contend are denied by the transaction.

Although the bankruptcy court need not turn every § 363(b) hearing into a mini-confirmation hearing, the bankruptcy court must not authorize a § 363(b) transaction if the transaction would effectively evade the "carefully crafted scheme" of the chapter 11 plan confirmation process, such as by denying §§ 1125, 1126, 1129(a)(7), and 1129(b)(2) rights.

If the bankruptcy court concludes that such rights are denied, then the bankruptcy court can only approve the transaction if it fashions an appropriate protective measure modeled on those which would attend a reorganization plan.

Transactions that explicitly release all (or virtually all) claims against the estate, predetermine the structure of a plan of reorganization, and explicitly obligate parties to vote for or against a plan are not authorized under § 363(b).

Id. at 422.

Judge Steen suggests a number of factors to consider when a § 363 motion is brought before the court. He identifies and discusses nine areas of concern presenting them as questions and discussion. The nine areas of concern provide a solid foundation to analyze § 363 sales. They are, without the discussion which is itself very helpful:

1. Is there evidence of a need for speed?

2. What is the business justification?

3. Is the case sufficiently mature to assure due process?

4. Is the proposed APA sufficiently straightforward to facilitate competitive bids or is the purchaser the only potential interested party?

5. Have the assets been aggressively marketed in an active market?

6. Are the fiduciaries that control the debtor truly disinterested?

7. Does the proposed sale include all of a debtor's assets and does it include the "crown jewel"?

8. What extraordinary protections does the purchaser want?

9. How burdensome would it be to propose the sale as part of confirmation of a chapter 11 plan?

Id. at 423–424.

The court considered these and other factors in approving the proposed sale in this case, but required certain provisions to be excised. The excised provisions all furthered a *sub rosa* plan of reorganization. None, especially the proposed unsecured creditors trust, had a good business reason.

The releases for the three key employees were removed. Integreon asserted that it did not want its newly acquired employees to be burdened by claims that could be made by the debtor. It would distract them from their new jobs at Integreon. The difficulty was that no one was able to articulate what the threatened claims were, the likelihood that the debtor would prevail or what they were worth. Moreover, Integreon agreed to carve-out up to $30,000 for tail directors and officers liability insurance. The relation or availability of the insurance to the hypothetical claims and the effect of releasing them was not explored.[6] The absence of this information suggests that a sound business reason had not been formulated. Such provisions are more appropriately sought in the context of a chapter 11 plan confirmation where the issues can be fully explored, evaluated and measured against the confirmation requirements.

The payment to the proposed general unsecured creditors trust was removed. This provision was inserted at the insistence of the Unsecured Creditors Committee. The debtor presented itself as uninterested in the outcome of this provision. Integreon was unaffected by it. It agreed to pay the money to either the debtor or the proposed general unsecured creditors trust. The modification to the debtor's sale agreement provided:

> Integreon and the Committee recognize that the creation of such a separate trust remains subject to approval by the Bankruptcy Court. If the Court does not approve the establishment of such a trust, it is understood and agreed that Integreon will not be expected or required to provide any further consideration for the sale and that the sale shall go forward with all the assets provided for herein being received by the On-Site Estate including, without limitation the Collateral Carve-Out.

Notice of Material Changes to Terms of Asset Purchase Agreement, Exhibit A at 3. (Docket Entry 251). While the language was at first somewhat confusing to the court, Integreon stated at the hearing that the language meant that it would pay the $132,000 in any event, but no more.

The Unsecured Creditors Committee argues that the intended payment to the general unsecured creditors trust is really a distribution of Integreon's property and Integreon can do anything it likes with its property. In fact, the proceeds from the sale of property of the estate are property of the estate. Bankruptcy Code § 541. This is not changed by the fact that the property sold is subject to an encumbrance. That just means that the proceeds are also subject to an encumbrance. The proceeds nonetheless remain property of the estate. They are subject to the jurisdiction of the court. Moreover, the Committee's argument is vitiated by the facts of this case. In this case, upon consummation of the sale Integreon released its lien on the remaining property of the estate and forgave its deficiency. The money paid by Integreon remained property of the estate as proceeds from the sale of property of the estate, but free and clear of Integreon's lien which it released and which was extinguished by the satisfaction of the indebtedness to it by forgiveness.

The Committee further argues, quite disingenuously, that the payment is a gift from Integreon to the general unsecured creditors. It more aptly describes the

---

[6] There is no provision for issuing injunctions in § 363. Injunctions may be available in the context of a § 363 sale, but must be obtained by commencing an adversary proceeding. Fed.R.Bankr.P. 7001(7). They may be available as a part of a chapter 11 plan. *See* Bankruptcy Code § 524(g). The extent of the release sought by Integreon, for example, to prevent creditors as opposed to the debtor from bringing actions against the three key employees, may implement Rule 7001(7).

circumstances of the "gift" elsewhere in its reply to the United States Trustee's objection to the modified terms:

> 41. . . . The resolution of all disputes as between the Committee and Integreon with respect to the sale process was critical to the Sale Motion going forward unopposed, paving the way for Integreon and the Debtors to consummate the sale within the expedited time frame desired by the parties as vital to preserve the value of the assets of the estate to be sold.
>
> 42. In the event that the Sale Motion was opposed by the Committee, and the Committee was successful with its objections, the Closing could have been seriously delayed, resulting in a substantial decline in value of Integreon's collateral. Clearly, the Collateral Carve-Out is not only in exchange for the release/waiver of "estate" causes of action, but also for the removal of the only serious impediment to the Debtors and Integreon effectuating a quick sale that, as originally proposed, would have provided little, if any, benefit to any party other than Integreon. Under these circumstances, the Committee's agreement to support the Sale Motion constitutes substantial consideration given by the Committee, not on behalf of the estates or the Debtors, in exchange for the Collateral Carve-Out.

The Official Committee of Unsecured Creditors' Reply to the Objection of the United States Trustee to Certain Changes Set Forth in the Notice Of Material Changes to Terms of Asset Purchase Agreement at PP41–42. (Committee's Reply) (Docket Entry 292).

There is a greater problem with the general unsecured creditors trust: the effect on the chapter 11 process. The provision effectively predetermines, in significant part, the structure of an as yet to be drafted plan of reorganization and effectively evades the "carefully crafted scheme" of the chapter 11 plan confirmation process. *In re Gulf Coast Oil Corp.*, 404 B.R. at 422 (quoting *Pension Benefit Guaranty Corp. v. Braniff Airways, Inc. (In re Braniff Airways, Inc.)*, 700 F.2d 935, 940 (5th Cir. 1983)).

The general unsecured creditors trust provision is contrary to the scheme of distribution envisioned in both a chapter 7 and chapter 11 liquidation. It would assure that the general unsecured creditors are paid in advance of the administrative and priority claims. At oral argument, the Committee's counsel candidly admitted that the purpose was to assure that the general unsecured creditors received a distribution. He admitted that if there were insufficient funds to pay all administrative expenses and priority claims, some administrative or priority claimants would go unpaid while the unsecured creditors received a distribution. The chapter 7 liquidation scheme is a matter of consideration because conversion of this case to chapter 7 and payment of creditors under § 726 is likely. Moreover, the chapter 7 liquidation scheme provides a comparison against which this chapter 11 liquidation plan may be compared.

The total amount that Integreon is paying the debtor for its assets represents the fair value of the assets purchased on the day they were purchased. Fair market value of an asset is the value at which a willing buyer is willing to pay and a willing seller is willing to sell where neither the purchaser nor the seller are under any compulsion to buy or to sell. Here, both Integreon and the debtor are under pressure. The debtor cannot continue in business without outside financial support and Integreon desires a prompt conclusion to the sale, it having already effectively expended the purchase price in buying the bank's notes. But, it does represent the fair value at the time. The debtor had marketed itself and had no other offers. The Unsecured Creditors Committee agreed to the sale, which includes the total price to be paid although it was to receive special consideration. Had it thought that the price was inadequate, it would not have consented to the sale. The court was satisfied as to the price, the price being the total amount being paid by Integreon which includes the $132,000 and other consideration proposed to be earmarked for the general unsecured creditors trust.

In the ordinary course of a chapter 11 case, the $132,000 and other consideration proposed to be earmarked for the general unsecured creditors trust would be part of the fund to be distributed to creditors of the estate. That distribution would be determined in a confirmed chapter 11 plan. A chapter 11 plan cannot be confirmed unless it complies with § 1129(a). . . . Two provisions . . . would most likely be violated by the proposed general unsecured creditors trust. Priority claimants are adversely affected. Section 1129(a)(7) requires that an impaired class of claims accept the plan or receive as much as they would receive under a distribution under chapter 7. Absent consent, this is not satisfied if the general unsecured creditors receive a distribution before the priority claims are paid in full. In addition, § 1129(a)(9) requires that all administrative claims be paid in full unless the holder of a particular claim has agreed to a different treatment. The consideration earmarked for the general unsecured creditors trust effectively evades this requirement by redirecting part of the purchase price from the administrative expense claimants to general unsecured creditors without the consent of the holders of the administrative claims.

It is true that consent to a chapter 11 plan could overcome the confirmation requirements of §§ 1129(a)(7) and (a)(9). Consent invokes the chapter 11 provisions relating to the preparation, approval and circulation of a disclosure statement. The disclosure statement is the mechanism by which creditors make informed choices on a proposed chapter 11 plan. This case has not progressed to the disclosure statement point, yet. Without consent, it does not appear that § 1129(b) would enable the court to confirm a plan containing the proposed general unsecured creditors trust. Moreover, the sale process was quick. The applicable terms were not filed with the court until April 9, 2009. The hearing approving the sale was held on April 28, 2009. It is not clear that the adversely affected parties had meaningful notice, if they received any notice of the proposed general unsecured creditors trust. Only the United States Trustee appeared and challenged the provision.

The end result of the proposed consideration for the general unsecured creditors trust would have been to divert a part of the proceeds of the sale of the debtor's assets to the general unsecured creditors to the detriment of administrative expense and priority creditors and thereby allow the general unsecured creditors to avoid some of the vicissitudes of the chapter 11 process or a conversion to chapter 7. All of this violates the protections chapter 11 seeks to provide for creditors, particularly administrative expense and priority creditors. They are effectively deprived of their rights under § 1129(a)(7) and (a)(9), their right to adequate information to make an informed decision on a proposed chapter 11 plan under § 1125, and their right to object to a proposed chapter 11 plan under § 1126.

There is another aspect that is troubling. Integreon paid the $132,000 as additional consideration so that it could obtain quick approval of the sale. The Committee stated as much. . . . There is nothing wrong with the Committee or any individual creditor examining a proposed transaction to determine whether it is fair and reasonable. Nor is there anything wrong in the Committee or any individual creditor objecting to a proposed transaction that is not fair or reasonable. Chapter 11 is a community action. It is hoped that through the analysis and action of the creditor body both collectively and individually that the best result for the most creditors within the confines of the Bankruptcy Code will be achieved. However, it is unfair to successfully increase an inadequate sales price to a fair sales price, but then keep that benefit for one's own constituency at the expense of other more senior classes of creditors. It is unfair to other creditors adversely affected. It is unfair to prospective purchasers. Prospective purchasers should defend their offers on the merits. The sale should benefit the estate. They should not be put in the position of succumbing to creditors seeking individual advantage. The court should not facilitate or encourage this type of action. It may discourage prospective purchases or cause them to underbid in the expectation that there will be objections that have to be resolved on an individual basis. This distorts the chapter 11 process.

The final consideration is the weight to be placed on the debtor's business judgment. The court returns to *In re Gulf Coast Oil Corp.* It discussed this matter:

> 6. Are the fiduciaries that control the debtor truly disinterested?
>
> As the Fifth Circuit discussed, a debtor-in-possession must exercise fiduciary duty in determining whether and how to propose a sale of assets. If entities that control the debtor will benefit, or will potentially benefit, from the sale the court must carefully consider whether it is also appropriate to defer to their business judgment.

In re Gulf Coast Oil Corp., 404 B.R. at 424.

In determining the weight to put on the debtor's business judgment in this case, the court recognizes the difficult positions in which the debtor was placed. The first was with the Committee. While the debtor benefitted from the Committee's success in having Integreon forgive its potentially huge deficiency claim, it opposed the Committee's request for a Rule 2004 examination of Integreon. In addition, the proposed consideration to the general unsecured creditors trust shows the not unusual situation where the debtor has a lot at stake and the particular controversy is relatively insignificant. The debtor was, as have been many other chapter 11 debtors, caught in the crossfire.

The debtor was in a difficult position when Integreon requested releases for the three key employees. The matter is somewhat clouded. It is not clear what role the three key employees played in the management of the debtor, the Integreon negotiations or the direction of the chapter 11 case. It is not clear what claims against the employees might have existed or the value of the claims. This situation is an uncomfortable one for a debtor-in-possession.

The general unsecured creditors trust provision illustrates another uncomfortable position for the debtor. The entire sale, worth over $28 million was placed in risk, and at least faced delay, over the additional consideration to the general unsecured creditors trust of $132,000 and other assets. No sound business reason was articulated by the debtor for the general unsecured creditors trust. Even the Unsecured Creditors Committee does not offer one other than it permitted the resolution of "all disputes as between the Committee and Integreon with respect to the sale process [which were] critical to the Sale Motion going forward unopposed, paving the way for Integreon and the Debtors to consummate the sale within the expedited time frame desired by the parties as vital to preserve the value of the assets of the estate to be sold." Committee's Reply at P41. This is a spoiler's argument.[7] The debtor faced the prospect of losing the sale over a relatively small amount, possibly one or two percent of the total deal.

Given the difficult positions in which the debtor found itself, the court cannot give much deference to the debtor's business judgment as applied to these additional provisions. The two provisions are not supported by legitimate business reasons.[8] They do not advance the debtor's chapter 11 efforts. They distort the chapter 11 process. They compromise the debtor's fiduciary duties which run to all creditors, not simply a portion of the creditors. It is difficult to imagine any business reason furthered by the proposed general unsecured creditors trust other than appeasement of "the hue and cry of the most vocal special interest groups." *In re Lionel Corp.*, 722 F.2d at 1071.

The court is satisfied that the overall sale was in the best interests of the debtor and that the debtor exercised its sound business judgment in proposing the sale. However, the court cannot give any significant weight to the debtor's business judgment as exercised by the inclusion of the general unsecured creditors trust or the release of the three key employees. The remedy was, with the consent of the debtor, Integreon and the Unsecured Creditors Committee, to excise these provisions and approve the sale without them.

Conclusion

The § 363(b) sale of substantially all of the assets of the debtor to Integreon was approved by the court despite the fact that it was for all practical purposes the predetermined purchaser. The debtor's pre-petition sales efforts and the absence of money in the credit market satisfied the court that this was the best deal — and the only one — available. Integreon came into the court with an exceptionally strong position as the sole pre-petition secured creditor with a significant undersecured

---

[7] The sale as originally proposed, "provided little, if any, benefit to any party other than Integreon." Committee's Reply at P42.

[8] There is a certain amount of pragmatism in caving in to a spoiler's arguments, particularly where the additional cost of the sale in relation to the potential benefit of the sale is relatively small. Pragmatism, though, does not convert a spoiler's argument into a legitimate business reason. The Unsecured Creditors Committee never developed its objections before the court. Whatever those objections might have been, the court cannot see why they would be unique to the general unsecured creditors. At best, they concerned the sales process or the sales price, matters of concern to all creditors and parties in interest.

claim. It sought additional leverage in the DIP Financing Motion. Much of the requested relief in the DIP Financing Motion, such as the roll-up of the pre-petition debt into a single post-petition debt was denied. The excesses in the Sales Motion were eliminated, such as the unnecessary break-up fee. The Unsecured Creditors Committee was successful in obtaining a major concession, the forgiveness of any deficiency claim. Whether this will be worth anything is unknown at this time, but without the concession, the unsecured creditors' claims would have been significantly diluted by Integreon's huge unsecured deficiency claim.

The principal relief denied was the Unsecured Creditors Committee's provision for a general unsecured creditors trust. That was excised from the sale for the reasons set out above.

§ 6.02 THE POWER TO SELL FREE AND CLEAR OF CLAIMS AND INTERESTS

Bankruptcy Code § 363(f) permits a trustee or debtor in possession to sell property of the estate free and clear of *interests* in the property if any one of five conditions is met:

(1) applicable nonbankruptcy law permits sale of such property free and clear of such interest;

(2) the entity asserting the interest consents;

(3) such interest is a lien, and the price at which such property is to be sold is greater than the aggregate value of all liens on such property;

(4) such interest is in bona fide dispute; or

(5) the entity asserting the interest could be compelled, in a legal or equitable proceeding, to accept a money satisfaction of such interest.

The sale free and clear powers have presented a number of issues that have been resolved by the courts and through statutory amendment during the period since § 363(f) was enacted in 1979. For example, the term "interest" — the group of things free of which an asset may be sold — is not defined in the Bankruptcy Code, despite the fact that detailed definitions for many similar foundational terms may be found in Code §§ 101 and 102. Both the Second and Third Circuits, which include the Southern District of New York and the District of Delaware, the nation's premiere Chapter 11 venues, have rejected a limiting definition of interest and held that "claims," such as successor liability claims that would otherwise follow the property, are in the category of interests that can be stripped off or washed away through a § 363(f) sale.

[A]　Conditions for Sale Free and Clear

[1]　Code §§ 363(f)(1), (2), (3) — Unsurprising Conditions Allowing Sale Free and Clear

The first three alternative preconditions for preplan sales free and clear under § 363(f) are straightforward. Under § 363(f)(1), if applicable nonbankruptcy law permits the sale, the Code also permits the sale. Essentially, this recognizes that there is no reason to limit preexisting rights and remedies in a liquidation or reorganization to benefit creditors and parties in interest. There may be an advantage to selling the assets under § 363(f)(1) rather than the applicable nonbankruptcy law, since under § 363(f)(1) there is no need to follow the procedures of applicable nonbankruptcy law. For example, in *In re Terrace Chalet Apartments, Ltd.*, 159 B.R. 821, 824–25 (N.D. Ill. 1993), the court held that the notice, manner, and timing of a sale free and clear are governed by Bankruptcy Rules 2002(a)(2) and 6004(f)(1) and not by otherwise applicable state foreclosure law. This may result in savings of time and money. Additionally, the protections of the bankruptcy court's findings of fact and conclusions of law and order approving the sale may make this method of sale desirable, especially if postsale litigation is foreseen.

Similarly, under § 363(f)(2), if the party asserting the interest consents to the sale free and clear of that interest, the Code permits the sale. The statute is generally construed to require actual consent, not "deemed consent" based upon a failure to object. *In re Roberts*, 249 B.R. 152 (Bankr. W.D. Mich. 2000) (When failure to object is the standard, the statute and rules use the phrase "after notice and a hearing," defined in § 102(1)(B)(i), which authorizes the no-hearing-without-objection-and-request-for-hearing procedure that is pervasive in bankruptcy practice and is colloquially known as "scream or die."); *but see Citicorp Home Owner Serv., Inc. v. Elliot (In re Elliot)*, 94 B.R. 343, 345–46 (E.D. Penn. 1988) (failure to object is not implied consent that will satisfy § 363(f)(2)). At minimum, § 363(f)(2) recognizes that there is no reason to bar a consensual transaction that will benefit the estate.

Finally, under § 363(f)(3), a sale free and clear of liens — a narrower category than "interests" — is authorized when such a sale will result in proceeds that exceed the aggregate value of all liens on the property. The liens exist to secure payment; if the payment is made, there is no need for the liens. A sale under § 363(f)(3) does, however, significantly change the rights of the parties and may negatively affect a lienholder who is forced to receive an accelerated prepayment of a long-term obligation under documents that lack prepayment fees and similar protective provisions.

The one controversial aspect of § 363(f)(3) concerns the amount of the payment that must be made to a purportedly secured creditor when the value of the collateral will not support full payment of the claim. Remember that 11 U.S.C. § 506(a)(1) bifurcates an undersecured claim into a secured claim equal to the value of the collateral and an unsecured deficiency claim. For example, if an undersecured creditor holds a note for $100 that is secured by property worth $60, under § 506(a)(1) she holds a secured claim of $60 and an unsecured claim of $40. In that case, does the sale of her collateral free and clear of her lien have to produce proceeds of $60 or $100 to be authorized under § 363(f)(3)? The courts have split on the issue. Even after the 1984 amendments, which attempted to resolve this question, the courts disagree as to whether the statute requires the payment of the economic value of the lien or the full amount of the obligation that the lien secured. For example, in *In re Beker Indus. Corp.*, 63 B.R. 474, 477 (Bankr. S.D.N.Y. 1986), the court held that the term "aggregate value of all liens" meant the actual economic value of the lien, which in the case of our example, would mean $60. In contrast, in *Richardson v. Pitt County (In re Stroud Wholesale, Inc.)*, 47 B.R. 999, 1002 (E.D.N.C. 1985), *aff'd*, 983 F.2d 1057 (4th Cir. 1986), the court held that "aggregate value of all liens" meant the full amount of all debt secured by the liens, which in our example would mean $100. The different approaches result from the wording of the statute, which uses the confusing concept of "valuing a lien" rather than referring to the amount of the debt secured, or purportedly secured, by the lien.

[2]   Code § 363(f)(4) — Sale When the Interest Is in Bona Fide Dispute

Although far-reaching, the fourth condition to the power of sale free and clear is pretty easily understood and applied. If the property interest is subject to bona fide dispute between the interested parties, the property can be sold free and clear of that interest, which will generally attach to the proceeds. This provision allows productive assets subject to deadlocking disputes to be transferred to a third party so that they can remain economically productive while the original parties may continue to litigate or otherwise proceed to resolve their dispute.

Although it is clear that the burden of demonstrating the existence of a bona fide dispute is borne by the proponent of the sale, *In re Octagon Roofing*, 123 B.R. 583, 590 (Bankr. N.D. Ill. 1991), the definition of "bona fide" is less than clear. In *Cheslock-Bakker & Assocs. v. Kremer (In re Downtown Athletic Club)*, 2000 U.S. Dist. LEXIS at *10 (S.D.N.Y. June 9, 2000) the court stated that showing the existence of a "bona fide" dispute requires "an objective basis for either a factual or legal dispute." The commencement of an adversary proceeding by either party challenging the priority, validity, and extent of the lien is not required, however. *In re Oneida Lake Dev, Inc.*, 114 B.R. 352, 357–58 (Bankr. N.D.N.Y. 1990); *In re Millerburg*, 61 B.R. 125 (Bankr. E.D.N.C. 1986).

A sale under § 363(f)(4) makes good sense in a simple case involving economically productive assets. It allows an asset to be sold and the proceeds to essentially be the subject of an interpleader-like proceeding in the bankruptcy court. The sale free and clear allows the asset to return to productivity, with attendant societal benefits, while the owners' and creditors' interests are adequately protected, generally by being transformed into an interest in the proceeds of the sale. Assuming something approaching a perfect market for the sale of the asset, the owners are not materially harmed and economic efficiency is served.

[3]   Code § 363(f)(5) — The Standard That Could Have Swallowed the Others

The final alternative condition for a sale free and clear under § 363(f) is potentially the broadest of all: § 363(f)(5). It provides for a sale free and clear of interests if the interest holder "could be compelled, in a legal or equitable proceeding, to accept a money satisfaction of such interest." A plain reading of the statute is: If an entity can be forced to accept money for the property interest at law or in equity, its interest can be stripped off the asset in a § 363 sale.

Public and private sales of collateral pursuant to Article 9 of the U.C.C., and real property foreclosure sales pursuant to state real property law, are the most common kinds of hypothetical proceedings contemplated by § 363(f)(5). If the claimant, generally a lienholder, could be forced to accept a monetary satisfaction through the process of foreclosure, the condition is satisfied and the sale may take place. It is not even clear that a senior lien must actually exist, as foreclosure of a hypothetical priming tax lien may conceivably satisfy the condition.[1]

Some courts hold that a hypothetical plan of reorganization cramdown scenario that would result in removal of the interest from the asset satisfies the § 363(f)(5) analysis. Under this theory, if the entity could be forced to accept a money satisfaction for its interest in a cramdown, then a sale free and clear is permitted. To date, reported cases dealing with Code § 1129(b)(2) cramdown as the mechanism used to extinguish an interest under § 363(f)(5) have involved liens, not ownership claims or traditional *in rem* interests that run with the land.

Some courts have considered and authorized sales free and clear of liens if those liens could be subordinated under Code § 724(b) and disallowed and stripped down under Code § 507(a)(1). One commentator has suggested that a hypothetical eminent domain proceeding should qualify, *see* Basil R. Mattingly, *Sale of Property of the Estate Free and Clear of Restrictions and Covenants in Bankruptcy*, 4 Am. Bankr. Inst. L. Rev. 431 (1996), but no court has adopted that position in a written ruling, probably either because the issue has never come up or because that interpretation would cause (f)(5) to swallow and make unnecessary the other § 363(f) subsections.

Now we return to the Second Circuit's *Chrysler* opinion to see how the sale free and clear process plays out in the face of objections by lienholders as well as product liability claimants.

INDIANA STATE POLICE PENSION TRUST V. CHRYSLER, LLC (IN RE CHRYSLER LLC, PART 2)
United States Court of Appeals, Second Circuit
576 F.3d 108 (2009)

Dennis Jacobs, Chief Judge:

The portion of the opinion in which the court holds that there was a good business justification for a prompt sale of the debtor's assets is reproduced in § 6.01 of this chapter. — Eds.]

---

[1] *Cf. In re Grand Slam U.S.A.*, 178 B.R. 460, 461–64 (E.D. Mich. 1995)(hypothetical administrative expense subordinating lien allowed sale without payment in full of subordinated debt).

II

The Indiana Pensioners next challenge the Sale Order's release of all liens on Chrysler's assets. In general, under § 363(f), assets sold pursuant to § 363(b) may be sold "free and clear of any interest" in the assets when, *inter alia*, the entity holding the interest consents to the sale. 11 U.S.C. § 363(f)(2). The bankruptcy court ruled that, although the Indiana Pensioners did not themselves consent to the release, consent was validly provided by the collateral trustee, who had authority to act on behalf of all first-lien credit holders.

We agree. Through a series of agreements, the Pensioners effectively ceded to an agent the power to consent to such a sale; the agent gave consent; and the Pensioners are bound. Accordingly, questions as to the status or preference of Chrysler's secured debt are simply not presented in this case.

The first-lien holders — among them, the Indiana Pensioners — arranged their investment in Chrysler by means of three related agreements: a First Lien Credit Agreement, a Collateral Trust Agreement, and a Form of Security Agreement. Together, these agreements create a framework for the control of collateral property. The collateral is held by a designated trustee for the benefit of the various lenders (including the Indiana Pensioners). In the event of a bankruptcy, the trustee is empowered to take any action deemed necessary to protect, preserve, or realize upon the collateral. The trustee may only exercise this power at the direction of the lenders' agent; but the lenders are required to authorize the agent to act on their behalf, and any action the agent takes at the request of lenders holding a majority of Chrysler's debt is binding on all lenders, those who agree and those who do not.

When Chrysler went into bankruptcy, the trustee had power to take any action necessary to realize upon the collateral — including giving consent to the sale of the collateral free and clear of all interests under § 363. The trustee could take such action only at the direction of the lenders' agent, and the agent could only direct the trustee at the request of lenders holding a majority of Chrysler's debt. But if those conditions were met — as they were here — then under the terms of the various agreements, the minority lenders could not object to the trustee's actions since they had given their authorization in the first place.

. . . .

Anticipating the consequence of this contractual framework, the Indiana Pensioners argue as a last resort that the majority lenders were intimidated or bullied into approving the Sale in order to preserve or enhance relations with the government, or other players in the transaction. Absent this bullying, the Pensioners suggest, the majority lenders would not have requested the agent to direct the sale of the collateral, and the Sale would not have gone through. The Pensioners argue that this renders the lenders' consent ineffective or infirm.

The record before the bankruptcy court, and the record before this Court, does not support a finding that the majority lenders were coerced into agreeing to the Sale. On the whole, the records (and findings) support the view that they acted prudently to preserve substantial value rather than risk a liquidation that might have yielded nothing at all. Moreover, it is not at all clear what impact a finding of coerced consent would have on the validity of the consent given, or whether the bankruptcy court would have jurisdiction — or occasion — to adjudicate the Indiana Pensioners' allegation. Because the facts alleged by the Indiana Pensioners are not substantiated in this record, their arguments based on those allegations provide no ground for relief in this proceeding, and we decline to consider whether the allegations might give rise to some independent cause of action.

. . . .

IV

Finally, several objectors appeal from that portion of the Sale Order extinguishing all existing and future claims against New Chrysler, that "(a) arose prior to the Closing Date, (b) relate[] to the production of vehicles prior to the Closing Date or (c) otherwise [are] assertable against the Debtors or [are] related to the Purchased Assets prior to the closing date." Sale Order at 40. The objectors can be divided into three groups: (1) plaintiffs with existing product liability claims against Chrysler; (2) plaintiffs with existing asbestos-related claims against Chrysler; and (3) lawyers undertaking to act on behalf of claimants who, although presently unknown and unidentified, might have claims in the future arising from Old Chrysler's production of vehicles. We consider each group's arguments in turn.

A. Existing Product Liability Claims

The Ad Hoc Committee of Consumer-Victims of Chrysler LLC and William Lovitz et al. challenge the foreclosing of New Chrysler's liability for product defects in vehicles produced by Old Chrysler.[15] Section 363(f) provides, in relevant part, that a "trustee may sell property . . . free and clear of *any interest in such property*," under certain circumstances. 11 U.S.C. § 363(f) (emphasis added). The objectors argue that personal injury claims are not "interests in property," and that the district court's reliance on *In re Trans World Airlines, Inc.*, 322 F.3d 283 (3d Cir. 2003) ("*TWA*"), which advances a broad reading of "interests in property," was misplaced.

We have never addressed the scope of the language "any interest in such property," and the statute does not define the term. *See, e.g., Precision Indus., Inc. v. Qualitech Steel SBQ, LLC*, 327 F.3d 537, 545 (7th Cir. 2003) ("The Bankruptcy Code does not define 'any interest,' and in the course of applying § 363(f) to a wide variety of rights and obligations related to estate property, courts have been unable to formulate a precise definition.").

In *TWA*, the Third Circuit considered whether (1) employment discrimination claims and (2) a voucher program awarded to flight attendants in settlement of a class action constituted "interests" in property for purposes of § 363(f). *See* 322 F.3d at 285. The Third Circuit began its analysis by noting that bankruptcy courts around the country have disagreed about whether "any interest" should be defined

---

[15] The Sale Order does not limit the right of tort plaintiffs to pursue existing claims against Old Chrysler. However, it is undisputed that little or no money will be available for damages even if suits against Old Chrysler succeed.

broadly or narrowly.[16] *Id.* at 288–89. The Third Circuit observed, however, that "the trend seems to be toward a more expansive reading of 'interests in property' which 'encompasses other obligations that may flow from ownership of the property.'" *Id.* at 289 (quoting 3 Collier on Bankruptcy P 363.06[1]); *see also* George W. Kuney, *Misinterpreting Bankruptcy Code § 363(f) and Undermining the Chapter 11 Process*, 76 Am. Bankr. L.J. 235, 267 (2002) ("[T]he dominant interpretation is that § 363(f) can be used to sell property free and clear of claims that could otherwise be assertable against the buyer of the assets under the common law doctrine of successor liability.").

The Third Circuit reasoned that "to equate interests in property with only *in rem* interests such as liens would be inconsistent with § 363(f)(3), which contemplates that a lien is but one type of interest." 322 F.3d at 290. After surveying its own precedents and the Fourth Circuit's decision in *United Mine Workers of Am. 1992 Benefit Plan v. Leckie Smokeless Coal Co. (In re Leckie Smokeless Coal Co.)*, 99 F.3d 573 (4th Cir. 1996),[17] the *TWA* court held that "[w]hile the interests of the [plaintiffs] in the assets of TWA's bankruptcy estate are not interests in property in the sense that they are not *in rem* interests. . . . they are interests in property within the meaning of § 363(f) in the sense that they *arise from the property* being sold." 322 F.3d at 290 (emphasis added).

Shortly after *TWA* was decided, the Southern District of California concluded that *TWA* applied to tort claimants asserting personal injury claims. *See Myers v. United States*, 297 B.R. 774, 781–82 (S.D. Cal. 2003). *Myers* involved claims arising from the negligent handling of toxic materials transported pursuant to a government contract. *Id.* at 781. Applying *TWA*, the *Myers* court ruled that the plaintiff's "claim for personal injury does arise from the property being sold, i.e. the contracts to transport toxic materials." *Id.*; *see also Faulkner v. Bethlehem Steel/Int'l Steel Group*, No. 2:04-CV-34 PS, 2005 U.S. Dist. LEXIS 7501 (N.D. Ind. April 27, 2005) (applying *TWA* to bar successor liability for racial discrimination claim).

Appellants argue that these decisions broadly construing the phrase "any

---

[16] For examples of bankruptcy courts' divergent rulings on this issue, compare, *e.g.*, *P.K.R. Convalescent Ctrs., Inc. v. Commonwealth of Va., Dept. of Med. Assistance Serv. (In re P.K.R. Convalescent Ctrs., Inc.)*, 189 B.R. 90, 94 (Bankr. E.D. Va. 1995) (holding that Virginia's depreciation-recoupment interest in the debtor's property was an "interest in property," even though the interest was not a lien), and *Am. Living Sys. v. Bonapfel (In re All Am. of Ashburn, Inc.)*, 56 B.R. 186, 189–90 (Bankr. N.D. Ga. 1986) (holding that § 363(f) permitted the sale of assets free and clear and precluded successor liability in product liability suit against purchaser for cause of action that arose prior to date of sale), with *Schwinn Cycling and Fitness, Inc. v. Benonis (In re Schwinn Bicycle Co.)*, 210 B.R. 747, 761 (Bankr. N.D. Ill. 1997) (holding that § 363(f) "in no way protects the buyer from current or future product liability; it only protects the purchased assets from lien claims against those assets"), and *Volvo White Truck Corp. v. Chambersburg Beverage, Inc. (In re White Motor Credit Corp.)*, 75 B.R. 944, 948 (Bankr. N.D. Ohio 1987) (stating that "[g]eneral unsecured claimants including tort claimants, have no specific interest in a debtor's property" for purposes of § 363(f)).

[17] In *Leckie*, the Fourth Circuit held that Coal Act premium payment obligations owed to employer-sponsored benefit plans were interests in property under § 363(f). 99 F.3d at 582. The Fourth Circuit explained "while the plain meaning of the phrase 'interest in such property' suggests that not all general rights to payment are encompassed by the statute, Congress did not expressly indicate that, by employing such language, it intended to limit the scope of § 363(f) to *in rem* interests, strictly defined, and [it would] decline to adopt such a restricted reading of the statute . . . ." *Id.*

interest in such property" fail to account for the language of 11 U.S.C. § 1141(c), a provision involving confirmed plans of reorganization. Section 1141(c) provides that "except as otherwise provided in the [reorganization] plan or in the order confirming the plan, after confirmation of a plan, the property dealt with by the plan is free and clear of *all claims and interests* of creditors, equity security holders, and of general partners in the debtor." 11 U.S.C. § 1141(c) (emphasis added). Appellants argue that Congress must have intentionally included the word "claims"[18] in § 1141(c), and omitted the word from § 363(f), because it was willing to extinguish tort claims in the reorganization context, but unwilling to do so in the § 363 sale context. Appellants account for this discrepancy on the basis that reorganization provides unsecured creditors procedural rights that are not assured in a § 363(b) sale.

We do not place such weight on the absence of the word "claims" in § 363(f). The language and structure of § 1141(c) and § 363(f) differ in many respects. Section 1141(c), for example, applies to all reorganization plans; § 363(f), in contrast, applies only to classes of property that satisfy one of five criteria. *See* 11 U.S.C. § 363(f)(1)–(5). Thus, while § 363 sales do not afford many of the procedural safeguards of a reorganization, § 363(f) is limited to specific classes of property.

Given the expanded role of § 363 in bankruptcy proceedings, it makes sense to harmonize the application of § 1141(c) and § 363(f) to the extent permitted by the statutory language. *See In re Golf, L.L.C.*, 322 B.R. 874, 877 (Bankr. D. Neb. 2004) (noting that, while § 363(f) requires less notice and provides for less opportunity for a hearing than in the reorganization process, "as a practical matter, current practice seems to have expanded § 363(f)'s use from its original intent"). Courts have already done this in other contexts. For example, § 1141(c) does not explicitly reference the extinguishment of liens, while § 363(f) does. Notwithstanding this distinction, courts have uniformly held that confirmation of a reorganization can act to extinguish liens. *See, e.g., JCB, Inc. v. Union Planters Bank, NA*, 539 F.3d 862, 870 (8th Cir. 2008) ("Confirmation of the reorganization plan replaces prior obligations, and a lien not preserved by the plan may be extinguished." (internal citation omitted)); *Elixir Indus., Inc. v. City Bank & Trust Co. (In re Ahern Enters., Inc.)*, 507 F.3d 817, 820–22 (5th Cir. 2007) (holding that § 1141(c) extinguishes liens that are not specifically preserved in a reorganization plan, and citing cases from the Fourth, Seventh, Eighth and Tenth Circuits reaching the same conclusion).

We agree with *TWA* and *Leckie* that the term "any interest in property" encompasses those claims that "arise from the property being sold." *See TWA*, 322 F.3d at 290. By analogy to *Leckie* (in which the relevant business was coal mining), "[appellants'] rights are grounded, at least in part, in the fact that [Old Chrysler's]

---

[18] The Bankruptcy Code defines "claim" as:

　(A) right to payment, whether or not such right is reduced to judgment, liquidated, unliquidated, fixed, contingent, matured, unmatured, disputed, undisputed, legal, equitable, secured, or unsecured; or

　(B) right to an equitable remedy for breach of performance if such breach gives rise to a right to payment, whether or not such right to an equitable remedy is reduced to judgment, fixed, contingent, matured, unmatured, disputed, undisputed, secured, or unsecured.

11 U.S.C. § 101(5).

very assets have been employed for [automobile production] purposes: if Appellees had never elected to put their assets to use in the [automobile] industry, and had taken up business in an altogether different area, [appellants] would have no right to seek [damages]." *Leckie*, 99 F.3d at 582.

"To allow the claimants to assert successor liability claims against [the purchaser] while limiting other creditors' recourse to the proceeds of the asset sale would be inconsistent with the Bankruptcy Code's priority scheme." *TWA*, 322 F.3d at 292. Appellants ignore this overarching principle and assume that tort claimants faced a choice between the Sale and an alternative arrangement that would have assured funding for their claims. But had appellants successfully blocked the Sale, they would have been unsecured creditors fighting for a share of extremely limited liquidation proceeds. Given the billions of dollars of outstanding secured claims against Old Chrysler, appellants would have fared no better had they prevailed.

The possibility of transferring assets free and clear of existing tort liability was a critical inducement to the Sale. As in *TWA*, "a sale of the assets of [Old Chrysler] at the expense of preserving successor liability claims was necessary in order to preserve some [55],000 jobs, . . . and to provide funding for employee-related liabilities, including retirement benefits [for more than 106,000 retirees]." *TWA*, 322 F.3d at 293; *see also* Sale Opinion at 3.

It is the transfer of Old Chrysler's tangible and intellectual property to New Chrysler that could lead to successor liability (where applicable under state law) in the absence of the Sale Order's liability provisions. Because appellants' claims arose from Old Chrysler's property, § 363(f) permitted the bankruptcy court to authorize the Sale free and clear of appellants' interest in the property.

. . . .

C. Future Claims

The Sale Order extinguished the right to pursue claims "on any theory of successor or transferee liability, . . . whether known or unknown as of the Closing, now existing or hereafter arising, asserted or unasserted, fixed or contingent, liquidated or unliquidated." Sale Order at 40–41. This provision is challenged on the grounds that: (1) the Sale Order violates the due process rights of future claimants by extinguishing claims without providing notice; (2) a bankruptcy court is not empowered to trump state successor liability law; (3) future, unidentified claimants with unquantifiable interests could not be compelled "to accept a money satisfaction," 11 U.S.C. § 363(f)(5); and (4) future causes of action by unidentified plaintiffs based on unknown events cannot be classified as "claims" under the Bankruptcy Code.

We affirm this aspect of the bankruptcy court's decision insofar as it constituted a valid exercise of authority under the Bankruptcy Code. However, we decline to delineate the scope of the bankruptcy court's authority to extinguish future claims, until such time as we are presented with an actual claim for an injury that is caused by Old Chrysler, that occurs after the Sale, and that is cognizable under state successor liability law.

. . . .

CONCLUSION

We have considered all of the objectors-appellants' contentions on these appeals and have found them to be without merit. For the foregoing reasons, we affirm the June 1, 2009 order of the bankruptcy court authorizing the Sale.

———————

In *Chrysler*, the Second Circuit avoided the issue of successor liability and the problems posed by future claims. These are the subjects considered in the next section.

[B]   Successor Liability and the Problem of Future Claims

"Successor liability" is a collective name for a group of state law doctrines that allow plaintiffs with claims against a defunct entity to assert those claims against the entity's successor, such as a purchaser of substantially all of the entity's assets. Although most often litigated in the context of products liability and other tort claims, the underlying claim can sound in tort or contract.

Successor liability consists of a number of different doctrines that are loosely categorized into five principal groups: (1) express or implied assumption, (2) fraudulent schemes to avoid liability, (3) de facto merger, (4) mere continuation and continuity of enterprise, and (5) product line liability. The requirements for each of these doctrines vary by jurisdiction, and the name by which each doctrine is known is not dispositive as to what is required for its application. *See* George W. Kuney, *A Taxonomy and Evaluation of Successor Liability*, 6 Fla. St. U. Bus. L. Rev. 9 (2007) (the state-by-state appendix to which is regularly updated and found on SSRN). Successor liability developed along with the rise in the corporate form of organization and was intended to ameliorate some of the harms and sharp practices that the rule of limited liability created.

Think, for example, of a late 19th or early 20th century railroad company. After it constructs all or part of the railroad and runs up secured and unsecured debts, it runs into serious financial difficulty — as railroads of that era frequently did. Often, what would happen in those failed railroad cases is that the company's insider investors would form a new company — let's call it New Railroad — to acquire the assets of the troubled company for the price of the secured debt, *i.e.*, the secured creditors that financed the acquisition of the assets were the same secured creditors that had provided financing to the old company. When the transaction closed and the dust settled, New Railroad would emerge as a financially stronger railroad, whose secured debt was held by the old secured creditors and whose shares were owned by the same insider investors. Unsecured creditors and non-insider investors in the old firm would be left holding the bag — or, more precisely, the empty shell. If those old creditors attempted to enforce their claims against New Railroad, and the principle of limited liability were strictly applied, there would be no relief. *See, e.g., Colorado Springs Rapid Transit Ry. Co. v. Albrecht*, 123 P. 957 (1912). This struck some courts as patently unfair. As one court observed, the notion that the purchaser cannot be held liable on claims against the seller "does not appeal to us; it is an attempt to dodge the damages that respondent has sustained by a quirk and technical question of law, and smacks too much of a skin game, and [a] hand stacked and dealt to dealer from the bottom of the deck." *Brabham v. So. Express Co.*, 117 S.E. 368 (S.C. 1922). As a result, in such circumstances, some courts developed theories to enable creditors of the old firm to assert their claims against the new firm.

The history of the development of successor liability doctrines is detailed, twisted, sometimes tortured, and always interesting, but the following summary will suffice for present purposes. The general rule was, and continues to be, that a purchaser of assets for fair consideration does not become liable for the seller's liabilities, even when the purchaser acquires substantially all of the seller's assets. *See* George W. Kuney, *A Taxonomy and Evaluation of Successor Liability*, 6 Fla. St. U. Bus. L. Rev. 9 (2007). Some courts, however, have held that if certain additional factors are present, successor liability will attach, and claims for the seller's liabilities can be made against the purchaser. Those additional factors are commonly said to include:

- An express or implied assumption of liability by the purchaser;

- A transfer for less than fair consideration or for the purpose of escaping liability;

- A transfer that amounts to a de facto merger of the seller and purchaser;

- Where the purchaser is merely a continuation of the seller, as where some or all of the owners and officers of the purchasing entity are identical to the owners and officers of the seller; and

- Where the purchaser continues to manufacture or market the product line of the seller.

Thus, if the requirements of a particular jurisdiction's successor liability doctrine are met with regard to a particular claim, then under applicable nonbankruptcy law, the purchaser would be liable for that claim to the same extent as the seller. That is the nonbankruptcy law side of things.

On the bankruptcy side of the matter is Code § 363(f) and the ability to sell free and clear of interests, which has been held by many courts to include claims, as was discussed in the previous section of this chapter. Counsel were quick to realize that, if the sale free and clear power included the ability to strip claims from the property and the business, this would increase the value of businesses.

Consider a California business that makes and sells ladders and scaffolding equipment. At some point, one of its very successful products, folding ladders — of which millions have been manufactured and sold nationally and internationally — is determined to be defective. Specifically, after about two years of service — fewer if the ladders are used and stored in a humid environment — the hinge pins weaken and are prone to snap when under a load. As a result, many injuries are being reported, and many substantial claims are being made. The company's insurance coverage is insufficient to cover all claims.

Suppose Ladder Company files a Chapter 11 petition in order to stay the lawsuits being brought against it, to preserve insurance proceeds, and to catch its breath and evaluate the prospects for continuing in business. If the company were sold in a nonbankruptcy setting, purchasers planning to stay in the ladder business would only be willing to purchase the assets at a very low price, if at all, given California's "product line" theory of successor liability. *See Ray v. Alad*, 19 Cal. 3d 22 (1977). But, with the § 363(f) power to sell free and clear of claims and interests, the company should be able to realize a higher price for its assets.[1] The sale may generate even more in the way of a purchase price, if it is sold to a new company in which members of the seller's management and workforce have a presence. After all, who knows the product lines and practices better than former managers and workers? In any case, after the assets are sold, the sales proceeds, which might consist of cash or a note from or stock in the new company, will then be divided up and distributed among the old company's existing creditors. Meanwhile, the business continues in its new form.

In such a scenario, as in *Chrysler*, one thinks about the successor liability claims in two categories. The first consists of claims that are known to exist because an injury has manifestly occurred. The second consists of potential, or "future," claims that may arise in the future, as injuries occur or are discovered. Once a court concludes that "interests" includes "claims," the *existing* claims easily fall victim to the purchaser's § 363(f) shield, just as they did in *Chrysler*. But treating *future* claims in the same fashion raises conceptual problems, including, not least of all, a collision of § 363(f) and fundamental notions of due process.

If you think this discussion is beginning to sound a lot like something you covered in your first year civil procedure class, you are absolutely right. In fact, the case of *Mullane v. Cent. Hanover Bank*, 339 U.S. 306 (1950), and its bankruptcy analog, *New York v. New York, New Haven & Hartford Ry. Co.*, 344 U.S. 293 (1953), lie at the crux of the matter. There are two fundamental subissues that create problems for those seeking to strip or otherwise affect future claims using § 363(f) or any other sections of the Bankruptcy Code: (1) the nonexistence of the claim at the time of the sale and (2) the inability to give adequate notice to future claimants.

[C] Future Claims Not in Existence at the Time of Sale or Plan Confirmation

As to the first issue, which has been most thoroughly litigated in the plan confirmation context, it is fairly clear (but not free from doubt) that claims arising after the confirmation of a plan of liquidation or reorganization cannot be barred, extinguished, or otherwise compromised in the bankruptcy. *See, e.g., In re Chance Indus., Inc.*, 367 B.R. 689 (Bankr. D. Kan. 2006) (plaintiff's tort claim based on injuries suffered on a carnival ride postconfirmation was not discharged in bankruptcy, and plaintiff could proceed in state court against the reorganized debtor); *Hexcel Corp. v. Stepman Co. (In re Hexcel Corp.)*, 239 B.R. 564, 570 (N.D. Cal. 1999) (postconfirmation claim against the debtor for contribution in a toxic tort

---

[1] The sale might fetch something approaching the discounted present value of the firm's expected profits for 20 years plus a discounted terminal value.

case was not contemplated by the parties preconfirmation and thus was not discharged via a confirmed plan); *Schwinn Cycling & Fitness, Inc. v. Benonis*, 217 B.R. 790, 795–96 (N.D. Ill. 1997) (postconfirmation products liability claim was not discharged via the confirmed plan and was not extinguished through the sale free and clear); *Kewanee Boiler Corp. v. Smith (In re Kewanee Boiler Corp.)*, 198 B.R. 519, 526–27 (Bankr. N.D. Ill. 1996) (successor liability claim based on a postconfirmation explosion of a boiler manufactured by the debtor cannot be barred under § 524(a)(2)); *see also In re Piper Aircraft Corp.*, 58 F.3d 1573, 1577 (11th Cir. 1995) (a representative filed a proof of claim on behalf of future claimants who might assert postconfirmation products liability claims against the debtor, which designed, manufactured, and sold aircraft and parts; held: possible future products liability claimants with no preconfirmation relationship with the debtor's product do not hold claims under Code § 101(5) and cannot participate in the bankruptcy proceedings via an appointed representative); *In re Hoffinger Indus., Inc.*, 307 B.R. 112 (Bankr. E.D. Ark. 2004) (purported class of future claimants who were unknown to the Chapter 11 debtor swimming pool manufacturer and who had not yet used or sustained injuries as a result of use of the pools did not have claims under § 101(5)(a) subject to estimation).

In determining when a claim arises, courts have developed and applied three approaches: the accrued state law test, the conduct test, and the prepetition relationship test.

The first, the accrued state law test, asks whether all triggering events necessary for the claimant's cause of action to have accrued under state law have occurred. If so, there is a claim. If not, there isn't. The accrued state law test was adopted by the Third Circuit in *In re M. Frenville Co.*, 744 F.2d 332 (3d Cir. 1984), *cert. denied*, 469 U.S. 1160 (1985). In that case, the court held that under New York law, a claim for indemnification did not accrue until the time that the indemnified party actually paid. This test was subsequently widely rejected as being too narrow by almost every court to consider the issue. *See Epstein v. Official Comm. of Unsecured Creditors of Piper Aircraft Corp. (In re Piper Aircraft Corp.)*, 58 F.3d 1573, 1576 n.2 (11th Cir. 1995). In 2010, the Third Circuit affirmatively overruled it. *In re Rodriguez*, 629 F.3d 136 (3d Cir. 2010).

The second test, the conduct test, is based on the principle that a claim arises when the conduct that gives or will give rise to the alleged liability occurs. The conduct test has been adopted in some mass tort cases, perhaps most notably in *Grady v. A.H. Robins Co.*, 839 F.2d 198 (4th Cir. 1988), dealing with liability for defective intrauterine birth control devices. In that case, the claim was held to have arisen prepetition, when the defective product was inserted into the plaintiff's uterus. In mass tort cases, from the standpoint of the reorganizing debtor, the conduct test is more desirable than the state law accrual test, because the conduct test sweeps more plaintiffs into the classes of claimants whose claims can be addressed by the plan or by the preplan sale order. From the perspective of potential plaintiffs, however, the conduct test can be less than optimal. Many product defects and contamination and exposure cases involve plaintiffs who have been exposed to a product or substance but have not yet developed any symptoms or discovered their injury. The conduct test allows their claims to be dealt with in the bankruptcy case, but holders of future claims may have no reason to participate in the case, because they do not know they have a claim.

The third test, the prepetition relationship test, is something of a middle way between the two and appears to be the dominant and better reasoned approach. It requires that the conduct that will give rise to the claim have occurred and that the claimants have some preconfirmation or possibly presale relationship with the debtor, so that they have some reason to be taking notice of the debtor's bankruptcy case. *See Epstein v. Official Comm. of Unsecured Creditors of Piper Aircraft Corp. (In re Piper Aircraft Corp.)*, 58 F.3d 1573, 1576 n.2 (11th Cir. 1995).

Although § 101(5)(a) defines "claim" broadly, as "any right to payment, whether or not the right is reduced to judgment, liquidated, unliquidated, fixed, contingent, matured, unmatured, disputed, undisputed, legal, equitable, secured, or unsecured," even this broad definition does not include claims that don't exist. Even under a broad construction, the definition of claim requires that "events occurring before confirmation create a relationship such as contact, exposure, impact, or privity between the claimant and the debtor's product" in order for there to be a claim under § 101(5)(a). *Piper*, 58 F.3d at 1577 (noting that courts applying the conduct test presume some prepetition relationship between the debtor's conduct and the claimant); *White v. Chance Indus. (In re Chance Indus., Inc.)*, 367 B.R. 689, 701–03 (Bankr. D. Kan. 2006) (collecting and reviewing cases and noting that the claimants each had some prepetition contact, exposure to, or relationship with the debtor or debtor's product); *see e.g., Grady v. A.H. Robins Co.*, 839 F.2d 198, 203 (4th Cir. 1988) (claim arose when the Dalkon Shield was inserted into the claimant); *In re Johns-Manville Corp.*, 36 B.R. 743, 750 (Bankr. S.D.N.Y. 1984) (exposure to asbestos).

In re Chance Industries provides a good example of a garden variety "non-claim" outside of the mass tort context, in which the urgency and the magnitude of the problems to be addressed may have a tendency to distort the law. In *Chance*, an 8-year-old boy was injured on a carnival ride called the "Zipper" that had been manufactured by Chance Industries before the company filed a bankruptcy petition. The injury occurred after Chance had confirmed a plan of reorganization. Prior to the date of the injury, the boy had not ridden the Zipper and had no contractual or other contact with Chance Industries. The court found that, under these circumstances, although the defect that allegedly caused the boy's injuries was created prepetition, because there was no prepetition or preconfirmation relationship at all between the claimant and the company, he did not hold a "claim" that could be discharged in bankruptcy.

So, what does this mean for the future claimants of the ladder company in our earlier example? The answer is unclear, at least in part. Does a future plaintiff's prepetition or preconfirmation purchase of the ladder in question create enough privity, enough of a relationship, to allow Code § 363(f) (in the case of a proposed sale) or Code § 1123(a)(5)(D) and Code § 1141 (in the case of a confirmed plan) to strip away the future claim? *Possibly*.

What does this mean for someone who first comes into contact with the ladder after the sale or after the confirmation of the plan, even though the ladder was originally sold presale or preconfirmation? For example, suppose that years after a defective ladder was sold, it injures someone who bought it used. Will a § 363 sale or confirmed plan strip away the claim? *Probably not, but there is little clarity on this point.*

[D] The Problem of Providing Adequate Notice to Future Claimants

Even if such postsale or postconfirmation injuries give rise to "claims" within the meaning of Code § 101(5)(a), a strong argument exists that they should not be stripped off or discharged in bankruptcy proceedings because notice by publication is not constitutionally adequate notice to a potential future claimant. This reasoning was adopted by the court in *In re J.A. Jones, Inc.*, 492 F.3d 242, 249 (4th Cir. 2007): "A claim asserted by a creditor against a debtor's estate cannot constitutionally be discharged in accordance with the Bankruptcy Code unless the debtor provides constitutionally adequate notice to the creditor of the debtor's bankruptcy proceeding, as well as the applicable filing deadlines and hearing dates." This reasoning draws upon the familiar words of *Mullane*:

> An elementary and fundamental requirement of due process in any proceeding which is to be accorded finality is notice reasonably calculated, under all the circumstances, to apprise interested parties of the pendency of the action and afford them an opportunity to present their objections.

Mullane v. Cent. Hanover Bank & Trust Co., 339 U.S. 306, 314 (1950); *see also New York v. New York, New Haven & Hartford Ry. Co.*, 344 U.S. 293 (1953) (bankruptcy analog to *Mullane*).

Under *Mullane*, creditors who are known to the debtor must be given actual notice, while constructive notice by publication is generally sufficient for creditors who are unknown to the debtor. *See, e.g., In re J.A. Jones, Inc.*, 492 F.3d 242, 249 (4th Cir. 2007), where the court explained that a creditor falls into the "unknown" category if the creditor is "one whose interests or whereabouts could not with due diligence be ascertained," or one "whose interests are either conjectural or future or, although they could be discovered upon investigation, do not in due course of business come to [the] knowledge [of the debtor]." 492 F.3d at 250 n. 7 (quoting *Mullane*, 339 U.S. at 317).

It does not necessarily follow from *Mullane* that publication provides constitutionally adequate notice *to potential future claimants*, such as individuals who might one day be injured by a defective ladder. Some courts addressing the issue have held that publication notice to potential future claimants is inadequate and does not comport with due process. *See e.g., Jones v. Chemetron Corp.*, 212 F.3d 199, 209–210 (3rd Cir. 2000) (*Chemetron II*); *In re Hoffinger Industries, Inc.*, 307 B.R. 112 (Bankr. E.D. Ark. 2004); *In re Hexcel Corp.* 239 B.R. 564, 571 (N.D. Cal. 1999); *In re Pettibone*, 162 B.R. 791, 808 (Bankr. N. D. Ill. 1994); *see also In re Chance Indus., Inc.*, 367 B.R. 689 (Bankr. D. Kan. 2006). These courts have, in essence, held that in *Mullane*, a case that involved notice to bondholders, the Court was concerned with holders of currently existing future interests or claims, such as remainders, rather than with persons who did not hold an interest or a claim but might acquire one in the future.

For example, in the *Chemetron II* case, which involved mass tort claims for injuries resulting from exposure to radioactive waste that the debtor had put in a landfill, the court held that notice by publication was sufficient with respect to a woman who had been exposed to the waste prior to confirmation of the plan, but that it was not sufficient with respect to the woman's child, who was conceived and born after the plan was confirmed. The court was troubled by the fact that no legal representative had been appointed to represent the interests of future claimants. The court also rejected the debtor's contention that the child had adequate notice because his mother had notice of the bankruptcy proceeding. *Chemetron II*, 212 F.3d at 210.

The court did not reach the issue of whether the child had a claim under § 101(5)(a), because it identified a "more fundamental problem." The court explained:

> Under fundamental notions of procedural due process, a claimant who has no appropriate notice of a bankruptcy reorganization cannot have his claim extinguished in a settlement pursuant thereto. *See, e.g., Mullane v. Central Hanover Bank & Trust Co.*, 339 U.S. 306, 314–19, 70 S. Ct. 652, 94 L. Ed. 865 (1950); *Chemetron I*, 72 F.3d at 346; *In re Savage Indus.*, Inc., 43 F.3d 714, 721 (1st Cir. 1994). Here, [the child] had no notice of or participation in the Chemetron reorganization plan. No effort was made during the course of the bankruptcy proceeding to have a representative appointed to receive notice for and represent the interests of future claimants. Therefore, whatever claim [the child] may now have was not subject to the bankruptcy court's bar date order . . . and was not discharged by that court's confirmation order.

Chemetron II, 212 F.3d at 209–10.

The court in *Chance* further explained the constitutional inadequacy of notice by publication to potential future claimants:

> Some of the future claimants may not be living persons at the time the notice is given, so they are not necessarily capable of seeing it. If they are alive and actually see the notice, they could not recognize themselves as affected in any way by the bankruptcy case and will, therefore, take no action to ensure their interests are represented. The purpose behind requiring notice to creditors is to provide them the "opportunity to be heard" which is "the fundamental requisite of due process of law." Such a notice by publication is an exercise in futility as applied to creditors who are not only unknown to the debtor, but are also unknown to themselves. It cannot possibly define the requirements of the Due Process Clause.

367 B.R. at 708 (citations omitted).

Other cases addressing the issue are in line with *JA Jones, Chemetron II*, and *Chance Industries*, holding that publication notice is not constitutionally adequate to potential future claimants because they could not know that they would have a claim. *See In re Hoffinger*, 307 B.R. at 122 (court held debtor's proposed class of future claimants who had not yet used or sustained injuries resulting from the pools manufactured by the debtor violated due process notice requirements: "If the debtor does not fully know who the claimants are, the claimants should at least know who they are."); *In re Hexcel Corp.* 239 B.R. at 571 (while notice by publication may be sufficient for creditors who could contemplate that they might have a claim, it is not for potential future creditors: "It is difficult to imagine, however, how the announcement of a bankruptcy proceeding published in the Wall Street Journal could possibly satisfy due process concerns for a potential creditor who had no way of knowing that it may have a claim against the debtor some time in the future."); *In re Pettibone*, 162 B.R. 791, 808 (Bankr. N.D. Ill. 1994) ("The Bankruptcy Code does not require a party . . . to monitor national financial papers and read notices about businesses against which they have no known claims to guard against the possibility they might later be held on notice of claim bar.").

One possible solution to this problem that has been attempted is the appointment of a "Future Claims Representative" to receive notice and appear and be heard on behalf of the future claimants. That is the subject of the next subsection of this chapter.

[E] Using a Future Claims Representative to Satisfy Due Process

IN RE ROMAN CATHOLIC ARCHBISHOP OF PORTLAND
United States Bankruptcy Court, District of Oregon
2005 Bankr. LEXIS 42 (Jan. 10, 2005)

Elizabeth L. Perris, Bankruptcy Judge.

MEMORANDUM RE APPOINTMENT OF FUTURE CLAIMS REPRESENTATIVE

At the November 19, 2004 hearing, I approved the appointment of a future claims representative ("FCR") to represent the interests of certain unknown individuals holding claims against debtor who will fail to formally assert those claims by the bar date. The pertinent claims result from "Tortious Misconduct[1] by any priest, representative, agent, volunteer, or employee of the Debtor which occurred prior to the Petition Date." . . . There is no dispute that the FCR should represent the interest of individuals who are currently minors and whose parent or legal guardian does not file a timely claim (hereinafter "minors") and those with repressed memory who have no knowledge of the wrongful conduct resulting in their claim against

---

[1] Debtor defines the phrase "Tortious Misconduct" to mean the following:

any claim, demand, suit, cause of action, proceeding, or any other rights or asserted right to payment against the Debtor, based upon or in any manner arising from or related to any tortious act or acts, including, but not limited to, personal injury, wrongful death, assault, battery, negligence, intentional infliction of emotional distress, defamation, conversion, child abuse as defined in ORS 419B.005(1)(a)(A)) [sic], or any sexual misconduct with a person which is alleged to be inappropriate or nonconsensual, including, without limitation, any of the offenses defined in ORS Chapter 163. . . .

debtor.[2]

Debtor's position is that the scope of the FCR's authority should be limited to minor and repressed memory claimants. The Tort Claimants Committee ("the TCC") advocated for a broader scope of representation. At the November 19 hearing, I sustained the TCC's objection and ruled that, in addition to minors and those with repressed memory, the FCR would represent the interests of those persons who know they were subjected to sexual contact as children but who have "not discovered the [resulting] injury or the causal connection between the injury and the child abuse, nor in the exercise of reasonable care should have discovered the injury or the causal connection between the injury and the child abuse[.]"[3] This language comes from an Oregon statute, ORS 12.117(1), which would be pertinent to all the possible Tortious Misconduct for which debtor may be liable, because of the geographic location of debtor's operations. ORS 12.117(1) states as follows:

> Notwithstanding ORS 12.110, 12.115 or 12.160, an action based on conduct that constitutes child abuse or conduct knowingly allowing, permitting or encouraging child abuse accruing while the person who is entitled to bring the action is under 18 years of age shall be commenced not more than six years after that person attains 18 years of age, or *if the injured person has not discovered the injury or the causal connection between the injury and the child abuse, nor in the exercise of reasonable care should have discovered the injury or the causal connection between the injury and the child abuse*, not more than three years from the date the injured person discovers or in the exercise of reasonable care should have discovered the injury or the causal connection between the child abuse and the injury, whichever period is longer.

(Emphasis added).

The purpose of this memorandum is to explain the basis for my decision and to point out that the scope of the FCR's representation is more limited than some of the lawyers' arguments would suggest.

A. All Alleged Victims of Prepetition Sexual Abuse Have Claims Within the Meaning of the Bankruptcy Code

As an initial matter, I acknowledge, and all parties appear to agree, that the alleged victims of prepetition sexual abuse by priests or other representatives of debtor are "creditors" holding "claims" against debtor as those terms are defined under the Bankruptcy Code.

A creditor includes an "entity that has a claim against the debtor that arose at the time of or before the" petition date. § 101(10). "While state law determines the existence of a claim based on a cause of action, federal law determines when the claim arises for bankruptcy purposes." *In re Hassanally*, 208 B.R. 46, 50 (9th Cir. BAP 1997). The Bankruptcy Code defines a claim to be a:

---

[2] Debtor has reserved the right to challenge the validity of the repressed memory theory.

[3] For ease of reference, I will hereafter refer to these individuals as "future claimants."

(A) right to payment, whether or not such right is reduced to judgment, liquidated, unliquidated, fixed, contingent, matured, unmatured, disputed, undisputed, legal, equitable, secured, or unsecured; or

(B) right to an equitable remedy for breach or performance if such breach gives rise to a right to payment, whether or not such right to an equitable remedy is reduced to judgment, fixed, contingent, matured, unmatured, disputed, undisputed, secured or unsecured[.]

§ 101(5). Congress adopted the expansive definition of claim set forth above to ensure that "all legal obligations of the debtor, *no matter how remote or contingent*, will be able to be dealt with in the bankruptcy case." H.R. Rep. No. 595, 95th Cong., 2d Sess. 1, 309 (1978), *reprinted in* 1978 U.S.C.C.A.N. 5963, 6266 (emphasis added)[.] *In re Jensen*, 995 F.2d 925, 929 (9th Cir. 1993). Indeed, the breadth of the definition of claim is essential to achieve the Bankruptcy Code's goal of providing debtors with a fresh start. *Id.* at 930.

In *Jensen*, the Ninth Circuit applied a "fair contemplation test" to determine when an environmental claim arose. The fair contemplation test has been described as equivalent to the test set forth in *In re Piper Aircraft Corp.*, 58 F.3d 1573 (11th Cir. 1995), *see Hassanally*, 208 B.R. at 52, which requires some prepetition or preconfirmation relationship, such as "contact, exposure, impact, or privity" between the debtor and the claimant. *Piper*, 58 F.3d at 1577. Under this test, "the debtor's prepetition conduct gives rise to a claim to be administered in a case only if there is a relationship established before confirmation between an identifiable claimant or group of claimants and that prepetition conduct."[5] *Id.* There is no dispute that this requirement is met in this case. Therefore, all the future claimants to be represented by the FCR, including the minors and those with repressed memory, hold claims against debtor within the meaning of § 101(5).

B. Scope of the FCR's Representation

As I stated at the hearing, the fact that the future claimants have claims does not answer the question of whether there should be a FCR or of the appropriate scope of the FCR's authority. The debtor sought the appointment of a FCR, because it had unknown creditors who might be unaware that they had claims . . . . Debtor recognized that, absent the appointment of a FCR, it was questionable whether it could accomplish through this bankruptcy a global resolution and discharge of the abuse claims. The narrow scope of representation proposed by debtor for the FCR is inconsistent with the approach taken in other bankruptcy cases, and with debtor's stated purpose in invoking the relief afforded under chapter 11.

In October of this year, the United States Bankruptcy Court for the District of Arizona entered an order approving the appointment of an Unknown Claims Representative ("the UCR") in the chapter 11 case of the Catholic Diocese of

---

[5] The fair contemplation and Piper tests are considered compromises between the "conduct" test, under which a claim arises at the time the conduct occurs, and the "accrued state law test," which provides that "a claim does not arise in bankruptcy until an action has accrued under relevant substantive nonbankruptcy law." *In re Hassanally*, 208 B.R. 46, 51 (9th Cir. BAP 1997).

Tucson ("the Tucson case"). The UCR in the Tucson case has wide-ranging duties, including the authority to file a proof of claim on behalf of the class he represents, which class is comprised of "those persons who are of adult age whose claims currently exist but who do not realize and who will not realize, prior to the April 15, 2005 deadline for filing claims, that they have claims against the estate[.]" The scope of representation approved by the court in the Tucson case is even broader than that which I approved. In this case, the FCR will represent only those individuals who, "in the exercise of reasonable care," have failed to discover that they have been injured by debtor's conduct or the causal connection between debtor's conduct and their injury. ORS 12.117(1). There is no such limitation imposed in the Tucson case.

The approach taken in the Tucson case, and in this case, is consistent with that taken in the "mass tort" asbestos bankruptcy cases. The seminal asbestos bankruptcy case is that of the Johns-Manville Corporation. In that case, the court, citing § 105(a)[7] and § 1109(b),[8] approved the appointment of a future claims representative to represent all persons who, on or before a certain date,

> came into contact with asbestos or asbestos-containing products mined, fabricated, manufactured, supplied or sold by Manville and who have not yet filed claims against Manville for personal injuries or property damage. These claimants may be unaware of their entitlement to recourse against Manville due to the latency period of many years characterizing manifestation of all asbestos related diseases.

In re Johns-Manville Corp., 36 B.R. 743, 745 (Bankr. S.D.N.Y. 1984), aff'd, 52 B.R. 940 (S.D.N.Y. 1985). Other bankruptcy courts followed suit, appointing representatives for those who, whether knowingly or not, had already been exposed to asbestos, but for whom injury had not yet manifested itself. *See, e.g., In re Forty-Eight Insulations, Inc.*, 58 B.R. 476 (Bankr. N.D. Ill. 1986); *In re UNR Indus., Inc.*, 46 B.R. 671 (Bankr. N.D. Ill. 1985).[9] *In In re Amatex Corp.*, 755 F.2d 1034 (3d Cir. 1985), the Third Circuit affirmed the bankruptcy court's appointment of a representative for future claimants who had been exposed to asbestos but who had not yet manifested an injury.

The possibility of a long latency period before which injury becomes manifest is an important factual similarity between this case and the asbestos cases. The Oxford English Dictionary Online (2002) defines "manifest" as follows: "Clearly revealed to the eye, mind, or judgment; open to view or comprehension; obvious."

---

[7] Section 105(a) states that "the court may issue any order, process, or judgment that is necessary or appropriate to carry out the provisions of this title." The court in the Manville case noted that the power to appoint a representative "for parties in interest whose identities are yet unknown . . . is inherent in every court." *In re Johns-Manville Corp.*, 36 B.R. 743, 757 (Bankr. S.D.N.Y. 1984), aff'd, 52 B.R. 940 (S.D.N.Y. 1985).

[8] Section 1109(b) states that "[a] party in interest . . . may raise and may appear and be heard on any issue in a case under this chapter."

[9] The courts in many of the early asbestos cases declined to decide whether the future claimants had bankruptcy claims against the debtors, holding that the future claimants were entitled to representation even if they did not have claims against the debtor. As I discuss above, there is no dispute in this case that the pertinent unknown claimants are creditors holding claims against debtor as those terms are defined in the Ninth Circuit. This is an additional factor weighing in favor of the appointment of a FCR with a broad scope of responsibility.

The evidence in this case is that, when childhood sexual abuse causes an injury, the injury may not be manifest for many years.[10]

Debtor cites *In re Dow Corning Corp.*, 211 B.R. 545 (Bankr. E.D. Mich. 1997), in support of its position that a future claims representative is not necessary to represent the interests of those potential claimants who know they have been subjected to abuse, but have not yet manifested an injury. The Dow Corning chapter 11 case arose out of a flood of lawsuits connected to the debtor's involvement with silicone breast implants. The court in that case explained that it had not appointed a future claims representative, because "all who have received a breast implant are cognizable of this fact." *Id.* at 598 n. 55. However, the court also explained that a future claims representative was unnecessary, because

> it has been the consistent view of the official committee representing all tort claimants that "any person who has received a silicone-gel breast implant . . . has already suffered an injury and is therefore a present, as opposed to a future claimant . . . ." Order Dismissing Motion of Alan B. Morrison for Appointment as the Legal Representative of Future Breast Implant Claimants, Oct. 10, 1995.

Id.

This case is distinguishable from the *Dow* case for at least two reasons. First, the very nature of the tortious conduct alleged in this case can result in cognitive and psychological injuries, making the injured person incapable of recognizing that he or she has been injured or of identifying the causal connection between the abuse and the injury. Declaration of Jon R. Conte, Ph.D., 8; 9; 13–14. The potential injuries resulting from exposure to silicone breast implants are not of this type. Second, in this case, unlike the *Dow* case, the TCC does not take the position that all those exposed to childhood sexual abuse have been damaged in a legal sense, or purport to represent the interests of such persons. The *Dow* court did not disapprove of the approach taken in the asbestos cases. In fact, the court in *Dow* acknowledged that "future tort claims problems come in all shapes and sizes[,]" and cautioned against an oversimplified approach to such problems. *Dow*, 211 B.R. at 598 n. 55.

In a chapter 11 case involving future claims, a court must "balance the competing interests of the debtor's fresh start with the creditor's right to compensation. Largely, the issue of adequate notice to inform and bind the future claimant and notions of fundamental fairness determine the outcome." *Hassanally*, 208 B.R. at 53 n. 9. As I discuss above, the appointment of a FCR is appropriate, given that the tortious conduct at issue in this case does not consistently produce injury, and that when injury does result, it can take many years for it to become manifest. In addition, childhood sexual abuse can result in cognitive and psychological injuries making the injured person incapable of currently recognizing that he or she has been injured or of identifying the causal connection between the abuse and the injury.

---

[10] Not everyone who is subjected to childhood sexual abuse will be damaged in a legal sense. As pointed out by debtor's expert witness, "some people are quite resilient and do not become psychologically disabled or traumatized by episodes of sexual abuse." Declaration of Kevin McGovern, Ph.D., 2:22–23.

ORS 12.117(1) recognizes the unique nature of the potential damages caused by childhood sexual abuse by providing an unusually extended period to assert claims based on such conduct. Oregon case law acknowledges that decades may pass between the childhood abuse and the date the victim either manifests the injury or reasonably should have known of the causal connection between the abuse and the injury. *See, e.g., P. H. v. F. C.*, 127 Ore. App. 592, 873 P.2d 465 (Or. Ct. App. 1994).

While counsel for ACE is correct that the bankruptcy claims bar dates operate regardless of state statutes of limitation, that does not address the question of whether a FCR is appropriate. When there is a class of claimants that is incapable of asserting a claim, either because of a long latency period between the wrongful conduct and the manifestation of damages, or because the nature of the wrongful conduct is such that it disables the claimant from being reasonably able to recognize the injury, it is appropriate for the court to appoint a FCR to protect the interests of the class.

It is important to point out that the FCR does not represent all alleged childhood abuse victims who do not assert claims. The representation is much more limited. The only claimants represented are (1) minors; (2) those with repressed memory; and (3) those persons who know they were subjected to sexual contact as children but who have "not discovered the [resulting] injury or the causal connection between the injury and the child abuse, nor in the exercise of reasonable care should have discovered the injury or the causal connection between the injury and the child abuse[.]" ORS 12.117(1). Counsel for debtor and the insurance companies argue that, by including the third category, the court effectively excuses from filing individual childhood abuse victim claimants "who know that the conduct took place, people who do have the memory of that conduct, but . . . are ashamed, embarrassed, reluctant, [or] don't want to come forward . . . ." Transcript of November 19, 2004 Hearing, 118:5-10. This is incorrect.

I am not authorizing the FCR to represent claimants who decline to assert their own claims because of embarrassment, shame or a desire not to come forward. It is only those child abuse claimants who are minors, have repressed memory, or who have not discovered, "nor in the exercise of reasonable care should have discovered" their injury or that the abuse caused the injury. ORS 12.117(1). The limited scope of the third category, qualified by the objective requirement of the exercise of reasonable care, prevents the wholesale vitiation of the claims bar date that counsel for the insurance companies and debtor assert may happen.

C. Conclusion

Debtor's representatives and counsel have stated on numerous occasions in this court, that debtor's purpose in filing a chapter 11 petition was to resolve, fairly, finally and in a global fashion, the sexual abuse claims asserted against it. For example, debtor's Director of Business Affairs stated as follows in connection with the November 19 hearing:

> One of the principal reasons for seeking relief under chapter 11 was to enable the Debtor to use the chapter 11 process to address in a comprehensive manner all tort claims asserted against it in one forum, determine

the extent of the Debtor's liability with respect thereto, and address such claims and all other claims against the Debtor in a fair and equitable manner.

The appointment of a FCR to represent the interests of those persons who know they were subjected to abuse but who have not discovered the resulting injury or the causal connection between the injury and the abuse will effectuate debtor's stated goals and will assure equitable treatment of future as well as present claimants.[11]

NOTES AND QUESTIONS

Even though the appointment of a future claims representative seems to be the best approach suggested to date for dealing with the future claims problem, it is not clear that such a proceeding would pass due process muster before the United States Supreme Court. Especially in the context of mass tort cases, the Court has not necessarily shown itself to be moved by pragmatism. *See* S. Elizabeth Gibson, *A Response to Professor Resnick: Will this Vehicle Pass Inspection?*, 148 U. Pa. L. Rev. 2095, 2116 (2000). In *Ortiz v. Fibreboard Corp.*, 527 U.S. 815, 846 (1999), in the context of mandatory, no-opt out class actions — a procedural device that is very similar to a Chapter 11 case for unknown future claimants — the Court observed:

> mandatory class actions aggregating damages claims implicate the due process "principle of general application in Anglo-American jurisprudence that one is not bound by a judgment *in personam* in a litigation in which he is not designated as a party or to which he has not been made a party by service of process," *Hansberry* v. *Lee*, 311 U.S. 32, 40, 61 S. Ct. 115, 85 L. Ed. 22 (1940), it being "our 'deep-rooted historic tradition that everyone should have his own day in court'" (citations omitted). Although "we have recognized an exception to the general rule when, in certain limited circumstances, a person, although not a party, has his interests adequately represented by someone with the same interests who is a party," or "where a special remedial scheme exists expressly foreclosing successive litigation by nonlitigants, as for example in bankruptcy or probate," *Martin, supra*, at 762, n. 2 (citations omitted), the burden of justification rests on the exception.

In light of this less than bright line standard, it is difficult to state with certainty in any particular case whether the future claims representative "solution" will survive a determined and protracted due process challenge. Although this was recognized by the National Bankruptcy Review Commission in 1997, it was not addressed in the legislative process that followed and culminated in the widely criticized 2005 amendments to the Bankruptcy Code.

---

[11] In addition, the TCC's position is that the limited scope of the FCR's representation and notice procedure proposed by debtor would not satisfy the requirements of due process. While I am not convinced that the extensive Victim Outreach Plan proposed by the TCC would be necessary to satisfy the requirements of due process, the appointment of a FCR will address the TCC's concerns, to the extent they have merit.

§ 6.03 THE USE OF FINDINGS OF FACT AND CONCLUSIONS OF LAW IN THE SALE PROCESS

The bankruptcy court opinion approving the sale in the *Chrysler* case that was appealed to the Second Circuit and that resulted in the opinion excerpted earlier in this chapter is 47 double-spaced pages long. It is filled with a description of the background of Chrysler's problems and the restructuring transactions it approved, the procedural history of the bankruptcy case, a discussion of the court's authority to approve a sale of substantially all the company's assets free and clear of claims and interests outside of a plan, a determination that the debtors were meeting their fiduciary duties in proposing and pursuing the transaction, a determination that the purchaser was a good faith purchaser for value that qualified for the protections of Code § 363(m) should an appeal be taken and any part of the order overturned, and rulings overruling a long list of objections. The opinion bears no signature but that of the judge and does not feature the typical law firm tracking number in its footer.

The order approving the sale is even longer and does contain the tracking number "NYI-4178439v24," which seems to indicate that it is the 24th version or draft of a document prepared by a law firm, with an assigned unique document number for document management purposes. It consists of 51 pages in which the court, in sum, finds or orders that:

- Chrysler needed to seek refuge in bankruptcy,
- the court had jurisdiction over the case and the sale,
- venue was proper,
- judicial notice was taken of certain out-of-court remarks by President Obama,
- notice by publication was afforded the public,
- the sale was for a sound business purpose,
- the purchaser had made the highest and best offer for the assets,
- the transaction was in the best interests of creditors,
- the purchaser was acting in good faith,
- notice was proper,
- one or more of the § 363(f) standards had been met, allowing a sale free and clear of claims and interests,
- the standards for assumption and assignment of the contracts and leases transferred to the purchaser had been met,
- the transfer was legal, valid, and effective,
- the sale of personally identifiable information involved in the sale was proper,
- the motion was granted,
- the purchase agreement was approved,
- the transfer of the assets was free and clear of all claims (except certain allowed claims),

- claim holders were enjoined from interfering in any way with the purchaser,

- government units were prohibited from revoking or suspending any permits or license relating to the business conducted with the purchased assets,

- the purchaser would honor claims made under state or federal consumer protection "lemon laws,"

- an allocation of property tax liability between the debtor and the purchaser was approved,

- the debtors would establish a tax escrow,

- various specific deals with creditors were approved, including a settlement with the United Automobile Workers regarding retiree benefits,

- the purchaser would not be liable as a successor to the debtor,

- creditors were deemed to have released the purchaser from their claims,

- the transaction was undertaken in good faith,

- the transaction was not a fraudulent or otherwise avoidable transfer,

- the parties were authorized to mutually agree to modify the transactional documents if the change will not materially affect the transaction,

- every federal, state, and local governmental agency was ordered to accept all documents needed to consummate the transaction,

- the debtor was required to change its name, and

- the order was not stayed and was to be immediately effective, among other things.

The practice of loading up sale orders is not confined to mega cases, as the case below indicates.

IN RE AUTOMATION SOLUTIONS INTERNATIONAL, LLC
United States Bankruptcy Court, Northern District of California
274 B.R. 527 (2002)

ALAN JAROSLOVSKY, U.S. BANKRUPTCY JUDGE

The court issued an oral ruling approving the sale of one of the debtor's businesses known as IDC to Danaher Corporation for $5.25 million. The sale was approved free and clear of five liens, and involves the assumption and assignment of six modest equipment leases. Everything was entirely unopposed. The sale has the support of an active, well-represented creditors' committee. There is no confirmed plan.

The court has been presented with a form of order running to some 15 pages, exclusive of exhibits and attachments. Drafted by the purchaser's counsel, it contains 30 paragraphs of findings and 32 paragraphs of decrees. If the court were drafting its own order, it would be less than two pages in length.

Even after culling out the patently improper provisions, such as injunctive relief without benefit of an adversary proceeding, or an attempt to have the order trump an order confirming a plan, or an order that the transfer is tax exempt under 1146(c) of the Bankruptcy Code even though it is not being sold as part of a plan of reorganization, or an order that the purchaser can have no successor liability under any circumstances whatsoever, the remaining order is still an imposing tome. While the court has decided to sign it with modifications, the court feels compelled to comment on its utility and effectiveness.

The court understands the importance of asset sales in bankruptcy cases. Purchasers of assets from bankruptcy estates must feel secure that they are purchasing only the debtor's assets and are not being exposed to the debtor's troubles. This court stands ready to adjudicate any disputes which may arise and protect the purchaser from improper claims against it or the assets it has purchased. However, the order as drafted is an attempt to adjudicate those claims before they arise. As such, it is useless for two reasons. First, minimum standards of procedural due process have not been met. Second, and most crucially, most of the findings and provisions of the order are not *necessary* and therefore cannot have the preclusive effect the purchaser desires.

Any time relief is sought against a particular party, it must be in the context of at least a contested matter pursuant to FRBP 9014. Some relief, such as injunctive or declaratory relief, must be obtained through an adversary proceeding. Both contested matters and adversary proceedings must be served in accordance with FRBP 7004. The simple notice procedure employed in this case is adequate for a sale and meets the requirements of FRBP 2002(a)(2) but cannot serve as a basis for obtaining the relief the purchaser seeks. In addition, principles of fairness require that when relief is being sought against that party the party must be told in unambiguous terms that its specific rights are to be adjudicated.

More importantly, the order is almost an entirely a "comfort order" with no substantive purpose. Section 363(b)(1) provides that after notice and the opportunity for a hearing the trustee (or debtor in possession in a Chapter 11 case) may sell property of the estate out of the ordinary course of business. There is no provision in the Code for an order approving the sale, and in fact the Code was designed so that an order would not be necessary if no objections were raised. The issuance of an order approving an uncontested sale is a creature of custom and local practice, not the Bankruptcy Code. Only those provisions of the order approving the assumption and assignment of the equipment leases and the sale free and clear of certain identified liens are truly necessary and appropriate under the Code; the rest is just a big comfort order.

The futility of the order is best exemplified by the stricken provision which purported to make the sale free from taxation pursuant to § 1146(c). That issue is not before the court. It is not a necessary part of an order approving the sale. No taxing authority has been explicitly told its rights are being adjudicated, nor have they been served pursuant to FRBP 7004(b)(5) or (6). There is no way such a provision would be binding on anyone if the court had left it in.

The court has left the bulk of the order intact, but knows that there may be some remaining provisions which are not enforceable. The court issues this memorandum to make it clear that it will not give preclusive effect to anything in the order which was not necessarily determined, nor will it apply the order to the prejudice of any party not afforded procedural due process.

. . . .

In response to the varied approaches tried by counsel, and in an effort to standardize the practice of out of the ordinary course sales of substantially all the assets of debtors, many courts have issued general orders or guidelines governing the sale motion and order practice. The guidelines from the Southern District of New York, below, are not atypical.

GUIDELINES FOR THE CONDUCT OF ASSET SALES
United States Bankruptcy Court, Southern District of New York
M-383, General Order Amending M-331, November 18, 2009

The United States Bankruptcy Court for the Southern District of New York (the "Court") has established the following guidelines (the "Guidelines") for the conduct of asset sales under § 363(b) of 11 U.S.C. §§ 101 *et seq.* (the "Bankruptcy Code"). The Guidelines are designed to help practitioners identify issues that typically are of concern to parties and the Court, so that, among other things, determinations can be made, if necessary, on an expedited basis.

By offering the Guidelines, this Court does not address the circumstances under which an asset sale or asset sale process is appropriate or express a preference for asset sales under § 363(b) of the Bankruptcy Code as opposed to those conducted in the context of confirming a chapter 11 plan, address other substantive legal issues, or establish any substantive rules. However, the Guidelines do require disclosure of the "Extraordinary Provisions," discussed below, pertaining to the conduct of asset sales, which ordinarily will not be approved without good cause shown for such Extraordinary Provisions, or compelling circumstances, and reasonable notice.

The Guidelines are intended to supplement the requirements of § 363(b) and 365 of the Bankruptcy Code, Rules 2002 and 6004 of the Federal Rules of Bankruptcy Procedure (the "Bankruptcy Rules"), and Rules 6004-1 and 6005-1 of the Court's Local Rules.

I. MOTIONS

A. Motion Content When an auction is contemplated, the debtor[1] should file a single motion seeking the entry of two orders to be considered at two separate hearings. The first order (the "Sale Procedures Order") will approve procedures for the sale process, including any protections for an initial bidder, or stalking horse buyer, and the second order (the "Sale Order") will approve the sale to the successful bidder at the auction. If no

---

[1] The term "debtor" includes "debtor in possession" and "trustee," as appropriate under the particular circumstances.

auction procedures or stalking horse buyer protection provisions are contemplated, only one order (the Sale Order) and one hearing is required. If no auction is contemplated or the debtor has not actively solicited or will not actively solicit higher and better offers, the motion seeking approval of the sale should explain why the debtor proposes to structure the sale in such manner.[2]

1. The proposed purchase agreement, or a form of proposed agreement acceptable to the debtor if the debtor has not yet entered into an agreement with a proposed buyer, should be attached to the motion.

2. The motion also should include a copy of the proposed order(s), particularly if the order(s) include any Extraordinary Provisions.

3. The motion must comply in form with the Local Rules.

4. If a hearing is required under § 363(b) of the Bankruptcy Code in connection with the sale of personally identifiable information subject to a privacy policy of the debtor, the motion should request appointment of a consumer privacy ombudsman under § 332 of the Bankruptcy Code.

B. Bidding Procedures. Generally, the Court will entertain a motion for approval, in a Sale Procedures Order, of proposed bidding procedures if such procedures are, as a matter of reasonable business judgment, likely to maximize the sale price. Such procedures must not chill the receipt of higher and better offers and must be consistent with the seller's fiduciary duties. It is recommended that such procedures include the following:[3]

1. Qualification of Bidders. An entity that is seeking to become a qualified bidder will deliver financial information by a stated deadline to the debtor and other key parties (ordinarily excluding other bidders)[4] reasonably demonstrating such bidder's ability to consummate a sale on the terms proposed. Such financial information, which may be provided confidentially, if appropriate, may include current audited or verified financial statements of, or verified financial commitments obtained by, the potential bidder (or, if the potential bidder is an entity formed for the purpose of acquiring the property to be sold, the party that will bear liability for a breach). To be qualified, a prospective bidder also may be required by a stated deadline to make a non-binding expression of interest and execute a reasonable form of non-disclosure agreement before being provided due diligence access to non-public information.

2. Qualification of Bids Prior to Auction.

---

[2] With the exception of providing for such disclosure, these Guidelines do not express a preference for public over private sales as a means to maximize the sale price.

[3] When multiple asset sales over time are expected, a debtor should consider seeking Court approval of global bidding procedures to avoid the need to obtain Court approval of procedures for each such sale. Similarly, the debtor should consider seeking Court approval of global notice and other appropriate procedures to facilitate sales of assets of limited value or *de minimis* sales that do not warrant an auction or a separate motion for each sale. What constitutes a *de minimis* sale will depend on the facts of each case. *See* Local Rule 6004-1.

[4] It is expected that the debtor will also share its evaluation of bids with key parties-in-interest, such as representatives of official committees, and that it will in its reasonable judgment identify the winning bidder only after consultation with such parties.

(a) The bidding procedures should state the criteria for a qualifying bid and any deadlines for (i) submitting such a bid and (ii) notification whether the bid constitutes a qualifying bid.

(b) The bidding procedures may require each qualified bid to be marked against the form of a stalking horse agreement or a template of the debtor's preferred sale terms, showing amendments and other modifications (including price and other terms) proposed by the qualified bidder. The proposed bidding procedures may, but are not required to, limit bidding to the terms of a stalking horse agreement or preferred form of agreement; for example, bidding on less than all of the assets proposed to be acquired by an initial, or stalking horse, bidder normally should be permitted, unless such bidding is inconsistent with the purpose of the sale.

(c) A qualified bid should clearly identify all conditions to the qualified bidder's obligation to consummate the purchase.

(d) A qualified bid should include a good faith deposit, which will be non-refundable if the bidder is selected as the successful bidder and fails to consummate the purchase (other than as a result of a breach by the seller) and refundable if it is not selected as the successful bidder (other than as a result of its own breach). The amount of, and precise rules governing, the good faith deposit will be determined on a case-by-case basis, but generally each qualified bidder, including any initial, or stalking horse, bidder, should be required to make the same form of deposit.

3. <u>Backup Buyer</u>. The Sale Procedures Order may provide that the debtor in the reasonable exercise of its judgment may accept and close on the second highest qualified bid received if the winning bidder fails to close the transaction within a specified period. In such case, the debtor would retain the second highest bidder's good faith deposit until such bidder was relieved of its obligation to be a back-up buyer.

4. <u>Stalking Horse or Initial Bidder Protections/Bidding Increments</u>.

(a) <u>No-Shop or No-Solicitation Provisions</u>. Limited no-shop or no-solicitation provisions may be permissible, in unusual circumstances, if they are necessary to obtain a sale, they are consistent with the debtor's fiduciary duties and they do not chill the receipt of higher or better offers. Such provisions must be prominently disclosed in the motion, with particularity. If the relevant documents do not include a "fiduciary out" provision, the debtor must disclose the fact of and the reason for the exclusion of the provision.

(b) <u>Break-Up/Topping Fees and Expense Reimbursement</u>. The propriety of any break-up or topping fees and other bidding protections (such as the estate's proposed payment of out-of-pocket expenses incurred by a bidder in connection with the proposed transaction or the compensation of a bidder for lost opportunity costs) will be determined on a case-by-case basis. Generally such obligations should be payable only from the proceeds of a higher or better transaction entered into with a third party within a reasonable time of the closing of the sale. Such provisions must be set forth with particularity, and conspicuously disclosed in the motion.

(c) Bidding Increments. If a proposed sale contemplates the granting of a break-up or topping fee or expense reimbursement, the initial bidding increment must be more than sufficient to pay the maximum amount payable thereunder. Additional bidding increments should not be so high that they chill further bids, or so low that they provide insubstantial consideration to the estate.

(d) Rebidding. If a break-up or topping fee is requested, the Sale Procedures Order should state whether the stalking horse will be deemed to waive the break-up or topping fee by rebidding. In the absence of a waiver, the Sales Procedure Order should state whether the stalking horse will receive a "credit" equal to the break-up or topping fee when bidding at the auction.

5. Auction Procedures.

(a) If an auction is proposed, the Sale Procedures Order generally should provide that the auction will be conducted openly, and that each bidder will be informed of the terms of the previous bid. The motion should explain the rationale for proposing a different auction format in the Sale Procedures Order.

(b) If a professional auctioneer will conduct the auction, the parties should refer to the statutory provisions and rules governing the conduct of professional auctioneers. *See* Bankruptcy Rule 6004 and Rules 6004-1 and 6005-1 of the Local Bankruptcy Rules for the Southern District of New York (the "Local Rules").

(c) If the auction is sufficiently complex or disputes can reasonably be expected to arise, it is advisable at the sale procedures hearing to ask the Court whether it will consider conducting the auction in open court, or otherwise be available to resolve disputes. If the debtor proposes to conduct the auction outside the presence of the judge, the actual bidding should be transcribed or videotaped to ensure a record, or the motion should explain why this is not advisable.

(d) Each bidder is expected to confirm at the auction that it has not engaged in any collusion with respect to the bidding or the sale.

(e) The Sale Procedures Order should provide that, absent irregularities in the conduct of the auction, or reasonable and material confusion during the bidding, the Court will not consider bids made after the auction has been closed, or the motion should explain why this is not advisable.

C. Sale Motion. With regard to the proposed sale, the motion and the evidence presented or proffered at any sale hearing should be sufficient to enable the Court to make the following findings: (1) a sound business reason exists for the transaction; (2) the property has been adequately marketed, the purchase price constitutes the highest or otherwise best offer and provides fair and reasonable consideration; (3) the proposed transaction is in the best interests of the debtor's estate, its creditors, and where relevant, its interest holders; (4) the transaction has been proposed and negotiated in good faith; (5) adequate and reasonable notice has been provided; (6) the "free and clear" requirements of § 363(f) of the Bankruptcy Code, if applicable, have been met; (7) if applicable, the sale is consistent with the debtor's privacy policy concerning personally identifiable information, or, after appointment of a consumer ombudsman in accordance with § 332 of the Bankruptcy Code and notice and a hearing, no showing was made that such sale would violate applicable nonbankruptcy law; (8) the requirements of § 365 of the Bankruptcy Code have been met in respect of the proposed assumption and assignment or rejection of any executory contracts and unexpired leases; (9) where necessary, the debtor's board of directors or other governing body has authorized the proposed transaction; and (10) the debtor and the purchaser have entered into the transaction without collusion, in good faith, and from arm's-length bargaining positions, and neither party has engaged in any conduct that would cause or permit the agreement to be avoided under § 363(n) of the Bankruptcy Code.

1. Sound Business Purpose. A debtor must demonstrate the facts that support a finding that a sound business reason exists for the sale.

2. Marketing Efforts. A debtor must demonstrate facts that support a finding that the property to be sold has been marketed adequately.

3. Purchase Price. A debtor must demonstrate that fair and reasonable value will be received and that the proffered purchase price is the highest or best under the circumstances. If a bid includes deferred payments or any equity component, a debtor should discuss its assessment of the creditworthiness of competing bidders, if any, and the proposed buyer's ability to realize the projected earnings upon which future payments or other forms of consideration to the estate are based. Any material purchase price adjustment provisions should be identified.

4. Assumption and Assignment of Contracts and Leases. A debtor must demonstrate at a minimum: (a) that it or the assignee/acquiror has cured or will promptly cure all existing defaults under the agreement(s), and (b) that the assignee/acquiror can provide adequate assurance that it will perform under the terms of the agreement(s) to be assumed and assigned under § 365 of the Bankruptcy Code. Additional notice and opportunity for a hearing may be required, if the offer sought to be approved at the sale hearing is submitted by a different entity than the initial, stalking horse bidder or the winning bid identifies different contracts or leases for assumption and assignment, or rejection, than the initial bid that was noticed for approval. If this possibility exists, the sale motion should acknowledge the debtor will provide such additional notice and opportunity to object under such circumstances.

D. Extraordinary Provisions. The following provisions must be disclosed conspicuously in a separate section of the sale motion and, where applicable, in the related proposed Sale Procedures Order or Sale Order, and the motion must provide substantial justification therefore:[5]

1. Sale to Insider. If the motion proposes a sale to an insider, as defined in the Bankruptcy Code, the motion must disclose what measures have been taken to ensure the fairness of the sale process and the proposed transaction.

2. Agreements with Management. The sale motion must disclose whether the proposed buyer has discussed or entered into any agreements with management or key employees regarding compensation or future employment, the material terms of any such agreements, and what measures have been taken to ensure the fairness of the sale and the proposed transaction in the light of any such agreements.

3. Private Sale/No Competitive Bidding. If no auction is contemplated, the debtor has agreed to a limited no-shop or no-solicitation provision, or the debtor has otherwise not sought or is not actively seeking higher or better offers, the sale motion must so state and explain why such sale is likely to maximize the sale price.

4. Deadlines that Effectively Limit Notice. If the proposed transaction includes deadlines for the closing or Court approval of the Sale Procedures Order or the Sale Order that have the effect of limiting notice to less than that discussed in II, below, the sale motion must provide an explanation.

5. No Good Faith Deposit. If any qualified bidder, including a stalking horse, is excused from submitting a good faith deposit, the sale motion must provide an explanation.

6. Interim Arrangements with Proposed Buyer. If a debtor is entering into any interim agreements or arrangements with the proposed purchaser, such as interim management arrangements (which, if out of the ordinary course, also must be subject to notice and a hearing under § 363(b) of the Bankruptcy Code), the sale motion must disclose the terms of such agreements.

7. Use of Proceeds. If a debtor proposes to release sale proceeds on or after the closing without further Court order, or to provide for a definitive allocation of sale proceeds between or among various sellers or collateral, the sale motion must describe the intended disposition of such amounts and the rationale therefore.

8. Tax Exemption. If the debtor is seeking to have the sale declared exempt from taxes under § 1146(a) of the Bankruptcy Code, the sale motion must prominently disclose the type of tax (e.g., recording tax, stamp tax, use tax, capital gains tax) for which the exemption is sought. It is not sufficient to refer simply to "transfer" taxes. In addition, the debtor must identify the state or states in which the affected property is located.

9. Record Retention. If the debtor proposes to sell substantially all of its assets, the sale motion must confirm that the debtor will retain, or

---

[5] The fact that a similar provision was included in an order entered in a different case does not constitute a justification.

have reasonable access to, its books and records to enable it to administer its bankruptcy case.

10. Sale of Avoidance Actions. If the debtor seeks to sell its rights to pursue avoidance claims under chapter 5 of the Bankruptcy Code, the sale motion must so state and provide an explanation of the basis therefore.

11. Requested Findings as to Successor Liability. If the debtor seeks findings limiting the purchaser's successor liability, the sale motion must disclose the adequacy of the debtor's proposed notice of such requested relief and the basis for such relief. Generally, the proposed Sale Order should not contain voluminous findings with respect to successor liability, or injunctive provisions except as provided in III, below.

12. Future Conduct. If the debtor seeks a determination regarding the effect of conduct or actions that may or will be taken after the date of the Sale Order, the sale motion must set forth the legal authority for such a determination.

13. Requested Findings as to Fraudulent Conveyance. If debtor seeks a finding to the effect that the sale does not constitute a fraudulent conveyance, it must explain why a finding that the purchase price is fair and reasonable is not sufficient.

14. Sale Free and Clear of Unexpired Leases. If the debtor seeks to sell property free and clear of a possessory leasehold interest, license or other right, the debtor must identify the non-debtor parties whose interests will be affected, and explain what adequate protection will be provided for those interests.

15. Relief from Bankruptcy Rule 6004(h). If the debtor seeks relief from the ten-day stay imposed by Bankruptcy Rule 6004(h), the sale motion must disclose the business or other basis for such request.

II. NOTICE

A. General. Notice is always required under § 363(b); however, a hearing is required only if there are timely objections or the Court otherwise schedules a hearing.

B. Notice of Proposed Sale Procedures.

1. Notice Parties. Notice should be limited to those parties-in-interest best situated to articulate an objection to the limited relief sought at this stage, including:

(a) counsel for official and informal committees of creditors, equity holders, retirees, etc.;

(b) office of the United States Trustee;

(c) postpetition lenders;

(d) indenture trustees;

(e) agent for prepetition lenders;

(f) entities who have requested notice under Bankruptcy Rule 2002;

(g) all entities known or reasonably believed to have asserted a lien, encumbrance, claim or other interest in any of the assets offered for sale; and

(h) parties to executory contracts and unexpired leases proposed to be assumed and assigned, or rejected as part of the proposed transaction.

To provide additional marketing of the assets, the debtor also should send a copy of the motion to entities known or reasonably believed to have expressed an interest in acquiring any of the assets offered for sale. Nothing herein is meant to imply that prospective bidders have standing to be heard with respect to the Sales Procedures.

2. Notice Period. As a general matter, the minimum 20-day notice period set forth in Bankruptcy Rule 2002(a) can be shortened with respect to the request for approval of a proposed Sale Procedures Order, that does not involve Extraordinary Provisions and complies with these Guidelines, without compromising the finality of the proposed transaction. The 10-day notice period provided for in Local Rule 9006-1(b) should provide sufficient time, under most circumstances, to enable any parties-in-interest to file an objection to proposed sale procedures.

3. Contents of Notice. Notice should comport with Bankruptcy Rules 2002 and 6004.

C. Notice of Sale.

1. Notice Parties. Generally the proposed sale requires more expansive notice than proposed sale procedures. (*But see* footnote 2, above, regarding omnibus procedures for *de minimis* sales.) Notice should ordinarily be given to:[6]

(a) counsel for official and informal committees of creditors, equity holders, retirees, etc.;

(b) office of the United States Trustee;

(c) entities who have requested notice under Bankruptcy Rule 2002[7] (and, if the proposed sale is of substantially all of the debtor's assets, all known creditors of the debtor);

(d) postpetition lenders;

(e) indenture trustees;

(f) agent for prepetition lenders;

(g) all entities known or reasonably believed to have asserted a lien, encumbrance, claim or other interest in any of the assets offered for sale;

(h) all parties to executory contracts or unexpired leases to be assumed and assigned, or rejected as part of the transaction;

(i) all affected federal, state and local regulatory (including, for example, environmental agencies) and taxing authorities,[8] including

---

[6] In larger cases, a sale of significant assets may also require notice of the proposed sale in publications of national circulation or other appropriate publications.

[7] In the case of publicly traded debt securities, notice to indenture trustees and record holders may be sufficient to the extent that the identity of beneficial holders is not known.

[8] Notice must be given to applicable taxing authorities, including the state attorney general or other

the Internal Revenue Service;

(j) if applicable, a consumer privacy ombudsman appointed under § 332 of the Bankruptcy Code; and

(k) the Securities and Exchange Commission (if appropriate).

If the contemplated sale implicates the anti-trust laws of the United States, or a debt (other than for taxes) is owed by the debtor to the United States government, notice also should be given to:

(l) the Federal Trade Commission;

(m) the Assistant Attorney General in charge of the Antitrust Division of the Department of Justice; and

(n) the United States Attorney's Office.

To provide additional marketing of the assets, notice also should be sent to any entities known or reasonably believed to have expressed an interest in acquiring any of the assets.

See I.C.4, above for circumstances in which it may be required, based on changes in the proposed transaction that had originally been noticed, to give additional notice to parties to executory contracts and unexpired leases proposed to be assumed and assigned or rejected under § 365 of the Bankruptcy Code.

2. Notice Period. The statutory 20-day notice period should not be shortened for notice of the actual sale without a showing of good cause. The service of a prior notice or order, that discloses an intention to conduct a sale but does not state a specific sale date, does not affect the 20-day notice period.

3. Contents of Notice. Proper notice should comport with Bankruptcy Rules 2002 and 6004 and should include:

(a) the Sale Procedures Order (including the date, time and place of any auction, the bidding procedures related thereto, the objection deadline for the sale motion and the date and time of the sale hearing);

(b) reasonably specific identification of the assets to be sold;

(c) the proposed form of asset purchase agreement, or instructions for promptly obtaining a copy;

(d) if appropriate, representations describing the sale as being free and clear of liens, claims, interests and other encumbrances (other than any claims and defenses of a consumer under any consumer credit transaction that is subject to the Truth in Lending Act or a consumer credit contract (as defined in 16 C.F.R. § 433.1, as amended)), with all such liens, claims, interests and other encumbrances attaching with the same validity and priority to the sale proceeds;

(e) any commitment by the buyer to assume liabilities of the debtor; and

(f) notice of proposed cure amounts and the right and deadline to object thereto and otherwise to object to the proposed assumption and

---

appropriate legal officer, affected by the relief requested under § 1146(a) of the Bankruptcy Code.

assignment, or rejection of executory contracts and unexpired leases (*see* I.C.4, above for additional notice that debtor may need to acknowledge may be required).[9]

III. SALE ORDER

The Court discourages unduly long sale orders that contain unnecessary and redundant provisions. In the typical case, the findings should be limited to those set out in I.C, *supra*, tailored to the particular case. The decretal paragraphs should also be limited, and if more than one decretal paragraph deals with the same subject matter or form of relief, the proponent of the Sale Order should explain the reason in a separate pleading. Finally, if the order contains a decretal paragraph that approves the purchase agreement or authorizes the debtor to execute the purchase agreement, it should not also contain separate decretal paragraphs that approve specific provisions of the purchase agreement or declare their legal effect.

With these admonitions, the Court may enter a Sale Order containing the following, if substantiated through evidence presented or proffered in the motion or at the sale hearing:

A. Approval of Sale and Purchase Agreement. The order should authorize the debtor to (1) execute the purchase agreement, along with any additional instruments or documents that may be necessary to implement the purchase agreement, provided that such additional documents do not materially change its terms; (2) consummate the sale in accordance with the terms and conditions of the purchase agreement and the instruments and agreements contemplated thereby; and (3) take all further actions as may reasonably be requested by the purchaser for the purpose of transferring the assets.[10]

B. Transfer of Assets. The assets will be transferred free and clear of all liens, claims, encumbrances and interests in such property, other than any claims and defenses of a consumer under any consumer credit transaction subject to the Truth in Lending Act or a consumer credit contract, as defined in 16 C.F.R. § 433.1 (and as may be amended), with all such interests attaching to the sale proceeds with the same validity and priority, and the same defenses, as existed immediately prior to the sale,[11] and the persons and entities holding any such interests will be joined from asserting such interests against the purchaser, its successors or assigns, or the purchased assets, unless the purchaser has otherwise

---

[9] This notice may be provided in a separate schedule sent only to the parties to such agreements.

[10] Each and every federal, state and local government agency or department may be directed to accept any and all documents and instruments necessary and appropriate to consummate the transactions contemplated by the purchase agreement.

[11] If any person or entity that has filed financing statements, mortgages, mechanic's liens, *lis pendens*, or other documents evidencing interests in the assets has not delivered to the debtor prior to the closing date termination statements, instruments of satisfaction, and/or releases of all such interests, the debtor may be authorized and directed to execute and file such statements, instruments, releases and other documents on behalf of such person or entity.

The debtor should try to anticipate whether there are any complex allocation issues presented by the proposed "free and clear" relief.

agreed.

C. <u>Assumption and Assignment of Executory Contracts and Leases to Purchaser</u>. The debtor will be authorized and directed to assume and assign to the purchaser executory contracts and leases free and clear of all liens, claims, encumbrances and interests, with all such interests attaching to the sale proceeds with the same validity and priority as they had in the assets being sold (provided, however, that in certain circumstances additional notice may be required before assumption and assignment or rejection of executory contracts and leases can be granted. *See* I.C.4, above.)

D. <u>Statutory Provisions</u>. The proposed order should specify those sections of the Bankruptcy Code and Bankruptcy Rules that are being relied on, and identify those sections, such as Bankruptcy Rule 6004(h), that are, to the extent permitted by law, proposed to be limited or abridged.

E. <u>Good Faith/No Collusion</u>. The transaction has been proposed and entered into by the debtors and the purchaser without collusion, in good faith, and from arm's-length bargaining positions. The proposed Sale Order should also specify that neither the debtor nor the purchaser have engaged in any conduct that would cause or permit the transaction to be avoided under Bankruptcy Code § 363(n).

Chapter 7

EXECUTORY CONTRACTS

§ 7.01 INTRODUCTION: WHAT IS AN EXECUTORY CONTRACT?

You arrive at Carol Charisma's office with two litigation bags in tow. They are stuffed with papers. Carol looks up from her desk and says, "What have you got there?"

"I have two bags full of contracts. We have to start thinking about what to do with them. I confess that on the way over here I gave myself a nasty little headache trying to figure out how best to explain the concept of executory contracts and their treatment in bankruptcy to Headley and you."

"Well, fortunately, Headley has gone fishing, so you only have to explain the concept to me," Carol says.

"That's good, because only a lawyer could possibly appreciate the intricacies of a subject that really could and probably should be considerably more straightforward."

"Do you mind if we start with a simple question?"

"Shoot."

"What is an executory contract?"

You take a deep, relaxing breath and begin.

You explain that when a debtor in possession or trustee takes stock of its liabilities and assets, it is likely to discover, in addition to cash, equipment, inventory, and real estate, yet another form of property: contracts and leases that the debtor entered into prior to the commencement of the case.

These contracts may be valuable. They may entitle a debtor such as Amphydynamics to purchase or sell something at an advantageous price. For example, a contract might entitle Amphydynamics to purchase a supply of sleek, flat panel monitors at a below-market price. Chances are, the debtor would want to perform such a contract, because the contract is profitable and performance will enhance the value of the bankruptcy estate.

On the other hand, some contracts may be of little or no value to the estate. Consider, for example, a contract that requires Amphydynamics to buy a truckload of clunky, black and white computer monitors at a price set in 1989. Chances are, the debtor would not want to perform such a contract, because the contract is not profitable and performance would deplete the value of the bankruptcy estate.

Recognizing that performance of a contract may enhance or diminish the value of the estate, Bankruptcy Code § 365 gives trustees and debtors in possession a considerable amount of flexibility in dealing with them. Code § 365(a) generally provides that "the trustee, subject to the court's approval, may assume or reject any executory contract or unexpired lease of the debtor." The essence of § 365, as one court has observed, is to "permit[] the trustee or debtor-in-possession, subject to the approval of the bankruptcy court, to go through the inventory of executory contracts . . . and decide which ones it would be beneficial to adhere to and which ones it would be beneficial to reject." *Orion Pictures Corp. v. Showtime Networks, Inc. (In re Orion Pictures Corp.)*, 4 F.3d 1095, 1098 (2d Cir. 1993).

Even though the trustee or debtor in possession makes a decision to reject after the Chapter 11 petition is filed, the Code treats rejection as if it occurred prepetition, and, as we will see in § 5.03, rejection is best understood as a breach of the contract. Thus, the general rule is that rejection of a contract gives rise to a prepetition, general unsecured claim for damages. In contrast, and as we will see in more detail in § 5.02, when the trustee or debtor assumes a contract, the cost of performance is an administrative expense. If a contract is assumed and subsequently breached (rejected), the damages flowing from that breach are entitled to priority as an administrative expense as well.

Assumption and rejection are not the debtor's only alternatives. Some contracts may have great value to the estate because the debtor can profitably assign its rights under the contracts. For example, Comp-U-All, the Amphydynamics subsidiary that operates retail computer stores in malls and shopping centers in several states, occupies those stores pursuant to long-term leases. Many of these leases were negotiated years ago and charge below-market rents. Assume that Comp-U-All decides to discontinue operations at some of those locations. Rejection of the unexpired leases, rather than assumption would seem to be in order. But the debtor has another choice: it may assume the leases and then assign (think "sell") them to third parties, capturing their full value for the benefit of the estate.

Finally, a trustee or debtor may do nothing. In a Chapter 7 case, if a contract is not timely assumed, it is automatically rejected. § 365(d)(1). As we will see in more detail in § 5.05, a Chapter 11 trustee or debtor in possession may assume or reject most kinds of contracts at any time prior to confirmation of a reorganization plan. What happens in a Chapter 11 case if a contract is neither expressly assumed nor rejected prior to plan confirmation? The contract will "ride through" the case and remain an obligation of the reorganized entity, if there is one. *In re BSL Operating Corp.*, 57 B.R. 945, 951 (Bankr. S.D.N.Y. 1986). This is why many reorganization plans contain boilerplate language rejecting all contracts not assumed previously or in the plan.

[A] The "Countryman" Definition of Executory Contract

Although Code § 365 is concerned with the treatment of "executory contracts," and although § 365 is more than 4,200 words long, it does not define the term "executory contract." Nor does any other section of the Code. Under the common law, as Professor Williston observed, "All contracts to a greater or lesser extent are executory. When they cease to be so, they cease to be contracts." 1 S. Williston,

Contracts § 14 (3d ed. 1957). In the context of bankruptcy law, courts and commentators have struggled to give meaning to the term.

The classic definition of an executory contract for bankruptcy purposes was coined by the late Professor Vern Countryman in the first of two celebrated law review articles published in the 1970s. *See* Vern Countryman, *Executory Contracts in Bankruptcy (Part I)*, 57 MINN. L. REV. 439 (1973), and Vern Countryman, *Executory Contracts in Bankruptcy (Part II)*, 58 MINN. L. REV. 479 (1974). According to the Countryman definition, an executory contract is:

> a contract under which the obligation of both the bankrupt and the other party to the contract are so far unperformed that the failure of either to complete performance would constitute a material breach excusing the performance of the other.

57 MINN. L. REV. at 460. The Supreme Court has offered a broader, though not necessarily inconsistent, definition. Citing the legislative history to § 365(a), the Court found:

> The Bankruptcy Code furnishes no express definition of an executory contract, but the legislative history . . . indicates that Congress intended the term to mean a contract "on which performance is due to some extent on both sides."

N.L.R.B. v. Bildisco and Bildisco, 465 U.S. 513, 522 n. 6 (1984) (citations omitted).

These definitions proceed from the notion that the proper case for *rejecting* a contract is when completion of performance by the debtor would be either burdensome or of no benefit to the estate, whereas the proper case for *assuming* a contract is when completion of performance would benefit the estate. A contract that requires no performance by the debtor could not possibly burden the estate, and a contract that requires no performance by the non-debtor party could not possibly benefit the estate. Hence, the need for "executoriness" on both sides. To see how the Countryman definition works in practice, consider the following examples.

Example 1

Amphydynamics agreed to sell 3,000 flat panel monitors to Buyer, a retailer, for $30,000. Amphydynamics has delivered, but Buyer has not yet paid. Debtor files a bankruptcy petition. Is the contract executory?

Under the Countryman definition, this contract would not be executory, because it is unperformed only on one side: the Buyer's. Nor is there any reason to treat it as executory. A rational trustee or debtor in possession would not reject the contract, because that would deprive the estate of the benefit of Buyer's performance. The estate would not get paid. On the other hand, there is no need to assume the contract, because the estate's right to payment is property of the estate. A rational trustee or debtor would await performance by the Buyer. If the Buyer does not pay, the trustee or debtor should take steps to enforce the contract. Section 365, however, is not implicated.

Example 2

Amphydynamics agreed to sell 3,000 flat panel monitors to Buyer, a retailer, for $30,000. Buyer paid for them in advance of shipment, but Amphydynamics has not yet delivered. Amphydynamics files a bankruptcy petition. Is the contract executory?

Once again, under the Countryman definition, this contract would not be regarded as executory, because performance is due only on one side: the debtor's. Nor is there any reason to treat it as executory, because, if the estate were to assume this contract and deliver the televisions to Buyer, the effect would be to prefer Buyer and elevate its claim over the claims of other unsecured creditors, including, for example, other buyers who did not receive the monitors they paid for, unpaid suppliers who sold goods on credit, and lenders whose loans are in default. If Amphy fails to deliver the monitors, Buyer will have a prepetition claim for damages, since Amphy's failure to perform is the breach of a claim that arose prepetition. Code § 101(5). That is the same remedy the Buyer would have if Amphy "rejected" the contract. In this context, rejection is superfluous, because it is the functional equivalent of breach.

Example 3

Amphydynamics promised to sell 3,000 flat panel televisions to Buyer for $30,000 C.O.D. At the time Amphydynamics filed its bankruptcy petition, it had not yet delivered the televisions, and Buyer had not yet paid. Is the contract executory?

According to the Countryman definition, this contract IS executory, because it is unperformed on both sides. Whether the estate should assume or reject it depends on which alternative benefits the estate. If the estate can turn a profit by performing the contract, the contract should be assumed. If the cost of performance exceeds the contract price, the contract should be rejected. If Amphy can sell the monitors to a different buyer for many times the contract price, the contract should be rejected. Here too, rejection of the contract is the functional equivalent of breach. Although rejection and breach are synonymous, in this context rejection may not be superfluous. Requiring the debtor to reject the contract expressly gives the court and creditors an opportunity to second guess the debtor's decision to forego the benefits of performance. It injects some certainty into the affairs of the nondebtor party, which otherwise would be called upon to perform without knowledge of the debtor's intentions. It prevents the obligation from riding through the case and binding the reorganized debtor.

In the following opinion, the court applies Professor Countryman's definition to a franchise agreement.

IN RE ROVINE CORP.

United States Bankruptcy Court, Western District of Tennessee
6 B.R. 661 (1980)

MEMORANDUM OPINION

WILLIAM B. LEFFLER, CHIEF BANKRUPTCY JUDGE.

I.

. . . .

On May 2, 1980 the defendant filed a petition under Chapter 11 of the Bankruptcy Code. Since that time the debtor has continued in possession of its property and has continued to operate its business without the intervention of a trustee. At the time of the filing, the defendant was a franchisee of the plaintiff, Burger King Corporation. On May 13, 1980, the plaintiff filed an application with the Court asking that the defendant be compelled to adopt or reject the franchise agreement as an executory contract under § 365(d) of the Bankruptcy Code.[1]

On July 18, 1980, the defendant rejected the franchise agreement. On July 28, 1980, the plaintiff filed a complaint with the Court seeking to enforce a covenant not to compete contained in the rejected franchise agreement. The covenant not to compete provided that upon termination of the franchise agreement and for a period of 18 months thereafter, the defendant would not engage in any business which was the same or similar to the plaintiff's business in a location within a 5-mile radius of the franchise premises.

On August 4, 1980, the Court entered a Memorandum Opinion holding that: (1) the covenant not to compete was executory in nature; (2) said covenant was rejected as a part of the defendant's prior rejection of the franchise agreement; and (3) the effect of rejection was to relieve the defendant and its estate of the obligations imposed via the covenant not to compete. The Court therefore refused the plaintiff's request for a temporary injunction. The plaintiff filed its instant motion on August 12, 1980, asking that the Court amend its prior judgment in this cause and grant the plaintiff's request for a temporary injunction enforcing the covenant not to compete.

II.

The plaintiff notes that the rejection of an executory contract not previously assumed gives rise to a claim against a debtor's estate under § 502(g) of the Bankruptcy Code. However, the plaintiff also notes that the definition of "claim" under § [101(5)] of the Code excludes a right to an equitable remedy for breach of performance if such breach does not give rise to a right of payment. The plaintiff

---

[1] The power of a Chapter 11 debtor in possession to assume or reject executory contracts stems from § 1107 of the Code, which grants such a debtor the rights and powers of a Chapter 11 trustee. One power of a trustee is the power to assume or reject executory contracts under § 365.

alleges that its remedy against the defendant is that of injunction and that the franchise agreement does not provide for monetary damages. Therefore, there is no right to payment that is a necessary element of the Code's definition of "claim." From these observations the plaintiff contends that Congress intended to retain the right of a nonbankrupt party to enforce covenants not to compete.

The plaintiff further contends that the covenant not to compete is fully executed in that it constituted an obligation of the defendant which immediately followed the termination of the franchise agreement. As such, the plaintiff contends that the covenant in question is a divisible part of the franchise agreement and may still be enforced via injunction notwithstanding the defendant's previous rejection under § 365 of the Code.

Finally, the plaintiff proposes an alternative argument. Despite the fact that it was the plaintiff's motion which brought about the defendant's rejection of the franchise agreement as an executory contract, the plaintiff now contends that the franchise agreement taken in its entirety is not an executory contract in the bankruptcy sense. As a basis for this alternative contention the plaintiff argues that the grant of a franchise is comparable to a license. The plaintiff would have this Court hold that as a license the franchise agreement was performed in material part by the plaintiff upon the granting of the franchise to the defendant and the agreement was, therefore, fully executed on the part of the plaintiff at that point, except for certain duties the plaintiff describes as administrative and therefore nonmaterial.

III.

This Court's decision to reconsider the instant case is further evidence of problems various courts have encountered in their struggle to define the term "executory contract" as used in the bankruptcy context. In this Court's prior decision, the Court considered only the covenant not to compete and the question of whether it was an executory provision of the franchise agreement. The question of the executory nature of the remaining provisions of the franchise agreement was not an issue. Now upon further reflection and in light of the plaintiff's contention that the agreement was fully executed on its part, the Court feels that the franchise agreement must be viewed in its entirety in order to decide the question of its executory nature.

IV.

The primary issues to be considered by the Court are as follows:

(1) Was the franchise agreement an executory contract within the meaning of § 365 of the Bankruptcy Code, and therefore subject to rejection by the defendant?

(2) If the franchise agreement was an executory contract under § 365, did the rejection of said agreement relieve the defendant and its estate of the obligations of the covenant not to compete, or may the plaintiff still enforce said covenant notwithstanding rejection?

V.

Probably the most comprehensive analysis of the term "executory contract" as used in the bankruptcy context is found in Professor Vern Countryman's two-part article appearing in 47 Minn. L. Rev. 436 (1973) and 58 Minn. L. Rev. 479 (1974). This article concerns executory contracts under § 70(b) of the Bankruptcy Act, the statutory predecessor to § 365 of the Bankruptcy Code.

Professor Williston in his work on contracts has stated that, "all contracts to a greater or lesser extent are executory. When they cease to be so, they cease to be contracts." 1 S. Williston, Contracts § 14 (3d ed. 1957). However, Professor Countryman notes that such an "expansive meaning can hardly be given to the term [executory contract] as used in the bankruptcy sense." Rather the term "executory contract" should be defined "in the light of the purpose for which the trustee is given the option to assume or reject." 57 Minn. L. Rev. 439, 450 (1973). Or in the words of the 6th Circuit Court of Appeals:

> The key, it seems, to deciphering the meaning of the executory contract rejection provisions, is to work backward, proceeding from an examination of the purposes rejection is expected to accomplish. If those objectives have already been accomplished, or if they can't be accomplished through rejection, then the contract is not executory within the meaning of the Bankruptcy Act.

In re Jolly, 574 F.2d 349, 351 (1978).

Professor Countryman goes on to analyze relevant court decisions on the subject of executory contracts in bankruptcy and states that that term does not encompass contracts fully performed by the nonbankrupt party, where the bankrupt party has only partially performed or not performed at all. 57 Minn. L. Rev. 439, 451 (1973). Nor does the term encompass contracts fully performed by the bankrupt party, but not fully performed by the nonbankrupt party. 57 Minn. L. Rev. 439, 458 (1973). The term executory contracts, however, does cover contracts where the obligations of both parties remain at least partially and materially unperformed at the time of bankruptcy. 57 Minn. L. Rev. 439, 460–461 (1973). The definition of executory contract offered by Professor Countryman and adopted by many courts is as follows:

> A contract under which the obligation of both the bankrupt and the other party to the contract are so far unperformed that the failure of either to complete performance would constitute a material breach excusing the performance of the other.

57 Minn. L. Rev. 460 (1973).

As an example of a case involving an executory contract under § 70(b) of the Bankruptcy Act, Professor Countryman cites *Wagstaff v. Peters*, 203 Kan. 108, 453 P.2d 120 (1969). This case involved a contract for the sale of a bankrupt's business. At the time of bankruptcy the buyers remained liable for a part of the purchase price and the bankrupt sellers remained obligated: (1) to pay certain accounts payable; (2) to advise and consult with the buyers; and, as in the instant case, (3) not to enter into a competing business. The trustee had failed to assume this contract within the time specified in § 70 of the Act. When the trustee subsequently brought an action against the buyers on the contract, the court in *Wagstaff* held that: (1) the contract was executory in nature because it involved future performance on both the buyers' and sellers' part and (2) the entire contract was conclusively presumed to be rejected due to the trustee's failure to affirm within the allotted time.

As noted previously, the plaintiff compares the instant franchise agreement to a license and contends that as a license the agreement was fully performed by it at the time of the execution of the agreement. A franchise agreement is in many respects similar to a license. In the typical franchise agreement a company (the franchisor) owns a trademark or trade name which it licenses to others (the franchisees) to use upon the condition that the franchisees conform their business to standards established by the franchisor. *Evans v. S. S. Kresge Co.*, 394 F. Supp. 817, 844 (W.D.Pa.1975). The franchise agreement between the plaintiff and defendant conforms to this general description. The plaintiff licensed the use of its systems, service marks, and trade marks to the defendant in return for the payment of a franchise fee. These mutual obligations were fully performed by both parties at the time of the Chapter 11 filing. During the term of the agreement the defendant agreed inter alia to make specified royalty payments to the plaintiff and also agreed not to compete with the plaintiff during the term of the agreement and for a specified time thereafter. These obligations remained to be performed by the defendant at the time of the filing. If there remained no other obligations or promises to be performed by the plaintiff under the term of the agreement, the contract in question would probably be executed in that the plaintiff would have fully performed prior to the filing date. However, this is not the case. The plaintiff agreed during the term of the franchise agreement to "use its best efforts to maintain the high reputation of Burger King Restaurants and in connection therewith to make available to franchisee" other services of the company. . . . The promise to make available these additional services was an obligation of the plaintiff that remained to be performed as of the filing date. In general these services included advising and consulting with the defendant in regards to merchandising, marketing, advertising research, special recipe techniques, food preparation, new restaurant services and other operational developments subsequently devised by the plaintiff. In essence the plaintiff agreed to continue to advise and consult with the defendant concerning the operation of its franchise and to afford said defendant the benefit of its expertise in the restaurant field as such aid was needed by the defendant. As is the case of most franchise agreements, the instant agreement required a continuing cooperative effort between franchisor and franchisee. *See Evans v. S. S. Kresge Co., supra*.

Returning to the plaintiff's license analogy, Professor Countryman in part two of his article discusses the executory nature of patent licenses and states:

> *The usual patent license, by which the patentee-licensor authorizes the licensee to exercise some part of the patentee's exclusive right to make, use and vend the patented item in return for payment of royalties, ordinarily takes the form of an executory contract.* A license simply to use patented equipment is typically a part of an agreement by which the equipment is leased to the licensee in return for royalty payments. Such an agreement is clearly within the Bankruptcy Act's concept of an executory contract. A

license merely to use a consumable patented product necessarily provides for the supplying of the product to the licensee. If the patentee-licensor is in any way responsible for supplying the product, the contract is executory. The same is true of a license to sell patented products manufactured by the patentee-licensor.

Where there is no express undertaking by the licensor, the agreement with the licensee may not be executory because the licensor may have fully performed merely by executing the license agreement. Thus a close question may be presented by a license to make and sell a patented product where another licensee undertakes to apply the product. Even in these close cases, however, there may be an implied undertaking by the licensor which brings all patent licenses within the ambit of an executory contract. It has been held in a patentee-licensor's infringement action against a third party that a final judgment adjudicating the patent invalid constitutes a "complete failure of consideration" amounting to an "eviction" which releases the licensee from any further obligation to pay royalties. Moreover, since the death of the doctrine of "licensee estoppel," the licensee can set up the invalidity of the patent as a defense when sued by the licensor for royalties due under the license. Hence, all patentee-licensors are now substantially in the position of having warranted to their licensees the validity of their patents. Although the sanction for the breach of such a warranty is only forfeiture of royalties rather than liability for damages, *this continuing undertaking by the licensor is enough to justify the treatment of all unexpired patent licenses as executory contracts.*

(Emphasis added) 58 Minn. L. Rev. 479, 501–502 (1974).

The Court is of the opinion that Professor Countryman's comments regarding patent licenses are applicable to the instant franchise agreement. The aforesaid comments recognize the interests of a licensee or franchisee in the continuing undertaking of the licensor or franchisor to cooperate in the operation of the franchised business and to insure that the license or franchise will not be infringed upon by third parties. These undertakings on the part of the instant plaintiff remained unperformed after the Chapter 11 filing and constituted a part of the consideration for the defendant's obligations under the franchise agreement. In other words, the franchise agreement in question was unperformed in material part by both the plaintiff and defendant as of the filing date of the defendant's Chapter 11. Therefore, the Court holds that said agreement was an executory contract within the meaning of § 365 of the Code and as such was subject to rejection by the defendant.

VI.

The remaining issue to be decided concerns the survivability of the covenant not to compete. The precise question may be phrased as follows: May a party to an executory contract, rejected by a debtor-in-possession pursuant to § 365 of the Bankruptcy Code, compel enforcement of a provision of that contract which restrains said debtor from competing with that party? The Court must answer this question in the negative. An executory contract must be rejected in its entirety or not at all. *In re Klaber Bros., Inc.*, 173 F. Supp. 83 (S.D.N.Y. 1959). It must be remembered that the purpose of both § 70(b) of the Act and § 365 of the Code is to allow the rejection of executory contracts which are burdensome to the estate and the assumption of executory contracts which would benefit the estate. These sections were intended to solve the problem of assumption of liabilities, i. e., excusing or requiring future specific performance by the debtor depending upon assumption or rejection. 4A, *Collier on Bankruptcy*, Par. 70.43(2), Page 523 (14th ed.); 2 *Collier on Bankruptcy*, Par. 365.01, pages through 365-10 (15th ed. 1979). The effect of rejection is to relieve a debtor and its estate of the obligation imposed under an executory contract. *In re Middleton*, 3 B.R. 610, 613. In the instant case the covenant not to compete was a part of the franchise agreement. Since the franchise agreement has been rejected by the defendant as an executory contract, the covenant not to compete must also be deemed rejected. The Court, therefore, must deny the plaintiff's request that the Court's prior judgment in this case be amended and must also refuse the plaintiff's request for a temporary injunction.

VII.

The Court must also disagree with the plaintiff's contention that it has no claim against the defendant's estate as that term is defined in § [101(5)] of the Code. Section 502(g) specifically grants the plaintiff a nonadministrative claim based upon the rejection of the franchise agreement. Any damages incurred by the plaintiff as a result of the rejection would constitute a "right to payment" sufficient under § [101(5)]. In fact the plaintiff has filed a proof of claim in the amount of $528,295.02.

. . . .

Counsel for the defendant is instructed to enter an order consistent with the Court's Memorandum Opinion.

[B] Other Approaches to Determining Whether a Contract is Executory

Although the Countryman definition is widely accepted, with increasing frequency, courts have departed from it in order to produce a result that enhances the value of the estate and, in Chapter 11 cases, enhances the prospects for rehabilitation of the debtor. In a sense, these courts extend Countryman's "functional approach" even further and turn it inside out by focusing on the effect of treating the particular contract in question as executory. If the estate benefits by treating the contract as executory, these courts will so treat it.

In *In re Booth*, 19 B.R. 53 (Bankr. D. Utah 1982), the Countryman definition was also disregarded, albeit, the court said, "reluctantly." The debtor in *Booth* was a real estate dealer who had contracted to buy a parcel of land from sellers. The debtor had made a down payment on the property, and the sellers were obliged to convey title to the debtor when the balance was paid. The debtor, meanwhile, had entered into a contract to re-sell the property to a third party. After the debtor filed its Chapter 11 petition, the sellers moved for an order directing the debtor to assume or reject the contract. Sellers contended that the contract was executory, because the debtor had yet to pay the balance of the purchase price and the sellers had yet to convey title. Failure of either side to perform, they said, would constitute material breach, excusing the other from performance. Judge Mabey disagreed. He found that the sellers should be regarded not as parties to an executory contract, but as holders of a lien on real estate that secured their claim for the unpaid balance of the purchase price.

First, Judge Mabey said that the Countryman definition was improperly fixated on the notion of benefit to the estate, whereas "[s]ection 365 . . . reflects a number of policies, including not only benefit to the estate but also protection of creditors." *Id.* at 55. The court nevertheless concluded that when a debtor is in the position of purchaser under a land sales agreement, the estate benefits more if the contract is regarded as a security agreement than if it is regarded as an executory contract. For one thing, if the seller's interest is regarded as a lien, then the estate is regarded as owner of the real estate. The estate is augmented. In addition, treating the seller as a lien holder spares the estate potential depletion. A debtor may not assume an executory contract unless it cures defaults and provides adequate assurance of future performance. Moreover, a debtor may not assume a contract piecemeal, *i.e.*, assume only the beneficial provisions and reject the burdensome ones. But, if the contract is not executory, then assumption is, in Judge Mabey's words, "irrelevant." Subject to the requirement that the seller's interest be adequately protected, the estate has the benefits — *i.e.*, the right to use, sell, or lease the property pursuant to Code § 363 — without all the burdens. The debtor may attempt to modify or scale down the seller's secured claim in the context of a plan.

The court then considered whether this approach also protected the non-debtor sellers, and concluded it did:

> Vendors have two rights under a contract for deed: the right to payment, which is not adequately protected, and the right to hold title as security, which is adequately protected. While the right to payment is suspended, the interest in property is adequately protected. This strikes a balance between vendors, other creditors, and the estate. Vendors are not preferred, for example, in terms of administrative claims, but are treated on a par with other mortgagees . . . who are protected against any decrease in the value of their liens.

Id. at 61.

In *Sipes v. Atlantic Gulf Cmtys. Corp. (In re General Development Corp.)*, 84 F.3d 1364 (11th Cir. 1996), the Eleventh Circuit adopted such a post-functional approach in a case involving rejection of an installment land sale contract by a debtor-seller. The purchasers were among thousands of buyers who had entered into contracts to purchase home sites from the debtor. The contracts provided that the purchasers would receive title upon payment of all installments. Seven years after the purchasers had completed making all required payments, but before the debtor had developed the home sites, the debtor filed a Chapter 11 petition. The purchasers took the position that the debtor could not reject the land sales contracts, because, since the purchasers had fully performed, the contracts were nonexecutory. The court disagreed. It found that the debtor was incapable of fulfilling its obligations under the thousands of outstanding purchase agreements, and that the only way to achieve "a meaningful reorganization for the benefit of hundreds of thousands of creditors who might not . . . otherwise receive any recovery" was to treat the contracts as executory subject to rejection. *Id.* at 1374.

By treating the contracts as executory, did the *Sipes* court empower the debtor to accomplish anything other than breach the contracts? Did the court have to find that the contracts were executory to enable the debtor to breach them? Would the purchasers have been entitled to specific performance in either case? These questions beg larger questions: what is the effect of assumption? What is the effect of rejection? We turn to those topics next.

§ 7.02   EFFECT OF ASSUMPTION

If (and only if) an executory contract is assumed by a trustee or debtor in possession, does the estate become bound by the debtor's contractual obligations. If the debtor fails to perform in accordance with the terms of an assumed contract, the other party to the contract will hold a claim for damages that will be entitled to priority as an administrative expense and rank ahead of general unsecured claims. Code §§ 503(b), 507(a)(1). *See, e.g., In re Marple Publishing Co.*, 20 B.R. 933 (Bankr. E.D. Pa. 1982). For example, assume that prior to filing its Chapter 11 petition, Amphydynamics agreed to purchase a thousand relay switches from Pouilly Fuse Co. The order has not yet shipped, and Amphydynamics has not paid. If, after filing its Chapter 11 petition, Amphydynamics assumes the contract, Pouilly's claim for goods sold and delivered would be treated as an administrative expense, with priority over general unsecured claims.

The concept embodied in Code § 365(a) — that a contract must expressly be assumed with the court's permission before it can become binding on the estate — is rooted in a concern, articulated by courts in some early bankruptcy cases, that because all of a debtor's property interests, including contract rights, pass to the bankruptcy estate, the estate could automatically become obligated to perform a contract even when performance was a losing proposition. *See Copeland v. Stephens*, 106 Eng. Rep. 218 (K.B. 1818), discussed in Michael T. Andrew, *Executory Contracts in Bankruptcy: Understanding "Rejection,"* 59 U. COLO. L. REV. 845, 856–61 (1988).

To avoid this result, courts devised the rule that a contract did not become binding on the estate unless the trustee "accepted" title to it. If the trustee "refused" title, the estate would not be bound. *Id.* More recently, some courts resorted to the fiction that the filing of a petition created a new entity — the debtor in possession — that was not a party to the erstwhile debtor's executory contracts until it assumed them. The Supreme Court rejected this "new entity theory" in *NLRB v. Bildisco & Bildisco*, 465 U.S. 513 (1984), but agreed that the estate is not bound by an executory contract unless the debtor in possession or trustee assumes it. Today, authorities disagree about whether a contract is technically property of the estate before it is assumed, but they do agree that the estate is not bound by a contract unless and until it is assumed. Charles J. Tabb, *The Law of Bankruptcy* § 8.3 at p. 580 (1997). *Compare* Michael T. Andrew, *Executory Contracts in Bankruptcy: Understanding "Rejection,"* 59 U. COLO. L. REV. 845, 856–66 (1988), *with* Jay L. Westbrook, *A Functional Analysis of Executory Contracts*, 74 Minn. L. Rev. 227, 250 (1989).

To say that the estate is not bound, however, is not to say that the nondebtor party to the contract does not hold a claim. That claim is, however, a general unsecured claim, not an administrative expense.

§ 7.03   EFFECT OF REJECTION

[A]   The General Rule

According to Code § 365(g)(1), the rejection of an executory contract constitutes a breach of the contract, and, if the contract has not been previously assumed, the breach is deemed to have occurred immediately before the filing of the bankruptcy petition. That rejection gives rise to a claim for damages that is allowable as a prepetition claim. The holder of a claim arising from the rejection of an executory contract holds a general unsecured claim that ranks on a par with other prepetition general unsecured claims. *See, e.g., In re Walnut Assocs.*, 145 B.R. 489, 494 (Bankr. E.D. Pa. 1992). Generally, nonbankruptcy law governs the measure of damages. *See, e.g., In re Besade*, 76 B.R. 845, 847 (Bankr. M.D. Fla. 1987).

For example, assume that Amphydynamics agrees to sell 10 flat panel monitors to Buyer One for $10 each. After entering into the contract, but before delivery or payment, Amphydynamics files a Chapter 11 petition. Due to unanticipated demand, the wholesale price of the monitors soars to $100 each. Amphydynamics, now a debtor in possession, obtains the court's permission to reject the executory contract so that the debtor can sell the monitors to Buyer Two for $100 each, enriching the estate by $900. As we've just seen, under Code § 365(g)(1), the rejection operates as a breach of the contract, and under Code § 502(g), Buyer One will have a claim for damages flowing from that breach that is allowable as a prepetition claim. Assuming the measure of damages is the contract/market price differential (see U.C.C. §§ 2-712 and 2-713), Buyer One will have a claim for $900. If rejection gives rise to a damage claim that is equal to the amount by which the estate is enriched, is the effect of rejection just a wash? The answer is no. The transaction is not the wash it might appear to be, because 100% of the appreciation in the value of the televisions is captured by the estate, and that added value is shared pro rata by all prepetition creditors, including Buyer One. The estate is enlarged by $900, but if, for example, creditors receive 10 cents on the dollar, Buyer One will recover only $90 on its $900 claim.

[B]   The Effect of Rejection on Specific Performance

The effect of rejection on the availability of the remedy of specific performance has caused the courts no end of trouble and confusion. Suppose that Amphydynamics, as seller, rejects a contract for the sale of a Van Gogh painting from its corporate art collection. The frustrated buyer is not going to be content with the prepetition claim for damages that Code § 502(g) gives her. The buyer wants the Van Gogh, and she will argue that under applicable nonbankruptcy law, she would be entitled to an injunction ordering the debtor to sell this unique masterpiece to her.

Professor Countryman would say that specific performance should not be available in this situation, because it is the functional equivalent of payment in full and offends the principle of equality of treatment of creditors who are similarly situated. Countryman, *Executory Contracts in Bankruptcy (Part I)*, 57 MINN. L. REV. 439, 465–66, 471 (1973). Another commentator has suggested that Countryman's reasoning is wrongheaded, because it ignores the fact that in other contexts, for example secured claims, "bankruptcy law recognizes that not all claimants are similarly situated; that those with rights to property, good as against competing claimants under state law, do not lose those rights." Michael T. Andrew, *Executory Contracts in Bankruptcy: Understanding "Rejection,"* 59 U. COLO. L. REV. 845, 926 (1988). He explains:

> [T]here is no elevation to priority. The non-debtor party started off differently situated as compared to other claimants, and the analysis simply takes account of and preserves that difference, consonant with the rest of bankruptcy law. Again, the point is that if such a right is good outside and inside bankruptcy as a general matter, its continued existence should not turn on the executoriness of a contract, a matter of pure happenstance. To hold otherwise does not preserve equality, it affirmatively demotes the non-debtor.

Id. If we follow this line of reasoning and want to figure out whether the buyer of the Van Gogh is entitled to specific performance, we need to figure out not only whether specific performance is available against the debtor, but also whether it is available against the debtor's other creditors. Remember Bankruptcy Code § 544(a) from your basic bankruptcy course? It embodies the so-called "strong arm" power of the trustee. It provides that, as of the date of the filing, a trustee or debtor in possession can avoid, for the benefit of the estate (and of all creditors) — any transfer that, as of the same date, could have been avoided by either a judicial lien creditor who levied on all the debtor's property or by a bona fide purchaser of all the debtor's real property who perfected title in the property before the bankruptcy case. If such a perfect, hypothetical lien creditor or bona fide purchaser could prime the buyer's right to the painting outside of bankruptcy, the buyer should not be entitled to specific performance inside of bankruptcy. In other words, if, under state law, the painting is subject to creditor levy as long as it remains in the possession of the seller, the buyer's interest in the painting is subordinate to the creditors' interest. *See* Douglas G. Baird, *The Elements of Bankruptcy* 119 (Fountain Press 1993); Charles J. Tabb, *The Law of Bankruptcy* § 8.8, at 595 (Fountain Press 1997).

A similar problem keeps cropping up in cases involving covenants not to compete. Courts have disagreed as to whether a covenant not to compete survives rejection of an executory contract. In the *Rovine* case, the court held that since a contract must be rejected in its entirety or not at all, rejection of a Burger King franchise agreement resulted in rejection of all terms, including the franchisee's covenant not to compete. But, in *In re Steaks to Go, Inc.*, 226 B.R. 35 (Bankr. E.D. Mo. 1998), the court held that a covenant not to compete was severable from the rest of the franchise agreement, and that the covenant remained enforceable against the debtor despite rejection. The court reasoned that "rejection operates as a breach of an existing and continuing legal obligation of the debtor, not as a discharge or extinction of the obligation itself," and that a covenant not to compete addresses the parties' responsibilities and actions *after* termination of the contract. Thus, the court held that rejection amounted to a breach and termination of the agreements but that the covenant remained enforceable against the debtor. *Id.* at 38, *citing In re Modern Textile, Inc.*, 900 F.2d 1184, 1191 (8th Cir. 1990).

One reason for the confused state of the law may be that the courts are asking the wrong question. Consider the following hypothetical. Burger King grants Rovine a franchise to operate a restaurant at 100 Main Street. Rovine agrees not to operate another fast food restaurant within a 50-mile radius of 100 Main Street. Rovine agrees to pay a monthly royalty to Burger King. Burger King has no continuing obligations to Rovine. A year later, Rovine opens another fast food restaurant three blocks away. Burger King brings an action to enforce the noncompete clause. Rovine files a Chapter 11 petition. The contract is not executory — remember, we assumed that Burger King has fully performed — so rejection is not possible. Thus, the issue will not be whether Rovine's promise not to open another restaurant survives rejection, but whether that promise survives discharge. Since confirmation of a reorganization plan discharges the debtor of liability on "claims," Code § 1141(d), the answer turns on whether Burger King's right to enforce the covenant not to compete is a "claim" within the meaning of Code § 101(5). Why should the analysis be different merely because Burger King owes Rovine an obligation to provide continuing marketing support and additional secret sauce formulas from time to time? Professor Westbrook, among others, has suggested that "the right to discharge is the correct place to tussle over this issue, rather than it being an offshoot of some special rule about executory contracts." Jay L. Westbrook, *A Functional Analysis of Executory Contracts*, 74 MINN. L. REV. 227, 277–78, 300 (1989). We will tussle with the dischargeability issue in § 8.06[C], *below*.

[C]　Damage Caps for Long Term Contracts

Although nonbankruptcy law generally governs the measure of damages flowing from rejection, in two situations involving what typically are long-term contracts — employment contracts and real property leases — the Code imposes damage "caps" in order to prevent the claim holders from garnering a disproportionate share of the estate. These damage caps might also be justified on the grounds that in the event of rejection, at least in theory, an employee can sell his services to another employer and a landlord can lease her premises to another tenant. These are advantages that other kinds of creditors do not usually enjoy.

The Code imposes a cap on damage claims arising from the rejection of an employment contract by a debtor-employer. The employee's claim is limited to compensation at the contract rate for one year following the filing of the petition or the termination of employment (whichever is earlier). *See* Code § 502(b)(7).

The other damage cap applies to claims arising from the rejection of unexpired real property leases. The landlord's claim for lost rent is limited to the rent reserved by the lease for the greater of one year or 15% of the remaining lease term, not to exceed three years' rent. *See* Code § 502(b)(6). For example, assume that a debtor-tenant rents office space pursuant to a 10-year lease at a rent of $1,000 per month. Two years later, when there are eight years left to run on the lease, the debtor-tenant files for bankruptcy. In the event that the debtor rejects that lease, the maximum damages that the lessor can claim are the *greater* of:

- rent for one year; or
- rent for 15% of the remaining lease term, not to exceed three years' rent.

To calculate the cap, do the following:

- First, calculate the total rent due under the lease from the earlier of either the date of filing or the date on which the lessor retook the premises. For purposes of this example, assume that the debtor was still in possession of the premises on the date the petition was filed. As of the date the petition was filed, there were eight years, or 96 months, left to run on the lease. Thus, the total rent due under the lease was 96 x $1,000, or $96,000.
- Second, calculate 15% of the total rent due. 15% of $96,000 is $14,500.
- Third, determine whether 15% of the total rent due ($14,500) is greater than the rent due for one year ($12,000). It is. Thus, $14,500 is the tentative damage cap.
- Fourth, calculate the rent reserved for three years following the filing. 36 x $1,000 is $36,000.
- Fifth, determine whether 15% of the total rent due (the $14,500 "tentative cap") exceeds the rent reserved for three years following the filing ($36,000). It does not. Thus, $14,500 is the damage cap.

This formula imposes a cap on damages, but not a floor. For example, if the landlord immediately relets the premises at a higher rent, it will have no allowable claim for damages under § 502(b)(6). The following opinion involves an interpretation of this provision, and it also considers what happens when an assumed contract is subsequently rejected.

IN RE KLEIN SLEEP PRODUCTS, INC.
United States Court of Appeals, Second Circuit
78 F.3d 18 (1996)

[Klein Sleep operated a chain of mattress and bedding stores. Shortly after commencing its Chapter 11 case, it assumed, with the court's approval, a store lease that had a remaining term of about 20 years. Two years later, a trustee was appointed in the Chapter 11 case. The trustee soon realized that the business was incapable of being reorganized and that the proceeds of liquidating the firm's assets would not cover even administrative expenses. In the jargon of bankruptcy lawyers, the estate was "administratively insolvent." The trustee rejected the lease and surrendered the premises to Nostas, the landlord. The bankruptcy court held that the landlord's claim for rents that accrued prior to the surrender of the premises would be entitled to administrative priority status. The bankruptcy court also found that the landlord's claim for rent due after surrender would be treated as a general unsecured claim and subject to the § 502(b)(6) cap. The district court affirmed, reasoning that the damages that resulted from the surrender of the premises to the landlord "bestowed no benefit upon the estate" and accordingly did not satisfy the basic criteria for treatment as administrative expenses. The Second Circuit reversed. Excerpts from its opinion follow. — Eds.]

CALABRESI, CIRCUIT JUDGE.

The liquidation provisions of the Bankruptcy Code contained in § 726 distribute a pro-rata share of a debtor's estate to each unsecured creditor so that similarly situated creditors may be treated alike. This pro-rata rule does not, however, always lead to an equitable distribution of the estate. When one claimant is a landlord holding a long-term lease, its single unsecured claim for twenty or thirty years of future rent could devour so much of the debtor's estate that only crumbs could be left for the other unsecured creditors. Recognizing the potentially distorting effect of claims arising out of long-term leases, Congress capped unsecured claims for future rent at one year. § 502(b)(6). This allows landlords to recover some of their losses from a bankrupt tenant, but sees to it that their recovery will not crowd out the claims of competing creditors.

Bankruptcy law also aims to avoid liquidation altogether when that is possible. Although the Code offers no magical potion to restore a debtor's financial health, it does provide some useful medicine designed to help a debtor get back on its feet and heading toward convalescence. It does this by allowing a debtor to attempt to reorganize rather than fold and by creating incentives for creditors to continue to do business with the debtor while reorganization proceeds. The Code does this, at least in part, by assuring these post-bankruptcy creditors that, if the debtor fails to rehabilitate itself and winds up in liquidation, they can move to the front of the distributive line, ahead of the debtor's pre-bankruptcy creditors. Special priority is therefore accorded to expenses incurred under new contracts with the debtor, as "administrative expenses" of the estate. The same priority is given to expenses arising under pre-existing contracts that the debtor "assumes" — contracts whose benefits and burdens the debtor decides, with the bankruptcy court's approval, are worth retaining.

These two competing bankruptcy policies — promoting parity among creditors and yet granting priority to the claims of creditors who continue to do business with an insolvent debtor — collide in the case before us. After entering bankruptcy, Klein Sleep (the debtor) assumed, with court approval, the unexpired lease it had with Nostas Associates (its landlord). Some eighteen months later, when it became apparent that the reorganization had failed, the newly appointed bankruptcy trustee decided to "reject" the lease. The landlord then sought to recover the future rent that was due under the lease. The bankruptcy court held, and the district court agreed, that Nostas was entitled to recover as an administrative expense only the rent that had come due before the trustee rejected the lease. Beyond that, Nostas could recover as a general unsecured claim only one year's worth of the rent coming due after rejection.

Two questions arise on appeal. We must first decide whether the future rent gives rise to a general unsecured claim that receives no priority or whether it is, instead, an administrative expense entitled to priority. If it is an administrative expense, we must then determine whether the claim is nonetheless capped at a year's worth of rent by § 502(b)(6).

Our task would be far easier if Congress had answered these questions explicitly in the Code, but unfortunately it left its intentions ambiguous. In order to resolve this ambiguity, we turn first to the various provisions of the Code that discuss the timing and priority of claims. Since we do not find an unmistakable Code directive, however, we also seek guidance from the practice prevailing under the Code's predecessor, the Bankruptcy Act. Adhering to that practice, we hold that damages arising from future rent under an assumed lease must be treated as an administrative expense, and we therefore reverse in part.

The conclusion we reach seems on its face to be unduly favorable to landlords. But it may in fact do no more than recognize the existence of a default rule, which the bankruptcy court can use in encouraging landlords and tenants alike to renegotiate leases in bankruptcy so as to treat all the parties, including general unsecured creditors, equitably.

. . . .

II. DISCUSSION

A. Administrative Expense Status

According to § 503(b)(1)(A), "the actual, necessary costs and expenses of preserving the estate" constitute administrative expenses entitled to priority status upon distribution of the estate. The crux of Nostas's argument is that a trustee's or debtor-in-possession's assumption of an unexpired lease transforms all liability under the lease, including damages that stem from a subsequent rejection of the lease, into administrative expenses. There is strong bankruptcy court precedent directly on point that supports this proposition. *See, e.g.,* . . . *In re Multech Corp.,* 47 Bankr. 747, 750 (Bankr. N.D. Iowa 1985); . . . 2 COLLIER ON BANKRUPTCY ¶ 365.08[01], at 365–65 (15th ed. 1995) ("[A] trustee must proceed cautiously in electing whether to assume or reject since an assumption will have the effect of making the expenses and liabilities incurred expenses of administration.").

Multech, the seminal case on this issue, offers the following rationale for this rule:

> By defining the time at which a rejection of an assumed contract or lease constitutes a breach, section 365(g) clearly indicates that the act of assumption creates an administrative expense obligation of the particular proceedings in which the contract or lease was assumed. Consequently, if a lease is assumed in Chapter 11 proceedings, the liabilities flowing from the rejection of that lease will ever after be regarded as a Chapter 11 administrative expense.

47 Bankr. at 750 (footnote omitted).

Citing our decision in [*Trustees of Amalgamated Ins. Fund v. McFarlin's, Inc.,* 789 F.2d 98 (2d Cir. 1986)] however, the district court declined to follow *Multech* and its progeny. The court stated that our decision in *McFarlin's* established that expenses fall within § 503(b)(1)(A) if they arise out of a transaction between the debtor and the creditor, and "only to the extent that the consideration supporting the claimant's right to payment was both supplied to and beneficial to the debtor-in-possession in the operation of the business." *McFarlin's*, 789 F.2d at 101 (quoting *In re Mammoth Mart, Inc.*, 536 F.2d 950, 953 (1st Cir. 1976)). It then asserted that Klein Sleep derived actual benefit not from its *assumption* of the lease, but only from its *occupation* of the leased premises.

Once the trustee gave the store back to Nostas, the court reasoned, Klein Sleep received no further benefit from the lease. As a result, the damages it sought for future rent did not meet the prerequisites for administrative expense status under § 503(b)(1)(A). . . .

At first glance, the bankruptcy court's approach has much to recommend it. By denying administrative expense status for all future rent under an assumed lease, the court followed our stated policy that priorities in bankruptcy should be narrowly construed and sparingly granted. *McFarlin's*, 789 F.2d at 100. And, the bankruptcy court's relegation of Nostas to the ranks of the unsecured creditors furthered this fundamental policy — based on the notion that individual creditors, whenever possible, should be prevented from seizing a disproportionate share of the estate — in a second way as well. Once future rent is treated merely as an unsecured claim, it is clearly capped by § 502(b)(6) at one year's worth of unpaid rent. As a result, the rent claims cannot absorb all the assets of the estate, no matter how long the lease.

Yet this approach has several deficiencies. First, it relies on an unduly narrow view of the benefit conferred on an estate when a trustee assumes an unexpired lease. Second, it does not adequately account for the Code's timing provisions, which explicitly provide that claims arise "postpetition," and therefore during the administration of the estate, if they are based on breaches of assumed leases. And finally, even if these two considerations did not resolve the matter, the district court's approach does not accord with prior practice under the Bankruptcy Act (practice which, in cases of ambiguity, stands as a decisive guidepost for interpreting today's Bankruptcy Code). Bankruptcy Act practice strongly directs us to treat the entire liability resulting from breach of an assumed lease as a cost of administering the estate.

1. Benefit

. . . .

The trustee argues that any inquiry as to "benefit" is foreclosed by the district court's factual finding that Klein Sleep did not benefit from its assumption of the lease. The opposite, however, is true: the bankruptcy court's earlier decision to let Klein Sleep assume the unexpired lease — a decision that was not appealed — precluded a subsequent finding that assuming the lease did not benefit Klein Sleep. That decision required a judicial finding — up-front — that it was in the best interests of the estate (and the unsecured creditors) for the debtor to assume the lease, pursuant to § 365(a). It is the same kind of finding that the bankruptcy court is required to make with regard to all new contracts entered into by the trustee without prior court approval during the administration of the estate in order for those contracts to qualify for priority pursuant to § 503(b). Compare *In re Orion Pictures Corp.*, 4 F.3d 1095, 1099 (2d Cir. 1993) ("[A] bankruptcy court reviewing a trustee's or debtor-in-possession's decision to assume or reject an executory contract [pursuant to § 365] should examine a contract and the surrounding circumstances and apply its best 'business judgment' to determine if it would be beneficial or burdensome to the estate to assume it."), cert. dismissed, 114 S. Ct. 1418 (1994) with *Mammoth Mart*, 536 F.2d at 954 (granting administrative expense status to postpetition claim only if consideration "was both supplied to and beneficial to the debtor-in-possession in the operation of the business").

As one bankruptcy court has explained:

> By requiring the court to determine the reasonable necessity of the newly entered contract under § 503(b), Congress has insured some judicial control over the determination of what executory contracts will be granted administrative expense priority. The Code, in order to streamline reorganization procedure, allows a debtor in possession to enter into contracts in the ordinary course of business without seeking court approval. Thus, contracts initially entered into during reorganization, unlike contracts assumed during reorganization, will not have undergone court scrutiny. By limiting automatic administrative expense treatment under § 365(g) to assumed contracts, and by requiring initially entered contracts to qualify under § 503(b) in order to be granted an administrative expense priority, Congress has insured both similar treatment and similar procedural safeguards for these fundamentally similar obligations.

In re Chugiak Boat Works, Inc., 18 Bankr. 292, 297–98 (Bankr. D. Alaska 1982) (footnotes omitted).

In short, we decline to find that Klein Sleep did not benefit by assuming its lease simply because the lease was no longer profitable at the time it stopped displaying mattresses on the premises. Such a holding would mean that any post-bankruptcy contract, entered into for the benefit of a bankrupt's estate, would cease to be entitled to priority the moment the deal turned sour. When the debtor-in-possession assumed the lease, it retained the right to occupy the leased premises immediately and in the future. Its ability to assign this immediate right of possession, as well as its ability to assign the future right of possession under the lease, had a present value at the time of assumption. Acquisition of those rights clearly constituted a benefit to the estate even if, later, the benefit turned to dust.

2. Timing

The Code's timing provisions also tilt in favor of Nostas's position that all future rent is an administrative expense. In allowing and assigning priority to claims arising from unexpired leases, the Code distinguishes between leases that have been assumed, and those that have not. Section 502(g) of the Code clearly instructs us that claims arising from unassumed leases are to be allowed as general unsecured claims. Section 502(g) has no analogue that tells us what to do with claims arising from assumed leases. But because § 502(g) limits its reach to unassumed leases, it is reasonable to infer that assumed leases are to be treated differently. Since it would be absurd to suppose that such leases would not qualify as claims at all, it follows that they must be considered administrative expenses of the estate.

This inference is further supported by § 365(g), which fixes the time at which a debtor's rejection of an unexpired lease is deemed to constitute a breach of the lease. When a debtor rejects an unassumed lease, breach is deemed to occur at the time the bankruptcy petition was filed. § 365(g)(1). If the lease has been assumed, however, breach is deemed to occur whenever the lease is later rejected. § 365(g)(2)(A).[5] According to the Code's legislative history, the purpose of § 365(g) is to treat claims arising from unassumed leases "as prepetition claims." H.R. REP. No. 595, 95th Cong., 2d Sess. 349 (1977); S. REP. No. 989, 95th Cong., 2d Sess. 63 (1978), reprinted in 1978 U.S.C.C.A.N. 5787, 6305, 5849. But the only way in which prepetition claims are treated differently from postpetition claims is that the former are classified as general claims, whereas the latter — arising, for example, from torts committed by the estate in bankruptcy, or from contracts entered into by the trustee or debtor-in-possession — are entitled to administrative expense priority. It would seem to follow that rejection of an assumed lease — that is, breach of contract committed by the trustee or debtor-in-possession while administering the estate — gives rise to a debt entitled to the same administrative expense priority.

The timing provisions of the Code were not, however, directly designed to answer the question we are asking today, and so we are hesitant to read too much into them. Indeed, because all of our previous discussion has essentially required us to read between the lines of Congress's directives, we conclude that the Bankruptcy Code, though it clearly leans in favor of administrative status for assumed leases, is still ambiguous. When that is the case, we are required to turn for further guidance to the prior practice under the Bankruptcy Act.

3. Practice Under the Bankruptcy Act

Were we writing on a clean slate, we might perhaps be persuaded by the district court's analysis — though, as we have discussed above, we think that the structure of the Code favors the landlord's position. We are not, however, permitted to start from scratch. In *Dewsnup v. Timm*, 502 U.S. 410, 112 S. Ct. 773, 116 L. Ed. 2d 903 (1992), the Supreme Court declined to resolve de novo an ambiguous interrelationship between certain Bankruptcy Code provisions, where accepted pre-Code bankruptcy practice existed. The Court stated:

> When Congress amends the bankruptcy laws, it does not write "on a clean slate." . . . Furthermore, this Court has been reluctant to accept arguments that would interpret the Code, however vague the particular language under consideration might be, to effect a change in pre-Code practice that is not the subject of at least some discussion in the legislative history.

---

[5] When a reorganization case is converted to a liquidation proceeding after the lease has been assumed but before it is rejected, breach is deemed to have occurred immediately before the conversion. § 365(g)(2)(B).

502 U.S. at 419 (citation omitted).

In the case before us, an ambiguity arguably exists as to whether claims arising from the rejection of assumed contracts by definition meet the "actual and necessary" requirements of § 503(b)(1)(A) and hence automatically enjoy administrative expense priority under § 507(a)(1). . . . Nostas and amicus argue, however, that the pre-Code practice was to grant administrative status automatically to all claims arising from the subsequent rejection of an assumed executory contract — and, therefore, that any ambiguity must be resolved in favor of granting administrative expense status.

Nostas points out in its reply brief that the relevant sections of the former Bankruptcy Act provided that "when a contract entered into or assumed in a superseded proceeding is rejected, *the resulting liability* should constitute a cost of administration of the superseded proceeding." Bankruptcy Act §§ 238(b), 378(b), 483(b) (emphasis added). In this context, the "resulting liability" would be the landlord's damages for future rent and, arguably, for related costs such as legal and brokerage fees.

. . . .

Moreover, even before Congress added this clarificatory language to the Bankruptcy Act, it was well-established in this Circuit that administrative priority was available either if the trustee assumed an executory contract or if the estate received demonstrable benefits under the contract.

. . . .

Absent a clear Code directive, or legislative history that directly addresses the issue and reaches a contrary result, the rule of construction set forth in Dewsnup dictates that Nostas's claim for post-rejection rental damages should be governed by Bankruptcy Act practice. That practice strongly supports the conclusion that Nostas's claim was entitled to administrative expense status. This result, moreover, agrees with our earlier analysis that the Code's timing provisions, together with the rules governing "benefit," indicate that all future rent accruing under an assumed lease is entitled to the status of an administrative expense. Accordingly, we so hold.

B. The § 502(b)(6) Cap on Damages for Future Rent

Because it determined that Nostas's claim was not an administrative expense, the district court never reached the issue of whether § 502(b)(6) limits Nostas's claim arising from the assumed leases to one year's worth of future rent. Since we conclude that such future rent is an administrative expense, we must now decide whether § 502(b)(6) caps the rent.

Section 502(b)(6) requires a court to allow a claim except to the extent that it exceeds one year's rent due under the lease.[6]

---

[6] Section 502(b)(6) provides, more fully, that the bankruptcy court shall allow a lessor's claim for damages arising from the termination of a lease of real property, except to the extent that the claim exceeds

(A) the rent reserved by such lease, without acceleration, for the greater of one year, or 15

This cap is designed to prevent a landlord's single unsecured claim — which, depending on the length of the lease, may be enormous — to elbow aside the other unsecured creditors. The trustee argues that "the policy underlying Code § 502(b)(6) applies equally to claims arising under leases that have been assumed and those that have not." Indeed, because the drafters of the Code took such care to prevent a monstrous unsecured claim from swallowing up the estate, it might seem odd not only to give an analogous type of claim priority over unsecured creditors, but also to allow such a claim in its entirety, merely because it arose from an assumed lease.

Sensible as this policy argument might be, we do not find the Code ambiguous on this point. Section 502, which contains the cap on future rent, applies only to "a claim or interest, proof of which is filed under section 501." § 502(a). Section 501 prescribes the method for filing proofs of prepetition claims against the debtor and certain postpetition claims that are deemed to have arisen prepetition. It does not apply to administrative expenses payable by the debtor, which must be requested pursuant to § 503. *See also id.* § 507 (referring to "expenses and claims"). And because § 502 does not apply to administrative expenses, it cannot cap future rent due under an assumed lease.

The legislative history of § 502(b)(6) confirms that, at least on this score, Congress said what it meant. H.R. Rep. No. 595, 95th Cong., 2d Sess. 353 (1977); S. Rep. No. 989, 95th Cong., 2d Sess. 63 (1978), 1978 U.S.C.A.A.N. 5849, 6309 (stating that § 502(b)(6) "does not apply to limit administrative expense claims for use of the leased premises to which the landlord is otherwise entitled"); *see also Multech*, 47 Bankr. at 751 (explaining that the policy of preventing landlord's unsecured claim from crowding out other unsecured creditors "is no longer germane in the case of an assumed contract or lease, since the resulting obligations and liabilities are elevated to a priority status and no longer fall in the class of general unsecured creditors"); *In re Johnston, Inc.*, 164 Bankr. at 555 (stating that § 502(b)(6) does not limit administrative expense claims); 2 COLLIER ON BANKRUPTCY ¶ 365.08, at 365–67 (15th ed. 1995) ("The limitation upon the amount of an allowed claim arising from breach of a lease in section 502(b)(6) of the Code does not apply to leases assumed and thereafter rejected in the case.") (footnotes omitted) (citing *Multech*).

. . . .

---

percent, not to exceed three years, of the remaining term of such lease, following the earlier of —

   (i) the date of the filing of the petition; and

   (ii) the date on which such lessor repossessed, or the lessee surrendered, the leased property; plus

(B) any unpaid rent due under such lease, without acceleration, on the earlier of such dates

. . . .

Because in the case before us § 506(b)(6) operates to limit rent claims to one year — rather than fifteen percent of all future rent capped at three years — we refer to this section as imposing a "one-year cap."

III. CONCLUSION

It would surely have been better if Congress had spelled out its intentions as to assumed leases in the Code, rather than leaving it up to the courts to clean up the ambiguities. But, under the circumstances, clean them up we must. The trustee complains that the rule we pick — a rule that accords administrative priority to claims for all future rent under an assumed lease — is overly generous to landlords, since it gives them a lion's share of estates upon liquidation. While that may seem to be the case, we doubt that it will work out that way in practice. Under the rule we adopt, bankruptcy courts will rarely find that assuming liability for all future rent under a long-term lease is in the best interests of the estate — including the interest of the general creditors — unless the rental terms are highly advantageous. They will therefore block assumption of such leases except in unusual cases. As a result, landlords will find themselves with unsecured claims capped at one year's worth of future rent.

This may also seem undesirable, especially since in some such cases the tenant properly wishes to continue the rental. But this too is not quite the end of the story, for bankruptcy courts may have another option open to them. Faced with the unattractive choice of either requiring a bankrupt tenant to reject its long-term lease (and thereby possibly dooming the reorganization to failure) or letting it assume the lease (and leaving the general creditors with a paltry recovery should liquidation ensue), one bankruptcy court suggested that it could instead put off the decision on whether or not to assume a long-term lease. It could delay, the court stated, until the moment of confirmation, when the debtor's chances of rehabilitation would finally be clear. [*See In re Monica Scott*, 123 B.R. 990, 993 (Bankr. D. Minn. 1991).] ("Unless the Congress addresses this situation, cause will undoubtedly be found to exist, as a matter of course, for extending to confirmation the time to assume or reject significant leases in Chapter 11 cases.") (citing § 365(d)(4), which permits bankruptcy courts to extend the 60-day assumption/rejection period "for cause"). The uncertainty engendered by such an approach would give the bankruptcy court significant leverage over both tenant and landlord, and might well lead to a renegotiation of the long-term lease. The tenant who wishes to retain control over the premises has an interest — arising out of fear that the court will force rejection of the original lease — in renegotiating the lease, though perhaps for a shorter term. The landlord also has an interest in renegotiating the lease to escape the limbo between assumption and rejection. In such circumstances the landlord might well prefer to recover some guaranteed amount of future rent, as an administrative expense, under a new contract rather than risk having the lease rejected and the recovery limited to a fractional share of one year's worth of future rent, as an unsecured claim, under the pre-existing contract.[7]

None of this is before us today. But we do note that the rule that we enunciate may not be quite as rigid as it looks. It may well operate, like so many other default rules in contract law, only as a backdrop against which the parties — here the landlord and tenant — can renegotiate to reach a satisfactory, middle solution.

---

[7] In either event, of course, the landlord is entitled to recover as an administrative expense the rent due while the debtor and the bankruptcy court debate whether to assume the lease. § 365(d)(3).

For the reasons stated above, we hold that claims for future rent arising out of assumed leases are administrative expenses of the debtor's estate, regardless of whether they are subsequently rejected, and that they are not capped at a year's worth of unpaid rent by § 502(b)(6). We reach this conclusion in light of the prior practice under the Bankruptcy Act, the timing provisions of the Code, and an understanding that debtors generally benefit from court-approved assumptions of executory contracts and unexpired leases.

Reversed to the extent that the court disallowed Nostas's claim for future rent as an administrative expense, and remanded for further proceedings consistent with this opinion.

IN RE ENERGY CONVERSION DEVICES, INC.

United States Bankruptcy Court for the Eastern District of Michigan, Southern Division
483 B.R. 119 (2012)

OPINION REGARDING LIQUIDATION TRUSTEE'S OBJECTION TO THE CLAIMS OF THE PEGASUS GROUP, AND BANKRUPTCY CODE § 502(b)(6)

I. Introduction

The dispute now before the Court concerns the meaning and scope of § 502(b)(6) of the Bankruptcy Code, 11 U.S.C. § 502(b)(6). That section sets a limit on "the claim of a lessor for damages resulting from the termination of a lease of real property."

. . . .

III. Background and facts

The two Pegasus claims at issue, which were amended on September 7, 2012, consist of one claim against each of the two Debtors' estates in these jointly-administered cases. The claims are identical in amount, and are based on the breach of a lease of commercial real property located at 2705 Commerce Parkway, Auburn Hills, Michigan (the "Lease"). Pegasus leased the property to the Debtor United Solar Ovonic, LLC ("USO"), and the Debtor Energy Conversion Devices, Inc. ("ECD") guaranteed USO's performance under the Lease. The Lease was an unexpired lease when the Debtors filed their bankruptcy petitions. Debtors continued to occupy and use the leased property for several months after filing their petitions. Ultimately, the Lease was rejected and Debtors surrendered the property back to Pegasus, before Debtors obtained confirmation of their Chapter 11 plan.

Pegasus's amended claims each total $1,933,113.38. Each claim consists of several components. These include a "Prepetition Default" amount of $332,337.25, and a credit to reflect a letter of credit balance in Pegasus's favor, as of the petition date, of $937,166.70. Another component, which Pegasus refers to as the "502(b) claim," is for $1,720,000.00. This amount, the parties agree, is one year's rent under the

Lease. Pegasus's amended claims describe this amount as "one year of lease payments (base rent plus other rent)." This component of Pegasus's claim is based on the formula in 11 U.S.C. § 502(b)(6)(A), discussed below. A final component of Pegasus's claim, which Pegaus refers to as the "Additional Damage Claim," is for a total of $817,942.83.

The "Additional Damages Claim" itself has numerous itemized sub-components, and it includes damages for USO's alleged breaches of the Lease for the following:

> removal of equipment and other personal property in violation of the Lease, . . . damage to the roof, damage to the parking lot, damage to HVAC and exhaust units and fire extinguishers, damage to the landscaping, environmental damage and liabilities, cleaning fees, plumbing damages and other costs to be incurred in restoring the property to the condition set forth in the Lease.

Pegasus and U.S. Bank say that in addition to breaching the Lease by rejecting it, *see* 11 U.S.C. § 365(g)(1), the Debtors also breached the Lease by failing to perform their obligations under several sections of the Lease, which among other things, essentially require USO to maintain and repair damage to the premises.

Among other lease provisions, Pegasus and U.S. Bank rely on sections 10.01 and 21.01 of the Lease, which provide, in part, as follows:

> 10.01 Tenant agrees at its own expense to keep the Improvements, including all structural, electrical, mechanical and plumbing systems at all times in good appearance and repair. Tenant shall keep the Premises (including all interior walls, overhead doors and doorways, the exterior and interior portion of all doors, door checks, windows, window frames, plate glass, all plumbing and sewage facilities, including free flow up to the main sewer line, fixtures, heating and air conditioning and sprinkler system, walls, floors and ceilings, all structural and nonstructural elements, craneways, cranes, electrical buss ducts, mechanical, electrical and plumbing systems, interior, exterior, and landscaped areas, sidewalks, driveway areas and all other systems and equipment) in good order, condition and repair during the Lease Term. . . . Tenant shall promptly replace any portion of the Premises or system or equipment in the Premises which cannot be fully repaired, regardless of whether the benefit of such replacement extends beyond the Lease Term, provided, however that Landlord agrees to perform at its expense any required replacement of the roof, unless replacement is required as a result of the act or omission of Tenant or the failure of Tenant to properly service and maintain same. . . . It is the intention of Landlord and Tenant that at all times during the Lease Term, Tenant shall maintain the Premises in a first-class and fully operative condition. . . .
>
> . . . .
>
> 21.01 At the expiration (or earlier termination) of the Term, Tenant will surrender the Premises broom clean and, subject to the provisions of Sections 9 and 14 of this Lease, in as good condition and repair as they were at the time Tenant took possession, reasonable wear and tear excepted, and

promptly upon surrender will deliver all keys and building security cards for the Premises to Landlord at the place then fixed for payment of rent. All costs and expenses incurred by Landlord in connection with repairing or restoring the Premises to the condition called for herein, together with liquidated damages in an amount equal to the amount of minimum net rental plus all other charges which would have been payable by Tenant under this Lease if term of this Lease had been extended for the period of time reasonably required for Landlord to repair or restore the Premises to the condition called for herein, shall be invoiced to Tenant and shall be payable as additional rent within five (5) days after receipt of invoice.

Pegasus claims that it is entitled to both the "502(b) claim" and the "Additional Damages Claim" components of its claim, as part of its allowed claim. The Trustee disagrees, and argues that all of Pegasus's Additional Damages Claim component must be disallowed, as a matter of law, because of § 502(b)(6). This opinion addresses the Trustee's argument.

IV. Discussion

Under § 502(b)(6), a claim of a lessor of real property is to be disallowed "to the extent that":

(6) *if such claim is the claim of a lessor for damages resulting from the termination of a lease of real property, such claim exceeds —*

(A) the rent reserved by such lease, without acceleration, for the greater of one year, or 15 percent, not to exceed three years, of the remaining term of such lease, following the earlier of —

(i) the date of the filing of the petition; and

(ii) the date on which such lessor repossessed, or the lessee surrendered, the leased property; plus

(B) any unpaid rent due under such lease, without acceleration, on the earlier of such dates[.]

11 U.S.C. § 502(b)(6) (emphasis added).

The Trustee argues that this section has the effect of eliminating the entire "Additional Damages Claim" component of Pegasus's claim, because all of the items in that component are subject to the cap established by the formula in § 502(b)(6). The parties agree that the formula in § 502(b)(6)(A) yields a cap in this case of $1,720,000.00, which is the amount of Pegasus's "502(b) claim" component. According to the Trustee, this sum, plus the amount referred to in § 502(b)(6)(B), which in this case means the amount of any unpaid rent due under the Lease, without acceleration, as of the petition date, is the maximum amount of Pegasus's claim that can be allowed. According to the Trustee, the entire "Additional Damages Claim" component is part of "the claim of a lessor for damages resulting from the termination of a lease of real property," within the meaning of § 502(b)(6).

Pegasus and U.S. Bank argue that none of the "Additional Damages Claim" component of Pegasus's claim is subject to the § 502(b)(6) cap, because none of it is part of "the claim of a lessor for damages resulting from the termination of a lease of real property," within the meaning of § 502(b)(6).

As the parties point out, there is a split in the case law regarding the meaning and scope of this statutory phrase. On the one hand, the Trustee relies on cases that interpret the phrase "claim . . . for damages resulting from the termination of a lease" broadly. These cases hold that a debtor's rejection of a real estate lease under 11 U.S.C. § 365(a) constitutes a breach of all covenants in the lease, including, for example, covenants requiring the debtor to maintain and repair the premises. From this, these cases reason, all damage claims by the lessor are subject to the cap of § 502(b)(6)(A) plus § 502(b)(6)(B).

The parties point out that there are no Sixth Circuit cases on this issue. Cases supporting the Trustee's position include the following three cases: *In re Foamex Int'l., Inc.*, 368 B.R. 383 (Bankr. D. Del. 2007); *Kuske v. McSheridan (In re McSheridan)*, 184 B.R. 91 (B.A.P. 9th Cir. 1995), overruled in part by *In re El Toro Materials Co., Inc.*, 504 F.3d 978 (9th Cir. 2007), cert. denied, *El Toro Materials Co., Inc. v. Saddleback Valley Cmty. Church*, 552 U.S. 1311, 128 S. Ct. 1875, 170 L. Ed. 2d 746 (2008); and *In re Mr. Gatti's, Inc.*, 162 B.R. 1004 (Bankr. W.D. Tex. 1994).

On the other hand, Pegasus and U.S. Bank argue for a narrower reading of § 502(b)(6). They cite cases holding that this section applies, as one case puts it, "to solely those damages arising as a consequence of the lease being terminated." *In re Brown*, 398 B.R. 215, 218 (Bankr. N.D. Ohio 2008) (citations omitted). Under this view, the application of § 502(b)(6) depends on the answer to the following question: " 'Assuming all other conditions remain constant, would the landlord have the same claim against the tenant if the tenant were to assume the lease rather than rejecting it?' " If the claim at issue "would still have existed even had the debtor 'accepted the lease and committed to finish its term' then the claim is not subject to the § 502(b)(6) cap." *Id.* at 218-19 (quoting, in part, *In re El Toro Materials Co., Inc.*, 504 F.3d 978, 981 (9th Cir. 2007), cert. denied, *El Toro Materials Co., Inc. v. Saddleback Valley Cmty. Church*, 552 U.S. 1311, 128 S. Ct. 1875, 170 L. Ed. 2d 746 (2008)).

Cases adopting this more narrow view of § 502(b)(6) include the following five cases: in addition to the *Brown* and *El Toro Materials* cases cited above, *In re Atlantic Container Corp.*, 133 B.R. 980 (Bankr. N.D. Ill.1991); *In re Bob's Sea Ray Boats, Inc.*, 143 B.R. 229 (Bankr. D.N.D. 1992); *In re Best Products Co., Inc.*, 229 B.R. 673 (Bankr. E.D. Va.1998). *See also* 4 Collier on Bankruptcy ¶ 502.03[7][a], at 502–40 (Alan N. Resnick & Henry J. Sommer eds., 16th ed. 2012) ("It is important to recognize that [§ 502(b)(6)] addresses only lease terminations. Claims for damages arising under a lease for items such as physical damages to the premises [are] not subject to the section 502(b)(6) limitation.") (citing *In re Bob's Sea Ray Boats, Inc.*).

. . . [T]he Court is persuaded that Pegasus and U.S. Bank have the better view of § 502(b)(6). The review of the background and legislative history of § 502(b)(6) and the wording of that section, and the other points made by the courts in the *El Toro Materials* and *Atlantic Container Corp.* cases, cited above, are particularly persuasive. First, the Court agrees with the following observations by the court in *Atlantic Container Corp.*:

[T]he phrase "damages resulting from the termination of a lease" does not seem to contemplate the type of damages being sought here. The phrase suggests that § 502(b)(6) is intended to limit only those damages which the lessor would have avoided but for the lease termination. Any damages caused to the Premises by the Debtor's failure to fulfill its repair and maintenance obligations are unrelated to the termination of the lease.

In addition, the formula for calculating the maximum allowable claim for termination damages under § 502(b)(6) suggests that the primary purpose of the section is to limit claims for *prospective* damages resulting from the lease termination. Under § 502(b)(6)(B), a lessor is permitted to claim, without limitation, the entire amount of rent which is due and owing under the lease as of the earlier of the bankruptcy filing date and the date the lessee ceased to occupy the premises. 11 U.S.C. § 502(b)(6)(B). Claims for *future rent* under the lease, however, are subject to a statutory limit.

In re Atlantic Container Corp., 133 B.R. at 987 (italics in original).

Second, the Court finds persuasive the opinion of the United States Court of Appeals in the *El Toro Materials* case, and will quote it at length:

Claims made by landlords against their bankrupt tenants for lost rent have always been treated differently than other unsecured claims. Prior to 1934, landlords could not recover at all for the loss of rental income they suffered when a bankrupt tenant rejected a long-term lease agreement; future lease payments were considered contingent and thus not provable debts in bankruptcy. *See Manhattan Props., Inc. v. Irving Trust Co.*, 291 U.S. 320, 332–36, 338, 54 S. Ct. 385, 78 L. Ed. 824 (1934).

The Great Depression created pressure to reform the system: A wave of bankruptcies left many landlords with broken long-term leases, buildings sitting empty and no way to recover from the estates of their former tenants. *See Oldden v. Tonto Realty Corp.*, 143 F.2d 916, 919–920 (2d Cir.1944). On the one hand, allowing landlords to make a claim for lost rental income would reduce the harm done to them by a tenant's breach of a long-term lease, especially in a down market when it was difficult or impossible to re-lease the premises. On the other hand, "extravagant claims for . . . unearned rent" could quickly deplete the estate, to the detriment of other creditors. *See In re Best Prods. Co.*, 229 B.R. 673, 676 (Bankr. E.D. Va. 1998). The solution was a compromise in the Bankruptcy Act of 1934 allowing a claim against the bankruptcy estate for back rent to the date of abandonment, plus damages no greater than one year of future rent. *See Oldden*, 143 F.2d at 920–21.

Congress dramatically overhauled bankruptcy law when it passed the Bankruptcy Reform Act of 1978. However, section 502(b)(6) of the 1978 Act was intended to carry forward existing law allowing limited damages for lost rental income. S. Rep. No. 95-989, at 63 (1978) as reprinted in 95th Cong., 2nd Sess. 1978, 1978 U.S. Code Cong. & Admin. News 5787, 5849 (the cap on damages is "derived from current law"). Only the method of calculating the cap was changed. Under the current Act, the cap limits damages "resulting from the termination of a lease of real property" to "the greater of one year, or 15 percent, not to exceed three years, of the remaining term of such lease." 11 U.S.C. § 502(b)(6). The damages cap was "designed to compensate the landlord for his loss while not permitting a claim so large (based on a long-term lease) as to prevent other general unsecured creditors from recovering a dividend from the estate." S. Rep. No. 95-989, at 63, 1978 U.S. Code Cong. & Admin. News at 5849.

The structure of the cap — measured as a fraction of the remaining term — suggests that damages other than those based on a loss of future rental income are not subject to the cap. It makes sense to cap damages for lost rental income based on the amount of expected rent: Landlords may have the ability to mitigate their damages by re-leasing or selling the premises, but will suffer injury in proportion to the value of their lost rent in the meantime. In contrast, collateral damages are likely to bear only a weak correlation to the amount of rent: A tenant may cause a lot of damage to a premises leased cheaply, or cause little damage to premises underlying an expensive leasehold.

One major purpose of bankruptcy law is to allow creditors to receive an aliquot share of the estate to settle their debts. Metering these collateral damages by the amount of the rent would be inconsistent with the goal of providing compensation to each creditor in proportion with what it is owed. Landlords in future cases may have significant claims for both lost rental income and for breach of other provisions of the lease. *To limit their recovery for collateral damages only to a portion of their lost rent would leave landlords in a materially worse position than other creditors. In contrast, capping rent claims but allowing uncapped claims for collateral damage to the rented premises will follow congressional intent by preventing a potentially overwhelming claim for lost rent from draining the estate, while putting landlords on equal footing with other creditors for their collateral claims.*

The statutory language supports this interpretation. The cap applies to damages "resulting from" the rejection of the lease. 11 U.S.C. § 502(b)(6). . . . [Here] the harm to [the landlord's] property existed whether or not the lease was rejected. A simple test reveals whether the damages result from the rejection of the lease: Assuming all other conditions remain constant, would the landlord have the same claim against the tenant if the tenant were to assume the lease rather than rejecting it? Here, Saddleback would still have the same claim it brings today had El Toro accepted the lease and committed to finish its term.

. . . .

Further, extending the cap to cover any collateral damage to the premises would allow a post-petition but pre-rejection tenant to cause any amount of damage to the premises — either negligently or intentionally — without fear of liability beyond the cap. If the tenant's debt to the landlord already exceeded the cap then there would be no deterrence against even the most flagrant acts in violation of the lease, possibly even to the point of the tenant burning down the property in a fit of pique. Absent clear statutory language supporting such an absurd result, we cannot suppose that Congress intended it.

In re El Toro Materials Co., Inc., 504 F.3d at 979–81 (emphasis added; footnotes omitted).

The Court adopts the views of the *Atlantic Container Corp.* and *El Toro Materials* court, and their more narrow interpretation of § 502(b)(6), discussed above. For this reason, to the extent the Trustee seeks disallowance of the entire $817,942.83 "Additional Damages Claim" component of Pegasus's claim, based on § 502(b)(6), that relief is denied, and the Court will enter an order to that effect.

The present procedural posture and record does not permit the Court to be more specific than this, at this time, in ruling on the numerous particular items that make up the "Additional Damages Claim" component of Pegasus's claim. That will have to await further briefing and argument, at a minimum, after discovery and further proceedings have been completed, all under the Scheduling Order already in place.

[D]   The Special Rule for Rejection of Real Property Leases by a Debtor-Landlord

In the preceding section, we considered what would happen if a debtor rejected a lease under which it was the *lessee*. We saw that the Code gives the landlord a claim for damages. What consequences flow from rejection of a lease if the debtor is not the tenant, but the landlord? Suppose that Amphydynamics owns a small manufacturing building that is no longer suitable for its expanded operations. Several years ago, it leased the building to Legal.bagel.com. Legal.bagel.com is doing well and so is the surrounding neighborhood. In fact, the area has become such a Mecca for e-businesses that real estate brokers now refer to it as "Silicon Alley." Headley knows that Legal.bagel.com is paying far less rent than what the market will currently bear. He knows that if he could get Legal.bagel.com out, Amphydynamics could re-lease the building for 10 times more than what Legal.bagel.com is paying. In fact, if he could get Legal.bagel.com out, he could sell the building at a handsome profit. The problem is that Legal.bagel.com has 10 years to run on its lease and an option for another 10-year term. Headley has a bright idea. He suggests that Amphydynamics can take advantage of the current hot market by rejecting the lease, ousting Legal.bagel.com, and selling or re-letting the building. Will his idea work?

It won't. Code § 365(h)(1) provides that if an unexpired lease of real property is rejected by a debtor-lessor, the lessee has the option of either treating the lease as terminated or remaining in possession of the property for the balance of the lease term, including any renewal or extension periods. *See, e.g., In re Child World, Inc.*, 142 B.R. 87, 89 (Bankr. S.D.N.Y. 1992). In the event the lessee remains in possession and the debtor fails to provide the services called for under the lease, such as heat, hot water, and repairs, the lessee may deduct the cost of these services from the rent. *Megafoods Stores, Inc. v. Flagstaff Realty Assoc. (In re Flagstaff Realty Assoc.)*, 60 F.3d 1031 (3d Cir. 1995). That is the lessee's exclusive remedy. The failure of the debtor to perform does not give rise to a claim that may be asserted against the estate except by way of setoff. See § 365(h)(2). *See also In re Taylor*, 198 B.R. 142 (Bankr. D.S.C. 1996); *In re J. H. Land & Cattle Co.*, 8 B.R. 237 (Bankr. W.D. Okla. 1981).

As originally enacted, § 365(h) provided merely that if a debtor-lessor rejected a lease, the tenant was entitled to "remain in possession" for the duration of the lease and any renewal terms. Courts had difficulty with this provision. Suppose that Legal.bagel.com wants to sublet the building (or part of it) to a third party. Does rejection of the lease by Amphydynamics affect Legal.bagel.com's ability to do that? In *In re Carlton Restaurant, Inc.*, 151 B.R. 353, 355 (Bankr. E.D. Pa. 1993), the bankruptcy court held that the tenant's right to "remain in possession" did not include the right to assign the lease, reasoning that § 365(h) "allows only a lessee the choice to remain in possession under the terms of the lease. It does not provide that the lease continues, but merely accords a lessee the choice to remain in a rented premises under the terms of the lease."

Other courts disagreed, holding that even a lessee not in possession could invoke the protections of § 365(h) and continue to sublet. *In re Lee Road Partners, Ltd.*, 155 B.R. 55 (Bankr. E.D.N.Y. 1993), *affirmed*, 169 B.R. 507 (E.D.N.Y. 1994).

Much of the confusion was eliminated by the Bankruptcy Reform Act of 1994, pursuant to which Code § 365(h) was substantially amended. No longer is the lessee merely entitled to "remain in possession." The statute now expressly (and expansively) provides that if a lessee opts to retain its rights under the lease, those rights include "those relating to the amount and timing of payment of rent and other amounts payable by the lessee and any right of use, possession, quiet enjoyment, subletting, assignment, or hypothecation . . . that are in or appurtenant to the real property." Code § 365(h)(1)(A)(ii). In addition, a new Code § 365(h)(1)(D) was added, which provides that for purposes of § 365(h), " 'lessee' includes any successor, assign, or mortgagee permitted under the terms of such lease." The purpose of the amendment was to overrule cases such as *Carlton* and to insure that when a lessor rejects a lease, the lessee may retain not only the right to possession, but also all rights appurtenant to the lease.

Bear in mind, however, that if the debtor is both a lessee and sublessor, rejection by the debtor of the prime lease either prior to or simultaneous with the rejection of the sublease will divest the sublessee of its rights under the lease because they derive from the rejected prime lease. *In re Child World, Inc.*, 142 B.R. 87, 89 (Bankr. S.D.N.Y. 1992). On the other hand, if the debtor assumes the prime lease and then rejects the sublease, the sublessee will enjoy the protections of § 365(h). *Id.*

NOTES AND QUESTIONS

A recent case highlights a potential issue regarding the acceptance or rejection of leases of importance especially to master landlords who lease their land to developers who, then, develop the property. In *In re Mervyn's Holdings*, the lease in question contained a provision that required a debtor/tenant to indemnify the landlord against liability for any mechanic's liens that were filed against the property. While construction on the real estate was underway, the debtor filed for bankruptcy, and the construction company filed two mechanic's liens against the landlord. The debtor had not accepted or rejected the lease when the landlord, in turn, filed two proofs of claim in the debtor's bankruptcy case claiming administrative priority for the claims. The debtor argued that the landlord's claims were pre-petition, general unsecured claims because the lease containing the provisions was signed prior to filing for bankruptcy. The court disagreed, finding that the claims arose post-petition and that, since the debtor had not yet rejected the lease, under 11 U.S.C. § 365(d)(3), the claim relating to the indemnification provision was entitled to administrative priority. *See WM Inland Adjacent v. Mervyn's (In re Mervyn's Holdings)*, 2013 Bankr. LEXIS 67 (Bankr. D. Del. Jan. 8, 2013).

[E]   The Special Rule for Rejection of Contracts for the Sale of Real Property or Timeshare Interests

A similar rule protects purchasers when the trustee or debtor in possession rejects a contract for the sale of real property *and* the purchaser is in possession. Section 365(i) gives the purchaser a choice. It may remain in possession, continue making payments due under the contract, and upon completion of payments, receive title to the property. In addition, the purchaser may offset against such payments of damages resulting from the debtor's nonperformance of any obligation after the date of the rejection. Alternatively, the purchaser may treat the contract as terminated. Code § 365(j) grants a purchaser, who treats the contract as terminated, a lien on the debtor's interest in the property to secure the recovery of any portion of the purchase price already paid to the debtor. *A purchaser who is not in possession* is not so blessed. It must treat a rejected contract as terminated and accept the § 365(j) lien. The purpose of the special treatment accorded purchasers in possession has been explained as follows:

> The purchaser in this kind of contract is likely to be the buyer of a home or farm or small business who has adjusted to a new location. Very often, especially in the case of a residential buyer, he will be poor. Certainly modern American bankruptcy policy places as high a value on relieving the poor for the consequences of their own and others' improvidence as in doing perfect justice between creditors.

Frank R. Lacy, *Land Sale Contracts in Bankruptcy*, 21 U.C.L.A. L. Rev. 477, 484 (1979).

[F] The Special Rule for Rejection of Intellectual Property Licenses

SUNBEAM PRODUCTS, INC. v. CHICAGO AMERICAN MANUFACTURING, LLC

United States Court of Appeals for the Seventh Circuit
686 F.3d 372 (2012)

EASTERBROOK, CHIEF JUDGE.

Lakewood Engineering & Manufacturing Co. made and sold a variety of consumer products, which were covered by its patents and trademarks. In 2008, losing money on every box fan, Lakewood contracted their manufacture to Chicago American Manufacturing (CAM). The contract authorized CAM to practice Lakewood's patents and put its trademarks on the completed fans. Lakewood was to take orders from retailers such as Sears, Walmart, and Ace Hardware; CAM would ship directly to these customers on Lakewood's instructions. Because Lakewood was in financial distress, CAM was reluctant to invest the money necessary to gear up for production — and to make about 1.2 million fans that Lakewood estimated it would require during the 2009 cooling season — without assured payment. Lakewood provided that assurance by authorizing CAM to sell the 2009 run of box fans for its own account if Lakewood did not purchase them.

In February 2009, three months into the contract, several of Lakewood's creditors filed an involuntary bankruptcy petition against it. The court appointed a trustee, who decided to sell Lakewood's business. Sunbeam Products, doing business as Jarden Consumer Solutions, bought the assets, including Lakewood's patents and trademarks. Jarden did not want the Lakewood-branded fans CAM had in inventory, nor did it want CAM to sell those fans in competition with Jarden's products. Lakewood's trustee rejected the executory portion of the CAM contract under 11 U.S.C. § 365(a). When CAM continued to make and sell Lakewood-branded fans, Jarden filed this adversary action. It will receive 75% of any recovery and the trustee the other 25% for the benefit of Lakewood's creditors.

The bankruptcy judge held a trial. After determining that the Lakewood-CAM contract is ambiguous, the judge relied on extrinsic evidence to conclude that CAM was entitled to make as many fans as Lakewood estimated it would need for the entire 2009 selling season and sell them bearing Lakewood's marks. *In re Lakewood Engineering & Manufacturing Co.*, 459 B.R. 306, 333–38 (Bankr. N.D. Ill. 2011). Jarden contends in this court — following certification by the district court of a direct appeal under 28 U.S.C. § 158(d)(2)(A) — that CAM had to stop making and selling fans once Lakewood stopped having requirements for them. The bankruptcy court did not err in reading the contract as it did, but the effect of the trustee's rejection remains to be determined.

Lubrizol Enterprises, Inc. v. Richmond Metal Finishers, Inc., 756 F.2d 1043 (4th Cir. 1985), holds that, when an intellectual-property license is rejected in bankruptcy, the licensee loses the ability to use any licensed copyrights, trademarks, and patents. Three years after *Lubrizol*, Congress added § 365(n) to the Bankruptcy

Code. It allows licensees to continue using the intellectual property after rejection, provided they meet certain conditions. The bankruptcy judge held that § 365(n) allowed CAM to practice Lakewood's patents when making box fans for the 2009 season. That ruling is no longer contested. But "intellectual property" is a defined term in the Bankruptcy Code: 11 U.S.C. § 101(35A) provides that "intellectual property" includes patents, copyrights, and trade secrets. It does not mention trademarks. Some bankruptcy judges have inferred from the omission that Congress codified *Lubrizol* with respect to trademarks, but an omission is just an omission. The limited definition in § 101(35A) means that § 365(n) does not affect trademarks one way or the other. According to the Senate committee report on the bill that included § 365(n), the omission was designed to allow more time for study, not to approve *Lubrizol*. See S. Rep. No. 100-505, 100th Cong., 2d Sess. 5 (1988). *See also In re Exide Technologies*, 607 F.3d 957, 966–67 (3d Cir. 2010) (Ambro, J., concurring) (concluding that § 365(n) neither codifies nor disapproves *Lubrizol* as applied to trademarks). The subject seems to have fallen off the legislative agenda, but this does not change the effect of what Congress did in 1988.

The bankruptcy judge in this case agreed with Judge Ambro that § 365(n) and § 101(35A) leave open the question whether rejection of an intellectual-property license ends the licensee's right to use trademarks. Without deciding whether a contract's rejection under § 365(a) ends the licensee's right to use the trademarks, the judge stated that she would allow CAM, which invested substantial resources in making Lakewood-branded box fans, to continue using the Lakewood marks "on equitable grounds". 459 B.R. at 345; *see also id.* at 343–46. This led to the entry of judgment in CAM's favor, and Jarden has appealed.

What the Bankruptcy Code provides, a judge cannot override by declaring that enforcement would be "inequitable." *See, e.g., Toibb v. Radloff*, 501 U.S. 157, 162, 111 S. Ct. 2197, 115 L. Ed. 2d 145 (1991); *In re Kmart Corp.*, 359 F.3d 866, 871 (7th Cir. 2004); *In re Sinclair*, 870 F.2d 1340 (7th Cir. 1989). There are hundreds of bankruptcy judges, who have many different ideas about what is equitable in any given situation. Some may think that equity favors licensees' reliance interests; others may believe that equity favors the creditors, who can realize more of their claims if the debtor can terminate IP licenses. Rights depend, however, on what the Code provides rather than on notions of equity. Recently the Supreme Court emphasized that arguments based on views about the purposes behind the Code, and wise public policy, cannot be used to supersede the Code's provisions. It remarked: "The Bankruptcy Code standardizes an expansive (and sometimes unruly) area of law, and it is our obligation to interpret the Code clearly and predictably using well established principles of statutory construction." *RadLAX Gateway Hotel, LLC v. Amalgamated Bank*, 132 S. Ct. 2065, 2073, 182 L. Ed. 2d 967 (2012).

Although the bankruptcy judge's ground of decision is untenable, that does not necessarily require reversal. We need to determine whether Lubrizol correctly understood § 365(g), which specifies the consequences of a rejection under § 365(a). No other court of appeals has agreed with *Lubrizol* — or for that matter disagreed with it. *Exide*, the only other appellate case in which the subject came up, was resolved on the ground that the contract was not executory and therefore could not be rejected. (*Lubrizol* has been cited in other appellate opinions, none of which concerns the effect of rejection on intellectual-property licenses.) Judge Ambro, who filed a concurring opinion in *Exide*, concluded that, had the contract been eligible for rejection under § 365(a), the licensee could have continued using the trademarks. 607 F.3d at 964–68. Like Judge Ambro, we too think *Lubrizol* mistaken.

Here is the full text of § 365(g):

Except as provided in subsections (h)(2) and (i)(2) of this section, the rejection of an executory contract or unexpired lease of the debtor constitutes a breach of such contract or lease —

(1) if such contract or lease has not been assumed under this section or under a plan confirmed under chapter 9, 11, 12, or 13 of this title, immediately before the date of the filing of the petition; or (2) if such contract or lease has been assumed under this section or under a plan confirmed under chapter 9, 11, 12, or 13 of this title —

(A) if before such rejection the case has not been converted under section 1112, 1208, or 1307 of this title, at the time of such rejection; or (B) if before such rejection the case has been converted under section 1112, 1208, or 1307 of this title —

(i) immediately before the date of such conversion, if such contract or lease was assumed before such conversion; or

(ii) at the time of such rejection, if such contract or lease was assumed after such conversion.

Most of these words don't affect our situation. Subsections (h)(2) and (i)(2) are irrelevant, and paragraph (1) tells us that the rejection takes effect immediately before the petition's filing. For our purpose, therefore, all that matters is the opening proposition: that rejection "constitutes a breach of such contract."

Outside of bankruptcy, a licensor's breach does not terminate a licensee's right to use intellectual property. Lakewood had two principal obligations under its contract with CAM: to provide CAM with motors and cord sets (CAM was to build the rest of the fan) and to pay for the completed fans that CAM drop-shipped to retailers. Suppose that, before the bankruptcy began, Lakewood had broken its promise by failing to provide the motors. CAM might have elected to treat that breach as ending its own obligations, *see* Uniform Commercial Code § 2-711(1), but it also could have covered in the market by purchasing motors and billed Lakewood for the extra cost. UCC § 2-712. CAM had bargained for the security of being able to sell Lakewood-branded fans for its own account if Lakewood defaulted; outside of bankruptcy, Lakewood could not have ended CAM's right to sell the box fans by failing to perform its own duties, any more than a borrower could end the lender's right to collect just by declaring that the debt will not be paid.

What § 365(g) does by classifying rejection as breach is establish that in bankruptcy, as outside of it, the other party's rights remain in place. After rejecting a contract, a debtor is not subject to an order of specific performance. *See NLRB v. Bildisco & Bildisco*, 465 U.S. 513, 531, 104 S. Ct. 1188, 79 L. Ed. 2d 482 (1984); *Midway Motor Lodge of Elk Grove v. Innkeepers' Telemanagement & Equipment*

Corp., 54 F.3d 406, 407 (7th Cir. 1995). The debtor's unfulfilled obligations are converted to damages; when a debtor does not assume the contract before rejecting it, these damages are treated as a pre-petition obligation, which may be written down in common with other debts of the same class. But nothing about this process implies that any rights of the other contracting party have been vaporized. Consider how rejection works for leases. A lessee that enters bankruptcy may reject the lease and pay damages for abandoning the premises, but rejection does not abrogate the lease (which would absolve the debtor of the need to pay damages). Similarly a lessor that enters bankruptcy could not, by rejecting the lease, end the tenant's right to possession and thus re-acquire premises that might be rented out for a higher price. The bankrupt lessor might substitute damages for an obligation to make repairs, but not rescind the lease altogether.

. . . .

Scholars uniformly criticize *Lubrizol*, concluding that it confuses rejection with the use of an avoiding power. *See, e.g.*, Douglas G. Baird, *Elements of Bankruptcy* 130–40 & n. 10 (4th ed. 2006); Michael T. Andrew, *Executory Contracts in Bankruptcy: Understanding "Rejection"*, 59 U. Colo. L. Rev. 845, 916–19 (1988); Jay Lawrence Westbrook, *The Commission's Recommendations Concerning the Treatment of Bankruptcy Contracts*, 5 Am. Bankr. Inst. L. Rev. 463, 470–72 (1997). *Lubrizol* itself devoted scant attention to the question whether rejection cancels a contract, worrying instead about the right way to identify executory contracts to which the rejection power applies.

Lubrizol does not persuade us. This opinion, which creates a conflict among the circuits, was circulated to all active judges under Circuit Rule 40(e). No judge favored a hearing en banc. Because the trustee's rejection of Lakewood's contract with CAM did not abrogate CAM's contractual rights, this adversary proceeding properly ended with a judgment in CAM's favor.

Affirmed.

NOTES AND QUESTIONS

Code § 365(n) provides that if a trustee or debtor in possession rejects an executory contract under which the debtor is a licensor of a right to intellectual property, the licensee has a choice. Bankruptcy Code § 365(n)(1)(A) provides that the licensee may choose to treat the agreement as terminated, if the rejection "amounts to such a breach as would entitle the licensee to treat such contract as terminated by virtue of its own terms, applicable nonbankruptcy law, or an agreement made by the licensee with another party" — in other words, if the breach amounts to a material breach. In such a case, the licensee in effect walks away from the property and asserts a claim for any damages resulting from the breach. As we've seen, under Code § 502(g), the claim will be treated as a prepetition claim.

Alternatively, Bankruptcy Code § 365(n)(1)(B) provides that the licensee may elect, for the duration of the agreement and any extensions thereof, to retain its rights to the "intellectual property" and any embodiment thereof under the license agreement and any supplemental agreements. The rights retained are "as such rights existed immediately before the case commenced." This means that although § 365(n) avoids the rescissionary effect of opinions such as *Lubrizol*, the licensee cannot compel specific performance of the debtor's affirmative duties under the rejected license. For example, the debtor cannot be compelled to maintain, enhance, or upgrade the technology. *See Biosafe Int'l, Inc. v. Controlled Shredders, Inc. (In re Szombathy)*, 1996 Bankr. LEXIS 888 (Bankr. N.D. Ill. July 9, 1996). If the licensee elects to retain its rights to the property, it must continue to pay royalties at the contract rate. The Code does not define "royalties," however, and at least one court has concluded that even though payments were described as "license fees," they were "royalties in the sense of section 365(n)." *Encino Bus. Mgmt. v. Prize Frize, Inc.*, 32 F.3d 426 (9th Cir. 1994).

Code § 101(35A) provides that for purposes of § 365(n), "intellectual property" includes, among other things, trade secrets, patented inventions, and copyrighted materials, but not trademarks. According to the legislative history of § 365(n), trademark "licensing relationships depend to a large extent on control of the quality of products or services sold by the licensee. Since these matters could not be addressed without more extensive study, it was proposed to postpone congressional action . . . and to allow the development of equitable treatment of this situation by bankruptcy courts." S. Rep. No. 100-505 (1988).

The special rules governing rejection of leases, land sale contracts, and intellectual property licenses do not apply to other kinds of transactions. Suppose that prior to filing its Chapter 11 petition, Amphydynamics leased computer equipment — such as servers, routers, and tools for designing web pages — to IPO.com. Now a debtor in possession, Amphydynamics decides to reject this equipment lease because it believes it can lease the equipment elsewhere for more. Does IPO.com have to return the equipment, even though the lease has several years to run before it expires? If rejection does result in rescission of the contract, it would have to return the equipment. In the following article, the author rejects the notion that rejection means rescission. He also explains why rejection should not deprive a nondebtor of its interest in the property that is the subject matter of the contract.

Bankruptcy: The Next Twenty Years, Report Of The National Bankruptcy Review Commission
Volume 1, pp. 460–61 (1997)

The Commission recommends a common-sense clarification of the term "rejection" by replacing it with "election to breach." The Commission further recommends that the Bankruptcy Code delineate the consequences of electing to breach to correct on a generic basis the contrary results reached by some courts. The bankruptcy trustee's election not to perform a contract is nothing more than or less than a breach of the contract and should be treated accordingly. Rejection does not "nullify," "rescind," or "vaporize" the contract or terminate the rights of the parties; it does not serve as an avoiding power separate and apart from the express avoiding powers already provided in the Bankruptcy Code. For example, if a debtor entered a contract prepetition and conferred rights in an asset to a nondebtor party, a trustee would not be entitled to repudiate the transfer and retrieve the property unless one of the other avoiding powers, not section 365, permitted it to do so. Under most circumstances, this means that the nondebtor party would be entitled to a claim for money damages, and the contract obligations themselves would be discharged. The claim would be paid in the bankruptcy pro rata with other unsecured creditors.

§ 7.04   TIME FOR ASSUMPTION AND REJECTION

In a Chapter 7 case, the general rule is that a trustee must assume an executory contract within 60 days after the order for relief, and a contract or lease that is not timely assumed is deemed rejected. Code § 365(d)(1). In contrast, in a Chapter 11 case, the general rule is that a trustee or debtor in possession may assume or reject an executory contract at any time prior to confirmation of the plan or in the plan itself. Thus, the decision to assume or reject can be postponed until the latest stages of a case, and, according to the court in *Klein Sleep*, in many cases it should be. However, the court may order a trustee or debtor in possession to assume or reject within a specified time. Code § 365(d)(2). *See, e.g., Theatre Holding Corp. v. Mauro*, 681 F.2d 102 (2d Cir. 1982).

A special timing rule applies to one subspecies of executory contract: the *nonresidential* (i.e., commercial) real property lease. Even in a Chapter 11 case, a trustee or debtor in possession must assume a nonresidential real property lease within 60 days after the order for relief. If the lease is not assumed, it is deemed rejected, and the premises are to be immediately surrendered to the lessor. Code § 365(d)(4). However, as the following opinion demonstrates, this time period may be extended by the court for cause. *See e.g., South Street Seaport Ltd. P'ship v. Burger Boys, Inc.*, 94 F.3d 755 (2d Cir. 1996).

NOTES AND QUESTIONS

(1) *Performance Pending Assumption or Rejection of Nonresidential Real Property Leases.* Unlike its companion provision, Code § 365(d)(4), Code § 365(d)(3) does not provide that the debtor's failure to perform these obligations will result in automatic termination or "deemed rejection" of the lease. Short of denying an extension motion, what remedies can a court impose?

(2) *Relationship of § 365(d)(3) and § 503(b)(1).* According to Code § 365(d)(3), the obligation to perform postpetition obligations under a nonresidential real property lease exists independently of Code § 503(b)(1), which otherwise governs the allowance of administrative expenses. A little history will help you understand the purpose of this cryptic clause. Over the years, in order to keep administrative costs down, a number of courts held that prior to the assumption of a lease, the claim of a lessor was merely an equitable right based upon the value of the benefits conferred on the estate, rather than the contract price. *In re United Cigar Stores*, 69 F.2d 513 (2d Cir. 1934). Thus, for example, a debtor that leased a large storeroom, but only occupied half of it postpetition, was only obligated to pay "what would be a fair return for the use of the store which he occupied." *In re J. Frank Stanton Co.*, 162 F. 169 (D. Conn. 1908). Code § 365(d)(3) was intended to overrule that approach. It requires the debtor to pay the entire rent due under the lease, irrespective of how

much (or how little) of the premises it occupied. The entire rent obligation is entitled to priority treatment as expenses of administration without any additional showing of benefit to the estate. *In re Amber's Stores, Inc.*, 193 B.R. 819 (Bankr. N.D. Tex. 1996).

(3) *Time for Seeking an Extension of the 60-day Period.* Courts generally agree that if a motion to extend the 60-day period for assuming or rejecting leases of nonresidential real estate is made within the 60-day period or any extensions thereof, the lease will not be deemed rejected even if the extension is not granted by the end of the period. *See, e.g., In re Wedtech Corp.*, 72 B.R. 464 (Bankr. S.D.N.Y. 1987). Some courts, however, have concluded that the debtor must not only seek, but actually obtain, an order within the 60-day period in order to keep the lease from being automatically rejected. *See, e.g., Debartolo Props. Mgmt., Inc. v. Devan (In re Merry-Go-Round Enter., Inc.)*, 194 B.R. 46 (D. Md. 1996).

(4) *Absolute Deadline.* Under proposed legislation, the 60-day period for assuming or rejecting nonresidential real property would be extended to 120 days, but the debtor would not be able to obtain an extension of these time periods, § 205, H.R. 833, 106th Cong., 2d Sess. (1999); § 405, S. 625, 106th Cong., 2d. Sess. (1999). The court would be authorized to extend the deadline upon motion of the lessor only. Any lease not assumed before the expiration of the deadline would be deemed rejected, and the debtor would have to surrender possession of the premises immediately.

(5) *What is a "Lease of Nonresidential Real Property"?* Interestingly, most courts have concluded that the phrase "lease of nonresidential real property" does not mean "commercial lease of real property," and that the adjective "nonresidential" modifies the word "real property" rather than the word "lease." *In re Independence Village*, 52 B.R. 715, 722 (Bankr. E.D. Mich. 1985). Thus, a nursing home lease was deemed to be a lease of residential property for § 365(d)(4) purposes, *In re Care Givers, Inc.*, 113 B.R. 263, 266–67 (Bankr. N.D. Tex. 1989), as was a 50-year ground lease on which an apartment building was built, *In re Bonita Glen II*, 152 B.R. 751 (Bankr. S.D. Cal. 1993), as was the lease of a cooperative apartment even though the apartment was rented by the debtor for the purpose of subletting it at a profit, *In re Lippman*, 122 B.R. 206 (Bankr. S.D.N.Y. 1990).

(6) *Performance Pending Assumption or Rejection of Personal Property Leases.* There was a time when the filing of a Chapter 11 petition by a lessee of personal property placed the nondebtor lessor in limbo. Even though the debtor had until confirmation of a plan to decide whether to assume or reject the lease, the debtor was not required to perform any of its obligations under the lease. At some later date, the lessor might recover as an administrative expense the value of the lease to the estate based on the debtor's actual use of the property, or it might recover the reasonable rental value of the property, neither of which might be as much as the rent required to be paid under the lease. *See, e.g., In re Fred Sanders Co.*, 22 B.R. 902 (Bankr. E.D. Mich. 1982). *See* discussion in note (2), above. The best the lessor could do was to ask the court to order the debtor to make up its mind about the lease sooner rather than later.

In 1994, a new § 365(d)(10) was added to the Code. Similar to § 365(d)(3), it provides that the trustee shall perform all obligations of the debtor under a personal property lease during the period running from 60 days after the order for relief until the lease is assumed or rejected. This section does not apply to leases of personal property for "personal, family, or household purposes."

Section 365(d)(10) requires the debtor to pay the rent reserved under the lease and treats this obligation as an administrative expense. However, the section also states that the court may, "based on the equities of the case, order otherwise." The effect of § 365(d)(10) is to shift the burden to the trustee or debtor to show why it should be excused from paying the lessor during this limbo period or why it should be permitted to pay less than the rent reserved under the lease. *In re Elder-Beerman Stores Corp.*, 201 B.R. 759 (Bankr. S.D. Ohio 1996). Lessors of personal property are now also entitled to "adequate protection" pursuant to Code § 363(e).

(7) *Performance Pending Assumption or Rejection of Other Kinds of Contracts.* Suppose, that Amphydynamics contracts with its supplier, MicroMax, for several shipments of microchips. At the time Amphydynamics files its Chapter 11 petition, MicroMax has not yet shipped and Amphydynamics has not yet paid. Amphydynamics decides to heed the *Klein Sleep* court's advice to postpone the assumption/rejection decision until reorganization is a certainty. MicroMax wants to know if, in light of the debtor's dithering, it still has to ship the goods. As we've just seen, Code §§ 365(d)(3) and (d)(1) require the debtor to perform its end of the bargain while it is deciding whether to assume or reject leases of nonresidential real property and leases of personal property. Nothing in the Code requires the debtor to perform its end of the bargain of other kinds of contracts during this limbo period.

What about the nondebtor? May it suspend performance in the meantime? The answer is no. During the period between filing of the petition and assumption or rejection, the contract continues in effect, and the nondebtor party — here MicroMax — is bound to honor it. *In re Public Serv. Co. of New Hampshire*, 884 F.2d 11, 14 (1st Cir. 1989). Some courts have reasoned that the unilateral termination of a contract by the nondebtor party amounts to an "act to obtain possession of property or the estate . . . or to exercise control over property of the estate" in violation of the automatic stay. *See* Code § 362(a)(3); *In re Computer Commc'ns., Inc.*, 824 F.2d 725 (9th Cir. 1987). The nondebtor party may, of course, ask the court to impose a deadline for assumption or rejection, but, as the *Burger Boys* opinion demonstrates, the failure of the debtor to perform its end of the bargain is only one factor the court will consider in deciding whether to force the debtor to fish or cut bait.

Thus, it is quite possible that the nondebtor will be compelled to perform during this limbo period, even though the debtor is not. If the nondebtor continues to provide goods or services — for example, if MicroMax ships microchips — and the debtor does not pay for them, the debt for goods or services actually provided would in theory be entitled to administrative expense priority status. However, some courts have held that a nondebtor who continues to perform without the court's blessing may find that it is not entitled to administrative priority if, when all is said and done, the transaction does not benefit the estate. *See, e.g., In re Jartran, Inc.*, 732 F.2d 584 (7th Cir. 1984). The Bankruptcy Review Commission has recommended that this "gap" in the Code be filled by a new provision that would expressly authorize the bankruptcy court to "grant an order governing temporary performance and/or providing protection of the interests of the nondebtor party until the court approves a decision to perform or breach a contract." The proposed new rule would insure that losses incurred by nondebtor parties to executory contracts during the limbo period be treated as administrative expenses.

§ 7.05 WHEN SHOULD A COURT APPROVE ASSUMPTION? THE GENERAL RULE.

Assumption of an executory contract by a trustee or debtor in possession requires court approval. *See* Code § 365(a).

ORION PICTURES CORP. v. SHOWTIME NETWORKS, INC. (IN RE ORION PICTURES CORP.)
United States Court of Appeals for the Second Circuit
4 F.3d 1095 (1993)

WALKER, CIRCUIT JUDGE

BACKGROUND

Orion is a producer and distributor of motion pictures. Showtime operates subscription cable services that show movies licensed from motion picture distributors. In 1986, Showtime and Orion entered into an agreement (the "Agreement"), which was essentially an output contract under which Showtime would license all films distributed by Orion without regard to their commercial success, provided they met certain criteria pertaining to matters such as advertising expenditures and theatrical releases. The Agreement contained a "key-man" clause that conditioned Showtime's performance on Orion's continued employment of at least two of four named Orion executives in their then-current or substantially similar positions.

In letters dated October 17, 1991, and November 20, 1991, Showtime notified Orion of its position that, due to various management changes at Orion that occurred in 1990 and 1991, Orion was in violation of the key-man clause beginning April 2, 1991. On December 11, 1991, Orion filed for reorganization under Chapter 11 of the United States Bankruptcy Code. On December 24, 1991, Showtime notified Orion that because it believed Orion to be out of compliance with the key-man clause, it would not license the various films it would otherwise be obligated to accept under the Agreement.

On March 20, 1992, Orion filed a motion to assume the Agreement in the bankruptcy court pursuant to § 365 (the "Motion to Assume"). Also on March 20, Orion filed an adversary proceeding in the bankruptcy court against Showtime (the "Adversary Proceeding"), claiming anticipatory breach of the Agreement, and seeking an order permitting Orion to assume the Agreement, declaratory relief setting forth the parties' rights and obligations, and specific performance of Showtime's obligations to make payments under the Agreement, or, alternatively, $77 million in damages for breach of contract.

. . . .

The bankruptcy court held hearings on both the Motion to Assume and the Adversary Proceeding on May 14 and 15. During the hearings, Orion withdrew its demand for specific performance in the Adversary Proceeding, leaving only the request for assumption of the contract and a prayer for declaratory relief. At the close of the hearings on the two matters, the bankruptcy court ruled that Orion had not violated the key-man clause. Then, having held that Orion had not violated the clause, the court reasoned that it would be beneficial to Orion to assume the Agreement, since an enforceable Agreement would entitle Orion to $77 million.

. . . .

Showtime appealed the bankruptcy court's order to the district court. On December 14, 1992, the district court upheld the bankruptcy court's order in its entirety. This appeal followed.

DISCUSSION

I. The Motion to Assume

After taking evidence on the issue, the bankruptcy court decided, in the context of deciding the Motion to Assume, that Orion had not violated the key-man clause. We hold that it was error for the bankruptcy court to decide a disputed factual issue between the parties to a contract in the context of determining whether the debtor or trustee should be permitted to assume that contract.

Under § 365(a), "[a] trustee, subject to the court's approval, may assume or reject any executory contract or unexpired lease term of the debtor." Since § 1107(a) gives debtors-in-possession the same rights and powers of a trustee, a debtor-in-possession, such as Orion, also may assume a contract with bankruptcy court approval.

The purpose behind allowing the assumption or rejection of executory contracts is to permit the trustee or debtor-in-possession to use valuable property of the estate and to "renounce title to and abandon burdensome property." 2 COLLIER ON BANKRUPTCY ¶ 365.01[1] (15th ed. 1993). If the trustee or debtor-in-possession rejects an executory contract pursuant to § 365, "the other party to the rejected contract becomes a general creditor of the estate for any damages flowing from the rejection." *In re Minges*, 602 F.2d 38, 41 (2d Cir. 1979). In short, § 365 permits the trustee or debtor-in-possession, subject to the approval of the bankruptcy court, to go through the inventory of executory contracts of the debtor and decide which ones it would be beneficial to adhere to and which ones it would be beneficial to reject.

The bankruptcy court erred because it misapprehended the fundamental nature and purpose of a motion to assume. At heart, a motion to assume should be considered a summary proceeding, intended to efficiently review the trustee's or debtor's decision to adhere to or reject a particular contract in the course of the swift administration of the bankruptcy estate. It is not the time or place for prolonged discovery or a lengthy trial with disputed issues. . . .

In *In re Minges* we held that a bankruptcy court reviewing a trustee's or debtor-in-possession's decision to assume or reject an executory contract should examine a contract and the surrounding circumstances and apply its best "business judgment" to determine if it would be beneficial or burdensome to the estate to assume it. 602 F.2d at 43. In reviewing a trustee's or debtor-in-possession's decision to assume an executory contract, then, a bankruptcy court sits as an overseer of the wisdom with which the bankruptcy estate's property is being managed by the trustee or debtor-in-possession, and not, as it does in other circumstances, as the arbiter of disputes between creditors and the estate. Although several bankruptcy courts have read § 365 as authorizing them to resolve questions involving the validity of contracts before deciding whether to permit the trustee or debtor-in-possession to assume the contracts, we believe that nothing in § 365 provides such authorization.

As we held in *Minges*, the process of deciding a motion to assume is one of the bankruptcy court placing itself in the position of the trustee or debtor-in-possession and determining whether assuming the contract would be a good business decision or a bad one. Every business person would like to control the end result of her projections and judgments: a stock analyst who had the power to cause stocks to rise and fall to meet her projections would have an enviable track record. This is essentially what the bankruptcy court did here. Permitting a bankruptcy court to rule conclusively on a decisive issue of breach of contract would render the use of "business judgment" required by *In re Minges* unnecessary, and is incompatible with the limited purpose of motions to assume of ensuring that valuable property is preserved and burdensome property discarded.

Finally, it is important to keep in mind that the bankruptcy court's "business judgment" in deciding a motion to assume is just that — a judgment of the sort a businessman would make. In no way is this decision a formal ruling on the underlying disputed issues, and thus will receive no collateral estoppel effect. In a given case, a bankruptcy court might decide that it would be beneficial for the trustee or debtor-in-possession to assume a certain contract because the court thinks it unlikely that a court would hold that the debtor had breached the contract, and thus assuming the contract would be a good "business judgment." This "business judgment" could turn out to be wrong, however, if a later fact finder in an adversary proceeding decides that the underlying contract was in fact breached. In such a case, the judge's wrong decision is simply an error of business judgment, not legal error.

Our conclusion that the bankruptcy court erred in adjudicating the key-man issue in deciding the Motion to Assume is also informed by the fact that motions to assume always involve contracts, and allowing a bankruptcy court to decide a disputed legal contract issue in the course of deciding a motion to assume could usurp litigants' Seventh Amendment jury-trial rights. Our holding that contract issues may not be decided as part of a motion to assume eliminates the possibility that any such constitutional problems will arise. We note that there is no prohibition on bankruptcy courts, for reasons of efficiency, hearing motions to assume and trying related adversary proceedings simultaneously. They merely must be treated as conceptually separate proceedings, which is to say that adversary proceeding issues are not to be decided as part of a motion to assume.

Because the bankruptcy court improperly decided the key-man issue in deciding the Motion to Assume, we vacate the bankruptcy court's holding on this issue. Since the bankruptcy court might not have granted the Motion to Assume if it had known that it was not empowered to decide the key-man issue, we vacate the grant of the Motion to Assume and remand it to the bankruptcy court for further proceedings consistent with this opinion.

§ 7.06   LIMITATIONS ON THE POWER TO ASSUME EXECUTORY CONTRACTS

[A]   Contracts that Have Terminated

A contract that has been rescinded or that, by its terms has expired or been completely and validly terminated prior to the commencement of a bankruptcy case, is no longer executory for purposes of § 365 and there is nothing to assume or reject. As one court put it: "Filing a Chapter 11 petition will not resuscitate a contract that has already been terminated." *In re Best Film & Video Corp.*, 46 B.R. 861, 869 (Bankr. E.D.N.Y. 1985).

In re Anne Cara Oil Co., Inc., 32 B.R. 643 (Bankr. D. Mass. 1983), is a case in point. Shell Oil Company granted Anne Cara Oil Company the right to use the Shell trademark and sell Shell products. The dealer agreement provided that Shell could terminate the agreement if Anne Cara failed to pay Shell or mixed Shell and non-Shell products. On January 12, Shell notified Anne Cara that it was canceling the agreement as of April 15, because of defaults under those provisions. Anne Cara Oil Co. filed a Chapter 11 petition on April 14. The court held that although "[a]t the time of the filing of the Chapter 11 petition the franchise relationship was executory. . . . As of the day after the petition was filed, the franchise agreement ceased to be executory and . . . could not therefore be assumed."

However, the steps required to terminate the contract must be complete as of the time of the bankruptcy filing and not subject to reversal under applicable nonbankruptcy law. Where notice of termination is not effective until received by the debtor and notice is not received until after commencement of the case, the contract is executory at the time of filing and the debtor may be given the opportunity to cure defaults and assume. *In re R. S. Pinellas Motel P'ship*, 2 B.R. 113 (Bankr. M.D. Fla. 1979). In *In re Waterkist Corp.*, 775 F.2d 1089 (9th Cir. 1985), a lease provided for automatic termination upon a default by the lessee. However, because under applicable Alaska law, a court could consider the "equities of the situation" and decline to enforce the termination provision on anti-forfeiture grounds, the lease remained executory. A debtor retains the right to assume or reject a lease even though a warrant of eviction has issued if the state court retains the power to vacate the order. *In re Sanshoe Worldwide Corp.*, 993 F.2d 300 (2d Cir. 1993). *See also In re Touloumis*, 170 B.R. 825 (Bankr. S.D.N.Y. 1994).

[B] Contracts in Default

Code § 365(b)(1) provides that if there has been a default under an executory contract or lease, a trustee or debtor may not assume it unless three requirements are first satisfied. These requirements apply only if there has been a default.

First, under § 365(b)(1)(A), before it may assume a contract or lease that is in default, the trustee or debtor must cure any default or provide adequate assurance that any default will be cured promptly. *Manhattan King David Rest. v. Levine*, 154 B.R. 423, 429 (S.D.N.Y. 1993). This obligation to cure relates to both pre- and postpetition defaults. Courts have concluded that "prompt" does not mean "immediate," and that the meaning of "prompt" may "vary according to the circumstances of a given case." *In re Coors of North Miss., Inc.*, 27 B.R. 918, 922 (Bankr. N.D. Miss. 1983). In that case, the debtor sought to assume and assign a beer distributorship agreement. At the time the petition was filed, the debtor was heavily indebted to the Coors brewery. The debtor proposed to assign the agreement to another distributor, who would pay the purchase price in installments over a period of three years. The debtor, in turn, proposed to cure its past-due indebtedness to the brewery by making installment payments over a period of three years. The court held that in light of the financial strength of the assignee, a three year cure was "prompt" enough:

> In short the issue as to prompt cure devolves on the question of whether or not, under the totality of circumstances in this case, a cure effectuated within three years would be prompt within the meaning of the statute. This court regards as persuasive on this point the legal principles recited as dicta in the case of *In re Berkshire Chem. Haulers, Inc.*, [6 C.B.C. 843, 847] 20 B.R. 454, 457, 9 B.C.D. 230, 232 [Bankr. D. Mass. 1982]. The opinion provides, in pertinent part, as follows:
>
> > The Bankruptcy Code speaks of a "prompt cure," or "adequate assurance of a prompt cure." In at least one case, prompt cure meant an immediate payment. However, what is a prompt cure can often vary according to the circumstances of a given case. I therefore would disagree with the holding of *General Motors Acceptance Corp. v. Lawrence*, 11 B.R. 44, 45 (Bktcy. N.D. Ga. 1981), where the court felt it unlikely that a period of time in excess of one year would ever be considered a "prompt cure." For instance, a debtor with 90 years remaining on a 99 year lease, who proposes to cure its arrearage by monthly payments over an 18 month period, might be found to have offered adequate assurance of a *prompt cure*. . . .
>
> In keeping with the rationale of the Bankruptcy Court in *Berkshire*, and buttressed by the additional circumstance that each proposed assignee in the case sub judice enjoys an earned reputation of outstanding financial strength and integrity, there are reasonable prospects that the distributorship rights, if so assigned, may well result in a long range business enterprise mutually profitable to each such assignee and to the Adolph Coors Company. So measured, particularly in view of the many years of successful operation of each proposed assignee's business enterprise up to

this time, the curing of the default within a period of three years may well be a comparatively short period of time as it relates to the prospective longevity of successful business operation.

27 B.R. at 922.

On the other hand, in *In re Berkshire Chem. Haulers, Inc.*, 20 B.R. 454 (Bankr. D. Mass. 1982), cited in *Coors*, the court concluded that a debtor could not take 18 months to cure defaults under a truck lease agreement. While conceding that it could "envision many cases where the promise to cure a default out of future profits might be sufficiently assured as to warrant approval of such a proposal," the court found it untenable to make the lessor wait where there was "no past history of profitability . . . no competent evidence of future profitability and the debtor's projections seem nothing more than pipe dreams." 20 B.R. at 458–459.

A debtor or trustee is not required to cure a so-called "bankruptcy default" clause, *i.e.*, a clause providing that a party is deemed to be in default if the party becomes insolvent or bankrupt. *See* Code § 365(b)(2).

Second, § 365(b)(1)(B) provides that in addition to curing defaults, the debtor or trustee must compensate, or provide adequate assurance that it will promptly compensate, the nondebtor party for any actual pecuniary loss resulting from the debtor's default. Code § 365(b)(2)(D), added by the 1994 Bankruptcy Reform Act, provides that to cure a default, the debtor does not have to satisfy "any penalty rate or provision relating to a default arising from any failure by the debtor to perform nonmonetary obligations" under the contract or lease.

In *Ford Motor Co. v. Claremont Acquisition Corp. (In re Claremont Acquisition Corp.)*, 186 B.R. 977 (C.D. Cal. 1995), the debtor, a car dealer, sought to assume and assign an automobile franchise agreement. The agreement provided that the manufacturer could terminate the franchise if the dealer failed to operate the business for seven business days. The court held that the debtor's failure to operate the business was the kind of nonmonetary default that did not have to be cured. Had the court held otherwise, the debtor could not possibly have assumed the contract because, given the limits of current transportation technology, it could not have traveled back in time to cure its past failure to operate the business.

Third, under § 365(b)(1)(C), in addition to curing existing defaults, the trustee or debtor must provide adequate assurance of its ability to perform its future obligations under the contract. Adequate assurance might take the form of payment of a security deposit. *Seidle v. Pan Am. World Airways, Inc. (In re Belize Airways, Ltd.)*, 5 B.R. 152 (Bankr. S.D. Fla. 1980). At least one court has found that a realistic possibility of successful reorganization was, in itself, adequate assurance. *In re Shelco, Inc.*, 107 B.R. 483 (Bankr. D. Del. 1989). This requirement is discussed in more detail later, in connection with the assumption and assignment of contracts.

[C] Contracts to Make a Loan

Code § 365(c)(2) provides that a debtor or trustee may not assume (nor assume and assign) a contract that requires the nondebtor party to make a loan or extend other financial accommodations to the debtor or to issue a security of the debtor.

Clearly, this section will prevent the assumption of a mortgage loan commitment or a line of credit agreement, *see, e.g., In re New Town Mall*, 17 B.R. 326 (Bankr. D.S.D. 1982), but what about a contract for the sale of goods on credit or a contract to deliver a manuscript in exchange for payment upon acceptance by the publisher? According to the Code's legislative history, "Characterization of contracts to make a loan, or extend other debt accommodations, is limited to the extension of cash or a line of credit and is not intended to embrace ordinary leases or contracts to provide goods or services with payments to be made over time." 124 Cong. Rec. H 11093 (Daily Ed. Sept. 28, 1978). Workout agreements, entered into in anticipation of a bankruptcy filing, have been held to be assumable, even though they are technically contracts of financial accommodation. *In re TS Indus., Inc.*, 117 B.R. 682 (Bankr. D. Utah 1990). *But see Steele v. Boutiette (In re Boutiette)*, 168 B.R. 474 (Bankr. D. Mass. 1994) (agreement not entered into in contemplation of bankruptcy filing held nonassumable).

[D] Nonresidential Real Estate Leases that Have Terminated

Code § 365(c)(3) expressly prohibits the assumption of a lease of nonresidential real estate that terminated under applicable nonbankruptcy law prior to the commencement of the bankruptcy case. One might reasonably wonder why this provision, which was added to the Code in 1984, was necessary considering as we have already seen, a contract that has expired is by definition not nonexecutory and nonassumable. The reason is that Code § 541 provides that the property of the debtor consists of "all legal or equitable interests of the debtor in property as of the commencement of the case," and courts have sometimes regarded a debtor-tenant's possessory interest in property (albeit under an expired lease) as a "slight" equitable interest under § 541, interference with which was protected by the automatic stay. *See, e.g., In re Maxwell*, 40 B.R. 231 (N.D. Ill. 1984). What gives this section real bite are two other provisions that were added by the 1984 amendments. One is Code § 541(b)(2), which provides that "property of the estate" does not include any interest of the debtor in nonresidential real property under a lease that has terminated at the expiration of its stated term. The other is Code § 362(b)(10), which contains an exception to the automatic stay. It provides that a lessor of nonresidential real estate may take action against a debtor to recover property if the stated term of the lease expired before commencement of the case or if the lease expires during the pendency of the case.

[E] Bankruptcy Termination Clauses

Except with respect to contracts for the extension of credit or for the issuance of securities of the debtor, so-called "ipso facto" bankruptcy clauses, which provide for the automatic termination of a contract in the event of a party's insolvency or bankruptcy, are not effective in bankruptcy. *See* Code § 365(e) and *Computer Commc'ns., Inc. v. Codex Corp. (In re Computer Commc'ns., Inc.)*, 824 F.2d 725 (9th Cir. 1987). Although § 365(e) makes such provisions unenforceable against a debtor once it files a bankruptcy petition, some courts have held that they are effective if they are invoked and the contract is effectively terminated before the debtor files a bankruptcy petition.

In re Comp III, Inc., 136 B.R. 636 (Bankr. S.D.N.Y. 1992), is a case in point. In 1984, Computerland granted the debtor a franchise to operate a store. The franchise agreement provided that Computerland could terminate the agreement in the event the debtor became insolvent or unable to pay its debts as they came due. For the next several years, the store operated profitably, but it began suffering losses in 1990 and 1991. In early April of 1991, Computerland learned that the debtor was in serious financial trouble. On April 29, the debtor informed Computerland that it was preparing to file a bankruptcy petition. Computerland responded by terminating the franchise agreement. The court held that the contract could not be resurrected and assumed by the debtor, explaining, "Where an executory contract has been terminated prior to bankruptcy, section 365(e)(1) does not authorize a bankruptcy court to reach beyond the veil of the petition to reinstate the contract."

[F]　Contracts that Are Non-Assignable Under Nonbankruptcy Law

IN RE PIONEER FORD SALES, INC.
United States Court of Appeals, First Circuit
729 F.2d 27 (1984)

BREYER, CIRCUIT JUDGE.

The Ford Motor Company appeals a federal district court decision, 30 Bankr. 458, allowing a bankrupt Ford dealer (Pioneer Ford Sales, Inc.) to assign its Ford franchise over Ford's objection to a Toyota dealer (Toyota Village, Inc.). The district court decided the case on the basis of a record developed in the bankruptcy court. The bankruptcy court, 26 Bankr. 116, had approved the transfer, which ran from Pioneer to Fleet National Bank (Pioneer's principal secured creditor) and then to Toyota Village. Fleet sought authorization for the assignment because Toyota Village will pay $10,000 for the franchise and buy all parts and accessories in Pioneer's inventory at fair market value (about $75,000); if the franchise is not assigned, Ford will buy only some of the parts for between $45,000 and $55,000. Thus, the assignment will increase the value of the estate. Fleet is the appellee here.

The issue that the case raises is the proper application of § 365(c)(1)(A), an exception to a more general provision, § 365(f)(1), that allows a trustee in bankruptcy (or a debtor in possession) to assign many of the debtor's executory contracts even if the contract itself says that it forbids assignment. The exception at issue reads as follows:

> (c) The trustee [or debtor in possession] may not assume or assign an executory contract . . . of the debtor, whether or not such contract . . . prohibits assignment

(1)(A) applicable law excuses [the other party to the contract] from accepting performance from . . . an assignee . . . whether or not [the] . . . contract . . . prohibits . . . assignment.

The words "applicable law" in this section mean "applicable non-bankruptcy law." *See* H.R. Rep. No. 95-595, 95th Cong., 1st Sess. 348 (1977). Evidently, the theory of this section is to prevent the trustee from assigning (over objection) contracts of the sort that contract law ordinarily makes nonassignable, *i.e.* contracts that cannot be assigned when the contract itself is silent about assignment. At the same time, by using the words in (1)(A) "whether *or not* the contract prohibits assignment," the section prevents parties from using contractual language to prevent the trustee from assigning contracts that (when the contract is silent) contract law typically makes assignable. *Id.* Thus, we must look to see whether relevant nonbankruptcy law would allow Ford to veto the assignment of its basic franchise contract "whether or not" that basic franchise contract itself specifically "prohibits assignment."

The nonbankruptcy law to which both sides point us is contained in Rhode Island's "Regulation of Business Practices Among Motor Vehicle Manufacturers, Distributors and Dealers" Act. R.I. Gen. Laws § 31-5.1-4(C)(7). It states that:

[N]o dealer . . . shall have the right to . . . assign the franchise . . . without the consent of the manufacturer, except that such consent shall not be unreasonably withheld.

The statute by its terms, allows a manufacturer to veto an assignment where the veto is reasonable but not otherwise. The statute's language also indicates that it applies "whether or not" the franchise contract itself restricts assignment. Thus, the basic question that the case presents is whether Ford's veto was reasonable in terms of the Rhode Island law.

Neither the district court nor the bankruptcy court specifically addressed this question. Their failure apparently arose out of their belief that § 365(c)(1)(A) refers only to traditional personal service contracts. But in our view they were mistaken. The language of the section does not limit its effect to personal service contracts. It refers *generally* to contracts that are not assignable under nonbankruptcy law. State laws typically make contracts for personal services nonassignable (where the contract itself is silent); but they make other sorts of contracts nonassignable as well. *See, e.g.,* N.Y. State Finance Law § 138 (1974) (making certain government contracts unassignable); N.Y. General Municipal Law § 109 (1977) (same); N.C. Gen. Stat. § 147-62 (1978) (same). The legislative history of § 365(c) says nothing about "personal services." To the contrary, it speaks of letters of credit, personal loans, and leases — instances in which assigning a contract may place the other party at a significant disadvantage. The history thereby suggests that (c)(1)(A) has a broader reach.

The source of the "personal services" limitation apparently is a bankruptcy court case, *In re Taylor Manufacturing, Inc.,* 6 B.R. 370 (N.D. Ga. 1980), which other bankruptcy courts have followed. The *Taylor* court wrote that (c)(1)(A) should be interpreted narrowly, in part because it believed that (c)(1)(A) conflicted with another section, (f)(1), which states in relevant part:

> Except as provided in subsection (c) . . . , notwithstanding a provision . . . in applicable law that prohibits . . . the assignment of [an executory] contract . . . the trustee may assign [it]. . . .

As a matter of logic, however, we see no conflict, for (c)(1)(A) refers to state laws that prohibit assignment "whether or not" the contract is silent, while (f)(1) contains no such limitation. Apparently (f)(1) includes state laws that prohibit assignment only when the contract is *not* silent about assignment; that is to say, state laws that enforce contract provisions prohibiting assignment. *See* 1 Norton, *Bankruptcy Law and Practice* § 23.14. These state laws are to be ignored. The section specifically excepts (c)(1)(A)'s state laws that forbid assignment even when the contract *is* silent; they are to be heeded. Regardless, we fail to see why a "conflict" suggests that (c)(1)(A) is limited to "personal services."

The *Taylor* court cites 2 *Collier on Bankruptcy* § 365.05 and the Commission Report, H.R. Doc. No. 93-137, 93rd Cong., 1st Sess. 199 (1973), in support. Both of these sources speak of personal services. However, they do not say that (c)(1)(A) was intended to be *limited* to personal services. Indeed, since it often is difficult to decide whether or not a particular duty can be characterized by the label "personal service," it makes sense to avoid this question and simply look to see whether state law would, or would not, make the duty assignable where the contract is silent. Thus, the Fifth Circuit has found no reason for limiting the scope of (c)(1)(A) to personal service contracts. *In re Braniff Airways, Inc.*, 700 F.2d 935, 943 (5th Cir. 1983). Fleet concedes in its brief that "the exception to assignment [of § 365(c)(1)(A)] is not limited to personal services contracts." We therefore reject the district court's conclusion in this respect.

Although the district court did not explicitly decide whether Ford's veto was reasonable, it decided a closely related question. Under other provisions of § 365 a bankruptcy court cannot authorize assignment of an executory contract if 1) the debtor is in default, unless 2) there is "adequate assurance of future performance." § 365(b)(1)(C). Pioneer is in default, but the bankruptcy and district courts found "adequate assurance." For the sake of argument, we shall assume that this finding is equivalent to a finding that Ford's veto of the assignment was unreasonable. And, we shall apply a "clearly erroneous" standard in reviewing the factual element in this lower court finding. Fed. R. Civ. P. 52. On these assumptions, favorable to Fleet, we nonetheless must reverse the district court, for, in our view, any finding of unreasonableness, based on this record, is clearly erroneous.

Our review of the record reveals the following critical facts. First, in accordance with its ordinary business practice and dealer guidelines incorporated into the franchise agreement, Ford would have required Toyota Village, as a dealer, to have a working capital of at least $172,000, of which no more than half could be debt. Toyota Village, however, had a working capital at the end of 1981 of $37,610; and its net worth was $31,747. Although the attorney for Fleet at one point in the bankruptcy proceedings said Toyota Village could borrow some of the necessary capital from a bank, he made no later reference to the point, nor did he ever specifically state how much Toyota Village could borrow. Since the tax returns of Toyota Village's owner showed gross income of $27,500 for 1981, there is no reason to believe that the owner could readily find the necessary equity capital.

Second, at a time when Japanese cars have sold well throughout the United States, Toyota Village has consistently lost money. . . .

At the same time, the record contains no significant evidence tending to refute the natural inference arising from these facts. The bankruptcy court mentioned five factors that it said showed that Toyota Village gave "adequate assurance" that it could do the job.

1) Toyota Village was an established dealership.

2) Toyota Village was "located within 500 yards of the present Ford dealership."

3) Toyota Village had a proven track record for selling cars.

4) Toyota Village was willing and able to pay $15,000 that Pioneer still owed Ford.

5) The owner and sole stockholder of Toyota Village testified that he was willing and able to fulfill the franchise agreement.

The first of these factors (dealer experience), while favoring Toyota Village, is weak, given the record of continuous dealership losses. The second (location) proves little, considering that Pioneer went bankrupt at the very spot. The third (track record) cuts against Toyota Village, not in its favor, for its track record is one of financial loss. The fourth (willingness to pay a $15,000 debt that Pioneer owed Ford) is relevant, but it shows, at most, that Toyota Village *believed* it could make a success of the franchise. The fifth (ability to act as franchisee) is supported by no more than a simple statement by the owner of Toyota Village that he could do the job.

We do not see how the few positive features about Toyota Village that the record reveals can overcome the problem of a history of losses and failure to meet Ford's capital requirements. In these circumstances, Ford would seem perfectly reasonable in withholding its consent to the transfer. Thus, Rhode Island law would make the franchise unassignable.

The Rhode Island authority we have found supports this conclusion. In *Dunne Leases Cars & Trucks v. Kenworth Truck Co.*, 466 A.2d 1153 (R.I. 1983), the Supreme Court of Rhode Island held that failure to meet a condition in the franchise agreement requiring a leasing business to be removed from the dealership site, provided due cause for the manufacturer's decision to *terminate* the dealership agreement. In *Scuncio Motors, Inc. v. Subaru of New England, Inc.*, 555 F. Supp. 1121 (D.R.I. 1982), *aff'd*, 715 F.2d 10 (1st Cir. 1983), the federal district court for the District of Rhode Island wrote that failure to meet a franchise requirement to provide additional selling space provided cause to terminate a dealer contract. Inability to meet capital requirements, as revealed here, would seem to provide reasonable grounds for objecting to a franchise transfer *a fortiori*. If not, a manufacturer would have to allow the transfer of its franchise to virtually any auto dealer.

One might still argue that under Rhode Island law the only "reasonable" course of action for Ford is to allow the transfer and then simply terminate Toyota Village if it fails to perform adequately. This suggestion, however, overlooks the legal difficulties that Ford would have in proving cause for termination under the Rhode

Island "Regulation of Business Practices Among Motor Vehicle Manufacturers, Distributors and Dealers" Act. R.I. Gen. Laws § 31-5.1-4(D)(2). The very purpose of the statute — protecting dealer reliance — suggests that it ought to be more difficult for a manufacturer to terminate a dealer who has invested in a franchise than to oppose the grant of a franchise to one who has not. In any event, the law does not suggest a manufacturer is "unreasonable" in objecting to a transfer unless he would have "good cause" to terminate the transferee. And, to equate the two standards would tend to make the "unreasonable" provision superfluous. Thus, we conclude that the Rhode Island law would make the franchise unassignable on the facts here revealed. Therefore, neither the bankruptcy court nor the district court had the power to authorize the transfer.

. . . .

For these reasons, the judgment of the district court is Reversed.

NOTES AND QUESTIONS

Bankruptcy Code § 365(f)(1) generally provides that a trustee or debtor in possession can assume and assign an executory contract, notwithstanding any contrary provision in the contract or applicable nonbankruptcy law. However, § 365(c)(1) contains an exception to § 365(f)(1). The gist of § 365(c)(1) is that if applicable nonbankruptcy law makes a contract nonassignable, then the debtor may not assume it, even if the contract itself is silent on the point. A companion provision, Code § 365(e)(2), provides that although so-called *ipso facto* clauses are generally unenforceable under § 365(e)(1), they are enforceable in the case of contracts that are nonassignable under nonbankruptcy law. Section 365(c)(1) is often said to bar the assumption of a personal service contract, because it is the classic example of the kind of contract that is nonassignable as a matter of state law, but the reach of § 365(c)(1) extends beyond the realm of personal service contracts. For example, in *Breeden v. Catron*, 158 B.R. 624 (Bankr. E.D. Va. 1992), the debtor was not permitted to assume a real estate partnership agreement. In *Rieser v. Dayton Country Club Co. (In re Magness)*, 972 F.2d 689 (6th Cir. 1992), the court held that a golf club membership could not be assumed and assigned.

The effect of § 365(c)(1) has been a major source of concern to debtors who are licensees of mission critical patents, copyrights, and other intellectual property. In *In re Alltech Plastics, Inc.*, 71 B.R. 686, 689 (Bankr. W.D. Tenn. 1987), the debtor manufactured plastic containers using a patented procedure pursuant to a license from the patent holder. The trustee sought to assume the license and assign it to another manufacturer. Noting that federal common law "classifies patent licenses as personal in nature and not assignable unless expressly made so," the court concluded that the trustee did not have power to assign the patent license absent consent of the patent holder. In *Everex Systems, Inc. v. Cadtrak Corp. (In re CFLC, Inc.)*, 89 F.3d 673 (9th Cir. 1996), the debtor sought to assume a license to use Cadtrak computer graphics and assign it to Everex, which had agreed to buy all of its assets. The court held that the license could not be assumed and assigned without the licensor's consent, because federal law holds a nonexclusive patent license to be personal and nonassignable. Federal law, therefore, would excuse the licensor from accepting performance from, or rendering it to, anyone other than the debtor. The court then explained why federal law regards a nonexclusive patent license as personal:

> The fundamental policy of the patent system is to "encourage the creation and disclosure of new, useful, and non-obvious advances in technology and design" by granting the inventor the reward of "the exclusive right to practice the invention for a period of years." Allowing free assignability . . . of nonexclusive patent licenses would undermine the reward that encourages invention because a party seeking to use the patented invention could either seek a license from the patent holder or seek an assignment of an existing patent license from a licensee. In essence, every licensee would become a potential competitor with the licensor-patent holder in the market for licenses under the patents. And while the patent holder could presumably control the absolute number of licenses in existence under a free-assignability regime, it would lose the very important ability to control the identity of its licensees. Thus, any license a patent holder granted even to the smallest firm in the product market most remote from its own would be fraught with the danger that the licensee would assign it to the patent holder's most serious competitor, a party whom the patent holder itself might be absolutely unwilling to license. As a practical matter, free assignability of patent licenses might spell the end to paid-up licenses such as the one involved in this case. Few patent holders would be willing to grant a license in return for a one-time lump-sum payment, rather than for per-use royalties, if the license could be assigned to a completely different company which might make far greater use of the patented invention than could the original licensee.

89 F.3d 673, at 679.

The rationale of *Alltech* and *Everex* has been applied with equal force to other kinds of intellectual property licenses. In *In re Patient Educ. Media, Inc.*, 210 B.R. 237 (Bankr. S.D.N.Y. 1997), the debtor was not allowed to transfer its nonexclusive license to use the copyrighted work over the copyright owner's objections. Thus, absent the licensor's consent, neither a trustee nor debtor in possession will be able to wring any value for the estate out of intellectual property licenses by assigning them.

Suppose, however, that the debtor intends to reorganize in Chapter 11 and seeks to assume (but not assign) a nonassignable contract? What result then? In *Perlman v. Catapult Entm't, Inc. (In re Catapult Entm't, Inc.)*, 165 F.3d 747 (9th Cir. 1999), the debtor sought to assume nonexclusive patent licenses for online video game technology. Perlman, the patent owner, objected on the grounds that the licenses were not assumable under federal patent law. The debtor argued that Congress never intended in § 365(c)(1) to bar debtors in possession from assuming their own contracts. The lower courts agreed and confirmed the debtor's plan. The Ninth Circuit reversed. It held that whether or not the debtor intended to assign the license to a third party, it could not assume it, if nonbankruptcy law prohibited assignment.

To understand how the court reached this conclusion, a little history is helpful. As originally drafted, § 365(c)(1) prohibited assignment if nonbankruptcy law excused the nondebtor party from accepting performance from or rendering it to *a trustee*. The opinion in *In re Midway Airlines, Inc.*, 6 F.3d 492, 495 (7th Cir. 1993), explains the purpose of this restriction. The issue in that case was whether the debtor, an airline, could assume and assign airport gate leases that contained anti-assignment provisions. En route to holding that the gate leases were assumable and assignable, the court observed:

> [The purpose of § 365(c)(1)] is rather narrow: to prevent a trustee from forcing a party to accept performance from, or provide performance to, someone other than the party with whom it contracted in those situations where the identity of the party is central to the obligation itself. . . . There can be little doubt, therefore, that, had [the airport] contracted with Luciano Pavarotti to sing in its passenger facilities in order to soothe the souls of weary travelers, it could not be compelled to accept performance from pop-star Michael Jackson in the event of the great tenor's bankruptcy. On the other hand, the payment of rent pursuant to a lease is hardly the type of performance that depends upon the identity of the party that is to perform, i.e., the lessee.

However, amendments in 1984 and 1986 have muddled the language of § 365(c)(1) and produced unintended and problematic results. As previously noted, § 365(c)(1) as originally enacted, prohibited assignment if nonbankruptcy law excused the nondebtor party from accepting performance from or rendering it to *a trustee*. Section 365(c)(1) was later amended to prohibit assumption and assignment if nonbankruptcy law excuses the party from accepting performance from or rendering it to a person *other than the debtor in possession*. The purpose of this amendment was not to prevent a debtor in possession such as Luciano Pavarotti in the preceding example from assuming a performance contract. On the contrary, it was intended to prevent the nondebtor airport in the example from terminating a contract and firing a debtor such as Pavarotti merely because he was in bankruptcy. However, it is now possible — and some courts believe necessary — to construe § 365(c)(1) as meaning that if nonbankruptcy law provides that the nondebtor party would have to consent to assignment of a contract to someone other than the debtor in possession, then even the debtor in possession cannot assume the contract. In other words, these courts hold that a contract is nonassumable if under nonbankruptcy law it is unassignable. This reasoning is said to employ a "hypothetical test," because it hypothesizes that a contract will be assigned whether or not it actually will be assigned. It has been employed by the Third, Fourth, Eleventh, and Ninth circuits. *In re James Cable Partners*, 27 F.3d 534 (11th Cir. 1994); *In re Catron*, 158 B.R. 629 (E.D. Va. 1993), *aff'd without opinion*, 25 F.3d 1038 (4th Cir. 1994); *In re West Elec., Inc.*, 852 F.2d 79 (3d Cir. 1988). *See also, In re Access Beyond Techs., Inc.*, 237 B.R. 32 (Bankr. D. Del. 1999).

Other courts have rejected the "hypothetical" approach as "hypertechnical," noting that the thrust of § 365 is to prevent the nondebtor party from terminating a contract simply because the debtor is in bankruptcy and that, in most cases, the prepetition debtor and the debtor in possession are identical. They have concluded that § 365(c)(1) should not bar a debtor in possession from assuming a contract merely because it is not assignable, and have employed an "actual" rather than a "hypothetical" test. *In re Cardinal Indust., Inc.*, 116 B.R. 964 (Bankr. S.D. Ohio

1990). One court has explained the difference between the "hypothetical" and "actual" tests this way:

> The hypothetical test prohibits assumption and performance by the debtor in possession if applicable law would excuse the nondebtor party from accepting performance from an entity other than the debtor. In other words, under the hypothetical test, if the debtor in possession cannot assign the contract to a third party, the debtor itself cannot assume the contract. . . . Under the actual test, however, assumption will be denied only if performance of the assumed contract by the debtor in possession will in fact deprive the nondebtor party to the contract of the benefit of the bargain. Since the debtor is the very party with whom the nondebtor party contracted, it is usually quite difficult for the nondebtor party to persuade the court that performance by the debtor will eviscerate its contractual expectations.

In re Edward G. Leroux, 1997 Bankr. LEXIS 971, at note 5 (Bankr. D. Mass. June 30, 1997), quoting *How to Transfer a Nonassignable Patent License*, 17 Bankr. L. Letter 1 No. 4 (Warren, Gorham & Lamont, 1997).

In *Institut Pasteur v. Cambridge Biotech Corp.*, 104 F.3d 489 (1st Cir. 1997), the First Circuit rejected the hypothetical test, holding instead that section 365(c) requires a:

> case-by-case inquiry into whether the nondebtor party . . . actually was being forced to accept performance from someone other than the debtor party with whom it originally contracted. Where the particular transaction envisions that the debtor-in-possession would assume and continue to perform under an executory contract, the bankruptcy court cannot simply presume as a matter of law that the debtor-in-possession is a legal entity materially distinct from the prepetition debtor with whom the nondebtor party contracted.

Id. at 493.

Interestingly, in the *Pasteur* case, the licensor argued that it was being forced to accept performance from a new party, because, under the plan, the debtor's stock was being transferred to a new parent company. The court disagreed.

> Stock sales are not mergers whereby outright title and ownership of the licensee-corporation's assets (including its patent licenses) pass to the acquiring corporation. Rather, as a corporation, [the debtor] is a legal entity distinct from its shareholders. Absent compelling grounds for disregarding its corporate form, [the debtor's] separate legal identity and its ownership of the patent cross-licenses, survive without interruption, notwithstanding repeated and even drastic changes in ownership.

Id. at 494.

The court distinguished between a sale of stock and an outright transfer of the license. A proposed amendment to the Code would resolve this conflict among the circuits by providing that a debtor's ability to assume a contract would not depend on its ability to assign it.

[G]   Adequate Assurance of Future Performance

IN RE U.L. RADIO CORP.
United States Bankruptcy Court, Southern District of New York
19 B.R. 537 (1982)

MEMORANDUM & ORDER

JOHN J. GALGAY, BANKRUPTCY JUDGE.

Debtor, U.L. Radio Corp., has moved for an order, pursuant to Bankruptcy Code section 365(f), authorizing it to assume its lease ("Lease") with Jemrock Realty Company ("Jemrock"), the landlord, and authorizing U.L. Radio to assign the Lease to Just Heaven Restaurant, Ltd. ("Just Heaven"). U.L. Radio operates the leasehold as a television sales and service store. Just Heaven, the prospective assignee, will operate the premises as a small bistro. Jemrock opposes such an assignment, citing a use clause in the Lease which provides that the lessee shall use the premises only for television service and sale of electrical appliances. Jemrock asserts that the assignment of the Lease to Just Heaven would unlawfully modify the Lease by violating the use clause. Such modification, Jemrock avers, is not permitted under section 365 without the landlord's consent, which consent Jemrock withholds.

. . . The Court grants debtor's motion to assume and assign the Lease to Just Heaven.

I. Background

On September 17, 1979, the debtor entered into the Lease with Jemrock for a store located at 2656 Broadway, New York, New York. The store is located in a building which is also occupied by a grocery store, a Chinese restaurant, a liquor store, and 170 apartments. The term of the Lease is for ten years. The rent required to be paid is as follows: $9600 per year from November 1, 1979, to October 31, 1982; $10,800 from November 1, 1982, to October 31, 1985; and $12,000 from November 1, 1985 to October 31, 1989. Paragraph 43 of the Rider to the Lease provides that the tenant may assign the Lease with the written consent of the Landlord, which consent is not to be unreasonably withheld.

On May 20, 1981, the debtor filed an original petition under Chapter 11 of the Bankruptcy Code and continues to operate its business as debtor in possession. No creditors' committee has been formed. The debtor intends to propose a liquidation plan of reorganization. The debtor is current in the payment of rent and related charges required by the terms of the Lease and is not in default of any of the Lease terms.

In furtherance of its intention to liquidate all of its assets and to propose a plan of reorganization, the debtor, subject to the approval of this Court, entered into an assignment of the Lease to Just Heaven. The proposed assignment provides, *inter alia*, that Just Heaven will pay to the Debtor as consideration for the assignment as follows: for the period commencing three months after this Court's approval of the assignment to October 31, 1988, the sum of $2000 per month. Such payments will fund a plan paying unsecured creditors 100 percent of their claims. Rockwell International, the largest creditor, recommends the assignment.

The president of Just Heaven has executed a personal guarantee for the payment of rent in favor of the landlord for the first two years of the assignment, together with a statement that her net worth exceeds $50,000.

The Lease provides . . . that "any noise emanating from said premises shall be deemed a breach of the terms and conditions of this Lease." Just Heaven has allocated $20,000 for construction, including soundproofing. David Humpal St. James, Vice President and Secretary as well as a director and a shareholder of Just Heaven, is a noted interior designer including the design of commercial restaurants. His design work has involved soundproofing.

II. Issues

Two issues confront this Court:

(1) Have the provisions of section 365, regarding assumption and assignment of leases, been satisfied?

(2) Can deviation from a use clause prevent the assignment of a lease, when the assumption and assignment otherwise comport with the requirements of section 365?

III. Assumption and Assignment Under Section 365

Code section 365 governs the assumption and assignment of executory contracts, providing broad authority to a trustee or debtor in possession to assume and assign an unexpired lease. . . . The aim of this statutory authority to assume a lease is to "assist in the debtor's rehabilitation or liquidation." [H.R. 95-595 ("*House Report*") at 348.]

. . . .

A. Requirements of Assumption

The first requirement of assignment under section 365(f)(2) is proper assumption under section 365. § 365(f)(2)(A). The broad authority of a trustee or debtor in possession to assume is limited in Code section 365 by subsections (b), (c), and (d). *House Report* at 347.

Section 365(b)(1) and (2) prescribe conditions to assumption of a lease if a default has occurred. "Subsection (b) requires the [debtor] to cure any default in the . . . lease and to provide adequate assurance of future performance . . . before he may assume." *House Report* at 347. No default exists under the Lease before this Court; therefore, the subsection (b) requirements for assignment are not applicable.

. . . .

B. Adequate Assurance of Future Performance

The second requirement of assignment is adequate assurance of future performance § 365(f)(2)(B). Adequate assurance also appears in [§ 365(b)(1)(C)] as a requirement of assumption if an executory contract is in default. The phrase "adequate assurance of future performance" is not found in the Bankruptcy Act.

. . . In the legislative history of section 365(b), Congress while discussing assumption under section 365(b) and the bankruptcy clause under section 365(f), provided this explanation of adequate assurance:

> If a trustee is to assume a contract or lease, the courts will have to insure that the trustee's performance under the contract or lease gives the other contracting party the full benefit of the bargain.

House Report at 348.

Beyond equating adequate assurance with the full benefit of the bargain, Congress offers no definition of adequate assurance except in the case of real property leases in shopping centers. The Lease at issue here is not located in a shopping center. Congress described a shopping center as "often a carefully planned enterprise, and though it consists of numerous individual tenants, the center is planned as a single unit, often subject to a master lease or financing agreement." *House Report* at 348. The building in which U.L. Radio is located is primarily a residential apartment building, with a liquor store, a grocery store, a restaurant, and U.L. Radio on the first floor. Thus the specific provisions of adequate assurance in the shopping center case do not apply to the assignment at issue here.

. . . Adequate assurance of future performance are not words of art, but are to be given practical, pragmatic construction. What constitutes "adequate assurance" is to be determined by factual conditions. The broad authorization of the trustee or debtor to assume or assign unexpired leases, notwithstanding anti-assignment or bankruptcy clauses, prompted the admonition from Congress that the courts must "be sensitive to the rights of the nondebtor party to . . . unexpired leases." *House Report* at 348.

The phrase "adequate assurance of future performance" was adopted from Uniform Commercial Code section 2-609. Report of the Commission on Bankruptcy Laws of the United States, H.R. Doc. No. 93-137, 93d Cong., 1st Sess. Pt. II 156–57 (1973). U.C.C. section 2-609 provides that a party with reasonable grounds for insecurity regarding another party's performance may demand "adequate assurance." Official Comment 4 to section 2-609 . . . indicates that "adequate assurance" focuses on the financial condition of a contracting party and his ability to meet his financial obligations.

In *In re Pin Oaks Apartments*, 7 Bankr. 364, 6 B.C.D. 1396 (Bkrtcy. S.D. Tex. 1980), the Court found that changes in financial provisions of a lease, a percentage rental clause and a sublease provision which protected that rental clause, precluded a finding that adequate assurance had been provided because of the drastic effect the changes would have on rentals received.

Thus, the primary focus of adequate assurance is the assignee's ability to satisfy financial obligations under the lease. In this case, the president of the assignee has executed a personal guarantee of the payment of rent in favor of the landlord for the first two years of the assignment, together with a statement that her net worth exceeds $50,000. The assignee has budgeted $20,000 for construction, enhancing the chances of success of the assignee's enterprise. The assignee will have operating capital of an additional $30,000. Upon these facts, the Court rules that adequate assurance of future financial performance has been provided by the assignee.

IV. Use Clause

However, adequate assurance of future financial performance is not the complete statutory requirement; adequate assurance of future performance is. The financial capability of an assignee may be sufficient for a finding of adequate assurance under an executory sales contract or a similar commercial transaction. In a landlord-tenant relationship, more than an assignee's ability to comply with the financial provisions of a lease may be required. More particularly, will compliance with a use clause be required in order to provide adequate assurance?

Congress indicates that adequate assurance will give the landlord the full benefit of his bargain. *House Report* at 348. In its case-by-case determination of those factors, beyond financial assurance, which constitute the landlord's bargain, the Court will generally consider the provisions of the lease to be assigned. . . . [A]s-sumption and assignment of a lease entails acceptance by the assignee of the burdens as well as the benefits of the lease[.]

However, it is equally clear that, by requiring provision of adequate assurance under section 365, i.e., "the lessor's receipt of the 'full benefit of his bargain' " Congress did not require the Court to assure "literal fulfillment by the lessee of each and every term of the bargain." . . . Section 365, by its own terms, empowers the court to render unenforceable bankruptcy clauses and anti-assignment clauses which permit modification or termination of a lease for filing in bankruptcy or assignment of the lease. § 365(e), (f)(3). Section 365(k) relieves the estate of liability for future breaches of a lease after assignment, notwithstanding lease provisions to the contrary.

The Court in *In re Pin Oaks Apartments* argued that court authority to abrogate lease provisions extends only to those provisions expressly stated by Congress:

> If Congress intended to give this Court or the trustee the power to abrogate any contractual rights between a debtor and non-debtor contract-ing party other than anti-assignment and "ipso facto" [i.e. bankruptcy] clauses, it would have expressly done so.

7 B.R. at 367, 6 B.C.D. at 1398.

Such a narrow view of court authority is not supported by the statute or the legislative history. First, such a narrow view would frustrate the express policy of Congress favoring assignment. Under the *Pin Oaks* reasoning, lessors could employ very specific use clauses to prevent assignment and thus circumvent the Code. Section 365(f), in broad language, empowers the Court to authorize assign-ment of an unexpired lease and invalidate any lease provision which would terminate or modify the lease because of the assignment of that lease. § 365(f)(1), (3). Any lease provision, not merely one entitled "anti-assignment clause," would be subject to the court's scrutiny regarding its anti-assignment effect. The court could render unenforceable any provision whose sole effect is to restrict assignment, "as contrary to the policy of [subsection (f)(3)]." *House Report* at 349.

. . . .

Thus, provision of adequate assurance of future performance does not require an assignee's literal compliance with each and every term of the lease. The court may permit deviations from strict enforcement of any provision including a use clause.

One commentator suggested that the court render completely invalid any use clause in a non-shopping center lease because: (1) "the lessor is seeking to protect his tenant mix with the lease provision, and the Code does not require the court to provide such protection"; and (2) a use clause "invalidly conditions assignment." Fogel, *Executory Contracts* at 364 (footnote omitted); *see* Simpson, *Leases* at 37 n. 45. The Court rejects this *"per se* unenforceable" reading of a use clause.

However, the Court will not go to the other extreme and adopt the "insubstantial" breach or disruption standard for non-shopping center cases that is applicable only to shopping center leases. The insubstantial breaches and disruptions language of section 365(b)(3) "clearly reflects an attempt to limit the effects of what was understood — and feared — to be the more expansive authority conferred by the balance of [s]ection 365(a)." The Court's authority to waive strict enforcement of lease provisions in the non-shopping center cases will permit deviations which would exceed those permitted in the shopping center cases.

Within the range between unenforceability of a use clause and insubstantial breaches of a use clause, the Code provides no specific standard by which to measure permissible deviations in use. Whatever standard is applied must serve the policy aims of Congress.

Section 365 expresses a clear Congressional policy favoring assumption and assignment. Such a policy will insure that potential valuable assets will not be lost by a debtor who is reorganizing his affairs or liquidating assets for distribution to creditors. This policy parallels case law which disfavors forfeiture. To prevent an assignment of an unexpired lease by demanding strict enforcement of a use clause, and thereby contradict clear Congressional policy, a landlord or lessor must show that actual and substantial detriment would be incurred by him if the deviation in use was permitted.

In this case, the contemplated deviation in use is from an appliance store to a small bistro. The building in which the unexpired leasehold is located already contains a restaurant, a laundry, and a liquor store. The landlord has failed to demonstrate any actual and substantial detriment which he would incur if the proposed deviation in use is permitted. The Court also notes that the contemplated use, along with the planned soundproofing, will have no adverse effect on other tenants in the building. Thus, this Court rules that the use clause may not be enforced so as to block assignment of this lease to Just Heaven. The fact that Jemrock withholds its consent to the proposed assignment will not prevent the assignment.

. . . .

Congress, in section 365, has stated a general policy favoring assignment. Balanced against this general policy is the requirement that the non-debtor contracting party receive the full benefit of his bargain. Jemrock Realty will receive the full benefit of its bargain under the proposed assignment of the leasehold from U.L. Radio to Just Heaven. No defaults exist under the lease. The lease has properly been assumed and Just Heaven has provided adequate assurance of future performance. The landlord has shown no actual or substantial detriment to him from the proposed assignment. The statutory requirements have been satisfied. The assignment is authorized.

It is so ordered.

NOTES AND QUESTIONS

Would the result in *U.L. Radio* have been different if the leases were for premises located in a suburban shopping mall rather than a freestanding, downtown commercial building? As the *U.L.* court noted, special rules govern the assumption (and assignment) of shopping center leases. Code § 365(b)(3) provides that before it may assume a shopping center lease that is in default, and before it may assign to a third party a shopping center lease whether or not it is in default, a trustee or debtor must give adequate assurance that it or the proposed assignee will be able to perform its obligations under the contract. The Code actually defines what it means by "adequate assurance of future performance" when that term is used in the context of a shopping center, but it does not define "shopping center," leaving that to the courts on a case-by-case basis. *See In re Joshua Slocum, Ltd.*, 922 F.2d 1081 (3d Cir. 1990).

The *Joshua Slocum* court discussed how location "is only one element in the determination of whether a group of stores can properly be described as a 'shopping center.'" However, more significant are the following criteria sketched in *Collier on Bankruptcy, In re Goldblatt Bros., Inc.*, 766 F.2d 1136, 1140-41 (7th Cir. 1985), and *In re 905 Int'l Stores, Inc.*, 57 B.R. 786, 788-89 (E.D. Mo. 1985):

(a) A combination of leases;

(b) All leases held by a single landlord;

(c) All tenants engaged in the commercial retail distribution of goods;

(d) The presence of a common parking area;

(e) The purposeful development of the premises as a shopping center;

(f) The existence of a master lease;

(g) The existence of fixed hours during which all stores are open;

(h) The existence of joint advertising;

(i) Contractual interdependence of the tenants as evidenced by restrictive use provisions in their leases;

(j) The existence of percentage rent provisions in the leases;

(k) The right of the tenants to terminate their leases if the anchor tenant terminates its lease;

(l) Joint participation by tenants in trash removal and other maintenance;

(m) The existence of a tenant mix; and

(n) The contiguity of the stores.

NOTES AND QUESTIONS

In *In re Jamesway Corp.*, 201 B.R. 73 (Bankr. S.D.N.Y. 1996), the court held that a provision requiring a debtor-lessee to share with the shopping center landlord the proceeds of subletting or assigning a store lease was unenforceable. Similarly, in *In re Office Products of Am., Inc.*, 140 B.R. 407 (Bankr. W.D. Tex. 1992), the court held that a lease provision requiring the debtor-tenant to pay its landlord the proceeds of assigning a lease was the functional equivalent of an anti-assignment clause.

§ 7.07   WHEN SHOULD A COURT AUTHORIZE REJECTION?

PROBLEM 7.1

Assume that several months prior to filing its Chapter 11 petition, Amphydynamics agreed to sell 1,000 flat panel computer monitors to Buyer One, a retailer, for $100 each. Due to unanticipated demand, the wholesale price of the monitors is now $200. To meet customer demand, Buyer Two, a larger retailer, has offered to buy as many monitors as Amphy can deliver within the next month for $200. Amphy would like to reject the contract with Buyer One and sell the monitors to Buyer Two instead. Can it do that?

IN RE CHI FENG HUANG
United States Bankruptcy Appellate Panel, Ninth Circuit
23 B.R. 798 (1982)

Elliott, Bankruptcy Judge.

FACTS

Florence Chi-Feng Huang ("Florence") filed her Chapter 11 petition in November of 1980; Florence's mother, Sheila Chen Huang ("Sheila"), filed her Chapter 11 petition in February 1981. Jerome E. Robertson was appointed trustee of each estate shortly after the respective filings. The debtors manage and operate a business known as The Kaleidescope, a California Corporation. The Kaleidescope is also before the same court, having filed a Chapter 11 case February 3, 1981.

The most significant asset in the estates is an apartment complex located in Menlo Park, California commonly known as the "Caroline Apartments." . . . For the purposes of this appeal, the parties stipulated the value of the complex is $2,400,000. The debtors' equity, deducting several deeds of trust, is approximately $320,000.

On June 13, 1979 the Huangs entered into a written contract to sell the complex to Robert L. Pierce, the Appellee in this proceeding, for $1,900,000. Pierce has not taken possession of the complex and no part of the purchase price has been paid. We assume for the purposes of this appeal that Pierce has a valid, specifically enforceable contract. Pierce sought relief from the automatic stay in order to prosecute a pending state court performance action. The trustee responded by seeking to reject the contract as to both estates.

The trial court considered the relief from stay issue and the rejection issue simultaneously. It refused to permit rejection of the contract and granted relief from stay. The court denied permission to reject the contract on the grounds that to do so would violate fundamental principles of fair dealing and that "the primary beneficiaries of rejection would be the debtors, not creditors, and that is not a proper use of the rejection device." At the heart of this conclusion is the trial court's apparent conviction that each estate is solvent and that most of the unsecured claims scheduled in the case are "questionable" debts owing to friends or relatives of the debtors or to The Kaleidoscope.

Although Sheila listed a total of $17,887.43 owing to unsecured creditors and Florence listed $660,187.43 in unsecured debts, the court disregarded the "questionable" debts and concluded that even assuming the two estates were forced to honor the specific performance contract, approximately $320,000 in equity in the apartment complex would be realized from the sale and that this amount exceeds the amount needed to pay in full all of the unquestioned unsecured creditors.

The principal issues are: Did the trial court err or abuse its discretion by refusing to permit rejection of the contract? Did the trial court err in disregarding for the purposes of the rejection issue the "questionable" claims against Florence? We conclude that based upon the record before it that the court did err in refusing permission to reject the contract and also in disregarding claims of creditors and reverse.

Standards Governing the Court's Power to Approve or Disapprove Rejection of Executory Contracts

. . . § 365(a) provides, in part, that the trustee, subject to court approval, may assume or reject an executory contract of a debtor. At 2 COLLIER ON BANKRUPTCY (15th Ed.) ¶ 365.03 (365-14) the editors state:

> There are several schools of thought concerning the standard to be applied in rejecting an executory contract. The rationale is often based in a rather haphazard way upon the nature of the contract in question. . . . [T]he concept of rejection of executory contracts had its roots in the principle that the trustee might abandon burdensome property. From this has grown one view that for the trustee to reject an executory contract, the contract must in fact be burdensome, i.e., involve some loss or detriment to the estate. What, however, of the situation where the contract, while profitable or

generally beneficial, could be, if rejected, replaced by a more attractive arrangement? The leading case is unquestionably *Group of Institutional Investors v. Chicago, Milwaukee, St. Paul & Pacific R. Co.*, 318 U.S. 523 [63 S. Ct. 727, 87 L. Ed. 959] (1943), which is the strongest statement of the "business judgment test."

The trial court held that it was not necessary for it to determine whether the "business judgment" or "burdensome" test should apply because it concluded to permit rejection under either test would, under the circumstances, violate fundamental principles of fair dealing and give the debtors a windfall.

We believe the "business judgment" rule is the standard which controls the court's right to disapprove the trustee's decision to reject an executory contract. In relying upon grounds of "fairness" to the party whose contract is rejected the trial court erred.

The great weight of modern authority holds that whether an executory contract should be rejected is a matter within the business judgment of the trustee. . . .

We believe rejection of the burdensome test in favor of the "business judgment" rule is dictated by logic as much as by precedent. We agree with Professor Krasnowiecki's view of the burdensome test:

> . . . The purpose of the power to reject is to augment the estate of the debtor. For this purpose, there seems to be no difference between an obligation which consumes cash, and an obligation which, because of its depressive effect on a particular asset or because of its undervaluation of that asset consumes a part of the value of that asset. In the end the latter will turn up as a net reduction in cash to pay the creditors.

Krasnowiecki, *The Impact of the New Bankruptcy Reform Act on Real Estate Development and Financing*, 53 Am. Bankr. L. J. 363, 382 (1979).

In short we find little judicial or logical support for the restrictive burdensome test and therefore cannot sustain the trial court's decision on the grounds that the contract with Pierce is not "burdensome."

Nature of the Business Judgment Test

What are the standards that are to guide the court and trustee in exercising their "business judgment?" Stated differently: What are the criteria which the court and trustee should legitimately consider in exercising their "business judgment?" The primary issue is whether rejection would benefit the general unsecured creditors. This may involve a balancing of interests. In *Matter of Minges*, 602 F.2d at 43, the Second Circuit noted the need for a flexible test, stating that, "the trustee and ultimately the court, must exercise their discretion fairly in the interest of all who have had the misfortune of dealing with the debtor." This statement illustrates that it is proper for the court to refuse to authorize rejection of a lease or executory contract where the party whose contract is to be rejected would be damaged disproportionately to any benefit to be derived by the general creditors of the estate as for example where most of the "benefit" of rejection of the contract would be captured by a third party at the expense of the unsecured creditors. This statement does not sanction rejection of a contract because of a generalized concern that a party whose contract is rejected will be damaged. The *Minges* court evidenced its view that "benefit to the unsecured creditors" was the primary concern by remanding the case for findings on whether in the trial court's judgment there was "a reasonable likelihood that general creditors will derive substantial or significant benefit from the proposed lease rejection." 602 F.2d at 44.

We now consider the application of these principles to the attempt to reject the contract with Pierce.

Application of the Business Judgment Test to Pierce's Contract

We do not view "principles of fair dealing" as a standard independent of the "business judgment" test. The trial court relied upon two underlying notions to support its view that to grant permission to reject the contract would work an injustice inconsistent with the intention of § 365(a). The first is that it is somehow unfair to Pierce to force him to give up the benefits of the appreciation in value of the apartment complex. The second and more important notion is that to permit rejection in this case would be unfair because it would result in a windfall to the debtors and their friends and relatives who hold "questionable" claims against the estate.

Unfairness of Rejecting Real Estate Sales Contracts

The fact that the expectations of a vendee are disappointed is not sufficient grounds standing alone to deny the trustee permission to reject. Any rejection will inevitably entail the disappointment of legitimate expectations. A basic policy of the Bankruptcy laws is to spread the burdens evenly among both those who may have loaned the debtor money and those who might have obtained a profit from dealing with him.

While it may seem inequitable to Pierce that he is deprived of the anticipated profit in the form of appreciation in value of the complex in favor of the other unsecured creditors of the estate, this result is required by well defined Bankruptcy policies. . . . To the extent the trial court's decision in refusing to authorize rejection of the contract relies upon Pierce's claim of unfairness, it is not consistent with the "business judgment" rule because it gives insufficient weight to the benefit accruing to the unsecured creditors arising from the rejection.

Whether The Debtors or Creditors Would Primarily Benefit from Rejection

The trial court's fundamental reason for declining to approve the proposed rejection was its conclusion that, "the primary beneficiaries of rejection would be the debtors, not creditors, and that is not a proper use of the rejection device." Thus, although it disclaimed any need to choose between the "burdensome" or "business judgment" tests, it applied the primary criterium of the "business judgment" test, benefit to the creditors. We hold that it did so incorrectly. It apparently viewed its conclusion as a corollary to its finding that:

Sale of the Caroline Apartments to Pierce, pursuant to the terms of the contract, would provide Florence and Sheila Huang with net proceeds of approximately $320,000.00. This amount exceeds the amount needed to pay in full all of the unquestioned unsecured creditors of Florence and Sheila Huang.

Appellant's Excerpts of Record at 45.

The conclusion that the debtors would be the primary beneficiaries of rejection and that rejection is therefore improper does not flow from the quoted findings for two reasons.

Exclusion From Consideration of Questioned Claims

First, by excluding the "questioned" claims from the computation, the court implicitly assumes that the claims of the "questioned" unsecured creditors are (1) invalid, or (2) that any benefit accruing to the friends and relatives of the debtors who hold those claims inures vicariously to the benefit of the debtors. Neither of these implicit assumptions is warranted.First, by excluding the "questioned" claims from the computation, the court implicitly assumes that the claims of the "questioned" unsecured creditors are (1) invalid, or (2) that any benefit accruing to the friends and relatives of the debtors who hold those claims inures vicariously to the benefit of the debtors. Neither of these implicit assumptions is warranted.

Although some evidence was taken at the time of the hearing on rejection relating to the various "questioned" claims, none of the holders of those claims had notice of, or were represented at the hearing. Florence and Sheila have personally guaranteed certain debts owed by Kaleidoscope, but the trial court has made no findings regarding the solvency of Kaleidoscope or the amount of any claim against the debtors with respect to Kaleidoscope obligations guaranteed by them. The failure to make findings regarding the Kaleidoscope related claims leaves in doubt whether the trial court considered those claims as "questioned" and if not whether it excluded them in reaching its conclusion that enough equity was available to pay the unsecured creditors. Under § 1111 . . . the scheduling of a claim or the filing of a proof of claim in a Chapter 11 case is prima facie evidence of the validity and amount of a noncontingent liquidated claim. Under § 502(a), a claim is deemed allowed unless objected to.

In light of these rules and the nonparticipation of the "questioned" creditors it was improper for the court to base its conclusion on the presumed invalidity of some of the claims against the estate. This is particularly so where the disapproval of the rejection request may have, depending upon the quantity of "questioned" claims ultimately allowed, a substantial effect on the net payout percentage to unsecured creditors. We also note that to the extent the "questioned" claims are ultimately allowed, the unquestioned claimants would be forced to accept a reduced payout.

Allowable claims of friends and relatives of the debtors are not given an inferior priority to all other unsecured claims. Title § 502(b)(5) limits allowable claims by insiders for services to the reasonable value of such services. By implication in all other respects, allowable claims of insiders should be treated as any other claim would be in the absence of inequitable conduct by them. . . . To the extent friends or relatives hold allowable unsecured claims, they are entitled to share in any enhanced value of the estate resulting from rejection of an executory contract with all other unsecured creditors.

Of course in determining whether a claim is allowable, the court may consider all relevant evidence, including the relationship of the parties. While some of the claims may appear open to question, it is not so self-evident that the claims could be disregarded without a hearing. We do not suggest that the court might not have temporarily refused to permit rejection pending consideration of the allowability of the "questioned" claims. Nor do we suggest that more summary treatment of the problem might not have been allowable if exigent circumstances had dictated. Here there were no such circumstances. Given the potential prejudice to holders of both "questioned" and unquestioned claims, the decision without a hearing on notice to the parties concerned, was improper.

Vendee's Damages

The debtors cannot directly become the primary beneficiaries of rejection either. Rejection of the executory contract by Pierce in this case would permit the estate to reap the benefits of the appreciation in value that has occurred in the three years since the contract was signed. Under § 365(g) the rejection of the executory contract would be treated as a breach of the contract and would entitle Pierce to present a claim against the estate for damages, presumably including the appreciation in value of the property. In effect the appreciation would be divided equally among all unsecured creditors including the vendee whose contract is rejected. The result is similar to the recovery of a preferential transfer or the voiding of a lien on property of the estate.

If without regard to rejection of the contract, the estate is solvent and the unsecured creditors would receive 100 percent of their claims, rejection would then accomplish nothing for the general unsecured creditors. We do not doubt that if in the judgment of the bankruptcy court, an estate is solvent in the sense that a 100 percent payout will occur in the event of liquidation, that it is within the discretion of the court to decline to authorize rejection of a contract on the grounds that no benefit would accrue to the creditors from the rejection. In such circumstances, rejection might only impose unwarranted administrative expenses or delay.

NOTES AND QUESTIONS

(1) *Tempering Business Judgment.* The business judgment standard notwithstanding, there is bountiful authority for the proposition that a bankruptcy court is a court of equity and has the power and duty to see that injustice and unfairness do not result from the exercise of its jurisdiction. *See e.g., Pepper v. Litton,* 308 U.S. 295 (1939). Thus, even in the *Chi-Feng Huang* case, the court acknowledged, "It is proper for the court to refuse to authorize rejection . . . where the party whose contract is to be rejected would be damaged disproportionately to any benefit to be derived by the general creditors of the estate."

Such a lopsided situation was presented in *In re Petur U.S.A. Instrument Co., Inc.,* 35 B.R. 561 (Bankr. W.D. Wash. 1983), where rejection of a 20-year license agreement would have destroyed the business of a company organized solely for the purpose of marketing the debtor's products. The court explained:

> [H]ere we are not only dealing with harm resulting from a mere disappointment of legitimate expectations. Rather we are dealing with the actual ruination of an otherwise profitable, successful and ongoing business. Equity will not permit such a result.

35 B.R. at 564. Interestingly, the *Petur* court said that its holding was also influenced by the seemingly dim prospects for the debtor's recovery whether it rejected the license or not. The court's skepticism was based not only on the debtor's continued operating losses and its failure to propose a reorganization plan, but on the fact — of which the court took judicial notice — that fewer than 4% of the Chapter 11 cases in its judicial district resulted in confirmed reorganization plans! *See also In re Monarch Tool & Mfg. Co.*, 114 B.R. 134 (Bankr. S.D. Ohio 1990).

(2) *Effect of Decree of Specific Performance.* A contract for the sale of land ceases to be executory — and rejectable in bankruptcy — at the instant a decree of specific performance is issued. *In re Sundial Asphalt Co.*, 147 B.R. 72 (E.D.N.Y. 1992). The theory is that once court has ordered specific performance, the parties' unperformed obligations are merely nonmaterial or ministerial acts through which they carry out the court's directive. *Roxse Homes, Inc. v. Roxse Homes Ltd. Partnership*, 83 B.R. 185 (D. Mass. 1988).

§ 7.08 REJECTION OF COLLECTIVE BARGAINING AGREEMENTS

PROBLEM 7.2

As you may recall from the story about Amphydynamics that appeared in a recent issue of *Mismanagement Week* (*see* "Meet Your Client: The Great Amphydynamics Business Disaster," in Chapter 1, § 1.01, *above*), Amphydynamics' business ills were attributed, in part, to a long strike by workers at the company's St. Louis assembly plant and high labor costs. Only a month or so before the company entered the congenial climate of Chapter 11, Headley Charisma testified before a congressional subcommittee investigating problems afflicting U.S. industry that "exorbitant labor costs and meddlesome government regulators have made it impossible for domestic businesses such as mine to compete effectively against foreign competitors."

Headley says that reductions in operating costs are essential if Amphydynamics is to survive. He also says expenses related to the collective bargaining agreement between Amphydynamics and the International Union of Electronics Workers account for "a significant portion" of the company's operating costs. Last week, he sent a letter to union president Evan Parter requesting certain modifications in the labor contract. He asked for: (1) a two-year freeze on all wages; (2) a reduction in overtime, vacation, and fringe benefit contributions; (3) a reduction in sick days from 10 to five per year. In addition, Headley wants a two year no-strike clause and a freeze on pension plan contributions with no additional coverage, and he wants union employees to make a larger contribution to medical insurance plan premiums.

Evan Parter wrote back saying that none of the proposed modifications were tenable.

Headley is in your office. He says he has decided to reject the labor contract. He plans to instruct the payroll department to make the necessary adjustments in checks that are to be distributed at the end of the week. He will announce the changes via a "letter from your president" insert in workers' paycheck envelopes that will be reprinted in the company's in-house e-news letter. He wants you to help draft the letter. "I want to make the point that all employees, managerial and non-managerial alike, must pull together and make sacrifices if our company is to survive," he says.

He asks whether his approach is appropriate, under the circumstances.

Is it?

To answer his question, you will need to look at Code § 1113. To understand § 1113, a little history is helpful. Prior to the enactment of Code § 1113, the rejection of collective bargaining agreements, like the rejection of any other kind of executory contract, was governed by § 365. Thus, a collective bargaining agreement, like any other kind of contract, could be rejected with the court's permission. All Courts of Appeals that considered the question agreed that, because of the special nature of collective bargaining agreements, they should apply something stricter than a routine business judgment standard in determining whether to authorize rejection. The question was, "How much stricter?" Some authorities suggested that a debtor should not be permitted to reject a collective bargaining agreement unless it could demonstrate that, absent rejection, the reorganization would fail. *Brotherhood of Ry. and Airline Clerks v. REA Express, Inc.*, 523 F.2d 164, 167–69 (2d Cir. 1975). Other authorities held that a showing that the labor contract burdened the estate and that the equities tipped in favor of rejection was sufficient. *In re Brada-Miller Freight System, Inc.*, 702 F.2d 890 (11th Cir. 1983).

In 1984, in *NLRB v. Bildisco & Bildisco*, 465 U.S. 513 (1984), the Supreme Court decided that the appropriate standard was "a higher one than that of the 'business judgment' rule, but a lesser one than that embodied in the *REA Express* opinion." *Id.* at 526. The Court essentially adopted the more liberal *Brada-Miller* standard. The Court also held that from the time a bankruptcy petition is filed and prior to formal assumption, a debtor in possession or trustee could unilaterally modify the terms and conditions of a collective bargaining agreement without committing an unfair labor practice.

Union leaders were alarmed by the *Bildisco* decision. On the day the Court rendered its decision, the president of the International Association of Machinists said, "It's outrageous. This was never to be the intent of Congress," and an attorney for the AFL-CIO said labor representatives would work with Congress to pass a law that would "prevent this kind of manipulation of collective bargaining agreements." William Serrin, *Labor Leaders Voice Concern*, The New York Times, Feb. 23, 1984, at D4.

The Congressional response to *Bildisco* is contained in Bankruptcy Code § 1113, which was added by the 1984 amendments. Although § 1113 does not preclude rejection of collective bargaining agreements, it imposes significant procedural and substantive hurdles that must be overcomed before rejection will be authorized.

Before seeking to reject a collective bargaining agreement, the debtor in possession or trustee must provide the union with a proposal to modify it. This proposal must be "based on the most complete and reliable information available at the time of such proposal . . . [and] provide[] for those necessary modifications in the employee benefits and protections that are necessary to permit the reorganization of the debtor and assure that all creditors, the debtor and all of the affected parties are treated fairly and equitably . . . ." Code § 1113(b)(1)(A). The debtor is required to give the union information necessary to evaluate the proposal. Code § 1113(b)(1)(B). After the proposal is delivered, the debtor and the union are required to attempt in good faith to reach an agreement. Code § 1113(b)(2).

The court may order rejection only if the foregoing procedural requirements are met, Code § 1113(c)(1), the union has rejected the debtor's proposal "without good cause," Code § 1113(c)(2), and "the balance of the equities clearly favors rejection . . . ." Code § 1113(c)(3).

Section 1113(b) raises some questions, too. For example, how will a court determine which modifications are truly "necessary"? *Compare Wheeling-Pittsburgh Steel Corp. v. United Steelworkers*, 791 F.2d 1074 (3d Cir. 1986) (necessary means minimum essential modifications) *with Truck Drivers Local 807 v. Carey Transp., Inc.*, 816 F.2d 82 (2d Cir. 1987) (modification need not be essential to be necessary.)

Is rejection available if the debtor intends to liquidate after rejection? Does it matter if the business is being sold as a going concern to a third party? If the third party is not in Chapter 11, how are such modifications "necessary to permit the reorganization of the debtor"? Consider the decision that follows.

IN RE PINNACLE AIRLINES CORP.
United States Bankruptcy Court for the Southern District of New York
483 B.R. 381 (2012)

DECISION ON DEBTORS' MOTION, PURSUANT TO BANKRUPTCY CODE SECTION 1113, TO REJECT COLLECTIVE BARGAINING AGREEMENT WITH AIR LINE PILOTS ASSOCIATION

Under section 1113 of the Bankruptcy Code, a chapter 11 debtor may reject an executory contract that is a collective bargaining agreement if, but only if, the Bankruptcy Court finds that rigid requirements imposed under that section have been satisfied. Section 1113 attempts to "reconcile the public policy that favors collective bargaining with the reality of bankruptcy, recognizing that Chapter 11 is not merely business as usual but an extremely serious process that can lead to liquidation and the loss of the jobs of all the debtor's employees as well as of the creditors' opportunity for any meaningful recovery." In this contested matter in the chapter 11 case of debtor Pinnacle Airlines, a regional air carrier (which, together with its affiliates, has been referred to variously in briefing and argument, and here, as "Pinnacle," the "Debtor" or the "Company"), the Company moves, pursuant to section 1113, for leave to reject its collective bargaining agreement with the Air Lines Pilots Association (referred to in briefing and argument, and here, as "ALPA" the "Union," or the "Pilots").

Pinnacle contends, among other things, that it is in a liquidity crisis that impairs its ability to survive. It further contends that the regional air transport industry has become commoditized (making pricing the determinant of ability to compete in the industry); that its Pilots' wages, benefits, and work rules are greatly above market; and that its labor costs must be reduced dramatically — to the extent of $59.6 million in cost savings — and quickly for Pinnacle to survive. In fact, Pinnacle argues, its labor costs must be reduced to make them the lowest in the industry — without which, Pinnacle contends, it can survive in neither the long or even the short term. As a result, the Company argues, the Pilots unjustifiably turned down the Company's proposal — an important element of a section 1113 motion showing.

The Pilots acknowledge the liquidity crisis, and that their labor costs need to be reduced. But they contend that the extent to which the Company needs the very major concessions the Company seeks has been overstated. And they further contend that the Company's demands — under which the Pilots' labor costs would drop below the lowest of any of Pinnacle's competitors — would portend a "Race to the Bottom" in employee labor costs under which employees would be the continual losers.

In that connection, the Pilots note that the Company dramatically increased its demands — by 78% — in August, after the Pilots had already responded to an earlier Company section 1113 proposal (then seeking $33 million in cuts) in a way that the Pilots contend should have met the Company's legitimate needs. The Pilots further argue that the Company's stated reason for the very large increase in its demands — that Delta Air Lines, Inc. ("Delta Airlines" or "Delta"), the Company's only present customer, told Company representatives in June that Pinnacle was not competitive with the other regional air carriers providing similar services to Delta — was insufficiently supported, when Delta did not provide copies of the contracts with others that would support that view.

The Pilots further argue that the Company showed no downward movement whatever in its aggregate demands. And the Pilots further argue (or at least proceed on the assumption) that it does not matter that their costs are above market, as Delta is locked into contracts with Pinnacle impairing Delta's ability to give its work to other regional air carriers.

For these reasons, and others, the Pilots argue that they were fully justified in turning down the Company's latest proposal.

. . . .

After hearing the evidence, and related argument, the Court is compelled to agree with the great bulk, but not all, of Pinnacle's contentions. The Court finds, with great regret, that immediate reductions in Pinnacle's pilot labor costs are essential not only to Pinnacle's reorganization, but also to its survival. The Court further finds that nearly all of Pinnacle's "Ask" was justified, even as it was increased by Pinnacle's proposal in August, after Pinnacle took measures to corroborate what Delta had said.

But Pinnacle has failed to meet burdens on this motion — including, most significantly, necessity for the proposed modifications and unjustified refusal to agree by the Pilots (as described more fully in the legal discussion that follows) — in three respects.

First, Pinnacle has failed to show that cutting costs to a level *below* that of any of the other regional airlines is justified and essential to the Company's survival — particularly given Pinnacle's failure to take into account (at least on the record before the Court) the costs Delta would incur to switch its business to other carriers. Pinnacle did not convince the Court that a "Race to the Bottom" was necessary.

Second, Pinnacle's proposal to protect the Pilots from windfalls others might enjoy after Pinnacle is nursed back to health fell short of that required for the Court to make necessary findings of "Necessity" and "Fair and Equitable Treatment." Pinnacle's need for cutting its Pilots' labor costs, very substantially, was overwhelmingly established. But under its proposal, the Pilots would share to only a very modest extent, through profit sharing or equity participation, in the restored profitability that would hopefully come after the Pilots' sacrifices. That failed to satisfy the requirement of Fair and Equitable Treatment, and they were fully justified in declining to agree to a proposal structured in that manner.

Third, the Court was troubled by Pinnacle's failure to make *any movement whatever* in its aggregate demands after filing its motion, and by Pinnacle's insistence on bargaining only with respect to *how* the Pilots would make the overall concessions that Pinnacle sought. While it is true, as Pinnacle argues, that a debtor seeking 1113 relief should not make demands at a high level in contemplation of reducing them thereafter, the Court is unwilling to endorse Pinnacle's position that its absolute refusal to make any concessions at all in its aggregate demand was required (or even justifiable), at least under the facts here. Though Pinnacle's misreading of the law in this area was excusable, and the Court does not, as a consequence, now find bad faith, the Court holds that Pinnacle's total lack of movement gave the Pilots additional good cause to reject Pinnacle's proposal.

Accordingly, Pinnacle's motion is denied without prejudice. If the parties cannot reach agreement with the assistance of the Court's analysis of the issues as set forth in this Decision, Pinnacle can file another motion based on a revised proposal. If any such motion addresses the concerns the Court has articulated here, it almost certainly will be granted.

Findings of Fact

With the exception of one of Pinnacle's witnesses (whose testimony the Court found in numerous respects to be unworthy of belief, but which was not particularly important), the Court found all witnesses whose demeanor it observed to be credible and candid. The Court's Findings of Fact as a consequence of the two sides' evidentiary showings — by direct testimony declaration, live cross-examination, redirect, and any subsequent examination, and exhibits — follow.

1. Background

Pinnacle is a regional airline that, at the time of its chapter 11 filing, operated over 1,300 flights per day to cities in the United States, Canada, and Mexico. Founded in 1985 as Express Airlines I, pre-merger Pinnacle ("Pinnacle I") was created to provide regional lift to Republic Airlines. Republic was acquired by Northwest Airlines Corporation ("Northwest") in 1986, and in 1997, Northwest also acquired Pinnacle I. In 2003, Pinnacle I was spun off by Northwest in an initial public offering although Pinnacle I continued to provide regional flying services to Northwest under a multi-year agreement. In 2007, Pinnacle I acquired Colgan Air ("Colgan"), and in July 2010, it acquired Mesaba Aviation, Inc. ("Mesaba").

Currently, Pinnacle's fleet consists of 140 50-seat Bombardier CRJ-200s and 57 76-seat Bombardier CRJ-900s. The aircraft operate as Delta Connection flights under agreements with Delta Airlines. Pinnacle provides short- and medium-haul flights to and from Delta's hub airports in Atlanta, Detroit, Memphis, New York City (John F. Kennedy Airport), and Minneapolis/St. Paul. Until recently, Colgan operated a fleet of 55 turboprops under regional lift agreements with United Airlines (or "United") and US Airways. Pinnacle wound down these operations as part of the restructuring, leaving Delta as Pinnacle's only remaining mainline customer, as discussed below in further detail. As of August 2012, Pinnacle had approximately 5,800 employees, including approximately 2,400 pilots, 1,500 flight attendants, and 80 flight dispatchers. More than 75% of Pinnacle's 5,800 employees are unionized.

(a) Regional Airline Industry

Regional carriers, like Pinnacle, are airlines that provide flying services to mainline carriers on routes where (or at times of day when) passenger demand is not sufficient to support using larger mainline aircraft. Though operated by a regional carrier, regional aircraft and flights display the livery and adopt the brand of the mainline partner. From the point of view of the passenger, therefore, the regional carrier flight represents an integrated service on a single carrier.

. . . .

Regional carriers are compensated by their mainline partners under one of two types of agreements. Under a pro-rate agreement, the fee paid by the mainline airline is dictated by ticket sales or the number of passengers, and the regional airline pays certain "Pass-Through Costs" like fuel, engine maintenance, ground handling, insurance, aircraft ownership costs, and other enumerated costs. Thus, both the regional and the mainline carrier share risks associated with fuel prices, passenger demand, and fares. Most pro-rate agreements today cover turboprop flying, and often for subsidized "Essential Air Services" routes (routes between small communities and larger hubs that receive a subsidy from the U.S. Department of Transportation).

By contrast, under a "Capacity Purchase Agreement," the mainline airline pays the regional airline a fixed dollar rate per block hour, day, or departure to operate regional aircraft (either turboprops or regional jets). Pass-Through Costs are also often covered by the mainline airline under such agreements, under which the regional carrier receives fixed fees, and the mainline carrier assumes all risk associated with passenger demand and fuel prices. In addition, the mainline carrier is solely responsible for determining the regional carrier's schedule (both routes and flight times) and for the sale and marketing of tickets. Profit under a Capacity Purchase Agreement is driven by a regional carrier's ability to control costs, since the regional carrier receives the fixed fees irrespective of ticket sales or fares charged. And because so many of the other costs (the Pass-Through Costs) are covered by the mainline airline, labor (which is not a Pass-Through Cost) is generally the largest controllable cost for regional airlines. By shifting most of the risks to the mainline airlines, Capacity Purchase Agreements (which now make up the bulk of agreements between regional and mainline airlines) have essentially made the regional airline industry a commoditized business, with major airlines generally relying on a number of different regional carriers to provide regional lift.

(b) Recent Challenges Facing the Mainline Airline Industry

In recent years, mainline carriers like American, Delta, United, and US Airways have faced increased pressure to control their costs as a result of several factors. "Low Cost Carriers," like JetBlue, Spirit, Virgin America, and Allegiant, have expanded rapidly both in terms of size and geographic coverage. Low Cost Carriers benefit from a lower cost structure as a result of simplified fleets of one or two types of aircraft only; more flexible work rules; quick turn-around times; and employee populations of lesser seniority than large network carriers because of their relatively recent entries to the market. This dramatic growth of Low Cost Carriers as well as widespread passenger acceptance of Low Cost Carriers has placed downward pressure on mainline carriers to provide cost-competitive lift. Internet-based airline search and booking tools have increased price transparency, resulting in further downward pressure on airfares. Higher fuel costs have forced mainline carriers to reduce services that cannot be operated economically. Carriers are unable to cover the higher fuel costs without raising fares to help offset the increased costs. But passenger demand decreases when fares are raised, forcing mainline carriers to reduce capacity, which results in decreased revenues. And more stringent and time-consuming passenger screening procedures following the September 11th terrorist attacks — what has become known as the "hassle factor" — have also resulted in decreased passenger demand.

These factors, among others, have contributed to over $30 billion in operating losses for large mainline carriers since 2001, and are at least in part what has forced all of the surviving mainline carriers (American, United, Delta, and US Airways) to file for chapter 11 protection and seek reduction of controllable costs, including their costs for regional lift.

(c) Recent Challenges Facing the Regional Airline Industry

Although regional airlines initially were largely immune from the factors affecting mainline carriers (due in large part to the protection regional carriers received under Capacity Purchase Agreements from both demand risk and increased fuel costs), regional carriers are now feeling the effects. The "hassle factor" has had a particularly harsh impact on short-haul flying (less than 500 miles), where regional aircraft are most commonly used, thus reducing demand by mainline carriers for regional carrier services. Although fuel is generally covered by the mainline carrier under a Capacity Purchase Agreement, increased fuel prices make regional aircraft — especially 50-seat regional jets — less cost effective. For example, 50-seat regional jets consume 55% to 126% more fuel per seat hour than small mainline jets like the Boeing 737 or Airbus A-320. Mainline airlines therefore have reduced the number of 50-seat regional jet block hours flown by regional partners by 24% since 2005, and further reductions are expected. During their chapter 11 restructurings, many mainline carriers reduced the number of less efficient regional aircraft, including those operated by independent regional carriers, and rejected or renegotiated unfavorable contracts with regional carriers. In addition, the large number of mergers between mainline carriers over the past several years has left independent regional carriers with fewer mainline airline customers for whom they can provide regional lift services. In 2011, these factors, among others, resulted in profit margins for regional carriers dropping to their lowest levels in a decade.

(d) Recent Challenges Specifically Facing Pinnacle

Pinnacle began experiencing financial difficulties in recent years as a result of a confluence of issues. In 2011, Pinnacle operated at a net loss of $31 million, and Pinnacle's profit margin (-2.6%) reached its lowest level since 1998. Pinnacle replaced its former Chief Executive Officer and Chief Operating Officer that year with Sean Menke and John Spanjers respectively. In July 2011, the new management conducted an assessment of Pinnacle's business and identified several factors that contributed to Pinnacle's questionable viability, including: (1) delays in integrating the flying of Pinnacle I and Mesaba; (2) unanticipated developments arising out of a new "Joint Collective Bargaining Agreement" with the Debtors' pilots; and (3) increasingly unprofitable contracts with mainline airline customers.

(i) Integration Delays

At the time it acquired Mesaba, Pinnacle announced its intention to merge the three carriers (Pinnacle I, Mesaba, and Colgan) into two, with one operating regional jet aircraft and the other operating turboprop aircraft. Although the pre-merger carriers operated some common aircraft types, the carriers had independent operating standards and procedures for those aircraft. To effectively merge the carriers, the operations needed to be combined on a single operating certificate issued by the Federal Aviation Administration ("FAA"). At the time, Pinnacle had three separate operating certificates for each of its three airlines. Moving Mesaba under the Pinnacle operating certificate was originally scheduled for May 2011, but Pinnacle was not able to obtain FAA approval in time, and the move was delayed until January 2012. The delays resulted in deferral of cost savings, and also required Pinnacle to hire additional employees and consultants to accomplish the consolidation. Full integration of maintenance and flight operations of the Pinnacle I and Mesaba jets is not expected to be completed until early 2013, even though the Mesaba jets have now been moved under the Pinnacle operating certificate.

(ii) Joint Collective Bargaining Agreement

Following the Mesaba acquisition, the Company and the Pilots entered into negotiations in the fall of 2010 in an effort to create a single collective bargaining agreement that would cover all three carriers. By February 2011, the Company reached an agreement with the joint representative of the pilots for all three subsidiaries — the Joint Collective Bargaining Agreement. But there were two problems that arose as a consequence of the Joint Collective Bargaining Agreement: (1) recent analysis showed the compensation of the pilots to be above market average with respect to wages, benefits, and work rules; and (2) under the Joint Collective Bargaining Agreement, an "integrated seniority list" had to be created that would merge the pilot seniority lists of all three subsidiaries.

With respect to the first of the problems (pilot costs), Pinnacle's pilots' compensation, in terms of wages, benefits, and work rules, is above market average. Pinnacle's pilot pay scale is among the highest in the regional airline industry, and this disadvantage is exacerbated by Pinnacle's "seniority disadvantage" — i.e., the relatively high seniority of its pilots compared to those of competitors — which leads to significantly higher costs. These higher costs, compared to younger airlines such as GoJet Airlines ("GoJet") and Compass Airlines ("Compass"), put Pinnacle at a disadvantage. Pinnacle's pilot work rules limit pilot productivity by a series of provisions, including work rules related to minimum day rigs, open time posting, and duty days. Pinnacle is also uncompetitive with respect to rules governing pilots' ability to take time off (*e.g.*, vacation accruals, vacation credit, extended sick leave, and use of the Family Medical Leave Act). Under these terms, Pinnacle pilots are less productive, requiring Pinnacle to utilize more pilots and more payable hours than competitors to fly comparable routes and aircraft. Under Pinnacle's current active medical plan, Pinnacle's employee contribution level is lower than that of employees at other carriers. Pinnacle is also one of only a handful of airlines to still offer medical plans to its retirees. In addition, Pinnacle's current 401(k) plan is one of the most generous in the regional industry. For Pinnacle's most senior employees, for example, Pinnacle matches employee contributions up to 12.5%.

With respect to the second of the problems (integration of the seniority lists), difficulties arose in connection with the development of one unified seniority list. Pilots bid on vacancies to obtain a new domicile, new aircraft, or new category, and bids are honored based on seniority. The integration of the three seniority lists into one resulted in new seniority relationships among thousands of pilots. Pilots undergo training each time they move to a new aircraft or category, and under the Joint Collective Bargaining Agreement, the pilots receive full salary during training. In addition, when a pilot moves to fill a vacancy, his or her position must also be filled through the bidding system. Prior to the integration, pilots at each airline were only permitted to bid on vacancies at their airline specifically. Following the integration, pilots were permitted to bid on vacancies at any of the three airlines, which opened up many new routes and different aircraft possibilities for the pilots, all of which necessitated additional training. The Joint Collective Bargaining Agreement did not contain safeguards (or "fences") that would keep training costs for this type of movement of pilots in check by essentially preventing pilots from bidding or being awarded positions at the other airlines before the companies were operationally merged.

The delayed integration (discussed previously) further added to the training costs associated with the Joint Collective Bargaining Agreement because pilots not only needed to be trained on transfers to different aircraft; they also needed to be trained for transfers even to the same aircraft type if the aircraft was under a different operating certificate.

The Joint Collective Bargaining Agreement does not become "amendable," within the meaning of the Railway Labor Act, until February 18, 2016.

(iii) Unprofitable Contracts

An analysis of Pinnacle's contracts in 2011 showed that non-compensable costs incurred by Pinnacle under their existing contracts with mainline carriers, including increased labor costs under the Joint Collective Bargaining Agreement and costs associated with maintaining an aging fleet, were in excess (or soon would be in excess) of fees received by Pinnacle under its contracts. Neither the pro-rate agreement under which Pinnacle was providing Saab 340 turboprop flying to US Airways nor the Capacity Purchase Agreement under which Pinnacle was providing Q400 turboprop flying to United were profitable. Also, the profitability of Pinnacle's three existing contracts with Delta to provide CRJ-200 and CRJ-900 flying was also in question.

2. Initial Cost Saving Measures

Prior to the filing, Pinnacle engaged in a number of cost saving measures in an effort to avoid bankruptcy. Pinnacle reduced the number of officers from 29 to 18, and 26 "director"-level positions were eliminated — a 40% reduction. The number of support staff and other employees was also reduced. Merit increases and discretionary bonuses scheduled for 2012 were eliminated, producing an estimated savings of approximately $3 million.

Pinnacle sought concessions from its lenders and other creditor concessions. Pinnacle was able to obtain some short-term liquidity in early 2012 as a result of an agreement reached with Export Development Canada, Pinnacle's lender in connection with mortgages for purchased Q400 and CRJ-900 aircraft, to defer payments until April 2012.

Pinnacle also reached out to its unions pre-filing to negotiate potential pay cuts and work-rule concessions, and to secure limitations on pilot transfers that would help mitigate the issues related to integration of the seniority lists. The parties ultimately were not able to come to an agreement.

3. Chapter 11 Filing and Immediate Aftermath

The cost saving measures were not sufficient to stave off bankruptcy, however, and on April 1, 2012, Pinnacle Airlines Corp. and its affiliates filed voluntary chapter 11 petitions. The following day, Pinnacle filed a motion requesting that the Court authorize assumption of Pinnacle's revised "Airline Service Agreements" (sometimes referred to in testimony or briefing as "ASAs") with Delta. Pinnacle also sought approval of an agreement with Delta, as lender, under which Pinnacle would receive debtor-in-possession ("DIP") financing from Delta (the "DIP Financing Agreement").

Under the DIP Financing Agreement, Delta provided a $74.285 million DIP facility, which, subject to various conditions, could be convertible to exit financing. The DIP Financing Agreement contained various milestones, financial covenants, and additional requirements with which Pinnacle would have to comply to avoid an event of default. The DIP Financing Agreement contained (among other financial covenants) a minimum unrestricted liquidity covenant that dictated that Pinnacle's unrestricted cash and cash equivalents could not fall below $25 million as of the last day of any calendar month, or the first day of the next month if the last day were to fall on a weekend.

In addition, the DIP Financing Agreement contained various milestones with which Pinnacle would have to comply relating to its collective bargaining agreements. Pinnacle was required under the DIP Financing Agreement to file a motion under section 1113 "reasonably acceptable" to Delta in both form and substance if Pinnacle could not reach a consensual agreement with its unions. The DIP Financing Agreement further dictated a time frame in which this was to occur, which was extended through amendments to the DIP Financing Agreement to a final deadline of September 13, 2012.

Additionally, any final order of the Court granting a section 1113 motion or approving consensual collective bargaining agreement modifications also needed to be "reasonably acceptable" to Delta. Violation of any of the financial covenants, milestones, or other requirements contained in the DIP Financing Agreement would trigger an automatic event of default, entitling Delta to accelerate all amounts due to it under the DIP Financing Agreement on five days' notice.

Although Pinnacle and its advisors had sought financing from a number of potential sources, in the end, Delta was the only option. The onerous milestones, financial covenants and other provisions in the DIP Financing Agreement and the associated DIP Financing Order had to be approved for lack of viable alternatives. They remain in the DIP Financing Agreement and DIP Financing Order to this day.

4. Initial May Proposal to Unions

On May 8, 2012, Pinnacle made an initial section 1113 proposal to its unions. More than 75% of Pinnacle's workforce is unionized, with the pilots represented by the Air Line Pilots Association ("ALPA"), the flight attendants represented by the Association of Flight Attendants ("AFA"), and the flight dispatchers represented by the Transport Workers Union ("TWU").

(a) Business Plan

At the May 8, 2012 meeting with Pinnacle's unions, Pinnacle presented the unions with a six-year business plan. Pinnacle's remaining contracts, upon which the business plan was based, involve two separate Capacity Purchase Agreements covering 50-seat CRJ-200 flying and 76-seat CRJ-900 flying for Delta. Pinnacle flies

140 CRJ-200s and 41 CRJ-900s for Delta pursuant to those agreements. The agreements extend through 2022, with termination of 78 of the CRJ-200s scheduled to begin in 2019, with rate resets in 2018.

In developing its business plan and calculating the initial labor "Ask," Pinnacle had three primary goals: (1) attaining a cost structure that would avoid losing money on its only existing contracts; (2) achieving a sufficient profit margin to attract an investor to allow Pinnacle to emerge from bankruptcy and to generate excess cash for future growth and protection against unforeseen fluctuations; and (3) achieving an overall competitive cost structure allowing the company to win future new business.

(b) Labor "Ask"

Based on these considerations, initially Pinnacle proposed a package of wage, benefit, and work rule concessions (from all of its unions) that would produce total savings of approximately $43 million annually. In developing the business plan and determining the amount of the initial "Ask," Pinnacle relied upon the rates agreed to in its recent amendments to its contracts with Delta so as to ensure that labor cost reductions would enable it to continue bidding for additional contracts at those rates. At the time, Pinnacle believed these rates to be industry-competitive given Delta's recent agreement to them. Because pricing terms of regional airline contracts are generally not publicly available, Pinnacle was not able to rely on competitors' rates in determining its initial $43 million "Ask."

Pinnacle first presented a general overview of the proposal to all of the unions, and then met with each union individually. Pinnacle provided the unions with an electronic "Data Room" and access to a "live" version of the model underlying Pinnacle's business plan, which the unions were free to manipulate.

Of the approximately $43 million initial ask of labor, Pinnacle sought approximately $33 million from pilots in revisions to wages, work rules, and benefits.

5. Delta's Price Gap Calculations

In May 2012, as a result of an agreement Delta reached with its pilot union on May 21, 2012, Delta announced that it would be adding 70 "dual class" regional aircraft (70- or 76-seat aircraft that provide first class seating, as well as coach) and substantially decreasing the number of 50-seat aircraft (single class) flown by its regional carriers. Delta plans to reduce its total number of 50-seat aircraft by at least 200 to 125 or fewer over the next two to three years. Pinnacle's fleet consists of 140 50-seat aircraft; therefore, at least some of the reduction will need to come from Pinnacle's fleet.

On June 15, following Delta's announcement of the new agreement with its pilot union, Pinnacle advisor Virginia Hughes, of Seabury Advisors LLC ("Seabury"); Pinnacle Chief Restructuring Officer Steven Rossum; and Pinnacle President and Chief Executive Officer ("CEO") John Spanjers met with Delta representatives in Minneapolis. The Delta representatives then informed Pinnacle that Pinnacle's rates for 76-seat flying per aircraft exceeded the average rates charged by Delta's other regional carriers for similar-gauge aircraft. The Delta representatives noted that the price spread amongst carriers providing 76-seat lift was narrow — ruling out the possibility that the price gap was driven by one or two outliers. They further reported that Pinnacle's rates for 50-seat flying also exceeded average rates charged by other Delta Connection carriers. The Delta representatives did not reveal the details of their analysis, however, citing confidentiality obligations to other Delta Connection providers.

Instead, Delta provided a letter to Mr. Spanjers, dated August 1, 2012, from Senior Vice President of Delta Connection Donald Bornhorst, that memorialized the conclusions and methodology Delta had employed in reaching the price gap calculation. Delta compared the estimated 2012 base rate amounts payable by Delta under its agreements with Pinnacle with the average estimated base rate amounts payable by Delta under its agreements with other Delta Connection carriers.

If the price gaps identified by Delta were in fact accurate, Pinnacle's management understood that Pinnacle would be hard pressed to win new flying from Delta or any other major carrier if Pinnacle could not achieve cost savings sufficient to bring its rates more in line with other regional carriers. The Court finds this not to be merely Pinnacle management's understanding; it is a fact. On June 22, 2012, Pinnacle suspended negotiations with its unions to reassess its business plan, and set out to corroborate the price gaps identified by Delta through Pinnacle independent analysis.

6. Corroborating the Price Gaps

Without access to information on rates other regional carriers charge mainline carriers, Pinnacle instead focused on validating Delta's price gap calculation through a comparison of Pinnacle's costs to those of competitors. Since Delta had announced its intention to dramatically scale back its 50-seat flying with 70- and 76-seat flying, Pinnacle chose to focus on the 76-seat flying price differential. To analyze the price gap, Pinnacle employed the services of Seabury's Virginia Hughes (which provides advisory services to financially troubled companies), and Daniel Kasper, an airline industry expert employed by consulting group Compass Lexecon.

. . . .

Ms. Hughes calculated that Pinnacle would need to obtain an additional $33.9 million in savings above that requested in Pinnacle's May labor "Ask" in order to bridge the price gaps — increasing the total annual required savings to $76.5 million.

. . . .

Mr. Kasper . . . determined that, based on pilot costs alone, Pinnacle had a cost disadvantage per 76-seat aircraft that exceeded the Delta price gap compared to Compass' annual E-175 pilot costs, and compared to the other carriers (Shuttle America, SkyWest, ExpressJet/ASA), constituted a substantial portion of the Delta price gap.

For smaller regional jets with 50 seats or fewer, Mr. Kasper computed Pinnacle's cost per pilot block hour to be just below the average for other Delta Connection carriers (excluding Comair). But Mr. Kasper believed that the methods used to assess Pinnacle's 76-seat cost disadvantage using publicly available Form 41 data were not a reliable basis for assessing Pinnacle's 50-seat cost disadvantage "due to the chaotic status of the current market for 50-seat flying" (*i.e.*, the large reductions in 50-seat regional jet block hours over the last several years by mainline carriers).

7. Revised Proposal

Pinnacle delivered a revised *section 1113* proposal to the unions on August 16, 2012, along with a revised business plan. The proposal consisted of wage, benefit, and work rule modifications totaling $76.5 million (the amount Pinnacle and its advisors determined would be required in aggregate labor savings per year to eliminate the Delta price gap (and, the Court infers, to get "a little more")). The August proposal contained all of the work rule and benefit modifications included in the May proposal, and in addition, various new items. Of the $76.5 million, $59.6 million was sought from the pilots; $6.5 million from the flight attendants; and a little less than $200,000 from flight dispatchers. An additional $10.1 million in annual savings was expected from salary cuts, benefit reductions, and work rule modifications for non-unionized employees.

Pinnacle reasoned that the Pilots were asked to contribute the greatest portion of the overall savings because (1) pilot costs constituted the largest component of Pinnacle's labor costs, and (2) Pinnacle's pilot costs were also furthest from the industry norm in comparison to the other labor groups — especially when factoring in seniority disadvantage. To specifically address the seniority disadvantage, the proposal included several changes to pay rates, generally reducing the premium in pay that would result from seniority. For example, longevity steps would be capped at twelve years for Captains, and four years for First Officers.

Although the new plan incorporated the higher labor "Ask," Pinnacle did not adjust the revenue projections on the long-range outlook. A profit sharing plan, however, was added to the plan.

8. Section 1113 Motion and Continued Negotiations

On August 30, 2012, Pinnacle reached a tentative agreement with the TWU on behalf of Pinnacle's flight dispatchers, and the agreement was ratified on September 11, 2012.

Unable to reach similar agreement with ALPA and the AFA on behalf of the flight attendants, Pinnacle filed its motion, under section 1113, for leave to reject its collective bargaining agreements with each union on September 13, 2012.

Negotiations continued following the filing of the motion, and Pinnacle and the AFA came to a tentative agreement late on Friday, October 12, four days before the scheduled trial. The agreement, which was later ratified by the AFA's membership, would achieve $6.4 million in savings.

The negotiations between Pinnacle and the Pilots continued, with both parties meeting with a mediator. But the two sides were unable to come to a resolution. The Pilots presented various counter-proposals to the Company's revised August proposal, both before and after the section 1113 motion filing. The Company responded with revised proposals, the last of which (prior to conclusion of the hearing) was presented to the Pilots on October 15, 2012. Although the Company informed the Pilots that it was willing to consider different means of attaining the $59.6 million total dollar ask, it was unwilling to reduce the dollar amount of the "Ask," and showed no movement with respect to the total "Ask" whatever.

9. Liquidity Crisis

The possibility of a liquidity shortfall was raised by Pinnacle as early as May 8, 2012, during its presentation to the unions. However, as the trial on this motion drew closer, Pinnacle grew more concerned about its cash levels and its ability to avoid events of default under various agreements. In her reply declaration submitted on October 12, 2012, Ms. Hughes explained that because Pinnacle does not have a "minimum utilization" requirement in any of its Delta agreements, Delta is free to reduce its use of Pinnacle services, and in fact Delta has reduced its use of Pinnacle aircraft, resulting in reduced revenues for Pinnacle and lower projected cash levels. As noted previously, specifics as to Pinnacle's liquidity situation appear in the Confidential Supplement.

10. Section 1113 Trial

The Court held a four-day trial beginning on October 16, 2012. Consistent with the Court's Case Management Order and its need to receive quantitative and technical information in writing, direct testimony was taken by declaration, and cross-examination, redirect, and any subsequent examination proceeded live. Also, certain witnesses supplemented their written declarations by providing oral direct testimony in Court as to events that occurred since they submitted their declarations.

. . . .

11. Ultimate Facts

The Court additionally makes the following findings of ultimate facts:

(1) Pinnacle has made a proposal to the authorized representative of the employees (i.e., the Pilots) covered by the collective bargaining agreement.

(2) The proposal was based on the most complete and reliable information available at the time of the proposal.

(3) Pinnacle provided the Pilots, to the extent Pinnacle could, with such relevant information as was necessary to evaluate the proposal.

(4) Pinnacle met, at reasonable times, with the Union to attempt to reach mutually satisfactory modifications of the collective agreement. Pinnacle did so in good faith.

(5) In nearly all respects, though not in every respect, Pinnacle's proposal was necessary to permit the reorganization of the Debtor.

(6) In nearly all respects, though not in every respect, Pinnacle's proposal assured that all creditors, the debtor, and all affected parties were treated fairly and equitably. To the extent it was not, it was by reason of its unfairness to the Pilots.

(7) The Pilots were justified in refusing to accept Pinnacle's proposal as the proposal was tendered to it — or, putting it in the terms of section 1113(c)(2), the Pilots did not refuse to accept Pinnacle's proposal "without good cause."

Discussion

Section 1113 of the Bankruptcy Code imposes special requirements for the rejection of a collective bargaining agreement, to reconcile the reorganization imperatives of a chapter 11 debtor with the collective bargaining interests of organized employees. It was enacted in 1984 in response to the Supreme Court's decision in *N.L.R.B. v. Bildisco & Bildisco*, in which the Supreme Court held that a debtor could reject a collective bargaining agreement as an executory contract by showing that the agreement "burdens the estate, and that after careful scrutiny, the equities balance in favor of rejecting the labor contract."

In the wake of the *Bildisco* decision, congressional concerns intensified that certain companies were misusing the bankruptcy system as an end-run around collective bargaining. Consequently, Congress, overruling *Bildisco* in part, provided that collective bargaining agreements would not be subject to the general provisions of section 365, and laid down procedural and substantive prerequisites to a debtor's rejection of a collective bargaining agreement.

These requirements are imposed on the debtor "to prevent it from using bankruptcy as a judicial hammer to break the union." The prerequisites, set forth in section 1113, are aimed at facilitating consensual modifications to collective bargaining agreements but include finite time periods in recognition of the fact that indefinite delay can doom a chapter 11 reorganization. If the efforts to negotiate a consensual resolution fail, the court can approve rejection when the statutory requirements have been met.

A.

Legal Standards

Section 1113 has three subsections relevant to this motion. Its subsection (a) provides that a collective bargaining agreement can be rejected only after compliance with the requirements of section 1113. Then its subsection (b) lays out steps with which a debtor or trustee must comply before a motion for approval of rejection can be filed, and (after any such motion has been filed) before the hearing on it. Then its subsection (c) lays out requirements for approval of any such motion.

Subsection (c) provides:

The court shall approve an application for rejection of a collective bargaining agreement only if the court finds that —

(1) the trustee has, prior to the hearing, made a proposal that fulfills the requirements of subsection (b)(1);

(2) the authorized representative of the employees has refused to accept such proposal without good cause; and

(3) the balance of the equities clearly favors rejection of such agreement.

Subsection (b)(1), referenced in subsection (c) as establishing the requirements for any satisfactory modification proposal, imposes both procedural and substantive requirements. As procedural matters, subsection (b)(1) requires that prior to rejecting a collective bargaining agreement, a debtor provide the union with a proposal for proposed modifications; that the proposed modifications be based on the most complete and reliable information available at the time of the proposal; that the debtor provide the union with all relevant information that is necessary to assist the union in evaluating the proposal; and that the debtor bargain in good faith with the union in attempting to reach mutually satisfactory modifications during the period from the date of the initial proposal to the date of the hearing before the Court.

. . . .

Effectively, then, by reason of the amalgam of the requirements of section 1113's subsections (b) and (c), a debtor must show, in addition to compliance with the procedural requirements, that:

(1)   the modifications it seeks are necessary to permit the reorganization of the debtor;

(2)   the proposal assures that all affected parties are treated "fairly and equitably;"

(3)   the authorized representative of the employees has refused to accept the proposal without good cause; and

(4)   the balance of the equities clearly favors rejection of such agreement.

The debtor bears the burden of proof, by preponderance of the evidence, on all elements of section 1113.

1. Necessity

"A debtor must show that its proposed modifications to the collective bargaining agreement are necessary for reorganization." Indeed, as Judge Gropper observed in *Northwest Airlines*, "[t]he *most fundamental* requirement for rejection of a collective bargaining agreement is that the rejection must be 'necessary.' "

In that connection, the Court agrees with Pinnacle's point, quoting Second Circuit authority, that a section 1113 proposal must contain "necessary, but not absolutely minimal, changes that will enable the debtor to complete the reorganization process successfully." In the Second Circuit, it is true, as Pinnacle argues, that the debtor's proposal "need not be limited to the bare bones relief that will keep it going."

On the other hand, the Court does not understand that to mean, and in any event the Court is unwilling to hold, that a necessity that exists as a general matter supports a proposal that goes beyond the demonstrated necessity. That is the teaching of Judge Lane's decision in *American Airlines*, and Judge Drain's decision in *Hostess Brands* — in each of which the court found that necessity for most of the proposed modifications had been shown, but that it did not support demands that went further. Though stated in another section 1113 context, an observation by the Tenth Circuit has broader application, and is equally applicable here: "[a] debtor may not overreach under the guise of proposing necessary modifications." Thus, necessity that has been established cannot be used as a Trojan Horse to support proposals that go beyond the necessity that has actually been shown.

But the necessity that may be shown includes necessity in the long term, as well as the short term. To determine whether changes are necessary for a successful reorganization, the court must "look[ ] into the debtor's *ultimate future* and estimate[e] what the debtor needs to attain financial health." And as Judge Lane observed in *American Airlines*, quoting earlier analysis by Judge Hardin in *Delta Airlines*:

> [A] court should focus "on the long-term economic viability of the reorganized debtor, as opposed to the debtor's short-term economics as they may have evolved during the course of the bankruptcy. . . . "

Caselaw in this area also requires the Court to consider not just the costs inherent in a debtor's ability to survive, but also in its ability to compete — at least in cases (like this one) where the debtor lacks the ability to charge its customers or its contract counterparties whatever the debtor's costs require, and the debtor's ability to survive depends on its ability to compete. As Judge Lane stated in *American Airlines*:

> It is self-evident that a debtor's long-term ability to compete in the marketplace for its product is essential for the viability of any reorganization. . . .

And like Judge Hardin ahead of him in *Delta Airlines*, Judge Lane noted the Second Circuit's recognition, in *Royal Composing Room*, of the necessity of rejection when a debtor's labor costs are higher than those of its competitors and where the debtor faces "enormous competitive pressure."

2. Fair and Equitable Treatment

Section 1113(c) — by reason of its incorporation, in section 1113(c)(1), of requirements of section 1113(b)(1) — also requires that the debtor's proposal "assure that all creditors, the debtor and all of the affected parties are treated fairly and equitably." This requirement "spread[s] the burden of saving the company to every constituency while ensuring that all sacrifice to a similar degree."

As Pinnacle correctly states, there are no bright-line rules indicating whether a proposal is fair and equitable. Instead, courts "apply a general, flexible standard" that cost-cutting burdens be shared among affected parties — and that to the extent some groups are asked to contribute more than others, the different contribution levels be justified under the circumstances. As Judge Lane put it in *American Airlines*:

> Courts take a flexible approach in considering what constitutes fair and equitable treatment due to the difficulty in comparing the differing sacrifices of the parties in interest. . . . A debtor can meet the requirement "by showing that its proposal treats the union fairly when compared with the burden imposed on other parties by the debtor's additional cost-cutting measures and the Chapter 11 process generally."

. . . .

3. Good Cause to Reject Debtor's Proposal

To grant section 1113 relief, the Court must also find, consistent with the requirements of section 1113(c)(2), that "the authorized representative of the employees has refused to accept such proposal without good cause . . . ." The requisite "good cause" in this context is not statutorily defined, nor are standards for finding it articulated in the Code. But "good cause" has been fleshed out in the caselaw. Findings that a proposed modification is necessary, fair and equitable do not by themselves compel an additional finding that a union's refusal to agree to a proposal is without "good cause." The requirement of section 1113(c)(2) is an additional one, and cannot be read to be surplusage.

As the Second Circuit observed in *Maxwell Newspapers*:

> What "good cause" means is difficult to answer in the abstract apart from the moorings of a given case. A more constructive and perhaps more answerable inquiry is why this term is in the statute. We think good cause serves as an incentive to the debtor trying to have its labor contract modified to propose in good faith only those changes necessary to its successful reorganization, while protecting it from the union's refusal to accept the changes without a good reason.

. . . .

4. Balance of Equities

Then, to grant section 1113 relief, the Court must additionally find, consistent with the requirements of section 1113(c)(3), that "the balance of the equities clearly favors rejection of such agreement." In applying that subsection, it is important to note the word "clearly" that appears as part of that clause; textual analysis tells us that considerably more than a minimal tipping in the balancing is required.

This requirement is a codification of the standard set out in *Bildisco*. In *Carey Transportation*, the Second Circuit identified "at least" six "permissible equitable considerations" (many of which also factor into the other substantive requirements imposed by section 1113) for use in determining if the equities favor rejection of a collective bargaining agreement:

(1) the likelihood and consequences of liquidation if rejection is not permitted;

(2) the likely reduction in the value of creditors' claims if the bargaining agreement remains in force;

(3) the likelihood and consequences of a strike if the bargaining agreement is voided;

(4) the possibility and likely effect of any employee claims for breach of contract if rejection is approved;

(5) the cost-spreading abilities of the various parties, taking into account the number of employees covered by the bargaining agreement and how various employees' wages and benefits compare to those of others in the industry; and

(6) the good or bad faith of the parties in dealing with the debtor's financial dilemma.

The equities must be examined in relation to the debtor's attempts to reorganize. "[T]he Bankruptcy Court must focus on the ultimate goal of Chapter 11 when considering these equities. The Bankruptcy Code does not authorize freewheeling consideration of every conceivable equity, but rather only how the equities relate to the success of the reorganization."

But in this Court's view, even recognizing that equitable considerations must be limited to those that relate to the success of the reorganization, there is an additional important matter to consider as well. In the past, when the Second Circuit has articulated factors for the courts in the Circuit to consider, it has not infrequently done so by use of expressly or impliedly nonexclusive lists. And in the past, as it did in *General Motors*, this Court, recognizing that the Circuit's list was not exclusive, has suggested additional factors to consider as well. That is appropriate here too, since the Circuit, in *Carey Transportation*, articulated "at least six permissible equitable considerations."

Another key equitable consideration — perhaps implied, but not expressly stated, in the considerations listed by the Circuit in *Carey Transportation* — is whether imposing the requested pay cuts or other concessions would still be preferable to the loss of everyone's jobs, those of union members and non-union members alike. That consideration is so important, in this Court's view, that it deserves separate mention and analysis.

B.

Application to Facts Here

The Court then turns to its application of those legal principles to the facts it found in the evidentiary hearing on this motion, rearranging them slightly for ease of discussion.

1. Procedural Matters

The Court turns initially to the procedural requirements for section 1113 relief, though they need only modest mention.

First, the Court has found as a fact, and now determines as a mixed question of fact and law, that Pinnacle satisfied the necessary procedural requirements to make a proposal; to provide any and all information that it could to enable the Pilots to evaluate the proposal; and to negotiate with the Union. As a matter of law on an issue that the Court believes to be one of first impression, the Court rules that to meet the procedural requirements of section 1113(b)(1), a debtor can only be required to provide information that is within the debtor's power to provide.

While section 1113(b)(1)(B) requires the debtor to provide "such relevant information as is necessary to evaluate the proposal" (and while information unavailable to the debtor could often be helpful, or even "necessary," at least in the sense of being the information that would be most helpful), section 1113(b)(1)(A) requires the proposal to be "based on the most complete and reliable information available at the time of such proposal." In the Court's view, all of the provisions of section 1113(b)(1) must be read together. And together they evidence, along with the remainder of section 1113 and section 1113 caselaw, Congress' intention that the parties try as hard as they can to reach a negotiated, and nonjudicial, resolution. But the parties can only do what is possible, and the statutory language, and common sense, require that the Court impose requirements consistent with reality.

The Court has little doubt that information available only to Delta — what its contracts with other regional carriers provide, and, perhaps, what Delta has to support its statements as to what other regional carriers' costs are — would be the best indication of what Pinnacle would need to do to compete and survive. But the Court is persuaded, after hearing all of the evidence, that Pinnacle does not have that information except in the form that Delta shared it, and in the form of the results of Pinnacle's own efforts to corroborate Delta assertions, which Pinnacle shared with the Pilots. Thus Pinnacle's inability to provide information that only Delta could provide is not fatal to Pinnacle's motion.

Second, as noted above and below, the Court was and still is troubled by Pinnacle's unwillingness to show any movement whatever in its aggregate demand. In some cases, refusal to move in any way could reasonably be argued to evidence a failure to negotiate in good faith, and might be found to be such in the future. But the Court recognizes some subtlety in the caselaw as to this issue. As a consequence, the Court is disinclined to rule that Pinnacle's refusal to move in negotiations based on advice that counsel may have given to Pinnacle with which this Court now disagrees rose to the level of either bad faith or a failure to satisfy statutory requirements for negotiation in good faith. Thus the Court assumes, for the purpose of the analysis that follows, that Pinnacle complied with the requirement under section 1113(b)(2) that Pinnacle meet to confer in good faith with the Union after making its proposal.

2. Necessity

As noted above, the most fundamental requirement for rejection of a collective bargaining agreement is that the rejection must be "necessary." The Court is compelled to find that in nearly every respect, Pinnacle has made the required showing.

Though the Court regards it as unnecessary and inappropriate to here set forth in detail evidence it heard in closed proceedings at trial, and findings it has set forth in the Confidential Supplement, the bottom line is clear — and the question is not in any way close. Pinnacle's liquidity crisis is acute, and its pilot labor costs are considerably over market. These are critical issues in the short run and the long run, and without correcting both, Pinnacle cannot reorganize. Indeed, without correcting the former, Pinnacle would quickly come to an end.

(a) Liquidity as Resulting in Necessity

The Court has addressed Pinnacle's liquidity situation in the Confidential Supplement. It is sufficient for purposes of this public discussion to state that Pinnacle's liquidity situation is serious. The issue is not that the liquidity situation is disputed in any way. To their credit, the Pilots acknowledge it. But they say that the liquidity problems are not their fault; that the liquidity problems were exacerbated, if not also caused, by one-time transitional costs in 2011 and 2012; and that the cost-cutting measures Pinnacle seeks would take so long as to be ineffectual in solving the liquidity problem that there is no point to asking the Pilots to make the requested sacrifices.

The Pilots are right with respect to the underlying facts, but not with respect to the conclusion or what needs to be done. Section 1113 determinations are not an exercise in finding fault; they are an exercise in problem solving — determining what measures are necessary to enable a debtor to reorganize, and, in extreme cases, what measures are necessary to enable a debtor to survive. It is not the Pilots' fault that the Debtor has serious liquidity issues, but it is only through sacrifices the Pilots will have to make that the liquidity problem may be resolved.

The Pilots are also correct that even if they make concessions — particularly concessions with respect to work rules — those concessions would not, by themselves, have a quick enough economic effect to respond to Pinnacle's liquidity crisis. All parties recognize that reality. The most likely source of a solution to that would be short term relief from Delta — which undoubtedly has an incentive to keep Pinnacle alive (as Delta has done through the duration of Pinnacle's chapter 11 cases through DIP financing) to keep Pinnacle's planes flying to meet Delta's own operational needs. But Delta has stated that it is not interested in talking to Pinnacle about help with Pinnacle's short term liquidity problems if Pinnacle doesn't first get its labor costs house in order. The Court takes Delta at its word.

The Court well understands, of course, that there is no guarantee that if Pinnacle does gets its labor house in order, Delta will assist. But the Court can and must make an informed judgment as to the likelihood of assistance if Pinnacle does not get its labor house in order. The most serious risk (if not also likelihood) is that Delta would keep Pinnacle alive until Delta could put in place satisfactory substitutes for Pinnacle's services, and that Delta will then switch to cheaper alternatives, leaving Pinnacle then to fail — with insufficient liquidity, no other customers, and no choice then but to liquidate. That would be a tragic consequence for the Pilots and, of course, all of Pinnacle's other employees, and makes an overwhelming showing of what the Necessity provision of section 1113 requires.

(b) Excessive Costs as Resulting in Necessity

The Court is also compelled to find that Pinnacle has shown the necessity for dramatically reducing its Pilots' labor costs even apart from its liquidity situation. The Court has no doubt, based on its earlier Findings of Fact, that Pinnacle's Pilot labor costs are dramatically over market. A significant part of that overage results from the Pilots' high average level of seniority, but it is no less a problem. Other regional airlines have dramatically lower costs.

The backup to Delta's calculation as to the extent to which Pinnacle's costs are way over market was not made available — not to the Pilots and not to Pinnacle. So appropriately, Pinnacle took steps to try to corroborate the Delta calculation. Pinnacle did so through the Seabury analysis, explained by Ms. Hughes, and the Compass Lexecon analysis, explained by Mr. Kasper — each of which the Court finds to have been performed competently and in good faith. The corresponding analysis of the Union's own financial expert, Ms. Eubanks, was consistent with Pinnacle's expert's analysis, after adjustment for a computational error which resulted in most of the discrepancy.

The dramatic extent to which Pinnacle's costs are higher than market affects both Pinnacle's ability to get future work from other carriers and even from Delta itself, at least in 2018 and thereafter. The evidence the Court heard as to the extent to which the regional air transport industry is commoditized was effectively undisputed, and in any event was unrefuted and highly persuasive. So was the evidence of Delta's ability to invoke the reset provisions of the Delta Connection Agreements. Pinnacle can offer no bases for choosing its services over those of its competitors except on the basis of price. It will need to be among the lowest-cost providers in the industry.

Additionally, the requirement that the Court look also to the long term prevents the Court from being satisfied with band-aid solutions. The Pilots cannot proceed on the assumption that Delta is now stuck with Pinnacle, and that it doesn't now matter that the Pilots' wages make Pinnacle grossly uncompetitive. The Court cannot find Pinnacle's proposal for wage cuts to be unnecessary simply because they will become most critical only at a later time. When that later time comes, unless Pinnacle is then competitive, it will almost certainly lose its Delta business — the business from its only present customer.

And there will be no reasonable basis for concluding that Pinnacle will secure business from anyone else, unless its costs (and thus the rates it will be able to charge and still make a profit) are at least near, if not also at the same level as, the rates of its competitors. Then, without the dramatic reduction in costs that is necessary to make Pinnacle competitive, the Court will find it impossible to find, as confirmation of a reorganization plan requires, that confirmation is not likely to be followed by liquidation. A future liquidation will be a certainty, or a likelihood very close to one.

Thus the Court has found the requisite necessity for nearly all of the cost savings that Pinnacle seeks. The Court cannot, however, find the requisite necessity for the entirety of Pinnacle's "Ask." That is so because Pinnacle's proposal at least seemingly sought to place the Pilots' aggregate labor costs *below* those of Pinnacle's lowest cost competitors. That was aptly characterized by the Pilots as a "Race to the Bottom," and was unsupported by the evidence presented to the Court. It was particularly unsupported with respect to the ongoing relationship with Delta, since there would undoubtedly be costs — very possibly more than minimal ones — that Delta would have to incur upon shifting from one regional carrier to another, which would at least seemingly have to be trumped by any difference in pricing to warrant a shift away from Pinnacle, at least until 2018. And there was similarly no evidence that being *below* competitors' cost levels — as contrasted to being at approximately the same level — would be necessary to compete. Pinnacle has met its burden to show the requisite necessity for the great bulk of the cost savings it seeks. But for this reason, it has not shown the need for all of them.

The Pilots should not read too much, however, from the Court's view that the necessity for a "Race to the Bottom" has not been shown. Even with Pinnacle's somewhat excessive demands, the requisite necessity was shown for nearly all of Pinnacle's request. While Pinnacle asked for cost savings of $59.6 million, the Pilots offered only $33 million, and the Court is not even confident that the Pilots' valuation of the savings under their offer could fairly be regarded as that much, or would continue for the requisite time. The savings for which necessity has been shown are very near to the Pinnacle figure, and not at all close to the Pilots'.

(c) Necessity Requirement Conclusions

Because the proposal as put forward by Pinnacle was to a certain extent overreaching, the Court cannot find that the Necessity requirement of section 1113(b)(1) was satisfied. But Pinnacle's proposal was not overreaching by very much. The failure to meet the Necessity requirement with respect to the proposal as put forward requires denial of the motion without prejudice. If negotiations do not otherwise lead to agreement, a somewhat modified proposal may be put forward, and if necessary a new motion may be filed.

3. Fair and Equitable Treatment

With one exception (but only one), the Court determines that the modifications Pinnacle seeks meet all of the requirements, discussed above, for Fair and Equitable Treatment.

The principal potential unfairness addressed in briefing was the extent to which the Pilots were asked to take pay cuts and make other concessions relative to other unionized employees — especially flight attendants — and non unionized personnel. But after review of the evidence, the Court is satisfied with the reason for the greater sacrifice asked from the Pilots. A greater market disparity exists for the Pilots as compared to other labor groups, both union and non-union.

Pinnacle presented unrebutted testimony that its two other unionized work groups, the flight attendants and the dispatchers, were at or below market before any labor concessions. That is a critical distinction, and it satisfactorily explains why the Pilots needed to sacrifice more.

Likewise, the Court regarded it as important to query whether Pinnacle's non-unionized personnel — and its senior management in particular — were likewise sharing in the sacrifices asked of the Pilots. The testimony was unrebutted that Pinnacle's management receives below-market compensation. And while the evidence of sacrifices management made did not come in as clearly as the Court would have hoped (and the Pilots were not given the information as to this as early as the Court would have hoped), the showing ultimately was made that management sacrificed too, with reductions in pay of from 8% to 10%. That is not as much as the Pilots were asked to bear, but was in the context of below-market compensation for management.

There was a fair and reasonable basis for the sacrifices the Pilots were asked to make. In that respect, the "Fair and Equitable Treatment" requirement was satisfied.

There is, however, another consideration relevant to "Fair and Equitable Treatment" — fairness with respect to other stakeholders — and in this respect the Court finds deficiencies. Pinnacle is asking the Court for leave to abrogate numerous contractual obligations. That would result in great pain to the Pilots. The need to dramatically reduce the costs associated with the contractual obligations has been shown to exist — but Fair and Equitable Treatment requires ameliorating the pain to the Pilots (insofar as possible) by giving them, by means of appropriate profit sharing, or issuance of equity, a share in the fruits of any profits that their sacrifice might entail, and avoiding windfalls to others.

The Court is not satisfied that such has been offered here. Any such profit sharing — not being a cost Pinnacle would have to bear, but having relevance only after Pinnacle would be showing a profit — would have no impact on Pinnacle's liquidity or ability to compete. The Court was not impressed by Pinnacle's less than wholly direct response to the Court's concerns with respect to "the windfall that might perhaps happen if we implement these cost savings," or its vague assertion that we have a "very serious" profit sharing proposal to Pinnacle's unions. To the extent that Pinnacle contends that its proposal for profit sharing is in any way significant, the Court is surprised by that contention. The Court considers it very modest given the sacrifices the Pilots will have to bear. This case contrasts with *Northwest Airlines*, in which substantial profit sharing was offered to flight attendants under the proposal that ultimately warranted section 1113 relief.

The words "fair and equitable" have, or may have, different meanings in at least three different contexts in bankruptcy law. But the combination of making the Pilots take such a large haircut with minimal sharing in the benefits would subject the Pilots to the risk, if not certainty, of others (such as Equity) securing a windfall at the expense of the Pilots — who have, at least until this motion is granted, contractual rights. That is neither "fair" nor "equitable," by any measure under which those words might be construed. The Pilots must receive, in the form of equity or profit sharing, a greater share of any benefits that result from the abrogation of their contractual rights before the Court can find that they have received "Fair and Equitable Treatment."

However, in *Northwest Airlines Corp. v. Association of Flight Attendants (In re Northwest Airlines Corp.)*, 483 F.3d 160, 170–73 (2d Cir. 2007) ("*Northwest-Circuit*"), a case dealing with the propriety of an anti-strike injunction after an 1113 motion was granted (and not the allowance of a union's claim), the panel's two judge majority stated that the rejection of the collective bargaining agreement under section 1113 would result not in the breach and resulting prepetition claim that results from the rejection of executory contracts generally, but rather a court authorized "abrogation," *id.* at 170, 174; *accord id.* at 169, which would not result in an allowable claim for the disclaimer of the debtor's obligations. The *Northwest-Circuit* majority also made several statements effectively compelling the conclusion that union claims for rejection damages could not lie after a decision approving rejection under section 1113. *See* 483 F.3d at 174 ("We thus conclude that a bankruptcy court acting pursuant to § 1113 may authorize a debtor to abrogate its [collective bargaining agreement], effectively shielding it from a charge of breach."); *id.* at 172 ("If a carrier that rejected a [collective bargaining agreement] simultaneously breached that agreement and violated the [Railway Labor Act], the union would be correspondingly free to seek damages or strike, results inconsistent with Congress's intent in passing § 1113."). The *Northwest-Circuit* majority also twice mentioned, though without substantive discussion, a Tennessee bankruptcy court decision, affirmed at the district court level, that had held there is no claim for breach of a collective bargaining agreement in light of section 1113. *Id.* at 169, 172 (citing *In re Blue Diamond Coal Co.*, 147 B.R. 720 (Bankr. E.D. Tenn. 1992), *aff'd*, 160 B.R. 574 (E.D. Tenn. 1993).

After the decision in *Northwest-Circuit*, Judge Gropper of this Court, with extensive consideration of what the Circuit panel's majority had said, understandably ruled that *Northwest-Circuit* required union claims for rejection damages to be expunged. *See Northwest-Claims*, 366 B.R. at 275–76. If Pinnacle can abrogate the Pilots' contractual rights and deny them even a prepetition claim, it is all the more important that the Court take appropriate measures to ensure that the Pilots are fairly and equitably treated in the section 1113 process, especially by means that do not impair Pinnacle's ability to survive.

4. Balance of Equities

As discussed above, in *Carey Transportation*, the Second Circuit identified "at least" six "permissible equitable considerations" for use in determining if the equities favor rejection of a collective bargaining agreement. Though as is common when courts articulate multi-factor tests, all are not equally applicable or significant, four of the named factors weigh in favor of rejection:

#1:   liquidation is effectively a certainty if rejection is not permitted;

#2:   there will be a dramatic reduction in the value of creditors' claims if the bargaining agreement remains in force;

#5:   the Pilots wages are above market with respect to those of others in the industry;

#6:   the Company dealt with the Union in good faith in dealing with the Company's financial dilemma.

Factors #1 and #5 favor rejection particularly strongly. Factors #3 and #4 are effectively addressed in law that has come down since *Carey Transportation* — in *Northwest-Circuit* (holding, in the Railway Labor Act context, that a union's strike after an adverse section 1113 determination was granted could be enjoined), and in *Northwest-Circuit* and *Northwest Claims* (effectively stating, and holding, respectively, that union members' rejection claims should be expunged). Factors #3 and #4 tend to cut against granting section 1113 relief here, because they cut off mechanisms that Pilots might otherwise employ to ameliorate the harm to them resulting from an adverse 1113 decision but they are insufficient to trump the other factors, especially #1, which in this Court's view is by far the most important of the *Carey Transportation* enumerated considerations.

The Court noted above that it was free to consider other factors as well. A critical equitable consideration, in the Court's view, is the consequences of inaction, and the consequences to the other employees. As harsh as the consequences of relief here would be to the Pilots, they pale in comparison to the loss of 5,800 jobs (including those of the Pilots themselves) — which the Court finds to be a certainty if Pinnacle's labor costs are not dramatically reduced. As Judge Gropper put it in *Northwest Airlines* (also in the context of the Balance of Equities analysis that section 1113(c)(3), and *Carey Transportation*, require):

> The Court would do the flight attendants and the Debtors' thousands of other employees no favor if it refused to grant the Debtors' § 1113 relief, and the Debtors joined the ranks of the many other airlines that have liquidated as a consequence of a Chapter 11 filing.

Three deficiencies that the Court has addressed above and below prohibit, at this time, section 1113 relief. But they do not go to the Balance of Equities. This requirement has been satisfied. If the deficiencies the Court has noted above and below are satisfactorily addressed, and Pinnacle and the Union still cannot reach agreement, the Balance of Equities will not in any way be an impediment to section 1113 relief.

5. Good Cause to Reject Company's Proposal

The final requirement to be addressed, as also discussed above, is that of section 1113(c)(2) that "the authorized representative of the employees has refused to accept such proposal without good cause . . . ." In this case, the Court finds that the Pilots had good cause for declining to accept Pinnacle's proposal as it was then put forward — though they would no longer have such good cause if Pinnacle revised and negotiated its proposal in the three respects the Court identifies here.

Two of those respects have already been addressed. As noted above, Pinnacle showed an overwhelming necessity for very major reductions in its Pilot labor costs — having shown, among many other things, that its Pilot labor costs are substantially over market, and are effectively going to kill Pinnacle. But Pinnacle overreached. Without showing that the necessity it had otherwise shown required the Pilots' labor costs to be *below* market, Pinnacle at least seemingly asked the

Pilots to agree to a proposal premised on that. Pinnacle sought what the Pilots aptly called a "Race to the Bottom," which was unjustified by Pinnacle's showing of necessity. The Court does not need to decide, and does not now decide, whether a "Race to the Bottom" would be appropriate upon an appropriate evidentiary showing that a continuing leapfrog toward lower and lower labor costs is necessary to compete or survive; it was not made here. The Pilots had good cause to reject Pinnacle's proposal for this reason.

The Court has also addressed Pinnacle's very modest proposal to assuage the pain the Pilots would suffer by means of profit sharing mechanisms. To the extent necessity could be shown (and as it was shown, with respect to the great bulk of Pinnacle's "Ask"), the Pilots would lack good cause to reject proposals for reduced compensation and benefits, as each would directly impact cash flow and Pinnacle's liquidity. But profit sharing would not impact Pinnacle's operating cash flow. It would have relevance only thereafter. Pinnacle could have, and should have, offered more to the Pilots to make up for their sacrifices in a way that would not have affected Pinnacle's ability to be profitable and survive. The Pilots had good reason to reject Pinnacle's proposal for this reason as well.

The Pilots also had good cause to reject Pinnacle's proposal by reason of Pinnacle's negotiating conduct. While Pinnacle was willing to secure the cost savings it wanted by flexible allocation between wages, benefits and work rules, it was unwilling to show any movement whatever in its aggregate demand.

Pinnacle says that it justified this approach by reason of its counsel's review of the underlying law in this area, and counsel's conclusion that the statutory framework, and earlier caselaw, did not permit movement in the overall "Ask" once Pinnacle's proposal was made — reasoning that if there was any room for negotiation, the proposal would not be "necessary." That view was incorrect. There is no requirement in section 1113 law that in order to show "Necessity," a debtor show no movement in its overall demand whatever — particularly in the period between the filing of the section 1113 motion and the time of hearing on it, during which section 1113(b)(2) requires continuing good faith efforts to try to reach agreement. If such stonewalling were in fact required, that would wholly frustrate the "entire thrust of section 1113" — as stated by the Second Circuit in *Maxwell Newspapers*, "to ensure that well-informed and good faith negotiations occur in the market place, not as part of the judicial process, and . . . to encourage such a negotiated voluntary modification."

Pinnacle articulated the bases for its view on what it asserted was language in *American Airlines*: a supposed statement — surrounded in quotes in the Closing Arguments transcript consistent with the way counsel described it in argument, as if it appeared in the *American Airlines* opinion, and following counsel's statement of "what does Judge Lane say?" — that "good faith is satisfied by remaining open to alternative saving approaches while adhering to a necessary cost saving target." But that is not in fact what Judge Lane said, nor was it even a fair paraphrase — especially with the failure to mention the other things Judge Lane said. Additionally, Pinnacle failed to consider the context of the statements that *were* made by Judge Lane on the pages to which Pinnacle referred; failed to address *other* things Judge Lane said, on those pages and earlier in his decision; and failed to consider other relevant analysis, by Judges Hardin and Gropper, in *Delta Airlines* and *Northwest Airlines*, the other cases on point.

First, Pinnacle gave insufficient attention to the context in which Judge Lane made his remarks. The time to which Judge Lane was referring was the time before the American motion was filed — not the time relevant here, between motion filing and hearing, where Pinnacle's failure to show any negotiating movement is of such concern to this Court. Second, Pinnacle ignored the fact-driven nature of Judge Lane's conclusion that the failure to move was there justified under the facts of that case, and also ignored Judge Lane's careful statement that, with respect to certain aspects of the American proposal, American's unwillingness to move was "not necessarily" a failure to confer in good faith.

Third, but no less important, Pinnacle failed to address rulings by other judges in this district, in *Delta Airlines* and *Northwest Airlines*, noted by Judge Lane, that as a general matter had recognized the importance (though not necessity in every case) of a debtor's willingness to show negotiating movement, at least in some respects, in the period after filing of a motion. In his earlier general discussion of the law, before his later, fact-driven, discussion of the facts there before him, Judge Lane analyzed Judge Gropper's and Hardin's earlier rulings in *Northwest Airlines*, and *Delta Airlines*, respectively. In significant reliance on those earlier holdings, Judge Lane observed, in *American Airlines*:

> Section 1113(b)(2) requires that after a proposal is made, but before a hearing on rejection, the debtor meet with the union at reasonable times to negotiate in good faith. To satisfy the requirement of negotiating in good faith, a debtor cannot approach negotiations with a "take it or leave it" mentality.
>
> . . . .

It was only then that Judge Lane went on to state an exception to the general rule:

> This should be determined, however, on a case by case basis. For "depending on the facts of the case, a debtor may not be obligated to reduce the total amount of cost savings requested in its original proposal to demonstrate good faith."

When the totality of what Judges Hardin, Gropper and Lane said is put together, a more accurate description of the general rule emerges. It starts with what Judge Hardin initially said in *Delta Airlines*, goes on to what Judge Gropper said in *Northwest Airlines*, and then goes on to what Judge Lane actually said in *American Airlines*: a debtor generally cannot be said to comply with its obligation to confer in good faith in attempting to reach mutually satisfactory modifications when it steadfastly maintains that its initial proposal is nonnegotiable. But parts of a debtor's section 1113 proposal may be non-negotiable if they are essential to a debtor's reorganization. It is *not necessarily* bad faith to adhere to a necessary cost-saving target, but this depends on the facts of the case, and *depending on the facts of the case*, a debtor may not be obligated to reduce the total amount of cost savings requested in its original proposal to demonstrate good faith.

But most importantly, there is no legal duty imposed on a debtor to stay put in negotiations, so as to preserve the debtor's showing of necessity or for any other reason. In fact, movement, and not stonewalling, should be the norm.

Ultimately, all of this depends on whether the *entirety* of the demand put forward by a debtor at the time of the filing of the motion is indeed necessary. As Judge Hardin recognized in *Delta Airlines*, the entirety generally will not be. And here the Court finds, on the facts of this case, that the entirety of Pinnacle's demand was not necessary, and that Pinnacle's insistence on no movement whatever in its aggregate demand, after it filed its motion, was error.

Given the need to synthesize several cases to get to the right result, and the false signals that apparently resulted when language was taken out of context, the Court is not of a mind to tag Pinnacle here with bad faith. But Pinnacle was wrong when it concluded that it had had an absolute right (or, worse yet, a duty) not to budge as to its aggregate demand in the negotiations following the filing of its motion. Under these circumstances, the Pilots certainly had good cause to reject Pinnacle's proposal when it evidenced no movement by Pinnacle whatever.

Conclusion

Pinnacle has come very close to making the showing it must make to reject its collective bargaining agreement with the Pilots. Pinnacle's need for significant reductions in labor costs is profound. Though Delta failed to do everything it could have done to document the extent to which Pinnacle's labor costs exceed those of other Delta regional carriers, Pinnacle's own efforts to investigate that issue satisfied the Court that Pinnacle's pilot labor costs are way over market. And Pinnacle's liquidity issues make it clear that Pinnacle cannot continue under the status quo. As unfortunate as pay cuts for the Pilots would be, the liquidation of Pinnacle, and the loss of 5,800 jobs, would be far worse.

Thus the necessity for dramatic cuts in Pilot labor costs has been shown. So have all of the other requirements for the relief Pinnacle seeks on this motion, with very limited exceptions. The only remaining issues are (1) the *full extent* of the necessary cuts in Pilot labor expense, by reason of failure to show necessity for a "Race to the Bottom" making the Pilots' costs *lower* than anyone else's; (2) whether the Pilots' pain should have been ameliorated, at least to some greater extent, by a better proposal to allow them to share, through equity or profit sharing, in fruits of concessions they were asked to make; and (3) whether Pinnacle properly could have shown no movement whatever in its overall cost savings demand.

With respect to each of these matters (but these matters alone), the Court finds Pinnacle's proposal insufficient to pass muster under sections 1113(b) and 1113(c). While necessity was shown for the great bulk of the requested pay cuts, necessity was not shown for all of them, resulting in a failure to satisfy section 1113(b)(1).

The failure to offer greater equity or profit sharing to better offset the Pilots' wage and benefits sacrifices — which, in the absence of any modification, would give others a windfall at the Pilots' expense — resulted in a failure of the section 1113(b)(1)'s requirement that Pilots be treated fairly and equitably.

And the three deficiencies just noted gave the Pilots good cause not to accept Pinnacle's proposal.

Pinnacle may be well served to present a new proposal that cures the deficiencies just noted. If Pinnacle does so, and if that does not by itself result in consensual agreement after negotiation with the Pilots, a subsequent motion for 1113 relief will almost certainly be granted.

NOTES AND QUESTIONS

Does the fact that a proposal to modify a collective bargaining agreement that violates federal labor law *per se* constitute good cause for its rejection? *See Sheet Metal Workers' Int'l Ass'n, Local 9 v. Mile Hi Metal Sys., Inc.*, 899 F.2d 887, 891 (10th Cir. 1990) ("fact that a proposal, if implemented, would violate federal labor law does not necessarily mean that the requirements of section 1113 are not satisfied, and therefore, the union is not relieved of the duty to bargain in good faith"). Code § 1113 also equips debtors with a tool a little blunter than outright rejection of the collective bargaining agreement. Section 1113(e) permits the court to authorize the interim modification of "terms, conditions, wages, benefits, or work rules" if such modifications are "essential to the continuation of the debtor's business, or . . . to avoid irreparable damage to the estate . . . ." This section has been construed to mean that "interim changes may only be authorized if the evidence establishes that, without such changes, the company will collapse and the employees will no longer have their jobs." *In re Salt Creek Freightways*, 46 B.R. 347, 350 (Bankr. D. Wyo. 1985). Notably, interim relief does not relieve the parties from their obligation under § 1113(c) to bargain in good faith toward modification or rejection of the contract. *Id.* at 351.

Chapter 8

CLAIMS AGAINST THE DEBTOR

§ 8.01 INTRODUCTION TO THE PROOF AND ALLOWANCE OF CLAIMS IN CHAPTER 11

You have asked Carol Charisma to set the day aside so that she can spend some time reviewing "proofs of claim" with you. Carol considers the mountain of papers on the conference table and sighs. "I take it those are the proofs of claim." You nod and explain that a proof of claim is the written statement that a creditor files with the bankruptcy court in order to present a demand for payment. Code § 501(a); Rule 3001. An equity security holder may file a document known as a "proof of interest," and many of the rules governing proofs of claim apply to proofs of interest as well. For administrative claims, the analog is usually styled "Request for Payment of Administrative Claim" and is prepared so that it mirrors the substance of a proof of claim, with a few changes as needed to reflect the administrative nature of the claim. At this point, you and Carol are concentrating on claims, not interests or administrative claims.

In a Chapter 11 case, proofs of claim must be filed before a deadline commonly referred to as a *bar date* that is set by the court upon motion of the debtor or other interested party. Rule 3003(c)(3). As one court observed:

> The creditors and bankruptcy court must be able to rely on a fixed financial position of the debtor in order to evaluate intelligently the proposed plan . . . . After initiating a carefully orchestrated plan of reorganization, the untimely interjection of an unanticipated claim, particularly a large one, can destroy the fragile balance struck by all the interested parties in the plan.

In re Analytical Sys., Inc., 933 F.2d 939, 942, n. 5. (11th Cir. 1991). Accordingly, bar dates are strictly enforced as long as sufficient notice to satisfy the requirements of due process has been given. Failure to timely file a proof of claim is grounds for disallowance of a claim. Code § 502(b)(9); Bankruptcy Rule 3003(c)(2). Interestingly, though, Code § 1111(a) makes filing unnecessary for claims that are listed in the debtor's schedules, *if* those claims are *not* listed as disputed, contingent, or unliquidated. If a claim is listed as disputed, contingent, or unliquidated, a proof of claim is required.[1]

Carol looks at the piles of documents on the table and shakes her head. "All those claims were scheduled as disputed, contingent, or unliquidated?" You explain that,

---

[1] *Pioneer Inv. Servs. Co. v. Brunswick Assocs.*, 507 U.S. 380, 384 (1993)

even when filing may not be necessary, § 1111(a) notwithstanding, many seasoned practitioners take the precaution of filing.[2]

Sensing from her groans that Carol is a little daunted by the number of claims that have to be reviewed, you try to explain why the task of reviewing these proofs of claim, though tedious, is so important:

1. Only holders of "claims" that are "allowed" are entitled to vote on reorganization plans, Code § 1126(a), to receive distributions under a plan.[3]

2. In order for a claim to be allowed under Code § 502, it must be evidenced by a timely filed proof of claim. Indeed, § 502(a) states that if a proof of claim is filed or is deemed filed under § 1111(a), the claim that it represents will be deemed *allowed*, unless a party in interest objects. This is why a trustee or debtor in possession is duty bound to "examine proofs of claims and object to the allowance of any claim that is improper." *See* Code §§ 704(5); 1106(a)(1); 1107(a).

3. When a debtor in possession or trustee objects to the allowance of a claim, the basis of the objection may be that the claim lacks merit. Code § 502(b)(1) provides that a claim is not allowable to the extent that the "claim is unenforceable against the debtor and property of the debtor, under any agreement or applicable law . . . ." Alternatively, the objection may be based on one of the more specific grounds described in the balance of § 502.[4]

"Slow down, a second," Carol says. "Isn't there a more basic objection that we also have to keep in mind as we review these proofs of claim? Before we consider whether a claim is allowable, shouldn't we be considering, at the outset, whether what we are looking at is even a 'claim' at all?"

"You're right. There are a few more dots that we have to connect to get the full picture."

"I'm waiting."

"I'm billing," you smile.

---

[2] Prudent practitioners may have several reasons for doing this. They may not know how a claim is scheduled (and they may not want to waste time finding out). They may know how a claim is scheduled but be concerned that a debtor will amend its schedules to recharacterize the claim as disputed, contingent, or unliquidated. They may have reason to worry that the case will be converted from Chapter 11 to Chapter 7 down the road. If that happens, only claims with respect to which proofs were *actually filed* (as opposed to *deemed filed*) in the superceded Chapter 11 case will be treated as having been automatically filed in the superceding Chapter 7 case. Rule 1019(3). Thus, prudence may dictate the filing of a proof of claim rather than relying on § 1111(a) to protect a creditor's interest. All of this might lead one to conclude that there is no reason not to file a proof of claim, but in fact there may be. A creditor that files a proof of claim waives its right to a jury trial in an action to recover a preference or fraudulent transfer. *See Langenkamp v. Culp*, 498 U.S. 42 (1990).

[3] Holders of administrative expenses allowed under Code § 503 are also entitled to receive distributions under the plan. *See* discussion in § 8.05, *supra*.

[4] Under § 502(a), any "party in interest" may object to the allowance of a claim, but typically such objections are made by the debtor in possession or trustee. When an objection is made, the court must rule on it. § 502(b). Generally, the hearing on the allowance or disallowance of a claim is a core proceeding under 28 U.S.C. § 157(b)(2)(B); hence it is the province of bankruptcy judges.

She doesn't.

"As I said, in order for a claim to be allowed, it must be evidenced by a timely filed proof of claim. Code § 501 says that a proof of claim is to be filed by a 'creditor.' A *creditor* is an entity that holds a 'claim' that arose before the order for relief.[5] And that brings us back to your question, and the definition of 'claim.' The Code's definition of claim is very broad. According to Code § 101(5), a claim is a:

> (A) right to payment, whether or not such right is reduced to judgment, liquidated, unliquidated, fixed, contingent, matured, unmatured, disputed, undisputed, legal, equitable, secured, or unsecured; or

> (B) right to an equitable remedy for breach of performance if such breach gives rise to a right to payment, whether or not such right to an equitable remedy is reduced to judgment, fixed, contingent, matured, unmatured, disputed, undisputed, secured, or unsecured.

"Note also that § 101(12) says that 'debt' means 'liability on a claim.' Thus, the Code seems to use the terms 'claim' and 'debt' to refer to the same concept." In the words of one court, "The terms 'debt' and 'claim' are synonymous and refer to a single obligation as seen from the point of view of the debtor and creditor; a debtor has 'debts' and a creditor has 'claims.' " *In re Jordan*, 166 B.R. 201, 202 (Bankr. D. Me. 1994). *See also Siegel v. Fed. Home Loan Mortg. Corp.*, 143 F.3d 525, 532 (9th Cir. 1998).

Finally, you point out that whether an obligation is a claim determines more than whether the holder will be entitled to vote on a reorganization plan or share in a distribution under it. It also determines whether the obligation will be discharged in Chapter 11. This is so because the confirmation of a reorganization plan discharges the debtor from "any debt that arose before the date of such confirmation," whether or not a proof of claim was filed, whether or not "such claim" was allowed, and whether or not the holder of such claim voted to accept the plan. Thus, a claim need not be allowed to be discharged. It needs only to have arisen prior to confirmation of the plan.

"The definition is so broad, it sounds as if almost anything can be a claim," Carol says.

There is no doubt that Congress intended to paint with a broad brush when it came up with that definition of claim. The purpose was to sweep as many of a debtor's legal obligations into a bankruptcy case as possible in order to provide debtors "the broadest possible relief," while also allowing creditors to recover something on their claims, no matter how remote or contingent. Although the concept of claim is elastic, it is not without limits, and those limits will be explored in the balance of this chapter.[6]

"Good." Carol says. "I think I'm beginning to get a handle on the meaning of claim. But what about all those adjectives — liquidated, unliquidated, contingent, matured, unmatured, etc. — that modify it? What do they mean?"

---

[5] Code § 101(10).

[6] H.R. Rep. No. 95-595 at 309 (1977).

You tell Carol that all will be revealed in the course of your analysis of the proofs of claim. "Let's dig in."

§ 8.02 ESTIMATION OF CONTINGENT AND UNLIQUIDATED CLAIMS AND TEMPORARY ALLOWANCE OF DISPUTED CLAIMS

You slide the first pile of papers over to Carol's side of the table and invite her to pick the first one.

"Hmm," she says. "This is interesting. This one was filed by Sound Solutions, and it claims we owe $150,000 for goods sold and delivered."

"Isn't Sound Solutions your sound card supplier?"

"It is. But I happen to know that this bill is for a bad shipment that caused us lots of problems. Half the cards turned out to be defective and we had to return them. It slowed down the line for a week. Our customers were really angry. We had a lot of products returned to us. We paid for a portion of the shipment, but when we discovered the problem we refused to pay the balance. I can't believe that now they're claiming we owe them for the entire shipment. In fact, I think we should take the position that they owe us for the disruption they caused."

You make a few notes. "All right. Let's start a pile of claims that we'll be objecting to on the grounds that they're *disputed* . . . "

"What exactly does that mean?"

You remind Carol that the Bankruptcy Code, in § 101(5), broadly defines the term claim as a right to payment, even though that right is unliquidated, contingent, unmatured, or disputed.

- A right to payment is said to be unliquidated if the existence of the claim is not in question, but the amount of the claim is. If the amount is easily ascertainable, the claim is liquidated.[7]

- A right to payment is said to be *contingent* if the debt is one that the debtor will be called upon to pay only upon the occurrence of an extrinsic event and if that occurrence or event was reasonably contemplated by the debtor and the creditor.[8] A classic example of a contingent liability is that of the guarantor of a promissory note who, under applicable state law, has no liability until the principal maker defaults.

- A right to payment is said to be *unmatured* if the time for payment has not arrived. For example, a promissory note that comes due one year from now gives rise to an unmatured claim.

---

[7] *U.S. v. Verdunn*, 89 F.3d 799, 802 (11th Cir. 1996) (debtor's tax liability was easily determined by reference to the government's notice of deficiency); *In re Teigen*, 228 B.R. 720, 723 (Bankr. D.S.D. 1998) (claim based on a guarantee was unliquidated because amount of debtor's liability depended on the amount creditor received under the principal maker's Chapter 11 plan)

[8] *In re All Media Properties, Inc.*, 5 B.R. 126, 133 (Bankr. S.D. Tex. 1980), aff'd, 646 F.2d 193 (5th Cir. 1981).

- A right to payment is said to be *disputed* if the existence of the liability or the amount of the liability is challenged.[9] A disputed claim may also be contingent, unliquidated, or both.[10] For example, the guarantor of a promissory note may assert the principal maker's *defenses* to payment if there are any.

"So I guess what you are telling me is that the Sound Solutions claim is at best disputed and unliquidated," said Carol. "But I have a question. Suppose that we object to the allowance of this claim. I understand that if Amphydynamics weren't in Chapter 11, Sound Solutions might just sue us and we might file a counterclaim and raise a defense of recoupment. If we couldn't settle, things would probably be sorted out in court. But the fact is that Amphy is in bankruptcy, and I don't understand how we're supposed to get a plan negotiated, voted on, and confirmed with a claim like this still pending."

You respond that several solutions are possible.

One is that Amphydynamics and Sound Solutions will be able to settle their dispute and stipulate as to the allowed amount of the Sound Solutions claim.[11] Another possibility is that the court will grant relief from the stay to permit the liquidation of the claim through litigation in nonbankruptcy court. There is yet another possibility. Code § 502(c)(1) requires the bankruptcy court to *estimate* the amount of any contingent or unliquidated claim, if fixing or liquidating the claim would unduly delay the administration of the case. Similarly, the court may temporarily allow a disputed claim under the last sentence of Rule 3018. Both estimation and temporary allowance are very fluid processes that can be tailored to match the needs of the parties and the court under the particular circumstances of the case at hand.

In *Bittner v. Borne Chem. Co.*, 691 F.2d 134 (3d Cir. 1982), the court explained the very fluid § 502(c) process and how it is subject to very deferential review on appeal:

> The Code [and the Rules] are silent as to the manner in which contingent or unliquidated claims are to be estimated. Despite the lack of express direction on the matter, we are persuaded that Congress intended the procedure to be undertaken initially by the bankruptcy judges, using whatever method is best suited to the particular contingencies at issue. The principal consideration must be an accommodation to the underlying purposes of the Code. It is conceivable that in rare and unusual cases arbitration or even a jury trial on all or some of the issues may be necessary

---

[9] *In the Matter of Knight*, 55 F.3d 231, 235 (7th Cir. 1995).

[10] *In re Barcal*, 213 B.R. 1008, 1012 (B.A.P. 8th Cir. Neb. 1997).

[11] Such a compromise or settlement is subject to court approval. Bankruptcy Rule 9019. Since Amphy appears to hold a claim against Sound Solutions, it is also important to note that a claim belonging to the debtor is property of the estate under Code § 541(a). In other words, a claim or, to use a somewhat dated expression, a "chose in action," is an asset of the debtor. Code § 1123(b)(3) provides for the settlement of such claims held by the estate in the context of a plan. Settlement of such a claim outside a plan is regarded as a use or sale of property under Code § 363. Accordingly, compliance with the notice and hearing provisions of § 363 may be required. *See* chapter 6 of the casebook and *In re Dow Corning Corp.*, 198 B.R. 214 (Bankr. E.D. Mich. 1996).

to obtain a reasonably accurate evaluation of the claims. *See* 3 *Collier on Bankruptcy* ¶ 502.03 (15th ed. 1981). Such methods, however, usually will run counter to the efficient administration of the bankrupt's estate and where there is sufficient evidence on which to base a reasonable estimate of the claim, the bankruptcy judge should determine the value. In so doing, the court is bound by the legal rules which may govern the ultimate value of the claim. For example, when the claim is based on an alleged breach of contract, the court must estimate its worth in accordance with accepted contract law. *See, e.g.,* 3 *Collier on Bankruptcy* ¶ 57.15[3.2] (14th ed. 1977). However, there are no other limitations on the court's authority to evaluate the claim save those general principles which should inform all decisions made pursuant to the Code.

In reviewing the method by which a bankruptcy court has ascertained the value of a claim under section 502(c)(1), an appellate court may only reverse if the bankruptcy court has abused its discretion. That standard of review is narrow. The appellate court must defer to the congressional intent to accord wide latitude to the decisions of the tribunal in question. Section 502(c)(1) of the Code embodies Congress' determination that the bankruptcy courts are better equipped to evaluate the evidence supporting a particular claim within the context of a particular bankruptcy proceeding.

. . . .

If the bankruptcy court estimated the value of the [stockholders'] claims according to the ultimate merits of their state court action, such a valuation method is not inconsistent with the principles which imbue Chapter 11. . . . According to the bankruptcy court's findings of fact, the [stockholders'] chances of ultimately succeeding in the state court action are uncertain at best. Yet, if the court had valued the [stockholders'] claims according to the present probability of success, the [stockholders] might well have acquired a significant, if not controlling, voice in the reorganization proceedings. The interests of those creditors with liquidated claims would have been subject to the [debtor's] interests, despite the fact that the state court might ultimately decide against those interests after the reorganization. The bankruptcy court may well have decided that such a situation would at best unduly complicate the reorganization proceedings and at worst undermine [the debtors] attempts to rehabilitate its business and preserve its assets for the benefit of its creditors and employees. By valuing the ultimate merits of the [stockholders'] claims at zero, and temporarily disallowing them until the final resolution of the state action, the bankruptcy court avoided the possibility of a protracted and inequitable reorganization proceeding while ensuring that Borne will be responsible to pay a dividend on the claims in the event that the state court decides in the [stockholders'] favor. Such a solution is consistent with the Chapter 11 concerns of speed and simplicity but does not deprive the . . . stockholders of the right to recover on their contingent claims against Borne.

NOTES AND QUESTIONS

(1) *Other Methods of Estimating Claims*. The "ultimate merits" approach adopted by the court in *Bittner v. Borne* is not the only way to estimate claims. For example, in *In re Baldwin United Corp.*, 55 B.R. 885 (Bankr. S.D. Ohio 1985), the court, after abbreviated discovery, conducted a two-day bench trial with a limit on the number of witnesses that could be called.   The "present value of the probability" test that the *Bittner* court rejected has been followed in other cases. *See, e.g., In re Farley, Inc.*, 146 B.R. 748 (Bankr. N.D. Ill. 1992). In light of the fact that a state court had previously denied the debtor's motion for summary judgment, the bankruptcy court reasoned:

> Barring settlement, the tort case will be going to trial before a state court jury. Therefore, the subject claims cannot and do not have a zero value in any legal or practical sense. Their more realistic value consists of the amount stipulated as damages in [the event the debtor] is found liable, discounted by the chance that [the debtor] will not be found liable.

Id. at 753.

(2) *Effect of Estimation*. In *Bittner*, the stockholder claims were estimated to be worthless and *temporarily* disallowed, pending an on-the-merits determination in state court. Accordingly, the stockholders were deprived of the opportunity to vote on Borne's reorganization plan. However, the court also required the debtor to waive discharge of the stockholder claims as a condition of confirming the plan. In the unlikely event that a state court ruled in favor of the stockholders, Borne would have been responsible "for paying a dividend on the claims." Would this sort of tentative approach work in cases involving unliquidated claims so large or numerous that their allowance would render a confirmed plan unfeasible? What is the effect of claims estimation in the absence of such a waiver of discharge?

As we will see, confirmation of a Chapter 11 plan discharges the debtor from liability on all debts that arose prior to confirmation, except to the extent that they are dealt with in the plan. Code § 1141(d). Accordingly, in the absence of *Bittner*-type limitations, estimation would amount to a final adjudication of the claim. As one court has observed, "it is apparent that the estimation of a claim conclusively sets the outer limits of a claimant's right to recover either from the debtor or the estate, and that estimated claims are covered by a debtor's discharge, subject only to a Code § 502(j) motion for reconsideration at a later time." *In re Baldwin-United Corp.*, 55 B.R. 885, 898 (Bankr. S.D. Ohio 1985). Section 502(j) provides that as long as a case is not closed, creditors may request to have any allowed or disallowed claim reconsidered for cause. Should the res judicata or collateral estoppel effect of an estimate depend on whether the estimating procedure that the court employs is an attempt (albeit summary) to get at the merits, rather than a "best guess" as to the probable outcome if the issue goes to trial?

(3) *Estimation of Personal Injury Claims*. Unless a claimholder consents, a bankruptcy court may not determine the amount of a personal injury or wrongful death claim for purposes of distribution. That must be done in the district court for the district in which the bankruptcy case is pending or in which the claim arose. 28

U.S.C. § 157(b)(5). This provision was a hard-fought-for success of the plaintiff's trial lawyer bar, which feared loss of a right to jury trial and other rights that are inherent in a normal district court proceeding but may be lost in the bankruptcy court's streamlined, "equitable" proceedings. However, a bankruptcy court may estimate the claims for purposes of establishing voting rights or determining the feasibility of a Chapter 11 plan. *A.H. Robins Co. v. Piccinin*, 788 F.2d 994, 1011–12 (4th Cir. 1986).

Consider the following case regarding estimation of disputed claims, which serves as the segue to the section of this chapter on grounds for disallowance of claims.

IN RE HARMONY HOLDINGS, LLC
United States Bankruptcy Court for the District of South Carolina
395 B.R. 350 (2008)

This matter comes before the Court upon the Motion for Temporary Allowance of Chapter 11 Claims for Voting Purposes ("Motion") filed by Barney Ng and R.E. Loans, LLC (collectively "Movants") on August 27, 2008. A hearing was held on the Motion September 18, 2008. Harmony Holdings, LLC, Spanish Moss Development, LLC (collectively "Debtors"), and Movants appeared by and through counsel. This Court has jurisdiction pursuant to 28 U.S.C. § 1334 and this is a core proceeding pursuant to 28 U.S.C. § 157(b)(2)(A) and (B). In compliance with Fed. R. Civ. P. 52, made applicable to this proceeding by Fed. R. Bankr. P. 7052 and 9014, the Court makes the following Findings of Fact and Conclusions of Law.

Findings of Fact

1. Debtors own approximately 780 acres of real property and seek to develop a planned community including both commercial and residential sections and a marina. Debtors filed voluntary petitions under chapter 11 of the Bankruptcy Code on January 31, 2008. Debtors' schedules filed with the petitions list Movants as creditors with disputed claims.

2. On May 23, 2008 Movants filed six proofs of claim, three in each case, evidencing secured claims against the bankruptcy estates. R.E. Loans filed a secured claim in the amount of $41,432,036.90 in each case. Barney Ng filed two $5,000,000.00 secured claims in each case, for a total claim of $10,000,000.00 in each case. The liabilities, if any, are joint and several such that a total of $51,432,036.90 is owed by the combined Debtors. The debts are secured by mortgages encumbering Debtors' real estate.

3. On June 13, 2008, Debtors objected to the claims and filed an adversary proceeding which includes the following causes of action: breach of contract and breach of implied covenant of good faith and fair dealing; fraud in the inducement to enter a contract; unconscionability; lender liability; unfair trade practices; rescission; conversion; fraudulent concealment; negligent misrepresentation; breach of contract accompanied by a fraudulent act; breach of fiduciary duty; demand for accounting; invalidation of the Defendant's liens; equitable subordination; setoff; and disallowance of Defendants' claims against the estate. (Adv. Proc.

C/A No. 08-80101-DD) (the "Litigation"). The objections to Movants' claims will be resolved through the adversary proceedings. The adversary proceeding will not be concluded before the deadline for voting on the plan of reorganization.

4. This Court determined the cases to be single-asset real estate cases, as defined by 11 U.S.C. § 101(51B), by order entered on June 20, 2008.

5. Debtors filed a Plan of Reorganization on July 23, 2008 and this Court established a deadline for objections to the Disclosure Statement and submission of ballots accepting or rejecting the plan of September 8, 2008.

6. Debtors' Plan of Reorganization provides a separate class for R.E. Loans, LLC and a separate class for Barney Ng. In each case the Movant is the only creditor in the respective class. The Plan of Reorganization provides that the allowed claims of the Movants, if any, will be paid in full with interest, albeit after some delay.

7. It appears that the continued operation of the Debtors, and thus the feasibility of reorganization, is dependent upon a loan from Kennedy Funding, Inc., which, if approved, is scheduled to close on October 29, 2008.

8. The confirmation hearing on Debtors' plan of reorganization is scheduled for October 28, 2008.

9. Barney Ng testified to the validity of Movants' claims and identified business records of R.E. Loans, LLC that support the amount of its claim.

10. Barney Ng testified that the two $5,000,000.00 notes in his favor are supported by the consideration of services he provided Debtors.

Conclusions of Law

Movants ask the Court to temporarily allow their claims for the purpose of voting on the Debtors' plan. Movants contend that their claims are impaired by the plan and the effect of allowing the claims, coupled with Movants' rejection of the plan, is to require consideration of 11 U.S.C. § 1129(b) at the time of the confirmation hearing.[4] Debtors contend that § 1126(a), coupled with § 502(a), is irreconcilably in conflict with Fed. R. Bankr. Proc. 3018 and that Movants should not be permitted to vote on the chapter 11 plan because their claims are not "allowed."[6] Alternatively Debtors argue that Movants do not meet the standard adopted by various courts for temporary allowance of claims pursuant to Rule 3018 and that the Court should exercise its discretion to deny the relief that has been requested.

Section 1126(a) states, "the holder of a claim or interest allowed under section 502 of this title may accept or reject a plan." Section 502(a) provides, "[a] claim or interest, proof of which is filed under section 501 of this title, is deemed allowed, unless a party in interest . . . objects." Authority to temporarily allow a claim comes, if at all, from Rule 3018(a) which states, "[n]otwithstanding objection to a

---

[4] Debtors contend that all other classes of creditors are either unimpaired or have accepted the plan. Movants did not dispute this.

[6] Debtors contend that Movants may otherwise raise objections to confirmation buy may not reject the plan.

claim or interest, the court after notice and hearing may temporarily allow the claim or interest in an amount which the court deems proper for the purpose of accepting or rejecting a plan." Our Court of Appeals has construed §§ 1126(a) and 502(a) stating, "[t]hese provisions allow only holders of claims to which no party has objected to vote on Chapter 11 plans." *Jacksonville Airport, Inc., v. Michkeldel, Inc.*, 434 F.3d 729, 731 (4th Cir. 2006).

Debtors contend that this analysis is dispositive and that the Bankruptcy Code conflicts with Rule 3018(a). Debtors ask the court to write the temporary claims allowance provision of Rule 3018(a) out of the Federal Rules of Bankruptcy Procedure. One court has opined:

> This Rule is obviously contrary to the seemingly clear provisions of the Code because it purports to give discretion to a court to permit a claim or interest to vote even though the claim is challenged and the objection is yet to be ruled on.

> It needs no elaborate citation of authorities for the proposition that the rulemaking power granted to the Supreme Court by 28 U.S.C. § 2075 on the subject of bankruptcy does not authorize adoption of rules which are in conflict with any Act of Congress.

In re Gardinier, Inc., 55 B.R. 601, 604 (Bankr. M.D. Fla. 1985). Interestingly, the *Gardinier* court decided the dispute on other grounds and no other court has followed its analysis in a published opinion. The *Gardinier* court itself recognizes,

> [O]ne can easily visualize a situation where it would be grossly unfair and unjust to disenfranchise any claim or interest just because the debtor interposed an objection to the allowance of the claim or interest. This is true especially in situations when the objection appears to be frivolous and without basis, and, because of time restraints, the court is not in the position to consider the objection on its merits prior to the confirmation hearing. It is not unusual in a Chapter 11 case that time is of the essence and frequently the success or failure hinges upon a prompt resolution of a debtor's right to obtain confirmation. This urgency, in turn, would not permit extensive hearings on objections to claims prior to the bar date fixed by the court for voting. To achieve justice, some discretion must be left to the court to deal with the problem just described.

Id. at 604.

The Fourth Circuit Court of Appeals has acknowledged the application of Bankruptcy Rule 3018(a). *See Jacksonville Airport, Inc. v. Michkeldel, Inc.*, 434 F.3d 729, 732 (4th Cir. 2006) ("Of course, the court upon motion could have temporarily allowed the claim for voting purposes or fully adjudicated [the] objection prior to the vote."). Although the statement is dicta, such statements by the Court of Appeals are persuasive authority and should be followed by a lower federal court absent well grounded reasons for following contrary authority.

The recognition of Rule 3018(a) as the basis for temporary allowance of claims for chapter 11 voting purposes by the Fourth Circuit finds statutory support in 28 U.S.C. 157(b)(2)(B) which provides the jurisdictional predicate for matters involving the, "allowance or disallowance of claims against the estate . . . and estimation of claims or interests for the purposes of confirming a plan under chapter 11, 12, or 13 of title 11 . . . ." Further support arises from the statutory scheme of § 502, which provides both for claims estimation (with respect to contingent or unliquidated claims where adjudication of the claim would unduly delay administration of the estate) and reconsideration of allowed and disallowed claims. *See* § 502(c), (j). This flexibility in dealing with claims suggests equitable authority to do just what Rule 3018 allows. There is, thus, no conflict of Rule 3018 with the statutory schemes weaving of voting rights and allowance of claims.

The question then remains whether, despite the objection to the claims of Movants, the court should temporarily allow the claims for voting purposes. The Bankruptcy Rules leave the determination of whether to temporarily allow a claim to the discretion of the court. Courts in other circuits have developed multi-factor tests for temporary allowance of claims. *See, e.g., In re Armstrong*, 294 B.R. 344, 354 (10th Cir. 2003) (Identifying three non-exclusive circumstances: (1) when an objection to the claim has been filed and the objection was filed too late to be heard prior to the confirmation hearing, (2) when fully hearing the objection would delay administration of the case, or (3) when the objection is frivolous or of questionable merit.); *In re Gardinier*, 55 B.R. 601, 604–05 (Bankr. M.D. Fla. 1985) (Considering (1) whether the objection to the claim at issue "appears to be frivolous or without basis," (2) the effective power which the holder of the disputed claim may have to "scuttle [the] reorganization proceeding, which is almost near completion[,]" and (3) given the facts of that case, that the debtor was willing to preserve funds to pay the disputed claim under the terms of the plan in the event the claim was ultimately allowed.). One judge in this District has stated "the Court must use its own discretion when deciding whether or not to allow the vote of a creditor whose claim has been objected to." *In re Remington Forest*, 1996 Bankr. LEXIS 1986 (Bankr. D.S.C. June 18, 1996) (internal citations omitted). When applying Rule 3018, courts often consider whether undue delay in case administration will result from delaying confirmation of a chapter 11 plan until after all claims objections can be heard. *In re Armstrong*, 294 B.R. at 354, *citing, 9 Collier on Bankruptcy* P 3018.01[5] (Lawrence P. King ed., 15th ed. 2003); *In re Gardinier*, 55 B.R. at 604–05.

Here, the Court has made the determination that these are single-asset real estate cases, triggering accelerated scheduling. There is complex litigation pending that will not be finalized before the balloting deadline or the confirmation hearing. Awaiting final adjudication of the adversary proceeding will delay the administration of the case.

Debtors' contention that Movants actions contributed to the delay in resolving the claims objections this case is not without basis. Movants filed a motion to dismiss the adversary proceeding rather than an answer. They withdrew the motion to dismiss and filed an answer shortly before a hearing on the motion to dismiss. Both parties have employed litigation strategies, including discovery disputes, which do not lend themselves a fast track. The truth, however, is that the litigation is complicated and it would be unrealistic to expect resolution in a few short months. There is a sound basis in advancing the administration of this case for the temporary allowance of Movants' claims.

At the hearing, Barney Ng testified on behalf of R.E. Loans and himself regarding the amounts of their claims. Mr. Ng testified as to the amount owing and due to R.E. Loans, and the court admitted into evidence the proofs of claim and attachments. Mr. Ng responded to earlier allegations made by the Debtors that R.E. Loans did not credit the underlying debt in the amount of $8.5 million for lots sold and released from the mortgage securing the debt to R.E. Loans. He testified that a percentage of each lot release was paid into an account established pursuant to the loan documents. Mr. Ng provided an accounting that reflects some $9.47 million was deposited into the account, of which approximately $5.97 million was returned to the Debtors and $3.5 million was applied to interest on the debt.

With regard to his own claim, Mr. Ng testified that the two $5 million non-interest-bearing notes were for the payment of services that he provided to the Debtors. He testified that he negotiated with the Debtors' then existing secured lender Western United Life Assurance ("WULA"). He testified that WULA was then in bankruptcy and it would not consent to new debt to be secured by the property. Mr. Ng's testimony indicated that he negotiated with WULA to restructure its debt and allow other new debt to be secured by the property. Mr. Ng further testified he negotiated the buyout of one of Harmony Holdings' members, Michael Chesser, for the benefit of the other member, Tim Casey. According to that testimony, the Debtors agreed to and did execute two $5 million non-interest-bearing notes for the services. The notes are secured by mortgages.

Rule 3018(a) provides for temporary allowance of claims, "in an amount which the court deems proper for the purpose of accepting or rejecting a plan." The temporary allowance of a claim under Rule 3018 is not dispositive as to the amount of the claim. Rather, Rule 3018 only provides limited voting authority to the creditor. *In re Armstrong*, 294 B.R. at 355. The evidence adduced at the hearing is sufficient to temporarily allow Movants' claims in the amounts filed.

For these reasons, the Court finds that R.E. Loans and Barney Ng have established their claims for the limited purpose of voting on the Debtors' Plan of Reorganization. This order does not otherwise adjudicate the claims or the adversary proceeding. The Movants claims are temporarily allowed, in the full amounts, for the purpose of voting on the plan of reorganization filed by the Debtors.

§ 8.03 OTHER GROUNDS FOR THE DISALLOWANCE OF CLAIMS

Bankruptcy Code § 502(b), (d), and (e) list several kinds of claims that, for a variety of practical and policy reasons, the Code makes nonallowable. You may already have studied these in your basic bankruptcy course. Read § 502 and consider the following problems.

(1) Prior to the time that Amphydynamics commenced its Chapter 11 case, a supplier sued it for breach of contract. In its answer, Amphydynamics asserted the affirmative defense that the supplier's claim was barred by the statute of limitations. If that is the case, is the supplier's claim allowable? What if the limitations period did not expire until after Amphydynamics

filed its petition? *See* Code § 502(b)(1) and Code § 108(c).

(2)   Assume that Amphydynamics borrowed $1.2 million on an unsecured basis from the bank. The loan agreement calls for monthly payments of $120,000 commencing January 1. Amphy defaults on the first payment and files a bankruptcy petition on January 15th. Amphy makes no payments to the bank during the pendency of the case. On May 1, the bank files a proof of claim. What is the amount of the bank's allowed claim? *See* Code § 502(b)(1).

(3)   Assume that Amphydynamics rents office space pursuant to a 10-year lease at a rent of $1,000 per month. Amphy files a Chapter 11 petition and rejects the lease. At the time of rejection, the lease term has eight years to run. What is the amount of the landlord's allowed claim? *See* Code § 502(b)(6) and (g). What if, the day after Amphy notified its landlord that it was rejecting the lease, the landlord relet the premises to a tenant that agreed to pay $1,500 a month for a 10-year term?

§ 8.04   SECURED CLAIMS

[A]   Introduction

As you may recall from your basic bankruptcy course, and although they may dispute it, secured creditors occupy an enviable position in a bankruptcy case. The commencement of a case and the imposition of the automatic stay may postpone the ability of a secured creditor to enforce its lien, but the lien remains in force. While the right to foreclose is suspended, a secured creditor is entitled to adequate protection of the value of its lien, Code § 362(d), and to the extent that the value of the collateral exceeds the amount of its claim, a secured creditor is entitled to postpetition interest, Code § 506(b). And as we will see in the next chapter, although a reorganization plan may modify the rights of secured creditors, Code § 1123(a)(5)(e), (b)(5), if a secured creditor objects to the treatment it receives under a plan, the court may not confirm the plan unless it satisfies the "cramdown" standard embodied in Code § 1129(b)(2)(A). That standard is required in order to meet the requirement of the Fifth Amendment's Takings Clause, which applies to property — as opposed to contract — rights. Unsecured claims are creatures of mere contract and are covered only by the modified absolute priority rule of § 1129(b)(2)(B). But secured claims are creatures of both contract (a promissory note, for instance) and property (the security interest in the collateral, for instance). The cramdown standard for secured claims is satisfied if a plan provides that the secured creditor: (i) will retain its lien on the collateral and receive a stream of payments having a present value equal to the allowed amount of the creditor's allowed secured claim, or (ii) will receive the proceeds of the sale of the collateral at a sale at which it has a credit bid right, or (iii) will receive the "indubitable equivalent" of its security. This standard will be explored in more detail in chapter 9.

[B]   Determining the Allowed Amount of a Secured Claim

PROBLEM 8.1

The next proof of claim form that Carol selects from the pile was filed by MegaBank. Three years ago, MegaBank made a $12,000,000 loan at 7.50% interest to Amphydynamics to finance the purchase of an assembly plant. The loan, which has a term of 20 years, is secured by a mortgage on the plant. The plant is located in an area of the city that has been particularly hard-hit by a real estate recession.

Carol hands the form to you. You note that according to the proof of claim, Amphydynamics owes MegaBank $11,101,018.17. MegaBank has checked the box that indicates the claim is a secured claim, and on the line where MegaBank is supposed to indicate the "value of collateral" MegaBank has written "$12,000,000 plus."

"I only wish that plant were worth '$12,000,000 plus,' " Carol sighs. "But I have a feeling that in today's market, it's worth $8,000,000 tops. At foreclosure, I think it would fetch even less."

"That's important information," you say. "We've already seen [in chapter 3, § 3.06] that Code § 506(a) defines a secured claim as 'an allowed claim of a creditor secured by a lien on property in which the estate has an interest . . . to the extent of the value of such creditor's interest in the estate's interest.' "

"In other words, the value of the collateral is the measure of the secured claim."

"That's essentially correct."

"And to the extent that there's a deficiency — to the extent that the value of the collateral is less than the amount of the allowed claim — the creditor holds an unsecured claim."

"That's right. This is the 'bifurcation of claims' principle that we've talked about before in connection with the concepts of *adequate protection* and *stay relief*." According to the legislative history, you explain, § 506(a) "separates an undersecured creditor's claim into two parts: He has a secured claim to the extent of the value of his collateral; and he has an unsecured claim for the balance of his claim." H.R. Rep. No. 95-595 at 356 (1977). You also tell her to keep in mind that Code § 101(37) broadly defines "lien" as any "charge or interest in property to secure payment of a debt or performance of an obligation." Thus the lien may arise by operation of contract (for example, a mortgage or security agreement); by operation of judicial process (for example, a judgment lien), or by statute (for example, a mechanic's lien).

"Pardon me for interrupting, but this is getting interesting. I seem to remember that earlier in the course — I mean case — secured creditors were taking the position that they were undersecured — that their collateral was worth less than the amount of their claims. Now they're saying its worth more? Why are they doing that? And how can they do that?"

You tell Carol she is right. Valuation of collateral is an issue that you've confronted before, most notably when secured creditors, including MegaBank, sought relief from the automatic stay in order to bring or continue foreclosure actions. At that point in the case, they had an incentive to *understate* collateral values so that they could prove that their interests in the collateral were not adequately protected (*see* Code § 361(d)(1)), or that the debtor had no equity in the collateral (*see* Code § 361(d)(2)). Debtors, of course, had an incentive to overstate collateral values in order to show that the creditors were protected by equity cushions. Now, as we approach the plan stage of the case, the positions are reversed. Creditors have an incentive to overstate collateral values in order to maximize the amount of their secured claims in order to secure better treatment under the plan and, as we will see in § 9.10, resist cramdown. Such inconsistent positions are possible, if not always plausible, because the valuation of property at one point in the case is "binding only for the purposes of the specific hearing and is not to have a res judicata effect." S. Rep. No. 95-589, 54 (1979).

Thus, the first step in determining whether a secured claim is receiving appropriate treatment under a plan requires determining the value of the collateral and fixing the allowed amount of the secured claim. § 506(a). Value is likely to be established through the testimony of appraisers, brokers, and other experts, but what measure of value is relevant in this context? Fair market value? Foreclosure or forced sale value? Replacement value? Retail value? Wholesale value?

The Code provides little guidance, apart from stating in § 506(a) that "value is to be determined in light of the purpose of the valuation and of the proposed disposition or use of such property." Interestingly, many of the significant case law developments in this area have involved Chapter 13 debtors seeking to retain cars and trucks over the objection of secured creditors by paying the present value and allowed amount of the secured claims pursuant to Code § 1325(a)(5), which parallels Code § 1129(b)(2)(A)(i) of Chapter 11. In the following short excerpt from a Supreme Court opinion on the issue, in which the Court considered how to value a truck that a Chapter 13 debtor proposed to keep and operate in order to make a living, the Court concluded that a "replacement value" standard was appropriate, rather than the "present or actual value" standard that the Fifth Circuit had adopted in the proceedings below.

ASSOCIATES COMMERCIAL CORP. v. RASH
Supreme Court of the United States
520 U.S. 953 (1997)

Justice Ginsburg delivered the opinion of the Court.

We resolve in this case a dispute concerning the proper application of § 506(a) of the Bankruptcy Code when a bankrupt debtor has exercised the "cram down" option for which Code § 1325(a)(5)(B) provides. Specifically, when a debtor, over a secured creditor's objection, seeks to retain and use the creditor's collateral in a Chapter 13 plan, is the value of the collateral to be determined by (1) what the secured creditor could obtain through foreclosure sale of the property (the "foreclosure-value" standard); (2) what the debtor would have to pay for comparable property (the "replacement-value" standard); or (3) the midpoint between these two measurements? We hold that § 506(a) directs application of the replacement-value standard.

. . . .

II

The Bankruptcy Code provision central to the resolution of this case is § 506(a), which states:

> "An allowed claim of a creditor secured by a lien on property in which the estate has an interest . . . is a secured claim to the extent of the value of such creditor's interest in the estate's interest in such property, . . . and is an unsecured claim to the extent that the value of such creditor's interest . . . is less than the amount of such allowed claim. Such value shall be determined in light of the purpose of the valuation and of the proposed disposition or use of such property . . . ." 11 U.S.C. § 506(a).

. . . [T]he Rashes' repayment plan proposed, pursuant to § 1325(a)(5)(B), continued use of the property in question, i.e., the truck, in the debtor's trade or business. In such a "cram down" case, we hold, the value of the property (and thus the amount of the secured claim under § 506(a)) is the price a willing buyer in the debtor's trade, business, or situation would pay to obtain like property from a willing seller.

Rejecting this replacement-value standard, and selecting instead the typically lower foreclosure-value standard, the Fifth Circuit trained its attention on the first sentence of § 506(a). In particular, the Fifth Circuit relied on these first sentence words: a claim is secured "to the extent of the value of *such creditor's interest* in the estate's interest in such property." The Fifth Circuit read this phrase to instruct that the "starting point for the valuation [is] what the creditor could realize if it sold the estate's interest in the property according to the security agreement," namely, through "repossessing and selling the collateral."

We do not find in the § 506(a) first sentence words — "the creditor's interest in the estate's interest in such property" — the foreclosure-value meaning advanced by the Fifth Circuit. Even read in isolation, the phrase imparts no valuation standard: A direction simply to consider the "value of such creditor's interest" does not expressly reveal how that interest is to be valued.

Reading the first sentence of § 506(a) as a whole, we are satisfied that the phrase the Fifth Circuit considered key is not an instruction to equate a "creditor's interest" with the net value a creditor could realize through a foreclosure sale. The first sentence, in its entirety, tells us that a secured creditor's claim is to be divided into secured and unsecured portions, with the secured portion of the claim limited to the value of the collateral. To separate the secured from the unsecured portion of a claim, a court must compare the creditor's claim to the value of "such property," i.e., the collateral. That comparison is sometimes complicated. A debtor may own only a part interest in the property pledged as collateral, in which case the court will be required to ascertain the "estate's interest" in the collateral. Or, a creditor may hold a junior or subordinate lien, which would require the court to ascertain the creditor's interest in the collateral. The § 506(a) phrase referring to the "creditor's interest in the estate's interest in such property" thus recognizes that a court may encounter, and in such instances must evaluate, limited or partial interests in collateral. The full first sentence of § 506(a), in short, tells a court what it must evaluate, but it does not say more; it is not enlightening on how to value collateral.

The second sentence of § 506(a) does speak to the how question. "Such value," that sentence provides, "shall be determined in light of the purpose of the valuation and of the proposed disposition or use of such property." § 506(a). By deriving a foreclosure-value standard from § 506(a)'s first sentence, the Fifth Circuit rendered inconsequential the sentence that expressly addresses how "value shall be determined."

As we comprehend § 506(a), the "proposed disposition or use" of the collateral is of paramount importance to the valuation question. If a secured creditor does not accept a debtor's Chapter 13 plan, the debtor has two options for handling allowed secured claims: surrender the collateral to the creditor, *see* § 1325(a)(5)(C); or, under the cram down option, keep the collateral over the creditor's objection and provide the creditor, over the life of the plan, with the equivalent of the present value of the collateral, *see* § 1325(a)(5)(B). The "disposition or use" of the collateral thus turns on the alternative the debtor chooses — in one case the collateral will be surrendered to the creditor, and in the other, the collateral will be retained and used by the debtor. Applying a foreclosure-value standard when the cram down option is invoked attributes no significance to the different consequences of the debtor's choice to surrender the property or retain it. A replacement-value standard, on the other hand, distinguishes retention from surrender and renders meaningful the key words "disposition or use."

Tying valuation to the actual "disposition or use" of the property points away from a foreclosure-value standard when a Chapter 13 debtor, invoking cram down power, retains and uses the property. Under that option, foreclosure is averted by the debtor's choice and over the creditor's objection. From the creditor's perspective as well as the debtor's, surrender and retention are not equivalent acts.

When a debtor surrenders the property, a creditor obtains it immediately, and is free to sell it and reinvest the proceeds. We recall here that ACC sought that very advantage. . . . If a debtor keeps the property and continues to use it, the creditor obtains at once neither the property nor its value and is exposed to double risks: The debtor may again default and the property may deteriorate from extended use. Adjustments in the interest rate and secured creditor demands for more "adequate protection," 11 U.S.C. § 361, do not fully offset these risks. *See* 90 F.3d at 1066 (Smith, J., dissenting) ("vast majority of reorganizations fail . . . leaving creditors with only a fraction of the compensation due them"; where, as here, "collateral depreciates rapidly, the secured creditor may receive far less in a failed reorganization than in a prompt foreclosure").

Of prime significance, the replacement-value standard accurately gauges the debtor's "use" of the property. It values "the creditor's interest in the collateral in light of the proposed [repayment plan] reality: no foreclosure sale and economic benefit for the debtor derived from the collateral equal to . . . its [replacement] value." *In re Winthrop Old Farm Nurseries*, 50 F.3d at 75. The debtor in this case elected to use the collateral to generate an income stream. That actual use, rather than a foreclosure sale that will not take place, is the proper guide under a prescription hinged to the property's "disposition or use."

The Fifth Circuit considered the replacement-value standard disrespectful of state law, which permits the secured creditor to sell the collateral, thereby obtaining its net foreclosure value "and nothing more." In allowing Chapter 13 debtors to retain and use collateral over the objection of secured creditors, however, the Bankruptcy Code has reshaped debtor and creditor rights in marked departure from state law. *See, e.g.*, Uniform Commercial Code §§ 9-504, 9-505, 3B U. L. A. 127, 352 (1992). The Code's cram down option displaces a secured creditor's state-law right to obtain immediate foreclosure upon a debtor's default. That change, ordered by federal law, is attended by a direction that courts look to the "proposed disposition or use" of the collateral in determining its value. It no more disrupts state law to make "disposition or use" the guide for valuation than to authorize the rearrangement of rights the cram down power entails.

. . . .

In sum, under § 506(a), the value of property retained because the debtor has exercised the § 1325(a)(5)(B) "cram down" option is the cost the debtor would incur to obtain a like asset for the same "proposed . . . use."[6]

For the foregoing reasons, the judgment of the Court of Appeals is reversed, and the case is remanded for further proceedings consistent with this opinion.

It is so ordered.

NOTES AND QUESTIONS

(1) *Not a Rash Decision, But Neither Is It a Balm.* Both before and after the Supreme Court's decision in *Rash*, courts have held in the Chapter 11 context that replacement value is the appropriate standard to apply when valuing property that a debtor proposes to retain and use in its ongoing business. *See, e.g., Winthrop Old Farm Nurseries, Inc. v. New Bedford Inst. for Savings (In re Winthrop Old Farm Nurseries, Inc.)*, 50 F.3d 72 (1st Cir. 1995); *Amresco New England II, L.P. v. Vescio (In re Vescio)*, 227 B.R. 352 (Bankr. D. Vt. 1998); *In re Am. Kitchen Foods, Inc.*, 1976 Bankr. LEXIS 6 (Bankr. D. Me. 1976), reprinted in chapter 3, § 3.07[B]. Hence, the *Rash* approach is not audacious. Nor does it shed much light on how replacement value is to be determined.

---

[6] Our recognition that the replacement-value standard, not the foreclosure-value standard, governs in cram down cases leaves to bankruptcy courts, as triers of fact, identification of the best way of ascertaining replacement value on the basis of the evidence presented. Whether replacement value is the equivalent of retail value, wholesale value, or some other value will depend on the type of debtor and the nature of the property. We note, however, that replacement value, in this context, should not include certain items. For example, where the proper measure of the replacement value of a vehicle is its retail value, an adjustment to that value may be necessary: A creditor should not receive portions of the retail price, if any, that reflect the value of items the debtor does not receive when he retains his vehicle, items such as warranties, inventory storage, and reconditioning. . . . Nor should the creditor gain from modifications to the property — e.g., the addition of accessories to a vehicle — to which a creditor's lien would not extend under state law.

The Supreme Court's suggestion in footnote 6 that "Whether replacement value is the equivalent of retail value, wholesale value, or some other value will depend on the type of debtor and the nature of the property," has raised concerns that the *Rash* approach will inspire litigation. Judge Frank Easterbrook has observed, "Replacement value cannot be looked up. It must be litigated; and in the process the value of the asset will be paid out to the lawyers rather than to the creditors." Hon. Frank H. Easterbrook, *Luncheon Address to the National Bankruptcy Review Commission Chicago Regional Hearing: Bankruptcy Reform* (July 17, 1997).

(2) *Measuring the Creditor's Interest.* Code § 506(a) says that a claim is a secured claim to the extent of "the value of such creditor's interest in the estate's interest in such property." Assume that MegaBank holds a mortgage on the Amphydynamics factory to secure its $11 million claim against Amphydynamics. Assume that Second Bank holds a second mortgage on the same factory to secure its $4 million claim against Amphydynamics. Assume that the factory has a value of $8 million. What is the value of MegaBank's interest in the estate's interest in the factory? What is the value of Second Bank's interest in the estate's interest in the factory? Does MegaBank hold an allowed secured claim? Does Second Bank?

[C]   Interest on Secured Claims

PROBLEM 8.2

Carol pulls another proof of claim form from the pile. "This is odd," she says. "This is another one filed by MegaBank."

"This explains it," you say, pointing to a notation indicating that "this claim amends a previously filed claim."

"They amended their claim? Why?"

"Well, according to this, you owe MegaBank $11,865,000 not $11,101,000 as they had indicated before."

"How is that possible?"

You look at the loan documents again. "It seems the bank is taking the position that you owe interest for the period during which the case has been pending. Not only that, since payment has been suspended, they're charging interest at the default rate provided for in the loan agreement of 18%."

"Can they do that?"

Read Code §§ 502(b)(2) and 506(b) and the opinion that follows.

KEY BANK v. MILHAM
United States Court of Appeals, Second Circuit
141 F.3d 420 (1998)

PER CURIAM:

The question presented on this appeal, which is one of first impression in this Circuit, is whether an oversecured creditor is entitled to be paid its contract rate of interest post-confirmation even if the payment of that rate of interest will enable the creditor to receive more than the present value of its claim as of the effective date of the plan. For the reasons that follow, we answer this question in the negative.

BACKGROUND

Ronald and Benedetta Milham filed a petition under Chapter 13 of the Bankruptcy Code on April 24, 1996. They were indebted to Key Bank under a retail installment contract secured by a 1991 Lincoln Town Car. The Milhams owed $3,163.07 on the contract, which has an interest rate of 9.5%. The collateral has a National Automobile Dealers Association value of $11,962.50. Key Bank is therefore an oversecured creditor: the value of the asset securing its payment exceeds the amount of the debt owed to it.

The plan proposed by the Milhams contemplated payment of $3,000 plus 8.5% interest per annum on the Key Bank loan. Key Bank objected, arguing that as an oversecured creditor it is entitled to the entire amount owed plus the 9.5% per annum contract rate of interest. The Bankruptcy Court confirmed the plan at the 8.5% rate, and Key Bank appealed to the Second Circuit Bankruptcy Appellate Panel on the limited question of the applicable rate of interest post-confirmation. The panel affirmed the confirmation in an opinion by Judge Lifland with a partial dissent by Judge Kaplan. This appeal followed.

DISCUSSION

"In a bankruptcy case, interest is the tail of the dog, but it is a long tail and it wags a lot." Dean Pawlowic, *Entitlement to Interest Under the Bankruptcy Code*, 12 Bankr. Dev. J. 149, 150 (1995). Directly or by implication, the Bankruptcy Code provides for three categories of interest: (1) interest accrued prior to the filing of the bankruptcy petition (prepetition interest); (2) interest accrued after the filing of a petition but prior to the effective date of a reorganization plan (pendency interest); and (3) interest to accrue under the terms of a reorganization plan (plan interest). *Id.* at 151. Prepetition interest is generally allowable to the extent and at the rate permitted under the applicable nonbankruptcy law, including the law of contracts. *Id.* Thus, for amounts accrued prior to the Milhams' filing, it is undisputed that Key Bank is entitled to interest at the contract rate.

Pendency interest presents a trickier question. In general, the Bankruptcy Code does not provide for pendency interest, because the filing of a bankruptcy petition usually stops interest costs from running. [*See* § 502(b)(2).] Section 506(b), however, provides an exception for oversecured creditors:

To the extent that an allowed secured claim is secured by property the value of which, after any recovery under subsection (c) of this section, is greater than the amount of such claim, there shall be allowed to the holder of such claim, interest on such claim, and any reasonable fees, costs or charges provided for under the agreement under which such claim arose.

In this passage, Key Bank places heavy weight on the phrase "to the extent"; essentially, Key Bank argues that this provision guarantees it interest at the contract rate, even after confirmation, until the equity cushion is exhausted (that is, until the value of the collateral no longer exceeds the creditor's claim). Key Bank's position is problematic, for several reasons.

First, as the panel in the present case correctly noted, section 506(b) does not say that the oversecured creditor collects pendency interest at the contractual rate. In *United States v. Ron Pair Enters., Inc.*, 489 U.S. 235, 241, 109 S. Ct. 1026, 1030, 103 L. Ed. 2d 290 (1989), the Supreme Court held that the phrase "provided for under the agreement under which such claims arose" does not modify the phrase "interest on such claim." Unlike prepetition interest, pendency interest is not based upon contract. *See Rake v. Wade*, 508 U.S. 464, 468, 113 S. Ct. 2187, 2190, 124 L. Ed. 2d 424 (1993) ("The right to postpetition interest under § 506(b) is unqualified and exists regardless of whether the agreement giving rise to the claim provides for interest."). The appropriate rate of pendency interest is therefore within the limited discretion of the court. Most courts have awarded pendency interest at the contractual rate; but nevertheless, however widespread this practice may be, it does not reflect an entitlement to interest at the contractual rate.

Even if Key Bank were entitled to pendency interest at 9.5%, that rate would apply only to the period bounded by the petition on one side and on the other by confirmation of the plan, because pendency interest does not continue to run post-confirmation. "It is generally recognized that the interest allowed by § 506(b) will accrue until payment of the secured claim or until the effective date of the plan." *Rake*, 508 U.S. at 468, 113 S. Ct. at 2190 (citing 3 Collier on Bankruptcy ¶ 506.05, pp. 506–43 and n. 5c (15th ed. 1993)).

On the date of confirmation, the allowed claim of an oversecured creditor is augmented by the inclusion of section 506(b) pendency interest. *See, e.g., Orix Credit Alliance, Inc. v. Delta Resources, Inc. (In re Delta Resources, Inc.)*, 54 F.3d 722, 729 (11th Cir.) ("An oversecured creditor . . . is entitled to receive postpetition interest as part of its claim at the time of confirmation of a plan or reorganization . . . .").

Section 506(b) thus defines the allowed claim of an oversecured creditor; treatment of that claim after confirmation is governed by Section 1325, which establishes the circumstances under which the court may confirm a Chapter 13 debtor's reorganization plan. . . . Under this provision, the court can confirm a plan if one of three conditions is satisfied with respect to secured creditors (a category which, of course, includes oversecured creditors): the secured creditor accepts the plan; the debtor surrenders the property securing the claim to the creditor; or the debtor invokes the so-called "cram-down" power . . . . The present case concerns the cram-down option, pursuant to which the debtor can keep the property over the objection of the creditor. The creditor then retains a lien securing the claim and the debtor must pay the creditor over the life of the plan . . . amounts totaling the present value of the allowed secured claim as of the effective date of the plan. [Section 1129(b)(2)(A) is to the same effect. — Eds.]

Postconfirmation interest, or plan interest, is a function of the present value requirement of the cram-down provision. The Code does not define the term "present value" but legislative history describes the mechanical process of determining present value in a manner consistent with the use of the term by the economic and financial community. . . . Thus, a bankruptcy court confirming a Chapter 13 plan that invokes the cram-down option would undertake the following calculation: first, the court would determine the sum of the principal amount (including section 506(b) interest) that would be due if it were to be paid in total on the date of confirmation; next, the court would determine the schedule of installment payments to be made pursuant to the plan; finally, the court would impose interest at a rate equal to that necessary to recoup the value of the secured claim determined in the first step.

We have previously determined that [postconfirmation or cram down] interest . . . "should be fixed at the rate on a United States Treasury instrument with a maturity equivalent to the repayment schedule under the debtor's reorganization plan." *In re Valenti*, 105 F.3d 55, 64 (2d Cir. 1997). However, "because the rate on a treasury bond is virtually risk-free, the [cram down] interest rate should also include a premium to reflect the risk to the creditor in receiving deferred payments under the reorganization plan." *Id.* The court below determined that in the Milhams' case, this equation resulted in an 8.5% postconfirmation interest rate.

Key Bank argues that it should receive a higher rate of interest postconfirmation than one that would assure it the present value of its claim as of the confirmation date for two reasons: (1) it is entitled to its contract rate of interest; and (2) the words "to the extent" in section 506(b) mean that it continues to receive contract interest even after confirmation up until the point at which the equity cushion in the Lincoln Town Car is exhausted.

As to the first point, Key Bank's repeated theme is that it should not be required to accept less than contract interest in the post-confirmation period because that is no more than its well-secured contract right. But Key Bank's allowed claim under section 506(b) includes both principal and interest. By seeking to apply the contract rate to both components, Key Bank in essence seeks to compound its interest. Were we to adopt its interpretation, Key Bank would receive substantially more than a stream of payments equal to the "present value" of its claim it would receive compound interest for which its contract does not provide. Moreover, section 1322(b)(2) of the Code [like section 1123(b)(5)] expressly authorizes debtors to modify the rights of secured claim holders (other than holders of claims secured only by the debtor's principal residence). As the Ninth Circuit has noted, "the cramdown route necessarily involves a modification of the creditor's rights with regard to such factors as number of payments *and the rate of interest*." *Shearson Lehman Mortgage Corp. v. Laguna (In re Laguna)*, 944 F.2d 542, 544–45 (9th Cir. 1991) (emphasis added) (citation omitted), *cert. denied*, 503 U.S. 966, 112 S. Ct. 1577, 118 L. Ed. 2d 219 (1992).

As to the second point, we prefer an interpretation of section 506(b) that accommodates section 1325, and we believe one is readily available. "To the extent" means that pendency interest runs (often, although not necessarily, at the contract rate) until the time of confirmation unless the equity cushion is exhausted before that; this makes perfect sense because at the point preconfirmation that the equity cushion is exhausted, the creditor ceases to be oversecured.

Accordingly, we hold that an oversecured creditor such as Key Bank is entitled to receive § 506(b) interest only until the confirmation date of the Chapter 13 reorganization plan. At that time, the accumulated pendency interest becomes a part of the allowed secured claim, and the plan must provide for payment of the present value of such allowed claim as of the effective date of the plan. Present value is achieved by the payment of interest at a rate calculated in accordance with our holding in *In re Valenti*. Because the postconfirmation rate in the confirmed plan at issue was so calculated, the bankruptcy court decision confirming the plan, and the decision of the Bankruptcy Appellate Panel affirming the confirmation, are affirmed.

NOTES AND QUESTIONS

1. *Calculating Cram Down Interest Rates.* Competing methods for calculating an appropriate cram down rate of interest are discussed more thoroughly in § 9.10 of chapter 9 of the text.

2. *Default Rates of Interest.* In the Bankruptcy Appellate Panel opinion in *Milham*, Judge Lifland observed that although the appropriate "pendency interest" rate is within the discretion of the bankruptcy court, courts "habitually" award interest at the contract rate. What if, as in the Amphydynamics problem, a contract provides that in the event of a default, interest on unpaid principal and interest will accrue at a default rate that is higher than the predefault rate? Although the Code is silent on the question, courts generally have been willing to enforce such provisions and have allowed pendency interest to accrue on oversecured claims at the default rate absent a showing that the stepped up rate is unenforceable under nonbankruptcy law or that equitable considerations militate against enforcing it. *See, e.g., In re Terry L.P.*, 27 F.3d 241, 243 (7th Cir. 1994). But in *In re DWS Inv., Inc.*, 121 B.R. 845 (Bankr. C.D. Cal. 1990), the court declined to enforce a postdefault interest rate for both reasons:

> A default rate of interest should not be a penalty. Rather, it should be a means for compensating the creditor for any loss resulting from the nonpayment of principal at maturity. Claimants have not shown that the 25% rate has any relationship to actual or projected loss as a result of nonpayment. . . . Usually, the court should apply the contract rate, but it has the power to apply a different rate depending upon equitable considerations. Claimants ask me to accept a default interest rate of 25%. This seems excessive. Claimants offer no evidence to justify this rate other than it is the rate they use for other transactions. I have no evidence that this rate approximates the market rate for similar loans with borrowers in similar circumstances at the time of the default. The estate is insolvent and the unsecured creditors are unlikely to receive a distribution unless the Plan is confirmed. In order for the Plan to consummate, substantial funding

is required from the principals. Furthermore, under California law I question whether this rate would be legal. . . . In California, the term "penalty" traditionally has been used to designate a charge which is deemed to be void because it cannot qualify as proper liquidated damages.

121 B.R. at 849.

Similarly, in *In re Hollstrom*, 133 B.R. 535, 539 (Bankr. D. Colo. 1991), the court refused to enforce a 36% postdefault interest rate where:

No evidence has been presented to justify the 36% rate of interest. There has been no showing that the rate approximates the market rate or default rate for similar loans with borrowers in similar circumstances. The default rate of interest has not been established as having any relationship to actual or projected loss as a result of nonpayment.

Considering why a secured creditor should not enjoy the benefit of its bargain, the court observed:

Sight must never be lost of the fact that these Debtors are in bankruptcy; there are too many creditors chasing too few dollars.

While it is clear that courts must look to the underlying contract as the initial focal point, it is equally clear that after bankruptcy, it is § 506(b), not state law, through which that look is focused, and that examination must view not only the contours of § 506(b) but also the broader penumbra of bankruptcy law. . . . Contracts do not exist in a vacuum. Their life and meaning depend upon the legal environment in which their enforcement is sought, and it is a fact of life that after bankruptcy a creditor's rights are more restricted because of the codified public policy of giving a debtor an opportunity to attempt to reorganize. "There may be situations in bankruptcy where giving a secured creditor an absolute right to his bargain may be impossible or seriously [detrimental] to the policy of the bankruptcy laws." . . . While a default rate may well not constitute a penalty, as between the secured creditor and the debtor, under state law and for state law purposes, that conclusion does not answer the federal question of relative distributive rights of creditors in a reorganization proceeding. . . . "Appropriate regard" should be given to the state law but the "distribution in bankruptcy" is in the last analysis a matter of federal law.

. . . .

It is reasonable to conclude that an excessive default interest rate imposed by a secured creditor serves as a penalty, . . . as against other creditors, not the debtor, and specifically against unsecured creditors. This is particularly true in a bankruptcy situation where the unsecured creditors are already probably taking a substantial hit on their claims.

133 B.R. at 540–41 (citations omitted).

Courts have also permitted oversecured creditors to seek interest on interest as part of their allowed secured claim, provided that their agreement or applicable nonbankruptcy law provides for it. *Compare Equitable Life Assurance Society v.*

Sublett (In re Sublett), 895 F.2d 1381 (11th Cir. 1990), *with In re Chateaugay Corp.*, 150 B.R. 529 (Bankr. S.D.N.Y. 1993), *aff'd*, 170 B.R. 551 (S.D.N.Y. 1994).

3. *Postpetition Interest and Nonconsensual Liens.* The rule currently embodied in Code § 502(b)(2) suspending the accrual of interest on unsecured claims is not new. It predates the Bankruptcy Code and has both a practical and philosophical basis:

> The age-old rule in bankruptcy, adopted from the English system, is that interest on claims stops accruing when the bankruptcy petition is filed. . . . One justification for the rule is that it promotes certainty and eases the administration of the estate by fixing a date when the affairs of the bankrupt are considered to be wound up. By setting a date when interest stops, the rule saves the trustee from having to continuously recalculate the amount due each creditor. It also saves the estate from having to pay extra for the delay in payment when that delay is necessary if the courts are to preserve and protect the estate for the benefit of all creditors. Further, the rule allows the trustee to fulfill the duty of objecting to questionable claims, without worrying that an unsuccessful objection will lead to claims for interest and increased administrative expense. Finally, the rule prevents any unmerited gain or loss by creditors whose claims have different interest rates or who are paid at different times by the bankruptcy court; all are treated equally.

In re Fesco Plastics Corp., 996 F.2d 152, 155 (7th Cir. 1993) (citations omitted).

The rule embodied in Code § 506(b) permitting oversecured creditors to recover postpetition interest out of their equity cushion is not new either. The underlying theory is that an oversecured creditor who has bargained for this cushion should not have it snatched out from under it in order to benefit other creditors. *See, e.g., In re Boston & Maine Corp.*, 719 F.2d 493, 496–97 (1st Cir. 1983). Whether the same boon should be accorded to holders of *nonconsensual* liens has been much debated over the years, but the issue was put to rest by the Supreme Court in *U.S. v. Ron Pair Enters.*, 489 U.S. 235 (1989). The answer, the Court held, turned on a plain reading of § 506(b), which provides:

> To the extent that an allowed secured claim is secured by property the value of which, after any recovery under subsection (c) of this section, is greater than the amount of such claim, there shall be allowed to the holder of such claim, interest on such claim, *and any reasonable fees, costs,* or charges *provided for under the* agreement *under which such claim arose.*

Id. at 240 n. 2 (emphasis added.) The Court held that the qualifying language "provided for under the agreement" modified only "reasonable fees, costs, or charges," but not "interest on such claim," since the latter phrase is set off by a comma. Thus, holders of claims secured by nonconsensual liens, such as statutory liens, tax liens, and judicial liens, are, like holders of consensual liens, entitled to accrue postpetition interest to the extent that their claims are oversecured.

4. *Timing Issues: When to Value Collateral.* As we have seen, § 506(b) provides that postpetition interest is added to a prepetition claim only to the extent that the claim is oversecured. What if the value of the collateral or the amount of a creditor's

claim fluctuate over the course of a case, with the result that at times the creditor is oversecured and at times it is not? Such fluctuations may result from market forces that affect the value of the collateral or interim payments to the creditor that affect the amount of the outstanding claim. In such a case, is the creditor entitled to add postpetition interest to its claim? Some courts have held that the date on which the collateral is to be valued and the outer limit of the allowed secured claim fixed is the date of the bankruptcy petition. Fluctuations that occur after filing are not taken into account. *See, e.g., In re Hulen Park Place Ltd.*, 130 B.R. 39, 43 (N.D. Tex. 1991); *In re Luchenbill*, 112 B.R. 204, 216 (Bankr. E.D. Mich. 1990). Other courts have agreed that a single valuation date is appropriate, but concluded that it should be the date a reorganization plan is confirmed. *See, e.g., In re Landing Assoc., Ltd.*, 122 B.R. 288, 297 (Bankr. W.D. Tex. 1990). The single valuation date was rejected in *Fin. Sec. Assurance Inc. v. T-H New Orleans Ltd. P'ship. (In re T-H New Orleans Ltd. P'ship.)*, 116 F.3d 790 (5th Cir. 1997), a case in which the creditor's claim was being reduced and the value of its collateral (a hotel) was appreciating during the time between the commencement of the case and the hearing on confirmation of the plan.

> [A]lthough we note that the lower courts that have faced this circumstance have selected a single valuation date . . . [w]e decline to follow such a narrow path. Therefore, we conclude that for purposes of determining whether a creditor is entitled to accrue interest under § 506(b) in the circumstance where the collateral's value is increasing and/or the creditor's allowed claim has been or is being reduced by . . . payments, such that at some point in time prior to confirmation of the debtor's plan the creditor may become oversecured, valuation of the collateral and the creditor's claim should be flexible and not limited to a single point in time, such as the petition date or confirmation date. We further hold that, notwithstanding the bankruptcy court's determination of a creditor's secured status as of the petition date (if such a finding is made), the party who contends that there is a dispute as to whether a creditor is entitled to interest under § 506(b) must [move] the bankruptcy court to make such a determination. The creditor though bears the ultimate burden to prove by a preponderance of evidence its entitlement to postpetition interest, that is, that its claim was oversecured, to what extent, and for what period of time. . . .

> A flexible approach recognizes the fact that a creditor's allowed claim, which is being reduced over time, may become entitled to accrue postpetition interest, and that under the plain language of § 506(b) there is nothing limiting that right. A flexible approach also recognizes that any increase over the judicially determined valuation during bankruptcy rightly accrues to the benefit of the creditor, and not to the debtor. Moreover, as the bankruptcy court in *In re Addison Properties* noted, the single valuation approach generally balances the bankruptcy process in favor of the debtor. *In re Addison Properties Ltd. P'ship*, 185 B.R. 766, 772 (Bankr. N.D. Ill. 1995). Because of the equitable nature of bankruptcy in seeking a balance between debtors and creditors (debtor's right to a fresh start versus the creditor's right to the value of its claim), we reject the single valuation approach under the particular facts of this case.

116 F.3d at 798 (citations omitted).

5. *Expenses of Preserving Collateral; Code § 506(c)*. Although an oversecured creditor is entitled to add postpetition interest, fees, costs, and charges to its allowed secured claim, 506(b) provides that in determining whether a creditor is oversecured, the expenses described in § 506(c) must be taken into account. Section 506(c) provides that a trustee, for the benefit of the estate, may recover from collateral the "reasonable, necessary costs and expenses of preserving, or disposing of such property to the extent of any benefit to the holder of such claim." This does not mean that a secured claim is subordinate to administrative expenses generally. To the contrary, the general rule is that administrative expenses cannot be charged against the collateral of a secured creditor but are chargeable only against unencumbered assets. It does mean that a secured claim is subordinate to administrative expenses that are incurred to preserve or dispose of the collateral that secures the claim, provided that the expenses were "reasonable" and only to the extent that they actually "benefitted" the secured creditor.

6. The premise of § 506(c) is that unsecured creditors should not be required to bear the cost of protecting a secured creditor's collateral, *In re Codesco, Inc.*, 18 B.R. 225, 230 (Bankr. S.D.N.Y. 1982), but the "key element" in applying § 506(c) is whether the expenditures resulted in a "direct benefit" to the secured creditor. *In re Evanston Beauty Supply, Inc.*, 136 B.R. 171, 177 (Bankr. N.D. Ill. 1992). For a more detailed analysis of this direct benefit requirement and the application of § 506(c) generally, see the discussion of the *Flagstaff Food Corp.* case that appears in chapter 5, §54.03[B] of the text.

Code § 506(c) provides that "the trustee" may recover the costs and expenses of preserving or disposing of collateral. Since a debtor in possession has the rights and powers of a trustee, Code § 1107, debtors in possession may also recover such costs and expenses. What about a creditor? Resolving a decade of controversy and a split in the circuits, the Supreme Court ruled in *Hartford Underwriters Ins. Co. v. Union Planters Bank*, 530 U.S. 1 (2000), that a non-trustee lacks standing to bring an action to surcharge a secured creditors' collateral. The debtor, Hen House Interstate, Inc., operated restaurants and service stations. It filed a Chapter 11 petition in 1991. Union Bank was Hen House's main pre- and postpetition lender. Its claim was secured by all of Hen House's assets. Hartford, which did not know that Hen House had filed a Chapter 11 petition, provided workers' compensation insurance to Hen House for more than two years while the case was pending, even though Hen House repeatedly missed monthly premium payments. When in late 1993 the case was converted from Chapter 11 to Chapter 7 and Hartford learned of the bankruptcy, it sought to recover on its administrative expense claim by surcharging the bank's collateral on the theory that by providing the workers' compensation insurance, it had preserved the value of the collateral. The Court held that even assuming the insurance coverage did benefit the secured creditor, the plain language of § 506(c) supported the conclusion that only a trustee had standing to bring an action to surcharge collateral.

The Court did not address whether a bankruptcy court can allow other interested parties, such as a creditors' committee, to act in place of the trustee when the trustee refuses to pursue recovery under § 506(c), explaining that "petitioner did not ask the trustee to pursue payment under § 506(c) and did not seek permission from the Bankruptcy Court to take such action in the trustee's stead. Petitioner asserted an independent right to use § 506(c), which is what we reject today."

In order to protect themselves from § 506(c) claims, lenders will generally ask for, and generally are able to receive, waivers of the Chapter 11 debtor's § 506(c) rights as part of a consensual cash collateral stipulation. Some of these stipulations also ask that the creditors' committee sign on to waive any right that it may have to a § 506(c) surcharge. It is unclear, but doubtful, that these sorts of waivers have any effect upon a subsequently appointed Chapter 7 or 11 trustee, although to the extent that the trustee intends to operate the business and needs to use cash collateral to do so, the same negotiation and same result could occur.

[D] Attorneys' Fees on Unsecured and Unsecured Deficiency Claims

We know, then, that interest and attorneys' fees, if provided for in the underlying transactional documents, are components of the allowed claim of a secured creditor, up to the amount of value in the collateral. With regard to postpetition attorneys' fees, there has been a hostility towards allowing them in the courts that follow the default "American Rule" that parties to a dispute bear their own costs and fees. Of course, this can be altered by contract, and attorneys' fees clauses, both of the "prevailing party" and "one way" types, are common. Prepetition, these clauses are enforceable subject to the limits of state law. *See, e.g.*, Cal. Civ. Code § 1717 (renders a one-way attorneys' fee clause into a prevailing party attorneys' fee clause).

But what of attorneys' fees incurred postpetition? They are not mentioned as objectionable items in Code § 502(b), and they are enforceable under state law, so they should be allowed, no? The answer is not so obvious, although after 30 years of litigation under the Bankruptcy Code, the answer is becoming more clear. One set of courts, fixating on § 506(b)'s express allowance of a secured creditor's fees up to the value of the collateral, found an implied disallowance of postpetition attorneys' fees for unsecured creditors, while other courts said § 502(b)'s lack of a provision disallowing these fees meant that they were enforceable. *See, generally,* George W. Kuney, *Issues in Litigation: Claims for Attorney Fees Under the Bankruptcy Code*, 4 J. Bankr. L. & Pract. 203 (1995) (collecting cases). In *Travelers Casualty & Surety Co. of Am. v. Pac. Gas & Elec. Co.*, 549 U.S. 443 (2007), the Court rejected the Ninth Circuit's rule barring attorneys' fees for matters particular to bankruptcy. The Court, however, did not address whether postpetition attorneys' fees were allowable categorically as part of unsecured claims and remanded the case, which has no public subsequent history.

Following this, in *In re SNTL Corp.*, 571 F.3d 826 (9th Cir. 2009), and *Ogle v. Fidelity & Deposit Co.*, 586 F.3d 143 (2d Cir. 2009), first the Ninth and then the Second Circuit concluded that the Bankruptcy Code permits an unsecured claim for postpetition attorneys' fees authorized by a valid prepetition contract due to the lack of a specific § 506(b) ground for disallowance. As this text goes to press, there is no other post-*Travelers* circuit-level authority, but when important circuit Courts of Appeals on both the west and east coasts agree, it may not be too soon to say that a trend is forming.

§ 8.05   ADMINISTRATIVE EXPENSE CLAIMS

"This is another interesting one," Carol says, passing a claim form to you. "This one was filed by someone named Ella Pyrenees. She says she purchased one of our video games a couple of months ago. She says that it short-circuited and blew up, damaging her television, a coffee table, a rug, and some drapes. She wants her money back plus $15,000 for property damage."

"Did you say she bought it a couple of months ago?" you ask.

"Yes, and there's a receipt attached. She bought it from one of our factory direct e-stores. Why does when she bought it matter?"

You explain to Carol that Ella Pyrenees may hold an administrative expense claim, and that this is important, because, as we will see in § 9.11[J] of the text, a reorganization plan must provide that administrative expense claims will be paid in full, in cash, on the effective date of the plan. Otherwise the plan cannot be confirmed by the court. Code § 1129(a)(9)(A). Code § 503(b) describes the kinds of claims that are entitled to administrative expense treatment. Read it now.

You will note that in contrast to the prepetition claims that we have been analyzing so far, administrative expenses are obligations that arise postpetition. That is why the date Ella Pyrenees purchased the video game is important. That is also why, technically, one does not file a "proof of claim" to obtain payment of an administrative expense. Instead, one "timely file[s] a request for payment of an administrative expense." § 503(a). "Timely" apparently means before the bar date set by the court. *Hall Fin. Group Inc. v. DP Partners Ltd. P'ship. (In re DP Partners Ltd. P'ship.)*, 106 F.3d 667 (5th Cir. 1997).

Code § 503(b)(1)(A) states the general proposition that administrative expenses include "the actual, necessary costs and expenses of preserving the estate, including wages, salaries, or commissions for services rendered after the commencement of the case." The balance of § 503 describes particular types of administrative expense claims. We have already encountered several examples of administrative expenses:

- In chapter 1 we saw that compensation for services rendered and expenses incurred by trustees, examiners, and their professional assistants are entitled to administrative expense treatment. Code § 503(b)(2). These fees are also subject to court approval. Code § 330. Similarly, expenses incurred in the performance of their duties by members of official creditors' and equity security holders committees appointed under Code § 1102 are entitled to administrative expense treatment, as are fees for services rendered by the committee's professional assistants. Code §§ 330, 503(b)(3)(F), 503(b)(2), 1102, 1103.

- In chapter 5, we saw that a lender who makes an unsecured loan to the debtor or a supplier who ships goods on credit will hold an administrative expense claim if the transaction is approved by the court or was entered into in the ordinary course of business and actually benefitted the estate.

Code § 364(a), (b). As a matter of practical necessity, these expenses are often paid as they come due in the ordinary course of the debtor's business pursuant to Code § 363(c). As we saw in chapter 4, § 363(c) provides that a trustee or debtor in possession presumptively may use estate property in the ordinary course of business. Thus, many of these debts will have been paid by the debtor before the plan stage of the case, and no request for payment will be necessary.

- In chapter 7, we saw that if an executory contract or unexpired lease is assumed by the trustee or debtor in possession, the contractual obligations are treated as administrative expenses.

Some obligations that might seem to qualify for administrative expense treatment don't. Consider this hypothetical. A company that is in the business of leasing trucks makes an irrevocable commitment to advertise its services in the Yellow Pages. Subsequently, the company files a Chapter 11 petition. During the period that the debtor is operating its business as a debtor in possession, the phone directories containing the advertisement are published. The publisher claims that the debtor's obligation to pay for the ads should be treated as an administrative expense. Should it?

In *In re Jartran, Inc.*, 732 F.2d 584 (7th Cir. 1984), the court held that the answer depended on whether the obligation both (1) arose from a transaction with the debtor in possession, and (2) arose out of a transaction that was beneficial to the debtor in possession in the operation of the business. The court held that the two-pronged test was not satisfied, because the debt did not arise out of a transaction with the debtor:

> There is no question that the appearance of ads in Yellow Page directories throughout the country is beneficial to Jartran, as a debtor-in-possession, in the operation of its business. . . . Therefore, the only serious question on appeal is whether the district court incorrectly concluded that the claim did not arise from a transaction with the debtor-in-possession.
>
> Stated this simply, we believe that the district court's conclusion was correct: the agreement among the parties was entered into, and the ads were placed without possibility of revocation, before the petition was filed.
>
> . . . .
>
> [T]he reason that inducement of the creditor's performance by the debtor-in-possession is crucial to a claim for administrative priority is rooted in the policies that gave rise to the creation of the priority. Thus, administrative priority is granted to post-petition expenses so that third parties will be moved to provide the goods and services necessary for a successful reorganization. In the case before us, no inducement by the debtor-in-possession was required because the liability for the costs of the ads was irrevocably incurred before the petition was filed. This construction of the requirements for the administrative priority provides as full an opportunity as can be furnished for rehabilitation of the debtor. And this approach simply carries out the teaching of the Supreme Court, "that fairness requires that any claims incident to the debtor-in-possession's

operation of the business be paid before those for whose benefit the continued operation of the business was allowed." *Mammoth Mart, supra* 536 F.2d at 954, *citing Reading Co. v. Brown*, 391 U.S. 471, 478, 88 S. Ct. 1759, 20 L. Ed. 2d 751 (1968).

Id. at 587–88.

Some obligations that do not seem to qualify for administrative expense treatment do. The Supreme Court case of *Reading Co. v. Brown*, cited by the court in *Jartran*, is an important example of a "transaction" that did not confer a "benefit" on the estate, at least not in the direct or usual sense. The debtor owned and leased an "industrial structure." It filed a Chapter 11 petition and a receiver was appointed to operate the business. While the receiver's employees were performing work on the building, a fire broke out, destroying not only the debtor's building, but several adjoining properties as well, including one owned by Reading Co. Asserting that the fire had been caused by the negligence of the receiver's workers, Reading and other adjoining property owners filed claims totaling $3.5 million, far more than the net worth of the debtor. Over a strenuous dissent by a minority of Justices who believed that administrative priority should be accorded to "only those costs required for a smooth and successful arrangement" incurred by those who directly deal with and directly benefit the estate, the majority of the Court held that the claims of the fire victims *were* entitled to administrative priority:

> [The fire victim] did not merely suffer injury at the hands of an insolvent business: it had an insolvent business thrust upon it by operation of law. That business will, in any event, be unable to pay its fire debts in full. But the question is whether the fire claimants should be subordinated to, should share equally with, or should collect ahead of those creditors for whose benefit the continued operation of the business (which unfortunately led to a fire instead of the hoped-for rehabilitation) was allowed.

> . . . .

> The "master," liable for the negligence of the "servant" in this case was the business operating under a Chapter XI arrangement for the benefit of creditors and with the hope of rehabilitation. That benefit and that rehabilitation are worthy objectives. But it would be inconsistent both with the principle of respondeat superior and with the rule of fairness in bankruptcy to seek these objectives at the cost of excluding tort creditors of the arrangement from its assets, or totally subordinating the claims of those on whom the arrangement is imposed to the claims of those for whose benefit it is instituted.

> . . . .

> Although there appear to be no cases dealing with tort claims arising during Chapter XI proceedings, decisions in analogous cases suggest that "actual and necessary costs" should include costs ordinarily incident to operation of a business, and not be limited to costs without which rehabilitation would be impossible. It has long been the rule of equity receiverships that torts of the receivership create claims against the receivership itself; in those cases the statutory limitation to "actual and

necessary costs" is not involved, but the explicit recognition extended to tort claims in those cases weighs heavily in favor of considering them within the general category of costs and expenses.

Reading Co. v. Brown 391 U.S. 471, 478–84 (1968).

Applying the rationale of *Reading*, a number of courts have held that the costs of environmental cleanup measures, whether undertaken by or on behalf of debtors, are entitled to administrative priority. For example, in *Matter of H.L.S. Energy Co.*, 151 F.3d 434 (5th Cir. 1998), the debtor operated oil and gas wells in Texas. While the case was pending, the state brought an action to compel the debtor to plug inactive oil wells as required by Texas law. Short of funds, the Chapter 11 trustee agreed that the state should plug the wells and charge the cost to the debtor. When the state sought reimbursement, the trustee argued that the claim was not a necessary administrative expense. The court disagreed:

> An "actual and necessary cost" must have been of benefit to the estate and its creditors. This requirement is in keeping with the conceptual justification for administrative expense priority: that creditors must pay for those expenses necessary to produce the distribution to which they are entitled. The "benefit" requirement has no independent basis in the Code, however, but is merely a way of testing whether a particular expense was truly "necessary" to the estate: If it was of no "benefit," it cannot have been "necessary."

> The trustee argues that the costs incurred by the state in connection with plugging the unproductive wells did not "benefit" the estate. Of course this is true — in the sense that the bankrupt estate and its creditors would have been happy to abandon the unproductive wells, leaving them un-plugged in abdication of HLS's obligations under Texas law. But bearing in mind that the "benefit" requirement is simply a gloss on the underlying concept of what is "necessary," our notion of "benefit" cannot be limited to the narrow sense that the trustee urges.

> Under federal law, bankruptcy trustees must comply with state law. *See* 28 U.S.C. § 959(b). Furthermore, a bankruptcy trustee may not abandon property in contravention of a state law reasonably designed to protect public health or safety. Thus, a combination of Texas and federal law placed on the trustee an inescapable obligation to plug the unproductive wells, an obligation that arose during the chapter 11 proceedings.

> The fulfillment of this, the estate's obligation, can only be seen as a benefit to the estate. In this sense, the state's action resembles the sort of "salvage" work that lies at the heart of the administrative expense priority. No one would challenge the expense of shoring up the sagging roof on a bankrupt's warehouse, for example, where carpentry was needed to prevent further damage to the structure or liability from injury to passers-by. . . . The laws of Texas compelled action in this case just as surely as would the laws of physics in that one. The unplugged unproduc-tive wells operated as a legal liability on the estate, a liability capable of

generating losses in the nature of substantial fines every day the wells remained unplugged.

 . . . .

 Of course, the chapter 11 trustee never did anything with the wells: The whole point of this case is that he neither produced oil from nor plugged them. Still, the bankrupt estate possessed the sole operating interest in the wells. Anyone possessing the sole operating interest in an unproductive well surely would be happy to abandon that interest, and the concomitant obligation to plug that well. But he cannot, for Texas law requires well operators to plug their wells when they are finished with production.

 It therefore matters not whether the bankrupt estate produced any oil or received any revenue from the wells. As the operator, it was required to plug them.

151 F.3d at 437–39 (citations omitted).

§ 8.06   REPRISE: WHAT IS A CLAIM AND WHEN DOES A CLAIM ARISE?

[A]   Special Problems in Products Liability Cases

Carol Charisma looks very perplexed. "I guess I can see why Ella Pyrenees ought to be entitled to — what did you call it? — an administrative priority. But what about all the people who bought video games from us *before* we filed our Chapter 11 petition. What happens if they explode today? Do they hold claims? Are they entitled to administrative priority? What about our customers who bought video games that haven't exploded but just may one of these days. Do they hold claims? What if the games don't explode until after this Chapter 11 case is over?"

Ever full of good news, you remind Carol not to forget the problem of the Hystereo plaintiffs: the people who claim they have developed that virtual illness as a result of exposure to the company's video games.

"Of course. How could I forget them?" Carol grouses. "We have plaintiffs who say they developed the illness *before we filed*. We have plaintiffs who say they developed the illness *after we filed*, and . . ." Carol stops talking mid-sentence. A quizzical expression crosses her face. "Hold on. Are you saying that we can deal with people who haven't even developed the illness yet?"

You remind Carol that this is a subject that is not entirely new. You have broached it before, most notably in the context of the scope of the automatic stay. You suggest that she reread the Fourth Circuit's opinion in *Grady v. A.H. Robins Co.* (reprinted in chapter 3 of the text). You also remind her to keep a few key principles in mind when thinking about Grady and the opinions that follow.

 (1) As we saw at the outset of this chapter, only holders of claims that are "allowed" under Code § 502 are allowed to vote on reorganization plans, Code § 1126(a), and only holders of claims or interests that are "allowed" under § 502 and holders of administrative expenses that are "allowed"

under Code § 503 are entitled to receive distributions under the plan.

(2) In order for a claim to be allowed under § 502, it must be evidenced by a timely filed proof of claim. According to Code § 501(a), a *creditor* may file a proof of claim. A creditor is an entity that holds a *claim* that arose before the order for relief. Code § 101(10).

(3) The concept of *claim* is defined very broadly in Code § 101(5), as including a "right to payment" whether or not such right is reduced to judgment, liquidated, contingent, unmatured, disputed, etc.

(4) The word *debt* means "liability on a claim." Code § 101(12).

(5) The confirmation of a reorganization plan discharges the debtor from "any debt that arose before the date of such confirmation," whether or not a proof of claim was filed, whether or not "such claim" was allowed, and whether or not the holder of such claim voted to accept the plan. Thus, a claim need not be allowed to be discharged. It need only have arisen prior to confirmation.

KANE v. JOHNS-MANVILLE CORP.
United States Court of Appeals for the Second Circuit
843 F.2d 636 (1988)

This appeal challenges the lawfulness of the reorganization plan of the Johns-Manville Corporation ("Manville"), a debtor in one of the nation's most significant Chapter 11 bankruptcy proceedings. Lawrence Kane, on behalf of himself and a group of other personal injury claimants, appeals from an order of the District Court for the Southern District of New York (Whitman Knapp, Judge) affirming an order of the Bankruptcy Court (Burton R. Lifland, Chief Judge) that confirmed a Second Amended Plan of Reorganization (the Plan). Kane and the group of 765 individuals he represents (collectively "Kane") are persons with asbestos-related disease who had filed personal injury suits against Manville prior to Manville's Chapter 11 petition. The suits were stayed, and Kane and other claimants presently afflicted with asbestos-related disease were designated as Class-4 creditors in the reorganization proceedings. Kane now objects to confirmation of the reorganization Plan on several grounds: it discharges the rights of future asbestos victims who do not have "claims" within the meaning of 11 U.S.C. § 101(4) [now § 101(5)], it was adopted without constitutionally adequate notice to various interested parties, the voting procedures used in approving the Plan violated the Bankruptcy Code and due process requirements. . . . The order of the District Court affirming the Bankruptcy Court's confirmation of the Plan is affirmed.

Background

Prior to its filing for reorganization in 1982, Manville was the world's largest miner of asbestos and a major manufacturer of insulating materials and other asbestos products. Beginning in the 1960's, scientific studies began to confirm that exposure to asbestos fibers over time could cause a variety of respiratory diseases, including certain forms of lung cancer. A significant characteristic of these asbestos-related diseases is their unusually long latency period. An individual might not become ill from an asbestos-related disease until as long as forty years after initial exposure. . . .

As a result of the studies linking respiratory disease with asbestos, Manville became the target in the 1960's and 1970's of a growing number of products liability lawsuits. By the early 1980's, Manville had been named in approximately 12,500 such suits brought on behalf of over 16,000 claimants. New suits were being filed at the rate of 425 per month. Epidemiological studies undertaken by Manville revealed that approximately 50,000 to 100,000 additional suits could be expected from persons who had already been exposed to Manville asbestos. On the basis of these studies and the costs Manville had already experienced in disposing of prior claims, Manville estimated its potential liability at approximately $2 billion. On August 26, 1982, Manville filed a voluntary petition in bankruptcy under Chapter 11. From the outset of the reorganization, all concerned recognized that the impetus for Manville's action was not a present inability to meet debts but rather the anticipation of massive personal injury liability in the future.

Because future asbestos-related liability was the *raison d'etre* of the Manville reorganization, an important question at the initial stages of the proceedings concerned the representation and treatment of what were termed "future asbestos health claimants" ("future claimants"). The future claimants were persons who had been exposed to Manville's asbestos prior to the August 1982 petition date but had not yet shown any signs of disease at that time. Since the future claimants were not yet ill at the time the Chapter 11 proceedings were commenced, none had filed claims against Manville, and their identities were unknown. An Asbestos Health Committee was appointed to represent all personal injury claimants, but the Committee took the position that it represented the interests only of "present claimants," persons who, prior to the petition date, had been exposed to Manville asbestos and had already developed an asbestos-related disease. The Committee declined to represent the future claimants. Other parties in the proceedings, recognizing that an effective reorganization would have to account for the future asbestos victims as well as the present ones, moved the Bankruptcy Court to appoint a legal guardian for the future claimants. The Bankruptcy Court granted the motion, reasoning that regardless of whether the future claimants technically had "claims" cognizable in bankruptcy proceedings, [§ 101(4)], they were at least "parties in interest" under section 1109(b) of the Code and were therefore entitled to a voice in the proceedings. The Court appointed a Legal Representative to participate on behalf of the future claimants. Additionally, the Court invited any person who had been exposed to Manville asbestos but had not developed an illness to participate in the proceedings, and two such persons appeared.

The Second Amended Plan of Reorganization resulted from more than four years of negotiations among Manville, the Asbestos Health Committee, the Legal Representative, the Equity Security Holders' Committee, and other groups interested in the estate.[1] The cornerstone of the Plan is the Asbestos Health Trust (the

---

[1] The Plan provides for nine classes of claims and interests: administrative expenses (Class 1), secured claims (Class 2), asbestos property damage claims (Class 3), present asbestos health claims (Class 4), employee and non-asbestos material claims (Class 5), other unsecured claims (Class 6), interests of preferred stockholders (Class 7), interests of common stockholders (Class 8), and interests

"Trust"), a mechanism designed to satisfy the claims of all asbestos health victims, both present and future. The Trust is funded with the proceeds from Manville's settlements with its insurers; certain cash, receivables, and stock of the reorganized Manville Corporation; long term notes; and the right to receive up to 20% of Manville's yearly profits for as long as it takes to satisfy all health claims. According to the terms of the Trust, individuals with asbestos-related disease must first try to settle their claims by a mandatory exchange of settlement offers with Trust representatives. If a settlement cannot be reached, the claimant may elect mediation, binding arbitration, or traditional tort litigation. The claimant may collect from the Trust the full amount of whatever compensatory damages he is awarded. The only restriction on recovery is that the claimant may not obtain punitive damages.

The purpose of the Trust is to provide a means of satisfying Manville's ongoing personal injury liability while allowing Manville to maximize its value by continuing as an ongoing concern. To fulfill this purpose, the Plan seeks to ensure that health claims can be asserted only against the Trust and that Manville's operating entities will be protected from an onslaught of crippling lawsuits that could jeopardize the entire reorganization effort. To this end, the parties agreed that as a condition precedent to confirmation of the Plan, the Bankruptcy Court would issue an injunction channeling all asbestos-related personal injury claims to the Trust (the "Injunction"). The Injunction provides that asbestos health claimants may proceed only against the Trust to satisfy their claims and may not sue Manville, its other operating entities, and certain other specified parties, including Manville's insurers. Significantly, the Injunction applies to all health claimants, both present and future, regardless of whether they technically have dischargeable "claims" under the Code. The Injunction applies to any suit to recover "on or with respect to any Claim, Interest or Other Asbestos Obligation." "Claim" covers the present claimants, who are categorized as Class-4 unsecured creditors under the Plan and who have dischargeable "claims" within the meaning of [§ 101(5)]. The future claimants are subject to the Injunction under the rubric of "Other Asbestos Obligation," which is defined by the Plan as asbestos-related health liability caused by pre-petition exposure to Manville asbestos, regardless of when the individual develops clinically observable symptoms. Thus, while the future claimants are not given creditor status under the Plan, they are nevertheless treated identically to the present claimants by virtue of the Injunction, which channels all claims to the Trust.

The Plan was submitted to the Bankruptcy Court for voting in June of 1986. At that time relatively few present asbestos health claimants had appeared in the reorganization proceedings. Approximately 6,400 proofs of claims had been filed for personal injuries, which accounted for less than half of the more than 16,000 persons who had filed pre-petition personal injury suits against Manville. Moreover, Manville estimated that there were tens of thousands of additional present asbestos victims who had neither filed suits nor presented proofs of claims. Manville and the creditor constituencies agreed that as many present claimants as possible should be brought into the proceedings so that they could vote on the Plan. However, the

---

of certain individual plaintiffs in pending lawsuits (Class 9). Future asbestos health claimants are not part of any class but are treated as "other asbestos obligations" under the Plan and are subject to the same claims handling facility as the present health claimants in Class 4.

parties were reluctant to embark on the standard Code procedure of establishing a bar date, soliciting proofs of claims, resolving all disputed claims on notice and hearing, and then weighting the votes by the amounts of the claims, as such a process could delay the reorganization for many years. To avoid this delay, the Bankruptcy Court adopted special voting procedures for [the present asbestos claim holders in] Class 4. Manville was directed to undertake a comprehensive multi-media notice campaign to inform persons with present health claims of the pendency of the reorganization and their opportunity to participate. Potential health claimants who responded to the campaign were given a combined proof-of-claim-and-voting form in which each could present a medical diagnosis of his asbestos-related disease and vote to accept or reject the Plan. For voting purposes only, each claim was valued in the amount of one dollar. Claimants were informed that the proof-of-claim-and-voting form would be used only for voting and that to collect from the Trust, they would have to execute an additional proof of claim establishing the actual value of their damages.

The notice campaign produced a large number of present asbestos claimants. In all, 52,440 such claimants submitted proof-of-claim-and-voting forms. Of these, 50,275 or 95.8% approved the Plan, while 2,165 or 4.2% opposed it. In addition to these Class-4 claimants, all other classes of creditors also approved the Plan. Class 8, the common stockholders, opposed the Plan.

A confirmation hearing was held on December 16, 1986, at which Manville presented evidence regarding the feasibility and fairness of the Plan. Objections to confirmation were filed by several parties, including Kane. On December 18, 1986, the Bankruptcy Court issued a Determination of Confirmation Issues in which it rejected all objections to confirmation. With respect to Kane's challenge to the Injunction and the voting procedures, the Court relied primarily on its broad equitable powers to achieve reorganizations. . . . The Court entered an order confirming the Plan on December 22, 1986. Kane and others appealed. By order dated July 15, 1987, the District Court affirmed the Bankruptcy Court's confirmation order "for substantially the reasons set forth" in the Bankruptcy Judge's Determination of Confirmation Issues. This appeal followed.

Discussion

. . . .

B. Voting Procedures

Consideration of Kane's challenge to the voting procedures requires a brief outline of pertinent provisions of the Bankruptcy Code. A plan of reorganization must either be accepted by each impaired class of claims or interests, 11 U.S.C. § 1129(a)(8), or meet certain rigid requirements with respect to each non-accepting class, 11 U.S.C. § 1129(b) (so-called "cram down" provision). A class of creditors has accepted a plan under the Code "if such plan has been accepted by creditors . . . that hold at least two-thirds in amount and more than one-half in number of the allowed claims of such class held by creditors . . . that have accepted or rejected such plan." 11 U.S.C. § 1126(c). Claims are "allowed" in the amount filed unless they are objected to by a party in interest, including the debtor or another creditor. 11 U.S.C. § 502(a); Bankruptcy Rule 3001(f). If a party in interest wishes to object to a claim, notice of the objection must be mailed to the claimant at least thirty days prior to a hearing at which the bankruptcy court determines the validity of the claim and the amount allowed. 11 U.S.C. § 502(b); Bankruptcy Rule 3007. However, objections to claims need not be finally resolved before voting on a plan may occur. Bankruptcy Rule 3018(a) provides that "notwithstanding objection to a claim or interest, the court after notice and hearing may temporarily allow the claim or interest in an amount which the court deems proper for the purpose of accepting or rejecting a plan."

Kane contends that the special Class-4 voting procedures adopted by the Bankruptcy Court violated his rights under the Code in several ways. First, since proofs of claims and votes were simultaneously solicited from present claimants in a combined mailing form, no creditor had an opportunity to object to the Class-4 members' claims before their votes were cast. Kane argues that this lack of opportunity to object prejudiced him because some of the claims might have been invalid and counting votes of those with invalid claims diluted his own vote. Second, Kane argues that the Bankruptcy Court improperly "allowed" claims for voting purposes in the arbitrary amount of one dollar, thereby depriving him of the opportunity to vote his claim weighted in the amount indicated in his proof of claim. By weighting all Class-4 votes equally, the Bankruptcy Court, in Kane's view, failed to adhere to the Code's voting scheme whereby a minority of class members with just over one third of the value of the total claims may reject a plan. Finally, Kane suggests that by assigning the one dollar value to all of the claims, the Bankruptcy Court might have discouraged Plan opponents with large claims from casting their votes since such opponents might have believed that, without the benefit of weighted voting, their opposition to the Plan would be futile.

Appellees respond that the Code is sufficiently flexible to accommodate the creative voting scheme used in this case. They argue primarily that the Code evinces a strong preference for facilitating reorganizations and that strict adherence to a weighted voting scheme would have been impractical in this case. Appellees point out that either the reorganization would have been delayed for years while the dollar value of every disputed health claim was determined or the vote would have been taken without contacting present health claimants other than the few who had voluntarily submitted proofs of claims, leaving a large group of important creditors disenfranchised. Additionally, appellees rely on Bankruptcy Rule 3018(a) as express authority for temporarily allowing claims for voting purposes only. Kane responds that Rule 3018(a) is not applicable because it permits temporary allowance only after formal filing of an objection and a hearing on the disputed claims, neither of which occurred in this case.

We need not decide whether the special Class-4 voting procedures violate the Code because, in view of the outcome of the vote, the alleged irregularities were at most harmless error.

None of the procedures that Kane contends were required would have changed the outcome of the vote. With respect to denial of the opportunity to object to the Class-4 claims before they were voted, no substantial rights were impaired because

Kane is unable to show that, had he been afforded a chance to object, any of the present health claims would have been excluded. The only objection Kane contends that he would have asserted is that the combined proof-of-claim-and-voting form approved by the Bankruptcy Court permitted a filing supported only by a written medical diagnosis of an asbestos-related condition without evidence that the claimant was exposed to Manville's product, as opposed to the product of some other company. However, it is clear from the record that this objection would have been unavailing. The combined proof-of-claim-and-voting form required anyone who had not already filed a lawsuit against Manville to submit a diagnosis of his disease and to represent that he had been exposed to Manville's product. Such a representation would have sufficed to warrant accepting the claim for voting purposes, especially in the absence of any particularized contrary evidence from Kane. In any event, since 95.8% of those Class-4 members who voted approved the Plan, the result would not have been different unless more than 90% of those who voted in favor had invalid claims, an improbable circumstance.[6] Similarly, Kane was not prejudiced by the assignment of a one dollar value to each claim. If we make the reasonable assumption that the percentage of claims that are valid is the same for "yes" votes and "no" votes, then the "no" votes would have to be at least ten times larger, on average, than the "yes" votes in order to change the result from what occurred with equal weighting of each vote.[7] Nothing in the record gives any indication that such a large variation in claims existed, much less that the "no" votes were the larger claims. Indeed, it is safe to assume that if the procedures insisted upon by Kane had been used, all the votes would have still been weighted roughly the same since significant variations would not likely occur in the damages sustained by similar groups of people from similar kinds of injuries. Even if Kane is correct that some Plan opponents with larger claims were discouraged from voting, no prejudice occurred. Even if we make the unlikely assumption, favorable to Kane, that Plan opponents in Class 4, on average, had claims twice the size of the claims of Plan proponents, the number of "no" votes in this class would have had to increase nearly six times, from 2,165 to 12,569, in order to change the result.[8] If there really were

---

[6] With all votes weighted equally, the number of "yes" votes would have to be less than two thirds of the total Class-4 votes cast in order for the Plan to lack approval by holders of two thirds of the aggregate value of the claims of this class. 11 U.S.C. § 1126(c). Since 2,165 opposed the Plan, the total of valid votes would have to be less than 6,495 in order to prevent the "yes" votes from constituting two thirds of the total votes cast; if the total is at least 6,495, the "yes" votes would be at least 4,330 (6,495 - 2,165), which is two thirds of 6,495. In order to reduce the total vote from the 52,440 cast to less than 6,495, the "yes" votes would have to be reduced from the 50,275 cast to less than 4,330 (6,495 - 2,165). To accomplish this result would have required invalidation of at least 91.4% of the "yes" votes (50,275 - 4,330 = 45,945, which is 91.4 % of 50,275).

[7] The aggregate value of the "no" votes would have to exceed one third of the aggregate value of all Class-4 claims in order to prevent this class from approving the Plan. 11 U.S.C. § 1126(c). Since 2,165 votes opposed the Plan and 50,275 favored it, the multiple by which the average value of each "no" vote would have to exceed the average value of each "yes" vote in order to change the result can be derived from the formula, 2,165 x (p) = 1/3(2,165 x (p) + 50,275(p)), where "x" equals the multiple and "p" equals the percentage of valid claims. In this equation, x = 11.6. Because we have assumed that the percentage of claims that are valid is the same for "yes" votes and "no" votes (i.e., "p" is the same throughout the equation), the multiple "x" is unaffected by the actual percentage of the claims that are valid.

[8] If the average value of an opponent's claim is twice the value of a proponent's claim, the number of opponents needed to have Class 4 oppose the Plan for lack of approval by holders of two thirds of the aggregate value of claims may be derived from the formula, 2(x) = 1/3(50,275 + (2x)), where "x" equals

12,569 Class-4 claimants opposed to the Plan, it is highly unlikely that 10,404 or 83% of them were discouraged from voting.

. . . .

MINER, CIRCUIT JUDGE, concurring:

Since the bankruptcy judge was empowered to estimate the claims of the Class-4 creditors, and did not abuse his discretion in doing so, I perceive no need to apply a harmless error analysis or to employ mathematical calculations to sustain the voting procedures adopted.

Acceptance of a plan of reorganization occurs when "such plan has been accepted by creditors . . . that hold at least two-thirds in amount and more than one-half in number of the allowed claims of such class held by creditors . . . that have accepted or rejected such plan." 11 U.S.C. § 1126(c). For the purpose of allowance, a bankruptcy court must estimate "any contingent or unliquidated claim, the fixing or liquidation of which, as the case may be, would unduly delay the administration of the case." 11 U.S.C. § 502(c)(1). Moreover, the court is authorized, after objections and notice and hearing, to allow a claim temporarily "in an amount which the court deems proper for the purpose of accepting or rejecting a plan." Bankruptcy Rule 3018(a).

By the time of the June 23, 1986 hearing held to consider the Disclosure Statement and the Second Amended and Restated Plan of Reorganization filed by the debtors, approximately 6,400 proofs of claim had been submitted by asbestos health claimants for personal injuries. It was apparent at that juncture in the proceedings that the administration of the case would be delayed unduly if each of those unliquidated claims were to be considered separately for allowance purposes. Referring to the number of actual lawsuits then pending on behalf of asbestos health claimants, the bankruptcy judge observed that more than 16,500 hearings would be necessary "to treat each individual claim discretely." In the words of the debtors' attorney, "the practical effect of having to value each and every claim individually would . . . be delay beyond anybody's reasonable expectations and probably lifetime." The problem of delay was even more apparent at the conclusion of the notice campaign, when proof-of-claim-and-voting forms had been received from 52,440 claimants.

Under the circumstances, the bankruptcy judge properly exercised his authority to estimate each of the claims at $1.00. The asbestos health claims were especially suited to estimation because of the uncertain nature of both liability and damages. Moreover, the very purpose of the reorganization would be defeated if each claim were to be considered separately for purposes of allowance and voting. Indeed, the delay entailed by such an approach would not only be fatal to the entire plan but might very well be fatal to any recovery for the claimants. Section 502(c)(1) is designed to forestall these types of consequences.

In any event, the assignment of a value of $1.00 per claim is merely the temporary allowance contemplated by Rule 3018(a), with the right reserved to each

---

the number of opponents. In this equation, "x" equals 12,569.

claimant to seek actual damages from the Asbestos Health Trust. Although the Rule calls for objections to the claims, followed by notice and hearing, before temporary allowances for voting purposes are made, there was substantial compliance with this requirement here.

EPSTEIN v. OFFICIAL COMMITTEE OF UNSECURED CREDITORS OF PIPER AIRCRAFT CORP. (IN RE PIPER AIRCRAFT CORP.)

United States Court of Appeals for the Eleventh Circuit
58 F.3d 1573 (1995)

[Piper began manufacturing airplanes in 1937, and at the time of this case, there were about 60,000 of them still in use. Periodically, these planes are involved in crashes. Although Piper has been named as a defendant in a number of lawsuits relating to these crashes, it has never acknowledged that its products are harmful or defective. In 1987, it made a decision to self-insure and stop carrying product liability insurance. In 1991, Piper filed a Chapter 11 petition. In 1993, Piper identified a company, Pilatus Aircraft Ltd., that wanted to buy its assets. Pilatus, concerned about a successor liability problem, insisted that Piper have a representative appointed in the Chapter 11 case to represent the interests of so-called future claimants (people who, in the future, might be injured in a Piper plane crash). The theory was that the representative would seek the establishment of a special fund to pay such claims if and when they arose. A legal representative ("Epstein") was appointed. The legal representative filed a $100,000,000 proof of claim on behalf of future claimants. The creditors' committee objected, asserting that the claimants did not hold claims cognizable under Code § 101(5). The bankruptcy court disallowed the claim and the district court affirmed. The Eleventh Circuit also affirmed. Portions of its opinion follow.]

BLACK, CIRCUIT JUDGE.

. . . .

II. DISCUSSION

The sole issue on appeal, whether any of the Future Claimants hold claims against Piper as defined in § 101(5) of the Bankruptcy Code, is one of first impression in this Circuit. . . .

A. Statute

Under the Bankruptcy Code, only parties that hold preconfirmation claims have a legal right to participate in a Chapter 11 bankruptcy case and share in payments pursuant to a Chapter 11 plan. 11 U.S.C.A. §§ 101(10), 501, 502. In order to determine if the Future Claimants have such a right to participate, we first must address the statutory definition of the term "claim." The Bankruptcy Code defines claim as:

(A) right to payment, whether or not such right is reduced to judgment, liquidated, unliquidated, fixed, contingent, matured, unmatured, disputed, undisputed, legal, equitable, secured, or unsecured; or

(B) right to an equitable remedy for breach of performance if such breach gives rise to a right to payment, whether or not such right to an equitable remedy is reduced to judgment, fixed, contingent, matured, unmatured, disputed, undisputed, secured, or unsecured.

11 U.S.C.A. § 101(5). The legislative history of the Code suggests that Congress intended to define the term claim very broadly under § 101(5), so that "all legal obligations of the debtor, no matter how remote or contingent, will be able to be dealt with in the bankruptcy case." H.R. Rep. No. 595, 95th Cong., 2d Sess. 309 (1978). . . .

B. Case Law

Since the enactment of § 101(5), courts have developed several tests to determine whether certain parties hold claims pursuant to that section: the accrued state law claim test, the conduct test, and the prepetition relationship test. The bankruptcy court and district court adopted the prepetition relationship test in determining that the Future Claimants did not hold claims pursuant to § 101(5).[2]

Epstein primarily challenges the district court's application of the prepetition relationship test. He argues that the conduct test, which some courts have adopted in mass tort cases,[3] is more consistent with the text, history, and policies of the Code.[4] Under the conduct test, a right to payment arises when the conduct giving rise to the alleged liability occurred. See *A.H. Robins*, 839 F.2d at 199; *Waterman*, 141 Bankr. 552 at 556. Epstein's position is that any right to payment arising out of the prepetition conduct of Piper, no matter how remote, should be deemed a claim and provided for, pursuant to § 101(5), in this case. He argues that the relevant conduct giving rise to the alleged liability was Piper's prepetition manufacture,

---

[2] The accrued state law claim theory states that there is no claim for bankruptcy purposes until a claim has accrued under state law. The most notable case adopting this approach is the Third Circuit's decision in *In re*: M. Frenville Co., 744 F.2d 332 (3d Cir.1984), cert. denied, 469 U.S. 1160, 105 S. Ct. 911, 83 L. Ed. 2d 925 (1985). This test since has been rejected by a majority of courts as imposing too narrow an interpretation on the term claim. *See e.g.*, Grady v. A.H. Robins Co., 839 F.2d 198, 201 (4th Cir.), cert. denied, 487 U.S. 1260, 109 S. Ct. 201, 101 L. Ed. 2d 972 (1988); *In re*: Black, 70 Bankr. 645 (Bankr. D. Utah 1986); Acevedo v. Van Dorn Plastic Machinery Co., 68 Bankr. 495 (Bankr. E.D.N.Y. 1986); *In re*: Edge, 60 Bankr. 690 (Bankr. M.D. Tenn. 1986); *In re*: Johns-Manville Corp., 57 Bankr. 680 (Bankr. S.D.N.Y. 1986); *In re*: Yanks, 49 Bankr. 56 (Bankr. S.D. Fla. 1985). We agree with these courts and decline to employ the state law claim theory.

[3] *See, e.g.*, A.H. Robins Co., 839 F.2d at 203 (Dalkon Shield); *In re*: Waterman Steamship Corp., 141 Bankr. 552, 556 (Bankr. S.D.N.Y. 1992) (asbestos), *vacated on other grounds*, 157 Bankr. 220 (Bankr. S.D.N.Y. 1993); *In re*: Johns-Manville Corp., 36 Bankr. 743, 750 (Bankr. S.D.N.Y. 1984) (asbestos).

[4] Epstein claims that the prepetition relationship test, by requiring identifiability of claimants, eliminates the words "contingent," "unmatured," "unliquidated," and "disputed" from the statute. He further argues that requiring a prepetition relationship is contrary to the Congressional objective that bankruptcy permit a complete settlement of the affairs of the debtor and a complete discharge and fresh start, as the claims of those persons whose injuries become manifest after the petition is filed could prove a drain on the reorganized debtor's assets for years to come.

design, sale and distribution of allegedly defective aircraft. Specifically, he contends that, because Piper performed these acts prepetition, the potential victims, although not yet identifiable, hold claims under § 101(5) of the Code.

The Official Committee and Piper dispute the breadth of the definition of claim asserted by Epstein, arguing that the scope of claim cannot extend so far as to include unidentified, and presently unidentifiable, individuals with no discernible prepetition relationship to Piper. Recognizing, as Appellees do, that the conduct test may define claim too broadly in certain circumstances, several courts have recognized "claims" only for those individuals with some type of prepetition relationship with the debtor. . . . The prepetition relationship test, as adopted by the bankruptcy court and district court, requires "some prepetition relationship, such as contact, exposure, impact, or privity, between the debtor's prepetition conduct and the claimant" in order for the claimant to hold a § 101(5) claim.

Upon examination of the various theories, we agree with Appellees that the district court utilized the proper test in deciding that the Future Claimants did not hold a claim under § 101(5). Epstein's interpretation of "claim" and application of the conduct test would enable anyone to hold a claim against Piper by virtue of their potential future exposure to any aircraft in the existing fleet. Even the conduct test cases, on which Epstein relies, do not compel the result he seeks. In fact, the conduct test cases recognize that focusing solely on prepetition conduct, as Epstein espouses, would stretch the scope of § 101(5). Accordingly, the courts applying the conduct test also presume some prepetition relationship between the debtor's conduct and the claimant. *See A.H. Robins*, 839 F.2d at 203; *Waterman*, 141 Bankr. at 556.

While acknowledging that the district court's test is more consistent with the purposes of the Bankruptcy Code than is the conduct test supported by Epstein, we find that the test as set forth by the district court unnecessarily restricts the class of claimants to those who could be identified prior to the filing of the petition. Those claimants having contact with the debtor's product post-petition but prior to confirmation also could be identified, during the course of the bankruptcy proceeding, as potential victims, who might have claims arising out of debtor's prepetition conduct.

We therefore modify the test used by the district court and adopt what we will call the "Piper test" in determining the scope of the term claim under § 101(5): an individual has a § 101(5) claim against a debtor manufacturer if (i) events occurring before confirmation create a relationship, such as contact, exposure, impact, or privity, between the claimant and the debtor's product; and (ii) the basis for liability is the debtor's prepetition conduct in designing, manufacturing and selling the allegedly defective or dangerous product. The debtor's prepetition conduct gives rise to a claim to be administered in a case only if there is a relationship established before confirmation between an identifiable claimant or group of claimants and that prepetition.

In the instant case, it is clear that the Future Claimants fail the minimum requirements of the Piper test. There is no preconfirmation exposure to a specific identifiable defective product or any other preconfirmation relationship between Piper and the broadly defined class of Future Claimants. As there is no preconfirmation connection established between Piper and the Future Claimants, the Future Claimants do not hold a § 101(5) claim arising out of Piper's prepetition design, manufacture, sale, and distribution of allegedly defective aircraft.

III. CONCLUSION

For the foregoing reasons, we hold that the Future Claimants do not meet the threshold requirements of the Piper test and, as a result, do not hold claims as defined in § 101(5) of the Bankruptcy Code.

AFFIRMED.

NOTES AND QUESTIONS

1.   What legitimate bankruptcy policy is served by dealing with future claims in a Chapter 11 case? Consider the following passage from Mark J. Roe, *Bankruptcy and Mass Tort*, 84 COLUM. L. REV. 846, 855 (1984):

> Another basic bankruptcy goal, that of debtor rehabilitation, justifies an early resolution of future tort claims. To preserve the firm's equity and pay early-maturing claims while huge but future claims hang over the firm could bring about the firm's operational collapse. Dissipation and diversion of assets are perhaps more likely when the future claims are of scattered, unknown tort victims than when the future claim are of contract creditors that monitor the debtor and have agreements, such as the bond indenture, that facilitate the defeat of efforts to divert assets. . . . [E]ven absent diversion, the enterprise is likely to be affected severely and adversely. Access to capital markets will be reduced. The enterprise will shrink; contract claims will mature and be paid. Worthwhile projects will be foregone. Stockholders will be motivated to march the firm down risky paths. Customers and suppliers will flee. Mergers will be barred; management, no longer fearful of ouster by merger, might slacken its performance. To the extent it performs, it must donate its time and energy to the resolution of the firm's financial troubles, not to operations.

2.   What is the fate of holders of so-called "future claims" if their claims are not dealt with in a reorganization plan? The answer depends on whether the debtor liquidates or reorganizes. If a debtor is forced to liquidate (as might be the case if continued threat of future lawsuits jeopardizes its standing in the capital markets or causes customers to shun its products), future claim holders will have no source of recovery other than insurance, if any. If the business reorganizes, the result will be different.

Consider the following facts. Winston, a manufacturer and seller of mobile homes, commences business in 1965. In 1982, Winston files a Chapter 11 petition. In 1983, its reorganization plan is confirmed. In 1985 a mobile home that Winston manufactured in 1970 catches fire, allegedly as a result of a design defect. Two men are killed in the fire. Their mother brings a wrongful death action against the reorganized entity. What result? In *Lemelle v. Universal Mfg. Corp.*, 18 F.3d 1268 (5th Cir. 1994), the court held that neither the mother nor her children, held a "claim" that could have been asserted or discharged in the debtor's Chapter 11 case. Hence she could bring her tort action against the reorganized debtor:

> The injury suffered, i.e., the death of the decedents, occurred simultaneously with the manifestation of that injury in December 1985, years after Winston's reorganization plan had been confirmed. The design and manufacture of the mobile home in question thus resulted in no tortious consequence until a fire started in that mobile home in December 1985. Further, there is no evidence in the record to indicate when [Lemelle] and her family acquired this mobile home or from whom they acquired it. There is no evidence to establish that Winston, as the manufacturer of the mobile home in question, should have even known of [Lemelle's] and her family's existence.

> Where, as here, the injury and the manifestation of that injury occurred simultaneously — more than three years after Winston filed its petition and more than two years after the plan was confirmed, we think that, at a minimum, there must be evidence that would permit the debtor to identify, during the course of the bankruptcy proceedings, potential victims and thereby permit notice to these potential victims of the pendency of the proceedings. . . . We think the absence of this evidence precludes a finding by the district court that the claims asserted by [Lemelle] were discharged in Winston's bankruptcy proceedings.

>   . . . .

> In our view, however, even the broad definition of "claim" cannot be extended to include [Lemelle] or the decedents as claimants whom the record indicates were completely unknown and unidentified at the time Winston filed its petition and whose rights depended entirely on the fortuity of future occurrences. We do not here decide whether if evidence of some pre-petition relationship between Winston and [Lemelle] or the decedents had been adduced, we might nonetheless conclude that neither [Lemelle] nor the decedents had a "claim" or that any such claim had not been discharged in bankruptcy. We need not reach that question on this record.

18 F.3d at 1277–78 (citations omitted). Would the result have been different if the existence of the design defect had been identified before the Chapter 11 petition was filed?

Suppose that Schwinn Bicycle Co. files a Chapter 11 petition in 1992. Nine months later, it sells all its assets to a new entity. In 1994, a plan is confirmed. The order confirming the plan provides that the purchaser of the assets will not be liable for any personal injury claims against the debtor "whether arising prior to or subsequent to the Confirmation Date." A year after the plan is confirmed, a child is injured while riding a bike manufactured by Schwinn in 1979. Is the successor company liable? *See Schwinn Cycling & Fitness Inc. v. Benonis*, 217 B.R. 790 (N.D. Ill. 1997).

3.   Although the Manville channeling injunction was upheld in *Kane v. Johns-Manville*, some members of the financial community continued to harbor doubts

about whether it would survive future challenges. To allay these fears, subsection (g) was added to Code § 524 in 1994. The new subsection, which has retroactive effect, applies only to asbestos cases. It expressly authorizes a bankruptcy court to enter an injunction barring any action to collect a claim or demand that is to be paid by a trust created pursuant to a plan of reorganization, provided that the requirements set forth in § 524(g) are satisfied. These requirements, among other things, describe a trust that is formed and funded exactly as the Manville trust was. The references in § 524(g) to "claims" and "demands" are noteworthy. Although the amendment provides for the channeling of existing and future liabilities to the trust, the drafters stopped short of treating future liabilities as "claims." Rather, the amendment refers to them as "demands."

4. In the teacher's manual that accompanied the first edition of this casebook, the authors suggested that students might want to ponder "what will happen if the assumptions on which the Manville trust fund contributions are based turn out to be incorrect, and, a few decades from now, the fund runs dry?" Ironically, only a few years passed before the problem surfaced. By 1990, the assumption that the trust would have sufficient funds to deal with all asbestos claims if they were liquidated over a period of time had proven incorrect. The trust received far more claims than anticipated, and the average payments to victims were far higher than predicted. The history and predicament of the Manville trust are chronicled in *Findley v. Blinken (In re Joint E. and S. Districts Asbestos Litig., In re Johns-Manville Corp.)*, 120 B.R. 648 (E.D.N.Y. and S.D.N.Y 1990). The situation eventually led to a restructuring of the trust so that claimants would receive a smaller recovery on their claims — 10% of a fixed amount based on the severity of the asbestos related injury — paid in a shorter amount of time.

[B] Reprise: Special Problems in Environmental Cases

You will recall that in *Penn Terra Ltd. v. Dep't of Envtl. Res.*, discussed in chapter 3, § 3.04[A][2], the Third Circuit held that an action brought by a state agency to compel a coal mining company to restore land that it had strip mined was not an "action to enforce a money judgment" within the meaning of Code § 362(b)(4), and therefore was not automatically stayed. The practical effect of the holding was that the trustee was required to expend estate funds to restore the land, at the expense of other creditors. What if Penn Terra nevertheless failed to restore the land that it had strip mined? Does its obligation to restore the land constitute a "debt" founded on a "claim" cognizable in a bankruptcy case? If so, is such a debt dischargeable? Consider the next two opinions.

OHIO v. KOVACS
United States Supreme Court
469 U.S. 274 (1985)

[Kovacs and his company, Chem-Dyne, were in the waste disposal business in Ohio. In the late 1970s, the state of Ohio sued Kovacs individually and in his capacity as an officer of the company for polluting public waters, maintaining a nuisance, and causing fish kills. In 1979, Kovacs and the company signed a consent decree ordering them to cease causing pollution and to remove all industrial wastes from a storage facility within 12 months. Kovacs and the company failed to comply with the consent decree, and, in 1980, the state had a receiver appointed to take charge of the properties and clean up the storage site. A few months later, in July of 1980, Kovacs filed an individual Chapter 11 petition. In September, the bankruptcy court converted the case to Chapter 7.

The state commenced an adversary proceeding in bankruptcy court seeking a declaration that Kovacs's obligation under the consent decree was nondischargeable and would survive the bankruptcy case. The bankruptcy court concluded that the obligation was a dischargeable debt. The state appealed. The Court of Appeals affirmed, reasoning that the installation of a receiver to clean up the site had converted Kovacs's obligation to clean up into an obligation to pay money. That obligation to pay money, the court concluded, was indeed dischargeable. The Supreme Court affirmed.]

[T]he State submits that the obligation to clean up the Chem-Dyne site is not a debt at all within the meaning of the bankruptcy law.

For bankruptcy purposes, a debt is a liability on a claim. § [101(12)]. A claim is defined by § 101(4) [now § 101(5)] as follows:

(4) [now (5)] "claim" means —

(A) right to payment, whether or not such right is reduced to judgment, liquidated, unliquidated, fixed, contingent, matured, unmatured, disputed, undisputed, legal, equitable, secured, or unsecured; or

(B) right to an equitable remedy for breach of performance if such breach gives rise to a right to payment, whether or not such right to an equitable remedy is reduced to judgment, fixed, contingent, matured, unmatured, disputed, undisputed, secured, or unsecured.

The provision at issue here is § [101(5)(B)]. For the purposes of that section, there is little doubt that the State had the right to an equitable remedy under state law and that the right has been reduced to judgment in the form of an injunction ordering the cleanup. The State argues, however, that the injunction it has secured is not a claim against Kovacs for bankruptcy purposes because (1) Kovacs' default was a breach of the statute, not a breach of an ordinary commercial contract which concededly would give rise to a claim; and (2) Kovacs' breach of his obligation under the injunction did not give rise to a right to payment within the meaning of § [101(5)(B)]. We are not persuaded by either submission.

There is no indication in the language of the statute that the right to performance cannot be a claim unless it arises from a contractual arrangement. . . .

The courts below also found little substance in the submission that the cleanup obligation did not give rise to a right to payment that renders the order dischargeable under § 727. The definition of "claim" in H.R. 8200 as originally drafted would have deemed a right to an equitable remedy for breach of performance a claim even if it did not give rise to a right to payment. The initial Senate definition of claim was narrower, and a compromise version, § [101(5)], was finally adopted. In that version, the key phrases "equitable remedy," "breach of performance," and "right to payment" are not defined. See 11 U.S.C. § 101. Nor are the differences between the successive versions explained. The legislative history offers only a statement by the sponsors of the Bankruptcy Reform Act with respect to the scope of the provision:

> Section [101(5)(B)] is intended to cause the liquidation or estimation of contingent rights of payment for which there may be an alternative equitable remedy with the result that the equitable remedy will be susceptible to being discharged in bankruptcy. For example, in some States, a judgment for specific performance may be satisfied by an alternative right to payment in the event performance is refused; in that event, the creditor entitled to specific performance would have a "claim" for purposes of a proceeding under title 11.[8]

We think the rulings of the courts below were wholly consistent with the statute and its legislative history, sparse as it is. The Bankruptcy Court ruled as follows, *In re Kovacs*, 29 B.R., at 818:

> There is no suggestion by plaintiff that defendant can render performance under the affirmative obligation other than by the payment of money. We therefore conclude that plaintiff has a claim against defendant within the meaning of 11 U.S.C. § [101(5)(B)], and that defendant owes plaintiff a debt within the meaning of 11 U.S.C. § [101(12)]. Furthermore, we have concluded that that debt is dischargeable.[9]

The Court of Appeals . . . affirmed, rejecting the State's insistence that it had no right to, and was not attempting to enforce, an alternative right to payment:

> Ohio does not suggest that Kovacs is capable of personally cleaning up the environmental damage he may have caused. Ohio claims there is no alternative right to payment, but when Kovacs failed to perform, state law gave a state receiver total control over all Kovacs' assets. Ohio later used

---

[8] 124 Cong. Rec. 32393 (1978) (remarks of Rep. Edwards); see also *id.* at 33992 (remarks of Sen. DeConcini).

[9] More fully stated, the Bankruptcy Court's observations were:

> What is at stake in the present motion is whether defendant's bankruptcy will discharge the affirmative obligation imposed upon him by the Judgment Entry, that he remove and dispose of all industrial and/or other wastes at the subject premises. If plaintiff is successful here, it would be able to levy on defendant's wages, the action prevented by our Prior Decision, after defendant's bankruptcy case is closed and/or the stay of 11 U.S.C. § 362 as interpreted by our Prior Decision is no longer in force. The parties have crystallized the issue here in simple fashion, plaintiff stoutly insisting that the just identified affirmative obligation is not a monetary obligation, while defendant says that it is. The problem arises, of course, because it is not stated as a monetary obligation. Essentially for this reason plaintiff argues that it is not a monetary obligation. Yet plaintiff in discussing the background for the Judgment Entry says that it expected that defendant would generate sufficient funds in his ongoing business to pay for the clean-up. Moreover, we take judicial notice that plaintiff sought discovery with respect to defendant's earnings, the matter dealt with in our Prior Decision, for the purpose of levying upon his wages, a technique which has no application other than in the enforcement of a money judgment. There is no suggestion by plaintiff that defendant can render performance under the affirmative obligation other than by the payment of money. We therefore conclude that plaintiff has a claim against defendant within the meaning of 11 U.S.C. § [101(5)(B)], and that defendant owes plaintiff a debt within the meaning of 11 U.S.C. § [101(12)]. Furthermore, we have concluded that that debt is dischargeable. 29 B.R., at 818.

state law to try and discover Kovacs' post-petition income and employment status in an apparent attempt to levy on his future earnings. In reality, the only type of performance in which Ohio is now interested is a money payment to effectuate the Chem-Dyne cleanup.

The impact of its attempt to realize upon Kovacs' income or property cannot be concealed by legerdemain or linguistic gymnastics. Kovacs cannot personally clean up the waste he wrongfully released into Ohio waters. He cannot perform the affirmative obligations properly imposed upon him by the State court except by paying money or transferring over his own financial resources. The State of Ohio has acknowledged this by its steadfast pursuit of payment as an alternative to personal performance.

717 F.2d, at 987–988. As we understand it, the Court of Appeals held that, in the circumstances, the cleanup duty had been reduced to a monetary obligation.

We do not disturb this judgment. The injunction surely obliged Kovacs to clean up the site. But when he failed to do so, rather than prosecute Kovacs under the environmental laws or bring civil or criminal contempt proceedings, the State secured the appointment of a receiver, who was ordered to take possession of all of Kovacs' nonexempt assets as well as the assets of the corporate defendants and to comply with the injunction entered against Kovacs. As wise as this course may have been, it dispossessed Kovacs, removed his authority over the site, and divested him of assets that might have been used by him to clean up the property. Furthermore, when the bankruptcy trustee sought to recover Kovacs' assets from the receiver, the latter sought an injunction against such action. Although Kovacs had been ordered to "cooperate" with the receiver, he was disabled by the receivership from personally taking charge of and carrying out the removal of wastes from the property. What the receiver wanted from Kovacs after bankruptcy was the money to defray cleanup costs. At oral argument in this Court, the State's counsel conceded that after the receiver was appointed, the only performance sought from Kovacs was the payment of money. Tr. of Oral Arg. 19–20. Had Kovacs furnished the necessary funds, either before or after bankruptcy, there seems little doubt that the receiver and the State would have been satisfied. On the facts before it, and with the receiver in control of the site, we cannot fault the Court of Appeals for concluding that the cleanup order had been converted into an obligation to pay money, an obligation that was dischargeable in bankruptcy.

IV

. . . .

It is well to emphasize what we have not decided. First, we do not suggest that Kovacs' discharge will shield him from prosecution for having violated the environmental laws of Ohio or for criminal contempt for not performing his obligations under the injunction prior to bankruptcy. Second, had a fine or monetary penalty for violation of state law been imposed on Kovacs prior to bankruptcy, § 523(a)(7) forecloses any suggestion that his obligation to pay the fine or penalty would be discharged in bankruptcy. Third, we do not address what the legal consequences would have been had Kovacs taken bankruptcy before a receiver had been appointed and a trustee had been designated with the usual duties of a bankruptcy trustee. Fourth, we do not hold that the injunction against bringing further toxic wastes on the premises or against any conduct that will contribute to the pollution of the site or the State's waters is dischargeable in bankruptcy; we here address, as did the Court of Appeals, only the affirmative duty to clean up the site and the duty to pay money to that end. Finally, we do not question that anyone in possession of the site — whether it is Kovacs or another in the event the receivership is liquidated and the trustee abandons the property, or a vendee from the receiver or the bankruptcy trustee — must comply with the environmental laws of the State of Ohio. Plainly, that person or firm may not maintain a nuisance, pollute the waters of the State, or refuse to remove the source of such conditions. As the case comes to us, however, Kovacs has been dispossessed and the State seeks to enforce his cleanup obligation by a money judgment.

NOTES AND QUESTIONS

(1) *Kovacs*, of course, involved a liquidation case, but insofar as the opinion deals with the meaning of the term "claim," it has impact on Chapter 11 cases as well. If you were a legislator and favored fresh air and water as much as you favored fresh starts for bankrupts, how might you avoid the *Kovacs* effect? In a concurring opinion not reprinted here, Justice O'Connor observed that a state might protect its interest in the enforcement of environmental laws by giving cleanup judgments the status of statutory liens.

(2) The intersection of bankruptcy law and environmental law has proven difficult to navigate. Occupying one corner of this intersection is *In re Chateaugay Corp.*, 944 F.2d 997 (2d Cir. 1991). In *Chateaugay*, the Second Circuit had to decide whether the Environmental Protection Agency's claims against the debtor, a producer of steel, aerospace products, and energy, were dischargeable.

The claims arose under the Comprehensive Environmental Response Compensation and Liability Act ("CERCLA"). Under CERCLA, the EPA has the option of obtaining an injunction ordering the party responsible for environmental contamination to remedy it, or undertaking the remedial action itself and seeking reimbursement from the polluter. In this case, the EPA obtained a two-pronged injunction directing Chateaugay Corp. not only to clean up existing contamination but also to clean up future contamination. Although the Second Circuit acknowledged that an injunction ordering a debtor to remedy prepetition pollution gave rise to a dischargeable claim, an "order that accomplishes the dual objectives of removing accumulated wastes and *stopping or ameliorating ongoing pollution* emanating from such wastes is not a dischargeable claim." *Id.* at 1008 (emphasis added). The court reasoned that the cost of remedying past pollution could be reduced to a money judgment to which the EPA would have a right to payment under CERCLA.

On the other hand, since CERCLA does not give the EPA the option of allowing a debtor to continue polluting in exchange for a cash payment, an injunction requiring a debtor to remedy ongoing contamination does not give rise to a right to payment and thus cannot be converted into a dischargeable claim. As a result, the cleanup obligation "rides through" the case and binds the entity that emerges from

Chapter 11. The *Chateaugay* case is analyzed in the opinion that follows.

TORWICO ELECTRONICS, INC. v. STATE OF NEW JERSEY DEPARTMENT OF ENVIRONMENTAL PROTECTION
United States Court of Appeals, Third Circuit
8 F.3d 146 (1993)

STAPLETON, CIRCUIT JUDGE.

This case involves an attempt by the State of New Jersey to force Torwico Electronics, a debtor in chapter 11 bankruptcy, to comply with its obligations under state and federal environmental laws. Torwico asserts that these obligations are "claims," within the meaning of 11 U.S.C. § 101(5), and that, because the state failed to timely file a proof of claim, it is no longer responsible for them. The state claims that what is involved here are regulatory obligations, not bankruptcy claims. The bankruptcy court decided the issue in Torwico's favor, but was reversed by the district court. We conclude that the district court adopted the correct approach to this issue and will affirm.

I.

Torwico Electronics conducted a manufacturing business from a location in Ocean County, New Jersey until September 1985 when it moved to a new location. The Ocean County site ("the property") was owned by George Allen Associates and was leased to Torwico during the time Torwico did business at that address.

On August 4, 1989, Torwico filed for chapter 11 bankruptcy and listed the New Jersey Department of Environmental Protection and Energy (NJDEPE) on its schedules as a creditor with a disputed and unliquidated claim. On October 4, 1989, the bankruptcy court sent notice to all creditors, including NJDEPE, of Torwico's Chapter 11 bankruptcy and informed them that the last day to file a proof of claim was January 2, 1990. The following month, on November 13, 1989, NJDEPE performed an on-site inspection of the property and found a hidden illegal seepage pit containing hazardous wastes — wastes which were allegedly migrating into local waters. NJDEPE also found that Torwico was operating at its new site without the identification number required by EPA. NJDEPE immediately issued three notices of violation to Torwico, one concerning the failure to obtain a new identification number at the new place of business, and the others concerning the hazardous wastes found at the property. Torwico claims no knowledge of the seepage pit and the wastes found there.

The January 2, 1990 deadline for filing a proof of claim passed without any filing by NJDEPE. While Torwico did obtain an ID number for its new place of business, it did nothing about the seepage pit at the property. On April 9, 1990, NJDEPE issued an Administrative Order and Notice of Civil Administrative Penalty Assessment to Torwico relating to the violation noted in November 1989. The Order required Torwico to submit a written closure plan for the seepage pit and assessed a $22,500 penalty for failure to take action following the November notice. The Order also stated: "No obligations imposed [by this order] . . . are intended to constitute a debt, damage claim, penalty or other civil action which should be limited or discharged in a bankruptcy proceeding. All obligations are imposed pursuant to the police powers of the State of New Jersey, intended to protect the public health, safety, welfare, and environment."

Torwico and NJDEPE filed cross-motions for summary judgment before the bankruptcy court, with Torwico seeking to avoid its obligations to the state by claiming that they were claims barred by the absence of a filing prior to the bar date. The court agreed with Torwico and released the company from its obligations because NJDEPE had failed to timely file a proof of claim. On appeal, the district court reversed. Torwico then filed this appeal.

II.

A.

Because debts are dischargeable in Chapter 11, critical to the resolution of this case is whether Torwico's obligations constitute a "debt" under the bankruptcy code. A "debt" is defined as a "liability on a claim." 11 U.S.C. § 101(12) (1988).

A "claim," in turn, is defined in part as a:

> (A) right to payment, whether or not such right is reduced to judgment, liquidated, unliquidated, fixed, contingent, matured, unmatured, disputed, undisputed, legal, equitable, secured, or unsecured; or

> (B) right to an equitable remedy for breach of performance if such breach gives rise to a right to payment, whether or not such right to an equitable remedy is reduced to judgment, fixed, contingent, matured, unmatured, disputed, undisputed, secured or unsecured.

11 U.S.C. § 101(5) (1988). Torwico contends that this broad definition clearly encompasses its obligations to the state under the administrative order and the state statute pursuant to which it was issued. NJDEPE, on the other hand, contends that it has no "right to payment"; rather, it has only the right to enforce laws requiring Torwico to clean up the hazardous wastes it is responsible for under state law.

Both sides agree that a proper interpretation of the Supreme Court decision in Ohio v. Kovacs, 469 U.S. 274, 105 S. Ct. 705, 83 L. Ed. 2d 649 (1985) is instrumental in resolving this case. . . .

. . . .

Torwico contends that *Kovacs* applies here: Torwico's "affirmative duty to clean up the site and the duty to pay money to that end" is a claim. In addition, Torwico is no longer in possession of the site and thus, the Court's admonition that parties in possession "must comply with the environmental laws of the State" and cannot "refuse to remove" hazardous wastes does not apply to it. NJDEPE contends that *Kovacs* is inapplicable here because it does not seek a monetary judgment, but rather seeks to remedy ongoing pollution by forcing Torwico to clean up the site.

B.

Considerable insight into the issue presented here may be gleaned from two recent appellate cases that have dealt with similar questions. In *In re CMC Heartland Partners*, 966 F.2d 1143 (7th Cir. 1992), the debtor owned a hazardous waste site and went through bankruptcy under the Bankruptcy Act of 1898. Subsequently, EPA issued an order pursuant to CERCLA § 106, 42 U.S.C. § 9606, to the debtor, who still owned the site, requiring removal and remediation activity. The Seventh Circuit Court of Appeals held that the order, which was based on ownership of the land, survived reorganization. The court noted that "to the extent [the relevant federal statutory sections] require a person to pay money today because of acts before or during the reorganization proceedings, CERCLA creates a 'claim' in bankruptcy." *Id.* at 1146. However, by authorizing cleanup orders to current owners, CERCLA § 106 creates a claim "running with the land," and a "statutory obligation attached to current ownership of the land survives bankruptcy." *Id.* at 1147. Thus, the court found in favor of EPA, but warned that EPA must show under § 106 that the releases were "threatened or ongoing"; otherwise, one might conclude that EPA merely "repackaged a forfeited claim for damages." *Id.*

In *In re Chateaugay*, 944 F.2d 997 (2d Cir.1991), the court faced the issue of what constituted a claim in the context of the bankruptcy of LTV, an entity that owned and operated literally dozens of hazardous waste sites. The Second Circuit held that the EPA's costs of responding to a release of hazardous waste, even if not yet incurred at the time of bankruptcy, involved claims; thus, EPA was forced to file a proof of claim with respect to these costs and stand in line with the other creditors. As to injunctions requiring the debtor to clean up a waste site, the court made the following distinction:

> EPA is entitled to seek payment if it elects to incur cleanup costs itself, but it has no authority to accept a payment from a responsible party as an alternative to continued pollution. Thus, a cleanup order that accomplishes the dual objectives of removing accumulated wastes and stopping or ameliorating ongoing pollution emanating from such wastes is not a dischargeable claim. It is true that, if in lieu of such an order, EPA had undertaken the removal itself and sued for the response costs, its action would have both removed the accumulated waste and prevented continued pollution. But it is only the first attribute of the order than can be said to remedy a breach that gives rise to a right to payment. Since there is no option to accept payment in lieu of continued pollution, any order that to any extent ends or ameliorates continued pollution is not an order for breach of an obligation that gives rise to a right of payment and is for that reason not a "claim." But an order to clean up a site, to the extent that it imposes obligations distinct from any obligation to stop or ameliorate ongoing pollution, is a "claim" if the creditor obtaining the order had the option, which CERCLA confers, to do the cleanup work itself and sue for response costs, thereby converting the injunction into a monetary obligation.

Id. at 1008.[2]

C.

We find *CMC* and *Chateaugay* to be both persuasive and consistent.[3] Applying the precepts outlined in those cases to the situation here present leads us to conclude that Torwico's obligations under the administrative order do not constitute a claim.

As *Kovacs* noted, a debtor cannot maintain an ongoing nuisance in direct violation of state environmental laws. The state can exercise its regulatory powers and force compliance with its laws, even if the debtor must expend money to comply. Under *Kovacs*, what the state cannot do is force the debtor to pay money to the state; at that point, the state is no longer acting in its role as regulator, it is acting as a creditor.[4]

Here it is clear that the state demanded not that Torwico pay money over to the state, but rather that it take action to ameliorate ongoing hazard.[5] This is not the end of the inquiry, however. As noted in *Kovacs*, even if an injunction does not facially require payment of money, it still may present a "claim." 469 U.S. at 274[, 105 S. Ct. at 705]. *Chateaugay* and *CMC* also both suggest that, at least in some circumstances, an injunction that requires a cleanup may still be considered a "claim." *CMC* held that the CERCLA § 106 order there involved must be in response to an ongoing and continuing threat, and not merely the repackaging of a forfeited claim for damages. 966 F.2d at 1146–47. *Chateaugay* states that where an order imposes "obligations distinct from any obligation to stop or ameliorate ongoing pollution," the order presents a claim if the government could have done the work itself and then sought reimbursement; under such circumstances there is a "breach of an obligation that gives rise to a right of payment." 944 F.2d at 1008.

The state here found that the seepage pit was a continuing problem that was leaking hazardous material into the surrounding environment. Thus, the state is not

---

[2] The parties here also devote considerable attention to our decision in *Penn Terra Ltd. v. Dept. of Environmental Resources*, 733 F.2d 267 (3d Cir.1984). In this pre-*Kovacs* case, the court examined whether attempts by the state to enforce a pre-bankruptcy injunction requiring Penn Terra to undertake certain cleanup actions was barred by the automatic stay provisions of § 362. The court concluded that because the injunction was an exercise of state regulatory power and was not an action for a "money judgment," the state could enforce the injunction. Because this case involved the automatic stay provision of the Bankruptcy Code and the court expressly declined to discuss whether the injunction constituted a "claim" or "debt," *see id.* at 277 n. 11, this case is of only marginal relevance in deciding the issue currently before us.

[3] We note that neither NJDEPE nor Torwico appears to challenge the correctness of *CMC* or *Chateaugay* but rather, they dispute the proper application of those decisions to the current situation.

[4] Were we to adopt the bankruptcy court's position that any order requiring the debtor to expend money creates a dischargeable claim, it is unlikely that the state could effectively enforce its laws: virtually all enforcement actions impose some cost on the violator.

[5] The Order requires Torwico to submit "a written closure plan . . . for closure of the seepage pit." App. at 210. An affidavit from an employee of NJDEPE discusses in detail the findings of contamination and the fact that wastes are migrating into the surrounding environment. *See* App. at 219–31 ("It is safe to assume, at the concentrations detected at the property boundary, that the contamination has migrated offsite.").

asserting a "repackaged claim for damages"; rather, there is an ongoing and continuing threat and, in the words of *Chateaugay*, an obligation on the part of the debtor "to ameliorate ongoing pollution emanating from [accumulated] wastes." *Chateaugay*, 944 F.2d at 1008. The state has no "right to payment" here. What it has is a right to force the debtor to comply with applicable environmental laws by remedying an existing hazard.

The single fact which Torwico relies on most heavily is that it is no longer in possession of the site, and has not been in possession for several years. Thus, Torwico argues that it is not maintaining a nuisance or participating in an ongoing release of hazardous substances into the environment. It notes that a prime factor in *Kovacs* was that the debtor was no longer in possession of the property and that a receiver was in possession and was conducting the cleanup. Similarly, unlike the debtor in *Chateaugay*, Torwico is not, in its view, "continuing to pollute" here. Finally, Torwico notes that *CMC* found a "statutory obligation running with the land"; Torwico no longer owns or occupies the land here.

We do not find Torwico's suggested distinction persuasive. Unlike the debtor in *Kovacs*, Torwico can (and in the state's view, must) conduct the cleanup: it has access to the site and the state has not, apparently, performed any cleanup on its own. . . .

D.

Unlike *Kovacs*, the state in this case neither seeks money nor has a right to payment under the statutory authority asserted or the Order imposed; the state seeks compliance with its laws through cleanup of a current hazardous situation. In the words of *Chateaugay*, "there is no option to accept payment in lieu of continued pollution," and there is an order intended to "ameliorate continued pollution"; thus, the Order "is not an order for breach of an obligation that gives rise to a right of payment and is for that reason not a 'claim.'" 944 F.2d at 1008. Under the circumstances here present, Torwico's obligations do not run with the land as did the debtor's in *CMC*; however, they run with the waste. To the extent that Torwico's waste poses a continuing hazard, Torwico is responsible for remedying the problem regardless of where the waste might be.[7] As in *CMC*, the release here is "threatened and ongoing"; as in *CMC*, this is not a "repackaging [of] a forfeited claim for damages" (966 F.2d at 1147) for past conduct, but rather an attempt to prevent additional future damage.

IV.

In conclusion, we hold that the state's attempt in this case to force a party to clean up a waste site which poses an ongoing hazard is not a "claim" as defined by the Bankruptcy Code. This is not a situation where the state is attempting to get money from the debtor but rather, it is an exercise of the state's inherent regulatory and police powers. We will therefore affirm the district court.

---

[7] *CMC* held that a "statutory obligation attached to current ownership of the land survives bankruptcy." 966 F.2d at 1147. Similarly, a statutory obligation attached to hazardous waste (i.e. to make sure it does no damage) also survives bankruptcy.

[C] Special Problems in Cases Involving Equitable Remedies

"All this discussion of what is and isn't a claim has me wondering about something," Carol says. "In *Ohio v. Kovacs*, the Supreme Court held that the debtor's obligation to clean up a hazardous waste site had been converted into an obligation to pay money because the state paid a receiver to do the cleanup work and then tried to recover the cleanup cost from the debtor."

"Right," you say. "The Court reasoned that under the circumstances, the obligation to pay money had been substituted for the obligation to clean up the site. The obligation to pay money was a 'claim' that could be discharged in bankruptcy."

"But in *Torwico*, the Third Circuit held that where the state had ordered the debtor to clean up a hazardous site but had not undertaken the cleanup job itself, the debtor's cleanup obligation had not been converted into an obligation to pay money, because the state was not seeking reimbursement from the debtor."

"Right," you say. "The court found that the state had no claim for damages, but rather a right to force the debtor to comply with state environmental regulations. That right to performance was not a 'claim' that could be discharged in bankruptcy."

"Let me ask you a question," Carol says. "Suppose that Kid-Vid enters into a joint venture agreement with RoboCoup, a manufacturer of toy robots. The agreement provides that the two companies will cooperate in the development of technology that is useful in manufacturing both toys and video games. The agreement also provides that the companies will not compete directly with one another. What I'm particularly concerned about is a provision that says that Kid-Vid will not make or sell toy robots that compete with RoboCoup's. It says that if Kid-Vid does attempt to sell toy robots, RoboCoup is entitled to an injunction to stop us, plus $5,000,000 in liquidated damages. Now, suppose that we've come up with a great idea for spinning off one of our video game characters into a robot toy. Can we escape our covenant not to compete by discharging it in bankruptcy?"

You call Carol's attention to yet another Third Circuit opinion, *In re Ben Franklin Hotel Assocs.*, 186 F.3d 301 (3d Cir. 1999). The debtor was a partnership that owned a well-known, landmark hotel in Philadelphia. The partnership issued a "cash call" requiring all partners to contribute a certain amount of capital to the partnership. When one of the partners refused to respond to the cash call, its partnership interest was terminated, in accordance with the terms of the partnership agreement. The ex-partner brought an action to have its interest equitably reinstated. The ex-partner claimed that the cash call was a sham employed to eject certain members of the partnership. In addition to reinstatement, the complaint sought $2,000,000 in damages. The debtor filed a Chapter 11 petition and confirmed a plan.

The issue was whether confirmation of the plan discharged the ex-partner's demand for reinstatement. The Court held that the applicable standard was articulated in *Ohio v. Kovacs*: If money damages were a viable alternative to the reinstatement demand, the demand was a "claim" under Code § 101(5)(B) that was discharged by confirmation of the plan. If money damages were not a viable alternative to reinstatement, the demand survived confirmation and discharge. The debtor argued that since the complaint sought both damages and equitable relief, damages were clearly a viable alternative to reinstatement. The Third Circuit disagreed. It noted that plaintiffs "routinely seek both [monetary] damages and equitable relief, arising from the same allegedly wrongful conduct, but that does not mean that one is an 'alternative' to the other. In many cases, prayed-for monetary and equitable relief will serve entirely distinct remedial purposes." *Id.* at 306. "The relevant issue here," the court said, "is not the form of relief that appellees most hoped to achieve in their state court action, but whether damages are an alternative to [the] proposed equitable remedy." *Id.* Examining the facts of the case and applicable state law, the court determined that because the interest in a unique hotel property constituted a unique business opportunity, it was impossible to calculate damages with any degree of certainty. Accordingly, it held that damages were not a viable alternative to reinstatement of the partnership interest and that the demand for reinstatement was not a claim that was discharged in the debtor's Chapter 11 case.

"Well," Carol says, "I think you are trying to tell me that RoboCoup's right to an injunction to enforce our covenant not to compete is not a claim that is dischargeable in bankruptcy. But aren't you ignoring the fact that our joint venture agreement *also* gives RoboCoup a right to money damages? Doesn't § 101(5)(b) say that a 'claim' includes a 'right to an equitable remedy for breach of performance if such breach gives rise to a right to payment'? Under the joint venture agreement, if Kid-Vid breaches the non-compete clause, RoboCoup has a right to payment."

"Ah!" you exclaim. "Did you hear what you said? You said that the joint venture agreement *also* gives RoboCoup a right to payment." In *In re Udell*, 18 F.3d 403 (7th Cir. 1994), the court held that where liquidated damages are not an *alternative* for specific performance of a covenant not to compete, but an *additional* remedy, the right to the equitable remedy is not a claim that can be discharged.

Do these opinions suggest that a creditor can avoid having its claim discharged in any case in which it can characterize its remedy as equitable and convince a court that money damages are difficult to ascertain?

§ 8.07 SUBORDINATION OF CLAIMS

[A] Equitable Subordination

PROBLEM 8.3

Scarlet's Web, a wholly-owned Amphydynamics subsidiary that operates a chain of internet coffee shops, has been losing money since it opened its doors a few years ago. Scarlet's Web was, however, the brain-child of Amphydynamics chairman Headley Charisma, who has a fair amount of ego invested in it. At a time when traditional lenders were not inclined to extend credit to Scarlet's Web, Headley decided that the time had come to invest more than ego. He personally loaned several hundred thousand dollars to the company. The loan was unsecured and bore an interest rate of 5 points above prime. The loan proceeds were quickly consumed by daily operating expenses and the need to purchase new equipment and software, much of which was manufactured by Amphydynamics.

Despite this cash infusion, Scarlet's Web's financial difficulties did not go away. The cost of purchasing and maintaining equipment was high, and customers were fickle. Scarlet's Web simply could not capture and hold the following that competitors enjoyed. Inept management, resources insufficient to allow it to expand quickly enough in a very competitive market, and lousy coffee were blamed. As a result, Scarlet's Web never made a payment on the Charisma loan, and Headley has regularly waived the defaults.

After it filed its Chapter 11 petition, Scarlet's Web auctioned off some of its more valuable leaseholds. The auction generated a substantial amount of cash to fund a reorganization plan, but not enough to pay all creditors in full on confirmation.

Today Headley Charisma received a call from the chairman of the subcommittee representing Scarlet's Web's creditors. She informed Headley that the subcommittee members "assume" that in light of his "self-dealing" any plan proposed by Scarlet's Web will subordinate Charisma's claim to the claims of other institutional and trade creditors. Headley is aghast. He says that he believed he was doing the correct — indeed noble — thing when he personally advanced monies to the ailing Scarlet's Web. When he agreed to auction the leases, he assumed — rightly, he thinks — that he would share the fruits of the lease auction on a par with other Scarlet's Web's unsecured creditors.

The subcommittee chair said that if the plan did not provide for subordination of the claims, he would have it subordinated by court order.

Headley can't believe this is happening to him. He wants to know whether such chicanery is possible. Read Code § 510 and the materials that follow.

IN THE MATTER OF LIFSCHULTZ FAST FREIGHT
United States Court of Appeals for the Seventh Circuit
132 F.3d 339 (1997)

CUDAHY, CIRCUIT JUDGE.

I. Background

A business is ailing. Revenues are down, profits gone. Rather than let it die, the owners decide to try reviving it. Doing so will require an infusion of new funds. The owners drum up the needed funds but face a choice: which legal form should the owners use, equity or debt?

If the business is closely held, the advantage will be to debt, preferably secured. Equity classically carries the right to the firm's residual earnings. But in a closely-held company, this advantage means little, for the owners already have it through their pre-existing equity stakes. A loan, on the other hand, will provide the firm with needed funds while limiting the owners' risk that the company will go bankrupt and the new funds will end up in the wallets of the unsecured creditors. Tax advantages might also accrue. Of course, in opting for debt, the owners also accept a trade-off: outside lenders will or ought to be more reluctant to extend credit to what is now a more heavily-leveraged firm.

An unfair advantage to the owners, allowing them to reap the benefits of both debt and equity? Maybe. Will a bankruptcy court respect this choice of form? Not always. The power of equitable subordination, codified at 11 U.S.C. § 510(c), allows a bankruptcy court to relegate even a secured claim to a lower tier, even to the lowest — the equity tier. This appeal centers on when a bankruptcy court may exercise this power based on the debtor's undercapitalization.

The debtor is Lifschultz Fast Freight Corporation. Its owners ran a shipping business dating from the turn of the century. Their company was Lifschultz Fast Freight, Inc. ("LFFI"). Its chief enterprise was freight forwarding: consolidating freight from customers and arranging for a shipper to haul it by road or rail. . . .

The second half of the 1980s was unkind to LFFI. Deregulation had unleashed rapacious competition in trucking, but LFFI stuck to a high-price, high-service track. The company lost hefty sums of money each year, starting at $400,000 in 1985 and rising more or less steadily to $5.5 million in 1989. The insiders decided against liquidating the losing business and instead tried to revive it. The revised business strategy was to focus on running trucks from the West Coast at full capacity. In early March 1990, the insiders set up a new corporation, the future debtor, with $1,000 in cash. Eighty percent of the debtor's stock was in five pairs of hands — Theodore Cohen, Salvatore Berritto, Anthony Berritto, Sebastián DeMarco and Michael DeMarco. The remaining 20% was LFFI's. These insiders transferred to the new company all of LFFI's operations outside New York City (including the customer list), a valuable lease to a California shipping terminal and Dodgers season tickets. The debtor's only assumed liability from LFFI was $232,000 of unpaid employee vacation.

As the list of initial assets shows, one thing the debtor lacked was cash — so sorely, in fact, that the debtor was short $91,000 for meeting its first payroll. The solution was the secured loan agreement (the "Loan Agreement"), dated March 13, 1990. The agreement linked the debtor and one of the insiders' affiliated companies, Salson Express Co., Inc. ("Salson Express"). By April, Salson Express had lent the debtor $862,841.30. Most of that money the insiders had themselves borrowed from First Fidelity Bank in exchange for personal guarantees from Salvatore Berritto, Sebastian DeMarco and Theodore Cohen. The insiders then lent the money on a secured basis to Salson Express, which lent it in turn to the debtor under the Loan Agreement. On August 10, 1990, the debtor found a fresh $1 million in the form of a factoring agreement from Ambassador Factors. Ambassador Factors required that its security interest super-ordinate that of the insiders under the Loan Agreement, and also extracted personal guarantees from the insiders. With some of this new money, the debtor paid off all but $300,000 of the insiders' secured loan at the time of the bankruptcy petition — the $300,000 at issue in this appeal.

The insiders never succeeded in staunching the losses. Administrative expenses ate up the debtor's operating margins month after month.[1] On revenues that fluctuated monthly between $1.7 million and $2.2 million, the debtor lost an average of $193,000 per month between March and October 1990. Its only monthly profit was in August, for $12,000. An involuntary chapter 11 petition brought the debtor into bankruptcy on November 20, 1990. Prepetition unsecured debt stood at $2.6 million. The trustee operated the business until May 1991, when the debtor proceeded to liquidation under chapter 7.

The insiders filed a claim in bankruptcy court for the remaining $300,000. (More precisely, Salson Express filed, but we refer to Salson Express and the insiders interchangeably, as the parties have stipulated.) In response, the trustee requested that the bankruptcy court equitably subordinate the insiders' secured interest and transfer the lien to the estate. The debtor had been undercapitalized, the trustee asserted, and therefore the insiders' claim should be subordinated to the general creditors.'

The bankruptcy court held that the debtor had not been undercapitalized as a matter of fact, but even if the debtor had been, undercapitalization by itself could not justify equitable subordination. To set aside Salson Express' lien would require that the insiders had been guilty of some other "inequitable conduct." Finding no other inequitable conduct, the bankruptcy court refused to subordinate the insiders' secured claim.

The district court saw the law and facts differently. Citing *In re Virtual Network Services Corp.*, 902 F.2d 1246 (7th Cir. 1990), the district court said that equitable subordination did not require proof of a creditor's inequitable conduct (or misconduct; the terms are often used synonymously in the case law). Undercapitalization alone was enough. Also, finding clear error, the district court concluded that the debtor had been patently undercapitalized. The district court reversed and ordered equitable subordination. The insiders (Salson Express) appeal.

. . . .

The crux of this case is undercapitalization — what the term means, whether it was present in this case, and if so, what consequences would follow. Undercapitalization is a poorly-defined phrase, and especially so in the context of bankruptcy. An undercapitalized firm is one without enough capital; but that tells us little. We try to define the meaning of "undercapitalization" in this opinion. First we clarify the controlling law. If the debtor was in fact undercapitalized, could undercapitalization alone justify equitable subordination of an insider's debt claim, absent misconduct by the insider? Absent extraordinary circumstances, we believe that it cannot.

II. Undercapitalization and equitable subordination

The trustee urges that undercapitalization is an independent basis on which a bankruptcy court may wield its power of equitable subordination. To explain why we disagree with this as a prevailing rule, we return to the first principles of equitable

---

[1] [The "administrative expenses" that the court is referring to here appear to be prepetition operating expenses, including salaries paid to officers and directors of Lifschultz, not postpetition expenses incurred by the debtor in possession. — Eds.]

subordination to show how the trustee's rule, if applied generally, would thwart the purpose of the doctrine.

The dominant theme of U.S. bankruptcy law for a business debtor is preservation of the state-law rights of claimants and their relative ordering. 11 U.S.C. § 507, 726, 1129; Douglas G. Baird, The Elements of Bankruptcy 15, 71 (rev. ed. 1993). A problem can arise if a claimant dresses up a claim she has on the firm as something else of higher priority. Equity holders come last in bankruptcy, which generally means they get nothing at liquidation. To avoid this, an owner might disguise her equity claim as debt. The doctrine of equitable subordination empowers a bankruptcy court to foil this queue-jumping, by reordering the formal rankings of the claimants to restore a just hierarchy.

Equitable subordination typically involves closely-held corporations and their insiders. *See Kham & Nate's Shoes No. 2, Inc. v. First Bank of Whiting*, 908 F.2d 1351, 1356 (7th Cir. 1990) ("Equitable subordination usually is a response to efforts by corporate insiders to convert their equity interests into secured debt in anticipation of bankruptcy."). This is so because elsewhere the suspicion does not easily arise that a claim is anything else but what it purports to be. Take the example of a bank loan. Under current law, banks in this country cannot own significant equity stakes in non-financial companies. The legal distinctions between debt and equity, creditor and owner, are therefore kept tidy. A loan from a bank is thus presumed to be a loan and the bank a creditor (although if the bank exerts de facto control of the firm, that presumption may be overturned).

A loan from a corporate insider muddles this conceptual clarity. The relationships start to add up: the same person can be an owner of a company, its creditor and, as in the instant case, its employee as well. So do the opportunities for self-dealing — and self-dealing would violate the insider's fiduciary duty to the corporation. *Pepper v. Litton*, 308 U.S. 295, 306, 60 S. Ct. 238, 84 L. Ed. 281 (1939). Suppose that as a firm is listing into insolvency, an insider arranges for the firm to confess a debt for her alleged unpaid salary (as in *Pepper*), with the idea that she, now a "creditor" and not just an owner, will jump ahead in the queue. The documents supporting the "debt" are unimpeachable, and she has observed all legal niceties. Strict adherence to claimants' formal rights would allow her ill-gotten gain at the other creditors' expense, because in liquidation there is rarely enough money left to pay off in full the claimants at the rear.

Equitable subordination allows a bankruptcy court to root out this sort of mischief. An insider is a fiduciary of the corporation. *Pepper*, 308 U.S. at 306. If her conduct breached the "rules of fair play and good conscience" vis-a-vis the company and its creditors, the bankruptcy court can send her back to the end of the line. The court will strip her of her debt claim and recharacterize it as what it truly is — equity. Courts subject the dealings of an insider to "rigorous scrutiny" for any such breach. *Id.* at 306. Once the trustee has offered "some substantial factual basis to support its allegation of impropriety," the insider must prove the loan's good faith and inherent fairness to the corporation. *In re Mobile Steel Co.*, 563 F.2d 692, 701 (5th Cir. 1977) (Clark, J.). If the loan cannot meet these exacting standards, the insider will be found to have breached her fiduciary trust, and the loan will be equitably subordinated. *Pepper*, 308 U.S. at 307.

What general principles guide a court's use of this power? We turn to the most influential discussion of equitable subordination, the magisterial *Mobile Steel*. . . . *Mobile Steel* laid out three conditions a bankruptcy court must find to exist before it equitably subordinates a claim. One, "the claimant must have engaged in some type of inequitable conduct." *Mobile Steel*, 563 F.2d at 700. Two, "the misconduct must have resulted in injury to the creditors of the bankrupt or conferred an unfair advantage on the claimant." *Id.* And three, "equitable subordination of the claim must not be inconsistent with the provisions of the Bankruptcy [Code]." *Id.*

Mobile Steel directs us to search for inequitable conduct as the first step. If there is none, then a bankruptcy court cannot subordinate a claim. This insistence on first finding inequitable conduct was the law before codification in 11 U.S.C. § 510(c), and it remained so afterwards. The creditor must have done something inequitable — a wrong or an unfairness or, at the very least, a masquerade of something for what it is not. In the context of equitable subordination, the type of conduct that has been considered "inequitable" generally falls within the following categories: "(1) fraud, illegality, breach of fiduciary duties; (2) undercapitalization; and (3) claimant's use of the debtor as a mere instrumentality or alter ego."

The alleged masquerade here is of the insiders' secured loan to the debtor. The trustee asserts that in truth, the loan was a capital contribution.[3] That the insiders made a secured loan to the company is not wrongful per se, and the trustee does not claim as much. An insider to a company is free to lend money to it, " 'provided he does not use his corporate position to defraud creditors or take unfair advantage of them.' " *Spach v. Bryant*, 309 F.2d 886, 889 (5th Cir. 1962) (quoting *In re Madelaine, Inc.*, 164 F.2d 419, 420 (2d Cir. 1947)).[4] The wrong must stem from the context in which the insiders made the loan. That context, the trustee says, was one of undercapitalization. We ask therefore how a loan (secured or unsecured) to an undercapitalized firm might breach the "rules of fair play and good conscience." *Pepper*, 308 U.S. at 310.

Undercapitalization sounds bad. It may not bear the harsh stigma of words like "fraud" and "deceit," but courts often seem to use "undercapitalization" as a term of opprobrium. Admittedly, some cases contain language suggesting that undercapitalization is in itself inequitable conduct. For example, some courts have justified equitable subordination by noting the presence of undercapitalization and "other inequitable conduct," . . . . While such language may be confusing, it has been established that equitable subordination requires "suspicious, inequitable conduct beyond mere initial undercapitalization." Because mere undercapitalization does not, and should not, justify equitable subordination, we think the better view

---

[3] As a technical matter, the appellee defends the judgment below only on the basis that equitable subordination is proper, not that the insiders' claim should be recast as equity. *Cf. In re Hyperion Enters.*, 158 B.R. 555, 560 (D.R.I. 1993) ("The issues of recharacterization of debt as equity capital and equitable subordination should be treated separately.").

[4] Not everyone agrees that insiders ought to be able to lend to their own companies. The criticism is that current law encourages the waste of scarce resources, because it permits already-failed business-people to flush good money after bad. *See* Leonard J. Long, Automatic Subordination as Incentive for Insider Creditors' Prudential Investing, 13 J.L. & Com. 97, 99 (1993). A counter-argument would be that insiders are best positioned (both in terms of knowledge and of incentives) to dispose wisely of their capital. Of course, whether the criticism has any merit is a matter for Congress, not the judiciary.

is that, while undercapitalization may indicate inequitable conduct, undercapitalization is not in itself inequitable conduct.

The source of the tainted connotation of "undercapitalization" is not self-evident. Under any definition, undercapitalization just means that a company does not have enough funds on its balance sheet or in the till. It is a common token of declining business fortune. Every firm in bankruptcy, and many outside, can in some sense be said to be undercapitalized — which is to say, to have insufficient funds on hand. Most often undercapitalization signifies nothing more than business failure, poor access to capital, or both. Centuries ago in Western Europe, bankruptcy was deemed "the single most scandalous phenomenon of commercial society," reviled everywhere as a "ghastly evil." James Q. Whitman, *The Moral Menace of Roman Law and the Making of Commerce: Some Dutch Evidence*, 105 Yale L.J. 1841, 1871 (1996). In 16th century northern Italy, for instance, a debtor seeking discharge would have to " 'go naked in a public and notorious place,' " like the piazza. *Id.* at 1873 (quoting Matteo Bruno, Tractatus Matthaei Bruni Arimineni de Cessione Bonoru 115[v] (Venice 1561)). There the debtor would have to " 'strike[] his backside' " three times against something called "The Rock of Shame," while "crying out, 'I DECLARE BANKRUPTCY.' " *Id.* Today we are a bit more relaxed about the mishaps of businesspeople. The word "bankrupt" may sting in lay language, but American law has jettisoned the idea that business failure and inadequate capital resources are inherently wrongful.

So what is wrong with undercapitalization in itself? The trustee argues that "insufficient capital leads to financing the operation with secured debt, and that exposes unsecured commercial creditors to a greater risk of loss." Quite so. But again, where is the wrong? Creditors extend credit voluntarily to a debtor. The debtor owes no duties to the creditor beyond those it promises in its contract (and beyond whatever common and statutory law may apply). A debtor decidedly does not owe a fiduciary duty to a creditor. *United States v. Jolly*, 102 F.3d 46, 48 (2d Cir. 1996) (citing *Katz v. Oak Indus., Inc.*, 508 A.2d 873, 879 (Del. Ch. 1986)). And a debtor is just as surely not obliged to be the lender's insurer. A lender will not offer a loan to a borrower unless the rate of return justifies the risk of default or underpayment. The same is true for the sub-class of lenders called trade creditors, for prudent businesspeople assess the risk of default before allowing customers to pay for goods or services on credit. The higher that risk, the more interest (or collateral) the lender will demand. If a firm is poorly capitalized, and thus less likely to repay than a better capitalized firm in the same line of business, the lender may require more security or more interest. But that a highly leveraged company exposes its creditors to serious risks is no new fact of commerce. Creditors are free to lend elsewhere. If they choose to lend to a company that then loses their investment, they cannot go to bankruptcy court and cry misconduct.

Trickery upsets this logic. Insiders cannot use their superior knowledge of a company to deceive outsiders. If the insider causes the borrowing company to lie to the lender about its financial health — by disguising a pre-existing debt, for instance — the insider is guilty of misconduct. Even the "morals of the market place" forbid deceit. The debtor's books must be open and its debts listed there, and it might be (although we do not so hold) that a security interest would have to be perfected (often by filing) to give notice of its existence. But if a creditor could have known about an insider's debt claim on a company, a bankruptcy court will not reward the creditor by lowering the insider's claim to equity status. Fairness then is primarily about disclosure. Absent "suspicious, inequitable conduct beyond mere initial undercapitalization," the creditor's loss is his own. And while it is true that the burden falls on the insider to prove the good faith of the loan and its inherent fairness, it is also true that the creditor must first proffer a challenge thereto with "some substantial factual basis to support its allegation of impropriety." *Mobile Steel*, 563 F.2d at 701 (citing *Pepper*, 308 U.S. 295 at 306). The mere presence of undercapitalization will not suffice.

The presumption of caveat creditor is certainly not absolute. For example, the situation could be different for a creditor who does not have "a meaningful opportunity given [it] to bargain for higher interest rates as compensation for the extreme risk of default." Robert C. Clark, The Duties of the Corporate Debtor to Its Creditors, 90 Harv. L. Rev. 505, 535–36 (1977). Consumer creditors would also generally fall into a more protected category. Some merchant-creditors might qualify, too. For minor transactions like buying a single office chair on 30-days' credit, businesspeople as a rule do not haggle over credit terms. If they did, the burden of inquiry and negotiation would quickly eat up the profits from the deal. Frank H. Easterbrook & Daniel R. Fischel, Limited Liability and the Corporation, 52 U. Chi. L. Rev. 89, 113 (1985). (Tort claimants, of course, typically have no opportunity to bargain at all.) As a general matter, the line is drawn at the point where a reasonably prudent merchant would check out her customer/debtor's creditworthiness before extending credit. In any particular case, the location of that point is a question of fact for the bankruptcy court's judgment.

The sense of these principles is shown in the instant case. The trustee objects to the $862,841.30 that the debtor's insiders supplied to the debtor under the Loan Agreement, or more precisely to the $300,000 secured claim the insiders still had against the company when the bankruptcy petition was filed. But we do not see the injury or inequity in this infusion of working capital. This case is not an example of the insiders' converting a pre-existing equity claim into debt. The insiders here contributed fresh working capital. They were under no obligation to do so. Assuming there was no deception, we see no reason to treat an insider's loan to a company more poorly than that of a third party's.

To hold otherwise would "discourage those most interested in a corporation from attempting to salvage it through an infusion of capital." *Mobile Steel*, 563 F.2d at 701. Equitable subordination means that a court has chosen to disregard an otherwise legally valid transaction. *Mobile Steel*, 563 F.2d at 702 ("It is important to remember that the issue is not whether the advances 'actually' were loans, but whether equity requires that they be regarded as if they were something else."). If the court incorrectly disregards a bona fide transaction, it commits a double wrong. First, the court has upset the legitimate expectations of a claimant, which in this case would be Salson Express (the insiders). The second wrong is less visible, but just as significant. Wrongful or unpredictable subordination spawns legal uncertainty of a particular type: the risk that a court may refuse to honor an otherwise binding agreement on amorphous grounds of equity. If a court wrongly subordinates a claim, other investors are sure to take heed. An investor will see that the chance she might not get her money back has gone up slightly. She will be less willing to lend or invest in the future; and the cost of credit will rise for all.[5]

III. "No-fault" equitable subordination

The trustee argues that under our decision in *Virtual Network*, equitable subordination no longer requires creditor misconduct. Virtual Network upheld the subordination of the IRS's non-pecuniary loss tax penalty claims to those of other unsecured creditors, even though the IRS had done nothing inequitable. See *In re Virtual Network*, 902 F.2d at 1250. "*Virtual Network* extends principles of equitable subordination to a penalty created by operation of law, where delay in collecting the penalty injured other creditors." *Kham & Nate's Shoes*, 908 F.2d at 1356. Other circuits have followed our lead in carving out this exception for tax penalties.[7] . . .

But the trustee mistakes the birth of an exception for the death of a rule. The rule is that equitable subordination is predicated upon creditor misconduct; the exception of Virtual Network is for a class of tardy tax penalties. . . .

. . . .

A bankruptcy court should be doubly wary of using its power of equitable subordination. There unfortunately cannot be perfect predictability for when a court will invoke the doctrine. Equitable subordination relies on courts' peering behind the veil of formally unimpeachable legal arrangements to detect the economic reality beneath. This task by nature "requires the court to make extremely subjective judgments as to whether a party has acted opportunistically." David A. Skeel, Jr., *Markets, Courts, and the Brave New World of Bankruptcy Theory*, 1993 Wis. L. Rev. 465, 506 (defending courts' power of equitable subordination). And easy, clear rules to find underhanded behavior are hard to come by, because the clever soon figure out ways around them. What courts can try to do,

---

[5] Recent bankruptcy scholarship has highlighted these ex ante effects of bankruptcy law — that is, "moving backward in time, how the law influences the parties' incentives to invest." Alan Schwartz, *The Absolute Priority Rule and the Firm's Investment Policy*, 72 Wash. U. L. Q. 1213, 1213 (1994). *See also* Susan Rose-Ackerman, *Risk Taking and Ruin: Bankruptcy and Investment Choice*, 20 J. Legal Stud. 277 (1991); David A. Skeel, Jr., *Markets, Courts, and the Brave New World of Bankruptcy Theory*, 1993 Wis. L. Rev. 465. This scholarship reiterates a theme of Adam Smith's. "When the law does not enforce the performance of contracts, it puts all borrowers nearly upon the same footing with bankrupts or people of doubtful credit in better regulated countries. The uncertainty of recovering his money makes the lender exact the same usurious interest which is usually required from bankrupts." Adam Smith, The Wealth of Nations, Bk. I, Chap. IX, P 14 (1776). *See also* Scott M. Browning, No Fault Equitable Subordination: Reassuring Investors That Only Government Penalty Claims Are at Risk, 34 Wm. & Mary L. Rev. 487, 524 (1993).

[7] The Supreme Court recently reversed two cases in which bankruptcy courts equitably subordinated federal tax penalties. *See United States v. Noland*, 517 U.S. 535, 116 S. Ct. 1524 (1996), ... The Supreme Court unanimously held that the bankruptcy court's exercise of its power of equitable subordination must not have the "inevitable result" of equitably subordinating "every tax penalty." *Noland*, 116 S. Ct. at 1527–28; *see also Reorganized CF & I Fabricators*, 116 S. Ct. at 2115; *id.* (Thomas, J., concurring in part and dissenting in part). The appellee suggests that these Supreme Court rulings "ratify" the approach of Appellee Br. at 13–14; the appellant contends that the Supreme Court held that "creditor misconduct was necessary to equitably subordinate the respective creditor claims in each case." Appellant Reply Br. at 6. Neither party's characterization of the holdings of these cases is accurate: the Supreme Court found it unnecessary to "decide . . . whether a bankruptcy court must always find creditor misconduct before a claim must be equitably subordinated." *Noland*, 116 S. Ct. at 1528.

however, is to mark off territory where there is generally no justification for equitable subordination. We attempt to do so here: undercapitalization alone, without evidence of deception about the debtor's financial condition or other misconduct, cannot justify equitable subordination of an insider's debt claim. Extraordinary circumstances might provide an exception, *see Pepper*, 308 U.S. at 309–11, but we believe that almost any such exception would arguably also involve other misconduct of some sort. In this case, the bankruptcy court did not recognize any extraordinary circumstances, and so without trying to be definitive as to every future contingency, we think that mere undercapitalization — if it exists in the present case — is not grounds for equitable subordination.

IV. The debtor and undercapitalization

A. Undercapitalization considered

But was the debtor here even undercapitalized? The insiders say no, and the bankruptcy judge agreed. The district court reversed. Undercapitalization is a question of fact, and we review the bankruptcy court's judgment for clear error. Before we can assess the debtor's undercapitalization, however, we must first confront the threshold issue of what undercapitalization denotes as a matter of law.

There really are two questions: what to measure, and how to measure it. The kind of capital a court is measuring has various names — shareholder equity, paid-in capital or equity capital — but whatever it is called, it means the excess of total assets over total liabilities. . . .

Shareholder equity should also be (but is not always) distinguished from working capital. Working capital is that portion of a firm's assets that are in relatively liquid form — the current assets such as cash, accounts receivable and inventory. Net working capital is the excess of current assets over current liabilities; it measures the ability of a firm to pay its debts as they mature. Working capital thus means something quite different from equity capital. The distinction is neatly shown with a balance sheet and the accounting identity $A = L + NW$ (assets = liabilities plus net worth, or equity capital). Working capital refers to a kind of asset that the firm holds; it shows up as an entry on the left-hand side of the balance sheet. Equity capital, on the other hand, refers to a kind of claim against the assets of the firm, the owners' stake, and is entered on the right-hand side. The other kind of claim against the firm's assets is debt (or liability); and once all the liabilities of a firm have been set off against its assets (and assuming there are still some assets left), the residuum is equity capital. A common transaction involves a firm's using its equity capital as a basis for acquiring working capital — as in the case before us.

Equitable subordination centers on sorting out the true nature of a claim against a firm. Thus it is the amount of equity capital, not working capital, that is the subject of our inquiry. . . . Take an example illustrating this distinction. Suppose a firm was set up with plenty of cash, more than enough to meet its current liabilities. Suppose also that the firm was encumbered from the start with non-current or longterm liabilities that dwarfed the firm's ability to repay them but that had yet to come due. That firm might have sufficient working capital, or liquidity; but it would also have zero equity capital, i.e., its liabilities would exceed its assets and its shares would be worthless. The firm would be undercapitalized from inception, no matter the adequacy of its initial working capital.

Equity and working capital are certainly not so cleanly separated in the daily workings of commerce. A shortage of working capital is often the mark of undercapitalization (i.e., inadequate equity capital). Take the case of a firm falling into arrears. By definition we know that the firm has too little working capital: it is failing to meet its current liabilities as they come due. Often the underlying reason will be inadequate equity capital. Whether a shortage of working capital actually does reveal undercapitalization turns on why the firm is in arrears. One possibility is that the firm does have enough assets to cover its debts, but cannot free them up just now. Perhaps the firm owns a new office building, the value of which could cover all the firm's liabilities, but which may take years to sell at a good price. In that instance, the firm's equity capital is more than sufficient; the deficiency is solely in working capital. A mortgage, backed by the building, might be the answer. If a firm cannot procure such a loan, a second possibility comes to the fore: the firm lacks enough equity capital (total assets minus total liabilities) to justify a creditor's lending it money. In that second possibility, a shortage of working capital would reveal a deficiency of equity capital, that is, undercapitalization. The point is that a shortage of working capital is neither a sufficient nor a necessary condition for undercapitalization. As noted above, a firm could have a surfeit of working capital and still be undercapitalized. And, conversely, if a firm lacks working capital, a court cannot automatically conclude that it is undercapitalized as well.

The case at bar illustrates these principles at least twice. The trustee points to the debtor's being almost cashless at inception as proof of undercapitalization. This does not necessarily follow: sometimes a dearth of working capital only suggests illiquidity. If the firm has no working capital but then raises sufficient liquid funds by borrowing against its illiquid assets, the firm is not undercapitalized. The bankruptcy court found that precisely this conversion of illiquid assets into liquid assets occurred in this case. The debtor obtained sufficient working capital by pledging its assets under the Loan Agreement. (That the loan was from the insiders is a matter we discuss below.) The trustee makes a similarly flawed objection to counting toward capitalization two assets the debtor held at inception: the bargain lease to a California shipping terminal and Dodgers tickets. Neither constitutes working capital, the trustee rightly says, for the assets are illiquid. Yet that observation determines nothing, because the trustee is measuring the wrong kind of capital. The tickets were sold during liquidation for $47,000, the lease for $292,500. Both represent hard value that the equityholders lost and the unsecured creditors gained in bankruptcy. They both should have been counted as contributions to equity capital.

How much equity capital is enough? There is no litmus test to sort firms into two neat piles, the adequately and inadequately capitalized. Numerous authorities have cautioned us not to be dogmatic or mechanical in assessing the adequacy of capital. As Judge Clark put it:

> Absolute measures of capital inadequacy, such as the amount of stockholder
> equity or other figures and ratios drawn from the cold pages of the

corporation's balance sheets and financial statements, are of little utility, for the significance of this data depends in large part upon the nature of the business and other circumstances.

Mobile Steel, 563 F.2d at 702–03. Instead a rule of reason governs. A firm is adequately capitalized for purposes of equitable subordination if its equity capital equals or exceeds "what reasonably prudent men with a general background knowledge of the particular type of business and its hazards would determine was reasonable capitalization in the light of any special circumstances which existed at the time of incorporation of the now defunct enterprise." *Mobile Steel*, 563 F.2d at 703 (citing N. Lattin, The Law of Corporations § 15, 77 (1971)).

To put this rule of reason into practical form, the approach finding the most favor is the two-pronged test enunciated in *Mobile Steel*. This test takes its cue from observable, formal changes in the firm's capital structure. The first prong looks to the moment of initial capitalization of the firm. Undercapitalization exists at inception "if, in the opinion of a skilled financial analyst, [the capitalization] would definitely be insufficient to support a business of the size and nature of the [debtor] in light of the circumstances existing at the time the bankrupt was capitalized." *Mobile Steel*, 563 F.2d at 703. The second prong looks to the time of the insider's loan, which may or may not be after inception. Undercapitalization at the time of the loan exists if the debtor "could not have borrowed a similar amount of money from an informed outside source." *Id.* If the debtor could have raised the funds elsewhere on similar or better terms, the inference would be that a third party thought that the firm had enough equity capital and was, in light of that fact and others, creditworthy. One can therefore safely conclude that such a firm is not undercapitalized. If the firm could not have borrowed elsewhere, however, the firm was undercapitalized at the time of the insider's loan.

The two-prong test avoids a tempting diagnostic error. When a business goes sour for whatever reason, its capitalization will necessarily suffer. Perhaps every firm that slips into insolvency can be termed undercapitalized. Testing by hindsight will thus turn up too many false positive results of undercapitalization. Owners owe no duty to recapitalize a failing firm, and courts should not introduce one through the back door by retrospectively finding undercapitalization by proof of "eventual failure." The *Mobile Steel* test prevents this error by directing a court's attention to what the owners could have reasonably known at a particular time. If the founders set up a clearly undercapitalized firm from the start, a court may with confidence find undercapitalization without risk of Monday morning quarterbacking. (We leave aside the possibility that the owners could subsequently cure their paltry initial contributions of equity capital, an uncommon event in undercapitalization cases. We also do not consider here the more typical cases of the owners' withdrawing equity capital as the business founders, or their transmogrifying an extant equity claim into a higher-tier claim.) And if, under prong two, the firm at the time the insiders advanced the debt could not have raised working capital elsewhere by leveraging its equity capital, that too is firm ground on which a court may find undercapitalization.

Either prong would suffice by itself. What if the prongs conflict? Concrete evidence based on the business judgment of merchants or bankers, we think, ought to triumph over the necessarily post hoc conjectures of judges. If the insiders can show convincingly that a firm could have got a loan elsewhere, the arm's-length prong should defeat a finding of initial undercapitalization. The finding at inception may be wrong, rooted as it must be in guesses and estimates; and even if the initial finding is right, later profits may have healed the foundational defect by boosting the value of the equity stakes.

B. Was the debtor undercapitalized?

When it comes to whether the debtor here was undercapitalized, the parties roughly agree upon the facts. Their interpretation fuels the dispute. The insiders and the trustee have struggled now in three courts over prong one of *Mobile Steel*, the debtor's initial capitalization. The parties cannot agree on how much equity capital the firm had at the start, much less whether it was enough. The trustee contends the debtor started operations with an initial capitalization of negative $131,013, which certainly sounds like undercapitalization; the insiders say the correct figure is over $1 million.[12] And even if they could agree on a number, they would still dispute how much equity capital a firm like the debtor ought to have had.

There is a less complicated way to resolve the debtor's putative undercapitalization: *Mobile Steel*'s second prong, the arm's-length test. At the time the insiders made the loan, we ask, would the debtor have been able to borrow a similar amount of money on comparable terms from an informed outside source? In this case, we need not speculate about what might have happened. We know what did happen. The debtor not only could have gotten a third-party loan, it actually did — from Ambassador Factors. The Ambassador Factors loan for $1 million came in August 1990, after the insiders' loan and with several financially gloomy months in between. Ambassador Factors was an informed outside source: its relationship with LFFI began well before the launching of the debtor. The insiders prudently had set the terms of their loan to match or beat those that Ambassador Factors had required from LFFI on an earlier occasion (before the debtor's creation). And like the insiders, it lent the money to the debtor on a secured basis (the insiders agreed to subordinate their secured interest to the loan from Ambassador Factors).

---

[12] For those curious about this wide divergence, the trustee says the debtor started business with an initial $1,000 in cash, plus $100,987 in depreciated property and equipment. The trustee would assign no value to LFFI's customer list, the Dodgers tickets and the lease to the California shipping terminal. Set against the accrued liability for unpaid vacation time for employees ($232,000), the trustee's figures yield an initial capitalization of negative $131,013. The insiders, on the other hand, would assign a value of $47,000 and $292,500 to the tickets and the lease respectively on the (correct) ground that illiquid assets count toward equity capital just as much as liquid ones.

The issue of the customer list is more difficult. The trustee says that a customer list should be valued as a multiple of profits. Because the firm was losing money, the customer list was supposedly worthless. The trustee's valuation method might make sense if the business were being transferred or sold whole. Here, though, only LFFI's customer list was transferred to the debtor. A better way to value the list would be as a percentage of gross earnings. *Kimball Laundry Co. v. United States*, 338 U.S. 1, 19 & n. 12, 69 S. Ct. 1434, 93 L. Ed. 1765 (1949). The fact is that the debtor's list was generating $22 million a year in revenue. Even if the debtor could not make money with it, maybe somebody else could. The debtor's customers were a premium bunch: all were willing to pay high prices for good service, and the list manifested that information. The precise value of the list is shrouded in an evidentiary tussle, one that we need not resolve for this appeal.

So far the two loans look indistinguishable. No, the trustee says: Ambassador Factors demanded a personal guarantee from several of the insiders, and that proves undercapitalization. Not so. Undercapitalization is a possible rationale for a lender's requiring a personal guarantee from the insider of a closely-held corporation, but it is far from the only one. The insiders control their own salary and the issuance of dividends. These two powers naturally make a lender wary that the insiders will siphon needed funds out of the company. A personal guarantee averts that risk. A personal guarantee also can align the entrepreneur's incentives more closely with the outside lenders by shifting risk of default back to the entrepreneur. And for a particularly risky enterprise, a lender may not wish to be saddled with the whole risk of business failure. (An example would be a bank's giving a recourse loan to a real estate developer: even if the bank gets a mortgage on the property, it may still require the ability to go after the developer if the project flops.) Which among these rationales or perhaps still others motivated Ambassador Factors, we do not know. At no time did the trustee offer evidence showing that undercapitalization even played a role in Ambassador Factor's demand for personal guarantees. Given the absence of factual proof, accepting the trustee's logic would amount to ruling that a personal guarantee denotes undercapitalization as a matter of law. That would be incorrect, and we do not so rule.

The two loans, however, would not be comparable — and the inference of adequate capitalization would be undermined — if Ambassador Factors had restricted the insiders' ability to pay off the older Salson Express loan with the new loan from Ambassador Factors. Had Ambassador Factors insisted on a condition like that, we could infer that Ambassador Factors was relying on the insiders' keeping the funds within the debtor so that a lender could rely on not just the solvency of the company, but of the owner as well. But Ambassador Factors did not; and the bankruptcy court did not err in likening the two loans to one another.

The law only asks of insiders that "under all the circumstances the transaction carries the earmarks of an arm's length bargain." *Pepper*, 308 U.S. at 306–07. It does not ask more. In this case, the insiders provided funds to the company on a footing comparable to that an outsider afforded. This conclusion supports the second prong of the *Mobile Steel* test, and thus the bankruptcy court's finding of adequate capitalization. On the matter of undercapitalization, we find no clear error and so reach a different conclusion on this point than the district court.

V. Final issues

We are almost — but not quite — done. The trustee has advanced two final grounds for justifying equitable subordination of Salson Express' claim. The first is that the insiders (specifically, Salvatore Berritto and Sebastian DeMarco) wronged the debtor by causing it to pay off $200,000 of the Salson loan in November 1990, just before the involuntary petition. The insiders then used that money to pay off their personal bank loans to First Fidelity. This withdrawal, the trustee says, is creditor misconduct. The bankruptcy judge rejected the trustee's argument, arguing that the withdrawal reduced the debtor's outstanding balance on the Salson Express loan, and thus conferred a benefit on the debtor. That's true; but as the district court noted in reversing the bankruptcy court, the benefit of reducing the balance was relatively trivial, and the debtor's need for funds great. The district court's conclusion would be more compelling, however, if the Salson Express loan were treated as equity capital and not a loan. Yet we have upheld the bankruptcy court's treatment of it as a loan and of Salson Express as a secured creditor. A consequence of respecting the insiders' choice of debt to contribute funds is that the insiders' withdrawal of those funds should be viewed on the same terms. A creditor is not obliged to forebear from calling its loan just because the debtor would find those funds useful. And in any case, no one has even argued that "a shortage of capital funds contributed to [the debtor's] financial demise," *Mobile Steel*, 563 F.2d at 703. Bankruptcy law empowers trustees with potent tools to avoid insiders' last-minute attempts to strip a debtor of capital. *See, e.g.*, 11 U.S.C. § 547 (preferences), 548 (fraudulent transfers). We are not inclined to create a superfluous mechanism that would posit that insider creditors are not "real" creditors.

On the second ground, we are far less sanguine about the insiders' conduct. In the bankruptcy court, the trustee pointed to a set of salary raises for insiders during the spring and summer of 1990. The bankruptcy judge decided the raises did not show creditor misconduct, and the district court expressed no opinion on the question (having already found independent grounds for equitable subordination).

The rationale for equitable subordination stems from the multiplicity of relationships that insiders may have with a firm. The insiders may own the firm, lend it money and, in the case of this debtor, work for it as employees. As we said above, one classic form of creditor misconduct is boosting the owner-employee's salary as the firm is drifting into financial collapse. *Pepper*, 308 U.S. at 306. The possibility of such misconduct inheres in the multiplicity of relationships, for in a closely held firm, "it is obvious that salaries must be fixed by the persons receiving them." *Spach*, 309 F.2d at 889. But just because the possibility is unavoidable does not make taking advantage of it right. If an insider did commit such salary inflating misconduct in this case, the salary inflation could justify equitably subordinating the (unrelated) secured claim of Salson Express. Any misconduct by an insider may be invoked to subordinate a particular claim of that insider, "irrespective of whether it was related to the acquisition or assertion of that claim." *Mobile Steel*, 563 F.2d at 700.

In the spring of 1990, the debtor's directors increased Theodore Cohen's salary from $75,000 to $125,000. Then, during the summer, the directors retroactively raised it to $130,000 a year. Also during the summer, the directors raised Michael DeMarco's initial salary retroactively from $73,000 to $130,000, and Anthony Berritto's from $31,000 to $55,000. The bankruptcy judge termed these instances of "questionable business judgment." We certainly agree. We would go further: the trustee, we think, has raised a "substantial factual basis" suggesting improper conduct through retroactive raises by and for the benefit of the insiders. The burden of proof therefore shifts to the insiders to show the inherent fairness and good faith of the transactions.

The evidence in the record is sketchy. The insiders, the trustee and both judges concentrated on the question of undercapitalization, and left the evidence (and arguments) about the salary raises underdeveloped. The salaries apparently reflected real, not fictive work; Cohen swore that he worked 70 to 100 hours a week as the debtor's chief executive, trying to turn the debtor around. Maybe the board of directors increased the salaries because Cohen, DeMarco and Berritto were Stakhanovite laborers. Maybe not. (It's also not obvious that overtime work by executives of a failing business justifies higher salaries.) In any event, the burden of evidence falls on the insiders, and if they fail to rebut, the court must presume misconduct. The bankruptcy court did not reach this question, as it thought the salary raises not so troubling as to flip the burden of persuasion to the insiders. We think otherwise; and from what little we can glean, the insiders did not rebut the allegation in the bankruptcy court. On such a piecemeal basis, however, we are not prepared to prejudge the question. We accordingly remand the case to the bankruptcy court to determine whether the insiders met (or can meet) their burden of rebuttal; we leave to the discretion of the bankruptcy court whether to hear additional evidence. If the insiders meet their burden of rebuttal, no portion of their claim should be equitably subordinated. And if the insiders fail, we leave it to the bankruptcy court's discretion to determine, depending on the insider's evidence, whether to equitably subordinate some or all of the insiders' claim, consistent with the principles of *Mobile Steel*, 563 F.2d at 700–02. The parties shall bear their own costs of this appeal.

REVERSED and REMANDED for further proceedings not inconsistent with this opinion.

NOTES AND QUESTIONS

(1) *DWU*. The "first step" in determining whether a claim should be equitably subordinated is to look for inequitable conduct by the claim holder. What kind of behavior will justify subordination? Consider the following examples:

- *In re Yellowstone Mountain Club, LLC.*, Case No. 08-61570-11, Adversary No. 09-00014, Partial and Interim Order, Docket No. 289 (Bankr. D. Mont. May 13, 2009).

  In 2005, Credit Suisse was offering a new financial product for sale. It was offering the owners of luxury second-home developments the opportunity to take their profits up front by mortgaging their development projects to the hilt. Credit Suisse would loan the money on a non-recourse basis, earn a substantial fee, and sell off most of the credit to loan participants. The development owners would take most of the money out as a profit dividend, leaving their developments saddled with enormous debt. Credit Suisse and the development owners would benefit, while their developments — and especially the creditors of their developments — bore all the risk of loss. This newly developed syndicated loan product enriched Credit Suisse, its employees and more than one luxury development owner, but it left the developments too thinly capitalized to survive. Numerous entities that received Credit Suisse's syndicated loan product have failed financially, including Tamarack Resort, Promontory, Lake Las Vegas, Turtle Bay and Ginn. If the [facts of those cases] were anything like this case, they were doomed to failure once they received their loans from Credit Suisse.

  The court equitably subordinated Credit Suisse's $232 million loan to the debtor, the once available balance of which had largely been drawn down by the debtor's insiders for their personal benefit.

- *In re McFarlin's*, 49 B.R. 550 (Bankr. W.D.N.Y. 1985).

McFarlin's was a men's retail clothing business. All the stock of McFarlin's was owned by a group of investors, who also happened to be the company's officers, directors, and lawyers. They decided that they wanted to expand the business by opening a new store. However, since no other financing was available, three of the owners formed a partnership that borrowed the money, purchased $74,400 worth of fixtures, and leased them to McFarlin's for a five-year term at a monthly rent of $3,000. The business floundered, and McFarlin's filed a Chapter 11 petition. The owners filed claims for the unpaid balance of the fixture lease. The court found that the owners had engaged in inequitable conduct that injured other creditors, and the court subordinated the owners' claims. The court explained:

> The first condition for equitable subordination is inequitable conduct by the claimants. In the case at bar, the debtor's officers informally inquired about a loan to McFarlin's to finance the purchase of the leasehold improvements and were unofficially denied such a loan. Instead of offering their personal guarantees on behalf of the debtor, the officers formed a separate partnership for the sole purpose of acquiring the capital to buy the leasehold improvements. F.G. & G. then leased the improvements to the debtor for five years at a total rental cost of $180,000. The officers were still personally liable for the loan obtained by F.G. & G., but now they were able to make a sizeable profit from the transaction and take tax deductions. If the debtor's officers had personally guaranteed a $75,000 loan to McFarlin's, the loan probably would have been granted and the debtor would have been able to buy the improvements and only pay a total of approximately $120,000; sixty monthly payments of approximately $2,000 at the then prevailing interest rates.

> What happened, however, was that the debtor's officers created a leasing arrangement costing the debtor an additional $60,000 over the five years, at the end of which the debtor would have no title to the improvements and no option to buy the improvements. . . . Assuming arguendo that the debtor's officers intended to transfer title of the improvements to McFarlin's at the end of the five year lease, the effective annual rate of interest on the $75,000 loan would be 42.36%. A loan at such an outrageous rate is unconscionable.

> . . . .

> If viewed as a lease, it is important to note that in five years the debtor is paying 150 percent of the financed cost of the improvements just to rent them. Instead of trying to save the debtor $60,000 by personally guaranteeing a loan in the debtor's name, the officers attempted to reap profits and reduce their risk of loss with a lease, exploiting their fiduciary position.

> The second condition for equitable subordination is an injury to the creditors or an unfair advantage to the claimant. In the case at bar,

there are both. The officers testified that one of the primary reasons . . . to lease improvements to the debtor was the accounting benefit of off-sheet financing. By using the off-sheet principle, the debtor was not required to show the leasehold improvements lease on its balance sheet. Therefore, creditors dealing with McFarlin's could not accurately appraise the debtor's financial condition and liabilities. With this somewhat distorted financial picture, creditors may have dealt with the debtor and incurred liabilities which they otherwise may not have incurred if they were aware of the debtor's financial situation. The officers purposefully created an inaccurate financial picture of the debtor to fool creditors and the public. Creditors who otherwise might have required cash on delivery terms continued to extend credit to the debtor and increase their unsecured losses.

Additionally, the claimants gained an unfair advantage over other creditors. The debtor's petition lists secured debts of $685,006.24 and unsecured debts of $272,992.41. Interestingly enough, [the insiders have] no pre-petition claim. Prior to filing its petition in bankruptcy, the debtor made every $3,000 payment due to [the insiders]. The decision by the officers to make these substantial payments [to insiders] and not to other creditors, conferred an unfair advantage on the officers to the detriment of other creditors.

In re McFarlin's, 49 B.R. 550, 554–55.

- *Matter of Herby's Foods, Inc.*, 2 F.3d 128 (5th Cir. 1993).

Herby's produced and distributed fast foods to convenience stores. At a time when "no third-party lender would make a working capital loan to Herby's on any terms," its parent company extended a $4 million line of credit secured by "basically everything" Herby's owned. The parent company did not file a UCC-1 to perfect its security interest for 13 months, during which period, the amount that Herby's owed to unsecured creditors increased from $929,000 to more than $4,600,000. The court found that the behavior of the parent company justified subordination of its claim:

> The Insiders never injected any equity capital into Herby's, electing instead to advance funds through tardily perfected secured loans made at times when no bona fide third-party lender would have done so. With full knowledge that Herby's was undercapitalized and insolvent, the Insiders persisted with their practice of advancing funds only in the form of loans.

> Further, the loan . . . was not initially reflected on Herby's books. When finally booked, it was listed as an unsecured loan.

> . . . .

> [T]he aggregate size of Herby's unsecured debt to its trade creditors increased from approximately $900,000 to over $4,600,000, and the average number of days outstanding for trade payables increased almost elevenfold, from approximately seven to approximately seventy-five, between the date [of the insider loan to] Herby's and its filing for relief in bankruptcy. Nevertheless, [the insiders] insist that no

evidence was presented to the bankruptcy court that any specific creditor was deceived or lured into extending additional unsecured credit by [their] actions.

. . . .

[T]he Insiders are not contesting the existence of inequitable conduct but, rather, whether such misconduct either produced injury to the arms-length creditors of the bankrupt or secured an unfair advantage for the miscreant claimants. Both injury and unfair advantage may be established by proving that a specific creditor was deceived or lured into extending additional credit to the bankrupt. Mere good faith on the part of the Insiders would not negate the harm sustained by Herby's creditors; neither would it lessen the advantage gained by the Insiders. The bankruptcy court found that the Insiders' conduct harmed Herby's outside creditors by significantly increasing their trade credit exposure and by reducing their ultimate dividend in the liquidation. Most importantly, the court found that the Insiders had secured an unfair advantage by structuring their cash contributions to Herby's as loans, rather than as equity capital. If the Insiders were allowed to retain their ranking as unsecured creditors, they would have gained an advantage in the priority scheme by encouraging outside creditors to increase their credit exposure to Herby's. Their efforts were successful; those trade creditors substantially increased their credit to Herby's during the period in question. We are persuaded that the inequitable conduct of the Insiders produced sufficient injury to the unsecured trade creditors and secured a sufficiently unfair advantage for the Insiders to warrant equitable subordination.

2 F.3d at 132–134.

(2) *Scope of Fiduciary Duties.* In *Lifschultz*, the court declared that "A debtor decidedly does not owe a fiduciary duty to a creditor." Is that decidedly so when the debtor is insolvent or is in the vicinity of insolvency? *See* the discussion in chapter 4, § 4.06[E] of the text.

(3) *Subordination of Non-Insider Claims.* Although, as the *Lifschultz* court pointed out, "equitable subordination typically involves closely-held corporations and their insiders," in a few cases, the claims of non-insider creditors have been subordinated. Since a creditor is not ordinarily a fiduciary of its debtor or its fellow creditors, subordination of non-insider claims has been confined to cases in which creditors have engaged in some form of overreaching or excessive control over the debtor. The behavior of a problematic bank creditor in *In re American Lumber, Co.*, 5 B.R. 470 (D. Minn. 1980), is a case in point. The court equitably subordinated the bank's claim after determining that:

[T]he bank "controlled" the debtor through its right to a controlling interest in the debtor's stock. The bank forced the debtor to convey security interests in its remaining unencumbered assets to the bank after the borrower defaulted on an existing debt. Immediately thereafter, the bank foreclosed on the borrower's accounts receivable, terminated the borrower's employees, hired its own skeleton crew to conduct a liquidation, and selectively honored the debtor's payables to improve its own position. The bank began receiving and opening all incoming mail at the borrower's office, and it established a bank account into which all amounts received by the borrower were deposited and over which the bank had sole control. The bankruptcy court found that the bank exercised control over all aspects of the debtor's finances and operation including: payments of payables and wages, collection and use of accounts receivable and contract rights, purchase and use of supplies and materials, inventory sales, a lumber yard, the salaries of the principals, the employment of employees, and the receipt of payments for sales and accounts receivable.

Despite its decision to prohibit further advances to the debtor, its declaration that the debtor was in default of its loans, and its decisions to use all available funds of the company to offset the company's obligations to it, the bank in American Lumber made two specific representations to the American Lumbermen's Credit Association that the debtor was not in a bankruptcy situation and that current contracts would be fulfilled. Two days after this second reassurance, the bank gave notice of foreclosure of its security interests in the company's inventory and equipment. Approximately two weeks later, the bank sold equipment and inventory of the debtor amounting to roughly $450,000, applying all of the proceeds to the debtor's indebtedness to the bank.

Matter of Clark Pipe and Supply Co., 893 F.2d 693, 701 (5th Cir. 1990) (describing the behavior of the bank in *In re American Lumber* and explaining why, absent such particularly egregious behavior, a creditor will not be held to a standard that exceeds the "morals of the marketplace.").

The court in *Waslow v. MNC Commercial Corp. (In re Paolella & Sons, Inc.)*, 161 B.R. 107, 119 (E.D. Pa. 1993), however, recognized that equitable subordination is seldom used in a non-insider, non-fiduciary scenario because, as Judge Easterbrook pointed out in *Kham & Nate's Shoes No. 2, Inc. v. First Bank*, 908 F.2d 1351, 1356 (7th Cir. 1990), "[c]ases subordinating the claims of creditors that dealt at arm's length with the debtor are few and far between." The dearth of cases subordinating the claims of non-insiders is readily explained by the high threshold of misconduct that the objectant must establish in non-insider cases. In *In re Osborne*, 42 B.R. 988, 996 (W.D. Wis. 1984), the court discussed the conduct required for equitable subordination in non-insider cases:

> [The degree of misconduct] has been variously described as "very substantial" misconduct involving "moral turpitude or some breach of duty or some misrepresentation whereby other creditors were deceived to their damage" or as gross misconduct amounting to fraud, overreaching or spoliation.

Accord In re Mayo, 112 B.R. 607, 650 (Bankr. D. Vt. 1990) ("There are few cases in which gross misconduct has actually been applied to non-insiders, and even fewer where inequitable misconduct has caused a claim to be subordinated."); *In re Dry Wall Supply, Inc.*, 111 B.R. 933, 938 (D. Colo. 1990) (noting that "when [the fiduciary] relationship is absent, the party seeking equitable subordination of a claim must demonstrate even more egregious conduct by the creditor").

Although courts have struggled to articulate the misconduct that must be established to subordinate non-insider claims, it is clear that the non-insider's misconduct must be "gross or egregious." *See* Benjamin Weintraub & Alan N. Resnick, *Bankruptcy Law Manual* ¶ 5.15 at 5-96 (3d ed. 1992); *see also In re Osborne*, 42 B.R. at 997 (stating that "plaintiffs are required to make a showing of gross or egregious misconduct"). Thus, "[a] mere statement that the creditor is guilty of 'inequitable conduct' will not suffice." *In re W. T. Grant*, 4 B.R. 53, 75–76 (Bankr. S.D.N.Y. 1980), *aff'd*, 699 F.2d 599 (2d Cir. 1983). Rather, the plaintiff must prove gross misconduct tantamount to "fraud, overreaching or spoliation." *Id.*; *see also In re Fabricators, Inc.*, 926 F.2d 1458, 1465 (5th Cir. 1991) ("If a claimant is not an insider, then evidence of more egregious conduct such as fraud, spoliation or overreaching is necessary."); *In re Dry Wall Supply, Inc.*, 111 B.R. 933, 938 (D. Colo. 1990) ("The degree of misconduct which the plaintiff must show in the case of a noninsider has been variously described as gross misconduct tantamount to fraud, misrepresentation, overreaching or spoliation."); *In re Teltronics*, 29 B.R. at 173 (holding that "it was incumbent upon the [objectant] to demonstrate that [the non-insider] engaged in very substantial misconduct tantamount to fraud, over-reaching or spoliation, which caused other creditors of [the debtor] to suffer damages"); *In re Pinetree Partners, Ltd.*, 87 B.R. 481, 488 (Bankr. N.D. Ohio 1988) ("Where the claimant is a non-insider, egregious conduct must be proven with particularity. It is insufficient for the objectant in such cases merely to establish sharp dealings; rather, he must prove that the claimant is guilty of gross misconduct tantamount to fraud, overreaching, or spoliation to the detriment of others."). In summary, the "gross or egregious misconduct" needed to subordinate claims of non-insiders is much greater than the "inequitable conduct" that warrants subordination of insiders and fiduciaries.

[B]   Subordination of Shareholder Claims for Rescission or Damages

PROBLEM 8.4

A few weeks before Amphydynamics filed its Chapter 11 petition, it was named as a defendant in a class action suit brought by shareholders who claimed their decision to purchase Amphydynamics shares was based on misleading financial statements. They sought rescission of the sale and damages.

Today, the attorney representing the plaintiff class called. He said that although he was not invited to the recent meeting at which the elements of an Amphydynamics reorganization plan were disclosed, he has received word that while the plan provides that common stockholders will retain their interest in the company, no other treatment has been accorded the defrauded shareholders he represents. He says that his clients, by virtue of their fraud claims, hold general, if disputed, claims against Amphydynamics and should be treated accordingly in the plan. In other words, he believes his defrauded security holders ought to be classified and treated on a par with bank and trade creditors of the debtor.

Is he correct? Read Code § 510(b) and the excerpt from the Code's legislative history which follows.

H.R. REP. NO. 95-595
at 194–96 (1977)

F. SUBORDINATION OF SECURITY PURCHASE RESCISSION CLAIMS

A difficult policy question to be resolved in a business bankruptcy concerns the relative status of a security holder who seeks to rescind his purchase of securities or to sue for damages based on such a purchase: Should he be treated as a general unsecured creditor based on his tort claim for rescission, or should his claim be subordinated? The issue of subordination must be resolved one way or the other; in any particular case there is no middle ground for compromise, though there may be a middle statutory ground. The argument for mandatory subordination is best described by Professors Slain and Kripke.[134]

The arguments against subordination were presented by the Securities and Exchange Commission.

A brief review of the case law in this area is appropriate. For many years, a security holder was precluded from asserting his rescission claim on a parity with general creditors. For example, *In re Racine Auto Tire Company* denied such claims on the basis of estoppel en pais. That case involved the issuance of preferred stock in violation of state Blue Sky laws. Three years after the issuance, the corporation was adjudicated bankrupt, and the stockholders attempted to file a claim for recovery of the consideration paid. The court noted that the four elements necessary for estoppel en pais were present. The stockholders knowingly assumed a position as equity security holders which is at variance with the position of a general creditor. The stockholders repeatedly ratified that position by accepting dividends and asserting to the world to be stockholders. The stockholders profited from their position to the extent of dividends paid. Finally, the stockholders did not attempt to change their position until more than two years had elapsed. Although the court concluded that the stockholders were estopped from asserting any claim, the interests of the general creditors would have been protected to the same extent by mandatory subordination.[136]

The law with respect to the rights of rescinding security holders was dramatically changed in 1937 by the decision of the Supreme Court in *Oppenheimer v. Harriman National Bank and Trust Co.*[137] That case, based on facts that occurred before passage of the Securities Acts, permits a rescinding security holder to share *pari passu* in the bankrupt estate with general creditors. The Supreme Court has not withdrawn from this position since 1937 but has specifically left the question open in Chapter X cases, *Protective Committee v. Anderson.*[138]

There is also authority under present law that if a security holder can trace the

---

[134] Slain & Kripke, *The Interface Between Securities Regulation and Bankruptcy: Allocating the Risk of Illegal Securities Issuance Between Security Holders and the Issuer's Creditors*, 48 N.Y.U. L. Rev. 261 (1973).

[136] 290 F.2d 939 (7th Cir. 1923).

[137] 301 U.S. 206 (1937).

[138] 390 U.S. 414, 453 (1968).

consideration paid into proceeds of the estate then he can, in straight bankruptcy, either reclaim the consideration or assert a security interest in the proceeds as a secured creditor.[139] That case involved an unincorporated individual oil and gas operator who sold working interests to investors, many of whom asserted rescission claims when the operator filed a petition in bankruptcy. It is possible that the case is analogous to a corporation selling investment contracts.[140]

Whether the rescinding security holder should be subordinated to, share *pari passu* with, or have priority over, unsecured creditors requires consideration of the elements of restitutionary relief. Generally, American law disfavors the general creditor whenever he competes with persons who have transferred property to a debtor in a voidable transaction. Professors Slain and Kripke argue that the general rule is premised on the assumption that the general creditor did not, in making his decision to extend credit, rely on the debtor's ownership of property transferred by the rescinding transferor. They point out that in the instant case, the unsecured creditor does rely on an apparent cushion of equity securities in making the decision to extend credit.

They conclude that allocation of assets in a bankruptcy case is a zero-sum situation, and that rules of allocation in bankruptcy should be predicated on allocation of risk. The two risks to be considered are the risk of insolvency of the debtor and the risk of an unlawful issuance of securities. While both security holders and general creditors assume the risk of insolvency. Slain and Kripke conclude that the risk of illegality in securities issuance should be borne by those investing in securities and not by general creditors. Placing rescinding share holders on a parity with general creditors shifts the risk of an illegal stock offering to general creditors. The general creditors have not had the potential benefit of the proceeds of the enterprise deriving from ownership of the securities and it is inequitable to permit shareholders that have had this potential benefit to shift the loss to general creditors. This conclusion is consistent with the equitable doctrine of laches which they characterize as "an anti-straddle rule." Laches will apply to cut off rescission rights if the security holders have failed to assert a known claim and such failure has caused detrimental reliance to an adverse party. In many cases, security holders of a bankrupt debtor will be aware of their rescission rights prior to bankruptcy.

The Securities and Exchange Commission supports the position that rescission claims of security holders should not be subordinated on a mandatory basis. The SEC argues that investors who are defrauded never bargained for the securities they received and therefore never consciously took the risk that the enterprise would become insolvent because of the illusion of investing in an enterprise of a different nature. The SEC is of the opinion that a security holder who has been defrauded should be treated the same as any other tort victim of the debtor. Mandatory subordination would result in different treatment to security holders whose fraud claims were reduced to judgment before bankruptcy, and those security holders whose claims had not reached that point.

---

[139] *In re Rhine*, 241 F. Supp. 86 (D. Colo. 1965).

[140] *Cf. Securities and Exchange Commission v. C. M. Joiner Leasing Corp.*, 320 U.S. 344 (1943).

Unfortunately, the SEC's desire to leave the issue to the courts on a case-by-case basis is not as clear cut as it may seem. Professor Kripke has made clear that leaving the issue to the courts to resolve on a case-by-case basis in effect means that rescission claims will not be subordinated because the doctrine of equitable subordination is inapplicable as between two innocent third parties. His statement is supported by the opinion of the Second Circuit in *In re Credit Industrial Corp.*, in which the court noted:

> Equitable subordination, which is founded upon estoppel, is the doctrine invoked by courts to deny equal treatment to creditors based on some inequitable or unconscionable conduct in which they have engaged, or a special position which they occupy vis-a-vis the bankrupt that justifies subordination of their claims. . . .

The bill generally adopts the Slain/Kripke position, but does so in a manner that is administratively more workable. The bill subordinates in priority of distribution rescission claims to all claims that are senior to the claim or interest on which the rescission claims are based. Thus, a rescission claim resulting from the purchase of a subordinated debenture would share in the proceeds of the estate before equity security holders but after general unsecured creditors. The bill also provides for some case-by-case adjustment. The court is given general authority to subordinate claims on equitable grounds. If those that would take before subordinated rescission claim holders had been involved in some activity that led to the fraudulent issue of the securities on which the rescission claims were based, the court would be able to subordinate those with dirty hands below the rescission claim holders, thus restoring the rescission claim holders to nearly a creditor position.

§ 8.08 SUBSTANTIVE CONSOLIDATION

PROBLEM 8.5

As you know, when Amphydynamics filed its Chapter 11 petition, so did several of its subsidiaries, including Kid-Vid, Inc., which manufactures coin-operated video games, and Comp-U-All, Inc., which operates a chain of brick-and-mortar electronics stores. Comp-U-All also operates Comp.com, a website where it markets electronic goods.

Kid-Vid always has operated profitably, and those profits have flowed "upstream" to Amphydynamics. Amphydynamics has deployed these earnings to help fund operations and acquisitions of other subsidiaries, including Comp-U-All. In addition, from time to time, Kid-Vid has guaranteed loans that others have made to Comp-U-All.

From the time that Amphydynamics acquired it, Comp-U-All has been operating at a loss. The stores have been poor performers, and huge amounts of capital have been consumed in an attempt to establish a strong market presence and brand identity for Comp.com. The e-tailing division has encountered brutal competition from other, better established firms with more marketing and advertising resources. Nevertheless, Comp-U-All does own some very valuable leaseholds for stores in some of the country's most desirable shopping malls.

Comp-U-All's creditors believe that those leases could be auctioned off to generate a "pot of cash" large enough to pay their claims in full.

The prospects for Kid-Vid creditors are not as bright. Although the books of Amphydynamics and its subsidiaries are in considerable disarray, Kid-Vid appears to be insolvent.

Pouilly Fuse Company is a longtime supplier of electronics parts to Kid-Vid. Earlier today, at a meeting of the Kid-Vid creditors' committee, Pouilly's credit manager, Ursula Cheape, asked whether the proceeds of liquidating the Comp-U-All leases could be used to help make payments to Kid-Vid's creditors. For that matter, she would like to know whether the assets of any other members of the Amphdynamics corporate family can be reached to fund a Kid-Vid reorganization plan.

Is it possible? Consider the following materials. The *Augie/Restivo* case is the gold standard of substantive consolidation court opinions and forms the basis and structure for most no-substantive-consolidation opinion letters that are issued by law firms in securitization and other transactions.

IN RE AUGIE/RESTIVO BAKING COMPANY, LTD.
United States Court of Appeals for the Second Circuit
860 F.2d 515 (1988)

WINTER, CIRCUIT JUDGE:

This appeal concerns the substantive consolidation of two bankruptcy proceedings. We reverse because the consolidation impairs the rights of certain creditors, principally Union Savings Bank ("Union"), which extended credit to Augie's Baking Company, Ltd. ("Augie's"), before Augie's had any relationship with Restivo Brothers Bakers, Inc. ("Restivo"). In turn, it also unfairly benefits later creditors of Restivo and Augie/Restivo, principally Manufacturers Hanover Trust Company ("MHTC"), who were aware of the debtors' separate corporate status.

BACKGROUND

Prior to 1985, Augie's and Restivo were two unrelated family-run wholesale bakeries. Augie's was located on Long Island in Central Islip and was a borrower of appellant Union. Restivo was based in Queens and was a borrower of MHTC. Between July 1983 and September 1984, Union loaned Augie's approximately $2.1 million, secured by a mortgage on Augie's real property in Central Islip, to finance an apparently improvident expansion.

In early November 1984, Augie's borrowed an additional $300,000 from Union, secured by its inventory, equipment and accounts receivable. Union was at the time unaware that Augie's had commenced negotiations with Restivo. On November 27, 1984, Augie's and Restivo entered into an agreement providing for Restivo's acquisition of all of Augie's stock in exchange for fifty percent of Restivo's stock. In the agreement, Augie's represented that it had receivables of over $630,000 and equipment and inventory valued at over $1.9 million. No provision for the legal transfer of Augie's real property or equipment to Restivo was made, and no such transfer occurred. Augie's thus remains the owner of that property.

After the exchange of stock on January 1, 1985, Restivo changed its name to Augie/Restivo Baking Company, Ltd. ("Augie/Restivo") and moved its manufacturing operations and some of its equipment from Brooklyn to Augie's plant in Central Islip. Augie's affairs were wound up and Restivo became the sole operating company, keeping a single set of books and issuing financial statements under the name Augie/Restivo. Augie's was not dissolved, however. From January through April 1985, MHTC extended further credit to Augie/Restivo in the amount of $750,000. MHTC also sought and received a guarantee of Augie/Restivo's obligations from Augie's, including a subordinated mortgage on Augie's real property in Central Islip in the sum of $750,000. By March 1986, MHTC had advanced a total of approximately $2.7 million to Augie/Restivo. During the period January 1985 through March 1986 various other firms extended trade credit to Augie/Restivo.

In April 1986, Augie/Restivo and Augie's were forced into bankruptcy. Union was listed as a creditor of Augie's only. Following the consolidation of the cases for procedural purposes, Augie/Restivo and MHTC entered into a series of more than twenty-five "cash collateral" stipulations, in which it was agreed that Augie/Restivo's accounts receivable constituted cash collateral [as defined in 11 U.S.C. § 363(a)]. The cash collateral was placed in a special account at MHTC from which MHTC agreed to make loans to Augie/Restivo in a sum equivalent to the cash collateral deposits. The loans were secured by the assets of Augie/Restivo, as debtor-in-possession, and carried a super-priority administrative expense status. Over time, the cash collateral stipulations were renewed in greater and greater amounts until eventually the entire amount of MHTC's pre-petition loans to Augie/Restivo, $2.7 million, had been converted to post-petition super-priority administrative debt, secured by Augie/Restivo's accounts receivable and by the subordinated mortgage on Augie's real property.

On November 30, 1987, the debtors agreed, conditioned upon confirmation of a reorganization plan, to sell their assets to Leon's Bakery for approximately $7.5 million. Apparently because Union could prevent confirmation of such a plan with regard to Augie's, the debtors moved for substantive consolidation of the two cases on December 17, 1987. Union opposed the motion. The bankruptcy court judge granted the motion on February 5, 1988, finding that Augie's and Restivo had merged and that the contemplated sale of assets to Leon's was in the interests of the creditors of both companies.

After the consolidation motion was granted, the proposed sale fell through because of difficulty in obtaining financing. If the consolidation stands, the equity in Augie's assets will be used to pay the debts of Augie/Restivo and Restivo, including the $2.7 million super-priority administrative debt to MHTC and certain priority tax liabilities in a sum over $1.2 million. Although Union's loan secured by the mortgage on Augie's real property will continue to have priority as to that property, Union's subsequent now undersecured $300,000 loan will be subordinated to MHTC's super-priority administrative debt. Union appealed the substantive consolidation to the district court, and Judge Weinstein affirmed.

DISCUSSION

Substantive consolidation has no express statutory basis but is a product of judicial gloss. . . . Substantive consolidation usually results in, *inter alia*, pooling the assets of, and claims against, the two entities; satisfying liabilities from the resultant common fund; eliminating inter-company claims; and combining the creditors of the two companies for purposes of voting on reorganization plans. *See* 5 *Collier on Bankruptcy* § 1100.06, at 1100–32 n. 1 (L. King ed. 15th ed. 1988). The effect in the present case is, as stated, to subordinate Union's undersecured claims against Augie's to MHTC's super-priority administrative claims. Because of the dangers in forcing creditors of one debtor to share on a parity with creditors of a less solvent debtor, we have stressed that substantive consolidation "is no mere instrument of procedural convenience . . . but a measure vitally affecting substantive rights," *Flora Mir Candy Corp. v. R.S. Dickson & Co.*, 432 F.2d 1060, 1062 (2d Cir. 1970), to "be used sparingly." *Chemical Bank New York Trust Co. v. Kheel*, 369 F.2d 845, 847 (2d Cir. 1966).

The sole purpose of substantive consolidation is to ensure the equitable treatment of all creditors. Numerous considerations have been mentioned as relevant to determining whether equitable treatment will result from substantive consolidation. *See, e.g., In re Continental Vending Machine Corp.*, 517 F.2d 997, 1001 (2d Cir. 1975) (whether creditors knowingly deal with corporations as unit), *cert. denied sub nom. James Talcott, Inc. v. Wharton, Trustee*, 424 U.S. 913 (1976); *Flora Mir*, 432 F.2d 1060 (whether one debtor was independent of other debtor when certain securities issued; whether creditor dealt only with one debtor and lacked knowledge of its relationships with others; whether interrelationships of group were closely entangled); *Kheel*, 369 F.2d 845 (whether entanglement of business affairs of related corporations was so extensive that the cost of untangling would outweigh any benefit to creditors); *In re Donut Queen, Ltd.*, 41 B.R. 706 (Bankr. E.D.N.Y. 1984) (presence or absence of consolidated financial statements; difficulty in segregating individual debtors' assets and liabilities; existence of parent and inter-corporate guarantees on loans; unity of interests and ownership; existence of transfers of assets without observance of corporate formalities; profitability of consolidation at single physical location) . . . . An examination of those cases, however, reveals that these considerations are merely variants on two critical factors:

   (i)   whether creditors dealt with the entities as a single economic unit and "did not rely on their separate identity in extending credit," or

   (ii) whether the affairs of the debtors are so entangled that consolidation will benefit all creditors. [Emphasis added.]

With regard to the first factor, creditors who make loans on the basis of the financial status of a separate entity expect to be able to look to the assets of their particular borrower for satisfaction of that loan. Such lenders structure their loans according to their expectations regarding that borrower and do not anticipate either having the assets of a more sound company available in the case of insolvency or having the creditors of a less sound debtor compete for the borrower's assets. Such expectations create significant equities. Moreover, lenders' expectations are central to the calculation of interest rates and other terms of loans, and fulfilling those expectations is therefore important to the efficiency of credit markets. Such efficiency will be undermined by imposing substantive consolidation in circumstances in which creditors believed they were dealing with separate entities.

The course of dealing and expectations in the instant case do not justify consolidation. It is undisputed that Union's loans to Augie's were based solely upon Augie's financial condition, and that, at the time the loans were made, Union had no knowledge of the negotiations between Augie's and Restivo. MHTC also operated on the assumption that it was dealing with separate entities. MHTC thus sought and received a guarantee from Augie's of MHTC's loans to Augie/Restivo in 1985, including a subordinated mortgage on Augie's real property. Union's claims against Augie's assets are thus clearly superior to those of MHTC. Given these circumstances, the fact that the trade creditors may have believed that they were dealing with a single entity does not justify consolidation. Upon a proper showing, the interests of the trade creditors can be protected by their participating in Augie's case as creditors of that entity. *See* 2 *Collier on Bankruptcy* § 101.04, at 101-20–21. The fact that they may have been unaware of Augie's separate corporate status is not cause for subordinating Union's claims to those of MHTC by substantively consolidating the two cases.

The second factor, entanglement of the debtors' affairs, involves cases in which there has been a commingling of two firms' assets and business functions. Resort to consolidation in such circumstances, however, should not be Pavlovian. Rather, substantive consolidation should be used only after it has been determined that all creditors will benefit because untangling is either impossible or so costly as to consume the assets. Otherwise, for example, a series of fraudulent conveyances might be viewed as resulting in a "commingling" that justified substantive consolidation. That consolidation, because it would eliminate all inter-company claims, would prevent creditors of the transferor from recovering assets from the transferee. Commingling, therefore, can justify substantive consolidation only where "the time and expense necessary even to attempt to unscramble them [is] so substantial as to threaten the realization of any net assets for all the creditors," *Kheel*, 369 F.2d at 847; *Commercial Envelope*, 3 B.C.D. at 648, or where no accurate identification and allocation of assets is possible. In such circumstances, all creditors are better off with substantive consolidation.

The evidence of commingling of assets and business functions in the instant case in no way approaches the level of "hopeless obscur[ity]" of "interrelationships of the group" found necessary to warrant consolidation in *Kheel*, 369 F.2d at 847. Business functions may have been commingled, but that hardly weighs in favor of consolidation in the instant case because the principal beneficiary of consolidation, MHTC, was not deceived and fully realized it was dealing with separate corporate entities. So far as the commingling of assets is concerned, Augie's real property and equipment appear to be traceable. The record also indicates that each company's inventory, liabilities and receivables as of January 1, 1985 are identifiable. It also appears that records exist of all transactions subsequent to that date.

A cornerstone of the bankruptcy court's decision with regard to the entanglement issue was its finding that there had been a merger between Augie's and Restivo. That finding is clearly erroneous. The two corporations were never legally merged because: (i) they failed to comply with the laws of merger under New York law; (ii) neither corporation was ever dissolved; and (iii) Augie's never formally transferred its assets and retains ownership of the Central Islip facility. Furthermore, the requirements for the finding of a *de facto* merger were not met. In *Ladjevardian v. Laidlaw-Coggeshall, Inc.*, 431 F. Supp. 834 (S.D.N.Y. 1977), the prerequisites for a de facto merger were summarized:

> To find that a *de facto* merger has occurred there must be a continuity of the selling corporation, evidenced by the same management, personnel, assets and physical location; a continuity of stockholders, accomplished by paying for the acquired corporation with shares of stock; a dissolution of the selling corporation, and the assumption of liabilities by the purchaser.

431 F. Supp. at 839 (citing *Shannon v. Samuel Langston Co.*, 379 F. Supp. 797, 801 (W.D. Mich. 1974)). Several of these requirements are unfulfilled in the instant case. First, there was no dissolution of Augie's, which remains an independent corporate entity. Second, Restivo did not assume Augie's liabilities. Third, no transfer of title to Augie's real property or equipment has ever taken place. Although there was continuity of shareholders in the transaction in the sense that the former shareholders of Augie's and Restivo became the new shareholders of Augie/Restivo, this alone does not sustain a finding of a *de facto* merger.

We turn now to the bankruptcy judge's finding that the proposed reorganization plan and sale justified the consolidation because consolidation would benefit the creditors of both companies. We do not pause to scrutinize her various speculations as to events that would occur if the proceedings were to continue separately because we do not believe that a proposed reorganization plan alone can justify substantive consolidation. Where, as in the instant case, creditors such as Union and MHTC knowingly made loans to separate entities and no irremediable commingling of assets has occurred, a creditor cannot be made to sacrifice the priority of its claims against *its* debtor by fiat based on the bankruptcy court's speculation that it knows the creditor's interests better than does the creditor itself. The rationale of the bankruptcy judge in the instant case would allow consolidation of two completely unrelated companies upon a finding that the creditors would be better off under some proposed plan involving the joint sale of their assets. The plan would then be approved under "cram-down" provisions that would subordinate the wishes of the creditors of one debtor to those of the other. We do not read the bankruptcy code to allow such a result. Where substantive consolidation is not otherwise justified, a proposed buyer can make contingent offers for each debtor so that priorities among creditors can be preserved.[2]

The plain fact is that Union's claim against Augie's assets is superior to that of MHTC, and, as a result, the undesirability of consolidation is as clear in the instant case as it was in our earlier decision in *Flora Mir*. In *Flora Mir*, a corporation and twelve of its subsidiaries filed for bankruptcy. The debtors moved to consolidate substantively the proceedings relating to the thirteen companies. The primary asset of Meadors, Inc., one of the subsidiaries, was a misappropriation claim against

---

[2] The recent falling through of the sale to Leon's reveals the bankruptcy court's decision to be all the more misguided, because the principal effect of consolidation is now a windfall for MHTC.

Flora Mir, which, as an inter-company claim, would have been eliminated in substantive consolidation. Certain debenture creditors of Meadors opposed the consolidation on the ground that they had extended credit to Meadors six years before it was acquired by Flora Mir and had relied solely on Meadors's balance sheet in making the loan. 432 F.2d at 1062. Even though there was some evidence of financial entanglement among the companies, we held that a consolidation was inequitable to Meadors' debenture creditors because, in consolidation, the assets of their debtor would be distributed to the creditors of all thirteen companies, robbing them of the benefit of their bargain. *Id.* at 1062–63. We did so even though the denial of consolidation would thwart an otherwise desirable arrangement among creditors under Chapter IX. As Judge Friendly stated in *Flora Mir*, "The nub of counsel's argument was that only consolidation will permit the quick consummation of an arrangement under Chapter IX. That may indeed be desirable *but not at the cost of sacrificing the rights of Meadors' debenture holders.*" *Id.* at 1063 (emphasis added).

Union is in the same position as were the debenture holders in *Flora Mir*. The result of substantive consolidation in the instant case would be to make the assets of Augie's available to pay the debts of Augie/Restivo, and to enrich MHTC (whose entire pre-petition loans to Augie/Restivo have been converted to fully-secured post-petition super-priority administrative debt pursuant to the cash collateral stipulations) at the expense of Union. Even if the reorganization and sale remained viable, moreover, there would be no justification for submitting Union to "cramdown" procedures dominated by creditors of Augie/Restivo.

Reversed.

NOTES AND QUESTIONS

(1)   Substantive consolidation is the judicially crafted mechanism by which affiliated entities, though legally separate, are treated as if they comprise a single economic unit. As a general rule, when substantive consolidation is ordered, assets of such related entities are pooled, interentity obligations are extinguished, and the resulting common pool of assets is subjected to the claims of creditors of the consolidated entities.

In a Chapter 11 reorganization case, consolidation results in a consolidated reorganization plan that, for purposes of voting on the plan and allowance of claims, treats claims against the separate entities as if they were claims against one debtor and one common fund. The effect of substantive consolidation is evident from a simple example: Assume that Comp-U-All has unsecured liabilities of $125,000 and stands to realize $150,000 from the sale of its leases. Assume further that Kid-Vid has unsecured liabilities of $300,000 and assets (mainly inventory and equipment) valued at $30,000. If there is no substantive consolidation, creditors holding claims against Comp-U-All might reasonably expect to be presented with a reorganization plan providing for payment of 100% of their claims over a reasonably short period of time. Kid-Vid creditors would fare considerably more poorly, since Kid-Vid has at best only 10 cents per claim dollar to fund a plan. Consolidation, however, would produce about 42 cents per claim dollar for creditors of both debtors, improving the position of Kid-Vid creditors at the apparent expense of Comp-U-All creditors. (For the sake of simplicity, this example does not take into account some variables, such as the cost of administering the cases or the cost of operating the business on an ongoing basis, which are important determinants of the amount and timing of payments to creditors.)

Although substantive consolidation has been characterized as "part of the warp and woof of the fabric of the bankruptcy process," *In re Commercial Envelope Co.*, 1977 Bankr. LEXIS 15, at *2 (Bankr. S.D.N.Y. Aug. 22, 1977), it has no specific statutory or rule basis, but is the product of judicial gloss. Some courts have found the power to order substantive consolidation in Code § 105(a), which provides that "The court may issue any order, process, or judgment that is necessary or appropriate to carry out the provisions of [Title 11]."

(2) *Substantive vs. Joint Administration.* When affiliated entities file Chapter 11 petitions, their cases, in the interests of judicial economy and efficiency, are often jointly administered, a form of *procedural* consolidation. Joint Administration is authorized by Bankruptcy Rule 1015(b), which provides, in part, that:

> If a joint petition or two or more petitions are pending in the same court by or against (1) a husband and wife, or (2) a partnership and one or more of its general partners, or (3) two or more general partners, or (4) a debtor and an affiliate, the court may order a joint administration of the estates.

The difference between substantive consolidation and joint administration has been explained this way:

> Whereas joint administration is designed in large part to promote procedural convenience and cost efficiencies which do not affect the substantive rights of claimants of the respective debtor estates, . . . substantive consolidation merges the assets and liabilities of the debtor entities into a unitary debtor estate to which all holders of allowed claims are required to look for distribution.

In re Hemingway Transp., Inc., 954 F.2d 1, 11–12 (1st Cir. 1992).

Although the majority of substantive consolidation cases appear to involve affiliated corporations, "In substantive consolidation cases, the relationship between entities with respect to which consolidation is sought is far more important than the nature of such entities." 5, *Collier on Bankruptcy* ¶ 105.09[1][c] (Lawrence P. King, ed., 15th rev. ed. 1999). *See also F.D.I.C. v. Colonial Realty Corp.*, 966 F.2d 57, 60 (2d Cir. 1992). Thus, the assets and liabilities of an individual debtor and an affiliated corporation can be consolidated, as an assets and liabilities of (i) an individual and one or more partnerships, (ii) affiliated partnerships, (iii) affiliated partnerships and corporations, and (iv) affiliated corporations. As is discussed in note (6) below, in rare cases, debtors that have filed bankruptcy petitions have been consolidated with nonfiling affiliates.

(3) *Entity vs. Enterprise Law; Consolidation vs. Veil Piercing.* The doctrine of substantive consolidation has been characterized as a triumph of enterprise law over entity law. Substantive consolidation recognizes that although related companies are distinct legal entities, they are often part of a unified economic enterprise and are so regarded by creditors. Substantive consolidation is a doctrinal descen-

dent of the more well known doctrines of corporate veil piercing and fraudulent transfer law. In some early cases that are now regarded as the progenitors of the current crop of consolidation cases, a fairly traditional veil piercing analysis was employed by the courts to erase corporate boundaries and compel turnover of property that had been fraudulently conveyed by one affiliate to another. For example, in *Fish v. East*, 114 F.2d 177 (10th Cir. 1940), the court held that certain assets, which had been transferred by a parent company to its subsidiary and then by the subsidiary to a partnership organized by the owners of the parent, were recoverable by the parent's bankruptcy trustee, because the other entities were "shams" or "mere alter egos," or "instrumentalities" of the parent. In so holding, the court observed that "a corporate entity may be disregarded where not to do so will defeat public convenience, justify wrong, or protect fraud," *id.* at 191, and explained that "The determination as to whether a subsidiary is an instrumentality is primarily a question of fact and degree." The court said the facts to be weighed included whether:

(1) The parent corporation owns all or majority of the capital stock of the subsidiary.

(2) The parent and subsidiary corporations have common directors or officers.

(3) The parent corporation finances the subsidiary.

(4) The parent corporation subscribes to all the capital stock of the subsidiary or otherwise causes its incorporation.

(5) The subsidiary has grossly inadequate capital.

(6) The parent corporation pays the salaries or expenses or losses of the subsidiary.

(7) The subsidiary has substantially no business except with the parent corporation or no assets except those conveyed to it by the parent corporation.

(8) In the papers of the parent corporation, and in the statements of its officers, "the subsidiary" is referred to as such or as a department or division.

(9) The directors or executives of the subsidiary do not act independently in the interest of the subsidiary but take direction from the parent corporation.

(10) The formal legal requirements of the subsidiary as a separate and independent corporation are not observed.

114 F.2d at 191. However, comparisons of veil piercing jurisprudence and substantive consolidation jurisprudence are "not entirely apt." *F.D.I.C. v. Colonial Realty*, 966 F.2d 57 (2d Cir. 1992). Although a finding that one entity is the alter ego or instrumentality of another entity will weigh in favor of substantive consolidation, courts have developed criteria for judging the appropriateness of consolidation that are considerably more flexible. These standards contain shards of the veil piercing tests, but they are less fixated on issues such as domination, capital adequacy, and fraud and more concerned with whether the separate entities behaved as an integrated economic unit, whether they were perceived by creditors as such, and

whether consolidation produces an equitable result. As Judge Winter pointed out in *Augie/Restivo*, over the years, courts have developed a catalog of factors that weigh in favor of consolidation, including:

(1) The presence or absence of consolidated financial statements.

(2) The unity of interests and ownership among the various corporate entities.

(3) The existence of parent and intercorporate guarantees on loans.

(4) The degree of difficulty in segregating and ascertaining individual assets and liabilities.

(5) The transfer of assets without the formal observance of corporate formalities.

(6) The commingling of assets and business functions.

(7) The profitability of consolidation at a single physical location.

See In re Vecco Constr. Indus., 4 B.R. 407, 410 (Bankr. E.D. Va. 1980). Thus, a finding that veil piercing is appropriate is not necessary to justify consolidation. As the court stated in *In re Gluckin Co.*, 457 F. Supp. 379, 384 (S.D.N.Y. 1978):

> While many of the considerations leading to a decision to consolidate may also lead to a conclusion that corporate identities should be disregarded, such a conclusion is not compelled. The standard for consolidation . . . that "the interrelationships of the group are hopelessly obscured and the time and expense necessary even to unscramble them so substantial as to threaten the realization of any net assets for all creditors, does not require 'piercing of the corporate veil.' " (Citations omitted.)

In *Augie/Restivo*, Judge Winter collapsed these factors into two basic tests: Did the creditors deal with the entities as a single unit and not rely on their separateness? Are the affairs of the debtors so hopelessly entangled that consolidation would benefit all creditors? Interestingly, although the existence of intercorporate guarantees has traditionally been regarded as evidence that creditors regarded affiliated firms as a unit, in *Augie/Restivo*, Judge Winter found that intercorporate guaranties were just the opposite: evidence that creditors understood that firms, though affiliated, were separate and thus required the guaranties in order to have both entities on the hook. He also rejected the proposition, occasionally expressed by other courts, that the goal of furthering the reorganization effort was, in and of itself, a sufficient justification for consolidation.

At least two circuits have adopted a more liberal and flexible standard that might produce a different result in some cases. Under this standard, the proponent of consolidation must show that (1) there is a substantial identity between the entities to be consolidated; and (2) consolidation is necessary to avoid some harm or realize some benefit. In determining whether these standards are met, the seven factors outlined above, among others, may be applied. Once this showing is made, a presumption arises that creditors did not rely on the separate credit of the entities, and the burden shifts to the creditor opposing consolidation to show that it did rely and that it will be prejudiced by consolidation. *In re Reider*, 31 F.3d 1102, 1107 (11th Cir. 1994); *Eastgroup Prop. v. S. Motel Assoc. Ltd.*, 935 F.2d 245, 249 (11th Cir. 1991); *Drabkin v. Midland-Ross Corp. (In re Auto-Train Corp.)*, 810 F.2d 270, 276

(D.C. Cir. 1987). How could such reliance be proven? Could a bank lender who had read the debtors' consolidated financial statements claim that it relied on the separate credit of a single affiliate? Could a paper clip supplier, not in the habit of reading anyone's financials, and accustomed to receiving payment 30 days after delivery, make such a claim? Into what category would a tort victim fall? A pedestrian injured in a collision with a Kid-Vid delivery truck is in no position to claim she dealt with Kid-Vid and its affiliated companies as a unit, because she engaged in no negotiations whatsoever. For the same reason, a pedestrian who collides with a Scarlet's Web truck could not claim reliance on that company's separate credit. Could a factory worker who collided with an asbestos fiber do so?

What would result if creditors of Kid-Vid could show the existence of factors militating for substantive consolidation of all members of the Amphydynamics family of companies, but one or more creditors of Comp-U-All could demonstrate that they relied on that company's separateness? One possibility is that, as in *Augie/Restivo*, the court should refuse to consolidate.

Another possibility is that the court should authorize consolidation of all entities, except Comp-U-All. This is what the Second Circuit did in *In re Flora Mir Candy Corp.*, 432 F.2d 1060 (2d Cir. 1970). The *Flora Mir* case involved an appeal from a bankruptcy court order authorizing consolidation of Flora Mir Candy Corp. and 12 affiliates. The debtors moved for consolidation on the same day that they filed separate Chapter 11 petitions. In support of the motion, an accountant and the secretary of Flora Mir (and all the subsidiaries) testified that there had been a "multitude of intercompany transactions, many without apparent business purpose" and they both attested to "the difficulty of disentangling them." Holders of debentures of one Flora Mir subsidiary, a company called Meadors, asserted that consolidation was unfair to them, and Judge Friendly agreed. First, Judge Friendly pointed out that the debentures had been issued six years before Meadors was acquired by Flora Mir; hence there was no question but that the debenture holders had extended credit without knowledge of Meadors' relationship with the Flora Mir family and only in reliance on Meadors' separate credit. In addition, Meadors' operations were discontinued shortly after it was acquired by Flora Mir, hence it had not been a participant in "the multitude of intercompany transactions" described by the witnesses. Moreover, some six months before the bankruptcy cases were commenced, the debenture holders had commenced a state court action charging Flora Mir and two former owners of Meadors with misappropriation of Meadors' assets. (Meadors had been sold to Keebler, which in turn sold it to Atlantic, which in turn sold it to Flora Mir. The debenture holders claimed fraud in connection with all three transfers.) Judge Friendly concluded that it would be grossly unfair to order consolidation of all the companies when the effect would be not only to wipe out Meadors' claim against Flora Mir (by canceling inter-company indebtedness), but also to permit creditors of other affiliates to share in any recovery from Keebler and Atlantic (by pooling assets and claims). Judge Friendly found that the creditors of the other companies "had not the slightest legitimate interest" in any damage award because the transaction giving rise to the lawsuit antedated the acquisition of Meadors by Flora Mir.

As an alternative to piecemeal consolidation, a court might order consolidation of all cases, but grant some kind of special treatment to those creditors able to prove they dealt with the companies as separate entities. This approach was recommended in *Flora Mir* by Judge Friendly himself, who counseled:

> [T]here is nothing to suggest that if . . . creditors, instead of attempting to profit from a quick consolidation, had sat down with the Meadors debenture holders in an effort to develop an equitable plan whereby Meadors' creditors would retain the assets particularly pertinent to them, with a reasonable adjustment to their own rights, the debenture holders would have turned a deaf ear.

Id. at 1063. Similarly, in *In re Gulfco Inv. Corp.*, 593 F.2d 921 (10th Cir. 1979), debtors mollified at least some objecting creditors by granting their claims priority status. Such accords are the result of give and take between debtors and creditors and among the creditors themselves. They are in keeping with the basic concept that a reorganization plan should be the product of negotiation. More recently, in *In re Jennifer Convertibles, Inc.*, 447 B.R. 713, 726 (Bankr. S.D.N.Y. 2011), the court suggested that the debtor might provide payment-in-full treatment to a group of small creditors who might be injured by consolidation.

The propriety and economic efficiency of consolidation are heatedly debated in a trilogy of law review articles. *See* J. Landers, *A Unified Approach to Parent, Subsidiary, and Affiliate Questions in Bankruptcy*, 42 U. CHI. L. REV. 589 (1975), and, in response, R. Posner, *The Rights of Creditors of Affiliated Corporations*, 43 U. CHI. L. REV. 499 (1976); and, in reply, J. Landers, *Another Word on Parents, Subsidiaries and Affiliates in Bankruptcy*, 43 U. CHI. L. REV. 527 (1976).

Professor Landers proposes that even though the owners of a business may choose to operate in the form of two or more separate but related corporations, their overall objective is to maximize the earnings of a unitary enterprise. As a result, the interests of creditors of any one constituent corporation may be prejudiced by efforts to enhance the profitability of the whole. Therefore, according to Professor Landers, to base a decision regarding consolidation on the criteria usually weighed by the courts — commingling of assets and business functions, adequacy of record keeping, cost of disentanglement — disregards the reality that even in the absence of these conditions, the entities are, except in name, one enterprise. Therefore, he proposes that, except when consolidation would do violence to the rights of a creditor who actually relied on the separateness of one entity (as in *Flora Mir* or when the corporations really did have separate existences), consolidation in bankruptcy should be the norm.

Professor (now Judge) Posner, accuses his colleague of "neglect of economic principles vital to an understanding of credit transactions, limited liability and corporate affiliation." 43 U. CHI. L. REV. at 500. He rejects the generalization that related corporations necessarily constitute a single enterprise, observing, "Even before the vogue of the 'conglomerate,' there were many highly diversified enterprises, comprising a number of distinct businesses, often separately incorporated and related only in the integration of a few headquarters functions . . . ." *Id.* at 510. He suggests that if consolidation becomes routine, the concept of limited liability will be forfeited and with it the inclination of investors to invest. He would, however, sanction consolidation in a case in which a proliferation of affiliated companies has misled creditors into believing that the company with which they did business was better capitalized than, in fact, it was.

(4)   *Consolidation by Consensus?* One should not assume that creditors such as those with claims against Comp-U-All will always object to consolidation because of its diluting effect. For the same reasons that creditors will endure any Chapter 11 case and consent to an extended payout rather than force prompt liquidation, even creditors that are facially prejudiced by consolidation may support it when the alternative is liquidation under Chapter 7. Thus, in *In re Richton Int'l Corp.*, 12 B.R. 555 (Bankr. S.D.N.Y. 1981), creditors unanimously supported consolidation because it treated "all unsecured creditors with the greater fairness and [was] the only alternative to a liquidation." The court and Richton's creditors recognized that "it would be impossible for [the] Debtor companies to operate on a stand-alone basis without the aid of the other operations."

One court has detected a more sinister explanation for creditor complacency in the face of consolidation motions. In *In re Parkway Calabasas, Ltd.*, 89 B.R. 832, 835 n. 6 (Bankr. C.D. Cal. 1988), Judge Bufford made this observation:

> One surprising feature of motions for substantive consolidation is the lack of opposition to such motions by unsecured creditors. . . . Perhaps the lack of opposition results from the fact that motions for substantive consolidation tend to be made after the cases have been pending for some time, and the unsecured creditors may have lost interest and given up hope for a substantial dividend.
>
> It appears to the Court, however, that there are often more sinister explanations . . . . While the unsecured creditors may have lost interest, the respective committees of unsecured creditors (if they are active) and their counsel should be actively involved in the process, and looking out for the interests of the disillusioned unsecured creditors. The respective trustees and their counsel should likewise be scrutinizing a substantive consolidation motion for fairness to the respective groups of unsecured creditors.
>
> None of these parties typically raises any concern about the possible prejudicial effects of substantive consolidation. The reason is that there is typically (as in this case) a single trustee, a single attorney or law firm representing the trustee (or the debtor, if the cases are under Chapter 11 and the debtor is in possession), a single committee of unsecured creditors, and a single attorney or law firm representing the committee.
>
> Where there are no separate trustees, creditors' committees or counsel, each has a hopelessly irresolvable conflict of interest on a motion for substantive consolidation. Each is required to support the substantive consolidation for the benefit of the less solvent estate and its creditors, and to oppose it for the benefit of the more solvent estate and its creditors.
>
> Curiously, the professionals do not typically find that this irresolvable conflict immobilizes them on the substantive consolidation issue. In fact, they almost universally support a motion for substantive consolidation. It appears to the Court that this support often arises from the selfish purpose of assuring a fund for the payment of all of their fees, and to avoid the

possibility that they will not be paid for the portion of their work performed for an administratively insolvent estate.

(5) *Consolidation of Filing and Nonfiling Affiliates.* Is it ever appropriate to order consolidation of an entity that has filed a Chapter 11 petition with one that has not? Although it is said to be possible, consolidation of a debtor and a nondebtor affiliate is very rare and is generally restricted to cases in which the nondebtor entity was on the receiving end of fraudulent transfers of the debtor's property, *Sampsell v. Imperial Paper Corp.*, 313 U.S. 215 (1941), and cases in which assets and business functions are so jumbled that corporate boundaries are hopelessly obscured, *In re Munford, Inc.*, 115 B.R. 390 (Bankr. N.D. Ga. 1990). Some courts have declined to consolidate nondebtors with debtors on the grounds that they lack the necessary subject matter and personal jurisdiction to do so, and because they regard pulling a nondebtor into the orbit of a bankruptcy case as an end run around Code § 303's requirements for commencing an involuntary case. *See, e.g., Helena Chem. Co. v. Circle Land and Cattle Corp. (In re Circle Land and Cattle Corp.)*, 213 B.R. 870 (Bankr. D. Kan. 1997).

(6) *Substantive Consolidation and Structured Finance.* Suppose that a few years ago, Amphydynamics realized that the company had outgrown its leased headquarters and that it needed to buy a larger building to house its operations. Management decided that in light of anticipated markets and revenues, the company should acquire the largest facility it could afford. Management then contacted an investment banker to discuss financing. The investment banker suggested that a type of entity sometimes referred to as a "special purpose vehicle" ("SPV" for short) be created to acquire and own the new facility and lease it back to Amphydynamics. To finance the cost of acquisition, this SPV would borrow $75,000,000 from the investment bank. The loan would be collateralized by a mortgage on the new facility. The investment bank would, in turn, package the loan with other debt instruments in a pool and issue mortgage-backed securities that would be sold to investors, such as insurance companies.

Why did the investment bank suggest structuring the deal this way? Were Amphydynamics to employ a more traditional funding approach (e.g., directly incurring debt secured by its inventory or receivables), lenders would evaluate the general credit of Amphydynamics, as well as the value of the collateral, in setting an interest rate. After all, even if the loan were fully secured, a bankruptcy filing by Amphydynamics could have a significant impact on a lender. To isolate the risks attributable to the collateral from the risks associated with the overall financial picture of Amphydynamics, the collateral is transferred to the SPV. Separating the risks attributable to the quality of the collateral from the risks attributable to the general creditworthiness of Amphydynamics should produce a lower interest rate for the loan. In essence, the goal of this structure is to render the assets "bankruptcy remote" by making it unlikely that, in the event of the bankruptcy of Amphydynamics, the building owned by the SPV will ever become a part of Amphy's bankruptcy estate.

As by now you may have surmised, this goal will be thwarted if the SPV is substantively consolidated with Amphy in the event of Amphy's bankruptcy. To limit this possibility, in a structured finance transaction, the organizational documents typically require that the SPV abide by so-called "separateness covenants." These covenants require that the SPV and its managers:

- maintain separate books and records;
- not commingle assets with those of any other entity;
- conduct its own business in its own name;
- maintain separate financial statements;
- pay its own liabilities using its own funds;
- observe all corporate (or partnership) formalities;
- maintain an arms' length relationship with affiliates;
- pay the salaries of its own employees;
- not guarantee the debts of any other entity;
- allocate fairly and reasonably any overhead for shared office space;
- use separate stationery, invoices, and checks; and
- hold itself out as a separate entity.

See Association of the Bar of the City of New York, Committee on Bankruptcy and Corporate Reorganization, *Structured Financing Techniques*, 50 Bus. Law. 527 (1995); Steven L. Schwarcz, *The Alchemy of Assets Securitization*, 1 Stan. J.L. Bus. & Fin. 133 (1994); Steven L. Schwarcz, *Structured Finance: A Guide to the Principles of Asset Securitization* (Practicing Law Institute 1993). Typically, the borrower's and lender's law firms will be required to give a non-consolidation opinion that performs an *Augie-Restivo* analysis as a condition to closing and funding the loan.

Chapter 9

THE CHAPTER 11 PLAN

§ 9.01 WHAT IS A PLAN?

The word "plan" appears in many places in the Bankruptcy Code. For example, Code § 1103(c)(3) says that one of the important duties of a creditors' committee is to participate in the formulation of "a plan." Code § 1106(a)(5) requires a trustee or debtor in possession, as soon as practicable after the commencement of the case, to file "a plan." Code §§ 1112(b)(4)(J)–(M) authorize dismissal or conversion of a Chapter 11 case for failure to propose, confirm, or carry out the provisions of "a plan." The confirmation of a plan is often described as the prime objective of a Chapter 11 case. But what is "a plan" and what does "confirmation" mean?

A plan is a contract between a Chapter 11 debtor and claim and interest holders that says what they will receive on account of their claims or interests and when they will receive it. As the court in *In re Lionel Corp.*, 722 F.2d 1063 (2d Cir. 1983) (reproduced in chapter 6) observed, "The plan of reorganization determines how much and in what form creditors will be paid, whether stockholders will continue to retain any interests, and in what form the business will continue." Generally speaking, a plan must be accepted by creditors and interest holders and confirmed by the court in order to become effective.

A confirmed plan redefines a debtor's obligations to its creditors and interest holders, and discharges a debtor's liability on debts arising prior to confirmation except to the extent that a debt is provided for under the plan. Code § 1141(d)(1). So, for example, if a plan provides that holders of unsecured claims will receive 40 cents on the dollar in satisfaction of their claims, to be paid in two equal installments, a creditor holding an allowed unsecured claim of $100 would be entitled to receive $40 under the plan. The debtor's liability for the $60 balance of the claim is discharged. Should the debtor make the first payment and default on the second, the original claim is not reinstated. The creditor could bring an action only to recover the $20 balance owed under the terms of the plan. In other words, a confirmed plan is not merely an executory accord that must be fully performed in order to result in a satisfaction and discharge of a debtor's obligations. A confirmed plan actually modifies the debtor's obligations. *In re Stratton Grp., Ltd.*, 12 B.R. 471 (Bankr. S.D.N.Y. 1981). The formulation of a plan is an exercise in business prognostication, valuation, and — not least of all — negotiation. Prognostication is required, because a plan is supposed to be feasible. Code § 1129(a)(11). Projections of sales, cash flow, earnings and expenses, and other items will be necessary to determine whether a reorganized debtor will be able to stay in business and fulfill its obligations under the plan. Valuation of the business may be required because it is precisely that — the value of the business — that is distributed to creditors and interest holders by the plan. Negotiation is the *sine qua non* of the plan process as the Code's drafters envisioned it. According to the legislative history, "negotiation among the parties after full disclosure will govern how the value of the reorganizing company will be distributed among creditors and stockholders." H.R. Rep. 95-595, 95th Cong., 1st Sess. 224 (1977). Don't be fooled by this language — the negotiations to which the House Report refers are often not the sort of polite, consensual negotiations that you might have in mind. Rather, the plan negotiation process often takes place against the backdrop of litigation over objections to disclosure statements and the plan itself, motions for relief from stay, motions to compel assumption or rejection of executory contracts and leases, objections to claims, and the like. Thus, while the parties are litigating to enforce their bankruptcy rights, they may also be negotiating to secure advantages that they could not obtain through litigation. The kinds of issues that routinely arise in the course of negotiations include the following; you can undoubtedly think of others:

How much, how soon, to whom? Creditors usually want the maximum recovery in the minimum amount of time. It is a rare debtor indeed who is, or believes that it is, in a position to pay off all its creditors in full immediately. Given that Chapter 11 debtors are rarely able to pay all creditors in full immediately or even over time, a common source of contention is whose claims will be provided for and whose will not. Since creditors and interest holders might be enticed to give up rights or share with others in order to achieve a workable plan, negotiation is the key. The Code itself provides some guidance by establishing certain priorities, Code §§ 503 and 507, and by recognizing the rank accorded creditors and interest holders by nonbankruptcy law or contract. Code §§ 510, 1129(b).

Form of compensation. Some creditors, because of their own particular needs, will settle for a smaller recovery in hard cash sooner, rather than wait for a larger recovery later. Debtors may want creditors to trade their claims for long-term notes, an equity stake in the company, or some combination of the two. Sometimes the negotiated result is a smorgasbord of compensation devices, some of which provide for quick payout, some of which promise a sum certain at a future date, and some of which (such as stock) create a contingent right to payment and hold creditors hostage to the future.

What assets will be used to fund the plan? A Chapter 7 liquidation case is often compared to the carving up of a pie and the distribution of the slices among claim holders. After the slices are distributed, all that is left is an empty shell (unless, of course, the debtor is an individual). This carving-up-of-the-pie metaphor does not quite fit Chapter 11, which contemplates the continuation of the business. The metaphor of the child who wanted to have her cake and eat it too works better, because in Chapter 11, we have to divide up the pie and have it, too. Some assets may be liquidated so that the proceeds may be distributed to creditors, but some assets have to be retained to form the core of the reorganized business without which there can be no business reorganization, at least in the traditional sense. As the *Lionel* case foretold, which assets the debtor will retain, and which it will liquidate in order to facilitate payments to creditors is an important issue for negotiation. Also, since Chapter 11 contemplates the continuation of the business, creditors are likely to feel that in addition to a fixed payment, they are entitled to a percentage of a debtor's future income stream. Debtors may feel differently and want to limit claims on their prospective cash flow.

For the most part, the Code refrains from dictating how issues such as these should be resolved. The Code does, however, provide some limited guidance concerning the form and content of plans. Code § 1123(a) contains a list of things a plan *must* do and § 1123(b) contains a list of things a plan *may* do, which is very broad. The possibilities under § 1123 are held in check by Code § 1129, which sets forth certain standards that a plan must satisfy in order to be confirmed by the court. We consider those confirmation standards in detail later in this chapter. You should read § 1123 now.

Sections 1123(a)(1)–(4) are fundamental to the process by which plans are submitted to creditors and interest holders for their approval, a process which is summarized in § 9.02, below.

- Sections 1123(a)(1) and (2) require a plan to designate "classes" of creditors and interests and specify which classes are *not "impaired"* by the plan. Section 1123(a)(3) is concerned with classes that *are "impaired."* It requires a plan to specify how each "impaired" class of claims or interests will be treated under the plan. These provisions need to be read in conjunction with § 1123(b)(1), which states that a plan may "impair" or leave "unimpaired" any class of claims or interests, and Code § 1124, which governs the concept of impairment. Section 1124 is considered in detail in § 9.04 of this chapter.

- As you will see, under § 1124, virtually any alteration in the rights of a creditor or interest holder constitutes impairment. Thus, § 1123(b)(1) appears to give a debtor or other plan proponent wide latitude in modifying the rights of creditors and stockholders. For example, a plan might provide for the payment of a percentage of each claim in a lump sum, or over time. A plan might provide for the exchange of debt for equity in the reorganized business. A plan might modify the terms of secured, as well as unsecured claims, by reducing the amount, extending maturity, altering the interest rate, or by doing all these things. On the other hand, by providing that a plan may leave claims or interests unimpaired, the Code makes it possible for a plan to affect only some classes of creditors, while leaving others untouched.

- Section 1123(a)(4) requires that a plan provide the same treatment for each and every claim or interest in a class (unless a particular holder agrees to less favorable treatment).

- Section 1123(a)(5) states that every plan must provide "adequate means for its implementation." Then this section sets forth a *non-exclusive* list of ways implementation might be achieved. Note the ability (and flexibility) this section gives plan proponents to restructure claims and interests. A plan might provide for retention by the debtor of all or part of its property or transfer of such property to others; merger or consolidation of the debtor with other entities; satisfaction or modification of any lien; curing or waiving of defaults, extension of maturity dates, adjustment of interest rates or any other term of the debtor's outstanding securities; and the issuance of new securities in exchange for new consideration or in exchange for claims or interests.

- Section 1123(a)(6) provides that, if the debtor is a corporation, a reorganization plan must provide for the insertion in the debtor's charter of a provision prohibiting the issuance of nonvoting securities. This section also requires that a plan provide for an "appropriate" distribution of voting power among the various classes of security holders of a debtor corporation. You will recognize the purpose of these requirements if you consider that reorganization plans may provide that creditors will receive new securities of the debtor in exchange for their claims. Section 1123(a)(6) apparently is intended to insure that the recipients of this new stock will have voting power proportionate to the size and rank of claims they surrender. The leading commentator has criticized this requirement as paternalistic and inflexible. *See* 7 King, *Collier on Bankruptcy*, ¶ 1123.01[6][a] (Matthew Bender 15th ed. Revised 2000). After you have learned more about the plan negotiation and voting process and after you have had the opportunity to think about the kinds of interests that must be accommodated in developing a plan, you may have some thoughts of your own about the desirability of this section.

- Finally, § 1123(a)(7) requires that plan provisions relating to the selection of officers and directors or trustees under the plan be consistent with public policy and the interests of creditors and equity security holders. This section dovetails with § 1123(a)(6) (just discussed) and Code § 1129(a)(5)(i). The latter requires that the proponent of a Chapter 11 plan disclose the identity of any individual who is to serve as an officer, director, or voting trustee of the reorganized entity. It also requires the court to determine that the appointment of any such individual be consistent with public policy and the interests of creditors and equity security holders.

In § 1123(b), the Code sets forth a nonexclusive list of provisions that a plan may, but is not required, to include:

- As discussed above, section 1123(b)(1) provides that a plan may "impair" or leave "unimpaired" any class of claims or interests.

- Section 1123(a)(2) gives debtors a second bite at the executory contract apple, allowing them to assume, reject, or assign such contracts as part of the plan.

- Section 1123(b)(3) authorizes a plan to provide for the settlement of a claim that belongs to the estate or to the debtor, or, alternatively for the enforcement of such a claim either by the debtor, the trustee, or a representative of the estate.

- Section 1123(b)(4) authorizes so-called "liquidating plans" that provide for the sale of most or all of the debtor's property and distribution of the proceeds to creditors and interest holders. When liquidation is necessary, there may be good reasons for undertaking it in Chapter 11, rather than in Chapter 7. The assets may yield a better return if they are sold as or by a going concern. An additional layer of Chapter 7 administrative expenses can be avoided by liquidating in Chapter 11, rather than in Chapter 7.

- Section 1123(b)(5) was added to the Code by the Bankruptcy Reform Act of 1994. It states an exception to the general rule that a plan may provide for the extension or modification of any lien. It provides that a plan may modify the rights of holders of secured claims, except a claim secured by the debtor's principal residence. Thus, an individual debtor may no longer do in Chapter 11 what he or she could never do in Chapter 13: restructure residential mortgage debt. Section 1123(c) provides a special rule for cases involving individual debtors. As you will see in § 9.03, below, a reorganization plan may be proposed by a debtor or, under certain circumstances, by any party in interest, such as a creditor. Section 1123(c) provides that, *if the debtor is an individual*, a plan may not provide for the disposition of the debtor's exempt property (Code § 522) unless the debtor is the proponent of the plan or gives his or her consent.

- The purpose of § 1123(d), also added by the 1994 Amendments, was to overrule the Supreme Court's decision in *Rake v. Wade*, 508 U.S. 464, 466 (1993). As we've seen, § 1123(a)(5)(G) provides that a plan may provide for the curing of any default. There is a similar provision in Chapter 13, Code § 1322(b)(3). In *Rake v. Wade*, a Chapter 13 case, the Court held that an oversecured mortgagee was entitled to receive, by way of cure, interest on missed payments, including interest on interest, whether or not such interest was provided for in the loan agreement or permitted under applicable nonbankruptcy law. Congress added § 1322(e) to Chapter 13 and the parallel provision, § 1123(d), to Chapter 11 to avoid this result. Section 1123(d) provides that if a plan proposes to cure a default, the amount necessary to cure the default will be determined in accordance with the underlying agreement and applicable nonbankruptcy law. As a result, payment of interest on interest is required only if the underlying agreement or applicable law compel it. This provision is examined in more detail in § 9.04 of this chapter.

A sample Amphydynamics plan of reorganization may be found at http://www.lexisnexis.com/lawschool/class/publications/pdf/Plan.pdf.

Code § 1145 of the Federal Bankruptcy Code provides a limited exemption from the registration requirements mandated by Section 5 of the Securities Act of 1933 when issuing securities in accordance with a Chapter 11 reorganization plan. The Securities Act of 1933 requires that companies file registration statements with the Securities Exchange Commission (SEC) before issuing securities to the public. Shortly after filing, the registration statements are released to the public in order to provide essential facts about the issuer, including "a description of the company's properties and business; a description of the security to be offered for sale; information about the management of the company; and financial statements certified by independent accountants." http://www.sec.gov/answers/regis33.htm. By relieving a reorganizing debtor of this requirement, § 1145 facilitates reorganizations. Filing a registration statement with the SEC is an expensive and time-consuming process that may take six months or more to complete and typically will cost an issuer several million dollars.

In order to qualify for the exemption, securities must be issued by the debtor itself, its affiliate, or its successor. Additionally, the securities must be exchanged for a claim or interest in the debtor or principally in such an exchange and partly for cash or other property. Securities issued in this manner are treated as "public offerings" for securities law purposes. 11 U.S.C. § 1145(c). Recipients of these securities are subsequently able to sell them for cash in order to fulfill a debtor's obligations. Generally, recipients of securities issued under § 1145 may resell these interests without registering them under the Securities Act; the same is typically true for subsequent purchasers from the recipients (as these interests are not considered "restricted securities" as defined in Rule 144 of the Securities Act). The legislative intent of Section 1145(b) was to create a "safe harbor" for resales by creditors and interest-holders that acquire securities under a confirmed plan of reorganization. There does, however, exist a significant caveat: persons or entities in "control" of the issuer of the securities are subject to additional requirements regarding the sale of interests received under a Chapter 11 reorganization plan. These individuals or entities, deemed "affiliates" or "underwriters," possess either the direct or indirect power to direct, or cause the direction of, the policies of the person or entity, whether through the ownership of voting securities, by contract, or otherwise. Those deemed to be "underwriters" or "affiliates" are allowed to sell their interests, but they must comply with the registration requirements set forth in the Securities Act.

The purpose of § 1145 is twofold: (1) to eliminate the cost and delay associated with the registration of securities at a time when there is still value left to preserve in the company and (2) to create an alternative for both debtors and creditors to obtain funds via the capital market instead of driving debtors to liquidate assets in order to satisfy their creditors.

§ 9.02 A BRIEF OVERVIEW OF THE PLAN ACCEPTANCE & CONFIRMATION PROCESS

You undoubtedly have noticed that it has been difficult to talk about what plans are and what they do without introducing the terms "acceptance" and "confirmation." These are important terms, because, in order for a plan to become effective, it must be accepted by the requisite number of a debtor's claim and interest holders and confirmed by the court.

To determine whether a plan is "accepted" by claim and interest holders, it is submitted to them for a vote. Federalist leader John Jay reportedly once remarked, "Those who own the country ought to govern it." The voting system set up by the Code embraces an analogous sentiment. Under the Code, votes are weighted in proportion to holders' economic interest in the debtor. The Code also employs a voting system that bears a certain resemblance to our indirect national election system. Every plan is required to group claims and interests into separate classes, § 1123(a)(1), and provide the same treatment for each claim or interest within a class (unless a particular holder agrees to less favorable treatment). § 1123(a)(4).

In order for a plan to be accepted, each class of claims that is impaired under the plan must vote to accept the plan. § 1129(a)(8). If a class is not impaired, it is conclusively presumed to have accepted the plan. § 1126(f). A class that receives nothing under the plan — for example, a class of equity holders whose interests are canceled — are deemed to have rejected the plan. § 1126(g). A class of claims accepts a plan if acceptance is voted by holders of at least two-thirds in dollar amount and more than one-half in number of allowed claims in the class that actually vote. § 1126(c). A class of *interests* accepts a plan if acceptance is voted by holders of at least two-thirds of the amount of interests in the class that actually vote. § 1126(d).

Note the use of the phrase "holders . . . that have accepted or rejected the plan" in §§ 1126(c) and (d). That phrase signifies that for purposes of determining whether the majorities are achieved, only votes actually cast are counted. In cases in which creditors are apathetic and fail to vote, this method of counting is a real boon to plan proponents. For example, if a class of claims contains 10 claims totaling $100, and all 10 claim holders vote on the plan, acceptance by the class will require the affirmative vote of at least six claim holders holding at least $66.66 in claims. If only six holders of claims totaling $60 vote on the plan, acceptance by the class will require the affirmative vote of only four holders holding at least $40. If a majority of holders within a class vote to accept a plan, the entire class is regarded as having accepted the plan and the dissenting minority is bound.

You will recall that in order for a plan to become effective, it must not only be accepted; it must also be confirmed by the court. Code § 1129, which governs plan confirmation, neatly dovetails with the preceding rules. It provides, among other things, that a plan may only be confirmed:

- if it has been accepted by each class of claims or interests that is impaired under the plan; § 1129(a)(8)(A), (B);

- if any class of claims is impaired under the plan, at least one impaired class of claims has voted to accept the plan. § 1129(a)(10);

- if any impaired class does not unanimously accept a plan (but has accepted by the requisite majorities), the non-consenting members in the class will receive property under the plan which is worth at least as much as they would receive if the debtor were liquidated. § 1129(a)(7)(A)(ii). This is known as the "best-interests-of-creditors test." Although the best interests test applies at the individual creditor level to protect dissenting creditors, inasmuch as the Code requires that all claims in a class receive the same treatment under the plan, it may also benefit creditors that vote in favor of the plan, unless they agree to less favorable treatment. § 1123(a)(4).

These rules seem straightforward. In application they raise some interesting and sometimes difficult problems, which are the focus of this chapter. For example:

A creditor's ability to demand better treatment in a plan may depend in part on the leverage he can obtain by voting against it. A creditor whose claim is grouped in a class containing other creditors who vote in favor of a plan may be bound by their assent. To what extent may a creditor's leverage be eliminated by the adroit gerrymandering of classes of claims? This issue is considered in § 9.06 of this chapter.

A plan must be accepted by every class of creditors that is *impaired*. What kind of treatment under a plan renders a class impaired? The meaning of impairment is examined in § 9.04 of this chapter.

Can a plan still be confirmed even though one or more classes vote to reject it? This question is answered in § 9.10 of this chapter.

However, before we turn to those questions, we first answer the threshold question, "Who may propose a reorganization plan?"

§ 9.03 WHO MAY PROPOSE A REORGANIZATION PLAN; EXCLUSIVITY

PROBLEM 9.1

Seven months have elapsed since Amphydynamics and its affiliates filed their Chapter 11 petitions. During this time, the companies have trimmed some of their unprofitable operations, assumed some contracts and rejected others, replaced some managerial personnel with "more qualified" individuals, auctioned off some valuable leases, and consolidated operations. The St. Louis plant has not yet been sold, but the expectation is that it will soon be purchased by a group of foreign investors who want to develop the site as an international dot-com complex. With the aid of consultants, Headley has developed a long-range business plan for Amphydynamics. According to the plan, the focus of the company will shift from the manufacture and sale of standard personal computers to a new generation product that combines flat panel high resolution display with direct Internet access technologies in such a way that users need not understand how to operate a computer or even a VCR to surf the net like an expert. After the closing of the St. Louis facility, manufacturing operations will be consolidated in San Diego.

Recognizing that it is now time to begin discussing the elements of a plan of reorganization, Headley asks you to call a joint meeting of the Amphydynamics creditors' committees and subcommittees. You already have told the attorneys for the committees that the plan will be item one on the meeting agenda, so you know that the committee members will be primed. You have suggested that Headley, assisted by Chief Financial Officer Emily Legerdemain and the outside accountants, present the plan. No other members of the board or the board audit committee are to be present. Although the meeting is being held in your firm's conference room, you plan to take a back seat at what you hope will be essentially a business person's meeting.

The meeting is called to order at 9:30 a.m. Headley greets the members, reintroduces Legerdemain and the accountants, and then makes a little joke. "I hope you enjoy the Danish and coffee," he says, "since you guys are paying for it."

When the chortles subside, the accountants distribute copies of something called a "Confidential Business Plan" that describes the company's revised marketing strategy and business plan. They also distribute some unaudited financial statements of assets and liabilities and some projections of cash flow and income from on-going business operations. At this point you decide that a brief reminder is in order. You say, "Since this meeting is a closed meeting not open to all creditors and stockholders, I'd just like to remind you that if any information is provided during the meeting or in the handouts that is material, confidential information not previously made public, you should be aware of the legal consequences of disclosing the information or trading Amphydynamics stock on the basis of such information." Then you return the floor to Headley who, alas, says that he "wants to talk turkey."

He provides the following rough description of what you have decided will be called "the principal elements of a plan":

(1)   The plan contemplates a substantive consolidation of Amphydynamics, Kid-Vid, Comp-U-All, and Scarlet's Web. All inter-company claims and cross-corporate guarantees will be eliminated.

(2)   The costs and expenses of administration of the Chapter 11 case and the allowed claim of each creditor entitled to priority in accordance with Code § 507 will be paid in full on the effective date of the plan. (As we will see, in order for a plan to be confirmed by the court, administrative expense claims must be paid in full on the effective date, priority tax claims may be paid over a period of years, and other priority claims must be paid in full unless the holders agree to a deferral. § 1129(a)(9).)

(3)   Secured creditors will retain their security interests in the debtors' property. Any defaults will be cured, and the original terms of credit and security agreements will be reinstated.

(4)   On the effective date of the plan, unsecured trade creditors and bank creditors will receive a cash payment equal to 25% of their allowed claims. Three additional interim distributions of 10% will be made to the creditors on the first, second, and third anniversaries of the plan effective date. Thus, creditors will receive 55% of their claims in cash over a period of three years.

(5)   Unsecured trade and bank creditors will receive shares of Amphydynamics common stock in exchange for the balance of their claims.

(6)   Holders of subordinated notes will receive 1% of their claims in cash on confirmation and shares of common stock in satisfaction of the balance.

(7)   Common stockholders will retain their interest in the company.

Ursula Cheape, credit manager of Pouilly Fuse and chairperson of the Kid-Vid creditors' committee, rises from her seat. For a scant moment, you think she is going to heave what's left of her Danish at Headley. However, she merely places it on the table and suggests that, although it is only half past 11, the meeting break for lunch so that the committee members can caucus. Everyone agrees to resume discussions at 2:30.

Three hours later, the meeting resumes. Ursula thanks you for directing the committee members to the French restaurant down the block. She says that, over drinks and a big plate of steak tartare, she and the members of the committee discussed the plan elements "candidly and sometimes heatedly because we are not necessarily of one mind on this" and that, "Frankly, the committee has some serious problems with the proposed plan, which leaves a lot to be desired." But she also says, "If we all approach this thing in good faith and the right spirit we can avoid the precipitous liquidation of the company."

First, she explains, the committee members and their constituents were naturally hoping for a plan that offered cash in full on confirmation. She concedes that she now doubts that the debtor can actually come up with the cash for a 100% plan now. However, she says, all members of the committee agree that they cannot recommend a plan that promises less than payment of 75% of the amount of their claims on confirmation and the balance within two years. "My company makes fuses. It isn't a holding company. We can't afford to become one by taking shares of your stock in satisfaction of our claims."

"I don't want you to get the idea I don't want to discuss options," Headley says, "but 75% up front just isn't a possibility. Also, I can't see how we can avoid giving you an equity position, there just isn't. . . . " Headley shrugs his shoulders and turns to Emily Legerdemain. "Really, Emily, is there?"

"Well," Emily begins, "I don't think 75% is really a viable option. I just don't see how we can get there from here . . . "

"If we can't get anyplace from here, then maybe we ought to talk about liquidating," Earnest Penney, credit manager of Ace Electronics, interrupts.

"I said *there*, not *anyplace*," Emily responds. "Look, I know you trade folks don't want to sit with stock, even though, I think I can say, we're talking about equity in a healthy company, and not a crapshoot. On the other hand, I think that I can assume that you banks would be more sanguine about an equity interest."

"Whoa, don't assume anything! I think we ought to hear from the banks on that one," Ursula says. "Josh, what do you say?"

Joshua Colman, vice president and problem loan manager of BigBank, clears his throat. "Ahem. I can't speak for every bank. I think there are some of us who at this point would be just as happy to write this thing off and be done with it. I know I can pretty well assure you that none of the banks I am in touch with is going to be satisfied with common stock. You say this is no crapshoot. May I remind you that at the organizational meeting at the beginning of this case, you said that a 100% plan was a distinct possibility if we all held tight. May I also remind you that Internet technology ventures are chancy. To my way of thinking, and I think I can speak for all the banks on this point, the only acceptable stock I can imagine would be something with a dividend and liquidation preference. Something that would give us control of the company. But you know, if you're not willing to forego control of the company, you might want to consider something that might even obviate the need for a distribution of stock to us creditors. Now, Headley, you're talking about funding this plan from . . . uh . . . what exactly?"

"I'm sorry, I thought we made that clear. The initial payment will be made from the proceeds of the disposition of our Comp-U-All and Scarlet's Web leases. The annual payments will be funded by operating income."

"Well, I have two questions then."

"Shoot."

"First, where are the proceeds from the sale of the St. Louis factory going? That amounts to several million. Second, why can't cash flow service more debt? If it can't, then these figures you've given us today are wrong, and I think we have to think about an alternative to a plan."

"No, I think our cash flow projections are right. Emily and the accounting team have really sweated those out. But the fact is, we need that cash for operating expenses, and we need to have enough liquidity to take advantage of opportunities as they arise. You folks, if you are holding equity, stand to benefit by our growth, and you also have a claim on our cash."

"If you pay a dividend."

"Right."

"*If.*"

"I hear you."

"And the St. Louis disposition proceeds?"

"Well, of course, even if the group that is looking at the property buys it, we're not going to be able to close until long after I'd like to have a plan in place, approved, and confirmed. There are all kinds of local and state and other governmental problems involved because of the foreign partners. I expect they will be resolved, but it's going to take some time. Okay, that's the first issue. The second is that, as the business plan shows, consolidating the operation in San Diego and getting new product production underway is going to require some re-tooling at the San Diego plant. We are also going to have to refurbish some of our stores. Extraordinary expenses, in other words. We want to have some opportunity cash around. I have thought a lot about this and I think it would be really shortsighted to sacrifice our growth potential for a quick payout now. Also, even if, and I think I'm correct on this, we were to dedicate all the St. Louis proceeds to the plan, it would not nearly bring all of you up to where you want to be on confirmation."

"No, but it might do that if the proceeds were spread among the trade only," says Max Matrix, another supplier.

"I can't really see a basis for distinguishing between the bank and trade here," says Josh Colman.

"Oh really," says Max. "What about the fact we've stepped up to the plate and shipped our products to this debtor? What about the banks' setoffs? Do we have figures on those? How much did your bank setoff on the day of the petition, Josh? You banks already have gotten 100% on some of your dollars. We haven't. I'll tell you what. If the banks return their bad setoffs, we'll be happy to share evenly."

"Could I speak for a moment?" asks Lauren Share, whose company was a supplier of materials to Comp-U-All. "I think you are all losing sight of an important issue here, and by that I mean substantive consolidation. We who are creditors of Comp-U-All should have first claim on the proceeds of the sale of the Comp-U-All leases. My figures indicate that we can get 100% plus interest on confirmation if you give Comp-U-All assets to Comp-U-All creditors first. We think we're entitled to that. We won't settle for less."

"Lauren, we've talked about this before, and I am simply going to repeat what I've already said. Our attorneys have reviewed the law and they tell me that this case is ripe for consolidation." Emily says.

"Well, these are things we can talk about," Headley says. "I'm glad we've been able to have this constructive chat. I think I know where we all stand, and I want you to know that we will try our darnedest to come up with a plan that is sensitive to all our requirements. Why don't we look at our electronic devices and see what would be a good time to meet next week? In the meantime, you might want to poll your respective constituencies. What's good for you Ursula, Lauren, Josh?"

At that moment the phone rings and you pick it up. You wince. "It's my associate. She says we've just received a copy of a proposed plan of reorganization for Amphydynamics and affiliates. Another copy has been filed with the court."

"What? Who did this?" Headley asks.

"She says it came from something called Avid Clip Company, a Baltimore outfit."

"Who the heck is Avid Clip Company?" Ursula asks.

"I think they supply us with paper clips," Headley says in utter disbelief. "Can they do this?" he asks.

Aren't you glad that you read Code § 1121 and the following case and notes and that you obtained an extension of exclusivity before convening the meeting?

IN RE EXPRESS ONE INTERNATIONAL, INC.
United States Bankruptcy Court, Eastern District of Texas
194 B.R. 98 (1996)

DONALD R. SHARP, BANKRUPTCY JUDGE.

FACTUAL AND PROCEDURAL BACKGROUND

On or about June 5, 1995, Express One International, Inc. ("Express One") filed a voluntary petition pursuant to Chapter 11 of the Bankruptcy Code. Since the filing of the voluntary petition, Express One has operated its business as a debtor-in-possession pursuant to §§ 1107 and 1108.

Express One's initial exclusivity period would have terminated on October 3, 1995, 120 days after the petition date, if it had not been extended by the Court. The Court has extended Express One's exclusivity period twice. The most recent extension provides that the exclusive period for Express One to file a plan would terminate on February 2, 1996. Further, the period in which Express One may obtain acceptances of a plan of reorganization [was] extended until April 2, 1996.

On January 18, 1996, within the exclusivity period, Express One filed its Plan of Reorganization and Disclosure Statement. Subsequent to the filing of the first plan, Express One and the Official Unsecured Creditors' Committee (the "Creditors' committee") negotiated certain modifications which were incorporated in an amended disclosure statement and plan of reorganization filed on March 14, 1996.

A hearing has been set on the Disclosure Statement for April 9, 1996.

On February 13, 1996, Kitty Hawk Charters, Inc. ("Kitty Hawk") moved to terminate Express One's exclusivity period so that Kitty Hawk could file a plan of reorganization. Kitty Hawk is a judgment creditor and direct competitor of Express One. Kitty Hawk introduced their proposed plan into evidence at the hearing and argued strenuously that it was superior in terms of recovery to creditors. It is clear that Kitty Hawk's involvement in this case is motivated solely by its desire to purchase this business.

On March 4, 1996, Express One filed an objection to the termination of its exclusivity period. On March 6, 1996, Express One filed its third Motion to Extend the Exclusivity Period. In this motion, Express One seeks an extension of the exclusivity period until the later of May 31, 1996, or the conclusion of the hearing on confirmation of Express One's Plan of Reorganization, as may be amended.

DISCUSSION OF LAW

The Bankruptcy Code provides debtors a limited period to propose a plan of reorganization and obtain acceptance without fear of competition. During the first 120 days of the Chapter 11 case, only the debtor-in-possession may file a plan of reorganization. If the debtor-in-possession files a plan of reorganization within the 120 days after the petition date, the debtor-in-possession has an additional 60 days (up to 180 days after the petition date) to obtain acceptance of the plan before any other party in interest may file a competing plan. If the debtor-in-possession files a plan but fails to obtain creditor acceptance within 180 days following the petition date, the exclusivity period automatically terminates. Any creditor or party in interest may then file a plan of reorganization. See § 1121(b) and (c). Upon the request of a party in interest, the Bankruptcy Court may extend or shorten the debtor's exclusivity period for cause. § 1121(d). The debtor-in-possession bears the burden of establishing "cause" for an extension of its exclusivity period.

Although § 1121(d) does not define "cause," the following factors, among others, have been identified by courts as being relevant in determining whether "cause" exists:

a. the size and complexity of the case;

b. the necessity of sufficient time to permit the debtor to negotiate a plan of reorganization and prepare adequate information;

c. the existence of good faith progress toward reorganization;

d. the fact that the debtor is paying its bills as they become due;

e. whether the debtor has demonstrated reasonable prospects for filing a viable plan;

f. whether the debtor has made progress in negotiations with its creditors;

g. the amount of time which has elapsed in the case;

h. whether the debtor is seeking an extension of exclusivity in order to pressure creditors to submit to the debtor's reorganization demands; and

i. whether an unresolved contingency exists.

See, e.g., In re Grand Traverse Development Co., Ltd., 147 Bankr. 418 (Bankr. W.D. Mich. 1992); *In re McLean Industries, Inc.*, 87 Bankr. 830 (Bankr. S.D.N.Y. 1988); *In re Wisconsin Barge Line, Inc.*, 78 Bankr. 946 (Bankr. E.D. Mo. 1987).

The traditional ground for cause is the large size of the debtor and the concomitant difficulty in formulating a plan of reorganization. *In re Pine Run Trust, Inc.*, 67 Bankr. 432, 435 (Bankr. E.D. Pa. 1986). Express One is a charter and cargo airline which operated a fleet of over 40 aircraft worldwide prior to filing it's [sic] petition. In this bankruptcy proceeding, there are several thousand creditors asserting pre-petition claims against the estate in an amount exceeding $100 million. In addition to the large number of claimants and the dollar amount of claims asserted against this estate, the fact that Express One is an airline further adds to the complexity of this case. Reorganization of an airline implicates the additional considerations of the involvement of governmental regulatory agencies such as the FAA, licensing requirements and standards for the transport of cargo and passengers, and the incidental impact on international and interstate commerce. The Court believes that Express One is the type of debtor for which the extension of exclusivity provisions of the Bankruptcy Code were contemplated. The Court does not believe it is necessary to be a Texaco, Johns-Manville Forest Products, or Ames Department Stores to be considered "large and complex" within the meaning of section 1121.

However, Express One has already obtained two extensions and is requesting a third extension that would provide the benefit of a full year of exclusivity. Where previous extensions have been allowed a showing of size and complexity must be accompanied by factors such as the likelihood of agreement on a consensual plan if debtor remains in control, the absence of alternative creditor plans which cannot be filed because of the debtor's exclusive right to propose and confirm a plan, and a showing that the debtor is not using exclusivity to force on its creditors its view of an appropriate plan.

Kitty Hawk would have the Court terminate exclusivity because they believe the Kitty Hawk plan is superior to Express One's plan. The issue to be determined, however, is not whether some other plan may exist which provides greater recovery; the issue is whether debtor has been diligent in its attempts to reorganize.

The Court believes that Express One has been diligent in its attempts to reorganize. It has a plan and disclosure statement on file. Moreover, Express One has negotiated with the Creditor's Committee. Counsel for Creditor's Committee appeared in support of the amended plan, but was neutral on the issue of exclusivity extension. Likewise, the major creditor appeared in general support of the plan but remained neutral on the question of exclusivity. This is not a case where the creditors are being held hostage by debtor.

Neither is this a case where the Court is asked to extend the exclusivity period for an indefinite period of time. The Court is heavily influenced by the fact that it is called upon to determine whether to terminate or extend exclusivity on the eve of Express One's Disclosure Statement hearing. The exclusivity period will expire on April 2, 1996. The Disclosure Statement hearing is currently set for April 9, 1996.

Under the circumstances, Express One should be allowed to proceed with obtaining approval of its Disclosure Statement unfettered by a competing plan.

Consequently, the Court believes cause exists to extend the exclusivity period to April 15, 1996. If Express One obtains approval of its Disclosure Statement on April 9, 1996, no other party will be permitted to file a plan unless and until confirmation of Express One's plan is denied. See Fed. R. Bankr. Proc. 3016(a).

If Express One fails to obtain approval of its Disclosure Statement on April 9, 1996, this case should not be further delayed.

NOTES AND QUESTIONS

(1)   Why Exclusivity?

Why should a debtor be given a "first shot" at proposing a reorganization plan? Why not open the field to all players from the outset of a case? In *Teachers Ins. and Annuity Assoc. v. Lake in the Woods*, 10 B.R. 338 (E.D. Mich. 1981), one of the earliest published opinions on exclusivity, the district court took pains to consider the rationale for debtor exclusivity. In that case, the district court held that the bankruptcy judge had abused his discretion in extending exclusivity for the seventh time over the objection of the debtor's largest creditor. The district court found that the record demonstrated that the debtor had been employing exclusivity as a stalling tactic to extort a settlement of pending litigation from the objecting creditor:

> As under the old Bankruptcy Act the purpose of a reorganization is to restructure the debtor's finances, if possible, so that the debtor may both continue to operate the enterprise and repay its creditors. To accomplish this goal, a plan of reorganization must be formulated, then filed and confirmed through the bankruptcy court. In the event a plan cannot be filed or confirmed under the provisions of Chapter 11, the case is either converted to one for liquidation or dismissed. Formulation of a plan that will be accepted by a party's creditors and confirmed by the bankruptcy court is therefore crucial to the concept of reorganization.
>
> . . . .
>
> The terms of the plan itself are necessarily a product of negotiation between the debtor and those with outstanding claims or interests, and Chapter 11 is drafted to afford maximum flexibility to the parties in the structuring of a plan of reorganization.
>
> . . . .
>
> Chapter 11 of the Code, and specifically Section 1121, represents a departure from the procedure under the old Act. While Section 1121 normally allows any party in interest to file a plan of reorganization once the initial 120-day period has passed, under Chapter XI of the Act only a debtor could file a "plan of arrangement." . . . The desire to allow other interested parties to file a plan was grounded in the philosophy that there should be a relative balance of negotiating strength between debtors and

creditors during reorganization of an enterprise. This goal was explained during the hearings before the House of Representatives on one of the drafts which preceded final passage of the new Code.

As indicated, under . . . Chapter XI the debtor may have unnecessary power to force creditors to yield to the terms of its proposal. Within certain limits, the Chapter XI debtor can effectively dictate the essential ingredients of a Chapter XI plan to its creditors. In many cases, the alternative to creditors may be to accept the proverbial "ten cents on the dollar" offered or be confronted with an adjudication in bankruptcy and the resultant liquidation. The bargaining power of creditors in such circumstances may be severely limited. The substantial loss that may be faced by creditors as a consequence of the forced auction sale of work in process, inventory, machinery and plant may be overwhelming.

In some Chapter XI cases, a settlement proposal is made on condition that a major and controlling stockholder be offered a substantial sum for his interest in the business while the return to creditors is minimal. Indeed, creditors may not be privy to the negotiations of such a stockholder and the arrangements which he may make concerning the financing of a Chapter XI plan and the sale of the principal's interest; a result which could not occur under Chapter X.

Of course, the bargaining position of the debtor under present Chapter XI may be further enhanced by the debtor's control of the business and the fear that a debtor through inter-manipulation may destroy or diminish the value of the business if creditors do not acquiesce to the debtor's Chapter XI plan. The take-it-or-leave-it attitude on the part of debtors as permitted by Chapter XI is fraught with potential abuse. The granting of authority to creditors to propose plans of reorganization and rehabilitation serves to eliminate the potential harm and disadvantages to creditors and democratizes the reorganization process.

[Bankruptcy Act Revision, Serial No. 27, Part 3, Hearings on H.R. 31 and H.R. 32 before the Subcomm. on Civil and Constitutional Rights of the Comm. on the Judiciary, 94th Cong., 2nd Sess., (March 29, 1976). (Prepared statement of Harvey R. Miller, William J. Rochelle and J. Ronald Trost) 1875–76.]

The legislative history of Section 1121 reflects congressional concern with two basic deficiencies of the old Act's reorganization provisions: their lack of flexibility, and the unfair leverage enjoyed by either debtors or creditors under the various chapters. Chapter X, originally designed for corporate reorganizations, was an unpopular procedure under the Bankruptcy Act both because it required the debtor to relinquish control of its enterprise, and because it imposed a rigid and formalized structure over the proceedings. [H.R. Rep. No. 595, 95th Cong., 2d Sess., 221–22 (1978).] While Chapter XI was designed to accommodate more flexibility during the reorganization, the sponsors of H.R. 8200 were dissatisfied with the undue bargaining advantage that debtors enjoyed by virtue of their exclusive right to file a plan of arrangement.

. . . .

Section 1121 of the new Code, which allows both debtors and creditors to file plans of reorganization after an initial 120-day period, represents the legislative solution to the problems created by Chapter XI's exclusive filing provision, and by Chapter X's inflexibility. Under Chapter 11 the debtor is not automatically required to turn its operation over to a trustee, nor is it permitted to retain control of the enterprise until an unwilling creditor agrees to accept a proposed plan of reorganization. Referring to Section 1121 of H.R. 8200, the committee report states:

> Proposed Chapter 11 recognizes the need for the debtor to remain in control to some degree, or else debtors will avoid the reorganization provisions in the bill until it would be too late for them to be an effective remedy. At the same time, the bill recognizes the legitimate interests of creditors, whose money is in the enterprise as much as the debtor's, to have a say in the future of the company. The bill gives the debtor an exclusive right to propose a plan for 120 days. In most cases, 120 days will give the debtor adequate time to negotiate a settlement, without unduly delaying creditors. The court is given the power, though, to increase or reduce the 120-day period depending on the circumstances of the case. For example, if an unusually large company were to seek reorganization under Chapter 11, the court would probably need to extend the time in order to allow the debtor to reach an agreement. If, on the other hand, a debtor delayed in arriving at an agreement, the court could shorten the period and permit creditors to formulate and propose a reorganization plan. Again the bill allows the flexibility for individual cases that is unavailable today.

Although the legislative goal behind Chapter 11 and Section 1121 is quite clear, neither the House nor the Senate committee reports discuss a definition of cause to reduce or increase the 120-day period under Section 1121(d). As the statement quoted above indicates, however, the drafters of Section 1121 in the House of Representatives believed that in most cases 120 days would accord the debtor sufficient time to negotiate a plan with its creditors. The report specifically cautions that the period could be shortened by the bankruptcy court if a debtor delays in arriving at an agreement. The senate drafters cautioned . . . that an extension should not be employed as a tactical device to put pressure on the parties to yield to a plan they considered unsatisfactory. [S. Rep. No. 989, 95th Cong., 2nd Sess., 118 (1978).]

10 B.R. at 343–345.

(2) Who Is the Debtor for Exclusivity Purposes?

For purposes of determining who can file a plan, who is the debtor? When a debtor is a corporation, operating as a debtor in possession, the board of directors has the authority to propose a plan of reorganization on behalf of the debtor. *In re Dark Horse Tavern*, 189 B.R. 576, 581 (Bankr. N.D.N.Y. 1995). Officers, acting without board approval, may not propose a plan. *In re New Orleans Paddlewheels, Inc.*, 350 B.R. 667 (Bankr. E.D. La. 2006).

(3) Size and Complexity Are Relative.

You will not be surprised to know that courts generally agree that extensions of exclusivity are appropriate in large and complex cases. For example, in the Texaco case to which the Express One court referred, that giant oil company sought an extension on the same day that its judgment creditor, Pennzoil (whose multi-billion dollar judgment against Texaco had driven it to file in the first place), sought to terminate the exclusive period. The court pointed out that Texaco was a publicly traded corporation whose 242,000,000 shares were in the hands of 278,000 stockholders; that Texaco was then the eighth largest corporation in the United States; that Texaco's was the largest Chapter 11 case ever filed; that Texaco had a complex financial structure, tens of thousands of creditors, a multitude of executory contracts with which to contend; and that the course of the case was likely to be determined by the resolution — still several months off — of Texaco's appeal from the Pennzoil judgment. Not surprisingly, against this backdrop, Judge Schwartzberg granted Texaco's motion. *In re Texaco, Inc.*, 76 B.R. 322, 326–27 (Bankr. S.D.N.Y. 1987).

Clearly, however, size and complexity are relative things, and a case need not be as large or complex as Texaco's, or even Express One's, to warrant an extension. For example, in *In re Perkins*, 71 B.R. 294 (W.D. Tenn. 1987), where the debtor proposed a plan within 120 days, but was still trying to get it confirmed more than two years later, the court held that extension of the exclusive period was proper because: "There are approximately 100 creditors holding approximately 225 claims . . . . The claims amount to roughly $10,000,000; the estate is valued at approximately $13,000,000." 71 B.R. at 296. The court also noted that the debtor's plan had been accepted by all but a few creditors.

Size and complexity, however, do not guarantee unlimited extensions of exclusivity. The debtor in *In re Public Serv. Co. of New Hampshire*, 88 B.R. 521 (Bankr. D.N.H. 1988), was a privately owned and publicly regulated utility company that was imploding financially because of delays in getting a nuclear power plant on line. The case was problematic not only because of its sheer size — $500 million in assets; $2 billion in liabilities; 350,000 customers; 2,700 employees; and a complex capital structure — but also because its operations and customer rates were subject to regulation by various state and federal agencies, and the case was thus highly politically charged. The court found that although size and complexity might *per se* justify an extension at the early stages of a case, something more than size alone would have to be shown to justify later stage extensions:

Such factors include . . . the likelihood of an imminent consensual plan if the debtor retains control, no alternate substantial plan being held off by debtor exclusivity, and the general balancing analysis to avoid allowing the debtor to hold the creditors and other parties in interest "hostage" so that the debtor can force its view of an appropriate plan upon the other parties.

88 B.R. 521, 537. The court granted the extension. However, less than a year later, the same court denied the debtor's motion for a further extension of exclusivity, because it was convinced that time was on no one's side:

I conclude that the debtor has not shown cause for a further extension of exclusivity to secure acceptance of its plan . . . . For one thing, the debtor itself indicates that the plan was not filed as a prelude to consensual acceptance, but only as a last resort in the event that further negotiations do not produce a consensual plan. More important, the stalemate between the debtor and the State of New Hampshire on rate levels, and the history of the negotiations following my prior exclusivity order . . . leave me with the view that further extension of exclusivity will not promote a consensual plan of reorganization within a reasonable time frame. The court must also consider the substantial administrative costs and delay costs being incurred as these proceedings drag on. I believe the time has come to return the parties to a "level playing field" as envisioned by Congress under the provisions of § 1121 of the Bankruptcy Code to occur at some state in even a complex reorganization proceeding. Indeed, I believe that the level playing field is *essential* to in the present circumstances of *this case* to foster a consensual plan.

99 B.R. 155, 176 (emphasis in the original). On the same date, the court ordered the appointment of an examiner for the purpose of resolving the deadlock over rate levels which, the court believed, was impeding progress toward a plan. *In re Public Serv. Co. of New Hampshire*, 99 B.R. 177 (Bankr. D.N.H. 1989).

As the *Public Service* opinion suggests, even in large cases, courts seem to be more comfortable about extending the exclusive period over other parties' objections when the debtor is making progress in formulating and negotiating a plan, when delay is not the product of the debtor's ineptitude or caginess, and rehabilitation seems possible. In *In re Southwest Oil Co.*, 84 B.R. 448 (Bankr. W.D. Tex. 1987), the court refused to grant even a first extension in the face of evidence that the debtors' financial condition had deteriorated during the initial exclusive period and was likely to continue to deteriorate. In *In re Sharon Steel Corp.*, 78 B.R. 762 (Bankr. W.D. Pa. 1987), the court denied an extension where the debtor had been unable to obtain financing, where the debtor's only operating blast furnace was in need of repair and in danger of being shut down, and the debtor seemed incapable of proposing a workable plan. The court explained:

The leverage accorded to the debtor by the period of exclusivity must give way to the legitimate interests of other parties in interest so that progress toward an effective reorganization of the debtor may be enhanced before it is too late. The proceeding must be opened up to substantial and significant input by the creditors in the event they can propose a means (possibly by proposal of a plan of reorganization) which will rescue the debtor from its precarious posture.

78 B.R. at 766. Ultimately, management was ousted and a trustee was appointed in the *Sharon Steel* case.

(4)   Terminating Exclusivity Does Not Mean Terminating the Case.

In exclusivity opinions, one occasionally can hear echoes of opinions such as *In re Victory Construction Co.* (reprinted in chapter 1) in which cases were converted or dismissed or stay relief was granted, because the debtors' prospects seemed hopeless. Note, though, that termination of exclusivity does not have the effect of conversion or dismissal, although it does open the door for a creditor or other party in interest to file a plan, including one that contemplates liquidation of the debtor. Nor does termination of exclusivity terminate the debtor's right to file a plan. Under Code § 1121(a) a debtor may file a plan at any time during a case, whether or not exclusivity has been terminated and whether or not another party has filed a plan. The Code contemplates the possibility that once the exclusivity period has expired or been terminated, competing plans may be proposed by parties in interest. *See In re East Redley Corp.*, 16 B.R. 429 (Bankr. E.D. Pa. 1982); *In re Rolling Green Country Club*, 26 B.R. 729 (Bankr. D. Minn. 1982).

(5)   Termination of Exclusivity as a Substitute for Appointment of Trustee.

Code § 1121(c)(1) provides that the debtor's exclusive right to file a plan terminates automatically if a trustee is appointed. Is termination of the exclusive period a useful alternative to the more drastic remedy of appointment of a trustee? In *In re Crescent Beach Inn, Inc.*, 22 B.R. 155 (Bankr. D. Me. 1982), the court doubted that management was guilty of *gross* mismanagement or fraud and was not eager to impose the expense of a trustee on creditors. The court did believe, however, that internecine warfare among the debtor's owners was preventing a plan from getting to the table. Rather than appoint a trustee, the court terminated exclusivity, "in order," said the court, to allow "parties with perhaps a more objective view of the debtor's circumstances, to file a plan." 22 B.R. at 161.

(6)   Early Termination of the Exclusive Period.

The potential for competing plans may be a good reason not to extend exclusivity, but does it justify cutting the period short? Although most of the case law relating to the exclusive period relates to requests to extend it, Code § 1121(d) also gives courts discretion to shorten the period. In *Geriatrics Nursing Home, Inc. v. First Fid. Bank (In re Geriatrics Nursing Home, Inc.)*, 187 B.R. 128 (D.N.J. 1995), the bankruptcy judge concluded that creditors should enjoy "the best of both worlds" and that the debtor's exclusive period should be cut short in light of the possibility that alternative plans might provide more favorable treatment for creditors.

The district court disagreed:

> This Court is not satisfied that statements made by creditors and parties in interest that they were prepared to offer more favorable plans if the court were to terminate the exclusivity period constitutes sufficient cause to cut short the debtor's window of opportunity opened by Congress. Like-

wise, the Court is not satisfied that the Bankruptcy Court's view that creditors' interests are paramount in Chapter 11 — at least during the exclusivity period — comports with Congressional intent. Further, the Court cannot conclude, based on reasoning of the Bankruptcy cases treating of "cause" under 11 U.S.C.§ 1121(d) that the fact that one creditor constituency is not happy with the debtor's plan constitutes cause to undermine the debtor's chances of winning final confirmation of its plan during the exclusivity period.

While the aim of expediting the process of reorganization is commendable, and the prospect of not getting confirmation of debtor's plan might make the potential for other plans appear inviting, this Court is not satisfied that such justifications rise to the level of "cause" for terminating the debtor's exclusivity period. Congress did indeed contemplate the discourse among debtors, creditor constituencies, and parties in interest which the existence of multiple plans can generate. But early termination of the statutorily prescribed period during which the debtor has the sole right to file a plan of reorganization is not the proper manner, absent a showing of sufficient cause, to facilitate such discourse.

187 B.R. at 134. How can "such discourse" be facilitated short of terminating exclusivity?

(7)   Modifying Exclusivity Without Terminating It.

A court may modify exclusivity without terminating it. In *In re United Press Int'l*, 60 B.R. 265 (Bankr. D.D.C. 1986), the bankruptcy judge had nothing but kind words for the debtor's conduct of the case and readily granted its application for a third extension of exclusivity. However, it also lifted the tent slightly to allow certain designated parties to file competing plans if they so choose:

All parties in a Chapter 11 case are usually best served by the speedy filing (and adoption) of a plan that both preserves the debtor as a going concern and realizes full going-concern value. Here, a major reason for permitting the Creditors' Committee to file a plan, even before expiration of the initial 120-day exclusivity period, was the prospect that continued conflict between management and [controlling] stockholder would lead to a stalemate in which no plan at all could feasibly be filed in the name of this Debtor. Later, WSG [the Wire Services Guild which represented many employees] was allowed to "join the exclusivity club" in the wake of serious conflict between management and labor (in which a disastrous complete shutdown was only narrowly averted) and in recognition of the special need by a wire service company for a dedicated, highly motivated reporters' work force.

This case involves several thousand creditors. "Opening the floodgates" to allow each and every one of them to file a plan, no matter how poorly conceived or supported, would not serve "to secure the expeditious and economical administration of" this case (see Bankruptcy Rule 1001) nor "to carry out the provisions of" the Bankruptcy Code (see § 105(a)).

Thus, this court adopted a middle approach, initially suggested by the parties themselves — opening up the right to file a plan on a limited basis to those two entities (besides the Debtor itself) that have the most at stake in this case and have shown themselves to be responsible parties, while refraining from opening the floodgates completely.

60 B.R. at 271 n.12.

(8)   Legislative Efforts to Curtail Exclusivity.

You should not leave this section believing that the majority of Chapter 11 debtors file plans within 120 days and manage to have them confirmed within another 60 days. In reality, in many cases, extensions are granted more routinely than the statements in some of the preceding cases would suggest. Indeed, repeated extensions of the exclusivity period are among the factors blamed for what critics perceived to be the unreasonable cost and duration of Chapter 11 cases, *see*, e.g., Lynn M. LoPucki, *The Trouble With Chapter 11*, 1993 Wis. L. Rev. 729; Kevin A. Kordana & Eric A. Posner, *A Positive Theory of Chapter 11*, 74 N.Y.U. L. Rev. 161 (1999), and the impetus behind several Code amendments.

In its first effort to curb the practice of granting extensions routinely, Congress, in 1994, amended 28 U.S.C. § 158 to provide for an immediate appeal, as of right, from an order extending or reducing the exclusive period. Since such an order is an interlocutory order, prior to the amendment, such an appeal required the permission of the district court. The amendment appears to have encouraged courts to scrutinize requests for extensions more carefully and to build better records to support their holdings and withstand appeal. *See* Karen Gross & Patricia Redmond, *In Defense of Debtor Exclusivity: Assessing Four of the 1994 Amendments to the Bankruptcy Code*, 69 Am. Bankr. L.J. 287 (1995). The 1994 amendments were actually a watered down version of original proposals that would have established a presumption against extending exclusivity in all cases.

In 2005, Congress acted again to curtail the debtor's exclusive period. Code § 1121(2)(A) now provides that a court may not extend the debtor's 120-day exclusive period beyond a date that is 18 months from the date of the Chapter 11 order for relief, which in voluntary cases is the date the petition was filed. Section 1121(2)(B) now provides that a court may not extend the debtor's 180-day exclusive period for obtaining plan acceptances beyond a date that is 20 months from the date of the order for relief. The time periods are different for debtors that are, and that elect to be treated as, "small business debtors." Section 1121(e)(1) provides that a small business debtor has a 180-day exclusive period in which to file a plan. Section 1121(e)(2) provides that a plan and disclosure statement "shall be filed not later than 300 days after the order for relief." This 300-day period may be extended if the debtor demonstrates, by a preponderance of the evidence, that "it is more likely than not that the court will confirm a plan within a reasonable period of time." Precisely what happens if no plan is filed before the expiration of the 300-day period is unclear. Apparently, this would be cause for dismissal or conversion of the case.

(9)   Extending the Acceptance Period.

Should a request for extending the exclusive period for getting a previously filed plan accepted be judged by the same standard as a request for extending the period for filing a plan? The court in *In re Perkins*, 71 B.R. 294 (W.D. Tenn. 1987), thought not:

> This court is of the opinion that an extension of the exclusive time in which to *file* a plan presents an enhanced potential for skewing the bargaining balance in favor of the debtor, contrary to the intent of the legislature. If no plan is filed, the creditor body has no information upon which to formulate either a positive or negative opinion. On the other hand, if the debtor has filed a plan, potential for upsetting the bargaining balance is more remote. No longer in the dark with respect to the debtor's intentions, the creditors have a basis for decision, and can either accept the plan or fight extensions of the exclusivity period, in order to file a competing plan. Therefore, extensions of the exclusivity period for gaining acceptances do not have the potential for detrimental impact upon the creditors' bargaining position occurring where no plan has been filed. Accordingly, cause may be measured by a more lenient standard in the determination to grant an enlargement of time in which to gain acceptances to a filed plan.

71 B.R. 294, 299.

Does the extension of the 120-day proposal period automatically extend the 180-day acceptance period? The courts disagree. *Compare In re Trainer's, Inc.*, 17 B.R. 246 (Bankr. E.D. Pa. 1982), *and In re Barker Estates, Inc.*, 14 B.R. 683 (Bankr. W.D.N.Y. 1981), *with In re Judd*, 173 B.R. 941 (Bankr. D. Kan. 1994), *and In re Ravenna Indus., Inc.*, 20 B.R. 886 (Bankr. N.D. Ohio 1982). The better practice is to move simultaneously for an extension of both the exclusivity and acceptance periods. *See* 7 King, *Collier on Bankruptcy* ¶ 1121.04 (Matthew Bender 15th ed. Revised 2000).

PROBLEM 9.2

If a trustee is appointed, or if exclusivity lapses for one of the reasons set forth in § 1121(c), then "any party in interest, including the debtor, the trustee, a creditors' committee, an equity security holders' committee, a creditor, an equity security holder, or any indenture trustee, may file a plan." That list is broadly inclusive, but not exclusive. Suppose that a private equity fund that is interested in acquiring ownership and control of Amphydynamics has purchased $15,000 in claims from several trade creditors. The fund now proposes a plan that provides that it will become the new owner of Amphydynamics. Does it have standing to propose a plan? Consider the following opinion.

IN RE EL COMANDANTE MANAGEMENT COMPANY, LLC

United States District Court, District of Puerto Rico

359 B.R. 410 (2006)

Enrique S. Lamoutte, U.S. Bankruptcy Judge.

Background

El Comandante Management Company, LLC ("ECMC"), Housing Development Associates, S.E. ("HDA"), El Comandante Capital Corporation ("ECCC") (collectively the "debtors"), filed for bankruptcy under Chapter 11 of the Bankruptcy Code on October 15, 2004. On January 25, 2006, Caribbean filed its disclosure statement. A hearing was held on February 21, 2006, to consider Caribbean's disclosure statement, and the objections filed by creditors and parties in interest (Minutes of February 21, 2006, Docket No. 921). [On March 3, 2006, the court denied Caribbean's request for approval of its disclosure statement because the proposed plan failed to classify creditors properly. We consider the classification issue in depth in § 9.06 of this chapter. — Eds.]

. . . .

Caribbean's Second Amended Disclosure Statement and Plan

Pursuant to the Second Amended Joint Plan Of Reorganization For Debtors And Debtors-In-Possession El Comandante Management Company, LLC, Housing Development Associates, SE, And El Comandante Capital Corp. ("Caribbean's Second Plan"), Caribbean will pay $67 million for the purchase of substantially all of debtors' assets ("Asset Purchase Agreement"),[3] and a deferred compensation under the Earn-Out Agreement ("Earn-Out Compensation").[4] The bondholders will receive $59–$60 million from Caribbean's purchase price for debtors' assets. The tentative breakdown provided by Caribbean is as follows:

Value of Wells Fargo's security interest:	$ 64,000,000
Adequate protection payments:	(8,700,000)
Face value of ECMC's notes:	(6,700,000)

---

[3] Caribbean's Asset Purchase Agreement is $3 million more than the one proposed by the Indenture Trustee in its proposed plan and sale to Camarero.

[4] The Earn-Out Agreement contemplates the creation of a trust by the purchaser of the racetrack and other assets. The funding of the trust is contingent on the Puerto Rico Government's approval of regulations to govern the installation and operation of the video-games machines. Otherwise the new owner will have to fund the trust. The trust must be established within five (5) years from the effective date of the plan. However, the Earn-Out Agreement requires that Caribbean must obtain a license to operate the racetrack. Distribution to the beneficiaries of the trust will be made within ten (10) years from the "Trigger Event" date, which is the date when the purchaser of the debtors' assets has installed at least 500 VGMs on or off the premises of the racetrack; provided, that the new legislation is enacted and the purchaser has obtained all the necessary governmental permits for the installation and operation of the equipment. The court notes that Caribbean's request for a license to operate El Comandante Racetrack has been denied by the Horse Racing Board.

Estimated Rent paid, as of September 2006:	(3,000,000)
Payment of deficiency claim:	13,700,000
(Unidentified funds)	750,000
Estimated total distribution amount:	$ 59–60 million

Caribbean's second plan also provides to pay in full all the allowed administrative claims, allowed other secured claims, allowed priority tax claims, and other allowed priority unsecured claims; and, an initial distribution to the allowed general unsecured claims against creditors of ECMC and HDA. The reserve funds to pay these claims have been increased under the second plan, and Caribbean has indicated that the company and its investors have the resources to adjust and/or increase the reserves, if necessary. . . . The source of funds to close the Asset Purchase Agreement is a credit facility by Westernbank Business Credit in the amount of $ 73 million dollars. The financing is not contingent on Caribbean obtaining a license to operate a racetrack.

. . . .

II. Standing to file a Chapter 11 Plan

A crucial issue before the court is whether or not Caribbean has standing to propose a plan of reorganization for HDA and ECCC, when Caribbean is not a creditor in these cases. Section 1109(b) provides that any party in interest "may raise and may appear and be heard on any issue in a case under this chapter." Section 1121(c) provides that any party in interest may file a plan provided that a trustee has been appointed; the debtor has not filed a plan within 120 days from the date of the order of stay; or the debtor's plan has not been accepted before 180 days after the date of the order of stay, by each class of claims or interests that is impaired under the plan. Section 1121(c) of the Bankruptcy Code provides the circumstances when a party in interest may file a plan. "If the debtor loses his or her exclusive right to file a plan, then 'any party in interest' may file one." 4 *Norton Bankr. L. & P. 2d* § 88:4. The Legislative History of section 1121(c) is silent as to who is a party in interest, aside from the persons or entities enumerated in the statute. Congress only states that the list that appears under section 1121(c) of the Code, is not exhaustive, allowing the courts a broad discretion to consider any relevant factors in order to determine who is a party in interest. *See* Bankruptcy Reform Act of 1978, P.L. 95-598, U.S. Code Cong. & Admin. News 1978, p.p. 5963 et seq.

Caribbean purchased a claim postpetition, thus becoming a creditor of ECMC's estate pursuant to section 101(10)(A) of the Bankruptcy Code.[6] A creditor is

---

[6] "The term [party in interest] has been held to include general and limited partners who owned over 99 percent of the debtor, a party who purchased a claim and became a creditor even if it was acquired postpetition for the express purpose of acquiring standing to file a plan, ... " *Id*. In *In re Rook Broadcasting of Idaho, Inc.*, 154 B.R. 970, 972 (Bankr. D. Idaho 1993), the court held that the term "party in interest is expandable, and its application must be determined on a case-by-case basis." (Citation omitted.) In *Rook*, the debtor and a creditor filed competing plans. The debtor alleged that the creditor did not have standing to file a plan, as it became a creditor by purchasing claims postpetition. The court

specifically listed as a party in interest in section 1109(b); thus, Caribbean is a party in interest in ECMC's case. The Indenture Trustee alleges that Caribbean is not a creditor of HAD's and ECCC's estates, and may not propose a plan in their cases. Caribbean argues that it is a party in interest in debtors' estates because it holds a direct financial stake in all the debtors' estates, as the proposed second amended plan contemplates the purchase of substantially all the debtors' assets, including HAD's and ECCC's. We agree.

The Bankruptcy Code does not define the term "party in interest," it only lists who may be a party in interest. Sections 1109(b) and 1121(c) provide that "party in interest" includes the debtor, a chapter 11 trustee, creditor, creditors' committee, equity security holders' committee or indenture trustee.[7] The list sections 1109(b) and 1121(c) is non-exclusive. . . . Generally, any person or entity, who holds a financial stake in the outcome of the debtor's estate, is a party in interest. *See* 7 Lawrence P. King, Collier on Bankruptcy, P1109.02[1] 15th Revised Edition 2006. A person who has a "significant legal stake" in the debtor's estate, as opposed to a financial stake, is also a party in interest. Collier ¶ 1109.02[1]. In *In re Overview Equities, Inc.*, 240 B.R. 683, 686–687 (Bankr. E.D.N.Y. 1999), the court followed the test set forth in *Amatex*, to determine whether a party qualifies as a "party in interest," a determination to be made on a case-by-case basis. "The test employed under section 1109(b) is 'whether the prospective party in interest has a sufficient stake in the outcome of the proceeding so as to require representation.' " (citing from *In re Amatex Corp.*, 755 F.2d 1034, 1042 (3d Cir. 1985)). Thus, the right of "individual stakeholders to have a voice in the chapter 11 process is fundamental." Collier ¶ 1102.02[2][a].

While the concept of "party in interest" should be interpreted broadly to allow parties affected by the outcome of the case, to appear and be heard, *Overview*, 240 B.R. at 686–687, "principles of standing do properly apply to limit the scope of section 1109(b)." Collier P 1109.01[3]. The concept of "party in interest" under sections 1109(b) and 1121(c) are the same. Collier P 1121.05[2]. The determination of who is a party in interest is made by the court on a fact-finding process, and it is determined on a case-by-case basis, after considering whether or not the person has sufficient stake in the outcome of the case. *Id.* Pursuant to Caribbean's plan, the outcome of each of the debtors' cases directly affects the outcome of ECMC's Chapter 11 case, wherein Caribbean is a creditor. Such combined effect places Caribbean within a "zone of interest" sufficient to grant it standing to appear in the three cases and propose a consolidated plan for the purchase of all assets. Collier P 1109.04[4].

---

held that the creditor was a party in interest with standing to file a plan under section 1121(c), regardless of whether the proponent of the plan became a creditor and a party in interest through transfers of claims postpetition. *Rook* followed the analysis of *In re First Humanics Corp.*, 124 B.R. 87, 91–93 (Bankr. W.D. Mo. 1991), and held that "a party who purchased claims against the debtor postpetition had standing to present a plan of reorganization, even though the sole reason for the purchase of the claims was to insure such standing." In *First Humanics*, the court also held that the determination of whether an entity qualifies as a party in interest "must be made in light of the specific reorganization context for which the determination is sought." (Citations omitted.) 124 B.R. at 90.

[7] Other parties not included in section 1109(b), but who may be considered a party in interest is "a regulatory agency with supervisory responsibilities over the debtor's business or financial affairs." Collier ¶ 1109.02[1]. Such is the case of the Horse Racing Administrator and the Horse Racing Board.

Caribbean became a creditor and a party in interest of ECMC's estate through a postpetition claim transfer. Clearly, Caribbean has standing to propose a plan for ECMC as a party in interest under section 1121(c). The plan proposed by Caribbean directly affects the estates of ECMC, HDA and ECCC, as the plan contemplates the purchase of substantially all the debtors' assets, and the purchase of the bondholders' notes. Caribbean's proposed plan cannot be effective without considering HDA's and ECCC's estates. Under Caribbean's Second Amended Disclosure Statement, the three estates are at stake. Upon the closing of the asset purchase agreement, the three estates will become one, with a new owner who will assume the claims of the debtors. Caribbean cannot purchase the assets of ECMC without having a direct impact on the estates of HDA and ECCC, who own and manage the premises where ECMC operates. Caribbean has sufficient financial stake in the debtors' estates, as the implementation of the plan depends in the outcome of all three bankruptcy cases. Based on the provisions of section 1109(b), a broad application of standing, and the zone of interest test, the court finds that Caribbean is a party in interest in the estates of HDA and ECCC, as Caribbean holds a direct financial stake in the outcome of the debtors' cases, and the feasibility of the plan. Therefore, the court finds that Caribbean has standing to propose a plan in all three cases (ECMC, HDA, and ECCC).

§ 9.04 IMPAIRMENT OF CLAIMS AND INTERESTS

[A] Introduction

The concept of "impairment" is fundamental to an understanding of the dynamics and mechanics of the Chapter 11 plan negotiation, acceptance, and confirmation process. As we already have seen:

> A plan must organize claims and interests into classes, provide the same treatment for each claim or interest in a particular class, specify any class that *is not impaired*, and specify the treatment of any class that *is impaired* under the plan. Code § 1123(a).

> In order for a plan to be confirmed by the so-called consensual route, each class of claims or interests that is *impaired* by the plan must vote to accept the plan. Code § 1129(a)(8). (A class of claims votes in favor of a plan if, of the allowed claims that vote, at least two-thirds in amount and more than one-half in number of allowed claims vote to accept.)

> Code § 1126(c). A class of interests votes in favor of a plan if, of the allowed interests that vote, at least two-thirds in amount vote in favor of the plan. Code § 1126(d).)

> If fewer than all impaired classes vote to accept a plan, the plan proponent may nevertheless seek to have the plan confirmed via the so-called "cramdown" route, *provided that at least one impaired class votes to accept the plan.* § 1129(a)(10). (Other standards for cramming a plan down are contained in § 1129(b).)

A class that is *not impaired* is conclusively presumed to have accepted the plan; a formal vote is not required. § 1126(f). Even if an unimpaired class actually votes against a plan, it is conclusively presumed to have accepted. *Farber v. 405 N. Bedford Drive Corp. (In re 405 N. Bedford Drive Corp.)*, 778 F.2d 1374 (9th Cir. 1985). Thus, a plan proponent can streamline the negotiation and voting process by leaving classes unimpaired.

A class that receives nothing under a plan on account of claims or interests is deemed to have rejected the plan, § 1126(g), and, as we will see, such a class is impaired.

The Bankruptcy Code defines the term "impaired" not by explaining what it is, but rather by explaining what it is not. Code § 1124, describes the kinds of treatment that will leave a claim or interest unimpaired. Section 1124 is reproduced in full, below. Read it carefully. As you do, keep in mind that unless a claim or interest is treated in precisely one of the two ways described in § 1124, it is impaired. Also, note that § 1124 formerly provided three ways of leaving a claim or interest unimpaired. However, subsection (3), which appears below in strikeout text, was repealed in 1994. The reasons for its repeal — and the unintended consequences of it — are discussed later in this section.

§ 1124.   Impairment of claims or interests

Except as provided in section 1123(a)(4) of this title, a class of claims or interests is impaired under a plan unless, with respect to each claim or interest of such class, the plan —

(1) leaves unaltered the legal, equitable, and contractual rights to which such claim or interest entitles the holder of such claim or interest; or

(2) notwithstanding any contractual provision or applicable law that entitles the holder of such claim or interest to demand or receive accelerated payment of such claim or interest after the occurrence of a default —

(A) cures any such default that occurred before or after the commencement of the case under this title, other than a default of a kind specified in section 365(b)(2) of this title;

(B) reinstates the maturity of such claim or interest as such maturity existed before such default;

(C) compensates the holder of such claim or interest for any damages incurred as a result of any reasonable reliance by such holder on such contractual provision or such applicable law;

(D) if such claim or such interest arises from any failure to perform a nonmonetary obligation, other than a default arising from failure to operate a nonresidential real property lease subject to section 365(b)(1)(A), compensates the holder of such claims or such interest (other than the debtor or an insider) for any actual pecuniary loss incurred by such holder as a result of such failure; and

(E) does not otherwise alter the legal, equitable, or contractual rights to which such claim or interest entitles the holder of such claim or interest.

~~(3) provides that, on the effective date of the plan, the holder of such claim or interest receives, on account of such claim or interest, cash equal to~~

~~(A) with respect to a claim, the allowed amount of such claim; or &cstrike;~~

~~(B) with respect to an interest, if applicable, the greater of~~

~~(i) any fixed liquidation preference to which the terms of any security representing such interest entitle the holder of such interest; and~~

~~(ii) any fixed price at which the debtor, under the terms of such security, may redeem such security from such holder.~~

Now that you've read § 1124, consider the questions and examples in the following section.

[B]   Leaving Rights Unaltered; Code § 1124(1)

Section 1124(1) provides that a class of claims or interests is not impaired, if the plan leaves "unaltered the legal, equitable, and contractual rights to which such claim or interest entitles the holder . . . "

Example 1

Suppose Amphydynamics borrowed $1,000,000 from the bank at 7.5% interest and agreed to repay the loan in 240 monthly installments of about $18,000. Assume that at the time of its Chapter 11 filing, Amphydynamics was current in its payments and that while the case was pending, perhaps pursuant to an adequate protection stipulation, Amphydynamics continued to make monthly payments in accordance with the terms of the loan agreement. The proposed plan provides that Amphydynamics will continue making payments in accordance with the original loan agreement. Is the bank's claim impaired?

Under § 1124(1), the claim is not impaired. Since the debtor did not default either before or after commencing the case, and since the plan provides that the debtor will assume the loan agreement according to its original terms, the legal, equitable, and contractual rights of the bank are unaltered.

Example 2

Assume the same facts as above, but also assume that instead of providing that Amphydynamics will continue making payments in accordance with the terms of the original loan agreement, the plan provides that the term will be extended from 240 to 360 months and the interest rate will be increased from 7.5% to 8.5%. Is the bank's claim impaired?

Under § 1124(1), the bank's claim is, of course, impaired. Its rights under the loan agreement have been altered. The fact that the interest rate has been increased to compensate for the extension of the term does not change the result.

Example 3

Suppose that instead of providing that Amphydynamics will continue making payments in accordance with the terms of the original loan agreement, the plan provides that Amphydynamics will repay the loan at a higher rate of interest (say 8.5% instead of 7.5%) over a shorter term (say 120 months instead of 240). Is the bank's claim impaired?

As unrealistic as this hypothetical is, and as counterintuitive as the result may strike you, under § 1124(1), the bank's claim is impaired. The terms of the original agreement have been changed; the bank's legal and contractual rights have been altered. To understand why even the enhancement of rights is treated as a form of impairment under the Code, an understanding of the problems that arose in connection with the former Act's counterpart of impairment is helpful.

Under §§ 107 and 179 of Chapter X of the former Bankruptcy Act (and under similar provisions of Chapters XI and XII), a creditor or interest holder was entitled to vote on a plan "only if their or its interest shall be materially and adversely affected thereby." The Act did not define the terms "interest" or "materially and adversely affected." This created uncertainty, and uncertainty invited litigation. Courts held that stockholders of apparently insolvent debtors were disqualified from voting on plans because they had no "interest" that could be "materially and adversely affected." In cases in which the debtor's property appeared to be worth less than the liens that encumbered it, unsecured creditors were similarly disenfranchised. The only way disenfranchised parties could regain their right to vote was by bringing costly and time consuming litigation to prove that the value of the reorganized debtor was in fact sufficient to justify their participation. Seeking to avoid valuation litigation and establish with greater certainty whether parties were affected by a plan and thus entitled to vote on it, the Code's drafters fashioned the broad concept of impairment. *See generally In re L&J Anaheim Associates*, 995 F.2d 940, 943 (9th Cir. 1993); *In re Barrington Oaks Gen. P'ship. and Starcrest Prop., Ltd.*, 15 B.R. 952 (Bankr. D. Utah 1981).

Example 4

Assume that Amphydynamics proposes a plan that scales down claims, with the result that it creates — where prior to reorganization there was none — a positive net worth for stockholders. Are the interests of the stockholders impaired?

No. The legal and equitable rights of the stockholders have not been altered, although the value of their shares has changed.

Example 5

You may recall from the plan negotiating session depicted at the beginning of this chapter that the bank representative said that the only stock that his constituents would be willing to swap for debt would have to have some kind of dividend and liquidation preference. Suppose that the plan proposes that bank creditors will exchange their claims for shares of a new class of preferred stock. Are the claims of the banks impaired?

Yes, clearly. The legal and contractual rights of the bank creditors have been altered by the substitution of equity for debt instruments.

Example 6

Is there another class whose claims or interests are being impaired by the plan described in Example 5?

Yes, the common stockholders, for several reasons. First, common stock dividends may not be paid until unpaid and current preferred dividends are paid. Second, whatever control stockholders exercise may be affected if, as is typically the case, preferred stockholders have a right to elect directors in the event dividends are unpaid. Third, in the event the corporation is liquidated, preferred stockholders receive a liquidation preference before any assets can be distributed to commons.

Example 7

What if the proposed plan provides that additional shares of common stock will be issued to the bank creditors in satisfaction of their claims? Assume that the stock has the same designation, rights, limitations, and other attributes of the common stock issued prior to the commencement of the Chapter 11 case. Are the interests of holders of stock that was issued prepetition impaired?

The issuance of new common shares will dilute stockholders' proportional voting and ownership interests, thus their legal and equitable rights appear to be altered. Would the result be different if the certificate of incorporation did not provide for preemptive rights? What if the debtor corporation is governed by a statute such as New York Business Corporation Law § 622(e)? It provides that unless the certificate of incorporation provides otherwise, shares are not subject to preemptive rights if they "[a]re to be issued under a plan of reorganization approved in a proceeding under any applicable act of Congress relating to reorganization of corporations."

[C]   Undoing Acceleration and Curing Defaults; Code § 1124(2)

PROBLEM 9.3

Assume that during the cash-short-months before it commenced its Chapter 11 case, Amphydynamics missed several payments to the bank. While the case was pending, Amphydynamics made no payments to the bank. As the bank's rights have been altered by the default, Amphydynamics cannot leave the legal, equitable, and contractual rights of the bank unaltered. Hence, it can't leave the bank's claim unimpaired under § 1124(1). Is there any other treatment that Amphydynamics can provide that will leave the bank unimpaired? What if the loan agreement provided for acceleration of the entire loan balance in the event of a default? What if the loan was secured by a mortgage on the Amphydynamics factory, and the bank obtained a foreclosure judgment before the Chapter 11 petition was filed?

Consider § 1124(2), and the case and notes that follow.

IN RE MADISON HOTEL ASSOCIATES
United States Court of Appeals, Seventh Circuit
749 F.2d 410 (1984)

Before Pell, Coffey, Circuit Judges, and Nichols, Senior Circuit Judge.

Coffey, Circuit Judge.

[Madison Hotel Associates ("MHA"), a limited partnership, owned and operated a hotel in Madison, Wisconsin. Prudential held a $7,000,000 mortgage on the property. Under the terms of the loan agreement, MHA was obligated to pay Prudential monthly installments of principal and interest in the amount of $59,360. The note and the mortgage also provided that in the event of a default, Prudential could immediate accelerate the entire balance, including principal and accrued interest, and reasonable attorney's fees. Shortly after the hotel opened, it began experiencing cash flow and operating problems. Two years later, MHA defaulted on its monthly loan installment payments to Prudential. Prudential exercised its right on default to accelerate the loan and declare the entire amount due. Prudential commenced a foreclosure action in the United States District Court and obtained a judicial order of foreclosure. MHA filed a Chapter 11 petition, staying the foreclosure. Four months later, MHA filed its proposed plan of reorganization. In the plan, MHA proposed to cure defaults by paying the missed payments, and to undo the acceleration and reinstate the original maturity date of the loan. MHA also proposed to compensate Prudential for attorney's fees and other costs incurred in connection with the foreclosure proceeding.

All MHA creditors, except Prudential, voted to accept the reorganization plan. Prudential claimed, among other things, that since its claim was impaired by the plan, the plan could not be confirmed over Prudential's dissent. The bankruptcy court entered an order confirming the plan, from which Prudential appealed. The appeal was assigned to the same district court judge who two years earlier had authorized Prudential to foreclose. The district judge reversed the bankruptcy judge's holding that Prudential was not impaired. According to the district court:

> MHA's plan impairs Prudential's claim because it does not restore Prudential's judicially-recognized right to proceed with foreclosure . . . . And, because Prudential's right to foreclosure does not arise merely from a contractual provision or applicable law but is created by court order and is not simply a right to accelerated payments which can be cured, Prudential's claim does not fall within the exception created by § 1124(a). Therefore, Prudential cannot be deemed to have accepted MHA's plan under § 1126(f)
>
> . . . .

MHA appealed. The question before the Court of Appeals, therefore, was whether or not the plan left Prudential's claim unimpaired.]

We initially address the legal issue of whether Prudential's claim against MHA is impaired for purposes of § 1129(a)(8), which provides in pertinent part:

> "The court shall confirm a plan only if *all* of the following requirements are met:
>
> (8) with respect to each class
>
>   (A) such class has accepted the plan; or
>
>   (B) such class is not impaired under the plan."

(Emphasis added). The parties agree that Prudential, as holder of the first mortgage on MHA's realty, is the sole member of its class. Furthermore, it is clear that Prudential has not affirmatively accepted MHA's plan of reorganization. Thus, in order for MHA's Chapter 11 plan to satisfy the requirement of confirmation set forth in § 1129(a)(8), Prudential's claim must be one that is "not impaired" under the plan.

. . . .

[In § 1124] Congress "define[s] impairment in the broadest possible terms" and then carves out three narrow exceptions to that expansive definition. *In re Taddeo*, 685 F.2d 24, 28 (2d Cir. 1982). *See also In re Forest Hills Associates*, 40 Bankr. 410, 414 (Bankr. S.D.N.Y. 1984). These three exceptions, though narrow in scope, are of vital importance in a Chapter 11 reorganization because, pursuant to § 1126(f) (1982), "a class that is not impaired under a plan is *deemed* to have accepted the plan." (Emphasis added.) In the present case, MHA began to default on its loan payments in early 1976, Prudential accelerated the maturity of the loan in October of 1978, and Prudential obtained a judicial order of foreclosure in August of 1981. Before Prudential reduced that order to a judgment of foreclosure, MHA filed a Chapter 11 petition for reorganization. MHA's plan of reorganization seeks to cure the default of Prudential's accelerated loan and reinstate the maturity of that loan as it existed before the default.

It is well-recognized that a Chapter 11 debtor's plan of reorganization may cure the default of an accelerated loan. Title § 1123(a)(5)(G) (1982) provides that:

> "A plan shall —
>
> (5) provide adequate means for the plan execution, such as —
>
>   (G) Curing or waiving any default."

Thus, the issue before this court is whether MHA's plan to cure the accelerated Prudential loan satisfies the four-prong test set forth in § 1124(2); if so, Prudential's claim is not impaired for purposes of § 1129(a)(8) and Prudential is deemed to have accepted the plan.

According to the bankruptcy court, MHA's plan of reorganization did, in fact, satisfy the four-prong test of § 1124(2). The bankruptcy court initially found that MHA's plan cures the default, providing "for full payment to Prudential of the claim it has filed based on default. . . . " The court next found that even though the district court had entered an order of foreclosure, MHA's plan reinstates the maturity of Prudential's accelerated loan as such maturity existed before the default. In support of this position the bankruptcy court relied upon language in *In re Hewitt*, 16 Bankr. 973 (Bankr. D. Alaska 1982), that a secured creditor is not "harmed by the reversal of acceleration, . . . where a . . . court has simply applied the contractual provision or applicable law requiring acceleration and has embodied this application in a judgment of foreclosure." 16 Bankr. at 977. The court next found that the plan properly "provides for payment of allowed costs and fees incurred [by Prudential] in enforcing the default." Finally, the bankruptcy court found that none of Prudential's alleged alterations in rights, neither "individually, nor all of them taken as a group, are sufficient to demonstrate that Prudential would be impaired by the confirmation of the plan."

The district court disagreed with the bankruptcy court's analysis of section 1124(2). According to the district court, "MHA's plan impairs Prudential's claim because it does not restore Prudential's judicially-recognized right to proceed with foreclosure of the real and personal property of the Concourse Hotel." *In re Madison Hotel Associates*, 29 Bankr. at 1009. Contrary to the language of *In re Hewitt*, the district court reasoned that "[a] judicially-recognized right to foreclosure is something different from a right to accelerated payments that arises by operation of a contractual provision or of applicable law." *In re Madison Hotel Associates*, 29 Bankr. at 1008. Thus, the district court concluded that "because Prudential's right to foreclosure does not arise merely from a contractual provision or applicable law but is created by court order and is not simply a right to accelerated payments which can be cured, Prudential's claim does not fall within the exception created by § 1124(2)." *Id.* at 1009.

The question that arises is what effect the district court's order of foreclosure, entered pursuant to Wisconsin state law, has upon MHA's attempt to cure the default of its accelerated loan and thereby render Prudential's claim "not impaired" under § 1124(2). To resolve this question, we initially review the relevant statutory language and Congress' intent in enacting the "impairment" exception set forth in section 1124(2). The general rule is that a claim is impaired unless it falls within one of the . . . exceptions set forth in § 1124. In the present case, the applicable exception is found in section 1124(2) which provides that "curing a default, even though it inevitably changes a contractual acceleration clause, does not thereby 'impair' a creditor's claim." *In re Taddeo*, 685 F.2d at 28–29. Indeed:

> "Section 1124(2) permits the plan to reverse a contractual or legal acceleration. In order for a class of claims or interest[s] to be unimpaired for purposes of section 1124(2), the plan must cure any default, other than an ipso facto default of a kind specified in section 365(b)(2), irrespective of whether such default occurred prior to or after commencement of the case. In addition, the plan must provide for the payment of compensation to the holder of the claim or interest for any damages incurred as a result of any reasonable reliance by such holder on the contractual provisions or applicable law which permitted acceleration. Provided that the plan does not otherwise alter the legal, equitable, or contractual rights to which the holder of the claim or interest is entitled, *section 1124(2) permits the plan to reinstate the original maturity of the claim or interest as it existed before the default without impairing such claim or interest.*"

5 L. King, Collier on Bankruptcy para. 1124.03[2] at 1124-14 (15th ed. 1979)

(emphasis added) (footnote omitted). *See also In re Otero Mills, Inc.*, 31 Bankr. 185, 8 Collier Bankr. Cas. 2d (MB) 1340, 1342 (Bankr. D.N.M. 1983). It is clear that section 1124(2) "provides the debtor in distress with the statutory tools necessary to effect a total healing of the scars of contractual default, by placing the parties into the same position they were in immediately before the default occurred." *In re Forest Hills Associates*, 40 Bankr. at 415.

Congress, when enacting section 1124(2), expressly provided that:

"A claim or interest is unimpaired by curing the effect of a default and reinstating the original terms of an obligation when maturity was brought on or accelerated by the default. The intervention of bankruptcy and the defaults represent a temporary crisis which the plan of reorganization is intended to clear away. *The holder of a claim or interest who under the plan is restored to his original position, when others receive less or get nothing at all, is fortunate indeed and has no cause to complain. Curing the default and the assumption of the debt in accordance with its terms is an important reorganization technique for dealing with a particular class of claims, especially secured claims.*"

S. Rep. No. 989, 95th Cong., 2d Sess. 120, reprinted in 1978 U.S. Code Cong. & Ad. News 5787, 5906 (emphasis added). There is no doubt that section 1124(2) embodies Congress' intent to allow the Chapter 11 debtor to cure the default of an accelerated loan and reinstate the original terms of the loan agreement, without impairing the creditor's claim. In sum, Congress:

"quite appropriately concluded that a person that receives the benefits of its original bargain is not impaired even if the plan modifies such person's rights by preventing such person from using a contractual or legal right of acceleration to terminate a valuable contract of the debtor in circumstances where the debtor is willing to cure past defaults and perform under the original terms of the agreement."

5 L. King, Collier on Bankruptcy, supra, at 1124–14. *See also In re Masnorth Corp.*, 28 Bankr. 892, 894 (Bankr. N.D. Ga. 1983). The rationale underlying Congress' enactment of Chapter 11, including the "impairment" exception of section 1124(2), is the simple fact that reorganization is economically more efficient than liquidation. According to Congress:

"Often, the return on assets that a business can produce is inadequate to compensate those who have invested in the business. Cash flow problems may develop, and require creditors of the business, both trade creditors and long-term lenders, to wait for payment of their claims. If the business can extend or reduce its debts, it often can be returned to a viable state. It is more economically efficient to reorganize than to liquidate, because it preserves jobs and assets."

H.R. Rep. No. 595, 95th Cong., 1st Sess. 220, reprinted in 1978 U.S. Code Cong. & Ad. News 5963, 6179. Frequently, the interest rates on long-term loans are substantially less than the current market rate. Section 1124(2) promotes the economic efficiency of reorganization by allowing the Chapter 11 debtor to reinstate the original terms of an accelerated long-term loan at this lower interest rate. *See*

5 L. King, Collier on Bankruptcy, supra, at 1124-16. See also *In re Jones*, 32 Bankr. 951, 955 (Bankr. D. Utah 1983) ("Section 1124(2) . . . enables . . . retention of advantageous contract terms.").

The legislative history of section 1124(2) reveals that a creditor who is prevented from exercising a contractual and/or legal right of acceleration, but who receives the complete benefit of its original bargain with the debtor, is "not impaired" for purposes of Chapter 11 analysis. Relying upon this policy consideration, various courts have reasoned that if a debtor cures the default of an accelerated loan in compliance with section 1124(2), the creditor who holds a judgment of foreclosure is not impaired, provided that . . . no sale of foreclosure has occurred.

[In a portion of the opinion not reproduced here, the court attached some importance to the fact that, under Wisconsin law, the judgment of foreclosure did not merge the mortgage and judgment, and hence there was still in existence a mortgage that could be reinstated. Most courts have found that this merger doctrine irrelevant to §§ 1124(2) and 1123(a)(5)(G), and that a debt that has merged into a foreclosure judgment may still be decelerated and reinstated. *See, e.g., In re Singer Island Hotel, Ltd.*, 95 B.R. 845 (Bankr. S.D. Fla. 1989); *In re Valente*, 34 B.R. 804 (Bankr. D. Conn. 1982); King, 7 Collier on Bankruptcy ¶ 1124.03[6] (Matthew Bender 15th Ed. Revised 2000). — Eds.]

[In the leading case, *In re Hewitt*, the Alaska bankruptcy] court . . . reasoned that:

> "The secured creditor is no more harmed by the reversal of acceleration, and thus has as little cause to complain, where a . . . court has simply applied the contractual provision or applicable law requiring acceleration and has embodied this application in a judgment of foreclosure. The Congressional policy to relieve Chapter 11 debtors of the burdens of acceleration clauses should not be thwarted by the formal obtaining of a judgment."

Id. at 977. Accordingly, the court held that, "since application of the Congressional policy of § 1124(2) will not further add to the uncertainties of the state system, particularly where, as here, no foreclosure sale has been held, the policy should be given effect." *Id.* at 979.

Similarly, in *In re Orlando Tennis World Development Co.*, 34 Bankr. 558 (Bankr. M.D. Fla. 1983), the debtor defaulted on a loan, the creditor accelerated payments, and the creditor then obtained a judgment of foreclosure, which was subsequently stayed upon the debtor's filing of a Chapter 11 petition for reorganization. The debtor's Chapter 11 plan of reorganization sought to cure the default of the accelerated loan. The Florida bankruptcy court confirmed the plan, reasoning that the debtor was not impaired for purposes of section 1124(2) because under Florida law, "the finality of the judgment of foreclosure is always subject to the exercise of the equity of redemption, and it is the foreclosure sale rather than the entry of judgment which cuts off the mortgagor's rights." *Id.* at 560.

The point to be gleaned from the relevant case law is that a creditor, holding a final judgment of foreclosure, is not impaired under section 1124(2) if the debtor's plan of reorganization cures the default of the accelerated loan before the foreclosure sale actually occurs . . . .

The intended purpose of § 1124(2) is to permit a Chapter 11 debtor to cure the default of an accelerated loan, reinstate the maturity of that loan as it existed before default, and thereby "reverse a contractual or legal acceleration." 5 L. King, Collier on Bankruptcy, supra, at 1124-14. MHA's plan of reorganization clearly complies with Congressional intent. According to the bankruptcy court, MHA's plan of reorganization will cure the default of Prudential's accelerated loan, reinstate the maturity of Prudential's accelerated loan as it existed previous to the default, compensate Prudential for damages incurred as a result of reasonable reliance on the acceleration, and not alter legal, equitable, or contractual rights between MHA and Prudential. Prudential's contention that the default is not cured under MHA's plan because Prudential has an order of foreclosure that will not be reduced to final judgment, directly contravenes the purpose of § 1124(2) to allow a Chapter 11 debtor to reverse a contractual or legal acceleration. Indeed, Congress provides that, *"the holder of a claim or interest who under the plan is restored to his original position, when others receive less or get nothing at all, is fortunate indeed and has no cause to complain."* S. Rep. No. 989, 95th Cong., 2d Sess. 120, reprinted in 1978 U.S. Code Cong. & Ad. News 5787, 5906 (emphasis added). Thus, in light of the fact that Prudential holds only a lien upon MHA's property, and that MHA's plan of reorganization satisfies the four-prong test of § 1124(2), we hold that Prudential's claim is "not impaired." Accordingly, Prudential, as the sole member of its class, is deemed to have accepted the plan for purposes of § 1129(a)(8).

NOTES AND QUESTIONS

(1) Does Reinstatement and Cure Require Payment of Default Rate Interest?

Suppose that a loan agreement provides that in the event the borrower defaults, the entire balance will become due and bear interest at a default rate that is 10% higher than the rate otherwise payable under the agreement. Clearly, Code § 1124(2) permits the debtor to undo acceleration and reinstate the terms of the loan agreement if the debtor cures defaults. Does the debtor have to pay the higher rate of interest on defaulted payments in order to effectuate a cure? A number of courts have held that cure and deceleration "nullify all consequences of default, including . . . default penalties such as higher interest." *In re Southeast Co.,* 868 F.2d 335, 338 (9th Cir. 1989); *In re Entz-White Lumber and Supply, Inc.,* 850 F.2d 1338 (9th Cir. 1988); *In re Udhus,* 218 B.R. 513, 517 (B.A.P. 9th Cir. 1998). As the bankruptcy court explained in *Levy v. Forest Hills Assocs. (In re Forest Hills Assocs.),* 40 B.R. 410, 415 (Bankr. S.D.N.Y. 1984):

> It is . . . clear that Code section 1124(2) provides the debtor in distress with the statutory tools necessary to effect a total healing of the scars of contractual default, by placing the parties into the same position they were in immediately before the default occurred. This healing is accomplished by paying the creditor whatever monies he would have received under the contract had the debtor not defaulted. Therefore, just as the debtor need not pay the post-default accelerated debt, he need not pay the post-default interest rate on the accelerated debt. The creditor is, nevertheless,

rightfully categorized as unimpaired, for he is returned to the same position he was in immediately prior to the default, and is thereby given the full benefit of his original bargain.

See also U.S. Trust Co. v. LTV Steel Co. (In re Chateaugay Corp.), 150 B.R. 529, 542–43 (Bankr. S.D.N.Y. 1993), *aff'd*, 170 B.R. 551 (S.D.N.Y. 1994).

Two 1994 amendments to the Code have raised still unsettled questions about the continued vitality of such holdings as these. To understand why, a brief detour to § 365, governing the assumption and rejection of executory contracts, is required. As we saw in chapter 7, Code § 365(b)(1) generally provides that before a trustee may assume an executory contract, it must cure (or provide assurances that it will promptly cure) any defaults under the contract. However, not every kind of default has to be cured. The kinds that do not have to be cured are the kinds described in § 365(b)(2) — those having to do with the insolvency or financial condition of the debtor, the commencement of a bankruptcy case, or the appointment of a trustee or other custodian of the debtor's property. For example, some agreements provide that if a debtor files a bankruptcy petition or becomes insolvent, that, in and of itself, will constitute a default. These are defaults that, as a practical matter, cannot be cured because, having occurred, they cannot be undone. Recognizing this, § 365(b)(2) says that they don't have to be.

In 1994, Code § 365(b)(2) was expanded by the addition of a new subsection (D). The new subsection clarifies that, for § 365 purposes, curing a default under an executory contract does not require "the satisfaction of any penalty rate or provision relating to a default arising from any failure by the debtor to perform nonmonetary obligations under the executory contract." The reason that all this is significant in the context of impairment is that § 1124(2) incorporates § 365(b)(2) by reference. Code § 1124(2) allows for deceleration even though a nonmonetary default of the kind specified in § 365(b)(2) is not cured. However, if new subsection (D), as incorporated into § 1124(2), means that the debtor is not required to satisfy a penalty rate or provision relating to a *nonmonetary* default in order to cure, does the same provision by negative implication mean that a penalty rate or provision relating to a *monetary* default must be satisfied? If so, then it would seem that a debtor that misses some installment payments must pay post-default interest if the loan agreement provides for it in order to cure and decelerate and leave the claim unimpaired. *See In re 139–141 Owners Corp.*, 306 B.R. 763 (Bankr. S.D.N.Y. 2004).

The meaning of "cure" in this context has also been confused by an amendment that resulted from the efforts of Congress to overrule the Supreme Court's decision in *Rake v. Wade*, 508 U.S. 464, 466 (1993). In that case, a Chapter 13 debtor proposed to cure mortgage defaults by paying missed payments over the life of his Chapter 13 plan. The Court held that under Code §§ 1322(b)(5), 1325(a)(5), and § 506(b), an oversecured mortgagee is entitled to receive interest on arrearages including interest on interest — whether or not such interest was provided for in the loan agreement or is permitted under applicable nonbankruptcy law. Since payment of this interest — which might not have been bargained for by the creditor — could spell the difference between the success and failure of a Chapter 13 case, Congress added Code § 1322(e) to Chapter 13 and a parallel provision, § 1123(d), to Chapter 11. Code § 1123(d) provides that:

> Notwithstanding subsection (a) of this section and sections 506(b), 1129(a)(7), and 1129(b) of this title, if it is proposed in a plan to cure a default the amount necessary to cure the default shall be determined in accordance with the underlying agreement and applicable nonbankruptcy law.

This provision, which governs agreements entered into after the October 22, 1994 effective date of the 1994 Amendments, also could mean that in a cure situation under § 1124(2), a plan must pay higher post-default interest on missed installments and interest on interest, if the underlying agreement provides for it and nonbankruptcy law permits it. *In re Johnston*, 2004 Bankr LEXIS 2055 (Bankr. N.D. Iowa Dec. 20, 2004). *See generally* David Gray Carlson, *Rake's Progress: Cure and Reinstatement of Secured Claims in Bankruptcy Reorganization*, 13 Bank. Dev. J. 273 (1997); Kenneth N. Klee, *Adjusting Chapter 11: Fine Tuning the Plan Process*, 69 Am. Bankr. L.J. 551 (1995). In New York, for example, default interest provisions are generally enforceable:

> Parties use default interest rates as a means to compensate a lender for the administrative expenses and inconvenience in monitoring untimely payments. Because the costs incurred in performing this task will vary from case to case, the increased interest rate is a compromise by the lender and the borrower in recognition of the fact that attempting to quantify the exact dollar amount of the lender's injury would be impractical.

In re Vest Assocs., 217 B.R. 696, 701 (Bankr. S.D.N.Y. 1998). These increased costs include the increased cost of collection; the increased risk of non-collection; and risk to the collateral if there is any.

(2) Deadline for Curing Defaults

Although the Code does not specify a deadline, courts agree that in order for a claim or interest to be left unimpaired under § 1124(2), defaults must be cured by the "effective date of the plan, because the creditor is impaired until the time the default is cured." *In re Otero Mills, Inc.*, 31 B.R. 185 (Bankr. D.N.M. 1983). However, the term "effective date of the plan" though used in several sections of the Code (*see, e.g.*, §§ 1129; 1145), is not defined. Some courts and commentators have suggested that the effective date should mean the date of confirmation, King, 7 *Collier on Bankruptcy* ¶ 1124.LH.[2][a] (15th Edition Revised 2000); others have simply suggested that the effective date must bear some reasonable relationship to the confirmation date, *In re Potomac Iron Works, Inc.*, 217 B.R. 170, 173 (Bankr. D. Md. 1997); *In re Jones*, 32 B.R. 951, 957 (Bankr. D. Utah 1983); while others have suggested that it should be the first day after which the order confirming the plan becomes final. Kenneth N. Klee, *All You Ever Wanted to Know About Cram Down Under the New Bankruptcy Code*, 53 Am. Bankr. L.J. 133, 137 n. 24 (1979). More recently, Prof. Klee made the following recommendation to the Bankruptcy Review Commission:

> A few key provisions of § 1129 of the Code use the term "effective date" of a plan of reorganization without defining it. It is clear to most practitioners and others in the bankruptcy arena that the "effective date" may be a different date than the date of confirmation of the plan, and often plans

define the effective date. Nevertheless, it would be useful [to] enact a provision defining the term "effective date" to be the date on which the provisions of a plan of reorganization become effective and binding on the parties. The statute might also specify that the effective date bear some reasonable relationship to the confirmation hearing date. At the very least, § 1123(a) should be amended to require a plan to define its effective date. This all-important date should not be left to conjecture or undue manipulation.

Kenneth N. Klee, *Adjusting Chapter 11: Fine Tuning the Plan Process*, 69 Am. Bankr. L.J. 551, 560–61 (1995).

(3) Compensation for Damages Caused by Default

In order to leave a claim or interest unimpaired under Code § 1124(2), a plan must do more than cure defaults. It must also compensate the claim or interest holder for damages incurred as a result of its reasonable reliance on a contract provision or law entitling the holder to demand or receive accelerated payment. § 1124(2)(c). These damages have been held to include attorneys' fees and other collection costs, but not lost opportunity costs or higher default interest. *See, e.g., In re Udhus*, 218 B.R. 513, 517 (B.A.P. 9th Cir. 1998); *In re Orlando Tennis World Dev. Co.*, 34 B.R. 558, 560 (Bankr. M.D. Fla. 1983). Default interest has been acknowledged to be a form of liquidated damages intended to compensate a lender for the cost and inconvenience of monitoring and collecting problem loans. *See, e.g., In re Vest Assocs.*, 217 B.R. 696, 701 (Bankr. S.D.N.Y. 1998). If that is the case, should default interest be recoverable as damages under § 1124(2)(c)?

[D] Payment in Cash on the Effective Date of the Plan; Former § 1124(3)

Prior to its deletion in 1994, § 1124(3) provided one more way of leaving a claim or interest unimpaired. The following opinion is the reason that subsection (3) was eliminated from the Code.

IN RE NEW VALLEY CORPORATION
United States Bankruptcy Court, District of New Jersey
168 B.R. 73 (1994)

Novalyn L. Winfield, J.

[An involuntary bankruptcy petition was filed against New Valley by three individual bondholders on November 15, 1991. New Valley obtained extensions of its time to answer the involuntary petition while it attempted to negotiate a prepackaged plan with its creditors. The negotiations failed and an order or relief was entered on March 31, 1993. On January 25, 1994, the court denied the New Valley request to further extend exclusivity in light of New Valley's continued inability to negotiate a plan acceptable to its creditors, the objection of all the creditor groups to a further extension, and the fact that the creditors' committee and the Pension Benefit Guaranty Corporation were prepared to jointly propose a plan that appeared to be a meaningful alternative to the Debtor's plan. On February 16, 1994, New Valley filed a reorganization plan that provided, *inter alia*, that unsecured creditors' allowed claims would be paid in full on the effective date of the plan. The creditors insisted that inasmuch as New Valley was solvent, they were entitled to postpetition interest on their claims. The debtor moved for an order declaring that payment of allowed claims in full renders such claims unimpaired under § 1124(3), and that, accordingly, the Debtor was not obliged to pay postpetition interest on unimpaired claims.]

All parties agree that operationally New Valley has done extremely well during the debtor-in-possession period and that its going concern value is increasing. The parties additionally agree that because New Valley has prospered postpetition, on a going concern basis its value presently exceeds its liabilities. Indeed, it is precisely because of the apparent solvency of New Valley that postpetition interest has become an issue between New Valley and its creditor constituencies in their negotiations as to the terms of a plan of reorganization.

In essence, the Debtor objects to allowance of postpetition interest on any claim except as may be permitted under Code § 506(b). The New Valley objection rests on analysis of the interplay of sections 502(b)(2), 1124(3) and 1129(a)(7)(A) of the Bankruptcy Code and can be summarized as follows:

    i. Bankruptcy Code section 502(b)(2) specifically disallows claims for "unmatured" interest as part of a creditor's "allowed" claim.

    ii. Payment to creditors in cash of the allowed amount of their prepetition claims renders such creditors unimpaired pursuant to Bankruptcy Code section 1124. Pursuant to section 1126(f) unimpaired claims are deemed to accept the plan.

    iii. The "best interest of creditors" test in section 1129(a)(7)(A)(ii) does not require the payment of postpetition interest by a solvent debtor since by its plain language section 1129(a)(7)(a)(ii) only applied to impaired classes.

    iv. The Bankruptcy Code has specifically addressed those instances where postpetition interest may be paid on a claim. Accordingly, to the extent that pre-Code common law provided broader rights to post-petition interest than the rights specifically set forth in the Bankruptcy Code, such pre-Code law was abrogated by the Bankruptcy Code.

The Debtor claims that a determination from the court as to whether it must pay postpetition interest to unsecured (including undersecured) creditors is of critical importance at this stage of the case. . . . [I]t asserts that if postpetition interest is required to be paid on allowed claims it affects the Debtor's reorganization effort including its ability (i) to consummate its agreements with equity investors, (ii) to obtain financing commitments from underwriters, (iii) to provide adequate information in its proposed disclosure statement and (iv) to meet its responsibilities as a debtor-in-possession to negotiate, prosecute its plan of reorganization.

The Unsecured Committee and the Noteholders Committee have filed objections to the Debtor's motion based on the solvent debtor rule established by courts under the Bankruptcy Act. Essentially, the rule recognized that in the event of a debtor's solvency the rationale for not computing interest on claims against the estate had little vitality. Though the rule was not codified by the Bankruptcy Code the committees and the PBGC argue that it has continuing application.

CONCLUSIONS OF LAW

The obligation to pay postpetition interest.

In large measure the statutory analysis urged by the Debtor is persuasive. Resolution of the issue before the court requires that we focus upon the language of the pertinent sections of the Bankruptcy Code. Construction of a statute must begin with the language of that statute.

Section 502(b) provides in relevant part that if an objection is made to a claim, "the court, after notice and a hearing, shall determine the amount of such claim in lawful currency of the United States as of the date of the filing of the petition, and shall allow such claim in such amount . . . 502(b)(2) further provides that a claim is disallowed to the extent that "such claim is for unmatured interest." Thus, by the very terms of the section of the Bankruptcy Code which treats allowance of claims against the estate, post-petition interest is not an authorized element of an allowed claim. . . .

At the time of enactment of the Bankruptcy Code, this largely judicially crafted rule had a long and well-established history. . . . As described in the case law, this general rule facilitated case administration because it simplified distribution calculations, it permitted the equitable pro rata distribution of the debtor's assets, and the payment delay resulted not from the debtor's actions but by application of the law for the mutual benefit of creditors. . . .

The Bankruptcy Act case law also recognized an exception to this general rule, and authorized the payment of interest where the debtor was solvent. . . .

Thus, the solvent debtor exception to non-payment of post-petition interest was equally well-established at the time of enactment of the Bankruptcy Code, and Congress can be presumed to have been fully aware of its existence. Interestingly, a related rule of Bankruptcy Act case law, which recognized the appropriateness of payment of post-petition interest to an oversecured creditor was codified in section 506(b). Importantly, while both the rule regarding unmatured interest and the rule regarding payment of interest to oversecured creditors are codified in a Bankruptcy Code chapter of general applicability, the solvent debtor exception is not so codified. Rather, the issue of a debtor's solvency is treated somewhat differently in the operative chapters of the Bankruptcy Code.

In Chapter 7, post-petition interest is paid as a fifth priority of distribution under section 726(a)(6). Consistent with section 502(b)(2) the post-petition interest is not a component of an allowed claim, but is paid from the petition date on claims allowed under subsections (a)(1) through (a)(4). Thereafter, pursuant to section 726(a)(5) any surplus is paid to the debtor.

A "best interest of creditors" test is codified in sections 1225(a)(4) and 1325(a)(4) so that a Chapter 12 plan or a Chapter 13 plan must provide that each allowed unsecured claim receive at least the amount that would be paid on such claim if the debtor's estate were liquidated under Chapter 7. Thus, if a debtor's estate is sufficient to pay post-petition interest in the event of liquidation, the debtor must similarly pay post-petition interest under a Chapter 12 or Chapter 13 plan.

The "best interest of creditors" test is activated somewhat differently in Chapter 11 than in Chapter 12 or Chapter 13. The test is found in section 1129(a)(7)(A). Pursuant to that subsection, to confirm a Chapter 11 plan each member of an impaired class of claims or interests must either have accepted the plan or retain or receive property that has a value not less than they would receive if the debtor were liquidated under Chapter 7.

Thus, post-petition interest must be paid to dissenting members of impaired classes under a Chapter 11 plan if they would receive post-petition interest pursuant to section 726(a)(5) in a Chapter 7 liquidation. The terms of the subsection are straightforward, and the court concurs with the debtor that a plain and sensible reading of section 1129(a)(7)(A)(ii) yields the conclusion that an unimpaired class is not protected by the "best interest of creditors" test.

This conclusion is reinforced if sections 1129(a)(7)(A), 1124(3), and 502(b)(2) are read together. When one does so, it is evident that the "best interest of creditors" test does not apply to require a solvent Chapter 11 debtor to pay post-petition interest to creditors whose allowed claims are unimpaired. As noted earlier, section 502(b)(2) disallows unmatured interest as a component of an allowed claim. Thus, by definition a creditor's allowed claim can equal no more than the principal amount of the claim together with such interest as accrued as of the date of the bankruptcy petition. Further, pursuant to section 1124(3) if each member of a class of claims receives full payment of its pre-petition allowed claim in cash, on the effective date of the plan, the class is unimpaired. Because the class is unimpaired by virtue of the full satisfaction of so much of its claim as is allowable against the bankruptcy estate by operation of section 502(b)(2), it does not receive the benefit of section 1129(a)(7)(A) which addresses only impaired classes.

The non-applicability of the "best interest of creditors" test to unimpaired classes is further evidenced by the modifications made to sections 1126(f) and 1129(a)(7) by the Bankruptcy Amendments and Federal Judgeship Act of 1984 (BAFJA). Section 1126(f) was amended to make it clear that not only is an unimpaired class conclusively presumed to have accepted the plan, but also each holder of a claim or interest is similarly conclusively presumed to have accepted the plan. The purpose of the amendment was to overrule the cases which had found the presumption of acceptance rebuttable if a majority of the unimpaired class nonetheless voted to reject the plan. 5 Collier on Bankruptcy Para. 1126.06[a][2] (15th ed. 1993). Congress also made a corresponding adjustment to section 1129(a)(7)(A). Prior to amendment, the section simply was applicable "with respect to each class of claims or interest." The BAFJA amendment modified the phrase so that it now is applicable "with respect to each *impaired* class of claims or interest." (emphasis supplied). The purpose of the amendment is to clarify that the provisions of the subsection and the "best interest of creditors" test apply only to impaired classes. 5 Collier on Bankruptcy Para. 1129.01[a] (15th ed. 1993).

Moreover, in light of the comprehensive statutory framework described above, this court can only conclude that the non-applicability of the "best interest of creditors" test to unimpaired classes of claims or interests was a deliberate policy choice by the framers of the Bankruptcy Code. This conclusion is reinforced by the fact that the other reorganization chapters, Chapters 12 and 13, include a statutory "best interest of creditors" provision which is not limited by whether a claim is impaired.

The fact that the legislative history does not contain a reference to modification of the solvent debtor rule does not compel the conclusion that Congress intended that it survive the enactment of the Code. Where Congress has fully addressed a matter in the statute there is no need to resort to the legislative history or pre-Code case law. Where the statutory language is clear, the "sole function . . . is to enforce it according to its terms." *United States v. Ron Pair Enters., Inc.*, 489 U.S. 235, 241, 109 S. Ct. 1026, 1030, 103 L. Ed. 2d 290 (1989) . . . .

Thus, this court concludes that a Chapter 11 debtor that proposes a plan that provides for payment of the allowed claims in full, in cash, on the effective date of its plan is not compelled to pay postpetition interest merely because it is solvent.

NOTES AND QUESTIONS

Although *New Valley* was correctly decided — only impaired classes whose members do not unanimously vote in favor of a plan are entitled to the protection of the best interests test embodied in § 1129(a)(7) — Congress believed the result was unfair to creditors in cases involving solvent debtors. To avoid the *New Valley* result in the future, Congress amended § 1124 by deleting subsection (3) in its entirety. The House Committee explained:

> As a result of this change, if a plan proposed to pay a class of claims in cash in the full allowed amount of the claims, the class would be impaired entitling creditors to vote for or against the plan of reorganization. If creditors vote for the plan of reorganization, it can be confirmed over the vote of dissenting individual creditors only if it complies with the "best interests of creditors" test under section 1129(a)(7) of the Bankruptcy Code. . . .

> With respect to section 1124(1) and (2), [the deletion] would not change the beneficial [1984 amendment] to section 1129(a)(7) . . . which excluded from application of the best interest of creditors test classes that are unimpaired under section 1124.

140 Cong. Rec. H10,764, H10,768 (daily ed. October 4, 1994).

§ 9.05 THE INTERSECTION OF IMPAIRMENT AND CLASSIFICATION: THE ONE IMPAIRED ACCEPTING CLASS REQUIREMENT; WHAT CODE § 1111(B) DOES TO CLAIMS, AND WHY

As we have seen, every reorganization plan is required to organize claims and interests into classes, Code § 1123(a)(1), and to specify the treatment of any class that is impaired under the plan, § 1123(a)(3). In § 9.04, above, we considered Code

§ 1124 and the meaning of impairment. In § 9.06, below, we will turn to Code § 1122 and the principles governing classification. Before we do, we first lift the curtain on Code §§ 1111(b) and 1129(a)(10), because some familiarity with those sections, and the case law that engendered them, is essential to understanding some of the problems that arise under the rubric of classification. In a sense, they are the bridge between impairment and classification.

Many students, and lawyers, find § 1111(b) difficult to fathom. We think this is not because the language of § 1111(b) is so cryptic (it is; however, law students are used to dealing with cryptic language), but rather because the effect of § 1111(b) is so counterintuitive. The discussion that follows should make it less so.

Sections 1111(b) and 1129(a)(10) are the products of two bankruptcy court opinions that sent shock waves through the real estate lending communities in the late 1970s. Both were decided under Chapter XII of the former Bankruptcy Act, which governed "Real Estate Arrangements." Chapter XII was a seldom-used hybrid of Chapters X and XI, designed for use by noncorporate debtors, including partnerships and individuals, for the restructuring of debts secured by real property. Noncorporate real estate debtors were ineligible for relief in Chapter X, because Chapter X was open only to corporations. They could not restructure mortgage debt in Chapter XI, because Chapter XI provided only for the restructuring of unsecured debt. Chapter XII was intended to fill the gap, but until the late 1970s it was, for several reasons, rarely invoked. One reason is that prior to that time, many distressed real estate debtors were corporations eligible for Chapter X relief; they did not need Chapter XII. Another reason is that Chapter XII contained some unappealing provisions. As originally enacted, Chapter XII required that a plan be filed with the petition. It also provided for the immediate appointment of a trustee. By the mid-1970s, however, the financial landscape had changed and Chapter XII had been liberalized. The trustee and contemporaneous plan filing requirements were eliminated. Limited partnerships had become a highly popular if not the dominant vehicle for investing in real estate, and, as one worried commentator at the time noted, "From one end of the country to the other real estate [was] in trouble." Robert K. Lifton, *Real Estate in Trouble: Lender's Remedies Need an Overhaul*, 31 Bus. Law. 1927 (1976).

The first of the controversial Chapter XII opinions that led to the enactment of §§ 1111(b) and 1129(a)(10) was *In re Pine Gate Assocs., Ltd.*, 1976 U.S. Dist. LEXIS 17366 (Bankr. N.D. Ga. Oct. 14, 1976). The debtor was a limited partnership that owned and operated an apartment complex. The debtor's plan divided creditors among several classes. The sole creditor in class one was the lender who held a nonrecourse mortgage on the apartment complex.

You may have noticed that then, as now, in most single asset real estate cases, the debtor is a limited partnership and the mortgage is nonrecourse. There is a reason that these two elements are present in so many cases. The popularity of the limited partnership is directly related to the "pass through" or "conduit" nature of the partnership's tax attributes. A partnership does not, itself, pay taxes. Instead, partnership income or loss is allocated among individual partners who do pay taxes. A nonrecourse mortgage is one that limits the mortgagee to the value of the collateral for the satisfaction of its claim. If the amount of the claim exceeds the value of the collateral — i.e., if the claim is undersecured — the mortgagee cannot pursue other assets of the debtor (or other assets of the partners, if the debtor is a partnership) to satisfy any deficiency. In contrast, a creditor that holds a recourse mortgage can pursue other assets of the partnership or its partners in addition to the collateral to satisfy any deficiency. You may be wondering why lenders would agree to a deal on nonrecourse terms. The answer is that for tax reasons, unless the mortgage is nonrecourse, there is no deal. If the mortgage is a recourse mortgage and there is a default, only the general partner is personally liable for a deficiency judgment; the limited partners are liable only to the extent of their cash investments in the limited partnership. Accordingly, the Internal Revenue Code limits the depreciation deduction that limited partners can use to shelter other income to the amount of their investment. The bulk of the deduction is allocated to the general partner who stands to bear the economic burden of satisfying a deficiency in the case of a default. On the other hand, if the mortgage is a nonrecourse mortgage and there is a default, the general partners are no more personally liable than the limited partners. As a result, if the mortgage is nonrecourse, the Internal Revenue Code permits the limited and general partners to share the depreciation deduction ratably, based on their share of profits of the partnership. This is why investors will not invest in a real estate limited partnership unless the mortgage is nonrecourse. *See* David Gray Carlson, *Artificial Impairment and the Single Asset Chapter 11 Case*, 23 Capital U.L. Rev. 339, 342 (1994).

In its plan, the debtor proposed to do a refinancing and cash out the mortgagee by paying it the appraised value of the apartment complex. The mortgagee contended that the plan could not be confirmed over its objection — could not be crammed down — unless the plan provided for the payment of the full amount of the debt, which far exceeded the value of the apartment complex that secured it. Bankruptcy Judge Norton, probably correctly interpreting the statute as it was then written, disagreed. The relevant Act section provided that in order for a Chapter XII plan of arrangement to be confirmed, it had to be accepted by "the creditors of each class, holding two-thirds in amount of such debts of such class," former Act § 468(1), but Chapter XII also provided that the plan could be confirmed even if fewer than two-thirds accepted, if the plan:

> shall provide for any class of creditors which is affected by and does not accept the arrangement . . . adequate protection for the realization by them of the *value of their debts* . . . by appraisal and payment in cash of the *value of such debts*.

Former Act § 461(11) (emphasis supplied). Judge Norton found that the *value* of the debt — as opposed to the *amount* of the debt — was all the nonaccepting mortgagee was entitled to receive:

> Clearly the property which is security for the debts owed to Class I creditors cannot result in those creditors being given greater protection than the value of the security. As a hypothetical example, if the security is worth $100,000 fairly valued, it is absurd to say that § 461(11)(c) requires payment of $200,000 because the debt is that amount. To arrive at such a result, one would have to contend that the property is worth more than the property is worth. . . . By specific provision in the loan agreements . . . the

Class I creditors have contractually limited themselves to looking to the value of their security to satisfy their debts. They may not look to other assets of the debtor. . . . The Class I creditors are not entitled to vote as unsecured creditors . . . because they have contractually limited their claim to the value of the property.

Id. at 595–602.

Judge Norton did express some reservations about whether a plan could be confirmed when the sole dissenting creditor is also the debtor's sole creditor. A few months later, in *In re Marietta Cobb Apartments*, 1977 Bankr. LEXIS 17 (Bankr. S.D.N.Y. Sept. 9, 1977), Judge Babitt strolled in where Judge Norton was reluctant to tread. He held that a Chapter XII plan could be confirmed via the cramdown route, even though the debtor's only creditor had voted against the plan. The debtor proposed to cash the secured creditor out not by paying the value of the debts in full, at once, but rather by a series of payments, plus interest, over time. The mortgagee voted to reject the plan and contended that since it was the only creditor in its class (and in fact the debtor's only creditor), the court could not confirm the plan over its dissent. Judge Babitt disagreed.

Although, as Judge Babitt pointed out, the statute was "not a model of sparkling, clear prose," he reasoned that if he could not confirm a plan over such a lone mortgagee's dissent, Chapter XII was inherently flawed, because:

> there can be no Chapter XII case where, as here, the sole secured creditor rejects the debtor's plan. And, moreover, a secured creditor, unlike Caesar's Gaul, cannot be divided into three parts to provide a two-thirds assent. Accordingly . . . the snug harbor of Chapter XII becomes unavailable to the harassed real estate partnership or individual dealing with but one recalcitrant mortgagee . . . . As Chapter X is unavailable because it deals with corporate debtors, as is Chapter XI because it is designed to deal with unsecured creditors, it follows that none of the debtor relief chapters of the National Act touching insolvency avails this debtor partnership in its hoped for dialogue with . . . its mortgagee.
>
>   . . . .
>
> The tyranny of such a situation is simply unacceptable for it cuts against the grain of the purpose of the debtor relief aspects of Chapter XII — its rehabilitation and emergence from this court at peace. That the words Congress wrote to achieve this desired result do not, at first blush, seem to accomplish this result, merely means that at second blush this court will. The rub is that Congress sought that end in 1938 in a different world. The end is the same although the world has changed. That end is achieved by my holding that, notwithstanding the dissent of the sole secured creditor, confirmation may still be had . . . .

14 C.B.C. at 510.

Now consider again Judge Norton's example of the creditor who holds a $200,000 claim secured by a mortgage on an apartment complex worth $100,000. Suppose that the debtor, anticipating or hoping that the real estate market will strengthen in a year, files a plan that provides that the debtor will pay the mortgagee $100,000 and that the debtor will retain the property. If the debtor's predictions are correct, then only the debtor will enjoy the benefits of the increase in value. One might argue that the secured creditor is getting what it bargained for — the price the property would have fetched in a foreclosure sale — since the mortgage was nonrecourse. On the other hand, outside of bankruptcy, the secured creditor would have had the option of selling the property in a down market or holding it for future appreciation. Of that choice, it was deprived. Real estate lenders attacked the *Pine Gate* and *Marietta Cobb* opinions as unfair because they permitted debtors to retain their interest in mortgaged real estate by paying mortgagees fire sale prices.

Code §§ 1129(a)(10) and 1111(b) were intended to prevent this result by making it much more difficult and in some cases impossible for a debtor to "cash out" a secured creditor by dealing only with the Code § 506(a) amount of the secured claim and ignoring the deficiency claim.

First, § 1129(a)(10) provides that if a class of claims is impaired under a plan, at least one impaired class must vote to accept the plan in order for the plan to be confirmable. Thus, the *Marietta Cobb* result no longer is possible: A plan cannot be confirmed even by means of cramdown, if all impaired classes reject it, or, as in a typical single asset case, the mortgagee votes no. As one court explained:

> Section 1129(a)(10) operates as a statutory gatekeeper barring access to cram down where there is absent even one impaired class accepting the plan. Cram down is a powerful remedy available to plan proponents under which dissenting classes are compelled to rely on difficult judicial valuations, judgments, and determinations. The policy underlying Section 1129(a)(10) is that before embarking upon the tortuous path of cram down and compelling the target of cram down to shoulder the risks of error necessarily associated with a forced confirmation, there must be some other properly classified group that is also hurt and nonetheless favors the plan. As a bankruptcy court so aptly summed up:

>> In short, [under § 1129(a)(10)] there must be someone other than the debtor, other than the insiders, and other than the target of the cram down, who cares enough about the reorganization and whose rights must also be considered to invoke the equitable grounds that justify resort to cram down. If cramdown is not available, it is pointless to further consider a plan which requires cramdown for its success. Because the reorganization which these Debtors contemplate is not possible, it follows as a matter of logic that the Debtors have failed to carry their burden that an effective reorganization is possible.

In re 266 Washington Assocs., 141 B.R. 275, 287 (Bankr. E.D.N.Y. 1992), *aff'd sub nom. 266 Washington Assocs. v. Citibank (In re 266 Washington Assocs.)*, 147 B.R. 827 (E.D.N.Y. 1992); *quoting In re Anderson Oaks (Phase I) Ltd. P'ship.*, 77 B.R. 108, 112–113 (Bankr. W.D. Tex. 1987).

Second, § 1111(b) makes it more difficult for debtors (or other plan proponents) to cash out a secured creditor by payment of the appraised value of the secured claim. Section 1111(b)(1)(A), which is applicable only in Chapter 11 cases, provides that except in certain situations, a secured claim will be treated as a recourse claim whether or not the claim is recourse or non-recourse in fact. This means that an undersecured non-recourse creditor will have an allowed unsecured claim against the debtor for the deficiency, notwithstanding that the underlying obligation was nonrecourse. So, to use Judge Norton's example once again, a creditor whose $200,000 claim is secured by a nonrecourse mortgage on an apartment building worth $100,000 would, under § 1111(b)(1)(A), hold a secured claim of $100,000 and an unsecured claim of $100,000.

Section 1111(b)(1)(A) provides that the right of a secured creditor to have its claim treated as a recourse claim terminates, if the creditor "elects" to have its claim treated in accordance with § 1111(b)(2). Section 1111(b)(2) in turn provides that if an "election" is made, then notwithstanding § 506(a) — which as by now we well know bifurcates an undersecured claim into a secured claim and an unsecured claim — that undersecured claim will be treated as if it were fully secured. This means that an electing undersecured creditor will lose its unsecured deficiency claim for the deficiency but that its secured claim will be measured not by the value of the collateral, but by the amount of the debt. To return to Judge Norton's example once again, a creditor whose $200,000 claim is secured by a nonrecourse mortgage on an apartment building worth $100,000 would, if it elects treatment under § 1111(b)(2), hold a secured claim of $200,000 and no unsecured claim.

Whether an undersecured creditor should elect to be treated as fully secured or to assert an unsecured deficiency claim is a strategic decision. The considerations that go into the decision will become apparent as the balance of this chapter unfolds.

§ 9.06 CLASSIFICATION

PROBLEM 9.4

You will recall that at the beginning of this Chapter, Headley Charisma met with creditors to outline the elements of a reorganization plan. Assume that in light of the resistance he encountered from unsecured creditors, he modified his proposal and called another meeting of the Unsecured Creditors' Committee. At the meeting, he explains that as much as he would like, the company obviously can't afford to pay all unsecured claims in cash, in full, immediately. However, Headley heard what was said at the last meeting, and he does want to propose a plan that takes into account the needs of particular creditors as well as their role in the company's future. Accordingly, Headley says that the debtor is now considering a plan that provides the following: Unsecured bank claims and trade claims will be placed in separate classes. On the effective date of the plan, unsecured trade creditors will receive not 25%, but 45% of their claims in cash. Bank creditors will receive 25% of their claims in cash, an additional 10% of their claims in 10-year notes, and an additional 20% in common stock of the reorganized company. Creditors holding claims of $3,000 or less and creditors holding larger claims who are willing to reduce their claims to $3,000 will be placed in a separate "convenience class" and receive payment in cash of the full amount of their claims on the plan's effective date.

Is this classification scheme permissible? Read Code § 1122 and the materials that follow.

PHOENIX MUTUAL LIFE INSURANCE COMPANY v. GREYSTONE III JOINT VENTURE
United States Court of Appeals for the Fifth Circuit
995 F.2d 1274 (1991)

JUDGE JONES, CIRCUIT JUDGE.

This appeal pits a debtor whose only significant asset is an office building in the troubled Austin, Texas real estate market against a lender who possesses a multi-million dollar lien on the property. After obtaining bankruptcy relief under Chapter 11, Greystone III proposed a "cramdown" plan of reorganization, hoping to force a write-down of over $3,000,000 on the secured lender's note and to retain possession and full ownership of the property. Over the secured lender's strenuous objections, the bankruptcy court confirmed the debtor's plan. *In re Greystone III Joint Venture*, 102 B.R. 560 (W.D. Tex. 1989). On appeal, the district court upheld the bankruptcy court's judgment. 127 B.R. 138.

[The term *cramdown* refers to the power of the Bankruptcy Court to confirm a plan even though one or more classes of claims or interests vote against the plan. Cramdown is discussed in detail in § 9.10 of this chapter. — Eds.]

[W]e must reverse. First, the Greystone plan impermissibly classified like creditors in different ways and manipulated classifications to obtain a favorable vote.

. . . .

I.

Appellant Phoenix Mutual Life Insurance Corporation ("Phoenix") lent $8,800,000, evidenced by a non-recourse promissory note secured by a first lien, to Greystone to purchase the venture's office building. When Greystone defaulted on the loan, missing four payments, Phoenix posted the property for foreclosure. Greystone retaliated by filing a Chapter 11 bankruptcy reorganization petition. No issue concerning the "good faith" of Greystone's Chapter 11 filing has been raised in the papers pertinent to this appeal.

At the date of bankruptcy Greystone owed Phoenix approximately $9,325,000 [and] trade creditors approximately $10,000 . . . . The bankruptcy court valued Phoenix's secured claim at $5,825,000, the appraised value of the office building, leaving Phoenix an unsecured deficiency of approximately $3,500,000 — the difference between the aggregate owed Phoenix and its secured claim.

As filed, Greystone's Second Amended Plan of Reorganization (the "Plan"), the confirmation of which is challenged in this appeal, separately classified the Code-created unsecured deficiency claim of Phoenix Mutual, *see* § 1111(b), and the unsecured claims of the trade creditors. The Plan proposed to pay Phoenix and the trade creditors slightly less than four cents on the dollar for their unsecured claims, but it also provided that Greystone's general partner would satisfy the balance of the trade creditors' claims after confirmation of the Plan.

. . . .

Finally, Greystone's Plan contemplated a $500,000 capital infusion by the debtor's partners, for which they would reacquire 100% of the equity interest in the reorganized Greystone.

Unsurprisingly, Phoenix rejected this Plan, while the trade creditors . . . voted to accept it. On January 27, 1989, the bankruptcy court held a confirmation hearing at which the Debtor orally modified its Plan to delete the statements that the general partner would pay the balance of trade debt . . . after confirmation. A Phoenix representative testified that the insurance company was willing to fund its own plan of reorganization by paying off all unsecured creditors in cash in full after confirmation. The bankruptcy court refused to consider this proposal and then confirmed Greystone's modified Plan. The district court upheld the confirmation.

Phoenix Mutual now appeals on several grounds: (a) the plan classified Phoenix's unsecured deficiency claim separately from that of other unsecured creditors for no valid reason. . . .

II.

Phoenix first attacks Greystone's classification of its unsecured deficiency claim in a separate class from that of the other unsecured claims against the debtor. This issue benefits from some background explanation.

Chapter 11 requires classification of claims against a debtor for two reasons. Each class of creditors will be treated in the debtor's plan of reorganization based upon the similarity of its members' priority status and other legal rights against the debtor's assets. § 1122. Proper classification is essential to ensure that creditors with claims of similar priority against the debtor's assets are treated similarly. Second, the classes must separately vote whether to approve a debtor's plan of reorganization. § 1129(a)(8), (10). A plan may not be confirmed unless either (1) it is approved by two-thirds in amount and more than one-half in number of each "impaired" class, §§ 1126(c), 1129(a)(8); or (2) at least one impaired class approves the plan, § 1129(a)(10), and the debtor fulfills the cramdown requirements of § 1129(b) to enable confirmation notwithstanding the plan's rejection by one or more impaired classes. Classification of claims thus affects the integrity of the voting process, for, if claims could be arbitrarily placed in separate classes, it would almost always be possible for the debtor to manipulate "acceptance" by artful classification.

In this case, Greystone's plan classified the Phoenix claim in separate secured and unsecured classes, a dual status afforded by § 1111(b) despite the nonrecourse nature of Phoenix's debt. Because of Phoenix's opposition to a reorganization, Greystone knew that its only hope for confirmation lay in the Bankruptcy Code's cramdown provision. § 1129(b). . . . Procedurally, Greystone faced a dilemma in deciding how to obtain the approval of its cramdown plan by at least one class of "impaired" claims, as the Code requires.

An impaired claim is defined at § 1124. For present purposes, it suffices to say that Phoenix was impaired both as a secured and unsecured creditor. § 1129(a)(10). Greystone anticipated an adverse vote of Phoenix's secured claim. If the Phoenix $3.5 million unsecured deficiency claim shared the same class as Greystone's other unsecured trade claims, it would swamp their $10,000 value in voting against confirmation. The only other arguably impaired class consisted of tenant security deposit claims, which, the bankruptcy court found, were not impaired at all.

Greystone surmounted the hurdle by classifying Phoenix's unsecured deficiency claim separately from the trade claims, although both classes were to be treated alike under the plan and would receive a cash payment equal to 3.42% of each creditor's claim. Greystone then achieved the required favorable vote of the trade claims class.

Phoenix contends that Greystone misapplied § 1122 by classifying its unsecured claim separately from those of trade creditors. The lower courts rejected Phoenix's argument in three steps. First, they held that § 1122 of the Code does not unambiguously prevent classification of like claims in separate classes. The only question is what types of class differentiations among like claims are acceptable. Second, Greystone's unsecured deficiency claim is "legally different" from that of the trade claims because it arises statutorily, pursuant to § 1111(b). Third, "good business reasons" justify the separate classification of these unsecured claims. We must address each of these arguments.

Section 1122 prescribes classification of claims for a reorganization as follows:

> (a) Except as provided in subsection (b) or this section, a plan may place a claim or an interest in a particular class only if such claim or interest is substantially similar to the other claims or interests of such claims.
>
> (b) A plan may designate a separate class of claims consisting only of every unsecured claim that is less than or reduced to an amount that the court approves as reasonable and necessary for administrative convenience.

We observe from this language that the lower courts' suggestion that § 1122 does not prevent classification of like claims in separate classes is oversimplified. It is true that § 1122(a) in terms only governs permissible inclusions of claims in a class rather requiring that all similar claims be grouped together. One cannot conclude categorically that § 1122(a) prohibits the formation of different classes from similar types of claims. But if § 1122(a) is wholly permissive regarding the creation of such classes, there would be no need for § 1122(b) specifically to authorize a class of smaller unsecured claims, a common feature of plans in reorganization cases past and present.

Greystone has never sought to justify its separate class of trade creditors under § 1122(b), nor did the lower courts employ that provision in their analysis. There is no suggestion in the Code, however, that a class may be created under § 1122(b) in order to manipulate the outcome of the vote on a plan, rather than simply to enhance administration of the plan.

The broad interpretation of § 1122(a) adopted by the lower courts would render

§ 1122(b) superfluous, a result that is anathema to elementary principles of statutory construction.

Section 1122 consequently must contemplate some limits on classification of claims of similar priority. A fair reading of both subsections suggests that ordinarily "substantially similar claims," those which share common priority and rights against the debtor's estate, should be placed in the same class. Section 1122(b) expressly creates one exception to this rule by permitting small unsecured claims to be classified separately from their larger counterparts if the court so approves for administrative convenience. The lower courts acknowledged the force of this narrow rather than totally permissive construction of § 1122 by going on to justify Greystone's segregation of the Phoenix claim. Put otherwise, the lower courts essentially found that Phoenix's unsecured deficiency claim is not "substantially similar" to those of the trade creditors.

Those courts did not, however, adhere to the one clear rule that emerges from otherwise muddled case law on § 1122 claims classification: thou shalt not classify similar claims differently in order to gerrymander an affirmative vote on a reorganization plan. As the Sixth Circuit observed:

> There must be some limit on a debtor's power to classify creditors in such a manner. . . . Unless there is some requirement of keeping similar claims together, nothing would stand in the way of a debtor seeking out a few impaired creditors (or even one such creditor) who will vote for the plan and placing them in their own class.

In re U.S. Truck Co., 800 F.2d 581, 586 (6th Cir. 1986). *See also . . . Hanson v. First Bank of South Dakota*, 828 F.2d 1310, 1313 (8th Cir. 1987) . . . . We agree with this rule, and if Greystone's proffered "reasons" for separately classifying the Phoenix deficiency claim simply mask the intent to gerrymander the voting process, that classification scheme should not have been approved.

We conclude that if § 1122(a) permits classification of "substantially similar" claims in different classes, such classification may only be undertaken for reasons independent of the debtor's motivation to secure the vote of an impaired, assenting class of claims. To those proffered reasons we now turn.

Greystone contends that the "legal difference" between Phoenix's deficiency claim and the trade creditors' claims is sufficient to sustain its classification scheme. The alleged distinction between the legal attributes of the unsecured claims is that under state law Phoenix has no recourse against the debtor personally. However, state law is irrelevant where, as here, the Code has eliminated the legal distinction between non-recourse deficiency claims and other unsecured claims. *See* § 1111(b)(1)(A); *In re Tampa Bay Associates, Ltd.*, 864 F.2d 47 (5th Cir.1989); *Hanson*, 828 F.2d at 1313.

Greystone argues that *Hanson* is not controlling because the issue there was whether it was clearly erroneous for the bankruptcy court to deny separate classification whereas the issue here is whether it was clearly erroneous for the court to approve the classification. The clearly erroneous rule has no application in this context. Whether a deficiency claim is legally similar to an unsecured trade claim turns not on fact findings but on their legal characteristics. This is an issue of law, freely reviewable on appeal. Subsidiary fact findings however, may be entitled to the deference of the clearly erroneous test. *Id.*

The purpose of § 1111(b) is to provide an undersecured creditor an election with respect to the treatment of its deficiency claim. Generally, the creditor may elect recourse status and obtain the right to vote in the unsecured class, or it may elect to forego recourse to gain an allowed secured claim for the entire amount of the debt. If separate classification of unsecured deficiency claims arising from non-recourse debt were permitted solely on the ground that the claim is non-recourse under state law, the right to vote in the unsecured class would be meaningless. Plan proponents could effectively disenfranchise the holders of such claims by placing them in a separate class and confirming the plan over their objection by cramdown. With its unsecured voting rights effectively eliminated, the electing creditor's ability to negotiate a satisfactory settlement of either its secured or unsecured claims would be seriously undercut. It seems likely that the creditor would often have to "elect" to take an allowed secured claim under § 1111(b)(2) in the hope that the value of the collateral would increase after the case is closed.

In this case, for example, Greystone proposed to extinguish Phoenix's $3,500,000 deficiency claim by the promised payment of $140,000. Under the valuation process, it confined Phoenix's secured claim to $5.8 million. § 506(a). Phoenix obviously objects to this arrangement because, in the future, it might ultimately receive more than the written-down value of the office building in a liquidation following foreclosure. Yet, with its voting rights effectively eliminated by separate classification, Phoenix has no leverage to persuade the Debtor to consider a more reasonable settlement. Had this scenario triumphed, Phoenix's most realistic option might have been to take an allowed secured claim in the hope that eventually the market value of the office building will increase by more than $140,000 over the presently estimated value of the collateral.

Thus, the election under § 1111(b) would be essentially meaningless. We believe Congress did not intend this result.

As the bankruptcy court viewed this issue, the debtor's ability to achieve a cramdown plan should be preferred over the creditor's § 1111(b) election rights because of the Code's policy of facilitating reorganization. The bankruptcy court resorted to policy considerations because it believed Congress did not foresee the potential impact of an electing creditor's deficiency claim on the debtor's aspiration to cramdown a plan. We disagree with this approach for three reasons. First, it results here in violating § 1122, by gerrymandering the plan vote, for the sake of allegedly effectuating a § 1129(b) cramdown. "Policy" considerations do not justify preferring one section of the Code, much less elevating its implicit "policies" over other sections, where the statutory language draws no such distinctions. Second, as shown, it virtually eliminates the § 1111(b) election for secured creditors in this type of case. Third, the bankruptcy court's concern for the viability of cramdown plans is overstated. If Phoenix's unsecured claim were lower and the trade debt were higher, or if there were other impaired classes that favored the plan, a cramdown plan would be more realistic. That Greystone's cramdown plan may not succeed on the facts before us does not disprove the utility of the cramdown provision. The state law distinction between Code-created unsecured deficiency claims and other unsecured claims does not alone warrant separate classification.

Greystone next argues that separate classification was justified for "good business reasons." The bankruptcy court found that the debtor "needs trade to maintain good will for future operations." *In re Greystone III Joint Venture, supra* at 570. The court further reasoned:

> If the expectation of trade creditors is frustrated . . . [they] have little recourse but to refrain from doing business with the enterprise. The resulting negative reputation quickly spreads in the trade community, making it difficult to obtain services in the future on any but the most onerous terms.

Id. Greystone argues that the "realities of business" more than justify separate classification of the trade debt from Phoenix's deficiency claim. This argument is specious, for it fails to distinguish between the classification of claims and the treatment of claims. Greystone's justification for separate classification of the trade claims might be valid if the trade creditors were to receive different treatment from Phoenix. Indeed, Greystone initially created a separate class of unsecured creditors that could be wooed to vote for the plan by the promise to pay their remaining claims in full outside the plan. Greystone then changed course and eliminated its promise. Because there is no separate treatment of the trade creditors in this case, we reject Greystone's "realities of business" argument.

Even if Greystone's Plan had treated the trade creditors differently from Phoenix, the classification scheme here is still improper. At the confirmation hearing, none of the Debtor's witnesses offered any reason for classifying the trade debt separately from Phoenix's unsecured deficiency claim. There is no evidence in the record of a limited market in Austin for trade goods and services. Nor is there is any evidence that Greystone would be unable to obtain any of the trade services if the trade creditors did not receive preferential treatment under the Plan. Thus, the bankruptcy court's finding that there were good business reasons for separate classification is without support in the record and must be set aside as clearly erroneous.

> Two standards of appellate review apply to the debtor's classification of claims. Issues such as the similarity in priority and legal attributes and the ultimate question whether treatment in the same or separate classes is necessary, are legal issues reviewable by our court de novo. Whether there were any good business reasons to support the debtor's separate classification of claims is a question of fact.

Phoenix's unsecured deficiency claim approximates $3,500,000, while the claims of the unsecured trade creditors who voted to accept the Plan total less than $10,000. Greystone's classification scheme, which effectively disenfranchised Phoenix's Code-created deficiency claim, is sanctioned neither by the Code nor by case law. The lower courts erred in approving it.

NOTE ON CLASSIFICATION IN SINGLE ASSET REAL ESTATE CASES

In the typical single asset real estate case, the mortgagee's deficiency claim is so large that unless the debtor can separately classify that deficiency claim, it will swamp the unsecured class and there is no way the debtor can overcome the one-impaired-accepting — class hurdle to confirmation. In the single asset context, the vast majority of courts — including the Courts of Appeals for the Second, Third, Fourth, Fifth, and Eighth Circuits — have adopted Judge Jones's approach and refused to permit gerrymandering for the purpose of manufacturing an accepting class. *Boston Post Road Ltd. P'ship. v. Federal Deposit Ins. Corp. (In re Boston Post Road Ltd. P'ship.)*, 21 F.3d 477 (2d Cir. 1994); *John Hancock Mutual Life Ins. Co. v. Route 37 Business Park Assocs.*, 987 F.2d 154 (3d Cir. 1993); *Travelers Ins. Co. v. Bryson Props., XVIII (In re Bryson Props., XVIII)*, 961 F.2d 496 (4th Cir. 1992); *Lumber Exch. Bldg. Ltd. P'ship. v. Mutual Life Ins. Co. of N.Y. (In re Lumber Exchange Bldg. Ltd. P'ship.)*, 968 F.2d 647 (8th Cir. 1992).

The Seventh Circuit has taken a less crowded path. In *In re Woodbrook Assocs.*, 19 F.3d 312 (7th Cir. 1994), the court held that separate classification of an unsecured deficiency claim is not only permissible, but required, because a § 1111(b) recourse claim is substantially different from a general unsecured claim. The reason is that it is purely a creature of Chapter 11, not contract. The court also reasoned that placing a § 1111(b) recourse claim in the same class as other unsecured claims would lead to "anomalous results." One anomalous result, the court said, was that a § 1111(b) claim holder, who would not be entitled to recover on its deficiency claim in a Chapter 7 case (indeed who would have no deficiency claim in a Chapter 7 case), could prevent confirmation of a Chapter 11 plan, and force conversion of the case to Chapter 7, by voting that same deficiency claim. Another anomalous result, the court said, is that, since the § 1111(b)(2) election is to be made by "the class of which such claim is a part," general unsecured creditors would have standing to vote on whether an undersecured creditor should elect to be treated as fully secured or assert a deficiency claim. Whoa! Is the court's reasoning correct? Read § 1111(b)(1)(A)(i) closely. Isn't it the class of which the *secured* claim is a part that decides whether to elect § 1111(b)(2) treatment? In the typical case, because there are no claims that are substantially similar to it, the secured claim will be in a class by itself. *See In re D&W Realty Corp.*, 165 B.R. 127, 128 (S.D.N.Y. 1994). The holder of the secured claim will thus decide whether to elect § 1111(b)(2) treatment.

The Seventh Circuit took its singular approach a step farther in *In re 203 N. LaSalle Street P'ship.*, 126 F.3d 955 (7th Cir. 1997). There, the court confirmed a plan that not only separately classified a mortgagee's $38.5 million deficiency claim, but also treated it differently from other unsecured claims. Under the *LaSalle* plan, trade creditors received 100 cents on the dollar while the mortgagee received only 16 cents on the dollar. The court reasoned that since, in a liquidation case, the trade creditors would have recovered the full amount of their unsecured claims while the mortgagee would have received nothing on account of its deficiency claim (since it would have had no deficiency claim in Chapter 7), the plan did not unfairly discriminate against the mortgagee. As we will see, the Supreme Court reversed

LaSalle on other grounds, but did not deal with the classification portion of the opinion.

Although most courts have shown little patience with "creative" classification schemes in the single asset real estate context, as the next two opinions suggest, in other kinds of cases, courts have been more flexible and in some cases questioned whether the debtor's motivation for separately classifying similar claims is relevant at all.

TEAMSTERS NATIONAL FREIGHT IND. NEGOTIATING COMM. v. U.S. TRUCK COMPANY (IN RE U.S. TRUCK COMPANY)
United States Court of Appeals for the Sixth Circuit
800 F.2d 581 (1986)

CORNELIA G. KENNEDY, CIRCUIT JUDGE.

The Teamsters National Freight Industry Negotiating Committee (the Teamsters Committee), a creditor of U.S. Truck Company, Inc. (U.S. Truck) — the debtor-in-possession in this Chapter 11 bankruptcy proceeding — appeals the District Court's order confirming U.S. Truck's Fifth Amended Plan of Reorganization.

I

[The court explained that the Teamsters Committee held a claim that arose when the debtor rejected and subsequently renegotiated an executory collective bargaining agreement between the debtor and the union local. The renegotiated agreement, which made it possible for the debtor to show monthly profits, reduced wages and required employees to buy their own trucking equipment and lease it back to the company. — Eds.]

II

Section 1129 contains two means by which a reorganization plan can be confirmed. The first way is to meet all eleven of the requirements of subsection (a), including (a)(8) which requires all impaired classes of claims or interests to accept the plan. The other way is to meet the requirements of subsection (b), which, first, incorporates all of the requirements of subsection (a), except for that contained in subsection (a)(8), and, second, imposes two additional requirements.

Subsection (b)(1) reads:

> Notwithstanding section 510(a) of this title, if all of the applicable requirements of subsection (a) of this section other than paragraph (8) are met with respect to a plan, the court, on request of the proponent of the plan, shall confirm the plan notwithstanding the requirements of such paragraph if the plan does not discriminate unfairly, and is fair and equitable, with

respect to each class of claims or interests that is impaired under, and has not accepted, the plan.

Confirmation under subsection (b) is commonly referred to as a "cram down" because it permits a reorganization plan to go into effect over the objections of one or more impaired classes of creditors. In this case, U.S. Truck sought approval of its plan under this "cram down" provision.

III

The Teamsters Committee's first objection is that the plan does not meet the requirement that at least one class of impaired claims accept the plan, *see* § 1129(a)(10), because U.S. Truck impermissibly gerrymandered the classes in order to neutralize the Teamsters Committee's dissenting vote. The reorganization plan contains twelve classes. The plan purports to impair five of these classes — Class VI (the secured claim of Manufacturer's National Bank of Detroit based on a mortgage); Class VII (the secured claim of John Graham, Trustee of Transportation Services, Inc., based on a loan); Class IX (the Teamsters Committee's claim based on rejection of the collective bargaining agreement); Class XI (all [unsecured] claims in excess of $200.00 including those arising from the rejection of executory contracts); and Class XII (the equity interest of the stockholder of the debtor). As noted above, section 1129(a)(10), as incorporated into subsection (b)(1), requires at least one of these classes of impaired claims to approve the reorganization plan before it can be confirmed. The parties agree that approval by Class XII would not count because acceptance must be determined without including the acceptance of the plan by any insider. *See* § 1129(a)(10). The Code's definition of "insider" clearly includes McKinlay Transport, Inc. *See* §§ 101 (25)(B)(iii), (30). Thus, compliance with subsection (a)(10) depends on whether either of the other three classes that approved the plan — Class VI, Class VII, or Class XI — was a properly constructed impaired class. The Teamsters Committee argues that Classes VI and VII were not truly impaired classes and that Class XI should have included Class IX, and hence was an improperly constructed class. . . .[6] Because we find that Class XI was a properly constructed class of impaired claims, we hold that the plan complies with subsection (a)(10).[7]

The issue raised by the Teamsters Committee's challenge is under what circumstances does the Bankruptcy Code permit a debtor to keep a creditor out of a class of impaired claims which are of a similar legal nature and are against the same property as those of the "isolated" creditor. The District Court held that the Code permits such action here because of the following circumstances: (1) the employees represented by the Teamsters Committee have a unique continued interest in the ongoing business of the debtor; (2) the mechanics of the Teamsters Committee's claim differ substantially from those of the Class XI claims; and (3) the

---

[6] Had the debtor included the Teamsters Committee's claim in Class XI, the Committee's vote to reject the plan would have swung the results of the Class XI vote from an acceptance to a rejection. See § 1126(c) (setting forth the requirement that creditors holding at least two-thirds in amount of allowed claims of a class accept).

[7] For this reason, we need not decide the challenge to the status of Class VI and Class VII.

Teamsters Committee's claim is likely to become part of the agenda of future collective bargaining sessions between the union and the reorganized company. *See* 47 Bankr. at 939–40. Thus, according to the court, the interests of the Teamsters Committee are substantially dissimilar from those of the creditors in Class XI. We must decide whether the Code permits separate classification under such circumstances.

Congress has sent mixed signals on the issue that we must decide. Our starting point is § 1122.

Section 1122, Classification of claims or interests

(a) Except as provided in subsection (b) of this section, a plan may place a claim or an interest in a particular class only if such claim or interest is substantially similar to the other claims or interests of such class.

(b) A plan may designate a separate class of claims consisting only of every unsecured claim that is less than or reduced to an amount that the court approves as reasonable and necessary for administrative convenience.

The statute, by its express language, only addresses the problem of dissimilar claims being included in the same class. It does not address the correlative problem — the one we face here — of similar claims being put in different classes. Some courts have seized upon this omission, and have held that the Code does not require a debtor to put similar claims in the same class.

. . . .

Section 1122(a) specifies that only claims which are "substantially similar" may be placed in the same class. It does not require that similar claims must be grouped together, but merely that any group created must be homogenous. *See* 5 Collier on Bankruptcy para. 1122.03[1][b] at 1122-6 (15th ed. 1982).

. . . .

Further evidence that Congress intentionally failed to impose a requirement that similar claims be classified together is found by examining the "classification" sections of the former Bankruptcy Act. The applicable former provisions were 11 U.S.C., sections 597 (from former Chapter X) and 751 (from former Chapter XI).

Section 597, Classification of creditors and stockholders

For the purposes of the plan and its acceptance, the judge shall fix the division of creditors and stockholders into classes according to the nature of their respective claims and stock. For the purposes of such classification, the judge shall, if necessary, upon the application of the trustee, the debtor, any creditor, or an indenture trustee, fix a hearing upon notice to the holders of secured claims, the debtor, the trustee, and such other persons as the judge may designate, to determine summarily the value of the security and classify as unsecured the amount in excess of such value.

Section 751, Classification of creditors

For the purposes of the arrangement and its acceptance, the court may fix the division of creditors into classes and, in the event of controversy, the court shall after hearing upon notice summarily determine such controversy.

Section 597 was interpreted to require all creditors of equal rank with claims against the same property to be placed in the same class. *See In re Los Angeles Land and Investments, Ltd.*, 282 F. Supp. 448, 453 (D. Hawaii 1968) (quoting *In re Scherk v. Newton*, 152 F.2d 747 (10th Cir. 1945), *aff'd*, 447 F.2d 1366 (9th Cir. 1971)). Congress' switch to less restrictive language in section 1122 of the Code seems to warrant a conclusion that Congress no longer intended to impose the now-omitted requirement that similar claims be classified together. *See Matter of Huckabee Auto Co.*, 33 Bankr. 132, 137 (Bkrtcy. M.D. Ga. 1981). However, the legislative history indicates that Congress may not have intended to change the prior rule. The Notes of the Senate Committee on the Judiciary state:

> This section [1122] codifies current case law surrounding the classification of claims and equity securities. It requires classification based on the nature of the claims or interests classified, and permits inclusion of claims or interests in a particular class only if the claim or interest being included is substantially similar to the other claims or interests of the class.

S. Rep. No. 989, 95th Cong., 2d Sess. 118, reprinted in 1978 U.S. Code Cong. & Ad. News 5787, 5904.

It is difficult to follow Congress' instruction to apply the old case law to the new Code provision. The old case law comes from two different sources. Chapter X of the old Act was designed for thorough financial reorganizations of large corporations. It imposed a very formal and rigid structure to protect the investing public. Chapter XI was designed for small nonpublic businesses, did not permit the adjustment of a secured debt or of equity, and thus contained few investor-protection measures. The idea behind Chapter 11 of the Code was to combine the speed and flexibility of Chapter XI with some of the protection and remedial tools of Chapter X. . . . Thus, Congress has incorporated, for purposes of interpreting section 1122, the case law from two provisions with different language, that were adopted for different purposes, and that have been interpreted to mean different things.

In this case, U.S. Truck is using its classification powers to segregate dissenting (impaired) creditors from assenting (impaired) creditors (by putting the dissenters into a class or classes by themselves) and, thus, it is assured that at least one class of impaired creditors will vote for the plan and make it eligible for cram down consideration by the court. We agree with the Teamsters Committee that there must be some limit on a debtor's power to classify creditors in such a manner. The potential for abuse would be significant otherwise. Unless there is some requirement of keeping similar claims together, nothing would stand in the way of a debtor seeking out a few impaired creditors (or even one such creditor) who will vote for the plan and placing them in their own class.[8]

---

[8] We need not speculate in this case whether the purpose of separate classification was to line up the votes in favor of the plan. The debtor admitted that to the District Court. *See* Debtor's Response to

We are unaware of any cases that deal with this problem as it arises in this case. As we noted above, the legislative history of the Code provides little assistance in determining what limits there are to segregating similar claims. Nevertheless, we do find one common theme in the prior case law that Congress incorporated into section 1122. In those pre-Code cases, the lower courts were given broad discretion to determine proper classification according to the factual circumstances of each individual case.

The District Court noted three important ways in which the interests of the Teamsters Committee differ substantially from those of the other impaired creditors. Because of these differences, the Teamsters Committee has a different stake in the future viability of the reorganized company and has alternative means at its disposal for protecting its claim. The Teamsters Committee's claim is connected with the collective bargaining process. In the words of the Committee's counsel, the union employees have a "virtually unique interest." *See* 47 Bankr. at 939. These differences put the Teamsters Committee's claim in a different posture than the Class XI claims. The Teamsters Committee may choose to reject the plan not because the plan is less than optimal to it as a creditor, but because the Teamsters Committee has a noncreditor interest — e.g., rejection will benefit its members in the ongoing employment relationship. Although the Teamsters Committee certainly is not intimately connected with the debtor, to allow the Committee to vote with the other impaired creditors would be to allow it to prevent a court from considering confirmation of a plan that a significant group of creditors with similar interests have accepted.

. . . .

IN RE DOW CORNING CORP.
United States Bankruptcy Court, Eastern District Of Michigan
244 B.R. 634 (1999), *aff'd*, 255 B.R. 445 (E.D. Mich. 2000), *aff'd*, 280 F.3d 648 (6th Cir. 2002)

[The following summary of facts is in part excerpted from the Sixth Circuit's opinion, which is reported at 280 F.3d 648. For nearly 30 years, Dow was the predominant producer of silicone gel breast implants. In the 1980s, medical studies indicated that the silicone gel might be the cause of various auto-immune tissue diseases. The Food and Drug Administration ordered that silicone gel implants be removed from the market and tens of thousands of implant recipients sued Dow. Dow filed a Chapter 11 petition in 1995. About four years later, Dow filed an amended reorganization plan. Under the Plan, a $2.35 billion fund was established for the payment of claims asserted by (1) personal injury claimants, (2) government health care payers, and (3) other creditors asserting claims related to silicone-implant products liability claims. The $2.35 billion fund was established with funds contributed by Dow's products liability insurers, Dow's shareholders, and Dow's operating cash reserves. As a quid pro quo for making proceeds available for the $2.35 billion fund, section 8.3 of the Plan releases Dow's insurers and shareholders from all further liability on claims arising out of settled personal injury claims, and

---

Objections to Confirmation Filed by the Teamsters National Freight Negotiating Committee, at 6 (Jan. 23, 1985).

section 8.4 permanently enjoins any party holding a claim released against Dow from bringing an action related to that claim against Dow's insurers or shareholders.

Under the Plan, claimants who choose to settle are channeled to the Settlement Facility, a legal entity created by the Plan and authorized to negotiate payments out of funds set aside for that purpose. Claimants who choose to litigate are channeled to the Litigation Facility, a legal entity created by the Plan that is essentially substituted for Dow as a defendant in the claimant's lawsuit.

The Plan divides claims and interests into 33 classes and subclasses, a number of which objected to the Plan's classification scheme. Classes 6.1 and 6.2 are composed of foreign breast-implant claimants who are given the opportunity to either settle or litigate their claims. Settlement payments to foreign breast implant claimants are between 35% and 60% of the amounts to be paid to domestic breast-implant claimants.

Under the Plan, a foreign claimant is defined as someone who (1) is not a United States citizen, (2) is not a resident alien, or (3) did not have his or her medical procedure performed in the United States. The Plan creates two classes for foreign claimants. Class 6.1 consists of claimants who are from a country that either (1) belongs to the European Union, (2) has a common law tort system, or (3) has a per capita Gross Domestic Product of greater than 60% of the United States per capita Gross Domestic Product. Class 6.2 consists of claimants from all other countries. Class 5 generally consists of domestic breast-implant claimants. Class 6.1 claimants receive settlement offers of 60% of analogous domestic claimants' settlements and Class 6.2 receive settlements of 35% of the domestic claimants' settlements. Members of both classes retain the option to litigate against the Litigation Facility for the full value of the claim should they deem the settlement offer inadequate.

Some groups of foreign claimants argued that that their claims were not worth less than those of the domestic tort claimants and, therefore, should not be classified separately from domestic claims. Expert witnesses testified that the highest tort awards in various other countries were significantly lower than in the United States. For example, one expert witness testified that the highest non-pecuniary award in injury cases in Australia is approximately $230,000.

Some groups of foreign claimants argued that their claims were more valuable than those of claimholders from other countries and that therefore their claims were not "substantially similar" as required by section 1122(a). They further argued that by giving identical consideration to class members whose claims are of different value, they are not being treated the same as other members of their class in violation of the Code's requirement that claimants within a class be treated equally. 11 U.S.C § 1123(a)(4).

Excerpts from the Bankruptcy Court's very lengthy classification opinion, which was affirmed by the Court of Appeals for the Sixth Circuit, follow.

ARTHUR J. SPECTOR, U.S. BANKRUPTCY JUDGE.

The Debtor and the Official Committee of Tort Claimants negotiated and on November 9, 1998 filed a Joint Plan of Reorganization. The plan (hereafter referred to simply as the "Plan") was subsequently amended on February 4, 1999 and modified various times. The hearing on confirmation of the Plan commenced on June 28, 1999 and closing arguments were heard on July 30, 1999. Several post-hearing briefs and other submissions were received and the Court took the matter under advisement.

On this date the Court issued its Findings of Fact and Conclusions of Law on the matter of the confirmation of the Plan. To supplement and explicate some of the findings and conclusions, the Court contemporaneously releases this opinion and several others.

A number of general unsecured creditors, whose claims arose from the Debtor's manufacture and sale of silicone-gel breast implants, objected to confirmation of the Plan. The objections addressed in this opinion assert that the Plan does not comply with 11 U.S.C. §§ 1122(a) and 1123(a)(4).[1] The Court disagrees, and for the reasons stated below these objections are overruled.

II. Classification of Claims Under the Plan

A. Standards Governing Classification

Claims may be classified together only if they are "substantially similar" to one another. 11 U.S.C. § 1122(a) ("[A] plan may place a claim or an interest in a particular class only if such claim or interest is substantially similar to the other claims or interests of such class."). "Substantially similar" means similar in legal nature, character or effect. 7 Collier on Bankruptcy P 1122.03[3] (15th ed. rev. 1999); *see also In re Johnston*, 21 F.3d 323, 327 (9th Cir. 1994).

Section 1122(a) speaks solely to the types of claims that can be classified together. It does not address the question of whether substantially similar claims may be classified separately. *In re U.S. Truck Co.*, 800 F.2d 581, 585 (6th Cir. 1986). Virtually every circuit that has encountered the issue, including the Sixth, has held that substantially similar claims may be classified separately. *Id.* at 585–86; *Clerk, U.S. Bankruptcy Court v. Aetna Cas. & Surety Co. (In re Chateaugay Corp.)*, 89 F.3d 942, 949 (2nd Cir. 1996); *In re Barakat*, 99 F.3d 1520, 1526 (9th Cir. 1996); *In re Woodbrook Assoc.*, 19 F.3d 312, 317–18 (7th Cir. 1994); *John Hancock Mutual Life Ins., Co. v. Route 37 Business Park Assoc.*, 987 F.2d 154, 158 (3rd Cir. 1993); *In re Bryson Properties, XVIII*, 961 F.2d 496, 502 (4th Cir. 1992); *In re Greystone III Joint Venture*, 995 F.2d 1274, 1278–79 (5th Cir. 1992); *Olympia & York Florida Equity Corp. v. Bank of New York (In re Holywell Corp.)*, 913 F.2d 873, 880 (11th Cir. 1990); *Hanson v. First Bank of South Dakota, N.A.*, 828 F.2d 1310, 1313 (8th Cir. 1987); *In re AOV Indus., Inc.*, 792 F.2d 1140, 1150, 253 U.S. App. D.C. 186 (D.C. Cir. 1986).

---

[1] Unless otherwise noted all statutory references are to the Bankruptcy Code, 11 U.S.C. § 101 *et seq.*

Most of these courts, however, also take the view that there are limits on a plan proponent's classification freedom. In short, they reason that substantially similar claims may not be classified separately when it is done for an illegitimate reason. Whether the reason proffered is legitimate is a factual determination that must be made on a case-by-case basis. *See U.S. Truck*, 800 F.2d at 586 (Bankruptcy courts have "broad discretion to determine proper classification according to the factual circumstances of each individual case.").

B. Comment on Classification Standards

Before applying the "legitimate reason" standard to the current objections, we pause to comment on this standard's correctness. We do so for two important reasons. First, as will be discussed below, this Court believes that the standard is wrong as a matter of law. And second, the real world costs of applying this legally incorrect standard can be enormous. In this case, for example, attorneys for a number of the foreign breast-implant claimants argued that the Proponents had not demonstrated a "legitimate reason" for classifying their claims separately from domestic breast-implant claims. Evidence and argument on the classification objections were presented to the Court during the confirmation hearing over the course of approximately six days. And as part of their case, the Proponents brought in a number of comparative law experts from countries such as England and Australia. It is safe to say that the costs incurred by the Debtor to properly respond to the classification objections ranged into the six-figures. It is bad enough that a debtor may be required to ante up this needless expense; it would be even worse if the debtor were insolvent and the money is taken from the pot established for creditors. In addition, the judicial resources involved in addressing such objections also can be substantial. Sadly, none of this time and expense would have been necessary if § 1122(a) were interpreted, as it should be, in accordance with its plain language.

The development of this standard occurred primarily in the context of cases where separate classification of substantially-similar claims had allegedly been done solely for the purpose of gerrymandering the vote on the plan.[5] In one of the first Code cases to address this issue, the Sixth Circuit stated that "there must be some limit on a debtor's power to classify" such claims separately when the singular reason for doing so is to ensure that at least one accepting class of impaired creditors exists for cramdown purposes. *U.S. Truck*, 800 F.2d at 586. Otherwise, the court reasoned, "the potential for abuse would be significant." *Id.*

Thereafter, the Eight and Eleventh Circuits agreed with this reasoning. *See*

---

[5] There is no evidence suggesting that the Plan's classification scheme was designed with such an objective in mind. In fact, such a conclusion would be counterintuitive. Twenty-four classes voted to accept it. And most of those 24 classes accepted by overwhelming margins. Not surprisingly, no meaningful allegation of gerrymandering was made by any of the objecting parties. Moreover, even if the Proponents admitted that they classified these similar claims separately in order to obtain an accepting impaired class, so long as there is another legitimate reason supporting separate classification, the separate classification can be upheld. *See In re U.S. Truck Co.*, 800 F.2d 581, 586 & n.8 (6th Cir. 1986) (Although the plan proponent admitted that it separately classified the Teamsters Committee's unsecured claims from the other unsecured claims in order to obtain at least one accepting impaired class of claims, the court held that independent justifications made the classification permissible).

Holywell Corp., 913 F.2d at 880; *Hanson*, 828 F.2d at 1313. The Fifth Circuit also agreed with U.S. Truck's "potential for abuse" assessment. *Greystone III*, 995 F.2d at 1279. But in the course of its analysis, *Greystone III* also suggested that a broad interpretation of § 1122(a) would render §§ 1122(b) and 1111(b) superfluous. *Id.* at 1278–80. *Greystone III*'s reasoning, which will be discussed in greater detail below, led to its frequently cited "one clear rule" pronouncement: "Thou shalt not classify similar claims differently in order to gerrymander an affirmative vote on a reorganization plan." *Id.*

Perhaps it is because the three words prefacing this statement convey the feel of a command set in stone, but for whatever reason, most courts have, with little question, accepted this judicial pronouncement as the supreme rule governing classification decisions.

Greystone III's "one clear rule" directive certainly has superficial appeal. But the reasoning which underlies it cannot withstand legal scrutiny. Even worse, its real world application actually makes the reorganization process, and classification issues in particular, needlessly complex, costly and unpredictable.

To see why, we must begin with the language of § 1122(a) which merely provides that "a plan may place a claim . . . in a particular class only if such claim . . . is substantially similar to the other claims . . . of such class." 11 U.S.C. § 1122(a). The plain language of this provision would seem to require a court to do nothing more than look at each individual class and determine whether the claims within that class are substantially similar.

As exemplified by the Sixth Circuit, however, courts have not done this. *See U.S. Truck*, 800 F.2d at 584 (stating, as justification for its reliance on § 1122(a)'s legislative history, that "Congress has sent mixed signals on the issue [of classification]"). The legislative history provides that § 1122(a) "requires classification based on the nature of claims . . . classified, and permits inclusion of claims . . . in a particular class only if such claim . . . being included is substantially similar to the other claims . . . of the class." S. Rep. No. 989. 95th Cong., 2d Sess. 118, *reprinted in* 1978 U.S. Code Cong. & Ad. News 5787, 5904. This piece of legislative history appears to fully support the plain language interpretation of § 1122(a) noted above. However, the legislative history also states that § 1122 (a) "codifies current case law surrounding the classification of claims." *Id.* Unfortunately, "it is difficult to follow Congress' instruction to apply old case law to the new Code provision." *U.S. Truck*, 800 F.2d at 586. In part, the reason for this is that there were three forms of business reorganizations under the Act, one each under Chapters X, XI and XII. *See* Linda J. Rusch, *Gerrymandering The Classification Issue In Chapter Eleven Reorganizations* (hereafter "*Gerrymandering*"), 63 U. Colo. L. Rev. 163, 189 (1992).

Case law under Chapters XI and XII, which contained identical classification provisions, apparently placed no limits on a plan proponent's ability to separately classify substantially similar claims. *Id.* at 190 nn. 128 & 130 (and cases cited therein). Under Chapter X, courts would generally allow separate classification of similar claims when doing so was "in the best interest of creditors; fostered reorganization efforts; did not violate the absolute priority rule; and did not uselessly increase the number of classes." *In re Ag Consultants Grain Div., Inc.*, 77 B.R. 665, 673 (N.D. Ind. 1987).

The first problem in applying cases decided under the Bankruptcy Act is knowing which case law Congress intended to codify. If it was case law interpreting Chapters XI and XII which Congress meant to codify, it would seem appropriate to use the plain-language interpretation of § 1122(a) since such cases permitted a plan proponent to separately classify substantially similar claims. Arguably this same result obtains if it is case law interpreting Chapter X that is pertinent because most of the factors considered under Chapter X, such as whether a plan is in the best interest of creditors and whether it satisfies the absolute priority rule, are addressed under Code provisions other than § 1122(a). *See* 11 U.S.C. § 1129(a)(7) (best interest of creditors' test) and § 1129(b)(2) ("fair and equitable" standard includes the absolute priority rule). And once these factors are removed from the equation, there would seem to be no reason not to apply § 1122(a) in accordance with its plain language. Thus, even assuming that the straightforward language of § 1122(a) is not plain and that there is justification for relying on legislative history, doing so would seem only to lead to the same interpretive result as the plain language construction already noted.

Another common rule of statutory construction is that every provision of a statute should be construed so that no other provision is rendered superfluous or meaningless. *Kawaauhau v. Geiger*, 523 U.S. 57, 118 S. Ct. 974, 977, 140 L. Ed. 2d 90 (1998). As noted above, *Greystone III* and others expressed concern that if limits are not placed on a plan proponent's ability to classify substantially similar claims separately, then §§ 1122(b), 1111(b) and 1129(a)(10) would be rendered meaningless. But these concerns are unfounded.

Greystone III stated that "if § 1122(a) is wholly permissive regarding the creation of . . . classes, there would be no need for § 1122(b) specifically to authorize a class of smaller unsecured claims." 995 F.2d at 1278; *see also* 11 U.S.C. § 1122(b) ("A plan may designate a separate class of claims consisting only of *every unsecured claim* that is less than or reduced to an amount that the court approves as reasonable and necessary for administrative convenience." (emphasis added)). For this reason, the court concluded that a broader interpretation of § 1122(a) than the one expressed in its holding would render § 1122(b) superfluous. One must presume, then, that *Greystone III* saw § 1122(b) as an expression of Congressional intent to circumscribe a plan proponent's ability to place substantially similar claims in different classes. But for this to be correct, one would also have to take the view that "every unsecured claim" is substantially similar to every other unsecured claim. It makes little sense to conclude that Congress intended for two phrases contained in the same statute — "substantially similar [claims]" and "every unsecured claim" — to carry identical meanings. Moreover, there seems to be little dispute that unsecured claims can be substantially dissimilar in nature. In this case for instance, there is no question that while disputed and unliquidated personal injury breast-implant claims and undisputed and liquidated commercial claims are both unsecured, they may be separately classified.[6] Fortunately, there is a more reasonable construction of § 1122(b) which enables it to co-exist perfectly with a

---

[6] Of course, had the Proponents wanted to, the Plan could have consisted of a single class of

plain-language interpretation of § 1122(a) — that is, as a general rule only substantially-similar claims may be classified together. 11 U.S.C. § 1122(a).

There will be times, however, when matters of administrative convenience make it "reasonable and necessary" to classify substantially dissimilar claims together. Section 1122(b) grants the court authority to do this when such circumstances arise. Thus, a broad interpretation (or more precisely a plain-language interpretation) of § 1122(a) in no way renders § 1122(b) meaningless.

As indicated, *Greystone III* also relied on § 1111(b) to support its interpretation of § 1122(a). Such reliance, too, was misplaced. Without § 1111(b), an undersecured non-recourse creditor's potential recovery would be limited to the value of the collateral securing its claim because its deficiency claim would be subject to disallowance pursuant to § 502(b)(1). 4 Norton Bankruptcy Law & Practice 2d § 89:2 at 89-5. Any subsequent appreciation in the collateral would be captured by the debtor. Under Chapter XII of the Bankruptcy Act, which was available only to individuals and partnerships, this in fact was how the process worked. *Id.* (discussing effect of ruling in *In re Pine Gate Assoc., Ltd.*, 1976 U.S. Dist. LEXIS 17366 (N.D. Ga. 1976)). Had this process carried over into the Bankruptcy Code, these same opportunities would have become available to corporate debtors. The potential for such a development was perceived to pose a substantial threat to non-recourse secured lenders in the form of unrealistically low valuations of collateral. *Id.*

To mitigate this risk, Congress enacted § 1111(b). *Id.* Section 1111(b) permits an undersecured non-recourse creditor to choose between two possible treatments with respect to its deficiency claim. The creditor can elect to have its deficiency claim treated as a recourse unsecured claim, whereby it will then have the right to vote its claim in a class composed of substantially similar unsecured claims. 11 U.S.C. § 1111(b)(1)(A). Alternatively, such a creditor can choose to have the entirety of its claim treated as fully secured by its collateral. 11 U.S.C. § 1111 (b)(2).

Greystone III postulated that if, any time an undersecured non-recourse creditor elects the § 1111(b)(1)(A) option, a plan proponent has the unfettered ability to place that claim in a class by itself, that creditor's "right to vote in the unsecured class would be meaningless." *Greystone III*, 995 F.2d at 1280–81. The result, according to *Greystone III*, would be as follows:

> Plan proponents could effectively disenfranchise the holders of such claims by placing them in a separate class and confirming the plan over their objection by cramdown. With its unsecured voting rights effectively eliminated, the electing creditor's ability to negotiate a satisfactory settlement of either its secured or unsecured claim would be seriously undercut. It seems that the creditor would often have to "elect" to take an allowed secured

---

unsecured claims, as each holder of an unsecured claim of either type would have the same priority on the assets of the Debtor. *See, e.g., In re U.S. Truck Co.*, 47 B.R. 932, 938 (E.D. Mich. 1985), *aff'd*, 800 F.2d 581 (6th Cir. 1986) ("As a general rule unsecured claims normally comprise one class."); *In re Apex Oil Co.*, 118 B.R. 683, 696 (Bankr. E.D. Mo. 1990) (Classifying all pre-petition general unsecured claims in one class is "the preferred course."). Our point is that the Code does not mandate a single class in such circumstances.

claim under § 1111(b)(2) in the hope that the value of the collateral would increase after the case is closed. Thus, the election under § 1111 (b) would be essentially meaningless.

Id. at 1280.

Based upon this passage it appears that *Greystone III* attributed a broader purpose to § 1111(b) than was intended by Congress. *See* Bruce A. Markell, *Clueless on Classification: Toward Removing Artificial Limits on Chapter 11 Claim Classification* (hereafter "*Clueless*"), 11 Bankr. Dev. J. 1, 21 (1994–95) (observing that "prohibiting separate classification for creditors who have . . . made the [§ 1111(b)(1)(A)] election . . . gives the secured creditor more than Congress provided"). As noted, § 1111(b) grants an undersecured non-recourse creditor the right to elect one of two types of treatment. This choice is an absolute right that cannot be denied by a plan proponent or the court. Consequently, if the creditor elects the § 1111(b)(1)(A) option — that is, if it opts to have a secured claim to the extent of the value of the collateral and to have the deficiency treated as a non-recourse unsecured claim — that is the treatment the creditor must receive under any plan that is confirmed. This is true whether confirmation of the plan is achieved on a consensual basis or through cramdown.

Moreover, the undisputed right to receive the selected treatment is all that § 1111(b) provides to the undersecured non-recourse creditor. There is nothing within the text of this section that suggests that it was intended to exclude such a creditor from the possibility of cramdown. Nor is there any language in this section suggesting that a creditor who chooses § 1111(b)(1)(A) must be placed in a class with every other unsecured creditor. And importantly, even if the plan proponent places such a creditor in its own class, this does not mean that the creditor is thereby disenfranchised from the bankruptcy process or that its vote somehow becomes meaningless. Markell, *Clueless*, 11 Bankr. Dev. J. at 20 ("Only a myopic view of bankruptcy law would see the partially-secured creditor as disenfranchised."). The creditor will still retain the ability to object to any aspect of the proposed plan. If the creditor votes to reject the plan, the plan can be confirmed only if the cramdown requirements are satisfied. And, despite intimation to the contrary by *Greystone III*, satisfying the cramdown requirements is no small hurdle for a plan proponent to overcome.

In addition, *Greystone III's* view of what constitutes a level field for purposes of negotiating a plan of reorganization is curious. Assume that there are two classes of unsecured creditors, one of which is composed entirely of the undersecured non-recourse creditor's deficiency claim. Such a plan could be confirmed over the objection of the creditor only if all of the requirements of § 1129(a) and (b) are satisfied — including the best-interest-of-creditors test and the absolute priority rule. Therefore, the undersecured creditor will likely be placed in a negotiating position of some strength. *See* Rusch, *Gerrymandering*, 63 U. Colo. L. Rev. at 197–98 (discussing aspects of the bankruptcy process that provide a dissenting undersecured non-recourse creditor with negotiating leverage). On the other hand, assume that the undersecured creditor is classified, as *Greystone III* requires, with all other unsecured creditors and that its claim is of sufficient value to control the class vote. In such a case, the undersecured creditor will have more than a strong bargaining position; it will have absolute veto power over the plan. Markell, *Clueless*, 11 Bankr. Dev. J. at 21; Rusch, *Gerrymandering*, 63 U. Colo. L. Rev. at 204. And this will be the case regardless of whether the proposed plan is capable of satisfying all requirements of confirmation save for § 1129(a)(10). *See* 11 U.S.C. § 1129(a)(10) (providing that at least one impaired class of claims must have accepted the plan before it is eligible for cramdown). The chapter 11 reorganization process serves a number of important policy objectives including "debtor relief, a preference for feasible reorganizations as opposed to liquidations, equality among similarly situated creditors, and loss distribution in an equitable way among the creditors and the debtor." Rusch, *Gerrymandering*, 63 U. Colo. L. Rev. at 200. Under the second scenario just discussed, these important policy objectives will clearly be defeated. *Id.* It is doubtful that this is the impact that Congress intended for § 1111(b). Therefore, a plain language interpretation of § 1122(a) would not render § 1111(b) meaningless.

Lastly, we are left with *John Hancock*'s reliance on § 1129(a)(10). Section 1129(a)(10) establishes the requirement that at least one class of impaired creditors must have accepted the plan before it can be eligible for cramdown. 11 U.S.C. § 1129(a)(10). Undoubtedly, it is this provision of the Code that sometimes causes plan proponents to place substantially similar claims in separate classes. In *John Hancock*, the court stated that

> where . . . the sole purpose and effect of creating multiple classes is to mold the outcome of the voting, it follows that the classification scheme must provide a reasonable method for counting votes. In a "cram down" case, this means that each class must represent a voting interest that is sufficiently distinct and weighty to merit a separate voice in the decision whether the proposed reorganization should proceed. Otherwise, the classification scheme would simply constitute a method for circumventing the requirement set out in . . . § 1129(a)(10).

John Hancock, 987 F.2d at 159.

John Hancock was correct that the cramdown process should not be undertaken unless the rejecting class is properly constituted. The problem with the court's statement, however, is that the classification determination is not made pursuant to § 1129(a)(10), but pursuant to § 1122(a), which is incorporated into the confirmation process through § 1129(a)(1). Section 1122(a) requires the claims within each class to be substantially similar in legal nature and character. It does not require a finding that "each class . . . represent a voting interest that is sufficiently distinct and weighty to merit a separate voice" in the confirmation process. And to this Court's knowledge there is nothing in the case law or legislative history that would require a court to ratchet the classification requirements up a notch whenever § 1129(a)(10) and cramdown come into play.

The above analysis demonstrates that § 1122(a) should not be circumscribed by judicially created limitations, but instead should be construed in accordance with its plain language. Classification objections should require a court to look only at whether the claims within a class are substantially similar. And importantly, § 1122(a) should not be viewed as prohibiting a plan proponent from placing substantially similar claims in different classes regardless of whether it has proven a "legitimate reason" for doing so. Such an interpretation of § 1122(a) does not conflict with or render meaningless any other provision of the Bankruptcy Code. Nor does such an interpretation work any inequities upon unsecured creditors.

Concerns as to whether a proposed plan is abusive of the bankruptcy process can be addressed through the good faith requirement of § 1129(a)(3).

This discussion demonstrates why § 1122(a) should be interpreted in accordance with its plain language. That is, when faced with a classification objection, a court's only task should be to ascertain whether the claims within that class are substantially similar in character to each other. Though we do not repeat them here, we emphasize again the enormous practical benefits that would result from a proper construction of this section. For these reasons, should forthcoming appeals on this matter reach the Sixth Circuit, we would encourage the court to reconsider the "legitimate reason" standard established in *U.S. Truck*. Irrespective of whether the "legitimate reason" standard is correct, however, this Court is bound by *U.S. Truck* to apply it to the current § 1122(a) objections.

. . . .

E. Classification Objections of Claimants in Classes 6.1 & 6.2

Classification objections were also filed by a number of foreign breast-implant claimants. Almost all of these objectors assert that their claims should be placed in Class 5 and that the settlement offers extended to them under the Plan should be exactly the same in amount as those offered to domestic breast-implant claimants.

. . . .

We begin by noting a fairly obvious point upon which there is virtually no disagreement: all breast-implant claims, both domestic and foreign, are substantially similar. All are unsecured, unliquidated and disputed tort claims arising out of the Debtor's sale and manufacture of silicone-gel breast implants. All such claimants allege that the breast implants caused or will cause them personal injuries.

Moreover, the claims within each class of breast-implant claims are substantially similar in legal nature and character. In addition to the common characteristics noted above, claims within each class possess certain other characteristics that are unique to that class. For instance, Class 5 claimants are all citizens of the United States or residents of the Greater U.S. All Class 6.1 claimants are residents of countries that either: belong to the European Union, have a common law tort system, or have a per capita GDP that is greater than 60% of the United States' per capita GDP. And all Class 6.2 claimants are residents of countries that: do not belong to the European Union; do not have a common law tort system; and do not have a per capita GDP that is greater than 60% of the United States' per capita GDP.

The real question is whether there is a legitimate reason for classifying breast-implant claims in three separate classes. As explained below, the answer to this question is yes.

In reaching this conclusion the Court need not determine, as urged by The Netherlands Claimants, whether the proposed settlement offers to foreign claimants satisfies the fair, adequate and reasonable requirements of Federal Rule of Civil Procedure 23(e). Quite simply, this is a bankruptcy case and the Court's decision is governed, not by the rules of class action proceedings, but by the requirements of the Bankruptcy Code.

Nor is it necessary for the Court to determine whether the settlement offers in question are unfairly discriminatory toward foreign claimants. The conditions of § 1129(a) must be satisfied before a plan can be confirmed. But that section does not contain a requirement that a plan not discriminate unfairly against a particular class of creditors. Rather, that issue arises only when an impaired class has rejected a proposed plan, thereby triggering the cramdown requirements under § 1129(b). 11 U.S.C. § 1129(b)(1) (A plan which meets all conditions of § 1129(a), save § 1129(a)(8), can be confirmed only if the court finds that the plan "does not discriminate unfairly" against the rejecting, impaired class.).

A class has accepted a plan if its members vote to accept the plan by more than one-half in number and two-thirds in amount. 11 U.S.C. § 1126(c). In this case, the Court temporarily allowed all breast-implant claims at an equal value for purposes of voting. [The court noted that Classes 6.1 and 6.2 had voted to accept the plan by the required majorities.] Therefore, whether the Plan unfairly discriminates against Class 6.2 claimants is no longer an issue. For these reasons, it is not necessary to decide the fairness of the proposed settlement offers to foreign breast-implant claimants.

Nonetheless, it merits noting that the Proponents presented overwhelming evidence tending to show that the costs of resolving tort claims in foreign legal systems is such that the settlement offers contained in the Plan are neither unfair, unreasonable nor discriminatory. The Proponents' chief evidence on this regard was the testimony of three expert witnesses: Professor Basil Markesinis,[13] Mr. Augustus Ullstein[14] and Professor Harold Luntz.[15]

---

[13] Professor Markesinis is a professor of law at the University of Oxford in England, the University of Leiden in The Netherlands and the University Of Texas School of Law. He holds chairmanships at each of these institutions and his areas of instruction include comparative law, comparative methodologies, tort law and European law. In addition, to holding seven Ph.D.'s (four earned and three honorary), Professor Markesinis is a Fellow of the British Academy, a Corresponding Fellow of the Royal Belgian Academy, a Fellow of the Academy of Athens, a Foreign Fellow of the Royal Dutch Academy and a Member of the American Law Institute. He is an expert in the tort systems of each of the major legal systems of Europe (Germanic, English and Romanesque/French) and is well versed on how those tort systems have spread to and been implemented by countries in virtually every part of the world (i.e., United States, Central and South America, Japan, Africa etc.). Professor Markesinis has authored approximately 20 books and over 100 legal articles, most of which pertain in some manner to comparative law. Finally, he served as a member of a panel appointed by United States District Judge Speigel (the "*Pfizer* Foreign Fracture Panel"), that was charged with determining fair settlement levels for foreign tort claimants in the class action case of *Bowling v. Pfizer*, No. C-1-91-256 (S.D. Ohio 1995).

[14] Mr. Augustus Ullstein is a Queen's Counsel and practicing barrister in the United Kingdom. In addition to specializing in products liability litigation in England, Mr. Ullstein is knowledgeable on tort systems and verdict values in the United Kingdom, Germany, The Netherlands and South Africa. Like Professor Markesinis, he also served on the *Pfizer* Foreign Fracture Panel.

[15] Professor Luntz, a professor of law at the University of Melbourne in Australia, is an expert in the

The conclusions offered by Professor Markesinis can be set forth rather summarily. He testified that there are a number of legal, economic, cultural and miscellaneous factors[16] which tend to cause tort recoveries in foreign legal systems to be markedly lower than tort recoveries in the United States. *Transcript*, July 1, 1999 at 12-41. For this reason, he believes it is appropriate for the Plan to differentiate between foreign and domestic breast-implant claimants. Professor Markesinis also testified that these same factors provide a reasonable and fair basis for further differentiating between the claimants in Classes 6.1 and 6.2.

Mr. Ullstein testified that a woman bringing a breast-implant case in the United Kingdom, Germany, The Netherlands or South Africa would face substantial legal and procedural obstacles that would not be present in the United States. Therefore, he concluded that the settlement offers extended to foreign breast-implant claimants under the Plan are fair in relation to those extended to domestic claimants.

Professor Luntz similarly opined that, based upon his knowledge of tort damage awards in Australia and New Zealand, the settlement offers extended under the Plan to breast-implant claimants are more than fair and reasonable.[18]

Through long hours of cross-examination, the foreign objectors doggedly, though ultimately unsuccessfully, attempted to cast doubt upon the testimony by the Proponents' witnesses. The foreign objectors' witnesses were also unhelpful in this regard. For instance, the Shainwald Claimants presented the testimony of Edward Kellogg.[19] It was apparent on cross-examination that Mr. Kellogg has minimal practice experience in the English tort system, *Transcript*, July 15, 1999 at 86–89, and minimal knowledge of average recovery amounts in the English tort system. *Id.* at 92–94. But more importantly, and despite the noted limitations on his expertise, implicit within his testimony was an acknowledgment that tort values in the United

---

tort systems and damage awards of both Australia and New Zealand. He is the author of a number of books and articles on tort law, including the leading torts textbook in Australia and "Assessment of Damages for Personal Injury and Death." As part of his preparation for updating this latter book, now in its fourth edition, Professor Luntz stays current on developments in tort law in the United States. He is the editor of the Torts Law Journal in Australia and was a member of the *Pfizer* Foreign Fracture Panel.

[16] These factors include: the availability of strong social security system payments in foreign countries; that most tort cases in foreign countries are tried by judges, not juries; that punitive damages are typically not available in foreign countries or are available in only limited instances; that foreign countries lack American-style contingency fees; that foreign countries exhibit lower tort awards, and different, less plaintiff-friendly standards of liability; that cultural factors in foreign countries lead to a diminished propensity to litigate; that more plaintiffs proceed in foreign countries on a *pro se* basis; and that significant weight is given in foreign countries to semi-official medical reports completed at the direction of the government.

[18] Like Professor Markesinis, Professor Luntz stated that there are a number of factors which lead to this result. They are: Australians tend to be less litigious; certain social benefits, such as universal health care, which are not available in United States are available in Australia; litigation costs rules are a significant deterrent to lawsuits; judges, not juries, usually decide product liability cases; strict liability is less frequently available in Australia than in the United States; damage awards in Australia and New Zealand are lower than in the United States; and punitive damages are rarely available.

[19] Mr. Kellogg is a practicing attorney in Atlanta, Georgia specializing in pharmaceutical products liability cases. In addition to being a member of the Georgia bar, he is admitted to the British bar as a barrister.

States do indeed tend to be considerably higher than those in England. *Id*. at 94–103.

The Australian Claimants proffered the testimony of Professor David Partlett.[20] Though Professor Partlett testified that substantial differences did not exist between tort values in the United States and Australia, he nevertheless agreed with many of the differentiating factors identified by Professor Luntz. His concurrence with Professor Luntz was bolstered by reference to a law review article which he co-authored and in which he reiterated his agreement with many of those differentiating factors. *Id*. at 238–43 (discussing Jeffery O'Connell and David F. Partlett, *An America's Cup for Tort Reform? Australia and America Compared*, 21 U. Mich. J.L. Ref. 443 (1988)). In this article, in fact, Professor Partlett went so far as to refer to Australia's tort system as a "defendant's pleasure dome." *Id*. at 243; *An America's Cup for Tort Reform?* at 457. Not surprisingly, Professor Partlett made no attempt to similarly characterize the United States' tort system.

Without question, the evidence on the record shows that tort recoveries in the United States tend to be significantly higher than those in foreign jurisdictions. The record further shows that it is appropriate to differentiate, as the Plan does, between categories of foreign claimants on this basis. There is, in fact, little dispute among the legal community over the correctness of these basic propositions. *Piper Aircraft Co.*, 454 U.S. at 252 & n.18 (observing that American courts are very attractive to foreign plaintiffs) . . . *see also* Howard M. McCormack, *Uniformity of Maritime Law, History, and Perspective from the U.S. Point of View*, 73 Tul. L. Rev. 1481, 1506 (1999); Douglas W. Dunham & Eric F. Gladbach, *Forum Non Conveniens and Foreign Plaintiffs in the 1990's*, 24 Brook. J. Int'l L. 665, 666 (1999).

The Court emphasizes once again that both classes of foreign breast-implant claimants voted to accept the Plan and that it is, therefore, not necessary for the Plan to satisfy the cramdown requirements of § 1129(b). And again, this means that the issue of whether the settlement offers extended to foreign claimants are fair is not at issue in this case. Were we required to decide this issue, however, the evidence demonstrates that the Plan easily passes muster in this respect.

NOTES AND QUESTIONS

(1) *One Clear Rule?* In *Phoenix v. Greystone*, the court said that one clear rule had emerged from the *U.S. Truck* case: "thou shalt not classify similar claims differently in order to gerrymander an affirmative vote on a reorganization plan." Is that what the *U.S. Truck* court held? Look at footnote 8 of the *U.S. Truck* opinion. Didn't the debtor acknowledge that its purpose in separately classifying the Teamster claim was to produce an accepting class of claims? Nevertheless, the court

---

[20] Professor Partlett originally hails from Australia where he taught at the Australian National University in Canberra, Australia for nine years. Prior to that he was the principal law reform officer of the Australian Law Reform Commission. For the past 14 years he has been a professor of law at Vanderbilt University Law School. He teaches advanced torts and remedies and has taught courses in areas such as comparative law and health law. Professor Partlett has also published books and articles on a variety of topics including professional negligence, child mental health and the law, medical malpractice, punitive damages and repressed memories. Australian Claimants' Exhibit 1, Curriculum vitae for David Frederick Partlett; *Transcript of Hearing*, July 14, 1999 at 151–56.

approved the classification scheme based on its finding that the union claim was not similar to other unsecured claims because the union had "a different stake in the future viability of the reorganized company and has alternative means . . . for protecting its claim." Does a determination that claims are not substantially similar prevent a debtor from engaging in precisely the kind of gerrymandering denounced in *Phoenix*? In determining whether a plan proponent engaged in improper gerrymandering, how does a court ascertain the proponent's intent?

(2) *Meaning of Substantially Similar.* As a comparison of the preceding opinions demonstrates, courts can differ in their application and interpretation of the term "substantially similar." Consider whether the following kinds of claims and interests are substantially similar to general unsecured claims and whether they could or should be separately classified and disparately treated:

- Claims that have been equitably subordinated. *See* Resnick & Sommer, 7 *Collier on Bankruptcy* ¶ 1122.03[3][d] (LexisNexis 2010).

- Claims that are contractually subordinated. Compare *In re Station Casinos, Inc.*, 2010 Bankr. LEXIS 5365, *335 (Bankr. D. Nev. Aug. 27, 2010) with, *In re Pierce Goods Shops Co., L.P.*, 188 B.R. 778, 788 (Bankr. M.D.N.C. 1995).

- Claims that have been personally guaranteed by Headley and Carol Charisma. *See, e.g., In re AOV Indus. Inc.*, 792 F.2d 1140, 1150 (D.C. Cir. 1986); *In re Frascella Enters., Inc.*, 360 B.R. 435, 442–43 (Bankr. E.D. Pa. 2007).

- Claims held by insiders, such as Headley and Carol Charisma. *See In re 11,111, Inc.*, 117 B.R. 471 (Bankr. D. Minn. 1990).

- "Claims" held by existing or future products liability claimants, such as victims of Hystereo. *See* Richard L. Epling, *Separate Classification of Future Contingent and Unliquidated Claims in Chapter 11*, 6 Bankr. Dev. J. 173 (1989); Resnick & Sommer, 7 *Collier on Bankruptcy* ¶ 1122.03[3][b] (LexisNexis 2010).

(3) *Good Business Justification.* In *Phoenix v. Greystone*, the debtor's argument that it had good business reasons for separately classifying the trade and deficiency claims was rejected by the court as jejune, because holders of both kinds of claims were receiving the same treatment under the plan. Judge Jones did acknowledge that separate classification of even substantially similar claims may be appropriate if the classification scheme is supported by a good business rationale. The Report of the National Bankruptcy Review Commission states, "Classification for business purposes is an important feature of Chapter 11 plans and in most cases perfectly legitimate." National Bankruptcy Review Commission, *Bankruptcy: The Next Twenty Years, Final Report 581* (1997). One bankruptcy judge has observed, "It is not unknown that a debtor will deal with its trade creditor in one way, its union creditor in another way, its institutional debt in still another, and so on. It is up to the debtor and all of its creditors to decide the extent to which the good graces of the trade creditors or the union will be needed if the rehabilitated debtor is to survive as a viable commercial entity particularly where long range promises are made in the plan." *In re Winston Mills*, 1 C.B.C.2d 121, 128, 1979 Bankr. LEXIS 770 (Bankr. S.D.N.Y. 1979). Consider whether, if you were judge, would uphold the

classification scheme that is described in the problem that introduced this section. Would you approve the following classification schemes?

- Suppliers and other trade creditors that are continuing to do business with Amphydynamics are placed in one class; suppliers and trade creditors that have ceased doing business with the debtor are placed in another class. The former demand and receive better treatment under the plan. *See In re AG Consultants Grain Div., Inc.*, 77 B.R. 665 (Bankr. N.D. Ind. 1987). Should your analysis be influenced by whether other suppliers are readily available? *Barakat v. The Life Ins. Co. of Virginia*, 99 F.3d 1520 (9th Cir. 1996).

- Headley Charisma has been told that the union employees who work on the company's assembly lines will not vote in favor of any plan that does not provide for payment of at least 75% of their allowed claims. Moreover, the union has threatened to strike if the plan provides for a lesser recovery. Amphydynamics cannot afford to pay all unsecured claims that amount. Accordingly, under the plan, union employee claims and other unsecured claims will be separately classified. On the effective date of the plan, union employees will receive 75% of their claims in cash; other unsecured creditors will receive 45% of their claims in cash. *See In re Kliegl Bros. Universal Elec. Stage Lighting Co.*, 149 B.R. 306 (Bankr. E.D.N.Y. 1992).

- Amphy's universe of unsecured claims includes holders of 10-year notes bearing below-market interest. The notes are in default. Amphy would like to place the noteholders in a separate class from other unsecured creditors. Under the plan, all defaults under the notes would be cured, the maturity date would be reinstated, and the legal and equitable rights of the noteholders would be otherwise unchanged. Other unsecured creditors would receive 45% of their claims in cash.

In evaluating these schemes, would you want to know whether the debtor could reorganize without resort to the separate classification and discriminatory treatment? Would you want to know whether the discrimination has been limited to the degree necessary to elicit support for the plan? *See, e.g., In re 11,111, Inc.*, 117 B.R. 471 (Bankr. D. Minn. 1990); *In re Richard Buick, Inc.*, 126 B.R. 840 (Bankr. E.D. Pa. 1991).

(4) *Other Clear Rules.* Although some of the case law on classification may fairly be described as "muddled," there really are some clear rules that have emerged from the muck of statutes and case law:

- Claims and interests are not *substantially* similar and may not be classified together.

- Priority claims and general unsecured claims are not substantially similar and may not be classified together.

- As a general rule, secured creditors will be separately classified. Claims secured by interests in different property are not substantially similar and may not be classified together. Claims that are secured by interests of equal priority in the same property may be classified together, even though the claims and interests arise out of different transactions.

- Claims secured by liens of different priority may not be classified together, even if the liens are on the same property.

See Brady v. Andrew (In re Commercial W. Fin. Corp.), 761 F.2d 1329 (9th Cir. 1985); *Morkava Corp. v. Dolan*, 147 F.2d 340 (2d Cir. 1945); *In re Palisades-on-the-Desplaines*, 89 F.2d 214 (7th Cir. 1937); *In re Martin's Point Ltd. P'ship.*, 12 B.R. 721 (Bankr. N.D. Ga. 1981); King, 7 *Collier on Bankruptcy* ¶ 1122.03 (Matthew Bender 15th Ed. Revised 2000).

(5) *Convenience Classes.* Code § 1122(b) provides that a plan may designate a separate class of claims consisting of every unsecured claim that is less than or reduced to an amount that the court approves as reasonable and necessary for administrative convenience. One purpose of the section was to enable a plan proponent to reduce the number of claim holders entitled to vote. For example, a plan might provide that creditors holding claims of $500 or less would be separately classified and that they would receive cash in full on the effective date of the plan. Under former § 1124(3), such treatment would have made the class unimpaired and its acceptance would have been conclusively presumed. However, § 1124(3) was eliminated from the Code in 1994. Today, an administrative class receiving such treatment would be impaired and entitled to vote on the plan, although class members might be inclined to vote favorably.

§ 9.07 IMPAIRMENT AND CLASSIFICATION REVISITED: ARTIFICIAL IMPAIRMENT

IN RE WINDSOR ON THE RIVER ASSOCIATES, LTD.
United States Court of Appeals, Eighth Circuit
7 F.3d 127 (1993)

MORRIS SHEPPARD ARNOLD, CIRCUIT JUDGE.

Balcor Real Estate Finance, Inc. ("Balcor"), appeals a district court confirmation of a Chapter 11 reorganization plan proposed by Windsor on the River Associates, Ltd. ("Debtor"), the debtor in this case. At issue is whether a debtor's voluntary Chapter 11 reorganization plan can be confirmed over the objections of a secured creditor holding a claim worth over 99% of the total value of the claims against the debtor's assets, when no other creditors are materially affected by the plan. We hold that confirmation under such circumstances is improper and therefore reverse.

I.

Windsor on the River is a 298-unit apartment complex situated on 23 acres adjacent to the Cedar River in Cedar Rapids, Iowa. The property is essentially the only asset of Debtor, a limited partnership formed in 1982 for the purpose of acquiring and owning the complex. In 1987, the Debtor refinanced the loan used to purchase the property with a $9.35 million mortgage loan from Balcor. In connection with the loan, Debtor executed a note, mortgage and security agreement, and assignment of rents, in favor of Balcor. The term of the note is four years, providing for a balloon payment at maturity in May, 1991, of all unpaid principal and deferred interest.

Debtor made payments to Balcor in accordance with the terms of the note until March, 1991. During the months preceding the maturity of the loan, Debtor tried unsuccessfully to negotiate a loan extension with Balcor, or to find refinancing elsewhere. Debtor then failed to make the payments due in April and May, 1991. On May 22, 1991, five days before the maturity date of the note, the Debtor filed a voluntary petition under Chapter 11 of the bankruptcy code.

At the hearing on the Debtor's first plan of reorganization, the bankruptcy court determined the value of the apartment complex to be $10,500,000, while the amount of Balcor's secured claim at that time was determined to be $9,879,927.81. The bankruptcy court declined, however, to confirm the Debtor's initial plan, in part because of the insufficiency of the $164,141 partners' contribution called for by that plan. The Debtor subsequently amended its plan, providing for a capital contribution of $1 million.

[This is an oblique reference to the "new value" issue that we will be confronting later in this chapter, in § 9.10. — Eds.]

The plan now before us, the Debtor's third amended plan, divides the creditors' claims into six classes. It designates Balcor's secured claim as Class 1. Class 4 consists of the claims of tenants for return of their tenant security deposits. The plan provides for payment of these deposits in accordance with the leases. The Class 5 and Class 6 interests are those held by the limited and general partners respectively. The total amount of all claims in the two remaining classes is less than 1% of the amount of Balcor's secured claim.

Class 2 consists of a claim held by Ms. Mary Niman in the amount of $59,249. This claim is purported by the Debtor to have arisen through a series of complex transactions, the legal effect of which is in dispute. The district court subsequently disallowed the Class 2 claim.

The final class of claims under the plan, designated Class 3, consists of the claims of several unsecured trade debts. The total amount of all claims in this class was roughly $13,000, which was originally owed to 34 creditors.

The plan of reorganization is structured so that three classes of claims — Classes 1, 2, and 3 — are impaired. Under the plan, Classes 2 and 3 are scheduled to be paid 60 days after the plan's effective date. Class 1, the Balcor claim, was scheduled to be reduced by a payment of $500,000 to Balcor on the plan's effective date, funded in part by $435,000 of the partners' $1 million capital contribution. The plan also modifies the terms of the loan agreement made between the Debtor and Balcor by extending the maturity date to 10 years after the plan's effective date. The plan calls for the Debtor to make monthly payments to Balcor consisting of principal and interest computed on a 30-year amortization schedule at an annual rate of 8.5%. At maturity, the plan calls for the Debtor to make a final balloon payment to Balcor consisting of the outstanding balance of principal and any accrued unpaid interest.

Because of the "impairment" of the Class 2 and 3 claims, Balcor feared that the plan of reorganization could meet the technical requirements for confirmation with the approval of just one of these two classes. Under § 1129(a)(10), the plan could be confirmed over the disapproval of a creditor if the plan received the approval of "at least one class of claims that is impaired under the plan." This fear led Balcor to attempt to avoid having the reorganization plan "crammed down" its throat. Accordingly, Balcor challenged the validity of the Class 2 claim held by Ms. Niman. Then, to secure an unfavorable vote on the confirmation of the plan by Class 3, Balcor purchased a majority of the Class 3 unsecured trade claims and attempted to cast or change the votes accompanying these claims to deny confirmation.

At the confirmation hearing on the third amended plan, the district court denied Balcor the right to vote as claims assignee of the unsecured trade creditors, in part because 13 of the votes had been cast before Balcor had acquired the claims. As a result, the Class 3 unsecured trade creditors were deemed by the district court to have approved the plan, providing the impaired claim approval required for a "cramdown."

The district court confirmed the plan over Balcor's objections. Balcor appealed the confirmation of the plan on the grounds that the plan was not approved by at least one class of impaired creditors as required by § 1129(a)(10). The Debtor cross-appealed on the district court's decision to disallow the vote cast by the Class 2 claimant, Ms. Niman.

II.

Bankruptcy is a creature of statute. Applications of the bankruptcy code must, therefore, be consistent with long established canons of statutory construction. One such established maxim is that "the starting point for interpreting a statute is the language of the statute itself." *Consumer Prod. Safety Comm. v. GTE Sylvania, Inc.*, 447 U.S. 102, 108, 100 S. Ct. 2051, 64 L. Ed. 2d 766 (1980). While the language is the starting point, it is equally true that it is the task of federal courts when engaging in statutory construction "to interpret the words of the statute in light of the purposes Congress sought to serve." *Norfolk Redevelopment & Housing Authority v. Chesapeake & Potomac Tel. Co.*, 464 U.S. 30, 36, 104 S. Ct. 304, 78 L. Ed. 2d 29 (1983), quoting *Chapman v. Houston Welfare Rights Org.*, 441 U.S. 600, 608, 99 S. Ct. 1905, 60 L. Ed. 2d 508 (1979). Accordingly, "we must avoid statutory interpretation that renders any section superfluous and does not give effect to all of the words used by Congress." *In re Oxborrow*, 913 F.2d 751, 754 (9th Cir. 1990).

Confirmation of the Debtor's plan of reorganization in this case is governed by § 1129, which provides that:

> (a) The court shall confirm a plan only if all of the following requirements are met:
>
> . . . .
>
>> (10) If a class of claims is impaired under the plan, at least one class of claims that is impaired under the plan has accepted the plan, determined without including any acceptance of the plan by any insider.

Under § 1124(1), a class of claims is "impaired" under a plan of reorganization unless, with respect to each claim in the class, the plan "leaves unaltered the legal, equitable, and contractual rights to which such claim or interest entitles the holder of such claim or interest." By this standard, any alteration of a creditor's rights, no matter how minor, constitutes "impairment." The central question presented by the instant case is whether such impairment may be manufactured at the will of the debtor "just to stave off the evil day of liquidation." Richard A. Posner, *Economic Analysis of Law* 378 (3rd ed. 1986). We think that the answer is no.

To allow manipulation of claims in a reorganization proceeding under Chapter 11 would be contrary to the purpose of the provisions of the bankruptcy code. Section 1129(a)(10) was created in 1984 to protect lenders from the potential inequities of the "cramdown" provisions of the Bankruptcy Act. *See* Peter E. Meltzer, *Disenfranchising the Dissenting Creditor through Artificial Classification or Artificial Impairment*, 66 Am. Bankr. L.J. 281, 311–12 (1992). Under the original section 461 of the act, a plan of reorganization for real property could be confirmed so long as the mortgagee received the appraised value of the subject property. § 861 (repealed 1978). The act was amended to address the concerns of lenders that in a depressed real estate market, a cash payment equal to the amount of the market value of the property would "prevent the creditor from recovering the full debt in the event of improved real estate conditions," even though "the creditor would belong to an unimpaired class and would thus be deemed to accept the plan." *In re Polytherm Industries, Inc.*, 33 Bankr. 823, 834 (W.D. Wis. 1983). The structure of this provision imposed "the entire risk of under-valuation by the bankruptcy court on the secured creditor and permits the debtor to receive all of the benefits of future appreciation of the property." *In re 222 Liberty Assoc.*, 108 Bankr. 971, 979 n.6 (Bankr. E.D. Pa. 1990).

To curb the inequities of such reorganization plans being "crammed down" the throat of secured lenders, Congress enacted section 1129(a)(10). The purpose of the section "is to provide some indicia of support by affected creditors and prevent confirmation where such support is lacking." *In re Lettick Typografic, Inc.*, 103 Bankr. 32, 38 (Bankr. D. Conn. 1989). Since Chapter 11 is designed to promote consensual reorganization plans, a proposal that has no support from impaired creditors cannot serve its purpose. It would be odd if an amendment designed to give secured creditors more protection were used as the means to rewrite their credit agreements without their consent. Confirmation of a plan where the debtor engineers the impairment of the only approving impaired class "so distorts the meaning and purpose of [section 1129(a)(10)] that to permit it would reduce (a)(10) to a nullity." *Id.*

It appears that the problems of artificial impairment and artificial classification have much in common. Artificial classification tends to arise where the principal creditor in a single-asset reorganization is undersecured. The extent to which the creditor's claim exceeds its security interest in the single asset of the debtor should be treated, absent the debtor's manipulation, as unsecured credit, and classified with the rest of the unsecured creditors. To achieve "cramdown" under section 1129(a)(10), however, many debtors have attempted to classify the often large unsecured portion of the principal creditor's claim separately from small unsecured trade claims. This is done to prevent the principal creditor from blocking approval of the debtor's plan, which a slightly impaired class of trade claimants might be persuaded to give, in light of the alternative specter of liquidation. *See In re Sandy Ridge Dev. Corp.*, 881 F.2d 1346 (5th Cir. 1989); *see also* Meltzer, *Disenfranchising the Dissenting Creditor*, 66 Am. Bankr. L.J. at 281.

Similarly, artificial impairment has arisen most commonly in single-asset reorganizations. The difference is that the debtor is dealing with an oversecured, rather than undersecured, creditor. Because the lender is oversecured, there is no unsecured portion of the claim to classify along with the unsecured trade creditors. The problem, however, is that the approving class of unsecured trade claimants must hold impaired claims. Impairment in such cases is more difficult, since the value of the asset exceeding the secured claim is often sufficient to satisfy the much smaller unsecured trade claims in full. *See* Meltzer, *Disenfranchising the Dissenting Creditor*, 66 Am. Bankr. L.J. at 283.

The possible effects of confirmation under such circumstances are somewhat unsettling. Confirmation might encourage similarly situated debtors to view the bankruptcy code as an alternative to refinancing. First, debtors with projects lacking the fiscal promise necessary to gain refinancing on the open market might resort to section 1129(a)(10) as the mechanism by which they might draft their own loans from existing lenders. Second, the very threat of such an alternative might coerce lenders into extensions of credit terms that might otherwise not be called for by market conditions.

Finally, such an outcome would directly undermine one of the primary functions of bankruptcy law: to discourage "side dealing" between the shareholders of a corporation and some creditors to the detriment of other creditors. *See* Posner, *Economic Analysis of Law* 375. A similarly situated debtor, with the knowledge that impairment under section 1129(a)(10) might be manufactured, would be encouraged to make arrangements with small, unsecured creditors, and to seek their approval when a plan is filed that leaves their interests only marginally affected. It is exactly such "side dealing" that prompted the adoption of a bankruptcy code, and to allow it would defeat "the purposes Congress sought to serve." *Norfolk Redevelopment*, 464 U.S. at 36, quoting *Chapman*, 441 U.S. at 608. Accordingly, we hold that, for purposes of § 1129(a)(10), a claim is not impaired if the alteration of rights in question arises solely from the debtor's exercise of discretion.

III.

Here, Debtor had no need to classify claims artificially to achieve its purpose. Debtor in the instant case had a reasonable basis for classifying the Balcor loan separately from the trade debt because it was secured. The difficulty, however, is that the separate, approving class must also be "impaired." One such impairment might be a delay in payment. Debtor proposed a plan that delayed payment to the trade creditors for 60 days after the effective date. If this impairment has been manufactured, then the plan must be regarded as having circumvented the purpose of the statute, namely, consensual reorganization.

Whether Debtor manipulated the terms of its plan for purposes of securing confirmation is a question of fact. Findings of fact made by the district court should not be disturbed unless determined to be clearly erroneous. We believe, however, that the trial court clearly erred when it determined that the Class 3 claims were impaired.

The face of Debtor's third amended plan of reorganization clearly shows that the unsecured trade creditors' claims of Class 3 and the disallowed Class 2 claim were arbitrarily and artificially impaired. Simple remanipulation of the plan demonstrates this. Had Debtor's plan allowed for a smaller payment to Balcor, say, $400,000 instead of $500,000, Debtor could have paid both the Class 2 and Class 3 claimants on the effective date. Balcor would have been the only impaired claimant. As the only impaired claimant, and as a secured claimant, it is likely that Balcor would have rejected Debtor's plan. Oddly, Balcor was placed in the position of possibly having to argue that it should receive less under the plan in the hope that its interests might be protected. The only purpose to be served by the delay in payment to the Class 2 and Class 3 claimants was, therefore, to ensure approval by at least one "impaired" class as required by section 1129(a)(10). Debtor never presented a plausible alternative explanation.

Once the arbitrary manipulation of claims is exposed, Balcor becomes the only creditor whose claim is impaired. Accordingly, confirmation of the plan without Balcor's approval was improper. § 1129(a)(10) . . . .

NOTES AND QUESTIONS

(1) *Effect of the 1994 Amendments to § 1124.* Is the sort of artificial impairment denounced in the *Windsor* opinion still possible? The basis of the opinion is that the debtor could have paid unsecured creditors cash in full on the effective date of the plan, leaving them unimpaired under § 1124(3). However, § 1124(3) was eliminated from the Code in 1994. As a result, a class of claims can no longer be left unimpaired by payment in full in cash on the effective date of the plan. Does the elimination of § 1124(3) make it easier for plan proponents in Windsor's position to create an impaired accepting class?

(2) Suppose that on the motion of BigBank, the bankruptcy court terminates Amphy's exclusive period. BigBank then files a plan that provides for payment of BigBank's claim in cash, in full, on the effective date of the plan. Is BigBank's claim impaired? If the class of which BigBank is a part votes in favor of the plan, will it qualify as an impaired accepting class under § 1129(a)(10)? *See In re Union Meeting Partners*, 160 B.R. 757 (Bankr. E.D. Pa. 1993) (holding that even where a creditor's rights are improved by a plan — even if the plan is the creditor's plan — the creditor's claim is impaired).

§ 9.08 THE PLAN ACCEPTANCE PROCESS — CONSENSUAL CONFIRMATION

[A] Disclosure of Adequate Information

After several additional, occasionally explosive meetings, the creditors' committee and representatives of large creditors and stockholders' reached a consensus about the basic provisions of a reorganization plan. You and Headley Charisma and Carol Charisma are now sitting quietly in your conference room.

"Finally," Headley says, "The home stretch. All we have to do is draft a plan and . . . ."

"Slow down, Headley," you say. "That is light that you see at the end of the funnel, but we still have a lot to do."

"Ho, you mean 'tunnel.' "

"No, Headley, I really mean 'funnel,' which is a much better metaphor for what's happening at this stage of the case. This is the point at which all the fruits of our labors over the past months converge. We've rationalized our operations and formulated a business plan. We've developed a vision of what the reorganized Amphydynamics will be. We've reached a tentative accord with our creditors. Now it's time for us to distill all of this, and more, into a formal plan and a disclosure statement."

"I suppose that if I ask you what a disclosure statement is, I will be in for another history lesson."

"Yes, but it will be brief," you say, "because we really have a lot to do."

You begin by reminding Headley that (as you explained at the beginning of this chapter) a plan is a contract between the debtor and claim and interest holders that provides what they will receive on account of their claims or interests and when they will receive it. Every first year law student has heard the cliché that the formation of a contract requires a "meeting of the minds." Whether this is a correct statement of contract law is doubtful; however, in a sense, the Code attempts to insure not just that minds have met, but that *informed* minds have met. It does this by authorizing plan proponents to solicit votes only after claim and interest holders have received a court-approved disclosure statement containing the information necessary to make an informed decision about whether to accept or reject a plan. The Code's "requirement for informed suffrage" is said to be "at the heart of Chapter 11." *In re Lionel Corp.*, 722 F.2d 1063, 1066 (2d Cir. 1983) (reprinted in chapter 6, § 6.01).

"Having the court approve the disclosure statement strikes me as a little paternalistic," Carol interrupts.

"So it might," you concede. You also suggest that Carol keep a few points in mind. One, unless a creditor can get relief from the stay, it, in essence, is held hostage during the case by the debtor, who at least initially has control over the plan process. Two, under the Chapter 11 regime, if a class accepts the plan by the required majorities, dissenting class members are also bound. Consequently, this paternalistic intrusion into the parties' freedom of contract may be warranted. The third point is that the Code's "informed suffrage" approach is considerably more hands-off than the approach that was followed under the former Act. The drafters of the Act seemed to believe that creditors and stockholders lacked the information (and perhaps the capacity) required to make an informed decision about a plan. That is why, under former Chapter X, the plan approval process was a highly ritualized, time-consuming, and costly affair in which the SEC, the court, and the Chapter X trustee were very much involved:

> Under . . . chapter X . . . a trustee is always appointed. The trustee is the prime agent in the formulation and presentation of a plan of reorganization. When the trustee files the plan, the court sets an approval hearing. At the approval hearing, the trustee and other interested parties develop financial information about the plan. The purpose of the hearing is to arrive at a going concern valuation of the debtor, in order to determine how much the debtor is worth, and whether the plan meets the standards for confirmation of the plan under chapter X.

> The valuation of the debtor arrived at during the approval hearing will be applied to the plan, to determine if the reorganization values distributed under the plan are distributed in such a way that the absolute priority rule is satisfied. The valuation consists of an estimate of the earning power of the reorganized debtor, and the appropriate market capitalization rate of that estimated income stream. The income stream thus estimated, capitalized as appropriate, is then distributed among the classes of creditors and equity security holders according to the absolute priority rule. The [valuation] process, however, is inherently uncertain. Professor Peter Coogan has frequently referred to it as "an estimate compounded by a guess."

> At the approval hearing, the court also determines whether the plan is worthy of consideration, and whether it meets the other confirmation standards of chapter X. If it does, the court approves the plan. If there is more than one plan proposed, the court will conduct the same approval process for each plan, and approve those that meet the standards. The approval process is generally a long and intricate process. The hearing frequently spans months.

> After the hearing on the plan, the plan, along with the evidence developed at the approval hearing, is sent to the Securities and Exchange Commission. The Commission develops an advisory report on the plan. This process may take anywhere from one to six months or more. The purpose of the advisory report is to inform the creditors and stockholders of the contents of the plan, and of the SEC's evaluation of the plan. Some have argued that creditors and stockholders simply are unable to make an intelligent or informed decision without the SEC's report, all of the valuation evidence developed at the disclosure hearing, and an order of the court finding the plan worthy of consideration and approving the plan. The purpose of the approval hearing, court approval, and an SEC report in chapter X was public investor protection.

H.R. Rep. 95-595, 95th Cong., 1st Sess. 224–225 (1977).

Under Chapter XI, trustees were not appointed, the absolute priority rule did not apply, no valuation hearings or SEC advisory reports were required, and the plan process was therefore considerably more streamlined and flexible. Yet, the Chapter XI approach, too, was subject to criticism, especially as Chapter XI became the favored haven for large companies in distress:

> The disclosure to creditors and stockholders is minimal at best. The original rationale of chapter XI provides the reason: chapter XI was designed to deal with trade debt, not secured or public debt or equity. Trade creditors are most often involved in the debtor's operations, and are familiar with them. They do not require the elaborate disclosure in order to make an informed decision with respect to a chapter XI plan. In practice, this is generally true, but it has permitted solicitation of acceptances of plans from creditors that are in the dark about the debtor's business, the prospect for success under the plan, and whether the offer under the plan is a reasonable offer. In addition, as chapter XI has grown, its effect has been to modify the rights of equity security holders, usually by dilution through issuance of additional equity to creditors in exchange for their claims. Chapter XI needs some form of investor protection in order to make it a fairer reorganization vehicle.

Id. Today's Chapter 11 is a hybrid of Chapters X and XI. Chapter 11 trustees are not routinely appointed and debtors in possession are the usual proponents of plans, although any party in interest may file a plan if the debtor's exclusive period has ended. § 1121. Under Chapter 11, the absolute priority rule has been relaxed and the role of the SEC has been curtailed significantly and its formal advisory role eliminated.

Who, then, is looking out for the creditors and investors and making sure they are not being euchred into voting in favor of a bad plan?

The theory of the Code is that given appropriate information, creditors and interest holders, both large and small, can look out for themselves. The drafters explained:

> In consolidating the two reorganization chapters, it is necessary to determine the extent of the disclosure to creditors and equity security holders required, and the extent of advance court determination of the propriety of the plan. The premise underlying the consolidated chapter 11 of this bill is the same as the premise of the securities law. If adequate disclosure is provided to all creditors and stockholders whose rights are to be affected, then they should be able to make an informed judgment of their own, rather than having the court or the Securities and Exchange Commission inform them in advance whether the proposed plan is a good plan. Therefore, the key to the consolidated chapter is the disclosure section.

H.R. Rep. 95-595, 95th Cong., 1st Sess. 226 (1977).

"The disclosure section" to which the House Report refers is Code § 1125. Read it, and the materials that follow now.

IN RE METROCRAFT PUBLISHING SERVICES, INC.
United States Bankruptcy Court, Northern District of Georgia
39 B.R. 567 (1984)

W. Homer Drake, Bankruptcy Judge.

This case is before the Court on the application by the above-named debtor for approval of its disclosure statement in accordance with § 1125 of the Bankruptcy Code. An objection to the disclosure statement was filed by the Creditors' Committee ("Committee"). Following a hearing on May 1, 1984, this matter was taken under advisement. As set forth below, the disclosure statement contains a number of deficiencies which must be corrected before the Court will approve the disclosure statement for distribution to creditors.

Section 1125(b) of the Bankruptcy Code states as follows:

> An acceptance or rejection of a plan may not be solicited after the commencement of the case under this title from a holder of a claim or interest with respect to such claim or interest, unless, at the time of or before such solicitation, there is transmitted to such holder the plan or a summary of the plan, and a written disclosure statement approved, after notice and a hearing, by the court as containing adequate information. The court may approve a disclosure statement without a valuation of the debtor or an appraisal of the debtor's assets.

"Adequate information" is defined in § 1125(a)(1) of the Bankruptcy Code to mean

> information of a kind, and in sufficient detail, as far as is reasonably practicable in light of the nature and history of the debtor and the condition of the debtor's books and records, that would enable a hypothetical reasonable investor typical of the holders of claims or interests of the relevant class to make an informed judgment about the plan.

Case law under § 1125 of the Bankruptcy Code has produced a list of factors disclosure of which may be mandatory, under the facts and circumstances of a particular case, to meet the statutory requirement of adequate information. Disclosure of all factors is not necessary in every case. Conversely, the list is not exhaustive, and a case may arise in which disclosure of all these enumerated factors is still not sufficient to provide adequate information for the creditors to evaluate the plan. Nevertheless, these factors provide a useful starting point for the Court's analysis of the adequacy of the disclosure statement. The Court will address the Committee's objections with an eye toward these enumerated factors as they pertain to this debtor's business and the proposed Chapter 11 plan of reorganization.

Factors (1) through (11) are taken from the case of *In re A. C. Williams Co.*, 25 B.R. 173 (Bkrtcy. N.D. Ohio 1982). Factors (12) through (13) and (14) through (15) appear in *In re William F. Gable Co.*, 10 B.R. 248 (Bankr. N.D. W. Va. 1981), and *In re Adana Mortg. Bankers, Inc.*, 14 B.R. 29 (Bkrtcy. N.D. Ga. 1981), respectively. This Court adds factors (16) through (19) in response to objections raised in the instant proceeding.

Relevant factors for evaluating the adequacy of a disclosure statement may include: (1) the events which led to the filing of a bankruptcy petition; (2) a description of the available assets and their value; (3) the anticipated future of the company; (4) the source of information stated in the disclosure statement; (5) a disclaimer; (6) the present condition of the debtor while in Chapter 11; (7) the scheduled claims; (8) the estimated return to creditors under a Chapter 7 liquidation; (9) the accounting method utilized to produce financial information and the name of the accountants responsible for such information; (10) the future management of the debtor; (11) the Chapter 11 plan or a summary thereof; (12) the estimated administrative expenses, including attorneys' and accountants' fees; (13) the collectability of accounts receivable; (14) financial information, data, valuations or projections relevant to the creditors' decision to accept or reject the Chapter 11 plan; (15) information relevant to the risks posed to creditors under the plan; (16) the actual or projected realizable value from recovery of preferential or otherwise voidable transfers; (17) litigation likely to arise in a nonbankruptcy context; (18) tax attributes of the debtor; and (19) the relationship of the debtor with affiliates.

[Having presented the legal background, and having made the necessary disclaimer, the Court proceeds to discuss the particulars of the case *sub judice*. — Eds.]

The disclosure statement describes the business of the debtor, Metrocraft Publishing Services, Inc. ("Metrocraft"), in the following terms:

> Metrocraft is a medium size commercial web printing company with its place of business at 1833 Lawrenceville Highway, Decatur, Georgia. Metrocraft offers to its customers a full spectrum of services from composition and typesetting to complete web offset press. These services[,] including camera ready preparations and sheet fed presses, are offered as separate services as well as a completely integrated package.

A separate entity, Metropolitan Advertising Associated ("MAA") was created to act as a sales organization to increase Metrocraft's business and, ultimately, to act as a broker to place business with other printers. The disclosure statement indicates that:

> In January, 1983, MAA supplied all of its business to Metrocraft. By February MAA was brokering some business, and by March MAA was brokering 80% of its business. The combined business of Metrocraft and the MAA brokering brought in some 26 million impressions, or $650,000.00 gross sales for the quarter ending March 31, 1983.

The disclosure statement points out that two experienced printing sales and marketing individuals left MAA during July, 1983 thereby causing a loss in sales momentum. Efforts to regain sales momentum have not been entirely successful. After filing the Chapter 11 petition, Metrocraft has concentrated on cutting variable operating costs, primarily in the area of payroll.

The Chapter 11 plan allocates a total of $48,000.00, plus nominal interest, to be distributed to all unsecured claimants. Neither the plan nor the disclosure statement suggests the percentage at which unsecured creditors will be paid under the plan.

The Committee legitimately desires more information before an intelligent decision can be rendered as to the acceptability of the Chapter 11 plan. The Court categorizes the Committee's objections according to the criteria set forth above under which such objections arise:

> (2) *A Description of the Available Assets and their Value.* The Committee notes that the disclosure statement fails to give the actual or projected realizable value from machinery, fixtures and equipment originally scheduled in the amount of $354,499.92. The Court agrees that creditors are entitled to such information or an explanation why such information has not been presented.
>
> . . . .
>
> (7) *The Scheduled Claims.* The Committee raises a number of objections relating to the disclosure of claims. First, the Committee points out that the plan proposes to pay . . . claims [that] are not scheduled. It is imperative that creditors be informed of the nature of these claims, the principal amount due on these claims and the monthly payments specified in the agreements under which these claims arise. Second, the Committee strongly desires to know the amount of unsecured claims so that some calculation can be made as to the percentage at which such claims shall be paid under the proposed pro rata distribution of $48,000.00. The debtor argues that the amount of unsecured claims is subject to the Court's determination of which claims are allowable. In addition, the debtor asserts that certain claims may be offset by preferential transfers. The Court concludes that the debtor cannot avoid all disclosure regarding unsecured claims simply because their exact amount cannot be determined at this time. Some discussion of the nature of unsecured claims, their approximate value and the approximate amount by which such claims may be subject to setoff for settlement purposes shall be disclosed to creditors. Third, the Committee objects that the disclosure statement fails to indicate the sums to be paid to other creditors, both on a monthly basis and in total amount. The Court agrees that disclosure in this regard is necessary to evaluate, *inter alia*, the debtor's cash flow and the amount of money being diverted to creditors which might be available to pay unsecured claims. Fourth, the Chapter 11 plan provides for payment of wage priority claims notwithstanding the fact that no such claims have been scheduled. The debtor argues that no disbursements are intended to be made to priority wage claimants, but that the wage priority provision was included in the plan to assure that the plan complies with the Bankruptcy Code. Rather than force creditors to ponder the discrepancy between the schedule and the plan, a short statement explaining why the wage priority provision is in the plan shall be provided to eliminate any confusion.

(8) *The Estimated Return to Creditors Under Chapter 7 Liquidation.* The Committee asserts that the disclosure statement should reveal the estimated return to creditors under a Chapter 7 liquidation as an alternative to the Chapter 11 reorganization. The debtor argues that the projected balance sheet shows that the debtor would be insolvent by the amount of $42,500.00 after subtracting from asset value the amount of secured claims, estimated administrative claims and unsecured claims in the reduced amount of $48,000.00. However, as the Committee's first objection illustrates, the debtor has not provided a valuation regarding the machinery and equipment. Absent a valuation of the assets with some factual basis, and absent a concise statement addressing the prospects of a Chapter 7 liquidation, the disclosure statement does not provide adequate information as required by the Bankruptcy Code.

. . . .

(13) *The Collectability of Accounts Receivable.* The debtor's Schedules list the amount of accounts receivable at $117,232.16. Related to the question of the value of assets is the question of the collectability of these accounts receivable. The debtor's accounting records should enable the debtor to offer at least a historical analysis as to the collectability of the outstanding accounts. Absent such disclosure, the statement of the amount of accounts receivable is nothing but raw data with little significance.

. . . .

(16) *The Actual or Projected Realizable Value from Recovery of Preferential or Otherwise Voidable Transfers.* The debtor acknowledges that the bankruptcy estate may have claims for preferential transfers, but no light is shed on the nature of these preferential transfers or their approximate amount. Admittedly, the precise amount of such preferential transfers cannot be stated prior to this Court's determination on such claims. Nevertheless, the debtor is not excused from discussing the amount of preferences in approximate terms and setting forth what steps have been taken toward settling or litigating these claims.

(17) *Litigation Likely to Arise in a Nonbankruptcy Context.* The debtor's Statement of Financial Affairs shows that a lawsuit has been filed against the debtor by Covington News, but the claim of Covington News is not discussed in the disclosure statement or provided for in the Chapter 11 plan. The creditors are entitled to information regarding the claim by Covington News. In addition, there is a possibility that the debtor may have claims against former principals. The debtor shall indicate what progress has been made or is expected to be made in furtherance of these claims.

(18) *Tax Attributes of the Debtor.* The disclosure statement makes no mention of net operating loss carry-overs which would seemingly be available to reduce the debtor's tax liability in the future. The Court will not impose upon the debtor the obligation to render a lengthy analysis of the law under the Internal Revenue Code. But, if such tax attributes are available for the debtor's use, they should be described so that creditors

may evaluate the actual after tax position of the debtor. If such tax attributes are not available to the debtor, a brief explanation of the reasons leading to that conclusion is sufficient.

(19) *The Relationship of the Debtor with Affiliates.* The Committee contends that the disclosure statement does not illuminate the relationship between the debtor and MAA and any potential claims that may exist between the debtor and MAA. Although the debtor makes reference to MAA at page 5 of the disclosure statement, the exact relationship of the two entities is not clearly set forth, and no discussion is made as to potential liability running to and from the entities. The Court concludes that this relationship and the possible claims shall be disclosed.

In accordance with the foregoing, approval of the debtor's disclosure statement shall be and is hereby DENIED. The debtor shall have thirty (30) days to file an amended disclosure statement which conforms with the directives stated herein.

It is so ordered.

NOTES AND QUESTIONS

(1) *Meaning of "Adequate Information."* Congress purposely left vague the standard for judging what constitutes adequate information in order to permit a case-by-case determination based on the circumstances of each case, including the cost of preparing a more detailed statement, the need for relative speed in soliciting votes and moving the case toward confirmation, and the need for creditor and investor protection. H.R. Rep. No.95-595, 95th Cong., 1st Sess. 225, 409 (1977). "A disclosure statement must contain all pertinent information bearing on the success or failure of the proposals in the plan of reorganization. A disclosure statement should likewise contain all material information relating to the risks posed to creditors and equity interest holders under the proposed plan of reorganization. The disclosure statement, on the other hand, should not be burdened with 'overly technical and extremely numerous additions,' where such information would serve only to diminish the understanding of a typical creditor or interest holder." *In re Cardinal Congregate I*, 121 B.R. 760, 765–66 (Bankr. S.D. Ohio 1990) (citations omitted). A disclosure statement is intended to be a source "of factual information upon which one can make an informed judgment about a reorganization plan," and not "an advertisement or a sales brochure." *In re Egan*, 33 B.R. 672, 676–77 (Bankr. N.D. Ill. 1983). When courts withhold approval of disclosure statements, it is frequently because they say too little or too much. For example, in the *Cardinal* case, the court found that the plan fell short in the following respects:

> The Court finds that the Disclosure Statement lacks certain necessary information. First, the Disclosure Statement contains an inadequate discussion of the claims held by various affiliates . . . for loans made and services provided to the debtor. The Disclosure Statement should contain more detailed information regarding the nature of these claims and should specifically identify the holders of such claims. Additionally, a more complete discussion of the Amended Plan's proposed treatment of these claims is necessary.

Second, the Disclosure Statement must contain more information regarding the debtor's operations postpetition. It is not enough that the Disclosure Statement refers its reader to the monthly operating reports filed by the debtor with this Court; the Disclosure Statement should contain a detailed textual description of the debtor's postpetition performance. . . .

Third, the Disclosure Statement should include a discussion of the anticipated future of the debtor's business. Merely attaching pro forma income calculations to the Disclosure Statement is insufficient. A more detailed analysis of the projected income, expenses, and surplus funds available for satisfaction of claims and interest is appropriate. Further, the Disclosure Statement should clearly identify all assumptions made in calculating pro forma information and should set forth those facts supporting all estimates. Information regarding the accounting and valuation methods used in preparation of the Disclosure Statement's financial exhibits must also be included.

Fourth, both the Disclosure Statement and Amended Plan of Reorganization identify "Net Cash Flow" as a source of funds for the satisfaction of allowed claims and interests. However, the Court can find no definition of Net Cash Flow in either document. The Disclosure Statement must clearly state how Net Cash Flow is defined and calculated.

Fifth, the Disclosure Statement and Amended Plan of Reorganization discuss as a potential source of funds those proceeds that will be realized upon the contemplated sale or refinancing of the retirement facility. The Disclosure Statement should more fully explain the consequences of any such sale or refinancing upon all allowed claims and interests. Additionally, the Disclosure Statement should contain a discussion of any efforts to date, as well as intended future efforts, to bring about a sale or refinancing of the property.

Sixth, the Disclosure Statement should provide a more detailed estimation of allowable administrative expenses. This should include, without limitation, all estimated fees for attorneys and accountants.

Finally, an identification and discussion of all causes of action which the debtor may pursue under the Bankruptcy Code or other applicable law should be included in the Disclosure Statement. The debtor's intentions as to these causes of action must also be disclosed.

The information required by the Court is neither unreasonable nor voluminous. Where, as here, the satisfaction of claims and interests is dependent upon the debtor's ability to improve its financial performance or to consummate contemplated transactions, it is not overly demanding for the Court to require detailed disclosure of the facts and assumptions underlying the debtor's belief that it will accomplish its reorganization effort.

121 B.R. at 767. On the other hand, particularly (but not exclusively) in cases of lesser complexity, courts have expressed frustration with disclosure statements that

obfuscate rather than inform and that test a court's patience and a reader's endurance:

> A disclosure statement must be meaningful to be understood, and it must be understood to be effective. Thus, what lawyers regard as useful information based upon their experience might be meaningless verbiage in the hands of a "typical" investor. Accordingly, by overburdening a proponent's disclosure statement with information significant and meaningful to lawyers alone may result ultimately in reducing the disclosure statement to an overlong, incomprehensible, ineffective collection of words to those whose interests are to be served by disclosure. Thus, compounding a disclosure statement for the sake of a lawyer's notion of completeness, or because some additional information might enhance one's understanding, may not always be necessary or desirable, and the length of a document should not be the test of its effectiveness.

In re Stanley Hotel, Inc., 13 Bankr. 926, 933–934 (Bankr. D. Co. 1981). Or, as another court more succinctly put it:

> [D]isclosure statements should not contain overly technical language that the average creditor cannot readily understand. . . . [A] proper disclosure statement must clearly and succinctly inform the average unsecured creditor what it is going to get, when it is going to get it, and what contingencies there are to getting its distribution.

In re Ferretti, 128 B.R. 16, 19 (Bankr. D.N.H. 1991).

(2)   *The Code Brooks Bad Books?* According to Code § 1125(a)(1), what constitutes "adequate information" may depend on "the condition of the debtor's books and records." The Senate report explains this standard this way:

> Reporting and audit standards devised for solvent and continuing businesses do not necessarily fit a debtor in reorganization. Subsection (a)(1) expressly incorporates consideration of the nature and history of the debtor and the condition of its books and records into the determination of what is reasonably practicable to supply. These factors are particularly pertinent to historical data and to discontinued operations of no future relevance.
>
> A plan is necessarily predicated on knowledge of the assets and liabilities being dealt with and on factually supported expectations as to the future course of the business sufficient to meet the feasibility standard in [Code § 1129(a)(11)] of this title. It may thus be necessary to provide estimates or judgments for that purpose. Yet it remains practicable to describe, in such detail as may be relevant and needed, the basis for the plan and the data on which supporters of the plan rely.

S. Rep. No. 989, 95th Cong., 2d Sess. 121 (1978). Code § 1129(a)(11) requires a plan proponent to demonstrate that confirmation of a reorganization plan is not likely to be followed by a liquidation of the debtor, or, in other words, that the plan is feasible. Notably, if the condition of the debtor's books and records makes it impossible for the debtor to provide reasonable projections of future income and expenses or to make an informed judgment about its ability to perform its obligations under the plan, confirmation may be denied on the grounds that the plan is not feasible. *See In re Ferretti*, 128 B.R. 16, 21 (Bankr. D.N.H. 1991).

(3) *Meaning of Typical Investor.* As we know, every plan is required to group claims and interests into separate classes, Code § 1123(a)(1), and provide the same treatment for each claim or interest within a class (unless a particular holder agrees to less favorable treatment). § 1123(a)(4). In order for a plan to be accepted, each class of claims that is impaired under the plan must vote by the required majorities to accept the plan. § 1129(a)(8).

Consistent with these principles, § 1125(c) requires that all members of a given class receive the same disclosure statement. According to § 1125(a)(1), the disclosure statement is to be pitched to the "typical" class member, and § 1125(a)(2) says typical means as one who has the same type of claim, relationship with the debtor, and access to other information about the debtor as other members of the class generally have. This can be tricky. As we've seen, a class of unsecured creditors might contain a panorama of creditors including large, sophisticated banks that have been tracking the debtor for years, small suppliers of the debtor who know something about the business, and retail customers and tort victims who know nothing about the debtor's financial affairs. Section 1125(a)(2) suggests that the disclosure statement should be drafted for the members of the class that are most typical, not for the most or least sophisticated members. As the legislative history explains, "the hypothetical investor against which the disclosure is measured must not be an insider if other members of the class are not insiders, and so on. In other words, the adequacy of disclosure is measured against the typical investor, not an extraordinary one." H.R. Rep. No. 95-595, 95th Cong., 1st Sess. 409 (1977).

(4) *Different Editions.* Section 1125(c) authorizes the transmittal of different disclosure statements to members of different classes. "This provision," according to the legislative history, "permits flexibility in the preparation and distribution of disclosure statements. It may be used, for example, where a very large class required only limited disclosure, while other classes required more extensive disclosure. To save preparation, printing, and mailing costs, it might be appropriate to send different statements to the different classes. On the other hand, in many cases, it will be a cheaper matter to send the most complete disclosure statement to all classes, instead of attempting to prepare separate ones." H.R. Rep. 95-595, 95th Cong., 1st Sess. 227 (1977).

(5) *Necessity for a Valuation.* Consistent with the Code's aim of facilitating the plan process and encouraging negotiated, consensual plans, § 1125(b) permits the court to approve a disclosure statement "without a valuation of the debtor or an appraisal of the debtor's assets." Nevertheless, the reorganization value of the debtor is what is being distributed under a plan, and as the legislative history points out, in some cases, a valuation or appraisal will be necessary to develop adequate information. H.R. Rep. 95-595, 95th Cong., 1st Sess. 409 (1977). A valuation of the debtor may be necessary, for example, if securities are issued in exchange for debt or other securities under the plan or if a consensus cannot be reached and the court's cramdown power is invoked. *See* discussion in § 9.10.

Notwithstanding § 1125(b), as the *Metrocraft* opinion demonstrates, courts routinely look for a comparison of what creditors will receive under the plan and what they would receive if the debtor were liquidated. Under the former Act, it was necessary to put a liquidation value on the debtor in virtually every case, because it was necessary to show that creditors would fare as well under the plan as they would in a prompt liquidation. This became known as the best interests of creditors test. Today a shard — actually a very big shard — of it remains in Code § 1129(a)(7)(A), which provides that if a class accepts by the required majorities, but not unanimously, then each claim holder within the class must receive treatment under the plan that is at least as good as what it would receive if the debtor were liquidated. Thus, today, the best interests test only comes into play if a class does not accept unanimously.

Consistent with the principle that all members of a class must be treated alike, this test must be satisfied with respect to accepting creditors as well as dissenting creditors. § 1123(a)(4). For plan proponents, a liquidation analyses can be an effective plan marketing tool, especially in cases in which the debtor has few unencumbered assets with which to satisfy unsecured claims. Courts still seem to view the best interests test as a litmus test. In *In re Crowthers McCall Pattern, Inc.*, 120 B.R. 279, 300–301 (Bankr. S.D.N.Y. 1990), the debtor's disclosure statement was approved by the court, transmitted to creditors, and votes were solicited. At the confirmation hearing, the court found that the disclosure statement contained an incorrect liquidation analysis. The court refused to accept the vote or confirm the plan and required the plan proponents to transmit a corrected liquidation analysis and ballots. The court explained, "Disclosure statements are required to contain liquidation analyses that enable creditors to make their own judgment as to whether a plan is in their best interests and to vote and object to a plan if they so desire. . . . The confirmation process and the protections of creditors are not to be denigrated by a liquidation analysis such as that presented in this case." *Id.*

(6) *A Problem of Gun-Jumping or Prior Restraint?* Dow Corning Corp. filed a Chapter 11 petition in May, 1995, after being named as a defendant in thousands of product liability suits arising out of its manufacture and sale of silicone breast implants. Three years later, after months of difficult negotiations, the debtor and the committee representing the product liability plaintiffs filed a joint plan of reorganization and disclosure statement. The debtor and the committee mentioned that they hoped to "generate some good publicity" with the filing of the plan. The unsecured creditors' committee asked the court to limit efforts of the debtor and the product liability committee to publicize the plan through the use of press releases and media appearances until the disclosure statement was approved. Is an attempt to put a little positive public relations spin on a plan a solicitation? Can a public relations campaign be restrained prior to approval of a disclosure statement? *See In re Dow Corning Corp.*, 227 B.R. 111 (Bankr. E.D. Mich. 1998).

(7) *Securities Disclosure Standards Rejected.* Section 1125(d) provides that the adequacy of a Chapter 11 disclosure statement is *not* to be judged according to the standards imposed by any otherwise applicable nonbankruptcy law, rule, or regulation. As you may have surmised, the primary targets of this rule are the federal securities laws and the SEC, although it applies to state laws and agencies as well. According to the House Report:

The bill also permits the disclosure statement to be approved without the necessity for compliance with the very strict rules of Section 5 of the Securities Act of 1933, section 14 of the Securities Exchange Act of 1934, or relevant State securities laws. Without such a provision, the court would have no discretion in approving disclosure statements that go to public classes, but would be required in every case to require a full proxy statement or prospectus whenever public classes were solicited. Such a statement requires certified audited financial statements and extensive information. The cost of developing a prospectus or proxy statement for a large company often runs well over $1 million. That cost would be nearly prohibitive in a bankruptcy reorganization. In addition, the information normally required under section 14 may simply be unavailable, because of the condition of the debtor. Finally, court supervision of the contents of the disclosure statement will protect the public investor from any serious inadequacies in the disclosure statement.

The provision does not prohibit a section 14-type statement or a prospectus. In some cases it may indeed be appropriate to go to that length in disclosure. The courts will have to determine the need on a case-by-case basis. The section merely does not require it in every public case.

Bankruptcy law cuts across many others area of the law. In the interaction between bankruptcy law and other laws, each bends somewhat to accommodate the policies of the other. The disclosure provisions in the bill are a compromise between the strict requirements of the securities laws and the near-absolute freedom of the present bankruptcy laws. A compromise is essential. If nothing is to change when a company becomes insolvent, then the bankruptcy laws can offer that company little help. The company would be no better off proceeding under the bankruptcy laws than under generally applicable law. The compromise proposed in this section is a reasonable one that accounts for both the interest of the creditors in a successful reorganization, and the interest of the public in preventing securities fraud.

H.R. Rep. 95-595, 95th Cong., 1st Sess. 227–228. In *Kirk v. Texaco, Inc.*, 82 B.R. 678 (S.D.N.Y. 1988), a Chapter 11 case of cosmic proportion and complexity, the district court flatly rejected one commentator's suggestion that "the closer the case comes to a major reorganization of a widely held debtor, the closer will be the requirement of the disclosure statement to that of a non-bankruptcy prospectus." *Id.* at 681. To the contrary, the court chided:

On a plain reading of § 1125(a) and (d), the bankruptcy judge is under no duty to analogize to the securities laws even in complex, securities-related bankruptcy cases, and the legislative history does not suggest that any such duty was intended. Congress knew that it could apply the securities laws to certain bankruptcy matters. It declined to require such application, choosing instead to give bankruptcy judges broad discretion in their supervision of corporate reorganizations. This Court should not undermine this important legislative policy.

Id. at 682.

Section 1125(d) states that an official or agency whose responsibility is to enforce such nonbankruptcy standards may be heard on the issue of the adequacy of the disclosure statement, but adds that such official or agency may not appeal from a court order approving a disclosure statement.

> The compromise contains certain protections, so that the public is not left entirely at the mercy of the debtor and its creditors. First and most important, the court will be required to approve a disclosure statement before there may be any solicitation of acceptances or rejections of a plan. . . . The other important protection provided in this section is that the Securities and Exchange Commission and any other regulatory agency or officers whose responsibility it is to enforce securities laws will have an absolute right to appear and be heard on whether a disclosure statement contains adequate information. Their arguments, on behalf of the public interest in an orderly securities market, will undoubtedly be heard and considered by the bankruptcy judges. . . .

> The S.E.C. and State agencies will not have a right of appeal on the adequacy of disclosure, either in the role of an advisor to the court in reorganization cases, or in the role of the agency responsible for the enforcement of the securities laws generally. The disclosure hearing is the central hearing in the case, and in a case of any size will be a relatively long process. An appeal by an agency that had no direct interest in the case when none of those with money involved can be persuaded to take an appeal could cause delay to the detriment of the debtor, the creditors, and the stockholders.

H.R. Rep. 95-595, 95th Cong., 1st Sess. 229.

(8) *Estoppel Effect of Disclosure Statement.* Among the items that a disclosure statement is supposed to disclose are the actual or projected value that can be obtained by avoidance of preferences and fraudulent transfers (item 19 in the *Metrocraft* list) and litigation likely to arise in the nonbankruptcy context (item 20). Suppose Amphydynamics files a disclosure statement that states that "the Debtor has discussed the nature of preferential payments and fraudulent transfers with its counsel and accountants. The Debtor's management does not believe any preferences or fraudulent transfers have occurred." Suppose the court approves the disclosure statement. Votes are solicited and creditor BigBank votes in favor of the plan. A week later, Amphydynamics brings an action against BigBank to recover alleged preferences it received. Does anything about this trouble you? In fact, Amphydynamics may be judicially estopped from asserting its claim against BigBank.

The proponent of a Chapter 11 plan has a duty to disclose the existence of potential claims against creditors before they vote on a plan. *See, e.g., Krystal Cadillac-Oldsmobile GMC Trucks v. General Motors Corp.,* 337 F.3d 314 (3d Cir. 2003); *Construction Mgmt. Servs., Inc. v. Manufacturers Hanover Trust Co. (In re Coastal Grp., Inc.),* 13 F.3d 81, 86 (3d Cir. 1994). As one court has noted, "The preparing and filing of a disclosure statement is a most important step in the reorganization of a Chapter 11 debtor. It is relied on by both the creditors of the debtor before they vote on the plan . . . and by the bankruptcy court before approving it. Given this reliance, it is crucial that a debtor be absolutely truthful so that the disclosure statement meets the Code standard in § 1125 . . . . [A] debtor who stated in its disclosure statement that it has no preference actions and thereby implies that it investigated the possibility of such claims, and failed to amend its disclosure statement upon discovering same may not thereafter reverse its field . . ." *Galerie Des Monnaies of Geneva, Ltd. v. Deutsche Bank, A.G. (In re Galerie Des Monnaies of Geneva, Ltd.)*, 55 B.R. 253, 259–60 (Bankr. S.D.N.Y. 1985).

(9)   *The Cost of Non-Disclosure.* If a disclosure statement is "wholly inadequate" under § 1125, and thus of no benefit to the estate, the professionals who drafted it may not be entitled to compensation for their services. *Hansen, Jones & Leta, P.C. v. Segal, (In re Bonneville Pac. Corp.)*, 220 B.R. 434 (D. Utah 1998). There is no requirement that an attorney sign a disclosure statement. In fact, Rule 9011(a) suggests that disclosure statements do not have to be signed by an attorney. However, an attorney who knowingly or recklessly signs and files a disclosure statement containing false information may be subject to Rule 9011 sanctions. *See, e.g., In re Ligon*, 50 B.R. 127 (Bankr. M.D. Tenn. 1985); *In re Beltrami Enters.*, 191 B.R. 303 (Bankr. M.D. Pa. 1995).

(10)   *The Disclosure Hearing.* A disclosure statement should be filed at the same time that a plan is filed or within a time fixed by the court. Bankruptcy Rule 3016(b). After the disclosure statement is filed, the bankruptcy court is required to hold a hearing to consider the statement and any objections to it. Bankruptcy Rule 3017(a). The debtor, the trustee, creditors, equity security holders, other parties in interest, committees, the SEC, the IRS, and the United States Trustee are entitled to receive notice of the hearing and of the deadline for filing objections to the disclosure statement. Bankruptcy Rule 2002. The disclosure statement and plan themselves are sent only to the debtor, the trustee, the SEC, official committees, and the United States trustee, Bankruptcy Rule 3017(d), the theory being that an unapproved disclosure statement might be misleading and should be prevented from reaching voting creditors and equity security holders. Other parties, though, may obtain a copy of the disclosure statement or plan by making a written request for one. Bankruptcy Rule 3017(a).

After the court has heard any objections to the disclosure statement, the court must decide whether or not to approve it as containing "adequate information." § 1125; Bankruptcy Rule 3017(b). If the court has not already done so, at the time it approves of the disclosure statement, it will set a date by which creditors and interest holders may vote on the plan. The court may also set a date for the hearing on confirmation of the plan. Bankruptcy Rule 3017(c). After the disclosure statement has been approved, the following items will be sent — usually by the plan proponent — to creditors and equity security holders who are entitled to vote on the plan, i.e., those who are impaired: (1) the disclosure statement, (2) the plan or a court-approved summary of the plan, (3) a ballot for voting on the plan, (4) notice of the time for accepting or rejecting the plan, (5) notice of any date fixed for a hearing on confirmation of the plan, and (6) whatever else the court orders, such as a copy of the court's opinion approving the disclosure statement.

(11)   *Notice to Unimpaired Creditors and Interest Holders.* Given that unimpaired classes of claims and interests are conclusively presumed to have accepted a

plan, § 1126(f), do they receive a copy of the disclosure statement and other materials described in Note (10), above? Bankruptcy Rule 3017(d) gives the court discretion to order that the solicitation materials not be sent to members of unimpaired classes "if to do so would not be feasible considering the size of the unimpaired classes and the expense of printing and mailing." Committee Note to 1991 Amendments. If the court does this, members of the unimpaired class must receive notice that they are designated as unimpaired along with information that will enable them to request a copy of the disclosure statement and plan or summary of the plan from the plan proponent.

(12) *Streamlined Procedure in Small Business Cases.* In cases in which the debtor qualifies as a "small business" under Code § 101(51C) and elects to be so treated, Code § 1125(f) authorizes the court to relieve the debtor of the need to file a separate disclosure statement if the plan itself provides adequate information. Or, the court may "conditionally approve" a disclosure statement without conducting a hearing. A plan proponent may then solicit votes on a plan on the basis of the conditionally approved statement. A hearing on the disclosure statement may then be combined with a hearing on confirmation of the plan.

[B]   Solicitation of Acceptances and Rejections

PROBLEM 9.5

After the last plan negotiating session was concluded, Josh Colman, the workout officer at BigBank, and Max Matrix, the credit manager of MicroMax, the computer chip manufacturer and one of Amphy's largest creditors, stopped at a restaurant for dinner.

"I've got something important to discuss with you," Josh says. "I think the plan that Headley is proposing is ridiculous. Look at these cash flow projections prepared by my staff. If Amphy pursues the new Internet venture they keep touting, there won't be enough cash flow to service plan payments and meet operating expenses."

"That's a recipe for disaster," Max says.

"It sure is. Not only that, but I've been having conversations with management at Yachoo.com."

"Didn't they just do a public offering?"

"A few months ago, and now they're in acquisition mode. I've spoken to the CEO."

"Ben McLoughlin. I went to school with him."

"Right, and he says that he's taken a hard look at Amphydynamics and he's convinced it's ripe to be taken over. He says that at the price Yachoo.com would be willing to pay to acquire Amphydynamics, we could have our claims paid in full or darn near close to it."

"That's amazing. Then why should we support a plan that pays us half our claims in dribs and drabs?"

"That's my point. Tomorrow I plan to get on the phone and start calling around, telling people that they should vote Headley's plan down. Ben gave me the go-ahead to say Yachoo's interested in buying the company. Who knows, we might even get an auction going. Do you want copies of these spreadsheets to take back to the office with you? I have others."

"I have a better idea. If you send them to me as an e-mail attachment, I'll forward them to other creditors. In fact, why don't I arrange for a teleconference call tomorrow morning so that we all can review them together. In fact, you can report on your conversation with Ben McLoughlin, and we can ask folks to vote against the plan."

"Sounds good to me. People really need to know what's going on here. That we have other options."

"Speaking of which, do you think I could get salad instead of rice with my short ribs?"

"It never hurts to ask."

Does it "never hurt to ask"? Is the strategy that Josh and Max are contemplating problematic in any way?

Consider this: Under Code § 1125(b), neither acceptances nor rejections of a plan may be solicited until a disclosure statement has been approved and distributed. Did Josh *solicit* a rejection of Headley's plan from Max, or were they just having a friendly conversation over short ribs? Can Josh and Max send their fellow creditors e-mails containing information that contradicts the financial information that Headley has presented at the last plan negotiation session? Does that constitute an improper solicitation? What if they expressly urge their fellow creditors to vote against the plan when it is put on the table? If the bankruptcy court has approved the Amphydynamics disclosure statement, is your analysis different? If the debtor's exclusive period has expired, is that relevant? If Josh and Max did solicit votes in violation of § 1125(b), what are the consequences? Since a plan proponent is not required to disclose the existence of competing plans, § 1125(a), if creditors think that another plan is preferable to the debtor's, what can they do?

Re-read Code §§ 1121, 1125, and the materials that follow.

CENTURY GLOVE v.
FIRST AMERICAN BANK OF NEW YORK
United States Court of Appeals, Third Circuit
860 F.2d 94 (1988)

HUNTER, CIRCUIT JUDGE.

I.

Century Glove filed its petition seeking reorganization in bankruptcy on November 14, 1985. On August 1, 1986, Century Glove filed its reorganization plan, along with a draft of the disclosure statement to be presented along with the plan. Arguing that Century Glove's largest claimed assets are speculative lawsuits (including one against FAB), FAB presented a copy of an alternative plan to the unsecured creditors' committee. FAB advised that it would seek court approval to present its plan as soon as possible. The committee ultimately rejected the plan in favor of that of the debtor. On December 2, 1986, the bankruptcy court approved Century Glove's disclosure statement. A copy of the plan, the statement, and a sample ballot were then sent to Century Glove's creditors entitled to vote on the plan's acceptance.

Between December 12 and December 17, 1986, an attorney for FAB, John M. Bloxom, telephoned attorneys representing several of Century Glove's creditors. Among these creditors were Latham Four Partnerships ("Latham Four") and Bankers Trust New York Corporation ("BTNY"). Bloxom sought to find out what these creditors thought of the proposed reorganization, and to convince them to vote against the plan. He said that, while there was no other plan approved for presentation, and thus no other plan "on the table," FAB had drafted a plan and had tried to file it. The creditors' attorneys then asked for a copy of the plan, which FAB provided. The copies were marked "draft" and covering letters stated that they were submitted to the creditors for their comments. The draft did not contain certain information necessary for a proper disclosure statement, such as who would manage Century Glove after reorganization.

With a copy of its draft plan, FAB also sent to Latham Four a copy of a letter written to the unsecured creditors' committee by its counsel. In the letter, dated August 26, 1986, counsel questioned the committee's endorsement of the Century Glove plan, arguing that the lawsuits which Century Glove claims as assets are too speculative. As stated, the committee endorsed the plan anyway. Upset with this decision, one of its members sent a copy of the letter to a former officer of Century Glove. The officer then sent a copy, unsolicited, to FAB. Uncertain whether the letter was protected by an attorney-client privilege, FAB asked the committee member whether he had disclosed the letter voluntarily. He said that he had, and furnished a second copy directly to FAB. FAB attached this letter to a motion before the bankruptcy court seeking to have the committee replaced. The bank-ruptcy court later held the letter a privileged communication.

BTNY had made a preliminary decision on September 12, 1986, to reject Century Glove's plan. It reaffirmed this decision on December 15, when it received a copy of the plan and disclosure. Counsel for BTNY spoke with Bloxom the next day, December 16, 1986, and Bloxom mailed a letter confirming the call, but by mistake Bloxom did not send a draft of the alternate plan until December 17. On that day, counsel for BTNY prepared its ballot rejecting Century Glove's plan, and informed Bloxom of its vote.

After receiving the several rejections, Century Glove petitioned the bankruptcy court to designate, or invalidate, the votes of FAB, Latham Four and BTNY. Century Glove argued that FAB had acted in bad faith in procuring these rejections.

II.

The bankruptcy court held that FAB had violated 11 U.S.C. § 1125(b), which allows solicitation of acceptance or rejections only after an approved disclosure statement has been provided the creditor. Though a statement had been filed and provided, the bankruptcy court stated that:

> solicitations . . . must be limited by the contents of the plan, the disclosure statement, and any other court-approved solicitation material. The solicitee may not be given information outside of these approved documents.

The bankruptcy court found that FAB violated the section by providing additional materials such as copies of its draft plan. 74 B.R. 952.

The bankruptcy court also concluded that FAB had violated "the spirit of § 1121(b)," since FAB was apparently seeking approval of a plan which was not yet filed and which it could not file."

This "impropriety" was "heightened" by the absence from the FAB plan of such information as "who will manage the debtor." The bankruptcy court also found "improper" the disclosure by FAB of the August 26, 1986 letter to the creditors' committee. The court found that FAB's "machinations" in procuring a second copy of the letter showed that it was "obviously wary" that the letter might be privileged.

The bankruptcy court held invalid Latham Four's vote. It allowed the vote of BTNY, however, finding that the creditor had proved it had not relied on FAB's statements in deciding to reject Century Glove's plan. The court declined to bar FAB from participating further in the reorganization, finding such a sanction "too harsh," but instead, ordered FAB to pay for "all costs incurred by [Century Glove] in prosecuting" its motions. The amount of these damages was not specified. Both parties appealed the decision to the district court.

In a decision dated January 5, 1988, the district court affirmed the bankruptcy court rulings allowing BTNY's vote, but reversed the designation of Latham Four and the imposition of money sanctions against FAB.

. . . .

IV.

Century Glove argues that the district court erred in holding FAB did not improperly solicit rejections of Century Glove's reorganization plan. The bankruptcy court based its finding that FAB had violated 11 U.S.C. § 1125(b) primarily on its determination that a solicitee may not be provided with materials not approved by the court. The district court disagreed with this reading of the law. . . .

Section 1125(b) states, in pertinent part, that:

> An acceptance or rejection of a plan may not be solicited after the commencement of the case under this title from a holder of a claim or interest with respect to such claim or interest, unless, at the time of or before such solicitation, there is transmitted to such holder the plan or

summary of the plan, and a written disclosure statement approved, after notice and a hearing, by the court as containing adequate information.

There is no question that, at the time of FAB's solicitations, the solicitees had received a summary of the plan and a court-approved statement disclosing adequate information. Also, the bankruptcy court's factual conclusion that FAB was seeking rejections of Century Glove's plan is not clearly erroneous, and so must be assumed. Century Glove argues that FAB also was required to get court approval before it could disclose additional materials in seeking rejections.

Century Glove's interpretation of the section cannot stand. Century Glove argues, and the bankruptcy court assumed, that only approved statements may be communicated to creditors. The statute, however, never limits the facts which a creditor may receive, but only the *time* when a creditor may be solicited. Congress was concerned not that creditors' votes were based on misinformation, but that they were based on no information at all. *See* H.R. 95-595, at pp. 225-25, 95th Cong., 2d Sess., 124 Cong. Rec. —, *reprinted in*, 1978 U.S.C.C.A.A.N. 5963, 6185 (House Report). Rather than limiting the information available to a creditor, § 1125 seeks to guarantee a minimum amount of information to the creditor asked for its vote. *See* S.R. 95-989, at pp. 121, 95th Cong., 2d Sess., 124 Cong. Rec. —, *reprinted in*, 1978 U.S.C.C.A.A.N. 5787, 5907 ("A plan is necessarily predicated on knowledge of the assets and liabilities being dealt with and on factually supported expectations as to the future course of the business. . . . ") (Senate Report). The provision sets a floor, not a ceiling. Thus, we find that § 1125 does not on its face empower the bankruptcy court to require that all communications between creditors be approved by the court.

As the district court pointed out, allowing a bankruptcy court to regulate communications between creditors conflicts with the language of the statute. A creditor may receive information from sources other than the disclosure statement. Section 1125 itself defines "typical investor" of a particular class in part, as one having "such ability to obtain such information from sources other than the disclosure required by this section" 11 U.S.C. § 1125(a)(C). In enacting the bankruptcy code, Congress contemplated that the creditors would be in active negotiations with the debtor over the plan. *See infra*, part V. The necessity of "adequate information" was intended to help creditors in their negotiations. *See In re Gulph Woods*, 83 B.R. 339 (Bankr. E.D. Pa. 1988). Allowing the bankruptcy court to regulate communications between creditors under the guise of "adequate information" undercuts the very purpose of the statutory requirement.

Lastly, Century Glove's reading of § 1125 creates procedural difficulties. Century provides this court no means to distinguish predictably between mere interpretations of the approved information, and additional information requiring separate approvals. Therefore, to be safe, the creditor must seek prior court approval for every communication with another creditor (or refrain from communication), whether soliciting a rejection or an acceptance. Congress can hardly have intended such a result. It would multiply hearings, hence expense and delay, at a time when efficiency is greatly needed.

We also note that, as expressed in the House Report, Congress evidently contemplated a single hearing on the adequacy of the disclosure statement. *See*

House Report, 1978 U.S.C.C.A.A.N. at 6186.

Century Glove argues that two additional instances show that FAB violated § 1125(b). First, it claims that FAB's draft plan contained material misrepresentations, mostly omissions. Second, it claims that FAB improperly disclosed to Latham Four a letter the bankruptcy court later found privileged. The bankruptcy court found both "improper" in support of its finding under § 1125(b), and Century Glove argues that the bankruptcy court's decision can be affirmed on these grounds. The problem with the argument is that it rests on an erroneous interpretation of the law. Once adequate information has been provided a creditor, § 1125(b) does not limit communication between creditors. It is not an antifraud device. Thus, the bankruptcy court erred in holding that FAB had violated § 1125(b) by communicating with other materials. The district court therefore properly reversed the bankruptcy court on this issue.

V.

Though FAB was not limited in its solicitation of rejections, § 1125 did prevent FAB from soliciting acceptances of its own plan. The bankruptcy court held that, "since FAB was apparently seeking approval of a plan which was not yet filed," FAB violated § 1125. The court also found that FAB's actions violated the spirit of § 1121, which provides the debtor with a limited, exclusive right to present a plan. Reversing, the district court held that solicitations barred by § 1125(b) include only the "specific request for an official vote," and not discussions of and negotiations over a plan leading up to its presentation. *In re Snyder*, 51 B.R. 432, 437 (Bankr. D. Utah 1985). Because Bloxom explained that he was sending the draft only for discussion purposes, the district court found that the transmittal "may only be fairly characterized as part of FAB's negotiations." We exercise plenary review over the proper interpretation of the legal term "solicitation."

We agree with the district court that "solicitation" must be read narrowly. A broad reading of § 1125 can seriously inhibit free creditor negotiations. All parties agree that FAB is not barred from honestly negotiating with other creditors about its unfiled plan. "Solicitations with respect to a plan do not involve mere requests for opinions." Senate Report, 1978 U.S.C.C.A.A.N. at 5907. The purpose of negotiations between creditors is to reach a compromise over the terms of a tentative plan. The purpose of compromise is to win acceptance for the plan. We find no principled, predictable difference between negotiation and solicitation of future acceptances. We therefore reject any definition of solicitation which might cause creditors to limit their negotiations.

A narrow definition of "solicitation" does not offend the language or policy of 11 U.S.C. § 1121(b). The section provides only that the debtor temporarily has the exclusive right to file a plan (and thus have it voted on). It does not state that the debtor has a right to have its plan considered exclusively.

A right of exclusive consideration is not warranted in the policy of the section. Congress believed that debtors often delay confirmation of a plan, while creditors want quick confirmation. Therefore, *unlimited* exclusivity gave a debtor "undue bargaining leverage," because it could use the threat of delay to force unfair concessions. House Report, 1978 U.S.C.C.A.A.N. at 6191. On the other hand, Congress evidently felt that creditors might not seek the plan fairest to the debtor. Therefore, Congress allowed a *limited* period of exclusivity, giving the debtor "adequate time to negotiate a settlement, without unduly delaying creditors." *Id.* Section 1121 allows a debtor the threat of limited delay to offset the creditors' voting power of approval. FAB did nothing to reduce Century's threat of limited delay, and so did not offend the balance of bargaining powers created by § 1121 or the "spirit" of the law.

On the contrary, Century Glove's reading of § 1121(b) would in fact give the debtor powers not contemplated by Congress. The ability of a creditor to compare the debtor's proposals against other possibilities is a powerful tool by which to judge the reasonableness of the proposals. A broad exclusivity provision, holding that only the debtor's plan may be "on the table," takes this tool from creditors. Other creditors will not have comparisons with which to judge the proposals of the debtor's plan, to the benefit of the debtor proposing a reorganization plan. The history of § 1121 gives no indication that Congress intended to benefit the debtor in this way. The legislative history counsels a narrow reading of the section, one which FAB's actions do not violate.

We recognize that § 1125(b) bars the untimely solicitation of an "acceptance or rejection," indicating that the same definition applies to both. A narrow definition might allow a debtor to send materials seeking to prepare support for the plan, "for the consideration of the creditors," without adequate information approved by the court. Though such preparatory materials may undermine the purpose of adequate disclosure, the potential harm is limited in several ways. First, a creditor still must receive adequate information before casting a final vote, giving the creditor a chance to reconsider its preliminary decision. The harm is further limited by free and open negotiations between creditors. Last, because they are not "solicitations," pre-disclosure communications may still be subject to the stricter limitations of the securities laws. 11 U.S.C. § 1125(e). Where, as here, the creditors are counseled and already have received disclosure about the debtor's business, there seems little need for additional procedural formalities. *See e.g., In re Northwest Recreational Activities, Inc.*, 4 B.R. 43 (Bankr. N.D. Ga. 1980) (negotiations between debtor and creditor precede § 1125(b) approvals).

Therefore, we hold that a party does not solicit acceptances when it presents a draft plan for the consideration of another creditor, but does not request that creditor's vote. Applying this definition, FAB did not solicit acceptances of its plan. Century Glove does not dispute that FAB never asked for a vote, and clearly stated that the plan was not yet available for approval. Bloxom communicated with lawyers for the creditors, and there is no suggestion by Century that these lawyers did not understand the limitations. Also as Century argues, FAB never sent its plan to Hartford Insurance because Hartford firmly opposed Century's plan. Contrary to Century's conclusion, though, this fact argues that FAB sent copies of its plan because it was interested in obtaining rejections, not acceptances. (An opponent of Century's plan would be an ideal person to solicit for acceptances.) These undisputed facts require a finding that FAB did not "solicit" acceptances within the meaning of § 1125(b).

VI.

We hold that the district court correctly determined that Century Glove failed to show that FAB violated 11 U.S.C. § 1125 by soliciting acceptances or improperly soliciting rejections. We therefore will affirm the district court's order reversing the imposition of costs against FAB. We do not decide, however, whether the circumstances merit designation of the votes of any creditors.

IN RE CLAMP ALL CORP.
United States Bankruptcy Court for the District of Massachusetts
233 B.R. 198 (1999)

HENRY J. BOROFF, UNITED STATES BANKRUPTCY COURT.

I. Facts

[Clamp-All manufactured stainless steel couplings for use in plumbing applications. Anthony Foresta was its president and controlling stockholder. In 1989, Clamp-All encountered financial difficulties and filed a Chapter 11 petition. It confirmed a plan in 1991. Pursuant to the plan, Foresta resigned his position as president, but in consideration of his resignation Clamp-All entered into a consulting agreement with him and a company that he owned, Caliber Consulting Corporation. By 1993, this consulting arrangement had soured. Clamp-All sued Foresta in state court for breach of contract and Foresta counterclaimed. Foresta and Caliber obtained judgments of approximately $740,000 against Clamp-All, making them the largest creditor. Clamp-All's claims against Foresta were dismissed for failure to prosecute the action. In 1997, Clamp-All sought relief in Chapter 11 for the second time. On July 24, 1998, after three extensions of the exclusivity period, the debtor filed its plan and disclosure statement. The plan organized creditors and equity security holders into seven classes. The Foresta and Caliber claims and other unsecured claims were separately classified. The plan proposed to pay Foresta and Caliber a combination of cash and preferred stock. Other unsecured creditors were to receive payment in full within a year after the plan effective date. Foresta and Caliber filed (1) an objection to the adequacy of the disclosure statement; (2) a motion to terminate the exclusivity period for obtaining plan acceptances; and (3) an objection to the classification of the Foresta and Caliber claims.]

Attached as an exhibit to the Objection to Disclosure Statement was a full copy of a disclosure statement and reorganization plan proposed by Foresta and Caliber. All three pleadings and attachments were served on the entire creditor body of the Debtor. The Foresta and Caliber plan offered far more attractive treatment of unsecured creditors than the plan proposed by the Debtor during its period of exclusivity. In fact, it offered all creditors payment in full on the effective date of the plan.

II. Positions of the Parties

The Debtor argues that Foresta and Caliber violated § 1125(b) by soliciting votes against its reorganization plan with false and misleading information and by promoting their own plan during the Debtor's exclusivity period and before a disclosure statement had been approved by the Court. Consequently, the Debtor requests that the Court invalidate Foresta and Caliber's right to vote on the Debtor's proposed plan pursuant to 11 U.S.C. § 1126(e) and disallow any plan which Foresta and Caliber might file in the future, pursuant to § 1129(a)(3). In addition, the Debtor asks this Court to impose sanctions against Foresta and Caliber and/or find them in contempt of court.

Foresta and Caliber contend that their actions did not constitute an improper "solicitation" under 11 U.S.C. § 1125(b). They argue that the term "solicitation" should be construed narrowly to mean nothing short of a specific request for an official vote. Under this definition, they maintain, their actions can not be construed as a solicitation because they did not request any votes on their disclosure statement and plan, marked and referred to only as proposals and/or drafts. Moreover, they assert that their actions were not in bad faith and did not taint the plan approval process.

III. Discussion

Under section 1125(b), neither acceptances nor rejections of a Chapter 11 plan of reorganization may be solicited after the filing of the petition unless a disclosure statement has been approved by the court. The purpose of requiring an approved disclosure statement is to ensure that all claim holders are provided with adequate information to enable them to make an informed judgment regarding whether to vote for or against a reorganization plan. *In re Ferretti*, 128 B.R. 16, 18 (Bankr. D.N.H. 1991). It is only after the court has determined that the information contained within a disclosure statement is adequate can claim holders receive solicitations requesting their acceptance or rejection of the plan.

The terms "solicit" and "solicitation" are not defined in the Bankruptcy Code or in its legislative history. Consequently, what constitutes a "solicitation" under § 1125(b) is a matter left for determination by case law. The few courts that have addressed the question have struggled to find a precise definition for the term. A definition too broad could limit a debtor's postpetition negotiations with its creditors. A definition too narrow could hinder the court's ability to ensure that claim holders receive adequate information before deciding how to vote on a plan or might eviscerate Congress' intention to provide the Chapter 11 debtor an exclusive period within which to propose a plan. As a result, distinguishing between permissible negotiations and prohibited solicitations has been a difficult task. Neither the First Circuit Court of Appeals nor the lower courts within this circuit have yet addressed the issue.

A number of courts have proffered a narrow reading of the term. In the leading case of *Century Glove v. First Am. Bank of New York*, 860 F.2d 94, 101 (3d Cir. 1988), the Court of Appeals for the Third Circuit construed "solicitation" narrowly, agreeing with the district court that the term referred "only to a specific request for an official vote." *Century Glove*, 860 F.2d at 101 (citing *Snyder*, 51 B.R. at 437). In *Century Glove*, the debtor filed its plan and sought acceptance of the plan from the creditor body, all within its exclusivity period. At the same time, a plan opponent transmitted a copy of its yet unfiled plan to one of the debtor's largest creditors. The debtor subsequently argued that the plan opponent had improperly solicited and procured the rejection vote of the subject creditor. The Third Circuit disagreed, ruling that a party does not solicit acceptances when it presents a draft plan for the consideration of another creditor, so long as the party does not request that creditor's vote. *Century Glove*, 860 F.2d at 102.

The Third Circuit opined that allowing a draft competing plan to be circulated during the debtor's exclusivity period did not offend the language or policy of 11 U.S.C. § 1121(b). *Century Glove*, 860 F.2d at 102. According to the court, § 1121 provides a debtor with the temporary exclusive right to file a plan, not a right to have its plan considered exclusively. *Id.* "The ability of a creditor to compare the debtor's proposals against other possibilities is a powerful tool by which to judge the reasonableness of the proposals." *Id.* A broad exclusivity provision allowing only the debtor's plan to be "on the table," the court explained, would give a debtor undue bargaining leverage and inhibit creditor negotiations. *Id.* Therefore, the court concluded that sections 1121(b) and 1125(b) ought to be interpreted narrowly to allow a party to present a draft plan for the consideration of another creditor so long as the plan proponent does not request the creditor's vote. *Id.*

A majority of courts have now adopted the narrow reading of "solicitation" proffered by *Century Glove.* . . .

Other courts, however, have criticized such a narrow definition of "solicitation" when a creditor's communication includes information not raised by an approved disclosure statement. In *In re Temple Retirement Comm.*, 80 B.R. 367, 369 (Bankr. W.D. Tex. 1987), the court concluded that a letter proposed by the indenture trustee to bondholders during the debtor's exclusivity period — suggesting that another plan awaited bondholders if they rejected the debtor's plan — violated §§ 1121(b) and 1125(b). The court ruled that furnishing information outside the scope of the debtor's plan and disclosure statement or other court approved solicitation materials during the debtor's period of exclusivity was impermissible, and allowing a plan opponent to provide creditors with a proposed competing plan and unapproved disclosure statement would violate the "clear advantage" the Bankruptcy Code was designed to give to the debtor. *Temple Retirement Comm.*, 80 B.R. at 369.

Other courts have also applied the term solicitation more expansively. *See In re Apex Oil Co.*, 111 B.R. 245, 249 (Bankr. E.D. Mo. 1990) ("Soliciting party may react to and present contrary views regarding the court-approved disclosure statement, but may not present or suggest an alternative plan which has not been subject to court scrutiny regarding the adequacy of disclosure."); *Colorado Mountain Express, Inc. v. Aspen Limousine Serv., Inc. (In re Aspen Limousine Serv., Inc.)*, 198 B.R. 341, 348–49 (D. Colo. 1996) (letter sent by plan opponent to all debtor's creditors apprizing them of its unapproved alternative plan and urging them to reject debtor's plan violated § 1125(b)); *In re Rook Broadcasting of Idaho*, 154 B.R. 970 (Bankr. D. Idaho 1993) (sanctions were imposed when party distributed unapproved disclosure statement and reorganization plan to debtor's entire creditor body); *In re Gulph Woods Corp.*, 83 B.R. 339, 342 (Bankr. E.D. Pa. 1988) (recognizing that there must be some limitation on communications, or else the entire process of requiring court approval of disclosure statements would be undermined).

This Court agrees that open negotiation by creditors is imperative. However, those negotiations must be conducted in a manner consistent with the policy goals intended by Congress to be effectuated through sections 1121(b) and 1125(b) of the Bankruptcy Code. This Court must, therefore, turn to those policy goals for guidance.

1. Debtor's Exclusive Plan Filing Rights under § 1121

Section 1121 of the Bankruptcy Code grants the debtor the exclusive right to file a plan during the first 120 days after entry of the order for relief. . . . Congress explicitly sought to achieve two goals [via § 1121]. It wanted to grant the debtor a reasonable time to obtain confirmation of a plan without the threat of a competing plan. And at the same time, Congress sought to ensure that a debtor would not use Chapter 11 as a mechanism through which to operate indefinitely without attempting to reorganize.

Section 1121 provides the debtor with a clear advantage early in the case. "It was intended that at the outset of a Chapter 11 case a debtor should be given the unqualified opportunity to negotiate a settlement and propose a plan of reorganization without interference from creditors and other interests." *In re Texaco, Inc.*, 81 B.R. 806, 809 (Bankr. S.D.N.Y. 1988) (citing H.R. Rep. No. 595, 95th Cong., 2d Sess. 221–22, reprinted in 1978 U.S.C.C.A.N. 5787). The exclusivity period gives the debtor the ability to stabilize its operations and the opportunity to retain control over the reorganization process. The adoption of a limited period of exclusivity also assures speed by motivating the debtor to be more fair and reasonable in its negotiations with creditors, because the debtor knows that the bargaining leverage of exclusivity will soon end.

This Court believes that the *Century Glove* analysis fails to sufficiently recognize Congress' intention to allow the debtor a reasonable time to obtain confirmation of a plan without the threat of a competing plan. Therefore, whether a creditor's action during the exclusivity period violates § 1121(b) must be evaluated not only in terms of its effect on the ability of a debtor to delay reorganization, but also in terms of its interference with the debtor's efforts to propose and confirm a plan of reorganization. When a party in interest proposes an unapproved draft plan to other creditors, it is in effect "soliciting rejections by dangling an alternative plan before other creditors, suggesting in essence that, if the debtor's plan were scuttled, then a better alternative could then be proposed." [Citations omitted.]

2. Adequate Disclosure under § 1125

The requirement of adequate disclosure to parties in interest is a key feature of the reorganization provisions of Chapter 11. . . . Congress recognized that if creditors and other parties in interest were provided with financial and other adequate information regarding a debtor's business and plan of reorganization, they would be in a far better position to make an informed decision about whether to accept or reject a proposed plan.

Section 1125 furthers those goals by requiring that a written disclosure statement, approved by the bankruptcy court as containing adequate information, be transmitted to creditors, together with a plan or a summary of the plan, prior to any post-petition solicitation of votes for or against the plan. 11 U.S.C. § 1125(b). The requirement of advance court approval ensures that adequate information is provided to creditors and parties in interest and "was thought to discourage the undesirable practice (under the former Bankruptcy Act of 1898, as amended) of soliciting acceptance or rejection at a time when creditors and stockholders were 'too ill-informed to act capably in their own interests.'" [Citation omitted.] Moreover, prohibiting solicitations before court approval of a disclosure statement "protect[s] against 'end-runs' around the disclosure requirements." H.R. Rep. No. 595, 95th Cong., 1st Sess. at 227 (1977), reprinted in 1978 U.S.C.C.A.N. 5963.

Bankruptcy Rule 3017 supplements § 1125 by establishing strict guidelines on the process of obtaining court approval of a disclosure statement:

> The plan and the disclosure statement shall be mailed with the notice of the hearing only to the debtor, any trustee or committee appointed under the Code, the Securities and Exchange Commission and any party in interest who requests in writing a copy of the statement or plan.

Fed. R. Bankr. P. 3017(a). The rule forbids sending copies of a plan and disclosure statements to any party other than those explicitly mentioned. "The Bankruptcy Code's requirement of court approval of a disclosure statement, combined with Rule 3017's restrictions on dissemination of an unapproved disclosure statement, clearly contemplates some creditors need to be protected against misinformation." *Rook Broadcasting*, 154 B.R. at 976. Undoubtedly this prohibition was intended to preclude yet another "end-run" by providing creditors with inadequate or misleading information in draft plans and disclosure statements. As one court aptly stated:

> Permitting a plan proponent to distribute proposed disclosure statements taints the voting process. Those creditors who are ignorant of the debtor and its affairs, the ones for whose protection section 1125 requires court approval of the disclosure statement, would instead be presented with numerous documents containing inconsistencies, omissions, and misleading or incorrect statements. The debtors and the Court would be forced to attempt to "chase down" these problems, with little real hope of undoing the damage.

Id.

This Court acknowledges the *Century Glove* court's concern that a broad reading of § 1125(b) could limit creditor communications and negotiations. However, negotiations among creditors may be fostered without discussing unapproved alternate plans. Parties opposing a debtor's plan are not prohibited from soliciting rejection of the proposed plan by "arguing that [a] debtor's plan does not exhaust the panoply of possibilities for reorganization, nor are they prohibited from pointing out failings which they perceive to be present in the debtor's plan." In addition, the hearing on approval of the disclosure statement gives interested parties the opportunity to challenge certain statements or information contained in the disclosure statement and an opportunity to request the inclusion of additional facts which makes apparent their objections to the debtor's plan. Therefore, to find "that prohibiting the distribution of an alternative plan without an approved disclosure statement, during the debtor's exclusivity period, would be fatal to effective negotiations or evaluation of a Chapter 11 plan, ignores all other methods by which plan opponents can fairly communicate and solicit rejections." Non-debtor parties must be prohibited from circulating solicitation materials before a disclosure statement has been approved by the court. Only then can adequate disclosure to creditors and other parties in interest be assured.

IV. Application

It is undisputed that Foresta and Caliber transmitted their proposed competing plan of reorganization and unapproved disclosure statement to all of the Debtor's creditors while the Debtor had the exclusive right to propose a reorganization plan and before the scheduled hearing to approve its disclosure statement. As a result, Foresta and Caliber's actions undermined the Debtor's ability to propose a confirmable plan and circumvented the adequate disclosure requirements of the Bankruptcy Code. In so doing, Foresta and Caliber violated sections 1121(b) and 1125(b) of the Bankruptcy Code and Bankruptcy Rule 3017(a).

More problematic is choosing the appropriate remedy for those violations. Courts have employed various solutions to ameliorate the harm. Some have imposed a monetary sanction under § 105(a). Where a creditor disobeyed a court order that a competing plan not be sent to creditors, one court found the creditor in civil contempt and sanctioned it accordingly. *See Aspen Limousine*, 198 B.R. at 349–51. The Debtor's Motion for Sanctions seeks similar relief.

Through its Plan Voting Motion, the Debtor also requests that the Court remedy the harm caused by Foresta's and Caliber's actions by disqualifying their votes, pursuant to 11 U.S.C. § 1126(e) on future plans to be submitted by the Debtor. Section 1126(e) permits a bankruptcy court to hold invalid any vote that was not made or solicited "in good faith and in compliance with the applicable provisions of this title[.]"

The remedies suggested by the Debtor are, for one reason or the other, inappropriate. Civil contempt is a remedy which should be used sparingly and should not be employed without more of a direct relationship between a specific order focused on an alleged contemnor and the suggested violation. . . . And . . . disqualification of any votes made in the future by Foresta and Caliber — and advance disapproval of any plans to be submitted by Foresta and Caliber — [is] premature and in fact may miss the mark.

No plan with an approved disclosure statement is now before the Court, no vote has been cast and no assessment can now be made as to whether vote disqualification would have any impact on confirmation of any plan or, more importantly, ameliorate the harm caused by Foresta and Caliber.

In the end, one truth remains. The secured and other unsecured creditors in this case have been told by Foresta and Caliber that rejection of the Debtor's plan will be followed by Foresta's and Caliber's plan offering prompt payment in full of their claims. Unsecured creditors are unlikely to forget the unapproved plan and disclosure statement mailed to them by Foresta and Caliber, albeit in purportedly draft form. The appropriate remedy therefore ought be designed to undo that harm, above all. It must be designed to make Foresta's and Caliber's offer to creditors no longer material.

This Court believes that the best remedy can be found in consideration of § 510(c); [which provides for equitable subordination of claims].

The seminal case on equitable subordination is *Benjamin v. Diamond (In re Mobile Steel Co.)*, 563 F.2d 692 (5th Cir. 1977), wherein that court established three requirements for the application of the doctrine of equitable subordination: (1) the claimant must have engaged in some type of inequitable conduct; (2) the misconduct must have resulted in injury to the creditors of the debtor or conferred an unfair advantage on the claimant; (3) equitable subordination of the claim must not be inconsistent with the provisions of the Bankruptcy Code. *Id.* at 699–700.

The *Mobile Steel* standards are clearly met here. Foresta and Caliber have engaged in grossly inequitable conduct, having violated no less than two sections of the Bankruptcy Code and one of the Bankruptcy Rules, all of which were promulgated by Congress to provide equitable treatment for the debtor and other creditors. Undoubtedly those violations conferred on Foresta and Caliber an unfair advantage — in fact precisely the advantage which those sections of the Bankruptcy Code were designed to preclude. And . . . it is difficult to conceive how subordination of the Foresta and Caliber debt is anything other than a facilitation of . . . Congress' important goals in fashioning Chapter 11 relief.

In view of the foregoing, the Court will subordinate the claims of Foresta and Caliber to the claims of all other creditors (other than any insider claims). Such subordination will assist the Debtor in approving its offer to creditors. That improvement, together with the unlikelihood that Foresta and Caliber will be able to submit a confirmable competing plan is the best remedy which the Court can craft among those available. Finally, the Court will order that Foresta and Caliber reimburse the estate for Debtor's counsel's attorneys fees in drafting and prosecuting the two Motions before the Court.

V. Conclusion

The bankruptcy court is obliged to give the Chapter 11 debtor every reasonable opportunity to present and confirm a plan reorganizing its financial affairs. Concomitantly, the Court is obliged to use its best efforts to ensure that, in the course of the debtor's reorganization effort, the rights of creditors are not prejudiced. But, most important, the Court has a duty to safeguard the integrity of the negotiation process which is at the heart of Chapter 11. Foresta and Caliber undermined that process by communicating to creditors information (right or wrong) which interfered with a negotiation between the Debtor and its creditors that Congress intended to be exclusive. The Court's expression of disapproval of that behavior must be unequivocal.

NOTES AND QUESTIONS

(1) If the *Century Glove* court had decided the *Clamp-All* case, would it have reached a different result? Would the *Century Glove* court be troubled by the fact that Clamp-All's disclosure statement had yet to be approved when the creditors surfaced their plan? How would the *Century Glove* court judge the behavior of Max and Josh?

(2) In *In re Apex Oil Co.*, 111 B.R. 245, 249 (Bankr. E.D. Mo. 1990), the court, trying to balance the goal of providing voters with as much information as possible with the need to prevent end-runs around the § 1125(b) shield against misinformation, suggested that once a debtor's exclusive period has expired and a disclosure statement has been approved, soliciting parties need not obtain prior court approval of other solicitation materials *"only if"*:

1) the information provided is truthful and not misleading;

2) the information is presented in good faith;

3) the soliciting party does not propose or suggest an alternative plan unless a disclosure statement for that plan has received court approval.

(3) *Other Ways to Skin a Plan?* Suppose Amphy moves for an extension of exclusivity on the grounds that it needs more time to develop a plan. Suppose that Bank opposes the extension, because it has a plan of its own that it would like to file. The Bank intends to submit its plan to the court in order to show that the debtor's foot dragging is preventing a viable plan from getting to the table. Should the Bank be permitted to do this? May it also send a draft of its plan to members of the creditors' committee? To creditors at large? Should the Bank be permitted to get a plan before creditors by moving for the appointment of a trustee or dismissal of the case on the grounds that the debtor in possession is making unsatisfactory progress toward the filing and confirmation of a plan?

(4) *Securities Law Safe Harbor.* Code § 1125(e) provides that a person who, in good faith, solicits acceptances or rejections of a plan in compliance with the provisions of the Code (or who participates in the offer, issuance, sale, or purchase of securities in connection with a plan) is exempt from liability for violations of federal or state securities laws related to those activities. "The purpose of the provision is to protect creditors, creditors' committees, counsel for committees, and others involved in the case from potential liability under the securities laws for soliciting acceptances of a plan by use of an approved disclosure statement." H.R. Rep. 95-595, 95th Cong., 1st Sess. 229 (1977). This section is said to codify the Supreme Court's holding in *Ernst & Ernst v. Hochfelder*, 425 U.S. 185 (1976), that civil liability under section 10(b) of the Securities Exchange Act of 1934 and Rule 10b-5 did not extend to good faith omissions or misstatements. Apparently, a person who solicits acceptances or rejections based on information that is not contained in a court approved disclosure statement would not, in the *Century Glove* court's view, run afoul of § 1125(b), but that person would apparently not enjoy the protection of the Code's safe harbor provision.

[C] Voting on the Plan

[1] Overview

As we saw at the beginning of this chapter, Code § 1126 sets forth the basic rules governing plan acceptance. Subsection (c) provides that a class of claims accepts a plan if acceptance is voted by holders of at least two-thirds in dollar amount and more than one-half in number of allowed claims in the class. Subsection (d) provides that a class of interests accepts a plan if acceptance is voted by holders of at least two-thirds in dollar amount of interests. In determining whether these majorities are achieved, only those claims or interests that actually vote are counted. Acceptances need not be solicited from a class that is unimpaired under the plan, because such a class is conclusively presumed to have accepted the plan. § 1126(f). A class that receives or retains nothing under the plan is deemed to have rejected it. The fact that members of such a class vote in favor of the plan is irrelevant. *In re Egan*, 142 B.R. 730, 732 (Bankr. E.D. Pa. 1992). In *Egan*, the court also found such a vote "puzzling."

What happens if, as a result of creditor apathy or for other reasons, no member of an *impaired* class votes on the plan? The Tenth Circuit has concluded that the result is that the class be deemed to have accepted the plan. *In re Ruti-Sweetwater, Inc.*, 836 F.2d 1263 (10th Cir. 1988). In that case, the debtor's reorganization plan provided for the treatment of 83 classes of secured creditors and 40 classes of time share owners. Twenty classes failed to vote. Following confirmation, a secured creditor in one of those non-voting classes challenged the plan. The objecting creditor argued that, under § 1129(a)(8), the court shall confirm a plan only if each impaired class voted in favor of the plan; since the class was impaired and the class did not actually vote, the plan was not confirmable. The court disagreed:

> We hold that the district court correctly affirmed the bankruptcy court's ruling that [the creditors'] inaction constituted an acceptance of the Plan. To hold otherwise would be to endorse the proposition that a creditor may sit idly by, not participate in any manner in the formulation and adoption of a plan in reorganization and thereafter, subsequent to the adoption of the plan, raise a challenge to the plan for the first time. Adoption of [that] approach would effectively place all reorganization plans at risk in terms of reliance and finality.

836 F.2d at 1266–67. The same result was reached in a case in which 30 of 30 impaired voting classes, with claims totaling billions of dollars, voted in favor of the plan and several classes of small creditors, with aggregate claims of less than $50,000, failed to vote one way or the other, and objected to confirmation of the plan. *In re Adelphia Commc'ns Corp.*, 368 B.R. 140 (Bankr. S.D.N.Y. 2007). The court explained:

> I recognize that some cases and commentators have criticized and distinguished *Ruti-Sweetwater* . . . . But *Ruti-Sweetwater* is the only authority at the Circuit Court of Appeals level. And more importantly, I think *Ruti-Sweetwater* is rightly decided, especially in a situation like that one (and here), where dozens of classes vote, where the effect of not voting is

announced in advance, and everyone else's will would be burdened by those who simply don't vote at all. Regarding non-voters as rejecters runs contrary to the Code's fundamental principle, and the language of section 1126(c), that only those actually voting be counted in determining whether a class has met the requirements, in number and amount, for acceptance or rejection of a plan, and subjects those who care about the case to burdens (or worse) based on the inaction and disinterest of others. A holding to the contrary would mean that a failure to vote isn't relevant in a case where *anyone* else in that class votes, but is enough to force cramdown if the lack of interest in that class is so extreme that nobody at all chooses to vote, one way or the other. As Mr. Mabey, debtors' counsel in *Rudi-Sweetwater*, successfully argued in *Ruti-Sweetwater*, that cannot be the law. Section 1126(c) recognizes the unlikelihood of everyone caring enough about the plan to vote — basing acceptances not on the total claims in the class, but only those voting. And that is a principle upon which the bankruptcy community often relies, as creditor democracy could otherwise be frozen as a consequence of the disinterest of others. On a matter where the Code is essentially silent, making an exception to the principle of section 1126(c) — that only votes actually cast count — makes no sense.

368 B.R. at 261–62 (citations omitted). The court noted, however, that it was not deciding "whether a like analysis would apply in a smaller case, where billions of dollars of claims hadn't been voted for and against acceptance of a plan and the nonvoting claims were only a tiny proportion of that amount." *Id.* at 263. Several other courts have declined to treat non-voting classes as deemed accepting classes. *See, e.g., In re M. Long Arabians*, 103 B.R. 211, 215 (B.A.P. 9th Cir. 1989), *In re Higgins Slacks Co.*, 178 B.R. 853, 855 (Bankr. N.D. Ala. 1995); *In re Friese*, 103 B.R. 90, 92 (Bankr. S.D.N.Y. 1989); *In re 7th Street and Beardsley P'ship.*, 181 B.R. 426 (Bankr. D. Ariz. 1994).

Will the existence of a *deemed* accepting class satisfy the § 1129(a)(10) requirement that in order for a plan to be confirmed there must be at least one impaired class that votes in favor of the plan? Even the *Ruti-Sweetwater* court believed that "*actual* acceptance of a plan by at least one class of impaired claims" is required. *In re Ruti-Sweetwater, Inc.*, 836 F.2d 1263, 1267 (10th Cir. 1988).

Code § 1126 provides that a plan may be accepted or rejected by any creditor holding a claim or interest allowed under Code § 502. Thus, as discussed in chapter 8, above, eligibility to vote depends in the first instance on whether a claim or interest is allowed under § 502.

Bankruptcy Rule 3018(a) provides that a plan may be accepted or rejected within the time fixed by the court. You will recall that Bankruptcy Rule 3017(c) provides that on or before the approval of the disclosure statement, the court must fix a time within which creditors and equity security holders may vote on a plan. Rule 3017(d) requires that notice of this date, along with the disclosure statement, the plan, and a ballot be sent to creditors and interest holders. Tardily returned ballots will not be counted. *In re Hills Stores Co*, 167 B.R. 348 (Bankr. S.D.N.Y. 1994).

In a case in which there are competing plans, Rule 3018(c) permits creditors and interest holders to accept or reject any number of them. A creditor or equity holder who votes to accept more than one plan may indicate which of the plans it prefers.

[2] Creditors Holding Multiple Claims

We know that a secured creditor that is undersecured holds two claims — one secured and one unsecured — that will be separately classified. Bankruptcy Rule 3018(d) makes clear that such a creditor votes in two capacities: as a secured creditor and as an unsecured creditor.

Suppose that on January 1, Avid Paper Clip Company sent Amphydynamics a large shipment of paper clips. Amphy failed to pay for the shipment. On June 1, Amphy ordered a second shipment of paper clips and again failed to pay. For purposes of determining whether more than one-half in number of the allowed claims in a class have voted to accept a plan, how many "claims" does Avid hold?

If Avid's right to payment arose out of two separate and unrelated transactions, Avid holds two claims and is entitled to one vote for each. *In re Gilbert*, 104 B.R. 206, 211 (Bankr. W.D. Mo. 1989). What if Avid had acquired one claim by shipping paper clips and had also purchased claims from three other creditors during the pendency of the case? Would Avid hold one claim or four? Would it be entitled to cast one vote or four? What if it had purchased the three claims for the avowed purpose of blocking acceptance of the debtor's plan? This raises not only the question of how to count votes, but also how to appraise the good faith of the voter. Consider the problem and case that follow.

[3] The Requirement of Good Faith in Voting.

PROBLEM 9.6

You will recall that earlier in this chapter, Avid Paper Clip Co. attempted to file a plan of its own, but was thwarted because the debtor's exclusivity period had been extended by the bankruptcy court. Headley Charisma believes that Abel Avid, president of the paper clip company, is rabidly opposed to the debtor's plan because it contemplates that Headley will continue as CEO of the company. It isn't that Avid seriously doubts Headley's managerial prowess, Headley insists. Rather, according to Headley, the animus stems from a personal affront having nothing whatsoever to do with the case or the merits of the plan. Apparently, a year or so ago, Abel Avid asked Headley to consider his son for a mid-level management position with the company. Headley interviewed the son, concluded that he was unqualified, and rejected him. Avid is so angry that he has been telephoning other creditors and lobbying fellow creditors to vote against the plan. Headley also thinks that Avid has offered to supply a large unsecured creditor with all the paper clips it needs at a very advantageous price if the creditor will vote to reject the plan. He believes that this creditor has agreed to vote no.

Headley asks whether such tactics are permissible. Read Code § 1126(e) and the materials that follow:

IN RE FEATHERWORKS CORP.

United States District Court, Eastern District of New York
36 B.R. 460 (1984)

[Featherworks, the debtor, was in the business of buying, processing, and selling down and feathers. Featherworks was the wholly-owned subsidiary of Windsor Trading Corp. The president of Featherworks and Windsor was Arthur Puro. Puro's wife and daughter owned Windsor. Farwest Garments, a manufacturer, was a customer of the debtor. It held a $384,577 judgment against Featherworks. Walter E. Heller & Co. was financing Featherworks up to the time the Chapter 11 petition was filed. At the time of the filing, Featherworks owed Heller more than $5,000,000. Heller's claim was secured by a lien on inventory and accounts receivable. The security was worth only $3,500,000, making Heller an unsecured creditor for the $1,500,000 deficiency. As such, Heller dominated the class of unsecured creditors. Featherworks proposed a plan which offered unsecured creditors 1.3% of their claims in cash. The $40,000 needed to fund the plan was to be supplied by Windsor, which would retain its ownership interest. Finally, Heller was to be given title to the debtor's accounts and inventory. A disclosure statement was approved, and the court set a deadline for the filing of acceptances and rejections. Although the plan was accepted by some unsecured creditors, it was rejected by Heller and Farwest. Shortly after the voting was concluded, Heller asked the court for permission to change its vote from a rejection to acceptance. In reaction, Farwest cross-moved for an order disqualifying Heller's acceptance under § 1126(e), alleging that Heller had been paid $25,000, coincidentally with the attempted change in its vote. Farwest also requested that the court refer the matter to the United States Attorney to determine whether a crime had been committed. Heller stoutly maintained that its acceptance had not been bought. Heller said that it had initially intended to vote in favor of the plan, but that, shortly before the ballot deadline, it discovered that the debtor's inventory was worth far less than what had been represented in the disclosure statement. Upon learning this, Heller said, it decided to reject the plan and sue the debtor, Arthur Puro, and Windsor. To avoid the litigation, Puro and Windsor paid Heller $25,000 in exchange for releases of liability. On the day the settlement was reached, Heller announced that it would change its vote.

In an opinion reported at 25 B.R. 634 (Bankr. E.D.N.Y. 1982), Bankruptcy Judge Goetz refused to let Heller change its vote on the grounds that Heller's acceptance had not been solicited, procured, or given in good faith. Judge Goetz reasoned, "A change in vote by the debtor's major unsecured creditor, coincidental with the receipt from the same source as the $40,000 funding the plan of an additional $25,000 over and above what other creditors are receiving, will not be allowed." 25 B.R. at 641. The bankruptcy judge did not find evidence to warrant referring the matter to the United States Attorney, however. The debtor appealed from the bankruptcy court's order. The opinion of the district court is reprinted below.

MEMORANDUM AND ORDER

NEAHER, DISTRICT JUDGE

Debtor first contends that the bankruptcy court erred in finding that Arthur Puro's payment of $25,000 to Heller was made to purchase Heller's change of vote.

Before the reorganization petition, Heller had financed the debtor's inventory and accounts receivable, which were pledged as security for its loans. It is owed approximately $1,500,000. Debtor asserts that the plan was drafted almost to Heller's specifications, but after the drafting, Heller discovered that representations made by Arthur Puro, the debtor's principal officer, about the quality of some of the inventory were inaccurate. In response, Heller, quite displeased, rejected the plan. It submitted evidence, a letter in which it had initially expressed an intention to approve the plan, in explanation of its change of heart. The change had materialized shortly after Arthur Puro paid Heller $25,000 for a general release and reassignment of the uncollected pre-petition accounts receivable. Understandably Farwest objected to Heller's changing its vote, asserting that the purported settlement of this collateral claim constituted a criminal offense under 18 U.S.C. § 152 and bad faith under 11 U.S.C. § 1126(e).

> [I]f a member of the majority, because of having been misled, or of new information, or a change in the condition of the debtor, or for other good reason, should *honestly alter* his opinion of what is good for himself and the dissenting minority, the judge ought at any time before the plan is confirmed to hear his reasons and, if found substantial, to permit withdrawal.

Continental Ins. Co. v. Louisiana Oil Refining Corp., 89 F.2d 333, 337 (5th Cir. 1937) . . . .

In its argument, debtor initially assumes that the bankruptcy court erred by giving more weight to the circumstantial timing of the transaction than to Heller's self-serving evidence of its motives. The timing aside, the absence of evidence of the quality of the inventory and the inaccuracy of Puro's representations thereof, which evidence should be in debtor's possession, further supports the bankruptcy court's conclusion that the payment was not in good faith.

The Court recognizes that good faith and self-dealing are not mutually exclusive. The issue is much more complex, however, because vote changing is the exception and not the rule. Thus, debtor must demonstrate the propriety of Heller's actions. The Court is satisfied that this burden has not been sustained, and that the authorities debtor relies upon are not to the contrary.

In *In re P-R Holding Corp.*, 147 F.2d 895 (2d Cir.1945), the Court stated:

> The mere fact that a purchase of creditors' interests is for the purpose of securing the approval or rejection of a plan does not of itself amount to "bad faith." When that purchase is in aid of an interest other than an interest as a creditor, such purchases may amount to "bad faith" under section 203 of the Bankruptcy Act [the predecessor to 11 U.S.C. § 1126(e)]. And certainly

there is "bad faith" when those purchases result in a discrimination in favor of the creditors selling their interests.

Id. at 897 (citations omitted).

Heller's claim for fraud, which arose from its interest in the debtor's inventory and accounts receivable, was treated more favorably than any other tort claim, and for a relatively small price, Puro was guaranteed the continuation of his business. More importantly, however, debtor's new life offered Heller the opportunity to finance debtor's accounts in the future. As the former financing entity, Heller possessed an interest in the continued operation of the debtor that was not shared by other creditors. It may well have settled for the costs of financing the accounts that were pledged as collateral. The other creditors, all of whom had already voted, were not similarly afforded a chance to convert their claims to immediate cash.

With respect to the denial of Heller's application to change its vote, the Court does not believe that the law countenances vote trafficking and assertedly otherwise innocent self-dealing *after the votes have been cast.*

> A year before the House Committee on the Judiciary held its extensive hearings on the Chandler Act, a Circuit Court of Appeals held that a creditor could not be denied the privilege of voting on a reorganization plan under § 77B, although he bought the votes for the purpose of preventing confirmation unless certain demands of his should be met. *Texas Hotel Corp. v. Waco Development Co.*, 87 F.2d 395 [5th Cir.1936]. The hearings make clear the purpose of the Committee to pass legislation which would bar creditors from a vote who were prompted by such a purpose. To this end they adopted the "good faith" provisions of § 203. Its purpose was to prevent creditors from participating who "by the use of obstructive tactics and hold-up techniques exact for themselves undue advantages from the other stockholders[/creditors] who are cooperating." Bad faith was to be attributed to claimants who opposed a plan for a time until they were "bought off"; those who "refused to vote in favor of a plan unless given some particular preferential advantage." Hearing on Revision of the Bankruptcy Act before the Committee on the Judiciary of the House of Representatives, 75th Cong., 1st Sess., on H.R. 6439, Serial 9, pp. 180–82.

Young v. Higbee Co., 324 U.S. 204, 211 n. 10, 65 S. Ct. 594, 598 n. 10, 89 L. Ed. 890 (1945). The Court finds no error in the bankruptcy court's ruling.

. . . Farwest complains about the failure of the bankruptcy court to refer the charge of a violation of 18 U.S.C. § 152 to the United States Attorney pursuant to 18 U.S.C. § 3057. The bankruptcy court disposed of this contention as follows:

> The Court does not know enough with respect to what occurred to find, as Farwest requests, that there are reasonable grounds for believing that there has been a violation of 18 U.S.C. § 152 and to refer the matter to the United States Attorney pursuant to 18 U.S.C. § 3057.

> Whatever either Heller or Puro did was apparently done with the advice and knowledge of their respective attorneys, who are among the most respected lawyers appearing in this Court. It has long been recognized with

respect to other types of violations of 18 U.S.C. § 152 that acting on the advice of counsel negates the presence of the necessary fraudulent intent. *E.g., Thompson v. Eck*, 149 F.2d 631, 633 (2d Cir. 1945).

25 B.R.. at 641. Farwest has presented nothing to demonstrate that those findings are clearly erroneous.

NOTES AND QUESTIONS

(1)   Is a vote to reject a plan cast in bad faith if the voter's purpose in defeating the plan is to acquire control of the debtor? What about an acceptance voted by a supplier that hopes to enjoy a continuing business relationship with the debtor? What if the debtor's management encouraged that vote with secret assurances that "there will be more business to come" if the plan is accepted and confirmed? *See In re Three Fling Hill Ltd. P'ship.*, 213 B.R. 292 (D. Md. 1997); *In re Landing Assocs. Ltd.*, 157 B.R. 791 (Bankr. W.D. Tex. 1993).

(2)   Does *Featherworks* present a case in which substantially similar creditors that have been placed in the same class are receiving different treatment under the plan in violation of § 1123(a)(4)?

(3)   In *Featherworks*, the court declined to refer the matter to the U.S. Attorney for prosecution under 18 U.S.C. § 152, which makes it a criminal offense to "knowingly and fraudulently receive any material amount of property from a debtor after the filing of a case under title 11, with the intent to defeat the provisions of title 11" or to "knowingly and fraudulently give, offer, receive, or attempt to obtain any money or property, remuneration, compensation, reward, advantage, or promise thereof for acting or forbearing to act in any case under title 11." Did the conduct of Avid Abel or the unsecured creditor who sold his vote for free paper clips run afoul of this provision? Would Avid Abel's solicitation activities be protected by the securities laws safe harbor of § 1125(e)?

(4)   Bankruptcy Rule 3018(a) does permit a creditor or interest holder to change a vote "for cause," but only with permission of the court. The purpose of requiring permission is to "avoid the possibility of an entity changing its vote based upon consideration or promises outside of the plan," or, in other words, to prevent what occurred in *Featherworks*. What does constitute cause for changing a vote? "Examples include a breakdown in communications at the voting entity, misreading the terms of the plan, or execution of the first ballot by one without authority. In such circumstance, the vote could be changed in order to allow *the voting entity to intelligently express its will*." *In re MCorp Fin., Inc.*, 137 B.R. 237, 238 (Bankr. S.D. Tex. 1992)(emphasis added).

FIGTER LIMITED v. TEACHERS INSURANCE AND ANNUITY ASSN. OF AMERICA (IN RE FIGTER LIMITED)
United States Court of Appeals for the Ninth Circuit
118 F.3d 635 (1997)

FERNANDEZ, CIRCUIT JUDGE.

BACKGROUND

Figter filed a voluntary petition under Chapter 11 of the Bankruptcy Code. It owns Skyline Terrace, a 198-unit residential apartment complex located in Los Angeles. [Teachers Insurance and Annuity Association] is a creditor. It holds a $15,600,000 promissory note executed by Figter. The note is secured by a first deed of trust on Skyline Terrace and by $1,400,000 of cash on hand. In fact, Teachers is Figter's only secured creditor and is the only member of Class 2 in a reorganization plan proposed by Figter. [The plan proposed by the debtor would have left Teachers' claim unimpaired.]

The plan calls for the impairment of Class 3 unsecured claims by payment at only 80% of their face value.

Teachers has opposed Figter's reorganization plan from its inception because, among other things, that plan contemplates the conversion of Skyline Terrace Apartments into condominiums, with payment to and partial releases by Teachers as the units sell. That could easily result in a property that was part condominium and part rentals, if the plan ultimately fails in operation.

Teachers proposed a plan of its own, which provided for the transfer of Skyline Terrace and the cash collateral to Teachers in satisfaction of its secured claim, as well as a payment of Class 3 unsecured claims at 90%. Teachers' plan was premised on the assumption that its claim was partly unsecured. However . . . before the purchases of other claims took place, the bankruptcy court determined that Skyline Terrace had a value of $19,300,000. Thus, Teachers' claim in the amount of $17,960,000 was fully secured. It did not thereafter pursue its plan. From October 27, 1994 until October 31, 1994, Teachers purchased twenty-one of the thirty-four unsecured claims in Class 3 at one hundred cents on the dollar, for a total purchase price of $14,588.62. Teachers had made the same offer to all of the Class 3 claim holders, but not all accepted it. The offer remained open. Teachers then filed notices of transfer of claims with the court, as is required under Bankruptcy Rule 3001(e)(2). Those notices were served on all affected parties, including Figter. No objections were filed by the unsecured creditors. The district court upheld the bankruptcy court's determination regarding Teachers' purchase of the unsecured claims. As a result, Figter's plan is unconfirmable because it is unable to meet the requirements of 11 U.S.C. § 1129(a)(10); there will not be an impaired, consenting class of claims.

That will preclude a "cram down" of Teachers' secured claim under 11 U.S.C. § 1129(b). Figter has appealed in an attempt to avoid that result.

STANDARD OF REVIEW

Here we are asked to review the bankruptcy court's determination that Teachers acted in good faith when it purchased the claims of certain creditors and that it can vote each one separately.

[A] decision that someone did or did not act in good faith is one where the determination is "an essentially factual inquiry" and is driven by the "data of practical human experience." For that reason, we have, in various contexts, declared that we will review good faith determinations for clear error. . . .

DISCUSSION

A. Good Faith.

The Bankruptcy Code provides that "on request of a party in interest, and after notice and a hearing, the court may designate any entity whose acceptance or rejection of [a] plan was not in good faith, or was not solicited or procured in good faith or in accordance with the provisions of this title." 11 U.S.C. § 1126(e). In this context, designate means disqualify from voting. The Bankruptcy Code does not further define the rather murky term "good faith." That job has been left to the courts.

The Supreme Court brought some clarity to this area when it decided *Young v. Higbee Co.*, 324 U.S. 204, 65 S. Ct. 594, 89 L. Ed. 890 (1945). In *Young*, the Court was discussing the predecessor to § 1126(e) when it declared that if certain persons "had declined to accept [the] plan in bad faith, the court, under section 203 could have denied them the right to vote on the plan at all." It went on to explain that the provision was intended to apply to those "whose selfish purpose was to obstruct a fair and feasible reorganization in the hope that someone would pay them more than the ratable equivalent of their proportionate part of the bankrupt assets." In other words, the section was intended to apply to those who were not attempting to protect their own proper interests, but who were, instead, attempting to obtain some benefit to which they were not entitled. While helpful, those reflections by the Court do not fully answer the question before us. Other courts have further illuminated the area.

If a person seeks to secure some untoward advantage over other creditors for some ulterior motive, that will indicate bad faith. But that does not mean that creditors are expected to approach reorganization plan votes with a high degree of altruism and with the desire to help the debtor and their fellow creditors. Far from it.

> If a selfish motive were sufficient to condemn reorganization policies of interested parties, very few, if any, would pass muster. On the other hand, pure malice, "strikes" and blackmail, and the purpose to destroy an enterprise in order to advance the interests of a competing business, all plainly constituting bad faith, are motives which may be accurately described as ulterior.

In re Pine Hill Collieries Co., 46 F. Supp. 669, 671 (E.D. Pa. 1942). That is to say, we do not condemn mere enlightened self interest, even if it appears selfish to those who do not benefit from it.

Thus, if Teachers acted out of enlightened self interest, it is not to be condemned simply because it frustrated Figter's desires. That is true, even if Teachers purchased Class 3 claims for the very purpose of blocking confirmation of Figter's proposed plan. That self interest can extend even further without being an ulterior motive. It has been held that a creditor commits no wrong when he votes against a plan of a debtor who has a lawsuit pending against the creditor, for that will not, by itself, show bad faith. See *Federal Support Co.*, 859 F.2d at 20. It has also been held that no bad faith is shown when a creditor chooses to benefit his interest as a creditor as opposed to some unrelated interest. And the mere fact that a creditor has purchased additional claims for the purpose of protecting his own existing claim does not demonstrate bad faith or an ulterior motive. "As long as a creditor acts to preserve what he reasonably perceives as his fair share of the debtor's estate, bad faith will not be attributed to his purchase of claims to control a class vote."

Courts, on the other hand, have been sensitive to situations where a company, which was not a preexisting creditor, has purchased a claim for the purpose of blocking an action against it. They have seen that as an indication of bad faith. The same has been true where creditors were associated with a competing business and desired to destroy the debtor's business in order to further their own. And when the debtor had claims against itself purchased by an insider or affiliate for the purpose of blocking a plan, or fostering one, that was seen as a badge of bad faith. Figter would have us add that in a single asset bankruptcy, claim purchasing activities, like those of Teachers, are in bad faith. It cites no authority for that, and we see no basis for establishing that as a per se rule.

In short, the concept of good faith is a fluid one, and no single factor can be said to inexorably demand an ultimate result, nor must a single set of factors be considered. It is always necessary to keep in mind the difference between a creditor's self interest as a creditor and a motive which is ulterior to the purpose of protecting a creditor's interest. Prior cases can offer guidance, but, when all is said and done, the bankruptcy court must simply approach each good faith determination with a perspicacity derived from the data of its informed practical experience in dealing with bankrupts and their creditors.

Here, the bankruptcy court did exactly that. It decided that Teachers was not, for practical purposes, the proponent of an alternate plan when it sought to purchase the Class 3 claims. Nor, it found, did Teachers seek to purchase a small number of claims for the purpose of blocking Figter's plan, while injuring other creditors, even if it could do that in some circumstances. Rather, Teachers offered to purchase all Class 3 claims, and only some of those claimants' refusals to sell precluded it from doing so. Moreover, Teachers was a lender, not a competing apartment owner. It acted to protect its interests as Figter's major creditor. It reasonably feared that it could be left with a very complex lien situation, if Figter went forward with its plan. Instead of holding a lien covering the whole of the property, it could have wound up with separate fractured liens on various parts of the property, while other parts were owned by others. That could create a very undesirable mix of owners and renters and of debtors and nondebtors. Added to that was the actual use of cash, which was collateral for the debt owed to Teachers. It cannot be said that Teachers' concerns were irrational.

Based on all that was before it, the bankruptcy court decided that in this case Teachers was a creditor which acted in a good faith attempt to protect its interests and not with some ulterior motive. We cannot say that it erred in making that ultimate determination.

B. Voting.

Figter's fallback position is that even if Teachers did act in good faith, it must be limited to one vote for its twenty-one claims. That assertion is answered by the language of the Bankruptcy Code, which provides that:

> A class of claims has accepted a plan if such plan has been accepted by creditors . . . that hold at least two-thirds in amount and more than one-half *in number of the allowed claims* of such class held by creditors . . . that have accepted or rejected such plan.

11 U.S.C. § 1126(c) (emphasis added). That language was interpreted in *Gilbert*, 104 B.R. at 211, where the court reasoned:

> The formula contained in Section 1126(c) speaks in terms of the number of claims, not the number of creditors, that actually vote for or against the plan . . . . Each claim arose out of a separate transaction, evidencing separate obligations for which separate proofs of claim were filed. Votes of acceptance . . . are to be computed only on the basis of filed and allowed proofs of claim . . . . [The creditor] is entitled to one vote for each of his unsecured Class X claims.

That same view was iterated in *Concord Square Apartments of Wood Cty, Ltd. v. Ottawa Properties, Inc. (In re Concord Square Apartments of Wood Cty., Ltd.)*, 174 B.R. 71, 74 (Bankr. S.D. Ohio 1994), where the court held that a creditor with "multiple claims, has a voting right for each claim it holds." We agree. It would not make much sense to require a vote by creditors who held "more than one-half in number of the allowed claims" while at the same time limiting a creditor who held two or more of those claims to only one vote. If allowed claims are to be counted, they must be counted regardless of whose hands they happen to be in.

NOTES AND QUESTIONS

You will recall that Code § 1129(a)(10) provides that if any class of claims is impaired under a plan, at least one impaired class must vote in favor of the plan in order for the plan to be confirmed by the court. In determining whether that requirement is met, votes of creditors who are "insiders" do not count. Suppose that the CEO of the debtor also holds a claim against the debtor. Suppose that he transfers his claim to a college friend, who votes to accept the debtor's plan. Should the college buddy's vote be designated and disqualified under § 1126(e)? *See In re Derby Dev. Corp.*, 2012 Bankr. LEXIS 3034 (Bankr. D. Conn. June 27, 2012). What if a creditor who extended prepetition credit to the debtor just happens to be a friend of the debtor and wants to see his friend's plan succeed. Should his vote be designated? *See In re Bataa/Kierland, LLC*, 476 B.R. 558 (Bankr. D. Ariz. 2012).

§ 9.09 TRADING IN CLAIMS AGAINST THE DEBTOR

[A] Introduction

Trading in claims against Chapter 11 companies has become big business in recent years. (So has trading in their stock.) "The creation of a market in bankruptcy claims" has been described as "the single most important development in the bankruptcy world since the Bankruptcy Code's enactment in 1978." Adam J. Levitin, *Bankruptcy Markets: Making Sense of Claims Trading*, 4 Brook. J. Corp., Fin. & Com. L. 67 (2009).

Why creditors would be willing to sell their claims, often at a steep discount, is not too difficult to fathom. As we've seen, in the context of motions to convert or dismiss reorganization cases, motions for relief from the stay, the formation of creditors' committees, and the scope of managers' fiduciary duties, creditors may have conflicting interests, goals, and agendas. Some creditors will favor giving a debtor time and a chance to rehabilitate while others will favor conversion or dismissal and a quick dismemberment, preferring to get what they can quickly, rather than wait for some speculative amount in the future. The patience of the first group may stem from some loyalty to the debtor, a desire to maintain on-going business relationships, or sheer frustration or disinterest. The impatience of the second group may reflect peevishness or a genuine business compulsion. For creditors who have their own cash flow problems, twenty cents on the dollar today may be preferable to payment in full years from now. Even banks may choose to sell their claims at a discount rather than yield to pressure from bank examiners to write the claims off as uncollectible.

Why an investor would want to buy a claim against (let alone stock in) a financially troubled company may seem less obvious. Were you to ask buyers of bankruptcy claims or stocks why they were practicing such risky business, they might give you the same answer that the renowned bank robber Willie Sutton gave a reporter who asked him why he robbed banks: "Because that's where the money is." Of course, a better answer is: "We think, based on our careful analysis, that that's where the money is." An earlier edition of this casebook contained a passage from a report published by R.D. Smith & Company, a "Brokerage Firm Specializing in Financially Troubled Companies."

> R.D Smith & Co., Inc. specializes in the research, trading, and sales of the securities of financially troubled companies . . . . Typically the securities tend to be debt instruments such as publicly-held bonds but may also include bank debt and other privately-held claims. Equity securities are also traded and indeed, most distressed securities tend to exhibit equity characteristics.
>
>   . . . .
>
> The market for financially troubled companies has increased substantially over the past few years. Indeed, there are forces and trends in place

which indicate this market will be one of the country's leading growth areas in the 1990s.[1] Among the macroeconomic factors driving this market are: (1) the substantial growth of the junk bond market to well over $150 billion, (2) an increase in the default rate on debt due to massive litigation awards, (3) a greater acceptability by management to file for Chapter 11 protection, (4) structural economic changes (e.g., the health care industry), (5) weak commodity prices (e.g., the oil and gas and steel industries), (6) the increase in leveraged buyout transactions during the past five years, and (7) the pressure on financial institutions, principally commercial banks and savings and loans, as well as federal agencies, such as the FDIC and FSLIC, to reduce their problem loan portfolios.

Modern portfolio theory describes an efficient portfolio as one which offers the maximum ratio of return for a given level of risk, in a marketplace where all that is known about a particular security is reflected in the price. The approach of R.D. Smith is to help construct a portfolio whose elements are market inefficient, that is, where prices do not reflect all that is known about them. This investment opportunity is presented by financially troubled companies. Perceived risk, caused by the unknowns of bankruptcy and other extraordinary corporate reorganizations, often varies substantially from the risk. The role of the firm is to properly identify and thoroughly research, for purposes of trading and sales, those securities (be they equity, debt or hybrid) where we believe real risk to be far different from the market perception.

. . . .

Our experience has proven that what appears from the outside to be risky can be indeed quite conservative **if** (1) astute on-going interpretation is conducted, **and** (2) a diversified portfolio is maintained.

. . . .

While every financially troubled situation is unique, we focus on three fundamental issues to arrive at a current and projected value of the securities: (1) what the company is worth on a liquidated and going-concern basis, (2) in the case of a bankruptcy, the likely distribution of assets among claimants, and (3) the length of time for resolution.

A 1987 *Time Magazine* article on the art of what had become known as "vulture investing" reported:

Known in some corporate boardrooms as "vultures," the traders at R.D. Smith specialize in buying and selling low-priced stocks and bonds issued by companies that have filed for bankruptcy protection or are perilously close to taking that step. This dishonor roll ranges from such well-known hard-luck cases as Texaco, Manville and LTV to obscure ailing firms like Crystal Oil. Smith and his growing legion of clients realize that investments in troubled companies may turn out to be worthless. But the prices of such cheap stocks and bonds can surge if the firms get out of difficulty. Only ten

---

[1] [The authors of this brochure were not being ironic. — Eds.]

years ago, for example, Toys "R" Us, then called Interstate Stores, was wallowing in bankruptcy proceedings, and its stock was selling for as low as 12.5 cents. Today a share of the resurgent toy-store chain goes for more than $38, a 300-fold increase. Windfalls can also be made from convalescing companies like LTV, the giant steel firm that is still reorganizing under Chapter 11 protection but has made strides toward renewed profitability. This year the price of LTV bonds maturing in 2003 has nearly tripled, from 11% of face value to 30%.

Eugene Linden, *Boom in The Bust Market: Taking Stock in Bankruptcy*, Time Magazine, October 12, 1987, available at http://www.time.com/time/subscriber/article/0,33009,965703,00.html.

If a distressed debt investor buys claims at 20 cents on the dollar and sells them to another distressed debt investor at, say, 30 cents on the dollar, it will have realized a tidy profit. Yet another reason that claims traders are able to profit by trading on the difference between the perceived and actual value of claims is that, as a general rule,[2] a bankruptcy claim is worth the same in the hands of a transferee as it is in the hands of the original claim holder. For example, were Abel to stay in the case to the finish, and were Amphydynamics to deliver a plan that paid, say, 50 cents on the dollar to unsecured creditors, then Abel would receive $5,000 in satisfaction of its $10,000 claim. If Abel chose to bail out of the case by selling its $10,000 claim to Lazarus for $2,000, then Lazarus would receive the $5,000 payment under the plan. Lazarus will make a tidy profit — provided, of course, that the payment is made quickly enough so that Lazarus's cost of funds does not exceed the gain.

In the early, Code-era, claims trading opinions, the main concern of bankruptcy courts was that unsophisticated claim holders were being taken to the cleaners by sophisticated purchasers. The opinion of Bankruptcy Judge Abrams, as she was then known, in the Chapter 11 case of Revere Copper & Brass, the famous maker of popular kitchen utensils, is one example. *In re Revere Copper and Brass, Inc.*, 58 B.R. 1 (Bankr. S.D.N.Y. 1985).

Revere filed its Chapter 11 petition in late 1982. In early November, 1984, a distressed debt investor, Phoenix Capital Corporation, sent the following letter to Revere creditors:

Dear Sir:

SUBJECT: Sale of your claim against Revere Copper and Brass Incorporated, Bankruptcy Case No. 82B 12073 (PA)

Phoenix Capital Corporation is prepared to pay immediate cash for your claim against the bankrupt Revere Copper and Brass Incorporated.

---

[2] This is the general rule. When, however, the purchasers are fiduciaries of the debtor's creditors, their claims may be equitably subordinated to limit their recovery to the purchase price of the claims. *Citicorp Venture Capital, Ltd. v. Committee of Creditors Holding Unsecured Claims (In re Papercraft Corp.)*, 160 F.3d 982 (3d Cir. 1998). For an early and excellent discussion of this and other aspects of claims trading, *see* Fortgang & Mayer, *Trading Claims and Taking Control of Corporations in Chapter 11*, 12 Cardozo L. Rev. 1 (1990).

The schedule of accounts payable filed with the U.S. Bankruptcy Court for the Southern District of New York, indicates that your company has a claim in the amount of [$_____]. Our offer is to pay twenty percent (20%) of the face amount of any valid, uncontested and unpaid claim.

If you wish to accept this offer, please acknowledge your acceptance in the space provided below and return one copy to me for my further handling. A check will be issued to your company at once. Claims will be purchased on a first offered, first bought basis.

58 B.R. 1–2. A number of creditors responded by tendering their claims and Phoenix bought them in late November and early December. On November 30, the Wall Street Journal reported that the elements of a plan had been agreed upon by Revere and its various constituencies. The proposed plan gave creditors three payment options. They could opt for (1) payment of 65% of their claims in cash upon confirmation of the plan; (2) 60% of their claim in cash and 10% of their claim in stock of the reorganized company; or (3) 39% in cash, 46% in notes, and 14% in stock of the reorganized company. Confirmation of the plan would occur, at the earliest, the following summer.

What was the issue before the court? That is an interesting question, because no party in interest had questioned the validity or fairness of the claims transfers. What happened is that Phoenix had taken steps to comply with Bankruptcy Rule 3001(e)(2), which at that time provided:

> *Unconditional Transfer After Proof Filed.* If a claim other than one based on a bond or debenture has been unconditionally transferred after the proof of claim has been filed, evidence of the terms of the transfer shall be filed by the transferee. The clerk shall immediately notify the original claimant by mail of the filing of the evidence of transfer and that objection thereto, if any, must be filed with the clerk within 20 days of the mailing of the notice or within any additional time allowed by the court. If the court finds, after a hearing on notice, that the claim has been unconditionally transferred, it shall enter an order substituting the transferee for the original claimant, otherwise the court shall enter such order as may be appropriate.

The rule made good sense. It was intended to make sure that a party that claimed to be the transferee of a claim was, in fact, the transferee and that the transferor had not retained an interest. If the court found that the claim had indeed been unconditionally transferred, the new creditor would be substituted for the creditor who had filed the proof of claim. No one objected to the claim transfers. No one suggested that the transfers to Phoenix were not unconditional. The judge, nevertheless, was concerned:

> The assignor-creditors may indeed prefer the certainty of the 20% cash in hand offered by Phoenix today over the possibility of 65% cash at an uncertain time in the future under Revere's announced plan of reorganization. However, the court is concerned that the assignor-creditors have not been plainly advised of their options. Bankruptcy Rule 3001(e)(2) contemplates that the court will enter the order of substitution only after a hearing

on notice and further permits the court to enter such an order as is appropriate. The Advisory Committee Note to this rule states in relevant part:

> "The interests of sound administration are served by requiring the post-petition transferee to file with the proof of claim a statement of the transferor acknowledging the transfer and the consideration for the transfer. Such a disclosure will assist the court in dealing with evils that may arise out of post-bankruptcy traffic in claims against an estate" (citations omitted).

> One of the evils attendant upon a solicitation of assignment of claims for a cash payment such as is being made by Phoenix is that solicited creditors may be unaware of their rights and options and fall prey to the belief that bankruptcy inevitably will result in their receiving the proverbial 10 cents on the dollar or worse. Creditors may not be aware of the difference between a straight bankruptcy case under Chapter 7 and a reorganization case under Chapter 11 of the Bankruptcy Code. Bankruptcy Code § 1125 prohibits solicitation of acceptances or rejections of a filed plan unless the solicitation is accompanied or preceded by a disclosure statement. The disclosure statement must contain adequate information which means information of a kind and in sufficient detail to enable a hypothetical reasonable investor typical of holders of claims to make an informed judgment about the plan. Code § 1125(a)(1). The assignor-claimant [sic] have not been shown to have been given sufficient information by Phoenix that they might make an informed judgment about the offer made to them. That much is required.

Id. at 2–3. The bankruptcy judge ruled that she would not approve the assignments until the claim sellers had been given a 30-day period in which to revoke the transfers. She also advised Phoenix that the court would not approve any future assignments "unless it appears that the claimants have been advised at the time of solicitation and again at the time a check in payment of Phoenix's offer is tendered of the pertinent terms of Revere's announced or any subsequently filed plan and the procedural status of the Chapter 11 case and plan, so that the solicited creditor may know where along the plan filing-disclosure statement hearing-confirmation line the case stands." *Id.* at 3.

That claims traders took note of the *Revere* opinion is apparent from the facts of *In re Allegheny Int'l, Inc.*, 100 B.R. 241 (Bankr. W.D. Pa. 1988). In that case, at a time that the debtor was on the verge of filing an amended plan that would pay creditors 100% of their claims, distressed debt buyers, including Phoenix, had purchased claims at prices ranging between 20% and 75% of their face value. In some cases, the sellers were sophisticated institutional lenders and the sales were well-lawyered. In some cases the sellers had signed "Big Boy Letters," in which they acknowledged that the buyers might have better information and that a richer recovery through a confirmed plan was possible. Still, the court's discomfort was palpable. The court mused that the claims purchasers might have been well-advised to have their solicitation materials approved by the court. The court was troubled that it had declined to allow the debtor to pay the claims of critical vendors, but in a sense, claims purchasers were doing just that. The court was uneasy, because some claim sellers were more sophisticated than others:

> We also remain concerned that some assignors were not aware of the implications of the assignment of their claims. Although it appears that the assignors were generally business entities, some of them were small businesses who may have lacked an understanding of Chapter 11 and ready access to the debtor's plan of reorganization. Many people in small businesses do not read the Wall Street Journal!
>
> By the filing of a bankruptcy case, a market in nonpublicly traded securities is created. Claimants are not protected by a disclosure statement. It is an undesirable practice. This court intends to continue to press the debtor in possession to file its modified disclosure statement and plan, and to move expeditiously to confirmation, to reduce the need of creditors to accept these offers. We do not believe that Congress intended the trafficking in claims such as has occurred in this case and others. Such concerns are evident from the 1983 Advisory Committee Note, although we recognize that the cases cited therein involved breaches of fiduciary duty. A breach of fiduciary duty implies inside knowledge. Although this case does not involve inside knowledge, it is colored with superior knowledge, and thus the assignments are similar to contracts of adhesion. We hope that Congress will address these concerns in the future.
>
> Prospective assignments will require compliance with Bankruptcy Rule 3001(e)(2), as modified by this order. We impose on the debtor the duty of advising the potential assignor of the debtor's estimate of the value of the claim. The prospective assignee, in addition to filing a copy of the information required by Rule 3001(e)(2) with the clerk, shall provide such information to the debtor. Within 15 days, the debtor shall provide the potential assignor with its best estimate of the value of the debtor's claim, until such time as a new plan of reorganization and disclosure statement are filed. The court explicitly grants the debtor permission to provide such information. The debtor shall be held harmless from any claims arising from such disclosure. After the plan of reorganization and disclosure statement are filed, the debtor shall provide the relevant information from the plan of reorganization and disclosure statement in lieu of its estimate of the claim. Proof that the debtor has provided the requisite information shall be filed with the court. The 20-day period for filing objections, as set forth in Rule 3001(e)(2), shall run from the filing of this notice by the debtor. If no objections are filed, the court will approve the assignment.

Id. at 243–44.

Less than a year later, a bankruptcy judge in the Southern District of New York issued a "Supplement to the Requirements of Fed. R. Bankr. P. 3001(e)(2)." The supplement, since rescinded, required that applications for Rule 3001(e) orders be accompanied by a statement of consideration paid for the assigned claims; and a representation that the purchaser did not solicit the claim holder by "the use of misinformation."

In the wake of the *Revere* and *Allegheny* opinions, Bankruptcy Rule 3001(e)(2) was amended — with the express goal of getting bankruptcy courts out of the business of regulating claims trading. Among other things, the amendments eliminated the requirement of a hearing, except in cases in which transferors filed objections to the transfer. Absent such an objection, the transferee is to be substituted for the transferor. This does not mean that courts have gotten out of the business of reviewing the terms of claims transfers entirely. Rule 3001(e)(2) still requires that "evidence of the transfer shall be filed by the transferee." The Bankruptcy Court for the Southern District of New York has issued a Guideline, "Claims Transfers — Importance of Compliance with the Federal Rules of Bankruptcy Procedure." It states, among other things, that to comply with Rule 3001(e)(2), parties involved may submit the actual agreement between the parties or other evidence of the transfer, provided that it includes a description of pertinent terms.

[B] Acquiring Claims to Take Control of the Debtor

Purchasing claims in the hope of cashing them in at a profit is not the only motivation for acquiring claims against a debtor. Purchasing claims is also a technique for acquiring ownership and control of troubled companies. The strategy, simply put, is to acquire claims and then, exchange them pursuant to a reorganization plan for a controlling equity interest in the debtor company.

Although, in the *Allegheny* case, the Bankruptcy Court's initial focus was on the effect of claims trading on unsophisticated claims sellers, a year later, the judge believed he was confronted with a dispute over the effect of claims trading on the integrity of the Chapter 11 process itself. Nearly two years into the case, as the hearing on the disclosure statement on the debtor's plan was concluding, Japonica Partners, which had purchased millions of dollars of claims against the debtor, filed its own plan. Japonica's holdings were sufficient to give it a blocking position, which it exercised by voting against the debtor's plan. The debtor and Japonica filed dueling motions to have votes designated and disqualified under Code § 1126(e). The court found that Japonica had a longstanding interest in acquiring Allegheny, that it had filed a competing plan that would give it control of Allegheny, and that it had strategically purchased claims in the two highest priority impaired classes in order to block acceptance of the plan. The court did designate and disqualify Japonica's votes. *In re Allegheny Int'l, Inc.*, 118 B.R. 282 (Bankr. W.D. Pa. 1990). The court's reasoning is discussed in further detail in the following, more recent opinions.

DISH NETWORK CORP. v. DBSD NORTH AMERICA CORP. ("DISH I")

United States Bankruptcy Court, Southern District of New York

421 B.R. 133 (2009)

Robert E. Gerber, United States Bankruptcy Judge.

Introduction

In this contested matter in the chapter 11 cases of DBSD North America, Inc. and its subsidiaries (the "Debtors"), the Debtors move, pursuant to section 1126(e) of the Bankruptcy Code, to designate the votes of DISH Network Corporation ("DISH"), now the sole holder of debt in the First Lien Debt (as defined below) class, rejecting the reorganization plan before the Court for confirmation. As described more fully below, DISH became involved in these cases when, after the Debtors proposed a plan of reorganization, DISH bought up all of the Debtors' First Lien Debt from its prior holders, *at par*, seeking by its acquisition of the Debtors' debt, "to acquire control of this strategic asset." Thereafter, literally on the eve of the plan confirmation hearing, DISH sought to terminate exclusivity and obtain permission to file its own plan, further to achieve its strategic objective.

The motion is granted. This is the paradigmatic case for the application of the Allegheny doctrine, described more fully below. . . .

Findings of Fact

The Debtors are a development-stage enterprise formed in 2004 to develop an integrated mobile satellite and terrestrial services network (the "Satellite System") to deliver wireless satellite communications services to mass-market consumers. To date, the Debtors have made significant progress in developing the Satellite System, including launching a satellite and obtaining frequency bands and related regulatory approval from the FCC for the Satellite System.

But the Debtors are still a development-stage enterprise and, as such, do not yet have significant operations from which to generate revenues or cash flow. However, the Satellite System, as developed to date, has substantial value.

In 1992, EchoStar Satellite LLC ("EchoStar"), a satellite television equipment distributor, acquired a Direct Broadcast Satellite license from the FCC. In early 1996, EchoStar established DISH as a provider of satellite television. Since then, EchoStar and DISH have launched a number of satellites to accommodate the enterprises' growth, and they now own and lease a total of 14 satellites. In addition to developing its proprietary satellite system, DISH has made significant investments in TerreStar Corporation ("TerreStar"), a development-stage telecommunications enterprise like the Debtors', which is likewise engaged in designing and developing a mobile satellite and terrestrial services network to deliver wireless satellite communications services . . . . TerreStar is a direct competitor of the Debtors.

On May 15, 2009, the Debtors filed for chapter 11 relief and, on June 26, 2009, filed an amended plan (as amended to that point and thereafter, the "Plan") and associated disclosure statement. Under the Plan, the Debtors proposed to satisfy their first lien secured prepetition debt of approximately $40 million (the "First Lien Debt") through issuance of a modified promissory note, under an amended first lien facility (the "Amended Facility").

On July 9, 2009, about two weeks after the Debtors filed the Plan and disclosure statement (each of which disclosed the proposed treatment for the First Lien Debt), DISH purchased all of the First Lien Debt, in a principal amount of approximately $40 million, at par. Additionally, also after the Debtors' chapter 11 filing, DISH through an affiliate purchased approximately $111 million in principal amount of the Debtors' "7.5% Convertible Senior Subordinated Notes," representing second lien debt (the "Second Lien Debt") — a fulcrum security that the Plan proposed to convert to equity. DISH purchased Second Lien Debt only from sellers who were not bound by a support agreement (the "Plan Support Agreement"), which would obligate its parties to vote their claims in favor of the Plan.

DISH's actions and intent may be observed and inferred from the circumstances and its own documents. DISH purchased its debt at par — *paying* the price for which most other creditors could only hope. DISH thought it was overpaying for debt it acquired in this case, but was willing to make that investment. It was willing to overpay for this investment:

> Because we have an interest generally in spectrum assets, and we were interested in having a relationship with [Debtor] that might allow us to, you know, reach some sort of transaction in the future if that spectrum could be useful in our business.

DISH's acquisition of First Lien Debt was not a purchase to make a profit on increased recoveries under a reorganization plan. Rather, the Court finds that DISH made its investments in the Debtors' First Lien and Second Lien Debts as a strategic investor. One of its documents stated, in a number of bullet points that were part of an "Executive Summary":

> DISH has invested [$32.9M] for [$111.6M] of Face Value 2nd Priority Convertible Notes at an average dollar price of [29.5].

> The Company is attempting to negotiate a proposal to equitize Bondholders in return for 95% of the restructured [DBSB] (subject to certain earnouts based on valuation).

> We believe there is a strategic opportunity *to obtain a blocking position* in the 2nd Priority Convertible Notes and *control the bankruptcy process for this potentially strategic asset.*

> We are seeking Board approval to invest up to an incremental [$100M] to purchase securities necessary *to gain control of the Unsecured (impaired) Class.*[9]

---

[9] Doc. DISH-002863 (brackets in original; emphasis added). While the language just quoted, and that in the following passage, appeared in documents that were produced to opposing counsel as "Highly

And another document, similar to but different from the one just quoted, said things similarly but in some respects even more explicitly:

> DISH has invested [$32.9M] for [$111.6M] of Face Value 2nd Priority Convertible Notes at an average dollar price of [29.5].
>
> The Company is attempting to negotiate a proposal to equitize Bondholders in return for 95% of a restructured [Debtor] (subject to certain earnouts based on valuation).
>
> We believe there is a strategic opportunity to obtain the remaining convertible bonds outstanding *in an attempt to convert to equity and acquire control of [DBSB]*.
>
> We are seeking board approval for up to [$200M] to acquire the remaining convertible bonds outstanding and *establish control of this strategic asset*.

DISH voted all of its claims, including all of its First Lien Debt and Second Lien Debt claims, to reject the Plan. With a single exception, all other impaired classes in which votes were cast voted to accept the Plan.

In response to DISH's rejection of the Plan, the Debtors filed a motion seeking to designate DISH's vote of its First Lien Debt to reject the Plan.[12] In its objection to such motion DISH noted, among other things, that its conduct was that of a "model bankruptcy citizen" and that it "has not moved to terminate exclusivity, and it has not proposed a competing plan." But on the morning before the scheduled confirmation hearing, September 21, 2009, DISH filed a motion seeking an order terminating the Debtors' 180 day exclusivity period for obtaining approval of the Plan and for authority to propose a competing plan.

DISH has made a proposal to enter into a major transaction with the Debtors, the specifics of which are inappropriate for disclosure in this public document. It is sufficient, for the purposes of this discussion, to say, and the Court finds, that DISH's proposal went far beyond the treatment of the First Lien Debt that DISH had recently acquired. DISH's proposal further evidences its strategic objective.

Based on the totality of the evidence, the Court finds DISH's efforts to understate its intent, as in some of its deposition testimony and counsel's argument, unpersuasive. The Court finds that DISH made its investment in this chapter 11 case, and has continued to act, not as a traditional creditor seeking to maximize its return on the debt it holds, but as a strategic investor, "to establish control over this strategic asset."

Confidential, For Attorneys' Eyes Only," the Court sees nothing in the quoted matter that is properly subject to protection under section 107(b) of the Code, and believes that the public interest in this motion affirmatively requires disclosure.

[12] Although DISH voted its Second Lien Debt to reject the Plan as well, its dissenting vote was insufficient to cause a rejection of the Plan by the Second Lien Debt class. Thus designation of DISH's voting with respect to the Second Lien Class would be academic, and presumably was not sought for this reason.

Discussion

Section 1126(e) of the Bankruptcy Code provides:

> On request of a party in interest, and after notice and a hearing, the court may designate any entity whose acceptance or rejection of such plan was not in good faith, or was not solicited or procured in good faith or in accordance with the provisions of this title.

Section 1126(e) is permissive in nature, and a bankruptcy judge has discretion in designating votes.

I.

Neither the expression "not in good faith," nor "good faith" itself, is defined in the Bankruptcy Code. Instead these concepts have been left to caselaw.[16] That caselaw goes back to cases under Chapter X of the former Bankruptcy Act,[17] section 203 of which provided for similar relief[18] and from which the present section 1126(e) emerged.[19] Under the caselaw, as Chief Judge Bernstein observed in *Dune Deck Owners*, and this Court observed in its earlier vote designation decision in *Adelphia*[21] (drawing upon *Dune Deck Owners* repeatedly), "bad faith" — i.e., an absence of the requisite good faith — may be found where a claim holder attempts to extract or extort a personal advantage not available to other creditors in the class, or, as relevant here, where a creditor acts in furtherance of an ulterior motive,

---

[16] *In re Dune Deck Owners Corp.*, 175 B.R. 839, 844 (Bankr. S.D.N.Y. 1995) (Bernstein, C.J.) ("*Dune Deck Owners*"). *See also In re Landing Assocs., Ltd.*, 157 B.R. 791, 802 (Bankr. W.D. Tex. 1993) (Leif Clark, J.) ("The term 'good faith' as used in [section 1126(e)] was intentionally left undefined, so that it might be defined and developed in accordance with cases as they arose.").

[17] One of those cases, *In re P-R Holding Corp.*, 147 F.2d 895 (2d Cir. 1945) ("*P-R Holding*"), was decided by the Second Circuit. In that case, the debtor owned a hotel in New York City. Various plans of reorganization were submitted, including one that included an offer made by two individuals to purchase the hotel. Shortly before the last day to vote on the plan, and to assure the success of the plan, they purchased a significant portion of the claims, most of which had been voted against the plan by the sellers. The Second Circuit held that the purchases were made in bad faith, and thus that their votes could not be voted in favor of the plan. Before so concluding, the Second Circuit stated:

> The mere fact that a purchase of creditors' interests is for the purpose of securing the approval or rejection of a plan does not of itself amount to "bad faith." When that purchase is in aid of an interest other than an interest of a creditor, such purchases may amount of "bad faith" under section 203 of the Bankruptcy Act.

Id. at 897.

[18] Section 203 then provided:

> If the acceptance or failure to accept a plan by the holder of any claim or stock is not in good faith, in the light of or irrespective of the time of acquisition thereof, the judge may, after hearing upon notice, direct that such claim or stock be disqualified for the purpose of determining the requisite majority for the acceptance of a plan. *See* 6 Collier on Bankruptcy P 9.21 (14th Ed. 1978) (that being the final edition of *Collier* covering the now superseded Bankruptcy Act).

[19] *See* 7 Collier on Bankruptcy P 1126.03[4] (15th Ed. Rev. 2009) This latter edition of Collier on Bankruptcy ("Collier"), a new version of which will be forthcoming shortly, is presently the latest edition covering the present Bankruptcy Code.

[21] *See In re Adelphia Commc'ns Corp.*, 359 B.R. 54 (Bankr. S.D.N.Y. 2006) (Gerber, J.) ("*Adelphia*").

unrelated to its claim or its interests as a creditor.[22]

In the latter connection, each of Chief Judge Bernstein in *Dune Deck Owners* and this Court in *Adelphia* observed that courts have developed several "badges of bad faith" which may justify disqualification. They include efforts to:

(1) assume control of the debtor;

(2) put the debtor out of business or otherwise gain a competitive advantage;

(3) destroy the debtor out of pure malice; or

(4) obtain benefits available under a private agreement with a third party which depends on the debtor's failure to reorganize.[23]

The preeminent case with respect to the first of the badges of fraud — efforts to assume control of the debtor — is *Allegheny*. There a plan proponent, Japonica Partners ("Japonica"), bought up claims against the debtor, at increasing prices (and indeed after the debtor had filed a plan of reorganization), to gain control of the reorganized debtor and to block confirmation of an alternative plan that would deny Japonica the opportunity to acquire the control for which Japonica had acquired its claims.

The *Allegheny* court ruled under section 1126(e) that Japonica's purchase of its claims was not in "good faith," and the court disqualified the Japonica vote against the debtor's plan. The *Allegheny* court observed, not surprisingly, that "[t]he particular claims that Japonica purchased, and the manner in which they were purchased, can be used to determine their intent."[25] And it found that Japonica did not acquire most of its claims until a plan had been proposed (and, indeed, a disclosure statement with respect to that plan had been approved); "knew what it was getting into when it purchased its claims"; was a " "voluntary claimant"; and that if Japonica "was unsatisfied by the proposed distribution, it had the option of not becoming a creditor," and "could have proposed its plan without buying these claims."[26]

Based on the evidence before it, the *Allegheny* court found that "Japonica's interest is to take over and control the debtor"[27] — a purpose fundamentally different than the understandable desire of any creditor to maximize the recovery on its claim. These were acts "in aid of an interest other than an interest as a creditor."[28] Noting that "[v]otes must be designated when the court determines that the 'creditor has cast his vote with an "ulterior purpose" aimed at gaining some advantage to which he would not otherwise be entitled in his position,'" the *Allegheny* court ruled that the purpose to take over the debtor was such an "ulterior

---

[22] *Dune Deck Owners*, 175 B.R. at 844; *Adelphia*, 359 B.R. at 61.

[23] *Dune Deck Owners*, 175 B.R. at 844–845; *Adelphia*, 359 B.R. at 61.

[25] *Allegheny*, 118 B.R. at 289. For example, the claims were acquired at prices as high as 95 [cents] on the dollar.

[26] *Id.* at 289.

[27] *Id.* at 289.

[28] *Id.* at 289 quoting *P-R Holding*.

motive," warranting vote disqualification.[29]

The *Allegheny* situation, the first listed of the badges of fraud as discussed by Chief Judge Bernstein in *Dune Deck Owners* and by this Court in *Adelphia*, has long been understood by the bankruptcy community to warrant vote designation. *Collier* recognizes the ability of creditors to vote "selfishly" to maximize the recovery on their claims,[30] and to act in their economic interest, "as long as the interest being served is that of a creditor as creditor, as opposed to creditor in some other capacity."[31] But *Collier* goes on to expressly state:

> On the other hand, a vote to block a reorganization plan in order to acquire the debtor company for one's self may justifiably result in disqualification of the vote.

II.

Here this is a classic case for application of the *Allegheny* doctrine. DISH's actions in this case, and its documents, demonstrate that DISH did not purchase and vote its claims in order to gain financially by way of a distribution in this case. Rather, as DISH's actions and documents make clear, its purpose was as a strategic investor — and, it may fairly be inferred, to use status as a creditor to provide advantages over proposing a plan as an outsider, or making a traditional bid for the company or its assets.

First, as the Court has found, and even more egregiously than Japonica did in *Allegheny* — where Japonica made its purchases at a maximum of 95 [cents] on the dollar — DISH purchased *all* of the First Lien Debt *at par*, knowing that the Plan proposed replacing the First Lien Debt with an Amended Facility that DISH did not want.[33] As this Court stated in its oral ruling, paraphrasing points made to it in argument,[34] "you can't do much better than get par."[35] In fact, Robert Rehg, DISH's Senior Vice President of Corporate Development, admitted that "there was no determination made that it made financial sense to buy this debt." DISH's purchase of the First Lien Debt at par even exceeds the 95 [cents] maximum that Japonica paid for the debt it acquired in *Allegheny*.

When an entity becomes a creditor late in the game paying 95 [cents] on the dollar (as in Japonica), or 100 [cents] on the dollar, as here, the inference is compelling that it has done so not to maximize the return on its claim, acquired only a few weeks earlier, but to advance an "ulterior motive" condemned in the caselaw. DISH's purpose, of course, was not that of the typical creditor — either a victim of

---

[29] *Id.* at 290.

[30] 7 *Collier* P 1126.06[2].

[31] *Id.* at P 1126.06[1].

[33] Courts in the future can decide whether strategic investors can circumvent the *Allegheny* doctrine if they buy up claims cheaply enough. The Court does not have to decide that here.

[34] *See* Hrg. Tr. at 21 ("one has to question how you pay par and expect to get a recovery . . . given that in many circumstances they're limited to getting full recovery on their claim and nothing more than that").

[35] *Id.* at 81.

financial distress left holding the bag when a debtor fails, or even an investor in distressed debt seeking to profit from the spread between its purchase price for the distressed debt and its ultimate distributions under a plan.

Second, the surrounding circumstances further demonstrate the similarity of this case to *Allegheny*. Like Japonica, DISH acquired claims after the Debtors proposed a plan of reorganization. Also like Japonica, DISH acquired claims that would give it voting power to resist the Debtors' reorganization efforts. . . .[37] Unlike Japonica, however, DISH did not stop when it acquired the minimum claims necessary for a blocking position; DISH acquired *all* of the First Lien Debt.

Lastly, the purpose to acquire debt in this case, and to use voting to advance the effort to take control, is as plain in this case as it was in *Allegheny*. As noted above, in the Court's Findings of Fact, one of DISH's own documents stated

> We believe there is a strategic opportunity *to obtain a blocking position* in the 2nd Priority Convertible Notes and *control the bankruptcy process for this potentially strategic asset.*

> We are seeking Board approval to invest up to an incremental [$100M] to purchase securities necessary *to gain control of the Unsecured (impaired) Class.*

And another stated, even more explicitly:

> We believe there is a strategic opportunity to obtain the remaining convertible bonds outstanding *in an attempt to convert to equity and acquire control of [DBSB].*

> We are seeking board approval for up to [$200M] to acquire the remaining convertible bonds outstanding and *establish control of this strategic asset.*

Additionally, Rehg admitted that DISH was willing to overpay and did overpay for its claims against the Debtors, "[b]ecause we have an interest generally in spectrum assets, and we were interested in having a relationship with [DBSD] that might allow us to, you know, reach some sort of transaction in the future if that spectrum could be useful in our business." While the Court is doubtful that Rehg's admission fully acknowledged the level of DISH's interest (particularly in light of the DISH proposal that the Court saw *in camera*), the Court need not make an ultimate credibility determination in this regard. It is sufficient, for the purposes of this analysis, to note what Rehg did admit, and (in addition to the surrounding circumstances) what DISH's documents said.

In its objection, DISH asserted that:

> DISH Network has been a model bankruptcy citizen. It announced in open Court at the Disclosure Statement hearing that it had a potential strategic

---

[37] DISH argues that the entities that sold it the First Lien Debt indicated their opposition to the Plan as well, and that in voting against the Plan, it did nothing different than they too would have done. It is possible that the former holders of the First Lien Debt would have voted against confirmation of the Plan, but if they had done so, it would have been for maximizing their recoveries on their claims — a goal they achieved when DISH bought their claims at par. When DISH voted against the Plan, it did in a wholly different context, and for wholly different reasons.

interest in the Debtors. Since that time, it has acted strictly within the confines of the bankruptcy process; among other things, it has not attempted to interfere with the Plan Support Agreement between the Debtors and the Ad Hoc Committee of Noteholders, it has not moved to terminate exclusivity, and it has not proposed a competing plan.

But the Court cannot agree that DISH has acted as a "model citizen," or that by not engaging in the acts it mentioned, DISH should be immune from application of the *Allegheny* doctrine. That is especially true here, since within days of saying what it said in its pleading, DISH *did* seek to terminate exclusivity, to propose a competing plan.

To be sure, DISH has not misbehaved as badly as some other investors in chapter 11 cases on this Court's watch — as, for example, one group of distressed debt investors moved for appointment of a trustee knowing that such would cause a default on the Debtors' DIP financing facility and a default on the sale of the company upon which all of the creditors' recoveries would rest, and then those distressed debt investor creditors put their motion on hold pending further plan negotiations. But those creditors were doing so to increase their recoveries as creditors holding long positions in debt — with a combined action and purpose that, while disgraceful, was insufficiently egregious to warrant disqualification of a creditor's vote.[42] Here, by contrast, DISH has acted to advance strategic invest-ment interests wholly apart from maximizing recoveries on a long position in debt it holds.

Moreover, virtually immediately after DISH noted, in connection with its "model citizen" contention, that it had not moved to terminate plan exclusivity, it did exactly that. Under these circumstances, the Court is unwilling to hold that DISH's failure to act as obnoxiously as creditors in other cases have acted somehow suggests that *Allegheny* should not apply.

III.

In *Adelphia*, this Court stated that:

---

[42] That was this Court's holding in *Adelphia. See* 359 B.R. at 56–57. One commentator has observed, without quarreling with this Court's ruling on the merits, that failing to punish, by vote designation, behavior of the type this Court saw in *Adelphia* "is likely to make the Chapter 11 process more contentious in some cases." Douglas, "Disenfranchising Creditors in Chapter 11: In Search of the Meaning of Bad Faith under *Section 1126(e)*," Pratt's Journal of Bankr. L. 2007.03-7 (Mar./Apr. 2007). Douglas observed:

> The message borne by *Adelphia* is that most kinds of overreaching or overly-aggressive creditor conduct designed to extract greater value, concessions or benefits under a plan may be objectionable, but are not sanctionable under section 1126(e). Given the reality that "distressed" investors involved in chapter 11 cases are more likely than most creditors to play hard ball at the plan negotiating table, *Adelphia* may actually encourage the sort of intractable conduct that the court found to be objectionable and unproductive, yet outside the scope of section 1126(e).

Douglas is unfortunately quite right in this regard, and the Court would encourage Congress to modify the Code to authorize Bankruptcy Judges to designate creditor votes for overly-aggressive and other egregious conduct even when the creditors are trying to increase returns on long positions. But in *Adelphia*, the Court had to rule under the Code and caselaw in their then-existing form.

The ability to vote on a reorganization plan is one of the most sacred entitlements that a creditor has in a chapter 11 case. And in my view, it should not be denied except for highly egregious conduct — principally, seeking to advance interests apart from recovery under the Plan, or seeking to extract plan treatment that is not available for others in the same class.[43]

But this Court made those observations in the context of a motion to designate creditors holding long positions in bonds of the various *Adelphia* debtors, who were acting to maximize their recoveries under a plan on the debt they held, and noted exceptions to that general rule that were not applicable there but are applicable here. Here, by contrast, DISH has indeed sought to advance interests apart from recovery under the Plan — as is evident from, *inter alia*, its purchase of claims at par, and the documents evidencing its strategic purpose, as contrasted to the normal desire of any creditor to be repaid. DISH's conduct is indistinguishable in any legally cognizable respect from the conduct that resulted in designation in *Allegheny*, and DISH's vote must be designated for the same reasons.

Conclusion

For the foregoing reasons, the Court rules that DISH did not act in good faith when it purchased its claims and voted to reject the Plan, and that its votes should be disqualified. The motion of the Debtors to designate the votes of DISH is granted.

Excerpts from the Second Circuit opinion affirming the Bankruptcy Court opinion follow.

DISH NETWORK CORP. v. DBSD NORTH AMERICA, INC. ("DISH II")
United States Court Of Appeals for the Second Circuit
634 F.3d 79, 102–105 (2011)

Judges: Before: POOLER, RAGGI, and LYNCH, CIRCUIT JUDGES. JUDGE POOLER concurs in part and dissents in part in a separate opinion.

GERARD E. LYNCH, CIRCUIT JUDGE:

We start with general principles that neither side disputes. Bankruptcy courts should employ § 1126(e) designation sparingly, as "the exception, not the rule." For this reason, a party seeking to designate another's vote bears the burden of proving that it was not cast in good faith. Merely purchasing claims in bankruptcy "for the purpose of securing the approval or rejection of a plan does not of itself amount to 'bad faith.'" Nor will selfishness alone defeat a creditor's good faith; the Code

---

[43] *Id.* at 56–57.

assumes that parties will act in their own self interest and allows them to do so.

Section 1126(e) comes into play when voters venture beyond mere self-interested promotion of their claims. . . .

Here, the debate centers on what sort of "ulterior motives" may trigger designation under § 1126(e), and whether DISH voted with such an impermissible motive. . . .

Clearly, not just any ulterior motive constitutes the sort of improper motive that will support a finding of bad faith. After all, most creditors have interests beyond their claim against a particular debtor, and those other interests will inevitably affect how they vote the claim. For instance, trade creditors who do regular business with a debtor may vote in the way most likely to allow them to continue to do business with the debtor after reorganization. And, as interest rates change, a fully secured creditor may seek liquidation to allow money once invested at unfavorable rates to be invested more favorably elsewhere. We do not purport to decide here the propriety of either of these motives, but they at least demonstrate that allowing the disqualification of votes on account of *any* ulterior motive could have far-reaching consequences and might leave few votes upheld.

The sort of ulterior motive that § 1126(e) targets is illustrated by the case that motivated the creation of the "good faith" rule in the first place, *Texas Hotel Securities Corp. v. Waco Development Co.*, 87 F.2d 395 (5th Cir. 1936). In that case, Conrad Hilton purchased claims of a debtor to block a plan of reorganization that would have given a lease on the debtor's property — once held by Hilton's company, later cancelled — to a third party. Hilton and his partners sought, by buying and voting the claims, to "force [a plan] that would give them again the operation of the hotel or otherwise reestablish an interest that they felt they justly had in the property." The district court refused to count Hilton's vote, but the court of appeals reversed, seeing no authority in the Bankruptcy Act for looking into the motives of creditors voting against a plan.

That case spurred Congress to require good faith in voting claims. As the Supreme Court has noted, the legislative history of the predecessor to § 1126(e) "make[s] clear the purpose of the [House] Committee [on the Judiciary] to pass legislation which would bar creditors from a vote who were prompted by such a purpose" as Hilton's. *Young*, 324 U.S. at 211 n.10. As then-SEC Commissioner Douglas explained to the House Committee:

> We envisage that "good faith" clause to enable the courts to affirm a plan over the opposition of a minority attempting to block the adoption of a plan merely for selfish purposes. The *Waco* case . . . was such a situation. If my memory does not serve me wrong it was a case where a minority group of security holders refused to vote in favor of the plan unless that group were given some particular preferential treatment, such as the management of the company. That is, there were ulterior reasons for their actions.

1937 Hearing, *supra*, at 181–82. One year after Commissioner Douglas's testimony, and two years after the *Waco* case, Congress enacted the proposed good faith clause as part of the Chandler Act of 1938. Pub. L. 75-575, § 203, 52 Stat. 840, 894. The

Bankruptcy Code of 1978 preserved this good faith requirement, with some rewording, as 11 U.S.C. § 1126(e).

Modern cases have found "ulterior motives" in a variety of situations. In perhaps the most famous case, and one on which the bankruptcy court in our case relied heavily, a court found bad faith because a party bought a blocking position in several classes after the debtor proposed a plan of reorganization, and then sought to defeat that plan and to promote its own plan that would have given it control over the debtor. *See In re Allegheny Int'l, Inc.*, 118 B.R. 282, 289–90 (Bankr. W.D. Pa. 1990). In another case, the court designated the votes of parties affiliated with a competitor who bought their claims in an attempt to obstruct the debtor's reorganization and thereby to further the interests of their own business. *See In re MacLeod Co.*, 63 B.R. 654, 655–56 (Bankr. S.D. Ohio 1986). In a third case, the court found bad faith where an affiliate of the debtor purchased claims not for the purpose of collecting on those claims but to prevent confirmation of a competing plan. *See In re Applegate Prop., Ltd.*, 133 B.R. 827, 833–35 (Bankr. W.D. Tex. 1991).

Although we express no view on the correctness of the specific findings of bad faith of the parties in those specific cases, we think that this case fits in the general constellation they form. As the bankruptcy court found, DISH, as an indirect competitor of DBSD and part-owner of a direct competitor, bought a blocking position in (and in fact the entirety of) a class of claims, after a plan had been proposed, with the intention not to maximize its return on the debt but to enter a strategic transaction with DBSD and "to use status as a creditor to provide advantages over proposing a plan as an outsider, or making a traditional bid for the company or its assets." *DBSD II*, 421 B.R. at 139–40. In effect, DISH purchased the claims as votes it could use as levers to bend the bankruptcy process toward its own strategic objective of acquiring DBSD's spectrum rights, not toward protecting its claim.

We conclude that the bankruptcy court permissibly designated DISH's vote based on the facts above. This case echoes the *Waco* case that motivated Congress to impose the good faith requirement in the first place. In that case, a competitor bought claims with the intent of voting against any plan that did not give it a lease in or management of the debtor's property. In this case, a competitor bought claims with the intent of voting against any plan that did not give it a strategic interest in the reorganized company. The purchasing party in both cases was less interested in maximizing the return on its claim than in diverting the progress of the proceedings to achieve an outside benefit. In 1936, no authority allowed disregarding votes in such a situation, but Congress created that authority two years later with cases like *Waco* in mind. We therefore hold that a court may designate a creditor's vote in these circumstances.

We also find that, just as the law supports the bankruptcy court's legal conclusion, so the evidence supports its relevant factual findings. DISH's motive — the most controversial finding — is evinced by DISH's own admissions in court, by its position as a competitor to DBSD,[12] by its willingness to overpay for the claims

---

[12] Courts have been especially wary of the good faith of parties who purchase claims against their competitors. *See In re MacLeod*, 63 B.R. at 655; *see also In re Figter*, 118 F.3d at 640 (finding no bad faith

it bought,[13] by its attempt to propose its own plan, and especially by its internal communications, which, although addressing the Second Lien Debt rather than the First Lien Debt at issue here, nevertheless showed a desire to "to obtain a blocking position" and "control the bankruptcy process for this potentially strategic asset."

The Loan Syndications and Trading Association (LSTA), as *amicus curiae*, argues that courts should encourage acquisitions and other strategic transactions because such transactions can benefit all parties in bankruptcy. We agree. But our holding does not "shut[] the door to strategic transactions," as the LSTA suggests. Rather, it simply limits the methods by which parties may pursue them. DISH had every right to propose for consideration whatever strategic transaction it wanted — a right it took advantage of here — and DISH still retained this right even after it purchased its claims. All that the bankruptcy court stopped DISH from doing here was using the votes it had bought to secure an advantage in pursuing that strategic transaction.

DISH argues that, if we uphold the decision below, "future creditors looking for potential strategic transactions with chapter 11 debtors will be deterred from exploring such deals for fear of forfeiting their rights as creditors." But our ruling today should deter only attempts to "*obtain* a blocking position" and thereby "control the bankruptcy process for [a] potentially strategic asset" (as DISH's own internal documents stated). We leave for another day the situation in which a *preexisting* creditor votes with strategic intentions. We emphasize, moreover, that our opinion imposes no categorical prohibition on purchasing claims with acquisitive or other strategic intentions. On other facts, such purchases may be appropriate. Whether a vote has been properly designated is a fact-intensive question that must be based on the totality of the circumstances, according considerable deference to the expertise of bankruptcy judges. Having reviewed the careful and fact-specific decision of the bankruptcy court here, we find no error in its decision to designate DISH's vote as not having been cast in good faith.

NOTE ON THE IMPACT OF CLAIMS TRADING ON CHAPTER 11 CASES

The impact of claims trading on the Chapter 11 process has been much debated. As Professor Levitin explains, "The changes wrought by claims trading have placed tremendous pressure on the bankruptcy reorganization structure set forth

---

in part because party was not competitor); *In re 255 Park Plaza Assocs.*, 100 F.3d at 1219 (same); *In re Pine Hill Collieries Co.*, 46 F. Supp. 669, 672 (E.D. Pa. 1942) (finding no bad faith even for a competitor, but only because competitor had a prior interest in the debtor).

[13] The fact that DISH bought the First Lien Debt at par is circumstantial evidence of its intent, though we do not put as much weight on the price as the bankruptcy court did. *See DBSD II*, 421 B.R. at 140. It is certainly true, as the Loan Syndications and Trading Association points out in an *amicus* brief, that purchasers may have many good business reasons for buying debt at par, especially when, as in this case, the debt is well secured and interest rates dropped between the original issuance of the debt and its purchase. Buying claims at or above par therefore could not provide the sole basis for designating a creditor's vote. Nevertheless, a willingness to pay high prices may tend to show that the purchaser is interested in more than the claim for its own sake. The weight to be given to such evidence is primarily an issue for the finder of fact, and we see no clear error in the bankruptcy court's reliance on the factor in this case.

in Chapter 11 . . . which was drafted with a relational creditor world in mind. Because of the changes that claims trading has unleashed on the bankruptcy process, it arouses passions unlike any other issue in the bankruptcy world." Adam J. Levitin, *Bankruptcy Markets: Making Sense of Claims Trading*, 4 Brook. J. Corp., Fin. & Com. L. 67, 68 (2009). As Professor Levitin, surveying the claims trading literature, explains, those who believe that claims trading has had a salutary effect on the process point out that it provides an exit strategy for creditors who want out of the bankruptcy process; it provides an entrance strategy for investors who are willing to devote their time, resources, and expertise to the reorganization process; it increases capital market liquidity and lowers the cost of credit; it streamlines the plan negotiation process by concentrating claims in the hands of fewer holders; it creates a market for control of troubled companies; and it incentivizes debtors to provide a higher and quicker return to creditors, who otherwise will flee the case by selling their claims. *Id.* at 73–74. Those who say that claims trading has had a negative impact on the process assert that it undermines the symbiotic relationship between debtors and their relationship creditors, which is the premise on which Chapter 11 is based; it facilitates greenmail and other unfair practices by creditors who will hold their votes hostage to unreasonable demands; it makes locking in a deal more difficult because the identity of creditors is continuously changing; it makes finding creditors who are willing to serve on official committees more difficult; and it encourages participation by creditors who value short-term returns over the long-term viability of the debtor. *Id.* at 75. Professor Levitin concludes, however, that the debate over claims trading "operates on a limited evidentiary base," and that attempts to regulate the claims trading market should be narrowly targeted.

§ 9.10 CRAMDOWN: TREATMENT OF DISSENTING CLASSES OF CLAIMS AND INTERESTS

[A] Introduction

Up to this point we have been concerned with the standards to be applied in confirming reorganization plans that have been accepted by all impaired classes of claims and interests. Although we have seen the protection the Code offers dissenting minorities — i.e., the assurance that they will receive under the plan no less than what they would receive on liquidation (*see* § 9.08[B], above, and Code § 1129(a)(7) — we have not yet considered what happens when a class fails to accept by the required majorities. In light of the requirement of § 1129(a)(8) that in order for a plan to be confirmed it must be accepted by each class that it impairs, one might reasonably conclude that debtors (or other plan proponents) who are unable to propound a winning plan must either propose or yield to a more acceptable plan or call it quits and liquidate.

This is not necessarily so. A plan may be confirmed by the court, notwithstanding the failure of one or more classes to accept it, *if* the requirements of Code § 1129(b) are met.

[B]   Treatment of Dissenting Classes of Secured Claims

[1]   Deferred Cash Payments — Rewriting the Loan; Code § 1129(b)(2)(A)(i)

PROBLEM 9.7

The Amphydynamics manufacturing plant is located in an area of the city that has been particularly hard-hit by a real estate recession. The plant is subject to a mortgage held by BigBank to secure a prepetition loan it made to Amphydynamics. Amphydynamics owes BigBank $10,000,000, and the plant is believed to be worth approximately $8,000,000. You know that Code § 506(a) divides the claim of an undersecured creditor such as BigBank into two claims: (1) a secured claim of $8,000,000, and (2) an unsecured claim of $2,000,000. You also know that even if under the terms of the loan and mortgage documents this is a nonrecourse claim, Code § 1111(b) gives BigBank a deficiency claim whether the bank bargained for recourse or not. Suppose that the plan organizes claims and interests in several classes, two of which are relevant for purposes of this problem. The plan provides that BigBank's secured claim of $8,000,000 will be placed in Class I, by itself, and that BigBank's unsecured claim of $2,000,000 will be placed in Class II, along with $12,000,000 in other unsecured claims. The plan provides that Amphydynamics will retain the manufacturing plant subject to the bank's mortgage, and that the bank will receive, on account of its secured claim, $8,000,000 plus 5% interest in 120 monthly installments. The plan provides that unsecured creditors will receive 55% of their claims in a series of cash payments over three years.

Headley predicts that even though BigBank opposes the plan, a majority of the claims in the unsecured creditor class will vote in favor of the plan. (In other words, BigBank's unsecured claim is not large enough to swamp the class.) Headley also has reason to believe that all the other impaired classes will vote in favor of the plan, with the exception of Class I, which contains (and only contains) BigBank's secured claim. Headley wants to know whether the plan can be confirmed even if Class I rejects it. In other words, can the plan be crammed down on Class I? Read Code §§ 1129(b)(2)(A) and 1111(b).

The effect of § 1129(b)(2)(A)(i) is essentially to allow a plan proponent "unilaterally to write a new loan." King, 7 *Collier on Bankruptcy* ¶ 1129.05[2][a] (Matthew Bender 15th Ed. Revised 2000). If you work through the statute you will see why. Under this section, a secured claim can be significantly modified — for example the term of a loan can be extended and the interest rate modified — so long as four requirements are met. Specifically, the plan must provide that:

1. The claim holder will retain its lien on the collateral to the extent of the allowed amount of its secured claim;

2. The claim holder will receive a series of "deferred cash payments";

3. Those deferred cash payments total at least the "allowed amount" of the secured claim; and

4. Those deferred cash payments have a "value" of "at least the value of such holder's interest in the estate's interest in such property." In other words,

the deferred cash payments must have a present value equal to the value of the collateral, i.e., the property that secures the claim.

If the phrase "the value of such holder's interest in the estate's interest in such property" sounds familiar, it is because it echoes Code § 506(a), which contains the Code's definition of a secured claim.

Applying this statutory formula to the facts of the problem that introduces this section, we see that the Amphydynamics plan provides that:

1. BigBank will retain its lien on the manufacturing plant, but that lien will be "stripped down" to the value of the plant;

2. BigBank will receive a series of 120 monthly deferred cash payments;

3. The sum of those payments will not only total, but exceed, the allowed amount of BigBank's secured claim, which is assumed to be $8,000,000.

So far, so good. Whether interest of 5% is sufficient to give this 10-year stream of payments a present value equal to the value of the collateral is an issue that we will turn to shortly. Before we do, we first need to consider the effect that a so-called "§ 1111(b)(2) election" would have on the formula that we have just outlined. That effect is explained in the following opinion.

IN RE HALLUM
United States Bankruptcy Court, Eastern District of Tennessee
29 B.R. 343 (1983)

MEMORANDUM

RALPH H. KELLEY, BANKRUPTCY JUDGE.

The debtors, A.P. and Bettye Hallum, are in the plant-nursery business. They filed a petition in bankruptcy for reorganization under Chapter 11 of the Bankruptcy Code (11 U.S.C.).

The Farmers Home Administration filed a claim for nearly $3,000,000 as of the date the bankruptcy petition was filed. The claim was filed as secured on the basis of deeds of trust on the debtors' real property and security interests in their equipment, crops, and livestock.

The debtors filed a disclosure statement and proposed plan of reorganization. The court approved the disclosure statement. The government rejected the proposal as to the claim of the Farmers Home Administration and objected to confirmation of the plan.

The plan provides that Farmers Home Administration will be paid on its secured claim the value of the collateral in which it has a validly perfected lien, plus interest at the rate provided in the earliest promissory note. This proposal was drafted to meet the requirements for confirmation of the plan without the consent of the government. 11 U.S.C. §§ 502, 506(a), 1124(3), 1129(a)(8), & 1129(b)(2).

Appraisals accompanying the disclosure statement and proposed plan valued the government's collateral at a maximum of about $1,400,000. Thus, the government would have an allowed secured claim of about $1,400,000 to be paid according to the provision mentioned above. The remaining claim of about $1,600,000 would be an unsecured claim. It would not be paid in full since the plan provides that only unsecured claims of less than $5,000 will be paid in full.

The government, however, gave notice that it elected to have its claim treated under § 1111(b)(2). It provides that a secured creditor who elects will have its claim allowed as secured to the full extent it is allowed. In other words, the amount of the allowed claim, rather than the value of the collateral, becomes the amount of the allowed secured claim. The government would have an allowed secured claim of about $3,000,000.

The court ordered a valuation hearing to determine the value of the government's collateral. The parties relied on the appraisals mentioned above. The court ordered the parties to submit briefs on the question of whether the government is entitled to elect treatment of its claim under § 1111(b)(2).

. . . .

The only question before the court is whether the government can elect under § 1111(b)(2). If it can, the proposed plan cannot be confirmed, and there is no need for further proceedings as to it. 11 U.S.C. § 1124 & § 1129(b)(2)(A).

Section 1111(b) provides:

(1)(A) A claim secured by a lien on property of the estate shall be allowed or disallowed . . . the same as if the holder of such claim had recourse against the debtor on account of such claim, whether or not such holder has such recourse, unless —

(i) the class of which such claim is part elects, by at least two-thirds in amount and more than half in number of allowed claims of such class, application of paragraph (2) of this subsection; or

(ii) such holder does not have such recourse and such property is sold under section 363 of this title or is to be sold under the plan.

(B) A class of claims may not elect application of paragraph (2) of this subsection if —

(i) the interest on account of such claims of the holders of such claims in such property is of inconsequential value; or

(ii) the holder of a claim of such class has recourse against the debtor on account of such claim and such property is sold under section 363 of this title or is to be sold under the plan.

(2) If such an election is made, then notwithstanding section 506(a) of this title, such claim is secured to the extent that such claim is allowed.

Subparagraph (1)(B) determines who may elect to be treated as fully secured. It eliminates inconsequential allowed secured claims and claims secured by property that has been sold or will be sold under the plan of reorganization.

The value of the government's collateral is not inconsequential. The property also has not been sold and is not to be sold under the proposed plan.

The result is that there is only one question regarding the government's right to elect to be treated as fully secured. Section 1111(b) refers to election by the class of secured claims. Does this mean that a single secured creditor cannot elect?

Section 1111(b) refers to election by a class of secured claims because there may be a class of secured claims. Generally, however, each secured claim is in a class by itself.

Ordinarily each holder of an allowed claim secured by a security interest in specific property of the debtor must be placed in a separate class. There are, however, exceptions to this rule. 5 Collier on Bankruptcy ¶ 1122.03[6] (15th ed. 1982).

Several creditors with liens of the same priority in the same property can be classified together. No doubt, there are other situations in which secured claims can be classified together, but the immediate question must be whether the government's secured claim can be classified by itself or is necessarily part of some class. . . . [T]he government's secured claim appears to be unique in that it alone is secured by first priority liens on all or almost all the debtors' business property.

The court concludes that the government was entitled to elect treatment of its secured claim under § 1111(b)(2). It follows that the plan as proposed cannot be confirmed, and the court will enter an order accordingly. Debtors will be allowed thirty days within which to file a new plan or the case will stand dismissed.

NOTE: WHY ELECT CODE § 1111(B)(2) TREATMENT?

As we saw in § 9.05, above, if a creditor holding a claim that is undersecured "elects" to have its claim treated in accordance with § 1111(b)(2), it will forego its deficiency claim, but its secured claim will be measured by the amount of the debt rather than by the value of the collateral. Thus, in the *Hallum* case, instead of a $1.4 million secured claim and a $1.6 million deficiency claim, the FHA was deemed to hold a secured claim of $3,000,000 and no deficiency claim. In our problem, instead of holding an $8,000,000 secured claim and a $2,000,000 deficiency claim, BigBank would be deemed to hold a $10,000,000 secured claim and no deficiency claim.

Thus, in order for the plan to be crammed down on BigBank, the plan would have to provide for deferred cash payments totaling $10,000,000 (instead of $2,000,000) and those deferred cash payments would have to have a present value of $8,000,000 not, as you might have expected, $10,000,000. Importantly, although the effect of the § 1111(b)(2) election is to increase the amount of the allowed secured claim, and hence the amount of the deferred cash payments required, it does not increase the present value of the return to the secured creditor, which is still pegged to the value of the collateral, not the allowed amount of the secured claim. Given that the election does not require an increase in the present value of the return to a secured creditor, you may be wondering why a secured creditor would forego a deficiency claim in exchange for a larger allowed secured claim. There are several reasons.

Consider the following hypothetical. BigBank's $10,000,000 claim is secured by a mortgage on the debtor's manufacturing facility. Although the value of the facility is believed to be $8,000,000, there is good reason to believe that the recession is about to end and that the value will soon rise. Or, perhaps there is good reason to believe that the area in which the facility is located has been targeted as an urban renewal zone. Suppose that the court confirms a plan that fixes BigBank's allowed secured claim at $8,000,000, provides that it will retain its lien on the manufacturing facility, and that it will receive deferred cash payments totaling $8,000,000 plus interest. Suppose that six months after the plan is confirmed, Amphdynamics sells the facility for $11,000,000. As Code § 1141(d) provides that an order confirming a plan discharges the debtor from liability on all claims except to the extent that they are provided for in the plan, the most that BigBank can recover out of the sales proceeds is $8,000,000 (less the principal payments received pursuant to the confirmed plan). On the other hand, if BigBank elected to be treated as fully secured, it would recover up to $10,000,000 out of the sales proceeds. The principle to be gleaned from this hypothetical is this: if an undersecured creditor suspects that the collateral has been undervalued or that its value may be increasing, and that the debtor is likely to sell the property in the future, the undersecured creditor may elect to be treated as fully secured in order to share in what otherwise would be a debtor's windfall. Similarly, if the undersecured creditor believes that the debtor is likely to default on its plan obligations, it may elect to be treated as fully secured in order to maximize its recovery when foreclosure ensues. Of course, if the value of the property does not rise, there will be no extra value to be captured by the creditor in the event of a sale or foreclosure.

An undersecured creditor may also be inclined to elect to be treated as fully secured and forego its unsecured deficiency claim when unsecured creditors are getting little or nothing under the plan, and when it can block confirmation of an undesirable plan by doing so because the debtor is unable to service the higher debt that results from increasing the "allowed amount" of the secured claim. Interestingly, in recent years, especially in single asset real estate cases, undersecured creditors have been able to exert more leverage and block the confirmation of plans by *not* electing to be treated as fully secured and, by dint of their huge deficiency claims, exerting voting control over the class of unsecured claims.

Obviously a debtor or other plan proponent cannot be left endlessly in the dark about a creditor's intentions with respect to making an election. In many cases, a creditor's intentions will become clear in the course of plan negotiations. In any case, Bankruptcy Rule 3014, which governs the timing and manner of § 1111(b)(2) elections, provides that, generally, an election may be made at any time prior to the conclusion of the disclosure hearing or a later deadline set by the court.

As we saw in chapter 8, determining the allowed amount of the secured claim and whether the present value test is satisfied will require a valuation of the collateral. In the *Hallum* case, the creditor did not challenge the debtor's appraisal. In our hypothetical we assumed that the Amphydynamics manufacturing plant was worth $8,000,000. In reality, in a cramdown setting, collateral value is an issue that is likely to be litigated.

As we saw in chapter 8, in *Associates Commercial Corp. v. Rash*, the Supreme Court held that where a debtor proposes to retain collateral and use it in the operation of the business, the appropriate valuation standard is replacement value.

The second step in determining whether the present value test is met is figuring out what rate of interest to apply in calculating the present value of the deferred cash payments. A number of approaches have been suggested, and they are explored in the opinions that follow.

TILL v. SCS CREDIT CORPORATION
United States Supreme Court
541 U.S. 465 (2004)

STEVENS, J., announced the judgment of the Court and delivered an opinion, in which SOUTER, GINSBURG, AND BREYER, JJ., joined. THOMAS, J., filed an opinion concurring in the judgment. SCALIA, J., filed a dissenting opinion, in which REHNQUIST, C. J., and O'CONNOR and KENNEDY, JJ., joined.

STEVENS, JUSTICE.

To qualify for court approval under Chapter 13 of the Bankruptcy Code, an individual debtor's proposed debt adjustment plan must accommodate each allowed, secured creditor in one of three ways: (1) by obtaining the creditor's acceptance of the plan; (2) by surrendering the property securing the claim; or (3) by providing the creditor both a lien securing the claim and a promise of future property distributions (such as deferred cash payments) whose total "value, as of the effective date of the plan, . . . is not less than the allowed amount of such claim." The third alternative is commonly known as the "cram down option" because it may be enforced over a claim holder's objection.

Plans that invoke the cram down power often provide for installment payments over a period of years rather than a single payment. In such circumstances, the amount of each installment must be calibrated to ensure that, over time, the creditor receives disbursements whose total present value[4] equals or exceeds that of the allowed claim. The proceedings in this case that led to our grant of certiorari identified four different methods of determining the appropriate method with which to perform that calibration. Indeed, the Bankruptcy Judge, the District Court, the Court of Appeals majority, and the dissenting Judge each endorsed a different approach. We detail the underlying facts and describe each of those approaches before setting forth our judgment as to which approach best meets the purposes of the Bankruptcy Code.

On October 2, 1998, petitioners Lee and Amy Till, residents of Kokomo, Indiana,

---

[4] In the remainder of the opinion, we use the term "present value" to refer to the value as of the effective date of the bankruptcy plan.

purchased a used truck from Instant Auto Finance for $6,395 plus $330.75 in fees and taxes. They made a $300 down payment and financed the balance of the purchase price by entering into a retail installment contract that Instant Auto immediately assigned to respondent, SCS Credit Corporation. Petitioners' initial indebtedness amounted to $8,285.24 — the $6,425.75 balance of the truck purchase plus a finance charge of 21% per year for 136 weeks, or $1,859.49. Under the contract, petitioners agreed to make 68 biweekly payments to cover this debt; Instant Auto — and subsequently respondent — retained a purchase money security interest that gave it the right to repossess the truck if petitioners defaulted under the contract.

On October 25, 1999, petitioners, by then in default on their payments to respondent, filed a joint petition for relief under Chapter 13 of the Bankruptcy Code. At the time of the filing, respondent's outstanding claim amounted to $4,894.89, but the parties agreed that the truck securing the claim was worth only $4,000. In accordance with the Bankruptcy Code, therefore, respondent's secured claim was limited to $4,000, and the $894.89 balance was unsecured.

Petitioners' proposed debt adjustment plan called for them to submit their future earnings to the supervision and control of the Bankruptcy Court for three years, and to assign $740 of their wages to the trustee each month.

The proposed plan also provided that petitioners would pay interest on the secured portion of respondent's claim at a rate of 9.5% per year. Petitioners arrived at this "prime-plus" or "formula rate" by augmenting the national prime rate of approximately 8% (applied by banks when making low-risk loans) to account for the risk of nonpayment posed by borrowers in their financial position. Respondent objected to the proposed rate, contending that the company was "entitled to interest at the rate of 21%, which is the rate . . . it would obtain if it could foreclose on the vehicle and reinvest the proceeds in loans of equivalent duration and risk as the loan" originally made to petitioners.

At the hearing on its objection, respondent presented expert testimony establishing that it uniformly charges 21% interest on so-called "subprime" loans, or loans to borrowers with poor credit ratings, and that other lenders in the subprime market also charge that rate. Petitioners countered with the testimony of an Indiana University-Purdue University Indianapolis economics professor, who acknowledged that he had only limited familiarity with the subprime auto lending market, but described the 9.5% formula rate as "very reasonable" given that Chapter 13 plans are "supposed to be financially feasible." Moreover, the professor noted that respondent's exposure was "fairly limited because [petitioners] are under the supervision of the court." The bankruptcy trustee also filed comments supporting the formula rate as, among other things, easily ascertainable, closely tied to the "condition of the financial market," and independent of the financial circumstances of any particular lender. Accepting petitioners' evidence, the Bankruptcy Court overruled respondent's objection and confirmed the proposed plan.

The District Court reversed. It understood Seventh Circuit precedent to require that bankruptcy courts set cram down interest rates at the level the creditor could have obtained if it had foreclosed on the loan, sold the collateral, and reinvested the proceeds in loans of equivalent duration and risk. Citing respondent's unrebutted testimony about the market for subprime loans, the court concluded that 21% was the appropriate rate.

On appeal, the Seventh Circuit endorsed a slightly modified version of the District Court's "coerced" or "forced loan" approach. *In re Till*, 301 F.3d 583, 591 (2002). Specifically, the majority agreed with the District Court that, in a cram down proceeding, the inquiry should focus on the interest rate "that the creditor in question would obtain in making a new loan in the same industry to a debtor who is similarly situated, although not in bankruptcy." *Id.*, at 592. To approximate that new loan rate, the majority looked to the parties' prebankruptcy contract rate (21%). The court recognized, however, that using the contract rate would not "duplicat[e] precisely . . . the present value of the collateral to the creditor" because loans to bankrupt, court-supervised debtors "involve some risks that would not be incurred in a new loan to a debtor not in default" and also produce "some economies." To correct for these inaccuracies, the majority held that the original contract rate should "serve as a presumptive [cram down] rate," which either the creditor or the debtor could challenge with evidence that a higher or lower rate should apply. *Ibid.* Accordingly, the court remanded the case to the Bankruptcy Court to afford petitioners and respondent an opportunity to rebut the presumptive 21% rate.

Dissenting, Judge Rovner argued that the majority's presumptive contract rate approach overcompensates secured creditors because it fails to account for costs a creditor would have to incur in issuing a new loan. Rather than focusing on the market for comparable loans, Judge Rovner advocated either the Bankruptcy Court's formula approach or a "straightforward . . . cost of funds" approach.

    . . . .

II

The Bankruptcy Code provides little guidance as to which of the rates of interest advocated by the four opinions in this case — the formula rate, the coerced loan rate, the presumptive contract rate, or the cost of funds rate — Congress had in mind when it adopted the cram down provision. That provision, 11 U.S.C. § 1325(a)(5)(B), does not mention the term "discount rate" or the word "interest." Rather, it simply requires bankruptcy courts to ensure that the property to be distributed to a particular secured creditor over the life of a bankruptcy plan has a total "value, as of the effective date of the plan," that equals or exceeds the value of the creditor's allowed secured claim — in this case, $4,000. § 1325(a)(5)(B)(ii).

That command is easily satisfied when the plan provides for a lump-sum payment to the creditor. Matters are not so simple, however, when the debt is to be discharged by a series of payments over time. A debtor's promise of future payments is worth less than an immediate payment of the same total amount because the creditor cannot use the money right away, inflation may cause the value of the dollar to decline before the debtor pays, and there is always some risk of nonpayment. The challenge for bankruptcy courts reviewing such repayment schemes, therefore, is to choose an interest rate sufficient to compensate the creditor for these concerns.

Three important considerations govern that choice. First, the Bankruptcy Code includes numerous provisions that, like the cram down provision, require a court to "discount[t] . . . [a] stream of deferred payments back to the[ir] present dollar value," *Rake v. Wade*, 508 U.S. 464, 472, n. 8, 113 S. Ct. 2187, 124 L. Ed. 2d 424 (1993), to ensure that a creditor receives at least the value of its claim.[10] We think it likely that Congress intended bankruptcy judges and trustees to follow essentially the same approach when choosing an appropriate interest rate under any of these provisions. Moreover, we think Congress would favor an approach that is familiar in the financial community and that minimizes the need for expensive evidentiary proceedings.

Second, Chapter 13 expressly authorizes a bankruptcy court to modify the rights of any creditor whose claim is secured by an interest in anything other than "real property that is the debtor's principal residence. . . . On the one hand, the fact of the bankruptcy establishes that the debtor is overextended and thus poses a significant risk of default; on the other hand, the postbankruptcy obligor is no longer the individual debtor but the court-supervised estate, and the risk of default is thus somewhat reduced. [In a Chapter 11 case, the court does not exercise supervision over the post-confirmation debtor. On the other hand, in both Chapters, a court should only confirm a plan that it believes is feasible. — Eds.]

Third, from the point of view of a creditor, the cram down provision mandates an objective rather than a subjective inquiry.[13] That is, although § 1325(a)(5)(B) entitles the creditor to property whose present value objectively equals or exceeds the value of the collateral, it does not require that the terms of the cram down loan match the terms to which the debtor and creditor agreed prebankruptcy, nor does it require that the cram down terms make the creditor subjectively indifferent between present foreclosure and future payment. Indeed, the very idea of a "cram down" loan *precludes* the latter result: By definition, a creditor forced to accept such a loan would prefer instead to foreclose.[14] Thus, a court choosing a cram down interest rate need not consider the creditor's individual circumstances, such as its

---

[10] *See* 11 U.S.C. § 1129(a)(7)(A)(ii) (requiring payment of property whose "value, as of the effective date of the plan" equals or exceeds the value of the creditor's claim); §§ 1129(a)(7)(B), 1129(a)(9)(B)(i), 1129(a)(9)(C), 1129(b)(2)(A)(ii), 1129(b)(2)(B)(i), 1129(b)(2)(C)(i), 1173(a)(2), 1225(a)(4), 1225(a)(5)(B)(ii), 1228(b)(2), 1325(a)(4), 1228(b)(2) (same).

[13] We reached a similar conclusion in *Associates Commercial Corp. v. Rash*, 520 U.S. 953, 117 S. Ct. 1879, 138 L. Ed. 2d 148 (1997), when we held that a creditor's secured interest should be valued from the debtor's, rather than the creditor's, perspective. *Id.*, at 963, 138 L. Ed. 2d, 148, 117 S. Ct. 1879 ("[The debtor's] actual use, rather than a foreclosure sale that will not take place, is the proper guide . . .").

[14] This fact helps to explain why there is no readily apparent Chapter 13 "cram down market rate of interest": Because every cram down loan is imposed by a court over the objection of the secured creditor, there is no free market of willing cram down lenders. Interestingly, the same is *not* true in the Chapter 11 context, as numerous lenders advertise financing for Chapter 11 debtors in possession. *See, e.g.,* Balmoral Financial Corporation, http://www.balmoral.com/bdip.htm (all Internet materials as visited Mar. 4, 2004, and available in Clerk of Court's case file) (advertising debtor in possession lending); Debtor in Possession Financing: 1st National Assistance Finance Association DIP Division, http://www. loanmallusa.com/dip.htm (offering "to tailor a financing program . . . to your business' needs and . . . to work closely with your bankruptcy counsel"). Thus, when picking a cram down rate in a Chapter 11 case, it might make sense to ask what rate an efficient market would produce. In the Chapter 13 context, by contrast, the absence of any such market obligates courts to look to first principles and ask only what rate will fairly compensate a creditor for its exposure.

prebankruptcy dealings with the debtor or the alternative loans it could make if permitted to foreclose. Rather, the court should aim to treat similarly situated creditors similarly, and to ensure that an objective economic analysis would suggest the debtor's interest payments will adequately compensate all such creditors for the time value of their money and the risk of default.

III

These considerations lead us to reject the coerced loan, presumptive contract rate, and cost of funds approaches. Each of these approaches is complicated, imposes significant evidentiary costs, and aims to make each individual creditor whole rather than to ensure the debtor's payments have the required present value. For example, the coerced loan approach requires bankruptcy courts to consider evidence about the market for comparable loans to similar (though nonbankrupt) debtors — an inquiry far removed from such courts' usual task of evaluating debtors' financial circumstances and the feasibility of their debt adjustment plans. In addition, the approach overcompensates creditors because the market lending rate must be high enough to cover factors, like lenders' transaction costs and overall profits, that are no longer relevant in the context of court-administered and court-supervised cram down loans.

Like the coerced loan approach, the presumptive contract rate approach improperly focuses on the creditor's potential use of the proceeds of a foreclosure sale. In addition, although the approach permits a debtor to introduce some evidence about each creditor, thereby enabling the court to tailor the interest rate more closely to the creditor's financial circumstances and reducing the likelihood that the creditor will be substantially overcompensated, that right comes at a cost: The debtor must obtain information about the creditor's costs of overhead, financial circumstances, and lending practices to rebut the presumptive contract rate. Also, the approach produces absurd results, entitling "inefficient, poorly managed lenders" with lower profit margins to obtain higher cram down rates than "well managed, better capitalized lenders." 2 K. Lundin, Chapter 13 Bankruptcy § 112.1, p 112-8 (3d ed. 2000). Finally, because the approach relies heavily on a creditor's prior dealings with the debtor, similarly situated creditors may end up with vastly different cram down rates.

The cost of funds approach, too, is improperly aimed. Although it rightly disregards the now-irrelevant terms of the parties' original contract, it mistakenly focuses on the creditworthiness of the *creditor* rather than the debtor . . . a creditworthy lender with a low cost of borrowing may obtain a lower cram down rate than a financially unsound, fly-by-night lender.

IV

The formula approach has none of these defects. Taking its cue from ordinary lending practices, the approach begins by looking to the national prime rate, reported daily in the press, which reflects the financial market's estimate of the amount a commercial bank should charge a creditworthy commercial borrower to compensate for the opportunity costs of the loan, the risk of inflation, and the relatively slight risk of default.[18] Because bankrupt debtors typically pose a greater risk of nonpayment than solvent commercial borrowers, the approach then requires a bankruptcy court to adjust the prime rate accordingly. The appropriate size of that risk adjustment depends, of course, on such factors as the circumstances of the estate, the nature of the security, and the duration and feasibility of the reorganization plan. The court must therefore hold a hearing at which the debtor and any creditors may present evidence about the appropriate risk adjustment. Some of this evidence will be included in the debtor's bankruptcy filings, however, so the debtor and creditors may not incur significant additional expense. Moreover, starting from a concededly *low* estimate and adjusting *upward* places the evidentiary burden squarely on the creditors, who are likely to have readier access to any information absent from the debtor's filing (such as evidence about the "liquidity of the collateral market," *post*, at ____, 158 L. Ed. 2d at 813 (Scalia, J., dissenting)). Finally, many of the factors relevant to the adjustment fall squarely within the bankruptcy court's area of expertise.

Thus, unlike the coerced loan, presumptive contract rate, and cost of funds approaches, the formula approach entails a straightforward, familiar, and objective inquiry, and minimizes the need for potentially costly additional evidentiary proceedings. Moreover, the resulting "prime-plus" rate of interest depends only on the state of financial markets, the circumstances of the bankruptcy estate, and the characteristics of the loan, not on the creditor's circumstances or its prior interactions with the debtor. For these reasons, the prime-plus or formula rate best comports with the purposes of the Bankruptcy Code.

We do not decide the proper scale for the risk adjustment, as the issue is not before us. The Bankruptcy Court in this case approved a risk adjustment of 1.5%, and other courts have generally approved adjustments of 1% to 3%, *see In re Valenti*, 105 F.3d 55, 64 (CA2) (collecting cases), abrogated on other grounds by *Associates Commercial Corp. v. Rash*, 520 U.S. 953, 117 S. Ct. 1879, 138 L. Ed. 2d 148 (1997). Respondent's core argument is that a risk adjustment in this range is entirely inadequate to compensate a creditor for the real risk that the plan will fail. There is some dispute about the true scale of that risk — respondent claims that more than 60% of Chapter 13 plans fail, Brief for Respondent 25, but petitioners argue that the failure rate for *approved* Chapter 13 plans is much lower, Tr. of Oral Arg. 9. We need not resolve that dispute. It is sufficient for our purposes to note that, under 11 U.S.C. § 1325(a)(6) [11 USCS § 1325(a)(6)], a court may not approve a plan unless, after considering all creditors' objections and receiving the advice of the trustee, the judge is persuaded that "the debtor will be able to make all payments under the plan and to comply with the plan." *Ibid.* Together with the cram down provision, this requirement obligates the court to select a rate high enough to compensate the creditor for its risk but not so high as to doom the plan. If the court determines that the likelihood of default is so high as to necessitate an "eye-popping" interest rate, 301 F.3d at 593 (Rovner, J., dissenting), the plan probably should not be confirmed.

---

[18] We note that, if the court could somehow be certain a debtor would complete his plan, the prime rate would be adequate to compensate any secured creditors forced to accept cram down loans.

NOTES AND QUESTIONS

(1) *Why a Cap?* Why, in *Till*, did the Supreme Court limit the risk premium to a maximum of 3%? Does imposing such a limit make more sense in the case of an individual — where we may harbor some residual concerns about usury — than in the case of a business debtor? Is there, perhaps, an unspoken fear that a plan is manifestly unfeasible if the premium needs to be higher in order to compensate for the risk of default?

(2) *Double Indemnity?* At least one court has suggested that if the formula prescribed by the Supreme Court in *Associates Commercial Corp. v. Rash* (*see* § 8.04[B], *supra*) is used to determine the value of collateral for cramdown purposes and the present value discount rate includes a risk premium, the secured creditor may be overcompensated. The court explained that both the formula for valuing collateral and the formula for calculating the present value of a stream of payments "require that secured creditors be protected from the 'double risks' of non-payment arising from cramdown under a Debtor's Plan — the risks of depreciation and default. *Rash* requires that the risk premium be built into the valuation process. Dealing with risk in this way, at least in the context of valuation of commercial real estate, is simple. It imposes no additional burdens on the Court or the parties, because identification of the risk factors is already part of the valuation process." *Amresco New England II, L.P. v. Pasquale*, 227 B.R. 352 (Bankr. D. Vt. 1998).

(3) *Risk Factors.* In a recap of the "expanding list of factors" that courts have applied in calculating risk premiums, one commentator came up with the following roster: "(1) the general circumstances of the estate; (2) the nature of the security; (3) the duration and feasibility of the reorganization plan, including adequacy of capital, earning power of the reorganized debtor, general economic conditions, and management's ability and its probability of continuation; (4) the current and future state of the debtor's operations; (5) any potential depreciation or appreciation of the collateral; (6) the size of any equity cushion; (7) the loan-to-value ratio; (8) the location, age, and condition of the collateral; (9) whether the local economy supports the particular type of development; (10) cash flow; and (11) the debt service coverage ratio." Adam Strochak, *Cram Session on Cramdown Interest Rates*, Weil Bankrutcy Blog, June 22, 2011, http://business-finance-restructuring.weil.com/chapter-11-plans/a-cram-session-on-cramdown-interest-rates/#axzz2Jsztc080.

(4) *Till*, of course, involved a Chapter 13 plan. Should the same methodology be employed in a Chapter 11 case? Did Justice Stevens think it should be? On one hand, Justice Stevens, referring to other sections and chapters of the Code said, "We think it likely that Congress intended bankruptcy judges and trustees to follow essentially the same approach when choosing an appropriate interest rate under any of these provisions." On the other hand, he suggested, in footnote 14, that Chapter 13 and Chapter 11 cases may be different, because, in Chapter 13, "there is no free market of willing cram down lenders. Interestingly, the same is *not* true in the Chapter 11 context, as numerous lenders advertise financing for Chapter 11 debtors in possession." Will there always be a market for loans to debtors that are attempting to emerge from Chapter 11? In the opinion that follows, the court concluded that, in Chapter 11 cases, because there may be a relevant "market rate," courts may depart from the *Till* formula. The first step, the court holds, is to

determine whether there is an efficient market rate. If so, that is the cramdown rate that should be applied. If there is no efficient market rate, then the *Till* approach should be employed.

BANK OF MONTREAL v. OFFICIAL COMMITTEE OF UNSECURED CREDITORS (IN RE AMERICAN HOMEPATIENT, INC.)
United States Court of Appeals for the Sixth Circuit
420 F.3d 559 (2005)

JUDGES: Before: CLAY, GILMAN, and COOK, CIRCUIT JUDGES.

OPINION BY: RONALD LEE GILMAN

In July of 2002, American HomePatient, Inc. (American) filed for relief under Chapter 11 of the Bankruptcy Code. Despite objections by a group of secured lenders to American's proposed plan of reorganization, the bankruptcy court imposed the plan on the lenders pursuant to the Bankruptcy Code's so-called "cramdown" provisions set forth in 11 U.S.C. § 1129(b). The bankruptcy court further concluded that the appropriate cramdown interest rate for the lenders was 6.785%, and it fixed their collateral value at $250 million.

. . . .

Background

American is a publicly-held company based in Brentwood, Tennessee. It specializes in providing home healthcare services and products and has more than 280 affiliates and subsidiaries in 35 states. Over the course of its operations, American borrowed a significant amount of money. Most of this debt was incurred between 1994 and 1998, when American invested in dozens of new branch offices. The lenders in this case are 24 entities that loaned money to American during this time frame. Although the parties disagree as to the exact total owed to the lenders, both sides acknowledge that the principal balance is in the range of $ 278 to $290 million.

. . . .

The bankruptcy court held a five-day hearing on the lenders' claims. During this hearing, the court heard from various witnesses who testified as to the appropriate cramdown interest rate to be applied to the lenders' allowed secured claim. The bankruptcy court was ultimately persuaded by the testimony of American's expert witness David Rosen, who opined that the appropriate cramdown interest rate was 6.785%, which was equal to the interest rate on a six-year Treasury note plus 3.5%. It determined that the lenders' proposed interest rate of 12.16% was inappropriate because it would result in a windfall to the lenders.

. . . .

On May 14, 2003, the bankruptcy court overruled the lenders' objections and directed American to submit a proposed order confirming the amended reorganization plan. This confirmation order was entered by the bankruptcy court on May 27, 2003. The lenders subsequently appealed to the district court and petitioned first the bankruptcy court and then the district court for a stay of the confirmation order. This request was denied by both courts, and the lenders did not seek a stay from this court. As a result, the amended reorganization plan became effective on July 1, 2003.

On August 15, 2003, American filed a motion to dismiss the lenders' appeal before the district court on the basis of equitable mootness. The district court denied the motion, but affirmed the bankruptcy court's decision to confirm the plan on the merits. This appeal by the lenders and cross-appeal by American followed.

II. ANALYSIS

[The portion of the opinion in which the court held that the appeal was not rendered equitably moot by the confirmation and substantial consummation of the reorganization plan is not reproduced here. En route to that holding, the court did find that the lenders had presented a plausible argument that American might be able to pay $290,000,000 at a 12.16% interest rate without affecting the success of the confirmed plan. The court then proceeded to the merits of the lenders' appeal.]

C. The cramdown interest rate

The lenders' first substantive argument is that the district court erred in applying the "coerced loan theory" to determine the appropriate cramdown interest rate. They further contend that the cramdown interest rate of 6.785% is too low. Instead, they submit that the bankruptcy court should have applied a blended interest rate of 12.16%. This complex issue is further complicated by the recent Supreme Court case of *Till v. SCS Credit Corp.*, 541 U.S. 465, 124 S. Ct. 1951, 158 L. Ed. 2d 787 (2004) (plurality opinion).

. . . .

In its pre-*Till* assessment, the bankruptcy court relied on several Sixth Circuit cases calling for the application of the coerced loan theory in determining cramdown interest rates. . . . Under the coerced loan theory, courts "treat any deferred payment of an obligation under a plan as a coerced loan and the rate of return with respect to such loan must correspond to the rate that would be charged or obtained by the creditor making a loan to a third party with similar terms, duration, collateral and risk." 7 Collier on Bankruptcy P 1129.06[1][c][ii][B]. Courts must therefore "use the current market rate of interest used for similar loans in the region." This court has concluded that "bankruptcy courts are generally familiar with the current conventional rates on various types of consumer loans. And where parties dispute the question, proof can easily be adduced." *Id.*

The bankruptcy court therefore proceeded to determine, "based on its assessment of the credibility and reliability of the expert witnesses, what best accomplishes the market rate under the . . . coerced loan theory." In this analysis, it was most persuaded by David Rosen, one of American's expert witnesses. Rosen testified that, "under the 'coerced loan' theory, the appropriate level of interest to provide the Lenders with the present value of their claim is the six-year Treasury Bill [interest rate] plus 350 basis points." This resulted in the appropriate interest rate under the coerced loan theory being fixed by the bankruptcy court at 6.785% per annum.

The lenders, however, contend that application of the coerced loan theory was improper in light of *Till*, 541 U.S. 465, 124 S. Ct. 1951, 158 L. Ed. 2d 787. In that Chapter 13 case, the Supreme Court evaluated the four widely used methods of calculating the cramdown interest rate (the coerced loan, presumptive contract rate, formula rate, and cost of funds approaches) and found that all but the formula rate suffered from serious flaws . . . .

Instead, the Court endorsed the use of the formula approach. Under this approach, the bankruptcy court

> begins by looking to the national prime rate, reported daily in the press, which reflects the financial market's estimate of the amount a commercial bank should charge a creditworthy commercial borrower to compensate for the opportunity costs of the loan, the risk of inflation, and the relatively slight risk of default. Because bankrupt debtors typically pose a greater risk of nonpayment than solvent commercial borrowers, the approach then requires a bankruptcy court to adjust the prime rate accordingly.

Id. at 478–79. The Court further observed that adopting "the formula approach entails a straightforward, familiar, and objective inquiry, and minimizes the need for potentially costly additional evidentiary proceedings." *Id.* at 479.

Till, however, was a Chapter 13 bankruptcy case. So even though the plurality is clear that the formula approach is the preferable method for Chapter 13 cases, the opinion is less clear about cases in the Chapter 11 context. On the one hand, the plurality noted that "the Bankruptcy Code includes numerous provisions that, like the [Chapter 13] cram down provision, require a court to 'discount . . . [a] stream of deferred payments back to their present dollar value' to ensure that a creditor receives at least the value of its claim." It further commented that "we think it likely that Congress intended bankruptcy judges and trustees to follow essentially the same approach when choosing an appropriate interest rate under any of these provisions." *Id.* Some commentators have taken this to mean that *Till*'s analysis of Chapter 13 cramdown interest rates might be applicable to Chapter 11 cramdowns as well. *See* 7 Collier on Bankruptcy P 1129.06[1][c][i].

In a footnote, however, the plurality noted that "there is no readily apparent Chapter 13 'cram down market rate of interest.'" *Id.* at 476 n.14. This follows from the fact that "because every cram down loan is imposed by a court over the objection of the secured creditor, there is no free market of willing cram down lenders." *Id.* But

> interestingly, the same is not true in the Chapter 11 context, as numerous lenders advertise financing for Chapter 11 debtors in possession. *Thus, when picking a cramdown rate in a Chapter 11 case, it might make sense to ask what rate an efficient market would produce.* In the Chapter 13

> context, by contrast, the absence of any such market obligates courts to look to first principles and ask only what rate will fairly compensate a creditor for its exposure.

Id. (emphasis added). This footnote suggests that a formula approach like the one adopted by the plurality is not required in the Chapter 11 context.

At least one court that has examined cramdown interest rates post-*Till* has concluded that *Till* does not apply in a Chapter 11 context. *See In re Prussia Assocs.*, 322 B.R. 572, 585, 589 (Bankr. E.D. Pa. 2005) (holding that "*Till* is instructive, but it is not controlling, insofar as mandating the use of the 'formula' approach described in *Till* in every Chapter 11 case," and noting that "[*Till's*] dicta implies that the Bankruptcy Court in such circumstances (i.e., efficient markets) should exercise discretion in evaluating an appropriate cramdown interest rate by considering the availability of market financing").

Several outside commentators, however, have argued that *Till's* formula approach should apply to Chapter 11 cases as well as to Chapter 13 cases, noting that the two are not all that dissimilar. . . . And at least one court has concluded that *Till* does apply in a Chapter 11 context. *See Official Unsecured Creditor's Comm. of LWD, Inc. v. K&B Capital, LLC (In re LWD, Inc.)*, 332 B.R. 543, 2005 Bankr. LEXIS 384, 2005; WL 567460 (Bankr. W.D. Ky. Feb. 10, 2005).

Taking all of this into account, we decline to blindly adopt *Till's* endorsement of the formula approach for Chapter 13 cases in the Chapter 11 context. Rather, we opt to take our cue from Footnote 14 of the opinion, which offered the guiding principle that "when picking a cram down rate in a Chapter 11 case, it might make sense to ask what rate an efficient market would produce." *Till*, 541 U.S. at 476 n.14. This means that the market rate should be applied in Chapter 11 cases where there exists an efficient market. But where no efficient market exists for a Chapter 11 debtor, then the bankruptcy court should employ the formula approach endorsed by the *Till* plurality. This nuanced approach should obviate the concern of commentators who argue that, even in the Chapter 11 context, there are instances where no efficient market exists.

While we accept Footnote 14's recommendation that the appropriate rate here is the one that "an efficient market would produce," we must still reconcile this principle with the coerced loan theory employed by the bankruptcy court. Indeed, the lenders make two related arguments against the bankruptcy court's determination of the appropriate interest rate, which they contend demonstrate that the court did not apply the rate that an efficient market would produce. They first claim that the 6.785% rate fixed by the bankruptcy court is not a realistic measure of what an efficient market would provide. According to the lenders' experts, an efficient market would have produced a rate of approximately 12%. One of their experts opined that this is because

> it is not feasible, using conventional funding sources, to provide the $309 million in financing needed by the Company with 100% debt. There is, however, an established market that can provide financing of $309 million to the Company. This market would provide a combination of senior debt,

mezzanine debt, and equity, with resulting yields priced in response to the inherent risks assumed by the holders of such instruments.

This dovetails with the lenders' second point of contention, which is that the bankruptcy court should have taken "loan-specific" criteria into account when adjusting the appropriate cramdown rate. In support of this argument, they cite to language in *Till* suggesting that the Supreme Court would look favorably on an analysis incorporating debtor-specific risks.

Our understanding of the bankruptcy court's methodology, however, is that it in fact sought to determine what an efficient market would have produced for the loan that the lenders provided, albeit under the rubric of the coerced loan theory. In its assessment of the coerced loan theory, the bankruptcy court accepted Rosen's testimony to the effect that the loan in question was "senior debt loan in the health care field . . . under a normalized capital structure." Rosen then proceeded to analyze the standard market rate for such a loan. The lenders' argument, on the other hand, is centered on the composite interest rate that a new loan (including "mezzanine" debt and equity) would command in the market, not what their loan to American (which was all senior debt) would require. But as the bankruptcy court properly noted:

> The Lenders' argument that the debtor could not obtain a "new loan" in the market place so highly leveraged might be so, but in actuality no new loan is being made here at all. Instead, the court is sanctioning the workout between the debtor and the Lenders. New funds are not being advanced without the consent of the claimants.

Indeed, the only type of debt contemplated by American's reorganization plan was senior secured debt. The inclusion of other types of financing — mezzanine debt and equity — is a pure hypothetical suggested by the lenders.

In addition, the bankruptcy court commented that, in its opinion, the 12.16% interest rate called for by the lenders would result in a "windfall." The court observed that

> the lenders are not entitled to a premium on their return because the debtor filed for bankruptcy. The blended rate suggested by the Lenders goes beyond protecting the value of its claim from dilution caused by the delay in payment. . . . Any windfall because of bankruptcy is neither contemplated nor required under the Code. The court's role is not to reward the creditor for the "new loan" to a bankrupt debtor, but instead only to provide the creditor with the present value of its claim.

This observation, that the lenders' request would result in a windfall, is further highlighted by *Till*. In *Till*, the plurality acknowledged that lenders ought to be compensated for their risk. The opinion, however, cited with approval the fact that other courts starting from the prime rate "have generally approved adjustments of 1% to 3%." *Till*, 541 U.S. at 480. It also commented that if a bankruptcy court "determines that the likelihood of default is so high as to necessitate an 'eye-popping' interest rate, the plan probably should not be confirmed." *Id.* at 480–81. The interest rate demanded by the lenders here — 12.16% — is nearly eight percentage points higher than the 4.25% prime rate in effect on May 27, 2003, the date that the confirmation order was entered by the district court. As such, the 12.16% rate appears to fall under the "eye-popping" category described unfavorably by *Till*.

In sum, *Till* provides the lower courts with the guiding principle that "when picking a cram down rate in a Chapter 11 case, it might make sense to ask what rate an efficient market would produce." *Till*, 541 U.S. at 476 n.14. Although the lenders argue that the rate chosen by the bankruptcy court was not the rate produced by an efficient market, this is a question that was fully considered by that court. Its conclusion that the appropriate market rate would be 6.785% was reached only after carefully evaluating the testimony of various expert witnesses. The fact that the bankruptcy court utilized the rubric of the "coerced loan theory" that was criticized in *Till* provides no basis to reverse the bankruptcy court's decision because *Till* pointed out that, if anything, the coerced loan theory "*overcompensates* creditors. . . . " *Till*, 542 U.S. at 477 (emphasis added). We therefore concur in the result reached by both the bankruptcy court and the district court on this issue.

NOTE ON *IN RE MACE*

As discussed earlier, Justice Stevens, writing for the plurality in *Till*, found evidence that there might be a free market of willing cram down lenders in the fact that "numerous lenders advertise financing for Chapter 11 debtors in possession." Would the existence of a market for Chapter 11 *exit financing* be even more relevant and compelling? In *In re Mace*, 2011 Bankr. LEXIS 280 (Bankr. M.D. Tenn. Jan. 25, 2011), the debtor was a residential homebuilder. The trustee's plan proposed that Regions Bank would retain its mortgage on certain properties, that its three secured claims would accrue interest at an annual rate of 6% for five years, and after that it would adjust to prime plus 2%, floating monthly with a floor of 6% and a ceiling of 11%. The claims would be amortized over 20 years. Regions Bank argued that an efficient market existed for the same type of loans, and in that efficient market, a normal repayment term (the market rate) would be five years with a twenty year or less amortization, not the twenty year repayment term proposed in the trustee's plan. The Bank also argued that even if the court found that no efficient market existed, the proposed interest rate was insufficient to compensate Regions for the riskier, longer repayment term. The court agreed that an efficient market existed for this type of loan, but disagreed that a twenty year amortization was not consistent with what the local market would bear. The court pointed out that the trustee had obtained exactly the same terms from four other similarly situated creditors who had accepted the plan. The court added that even if it was mistaken in its finding that an efficient market existed, Regions was being treated fairly and equitably under the *Till* formula approach and that a higher risk premium was not required. The court noted that the debtor had never "missed, or even been late on a single payment to Regions. Furthermore, there has been no challenge to the feasibility of the Trustee's plan. Regions' risk of spreading payments over the twenty years rather than five years is fairly compensated by the Trustee's proposed plan." *Id.* at *9–10.

[2]   Sale of Collateral with Liens Attaching to the Proceeds; Providing the Indubitable Equivalent; Code §§ 1129(b)(2)(A)(ii) and (iii)

There are two other ways to cram a plan down on a secured creditor.

Code § 1129(b)(2)(A)(ii) provides that a plan can be confirmed even over the objection of a secured creditor if the plan provides for the sale of the collateral free and clear of the secured creditor's lien with the lien attaching to the proceeds of sale. Such sales are expressly subject to Code § 363(k), which provides that "unless the court for cause orders otherwise, the holder of such claim may bid at such sale, and, if the holder of such claim purchases such property, such holder may offset such claim against the purchase price of such property." In other words, the secured creditor may "credit bid." If, for example, the collateral is a hotel valued at $1,000,000 that secures a $1,500,000 claim, the bank that holds the mortgage may purchase the hotel later at auction for, say, $1,100,000 without going out-of-pocket. This means that secured creditors can usually outbid cash bidders, and, in single asset real estate cases, scuttle a debtor's plan.

If the property is sold to a third party, then the secured creditor's lien attaches to the proceeds of sale and its claim must be dealt with in one of the other two ways described in § 1129(b)(2)(A). In other words, the debtor may retain the sales proceeds, subject to the secured creditor's lien, while making deferred cash payments that satisfy the allowed amount and present value tests. § 1129(b)(2)(A)(i). Alternatively, the debtor might choose to exercise the third "fair and equitable" treatment option set forth in § 1129(b)(2)(A)(iii), which says that a plan can be crammed down on dissenting holders of secured claims, if the plan provides "for the realization by such holders of the indubitable equivalent" of their claims. The Code does not define the term "indubitable equivalent," used in § 1129(b)(2)(A)(iii), but the Code's legislative history does state that "abandonment of the collateral to the creditor would clearly satisfy indubitable equivalence, as would a [replacement] lien on similar collateral." *See* 124 Cong. Rec. H 11104 (daily ed. Sept. 28, 1978). Presumably, so would an abandonment to the creditor of the proceeds of the § 1129(b)(2)(A)(ii) sale.

The term "indubitable equivalent" is derived from an old Second Circuit opinion written by Judge Learned Hand, *In re Murel Holding Corp.*, 75 F.2d 941 (2d Cir. 1935). In *Murel*, a mortgagee rejected the debtor's plan, which provided for a ten-year moratorium on amortization payments on a mortgage which already was in default. During the moratorium, interest was to be paid at the contract rate. The applicable statute, one of the predecessors of today's cramdown provisions, stated that a plan could be confirmed despite a dissenting class, if the plan treated the dissenting class members in one of several ways:

First, the liens might be kept in status quo. (Does this have a familiar ring? Would the lienholders be impaired if they were so treated? *See* Code §§ 1124 and 1129(b)(2)(A)(i).)

Second, the collateral could be sold with the lien attaching to the proceeds. (This should also sound familiar. *See* Code § 1129(b)(2)(A)(ii).)

Third, the value of the liens could be appraised and paid in full. (This concept too survived. *See* § 1129(b)(2)(A)(i)(II).)

Finally, the old law included a "catch-all" cramdown provision that stated that a plan could be confirmed, notwithstanding the dissent of an entire class, if the plan provided members of the dissenting class "adequate protection for the realization by them of the full value of their claims, or liens . . . by such method as will . . . equitably and fairly provide such protection."

The debtor maintained that its plan conformed to the last standard. Judge Hand disagreed:

> In construing so vague a grant we are to remember not only the underlying purposes of the section, but the constitutional limitations to which [they] must conform. It is plain that "adequate protection" must be completely compensatory; and that payment ten years hence is not generally the equivalent of payment now. Interest is indeed the . . . measure of the difference; but a creditor who fears the safety of his principal will [hardly] be content with that; he wishes to get his money or at least [his] property. We see no reason to suppose that the statute was intended to deprive him of that in the interest of junior holders, *unless by a substitute of the most indubitable equivalence.*

75 F.2d at 942 (emphasis added). Judge Hand found that the creditor had good reason to "fear the safety of his principal." The debtor had very little equity in the property above the amount of the debt it secured. The debtor's predicted turn-around of the enterprise was not impressively substantiated.

For decades, the conventional wisdom was that secured creditors had a nearly absolute right to credit bid if their collateral were sold pursuant to a plan. However, in *In re Philadelphia Newspapers, LLC*, 599 F.3d 298 (3d Cir. 2010), the Third Circuit held that a plan can be crammed down on a secured creditor when the creditor's collateral is sold even if the secured creditor is not given an opportunity to credit bid. The court relied on Code § 1129(b)(2)(A)(iii), which, as noted above, provides an alternative way to cram a plan down. It provides that a plan can be crammed down on holders of secured claims, if the plan "provides . . . for the realization by such holders of the indubitable equivalent of such claims." The court reasoned that a sale of collateral with the lien attaching to the proceeds — whether or not the secured creditor had the right to credit bid — provided the indubitable equivalent of the secured creditor's claim. The Fifth Circuit reached the same result in *Bank of New York Trust Co., NA v. Official Unsecured Creditors' Comm. (In re Pacific Lumber Co.)*, 584 F.3d 229 (5th Cir. 2009).

In *River Road Hotel Partners, LLC v. Amalgamated Bank (In re River Road Hotel Partners, LLC)*, 651 F.3d 642 (7th Cir. 2011), however, the Seventh Circuit held that secured creditors have an absolute right to credit bid under § 1129(b)(2)(A)(ii), and that to hold that § 1129(b)(2)(A)(iii) suggested otherwise would be to render subsection (ii) (not to mention subsection (i)) a nullity.

The Supreme Court resolved the disagreement in the opinion that follows:

RADLAX GATEWAY HOTEL, LLC v. AMALGAMATED BANK
Supreme Court of the United States
132 S. Ct. 2065, 182 L. Ed. 2d 967 (2012)

JUSTICE SCALIA delivered the opinion of the Court.

We consider whether a Chapter 11 bankruptcy plan may be confirmed over the objection of a secured creditor pursuant to 11 U.S.C. § 1129(b)(2)(A) if the plan provides for the sale of collateral free and clear of the creditor's lien, but does not permit the creditor to "credit-bid" at the sale.

I

In 2007, petitioners RadLAX Gateway Hotel, LLC, and RadLAX Gateway Deck, LLC (hereinafter debtors), purchased the Radisson Hotel at Los Angeles International Airport, together with an adjacent lot on which the debtors planned to build a parking structure. To finance the purchase, the renovation of the hotel, and construction of the parking structure, the debtors obtained a $142 million loan from Longview Ultra Construction Loan Investment Fund, for which respondent Amalgamated Bank (hereinafter creditor or Bank) serves as trustee. The lenders obtained a blanket lien on all of the debtors' assets to secure the loan.

Completing the parking structure proved more expensive than anticipated, and within two years the debtors had run out of funds and were forced to halt construction. By August 2009, they owed more than $120 million on the loan, with over $1 million in interest accruing every month and no prospect for obtaining additional funds to complete the project. Both debtors filed voluntary petitions for relief under Chapter 11 of the Bankruptcy Code.

A Chapter 11 bankruptcy is implemented according to a "plan," typically proposed by the debtor, which divides claims against the debtor into separate "classes" and specifies the treatment each class will receive. *See* 11 U.S.C. § 1123. Generally, a bankruptcy court may confirm a Chapter 11 plan only if each class of creditors affected by the plan consents. *See* § 1129(a)(8). Section 1129(b) creates an exception to that general rule, permitting confirmation of nonconsensual plans — commonly known as "cramdown" plans — if "the plan does not discriminate unfairly, and is fair and equitable, with respect to each class of claims or interests that is impaired under, and has not accepted, the plan." Section 1129(b)(2)(A), which we review in further depth below, establishes criteria for determining whether a cramdown plan is "fair and equitable" with respect to secured claims like the Bank's.

In 2010, the RadLAX debtors submitted a Chapter 11 plan to the United States Bankruptcy Court for the Northern District of Illinois. The plan proposed to dissolve the debtors and to sell substantially all of their assets pursuant to procedures set out in a contemporaneously filed "Sale and Bid Procedures Motion." Specifically, the debtors sought to auction their assets to the highest bidder, with the initial bid submitted by a "stalking horse" — a potential purchaser who was willing to make an advance bid of $47.5 million. The sale proceeds would be used to

880 THE CHAPTER 11 PLAN CH. 9

fund the plan, primarily by repaying the Bank. Of course the Bank itself might wish to obtain the property if the alternative would be receiving auction proceeds that fall short of the property's full value. Under the debtors' proposed auction procedures, however, the Bank would not be permitted to bid for the property using the debt it is owed to offset the purchase price, a practice known as "credit-bidding." Instead, the Bank would be forced to bid cash. Correctly anticipating that the Bank would object to this arrangement, the debtors sought to confirm their plan under the cramdown provisions of § 1129(b)(2)(A).

The Bankruptcy Court denied the debtors' Sale and Bid Procedures Motion, concluding that the proposed auction procedures did not comply with § 1129(b)(2)(A)'s requirements for cramdown plans. The Bankruptcy Court certified an appeal directly to the United States Court of Appeals for the Seventh Circuit. That court accepted the certification and affirmed, holding that § 1129(b)(2)(A) does not permit debtors to sell an encumbered asset free and clear of a lien without permitting the lienholder to credit-bid. . . .

II

A

A Chapter 11 plan confirmed over the objection of a "class of secured claims" must meet one of three requirements in order to be deemed "fair and equitable" with respect to the nonconsenting creditor's claim. The plan must provide:

> "(i)(I) that the holders of such claims retain the liens securing such claims, whether the property subject to such liens is retained by the debtor or transferred to another entity, to the extent of the allowed amount of such claims; and (II) that each holder of a claim of such class receive on account of such claim deferred cash payments totaling at least the allowed amount of such claim, of a value, as of the effective date of the plan, of at least the value of such holder's interest in the estate's interest in such property;

> "(ii) for the sale, subject to section 363(k) of this title, of any property that is subject to the liens securing such claims, free and clear of such liens, with such liens to attach to the proceeds of such sale, and the treatment of such liens on proceeds under clause (i) or (iii) of this subparagraph; or

> "(iii) for the realization by such holders of the indubitable equivalent of such claims." 11 U.S.C. § 1129 (b)(2)(A).

Under clause (i), the secured creditor retains its lien on the property and receives deferred cash payments. Under clause (ii), the property is sold free and clear of the lien, "subject to section 363(k)," and the creditor receives a lien on the proceeds of the sale. Section 363(k), in turn, provides that "unless the court for cause orders otherwise the holder of such claim may bid at such sale, and, if the holder of such claim purchases such property, such holder may offset such claim against the purchase price of such property" — i.e., the creditor may credit-bid at the sale, up to the amount of its claim.[2] Finally, under clause (iii), the plan provides the secured creditor with the "indubitable equivalent" of its claim.

The debtors in this case have proposed to sell their property free and clear of the Bank's liens, and to repay the Bank using the sale proceeds — precisely, it would seem, the disposition contemplated by clause (ii). Yet since the debtors' proposed auction procedures do not permit the Bank to credit-bid, the proposed sale cannot satisfy the requirements of clause (ii).[3] Recognizing this problem, the debtors instead seek plan confirmation pursuant to clause (iii), which — unlike clause (ii) — does not expressly foreclose the possibility of a sale without credit-bidding. According to the debtors, their plan can satisfy clause (iii) by ultimately providing the Bank with the "indubitable equivalent" of its secured claim, in the form of cash generated by the auction.

We find the debtors' reading of § 1129(b)(2)(A) — under which clause (iii) permits precisely what clause (ii) proscribes — to be hyperliteral and contrary to common sense. A well established canon of statutory interpretation succinctly captures the problem: "[I]t is a commonplace of statutory construction that the specific governs the general." *Morales v. Trans World Airlines, Inc.*, 504 U.S. 374, 384, 112 S. Ct. 2031, 119 L. Ed. 2d 157 (1992). That is particularly true where, as in § 1129(b)(2)(A), "Congress has enacted a comprehensive scheme and has deliberately targeted specific problems with specific solutions." *Varity Corp. v. Howe*, 516 U.S. 489, 519, 116 S. Ct. 1065, 134 L. Ed. 2d 130 (1996) (Thomas, J., dissenting); *see also HCSC-Laundry v. United States*, 450 U.S. 1, 6, 101 S. Ct. 836, 67 L. Ed. 2d 1 (1981) *(per curiam)* (the specific governs the general "particularly when the two are interrelated and closely positioned, both in fact being parts of [the same statutory scheme]").

The general/specific canon is perhaps most frequently applied to statutes in which a general permission or prohibition is contradicted by a specific prohibition or permission. To eliminate the contradiction, the specific provision is construed as an exception to the general one. *See, e.g., Morton v. Mancari*, 417 U.S. 535, 550–551, 94 S. Ct. 2474, 41 L. Ed. 2d 290 (1974). But the canon has full application as well to statutes such as the one here, in which a general authorization and a more limited, specific authorization exist side-by-side. There the canon avoids not contradiction but the superfluity of a specific provision that is swallowed by the general one, "violat[ing] the cardinal rule that, if possible, effect shall be given to every clause and part of a statute." *D. Ginsberg & Sons, Inc. v. Popkin*, 285 U.S. 204, 208, 52 S. Ct. 322, 76 L. Ed. 704 (1932). The terms of the specific authorization must be complied with. For example, in the last cited case a provision of the Bankruptcy Act prescribed in great detail the procedures governing the arrest and detention of

---

[2] The ability to credit-bid helps to protect a creditor against the risk that its collateral will be sold at a depressed price. It enables the creditor to purchase the collateral for what it considers the fair market price (up to the amount of its security interest) without committing additional cash to protect the loan. That right is particularly important for the Federal Government, which is frequently a secured creditor in bankruptcy and which often lacks appropriations authority to throw good money after bad in a cash-only bankruptcy auction.

[3] Title 11 U.S.C. § 363(k) — and by extension clause (ii) — provides an exception to the credit-bidding requirement if "the court for cause orders otherwise." The Bankruptcy Court found that there was no "cause" to deny credit-bidding in this case, and the debtors have not appealed that disposition.

bankrupts about to leave the district in order to avoid examination. The Court held that those prescriptions could not be avoided by relying upon a general provision of the Act authorizing bankruptcy courts to " 'make such orders, issue such process, and enter such judgments in addition to those specifically provided for as may be necessary for the enforcement of the provisions of [the] Act.'"*Id.*, at 206, 52 S. Ct. 322, 76 L. Ed. 704 (quoting Bankruptcy Act of 1898, § 2(15), 30 Stat. 546). The Court said that "[g]eneral language of a statutory provision, although broad enough to include it, will not be held to apply to a matter specifically dealt with in another part of the same enactment." 285 U.S., at 208, 52 S. Ct. 322, 76 L. Ed. 704. We recently quoted that language approvingly in *Bloate v. United States*, 559 U.S. ___, ___, 130 S. Ct. 1345, 1354, 176 L. Ed. 2d 54, 65 (2010). Or as we said in a much earlier case:

> "It is an old and familiar rule that, where there is, in the same statute, a particular enactment, and also a general one, which, in its most comprehensive sense, would include what is embraced in the former, the particular enactment must be operative, and the general enactment must be taken to affect only such cases within its general language as are not within the provisions of the particular enactment. This rule applies wherever an act contains general provisions and also special ones upon a subject, which, standing alone, the general provisions would include." *United States v. Chase*, 135 U.S. 255, 260, 10 S. Ct. 756, 34 L. Ed. 117 (1890) (citations and internal quotation marks omitted).

Here, clause (ii) is a detailed provision that spells out the requirements for selling collateral free of liens, while clause (iii) is a broadly worded provision that says nothing about such a sale. The general/specific canon explains that the "general language" of clause (iii), "although broad enough to include it, will not be held to apply to a matter specifically dealt with" in clause (ii). *D. Ginsberg & Sons, Inc., supra*, at 208, 52 S. Ct. 322, 76 L. Ed. 704.

Of course the general/specific canon is not an absolute rule, but is merely a strong indication of statutory meaning that can be overcome by textual indications that point in the other direction. The debtors point to no such indication here. One can conceive of a statutory scheme in which the specific provision embraced within a general one is not superfluous, because it creates a so-called safe harbor. The debtors effectively contend that that is the case here — clause (iii) ("indubitable equivalent") being the general rule, and clauses (i) and (ii) setting forth procedures that will always, *ipso facto*, establish an "indubitable equivalent," with no need for judicial evaluation. But the structure here would be a surpassingly strange manner of accomplishing that result — which would normally be achieved by setting forth the "indubitable equivalent" rule first (rather than last), and establishing the two safe harbors as provisos to that rule. The structure here suggests, to the contrary, that (i) is the rule for plans under which the creditor's lien remains on the property, (ii) is the rule for plans under which the property is sold free and clear of the creditor's lien, and (iii) is a residual provision covering dispositions under all other plans — for example, one under which the creditor receives the property itself, the "indubitable equivalent" of its secured claim. Thus, debtors may not sell their property free of liens under § 1129(b)(2)(A) without allowing lienholders to credit-bid, as required by clause (ii).

B

None of the debtors' objections to this approach is valid. The debtors' principal textual argument is that § 1129(b)(2)(A) "unambiguously provides three distinct options for confirming a Chapter 11 plan over the objection of a secured creditor." Brief for Petitioners 15 (capitalization and bold typeface removed). With that much we agree; the three clauses of § 1129(b)(2)(A) are connected by the disjunctive "or." The debtors contend that our interpretation of § 1129(b)(2)(A) "transforms 'or' into 'and.'" Reply Brief for Petitioners 3. But that is not so. The question here is not whether debtors must comply with more than one clause, but rather which one of the three they must satisfy. Debtors seeking to sell their property free of liens under § 1129(b)(2)(A) must satisfy the requirements of clause (ii), not the requirements of both clauses (ii) and (iii).

The debtors make several arguments against applying the general/specific canon. They contend that clause (ii) is no more specific than clause (iii), because the former provides a procedural protection to secured creditors (credit-bidding) while the latter provides a substantive protection (indubitable equivalence). As a result, they say, clause (ii) is not "a limiting subset" of clause (iii), which (according to their view) application of the general/specific canon requires. Brief for Petitioners 30–31; Reply Brief for Petitioners 5–6. To begin with, we know of no authority for the proposition that the canon is confined to situations in which the entirety of the specific provision is a "subset" of the general one. When the conduct at issue falls within the scope of *both* provisions, the specific presumptively governs, whether or not the specific provision also applies to some conduct that falls outside the general. In any case, we think clause (ii) is entirely a subset. Clause (iii) applies to all cramdown plans, which include all of the plans within the more narrow category described in clause (ii).[4] That its requirements are "substantive" whereas clause (ii)'s are "procedural" is quite beside the point. What counts for application of the general/specific canon is not the nature of the provisions' prescriptions but their scope.

Finally, the debtors contend that the Court of Appeals conflated approval of bid procedures with plan confirmation. Brief for Petitioners 39. They claim the right to pursue their auction now, leaving it for the Bankruptcy Judge to determine, at the confirmation stage, whether the resulting plan (funded by auction proceeds) provides the Bank with the "indubitable equivalent" of its secured claim. Under our interpretation of § 1129(b)(2)(A), however, that approach is simply a nonstarter. As a matter of law, no bid procedures like the ones proposed here could satisfy the requirements of § 1129(b)(2)(A), and the distinction between approval of bid procedures and plan confirmation is therefore irrelevant.

III

The parties debate at some length the purposes of the Bankruptcy Code, pre-Code practices, and the merits of credit-bidding. To varying extents, some of

---

[4] We are speaking here about whether clause (ii) is a subset for purposes of determining whether the canon applies. As we have described earlier, *after* applying the canon — *ex post*, so to speak — it ceases to be a subset, governing a situation to which clause (iii) will no longer be deemed applicable.

those debates also occupied the attention of the Courts of Appeals that considered the question presented here. *See, e.g., In re Philadelphia Newspapers, LLC*, 599 F.3d 298, 314–317 (CA3 2010); *id.* at 331–337 (Ambro, J., dissenting). But nothing in the generalized statutory purpose of protecting secured creditors can overcome the specific manner of that protection which the text of § 1129(b)(2)(A) contains. As for pre-Code practices, they can be relevant to the interpretation of an ambiguous text, but we find no textual ambiguity here. And the pros and cons of credit-bidding are for the consideration of Congress, not the courts.

The Bankruptcy Code standardizes an expansive (and sometimes unruly) area of law, and it is our obligation to interpret the Code clearly and predictably using well established principles of statutory construction. *See United States v. Ron Pair Enterprises, Inc.*, 489 U.S. 235, 240–241, 109 S. Ct. 1026, 103 L. Ed. 2d 290 (1989). Under that approach, this is an easy case. Because the RadLAX debtors may not obtain confirmation of a Chapter 11 cramdown plan that provides for the sale of collateral free and clear of the Bank's lien, but does not permit the Bank to credit-bid at the sale, we affirm the judgment of the Court of Appeals.

It is so ordered.

Justice Kennedy took no part in the decision of this case.

NOTES AND QUESTIONS

Justice Scalia did not explore the meaning of the term "indubitable equivalent," because he found that the issue was resolved by the plain language of § 1129(b)(2)(A)(ii). Do you think that Judge Learned Hand, who coined the term in his *Murel Holding Corp.* opinion, would have been inclined to reserve the right of secured creditors to credit bid their claims?

[3] Dirt-for-Debt Plans

Transfer of the entire collateral to the secured creditor has been held to satisfy the § 1129(b)(2)(A)(iii) indubitable equivalent standard, *Sandy Ridge Dev. Corp. v. Louisiana Nat'l Bank (In re Sandy Ridge Development Corp.)*, 881 F.2d 1346 (5th Cir. 1989), but courts have been reluctant to hold that transfer of only a portion of the collateral does. In *Arnold & Baker Farms v. United States ex rel Farmers Home Admin. (In re Arnold & Baker Farms)*, 85 F.3d 1415 (9th Cir. 1996), the debtor proposed to transfer 566.5 of about 1,500 mortgaged acres of farm property to the FHA on the theory that, at current market values, it would enable the FHA to realize the indubitable equivalence of its claim. The court held that this "dirt-for-debt" arrangement did not do the trick:

> The determination of whether a partial dirt for debt distribution will provide the creditor with the indubitable equivalence of its secured claim must be made on a case-by-case basis . . . . Experience has taught us that determining the value of real property at any given time is not an exact science. Because each parcel of real property is unique, the precise value of land is difficult, if not impossible, to determine until it is actually sold. Nevertheless, bankruptcy courts have traditionally been requested, out of

necessity, to determine the value of various types of property, including real property, and yet courts have recognized the difficulty of being able to determine accurately the value of land. . . . [W]e concede to doubts about our ability to fix the "value" of the land in question. We need not make a pronouncement that no plan proposing the surrender of a portion of mortgaged land to a mortgagee in return for a compelled release of the lien on the remainder of the property will ever be confirmed. Suffice it to say, however, that no matter how hot the market for real estate may become in the future, the market for farm real estate here and now is not such which would permit us to hold that the value of the land being offered is the indubitable equivalent of [the mortgagee]'s claim. "Indubitable" means "too evident to be doubted." *Webster's Ninth New Collegiate Dictionary* (1985). We profess doubt on the facts of this case.

Id. at 1421 (quotations and citations omitted).

In *In re Investors Lending Group, LLC*, 489 B.R. 307 (Bankr. S.D. Ga. 2013), the debtor and the creditors' committee jointly filed a plan that provided that five of 12 mortgaged properties would be surrendered to the lender in full satisfaction of its claim. The remaining seven properties would be retained by the debtor to fund its future operations and payments to other creditors. The lender objected, asserting that the properties had been overvalued. The debtor and the committee responded by amending the plan to provide for the surrender of two more properties. First the court considered how the collateral should be valued, noting that Code § 506(b) provides that "Such value shall be determined in light of the purpose of the valuation and of the proposed disposition or use of such property." The court noted that in *Associates Commercial Corp. v. Rash*, the Supreme Court had concluded that when a debtor proposes to retain collateral, the proper measure is replacement value. Conversely, the bankruptcy court held, when the debtor proposes to surrender the collateral, the proper measure is liquidation value, reduced by costs that the lender would incur in marketing and selling the collateral. The court approved the partial dirt-for-debt plan, but noted that when all collateral is not being surrendered to the lender, conservatism is key:

> Precedent in "dirt for debt" cases . . . generally leads to the conclusion that if a Plan is to be confirmed which approves "dirt-for-debt" or "partial dirt for debt," the decision must be so conservatively or sparingly applied as to ensure that the lender forced over its objection to accept property in satisfaction of a claim receives the indubitable equivalent of cash. . . . *In re Bannerman Holdings, LLC*, 2010 Bankr. LEXIS 3752, 2010 WL 4260003 (Bankr. E.D.N.C. 2010) ("[V]aluation is not an exact science, and the chance for error always exists. A conservative approach should, therefore be taken in order to protect the secured creditor in this regard.").

Id. at 18.

PROBLEM 9.8

These problems are based in part on exercises appearing in the excellent article, Klee, *All You Ever Wanted to Know About Cram Down Under the New Bankruptcy Code*, 53 Am. Bankr. L.J. 133 (1979).

(1) Assume that Amphydynamics owes the bank $10,000,000 and that this obligation is secured by a mortgage on the company's assembly plant. All appraisals indicate that the plant is worth about $8,000,000. Assume that BigBank has not elected to be treated as fully secured pursuant to Code § 1111(b)(2). Thus, the amount of its allowed secured claim will be governed by § 1111(b)(1)(A). Assume further that Amphy proposes a plan that provides as follows:

Expenses of Administration. These will be paid in full, in cash, on the effective date of the plan. The Code does not require these claims to be classified under a plan of reorganization. *See* Code §§ 1123(a)(1); 1129(a)(9)(A).

Class I. Secured Creditor. BigBank will retain its lien on the assembly plant to secure its allowed secured claim of $8,000,000. The bank will be paid $8,000,000 in four installments of $2,000,000. The first installment will be paid on the effective date of the plan. The other installments will be paid on the first, second, and third anniversaries of the effective date.

Class II. Unsecured Creditors. Assume that this class consists of $25,000,000 in bank and trade claims plus BigBank's deficiency claim of $2,000,000. The plan provides that members of this class will receive 36 cents on the dollar in three equal annual installments.

Class III. Stockholders. Members of this class will retain their interest in the corporation.

A. Which classes, if any, are impaired under this plan?

B. Assume further that although the Bank votes against the plan, more than one-half in number and at least two-thirds in the amount of unsecured claims in Class II vote to accept the plan. Can this plan be confirmed even though the Bank votes to reject it? *See* Code § 1129(b)(2)(A).

(2) Assume that the bank has elected to be treated as fully secured pursuant to § 1111(b)(2), and that Amphy now proposes a plan that classifies and treats the parties as follows:

Class I. Secured Creditor. BigBank will retain its lien on the assembly plant to secure its allowed secured claim. What is the amount of its allowed secured claim? BigBank will be paid $10,000,000 in four equal installments of $2,500,000. The first installment will be paid on the first anniversary of the effective date of the plan. The remaining three installments will be paid on the second, third, and fourth anniversaries of the effective date.

Class II. Unsecured Creditors. Assume that this class consists of $3,500,000 in bank and trade claims. The plan provides that members of this class will receive 36 cents on the dollar in three equal annual installments. The class votes to accept the plan.

Class III. Stockholders. Members of this class will retain their interest in the corporation.

A. Which classes are impaired under this plan?

B. What is the amount of the Bank's allowed secured claim?

C. Can this plan be confirmed even though the Bank votes to reject it? *See* Code § 1129(b)(2)(A). Assume that the court decides that an interest rate of 10 % would give the Bank the present value of its secured claim. To assist you in answering this question, a present value chart is provided below.

D. What if the plan provides for an initial $2,500,000 payment to the Bank on the effective date of the plan, followed by three equal installments of $2,500,000. The first installment will be paid on the first anniversary of the effective date of the plan. The remaining two installments will be paid on the second and third anniversaries of the effective date. Assuming again that the court decides that an interest rate of 10 % would give the Bank the present value of its secured claim, can this plan be confirmed even though the Bank votes to reject it?

Present Value of $1: What a Dollar at End of Specified Future Year is Worth Today

Year	3%	4%	5%	6%	7%	8%	10%	12%	15%	20%
1	0.971	0.962	0.952	0.943	0.935	0.926	0.909	0.893	0.870	0.833
2	0.943	0.925	0.907	0.890	0.873	0.857	0.826	0.797	0.756	0.694
3	0.915	0.889	0.864	0.840	0.816	0.794	0.751	0.712	0.658	0.579
4	0.888	0.855	0.823	0.792	0.763	0.735	0.683	0.636	0.572	0.482
5	0.863	0.822	0.784	0.747	0.713	0.681	0.621	0.567	0.497	0.402
6	0.837	0.790	0.746	0.705	0.666	0.630	0.564	0.507	0.432	0.335
7	0.813	0.760	0.711	0.665	0.623	0.583	0.513	0.452	0.376	0.279
8	0.789	0.731	0.677	0.627	0.582	0.540	0.467	0.404	0.327	0.233
9	0.766	0.703	0.645	0.592	0.544	0.500	0.424	0.361	0.284	0.194
10	0.744	0.676	0.614	0.558	0.508	0.463	0.386	0.322	0.247	0.162
11	0.722	0.650	0.585	0.527	0.475	0.429	0.350	0.287	0.215	0.135
12	0.701	0.625	0.557	0.497	0.444	0.397	0.319	0.257	0.187	0.112
13	0.681	0.601	0.530	0.469	0.415	0.368	0.290	0.229	0.163	0.093
14	0.661	0.577	0.505	0.442	0.388	0.340	0.263	0.205	0.141	0.078
15	0.642	0.555	0.481	0.417	0.362	0.315	0.239	0.183	0.123	0.065
16	0.623	0.534	0.458	0.394	0.339	0.292	0.218	0.163	0.107	0.054
17	0.605	0.513	0.436	0.371	0.317	0.270	0.198	0.146	0.093	0.045
18	0.587	0.494	0.416	0.350	0.296	0.250	0.180	0.130	0.081	0.038
19	0.570	0.475	0.396	0.331	0.277	0.232	0.164	0.116	0.070	0.031
20	0.554	0.456	0.377	0.312	0.258	0.215	0.149	0.104	0.061	0.026
25	0.478	0.375	0.295	0.233	0.184	0.146	0.092	0.059	0.030	0.010
30	0.412	0.308	0.231	0.174	0.131	0.099	0.057	0.033	0.015	0.004
35	0.355	0.253	0.181	0.130	0.094	0.068	0.036	0.019	0.008	0.002
40	0.307	0.208	0.142	0.097	0.067	0.046	0.022	0.011	0.004	0.001
50	0.228	0.141	0.087	0.054	0.034	0.021	0.009	0.003	0.001	0.000

(3)   Suppose that the parties agree that an interest rate of 10% is required to give a series of deferred cash payments a present value equal to the allowed amount of the Bank's secured claim. Suppose however, that the debtor's projected cash flow for the first three years following confirmation will be insufficient to enable it to make payments at that rate of interest. Accordingly, the debtor's plan provides that

for the first three years, interest will be paid at 8% and the balance of the interest will be deferred and added to the principal to be paid later, when the debtor's income will be higher. Is such treatment fair and equitable to the secured creditor? These sorts of so-called "negative amortization plans" have been viewed with suspicion by the courts. The general rule with regard to them is that they will not be approved over creditor objection except in extraordinary circumstances, and a high level of creditor protection in the form of additional or appreciating collateral will be required. *See, e.g., Great Western Bank v. Sierra Woods Group*, 953 F.2d 1174 (9th Cir. 1992); *In re Apple Tree Partners*, 131 B.R. 380 (Bankr. W.D. Tenn. 1991) (providing a non-exclusive list of some of the factors that should be considered when confronted with a request to confirm a negative amortization plan: (1) Does the plan offer a market rate of interest and present value of the deferred payments; (2) Is the amount and length of the proposed deferral reasonable; (3) Is the ratio of debt to value satisfactory throughout the plan; (4) Are the debtor's financial projections reasonable and sufficiently proven, or is the plan feasible; (5) What is the nature of the collateral, and is the value of the collateral appreciating, depreciating, or stable; (6) Are the risks unduly shifted to the creditor; (7) Are the risks borne by one secured creditor or class of secured creditors; (8) Does the plan preclude the secured creditor's foreclosure; (9) Did the original loan terms provide for negative amortization; and (10) Are there adequate safeguards to protect the secured creditor against plan failure?).

(4) *Deferred Principal.* Suppose that the debtor proposes to make payments of interest only for the first five years following confirmation of its plan. The plan provides that at the end of that period, when the debtor's income is projected to be higher, the debtor will make a balloon payment of the entire balance. Courts have found that the approach adopted in *Great Western* should also be followed in evaluating plans that propose a deferral of principal payments. *See In re Sunflower Racing, Inc.*, 226 B.R. 673 (D. Kan. 1998).

(5) *Too Little, or Just Too Late?* Nothing in the Code or case law expressly prohibits a debtor from proposing (nor a court from confirming) a plan that contemplates long term payouts of loans, even if the loans originally were short term. However, courts generally agree that as the period of repayment grows longer, the burden on the debtor to prove feasibility grows heavier. For example, in *In re Macon Uplands Venture*, 7 B.R. 293 (M.D. Ga. (1980), wherein the debtor proposed to extend payment of a mortgage on a hotel from 32 to 48 years, the court refused to confirm the plan because the debtor was unable to project its financial condition for more than 10 years and the useful life of the hotel was 25 to 30 years. The court explained:

> The debtor's plan of arrangement is wholly speculative. The debtor can be enthusiastic about tomorrow today; but that is not sufficient. Ideas are noble, but it is mind boggling to think of the potential hazards that are probable in the future which would prevent the execution of the plan. The seeds in an apple can be counted, but the apples in a seed cannot be counted.

7 B.R. at 314.

Moreover, sometimes an extension is just too long. Code § 1129(b)(2) states that "the condition that a plan be fair and equitable *includes the . . . requirements*" set forth in subsections (A) through (C). Use of the word "includes" indicates that technical compliance with the requirements of § 1129(b)(2) will not insure that a plan will be crammed down if it is unfair and inequitable for some other reason, and in a number of cases, this other reason is that the term of a loan is extended to its breaking point. For example, in *In re VIP Motor Lodge, Inc.*, 133 B.R. 41 (Bankr. D. Del. 1991), the debtor proposed to extend a five-year loan to 30 years and compensate the lender by paying additional interest. The court refused to cram the plan down, explaining:

> Here, VIP attempts to provide fair and equitable treatment to the Bank primarily through deferred cash payment amortized over a 30-year term under subsection (b)(2)(A)(i) at a 10% interest rate. Nevertheless, the length of time for which payments are deferred under the plan is simply too long. Thirty years is an extraordinarily long payout period and, though Chapter 11 has no express limitation on the length of a plan (unlike Chapter 13 which has a five-year limit), the court must find a 30-year payback term unreasonably long based upon the facts on the record.

> At the confirmation hearing, the expert testimony revealed that very few bank loans are being made for hotel/motel ventures and, typically, such loans are several years long with 10 or 15 years being the longest possible commercially available. The proposed plan seeks to extend the Bank's original loan for over 25 years beyond its original term. No evidence was presented suggesting that present market conditions would permit such favorable financing terms as VIP's treatment of the Bank's secured claim, especially with respect to the length of the loan. Unlike a loan against residential property where a 30-year mortgage term is somewhat of a standard, the record shows that commercial loans secured against lodging or similar-type real estate are usually only a short term of years in length. . . . The interest rate and other factors do not compensate for the extended period of deferred cash payments under this plan. Thus, the court finds that the plan does not meet the requirements of subsection (b)(2)(A)(i)(I) and (II). . . . A a result, due to the excessive length of time in repaying the Bank its $1.9 million secured claim, the court must deny confirmation because the cramdown does not treat the Bank's secured claim equitably or fairly under § 1129(b)(2)(A).

133 B.R. at 45. *Accord: In re Manion*, 127 B.R. 887 (Bankr. N.D. Fla. 1991); *In re White*, 36 B.R. 199 (Bankr. D. Kan. 1983); *In re 750 Ave. Assocs.*, 1979 U.S. Dist. LEXIS 15385 (Bankr. S.D.N.Y. May 21, 1979); *In re KRO Assocs.*, 1978 Bankr. LEXIS 14 (Bankr. S.D.N.Y. June 7, 1978); *In re Country Green Ltd. P'ship.*, 3 Bankr. Ct. Dec. 427 (Bkrtcy. W.D. Va. 1977).

[C] Cramdown: Treatment of Dissenting Classes of Unsecured Claims and Equity Interests

[1] Historical Note: Absolute Priority Under the Former Bankruptcy Act

In 1980, when District Judge Kevin Duffy of the Southern District of New York was presiding over the Chapter X reorganization of a company then known as the Duplan Corporation, he received a number of letters from shareholders who were distressed about the direction in which the three-year-old case was heading. The court-appointed trustee had proposed a plan of reorganization that provided for a distribution of cash and stock in the reorganized company to general creditors, note holders, and debenture holders, but the plan provided nothing for stockholders, whose interests were to be extinguished. One correspondent complained that no one seemed to be minding the case on behalf of stockholders; that no one — not the court, not the trustee, not the company's creditors, not even the Securities and Exchange Commission — was "protecting the small investor." The letter read, in part:

> April 10, 1980
>
> Dear Judge Kevin T. Duffy,
>
> As a judge, it is you who has the last word — but it is the judge who must accept the fact that "the buck stops here".
>
> It is quite easy for some involved individuals at the S.E.C. to make an analysis on paper and then submit their findings to you, based upon cold numbered facts.
>
> It is the judge who must look into his own [conscience] and consider certain matters, not just the cold numbers.
>
> The S.E.C. is truly not the protector of the investor — when it really matters it is the judge who will, in the end, be responsible for the little man's plight.
>
> As you can realize my letter is just an appeal to reason and fairness regarding your final decision in the Duplan Corp. case.
>
> I know all about the greater debits vs. the assets — but I also know that the company has been making giant strides in its recovery. It is also quite obvious that if the company had been left to survive in its present state, it would have fully recovered and been able to be a viable organization.
>
> However, this is water under the bridge. All I ask is that you do not wipe out completely the rights of the present stockholders. The least that can be done, is to give them some option to partake in the new organization.
>
> To wipe them out altogether would truly be an injustice. These were investors who believed in our principles of business and in most cases understood the risks of investing.

Common stocks go up and down, but still they represent an equity in a public company. If a company fails, there still remain some values — whether it be good will or the potential [for] future earnings.

Therefore, to say that the common stockholders own nothing is not logical — it is a sell out to the professionals and bankers.

You as the judge, will be the only one who will be responsible. They will point to you and say it was his decision — "we only gave him our opinions based on facts."

The investor must be protected, just as the creditor is. He also takes risks and should have a chance to recover his losses.

Sincerely,

David Gilder

The reason for David Gilder's letter, and the source of his angst, was the fact that in order to be confirmed by the court, a Chapter X plan not only had to be accepted by creditors and satisfy the "best interests" test, it also had to satisfy a far more stringent financial standard known as the "absolute priority rule." As we saw in text § 4.01 when we touched briefly on the subject, the absolute priority rule meant that under a Chapter X reorganization plan, each class of claims or interests had to be satisfied in full (but no more than in full) before the next lower class could receive or retain any property under a plan.

The rule was first articulated by the Supreme Court a century ago in an equity receivership case, *Northern Pacific Ry. v. Boyd*, 228 U.S. 482 (1913). The Northern Pacific was just one of a large number of railroads that fell on hard times in the late nineteenth and early twentieth centuries. These railroads were huge operations with massive assets encumbered by equally or even more massive debt. The secured creditors quickly discovered that the traditional remedy of foreclosure and auctioning off the assets was useless, because the market for distressed railroads was so thin. As a result, they invoked the equity receivership process — a forerunner of today's Chapter 11. A secured creditor — usually a bondholder — who was friendly with management would file a petition in federal court to have a receiver appointed to take charge of the railroad. Then, with the consent of the secured creditors, the receiver would sell the assets at foreclosure prices to a new entity. The proceeds of sale would go to the secured creditors, and if, as was typically the case, the sale did not produce enough cash to pay off their claims, the secured creditors would receive debt and equity issued by the new entity to satisfy the old debt. They would also retain a lien on the assets after they were transferred to the new entity. Of course, if the railroad was going to continue to operate, someone had to operate it, and in exchange for their willingness to provide this service and their willingness to put in new cash to salvage their old investment, old stockholders were permitted by the secured creditors to subscribe to stock in the new enterprise at a bargain price. When the dust settled, there would be a new railroad holding the assets of the old railroad. The owners of the new railroad were largely identical to the owners of the old railroad. The secured creditors were identical to the secured creditors of the old railroad. Only the unsecured creditors were gone. They were squeezed out and given nothing.

When these transactions were challenged by unsecured creditors, the schemes were sometimes denounced by the courts as fraudulent transfers, *see Chicago Rock Island & Pac. R.R. v. Howard*, 74 U.S. 392 (1868), and the unsecured creditors were permitted to reach the assets in the hands of the stockholders. In *Northern Pacific Ry. Co. v. Boyd*, however, the stockholders argued that there was nothing unwholesome about such a transaction, because, since the assets of the railroad were demonstrably worth less than the amount of debt they secured, there was no equity in the property out of which unsecured creditors could ever have been paid. Accordingly, secured creditors were entitled to allow value to trickle down to stockholders, even if unsecured creditors were squeezed out in the process.

Interestingly, these transactions have been described as essentially the equivalent of a modern day leveraged buyout. Northern Pacific Railroad Company defaulted on its secured bonds. The reorganization plan transferred the Northern Pacific Railroad assets to a newly created Northern Pacific Rail*way*. Stockholders of the railroad were permitted to subscribe to shares of the rail*way* at bargain prices. *See* King, 7 *Collier on Bankruptcy* ¶ 1129.LH[4][a] (15th ed. rev. 1997).

The Supreme Court disagreed. It held that a reorganization plan could not preserve the interests of stockholders unless unsecured creditors' claims were first satisfied in full:

> If the value of the road justified the issuance of stock in exchange for old shares, the creditors were entitled to the benefit of that value, whether it was present or prospective, for dividends or only for purposes of control. In either event it was a right of property out of which the creditors were entitled to be paid before the stockholders could retain it for any purpose whatever.

Id. at 508. In other words, the Court believed that if there was sufficient value to justify the stockholders' continued participation, the value of the reorganized business was being diverted to stockholders in derogation of the unsecured creditors' prior claim to the value of corporate property. However, the Court added that its ruling did not require "the impossible and make it necessary to pay an unsecured creditor in cash as a condition of stockholders retaining an interest in the reorganized company." *Id.* The court explained:

> His interest can be preserved by the issuance, on equitable terms, of income bonds or preferred stock. If he declines a fair offer he is left to protect himself as any other creditor of a judgment debtor, and, having refused to come into a just reorganization, could not thereafter be heard in a court of equity to attack it. If, however, no such tender was made and kept good he retains the right to subject the interest of the old stockholders in the property to the payment of his debt. If their interest is valueless, he gets nothing. If it be valuable, he merely subjects that which the law had originally and continuously made liable for the payment of corporate liabilities.

Id.

Three decades later, Congress enacted § 77B(f)(1) of the Bankruptcy Act, the nation's first corporate reorganization statute. That section provided that before a reorganization plan could be confirmed, the court had to find that it "is fair and equitable." In 1938, Congress enacted Chapter X, in which § 221(2) contained the same requirement. In 1939, in *Case v. Los Angeles Lumber Co.*, 308 U.S. 106 (1939), Justice Douglas concluded that when Congress provided that a plan had to be "fair and equitable," it intended to import the absolute priority rule of *Northern Pacific Railway* into § 77B, and in *Consolidated Rock Prods. Co. v. DuBois*, 312 U.S. 510 (1941), held that by use of the same language, it had signaled its intention that the absolute priority rule apply to Chapter X plans.

In *Case v. Los Angeles Lumber Co.*, the Court refused to confirm a plan that permitted stockholders of an insolvent corporation to retain a 23 percent ownership interest in the reorganized debtor. Writing for a unanimous court, Justice Douglas rejected the contention that the continued participation of the stockholders was justified by their familiarity with the business, their standing and influence in the financial community, and their promise of continuity of management. He reasoned that if stockholders were to retain an interest, a larger, more concrete contribution would be required:

> [W]e believe that to accord "the creditor his full right of priority against the corporate assets" where the debtor is insolvent, the stockholder's participation must be based on a contribution in money or in money's worth, reasonably equivalent in view of all the circumstances of the stockholder.

> The alleged consideration furnished by the stockholders in this case falls short of meeting those requirements.

> The findings below that participation by the old Class A stockholders will be beneficial to the bondholders because those stockholders have "financial standing and influence in the community" and can provide "continuity of management" constitute no legal justification for issuance of new stock to them. . . . On the facts of this case they cannot possibly be translated into money's worth reasonably equivalent to the participation accorded the old stockholders. They have no place in the asset column of the balance sheet of the new company. They reflect merely vague hopes or possibilities. As such, they cannot be the basis for issuance of stock to otherwise valueless interests. The rigorous standards of the absolute or full priority doctrine of the *Boyd* case will not permit valueless junior interests to perpetuate their position in an enterprise on such ephemeral grounds.

308 U.S. at 122. Moreover, the Court held that the reorganization plan ran afoul of the absolute priority rule even though 80 percent of the bondholders and 90 percent of the stockholders had assented to it. Absolute meant absolute. Classes of senior creditors could not give up value to junior creditors and interests even if they chose to do so. The Court feared that even the mere possibility of such an arrangement would give insider stockholders leverage to demand the kind of treatment that led to the passage of Chapter X in the first place:

> If the reorganization court were bound by such conventions of the parties, it would be effectively ousted of important duties which the Act places on it. Federal courts would be required to place their imprimatur on plans of reorganization which disposed of the assets of a company not in

accord with the standards of "fair and equitable" but in compliance with agreements which the required percentages of security holders had . . . made. Such procedure would deprive scattered and unorganized security holders of the protection which the Congress has provided them.

. . . .

The scope of the duties and powers of the Court would be delimited by the bargain which reorganizers had been able to make with the security holders before they asked the intercession of the court in effectuating their plan. Minorities would have their fate decided not by the court in application of the law of the land . . . but by the forces utilized by reorganizers in prescribing the conditions precedent on which the benefits of the statute could be obtained. No conditions precedent to the enjoyment of the benefits of [bankruptcy law] can be provided except by Congress. To hold otherwise would be to allow reorganizers to rewrite it so as to best serve their own ends.

308 U.S. at 128–129, 60 S. Ct. at 13–14, 84 L. Ed. at 126.

Notably, Chapter XI of the former Bankruptcy Act did not contain an absolute priority rule. In fact, § 366 of former Chapter XI that "Confirmation of an arrangement shall not be refused solely because the interest of a debtor, or if the debtor is a corporation, the interests of its stockholders or members will be preserved under the arrangement." This provision was added to Chapter XI in 1952 in the belief that if the absolute priority rule were to be applied in Chapter XI cases, "no individual or corporate debtor (where stock ownership is substantially identical with management) . . . can effectuate a plan." Sen. Rep. No. 1395, 82d Cong., 2d Sess. (1952).

Over the years, dissatisfaction with the absolute priority rule grew for several reasons. One reason was the belief that, as a result of shifting investment patterns, "the rule strikes hardest at those it was designed to protect — the public investor and the public creditor."

Another problem with the rule was the perceived difficulty of applying it. Determining whether equity holders were entitled to retain an interest in the reorganized company required determining whether the going concern value of the debtor exceeded the debtor's liabilities. If it did, then equity holders would be entitled to participate in the reorganization. If it did not, equity interests would be wiped out. As we saw in chapter 1, § 1.09, determining the going concern value of a business requires capitalizing projected earnings at the appropriate rate, a process that critics have characterized as "fictional," and as "a guess compounded by an estimate."

The third problem with the rule was that although it was "theoretically correct and desirable, [it did] not work well on a practical level. The rule of absolute priority often serves only to prevent reasonable compromises and to wipe out the interest of shareholders. The rule leads to a large amount of useless litigation and should be replaced by a more flexible standard."

The *Duplan* case, 9 B.R. 921, 935 (S.D.N.Y. 1980), demonstrates both the difficulty of applying the absolute priority rule and its adverse impact on stockholders such as David Gilder, who wrote the poignant letter that introduced this topic. Duplan was a manufacturer of double knit fabrics. Students who were born after, say, 1964 are too young to remember the fashion abomination known as double-knit leisure suits, but their parents will. When the double knit leisure suit market came unraveled, Duplan sought refuge in Chapter XI. The SEC moved the case into Chapter X in October of that year, and a trustee was appointed. Three years later, the trustee proposed a reorganization plan that provided that in satisfaction of their claims, general creditors would receive a combination of cash and stock in the reorganized company, that subordinated note holders would receive only stock, and that the interests of existing stockholders would be eliminated. The note holders objected to the plan on the grounds that in determining the going concern value of the reorganized company (and thus the value of its shares) the trustee had either inflated projected earnings or used an excessive capitalization rate, with the result that the net worth of the reorganized company had been overstated.

To determine the going concern value of the reorganized company — and thus the value of the stock that was being traded to general creditors and note holders — the trustee multiplied projected earnings by a capitalization rate of 5. The multiple was determined by reference to the average earnings per share of 15 "comparable" companies. The note holders maintained that the calculation overstated earnings and produced a going concern value that was too high. They took the position that since both the trustee's earnings projections and capitalization rate reflected a performance expectation, the "expectancy" factor had been counted twice. They argued that either historical earnings (rather than projected earnings) or a lower ratio should be used to avoid this double dipping effect.

Duplan stockholders, not surprisingly, believed that the value of the reorganized company had been underestimated. Shareholders were joined in their dissent by Edward I. Altman, a professor of finance at New York University's Graduate School of Business. He insisted that Duplan's future was even brighter than the trustee's projections suggested. Based on the company's earnings during the months following the filing of the proposed reorganization plan, he predicted that future earnings would surpass the trustee's estimates and that the value of the company's tax loss carryover would be enhanced as a result. He concluded that Duplan's going concern value was about $10 million more than the trustee estimated — enough to allow the stockholders to retain an interest and participate in the future of the company. Metz, *A Restructured Plan for Duplan*, N.Y. Times, Aug. 15, 1980, at D6, col. 3.

The SEC suggested a capitalization rate somewhere in between. The SEC believed that the capitalization rate should reflect the emerging company's debt free capital structure and that therefore a rate slightly higher than the one employed by the trustee's investment bankers should be employed.

After hearing several days of testimony from several expert investment bankers and the SEC, Judge Duffy found that the trustee's analysis, which proved the emerging company to be insolvent, was the most realistic.

Judge Duffy found that historical earnings might be a useful reference point for calculating future earnings, but that they were a starting point only. He found that the trustee's earnings projections properly took into account market position, inflation rates, an anticipated recession, and the company's business plan. He also found that the trustee's capitalization rate was appropriate in light of the trustee's "conservative earnings projections." Judge Duffy rejected the SEC's contention that a higher capitalization rate should be used to reflect the company's debt-free capital structure, reasoning that the SEC's approach failed to take into account "the uncertainties which underlay the trustee's projections." 9 B.R. at 927–929.

As a result, the note holders took stock and the stockholders took nothing, except umbrage which they expressed to the court in letters such as Mr. Gilder's. Judge Duffy explained to the hapless stockholders that his hands were tied by the absolute priority rule:

> I have received several letters from stockholders reminding me of their investment in Duplan and their exclusion from the plan. Unfortunately, I cannot change the fact that the debtor is insolvent, nor the fact that the law excludes shareholder participation in a reorganization plan where insolvency exists. I recognize that the stockholders have invested large sums of money into a company whose prospects now seem bright. For many stockholders, that investment constituted a major portion of their savings. But, as anyone who purchases stock understands, their investment is not guaranteed. Furthermore, it is clear that creditors of the company must come before stockholders when distributing assets in reorganization under bankruptcy laws. If this were not so, it would be impossible for even the healthiest of companies to raise needed capital. The fact remains that despite the new Duplan's encouraging earnings figures, there are not enough funds to pay creditors. Regrettably, the Trustee's plan must exclude former stockholders of Duplan.

9 B.R. at 935.

The trustee's valuation approach was not validated by time. Soon after confirmation, the company — which had changed its name to Panex — had been transformed from a black hole to a shining star of the domestic apparel industry. The company was operating profitably and management was offering to buy back 1 million of the company's 21.7 million outstanding shares for $12 a share — cash.

The performance of the resuscitated company led some observers to believe that the higher valuation was indeed the correct one, and that the reorganization plan could have allowed stockholders to retain an interest.

Certainly it does make sense to eliminate junior interests when a going concern valuation fails to find even a conjectural value in excess of senior claims. However, as the *Duplan* case demonstrates, the valuation process is so inherently uncertain that it does not always produce a fair result. Also, the absoluteness of the rule tended to harden parties into recalcitrance. Since the rule had to be observed, there was no incentive or freedom on the part of senior interests to negotiate with junior interests. Even seniors who might for the sake of moving the case along choose to give junior interests a continued stake in the debtor's future could not do so, unless a valuation demonstrated that the net worth was there.

Professor Edward I. Altman, the Max L. Heine Professor of Finance at the NYU School of Business, studied the *Duplan* case as it was unfolding. He insisted that the Chapter X trustee's valuation of the company was too low and that it shortchanged the stockholders. He believed that during the period after the plan had been filed — but before it was confirmed by the court — Duplan's financial condition and prospects had so substantially improved that a new plan — one that allowed stockholders to retain an interest — was appropriate. Although the court disagreed, and adopted the trustee's valuation, time proved Professor Altman's more optimistic view of Duplan's going concern value to be correct. The *Duplan* case produced several interesting *New York Times* articles, which can be found at the following links:

> Metz, *Bankrupt — And in the Chips*, The New York Times, August 7, 1980, p. D6, col. 1 http://query.nytimes.com/mem/archive/pdf?res= FA0D11FF3A5F12728DDDAE0894D0405B8084F1D3

> Metz, *A Restructured Plan for Duplan*, The New York Times, August 15, 1980, p. D6, col. 3 http://query.nytimes.com/mem/archive/pdf?res= F50D1FFA3A5F12728DDDAC0994D0405B8084F1D3

> Metz, *A Vital Panex From Duplan*, The New York Times, April 29, 1982, p. D8 col. 1

[2] The Absolute Priority Rule and Cramdown Under the Bankruptcy Code

This disenchantment with the absolute priority rule as it was applied under the former Bankruptcy Act was addressed by the drafters of the current Bankruptcy Code. Their response, contained in Code § 1129(b), embodies the principle that the absolute priority standard should come into play only when a class rejects a plan, to insure that members of the dissenting class are fairly and equitably treated. By giving senior classes the option of giving up value to junior classes, the Code encourages a negotiated restructuring and eliminates the necessity of establishing the going concern value of a company in every case. The legislative history describes this relaxed version of the fair and equitable rule this way:

> The premise of the bill's financial standard for confirmation is the same as the premise of the securities law: parties should be given adequate disclosure or relevant information, and they should make their own decision on the acceptability of the proposed plan or reorganization. The bill does not impose a rigid financial rule for the plan. The parties are left to their own to negotiate a fair settlement. The question of whether creditors are entitled to the going-concern or liquidation value of the business is impossible to answer. It is unrealistic to assume that the bill could or even should attempt to answer that question. Instead, negotiation among the parties after full disclosure will govern how the value of the reorganizing company will be distributed among creditors and stockholders. The bill only sets the outer limits on the outcome: it must be somewhere between the going-concern value and the liquidation value.

Only when the parties are unable to agree on a proper distribution of the value of the company does the bill establish a financial standard. If the debtor is unable to obtain the consents of all classes of creditors and stockholders, then the court may confirm the plan anyway on request of the plan's proponent, if the plan treats the nonconsenting classes fairly. The bill defines "fairly" in terms of the relative rights among the classes. Simply put, the bill requires that the plan pay any dissenting class in full before any class junior to the dissenter may be paid at all. The rule is a partial application of the absolute priority rule now applied under chapter X and requires a full valuation of the debtor as the absolute priority rule does under current law. The important difference is that the bill permits senior classes to take less than full payment, in order to expedite or insure the success of the reorganization. H.R. Rep. No. 95-595, 95th Cong., 1st Sess. 224 (1977).

DEBATES ON UNIFORM LAW ON BANKRUPTCY
124 Cong. Rec. H 11104–11105
(Daily edition Sept. 28, 1978) (Remarks of Rep. Edwards)

Section 1129(b)(2)(B) applies to a dissenting class of unsecured claims. The court must confirm the plan notwithstanding the dissent of a class of impaired unsecured claims if the plan provides for such claims to receive property with a present value equal to the allowed amount of the claims. Unsecured claims may receive any kind of "property," which is used in its broadest sense, as long as the present value of the property given to the holders of unsecured claims is equal to the allowed amount of the claims. Some kinds of property, such as securities, may require difficult valuations by the court; in such circumstances the court need only determine that there is a reasonable likelihood that the property given the dissenting class of impaired unsecured claims equals the present value of such allowed claims.

Alternatively, under clause (ii), the court must confirm the plan if the plan provides that holders of any claims or interests junior to the interests of the dissenting class of impaired unsecured claims will not receive any property under the plan on account of such junior claims or interests. As long as senior creditors have not been paid more than in full, and classes of equal claims are being treated so that the dissenting class of impaired unsecured claims is not being discriminated against unfairly, the plan may be confirmed if the impaired class of unsecured claims receives less than 100 cents on the dollar (or nothing at all) as long as no class junior to the dissenting class receives anything at all. Such an impaired dissenting class may not prevent confirmation of a plan by objection merely because a senior class has elected to give up value to a junior class that is higher in priority than the impaired dissenting class of unsecured claims as long as the above safeguards are met.

Subparagraph (C) applies to a dissenting class of impaired interests. Such interests may include the interests of general or limited partners in a partnership, the interests of a sole proprietor in a proprietorship, or the interest of common or preferred stockholders in a corporation. If the holders of such interests are entitled to a fixed liquidation preference or fixed redemption price on account of such interests then the plan may be confirmed notwithstanding the dissent of such class of interests as long as it provides the holders property of a present value equal to the greatest of the fixed redemption price, or the value of such interests. In the event there is no fixed liquidation preference or redemption price, then the plan may be confirmed as long as it provides the holders of such interests property of a present value equal to the value of such interests. If the interests are "under water" then they will be valueless and the plan may be confirmed notwithstanding the dissent of that class of interests even if the plan provides that the holders of such interests will not receive any property on account of such interests.

Alternatively, under clause (ii), the court must confirm the plan notwithstanding the dissent of a class of interests if the plan provides that holders of any interests junior to the dissenting class of interests will not receive or retain any property on account of such junior interests. Clearly, if there are no junior interests junior to the class of dissenting interests, then the condition of clause (ii) is satisfied. The safeguards that no claim or interest receive more than 100 percent of the allowed amount of such claim or interest and that no class be discriminated against unfairly will insure that the plan is fair and equitable with respect to the dissenting class of interests.

. . . .

[A] senior class will not be able to give up value to a junior class over the dissent of an intervening class unless the intervening class receives the full amount, as opposed to value, of its claims or interests.

———

The Bankruptcy Code is said to contain a "relaxed" or "modified" absolute priority rule, because nothing in the Code prevents senior classes of creditors from waiving their priority rights to allow value to trickle down to junior classes of claims or interests. Senior classes are not obliged to do this, but they can, if a majority of claims within the class decides to do so.

Only if the required majorities of claims or interests in a class does not vote to accept a plan does the Code's version of the absolute priority rule — as embodied in § 1129(b)(2) — come into play. Even though a class of unsecured claims votes to reject a plan, the plan can still be confirmed over that class's dissent — can be crammed down — if the plan's treatment of unsecured claims is "fair and equitable." It is, if it complies with § 1129(b)(2)(B). Please read that section now. As you will see, it provides two alternative forms of treatment, the first of which is sometimes described as "payment in full," a characterization that is a little misleading.

Although payment of the full amount of unsecured claims, in cash, on the effective date, will satisfy § 1129(b)(2)(B)(i), such treatment is not required. A plan that provides that unsecured claim holders will receive deferred cash payments having a present value equal to their allowed unsecured claims also would satisfy § 1129(b)(2)(B)(i), as would a distribution of stock in the reorganized debtor or, theoretically, some other form of property, provided that the stock or property had a value equal to the allowed amount of the claims. As you have undoubtedly noticed, if a plan proposes that creditors will receive a stream of deferred payments, the present value of those payments will have to be determined by the methods discussed in §§ 1.09 and 9.10[B], above. If stock is going to be distributed, the value of the shares will have to be determined, and that will require a going concern valuation of the debtor of the kind that the Code's drafters sought to avoid by relaxing the absolute priority rule.

Even if the debtor cannot satisfy the "full value" requirement of § 1129(b)(2)(B)(i), the plan can still be crammed down on a dissenting class of claims provided that the buck stops there. No holder of a claim or interest junior to the claims of the dissenting class may receive or retain any property under the plan on account of its junior claim or interest. In the opinions that follow, this requirement is described as "the core of what is known as the 'absolute priority rule.' "

The Code provides similar treatment for dissenting classes of interests. Under § 1129(b)(2)(C)(i), a plan is "fair and equitable" with respect to a class of interest holders if holders will receive under the plan property of a value equal to the greater of (1) the value of their interest, (2) the amount of any fixed liquidation preference, or (3) any fixed redemption price. Even if the plan does not satisfy this requirement, it can still be crammed down on a dissenting class of interests if no holder of an interest junior to the dissenting class is receiving or retaining any property under the plan on account of its junior claim or interest. § 1129(b)(2)(C)(ii).

NORWEST BANK WORTHINGTON v. AHLERS
Supreme Court of the United States
485 U.S. 197 (1988)

JUSTICE WHITE delivered the opinion of the Court.

In this case, the Court of Appeals found that respondents' promise of future "labor, experience and expertise" permitted confirmation of their Chapter 11 reorganization plan over the objections of their creditors, even though the plan violated the "absolute priority rule" of the Bankruptcy Code. Because we find this conclusion at odds with the Code and our cases, we reverse.

I

Respondents operate a failing family farm in Nobles County, Minnesota. Between 1965 and 1984 they obtained loans from petitioners, securing the loans with their farmland, machinery, crops, livestock, and farm proceeds. In November 1984, respondents defaulted on their loan payments to petitioner Norwest Bank Worthington; at the time, the aggregate loan balance owed the petitioners exceeded $1 million.

Following the default, Norwest filed a replevin action in Minnesota state court seeking possession of the farm equipment respondents had pledged as security. However, two weeks later respondents obtained an automatic stay of the replevin proceedings, when they filed a petition for reorganization under Chapter 11 of the Bankruptcy Code.

Petitioners filed motions in the Bankruptcy Court for relief from the automatic stay. After decisions by the bankruptcy and the District courts, these motions were ultimately considered by the Court of Appeals, which prohibited petitioners from repossessing any equipment, pending a determination by the District Court of the probability of success of a reorganization plan to be filed by respondents. On remand, the District Court found respondents' reorganization plan to be "utterly unfeasible." *Id.* It therefore affirmed the Bankruptcy Court's initial decision to grant petitioners relief from the automatic stay.

On appeal, the Court of Appeals reversed. It found that respondents could file a feasible reorganization plan. 794 F.2d 388, 399 (CA8 1986). Consequently, the Court of Appeals remanded the case with instructions that the Bankruptcy Court entertain and confirm a reorganization plan which comported with an outline suggested in a lengthy appendix to the Eighth Circuit's opinion. *Id.* at 408–414.

In reaching this conclusion, the Court of Appeals rejected petitioners' contention that, because of the "absolute priority rule" in the Bankruptcy Code, 11 U.S.C. § 1129(b) their legitimate objections to any reorganization plan which allowed respondents to retain an interest in the farm property was sufficient to bar confirmation of such a plan. Petitioners contended that the absolute priority rule prohibited respondents from retaining their equity interest in the farm, which is junior to the creditors' unsecured claims. But the Court of Appeals, relying on this Court's decision in *Case v. Los Angeles Lumber Products Co.*, 308 U.S. 106 (1939), held that the absolute priority rule did not bar respondents from retaining their equity interest in the farm if they contributed "money or money's worth" to the reorganized enterprise. It further concluded that respondents' "yearly contributions of labor, experience, and expertise" would constitute a contribution of "money or money's worth," and therefore would permit confirmation of a reorganization plan over petitioners' objections. Judge John Gibson, in dissent, criticized the majority's application of the absolute priority rule and its reading of *Los Angeles Lumber* as "unprecedented, illogical, and unfair." 794 F.2d, at 406. He concluded that the absolute priority rule barred respondents' retention of an equity interest in the farm over petitioners' legitimate objections.

After the Eighth Circuit — sharply divided — denied rehearing en banc, petitioners sought review by this Court. We granted certiorari to consider the Court of Appeals' application of the absolute priority rule . . . and now reverse.

II

As the Court of Appeals stated, the absolute priority rule "provides that a dissenting class of unsecured creditors must be provided for in full before any junior class can receive or retain any property [under a reorganization] plan." The rule had its genesis in judicial construction of the undefined requirement of the early bankruptcy statute that reorganization plans be "fair and equitable." See *Northern Pacific R. Co. v. Boyd*, 228 U.S. 482, 504–505 (1913); *Louisville Trust Co. v. Louisville, N.A & C.R. Co.*, 174 U.S. 674, 684 (1899). The rule has since gained express statutory force, and was incorporated into Chapter 11 of the Bankruptcy Code adopted in 1978. See 11 U.S.C. § 1129(b)(2)(B)(ii) (1982 ed., Supp. IV). Under current law, no Chapter 11 reorganization plan can be confirmed over the creditors' legitimate objections (absent certain conditions not relevant here) if it fails to comply with the absolute priority rule.

There is little doubt that a reorganization plan in which respondents retain an equity interest in the farm is contrary to the absolute priority rule. The Court of Appeals did not suggest otherwise in ruling for respondents, but found that such a plan could be confirmed over petitioners' objections because of an "exception" or "modification" to the absolute priority rule recognized in this Court's cases.

The Court of Appeals relied on the following dicta in *Case v. Los Angeles Lumber Products Co., supra,* at 121–122:

> It is, of course, clear that there are circumstances under which stockholders may participate in a plan of reorganization of an insolvent debtor.
>
> . . . .
>
> [W]e believe that to accord 'the creditor of his full right of priority against the corporate assets' where the debtor is insolvent, the stockholder's participation must be based on a contribution in money or money's worth, reasonably equivalent in view of all the circumstances to the participation of the stockholder.

The Court of Appeals found this language applicable to this case, concluding that respondents' future contributions of "labor, experience, and expertise" in running the farm — because they have "value" and are "measurable" – are "money or money's worth" within the meaning of *Los Angeles Lumber.* We disagree.[3]

Los Angeles Lumber itself rejected an analogous proposition, finding that the promise of the existing shareholders to pledge their "financial standing and influence in the community" and their "continuity of management" to the reorganized enterprise was "[in]adequate consideration" that could not possibly be deemed "money's worth." *Los Angeles Lumber,* 308 U.S. at 122. No doubt, the efforts promised by the *Los Angeles Lumber* equity-holders — like those of respondents — had "value" and would have been of some benefit to any reorganized enterprise. But ultimately, as the Court said in *Los Angeles Lumber,* "They reflect merely vague hopes or possibilities." *Id.* at 122–123. The same is true of respondents' pledge of future labor and management skills.

Viewed from the time of approval of the plan, respondents' promise of future services is intangible, inalienable, and, in all likelihood, unenforceable. It "has no

---

[3] The United States, as *amicus curiae,* urges us to reverse the Court of Appeals ruling and hold that codification of the absolute priority rule has eliminated any "exception" to that rule suggested by *Los Angeles Lumber,* 308 U.S. 106 (1939). *See* Brief for United States as *Amicus Curiae* 17–23. Relying on the statutory language and the legislative history, the Solicitor General argues that the 1978 Bankruptcy Code "dropped the infusion-of-new-capital exception to the absolute priority rule." *Id.* at 22.

We need not reach this question to resolve the instant dispute. As we discuss infra, we think it clear that even if the *Los Angeles Lumber* exception to the absolute priority rule has survived enactment of the Bankruptcy Code, this exception does not encompass respondents' promise to contribute their "labor, experience, and expertise" to the reorganized enterprise.

Thus, our decision today should not be taken as any comment on the continuing vitality of the *Los Angeles Lumber* exception — a question which has divided the lower courts since passage of the Code in 1978. Rather, we simply conclude that even if an "infusion-of-'money-or-money's-worth' " exception to the absolute priority rule has survived the enactment of § 1129(b), respondents' proposed contribution to the reorganization plan is inadequate to gain the benefit of this exception.

place in the asset column of the balance sheet of the new [entity]." *Los Angeles Lumber, supra,* at 122–123. Unlike "money or money's worth," a promise of future services cannot be exchanged in any market for something of value to the creditors today. In fact, no decision of this Court or any Court of Appeals, other than the decision below, has ever found a promise to contribute future labor, management, or expertise sufficient to qualify for the *Los Angeles Lumber* exception to the absolute priority rule. In short, there is no way to distinguish between the promises respondents proffer here and those of the shareholders in *Los Angeles Lumber*; neither is an adequate contribution to escape the absolute priority rule.

Respondents suggest that, even if their proposed contributions to the reorganized farm do not fit within the *Los Angeles Lumber* dicta, they do satisfy some broader exception to the absolute priority rule. But no such broader exception exists. Even if Congress meant to retain the *Los Angeles Lumber* exception to the absolute priority rule when it codified the rule in Chapter 11 — a proposition that can be debated, *see* n.3, *supra* — it is clear that Congress had no intention to expand that exception any further. When considering adoption of the current Code, Congress received a proposal by the Bankruptcy Commission to modify the absolute priority rule to permit equity-holders to participate in a reorganized enterprise based on their contribution of "continued management . . . essential to the business" or other participation beyond "money or money's worth." *See* H. R. Doc. No. 93-137, pt. 1, pp. 258–259 (1973). This proposal — quite similar to the Court of Appeals' holding in this case — prompted adverse reactions from numerous sources. Congress ultimately rejected the proposed liberalization of the absolute priority rule and adopted the codification of the rule now found in 11 U.S.C. § 1129(b)(2)(B). "This [section] codifies the absolute priority rule from the dissenting class on down." *See* H. R. Rep. No. 95-595, p. 413 (1977). We think the statutory language and the legislative history of § 1129(b) clearly bar any expansion of any exception to the absolute priority rule beyond that recognized in our cases at the time Congress enacted the 1978 Bankruptcy Code.

In sum, we find no support in the Code or our previous decisions for the Court of Appeals' application of the absolute priority rule in this case. We conclude that the rule applies here, and respondents' promise of future labor warrants no exception to its operation.

III

Respondents advance two additional arguments seeking to obviate the conclusion mandated by the absolute priority rule.

A

Respondents first advance a variety of "equitable arguments" which, they say, prevent the result we reach today. Respondents contend that the nature of bankruptcy proceedings — namely, their status as proceedings in "equity" — prevents petitioners from inequitably voting in the class of unsecured creditors, and require that a "fair and equitable" reorganization plan in the best interests of all creditors and debtors be confirmed. Similarly, the Court of Appeals found it significant that — in its view — respondents' wholly unsecured creditors (as opposed to petitioners, who have partially secured claims) would fare better under the proposed reorganization plan than if the farm was liquidated.

The short answer to these arguments is that whatever equitable powers remain in the bankruptcy courts must and can only be exercised within the confines of the Bankruptcy Code. The Code provides that undersecured creditors can vote in the class of unsecured creditors, 11 U.S.C. § 506(a), the Code provides that a "fair and equitable" reorganization plan is one which complies with the absolute priority rule, 11 U.S.C. § 1129(b)(2)(B), and the Code provides that it is up to the creditors — and not the courts — to accept or reject a reorganization plan which fails to provide them adequate protection or fails to honor the absolute priority rule, 11 U.S.C. § 1126.

The Court of Appeals may well have believed that petitioners or other unsecured creditors would be better off if respondents' reorganization plan was confirmed. But that determination is for the creditors to make in the manner specified by the Code. 11 U.S.C. § 1126(c). Here, the principal creditors entitled to vote in the class of unsecured creditors (*i.e.*, petitioners) objected to the proposed reorganization. This was their prerogative under the Code, and courts applying the Code must effectuate their decision.

B

Respondents further argue that the absolute priority rule has no application in this case, where the property which the junior interest holders wish to retain has no value to the senior unsecured creditors. In such a case, respondents argue, "the creditors are deprived of nothing if such a so-called interest' continues in the possession of the reorganized debtor." Here, respondents contend, because the farm has no "going concern" value (apart from their own labor on it), any equity interest they retain in a reorganization of the farm is worthless and therefore is not "property" under 11 U.S.C. § 1129(b)(2)(B)(ii).

We join with the overwhelming consensus of authority which has rejected this "no value" theory. Even where debts far exceed the current value of assets, a debtor who retains his equity interest in the enterprise retains "property." Whether the value is "present or prospective, for dividends or only for purposes of control" a retained equity interest is a property interest to "which the creditors [are] entitled . . . before the stockholders [can] retain it for any purpose whatever." *Northern Pacific R. Co. v. Boyd*, 228 U.S. at 508. Indeed, even in a sole proprietorship, where "going concern" value may be minimal, there may still be some value in the control of the enterprise; obviously, also at issue is the interest in potential future profits of a now-insolvent business. *See SEC v. Canandaigua Enterprises Corp.*, 339 F.2d 14, 21 (CA2 1964) (Friendly, J.). And while the Code itself does not define what "property" means as the term is used in § 1129(b), the relevant legislative history suggests that Congress' meaning was quite broad. " '[P]roperty' includes both tangible and intangible property." *See* H. R. Rep. No. 95-595, at 413.

Moreover, respondents' "no value" theory is particularly inapposite in this case. This argument appears not to have been presented to the Eighth Circuit, which implicitly concluded — to the contrary of respondents' position here — that the equity interest respondents desire to retain has some value. Even cursory consideration reveals that the respondents' retained interest under the plan might be "valuable" for one of several reasons. For example, the Court of Appeals provided that respondents would be entitled to a share of any profits earned by the sale of secured property during the reorganization period, an interest which can hardly be considered "worthless." And there is great common sense in petitioners' contention that "obviously, there is some going concern value here, or the parties would not have been litigating over it for the last three years."

Consequently, we think that the interest respondents would retain under any reorganization must be considered "property" under § 1129(b)(2)(B)(ii), and therefore can only be retained pursuant to a plan accepted by their creditors or formulated in compliance with the absolute priority rule. Since neither is true in this case, the Court of Appeals' judgment for respondents cannot stand.

. . . .

In sum, because we find the decision below to be contrary to the Bankruptcy Code and this Court's previous cases, the judgment of the Court of Appeals is reversed, and the case is remanded for further proceedings consistent with this opinion.

It is so ordered.

PROBLEM 9.9

In *Ahlers*, the Supreme Court rejected the "no value" theory. It also rejected the Ahlers's fallback position: that their future contributions of labor, experience, and expertise constituted consideration sufficient to justify their retaining an interest in the farm. But what if the Ahlers had offered to pay real money in exchange for an interest in the farm? Would the result have been different? Should it have been? Consider the opinions that follow:

IN RE LANDAU BOAT CO.
(LANDAU I)
United States Bankruptcy Court, Western District of Missouri
8 B.R. 436 (1981)

ORDER DENYING MOTION UNDER § 1129(b)

Joel Pelofsky, Bankruptcy Judge.

In this Chapter 11 proceeding, the debtor has proposed a plan with four classes of creditors. Administrative costs constitute Class One; Secured claims constitute Class Two. Both of these classes are to be paid in full. Class Three is composed of unsecured creditors. This class is to be paid 10% of their allowed claims. Class Four is composed of stockholders who are to receive no distribution under the plan but will retain their interest in the corporation.

The plan did not receive the votes necessary to be confirmed. . . . At the time debtor filed its plan, it moved the Court to confirm the plan under 1129(b) of the Code, Title 11, U.S.C. Premature at that time, the Motion is now timely and will be considered.

Section 1129(b) provides, in part, that

> Notwithstanding section 510(a) of this title, if all of the applicable requirements of subsection (a) of this section other than paragraph (8) are met with respect to a plan, the court, on request of the proponent of the plan, shall confirm the plan notwithstanding the requirements of such paragraph if the plan does not discriminate unfairly, and is fair and equitable, with respect to each class of claims or interests that is impaired under, and has not accepted the plan.

Paragraph 8 refers to classes which have accepted or are not impaired under the plan. In this plan, the unsecured class is impaired and has not accepted the plan. Section 1129(b)(2) sets out criteria for "cram down" as it affects unsecured creditors.

> For the purpose of this subsection, the condition that a plan be fair and equitable with respect to a class includes the following requirements:
>
>   . . . .
>
> (B)With respect to a class of unsecured claims
>
>   (i) the plan provides that each holder of a claim of such class receive or retain on account of such claim property of a value, as of the effective date of the plan, equal to the allowed amount of such claim; or
>
>   (ii) the holder of any claim or interest that is junior to the claims of such class will not receive or retain on account of such junior claim or interest any property.

The issue of priority in corporate reorganization has a long history, originating in the railroad reorganizations of the turn of the century. In *Louisville Trust Co. v. Louisville, N. A. & C. Ry. Co., et al.*, 174 U.S. 674, 19 S. Ct. 827, 43 L. Ed. 1130 (1899), the bondholders and the mortgage holders arranged a foreclosure of the railroad property. The Supreme Court condemned the transaction in no uncertain terms.

>   . . . .
>
> a foreclosure which attempts to preserve any interest or right of mortgagor in the property after the sale must necessarily secure and preserve the prior rights of general creditors thereof. This is based upon the familiar rule that the stockholder's interest in the property is subordinate to the rights of creditors. And any arrangement of the parties by which the subordinate rights and interests of the stockholders are attempted to be secured at the expense of the prior rights of either class of creditors comes within judicial denunciation.

174 U.S. at 684, 19 S. Ct. at 830.

This statement of principle was broadened to reach reorganization foreclosures in *Northern P. R. Co. v. Boyd*, 228 U.S. 482, 33 S. Ct. 554, 57 L. Ed. 931 (1913). Here again the bondholders and stockholders agreed to create a new company, eliminating the claims of general creditors.

> As between the parties . . . the sale was valid. As against creditors, it was a mere form.
>
> . . . .
>
> The invalidity of the sale flowed from the character of the reorganization agreement regardless of the value of the property, for in cases like this the question must be decided according to a fixed principle, not leaving the rights of the creditors to depend upon the balancing of evidence as to whether, on the day of sale, the property was insufficient to pay prior encumbrances
>
> . . . .
>
> If the value of the road justified the issuance of stock in exchange for old shares, the creditors were entitled to the benefit of that value, whether it was present or prospective, for dividends or only for purposes of control. In either event it was a right of property out of which the creditors were entitled to be paid before the stockholders could retain it for any purpose whatever.

228 U.S. at 506–508, 33 S. Ct. at 561.

The fixed principle, set out in *Louisville Trust Co.* and restated in *Boyd*, was further explicated in *Case v. Los Angeles Lumber Products Co. Ltd.*, 308 U.S. 106, 60 S. Ct. 1, 84 L. Ed. 110 (1939). The Court noted that creditors were entitled to priority over stockholders to the extent of their debt and that the continued participation of stockholders in a reorganization would depend upon new equity contributions. The Court went on to comment upon the notion that benefit under the plan to creditors was immaterial. "The fact that bondholders might fare worse as a result of a foreclosure and liquidation than they would by taking a debtor's plan under Section 77B can have no relevant bearing on whether a proposed plan is " 'fair and equitable' under that section." 308 U.S. at 123, 60 S. Ct. at 11.

The Eighth Circuit follows the reasoning of these cases.

> Stockholders may not better their position at the cost of bondholders or other creditors and to justify a retention of stock interest by stockholders of a debtor it must appear that they have furnished some compensatory additional consideration or have an equity in the estate of the debtor after the rights of creditors are fully provided for.

Sophian v. Congress Realty Co., 98 F.2d 499, 502 (8th Cir. 1938).

Here the plan proposes to compromise the unsecured debts at 10%. The fund to pay this amount is to be received from outside investors, otherwise unidentified. There is nothing in the plan to suggest that the existing stockholders will provide new equity as a condition of retaining their interest. It is apparent from the schedules that the assets of the debtor are insufficient to pay the unsecured creditors in full and, therefore, the stockholders have no equity in the debtor.

The absolute priority rule of *Boyd*, as embodied in Section 1129(b), requires that a senior class of debt is to be paid in full if a junior class is to receive any property. Here, the unsecured debt is not being paid in full, while the stockholders, a class junior to the unsecured, retains its equity interest. Does the retention of an equity interest constitute the receiving of property if the interest, as here, has no value? The answer seems to be clearly yes.

In *Boyd*, the Court suggested that the value of the property received by the junior class need not be cash but could also be "prospective, for dividends or only for purposes of control." Quite clearly, retention of the stockholders' interest in this case is for prospective earnings and for control. But also, although this is more speculative, if the debts of the unsecured creditors are compromised, the stockholders may realize some immediate equity value. The statute prohibits such a result.

IN RE LANDAU BOAT CO.
(LANDAU II)
United States Bankruptcy Court, Western District of Missouri
13 B.R. 788 (1981)

MEMORANDUM OPINION AND ORDER

JOEL PELOFSKY, BANKRUPTCY JUDGE.

In this Chapter 11 proceeding, debtor's original plan was rejected by the impaired class of unsecured creditors. Debtor's request that the plan be "crammed down" under Section 1129(b) was denied by the Court, holding that the plan did not meet the "fair and equitable" test where unsecured creditors were not paid in full and shareholders retained their interest in the debtor, the corporation having some value as a going concern and with a reasonable expectation of future profit.

Debtor then filed an amended plan in which it was proposed that the existing common stock be cancelled and a new class of common stock be issued and be made available to purchasers, including creditors, at par of $1.00 per share. The plan also required subscribers to "offer an irrevocable loan commitment in the sum of Three ($3.00) Dollars for each dollar ($1.00) of stock purchased." The plan stated the shareholders of the corporation presently holders of debtor's stock had offered to purchase the issue in its entirety but that the Court had the right to allocate the division of the stock if some creditors subscribed. Unsecured creditors were to be paid from this fund and were still impaired under the plan.

This plan and an amended disclosure statement approved by the Court were distributed to creditors. The unsecured creditors again rejected the plan.

Section 1129(b) provides, in part, that:

> If all of the applicable requirements of subsection (a) of this section other than paragraph (8) are met with respect to a plan, the court, on request of the proponent of the plan, shall confirm the plan notwithstanding the requirements of such paragraph if the plan does not discriminate unfairly, and is fair and equitable with respect to each class of claims or interests that is impaired under, and has not accepted, the plan.

The Court finds that the plan meets the requirements of Section 1129(a) except for Section 1129(a)(8). The plan, therefore, may be "crammed down" if it is fair and equitable to the rejecting class. As to the class of unsecured claims, the plan is fair and equitable if:

> (i) the plan provides that each holder of a claim of such class receive or retain on account of such claim property of a value, as of the effective date of the plan, equal to the allowed amount of such claim; or (ii) the holder of any claim or interest that is junior to the claims of such class will not receive or retain on account of such junior claim or interest any property.

Section 1129(b)(2)(B).

The plan provides that the class [of unsecured creditors] receive only 10% of its allowed claims. The question then is whether any junior claim or interest receives any property. In denying cram down in the earlier proceeding, this Court found that the shareholders clearly retained an interest "for prospective earnings and for control," and with some possibility of the realization of immediate equity. Over the course of this proceeding, the testimony has been that the value of the real property does not exceed the amount of the lien against it. There is some question whether the value of the machinery and equipment exceeds the amount of the lien. An independent appraisal sets the value at half the amount of the lien. The scheduled values exceed that amount but debtor's representatives testified that many of the scheduled items have been sold or otherwise disposed of. The evidence does not permit the Court to set a precise value on the machinery and equipment but does permit the conclusion that the value by which such property exceeds the amount of the lien is nominal at best, leaving little or no equity to be realized by the shareholders.

Under the first plan, debtor did not make clear whether there was to be new equity contributions such as would justify retention of an interest by the shareholders. The amended plan specifically calls for new investment and an irrevocable commitment to a loan for operating funds from the investors.

> to justify a retention of stock interest by stockholders of a debtor it must appear that they have furnished some compensatory additional consideration or have an equity in the estate of the debtor after the rights of creditors are fully provided for.

Sophian v. Congress Realty Co., 98 F.2d 499, 502 (8th Cir. 1938).

The Court in *Marston, supra*, deals with retention of interests by existing shareholders where new investment is made.

Section 1129 . . . requires that where the dissenting class receives less than the full amount of its claim, no inferior class may retain any interest or receive any distribution. Thus, if no new money were contributed or the amount contributed a trivial sum, the retention of an interest by an inferior class would be a fatal defect.

> There is no reason why investors of new capital who happen to be shareholders, whose equity interest as old shareholders is extinguished, should be disqualified from investment in the reorganized corporation, where their contribution is substantial.
>
>   . . . .

Marston, supra.

Reynolds [an unsecured creditor] asserts that the contribution is not substantial. The new money will permit payment of the unsecured debt at the rate set out in the plan and leave $35,000 for capital uses. In addition, the commitment to invest requires the investor to make a loan to the debtor. Since the stock issue is fully subscribed, the new investors will be required to loan an additional substantial sum to the debtor. And, while the plan proposes that such loans be embodied in 90 day notes, there is no evidence that debtor would have the ability to repay such amounts in that period. In fact, debtor's reports over the year suggest that repayment within 90 days will be impossible. Thus, the amount of funds to be made available by the new investors is substantial.

Reynolds also asserts that the investment, even if substantial, allows the new investors to have equity value without consideration because debtor, as a going business, is worth more than the investors are paying. Reynolds points to the testimony of Heck, the witness offered by debtor, who stated that a boat builder should be capitalized at 4 to 8 times earnings in these times. Since other testimony predicted profits in 1982 and 1983, Reynolds contends that the true value of the debtor is about $240,000 and therefore the investment is insufficient.

The commercial value of property consists in the expectation of income from it. . . . Such criterion is the appropriate one here, since we are dealing with the issue of solvency arising in connection with reorganization plans involving productive properties. . . . The criterion of earning capacity is the essential one . . . if the allocation of securities among the various claimants is to be fair and equitable. . . . Since its application requires a prediction as to what will occur in the future, an estimate, as distinguished from mathematical certitude, is all that can be made. But that estimate must be based on an informed judgment which embraces all facts relevant to future earnings capacity and hence to present worth, including, of course, the nature and condition of the properties, the past earnings record, and all circumstances which indicate whether or not that record is a reliable criterion of future performance. *Consolidated Rock Products v. DuBois*, 312 U.S. 510, 526, 61 S. Ct. 675, 685, 85 L. Ed. 982 (1941).

Debtor presently rents a portion of its manufacturing facility to another aluminum boat maker, who is apparently profitable. There is no evidence as to that other boat maker's gross sales or whether its product competes with that produced by debtor. Debtor has stated that it will evict the other boat maker at the end of 1981 if the plan is confirmed for it will need all the space for projected manufacturing. Debtor projects that in the 1982 manufacturing season, it will earn $16,000 before taxes and in the 1983 manufacturing season it will earn $80,000 before taxes.

Both of these estimates are based upon gross of $2,000,000 or over and profits are calculated before debt service. The debt is to be paid at market rates of interest. Debt service will leave no projected profit in 1982 and only a small projected profit in 1983.

Debtor's financial report for the eleven month period ending May 31, 1981 shows gross sales of $569,526.11 and a net loss of $144,170.87. At an annual rate, debtor's gross sales will be about $620,000 with a net loss of $156,000. Heck, testifying on behalf of the new investors, seems confident that sales could be raised to $2,000,000 in 1982 and $2.5 million in 1983. He gave no specifics as to how this was to be achieved but did indicate that substantial operating funds would be necessary.

On February 9, 1981, the Court authorized debtor to borrow $35,000 to enable it to purchase materials to fill various orders. Debtor represented that it would make a profit on this activity. The funds were not to be used for the payment of secured debt but only for payment of expenses related to production. Weekly reports were required. The first report was filed March 13, 1981. Reports through early July 1981, a period of 17 weeks, and in the height of the selling season, show gross receipts of $326,803.09 and expenditures of $321,750.27. No payment for secured debt was charged against this activity. While it thus appears that, at this level, gross sales would be very close to $1 Million, there would be no profit.

This examination of the financial reports and the operating experience of debtor show that debtor has the potential to be profitable. However, in light of debtor's financial needs, the state of the economy and the fact that debtor is in a highly competitive business, the Court can only conclude that the probability of debtor making a profit in the next two years is unlikely. The Court, therefore, finds that the new investors are making a substantial investment which exceeds any value which can be realized from the business in the foreseeable future.

. . . .

On the basis of the foregoing, the Court finds that the "plan does not discriminate unfairly, and is fair and equitable with respect to the class of claims that is impaired under and has not accepted the plan." Section 1129(b)(1). The motion of debtor to confirm is SUSTAINED. The Plan is CONFIRMED effective September 1, 1981.

BANK OF AMERICA NATIONAL TRUST AND SAVINGS ASSOCIATION v. 203 NORTH LASALLE STREET PARTNERSHIP
Supreme Court of the United States
526 U.S. 434 (1999)

JUSTICE SOUTER delivered the opinion of the Court.

The issue in this Chapter 11 reorganization case is whether a debtor's prebankruptcy equity holders may, over the objection of a senior class of impaired creditors, contribute new capital and receive ownership interests in the reorganized entity, when that opportunity is given exclusively to the old equity holders under a plan adopted without consideration of alternatives. We hold that old equity holders are disqualified from participating in such a "new value" transaction by the terms of 11 U.S.C. § 1129(b)(2)(B)(ii), which in such circumstances bars a junior interest holder's receipt of any property on account of his prior interest.

I

Petitioner, Bank of America National Trust and Savings Association (Bank), is the major creditor of respondent, 203 North LaSalle Street Partnership (Debtor or Partnership), an Illinois real estate limited partnership.

The limited partners in this case are considered the Debtor's equity holders under the Bankruptcy Code, *see* 11 U.S.C. §§ 101(16), (17), and the Debtor Partnership's actions may be understood as taken on behalf of its equity holders.

The Bank lent the Debtor some $93 million, secured by a nonrecourse first mortgage on the Debtor's principal asset, 15 floors of an office building in downtown Chicago. In January 1995, the Debtor defaulted, and the Bank began foreclosure in a state court.

In March, the Debtor responded with a voluntary petition for relief under Chapter 11 of the Bankruptcy Code, which automatically stayed the foreclosure proceedings, *see* § 362(a). The Debtor's principal objective was to ensure that its partners retained title to the property so as to avoid roughly $20 million in personal tax liabilities, which would fall due if the Bank foreclosed. The Debtor proceeded to propose a reorganization plan during the 120-day period when it alone had the right to do so . . . . The Bankruptcy Court rejected the Bank's motion to terminate the period of exclusivity to make way for a plan of its own to liquidate the property, and instead extended the exclusivity period for cause shown, under § 1121(d).

The value of the mortgaged property was less than the balance due the Bank, which elected to divide its undersecured claim into secured and unsecured deficiency claims under § 506(a) and § 1111(b).

Under the plan, the Debtor separately classified the Bank's secured claim, its unsecured deficiency claim, and unsecured trade debt owed to other creditors. *See* § 1122(a).

The Bankruptcy Court found that the Debtor's available assets were prepetition rents in a cash account of $3.1 million and the 15 floors of rental property worth $54.5 million. The secured claim was valued at the latter figure, leaving the Bank with an unsecured deficiency of $38.5 million.

So far as we need be concerned here, the Debtor's plan had these further features:

(1) The Bank's $54.5 million secured claim would be paid in full between 7 and 10 years after the original 1995 repayment date.

(2) The Bank's $38.5 million unsecured deficiency claim would be discharged for an estimated 16% of its present value.

(3) The remaining unsecured claims of $90,000, held by the outside trade creditors, would be paid in full, without interest, on the effective date of the plan.

(4)   Certain former partners of the Debtor would contribute $6.125 million in new capital over the course of five years (the contribution being worth some $4.1 million in present value), in exchange for the Partnership's entire ownership of the reorganized debtor.

The last condition was an exclusive eligibility provision: the old equity holders were the only ones who could contribute new capital.

The Bank objected and, being the sole member of an impaired class of creditors, thereby blocked confirmation of the plan on a consensual basis. *See* § 1129(a)(8). The Debtor, however, took the alternate route to confirmation of a reorganization plan, forthrightly known as the judicial "cramdown" process for imposing a plan on a dissenting class. § 1129(b). See generally Klee, *All You Ever Wanted to Know About Cram Down Under the New Bankruptcy Code*, 53 Am. Bankr. L. J. 133 (1979).

There are two conditions for a cramdown. First, all requirements of § 1129(a) must be met (save for the plan's acceptance by each impaired class of claims or interests, *see* § 1129(a)(8)). Critical among them are the conditions that the plan be accepted by at least one class of impaired creditors, *see* § 1129(a)(10), and satisfy the "best-interest-of-creditors" test, *see* § 1129(a)(7). Here, the class of trade creditors with impaired unsecured claims voted for the plan, and there was no issue of best interest. Second, the objection of an impaired creditor class may be overridden only if "the plan does not discriminate unfairly, and is fair and equitable, with respect to each class of claims or interests that is impaired under, and has not accepted, the plan." § 1129(b)(1). As to a dissenting class of impaired unsecured creditors, such a plan may be found to be "fair and equitable" only if the allowed value of the claim is to be paid in full, § 1129(b)(2)(B)(i), or, in the alternative, if "the holder of any claim or interest that is junior to the claims of such [impaired unsecured] class will not receive or retain under the plan on account of such junior claim or interest any property," § 1129(b)(2)(B)(ii). That latter condition is the core of what is known as the "absolute priority rule."

The absolute priority rule was the basis for the Bank's position that the plan could not be confirmed as a cramdown. As the Bank read the rule, the plan was open to objection simply because certain old equity holders in the Debtor Partnership would receive property even though the Bank's unsecured deficiency claim would not be paid in full. The Bankruptcy Court approved the plan nonetheless, and accordingly denied the Bank's pending motion to convert the case to Chapter 7 liquidation, or to dismiss the case. The District Court affirmed, as did the Court of Appeals.

The majority of the Seventh Circuit's divided panel found ambiguity in the language of the statutory absolute priority rule, and looked beyond the text to interpret the phrase "on account of" as permitting recognition of a "new value corollary" to the rule. According to the panel, the corollary, as stated by this Court in *Case v. Los Angeles Lumber Products Co.*, 308 U.S. 106, 118, 60 S. Ct. 1, 84 L. Ed. 110 (1939), provides that the objection of an impaired senior class does not bar junior claim holders from receiving or retaining property interests in the debtor after reorganization, if they contribute new capital in money or money's worth, reasonably equivalent to the property's value, and necessary for successful reorganization of the restructured enterprise. The panel majority held that "when an old equity holder retains an equity interest in the reorganized debtor by meeting the requirements of the new value corollary, he is not receiving or retaining that interest 'on account of' his prior equitable ownership of the debtor. Rather, he is allowed to participate in the reorganized entity 'on account of' a new, substantial, necessary and fair infusion of capital."

126 F.3d at 964.

In the dissent's contrary view, there is nothing ambiguous about the text: the "plain language of the absolute priority rule . . . does not include a new value exception." 126 F.3d at 970 (opinion of Kanne, J.). Since "the Plan in this case gives [the Debtor's] partners the exclusive right to retain their ownership interest in the indebted property because of their status as . . . prior interest holders," 126 F.3d at 973, the dissent would have reversed confirmation of the plan.

We granted certiorari, to resolve a Circuit split on the issue. The Seventh Circuit in this case joined the Ninth in relying on a new value corollary to the absolute priority rule to support confirmation of such plans. *See In re Bonner Mall Partnership*, 2 F.3d 899, 910–916 (CA9 1993), *cert. granted*, 510 U.S. 1039, *vacatur denied and appeal dism'd as moot*, 513 U.S. 18, 115 S. Ct. 386, 130 L. Ed. 2d 233 (1994). The Second and Fourth Circuits, by contrast, without explicitly rejecting the corollary, have disapproved plans similar to this one. *See In re Coltex Loop Central Three Partners, L. P.*, 138 F.3d 39, 44–45 (CA2 1998); *In re Bryson Properties, XVIII*, 961 F.2d 496, 504 (CA4), cert. denied, 506 U.S. 866, 113 S. Ct. 191, 121 L. Ed. 2d 134 (1992).[15] We do not decide whether the statute includes a new value corollary or exception, but hold that on any reading respondent's proposed plan fails to satisfy the statute, and accordingly reverse.

II

The terms "absolute priority rule" and "new value corollary" (or "exception") are creatures of law antedating the current Bankruptcy Code, and to understand both those terms and the related but inexact language of the Code some history is helpful. The Bankruptcy Act preceding the Code contained no such provision as subsection (b)(2)(B)(ii), its subject having been addressed by two interpretive rules. The first was a specific gloss on the requirement of § 77B (and its successor, Chapter X) of the old Act, that any reorganization plan be "fair and equitable." 11 U.S.C. § 205(e) (1934 ed., Supp. I) (repealed 1938) (§ 77B); 11 U.S.C. § 621(2) (1934 ed., Supp. IV) (repealed 1979) (Chapter X). The reason for such a limitation was the danger inherent in any reorganization plan proposed by a debtor, then and now, that the plan will simply turn out to be too good a deal for the debtor's owners. *See* H. R. Doc. No. 93-137, pt. I, p. 255 (1973) (discussing concern with "the ability of a few

---

[15] All four of these cases arose in the single-asset real estate context, the typical one in which new value plans are proposed. See 7 Collier on Bankruptcy ¶ 1129.04[4][c][ii][B], p. 1129-113 (15th ed. rev. 1998). See also Strub, Competition, Bargaining, and Exclusivity under the New Value Rule: Applying the Single-Asset Paradigm of *Bonner Mall*, 111 Banking L.J. 228, 231 (1994) ("Most of the cases discussing the new value issue have done so in connection with an attempt by a single-asset debtor to reorganize under chapter 11").

insiders, whether representatives of management or major creditors, to use the reorganization process to gain an unfair advantage"); *ibid.* ("It was believed that creditors, because of management's position of dominance, were not able to bargain effectively without a clear standard of fairness and judicial control"); Ayer, *Rethinking Absolute Priority After Ahlers*, 87 Mich. L. Rev. 963, 969–973 (1989). Hence the pre-Code judicial response known as the absolute priority rule, that fairness and equity required that "the creditors . . . be paid before the stockholders could retain [equity interests] for any purpose whatever." *Northern Pacific R. Co. v. Boyd*, 228 U.S. 482, 508, 33 S. Ct. 554, 57 L. Ed. 931 (1913). *See also Louisville Trust Co. v. Louisville, N. A. & C. R. Co.*, 174 U.S. 674, 684, 19 S. Ct. 827, 43 L. Ed. 1130 (1899) (reciting "the familiar rule that the stockholder's interest in the property is subordinate to the rights of creditors; first of secured and then of unsecured creditors" and concluding that "any arrangement of the parties by which the subordinate rights and interests of the stockholders are attempted to be secured at the expense of the prior rights of either class of creditors comes within judicial denunciation").

The second interpretive rule addressed the first. Its classic formulation occurred in *Case v. Los Angeles Lumber Products Co.*, in which the Court spoke through Justice Douglas in this dictum:

> It is, of course, clear that there are circumstances under which stockholders may participate in a plan of reorganization of an insolvent debtor.
>
> . . . .
>
> Where the necessity [for new capital] exists and the old stockholders make a fresh contribution and receive in return a participation reasonably equivalent to their contribution, no objection can be made.
>
> . . . .
>
> We believe that to accord the creditor his full right of priority against the corporate assets' where the debtor is insolvent, the stockholder's participation must be based on a contribution in money or in money's worth, reasonably equivalent in view of all the circumstances to the participation of the stockholder.

308 U.S. at 121–122.

Although counsel for one of the parties here has described the Case observation as " 'black-letter' principle," it never rose above the technical level of dictum in any opinion of this Court, which last addressed it in *Norwest Bank Worthington v. Ahlers*, holding that a contribution of " 'labor, experience, and expertise" ' by a junior interest holder was not in the " 'money's worth' " that the *Case* observation required. Nor, prior to the enactment of the current Bankruptcy Code, did any court rely on the *Case* dictum to approve a plan that gave old equity a property right after reorganization. *See Ayer, supra*, at 1016; Markell, *Owners, Auctions, and Absolute Priority in Bankruptcy Reorganizations*, 44 Stan. L. Rev. 69, 92 (1991). Hence the controversy over how weighty the *Case* dictum had become, as reflected in the alternative labels for the new value notion: some writers and courts (including this one, *see Ahlers*) have spoken of it as an exception to the absolute priority rule

. . . while others have characterized it as a simple corollary to the rule.

Enactment of the Bankruptcy Code in place of the prior Act might have resolved the status of new value by a provision bearing its name or at least unmistakably couched in its terms, but the Congress chose not to avail itself of that opportunity.

[After an extensive analysis of the Code's legislative history and some provisions that were never enacted, the Court concluded that there was nothing in the history "to disparage the possibility, apparent in the statutory text, that the absolute priority rule now on the books . . . may carry a new value corollary."]

III

Three basic interpretations have been suggested for the "on account of" modifier. The first reading is proposed by the Partnership, that "on account of" harks back to accounting practice and means something like "in exchange for," or "in satisfaction of." On this view, a plan would not violate the absolute priority rule unless the old equity holders received or retained property in exchange for the prior interest, without any significant new contribution; if substantial money passed from them as part of the deal, the prohibition of subsection (b)(2)(B)(ii) would not stand in the way, and whatever issues of fairness and equity there might otherwise be would not implicate the "on account of" modifier.

This position is beset with troubles, the first one being textual. Subsection (b)(2)(B)(ii) forbids not only receipt of property on account of the prior interest but its retention as well. *See also* §§ 1129(a)(7)(A)(ii), (a)(7)(B), (b)(2)(B)(i), (b)(2)(C)(i), (b)(2)(C)(ii). A common instance of the latter would be a debtor's retention of an interest in the insolvent business reorganized under the plan. Yet it would be exceedingly odd to speak of "retaining" property in exchange for the same property interest, and the eccentricity of such a reading is underscored by the fact that elsewhere in the Code the drafters chose to use the very phrase "in exchange for," § 1123(a)(5)(J) (a plan shall provide adequate means for implementation, including "issuance of securities of the debtor . . . for cash, for property, for existing securities, or in exchange for claims or interests"). It is unlikely that the drafters of legislation so long and minutely contemplated as the 1978 Bankruptcy Code would have used two distinctly different forms of words for the same purpose.

The second difficulty is practical: the unlikelihood that Congress meant to impose a condition as manipulable as subsection (b)(2)(B)(ii) would be if "on account of" meant to prohibit merely an exchange unaccompanied by a substantial infusion of new funds but permit one whenever substantial funds changed hands. "Substantial" or "significant" or "considerable" or like characterizations of a monetary contribution would measure it by the Lord Chancellor's foot, and an absolute priority rule so variable would not be much of an absolute. Of course it is true (as already noted) that, even if old equity holders could displace the rule by adding some significant amount of cash to the deal, it would not follow that their plan would be entitled to adoption; a contested plan would still need to satisfy the overriding condition of fairness and equity. But that general fairness and equity criterion would apply in any event, and one comes back to the question why Congress would have bothered to add a separate priority rule without a sharper edge. Since the "in exchange for" reading merits rejection, the way is open to recognize the more common under-standing of "on account of" to mean "because of." This is certainly the usage meant for the phrase at other places in the statute, see § 1111(b)(1)(A) (treating certain claims as if the holder of the claim "had recourse against the debtor on account of such claim"); § 522(d)(10)(E) (permitting debtors to exempt payments under certain benefit plans and contracts "on account of illness, disability, death, age, or length of service"); § 547(b)(2) (authorizing trustee to avoid a transfer of an interest of the debtor in property "for or on account of an antecedent debt owed by the debtor"); § 547(c)(4)(B) (barring trustee from avoiding a transfer when a creditor gives new value to the debtor "on account of which new value the debtor did not make an otherwise unavoidable transfer to . . . such creditor"). So, under the commonsense rule that a given phrase is meant to carry a given concept in a single statute, the better reading of subsection (b)(2)(B)(ii) recognizes that a causal relationship between holding the prior claim or interest and receiving or retaining property is what activates the absolute priority rule.

The degree of causation is the final bone of contention. We understand the Government, as amicus curiae, to take the starchy position not only that any degree of causation between earlier interests and retained property will activate the bar to a plan providing for later property, but also that whenever the holders of equity in the Debtor end up with some property there will be some causation; when old equity, and not someone on the street, gets property the reason is *res ipsa loquitur*. An old equity holder simply cannot take property under a plan if creditors are not paid in full.

There are, however, reasons counting against such a reading. If, as is likely, the drafters were treating junior claimants or interest holders as a class at this point, then the simple way to have prohibited the old interest holders from receiving anything over objection would have been to omit the "on account of" phrase entirely from subsection (b)(2)(B)(ii). On this assumption, reading the provision as a blanket prohibition would leave "on account of" as a redundancy, contrary to the interpre-tive obligation to try to give meaning to all the statutory language. One would also have to ask why Congress would have desired to exclude prior equity categorically from the class of potential owners following a cramdown. Although we have some doubt about the Court of Appeals's assumption that prior equity is often the only source of significant capital for reorganizations, *see, e.g.,* Blum & Kaplan, *The Absolute Priority Doctrine in Corporate Reorganizations,* 41 U. Chi. L. Rev. 651, 672 (1974); Mann, *Strategy and Force in the Liquidation of Secured Debt,* 96 Mich. L. Rev. 159, 182–183, 192–194, 208–209 (1997), old equity may well be in the best position to make a go of the reorganized enterprise and so may be the party most likely to work out an equity-for-value reorganization.

A less absolute statutory prohibition would follow from reading the "on account of" language as intended to reconcile the two recognized policies underlying Chapter 11, of preserving going concerns and maximizing property available to satisfy creditors, *see Toibb v. Radloff,* 501 U.S. 157, 163, 111 S. Ct. 2197, 115 L. Ed. 2d 145 (1991). Causation between the old equity's holdings and subsequent property substantial enough to disqualify a plan would presumably occur on this view of things whenever old equity's later property would come at a price that failed to provide the greatest possible addition to the bankruptcy estate, and it would always come at a price too low when the equity holders obtained or preserved an ownership interest for less than someone else would have paid.

A truly full value transaction, on the other hand, would pose no threat to the bankruptcy estate not posed by any reorganization, provided of course that the contribution be in cash or be realizable money's worth, just as *Ahlers* required for application of *Case*'s new value rule.

IV

Which of these positions is ultimately entitled to prevail is not to be decided here, however, for even on the latter view the Bank's objection would require rejection of the plan at issue in this case. It is doomed, we can say without necessarily exhausting its flaws, by its provision for vesting equity in the reorganized business in the Debtor's partners without extending an opportunity to anyone else either to compete for that equity or to propose a competing reorganization plan. Although the Debtor's exclusive opportunity to propose a plan under § 1121(b) is not itself "property" within the meaning of subsection (b)(2)(B)(ii), the respondent partnership in this case has taken advantage of this opportunity by proposing a plan under which the benefit of equity ownership may be obtained by no one but old equity partners. Upon the court's approval of that plan, the partners were in the same position that they would have enjoyed had they exercised an exclusive option under the plan to buy the equity in the reorganized entity, or contracted to purchase it from a seller who had first agreed to deal with no one else. It is quite true that the escrow of the partners' proposed investment eliminated any formal need to set out an express option or exclusive dealing provision in the plan itself, since the court's approval that created the opportunity and the partners' action to obtain its advantage were simultaneous. But before the Debtor's plan was accepted no one else could propose an alternative one, and after its acceptance no one else could obtain equity in the reorganized entity. At the moment of the plan's approval the Debtor's partners necessarily enjoyed an exclusive opportunity that was in no economic sense distinguishable from the advantage of the exclusively entitled offeror or option holder. This opportunity should, first of all, be treated as an item of property in its own right. *Cf. In re Coltex Loop Central Three Partners, L. P.*, 138 F.3d at 43 (exclusive right to purchase post petition equity is itself property); *In re Bryson Properties, XVIII*, 961 F.2d at 504; *Kham & Nate's Shoes No. 2, Inc. v. First Bank*, 908 F.2d 1351, 1360 (CA7 1990); D. Baird, The Elements of Bankruptcy 261 (rev. ed. 1993) ("The right to get an equity interest for its fair market value is 'property' as the word is ordinarily used. Options to acquire an interest in a firm, even at its market value, trade for a positive price"). While it may be argued that the opportunity has no market value, being significant only to old equity holders owing to their potential tax liability, such an argument avails the Debtor nothing, for several reasons. It is to avoid just such arguments that the law is settled that any otherwise cognizable property interest must be treated as sufficiently valuable to be recognized under the Bankruptcy Code. *See Ahlers*, 485 U.S. at 207–208. Even aside from that rule, the assumption that no one but the Debtor's partners might pay for such an opportunity would obviously support no inference that it is valueless, let alone that it should not be treated as property. And, finally, the source in the tax law of the opportunity's value to the partners implies in no way that it lacks value to others. It might, indeed, be valuable to another precisely as a way to keep the Debtor from implementing a plan that would avoid a Chapter 7 liquidation.

Given that the opportunity is property of some value, the question arises why old equity alone should obtain it, not to mention at no cost whatever. The closest thing to an answer favorable to the Debtor is that the old equity partners would be given the opportunity in the expectation that in taking advantage of it they would add the stated purchase price to the estate. But this just begs the question why the opportunity should be exclusive to the old equity holders. If the price to be paid for the equity interest is the best obtainable, old equity does not need the protection of exclusiveness (unless to trump an equal offer from someone else); if it is not the best, there is no apparent reason for giving old equity a bargain. There is no reason, that is, unless the very purpose of the whole transaction is, at least in part, to do old equity a favor. And that, of course, is to say that old equity would obtain its opportunity, and the resulting benefit, because of old equity's prior interest within the meaning of subsection (b)(2)(B)(ii). Hence it is that the exclusiveness of the opportunity, with its protection against the market's scrutiny of the purchase price by means of competing bids or even competing plan proposals, renders the partners' right a property interest extended "on account of" the old equity position and therefore subject to an unpaid senior creditor class's objection.

It is no answer to this to say that the exclusive opportunity should be treated merely as a detail of the broader transaction that would follow its exercise, and that in this wider perspective no favoritism may be inferred, since the old equity partners would pay something, whereas no one else would pay anything. If this argument were to carry the day, of course, old equity could obtain a new property interest for a dime without being seen to receive anything on account of its old position. But even if we assume that old equity's plan would not be confirmed without satisfying the judge that the purchase price was top dollar, there is a further reason here not to treat property consisting of an exclusive opportunity as subsumed within the total transaction proposed. On the interpretation assumed here, it would, of course, be a fatal flaw if old equity acquired or retained the property interest without paying full value. It would thus be necessary for old equity to demonstrate its payment of top dollar, but this it could not satisfactorily do when it would receive or retain its property under a plan giving it exclusive rights and in the absence of a competing plan of any sort.

Under a plan granting an exclusive right, making no provision for competing bids or competing plans, any determination that the price was top dollar would necessarily be made by a judge in bankruptcy court, whereas the best way to determine value is exposure to a market. *See* Baird, Elements of Bankruptcy at 262; Bowers, *Rehabilitation, Redistribution or Dissipation: The Evidence for Choosing Among Bankruptcy Hypotheses* 72 Wash. U. L.Q. 955, 959, 963 n. 34, 975 (1994); Markell, 44 Stan. L. Rev., at 73 ("Reorganization practice illustrates that the presence of competing bidders for a debtor, whether they are owners or not, tends to increase creditor dividends"). This is a point of some significance, since it was, after all, one of the Code's innovations to narrow the occasions for courts to make valuation judgments, as shown by its preference for the supramajoritarian class creditor voting scheme in § 1126(c), *see Ahlers, supra,* at 207 ("The Code provides that it is up to the creditors — and not the courts — to accept or reject a reorganization plan which fails to provide them adequate protection or fails to honor the absolute priority rule").

In the interest of statutory coherence, a like disfavor for decisions untested by competitive choice ought to extend to valuations in administering subsection (b)(2)(B)(ii) when some form of market valuation may be available to test the adequacy of an old equity holder's proposed contribution.

Whether a market test would require an opportunity to offer competing plans or would be satisfied by a right to bid for the same interest sought by old equity, is a question we do not decide here. It is enough to say, assuming a new value corollary, that plans providing junior interest holders with exclusive opportunities free from competition and without benefit of market valuation fall within the prohibition of § 1129(b)(2)(B)(ii).

The judgment of the Court of Appeals is accordingly reversed, and the case is remanded for further proceedings consistent with this opinion.

It is so ordered. Concurring opinion of JUSTICE THOMAS, with whom JUSTICE SCALIA joins, and dissenting opinion of JUSTICE STEVENS omitted.

NOTES AND QUESTIONS

(1) *The Price is Right.* Did the Supreme Court, in its long anticipated *LaSalle* decision, settle the question of whether the new value exception survived the enactment of the Bankruptcy Code? The Court did state that, assuming the new value exception does exist, a plan cannot satisfy it if it gives old equity holders an exclusive opportunity to contribute new value "free from competition and without benefit of a market valuation." But how should the market be tested? What mechanism will insure that old equity is paying top dollar? In *Landau II*, the debtor's plan gave creditors an opportunity to subscribe to stock in the reorganized debtor. Does that solve the problem? If old equity in *LaSalle* had done a better job of exposing the office building to the market and shopping it around, would the Court have approved of a new value plan? Is an actual auction required? Will termination of plan exclusivity actually encourage others to propose competing plans that ratchet up the price? If no one else is interested in bidding, does that suggest the possibility of a feasibility problem? If others are willing to bid, does that suggest that the debtor was incorrectly valued in the first place? If the debtor were not correctly valued, what incentive would old equity have to contribute new value? One incentive, as we saw in § 9.05 is tax avoidance. In many single asset real estate cases, the primary motivation for filing a petition, and for coughing up enough cash to invoke the new value exception, is to shield partners from the tax liability that would result from foreclosure. *See, e.g., In re 203 N. LaSalle St. P'ship.*, 126 F.3d 955, 969 (7th Cir. 1997).

(2) *Show Me the Money.* According to Justice Douglas's famous dictum in *Case v. Los Angeles Lumber*, to satisfy the new value exception, old equity must contribute real money, or money's worth, that is reasonably equivalent to the value of the interest retained, and the contribution must be necessary for the reorganization of the debtor. Where does the money go? Who gets it? Does the fact that equity (and possibly others) are willing to contribute new value suggest that there

is some going concern value to buy? Unless creditors have been satisfied in full, doesn't that going concern value belong to them? If the new value does go into the pockets of creditors, rather than into the business to fund future operations, can one say that the new value is necessary for the reorganization of the debtor? *See* John D. Ayer, *Rethinking Absolute Priority After Ahlers*, 87 Mich. L. Rev. 963, 1015–16 (1989); Bruce A. Markell, *Owners, Auctions, and Absolute Priority in Bankruptcy*, 70 Stan. L. Rev. 69, 97–98 (1991). Similarly, if, as suggested above, old equity's sole purpose in contributing new value is merely to forestall the tax consequences of foreclosure, what does that signify about the necessity of the new value infusion?

(3) *Back to the Future.* We approach the end of this book by revisiting one of the questions that we pondered at the beginning of it: Why Chapter 11? One of the theories that has been advanced in support of allowing old equity to "purchase" an interest in a reorganized entity is that the alternative is liquidation of the debtor. According to this theory, the new value exception, properly applied, advances the purposes of Chapter 11 by allowing a debtor "to restructure a business's finances so that it may continue to operate, provide its employees with jobs, pay its creditors, and produce a return for its stockholders," and preserve asset values. H.R. Rep. No. 95-595, 95th Cong., 1st Sess. 220 (1977).

Does the new value exception really advance these lofty goals, or is the new value exception needed the most in cases where these goals are served the least? As Justice Souter pointed out in footnote 15 to *LaSalle*, cases such as *Landau* notwithstanding, the vast majority of reported new value cases have involved single asset real estate debtors. In the typical SARE case, the debtor's only significant creditor is its mortgagee, and the debtor has few, if any, employees. The *raison d'etre* for filing is not the resuscitation of a failing business, but avoidance by the debtor's equity holders of the dire tax consequences of foreclosure. The estate has a value that is quite independent of the goodwill, managerial expertise, and personal relationships of the owners.

In the typical SARE case, permitting old equity to retain an interest and a managerial role will do nothing to advance the revitalization of the debtor, save jobs, or enhance asset values. By comparison, in the typical large corporate case, where the broad purposes of Chapter 11 might be served, cramdown is a rarity. In such cases, allowing equity to retain a small interest is accepted as the price of a consensual plan. In small business cases, creditors may allow the owners to retain an interest because the continuation of the business actually depends on the continued participation of the owners. Lynn M. LoPucki & William C. Whitford, *Bargaining Over Equity's Share in the Bankruptcy Reorganization of Large, Publicly Held Companies*, 139 U. Pa. L. Rev. 125, 144 (1990). Does this suggest that recognition of a new value exception makes the most sense in the context of cases where it is least needed, i.e., in cases where continued participation of old equity is least likely to be opposed by creditors? Does it suggest that the utility of the new value exception is exceptionally limited? *See* David Gray Carlson and Jack F. Williams, *The Truth About the New Value Exception to Bankruptcy's Absolute Priority Rule*, 21 Cardozo L. Rev. 101 (2000).

Interestingly, the National Bankruptcy Review Commission made two recommendations with respect to new value plans. The first is that a debtor's exclusive right to propose a plan terminate upon the submission of a new value plan by the debtor. National Bankruptcy Review Commission, *Bankruptcy: The Next Twenty Years, Final Report* 545 (1997). The second, applicable in SARE cases, is that the new value contribution be applied to pay down the mortgagee's secured claim so that the principal amount of debt secured by the real property is no more than 80% of the court-determined fair market value of the property. In addition, the payment terms for the secured claim must not only satisfy all requirements of § 1129, but also "satisfy then-prevailing market terms in the same locality regarding maturity date, amortization, interest rate, fixed-charge coverage and loan documentation." *Id.* at 674. The Commission's proposals are criticized in Robert N. Zinman, *New Value and the Commission: How Bizarre!*, 5 Am. Bankr. Inst. L. Rev. 477, 501–02 (1997).

[3]   Gifting Plans

DISH NETWORK CORP. v. DBSB NORTH AMERICA, INC.
United States Court of Appeals for the Second Circuit
634 F.3d 79 (2011)

Before: POOLER, RAGGI, and LYNCH, CIRCUIT JUDGES. JUDGE POOLER concurs in part and dissents in part in a separate opinion.

GERARD E. LYNCH, CIRCUIT JUDGE.

On May 15, 2009, DBSD (but not its parent ICO Global), filed a voluntary petition in the United States Bankruptcy Court for the Southern District of New York, listing liabilities of $813 million against assets with a book value of $627 million. Of the various claims against DBSD, three have particular relevance here:

1. *The First Lien Debt*: a $40 million revolving credit facility that DBSD obtained in early 2008 to support its operations, with a first-priority security interest in substantially all of DBSD's assets. It bore an initial interest rate of 12.5%.

2. *The Second Lien Debt*: $650 million in 7.5% convertible senior secured notes that DISH issued in August 2005, due August 2009. These notes hold a second-priority security interest in substantially all of DBSD's assets. At the time of filing, the Second Lien Debt had grown to approximately $740 million. It constitutes the bulk of DBSD's indebtedness.

3. *Sprint's Claim*: an unliquidated, unsecured claim based on a lawsuit against a DBSD subsidiary. Sprint had sued seeking reimbursement for DBSD's share of certain spectrum relocation expenses under an FCC order. At the time of DBSD's filing, that litigation was pending in the United States District Court for the Eastern District of Virginia and before the FCC. In the bankruptcy case, Sprint filed a claim against each of the DBSD entities jointly and severally, seeking $211 million. The bankruptcy court temporarily allowed Sprint's claim in the amount of $2 million for voting purposes.

After negotiations with various parties, DBSD proposed a plan of reorganization which, as amended, provided for "substantial de-leveraging," a renewed focus on "core operations," and a "continued path as a development-stage enterprise." The plan provided that the holders of the First Lien Debt would receive new obligations with a four-year maturity date and the same 12.5% interest rate, but with interest to be paid in kind ("PIK"), meaning that for the first four years the owners of the new obligations would receive as interest more debt from DBSD rather than cash. The holders of the Second Lien Debt would receive the bulk of the shares of the reorganized entity, which the bankruptcy court estimated would be worth between 51% and 73% of their original claims. The holders of unsecured claims, such as Sprint, would receive shares estimated as worth between 4% and 46% of their original claims. Finally, the existing shareholder (effectively just ICO Global [the parent corporation], which owned 99.8% of DBSD) would receive shares and warrants in the reorganized entity.

Sprint objected to the plan, arguing among other things that the plan violates the absolute priority rule of 11 U.S.C. § 1129(b)(2)(B). That rule requires that, if a class of senior claim-holders will not receive the full value of their claims under the plan and the class does not accept the plan, no junior claim — or interest-holder may receive "any property" "under the plan on account of such junior claim or interest." *Id.* In making its objection, Sprint noted that the plan provided for the existing shareholder, whose interest is junior to Sprint's class of general unsecured claims, to receive substantial quantities of shares and warrants under the plan — in fact, much more than all the unsecured creditors received together. Sprint argued that "[b]ecause the Plan fails to satisfy" the absolute priority rule, "it cannot be confirmed."

The bankruptcy court disagreed. It characterized the existing shareholder's receipt of shares and warrants as a "gift" from the holders of the Second Lien Debt, who are senior to Sprint in priority yet who were themselves not receiving the full value of their claims, and who may therefore "voluntarily offer a portion of their recovered property to junior stakeholders" without violating the absolute priority rule. *DBSD I*, 419 B.R. at 210. It held that it would permit such gifting "at least where, as here, the gift comes from secured creditors, there is no doubt as to their secured creditor status, where there are understandable reasons for the gift, where there are no ulterior, improper ends . . . and where the complaining creditor would get no more if the gift had not been made." *Id.* at 212 (footnotes and quotation marks omitted).

DISCUSSION

I. Sprint's Appeal

Sprint raises only one issue on appeal: it asserts that the plan improperly gives property to DBSD's shareholder without fully satisfying Sprint's senior claim, in violation of the absolute priority rule. *See* 11 U.S.C. § 1129(b)(2)(B). That rule provides that a reorganization plan may not give "property" to the holders of any junior claims or interests "on account of those claims or interests, unless all classes of senior claims either receive the full value of their claims or give their consent."

Id.; see In re Coltex Loop Cent. Three Partners, L.P., 138 F.3d 39, 42 (2d Cir. 1998); *see also In re Armstrong World Indus., Inc.*, 432 F.3d 507, 512 (3d Cir. 2005). Because the existing shareholder received shares and warrants on account of its junior interest, Sprint argues, Sprint's class of general unsecured creditors had a right to receive "full satisfaction of their claims" or at least "an amount sufficient to obtain approval from the class." But the plan provided neither, and so Sprint asks us to vacate the order confirming it or to provide other relief that would satisfy Sprint's claim.

[The court turned first to the question of whether Sprint had standing to appeal from the bankruptcy court's order confirming the plan. The debtor contended that Sprint lacked standing, because the confirmed plan did not harm Sprint's interest, which was worthless. The court disagreed, reasoning that Sprint was the holder of an allowable claim that was impaired by the plan and therefore had standing to appeal from the confirmation order. — Eds.]

B. Gifting and the Absolute Priority Rule

Sprint argues that the plan violated the absolute priority rule by giving shares and warrants to a junior class (the existing shareholder) although a more senior class (Sprint's class) neither approved the plan nor received the full value of its claims. *See* 11 U.S.C. § 1129(b)(2)(B). The appellees respond, and the courts below held, that the holders of the Second Lien Debt, who are senior to Sprint and whom the bankruptcy court found to be undersecured, were entitled to the full residual value of the debtor and were therefore free to "gift" some of that value to the existing shareholder if they chose to. . . . We recently avoided deciding the viability of this "gifting doctrine" in a similar context, *see In re Iridium Operating LLC*, 478 F.3d 452, 460–61 (2d Cir. 2007), but we now face the question squarely. We look through the district court to the bankruptcy court's decision, and review its analysis of law *de novo*.

          . . . .

Long before anyone had imagined such a thing as Chapter 11 bankruptcy, it was already "well settled that stockholders are not entitled to any share of the capital stock nor to any dividend of the profits until all the debts of the corporation are paid." *R.R. v. Howard*, 74 U.S. (7 Wall) 392, 409–10, 19 L. Ed. 117 (1868). In the days of the railroad barons, however, parties observed this rule in the breach. Senior creditors and original shareholders often cooperated to control the reorganization of a failed company, sometimes to make the process go smoothly — to encourage the old shareholders to provide new capital for the reorganization or to keep them from engaging in costly and delaying litigation — or sometimes simply because the senior creditors and the old shareholders were the same parties. For their cooperation, the old owners would often receive or retain some stake in whatever entity arose from the reorganization. Junior creditors, however, often received little or nothing even though they technically stood above the old shareholders in priority. *See* John D. Ayer, Rethinking Absolute Priority After *Ahlers*, 87 Mich. L. Rev. 963, 970–71 (1989).

In response to this practice, the Supreme Court developed a "fixed principle" for reorganizations: that all "creditors were entitled to be paid before the stockholders could retain [shares] for any purpose whatever." *N. Pac. Ry. Co. v. Boyd*, 228 U.S. 482, 507–08, 33 S. Ct. 554, 57 L. Ed. 931 (1913). "[A] plan of reorganization," the Court later stated, "would not be fair and equitable which . . . admitted the stockholders to participation, unless" at very least "the stockholders made a fresh contribution in money or in money's worth in return for 'a participation reasonably equivalent to their contribution.'" *Marine Harbor Props., Inc. v. Mfrs. Trust Co.*, 317 U.S. 78, 85, 63 S. Ct. 93, 87 L. Ed. 64 (1942), quoting *Case v. L.A. Lumber Prods. Co.*, 308 U.S. 106, 121, 60 S. Ct. 1, 84 L. Ed. 110 (1939). Courts came to call this the "absolute priority rule."

The Bankruptcy Code incorporates a form of the absolute priority rule in its provisions for confirming a Chapter 11 plan of reorganization. For a district court to confirm a plan over the vote of a dissenting class of claims, the Code demands that the plan be "fair and equitable, with respect to each class of claims . . . that is impaired under, and has not accepted, the plan." 11 U.S.C. § 1129(b)(1). The Code does not define the full extent of "fair and equitable," but it includes a form of the absolute priority rule as a prerequisite. According to the Code, a plan is not "fair and equitable" unless:

With respect to a class of unsecured claims —

(i) the plan provides that each holder of a claim of such class receive or retain on account of such claim property of a value, as of the effective date of the plan, equal to the allowed amount of such claim; or

(ii) the holder of any claim or interest that is junior to the claims of such class will not receive or retain under the plan on account of such junior claim or interest any property

Id. § 1129(b)(2)(B). Absent the consent of all impaired classes of unsecured claimants, therefore, a confirmable plan must ensure either (i) that the dissenting class receives the full value of its claim, or (ii) that no classes junior to that class receive any property under the plan on account of their junior claims or interests.

Under the plan in this case, Sprint does not receive "property of a value . . . equal to the allowed amount" of its claim. Rather, Sprint gets less than half the value of its claim. The plan may be confirmed, therefore, only if the existing shareholder, whose interest is junior to Sprint's, does "not receive or retain" "any property" "under the plan on account of such junior . . . interest." We hold that the existing shareholder did receive property under the plan on account of its interest, and that the bankruptcy court therefore should not have confirmed the plan.

First, under the challenged plan, the existing shareholder receives "property" in the form of shares and warrants in the reorganized entity. The term "property" in § 1129(b)(2)(B) is meant to be interpreted broadly. *See Ahlers*, 485 U.S. at 208. But even if it were not, there is no doubt that "any property" includes shares and warrants like these.

Second, the existing shareholder receives that property "under the plan." The disclosure statement for the second amended plan, under the heading "ARTICLE IV: THE JOINT PLAN," states:

Class 9 — Existing Stockholder Interests

> In full and final satisfaction, settlement, release, and discharge of each Existing Stockholder Interest, and on account of all valuable consideration provided by the Existing Stockholder, including, without limitation, certain consideration provided in the Support Agreement . . . *the Holder of such Class 9 Existing Stockholder Interest shall receive the Existing Stockholder Shares and the Warrants.*

(emphasis added). We need not decide whether the Code would allow the existing shareholder and Senior Noteholders to agree to transfer shares outside of the plan, for, on the present record, the existing shareholder clearly receives these shares and warrants "under the plan."

Finally, the existing shareholder receives its shares and warrants "on account of" its junior interest. The Supreme Court has noted that "on account of" could take one of several interpretations. *See Bank of Am. Nat'l Trust & Sav. Ass'n v. 203 N. LaSalle St. P'ship*, 526 U.S. 434, 449, 119 S. Ct. 1411, 143 L. Ed. 2d 607 (1999). The interpretation most friendly to old equity — which the Supreme Court rejected as "beset with troubles . . . exceedingly odd . . . [and] unlikely" — reads "on account of" as "in exchange for." *Id.* at 449–50. Even under this generous test, the existing shareholder here receives property "on account of" its prior junior interest because it receives new shares and warrants at least partially "in exchange for" its old ones. The passage from the plan quoted above states as much: the existing shareholder receives shares and warrants "[i]n full and final satisfaction, settlement, release, and discharge of each Existing Stockholder Interest."

The gift here even more easily satisfies the two less restrictive tests the Supreme Court examined (and viewed more favorably) in *203 North LaSalle*, both of which read "on account of" to mean some form of "because of." *Id.* at 450. The existing shareholder received its property "because of," and thus "on account of," its prior interest, for the same reasons set forth above.

This conclusion is not undermined by the fact that the disclosure statement recites, and the district court found, additional reasons why the existing shareholder merited receiving the shares and warrants. First, a transfer *partly* on account of factors other than the prior interest is still partly "on account of" that interest. "If Congress had intended to modify ['on account of'] with the addition of the words 'only,' 'solely,' or even 'primarily,' it would have done so." *In re Coltex Loop*, 138 F.3d at 43. Upholding this principle in *203 North LaSalle*, the Supreme Court refused to characterize a benefit given to existing shareholders "merely as a detail of the broader transaction" in which those shareholders also contributed new capital. 526 U.S. at 456. Instead, receipt of property partly on account of the existing interest was enough for the absolute priority rule to bar confirmation of the plan. *See id.* at 456–58.

Second, the other reasons that the appellees assert drove the award of warrants and shares to old equity here are themselves "'on account of" the existing shareholder's prior interest. The existing shareholder did not contribute additional capital to the reorganized entity, *see, e.g., id.* at 443 (suggesting uncertainty about whether even new capital may suffice); rather, as the bankruptcy court explained, the gift aimed to ensure the existing shareholder's "continued cooperation and assistance" in the reorganization. The "continued cooperation" of the existing shareholder was useful only because of the shareholder's position as equity holder and "the rights emanating from that position," *In re Coltex Loop*, 138 F.3d at 43; an unrelated third party's cooperation would not have been useful. And "assistance" sounds like the sort of "future labor, management, or expertise" that the Supreme Court has held insufficient to avoid falling under the prohibition of the absolute priority rule. *Ahlers*, 485 U.S. at 204. Thus, notwithstanding the various economic reasons that may have contributed to the decision to award property to old equity here, it is clear that the existing shareholder "could not have gained [its] new position but for [its] prior equity position." *In re Coltex Loop*, 138 F.3d at 44.

In sum, we conclude that the existing shareholder received "property," that it did so "under the plan," and that it did so "on account of" its prior, junior interest.

The Supreme Court's interpretations of § 1129(b)(2)(B) give us confidence in ours. Although that Court has not addressed the exact scenario presented here under the codified absolute priority rule, its two post-Code cases on the rule are instructive. In both cases, the prior owners tried to avoid the absolute priority rule by arguing that they received distributions not on account of their prior interests but rather on account of the new value that they would contribute to the entity. *See 203 N. LaSalle*, 526 U.S. at 437; *Ahlers*, 485 U.S. at 199. In both cases, the Supreme Court rejected those arguments. Although dictum in an earlier case had suggested that contributing new value could allow prior shareholders to participate in the reorganized entity, *see Case*, 308 U.S. at 121, the Court refused to decide whether § 1129(b)(2)(B) permitted such new-value exchanges. Instead, the Court held that neither "future labor, experience and expertise," *Ahlers*, 485 U.S. at 199 (quotation marks omitted), nor capital contributions "without benefit of market valuation," *203 N. LaSalle*, 526 U.S. at 458, could suffice to escape the absolute priority rule, even assuming the ongoing validity of the *Case* dictum.

203 North LaSalle and *Ahlers* indicate a preference for reading the rule strictly. Given that the Supreme Court has hesitated to allow old owners to receive new ownership interests even when contributing new value, it is doubtful the Court would allow old owners to receive new ownership without contributing any new value, as in this case. As the Court explained in *Ahlers*, "the statutory language and the legislative history of § 1129(b) clearly bar any expansion of any exception to the absolute priority rule beyond that recognized in our cases at the time Congress enacted the 1978 Bankruptcy Code." *Ahlers*, 485 U.S. at 206. The Supreme Court has never suggested any exception that would cover a case like this one.

The appellees, unsurprisingly, see the case in a different light. They contend that, under the "gifting doctrine," the shares and warrants rightfully belonged to the secured creditors, who were entitled to share them with the existing shareholder as they saw fit. Citing *In re SPM Mfg. Corp.*, 984 F.2d 1305 (1st Cir. 1993), the appellees argue that, until the debts of the secured creditors "are paid in full, the Bankruptcy Code's distributional priority scheme, as embodied in the absolute priority rule, is not implicated." DBSD was not worth enough, according to the bankruptcy court's valuation, to cover even the secured lenders' claims, much less those of unsecured creditors like Sprint. Therefore, as the bankruptcy court stated in ruling for the appellees, "the 'Gifting' Doctrine — under which senior secured creditors voluntarily offer a portion of their recovered property to junior stake-holders (as the Senior Noteholders did here) — defeats defeats Sprint's Absolute Priority Rule objection." *DBSD I*, 419 B.R. at 210. We disagree.

Most fatally, this interpretation does not square with the text of the Bankruptcy Code. The Code extends the absolute priority rule to "any property," 11 U.S.C. § 1129(b)(2)(B)(ii), not "any property not covered by a senior creditor's lien." The Code focuses entirely on who "receive[s]" or "retain[s]" the property "under the plan," *id.*, not on who *would* receive it under a liquidation plan. And it applies the rule to any distribution "under the plan on account of a junior interest," *id.*, regardless of whether the distribution could have been made outside the plan, and regardless of whether other reasons might support the distribution in addition to the junior interest.

We distinguish this case from *In re SPM* on several grounds. In that case, a secured creditor and the general unsecured creditors agreed to seek liquidation of the debtor and to share the proceeds from the liquidation. 984 F.2d at 1307–08. The bankruptcy court granted relief from the automatic stay and converted the case from Chapter 11 to a Chapter 7 liquidation. *Id.* at 1309. The bankruptcy court refused, however, to allow the unsecured creditors to receive their share under the agreement with the secured creditor, ordering instead that the unsecured creditors' share go to a priority creditor in between those two classes. *Id.* at 1310. The district court affirmed, but the First Circuit reversed, holding that nothing in the Code barred the secured creditors from sharing their proceeds in a Chapter 7 liquidation with unsecured creditors, even at the expense of a creditor who would otherwise take priority over those unsecured creditors. *Id.* at 1312–19.

The first and most important distinction is that *In re SPM* involved Chapter 7, not Chapter 11, and thus involved a liquidation of the debtor, not a reorganization. *Id.* at 1309. Chapter 7 does not include the rigid absolute priority rule of § 1129(b)(2)(B). *See In re Armstrong*, 432 F.3d at 514. As the First Circuit noted, "the distribution scheme" of Chapter 7 "does not come into play until all valid liens on the property are satisfied." *In re SPM*, 984 F.2d at 1312; *see* 11 U.S.C. § 726(a) . . . . *In re SPM* repeatedly emphasized the "lack" of "statutory support" for the argument against gifting in the Chapter 7 context. 984 F.2d at 1313; *see id.* at 1313–14 (finding "no support in the Code for" rejecting gifting). Under Chapter 11, in contrast, § 1129(b)(2)(B) provides clear "statutory support" to reject gifting in this case, and the distribution scheme of Chapter 11 ordinarily distributes *all* property in the estate (as it does here), including property subject to security interests, *see* 11 U.S.C. § 1129(b)(2)(A).

Furthermore, the bankruptcy court in *In re SPM* had granted the secured creditor relief from the automatic stay, 984 F.2d at 1309, and treated the property in question as no longer part of the estate, *id.* at 1313. In a very real sense, the property belonged to the secured creditor alone, and the secured creditor could do what it pleased with it. Here, however, the relevant property has remained in the estate throughout, and has never belonged to the secured creditors outright. For these reasons, therefore, assuming without deciding that the First Circuit's approach was correct in the context of Chapter 7 — a question not before us — we do not find it relevant to this case.

. . . .

Even if the text of § 1129(b)(2)(B) left any room for the appellees' view of the case, we would hesitate to accept it in light of the Supreme Court's long history of rejecting such views. That history begins at least as early as 1868, in *Howard*, 74 U.S. (7 Wall) 392, 19 L. Ed. 117. In that case, the stockholders and mortgagees of a failing railroad agreed to foreclose on the railroad and convey its property to a new corporation, with the old stockholders receiving some of the new shares. *Id.* at 408–09. The agreement gave nothing, however, to certain intermediate creditors, who sought a share of the distribution in the courts. *Id.* at 408.

The stockholders defended their agreement with nearly the exact logic the appellees employ here:

> The road was mortgaged for near three times its value . . . . If, then, these stockholders have got anything, it must be because the bondholders have *surrendered* a part of *their* fund to them. If the fund belonged to the bondholders, they had a right so to surrender a part or a whole of it. And if the bondholders did so surrender their own property to the stockholders, it became the private property of these last; a gift, or, if you please, a transfer for consideration from the bondholders.

> . . . .

> What right have these complainants to *such* property in the hands of the stockholders?

Id. at 400. Even in 1868, however, the Supreme Court found that "[e]xtended discussion of that proposition is not necessary." *Id.* at 414. "Holders of bonds secured by mortgages as in this case," the Court noted, "may exact the whole amount of the bonds, principal and interest, or they may, if they see fit, accept a percentage as a compromise in full discharge of their respective claims, but whenever their lien is legally discharged, the property embraced in the mortgage, or whatever remains of it, belongs to the corporation" for distribution to other creditors. *Id.* Similarly, in this case, the secured creditors could have demanded a plan in which they received all of the reorganized corporation, but, having chosen not to, they may not "surrender" part of the value of the estate for distribution "to the stockholder," as "gift." *Id.* at 400. Whatever the secured creditors here did not take remains in the estate for the benefit of other claim-holders.

As the Court built upon *Howard* to develop the absolute priority rule, it continued to reject arguments similar to the ones the appellees make before us. For example, in *Louisville Trust Co. v. Louisville, New Albany & Chicago Railway Co.*, the Court noted that "if the bondholder wishes to foreclose and exclude inferior lienholders or general unsecured creditors and stockholders, he may do so; but a foreclosure which attempts to preserve any interest or right of the mortgagor in the property after the sale must necessarily secure and preserve the prior rights of general creditors thereof." 174 U.S. 674, 683–84, 19 S. Ct. 827, 43 L. Ed. 1130 (1899). The Court rejected another similar argument in 1913 in *Boyd*, where it finally set down the "fixed principle" that we now call the absolute priority rule. 228 U.S. at 507.

Those cases dealt with facts much like the facts of this one: an over-leveraged corporation whose undersecured senior lenders agree to give shares to prior shareholders while intermediate lenders receive less than the value of their claim. *See* Douglas G. Baird & Thomas H. Jackson, Bargaining After the Fall and the Contours of the Absolute Priority Rule, 55 U. Chi. L. Rev. 738, 739–44 (1988). And it was on the basis of those facts that the Supreme Court developed the absolute priority rule, with the aim of stopping the very sort of transaction that the appellees propose here. *See In re Iridium*, 478 F.3d at 463 n.17. These old cases do not bind us directly, given that Congress has now codified the absolute priority rule. But if courts will not infer statutory abrogation of the common law without evidence that Congress intended such abrogation, *see United States v. Texas*, 507 U.S. 529, 534, 113 S. Ct. 1631, 123 L. Ed. 2d 245 (1993), it would be even less appropriate to conclude that Congress abrogated the more-than-a-century-old core of the absolute priority rule by passing a statute whose language explicitly adopts it.

We recognize the policy arguments against the absolute priority rule. Gifting may be a "powerful tool in accelerating an efficient and non-adversarial . . . chapter 11 proceeding," Leah M. Eisenberg, Gifting and Asset Reallocation in Chapter 11 Proceedings: A Synthesized Approach, 29 Am. Bankr. Inst. J. 50, 50 (2010), and no doubt the parties intended the gift to have such an effect here. *See DBSD I*, 419 B.R. at 214. As one witness testified below, "where . . . the equity sponsor is out of the money, . . . a tip is common to [e]nsure a consensual bankruptcy rather than a contested one." Enforcing the absolute priority rule, by contrast, "may encourage hold-out behavior by objecting creditors . . . even though the transfer has no direct effect on the value to be received by the objecting creditors." Harvey R. Miller & Ronit J. Berkovich, The Implications of the Third Circuit's *Armstrong* Decision on Creative Corporate Restructuring: Will Strict Construction of the Absolute Priority Rule Make Chapter 11 Consensus Less Likely?, 55 Am. U. L. Rev. 1345, 1349 (2006).

It deserves noting, however, that there are substantial policy arguments in favor of the rule. Shareholders retain substantial control over the Chapter 11 process, and with that control comes significant opportunity for self-enrichment at the expense of creditors. *See, e.g.*, 11 U.S.C. § 1121(b) (giving debtor, which is usually controlled by old shareholders, exclusive 120-day period in which to propose plan). This case provides a nice example. Although no one alleges any untoward conduct here, it is noticeable how much larger a distribution the existing shareholder will receive under this plan (4.99% of all equity in the reorganized entity) than the general unsecured creditors put together (0.15% of all equity), despite the latter's technical seniority. Indeed, based on the debtor's estimate that the reorganized entity would be worth approximately $572 million, the existing shareholder will receive approximately $28.5 million worth of equity under the plan while the unsecured creditors must share only $850,000. And if the parties here were less scrupulous or the bankruptcy court less vigilant, a weakened absolute priority rule could allow for serious mischief between senior creditors and existing shareholders.

Whatever the policy merits of the absolute priority rule, however, Congress was well aware of both its benefits and disadvantages when it codified the rule in the

Bankruptcy Code. The policy objections to the rule are not new ones; the rule has attracted controversy from its early days. Four Justices dissented from the Supreme Court's 1913 holding in *Boyd, see* 228 U.S. at 511, and that decision "was received by the reorganization bar and bankers with something akin to horror," James N. Rosenberg, Reorganization — The Next Step, 22 Colum. L. Rev. 14, 14 (1922). The Commission charged with reviewing the bankruptcy laws in the lead-up to the enactment of the Bankruptcy Code suggested loosening the absolute priority rule to allow greater participation by equity owners. *See* Bruce A. Markell, Owners, Auctions, and Absolute Priority in Bankruptcy Reorganizations, 44 Stan. L. Rev. 69, 87–89 & n.117 (1991). Yet, although Congress did soften the absolute priority rule in some ways,[1] it did not create any exception for "gifts" like the one at issue here. *See also* H.R. Rep. 95-595, 1978 U.S.C.C.A.N. 5963, 6372 (1977) (noting that absolute priority rule was "designed to prevent a senior class from giving up consideration to a junior class unless every intermediate class consents, is paid in full, or is unimpaired"). We therefore hold that the bankruptcy court erred in confirming the plan of reorganization.

[The balance of the opinion (portions of which are reprinted in § 9.09 of the text) and the dissenting opinion of Judge Pooler on the issue of standing are omitted. — Eds.]

NOTES AND QUESTIONS

In *Dish Network*, the bankruptcy judge took pains to distinguish the case before him from *In re SPM Manufacturing Corp.*, 984 F.2d 1305 (1st Cir. 1993). *SPM* was a Chapter 7 case, the creditor that allowed value to trickle down was a secured creditor, and the arrangement was made in a side agreement. Do you think the *Dish Network* judge would have decided the case differently had the gifting arrangement been implemented pursuant to a side deal that was struck outside the reorganization plan? How would the bankruptcy judge who decided the *Featherworks* case (reprinted in § 9.08[C][3] *supra*) regard such an agreement?

[4]   Unfair Discrimination

Code § 1129(b)(1) provides that even though one or more classes of claims or interests have not accepted a plan, the plan may still be confirmed if all the requirements of § 1129(a) are met — other than the§ 1129(a)(8) requirement that all impaired classes accept — and if the plan does not "discriminate unfairly" and "is fair and equitable" with respect to dissenting classes. As we have seen, Code § 1129(b)(2) provides examples of treatment that satisfy the "fair and equitable," standard, but it provides no examples of treatment that is (or is not) unfairly discriminatory. As a result, it has been up to the courts to give meaning to the term.

The commandment that a plan not discriminate unfairly is said to require that "[n]o class can be selected involuntarily for sacrifice to the benefit of everyone else," and that "[t]he plan must allocate value to the dissenting class consistent with the

---

[1] Most importantly, the Code now determines objections on a class-by-class basis, not creditor-by-creditor. *See* 11 U.S.C. § 1129(b)(2)(B); Markell, 44 Stan. L. Rev. at 88.

value allowed other classes with similar legal claims." *In re Mcorp Financial, Inc.*, 160 B.R. 941, 960 (S.D. Tex. 1993).

Suppose that a class of senior bondholders agrees to take less under a plan so that a class of unsecured creditors — whose support of the plan is desired — may recover more. Does such a plan discriminate unfairly with respect to an intervening class of junior bondholders? In *Mcorp*, the court held that it did not, explaining, "The juniors argue that, because they are not subordinate to the FDIC [the unsecured creditor], the FDIC's receiving anything before the juniors are paid in full violates the code. . . . The seniors may share their proceeds with creditors junior to the juniors, so long as the juniors continue to receive at least as much as what they would without the sharing." 160 B.R. at 960. Would Judge Gerber, who wrote the *Dish Newtork* opinion agree?

Suppose that Amphydynamics proposes a plan that provides that union employee claims and other unsecured claims will be separately classified. On the effective date of the plan, union employees will receive 75% of their claims in cash; other unsecured creditors will receive 45% of their claims in cash. This is discrimination, of course, but is it "unfair"? If this sounds familiar to you, it is because we touched on the issue of unfair discrimination when we considered classification of claims and interests. Since § 1123(a)(4) requires that a plan provide the same treatment for all members of a particular class, only if claims are separately classified can they receive differing — and hence discriminatory — treatment. For this reason, unfair discrimination and unfair classification sometimes appear to be two sides of the same coin, although they are separate issues.

The treatment described in the preceding example was approved in *In re Kliegl Bros. Universal Electric Stage Lighting Co.*, 149 B.R. 306 (Bankr. E.D.N.Y. 1992). In that case, the court found that the separate classification and superior treatment of the union employee claims was not "unfair," because the debtor's ability to operate a union shop was critical to its ability to stay in business, and the union threatened to vote against the plan, and strike, if members did not receive at least 75% of their claims. The court held that it was "appropriate" to classify the claims separately and treat them differently "if the differences in classification are in the best interest of the creditors, foster reorganization efforts, do not violate the absolute priority rule, and do not needlessly increase the number of classes." 149 B.R. at 308.

Some courts have employed the analytical approach adopted in *In re Aztec Co.*, 107 B.R. 585 (Bankr. M.D. Tenn. 1989). In *Aztec*, the court, en route to holding that a plan that separately classified a mortgagee's deficiency claim was unfairly discriminatory, proposed a four-part test for evaluating the fairness of treatment that is patently discriminatory. It suggested that courts consider:

1. whether the discrimination is supported by a reasonable basis;

2. whether the debtor can confirm and consummate a plan without the discrimination;

3. whether the discrimination is proposed in good faith; and

4. the treatment of the classes discriminated against.

107 B.R. at 590. Other courts have boiled those tests down to two: Is there a rational or legitimate basis for the discrimination? Is the discrimination necessary for a successful reorganization. *See In re Dow Corning Corp.*, 244 B.R. 696 (Bankr. E.D. Mich. 1999); Denise R. Polivy, *Unfair Discrimination in Chapter 11: A Comprehensive Compilation of Current Case Law*, 72 Am. Bankr. L.J. 191, 225 n.102 (1998). Consider the following cases. What factors would you take into account in determining the wholesomeness of the treatment schemes?

(a) A plan proposed by a debtor-hospital separately classifies the claims of doctors, malpractice claimants, and other unsecured creditors. The plan provides that doctors will be paid 100% of their claims; that the others will be paid only 30%. *See In re Jersey City Medical Center*, 817 F.2d 1055 (3d Cir. 1987).

(b) A plan proposes that insiders will receive 100% of their claims in installments over ten years, and that trade creditors will be paid 15% in cash within 90 days of confirmation. *In re Barney & Carey Co.*, 170 B.R. 17 (Bankr. D. Mass. 1994).

(c) A plan provides that claims of creditors who are also equity holders will receive less than other unsecured creditors. *In re Arn Ltd. P'ship.*, 140 B.R. 5 (Bankr. D.D.C. 1992).

(d) A plan provides that the holder of a first mortgage on debtor's real property will be paid a slightly lower rate of interest on its claim than the rate of interest to be paid to the holder of a second mortgage on the same property. *In re Buttonwood Partners, Ltd.*, 111 B.R. 57 (Bankr. S.D.N.Y. 1990).

Before he became a Bankruptcy Judge, Professor Bruce Markell suggested that the four-point *Aztec* test be rejected in favor of a rebuttable presumption that a plan is unfairly discriminatory and unconfirmable "if there is: (1) a dissenting class; (2) another class of the same priority; (3) a difference in the plan's treatment of the two classes that results in [a] a materially lower percentage recovery for the dissenting class, or [b] an allocation of materially greater risk to the dissenting class . . . ." The proponent of the plan could overcome the presumption "by showing that a lower recovery for the dissenting class is consistent with the results that would be obtained outside of bankruptcy, or that a greater recovery for the other class is offset by contributions from that class to the reorganization. The presumption of unfairness based on differing risks may be overcome by showing that the risks are allocated in a manner consistent with the bankruptcy expectations of the parties." Bruce A. Markell, *A New Perspective on Unfair Discrimination in Chapter 11*, 72 Am. Bankr. L.J. 227, 228 (1998). The Markell approach was followed in *In re Dow Corning Corp.*, 244 B.R. 696 (Bankr. E.D. Mich. 1999). The District of Delaware also appears to have adopted the rebuttable presumption approach, at least with regard to asbestos tort claimants. *See In re Armstrong World Indus., Inc.*, 348 B.R. 111 (D. Del. 2006). *See also In re United States Mineral Prods. Co.*, 2005 Bankr. LEXIS 3259 (Bankr. D. Del. Nov. 29, 2005) (separate classification of unliquidated tort claimants permissible and not unfair discrimination based, in part, on availability of insurance to satisfy those claims); *In re Hoffinger Indus., Inc.*, 321 B.R. 498 (Bankr. E.D. Ark. 2005) (where insurance for tort claims is dwindling or illusory, separate classification will constitute unfair discrimination).

PROBLEM 9.10
Cramdown of Unsecured Claims and Equity Interests

These problems are based in part on exercises appearing in the excellent article, Klee, *All You Ever Wanted to Know About Cram Down Under the New Bankruptcy Code*, 53 Am.Bankr. L.J. 133 (1979).

Assume that the consolidated balance sheet of Amphydynamics and its subsidiaries looks like this:

Assets		Liabilities	
Cash	$3,000,000	Secured Debt	$5,000,000
Receivables	1,000,000	Unsecured Debt	3,500,000
Inventory	1,000,000		
Fixed Assets	3,000,000	Total Liabilities	$8,500,000
Total Assets	$8,000,000		

Shareholders' Equity (100,000 shares of common stock issued and outstanding: $500,000)
Total Liabilities & Shareholders' Equity $8,000,000

The unsecured debt includes $2,000,000 owed to the banks and $1,500,000 owed to trade creditors. The company is believed to have a liquidation value of $6,000,000. The going concern value of the assets has not been established.

Plan (1)

Now assume that the *debtors* propose a consolidated plan that classifies and treats creditors and shareholders as follows:

> *Class I: Secured Creditors.* All defaults under loan agreements will be cured and the original maturity dates of all obligations will be reinstated. Payments will be made in accordance with the original terms.

> *Class II: Unsecured Creditors.* Creditors will receive their *pro rata* share of a lump sum payment of $2,500,000 on the date of confirmation (i.e., approximately 72 cents on the dollar).

> *Class III: Common Stockholders.* The shareholders will retain their interest in the reorganized corporation.

(a) Which classes are impaired under this plan?

(b) If the creditors in Class II vote unanimously to reject the plan, can the plan nevertheless be confirmed? *See* Code § 1129(a)(10).

(c) Assume that there is an impaired, accepting class of claims that are senior to the claims in Class II. If Class II rejects the plan, can it nevertheless be confirmed? *See* Code § 1129(b)(2)(B).

Plan (2)

The renegade Avid Paper Clip Company, a supplier of paper clips to Amphydynamics, on the basis of the same balance sheet, has proposed a plan that treats creditors and shareholders as follows:

Class I: Secured Creditors. All defaults under loan agreements will be cured and the original maturity dates of all obligations will be reinstated. Payments will be made in accordance with the original terms.

Class II: Trade Creditors. Trade creditors will receive their *pro rata* share of $1,500,000 in cash on confirmation (i.e., 100 cents on the dollar).

Class III: Bank Creditors. Bank creditors (who hold $2 million in claims) will receive their *pro rata* share of $1,400,000 in cash on confirmation (i.e., 70 cents on the dollar) and their *pro rata* share of 100,000 shares of new common stock in the reorganized company.

Class IV. Common Stockholders. Their interest in the corporation will be canceled.

(a) What classes are impaired under this plan?

(b) Can this plan be confirmed if creditors in Classes II (trade) and Class III (bank) vote to accept it? *See* Code §§ 1126(g) and 1129(b)(2)(C).

(c) Can this plan be confirmed if a majority of the bank creditors oppose it? On what ground might they object to confirmation? *See* Code § 1129(b)(1) and (2)(B).

Plan (3)

Assume that the stockholders are able to present credible testimony demonstrating that the going concern value of the company is $10,500,000. How does this advance their position? Assume that in light of the stockholder's contention that the going concern value of the company is $10,500,000, the banks propose the following plan:

Class I: Secured Creditors. All defaults under loan agreements will be cured and the original maturity dates of all obligations will be reinstated. Payments will be made in accordance with the original terms.

Class II: Unsecured Creditors. Creditors (banks *and* trade) will receive their *pro rata* share of a lump sum payment of $2,700,000 on the date of confirmation (*i.e.*, approximately 77 cents on the dollar), plus 100,000 shares of newly issued common stock in satisfaction of the balance of their claims.

Class III: Common Stockholders. The shareholders will retain their interest in the corporation.

(a) What classes are impaired under this plan?

(b) Can the plan be crammed down if stockholders vote against it?

Plan (4)

Now assume that the debtor, with the support of the creditors' committee proposes the following plan:

Class I: Secured Creditors. The plan provides that the term of the loan will be extended from 10 to 15 years, and the interest rate will be increased from 7% to 8%.

Class II: Unsecured Creditors. Creditors will receive their *pro rata* share of $2,400,000 in cash on the effective date of the plan (i.e., approximately 68 cents on the dollar) plus their *pro rata* share of $500,000 each year for the next three years, payable on the anniversary of the effective date.

Class III: Common Stockholders. The shareholders will retain their interest in the corporation.

Assume that Class I votes to accept the plan and that Class II votes against the plan.

(a) Which classes are impaired under this plan?

(b) Can the plan be confirmed despite Class II's rejection of the plan? *See* Code § 1129(b)(2)(B) and assume that the court decides that an interest rate of 12% would give Class II creditors the present value of their claims.

§ 9.11   THE STANDARDS FOR CONFIRMING A PLAN

[A]   Introduction

As we have seen, in order for a plan to become effective, it must be confirmed by the bankruptcy court. Code § 1128(a) states that "after notice the court shall hold a hearing on confirmation of a plan." The purpose of the hearing is to determine whether the plan satisfies the requirements for confirmation set forth in Code § 1129. The burden is on the plan proponent to demonstrate that it does.

The confirmation hearing is the apex of a Chapter 11 case, and the importance the Code's drafters attached to the confirmation hearing is apparent from the fact that § 1128(a) *does not* employ the phrase — used elsewhere throughout the Code — "after notice and a hearing." Remember, according to Code § 102, the phrase "after notice and a hearing" means only "such notice as is appropriate in the particular circumstances," and a hearing only if one is actually requested by a party in interest. In other words, sometimes "notice and a hearing" means truncated notice and no hearing at all. That abbreviated process is not available here. Bankruptcy Rule 2002(b) and 2002(d) require that notice of the confirmation hearing be given to the debtor, the trustee, all creditors, all indenture trustees, and all equity security holders. Moreover, the court *must* hold a confirmation hearing whether a party in interest requests one or not, and the court must take evidence to assist it in determining whether the plan passes muster under § 1129. *Williams v. Hibernia National Bank (In re Williams)*, 850 F.2d 250, 253 (5th Cir. 1988).

Code § 1128(b) provides that any party in interest may object to confirmation of a plan. What happens if no one objects? Courts disagree. In *In re White*, 41 B.R. 227, 229 (Bankr. M.D. Tenn. 1984), the bankruptcy judge found that he had "a duty to determine whether or not the plan conforms to the requirements of 11 U.S.C. § 1129, regardless of whether objections are filed." In *Seaport Auto. Warehouse, Inc. v. Rohnert Park Auto Parts, Inc. (In re Rohnert Park Auto Parts, Inc.)*, 113 B.R. 610, 614 (B.A.P. 9th Cir. 1990), the court found that it had "no independent duty to insure that the plan satisfies the requirements of the Code."

Code § 1129(a) sets forth 13 requirements that a plan must satisfy in order to be confirmed by the court. We have already alluded to several of these requirements and we have considered two at length:

- The plan must be accepted by each class of claims or interests that is impaired under the plan; § 1129(a)(8). *See* §§ 9.02 and 9.08, *above*.

- If any class of claims is impaired under the plan, at least one impaired class must have accepted the plan. § 1129(a)(10). *See* §§ 9.04 and 9.05 of this chapter.

Now we turn to the others, beginning with two key standards.

[B]   Best Interests of Creditors

You will recall from the first plan negotiating session depicted in § 9.03 that Headley's opening gambit was to offer unsecured creditors 55% of their claims in cash payments spread over a period of three years plus some stock in the reorganized company. You will also recall that the meeting ended on a sour note when Avid Paper Clip Company announced that it was proposing an alternative plan that contemplated a prompt liquidation of the debtors. Abel Avid, president of the paper clip company, has maintained from the outset of the case that liquidation would produce a faster, better recovery for creditors. Avid is only one of many unsecured creditors, and its claim represents a tiny fraction of total unsecured indebtedness. As a result, Avid's negative vote will not carry the day.

"So, let Avid vote no, that's his right," Headley muses. "We'll get a majority of claims to vote to accept and get this plan confirmed whether Avid likes it or not. Thank heaven for democracy. Right?" Headley looks at you.

Before you answer this one, re-read § 1126(c) and then read § 1129(a)(7) and the materials that follow.

IN RE MERRIMACK VALLEY OIL CO.
United States Bankruptcy Court, District of Massachusetts
32 B.R. 485 (1983)

DECISION IN THE MATTER OF THE REQUEST FOR AN ORDER CONFIRMING THE DEBTORS' FIRST AMENDED PLAN OF REORGANIZATION

JAMES N. GABRIEL, BANKRUPTCY JUDGE.

This matter arises out of the application for confirmation of the Chapter 11 plans proposed by these five jointly administered debtors. At the hearings on confirmation the Court received into evidence the testimony of the individual debtor Thomas Fay, also the principal officer of the corporate debtors, the testimony of two accountants, as well as supporting exhibits. There was substantial cross-examination of the witnesses as well as contradictory testimony by the objecting party's accountant and exhibits received in support of and in opposition to the confirmation of the debtors' plan.

Findings Of Fact

The five debtors in these cases are: Thomas F. Fay, Jr., Oil Sales, Inc. ("Fay Oil"), Merrimack Valley Oil Co., Inc. ("Merrimack"), The Fay Group, Inc. ("Fay Group"), and Thomas F. Fay, Jr. and Mary B. Fay, husband and wife ("The Fays"). The three corporations filed voluntary Chapter 11 petitions on November 18, 1981. The Fays filed on December 30, 1981.

Fay Oil, the parent company, is engaged in the wholesale purchase and sale of industrial and home heating oil in North Andover, Massachusetts. Merrimack, a wholly-owned subsidiary, is a retailer of home heating fuel in North Andover. The other wholly-owned subsidiary, the Fay Group, buys, sells, raises and races standard-bred horses. The Fays, husband and wife, reside in Windham, New Hampshire.

Since the commencement of these cases, the debtors have operated their businesses as debtors-in-possession. They have incurred substantial losses and approximately $400,000 in post-petition debt that is entitled to priority pursuant to 11 U.S.C. Section 503. Approximately $390,000 of the post-petition indebtedness represents new purchases of oil from Global Petroleum Corporation ("Global") which has extended the oil company debtors a line of credit of $500,000. The indebtedness to Global is secured by a security interest in all assets of the debtors.

The debtors' major unsecured creditor is Belcher New England, Inc. ("Belcher"), a former supplier, which alleges it is owed approximately two million dollars for goods sold and delivered and opposes confirmation of the debtors' plan.

The debtors' consolidated First Amended Plan of Reorganization ("Plan"), filed on October 5, 1982, provides for a thirty-five per cent (35%) dividend to unsecured creditors, to be paid over three years, and an extra five per cent (5%) to Belcher.

Administrative expenses ($157,000) are to be paid on confirmation together with a five per cent (5%) dividend to unsecured creditors ($159,700) and a partial tax dividend ($20,875) for a total $447,575. For the next two years the debtors must pay $339,400 each year in cash on the anniversary of confirmation. The third deferred payment is to be combined with a bonus of $136,350 to Belcher for a required fourth payment of $475,750 on the third anniversary of confirmation. Total payments required under the plan are $1,492,125 assuming that all claims are allowed in full.

. . . .

One prerequisite of confirmation is that creditors receive as much under the plan as they would under a Chapter 7 liquidation. Unless there is unanimous acceptance of the plan by each member of each class, the Court must find that each creditor:

> . . . will receive or retain under the plan on account of such claim or interest property of a value, as of the effective date of the plan, that is not less than the amount that such holder would so receive or retain if the debtor were liquidated under Chapter 7 of this title on such date;

11 U.S.C. Section 1129(a)(7). The liquidation values are found to be as follows:

Cash Inventories	$63,600
Real Estate — Business	$100,000
Real Estate — Residential	$340,000
Transportation Equipment	$294,000
Furniture and Fixtures	$10,000
Race Horses	$173,000
Accounts Receivable	$282,400
Other Assets	$14,000
TOTAL NET REALIZABLE VALUE	$1,587,900

The value of goodwill and customer list is found to be highly speculative in the light of the restrictions and covenants required for their sale to be of any consequence.

The secured and priority claims are as follows:

Notes and mortgages	$126,100
Chapter 11 fees and expenses	157,500
Priority claims under Chapter 11	113,100
Post-filing debt	394,900
Estimated Chapter 7 expenses	160,000
TOTAL	$951,600

The net amount available on liquidation is therefore $636,000 or approximately twenty per cent (20%) of unsecured debt of $3,193,975.

The plan provides for thirty-five per cent (35%) to unsecured creditors and forty per cent (40%) to Belcher for its allowed claim. The present value of said payments is twenty-nine per cent (29%) (32% to Belcher). In liquidation, payment would not be made for at least six months of conversion to Chapter 7 because creditors have six months to file proofs of claims pursuant to Bankruptcy Rule 302(e). Secured creditors and administrative claimants are not impaired under the plan. Accordingly, I find that the debtors' plan which offers creditors 35% to 40% over three years, which amounts to a present value of 29% to 32%, is in the best interests of creditors, and complies with the requirements of 11 U.S.C. Section 1129(a)(7).

NOTES AND QUESTIONS

(1)   Determining what creditors and interest holders would recover in the event of Chapter 7 liquidation requires more than an appraisal of a debtor's assets. Other factors that might have to be considered include:

(a)   *The value of property that a Chapter 7 trustee might recover by bringing actions to recover preferences and fraudulent transfers.* You may recall that the failure of the debtor to provide an estimate of this was one of the reasons the court rejected a disclosure statement in the *Metrocraft* opinion, which is reprinted in § 9.08[A] of this chapter.

(b)   *The nature, costs, and timing of a liquidation sale.* A forced sale will usually fetch lower prices than one that is conducted at less hurried pace. The costs of the sale must also be taken into account. Indeed, some Chapter 11 plans create a liquidating trust that allows a debtor to liquidate in an orderly fashion.

(c)   *Whether a creditor would have an allowable claim in a Chapter 7 case.* For example, § 1111(b)(1)(A) provides that in a Chapter 11 case, a secured claim will be treated as a recourse claim whether or not the claim is in fact a recourse claim. Thus, an undersecured creditor will hold a deficiency claim whether the creditor bargained for it or not. Code § 1111(b) operates in Chapter 11 only. The same undersecured, nonrecourse creditor would have no allowable recourse claim in Chapter 7. *See, e.g., CC Britain Equities L.L.C. v. Allen-Main Assoc. (In re Allen-Main Assoc.)*, 223 B.R. 59 (B.A.P. 2d Cir. 1998).

(d)   *The present value of property received under the plan.* If the plan provides that creditors will receive one lump sum payment of cash on the effective date of the plan, this calculation is easy. If, however, the plan provides for a series of payments over time, then, as the *Merrimack Valley* case suggests, the present value of those payments must be estimated. How to determine the present value of a stream of payments is described in chapter 1, § 1.09[A], above and § 9.10[C]. How to identify the appropriate discount rate for present value purposes is discussed in detail in and § 9.10 of this chapter.

(e)   *The value of stock of the reorganized debtor.* If the property to be distributed to creditors under a plan includes shares of stock in the reorganized debtor, the value of those shares will have to be determined, and that will require a going concern valuation of the debtor. Techniques for estimating the going concern value of a business are described in chapter 1, § 1.09[D]. *See also In re Piece Goods Shops Co.*, 188 B.R. 778 (Bankr. M.D.N.C. 1995).

(2)   *Accepting, as well as Dissenting Class Members Protected.* The best interests test is invoked if even a single member of a class votes against a plan, but it protects every member of the class, not just the dissenters. This is clear from the

reference to "each holder . . . of such class" in § 1129(a)(7), and it is consistent with the principle that all claims or interests in a class be treated alike. § 1123(a)(4).

(3) *Only Impaired Classes Need Apply.* The "best interests" test only applies to impaired classes. If a class is unimpaired under § 1124, it is not entitled to vote on a plan and its acceptance is conclusively presumed. § 1126(f). *See In re New Valley Corp.*, reprinted in § 9.04[D] of this chapter.

(4) *Undoing an Election.* As we have just seen, Code § 1111(b)(1)(A) provides that a secured claim will be treated as a recourse claim whether or not the claim is recourse or non-recourse in fact. This means that an undersecured non-recourse creditor will have an allowed unsecured claim against the debtor for the deficiency, notwithstanding that the underlying obligation was nonrecourse. The right of a secured creditor to have its claim treated as a recourse claim terminates, if the creditor "elects" to have his claim treated in accordance with § 1111(b)(2). Section 1111(b)(2) in turn provides that if an "election" is made, an undersecured claim will be treated as if it were fully secured. Thus, for example, a creditor whose $200,000 claim is secured by a nonrecourse mortgage on an apartment building worth $100,000 would, if it elects treatment under § 1111(b)(2), hold a secured claim of $200,000 and no unsecured claim.

Code 1129(a)(7)(B) provides a special rule for classes of claims to which § 1111(b)(2) applies. To satisfy the best interests test with respect to such an electing creditor, § 1129(a)(7)(B) requires that the creditor receive not less than "the value of the holder's interest in the estate's interest in the property" securing the claim. In our example, this means that the creditor receive property of a value not less than $100,000. This makes sense, because in a liquidation case, the undersecured creditor would not have the option of electing to be treated as fully secured, and its claim could not exceed the value of the collateral.

(5) *Origins of the Best Interests Test.* Under the former Bankruptcy Act, one of the requirements for confirming a Chapter XI plan was that the court be "satisfied that [the plan] is for the best interests of the creditors." Act § 366(2). This language was consistently interpreted as requiring that the plan not pay creditors considerably less than what they would receive if the debtor were liquidated. *See, e.g., Technical Color & Chem. Works v. Two Guys From Massapequa, Inc.*, 327 F.2d 737, 741 (2d Cir. 1964). Code § 1129(a)(7) is said to be derived from this standard, H.R. Rep. 95-595, 95th Cong., 1st Sess. 412 (1977).

[C]   One Impaired Accepting Class

As explained in depth in §§ 9.05 and 9.08[C][1] of this chapter, Code § 1121(a)(10) provides that if any class of claims is impaired under a plan, at least one impaired class must vote to accept the plan in order for the plan to be confirmable.

Even when related debtors are not substantively consolidated, they may file a "joint plan." This means that a single disclosure statement is filed, a single plan is proposed for all of the related debtors, and votes are solicited with respect to that plan. Since no substantive consolidation has occurred, the plan must presumably satisfy the best interests test, § 1129(a)(7), on a debtor-by-debtor basis. In other words, creditors who vote against a plan must receive at least as much as they would have received if *their* debtor were liquidated. But how is the § 1129(a)(10) requirement that the plan must be accepted by at least one impaired class applied? Some courts have held that in such a multi-debtor plan, § 1129(a)(10) requires acceptance by at least one impaired class of creditors *per debtor*. Thus, a joint plan filed by ten related debtors must be accepted by ten impaired classes. Other courts have held that only one accepting class of creditors per plan must accept. Thus, even if a joint plan is filed by ten related debtors, only one impaired accepting class is required. *Compare In re Tribune Co.*, 464 B.R. 126, 183 (Bankr. D. Del. 2011) *with In re Charter Commc'ns*, 419 B.R. 221, 267 (Bankr. S.D.N.Y. 2009).

[D] Feasibility

Chapter X of the former Bankruptcy Act required that a reorganization plan be "feasible." Act § 212(2). In one of the last cases decided under Chapter X, the court explained, "For reorganization purposes, feasibility simply means that a plan must structure a debtor to insure its viability as a reorganized company. This includes providing the ability to service any debt included in the plan and providing enough working capital for continuation of the business." *In re Duplan Corp.*, 9 B.R. 921, 924 (S.D.N.Y. 1980). Today, the feasibility principle is embodied in Code § 1129(a)(11), which requires a court to find that:

> Confirmation of the plan is not likely to be followed by the liquidation, or the need for further financial reorganization of the debtor . . . unless such liquidation or reorganization is proposed in the plan.

This is a reality check on the ability of a debtor to deliver what the plan promises. As more than one court has observed, "The purpose of § 1129(a)(11) is to prevent confirmation of visionary schemes [that] promise creditors and equity security holders more under a proposed plan than the debtor can possibly attain after confirmation. . . . [T]he bankruptcy court has an obligation to scrutinize the plan carefully to determine whether it offers a reasonable prospect of success and is workable." *Travelers Ins. Co. v. Pikes Peak Water Co. (In re Pikes Peak Water Co.)*, 779 F.2d 1456, 1460 (10th Cir. 1985); quoting *Pizza of Hawaii, Inc. v. Shakey's Inc. (In re Pizza of Hawaii, Inc.)*, 761 F.2d 1374, 1382 (9th Cir. 1985), citing 5 *Collier on Bankruptcy* ¶ 1129.02 [11] at 1129–34 (15th ed. 1984).

The factors that courts are likely to consider in evaluating feasibility include (1) the adequacy of the debtor's capital structure; (2) the earning power of the business; (3) the economic environment in which the debtor will be operating; (4) the ability of management; and (5) any other factors that would affect the debtor's ability to perform its obligations under the plan. *In re Landmark at Plaza Park, Ltd.*, 7 B.R. 653 (Bankr. D.N.J. 1980). In the *Landmark* case, which involved a debtor that owned and operated an apartment complex, the court concluded that the debtor's plan was not feasible, because the debtor had overstated income and underestimated vacancies, operating expenses, and the cost of catching up with deferred maintenance. Cases such as *Landmark* notwithstanding, there seems to be general agreement that a showing of feasibility falls way short of a guarantee of success:

As with many provisions of the Bankruptcy Code, the statutory language articulating the feasibility requirement is sufficiently broad so as to have provided a great deal of latitude to Courts interpreting its provisions. Thus, in contrast to the decisions upon which the Objectors rely, the Plan Proponents point to decisions the language of which underscores that a reorganization plan, to be feasible, need not include a guarantee of success. Rather, a plan satisfies 11 U.S.C. § 1129(a)(11) so long as there is a reasonable prospect for success and a reasonable assurance that the proponents can comply with the terms of the plan. At bottom, it is clear that the feasibility inquiry is peculiarly fact-intensive and requires a case by case analysis, using as a backdrop the relatively broad parameters articulated in the statute. In this respect, however, it is clear that there is a relatively low threshold of proof necessary to satisfy the feasibility requirement . . . . The Bankruptcy Judge must simply find that the proposed plan provides a reasonable assurance of commercial viability by a preponderance of the evidence.

In re Eddington Thread Mfg. Co., 181 B.R. 826, 832–33 (Bankr. E.D. Pa. 1995) (citations omitted).

Although U.S. courts, attorneys, and other professionals have vast experience in restructuring firms in bankruptcy, Professor Edward Altman believes that there is a persistent tendency for many firms to emerge from bankruptcy with too much debt and negative profitability. In his article, *Post-Chapter 11 Bankruptcy Performance: Avoiding Chapter 22*, 8 Brook. J. Corp., Fin. & Comm L. (forthcoming 2014), he assesses the prognosis for firms just as they exit the bankruptcy reorganization process, specifically in terms of whether they are likely to file again. This is the so-called "Chapter 22" phenomenon, which is considered in chapter 10, § 10.07 of the text.

Professor Altman believes that by using a variant of the Z-Score model, one can predict quite well the post-bankruptcy performance of publicly-owned industrial firms. He found that firms that filed another bankruptcy petition after emerging from Chapter 11 exited bankruptcy with financial profiles that were much weaker than the profiles of firms that emerged from bankruptcy and stayed out. According to his investigation, firms that file for bankruptcy a second time were, at the time that they exited their first cases, significantly less profitable and significantly more leveraged than their more viable counterparts. Professor Altman concludes that careful screening of firms that exit bankruptcy can improve on the estimation of plan feasibility and the effectiveness of the reorganization process.

[E] Compliance with Provisions of Title 11

As a condition precedent to the confirmation of a plan, §§ 1129(a)(1) and (2) require that both the plan and the plan proponent comply with the applicable provisions of Title 11. These catch-all sections incorporate requirements stated in other sections of the Code and, no doubt for that reason, have not received a great deal of attention. The legislative history states that the purpose of § 1129(a)(1) is to insure "that the plan comply with the applicable provisions of Chapter 11, such as section 1122 and 1123, governing classification and contents of the plan." House

Report H.R. 95-595, 95th Cong., 1st Sess. 412 (1977). The section has been invoked to deny confirmation of a plan that improperly classified creditors. *Bustop Shelters of Louisville, Inc. v. Classic Homes, Inc.*, 914 F.2d 810 (6th Cir. 1990); *In re S & W Enterprise*, 37 B.R. 153 (Bankr. N.D. Ill. 1984). Courts have been reluctant to invoke this section to sacrifice fundamentally sound plans on the altar of technicality. *See, e.g., Kane v. Johns-Manville Corp.*, 843 F.2d 636, 648 (2d Cir. 1988), where the court said, "Where Code violations are so insubstantial that they constitute harmless error, they do not warrant overturning an entire plan of reorganization under subsection 1129(a)(1)."

The purpose of § 1129(a)(2), according to the drafters, is to insure "that the proponent of the plan comply with the applicable provisions of Chapter 11, such as section 1125 regarding disclosure." House Report H.R. 95-595, 95th Cong., 1st Sess. 412 (1977).

[F] Good Faith

Section 1129(a)(3) requires that a plan be "proposed in good faith" and not be proposed "by any means forbidden by law." The term "good faith" is not defined in the Code. The term has generally been interpreted to mean that there exists "a reasonable likelihood that the plan will achieve a result consistent with the objectives and purposes of the Bankruptcy Code." *In re Madison Hotel Assocs.*, 749 F.2d 410, 425 (7th Cir. 1984). You may recall that in that case, which is reprinted in § 9.04[C] of the text, the debtor proposed to leave its mortgagee unimpaired by curing defaults and reinstating the original terms in order to preserve desirable interest rates. The mortgagee argued that the debtor's initial filing, as well as its plan, were tainted by bad faith. The court disagreed.

A plan proposed solely for the purpose of avoiding taxes, rather than revitalizing a business has been found to violate the good faith requirement, *In re Maxim Indus., Inc.*, 22 B.R. 611 (Bankr. D. Mass. 1982), as has a plan — proposed by a competitor of the debtor — that provided for the liquidation of the debtor. *In re Unichem Corp.*, 72 B.R. 95 (Bankr. N.D. Ill. 1987), *aff'd*, 80 B.R. 448 (N.D. Ill. 1987). In *Hansen, Jones & Leta, P.C. v. Segal*, 220 B.R. 434 (D. Utah 1998), the court held that a palpably unfeasible plan filed solely for the purpose of extending the stay was filed in bad faith, and exposed the debtor's attorney to loss of fees and sanctions. The sensibility that if a "plan is proposed with the legitimate and honest purpose to reorganize and has a reasonable hope of success, the good faith requirements . . . are satisfied," *McCormick v. Banc One Leasing Corp. (In re McCormick)*, 49 F.3d 1524, 1526 (11th Cir. 1995), suggests that there is some overlap of the good faith and feasibility standards. However, the court must make a finding of feasibility whether a party in interest raises the feasibility issue or not. Bankruptcy Rule 3020(b)(2) provides that if no objection to confirmation is filed, the court may determine that the plan has been filed in good faith and not by any means forbidden by law without receiving evidence on the issue.

If the principal purpose of a plan is the avoidance of taxes or the avoidance of federal securities registration and blue sky laws, it may run afoul of Code § 1129(d) as well as the good faith standard. Code § 1129(d) provides that "on request of a party in interest that is a governmental unit, the court may not confirm a plan if the principal purpose of the plan is the avoidance of taxes or the avoidance of the application of section 5 of the Securities Act of 1933." *See In re Main Street AC, Inc.*, 234 B.R. 771 (Bankr. N.D. Cal. 1999). In the *Maxim Industries* case, discussed above, the court raised the issue *sua sponte* under the rubric of good faith even though no government unit objected.

[G] Approval of Costs and Expenses

Section 1129(a)(4) requires that the court approve professional and other fees and costs incurred in connection with the case or the plan. In most cases these will already have been approved by the court in connection with, for example, the retention of professionals. *See* discussion in chapter 2, § 2.02.

[H] Identity of Prospective Management and Insiders

Section 1129(a)(5)(A)(i) requires that the proponent of a Chapter 11 plan disclose the identity and affiliation of any individual proposed to serve, after confirmation, as a director, officer, or voting trustee of the debtor, of any affiliate of the debtor participating in a consolidated plan with the debtor, or of any successor to the debtor. Section 1129(a)(5)(A)(ii) further requires that the appointment or continuation in office of any such individual be consistent with public policy and the interests of creditors and equity security holders.

One court has explained the purpose of the section as follows:

> [T]he court has a duty to insure that the initial management and board of directors of the reorganized corporation will be sufficiently independent and free from conflicts and the potential of post-reorganization litigation so as to serve *all* creditors and interested parties on an even and loyal basis. The fiduciary duties of the board members and officers should not be hampered by conflicts of interest.

In re W. E. Parks Lumber Co., Inc., 19 B.R. 285, 292 (Bankr. W.D. La. 1982).

If there is no proposed slate of future board members, the plan is not required to "do the impossible" and specifically identify future board members. If the selection is to be made in accordance with applicable corporate governance law, § 1129(a)(5)(A)(i) is satisfied. *In re American Solar King Corp.*, 90 B.R. 808, 815 (Bankr. W.D. Tex. 1988).

Section 1129(a)(5)(B) provides that if an insider, as defined in § 101 of the Code, is to be employed or retained by the reorganized debtor, the insider's identity and the nature of any compensation to be paid, must be disclosed.

Section 1129(a)(5)(A)(ii) requires a finding that the appointment of prospective management "is consistent with the interests of creditors, equity security holders, and with public policy."

[I] Regulatory Approvals

Code § 1129(a)(6) provides that a plan may not be confirmed unless "any governmental regulatory commission with jurisdiction, after confirmation of the plan, over the rates of the debtor has approved any rate change provided for in the plan, or such rate change is expressly conditioned on such approval." The aim of this provision is obvious. It is to prevent Chapter 11 from becoming a haven from government regulation for regulated industries. *See In re Auto-Train Corp.*, 6 B.R. 510 (Bankr. D.D.C. 1980).

[J] Payment of Administrative Expenses

Code § 1129(a)(9)(A) provides that in order for a plan to be confirmed, § 507(a)(1) administration expense claims and § 507(a)(2) "involuntary gap" claims must be paid in full, in cash on the effective date of the plan — unless an individual claim holder agrees to different treatment. Administrative expense claims include monies owed for goods and services supplied to the debtor in the ordinary course of business after the filing, most taxes incurred by the debtor, and compensation owed to any trustee or examiner and compensation owed to any professional persons employed by a trustee, debtor, or creditors' committee. Involuntary gap claims arise from debts incurred in the ordinary course of business by a debtor after an involuntary petition is filed against it, but before an order for relief is entered. You may recall that under Code § 1123(a)(1), claims which fall into these categories need not be separately classified. Section 1129(a)(9)(A) is the reason. *See In re Polytherm Indus., Inc.*, 33 B.R. 823 (W.D. Wis. 1983).

Suppose that during the pendency of the case, the debtor purchases, on standard credit terms, component parts from a supplier. Does § 1129(a)(9)(A) mean that, even if payment for the shipment does not actually come due until after the effective date of the plan, payment must be made on the effective date? The answer appears to be yes, because such a claim is an administrative expense. This result can be avoided by setting an effective date that is past the time that such payments come due, or by inserting a plan provision which provides that "in the absence of objection such claims will be paid in the ordinary course of business." *See* ¶ 1129.02[8] *Collier on Bankruptcy* (16th ed. Rev. 2009).

Section 1129(a)(9)(B) treats holders of, among other things, § 507(a)(3) priority wage claims, § 507(a)(4) priority employee benefit plan claims, and § 507(a)(6) priority consumer deposit claims a little differently. This subsection requires that these types of claims be paid in full in cash on the effective date of the plan, unless a majority of holders in each class agree to accept deferred payments. Since a majority may bind a minority, these claims must be separately classified.

Finally, § 1129(a)(9)(C) authorizes a debtor to stretch out, for a period not to exceed five years measured from the date of the order for relief, repayment of the kinds of unsecured priority tax claims described in § 507(a)(7).

Deferred payments made under § 1129(a)(9)(B) or (C) must conform to the same valuation standard that governs deferred payments to dissenting classes of general unsecured creditors under the cramdown provision, § 1129(b)(2)(B). In other words, the sum of the deferred payments must have a present value at the effective date of the plan that would equal the amount of the allowed claim. Methods of calculating a discount rate that will produce the appropriate recovery are described in detail in chapter 1, § 1.09 and § 9.10 of this chapter. *See also In re Fi-Hi Pizza, Inc.*, 40 B.R. 258, 11 B.C.D. 1201 (Bankr. D. Mass. 1984).

Notwithstanding the foregoing, § 1129(a)(9)(C) provides that the deferred payment scheme must be in a "manner not less favorable than the most favored nonpriority unsecured claim provided by the plan," other than payments to members of so-called convenience classes created pursuant to § 1122(b). So, for example, if holders of unsecured nonpriority trade claims are to be paid in a stream of deferred cash payments over a period of four years, priority unsecured tax claims must also be paid over a period of four years or less, even though the Code otherwise permits a five-year stretch-out.

Section 1129(a)(9)(D), which was added by BAPCPA, requires the plan to treat secured tax claims in the same manner as unsecured tax claims, if but for the fact that they are secured, the claims would have the same characteristics as an unsecured priority tax claim under § 507(a)(8).

[K]   Payment of United States Trustee System Fees

Code section 1129(a)(12) requires that fees assessed pursuant to 28 U.S.C. § 1930, to fund the United States Trustee system, be paid prior to confirmation or that the plan provide that they will be paid on the effective date of the plan.

[L]   Payment of Certain Retiree Benefits

As we saw in chapter 7, Bankruptcy Code § 1114 prohibits a debtor from unilaterally terminating or modifying certain benefits for retired employees. These include medical and disability insurance benefits, among others. It also provides that a debtor in possession "shall timely pay and shall not modify any retiree benefits." § 1114(e). Section 1129(a)(13) dovetails with § 1114. It requires a plan to provide for the continued payment of such benefits.

§ 9.12   PREPACKAGED CHAPTER 11 CASES

You undoubtedly recall that at the beginning of this book, Amphydynamics tried to avoid the necessity of filing a Chapter 11 petition by negotiating an out-of-court restructuring — a so-called "workout" — with creditors. Headley and Carol Charisma had several reasons for wanting to avoid Chapter 11:

- They were afraid that they would lose control of the case, and the business, if a trustee were appointed.

- They were concerned about the cost of a protracted Chapter 11 case.

- They were worried about the stigma of bankruptcy and the possible erosion of creditor and customer confidence.

- They were concerned that a creditor or other party might propose a plan that provided for the sale or liquidation of the business.

We also saw that as advantageous as workouts might be, they do not always work out, and that some debtors need the assistance of tools that are not available outside of bankruptcy — such as the relief afforded by the automatic stay and the power to bind holdout creditors, to achieve their rehabilitative goals.

Now that we are familiar with the promise and the perils of Chapter 11, the time has come to take note of the fact that there is a technique that blends elements of an out-of-court workout with a Chapter 11 filing that can enable debtors to reduce the risks associated with a traditional Chapter 11 case, enhance their prospects of exiting Chapter 11 successfully, and still provide some of the economies of an extrajudicial workout. The technique is known as a "prepackaged Chapter 11 case" or "prepack."

The essence of a prepack is that a reorganization plan is negotiated and voted on *before* the debtor commences its Chapter 11 case. The court is asked to confirm the plan immediately after the case is commenced. If all goes according to design, the process is faster, cheaper, and carries less stigma than a conventional filing. In a prepackaged case, the time actually spent in Chapter 11 can be less than 30 days, although 45 to 90 days is more typical. Of course, these time periods do not include the time spent prior to filing negotiating and drafting the plan and soliciting acceptances.

The key to the prepack process is Code § 1126(b). It provides that acceptances and rejections obtained prior to the filing of a Chapter 11 petition are valid and binding, if:

> (1) the solicitation of such acceptance or rejection was in compliance with any applicable nonbankruptcy law, rule, or regulation governing the adequacy of disclosure in connection with such solicitation; or

> (2) if there is not any such law, rule, or regulation, such acceptance or rejection was solicited after disclosure to such holder of adequate information as defined in section 1125(a) of [the Code].

There are two types of prepackaged cases and a third variation on the prepack scheme.

Single Track Fully Prepackaged Case

In a fully prepackaged or "single track" case, the debtor negotiates and drafts a Chapter 11 plan and disclosure statement. Then the debtor solicits votes on the plan. Once it has solicited enough votes to insure acceptance of the plan, it commences a Chapter 11 case for the purpose of having the plan confirmed.

Dual Track Fully Prepackaged Cases

In order to understand how dual track cases work, a little background is helpful. Typically, when a debtor attempts an out-of-court restructuring of public debt instruments, it offers to exchange new securities with different payment terms for the old securities. This is known as an "exchange offer."

Most publicly held debt instruments by their terms cannot be modified without the consent of all debt holders. Obtaining unanimous consent can be very difficult for at least two reasons. One is that the holders are often difficult to identify, because the debt is held in "street name" by brokers. Another is that small holders have no incentive to agree to a restructuring, because they are aware that if they hold out, they must either be cashed out or paid in accordance with the original terms. Typically, debtors will condition an exchange offer on the consent of at least 90 to 95% of the holders, on the theory that a small dissenting minority can be accommodated. In contrast, in Chapter 11, a debtor needs to obtain only a majority of the number and at least two-thirds of the amount of claims actually voted to confirm a Chapter 11 debt restructuring plan. Code §§ 1126(c), 1129(a)(8).

Indeed, a debtor may even be able to cram a plan down if the required majorities fail to accept. Code § 1129(b)(2). When a debtor undertakes a "dual track" prepackaged case, it makes an exchange offer, but declares that if a stated percentage of acceptances (say 95%) is not received, the debtor will file a Chapter 11 petition. In that event, acceptances that were received prior to the Chapter 11 filing will be treated as acceptances of a reorganization plan embodying the terms of the exchange offer. If the debtor manages to secure enough acceptances, it avoids Chapter 11 altogether. If the debtor secures only enough acceptances to confirm a Chapter 11 plan, it does not avoid filing, but it can shorten the time it spends in Chapter 11 and, moreover, bind the holdouts to the terms of the exchange offer without having to buy them out. For an example of a dual track case, *see In re Sunshine Precious Metals, Inc.*, 142 B.R. 918 (Bankr. D. Idaho 1992).

The prepack approach, though expeditious, is neither cost- nor risk-free.

Code § 1126(b) provides that votes solicited prior to filing are valid and binding if the solicitation was in compliance with applicable nonbankruptcy law, or, in the absence of any applicable nonbankruptcy law, the vote was solicited in compliance with the Code's disclosure requirements. Although there is no nonbankruptcy law that expressly applies to Chapter 11 plans, the antifraud provisions of the securities laws would appear to apply to a prepackaged plan that proposes the exchange or issuance of securities. Thus, in many prepack cases, the prudent course will be to satisfy both nonbankruptcy and Bankruptcy Code disclosure standards. A debtor soliciting votes prepetition may have to comply with applicable registration and disclosure requirements under the Securities Act of 1933, the Securities Exchange Act of 1934, and state securities and blue sky laws.

In addition, the debtor will have to comply with the more flexible, but inconsistent disclosure standards imposed by the Code. As we saw earlier in this chapter, Congress adopted a flexible standard for judging the sufficiency of information that is provided to claim and interest holders before they vote on a plan. Code § 1125(b,) requires that they receive a disclosure statement that has been approved by the court as containing "adequate information," and § 1125(d) provides that whether a disclosure statement contains "adequate information" is not governed by nonbankruptcy law.

If a bankruptcy court finds that prepetition disclosure was inadequate or that the prepetition solicitation process was defective, it may order the debtor to cure the problem and repeat the process, defeating the purpose of a prepack. *See In re Southland Corp.*, 124 B.R. 211 (Bankr. N.D. Tex. 1991). In *Vista Del Mar Assocs., Inc. v. West Coast Land Fund (In re Vista Del Mar Assocs., Inc.)*, 181 B.R. 422

(B.A.P. 9th Cir. 1995), the debtor filed a petition with a prepackaged plan and disclosure statement. The court found that the statement was inadequate and ordered the debtor to revise it. Meanwhile, a creditor filed a competing plan and disclosure statement. The court approved the creditor's disclosure statement, but not the debtor's, and ultimately confirmed the creditor's plan, which provided for the liquidation of the debtor.

Bankruptcy Rule 3018(b), which implements Code § 1126(b), provides that prepetition votes will not be binding if "an unreasonably short time was prescribed for . . . creditors and equity security holders to accept or reject the plan." In *In re Southland Corp.*, 124 B.R. 211 (Bankr. N.D. Tex. 1991), the court found that eight days for responding to a solicitation fell into the "unreasonably short" amount of time category.

Another problem is potential liability under the securities laws. Code § 1125(e) provides a "safe harbor" from liability under federal and state securities laws for those who solicit votes on a Chapter 11 plan in good faith and in compliance with the Code. Whether the § 1125(e) safe harbor protects those who solicit votes prepetition is not clear. The title of § 1125, "Postpetition disclosure and solicitation," suggests that it does not. Yet, by its terms, § 1125(e) applies to *all* solicitations conducted in good faith an in compliance with other provisions of the Code.

The Bankruptcy Review Commission has recommended that the Bankruptcy Code disclosure requirements be applied to prepetition solicitations conducted within 120 days prior to filing a Chapter 11 petition. National Bankruptcy Review Commission, *Bankruptcy: The Next Twenty Years, Final Report 589* (1997).

Prenegotiated Plans

Debtors who want to eliminate the risk that a court will decide that a prepetition solicitation was defective might employ a variation on the prepack technique, known as a prenegotiated plan. After the debtor and its claim and interest holders have negotiated the terms of a plan, but before votes are solicited, the debtor files a Chapter 11 petition along with its plan and disclosure statement. The debtor immediately requests that the court approve the disclosure statement. Once the disclosure statement is approved, the debtor solicits votes on the plan. This approach differs from the single track, fully prepackaged case in that the debtor commences the Chapter 11 case with no assurance that creditors will actually vote to accept the plan. This process is also likely to take longer, because, once the debtor files a petition, it cannot solicit votes until the court approves a disclosure statement. Code § 1125(b). Thus, the process begins on a prepackaged fast track, but then converts to a traditional slow track. The Bankruptcy Review Commission has recommended a partial solution to this problem by proposing that if a debtor started to solicit votes from any class of claim or interest holders prior to filing its Chapter 11 petition, the debtor may continue to solicit votes from members of that class even before the court approves the disclosure statement. National Bankruptcy Review Commission, *Bankruptcy: The Next Twenty Years, Final Report 595* (1997).

Finally, those who are contemplating a prepackaged case need to keep in mind that a prepackaged plan must satisfy the same confirmation standards as a conventional plan. For example, a prepackaged plan is subject to attack on the grounds that it is not feasible, or in the best interests of creditors, or that it employs an improper classification scheme, or is unfairly discriminatory.

When all is said and done, the conventional wisdom is that a prepackaged case works best "only in those situations in which the debtor's financial distress primarily is traceable to burdensome debt levels and the company does not need a comprehensive rehabilitation of its business operations."

In other words, if a debtor needs the assistance of too many of the tools that are available only after filing a Chapter 11 petition, such as the power to reject executory contracts, or subordinate existing indebtedness, or renegotiate collective bargaining agreements, or avoid problematic transfers, the prepackaged approach is not the solution. The use of those tools is likely to result in litigation that would frustrate the principal benefit of a prepackaged case by prolonging the debtor's time in Chapter 11.

Chapter 10

THE EFFECT OF CONFIRMATION: POST CONFIRMATION CONCERNS

§ 10.01 THE EFFECT OF PLAN CONFIRMATION

"That's it, we're confirmed. We're home free!" Headley manages to say between breaths. Headley insisted that you and Carol join him for a three-mile run. He said he needed to burn off all the cortisol he's been pumping during these last tense weeks.

"Headley," you gasp — long hours under the florescent lights have taken their toll — "Confirmation does certainly mark the highpoint of a Chapter 11 case, but it doesn't mark the end of it."

"That's right," Carol says. "Many things go on — and I hate to say it, many things can go wrong — even after a plan is confirmed."

Headley stops. "Alright. Why don't we catch our breaths while you tell me exactly what we mean when we say that a plan is confirmed. Then we can talk about what can go on and what can go wrong."

[A] A Confirmed Plan Binds All Parties; Code § 1141(a)

You begin by reminding Headley that at the beginning of this process, when you and he and Carol were contemplating how to salvage their troubled business, one of the options that you and he considered was an out-of-court restructuring, or workout. Ultimately, the workout idea had to be discarded as unworkable, because Headley doubted that he could get a sufficient number of creditors to sign on. At that point you suggested that Headley consider the Chapter 11 alternative, because, as you correctly observed, "Chapter 11 enables a debtor to develop a debt restructuring plan that may bind even creditors who do not accept it." Code § 1141(a) is the reason. Generally, § 1141(a) provides that the provisions of a confirmed plan are binding on the debtor, creditors, and equity security holders, whether or not their claims or interests are impaired by the plan and whether or not they voted in favor of the plan. In other words, a confirmed plan has res judicata effect:

> An arrangement confirmed by a bankruptcy court has the effect of a
> judgment rendered by a district court . . . and any attempt by the parties
> or those in privity with them to relitigate any of the matters that were
> raised or could have been raised therein is barred under the doctrine of res
> judicata.

Miller v. Meinhard-Commercial Corp., 462 F.2d 358, 360 (5th Cir. 1972). *See also Stoll v. Gottlieb*, 305 U.S. 165 (1938); and *Republic Supply Co. v. Shoaf*, 815 F.2d 1046, discussed in § 9.04 of this text. In the opinion that follows, the Supreme Court considers whether actions brought against the debtor's insurers amounted to attempts to relitigate issues disposed of in the debtor's reorganization plan.

TRAVELERS INDEMNITY CO. v. BAILEY
Supreme Court of the United States
557 U.S. 137 (2009)

Justice Souter delivered the opinion of the Court.

As an element of the 1986 reorganization plan of the Johns-Manville Corporation (Manville), the United States Bankruptcy Court for the Southern District of New York enjoined certain lawsuits against Manville's insurers, including The Travelers Indemnity Company and its affiliates (Travelers). The question is whether the injunction bars state-law actions against Travelers based on allegations either of its own wrongdoing while acting as Manville's insurer or of its misuse of information obtained from Manville as its insurer. We hold that the terms of the injunction bar the actions and that the finality of the Bankruptcy Court's orders following the conclusion of direct review generally stands in the way of challenging the enforceability of the injunction.

I

From the 1920s to the 1970s, Manville was, by most accounts, the largest supplier of raw asbestos and manufacturer of asbestos-containing products in the United States, . . . and for much of that time Travelers was Manville's primary liability insurer. . . . As studies began to link asbestos exposure to respiratory disease and thousands of lawsuits were filed against Manville, Travelers, as the insurer, worked closely with Manville to learn what its insured knew and to assess the dangers of asbestos exposure; it evaluated Manville's potential liability and defenses, and paid Manville's litigation costs. In 1982, the prospect of overwhelming liability led Manville to file for bankruptcy protection in the Southern District of New York.

It thus became incumbent on the Bankruptcy Court to devise "a plan of reorganization for [Manville] which would provide for payment to holders of present or known asbestos health related claims . . . and [to] those persons who had not yet manifested an injury but who would manifest symptoms of asbestos-related illnesses at some future time." *In re Johns-Manville Corp.*, 97 B.R. 174, 176 (Bkrtcy. Ct. SDNY 1989). The ensuing reorganization plan created the Manville Personal Injury Settlement Trust (Trust) to pay all asbestos claims against Manville, which would be channeled to the Trust. *See Kane v. Johns-Manville Corp.*, 843 F.2d 636, 640–641 (CA2 1988); *In re Johns-Manville Corp.*, 340 B.R. 49, 54 (SDNY 2006). The Trust has since paid out more than $3.2 billion to over 600,000 claimants.

In the period leading up to the reorganization, Manville and its insurers litigated over the scope and limits of liability coverage, and Travelers faced suits by third parties, such as Manville factory workers and vendors of Manville products, seeking compensation under the insurance policies. There was also litigation among the insurers themselves, who brought various indemnity claims, contribution claims, and cross-claims. In a settlement described as the "cornerstone" of the Manville reorganization, the insurers agreed to provide most of the initial corpus of the Trust, with a payment of $770 million to the bankruptcy estate, $80 million of it from Travelers. *MacArthur Co. v. Johns-Manville Corp.*, 837 F.2d 89, 90 (CA2 1988).

There would have been no such payment without the injunction at the heart of the present dispute. The December 18, 1986, order of the Bankruptcy Court approving the insurance settlement agreements (Insurance Settlement Order) provides that, upon the insurers' payment of the settlement funds to the Trust, "all Persons are permanently restrained and enjoined from commencing and/or continuing any suit, arbitration or other proceeding of any type or nature for Policy Claims against any or all members of the Settling Insurer Group." The Insurance Settlement Order goes on to provide that the insurers are "released from any and all Policy Claims," which are to be channeled to the Trust. The order defines "Policy Claims" as "any and all claims, demands, allegations, duties, liabilities and obligations (whether or not presently known) which have been, or could have been, or might be, asserted by any Person against . . . any or all members of the Settling Insurer Group based upon, arising out of or relating to any or all of the Policies." The insurers were entitled "to terminate the settlements if the injunctive orders [were] not issued or if they [were] set aside on appeal." *MacArthur, supra,* at 90.

The Insurance Settlement Order was incorporated by reference in the Bankruptcy Court's December 22, 1986, order confirming Manville's Second Amended and Restated Plan of Reorganization Confirmation Order).[1] Both the Confirmation Order and the Insurance Settlement Order (collectively, 1986 Orders) were affirmed by the District Court, *see In re Johns-Manville Corp.*, 78 B.R. 407 (SDNY 1987), and the Court of Appeals for the Second Circuit, *see MacArthur, supra*; *Kane, supra.*

Nonetheless, over a decade later plaintiffs started filing asbestos actions against Travelers in various state courts, cases that have been spoken of in this litigation as Direct Actions. They are of two sorts. The Statutory Direct Actions are brought under state consumer-protection statutes, and allege that Travelers conspired with other insurers and with asbestos manufacturers to hide the dangers of asbestos and to raise a fraudulent "state of the art" (or "no duty to warn") defense to personal injury claims. The Common Law Direct Actions claim that Travelers violated common law duties by failing to warn the public about the dangers of asbestos or by acting to keep its knowledge of those dangers from the public. It is undisputed that many of the plaintiffs seek to recover from Travelers, not indirectly for Manville's wrongdoing, but for Travelers' own alleged violations of state law. *See* 517 F.3d at 63.[2]

---

[1] The Confirmation Order itself contains an additional injunction barring certain claims against the settling insurance companies. Bkrtcy. Ct. Op. 286a–288a. That injunction does not bear on our decision, and we do not consider it.

[2] A true "direct action" suit is "[a] lawsuit by a person claiming against an insured but suing the insurer directly instead of pursuing compensation indirectly through the insured." Black's Law Dictionary 491 (8th ed. 2004). Because many of the suits at issue seek to hold Travelers liable for

In 2002, Travelers invoked the terms of the 1986 Orders in moving the Bankruptcy Court to enjoin 26 Direct Actions pending in state courts. The court issued a temporary restraining order, repeatedly extended, and referred the parties to mediation, which led to settlements between Travelers and three sets of plaintiffs in both Statutory and Common Law Direct Actions. Under the settlement terms Travelers would pay more than $400 million to settlement funds to compensate Direct Action claimants, contingent upon the entry of an order by the Bankruptcy Court clarifying that the Direct Actions were, and remained, prohibited by the 1986 Orders. The settlement requires claimants seeking payment from the settlement funds to grant Travelers a release from further liability, separate and apart from Travelers' protection under the 1986 Orders.

After notice of the settlement was given to potential claimants, the Bankruptcy Court (the same judge who had issued the 1986 Orders) held an evidentiary hearing and made extensive factual findings that are not challenged here. . . . In sum, the Bankruptcy Court found that "Travelers learned virtually everything it knew about asbestos from its relationship with Manville."

As for the Direct Actions, the court saw "[t]he gravamen of the Statutory Direct Action Lawsuits" as "center[ing] on Travelers['] defense of Manville in asbestos-related claims." *Id.*, at 142a. The court read the "alleged factual predicate" of the Common Law Direct Actions as being "essentially identical to the statutory actions: Travelers . . . influence[d] Manville's purported failure to disclose knowledge about asbestos hazards; Travelers defended Manville; Travelers advanced the state of the art defense; and Travelers coordinated Manville's national defense effort."

. . . .

Hence, the court's conclusion that "[t]he evidence in this proceeding establishes that the gravamen of Direct Action Claims were acts or omissions by Travelers arising from or relating to Travelers['] insurance relationship with Manville." . . . Finding that the "claims against Travelers based on such actions or omissions necessarily 'arise out of' and [are] 'related to'" the insurance policies, which compelled Travelers to defend Manville against asbestos-related claims, id., at 173a–176a, the Bankruptcy Court held that the Direct Actions "are — and always have been — permanently barred" by the 1986 Orders.

The settlement was accordingly approved and an order dated August 17, 2004 (Clarifying Order), was entered, providing that the 1986 Orders barred the pending Direct Actions and "[t]he commencement or prosecution of all actions and proceedings against Travelers that directly or indirectly are based upon, arise out of or relate to Travelers['] insurance relationship with Manville or Travelers['] knowledge or alleged knowledge concerning the hazards of asbestos," including claims for contribution or indemnification. *Id.*, at 95a. The Clarifying Order does not, however, block "the commencement and prosecution of claims against Travelers by policyholders other than Manville . . . for insurance proceeds or other obligations arising

---

independent wrongdoing rather than for a legal wrong by Manville, they are not direct actions in the terms of strict usage. Nonetheless, because the suits are referred to as "direct actions" in the decisions of the Bankruptcy Court, the District Court, and the Court of Appeals, we call them that as well, in the interest of simplicity. *See* 517 F.3d at 55, n. 4.

under any policy of insurance provided by Travelers to a policyholder other than Manville." The Clarifying Order also separately disclaims that it enjoins bringing

"claims arising from contractual obligations by Travelers to policyholders other than Manville, as long as Travelers['] alleged liability or the proof required to establish Travelers['] alleged liability is unrelated to any knowledge Travelers gained from its insurance relationship with Manville or acts, errors, omissions or evidence related to Travelers['] insurance relationship with Manville."

Some individual claimants and Chubb Indemnity Insurance Company (Chubb), respondents before this Court, objected to the settlement and subsequently appealed.[3] So far as it matters here, the District Court affirmed, but the Court of Appeals for the Second Circuit reversed. In presenting the case to the Second Circuit the objectors argued that the Direct Actions fall outside the scope of the 1986 Orders and that the Clarifying Order erroneously expands those orders to bar actions beyond the Bankruptcy Court's subject-matter jurisdiction and statutory authority. Travelers and the settling claimants responded that the Clarifying Order is consistent with the terms of the 1986 Orders, that this reading of the 1986 Orders does not generate any jurisdictional or other statutory concerns, and that the Second Circuit's prior rejection of a challenge to the Insurance Settlement Order in *MacArthur*, 837 F.2d 89, is controlling.

In its opinion explaining the judgment under review here, the Second Circuit recognized that "[i]t is undisputed that the bankruptcy court had continuing jurisdiction to interpret and enforce its own 1986 orders," and that "there is no doubt that the bankruptcy court had jurisdiction to clarify its prior orders." 517 F.3d at 60–61. It also had "little doubt that, in a literal sense, the instant claims against Travelers 'arise out of' its provision of insurance coverage to Manville," . . . and the court emphasized that "[t]he bankruptcy court's extensive factual findings regarding Manville's all-encompassing presence in the asbestos industry and its extensive relationship with Travelers support this notion" that the subjects of the Clarifying Order fall within the scope of the 1986 Orders. The Circuit nevertheless held that the Bankruptcy Court could not, in enforcing the 1986 Orders, "enjoin claims over which it had no jurisdiction," *id.*, at 61, and that "[t]he ancillary jurisdiction courts possess to enforce their own orders is itself limited by the jurisdictional limits of the order sought to be enforced," *id.*, at 65, n. 22 (internal quotation marks omitted). *See also id.*, at 65 ("The fact that our case involves a clarification of the bankruptcy court's prior order does not alter the jurisdictional predicate necessary to enjoin third-party non-debtor claims").

The Court of Appeals found that "the jurisdictional analysis by the lower courts falls short," in failing to recognize the significance of the fact that the Direct Actions "do not seek to collect on the basis of Manville's conduct," but rather "seek to recover directly from Travelers, a non-debtor insurer, for its own alleged misconduct." The Court of Appeals held that the Bankruptcy Court mistook its jurisdiction

---

[3] Chubb is a codefendant with Travelers in certain Common Law Direct Actions, and the Clarifying Order prevents it from bringing contribution and indemnity claims against Travelers under certain circumstances. *See* Brief for Respondent Chubb 16.

when it enjoined "claims brought against a third-party non-debtor solely on the basis of that third-party's financial contribution to a debtor's estate," because "a bankruptcy court only has jurisdiction to enjoin third-party non-debtor claims that directly affect the *res* of the bankruptcy estate."

. . . .

We granted certiorari, 555 U.S. 1083, 129 S. Ct. 761, 172 L. Ed. 2d 752 (2009) and now reverse.

II

The Bankruptcy Court correctly understood that the Direct Actions fall within the scope of the 1986 Orders, as suits of this sort always have. The Court of Appeals, however, believed it was free to look beyond the terms of the 1986 Orders and so treated the action as one "concern[ing] the outer reaches of a bankruptcy court's jurisdiction." 517 F.3d at 55. This, we think, was error. If this were a direct review of the 1986 Orders, the Court of Appeals would indeed have been duty bound to consider whether the Bankruptcy Court had acted beyond its subject-matter jurisdiction. . . . But the 1986 Orders became final on direct review over two decades ago, and Travelers' response to the Circuit's jurisdictional ruling is correct: whether the Bankruptcy Court had jurisdiction and authority to enter the injunction in 1986 was not properly before the Court of Appeals in 2008 and is not properly before us.

A

We begin at our point of agreement with the Second Circuit, that the Direct Actions are "Policy Claims" enjoined as against Travelers by the language of the 1986 Orders, which covered "claims, demands, allegations, duties, liabilities and obligations" against Travelers, known or unknown at the time, "based upon, arising out of or relating to" Travelers' insurance coverage of Manville.

. . . .

The Bankruptcy Court's uncontested factual findings drive the point home. In substance, the Bankruptcy Court found that the Direct Actions seek to recover against Travelers either for supposed wrongdoing in its capacity as Manville's insurer or for improper use of information that Travelers obtained from Manville as its insurer. These actions so clearly involve "claims" (and, all the more so, "allegations") "based upon, arising out of or relating to" Travelers' insurance coverage of Manville, that we have no need here to stake out the ultimate bounds of the injunction. There is, of course, a cutoff at some point, where the connection between the insurer's action complained of and the insurance coverage would be thin to the point of absurd. . . . But the detailed findings of the Bankruptcy Court place the Direct Actions within the terms of the 1986 Orders without pushing the limits.

. . . .

B

Given the Clarifying Order's correct reading of the 1986 Orders, the only question left is whether the Bankruptcy Court had subject-matter jurisdiction to enter the Clarifying Order. The answer here is easy: as the Second Circuit recognized, and respondents do not dispute, the Bankruptcy Court plainly had jurisdiction to interpret and enforce its own prior orders. *See Local Loan Co. v. Hunt*, 292 U.S. 234, 239, 54 S. Ct. 695, 78 L. Ed. 1230 (1934). What is more, when the Bankruptcy Court issued the 1986 Orders it explicitly retained jurisdiction to enforce its injunctions. *See* App. to Pet. for Cert. in No. 08-295, at 284a–286a.

The Court of Appeals, however, went on to a different jurisdictional enquiry. It held that the 1986 Orders could not be enforced according to their terms because, as the panel saw it, the Bankruptcy Court had exceeded its jurisdiction when it issued the orders in 1986. We think, though, that it was error for the Court of Appeals to reevaluate the Bankruptcy Court's exercise of jurisdiction in 1986.

On direct appeal of the 1986 Orders, anyone who objected was free to argue that the Bankruptcy Court had exceeded its jurisdiction, and the District Court or Court of Appeals could have raised such concerns *sua sponte*. In fact, one objector argued just that. In *MacArthur*, a distributor of Manville asbestos claimed to be a coinsured under certain Manville insurance policies and argued that the 1986 Orders exceeded the Bankruptcy Court's jurisdiction by preventing the distributor from recovering under the policies; the Second Circuit disagreed, concluding that the Bankruptcy Court had not stepped outside its jurisdiction or statutory authority. *See* 837 F.2d at 91–94. But once the 1986 Orders became final on direct review (whether or not proper exercises of bankruptcy court jurisdiction and power), they became res judicata to the " 'parties and those in privity with them, not only as to every matter which was offered and received to sustain or defeat the claim or demand, but as to any other admissible matter which might have been offered for that purpose.' "

. . . .

Those orders are not any the less preclusive because the attack is on the Bankruptcy Court's conformity with its subject-matter jurisdiction, for "[e]ven subject-matter jurisdiction . . . may not be attacked collaterally." *Kontrick v. Ryan*, 540 U.S. 443, 455, n. 9, 124 S. Ct. 906, 157 L. Ed. 2d 867 (2004). *See also Chicot County Drainage Dist. v. Baxter State Bank*, 308 U.S. 371, 376, 60 S. Ct. 317, 84 L. Ed. 329 (1940) ("[Federal courts] are courts with authority, when parties are brought before them in accordance with the requirements of due process, to determine whether or not they have jurisdiction to entertain the cause and for this purpose to construe and apply the statute under which they are asked to act. Their determinations of such questions, while open to direct review, may not be assailed collaterally"). So long as respondents or those in privity with them were parties to the Manville bankruptcy proceeding, and were given a fair chance to challenge the Bankruptcy Court's subject-matter jurisdiction, they cannot challenge it now by resisting enforcement of the 1986 Orders. *See Insurance Corp. of Ireland v. Compagnie des Bauxites de Guinee*, 456 U.S. 694, 702, n. 9, 102 S. Ct. 2099, 72 L. Ed. 2d 492 (1982) ("A party that has had an opportunity to litigate the question of subject-matter jurisdiction may not . . . reopen that question in a collateral attack upon an adverse judgment"); *Chicot County, supra,* at 375, 60 S. Ct. 317, 84 L. Ed. 329 ("[T]hese bondholders, having the opportunity to raise the question of invalidity, were not the less bound by the decree because they failed to raise it").

The willingness of the Court of Appeals to entertain this sort of collateral attack cannot be squared with res judicata and the practical necessity served by that rule. "It is just as important that there should be a place to end as that there should be a place to begin litigation," *Stoll v. Gottlieb,* 305 U.S. 165, 172, 59 S. Ct. 134, 83 L. Ed. 104 (1938), and the need for finality forbids a court called upon to enforce a final order to "tunnel back . . . for the purpose of reassessing prior jurisdiction de novo," *Finova Capital Corp. v. Larson Pharmacy Inc. (In re Optical Techs., Inc.),* 425 F.3d 1294, 1308 (CA11 2005). If the law were otherwise, and "courts could evaluate the jurisdiction that they may or may not have had to issue a final judgment, the rules of res judicata . . . would be entirely short-circuited." *Id.,* at 1307; *see Willy v. Coastal Corp.,* 503 U.S. 131, 137, 112 S. Ct. 1076, 117 L. Ed. 2d 280 (1992) ("[T]he practical concern with providing an end to litigation justifies a rule preventing collateral attack on subject-matter jurisdiction"). Almost a quarter-century after the 1986 Orders were entered, the time to prune them is over.

III

Our holding is narrow. We do not resolve whether a bankruptcy court, in 1986 or today, could properly enjoin claims against nondebtor insurers that are not derivative of the debtor's wrongdoing. As the Court of Appeals noted, in 1994 Congress explicitly authorized bankruptcy courts, in some circumstances, to enjoin actions against a nondebtor "alleged to be directly or indirectly liable for the conduct of, claims against, or demands on the debtor to the extent such alleged liability . . . arises by reason of . . . the third party's provision of insurance to the debtor or a related party," and to channel those claims to a trust for payments to asbestos claimants. 11 U.S.C. § 524 (g)(4)(A)(ii). On direct review today, a channeling injunction of the sort issued by the Bankruptcy Court in 1986 would have to be measured against the requirements of § 524 (to begin with, at least). But owing to the posture of this litigation, we do not address the scope of an injunction authorized by that section.

. . . .

IV

We reverse the judgment of the Court of Appeals and remand the case for further proceedings consistent with this opinion.

[The dissenting opinion of Mr. Justice Stevens is omitted.]

[B]   A Confirmed Plan Vests Property in the Reorganized Debtor; Code § 1141(b), (c)

Consistent with the notion that confirmation marks the birth — or rebirth — of a reorganized debtor, Code § 1141(b) makes clear that except as otherwise provided in the plan or in the order confirming it, confirmation of a plan vests all property of the estate in the new, reorganized debtor. Moreover, § 1141(c) provides that "the property *dealt with by the plan* is free and clear of all claims and interests of creditors, equity security holders, and of general partners of the debtor." The meaning of the phrase "dealt with by the plan," and the effect of § 1141(c) on holders of secured claims are considered in the opinion that follows.

IN RE PENROD
United States Court of Appeals for the Seventh Circuit
50 F.3d 459 (1995)

Posner, Chief Judge.

This appeal raises an issue of bankruptcy law that one might have supposed had been settled long ago. It is whether, when a plan of reorganization makes provision for the payment of a secured creditor's claim but does not say whether the creditor's security interest (lien) is extinguished, the security interest survives, in accordance with the old saw that "liens pass through bankruptcy unaffected."

Hog farmers named Penrod executed a promissory note to Mutual Guaranty Corporation (actually to its predecessor, but we can ignore that detail) for $150,000, secured by the Penrods' hogs. A year later, the Penrods filed for bankruptcy under Chapter 11, owing Mutual Guaranty $132,000. Mutual Guaranty filed a proof of claim in the bankruptcy proceeding. The Penrods, neither objecting to the claim nor questioning the validity of Mutual Guaranty's lien, filed a plan of reorganization which designated Mutual Guaranty as a "Class 3 creditor" — in fact as the only Class 3 creditor. Class 3 creditors, the plan states, "will be paid in full, with interest at the rate of eleven percent (11 percent) per annum. Payments to this Class shall be paid on a monthly basis commencing sixty (60) days after Confirmation. Furthermore, said payments shall be based upon a seven (7) year amortization." That is all that the plan, or the order confirming it, says about Mutual Guaranty's interest.

Shortly after the plan went into effect, the Penrods' hogs became infected with "pseudo-rabies" virus, a disease of the reproductive system that causes the females infected with it to miscarry. Hogs so stricken cannot be kept for breeding purposes; all they are good for is food (human food, we note with some anxiety). So the Penrods sold their hogs for slaughter — without remitting the proceeds to Mutual Guaranty, as the security agreement accompanying the promissory note had required. Mutual Guaranty brought suit in a state court to enforce a lien in the proceeds. The Penrods responded by asking the bankruptcy court to hold Mutual Guaranty in contempt for violating the order confirming the plan of reorganization, which the Penrods claim extinguished Mutual Guaranty's lien. The bankruptcy court agreed that the lien had been extinguished and enjoined (the court's term was "precluded," but as far as we can tell it meant the same thing) Mutual Guaranty from attempting to enforce it. The district court affirmed.

A secured creditor can bypass his debtor's bankruptcy proceeding and enforce his lien in the usual way, which would normally be by bringing a foreclosure action in a state court. This is the principle that liens pass through bankruptcy unaffected.

Long v. Bullard, 117 U.S. 617, 620–21, 6 S. Ct. 917, 29 L. Ed. 1004 (1886); *Dewsnup v. Timm*, 502 U.S. 410, 112 S. Ct. 773, 116 L. Ed. 2d 903 (1992); *In re James Wilson Associates*, 965 F.2d 160, 167 (7th Cir. 1992). If the creditor follows this route, the discharge in bankruptcy will not impair his lien. *Dewsnup v. Timm, supra*, 112 S. Ct. at 778; *In re Tarnow*, 749 F.2d 464 (7th Cir. 1984). Alternatively, he may decide to collect his debt in the bankruptcy proceeding, and to this end may file a proof of claim in that proceeding. § 501(a). He will do this if he is undersecured, for in that case merely enforcing his lien would not enable him to collect the entire debt owed him. His only chance of recovering any part of the amount by which the debt exceeds the value of the lien would be to share in the distribution of the debtor's estate to the unsecured creditors. § 506(a); *In re Tarnow, supra*, 749 F.2d at 465.

A secured creditor may be dragged into the bankruptcy involuntarily, because the trustee or debtor (if there is no trustee), or someone who might be liable to the secured creditor and therefore has an interest in maximizing the creditor's recovery, may file a claim on the creditor's behalf. §§ 501(b), (c). He may participate in the bankruptcy in order to try to get the automatic stay (§ 362(d)) lifted to the extent of allowing him to enforce his lien; for the stay applies to the enforcement of liens. He may want to participate in the bankruptcy proceeding (and so may decide to file a claim) simply because he wants to make sure that the debtor's estate is not administered in a way that will diminish the value, as distinct from threatening the existence, of his lien.

The secured creditor does not, by participating in the bankruptcy proceeding through filing a claim, surrender his lien. But this is not to say that the lien is sure to escape unscathed from the bankruptcy. We have mentioned the automatic stay. If the secured creditor's claim is challenged in the bankruptcy proceeding and the court denies the claim, the creditor will lose the lien by operation of the doctrine of collateral estoppel. He may be forced in the plan of reorganization to swap his lien for an interest that is an "indubitable equivalent" of the lien. § 1129(b)(2)(A)(iii). And in some circumstances he may even be compelled to surrender his lien without receiving anything in return. See §§ 1126(d), 1129(a)(10), (b)(1). And, of course, he can consent to its discharge. The right is implicit in § 1126, and is anyway obvious. It is a frequent element of a plan of reorganization, as we are about to see.

Nothing we have said so far is controversial, and we can take one more step without inviting controversy. A plan of reorganization can expressly preserve preexisting liens, such as that of Mutual Guaranty in this case. § 1123(b)(1). Conversely, it can expressly abrogate some or all of those liens with the full consent of the lienholders; and this is common. A reorganization alters the capital structure of the bankrupt enterprise. Bondholders and other creditors, along with shareholders, exchange their notes, claims, and shares for new securities in the reorganized firm. Bondholders often give up their bonds and associated security agreements in exchange for common stock in the reorganized corporation, thus exchanging a secured for an unsecured interest. By now it should be clear that like most generalizations about law, the principle that liens pass through bankruptcy unaffected cannot be taken literally.

The question we must decide in this case is whether preexisting liens survive a reorganization when the plan (or the order confirming it) does not mention the liens.

What in other words is the default rule when the plan is silent? We acknowledge this to be a difficult question. Liens are property rights and the forfeiture of such rights is disfavored. But when lienholders participate in a bankruptcy proceeding, and especially in a reorganization, they know that their liens are likely to be affected, and indeed altered. The issue here, moreover, is what the proper rule for interpreting silence is rather than in what circumstances a lien can be taken away from someone who has expressed his desire to retain it.

We have concluded that the default rule for secured creditors who file claims for which provision is made in the plan of reorganization is extinction and is found in the Code itself. Section 1141(c) provides with immaterial exceptions that "except as provided in the plan or in the order confirming the plan, after confirmation of a plan, the property dealt with by the plan is free and clear of all claims and interests of creditors, equity security holders, and of general partners in the debtor." The term "interest" is not defined in the Code, but a lien is defined as an interest in property, § 101(37), and there is no doubt that a security interest is an interest, and it is defined as a "lien created by an agreement." § 101(51). So section 1141(c) must cover liens, and must mean, therefore, that unless the plan of reorganization, or the order confirming the plan, says that a lien is preserved, it is extinguished by the confirmation. This is provided, we emphasize, that the holder of the lien participated in the reorganization. If he did not, his lien would not be "property dealt with by the plan," and so the section would not apply. One could argue that the quoted phrase should be equated to "property of the estate," defined in section 541 to include "all legal or equitable interests of the debtor in property *as of the commencement of the case*" (emphasis added), and that at the start of the bankruptcy proceeding the liens of the secured creditors are not the debtor's property — which indeed they are not. But the suggested equation is not especially plausible. Property dealt with by the plan is property dealt with by the plan, whether it was part of the debtor's estate when bankruptcy was first declared or was tossed into the pot later. As we have said, secured creditors commonly give up their preexisting liens for other interests in the reorganized firm. A plan of reorganization that does this "deals with" the liens. Or does it? For it could be argued that the plan in this case dealt with the secured creditor's claim, but not with its lien. But this interpretation would be inconsistent with the rest of section 1141(c) — that the property dealt with by the plan is, after confirmation of the plan, to be "free and clear of all claims and interests of creditors" (and others). On the view pressed by Mutual Guaranty, the assets of the reorganized entity would continue to be burdened by secured creditors' claims by virtue of their liens even if the plan made provision for those claims.

Our suggested interpretation reconciles the language of section 1141(c) with the principle, which we have pointed out cannot be maintained without careful qualification, that liens pass through bankruptcy unaffected. They do — unless they are brought into the bankruptcy proceeding and dealt with there. The interpretation makes practical sense as well. It lowers the costs of transacting with the reorganized firm, thus boosting the chances that the reorganization will succeed. By studying the plan of reorganization a prospective creditor of or investor in the reorganized firm can tell whether any liens that creditors whose interests in the new entity are defined in the plan may have had against its bankrupt predecessor survive as encumbrances on the assets of the new firm. The cases that support a contrary interpretation are cases in which the courts were, we respectfully suggest, mesmerized by a formula ("liens pass through bankruptcy unaffected"). Oddly, none of the cases on either side is an appellate case, the ones cited by Mutual Guaranty being readily distinguishable. The secured creditor in *In re Tarnow, supra*, did not participate in the reorganization, except to file a late claim against the debtor. The bankruptcy court disallowed the lien because the claim was late — an excessive punishment — not because the plan of reorganization had dealt with the property constituted by the creditor's lien. It had not; in fact no plan had yet been confirmed. Nor had the plan in *Estate of Lellock v. Prudential Ins. Co.*, 811 F.2d 186, 188–89 (3d Cir. 1987), made provision for the secured creditor; the debtor had never even listed the property subject to the lien as an asset of the estate. In *General Electric Credit Corp. v. Nardulli & Sons Inc.*, 836 F.2d 184, 188–89 (3d Cir. 1988), the plan denominated the creditor as a "secured creditor" and explicitly recognized its security interest.

. . . .

There is nothing to Mutual Guaranty's suggestion that our interpretation raises a question under the due process or takings clauses of the Fifth Amendment because a lien is property within the meaning of the clause. It is, *United States v. Security Industrial Bank*, 459 U.S. 70, 76–77, 103 S. Ct. 407, 74 L. Ed. 2d 235 (1982), but Mutual Guaranty could have protected it by appealing from the order confirming the plan of reorganization. We recognize that since the law was not clear with respect to the survival of the lien of a creditor who is provided for in the plan without mention of his lien, Mutual Guaranty may not have realized when the plan was adopted that its lien was in jeopardy. Conceivably this might give Mutual Guaranty an equitable defense to the complete extinction of the lien, but it has not presented such a defense. It has staked its all on persuading us that its lien survived the bankruptcy proceeding intact.

AFFIRMED.

NOTES AND QUESTIONS

What pre-confirmation strategy could Mutual Guaranty have adopted to protect its lien? What language, if inserted in the plan, would have avoided the extinction of the lien? If Mutual Guaranty had not filed a proof of claim, but the debtor had filed one on Mutual Guaranty's behalf, would the analysis be any different? Should it be? In the context of a Chapter 13 case, the Fourth Circuit has suggested that where a creditor has not filed a proof of claim or participated in a case, a debtor must take some "affirmative step," such as "initiation of an adversary proceeding to determine the validity, priority or extent of a lien" in order to avoid a lien. *Cen-Pen Corp. v. Hanson*, 58 F.3d 89, 93 (4th Cir. 1995). What if the confirmed plan unambiguously provides that a lien will not be preserved? If a creditor receives notice about how the plan purports to treat — or mistreat — its claim, and the creditor fails to object to confirmation, should the confirmed plan bind the creditor? *See Winchell v. Town of Wilmington (In re Winchell)*, 200 B.R. 734 (Bankr. D. Mass. 1996); *In re Rodgers*, 180 B.R. 504 (Bankr. E.D. Tenn. 1995).

[C]   A Confirmed Plan Discharges the Debtor; Code § 1141(d)

As you know from your basic bankruptcy course, the goal of a Chapter 7 liquidation case is to provide for an equitable distribution of the debtor's property among its creditors, and, if the debtor is an individual, to give the debtor a fresh start in the form of a discharge. Accordingly, in a liquidation case, a bankruptcy trustee marshals a debtor's assets, liquidates those that are not exempt, and distributes the proceeds among the debtor's creditors. Then, an *honest, individual* debtor will be granted a discharge. Bankruptcy Code § 727 generally provides that, subject to certain exceptions, a debtor is to be discharged from all debts that arose before the date of the order for relief. Code § 523. The effect of a bankruptcy discharge is to relieve the debtor of any liability for the debts discharged and to enjoin creditors from pursuing the debtor to collect discharged debts. Code § 524. Note the emphasis on the words individual and honest. In a liquidation case, corporate and partnership debtors are not entitled to a discharge. Also, in a liquidation case, an individual debtor who is not honest — at least in the sense that he or she has engaged in the kind of misbehavior described in § 727(a) — is not entitled to a discharge. Finally, recall that even though an individual debtor might otherwise be entitled to a discharge under § 727, there are certain types of debts, that, for a variety of policy reasons, Congress has determined should not be dischargeable. These so-called "exceptions to discharge" are listed in § 523(a).

In several important respects, the Chapter 11 discharge is different, and these differences reflect inherent differences in the liquidation and reorganization processes and philosophies. Code § 1141(d) governs the scope and effect of a Chapter 11 discharge. The general rule is that confirmation of a plan discharges a debtor from all debts that arose prior to confirmation, except to the extent that provision is made for those debts in the plan or in the order confirming it. § 1471(d)(1)(A). Thus, in contrast to the Chapter 7 discharge, which reaches only debts arising prepetition, the Chapter 11 discharge reaches debts arising postpetition (but prior to confirmation) as well. According to § 1141(d)(1)(A), a claim is discharged whether or not a proof of claim is filed, whether or not the claim is allowed, and whether or not the claim holder voted in favor of the plan.

The general rule is that the confirmation of a plan discharges the debtor from any debt that arose before the date of the order confirming the plan. § 1141(d)(1)(A). That has always been the rule for corporate debtors and, until 2005, the same rule applied in cases involving individual debtors. In 2005, however, a new § 1141(d)(5) was added to the Code. Following the Chapter 13 approach (*see* Code § 1328(a)), it provides that an individual Chapter 11 debtor receives a discharge only on completion of all payments under the plan.

Moreover, an individual debtor who would not be entitled to a discharge in a Chapter 7 case is not entitled to a discharge in a Chapter 11 case either. Section 1141(d)(3) withholds the benefits of discharge from an individual Chapter 11 debtor who is guilty of the conduct described in § 727(a). Similarly, just as § 727 denies discharge to a corporation or partnership that liquidates in Chapter 7, § 1141(d)(3) denies a discharge to a corporation or partnership that ceases doing business and liquidates in Chapter 11. (Remember that § 1123(b)(4) makes liquidating plans possible.) The Chapter 11 discharge does not discharge an individual debtor from liability on the kinds of debts that are nondischargeable in a liquidation case. See Code §§ 1131(d)(3), 523. For example, an individual debtor cannot by invoking Chapter 11 avoid obligations in the nature of alimony or support owed to a spouse or former spouse. Nor can an individual Chapter 11 debtor avoid obligations arising out of the debtor's fraud. If, however, the Chapter 11 debtor is a firm — a corporation or partnership — then the § 523 exceptions to discharge do not apply. Confirmation will discharge the corporate or partnership debtor from liability even on debts arising from, for example, fraud or willful and malicious injury. In *In re Kuempel Co.*, 14 B.R. 324 (Bankr. S.D. Ohio 1981), the court held that a fraud claim against the corporate debtor was discharged and explained why the discharge exceptions do not apply to corporate debtors that reorganize in Chapter 11:

> A corporate debtor's ability to provide interested parties with a definite list of liabilities is essential to an informed judgment regarding the debtor's financial standing. To make nondischargeable to a corporate debtor debts based upon the type of conduct described in section 523(a)(2) would . . . effectively thwart the objective sought by Congress — certainty of a corporate debtor's Chapter 11 liabilities prior to submission of the plan to creditors.

14 B.R. at 327.

There are, however, some exceptions to this broad discharge. Section 1141(d)(6)(A) provides that a corporation may not discharge a debt owed to a domestic governmental unit "to the extent obtained by . . . false pretenses, a false representation, or actual fraud," or by a false financial statement. A fraudulently procured Small Business Administration loan, for example, would be nondischargeable under this section of the Code. In addition, Code § 1141(d)(6)(A) provides that a debt that is owed to an individual as the result of a *qui tam* action (a false claim action brought by a private individual on behalf of the government) is nondischargeable. Similarly, § 1141(d)(6)(B) makes nondischargeable "a tax or customs duty with respect to which the debtor (i) made a fraudulent return; or (ii) willfully attempted in any manner to evade or defeat."

§ 10.02 NOTICE TO CREDITORS

PROBLEM 10.1

Suppose that shortly before the commencement of the Amphydynamics Chapter 11 case, when Headley Charisma was interviewed by a reporter from *Mismanagement Week*, he referred to Evan Essence, the president of the union representing Amphydynamics' assembly line workers, as a "gangster, thug, and thief guilty of every crime imaginable, plus some too horrible to imagine." The next day, the statement was repeated in a press release issued by Amphydynamics. Hours after the statement was picked up by various news services, Essence commenced a defamation action against Amphydynamics in state court. The complaint charged that the company had published the statement "maliciously, willfully, wantonly, and wickedly, and intending to injure the plaintiff in his good name, and to cause the public to believe that the union was being presided over by criminals." Essence sought $1,000,000 in damages. Two days later, Amphydynamics filed its Chapter 11 petition, and the action was automatically stayed.

Essence never raised the issue of the lawsuit with Headley or the creditors' committee. Essence and Headley met face-to-face to discuss union representation on the creditors' committee, to negotiate modifications in the terms of the collective bargaining agreement, and to negotiate treatment of employee wage and benefit claims under the plan, and their relationship appeared to be cordial. Essence was not scheduled as a creditor of Amphydynamics. His vote on the plan was not solicited.

However, two weeks after the court entered its order confirming the consolidated reorganization plans of Amphydynamics and its subsidiary companies, Essence's attorneys resumed the state court action by serving notices of deposition on Headley and the vice president for public relations of Amphydynamics.

What effect, if any, did confirmation of the plan have on Evan Essence's damage claim? To what relief, if any, is he now entitled?

<h1 style="text-align:center">RELIABLE ELECTRIC CO., INC. v.
OLSON CONSTRUCTION COMPANY</h1>

United States Court of Appeals, Tenth Circuit
726 F.2d 620 (1984)

Before BARRETT and MCKAY, CIRCUIT JUDGES, and BROWN

HONORABLE WESLEY E. BROWN, SENIOR JUDGE, United States District Court for the District of Kansas, sitting by designation

BARRETT, CIRCUIT JUDGE.

Reliable Electric Company (Reliable), the debtor, appeals from a final order of the federal district court affirming a decision of the United States Bankruptcy Court for the District of Colorado that the prepetition unsecured claim of Olson Construction Company (Olson), the creditor, is not subject to Reliable's confirmed Plan of Reorganization. The bankruptcy court found that although Olson possessed actual knowledge of the reorganization proceeding in general, it did not receive adequate notice of the confirmation hearing. Thus, Olson's claim was found not to be discharged pursuant to the provisions of the Plan as provided by 11 U.S.C. § 1141. The pertinent facts are undisputed, but a detailed presentation of them is necessary to adequately address the question before us.

Between June, 1979, and December, 1979, Reliable was the electrical subcontractor on a construction project; Olson was the general contractor. On December 26, 1979, Reliable withdrew from the project because it felt Olson had breached the subcontract. On January 30, 1980, Reliable filed a petition for voluntary Chapter 11 reorganization in the United States Bankruptcy Court. Reliable filed a schedule of creditors on February 14, 1980, and amended that schedule on August 28, 1980. Within the schedule, Olson was listed under "Accounts Receivable," but never as a "Creditor."

Sometime between January, 1980, and November, 1980, Jon Clarke, Reliable's attorney, telephoned Charles H. Haines, Jr., Olson's attorney, and informed Mr. Haines that Reliable had instituted Chapter 11 proceedings. However, Olson did not receive any further information from Reliable concerning the proceedings. On November 9, 1980, Reliable filed suit against Olson in Colorado State District Court seeking damages for breach of the subcontract. On or about December 16, 1980, Olson removed the cause to federal bankruptcy court. Thereafter, on December 23, 1980, Olson responded to Reliable's complaint through an Answer and Counterclaim for damages based upon Reliable's alleged prepetition breach of the subcontract.

On January 6, 1981, Reliable filed its Third Amended Plan of Reorganization. The Disclosure Statement attached to this Plan stated that both documents were sent to all of Reliable's known creditors.

The Third Amended Plan of Reorganization defines "creditors" as all of those "holding claims for unsecured debts, liabilities, demands or claims of any character whatsoever." Reliable, however, failed to send a copy of these documents to Olson.

On January 13, 1981, the bankruptcy court mailed a notice to the scheduled creditors informing them of the time for filing acceptances or rejections of the Plan, of the confirmation hearing, and of the time for filing objections to confirmation. The confirmation hearing was conducted on March 9, 1981, after which the court entered an order confirming Reliable's Third Amended Plan. On March 12, 1981, the court mailed to the scheduled creditors notice of the confirmation order and discharge of Reliable. Because Olson was not a scheduled creditor, it did not receive any of these notices.

On March 30, 1981, the bankruptcy court issued an order to allow specific claims and authorize payment. The court ordered "the claim of any Class 4 unsecured creditor who failed to timely file a Proof of Claim and/or ballot in the bankruptcy proceeding and whose claim was *scheduled as disputed by the debtor is hereby disallowed*." Brief of Defendant-Appellee at 3 (quoting Trans., Vol. I at 35) (emphasis added by Defendant-Appellee).

On August 6, 1981, trial was held on the subcontract dispute between Reliable and Olson. On August 10, 1981, the bankruptcy court entered judgment dismissing Reliable's complaint and granting Olson recovery against Reliable in the amount of $10,378.00. Reliable then filed a claim in the Chapter 11 proceeding on behalf of Olson for $10,378.00 pursuant to Bankruptcy Interim Rule 3004. Reliable also filed a motion in the same proceeding to allow the claim of Olson. Further, Reliable filed a motion in the subcontract litigation to amend the judgment, requesting that the court specifically find the $10,378.00 judgment for Olson be determined a prepetition debt subject to compromise and payment as a general unsecured claim under the confirmed Plan of Reorganization and, thus, subject to discharge. The bankruptcy court issued an order, containing findings of fact and conclusions of law, denying Reliable's motions. The court found that because Reliable failed to schedule Olson as a creditor and failed to notify Olson of the confirmation hearing and because Olson's claim would be substantially impaired without due process of law if it were forced to comply with the Plan, Olson's claim was not subject to the confirmed Plan and, therefore, not discharged. The district court denied Reliable's petition for review of the bankruptcy court's ruling.

The issues on appeal are (1) whether Reliable's failure to give Olson reasonable notice of the bankruptcy confirmation hearing constituted a denial of due process, and (2) if we find a denial of due process, whether the district court erred by finding Olson's claim not to be subject to the Plan and, thus, not dischargeable.

I.

11 U.S.C. § 1128(a) provides: "After notice, the court shall hold a hearing on confirmation of a plan." This section requires notice to be given to all parties in interest. 5 Collier on Bankruptcy Para. 1128.01[2] (15th ed. 1983). After Olson filed the counterclaim against Reliable on December 23, 1980, Reliable was put on notice of Olson's status as a potential creditor. Despite this, no formal notice of any kind regarding the reorganization proceedings, or the time and manner of filing a claim, was ever given to Olson prior to the confirmation hearing. The apparent notice given to Olson prior to the counterclaim filing was inadequate notice of the confirmation hearing.

In the district court, Reliable did not dispute the inadequacy of the notice given to Olson regarding the confirmation hearing. *See* R., Vol. I at pp. 61–62, 65; R., Vol. III at p. 81. However, at oral argument on appeal, Reliable contended that Olson was adequately notified because its attorney had actual knowledge of the reorganization proceeding. We do not normally consider a contention raised for the first time on appeal, however, we will address this point in order to more fully discuss and decide the serious due process question involved.

Although Olson's attorney was generally aware of Reliable's involvement in reorganization proceedings, Olson was essentially denied the opportunity to be heard at the confirmation hearing.

The Supreme Court has repeatedly held that "[a]n elementary and fundamental requirement of due process in any proceeding which is to be accorded finality is notice reasonably calculated, under all the circumstances, to apprise interested parties of the pendency of the action and afford them an opportunity to present their objections." *Mullane v. Central Hanover Trust Co.* 339 U.S. 306, 314, [70 S. Ct. 652, 657, 94 L. Ed. 865] (1950) . . . . As specifically applied to bankruptcy reorganization proceedings, the Court has held that a creditor, who has general knowledge of a debtor's reorganization proceeding, has no duty to inquire about further court action. The creditor has a "right to assume" that he will receive all of the notices required by statute before his claim is forever barred. *New York v. New York, New Haven & Hartford R.R. Co.*, 344 U.S. 293, 297, 73 S. Ct. 299, 301, 97 L. Ed. 333 (1953). *See also In re Intaco Puerto Rico, Inc.*, 494 F.2d 94, 99 (1st Cir. 1974); *In re Harbor Tank Storage Co., Inc.*, 385 F.2d 111, 115 (3d Cir. 1967). Thus, Olson acted reasonably when it expected the same formal notice of the confirmation hearing which was sent to other identifiable creditors. Inasmuch as Olson was deprived of the opportunity to comment on Reliable's Third Amended Plan of Reorganization, it was denied due process of law.

II.

Reliable's primary contention is that, even if Olson was not given the requisite notice, Olson is still subject to the confirmed Plan as are all of the other creditors. Reliable argues that 11 U.S.C. § 1141(d) discharges all claims, whether a proof of claim has been filed, whether such claim is allowed, or whether the claim holder has accepted the plan. Further, Reliable contends that an "all-encompassing" discharge is necessary to meet the purpose of reorganization to give the debtor a "fresh start." Thus, Reliable urges that the only remedy available to Olson is to file a late claim under the confirmed Plan.

Sections 1141(c) and (d) ostensibly allow any claim to be discharged even though the claim holder has not received notice of the proceeding or of the confirmation hearing. However, we hold that notwithstanding the language of section 1141, the discharge of a claim without reasonable notice of the confirmation hearing is violative of the fifth amendment to the United States Constitution. *See* 5 Collier on Bankruptcy Para. 1141.01[b], at 1141-12. In our view, this holding is supported by the Supreme Court's decisions in *Mullane, supra,* and *New York, supra,* and by two other circuit court opinions which applied this reasoning specifically to bankruptcy reorganization proceedings. *See In re Intaco, supra; In re Harbor Tank, supra.* Inasmuch as we have held the notice by Reliable to Olson was deficient, the district court's decision was not contrary to law; Olson's claim cannot be bound to the Plan and, thus, it is not dischargeable.

A fundamental right guaranteed by the Constitution is the opportunity to be heard when a property interest is at stake. Specifically, the reorganization process depends upon all creditors and interested parties being properly notified of all vital steps in the proceeding so they may have the opportunity to protect their interests.

Reliable asserts that even if Olson had voted to reject the Third Amended Plan, the Plan would still have been approved. This overwhelming approval of the Plan by other creditors does not justify depriving Olson of its guaranteed due process right. *See Coe v. Armour Fertilizer Works,* 237 U.S. 413, 424, [35 S. Ct. 625, 629, 59 L. Ed. 1027] (1915).

We will not require Olson to subject its claim to a confirmed reorganization plan that it had no opportunity to dispute.

We affirm.

NOTES AND QUESTIONS

(1)   Assume that Reliable's reorganization plan gave creditors 25 cents per claim dollar in cash on confirmation and an additional 25 cents over time. Why should Olson be entitled to 100-cent dollars when other prepetition unsecured creditors are required to content themselves with 50-cent dollars?

(2)   Reliable filed a proof of claim on behalf of Olson. It was permitted to do this under Code § 501(c) which authorizes a debtor or trustee to file a proof of claim for a creditor who does not timely file a claim on its own behalf. Why would Reliable want to file a claim on behalf of Olson or, for that matter, any creditor? Inasmuch

as a claim in the amount of the judgment was filed, how was Olson prejudiced by the failure of Reliable to schedule Olson as a creditor or notify it of the bar date for filing proofs of claim or the date of the confirmation hearing? (Note that Bankruptcy Rule 3004 provides that in the event a debtor files a claim for a creditor, the clerk of the court shall notify the creditor, giving it an opportunity to file a superseding claim. Why isn't such notice, if received prior to the confirmation hearing, adequate notice?)

(3)   Olson held a $10,375 judgment. Assume that Olson's claim was not large enough to control the class of claims in which it was placed, nor even block an affirmative vote. How was Olson prejudiced by the debtor's failure to notify it of the confirmation hearing?

(4)   Reliable, the debtor, filed a proof of claim on behalf of Olson, but failed to give Olson notice of the confirmation hearing. As you might expect, the failure to give creditors reasonable notice of the deadline for filing proofs of claim also will prevent their claims from being discharged. In an old railroad reorganization case, *New York v. New York, New Haven & Hartford R.R. Co.*, 344 U.S. 293 (1953), the Supreme Court held that even though the creditor, New York City, had general knowledge of the pending case, and even though the debtor had published notice of the bar date for filing proofs of claim, the City was not barred from asserting its claim following confirmation. The Court explained:

> Nor can the bar order against New York be sustained because of the city's knowledge that reorganization of the railroad was taking place in the court. The argument is that such knowledge puts a duty on creditors to inquire for themselves about possible court orders limiting the time for filing claims. But even creditors who have knowledge of a reorganization have a right to assume that the statutory "reasonable notice" will be given them before their claims are forever barred. When the judge ordered notice by mail to be given the appearing creditors, New York City acted reasonably in waiting to receive the same treatment. The statutory command for notice embodies a basic principle of justice — that a reasonable opportunity to be heard must precede judicial denial of a party's claimed rights. New York City has not been accorded that kind of notice.

344 U.S. at 297.

Suppose that a creditor's $1 million claim is listed in the debtor's schedules. The creditor receives notice of the Chapter 11 filing and all other pertinent notices, including notice of the deadline for filing proofs of claim. The creditor participates actively in the case, but fails to file a proof of claim. Votes are solicited; the plan is accepted and confirmed. May the creditor now obtain an extension of time in which to file its proof of claim? In *In re St. James Mech., Inc.*, 434 B.R. 54 (Bankr. E.D.N.Y. 2010), such a creditor asked the court to extend the time period pursuant to Bankruptcy Rule 9006(b), which provides:

> [W]hen an act is required or allowed to be done at or within a specified period by these rules or by a notice given thereunder or by order of court, the court for cause shown may at any time in its discretion (1) with or without motion or notice order the period enlarged if the request therefor

is made before the expiration of the period originally prescribed or as extended by a previous order or (2) on motion made after the expiration of the specified period permit the act to be done where the failure to act was the result of excusable neglect.

The court concluded that the issue was not whether the creditor's failure to file a claim was the result of "excusable neglect," but rather whether the creditor still had a claim to file and prove. The court explained:

> Confirmation of a debtor's plan of reorganization is the seminal event in the Chapter 11 bankruptcy process. The entry of a final order of confirmation discharges the debtor of its prepetition obligations to a creditor whether or not a proof of claim has been filed. The United States Supreme Court recognized the consequential effect of plan confirmation in Chapter 11 cases, remarking that "[u]nder the Bankruptcy Code, a proof of claim must be presented to the Bankruptcy Court for administration or be lost when a plan of reorganization is confirmed." *NLRB v. Bildisco and Bildisco*, 465 U.S. 513, 529, 104 S. Ct. 1188, 79 L. Ed. 2d 482 (1984) (citing 11 U.S.C. § 1141). If creditors have 'been given notice [of a bar date] sufficient to satisfy due process,' their pre-petition claims are supplanted by the new contractual obligations reflected in the plan, which obligations are binding on the debtor and all creditors. *DePippo v. Kmart Corp.*, 335 B.R. 290, 295 (S.D.N.Y. 2005).

> . . . .

> Because of the post-confirmation discharge granted by section 1141, a creditor, who has received notice which satisfies the due process requirements imposed by the Constitution, can no longer be viewed as having a claim. It is axiomatic that a creditor cannot rely upon Rule 9006(b)(1) to extend the time period within which to file a proof of claim if that creditor no longer has an enforceable claim to assert against the debtor. The language "at any time" in Rule 9006(b)(1) denotes any time during which a creditor holds an enforceable claim against the debtor. Post-confirmation, a creditor has no claim against the debtor. A court may not resurrect through the use of Rule 9006 that which no longer exists by operation of Bankruptcy Code § 1141.

434 B.R. 54, 61–62. The court noted that other courts have applied the "excusable neglect" standard and granted relief in cases in which creditors' due process rights were violated. The court was dubious, however, that allowing such creditors to file belatedly was the correct approach. The court observed:

> [T]he fact that a creditor did not receive proper notice of the bar date does not give the creditor the right to file a claim post-confirmation. [Bankruptcy] Rule 9006 is the incorrect vehicle by which to provide relief to such creditor. The correct remedy for such creditor is to treat the discharge as having no effect against the creditor's claim.

Id. at 62.

In both the *Reliable* and *New York* cases, the debtors failed to give notice to creditors whose existence was known to the debtor. What if a debtor has no knowledge of the existence of a claim, and fails to schedule that claim or send notices to the claim holder? Consider the opinion that follows.

BERK v. BROOKS FASHION STORES, INC.
(IN RE BROOKS FASHION STORES, INC.)
United States District Court for the Southern District of New York
1994 U.S. Dist. LEXIS 4779 (1994)

KEVIN THOMAS DUFFY, D.J..

BACKGROUND

Berk was hired by Brooks Fashion in December 1985, as a Production Manager. In her complaint, Berk alleged that, pursuant to an oral contract with Brooks Fashion, her salary for 1986 was $50,000, plus a guaranteed 25% bonus, which was to be paid at the end of the year. Moreover, Berk claims that Barry Avid, Brooks Fashion's President, also offered her a new position for 1987 as head of a new department. Further, he purportedly told Berk that her salary for 1987 would be the same as her 1986 salary, including the 25% bonus, and that he would "try to get [her] more money."

In December 1986, two months after this alleged conversation, Berk received an evaluation report that was extremely critical of her overall job performance. The evaluation expressed dissatisfaction with Berk's lack of technical knowledge as well as her poor work habits. In addition, the report required Berk to improve her job performance or risk being terminated. Berk refused her supervisor's request to sign the critical evaluation, believing its contents to be false, distorted and exaggerated. Instead, Berk responded to the evaluation with a written letter to her supervisors in which she objected to the review and expressed a desire to establish a future relationship of mutual cooperation.

On approximately January 19, 1987, Berk received a follow-up evaluation in which Brooks Fashion expressed its continued dissatisfaction with her technical and professional abilities. Shortly thereafter, Berk was fired. Berk claims that at the time she was fired she made a demand for the unpaid 1986 bonus.

In December 1987, Brooks Fashion filed a voluntary petition under Chapter 11 of the Bankruptcy Code. In March 1989, a confirmed plan of reorganization was established by the Bankruptcy Court for the Southern District of New York, pursuant to § 1129 of the Bankruptcy Code. Berk received no formal notice of the filing of the petition or of any proceedings involved therewith.

In September 1991, Berk commenced this action against Brooks Fashion in New York Supreme Court. The complaint included claims of: (1) libel for the alleged dissemination of the evaluation reports, and (2) breach of contract for the non-payment of the 1986 bonus, 1987 base salary and 1987 bonus. Pursuant to 28 U.S.C. § 1452(a), the action was removed to the Bankruptcy Court of the Southern

District of New York. Contemporaneously, Brooks Fashion filed a Motion to Dismiss which was converted into a Summary Judgment Motion.

The Bankruptcy Court determined that Berk was an "unknown" creditor and, therefore, not entitled to formal notice of the bankruptcy proceedings. The Bankruptcy Court held that Berk was bound by the Confirmation Order dated February 2, 1989, and that Berk's claims had been discharged by the Confirmation Order. Accordingly, the Court granted Brooks Fashion motion for summary judgment.

DISCUSSION

Due process requires that actual written notice of a debtor's bankruptcy filing and the "bar date" for filing claims be provided to "known" creditors. Publication notification, however, is sufficient for the debtor's "unknown" creditors. A "known" creditor is one whose identification as such is either known or "reasonably ascertainable" by the debtor. Conversely, an "unknown" creditor is one whose identity is not "reasonably ascertainable" and whose claim is merely conceivable, conjectural or speculative.

Due process also requires the debtor to undertake "reasonably diligent efforts" to determine the identity and claims of any such creditors. Such an endeavor, however, does not require the debtor to undertake "impracticable and extended searches . . . in the name of due process." *Mullane*[*v. Central Hanover Bank & Trust Co.*], 339 U.S. at 317. . . . This standard, however, does not require the debtor to "search out each conceivable or possible creditor and urge that person or entity to make a claim against it." *Charter Crude*[*Oil Co. v. Petroleos Mexicanos*], 125 Bankr. at 655. Thus, the accepted standard for determining a creditor's status is one of reasonableness.

The dispositive issue identified and decided by the Bankruptcy Court was whether Berk was a "known" or "unknown" creditor. On a motion for summary judgment, the Bankruptcy Court determined that Berk failed to provide her former employer with any indication that she intended to commence a future action against Brooks Fashion, and, [the debtor] therefore, had no reason to identify Berk as a creditor entitled to notice of its bankruptcy proceedings.

. . . .

The evidence presented demonstrates that Berk was an "unknown" creditor entitled only to constructive notice. Berk failed to provide Brooks Fashion with any reason to believe that it would be the target of a future lawsuit. Berk argues that Brooks Fashion knew or should have known of her potential claims as they were "clearly ascertainable." In particular, Berk claims that she notified her supervisors, both orally and in writing, of her objections to the negative evaluations she received. Moreover, she maintains that at the time of her firing, she made a demand for the unpaid 1986 bonus. Finally, Berk alleges that Brooks Fashion knew or should have known of her claim particularly in light of the fact that she was not an employee at will but had an oral contract for a specified time period and that her firing was prior to the expiration date of the contract.

Even when assuming the truth of these assertions, Berk's claims nevertheless fail to alert Brooks Fashion of a future claim against it. Berk never informed Brooks Fashion of its potential liability nor did she ever threaten to commence an action for breach of contract or libel. Berk's single demand for the 1986 bonus cannot be said to put Brooks Fashion on notice of a future claim. Simply, further action by Berk was necessary in order for her to be a "known" creditor.

As the Bankruptcy Court notes, "anger and disagreement" are two emotions commonly exhibited when an individual is fired. An exhibition of these emotions, however, cannot be said to provide an employer with reason to believe that it will be the subject of a future lawsuit brought by that employee. As far as Brooks Fashion was concerned, any purported claims by Berk against it were entirely conjectural and speculative. It simply is not "reasonable," therefore, to require Brooks Fashion to identify and notify every potential plaintiff, regardless of how speculative or remote their claims might be of its bankruptcy proceedings. As the Court noted in Tulsa, not everyone who may conceivably have a claim is properly considered a creditor entitled to actual notice. *Tulsa [Professional Collection Services. Inc. v. Pope*, 485 U.S. 478, 490 (1988)].

. . . .

In sum, even if all the claims Berk asserts are true, she is still an "unknown" creditor. As such, she was entitled only to constructive notice. Neither party disputes that Brooks Fashion provided constructive notice of the claims bar date in satisfaction of both the Bankruptcy Law and constitutional due process considerations. Accordingly, the decision of the Bankruptcy Court is affirmed.

NOTES AND QUESTIONS

(1) A number of courts have held that notice by publication to creditors who are not readily ascertainable satisfies due process requirements. *See, e.g., Chemetron Corp. v. Jones*, 72 F.3d 341 (3d Cir. 1995); *In re Chicago, Milwaukee, St. Paul, & Pac. R.R. Co.*, 974 F.2d 775 (7th Cir. 1992); *Vancouver Women's Health Collective Soc. v. A.H. Robins Co. (In re A.H. Robins Co.)*, 820 F.2d 1359 (4th Cir. 1987). Most courts have suggested that the "reasonably ascertainable" standard requires only a careful examination of the debtor's own books and records, not an attempt to identify and contact every person that might conceivably hold a claim. *See, e.g., In re Best Prods. Co.*, 140 B.R. 353, 358 (Bankr. S.D.N.Y. 1992).

(2) Berk knew that she had a claim against Brooks Fashion Stores. Brooks did not know about Berk's claim. Had the court concluded that Berk's claim was not discharged, would that mean that any creditor whose existence is unknown to a debtor would have the option of "opting out" of the bankruptcy process in the hope of recovering more from the entity that emerges from Chapter 11? Would that result be fair to so-called "known" creditors, who either file proofs of claim or who, in Judge Posner's words, are "dragged into" the case by debtors who file proofs of claim on their behalf?

(3) What constitutes adequate notice to claim holders whose existence as such is not only unknown to the debtor, but to themselves? Is notice possible? Should

such claims be discharged by a confirmed plan? Consider the opinion in *Hexcel Corp. v. Stepan Co.* that follows.

HEXCEL CORP. v. STEPAN COMPANY
(IN RE HEXCEL CORP.)
United States District Court, Northern District of California
239 B.R. 564 (1999)

CHARLES R. BREYER, UNITED STATES DISTRICT JUDGE.

The issue presented on this appeal is whether the bankruptcy court applied the correct legal standard when it used the "fair contemplation" test set forth in *In re Jensen*, 995 F.2d 925 (9th Cir. 1993) (per curiam), to determine whether Stepan's third-party contribution claim against Hexcel was discharged in a prior bankruptcy proceeding. For the reasons set forth below, the ruling of the bankruptcy court is affirmed.

I.

On December 6, 1993, Hexcel Corporation, plaintiff and appellant in this action, petitioned for bankruptcy. On January 12, 1995, the plan of reorganization was approved by the bankruptcy court.

On December 9, 1997, a group of New Jersey residents filed a class action lawsuit in New Jersey state court against Stepan Company, defendant and appellee in this action. The complaint alleges that Stepan discharged toxic pollutants in the area, and that the resulting contamination has caused the plaintiffs bodily injury, death, and property damage. The plaintiffs in the class action seek compensatory and punitive damages as relief for their injuries.

On September 11, 1998, Stepan filed a third-party complaint in the New Jersey action against all those who could have contributed to the contamination. Stepan's complaint included Hexcel, because public records indicated that Hexcel had owned and operated a plant in the area that was the subject of a 1986 state cleanup order.

Hexcel sought an injunction in the bankruptcy court to prevent Stepan from pursuing this third-party complaint against it. Hexcel contended that Stepan's claim "arose" prior to Hexcel's bankruptcy petition in 1993, and therefore any debt resulting from this claim was discharged by the reorganization pursuant to § 1141.

The bankruptcy court rejected this argument and denied Hexcel's motion for a preliminary injunction, finding that Hexcel had failed to show a likelihood of success on its assertion that Stepan's claim arose prior to the 1993 petition. In making this determination, the court applied the test from the Ninth Circuit case of *In re Jensen*, 995 F.2d 925 (9th Cir. 1993), which held that, at least in cases involving the Comprehensive Environmental Response, Compensation and Liability Act of 1980 ("CERCLA") or similar state-law statutes, a claim "arises" for bankruptcy purposes when the claimant has a fair basis for contemplating that it might have a claim against the debtor prior to the discharge. The bankruptcy court found that the mere fact that Hexcel had been the subject of a state cleanup order in 1986 did not give the parties a fair basis for contemplating that Stepan might be sued in mass tort litigation some time in the future, and might have a third-party claim against Hexcel in connection with that litigation. In so holding, the bankruptcy court rejected Hexcel's argument that it should have applied the "debtor's conduct" test, which appears to provide that any claim arising from the debtor's pre-bankruptcy conduct must be discharged, regardless of whether that claim could fairly be contemplated by the parties.

This Court granted Hexcel leave to appeal this ruling pursuant to 28 U.S.C. § 158(a)(3).

. . . .

III.

§ 1141 provides, with limited exceptions not applicable here, that all claims against the debtor that "arose" prior to the debtor's bankruptcy proceedings are discharged. This discharge is effective regardless of whether the claimant has accepted the plan or has even filed a claim in the bankruptcy case. § 1141(a).

However, potential claimants must be given notice that their interests may be affected by the bankruptcy proceeding. *See, e.g.*, §§ 1109(b), 1128(a).

The Code defines a pre-petition claim as a "right to payment, whether or not such right is reduced to judgment, liquidated, unliquidated, fixed, contingent, matured, unmatured, disputed, undisputed, legal, equitable, secured or unsecured." § 101(5)(A). Congress indicated that the word "claim" is to be given the "broadest possible definition" to ensure that "all legal obligations of the debtor, no matter how remote or contingent, will be able to be dealt with in the bankruptcy case." H.R. Rep. No. 95-595 (1977) reprinted in 1978 U.S.C.C.A.N. 5963, 6266. Thus, if Stepan can be deemed to have had a "contingent" claim against Hexcel prior to Hexcel's bankruptcy proceedings, Stepan's present indemnity action against Hexcel must be discharged pursuant to section 1141.

However, despite the broad reach of section 101(5), the definition of a "claim" for bankruptcy purposes is not boundless. For example, this section does not include future rights to payment that are "unknown" and "unforeseeable." Indeed, the Ninth Circuit has explicitly recognized, albeit in a different context, that the definition of a "contingent" claim under section 101(5) is more limited: "claims are contingent . . . if the debt is one which the debtor will be called upon to pay only upon the occurrence or happening of an extrinsic event which will trigger the liability of the debtor to the alleged creditor *and if such triggering event or occurrence was one reasonably contemplated by the debtor and creditor at the time the event giving rise to the claim occurred.*" *In re Dill*, 731 F.2d 629, 631 (9th Cir. 1994) (quoting *In re All Media Properties, Inc.*, 5 B.R. 126, 133 (Bankr. S.D. Tex. 1980)) (emphasis added). Under this definition, a claim cannot fall within the purview of section 101(5) — and thus cannot be discharged as a pre-petition claim — unless that claim could have been contemplated by the parties prior to the bankruptcy proceedings. Any future, unknown claim that could not have been reasonably contemplated does not fall within the purview of section 101(5) and must not be discharged, even if the conduct giving rise to the claim took place before the bankruptcy proceedings.

This position is further supported by the Ninth Circuit decision of *In re Jensen*, relied on by the bankruptcy court in this case. In *Jensen*, the court stated that "nothing in the legislative history or the Code suggests that Congress intended to discharge a creditor's rights before the creditor knew or should have known that its rights existed." 995 F.2d at 930 (citation omitted).

An examination of the statutory scheme embodied in the Bankruptcy Code further supports this reading of section 101(5). As the courts have recognized, "notice is the cornerstone underpinning Bankruptcy Code procedure." *In re Savage Industries, Inc.*, 43 F.3d 714, 719 (1st Cir. 1994). For example, it provides that a bankruptcy trustee must ensure "parties in interest" adequate notice an opportunity to be heard before their interests may be adversely affected. § 363(b). Further, parties that would be bound by a proposed reorganization plan must be given notice of the plan, § 1128(a), and parties in interest are given the "right to be heard" in chapter 11 cases. § 1109(b). It would be incongruent for the Code to provide so extensively for notice to parties affected by the bankruptcy proceedings, yet to define a pre-petition claim under section 101(5) so broadly as to adversely affect the interests of those who could not possibly have notice of their rights and interests.

IV.

Although this distinction between future claims not subject to contemplation by the parties that fall outside the purview of section 101(5) and contingent, foreseeable claims that fall within the Code appears straightforward, the case law has created some confusion regarding the circumstances under which a claim may be discharged. Courts throughout the country have applied a number of different legal tests to conduct this inquiry. However, although these different tests might at first appear to support different outcomes with respect to the case at hand, closer examination reveals that a common thread runs through the large majority of these cases: the claim of a creditor which stems from the pre-petition conduct of the debtor should not be discharged if the parties could not reasonably contemplate the potential existence of the future claim prior to the reorganization.

For example, one test that courts have used in evaluating the dischargeability of future claims is the "relationship" or "Piper" test, which requires either a pre-petition or pre-confirmation relationship, "such as contact, exposure, impact, or privity, between the debtor's pre-petition conduct and the claimant." *Epstein v. Official Committee of Unsecured Creditors of Estate of Piper Aircraft Corp. ("In re Piper")*, 58 F.3d 1573, 1577 (11th Cir. 1995). [Reprinted in § 8.06 of the casebook. — Eds.] In *Piper*, an aircraft manufacturer filed a petition for bankruptcy. The court held that possible future holders of product liability claims — i.e., individuals who might some day be injured or killed in an airplane accident — did not hold pre-petition claims within the meaning of section 101(5) if they had not had any contact with Piper prior to the bankruptcy. As the Court stated, "the debtor's prepetition conduct gives rise to a claim to be administered in a case only if there is a relationship established before confirmation between an identifiable claimant or group of claimants and that prepetition conduct." *Id.*

This test appears to incorporate, at least implicitly, the notion that a future claim must be within the reasonable contemplation of the parties. If a relationship exists between the pre-petition conduct of the debtor and an identifiable potential claimant, it typically follows that the parties can fairly contemplate the possible existence of a claim against the debtor. This proposition was made explicit in *In re Russell*, 193 B.R. 568, 571–72 (Bankr. S.D. Cal. 1996), in which the court stated: "where the claimants had a pre-petition relationship to the debtor and the circumstance which gives rise to their claim, *it is within the fair contemplation of the parties that a contingent claim exists at that point in time.*" (emphasis added).

To the extent that the relationship test might be defined so broadly as to include future claims that cannot be contemplated, the Ninth Circuit has criticized it: "The relationship approach, when defined . . . broadly, undermines the rationale for considering whether or not a relationship exists," namely, "that a creditor with a relationship *may anticipate its potential claim.*" *Jensen*, 995 F.2d at 930 (emphasis added). This important caveat precludes the legally unsupportable and patently unfair result reached in *In re Edge*, 60 B.R. 690, 705 (M.D. Tenn. 1986), where the claim of a victim of a bankrupt dentist's pre-petition malpractice was discharged, notwithstanding the fact that the injury was not discoverable until after the completion of the bankruptcy.

A second method for determining whether a claim arose pre-petition or post-petition is the test urged by Hexcel here — the debtor's conduct test. This test provides that a claim, for bankruptcy purposes, arises upon the occurrence of the debtor's conduct that ultimately gave rise to the subsequent cause of action. For example, this test was applied in the asbestos liability case of *In re Johns-Manville Corp.*, 57 B.R. 680, 690 (Bankr. S.D.N.Y. 1986), where the court held that plaintiffs' claims "arose" at the time of asbestos exposure, and not the manifestation of their injuries. And, in *Grady v. A.H. Robins Co.*, 839 F.2d 198, 203 (4th Cir. 1988) [reprinted in chapter 3. — Eds.], a plaintiff who sued the debtor post-petition for an injury arising from the pre-petition insertion of an interuterine contraceptive device was denied relief on the grounds that her claim arose, for bankruptcy purposes, when the device was inserted into her body, not when her legal claim actually accrued.

The debtor's conduct test would appear to allow for the possibility that a creditor's claim is automatically discharged if the conduct giving rise to the claim occurred pre-petition, even if the creditor had no way of knowing of the claim at the time. However, even in these cases, courts applying the debtor's conduct test left room for protection of individuals with future, unknown claims. In both cases, the debtors were well aware of the damage their products had caused by the time of the bankruptcy proceeding; thus, the debtors and the bankruptcy courts anticipated that future claims would arise from unknown individuals who had been exposed to the harmful product, but who would not become aware of their claims until after the reorganization. Accordingly, trust funds were created during reorganization in order to compensate these prospective injuries, and representatives were appointed to articulate the interests of the future claimants during the proceedings. In applying the debtor's conduct test to determine that plaintiffs' claims were discharged in bankruptcy, the respective courts were not holding that the plaintiffs would be prevented from recovering at all. Rather, the claimants' interests had already been represented in the bankruptcy proceedings through the creation of the trust funds and the appointment of class representatives. Had this not been the case, it is doubtful that plaintiffs' claims could properly be deemed to have been discharged in bankruptcy.

The Ninth Circuit bankruptcy appellate panel has also recently applied the debtor's conduct test, holding that a lender bank's claim for negligent construction was a contingent claim falling within the scope of section 101(5) since the defective construction occurred pre-petition, even though the bank did not discover the defect until after the debtor's bankruptcy proceedings had been completed. *In re Hassanally*, 208 B.R. 46, 51 (Bankr. 9th Cir. 1997). In so holding, however, the court again lent support to the notion that the concept of "fair contemplation" is always implicit in the question whether a cause of action may be discharged as a pre-petition claim:

> It would not be inequitable to apply the conduct test to these facts. . . . *Lenders should fairly contemplate the possibility of negligent construction.* They have the opportunity to protect against that risk through their inspections . . . in spanned ought to have constructive notice that there might be defects.

Id. at 54 n. 11 (emphasis added).

Finally, the Ninth Circuit in Jensen adopted the "fair contemplation" test, at least in the context of claims brought pursuant to CERCLA or similar state statutes.

Actually, a fourth major test used by the courts to determine whether a claim arises pre-petition or post-petition is the "state-law accrual" test articulated by the Third Circuit in *In re Frenville Co.*, 744 F.2d 332 (3rd Cir. 1984), which provides that a claim only "arises" once the claimant has the right to obtain payment. This test, of course, automatically ensures that a creditor's claim will not be discharged if the claim could not be contemplated. However, the Ninth Circuit has rejected the Frenville test as "ignoring the breath of the statutory definition of claim." *Jensen*, 995 F.2d at 929. [The Third Circuit itself repudiated the *Frenville* test in *Jeld-Wen v. Van Brunt (In re Grossman's Inc.)*, 607 F.3d 114 (3d Cir. 2010). — Eds.]

In *Jensen*, the State of California brought a claim against the bankrupt debtor for hazardous waste cleanup costs pursuant to a state statute similar to CERCLA.

For the purpose of simplicity, the Court shall hereinafter follow the *Jensen* court's lead and refer to the state's claim in *Jensen* as a "CERCLA claim."

Although the state incurred the costs of the cleanup after the debtor's bankruptcy proceedings, the conduct that caused the harm occurred pre-petition. The Bankruptcy Appellate Panel ("BAP") ruled that the state's claim against the debtor arose pre-petition and had therefore been discharged in bankruptcy, on the grounds that "claims in bankruptcy arise based upon the debtor's conduct."

The Ninth Circuit rejected the BAP's application of the debtor's conduct test, ruling instead that, at least in the CERCLA context, a claim may only be deemed to have arisen pre-petition if it is "based upon pre-petition conduct that can fairly be contemplated by the parties at the time of the debtors' bankruptcy." Quoting *In re Nat'l Gypsum Co.*, 139 B.R. 397, 404 (N.D. Tex. 1992). The Court suggested that the application of this test, which is less protective of the debtor, on its face, than the test applied by the BAP, was dictated by the unique intersection of environmental cleanup law and federal bankruptcy statutes. On the one hand, the Court pointed out, the Bankruptcy Reform Act of 1978 was designed to provide debtors with a "fresh start" by discharging as many claims against them as possible. On the other hand, CERCLA embodies a strict Congressional mandate "to protect public health and the environment by facilitating the cleanup of environmental contamination and imposing costs on the parties responsible for the pollution." In light of the competing public policy concerns expressed by Congress, the Court stated, it would be inappropriate to bar a CERCLA claimant from recovery if the claimant could not reasonably contemplate, prior to the bankruptcy proceedings, that it might have a cause of action against the debtor.

The Court then went on to affirm the BAP's ruling that the claim was discharged, on the grounds that the state could have fairly contemplated, prior to the reorganization, that it may have had a claim against the debtor.

By holding that the fair contemplation test must be applied in the CERCLA context, it appears that the *Jensen* court was implying that the debtor's conduct test should be applied under most other circumstances. Hexcel seizes upon this apparent implication by arguing that outside the CERCLA context, the debtor's conduct test must be applied, and claims stemming from pre-petition conduct must be discharged, even if this would result in the discharge of a claim that the parties would had no way of contemplating prior to the bankruptcy. However, nothing in the *Jensen* decision supports this extreme conclusion. In fact, as mentioned above, the court explicitly stated that "nothing in the legislative history or the Code suggests that Congress intended to discharge a creditor's rights before the creditor knew or should have known that its rights existed." *Jensen*, 995 F.2d at 930 (citation omitted).

Therefore, although it is generally true that "claims in bankruptcy arise from the debtor's conduct," the common thread running through the case law is that the Code does not suggest that a creditor's claim is to be discharged if the parties could not reasonably contemplate the existence of that claim prior to the reorganization.

Accordingly, it would have been error for the bankruptcy court to discharge Stepan's indemnity claim against Hexcel without first determining that the parties could fairly contemplate the claim prior to the termination of the bankruptcy proceedings.

V.

This conclusion is further supported by the potential constitutional problems that could arise if the Court were to interpret the Bankruptcy Code in a manner that required the discharge of Stepan's claim. It is possible that such an interpretation could deprive Stepan of a property interest (its state law tort claim against Hexcel) without adequate notice in violation of the Due Process Clause of the Fifth Amendment.

Again, this analysis assumes the correctness of the bankruptcy court's factual finding that the parties could not fairly contemplate the existence of a future claim by Stepan against Hexcel. The Court expresses no opinion in this regard. Nothing in this decision should influence the bankruptcy court's resolution of this factual question at the permanent injunction stage of the litigation.

Due process concerns usually arise in the bankruptcy context when the debtor has failed to provide adequate notice to potential creditors that it has filed for bankruptcy. . . .

Hexcel argues that it addressed these concerns during bankruptcy by publishing notice of the proceedings in the Wall Street Journal so that any potential claimant that Hexcel could not identify would be alerted of the need to assert its interests in the bankruptcy court. Hexcel may be correct that this publication was sufficient to satisfy its notice obligation to creditors who could contemplate that they might have a claim. It is difficult to imagine, however, how the announcement of a bankruptcy proceeding published in the Wall Street Journal could possibly satisfy due process concerns for a potential creditor who had no way of knowing that it may have a claim against the debtor some time in the future. *See, e.g., In re Pettibone*, 162 B.R. 791, 808 (Bankr. N.D. Ill. 1994) ("The Bankruptcy Code does not require a party . . . with no known interest in a bankruptcy proceeding to monitor national financial papers and read notices about businesses against which they have no known claims to guard against the possibility they might later be held on notice of claim bar."). In short, Hexcel confuses the requirement that creditors be given notice of the bankruptcy proceeding (which it satisfied) with the requirement that parties must have some notice of potential claims they might have against the bankruptcy petitioner before those claims are discharged (which could not possibly have been satisfied).

Courts have discussed the due process problems that could arise from the discharge of a creditor's claim before the parties could contemplate that the claim existed. For example, in *In re Kewanee Boiler Corp.*, 198 B.R. 519 (N.D. Ill. 1996), plaintiff was injured in a post-petition [and post-confirmation — Eds.] boiler room accident as a result of alleged defects in a boiler manufactured pre-petition by the bankrupt debtor. The court found, for reasons similar to those expressed in Sections III and IV, *supra*, that even though plaintiff's cause of action stemmed from the debtor's pre-petition conduct, it did not fall within the Code's definition of "claim" and therefore was not discharged in bankruptcy. *Id.* at 528. In addition, the court stated as follows:

> Even if a contingent "claim" could by some stretch of § 101(5) be held by Smith pre-petition, this would raise other serious questions under the Code and Constitution. Such ruling would force Smith to be bound by proceedings in which he did not and could not participate. Fifth Amendment Due Process concerns are clearly at issue in a case like this. . . .

Id. at 528–29. The court went on to point out that although some courts have ruled that this due process concern may be adequately addressed by the establishment of a trust fund for future claimants and the appointment of a representative to articulate the interests of future claimants during the confirmation process, no such mechanism was created in connection with the boiler manufacturer's bankruptcy proceedings. *Id.* at 531. The court concluded that "procedural due process and requirements of meaningful notice are indeed a limitation on what possible 'claims' may be controlled by a confirmed plan in bankruptcy." *Id.* at 534.

The Second Circuit, in dicta, has also recognized the potential due process problems associated with the discharge of future claims that could not be contemplated by the parties pre-petition:

> Defining claims to include any ultimate right to payment arising from pre-petition conduct by the debtor comports with the theoretical model of assuring that all assets of the debtor are available to those seeking recovery for pre-petition conduct. But such an interpretation of "claim" yields questionable results. Consider, for example, a company that builds bridges around the world. It can estimate that of 10,000 bridges it builds, one will fail, causing 10 deaths. Having built 10,000 bridges, it becomes insolvent and files a petition in bankruptcy. Is there a "claim" on behalf of the 10 people who will be killed when they drive across the one bridge that will fail someday in the future? If the only test is whether the ultimate right to payment will arise out of the debtor's pre-petition conduct, the future victims have a [pre-petition] "claim." Yet it must be obvious that enormous practical and perhaps constitutional problems would arise from recognition of such a claim. The potential victims are not only unidentified, but there is no way to identify them. Sheer fortuity will determine who will be on that one bridge when it crashes.

In re Chateaugay Corp., 944 F.2d 997, 1003 (2nd Cir. 1991). . . .

Here, according to the preliminary factual findings of the bankruptcy court, the parties could not have contemplated the possibility that Stepan might have a right to payment from Hexcel in the future. Neither the New Jersey class plaintiffs nor Stepan knew or should have known of the potential health and property damage allegedly caused by Hexcel. Even Hexcel admits that it could not identify Stepan pre-petition as a future claimant, nor could it conceive of the set of facts that gave rise to Stepan's present indemnity claim. Accordingly, the due process concerns raised by the courts in Kewanee and Chateaugay are equally applicable here. The existence of these concerns bolsters the conclusion that a future claim that cannot be contemplated by the parties is not discharged under the Bankruptcy Code, even if that claim stems from the pre-petition conduct of the debtor.

VI.

This holding is not at odds with the basic notion that a claim in bankruptcy stems from the debtor's conduct. *See In re* Zelis, 66 F.3d 205, 209 (9th Cir. 1995). Clearly, the preliminary task for the bankruptcy court is to ask when the conduct giving rise to the claim occurred — the claim may not be discharged if the conduct did not occur pre-petition. The import of this ruling is simply that even if a claim stems from pre-petition conduct, it still may not be discharged if the parties could not fairly contemplate its potential existence during the bankruptcy proceedings. This conclusion is compelled by the Bankruptcy Code and the case law, and is bolstered by the potential constitutional problems that could arise from a contrary result. Accordingly, the decision of the bankruptcy court is AFFIRMED.

IT IS SO ORDERED.

NOTES AND QUESTIONS

(1)   Are the *Hexcel* and *Brooks* holdings reconcilable? Is the dispositive factor what the claimants knew about their status? Doesn't the *Hexcel* court acknowledge that notice by publication would have been sufficient to claim holders who could reasonably contemplate that they might hold claims?

(2)   In the *Kewanee Boiler* case, cited by the court in *Hexcel*, the debtor filed its petition in 1986 and confirmed its plan in 1988. Nearly two years after the plan had been confirmed, Smith was scalded when a boiler that the debtor had manufactured in 1952 exploded. In 1991, Smith brought a lawsuit against the reorganized debtor. The court held that Smith's claim had not been discharged:

> [T]he Kewanee confirmed Plan did not take steps to limit its liability to future tort victims through the bankruptcy either by any attempt to notice them or through any special provision for them in the Plan. No fund was provided for distribution to these future claimants. No claims were ever filed on behalf of possible future claimants and never was a legal representative appointed. The Plan itself never expressly provided for payment to a future class of claimants who had at that time not been injured by Kewanee's products manufactured before bankruptcy was filed, but would or might be injured thereafter.

> Because no such provision was made in the Plan, and because future victims of torts were not represented in the bankruptcy or noticed, these persons cannot be forced into participating in the limited distribution that unsecured creditors are entitled to receive under the Plan here. Whether Smith had a "claim" under § 101(5) is doubtful because he had no right to payment prior to confirmation. But even if he did, his right to notice under bankruptcy law and the Constitution were not met.

> . . . .

> Even where confirmed Chapter 11 plans have dealt with future liability, no case has been found that forced persons injured entirely post-petition to be bound by the bankruptcy because they were merely in the vicinity of the product manufactured pre-petition. A.H. Robins and Johns-Manville are cases where such proximity to a defective and harmful product forced a post-petition claimant to share in past bankruptcy settlement. There, some physical contact between the victim and the product actually occurred with some injury pre-petition. In those cases, however, exhaustive procedures were undertaken in an effort to assure constitutionality of trusts created for future claimants.

> In all cases found where a trust was created out of which future claims against the estate were to be paid, some assertedly injurious contact between the future victim and the product occurred pre-petition. Only the manifestation of a disease was lacking. In those cases, the existence of pre-petition physical contact, such as inhalation of asbestos, *Johns-*

Manville, . . . or insertion of a contraceptive, *A.H. Robins*, or implantation of a breast implant, *Dow-Corning*, more or less fixed the class of potential victims. In cases like . . . the case at bar, where absolutely no physical harm was suffered pre-bankruptcy and only some proximity to the product could be shown, a different practical and constitutional issue is presented.

Should Kewanee's Plan be read to apply to post-confirmation injuries, enjoining of Smith's efforts to liquidate his claim against the reorganized debtor and forcing him to partake in Kewanee's bankruptcy would be an inadmissible deprivation of his property interest in that claim, wholly without prior due process notice or bankruptcy notice.

Kewanee Boiler Corp. v. Smith (In re Kewanee Boiler Corp.), 198 B.R. at 539–540 (Bankr. N.D. Ill. 1996).

§ 10.03   THE EFFECT OF CONFIRMATION ON THE LIABILITY OF NON-DEBTORS

PROBLEM 10.2

"I probably should have mentioned this earlier," Headley says, "But I forgot. This morning we received a phone call from one of the banks whose loan to Amphydynamics I personally guaranteed. They say the bank wants me to make good on the guarantee or it will go to court to enforce it."

"I thought we took care of that in the plan," Carol interrupts. There's a provision in the plan that releases you from liability on those guarantees."

"That's what I told him," Headley says. "And he told me to go look at Code § 1141(d) and Code § 524(e). Is he right?"

Read those sections, and the opinion and materials that follow.

IN RE MASTER MORTGAGE INVESTMENT FUND, INC.
United States Bankruptcy Court for the Western District of Missouri
168 B.R. 930 (1994)

[Master Mortgage, the debtor, was a real estate investment fund. Skopbank, which held a $19 million secured claim, was Master Mortgage's largest creditor. Master Mortgage sought permission to use the cash proceeds of Skopbank's collateral pursuant to § 363(c)(2)(B), and to subordinate Skopbank's lien in order to obtain postpetition financing under § 364(d). Skopbank opposed these applications. Ultimately, Skopbank and Master Mortgage reached an agreement settling a number of disputes, including the postpetition financing issues. The settlement agreement also provided that in consideration of Skopbank's release of its interest in certain notes and mortgages, Master Mortgage would relinquish any claims that it had against Skopbank. In addition to this mutual release, Master Mortgage agreed to include in its reorganization plan a permanent injunction barring all of its creditors and equity security holders from asserting against Skopbank any claim arising from Skopbank's transactions with Master Mortgage. Master Mortgage also entered into settlement agreements with certain non-debtor affiliates. The affiliates released over $3 million in claims against Skopbank, released liens on Master Mortgage property, and agreed to contribute funds to enable Master Mortgage to settle a pending lawsuit. In exchange, the affiliates received a release from Master Mortgage, and Master Mortgage agreed to include in its reorganization plan a permanent injunction barring its creditors and equity security holder form asserting claims against the affiliates. Four out of five impaired classes voted to accept the plan. The Securities and Exchange Commission objected to confirmation of the plan on the grounds that the permanent injunction in favor of Skopbank and the non-debtor Affiliates violated § 524(e) of the Code, and that consequently, the Plan did not comply with § 1129(a)(1). — Eds.]

FRANK W. KOGER, BANKRUPTCY JUDGE.

Discussion

. . . .

I. Section 1129(a)(1): The SEC Objection

The SEC has statutory standing to appear and be heard on any issue in a Chapter 11 proceeding. 11 U.S.C. § 1109(1). The SEC objected to the confirmation of the Debtor's Fourth Amended Plan of Reorganization on the grounds that it violates § 1129(a)(1). That section requires a reorganization plan to comply with all applicable provisions of the Code; if it violates any provision of the Code, then a bankruptcy court has no statutory authority to confirm the plan. The SEC claims that Master Mortgage's plan, insofar as it provides for a permanent injunction protecting Skopbank and other non-debtor affiliates from creditors and interest holders, runs afoul of § 1129(a)(1) because the injunction violates § 524(e) by impermissibly discharging third parties. The issue is whether a bankruptcy court has the power and authority to issue a permanent injunction or whether § 524(e) prohibits the Court from acting. If the Court concludes that it has the authority to issue such an injunction, then the Court must determine when it is appropriate to issue such an injunction and if it is appropriate in this case.

A. Section 105 v. 524

The SEC contends that § 524(e) removes all authority from the bankruptcy court to issue a permanent injunction, release non-debtor third parties or otherwise discharge third party liabilities. Skopbank and the non-debtor affiliates argue that § 105 grants the necessary authority to issue an injunction, and § 524(e), on its face, does not restrict a bankruptcy court's power to issue a permanent injunction. Section 105(a) provides in part:

> The court may issue any order, process, or judgment that is necessary or appropriate to carry out the provisions of this title.

Section 524(e) provides:

Except as provided in subsection (a)(3) of this section, discharge of a debt of the debtor does not affect the liability of any other entity on, or the property of any other entity for, such debt.

Courts have split on the issue of permanent injunctions and third party releases. Those courts that have allowed injunctions or releases rely on the plain language of § 524 noting that the language:

does not purport to limit or restrain the power of a bankruptcy court to otherwise grant a release of third parties.

In re Specialty Equip. Co., 3 F.3d 1043, 1047 (7th Cir. 1993); *see also*, *In re A.H. Robins Co.*, 880 F.2d 694, 702 (4th Cir. 1989), cert. denied, 493 U.S. 959, 110 S. Ct. 376, 107 L. Ed. 2d 362 (1989); *Republic Supply Co. v. Shoaf*, 815 F.2d 1046, 1050 (5th Cir. 1987). Section 105 on the other hand is broadly written allowing all orders that are necessary and proper to effectuate a reorganization which may, at times, require the issuance of an injunction or release. *MacArthur Co. v. Johns-Manville Corp.*, 837 F.2d 89, 93 (2d Cir. 1988). Thus, while an injunction or release may not be warranted in all cases, a per se rule prohibiting injunctions and releases is "similarly unwarranted, if not a misreading of the statute." *In re Specialty Equip. Co.*, 3 F.3d at 1047.

Those courts adopting this permissive view note that injunctions or releases can create some "knotty problems," but have allowed them in specific factual contexts. Factors that courts have considered include:

(1) There is an identity of interest between the debtor and the third party, usually an indemnity relationship, such that a suit against the non-debtor is, in essence, a suit against the debtor or will deplete assets of the estate. *In re A.H. Robins Co.*, 880 F.2d at 701 (indemnity); *MacArthur Co. v. Johns-Manville Corp.*, 837 F.2d at 92 (indemnity); *In re AOV Indus., Inc.*, 792 F.2d 1140, 1142, 253 U.S. App. D.C. 186 (D.C. Cir. 1986) (indemnity); *In re Heron, Burchette, Ruckert & Rothwell*, 148 Bankr. 660, 669 (Bankr. D.D.C. 1992) (partner right to reimbursement by partnership); *In re G.S.F. Corp.*, 938 F.2d 1467, 1475 (1st Cir. 1991) (indemnity); *In re Kasual Kreation, Inc.*, 54 Bankr. 915, 917 (Bankr. S.D. Fla. 1985) (suit against officers would result in severe and irreparable harm to the bankruptcy estate); *In re MacDonald Assocs., Inc.*, 54 Bankr. 865, 867 (Bankr. D.R.I. 1985) (failure to enjoin action against debtor company's two sole shareholders would adversely affect the estate).

(2) The non-debtor has contributed substantial assets to the reorganization. *In re Specialty Equip. Co.*, 3 F.3d at 1045 (third party creditor extended additional $10 million in credit); *In re Drexel Burnham Lambert Group, Inc.*, 960 F.2d 285, 288–89 and n. 2 (2d Cir. 1992) (creditor and debtor pooled their rights to collect judgments from the debtor's former officers and director into a $1.3 billion dollar fund); *In re A.H. Robins Co.*, 880 F.2d at 696 (third party insurer contributed assets to a claimant fund); *MacArthur Co. v. Johns-Manville Corp.*, 837 F.2d at 90 (third party insurer contributed $770 million to a claimant fund); *Republic Supply v. Shoaf*, 815 F.2d at 1048 (third party guarantor contributed $850,000 in insurance proceeds to fund the plan); *In re AOV Indus., Inc.*, 792 F.2d at 1142 (creditor released $51 million in claims and contributed an additional $4.5 million); *In re Heron, Burchette,*

Ruckert & Rothwell, 148 Bankr. at 665–66 (plan funded exclusively by contributions of non-debtors); *In re Monroe Well Serv., Inc.*, 80 Bankr. 324 (Bankr. E.D. Pa. 1987) (largest creditor contributed 6.45 million and other creditors paid additional $1.2 million to fund plan).

(3) The injunction is essential to reorganization. Without the it, there is little likelihood of success. *In re Drexel Burnham Lambert Group, Inc.*, 960 F.2d at 289 (no reorganization without principal creditor settlement, including injunction); *In re A.H. Robbins Co.*, 880 F.2d at 702 (injunction essential to reorganization); *MacArthur Co. v. Johns-Manville Corp.*, 837 F.2d at 90 (injunction the "cornerstone" of the proposed plan); *In re Heron, Burchette, Ruckert & Rothwell*, 148 Bankr. at 667 (injunction the "sine qua non" of the plan); *In re Ionosphere Clubs, Inc.*, 124 Bankr. 635, 642 (S.D.N.Y. 1991) (injunction necessary for successful reorganization); *In re Johns-Manville Corp.*, 68 Bankr. 618, 625 (Bankr. S.D.N.Y. 1986) (no meaningful reorganization unless plan protects the equitable rights of parties in interest); *In re MacDonald Assocs., Inc.*, 54 Bankr. at 870 (debtor unable to reorganize without injunction).

(4) A substantial majority of the creditors agree to such injunction, specifically, the impacted class, or classes, has "overwhelmingly" voted to accept the proposed plan treatment. *In re Specialty Equip. Co.*, 3 F.3d at 1045 (creditors and interest holders entitled to vote "overwhelmingly" accepted the proposed plan treatment); *In re A.H. Robbins Co.*, 880 F.2d at 698 (94% of tort claimants affected by the injunction vote to accept the plan); *In re AOV Indus., Inc.*, 792 F.2d at 1143 (creditor's "overwhelmingly" accepted plan with over 90% of the creditors in each class voting to accept the plan); *In re Heron, Burchette, Ruckert & Rothwell*, 148 Bankr. at (only 1 of 63 creditors and 8 of 93 partners objected to injunction); *In re Johns-Manville Corp.*, 68 Bankr. at 621 (plan overwhelmingly accepted).

(5) The plan provides a mechanism for the payment of all, or substantially all, of the claims of the class or classes affected by the injunction. *In re Specialty Equip. Co.*, 3 F.3d at 1044–45 (plan provided for payment in full of priority and general unsecured claims); *In re Drexel Burnham Lambert Group, Inc.*, 960 F.2d at 288 (impaired parties received a pro rata share in fund established to satisfy their claims and estimated by the court to satisfy them in full); *In re A.H. Robbins Co.*, 880 F.2d at 697 (plan create claimant fund estimated to pay in full all tort claimants affected by injunction); *In re Johns-Manville Corp.*, 68 Bankr. at 621 (plan create a trust out of which claims were to be paid).

No court has set out a rigid "factor test" to be applied in every circumstance. Rather, the courts have engaged in a fact specific review, weighing the equities of each case. The courts seem to have balanced the five listed factors most often. However, these factors do not appear to be an exclusive list of considerations, nor are they a list of conjunctive requirements.

Other courts have reached a contrary result. Those cases advocating a restrictive view of § 524(e) emphasize that § 524(e) discharges the debtor only, not third parties. *See, e.g., In re Western Real Estate Fund, Inc.*, 922 F.2d 592, 601 (10th Cir. 1990), as amended, *Abel v. West*, 932 F.2d 898 (10th Cir. 1991); *In re American Hardwoods, Inc.*, 885 F.2d 621, 625 (9th Cir. 1989). The current § 524(e) is a reenactment of § 16 of the Bankruptcy Act of 1989 which more specifically provided that:

> The liability of a person who is a co-debtor with, or guarantor or in any manner a surety for, a bankrupt shall not be altered by the discharge of such bankrupt.

Act of July 1, 1898, ch. 541, § 16, 30 Stat. 550 (formerly codified at 11 U.S.C. § 34 (1976)). *See Underhill v. Royal*, 769 F.2d 1426, 1432 (9th Cir. 1985). Relying on Act precedent, the courts conclude that any effort to release or protect a non-debtor third-party contravenes the mandates of the Code. *See, e.g., Union Carbide Corp. v. Newboles*, 686 F.2d 593, 595 (7th Cir. 1982).

. . . .

The Court finds the permissive view more persuasive, and concludes that the Court has the authority to issue a permanent injunction or third-party release. The Court does so for three reasons: (1) the plain language of the statute supports this position, (2) an important case relied upon by the restrictive view courts has been overturned, and (3) the factors important to the permissive view courts were not present in restrictive view cases.

First, the clear pattern that has emerged from recent Supreme Court rulings is that an analysis of the plain meaning of the statute is to be used in construing the Bankruptcy Code. . . . When the plain language is clear, the court need go no further in its inquiry. *United States v. Ron Pair Enter. Inc.*, 489 U.S. 235, 113 S. Ct. at 1030. Moreover, the court should interpret the Code in a manner that avoids conflict. *Id.* at, 489 U.S. 235, 109 S. Ct. at 1033.

To the extent that § 524(e) does not explicitly prohibit the court from issuing a permanent injunction, the language is clear, and the Court need not look to the statutory precursor of § 524. . . .

To interpret the section as prohibiting all permanent injunctions would create a conflict with § 105 where there need be none.

Second, the courts using § 524(e) to limit § 105 relied on the Seventh Circuit's *Union Carbide Corp. v. Newboles*, 686 F.2d 593, decision for the proposition that § 524 can never alter the rights of third-party non-debtors. The Union Carbide rule has been substantially revised by the Seventh Circuit in *In re Specialty Equip. Co.*, 3 F.3d at 1046. The Seventh Circuit explained that Union Carbide stands only for the proposition that a gratuitous release of a third party who did not contribute to a reorganization plan was invalid. A third party release where the creditors "overwhelmingly" accept the plan and the party to be released pledges additional credit to the reorganized debtor is valid. Thus, the seminal ruling prohibiting permanent injunctions and releases has been revised.

Third, the five factors considered important to permissive view courts were not present in the restrictive view cases. For example in *In re Western Real Estate*, the Tenth Circuit refused to endorse a plan that proposed to enjoin a single attorney from the collection of his contingency fee against a third party. The third party protected by the injunction did not provide new and substantial contributions to the reorganized debtor, the injunction was not essential to the reorganization, and the only affected creditor, the attorney, did not agree to the plan's treatment of his claim and the concomitant injunction. Similarly in *In re American Hardwoods*, the Ninth Circuit invalidated a plan that proposed to insulate non-debtor guarantors of a secured debt by use of a permanent injunction. The non-debtor guarantors "did not offer to contribute assets to [the] bankruptcy estate," the injunction was not alleged to be essential to the reorganization, and the sole affected creditor did not acquiesce to its treatment.

The Court believes that under appropriate, limited circumstances a bankruptcy court has the power to issue a permanent injunction or third party release. Consequently, the Court adopts the permissive view as espoused in the 2nd, 4th, 5th, 7th and D.C. Circuits. While recognizing a bankruptcy court's power to issue the injunction or release, the Court agrees with the 7th Circuit that a permanent injunction can pose some "knotty" problems. *See In re Specialty Equip. Co.*, 3 F.3d at 1047. Because of these problems, the Court believes that the exercise of that power is discretionary. The Court cautions the Gentle Reader that a permanent injunction is a rare thing, indeed, and only upon a showing of exceptional circumstances in which the factors outlined above are present will this Court even entertain the possibility of a permanent injunction.

B. Application to Skopbank and Non-debtor Affiliates

The Court now turns to the facts at hand. The first factor to be considered is whether there is an identity of interest between Master Mortgage and the entities to be protected by the injunction. The settlement agreement between Skopbank and Master Mortgage creates a right of indemnity between the parties. Thus, any post-petition action against Skopbank would result in a right of contribution against Master Mortgage. Such action would seriously affect Master Mortgage's ability to successfully reorganize. However, the indemnity relationship did not exist prior to the bankruptcy, rather it was negotiated in conjunction with the permanent injunction. Thus, this factor weighs in favor of an injunction benefitting Skopbank, but only marginally because the injunction and indemnity provisions arose contemporaneously.

The non-debtor Affiliates have a right of indemnification against Master Mortgage pursuant to pre-petition contracts. This indemnity relationship extends to all of the possible lawsuits proposed to be enjoined by the permanent injunction. Factor one weighs in favor of an injunction favoring the non-debtor Affiliates.

The second factor to be considered is whether the non-debtor has contributed substantial assets to the reorganization. The Skopbank settlement compromised and settled all of Skopbank's claims against the estate. Under that agreement, Skopbank assigned participation interests and released its collateral interest in various notes and mortgages. These contributions have permitted, for example, a distribution to Class 3A, the holders of interest in Secured Note, who will receive an interest in the liquidation of some 2000 acres of lake front property from . . . collateral [that] was previously part of Skopbank's collateral package. In effect, the contributions of Skopbank valued at more than $4 million dollars have allowed for a distribution to other creditors. This is a substantial contribution of assets, and factor two weighs in Skopbank's favor.

The non-debtor Affiliates have also contributed substantial assets. They have released $3 million in claims against Skopbank, and such release allowed Master Mortgage to settle with Skopbank. Moreover, the non-debtor Affiliates are to contribute 80% of their payment under post-petition contracts to the reorganization. Factor two weighs in favor of an injunction for the non-debtor Affiliates.

Factor three considers whether the injunction is essential to the reorganization. There is little debate among the creditors that without the Skopbank settlement, Master Mortgage could not have reorganized. Skopbank was the single largest creditor, holding more than $19 million in claims. Without the settlement, little could be offered to satisfy other creditor's claims. The assets contributed by Skopbank form the foundation of the Plan. Just as the settlement is the linchpin of the Plan, the injunction is the cornerstone of the settlement. Without the settlement, Skopbank would not have been willing to settle. Thus, the Skopbank settlement and the injunction were essential to the reorganization. Factor three weighs in Skopbank's favor.

The non-debtor Affiliates released over $3 million in claims against Skopbank to facilitate the settlement. As mentioned before, without a release of claims and an injunction Skopbank would not have been willing to settle. Thus, the non-debtor Affiliates' release was also essential to the settlement. Factor three favors their injunction as well.

Factor four considers creditor approval of the injunction. The Court considers this the single most important factor. As shown by the table above, the creditors have overwhelmingly voted to approve the plan. Specifically, Class 5 which is impaired only by virtue of the injunction voted 94.8% in favor of the plan. The members of Class 3A, interest holders in Secured Note, voted 93.4% in number and 96.2% in amount in favor of the plan. Thus, the classes most affected by the permanent injunction have overwhelmingly accepted the proposed Plan treatment. Additionally, the Court notes that the only rejecting class, Class 2B containing the FDIC, settled its claims with Master Mortgage and no longer opposes the Plan. Thus, factor four weighs heavily in favor of the injunction.

Finally, factor five considers whether the Plan provides for the payment of all, or substantially all, of the claims of the class or classes affected by the injunction. The Plan proposes to pay in full all members of Class 3A under two alternative treatments. The first alternative would provide claimants 6% debentures to be paid periodically from specific sources, and to be paid in full by 2003. The second alternative would assign loan participation interests in the full amount of the claim with interest. Class 4, the general unsecured creditors, also are to receive full payment with interest over time. Class 5, the equity interest holders impaired solely by the injunction, will retain the full amount of their equity interest in the reorganized company. Therefore, the Plan proposes to pay in full all of the claims impaired by the injunction. Factor five weighs in favor of the injunction.

All five factors weigh towards the issuance of a permanent injunction in this case. Most significantly the injunction enjoys the support of virtually all creditors. Section 524(e) does not prohibit the issuance of a permanent injunction. That power is within the sound discretion of the Court, and after a close examination of the facts in this case, the Court has concluded that the issuance of a permanent injunction is appropriate here. Therefore, the SEC objection to confirmation must be OVER-RULED. Thus, the Plan complies with all applicable provisions of the Code in accordance to § 1129(a)(1).

DEUTSCHE BANK v.
METROMEDIA FIBER NETWORK, INC.
(IN RE METROMEDIA FIBER NETWORK, INC.)
United States Court of Appeals for the Second Circuit
416 F.3d 136 (2005)

DENNIS JACOBS, CIRCUIT JUDGE:

Creditors Deutsche Bank AG (London Branch) and Bear, Stearns & Co., Inc. (collectively, "appellants") challenge the now-largely implemented Plan of Reorganization ("Plan") confirmed in the Chapter 11 bankruptcy proceeding of Metromedia Fiber Network, Inc. and its subsidiaries (collectively, "Metromedia"). This appeal is taken from a March 18, 2004 judgment of the United States District Court for the Southern District of New York (Brieant, J.), affirming the August 21, 2003 confirmation order of the Bankruptcy Court (Hardin, Jr., B.J.).

. . . .

[A]ppellants argue that releases in the Plan improperly shield certain nondebtors from suit by the creditors.

AboveNet, Inc., f/k/a Metromedia Fiber Network, Inc., and its subsidiaries (collectively, "appellees" or "the Reorganized Debtors") refute these claims on the merits, and also argue that this appeal should be deemed equitably moot because numerous transactions have occurred since the Plan's September 8, 2003 effective date, and because appellants failed to ask the bankruptcy court or the district court for a stay of confirmation pending this appeal.

Appellants' objections to the Plan were rejected on the merits by the bankruptcy court and the district court. At the same time, the district court ruled that relief (if justified by the merits) would not have been barred by the doctrine of equitable mootness because effective relief could have been afforded without "unraveling the Plan."

We conclude that . . . the bankruptcy court erred in approving the nondebtor releases. Nevertheless, we affirm because this appeal is equitably moot.

. . . .

II. The Nondebtor Releases

Among the claims settled in the Plan are those of the Kluge Trust. Under the Plan, the Kluge Trust would [i] forgive approximately $150 million in unsecured claims against Metromedia; [ii] convert $15.7 million in senior secured claims to equity in the Reorganized Debtors; [iii] invest approximately $12.1 million in the Reorganized Debtors; and [iv] purchase up to $25 million of unsold common stock in the Reorganized Debtors' planned stock offering (collectively, "Kluge

Consideration"). In return, the Kluge Trust would receive [i] 10.8% of the Reorganized Debtors' common stock and [ii] the "Kluge Comprehensive Release," which provides that

> the Kluge Trust and each of the Kluge Insiders shall receive a full and complete release, waiver and discharge from . . . any holder of a claim of any nature . . . of any and all claims, obligations, rights, causes of action and liabilities arising out of or in connection with any matter related to [Metromedia] or one or more subsidiaries . . . based in whole or in part upon any act or omission or transaction taking place on or before the Effective Date.

Appellants challenge this release, as well as two other releases that permanently enjoin creditors from suing various nondebtors.[5] Appellants' sole argument — and the only argument that we consider — is that these nondebtor releases were unauthorized by the Bankruptcy Code, 11 U.S.C. § 101 et seq., at least on the findings made by the bankruptcy court.

We have previously held that "in bankruptcy cases, a court may enjoin a creditor from suing a third party, provided the injunction plays an important part in the debtor's reorganization plan." *In re Drexel Burnham Lambert Group, Inc.*, 960 F.2d 285, 293 (2d Cir. 1992). While none of our cases explains when a nondebtor release is "important" to a debtor's plan, it is clear that such a release is proper only in rare cases. *See, e.g., In re Dow Corning Corp.*, 280 F.3d 648, 657–58 (6th Cir. 2002) ("Such an injunction is a dramatic measure to be used cautiously . . . ."); *In re Cont'l Airlines*, 203 F.3d 203, 212–13 (3d Cir. 2000) (recognizing that nondebtor releases have been approved only in "extraordinary cases"). The Ninth and Tenth Circuits have held that nondebtor releases are prohibited by the Code, except in the asbestos context.

At least two considerations justify the reluctance to approve nondebtor releases. First, the only explicit authorization in the Code for nondebtor releases is 11 U.S.C. § 524(g), which authorizes releases in asbestos cases when specified conditions are satisfied, including the creation of a trust to satisfy future claims. . . . True, 11 U.S.C. § 105(a) authorizes the bankruptcy court to "issue any order, process, or judgment that is necessary or appropriate to carry out the provisions of [the Code]"; but section 105(a) does not allow the bankruptcy court "to create substantive rights that are otherwise unavailable under applicable law." *In re Dairy Mart Convenience Stores, Inc.*, 351 F.3d 86, 92 (2d Cir. 2003) (quotations and citation omitted). Any "power that a judge enjoys under § 105 must derive ultimately from some other provision of the Bankruptcy Code." Douglas G. Baird, Elements of Bankruptcy 6 (3d ed. 2001); accord *Dairy Mart*, 351 F.3d at 92 ("Because no provision of the Bankruptcy Code may be successfully invoked in this case, section 105(a) affords [appellant] no independent relief.").

---

[5] One release bars claims against former or current Metromedia personnel (among others), that are related to Metromedia's bankruptcy and based on acts or omissions taking place on or before the Plan's Effective Date, unless based upon "gross negligence or willful misconduct." A second (similar) release shields former or current Metromedia personnel from any claim relating to Metromedia, the Reorganized Debtors, or the Plan.

Second, a nondebtor release is a device that lends itself to abuse. By it, a nondebtor can shield itself from liability to third parties. In form, it is a release; in effect, it may operate as a bankruptcy discharge arranged without a filing and without the safeguards of the Code. The potential for abuse is heightened when releases afford blanket immunity. Here, the releases protect against any claims relating to the debtor, "whether for tort, fraud, contract, violations of federal or state securities laws, or otherwise, whether known or unknown, foreseen or unforeseen, liquidated or unliquidated, fixed or contingent, matured or unmatured."

Courts have approved nondebtor releases when: the estate received substantial consideration, the enjoined claims were "channeled" to a settlement fund rather than extinguished, *MacArthur Co. v. Johns-Manville Corp.*, 837 F.2d 89, 93–94 (2d Cir. 1988); . . . the enjoined claims would indirectly impact the debtor's reorganization "by way of indemnity or contribution," *id.*; and the plan otherwise provided for the full payment of the enjoined claims, *id.* Nondebtor releases may also be tolerated if the affected creditors consent.

But this is not a matter of factors and prongs. No case has tolerated nondebtor releases absent the finding of circumstances that may be characterized as unique. *See Dow Corning*, 280 F.3d at 658; *accord Gillman v. Continental Airlines (In re Continental Airlines)*, 203 F.3d 203 at 212–13 (3d Cir. 2000) ("A central focus of these . . . reorganizations was the global settlement of massive liabilities against the debtors and co-liable parties. Substantial financial contributions from non-debtor co-liable parties provided compensation to claimants in exchange for the release of their liabilities and made these reorganizations feasible."); *see also, e.g.*, *Drexel Burnham*, 960 F.2d at 288–93 (approving multi-billion dollar settlement of 850 securities claims against Drexel, involving $1.3 billion payment into fund by Michael Milken and other co-liable Drexel personnel).

Here, the sole finding made to justify the Kluge Comprehensive Release is that the Kluge Trust made a "material contribution" to the estate. But there is no finding (or evidence presented) that the Kluge Comprehensive Release was itself important to the Plan[7] — which is what *Drexel Burnham* at minimum requires. *See* 960 F.2d at 293 (question is whether "the injunction plays an important part in the debtor's reorganization plan"). Nor was any inquiry made into whether the breadth of the Kluge Comprehensive Release — which covers numerous third parties in addition to the Kluge Trust, and which covers any and all claims relating to Metromedia — was necessary to the Plan. (The two other releases were not separately considered.)

The bankruptcy court's findings were insufficient. A nondebtor release in a plan of reorganization should not be approved absent the finding that truly unusual circumstances render the release terms important to success of the plan, focusing on the considerations discussed above, *see supra* at 14–16. *Cf. Dow Corning*, 280 F.3d at 658 (requiring bankruptcy court to make "specific factual findings that support its conclusions" before authorizing nondebtor releases).

Appellants also claim that notwithstanding any other limitation on nondebtor

---

[7] AboveNet's chief operating officer was asked at the confirmation hearing if he knew "what happens with respect to [the Kluge Settlement] in the event the [Kluge Comprehensive Release] is not granted." He answered, "No, not really."

releases, good and sufficient consideration must be paid to any enjoined creditor. Such consideration has weight in equity, but it is not required. In *Drexel Burnham*, the complaining creditors received none of the proceeds of the settlement with Drexel's personnel. 960 F.2d at 289, 293.

By the same token, we reject appellees' argument that because appellants were allocated a Plan distribution, they received consideration, and therefore cannot be heard to complain about the nondebtor releases. Appellants' Plan distribution (ultimately re-distributed to other creditors, see supra, at 4–5), was on account of appellants' Notes, not on account of their claims against any nondebtor. *See Cont'l Airlines*, 203 F.3d at 215 & n. 13 (differentiating between plan distribution and consideration for enjoined claims). In any event, a nondebtor release is not adequately supported by consideration simply because the nondebtor contributed something to the reorganization and the enjoined creditor took something out.

III. Equitable Mootness

Insufficient findings would ordinarily be remedied by remand to the bankruptcy court. However, appellees argue that this appeal should be dismissed because it is equitably moot. We agree. This court has held that in bankruptcy cases, "an appeal should . . . be dismissed as moot when, even though effective relief could conceivably be fashioned, implementation of that relief would be inequitable." *Official Comm. of Unsecured Creditors of LTV Aerospace and Def. Co. v. Official Comm. of Unsecured Creditors of LTV Steel Co. (In re Chateaugay Corp.)*, 988 F.2d 322, 325 (2d Cir. 1993) [hereinafter *Chateaugay I*].

Equitable mootness is a doctrine distinct from constitutional mootness, though they have been discussed in the same breath. . . . Equitable mootness is a prudential doctrine that is invoked to avoid disturbing a reorganization plan once implemented. *See, e.g., In re UNR Indus.*, 20 F.3d 766, 769 (7th Cir. 1994) ("There is a big difference between inability to alter the outcome (real mootness) and unwillingness to alter the outcome ('equitable mootness')."); *see also MAC Panel Co. v. Va. Panel Corp.*, 283 F.3d 622, 625 (4th Cir. 2002) ("Equitable mootness is a pragmatic principle, grounded in the notion that, with the passage of time after a judgment in equity and implementation of that judgment, effective relief on appeal becomes impractical, imprudent, and therefore inequitable." (emphasis omitted)); *In re Envirodyne Indus.*, 29 F.3d 301, 304 (7th Cir. 1994) (defining the doctrine as "merely an application of the age-old principle that in formulating equitable relief a court must consider the effects of the relief on innocent third parties").

Because equitable mootness bears only upon the proper remedy, and does not raise a threshold question of our power to rule, a court is not inhibited from considering the merits before considering equitable mootness. . . . Often, an appraisal of the merits is essential to the framing of an equitable remedy.

As to the merits of the mootness argument, a plan is "substantially consummated" upon [i] transfer of substantially all of the property proposed by the plan to be transferred; [ii] the reorganized debtor's assumption of the debtor's business; and [iii] commencement of distribution under the plan. 11 U.S.C. § 1101(2). In that context, appellees cite the transactions completed since the Plan's September 8,

2003 effective date, including the issuance of substantially all of the Reorganized Debtors' stock (AboveNet, Inc., now publicly traded on NASDAQ), the full receipt of the Kluge Consideration, the cash distributions, and entry into a host of contracts, leases, and other arrangements as part of AboveNet's day-to-day operations. We conclude that Metromedia's Plan has been "substantially consummated" as that term is defined by the Code. Appellants have not argued otherwise on appeal.

"The ability to achieve finality is essential to the fashioning of effective remedies." *Chateaugay I*, 988 F.2d at 325. When a plan has been substantially consummated, an appeal should be dismissed unless several enumerated requirements are satisfied. *See Frito-Lay, Inc. v. LTV Steel Co. (In re Chateaugay Corp.)*, 10 F.3d 944, 952–53 (2d Cir. 1993) [hereinafter *Chateaugay II*]; *see also UNR Indus.*, 20 F.3d at 769 ("In common with other courts of appeals, we have recognized that a plan of reorganization, once implemented, should be disturbed only for compelling reasons."). A chief consideration under *Chateaugay II* is whether the appellant sought a stay of confirmation. If a stay was sought, we will provide relief if it is at all feasible, that is, unless relief would "knock the props out from under the authorization for every transaction that has taken place and create an unmanageable, uncontrollable situation for the Bankruptcy Court." *Chateaugay II*, 10 F.3d at 953 (quotation omitted). But if the appellant failed to seek a stay, we consider additionally whether that failure renders relief inequitable. *Id.* We insist that a party seek a stay even if it may seem highly unlikely that the bankruptcy court will issue one. *See Chateaugay I*, 988 F.2d at 326 ("A party cannot escape the obligation to protect its litigation position by so facile an argument.").

Here, appellants sought no stay of the confirmation order, and sought no expedited review in this appeal, which was filed over a year ago. Never mind, appellants argue, because (as the district court found) we can provide effective relief without "unraveling the Plan." Specifically, appellants may be permitted in all equity to pursue any claim barred by the releases. We disagree. In the absence of any request for a stay, the question is not solely whether we can provide relief without unraveling the Plan, but also whether we should provide such relief in light of fairness concerns.

Even if we could carve out appellants' claims from the nondebtor releases, we would not do so. If appellants' claims are substantial (as they urge), it is as likely as not that the bargain struck by the debtor and the released parties might have been different without the releases. . . . We therefore would not grant relief in any event without vacatur and remand for further findings and proceedings.

Vacatur and remand would, however, unsettle the settlement of the Kluge Trust's claims, a critical component of the Plan: in exchange for the Kluge Comprehensive Release and a 10.8% stake in the Reorganized Debtors, the Kluge Trust forgave about $150 million of unsecured claims, converted to equity another $15 million, invested a further $12.1 million in the Reorganized Debtors, and committed itself to purchase up to $25 million of unsold stock. It appears that all these things have been done, and that none of the completed transactions can be undone without violence to the overall arrangements. In any event, we cannot predict what will happen if this settlement is in any part altered.

Having sought no stay of the bankruptcy court's order (and no expedited appeal), appellants bear the burden of this uncertainty. *See Chateaugay I*, 988 F.2d at 326 ("The party who appeals without seeking to avail himself of that protection does so at his own risk.")

. . . .

This appeal is equitably moot.

CONCLUSION

For the foregoing reasons, the judgment of the district court is AFFIRMED.

NOTES AND QUESTIONS

(1) *Consideration.* As you undoubtedly recall from your first year of law school, the role of consideration in contract law is to provide evidence that one who made a promise intended to be bound by it. You probably also recall that, over time, the law found substitutes for consideration, such as signed writings, that fulfilled the same evidentiary purpose. *See, e.g.*, § 1-107 of the Uniform Commercial Code, which provides that "Any claim or right arising out of an alleged breach can be discharged in whole or in part without consideration by a written waiver or renunciation signed and delivered by the aggrieved party." Finally, you probably also remember that in most cases, courts will refrain from measuring the adequacy of consideration on the theory that "a cent or a pepper corn" if bargained for, would constitute a valuable consideration. *Whitney v. Stearns*, 16 Me. 394, 397 (1839).

Yet, in the *Master Mortgage* case, Judge Koger took pains to point out that in exchange for its "third party discharge," Skopbank contributed more than $4 million to the reorganization effort and that this constituted a "substantial contribution." Why is it appropriate to evaluate the adequacy of consideration in this context?

One reason may be that, because a Chapter 11 plan may be confirmed over the objection of dissenting creditors, some creditors may be bound by a release even though they do not intend to be. To them, a pepper corn isn't sufficient, because *they* did not bargain for it. Another reason is that in third-party release cases, courts are asked to confer the benefit of a discharge on parties that have not subjected themselves to the scrutiny and burdens of the bankruptcy process. The policy justification for doing so is that in exchange for the discharge, the third parties are making a substantial contribution to the reorganization effort, without which it would fail. Notably, this is not the only context in which bankruptcy courts are called upon to weigh the adequacy of consideration. They also do so when they apply the best interests of creditors test embodied in Code § 1129(a)(7), the cramdown standards of § 1129(b), and the judicially developed standard for confirming a new value plan. *See Bank of America Nat'l Trust and Savings Assoc. v. 203 North LaSalle Street P'ship.*, 526 U.S. 434, 119 S. Ct. 1411 (1999), reprinted in chapter 9, § 9.10.

(2) *Classification Issues.* Assume that among a population of unsecured creditors there are some creditors who hold guarantees provided by the debtor's principals and some who do not. Assume that the debtor proposes a plan that

provides for a release of the principals' liability on those guarantees. Should the claims of creditors who hold guarantees be placed in the same class as the claims of creditors who do not hold guarantees? Are such claims "substantially similar" within the meaning of Code § 1122? Would a plan that releases the guarantors subject creditors who do hold guarantees to unequal treatment in violation of § 1123(b)(4)? In *In re AOV Indus.*, 792 F.2d 1140, 1151 (D.C. Cir. 1986), the court said:

> [T]he most conspicuous inequality that Code § 1123(a)(4) prohibits is payment of different percentage settlements to co-class members. The other side of the coin of unequal payment, however, has to be unequal consideration tendered for equal payment. It is disparate treatment when members of a common class are required to tender more valuable consideration — be it their claim against specific property of the debtor or some other cognizable chose in action — in exchange for the same percentage of recovery.

(3) *Voluntary Releases.* Courts are, for obvious reasons, most comfortable with releases that are consensual and in theory actually bargained for. In *In re Specialty Equipment Cos.*, 3 F.3d 1043 (7th Cir. 1993), creditors were given the option of granting releases to the debtor's officers and underwriters who structured a leveraged buyout involving the debtor. Creditors who voted against the plan, or who abstained from voting, were deemed not to have granted releases. Irrespective of how a majority of claims in the class of which it was a part voted, a creditor who voted against the plan, or who abstained, could pursue its claims against the third parties. The Seventh Circuit refused to invalidate the releases, reasoning:

> The Plan, including the Releases, represents a consensual arrangement arrived at . . . lengthy negotiation and designed to serve a number of goals. The vast majority of interest holders in the same class as [the objecting interest holders], privy to the same information in the disclosure statement, voted to accept this Plan. [The objecting interest holders] have not shown that the Releases are not an essential part of the Plan nor have they offered any compelling reason for us to upset the bargain already struck. Nullification of the Releases at this juncture would amount to imposing a different plan of reorganization on the parties.

Id. at 1049.

In a number of cases, courts have approved third-party discharges given by creditors in exchange for additional distributions under the plan. For example, in *In re Monroe Well Service, Inc.*, 80 B.R. 324 (Bankr. E.D. Pa. 1987), unsecured creditors were placed in one class for voting purposes, but given the opportunity to opt into other classes. If they did, they received additional distributions in return for granting releases to the plan funders, who included the CEO of the debtor. The court held that because the releases were "purely voluntary" and given in exchange for consideration provided by a nondebtor plan funder, the plan was confirmable.

What happens when a creditor votes in favor of a plan that contains a third-party release, but expressly objects to that release? In *In re Rohnert Park Auto Parts*, 113 B.R. 610 (B.A.P. 9th Cir. 1990), the court held that a creditor who voted in favor of a plan but who objected at the confirmation hearing to the provisions of the plan that released claims against guarantors and who stated in its proof of claim that it was not waiving any claims against third parties, was not bound by the release. The National Bankruptcy Review Commission recommended that the Bankruptcy Code be amended to expressly provide for third party releases. However, the commission also has recommended that only voluntary releases be permitted; that consents to third party releases be separately solicited; and that a vote in favor of a plan containing a release not be deemed to be consent to the release. Thus, an accepting majority could not bind a dissenting minority to a third party release. The Commission also would require a finding that such a release is necessary for the effective reorganization of the debtor. *Bankruptcy the Next Twenty Years: Report of the National Bankruptcy Review Commission* at 534 (1997).

(4)   *Derivative vs. Direct Claims.* The controversial release cases generally involve so-called "direct" claims that *creditors hold* against third parties. A plan may also provide for the release of claims that the *debtor holds* against third parties. Release of these claims is governed by Code § 1123(b), which states that "a plan may . . . provide . . . for the settlement or adjustment of any claim or interest belonging to the debtor or to the estate." *See In re Texaco, Inc.*, 84 B.R. 893 (Bankr. S.D.N.Y. 1988), *appeal dismissed as moot*, 92 B.R. 38 (S.D.N.Y. 1988).

The distinction between a direct and derivative claim is apparent in *In re Inforex, Inc.*, 26 B.R. 515 (Bankr. D. Mass. 1983). The plan in that case released all derivative claims against the debtor's officers and directors and enjoined all creditors and stockholders from "instituting or continuing any action, derivative or otherwise, in the name of or on behalf of, or in the right of the debtors." *Id.* at 516–17. After confirmation, a group of former stockholders sued the debtor's current and former officers and directors under Rule 10b-5 and § 10(b) of the Securities Exchange Act of 1934. The directors argued that their liability had been discharged by the confirmed plan. The court disagreed. It explained that the complaint "alleges direct tortious conduct . . . and as such is not a shareholder derivative suit against Inforex's officers and directors for breach of their fiduciary duties owed to the corporation." *Id.* at 518.

(5)   *Mass Tort Bankruptcies.* Debtors faced with mounting claims for asbestos-related personal injury claims have a special protection in Chapter 11: The Code § 524(g) channeling injunction. Section 524(g) is only applicable to mass tort asbestos claims and allows a plan of reorganization to permanently prevent recovery from certain protected parties, such as the debtor and parties that are co-liable on the claims that make a substantial contribution to the reorganization, such as the debtor's insurers. Instead, plaintiffs are required to submit personal injury claims to a settlement trust that will evaluate and pay all present and future claims.

The goal of Code § 524(g) is to create a plan of reorganization that provides for an asbestos bodily injury claim settlement trust that is funded by the debtor, its insurers, and other co-liable third parties. In consideration for the contribution of funds to the claim settlement trust, the debtor and the non-debtor third parties receive the protection of an injunction that "channels" all current and future asbestos claims to the trust for resolution. In order to meet the requirements of

Article III of the United States Constitution, the plan confirmation order must be issued or affirmed by a United States District Court judge.

When issued, the channeling injunction results in the debtor and non-debtor third parties becoming protected parties. All entities that hold current or assert future asbestos claims are permanently enjoined from directly or indirectly recovering or otherwise receiving payment if the claims are against a protected party. Their only remedy is to submit their claims to the settlement trust and seek redress under its provisions, which often involve multiple layers of review, with the opportunity to accept a settlement at each juncture. The settlement trust will evaluate and pay all previously filed asbestos bodily injury claims and is intended to reserve adequate funds for future claims (those arising after the plan and settlement trust are in place).

Section 524(g) is the codification of the channeling injunction/settlement trust mechanism that was approved without specific statutory authorization in the *Johns-Manville and UNR Industries* bankruptcy cases. *See Kane v. Johns-Manville Corp.*, 843 F.2d 636 (2d Cir. 1988). The section was enacted to calm the capital markets, which appeared concerned with the lack of any statutory basis for the channeling injunctions that were being employed in asbestos cases. As stated in *Federal Insurance Co. v. Grace*, Slip Copy, 2004 WL 5517843 at 4 (D. Del. 2004):

> In 1994, with the enactment of the Bankruptcy Reform Act of 1994, the trust-injunctions and related procedures developed by the courts in the bankruptcies of *In re Johns-Manville Corp.* [36 B.R. 743 (Bank.S.D.N.Y.1984); 52 B.R. 940 (S.D.N.Y.1985)] and *In re UNR Industries, Inc.* [46 B.R. 671 (Bank.N.D.Ill.1985); 71 B.R. 467 (Bank. N.D. Ill.1 987)] were codified at 11 U.S.C. § 524(g). This new section, § 524(g), was added to the Code for handling "chapter 11 reorganization proceeding[s] with future personal injury claims against the debtor based on exposure to asbestos-containing products" H.R. Rep. No. 103-835, at 40 (1994), *reprinted in* 1994 U.S.C.C.A.N. 3340. In Chapter 11 asbestos cases, § 524(g) authorizes the appointment of a legal representative to "protect the rights of persons that might subsequently assert demands of such kind [future claims]." 11 U.S.C. § 524(g)(4)(B)(i) (2004). With respect to the legislative history of the Bankruptcy Reform Act of 1994, specifically the reasons for the addition of § 524(g) to the Bankruptcy Code, the House of Representatives Committee on the Judiciary wrote that § 524(g) was included "to offer similar certitude to other asbestos trust-injunction mechanisms that meet the same kind of high standards with respect to regard for the rights of claimants, present and future, as displayed in the two pioneering cases [*Johns-Manville* and *UNR Industries*]." H.R. Rep. No. 103-835, at 40 (1994), *reprinted in* 1994 U.S.C.C.A.N. 3340. The trust-injunctions of *Johns-Manville* and *UNR* were the models for § 524(g), and this Court will review the cases for guidance in the absence of explicit statutory instruction.

The tension in § 524(g) cases is between extracting sufficient value from the estate and those co-liable on the claims to fund the trust adequately in the face of an unknown amount of future claims and the desire of the contributors to minimize their contributions.

(6) *Partnership Bankruptcies.* Third party releases have also been used in partnership cases as a carrot to induce partners to help fund payments to creditors instead of seeking individual bankruptcy protection to extinguish their personal liability on partnership debts. *See, e.g., In re Heron, Burchette, Ruckert & Rothwell*, 148 B.R. 660 (Bankr. D.D.C. 1992).

§ 10.04   POST-CONFIRMATION APPEALS; MOOTNESS

The confirmation of a plan is a final order and therefore appealable. If a creditor or other party in interest is dissatisfied with a plan, and can shape its dissatisfaction into a plausible legal argument, that party can appeal from the order confirming the plan, provided that it made a timely objection to confirmation. *See, e.g. Heins v. Ruti-Sweetwater, Inc. (In re Ruti-Sweetwater, Inc.)*, 836 F.2d 1263 (10th Cir. 1988); *Republic Supply Co. v. Shoaf*, 815 F.2d 1046 (5th Cir. 1987). What happens if a creditor raises an objection prior to confirmation, gets an adverse decision, and takes an appeal, but, in the meantime, the debtor has begun to perform in accordance with the confirmed plan by, for example, making payments to creditors or selling assets. Can performance be unwound? Should it be? These issues, which were briefly addressed in the *Metromedia* opinion are more fully considered in the opinion that follows.

INSURANCE SUBROGATION CLAIMANTS v.
U.S. BRASS CORP.
(IN RE U.S. BRASS CORP.)
United States Court of Appeals for the Fifth Circuit
169 F.3d 957 (1999)

HIGGINBOTHAM, CIRCUIT JUDGE.

Insurance Subrogation Claimants appealed an order of confirmation of a Chapter 11 reorganization plan proposed by U.S. Brass, the debtor. . . .

The ISC contend that the plan violates § 1123(a)(4), which requires all creditors within a class be treated the same, unless the creditor who is being treated less favorably agrees to less favorable treatment. The ISC also argue that the plan was not proposed in good faith under § 1129(a) and should not have been approved.

Shell and U.S. Brass have moved to dismiss ISC's appeal as moot. We agree, and finding the plan substantially implemented and effective relief unattainable, dismiss the appeal.

I

On May 23, 1994, U.S. Brass filed for Chapter 11 relief in the Eastern District of Texas. Prior to the petition date, U.S. Brass had been sued in hundreds of cases seeking damages from alleged defects associated with a polybutylene plumbing system. During the pendency of the Chapter 11 case, a global settlement of the PB litigation was fashioned in an action styled *Tina Cox, et al. v. Shell Oil Co.* . . . with the Chancery Court for Obion County, Tennessee. The *Cox* court certified the Cox Plaintiffs as a national settlement class. The [Insurance Subrogation Claimants ("ISC")] were not members of the settlement class.

In November 1995, the *Cox* court approved a settlement agreement between the *Cox* Plaintiffs and Shell and Celanese and authorized the parties to pursue contributions from U.S. Brass. A contribution plan was negotiated and is incorporated into the plan as the *Cox* Plaintiffs' Settlement Agreement.

The *Cox* Plaintiffs and the ISC are designated as Class 5 claimants in the reorganization plan. The *Cox* Plaintiffs' Settlement Agreement, however, provides a settlement of all *Cox* Plaintiffs' claims in exchange for a cash contribution from the Brass Trust of $37.4 million and 80% of the Brass Trust's recoveries from insurance coverage to the settlement fund. The remaining 20% is available for the other Class 5 claimants like the ISC.

On September 30, 1997, the bankruptcy court approved U.S. Brass' Fourth Amended Disclosure Statement and on January 27–29, 1998, held a confirmation hearing. The bankruptcy court overruled the ISC's objections and confirmed the plan and the incorporated settlements, including the *Cox* Plaintiffs' Settlement Agreement. The *Cox* court in Tennessee, in turn, entered a final order on February 5, 1998, approving the Cox Plaintiffs' Settlement Agreement and authorizing the Cox Plaintiffs to consummate the transactions contemplated in the plan.

On February 24, 1998, the bankruptcy court entered its order confirming the reorganization plan and it became effective March 6, 1998. On the same day, the ISC filed a notice of appeal to the district court of the confirmation order. Here begins the path to mootness. The ISC also filed a motion for limited stay pending appeal with the bankruptcy court requesting the bankruptcy court to enjoin any funding from the Brass Trust to the *Cox* Plaintiffs or to the Consumer Plumbing Recovery Center, the entity that administers the $950 million settlement from Shell and Celanese. The ISC did not seek emergency or expedited consideration of the bankruptcy court's order.

The reorganization plan proceeded, and on March 19, 1998 the following events occurred:

(1) The Brass Trust was created pursuant to § 7.1 of the plan;

(2) nearly $5 million was distributed to pay the holders of allowed administrative, priority and general unsecured claims;

(3) Eljer [the parent company of U.S. Brass] wired more than $48 million into the Brass Trust;

(4) the Brass Trust paid more than $32 million to the CPRC for distribution to holders of allowed plumbing claims;

(5) various global settlement agreements and releases were signed by the major participants in the Chapter 11 case, such as the Cox Plaintiffs'

Settlement Agreement, the Shell/Celanese Settlement Agreement, and the Brass Settlement Agreement;

(6) [a note from the parent company] was executed; and

(7) U.S. Brass and its parents assigned all their right, title, and interest to certain insurance proceeds to the Brass Trust.

On March 26, 1998, U.S. Brass filed an objection to the ISC's motion to stay, urging that the plan was now substantially consummated. The bankruptcy court held a hearing on the stay motion on May 6, 1998. Although no ruling came forth, the ISC did nothing and on July 27, 1998, the district court affirmed the bankruptcy court's confirmation of the plan.

On August 25, 1998, the ISC filed a notice of appeal to this court. Then finally on September 17, 1998, the ISC filed a motion to stay and a request for expedited consideration with the district court. The district court never ruled on the stay motion.

The ISC did nothing until January 21, 1999, almost four months after appealing the confirmation of the plan to this court. The ISC requested that this court stay further proceedings pending appeal in this court. We must determine whether this appeal is moot considering the failure of the ISC to obtain a stay, the action taken toward implementing the plan, and the potential effect of the ISC's requested relief on the plan.

II

When evaluating whether an appeal of a reorganization plan in a bankruptcy case is moot, this court examines whether (1) a stay has been obtained, (2) the plan has been substantially consummated, and (3) the relief requested would affect either the rights of parties not before the court or the success of the plan. Shell and U.S. Brass argue that each of the factors favor finding the ISC's appeal moot.

1. *Failure to Obtain a Stay*

To date, the ISC have not obtained a stay. U.S. Brass and Shell argue that the ISC's efforts in pursuing a stay have not been diligent. For example, the first stay requested by the ISC, on March 6, 1998, was made without a request for expedited consideration even though the bankruptcy court had already confirmed the plan on January 29, 1998. Similarly, although the district court affirmed the plan on July 27, 1998, the ISC waited until September 17, 1998 to seek a stay from the district court. The district court never ruled, and the ISC never sought further action on this second stay request until January 21, 1999, when the ISC filed a motion for stay with this court. U.S. Brass and Shell maintain that the ISC's failure to obtain a stay and its lack of diligence militates in favor of dismissal for mootness.

This court has recognized that "the failure or inability to obtain a stay pending appeal carries the risk that review might be precluded on mootness grounds." *Manges*, 29 F.3d at 1040. In this case, it is undisputed that the ISC have failed to obtain a stay. We turn to the transactions that have taken place as a consequence to determine the extent to which the plan has been implemented.

2. *Substantial Consummation of the Plan*

The second question in the mootness inquiry is whether the plan has been substantially consummated. According to 11 U.S.C. § 1102(a):

"Substantial consummation" means —

(A) transfer of all or substantially all of the property proposed by the plan to be transferred;

(B) assumption by the debtor or by the successor to the debtor under the plan of the business or of the management of all or substantially all of the property dealt with by the plan; and

(C) commencement of distribution under the plan.

"'Substantial consummation' is a statutory measure for determining whether a reorganization plan may be amended or modified by the bankruptcy court." *Manges*, 29 F.3d at 1040. This court may "decline to consider the merits of confirmation when a plan has been so substantially consummated that effective judicial relief is no longer available — even though the parties may have a viable dispute on appeal." *Berryman*, 159 F.3d at 944.

The parties dispute whether the plan has been substantially consummated. In the absence of a stay pending appeal, U.S. Brass, the Brass Trust, the CPRC, and various other parties in interest have proceeded to implement the plan. Shell and U.S. Brass argue that the events following the March 1998 confirmation demonstrate how extensively the plan has been implemented. The following actions, for example, have occurred since the ISC sought a stay pending appeal in the district court:

(1) U.S. Brass has continued to operate as a reorganized entity;

(2) U.S. Brass has paid in full all of the outstanding debt owed to its debtor-in-possession financing lender;

(3) U.S. Brass and [its parent company] have implemented a new financing arrangement whereby [its parent company] provides operating funds to U.S. Brass;

(4) the bankruptcy court has entered orders providing the final allowance to Class 4 general unsecured claims;

(5) U.S. Brass has amended its state charter and by-laws as required by the plan;

(6) a number of state lawsuits against [its parent company] asserting plumbing claims have been dismissed with prejudice;

(7) the Brass Trust has transmitted checks in the sum of $267,978.45 as offers of full settlement to the convenience class claimants;

(8) the Brass Trust has opened bank accounts, established an account record system, implemented an investment program for excess funds, obtained insurance coverage, established by-laws, and retained professionals to carry out its duties;

(9) the Brass Trust, the CPRC, and Goldin Associates, the financial advisors to the Brass Trust, have established a claim resolution system to process allowed claims;

(10) the CPRC has distributed to holders of allowed plumbing claims all of the funds transferred by the Brass Trust to the CPRC;

(11) Shell and Celanese, in reliance on the Confirmation order and pursuant to the terms of the Shell/Celanese Settlement Agreement, which was incorporated into the plan, have released asserted claims against U.S. Brass in excess of $1 billion for a payment of $2.5 million and have increased their commitment to the Cox Settlement from $850 million to $950 million.

U.S. Brass claims that all of the elements of "substantial consumption" have occurred because on March 19, 1998, U.S. Brass emerged as a newly reorganized entity and, as the Closing Binders make clear, "(i) distributions commenced (with the transfer of more than $48 million to the CPRC and the payment if more than $5 million to holders of allowed administrative, priority and general unsecured claims), and (ii) substantially all the property to be transferred under the plan was transferred (i.e., U.S. Brass assigned to the Brass Trust all of their right, title and interest to certain insurance recoveries)." Shell and U.S. Brass maintain that these transactions cannot be "unscrambled" and should weigh in favor of mootness.

The ISC reply that the plan has not been so substantially consummated that effective relief is no longer available. The relief the ISC seek would require the Brass Trust to reallocate its future disbursements of insurance recoveries pro-rata among all Class 5 claimants, instead of the present 80%/20% plan. In order to effectuate this relief, the ISC propose removing the *Cox* Plaintiffs' Settlement Agreement from the plan. Shell and U.S. Brass contend that removing the *Cox* Plaintiffs' Settlement Agreement from the plan would dismantle the plan.

We find the transactions that have taken place to date, the exchange of mutual releases, the disbursements already made, and the general implementation of the plan by all the involved parties evidence substantial consummation of the plan. This determination, however, does not end the mootness inquiry. "Substantial consummation of a reorganization plan is a momentous event, but it does not necessarily make it impossible or inequitable for an appellate court to grant effective relief." *Manges*, 29 F.3d at 1042–43 (quoting *Frito-Lay, Inc. v. LTV Steel Co., Inc. (In re Chateaugay Corp.)*, 10 F.3d 944, 952 (2nd Cir. 1993)). Rather, we must also consider whether the remedy the ISC seek will affect the success of the plan or alter the rights of third parties that have been achieved by its substantial consummation. More specifically, we must determine whether the plan has been implemented to a point that the removal of the *Cox* Plaintiffs' Settlement Agreement would jeopardize the plan's success.

3. *Granting Relief Would Affect Third Parties and Plan*

Shell and U.S. Brass maintain that the Cox Plaintiffs' Settlement Agreement is an essential element of the plan, and its removal would detrimentally affect confirmation. They argue that the various settlement agreements between and among the major parties with an interest in the Chapter 11 case — U.S. Brass, Shell, Celanese, and the Cox Plaintiffs — were found by the bankruptcy court to be essential to the debtor's reorganization. Without the inclusion of the Cox Plaintiffs' Settlement Agreement, Shell and U.S. Brass argue that the plan would not have been confirmed.

Section 13.1 of the plan expressly provides that certain events, including the approval of the Cox Plaintiffs' Settlement Agreement, the Shell/Celanese Settlement Agreement, and the Brass Settlement Agreement, are conditions precedent to confirmation of the plan. These settlements reflect the negotiations of the parties interested in the Chapter 11 case and the bargains they secured by voting in favor of the plan. Shell and U.S. Brass argue that if the 80%/20% split provided by the Cox Plaintiffs' Settlement Agreement was altered, the change would affect the interdependence of all the settlements. The plan also provides that any of the settling parties may withdraw from the plan in the event there are modifications to which the parties have not agreed. In short, U.S. Brass and Shell maintain that the Cox Plaintiffs Agreement cannot be eliminated from the plan without unraveling the entire plan. In addition, U.S. Brass and Shell oppose any modification of the plan by judicial fiat because 11 U.S.C. § 1127 provides that only the proponent of a plan or the reorganized debtor may modify a confirmed plan.

The ISC, on the other hand, contend that the plan will not unravel if the court affords them relief by modifying the 80%/20% split with the Cox Plaintiffs to a pro rata distribution. According to the ISC, the only effect of removing the *Cox* Plaintiffs' Settlement Agreement would be to alter the Brass Trust's distribution to holders of Class 5 claims.

III

While the ISC's proposed surgery appears at first blush to be possible, we are persuaded it would excise parts to which other vitals of the plan are attached. To remove the *Cox* Plaintiffs' Settlement Agreement from the plan at this point would dismantle a substantially consummated plan, requiring, for example, a restoration of the rights of the *Cox* Plaintiffs to pursue claims against U.S. Brass, now a reorganized entity. In addition, the releases and settlements that were negotiated among the parties would have to be undone because removal of the *Cox* Plaintiffs' Settlement Agreement would consequently require giving each settling party the right to withdraw from the plan. Removal of the Cox Plaintiffs' Settlement Agreement would also require that the money contributed by U.S. Brass' parent corporations to fund the plan be recovered. These circumstances persuade us that it would be inequitable for this court to consider the merits of the ISC's appeal. Accordingly, we dismiss this appeal as MOOT.

NOTES AND QUESTIONS

(1) *Overcoming Mootness.* As more than one court has pointed out,

> Where a plan has been substantially consummated there fairly exists a strong presumption that appellants' challenges have been rendered moot due to their inability or unwillingness to seek a stay. This presumption is undergirded by the common sense notion that the piecemeal dismantling of the Reorganization Plan in subsequent appeals of individual transactions is, in practical terms if nothing else, a virtually impossible task. The policy reasons underlying the mootness doctrine is simply that where substantial elements of the reorganization plan have been implemented in the absence of a stay, any appeal of the confirmation order is moot because it is very doubtful that effective relief could be afforded.

In re Best Prods. Co., 177 B.R. 791, 803 (S.D.N.Y. 1995). Still, as the *U.S. Brass* court cautioned, substantial consummation in the absence of a stay does not automatically spell mootness. In *Frito-Lay, Inc. v. LTV Steel Co., Inc. (In re Chateaugay Corp.)*, 10 F.3d 944, 952 (2d Cir. 1993), the Second Circuit explained,

> Constitutional and equitable considerations dictate that substantial consummation will not moot an appeal if all of the following circumstances exist: (a) the court can still order some effective relief; (b) such relief will not affect the re-emergence of the debtor as a revitalized corporate entity; (c) such relief will not unravel intricate transactions so as to knock the props out from under the authorization for every transaction that has taken place and create an unmanageable uncontrollable situation for the Bankruptcy Court; (d) the parties who would be adversely affected by the modification have notice of the appeal and an opportunity to participate in the proceedings; and (e) the appellant pursued with diligence all available remedies to obtain a stay of execution of the objectionable order . . . if the failure to do so creates a situation rendering it inequitable to reverse the orders appealed from.

10 F.3d at 952–53 (citations and internal quotations omitted).

(2) *No End Runs.* A party that fails to obtain stay pending appeal cannot avoid the mootness problem by collaterally attacking a confirmation order. As discussed at the beginning of this chapter, a confirmation order has res judicata effect; parties may not re-litigate issues that were or could have been decided by the bankruptcy court. *Miller v. Meinhard-Commercial Corp.*, 462 F.2d 358, 360 (5th Cir. 1972). In *Republic Supply Co. v. Shoaf*, 815 F.2d 1046, 1051 (5th Cir. 1987), the bankruptcy court confirmed a plan that provided for the release of a third-party guarantor. Notwithstanding the release, a creditor continued to prosecute an action against the guarantor. The district court held that the confirmed plan did not release the guarantor, because the bankruptcy court had no authority under the Bankruptcy Code to release a nondebtor, and that, accordingly, the confirmation order was not res judicata of the suit on the guaranty. The Fifth Circuit reversed. It held that whether or not the Code authorized the release, it had been incorporated into a confirmed plan without objection or appeal and that it could not be collaterally attacked. The Fifth Circuit found that all the elements necessary for application of

res judicata were present: the parties were identical in both suits; the bankruptcy court had jurisdiction to determine the extent of its own jurisdiction over the parties and the subject matter (i.e., the release); the same cause of action was involved in both actions; and the confirmation order was a final judgment on the merits. *See also Stoll v. Gottlieb*, 305 U.S. 165 (1938).

(3) *Practical Effect of a Stay.* Why not issue a stay whenever one is requested? What harm could it do? Consider the following hypothetical: Suppose that a plan provides that shares of stock in the reorganized debtor will be distributed to creditors. Suppose that the shares are held in escrow pending the outcome of the appeal. What if the value of the shares in escrow declines while the appeal is pending, and at least some of the creditors would have sold those shares immediately — who bears the loss?

§ 10.05 REVOCATION OF CONFIRMATION

TENN-FLA PARTNERS v. FIRST UNION NATIONAL BANK OF FLORIDA
United States District Court, Western District of Tennessee
229 B.R. 720 (1999), *affirmed* 226 F.3d 746 (2000)

JEROME TURNER, UNITED STATES DISTRICT JUDGE.

I. Standard of Review

A district court reviews the bankruptcy court's findings of fact for clear error and the bankruptcy court's conclusions of law de novo.

. . . .

II. Background

TFP is a Tennessee general partnership whose primary asset was an apartment property located in Florida ("the property"). TFP acquired the property in 1984 and refinanced the first mortgage in 1989 through $12,685,000 worth of tax-exempt bonds issued by Florida Housing Finance Agency. The appellee, First Union National Bank of Florida, is the bond trustee.

TFP filed a Chapter 11 petition and related schedules on July 17, 1992. The schedules listed its major secured debt as the bonds, and its only substantial asset as the property with an estimated value of $6,000,000. On December 16, 1992, TFP filed its original plan of reorganization.

First Union challenged TFP's valuation of the property, and on April 22, 1993, the bankruptcy court found the value of the property to be $9,100,000.

The bonds were non-recourse, leaving any potential recovery to be determined by the value of the property.

First Union subsequently filed its own plan of reorganization.

Both the TFP and First Union plans were amended several times, with each amendment reflecting additional cash to be paid for the property and the bonds. TFP's amended plan also provided that upon acceptance the bondholders would rescind their § 1111(b)(2) election. . . .

The bankruptcy court approved the disclosure statements . . . and the competing plans and solicitation materials were mailed to creditors for their acceptance or rejection. The bondholders accepted both plans.

At a recess from the confirmation hearing . . . , TFP agreed to increase its monetary offer to match the offer contained in First Union's plan. First Union withdrew its objection to the confirmation of TFP's plan and recommended confirmation. After an oral offer of proof with respect to TFP's compliance with the requirements of § 1129(a), the bankruptcy court confirmed TFP's plan. Under the confirmed plan, TFP agreed to pay $9,885,000 (about $350,000 of which would go to First Union as part of an administrative claim) for the property and the bonds. This resulted in an approximate 75% recovery to the bondholders, with the shortfall being discharged.

Shortly after confirmation, TFP contracted to sell the bonds and the property to United Dominion for $12,443,547, resulting in an apparent net recovery to TFP of approximately $2,500,000 over the amounts necessary to pay the bondholders and other creditors under its plan. First Union subsequently filed suit to revoke the bankruptcy court's order of confirmation so that First Union might recover the excess proceeds for the bondholders. First Union claimed TFP knew of the property's true value and under-represented that value at the confirmation proceeding so that any excess proceeds from the sale of the property would benefit TFP's equity holders.

The bankruptcy court allowed TFP to proceed with the sale of the bonds and property to United Dominion and to make certain distributions required under the plan, but required TFP to place the excess in escrow pending a determination on First Union's claim.

The bankruptcy court made several factual findings, based on documentary and testamentary evidence, including:

a) First Union's interest was in getting the highest possible price for the property.

b) United Dominion, through its representative Benjamin Norbom, was told about the property in the fall of 1993. TFP and United Dominion had continuous discussions between August 1993 and October 1993 concerning United Dominion's interest in the property. . . .

c) Ray Coleman, the property manager, was told in November of 1993 by Jack Friedman, a broker, that Colonial Properties was interested in purchasing the property. Coleman told Colonial's representative that the property was in bankruptcy and would not be available for sale until after bankruptcy. Colonial kept in constant contact with Coleman, and ultimately made a $12,250,000 offer for the property on or about February 4, 1994.

d) Coleman was told by Cole Whitaker, a broker, in late 1993 that JMB Institutional Realty wanted an exclusive right to purchase the property. Coleman told a JMB representative that the property was in bankruptcy and that no offers could be accepted until TFP's plan had been accepted by the bankruptcy court. During these discussions, JMB indicated an interest in paying in the mid-$11,000,000 range for the property. JMB's interest continued right through the confirmation process, and a JMB representative testified the only reason for their delay in making a firm offer was Coleman's refusal to deal until after TFP's plan was confirmed.

e) In November of 1993, Coleman sent a solicitation letter to the bondholders urging them to accept the TFP plan. The letter represented that absent their acceptance of TFP's plan, there was a possibility that the bondholders "could be left without a buyer."

f) Coleman believed he would not get a real estate commission if the property was sold during bankruptcy. The bankruptcy court inferred from this that Coleman's primary concern may have been his own best interest.

g) Coleman told Robert Smith, the broker who eventually produced the successful offer from United Dominion, not to place further offers on the property until it was out of bankruptcy, and to have his main buyer ready as soon as TFP was out of bankruptcy.

h) TFP's partners had a personal obligation to First Tennessee Bank for approximately $2,500,000 they had borrowed to fund operating shortfalls of the property. Bryson Randolph, a consultant to TFP, testified that TFP intended to pay the bondholders a minimum amount of cash as quickly as possible and to create an investment recovery for its partners. An internal memorandum prepared by Norbom noted that United Dominion could not participate in TFP's plan of reorganization because TFP's goal was to receive approximately two million dollars in excess of the discounted value of the bonds. If United Dominion participated, First Union would seek the excess for the bondholders. The bankruptcy court inferred from the above that TFP intended to hide the true value of the property and sell soon after confirmation, using the excess proceeds to satisfy the personal obligations of TFP's equity holders.

i) Coleman was aware that he was under a duty to disclose any offers to purchase the property. While TFP did disclose an $8,000,000 offer on the property from FRM Properties, TFP did not disclose its contact with United Dominion, Colonial Properties or JMB. The bankruptcy court inferred from this that the lower offer was disclosed to play down the value of the property, while the more serious interest was hidden so the equity holders might take advantage post-confirmation.

The bankruptcy court summarized its factual findings as follows:

The court has considered all of the proof, disputed and undisputed, and has weighed the interest and credibility of witnesses. From its discussion of the proof, it is evident to the court that the debtor provided misleading and incomplete disclosures, that the debtor had serious contacts with several motivated and qualified purchasers at prices far exceeding what the debtor was offering to the bondholders, that the effect of the debtor's actions was to misrepresent the market for and market value of the property, that the debtor intentionally discouraged the submission of offers prior to confirmation, that the debtor concealed or "parked" purchasers until after the confirmation, that the debtor was motivated to accomplish its goal of protecting the investment of its insider partners by assuring payment of their recourse First Tennessee Bank debt, and that the debtor misrepresented to the court at the confirmation hearing that it was in compliance with all elements of § 1129(a). In summary, the debtor violated its debtor in possession obligations and engaged in self-dealing to the expense of the bondholders, who had been induced by the debtor's misrepresentations to give up their § 1111(b)(2) election. All of this was accomplished by the debtor without adequate disclosure to the court or to creditors until after the confirmation hearing and order.

170 B.R. at 963.

The bankruptcy court also found the undisclosed information to be material and that TFP was under a duty to disclose it. The bankruptcy court based this duty of disclosure on three separate grounds: a plan proponent's duty to comply with the disclosure requirements of § 1125; a plan proponent's duty to propose a plan in good faith; and the fiduciary duty of a debtor in possession. The court also found that as a fiduciary, TFP was not only obligated to disclose pre-confirmation interest in the property, but was obligated to maximize the value of the property for all creditors. The court found the failure to disclose the true value of the property was fraudulent within the meaning of § 1144, in that by concealing the true value of the property TFP induced the court to believe at the confirmation hearing that TFP had fully disclosed all material information and that it had proposed its plan in good faith. The bankruptcy court revoked the order of confirmation and awarded First Union attorney's fees and expenses. The court refused to impose punitive damages on TFP, however, and did not award to First Union as compensatory damages all sums paid out of the proceeds of the sale of the property to subordinate secured and unsecured creditors. The court also converted the case to a Chapter 7 proceeding and directed the United States Trustee to appoint an interim trustee.

. . . .

IV. The Elements of Fraud Under Section 1144

Section 1144 is the only provision under the Bankruptcy Code that allows a court to revoke an order confirming a plan of reorganization. Section 1144 allows a court to revoke the order "if and only if such order was procured by fraud." For the order of confirmation to be revocable, therefore, fraud must be directed at the court. There is no requirement that a creditor rely on the fraud.

While § 1144 does not define the term "fraud," "fraud on the court" has been defined as "a fraud perpetrated by officers of the court so that the judicial machinery cannot perform in the usual manner its impartial task of adjudging cases that are presented for adjudication." *Harbold v. Commissioner*, 51 F.3d 618, 622

(6th Cir. 1995) (internal quotations and citations omitted). In the context of revoking an order of confirmation under § 1144, this can be restated as requiring:

(1) a representation by the debtor regarding compliance with § 1129;

(2) which was materially false;

(3) that was either known by the debtor to be false, or was made without belief in its truth, or was made with reckless disregard for the truth;

(4) that was made to induce the court to rely upon it;

(5) that the court did rely upon; and

(6) that as a consequence of such reliance, the court entered the confirmation order.

Ordinarily, a party's failure to disclose material facts to the court does not rise to the level of fraud on the court. More egregious conduct, such as the fabrication of evidence or the bribery of a judge or jury is generally required. In actions to revoke a bankruptcy court's order, however, courts have been more willing to examine the disclosures of a party with the duty to disclose for fraudulent omissions. . . . These courts have determined fraudulent intent can be shown where "a person who (1) is obligated to disclose, (2) knows of the existence of material information, and (3) does not disclose it." *In re Giguere*, 165 B.R. at 534 (quoting *In re Michelson*, 141 B.R. at 725). This broader examination of a plan proponent's conduct is based on good reason. The integrity of the confirmation process is dependent on a plan proponent's honest compliance with the requirements of § 1129.

The test for fraud under § 1144 can be restated to account for a party's non-disclosures as follows:

(1) an intentional omission;

(2) by a party with a duty to disclose;

(3) of facts that would be material to finding the party complied with § 1129;

(4) that were withheld so that the court would find the party complied with § 1129;

(5) and that as a consequence of such non-disclosure, the court entered the confirmation order.

The court finds the burden of establishing these elements falls on the party challenging the confirmation.

. . . .

V. The Bankruptcy Court's Findings of Fraud

The bankruptcy court found that through non-disclosures TFP intentionally misrepresented at the confirmation hearing that it proposed its plan in good faith, that it complied with the Code's disclosure requirements, and that it complied with its fiduciary duty to its creditors, as required by § 1129(a)(2)–(3).

The transcript of the confirmation hearing shows the bankruptcy court asking for an oral offer of proof that the elements of § 1129 were met. TFP's attorney responded "Yes sir, good faith and all identities disclosed and all classes accept and better than liquidation."

The court further found that the misrepresentations were directed at the court, and that the misrepresentations impaired the court's ability to confirm the plan in an impartial manner. In light of the above standards, this court must determine whether the bankruptcy court was in clear error in finding a preponderance of the evidence supported its factual determinations, and must examine de novo whether the bankruptcy court's factual determinations were legally sufficient to fulfill the elements of fraud under § 1144.

1. An Intentional Omission

The question of intent is generally considered to be one of fact. *United States v. Hopkins*, 357 F.2d 14, 18 (6th Cir. 1966). The bankruptcy court found that prior to confirmation, TFP knew of several qualified purchasers who were actively interested in purchasing the property and the bonds for more than TFP was offering in its plan. Rather than disclosing this interest, the bankruptcy court found TFP intentionally concealed it so that it could sell the property after confirmation at a price far exceeding its obligations under the plan, thus retaining the excess proceeds for the benefit of the equity holders. In effect, the bankruptcy court found TFP had engaged in a form of self-dealing.

This court has reviewed the record and has set out earlier in this order several factual findings of the bankruptcy court. These facts offer strong support for the bankruptcy court's conclusion that TFP intentionally concealed the true interest in the property for its own benefit. . . .

TFP disagrees with the bankruptcy court's related conclusion that it was TFP's strategy to hide the true interest in the property so it could sell the property at an excess value shortly after confirmation. TFP argues there was no evidence of an intent to sell or evidence of a pre-confirmation deal. Evidence of a pre-confirmation deal is not necessary to find that TFP intended to make a deal with one of several interested buyers shortly after confirmation. The bankruptcy court found TFP put off several interested buyers in an attempt to take advantage of their interest for TFP's equity holders, who needed the excess funds to bail them out from recourse debt they had incurred to float operating shortfalls of the property. Several of the many pieces of evidence in support of this finding are set out earlier in this opinion, and are enough that this court cannot find clear error in the bankruptcy court's determination that TFP intended to sell the property shortly after confirmation.

Accordingly, the court finds the bankruptcy court did not clearly err in finding by a preponderance of the evidence that TFP intentionally concealed the true interest in the property, and that it intended to take advantage of this interest by selling the property shortly after confirmation.

TFP argues that the Code provides adequate protection of disclosures because they are tested twice in a normal bankruptcy case: once when the disclosure statement is approved, and again at confirmation, and that relitigation of the property's value, which First Union had previously contested, is unwarranted. *See In re Szostek*, 886 F.2d 1405 (3d Cir. 1989). This argument is without merit. Where the plan proponent intentionally does not make a full disclosure the protections of §§ 1125 and 1129 are inadequate, and an injured party may seek to revoke confirmation under § 1144. *"Absent substantial new evidence of fraud*, there is no reason why Congress would have wished, or the courts should permit, participants who actively participated in the reorganization to relitigate in later civil actions previously raised issues about the adequacy of the disclosure statement, or to reserve for such actions claims that feasibly could have been made in the reorganization." *Kaufman v. Public Service Co. (In re Public Service Co.)*, 43 F.3d 763, 768 (1st Cir. 1995) (emphasis added). The bankruptcy court found the evidence "does not support the argument that knowledge of the property's potential was equally available prior to confirmation to First Union or the court." The court finds no clear error in the bankruptcy court's determination and finds First Union may proceed under § 1144.

2. Duty to Disclose

It is axiomatic that the person charged with fraud on the court for non-disclosure must have had an obligation to disclose those facts to the court. As discussed above, the duty under this factor contemplates the debtor in possession's duty to the court, not to the creditors.

. . . .

A. Section 1125

The bankruptcy court found that § 1129(a)(2) requires that the plan proponent comply with all other applicable provisions of the Bankruptcy Code, including the adequate disclosure requirements of § 1125. This court agrees with the bankruptcy court's conclusion that § 1125 required TFP to make adequate disclosures.

Courts have found § 1125 to be one of the applicable provisions of the Code referred to in § 1129. *See, e.g., In re Trans World Airlines, Inc.*, 185 B.R. 302, 313 (Bankr. E.D. Mo. 1995) ("The principal purpose of section 1129(a)(2) of the Bankruptcy Code is to assure that the plan proponents have complied with the disclosure requirements of section 1125 of the Bankruptcy Code in connection with the solicitation of acceptances of the plan.").

The bankruptcy court also found that under the circumstances, TFP's disclosures were not adequate. This is a question of fact that will only be reversed if in clear error. Section 1125 defines "adequate information" as "information of a kind, and in sufficient detail, as far as is reasonably practicable . . . that would enable a hypothetical reasonable investor typical of holders of claims or interests of the relevant class to make an informed judgment about the plan." § 1125(a)(1). "Adequate information" generally includes a complete description of the available assets and their value and the anticipated future of the debtor. *In re Scioto Valley Mortgage Co.*, 88 B.R. 168, 170 (Bankr. S.D. Ohio 1988).

. . . .

This court agrees with the bankruptcy court's factual conclusion that the existence of purchasers who potentially were willing to pay substantially more than was being offered by the proposed plan is information that would be needed by a hypothetical investor to make an informed judgment about the plan. Accordingly, the court finds TFP had a duty under § 1125 to disclose the information.

B. Good Faith

Although the term "good faith" is not defined by the Code, there is substantial case law interpreting the requirements of good faith.

Under one view, the good faith requirement of § 1129(a)(3) is met if the plan will fairly achieve a result consistent with the objectives and purposes of the Bankruptcy Code. Under another view, the good faith requirement is met if the plan was proposed with honesty and good intentions, and with a basis for expecting that a reorganization can be effected. Under a third view, good faith requires fundamental fairness in dealing with one's creditors.

. . . .

The bankruptcy court found that TFP was obligated to disclose the true interest in the property in order to comply with the Bankruptcy Code's requirement that a plan be proposed in good faith. *See* § 1129(a)(3). TFP argues it could not have been in bad faith because it "subjectively thought it was achieving an end permitted by the Bankruptcy Code." The bankruptcy court, however, found TFP "knew of willing and able buyers but temporarily spurned their offers and 'parked' their interests, all for the purpose of preventing the secured bondholders from realizing or capturing the true value of their collateral. The court may not simply call this creative reorganization, when the debtor's strategy, inter alia, undermines the integrity of the chapter 11 process." This court finds no clear error in the bankruptcy court's determination, and accordingly finds TFP was required to disclose the true interest in the property to comply with § 1129(a)(3).

C. Section 1107

The bankruptcy court also found that § 1129(a)(2) placed TFP, as a debtor in possession, in a fiduciary relationship with creditors of the debtor under § 1107, and that as a fiduciary TFP had the duty to disclose the interest in the property. This court agrees.

Section 1107 places upon a debtor in possession the duties of a trustee, and a debtor in possession must comply with § 1107 to be in compliance with § 1129. As a debtor in possession, TFP owed a fiduciary duty to both the estate and the court. This fiduciary duty included a duty to disclose all known material information. *F & M Marquette Co. v. Emmer Bros. Co. (In re Emmer Bros. Co.)*, 52 B.R. 385, 394 (D. Minn. 1985) (finding that a debtor in possession "who fraudulently conceals an asset during the course of the bankruptcy proceedings surely violates" the "fiduciary responsibility to the bankruptcy court and its creditors"). Accordingly, the court finds that TFP was required by § 1107 to disclose the known interest in the property.

3. Material Facts

A bankruptcy court may only confirm a plan of reorganization if all the requirements of § 1129 are met. Thus, material information is information that is necessary for a court to decide whether the elements prescribed for confirmation have been satisfied. The bankruptcy court found information on the true value of the property would be material to a finding of compliance with § 1129.

In order to confirm the proposed plan, the court must be able to make "an informed, independent judgment regarding each element of confirmation." *In re Michelson*, 141 B.R. at 720. This court finds that information on TFP's failure to disclose the true interest in the property would be material to a determination on whether TFP's plan met the Code's disclosure requirements, was proposed in good faith, and on whether TFP complied with its fiduciary duty as a debtor in possession.

4. Withheld from the Court

The bankruptcy court found that TFP's "lack of disclosure and bad faith misrepresentations were made for the purpose of obtaining an order of confirmation and the court relied upon the debtor's representations that all § 1129(a) elements were satisfied."

Why TFP withheld information is a factual inquiry that will not be reversed absent clear error. This court finds the bankruptcy court was not in clear error in finding that TFP's omissions were directed at the court so that it might obtain an order of confirmation.

5. Causing the Plan to be Confirmed

A bankruptcy court must confirm a plan of reorganization if all the requirements of § 1129 are met. Thus, an order of confirmation can only be procured by fraudulent non-disclosures if the court would not have issued the order had it been aware of the undisclosed information.

This court has upheld the bankruptcy court's determination that TFP intentionally concealed facts from the court that would have been material to the confirmation process so that TFP's plan would be confirmed. The bankruptcy court also held "it would not have confirmed the debtor's plan had the court known that the debtor knew of an immediate $2,300,000 equity return to insiders of the debtor." The bankruptcy court based this determination on its finding that the undisclosed interest in the property would preclude the court from confirming the plan under § 1129(a) because of inadequate disclosure, bad faith, and breach of fiduciary duty.

Whether the bankruptcy court would be required to confirm TFP's plan in light of its non-disclosures is a question of law that this court reviews de novo. This court finds that if the bankruptcy court knew of TFP's true intentions at the time of confirmation it would be precluded from confirming TFP's plan because of inadequate disclosure, bad faith, and breach of fiduciary duty.

"The suppression of material facts that likely would have led to a different result unambiguously constitutes an impairment of the adjudicatory process." *In re Michelson*, 141 B.R. at 729. Accordingly, the court finds the bankruptcy court correctly held it would not have confirmed TFP's plan but for TFP's fraudulent omissions.

Non-disclosure of facts can amount to an interference with judicial machinery because the court's duty to make an informed, independent judgment regarding confirmation issues puts the court at center stage during the confirmation process. Recalling that the statute requires that the order confirming the plan have been "procured by fraud," it is apparent that pulling the wool over the eyes of the court impairs the judicial machinery in the performance of its duty. *In re Michelson*, 141 B.R. at 725.

6. Summary

The court finds all elements of the test for fraud upon the court via non-disclosure under § 1144 have been met. Accordingly, the bankruptcy court's decision to revoke its prior confirmation of TFP's plan of reorganization is affirmed.

VI. Duty to Maximize

The bankruptcy court found that as a party with fiduciary duties, TFP was under a duty to maximize the value of the estate. TFP argues that the fiduciary duty of a debtor in possession is owed to both creditors and equity holders, and that it took a course of action that recognized both of those interests. Even ignoring TFP's failure to account for its fiduciary duty to the court, the court finds TFP's failure to maximize the value of the estate was a breach of its fiduciary duty.

"The purpose of [Chapter 11] is to provide a debtor with legal protection in order to give it the opportunity to reorganize, and thereby to provide creditors with going-concern value rather than the possibility of a more meager satisfaction through liquidation. Therefore, the maximization of the value of the estate is not necessarily the primary goal of a Chapter 11 reorganization as it would be in a Chapter 7 liquidation." *Canadian Pacific Forest Products Ltd. v. J.D. Irving, Ltd. (In re The Gibson Group, Inc.)*, 66 F.3d 1436, 1442 (6th Cir. 1995). However, in this case the bankruptcy court found TFP intended to liquidate the property shortly after confirmation so that its equity holders could take advantage of the true value of the property. Thus, in this case, maximization of value should have been the primary concern of TFP.

Although not discussed by the bankruptcy court, in light of the true value of the property it would appear that the creditors did not receive under TFP's Chapter 11 plan what they would have received under a Chapter 7 liquidation, as required by § 1129(a)(7). The court need not discuss whether TFP's plan complied with this requirement, however, because the court has already found the plan failed to comply with several other requirements of § 1129.

The court does note, however, that TFP specifically told the bankruptcy court that all creditors would receive under its plan what they would in a Chapter 7 liquidation. Thus, contrary to numerous arguments in its brief, TFP did make an affirmative representation to the court on the value of the property.

"The willingness of courts to leave debtors in possession is premised upon an assurance that the officers and managing employees can be depended upon to carry out the fiduciary responsibilities of a trustee." *CFTC v. Weintraub*, 471 U.S. 343, 355, 105 S. Ct. 1986, 85 L. Ed. 2d 372 (1985). It is true that a debtor in possession owes a fiduciary duty to both creditors and equity holders. *Id.* This does not allow a debtor in possession to favor equity holders over creditors, however, or to engage in conduct that essentially amounts to concealing assets and self-dealing.

The [debtor in possession] does not act in his own interests until he reverts to his former status upon discharge and confirmation of the plan. The extent of the fiduciary duties should not vary with the identity of the one who performs that role.

The dangers resulting from the concealment of assets are greater when the debtor remains in possession than in cases in which a third party acts as trustee. An outside trustee is a separate mechanism for discovering unlisted claims or assets. If a debtor in possession were permitted to omit claims in bankruptcy and later assert title to them, there might be an inducement to do so, to the prejudice of creditors' interests. Such a rule would undermine the fiduciary status of the debtor in possession. *Stein v. United Artists Corp.*, 691 F.2d 885, 892 (9th Cir. 1982).

To the contrary, the hierarchy of the Bankruptcy Code provides that the interests of creditors are paramount to the interests of the equity holders, and a trustee must act in accordance with this hierarchy. *See id.* ("One of the painful facts of bankruptcy is that the interests of shareholders become subordinated to the interests of creditors."). Thus, the court finds that TFP had a duty to maximize the estate under § 1107. The court finds TFP breached this duty by not obtaining the known highest available price for the property prior to confirmation.

VII. Conversion to Chapter 7

TFP argues that if the bankruptcy court erred in revoking the order of confirmation, it also must have erred in converting the Chapter 11 proceeding to a proceeding under Chapter 7. This court has found that the bankruptcy court did not err in revoking the order of confirmation, however, and finds that the bankruptcy court was well within its discretion in converting the proceeding for cause under § 1112(b). Accordingly, the court finds the proceeding was properly converted to a Chapter 7 proceeding.

VIII. Attorney's Fees

The bankruptcy court awarded First Union attorney's fees and expenses incurred in this action. TFP protests that § 1144 makes no provision for an award of attorney's fees, and that under the "American Rule" a prevailing party does not receive attorney's fees in the absence of a statute or contract providing for such recovery.

While TFP is correct that ordinarily a court may not award attorney's fees in the absence of statutory or contractual authority, an exception exists where fraud has been practiced upon the court. The bankruptcy court found TFP had committed a fraud upon the court and this court has agreed with that determination. Accordingly, the court finds that the bankruptcy court was within its discretion to award attorney's fees to First Union.

IX. Compensatory Damages

First Union has cross-appealed the bankruptcy court's refusal to reimburse it for funds paid out of the proceeds of the sale of the property. After First Union filed a motion seeking to enjoin TFP's sale of the property to United Dominion, the parties entered into a consensual order whereby TFP was allowed to proceed with the sale of the property. Under that order, TFP was allowed to use the proceeds to pay ordinary closing costs and to satisfy the claims of classes 4, 5, 6, and 7 as provided in the challenged and confirmed plan while placing the rest of the funds in escrow. At issue is TFP's $10,000 payment to Sunburst Bank of Georgia and roughly $80,000 in payments to unsecured trade creditors.

First Union asked the bankruptcy court to reimburse it for those payments, because the claims of both Sunburst Bank and the trade creditors were subordinate to the claim of the bondholders. The bankruptcy court agreed that absent a confirmed plan neither Sunburst nor the trade creditors would have received any value for their claims because they were junior to the bondholders' secured claim. The bankruptcy court also recognized that to be compensated for the full value of their secured claim, the bondholders would have to be compensated in the amount of those payments. Nevertheless, the bankruptcy court refused to compensate First Union because it found that under First Union's plan First Union would have made the payments anyway.

Section 1144 is designed to put the parties back to their pre-confirmation positions, as long as the rights of third parties who in good faith relied on the plan are protected. § 1144. The bankruptcy court understood its task was to try and return the parties to their pre-confirmation positions. However, the bankruptcy court took one step further and essentially put the parties in the position it found they would be in pre-confirmation of TFP's plan and post-confirmation of First Union's plan.

There are several problems with this reasoning. First, it is unclear if First Union's plan would ever have been confirmed. The bankruptcy court itself noted if First Union had been advised of the true value of the property, it "probably would have withdrawn its plan, sought to negotiate a sale to [the interested buyers], or sought conversion or dismissal in order to foreclose and sell after bankruptcy." Second, even if First Union's plan had been confirmed, while that plan called for the payment of the unsecured trade creditors, it also provided that their claims against TFP would be assigned to First Union. These were recourse claims, and there is evidence in the record that the partners of TFP had personal assets sufficient to cover them. Thus, under First Union's plan the partners of TFP would ultimately have been liable for the $80,000 in unsecured trade claims. The bankruptcy court's refusal to compensate First Union for the payments made to the unsecured creditors therefore has the troubling effect of releasing TFP's partners from personal liability at the expense of sale proceeds First Union was entitled to. Third, the bankruptcy court's order essentially put the parties in their pre-confirmation positions and then directed that First Union pay Sunburst and the unsecured creditors in accordance with what the court believed was required by First Union's plan. It is unclear, however, where the bankruptcy court obtained the power to take this action. Section 105 empowers a court to take action necessary to carry out other provisions of the Bankruptcy Code. But neither § 1144 nor any other provision of the Code would seem to allow the court to direct First Union to proceed in accordance with First Union's proposed plan after TFP's confirmed plan had been revoked.

The court disagrees with the bankruptcy court's legal determination that the bondholders' willingness to make the payments under its plan was relevant in its attempt to restore the parties to their pre-confirmation positions. Accordingly, the court finds that TFP must reimburse First Union for the payments made to Sunburst and the unsecured trade creditors out of the property sale proceeds.

X. Punitive Damages

First Union has also cross-appealed the bankruptcy court's refusal to award punitive damages. The bankruptcy court found that punitive damages are often appropriate as punishment or to deter future inappropriate conduct. The court refused to award punitive damages in this case because it had converted the case to a Chapter 7 proceeding and there was no danger of the debtor repeating its abuses.

First Union argues the bankruptcy court should have considered the effect of an award of punitive damages on other debtors. First Union also asserts that the bankruptcy court's award does nothing to prevent the partners of the debtor from forming another entity and engaging in the same conduct.

The court agrees with First Union that the deterrence of conduct by other similarly situated parties, including the partners of the now bankrupt TFP, is a consideration that may be taken into account by a bankruptcy court in its decision on whether to award punitive damages. First Union has cited no case, and this court has found none, however, which holds that a bankruptcy court must consider the effect of punitive damages on other parties. An award of punitive damages is at the discretion of the bankruptcy court. The court finds the bankruptcy court was not required to explore the potential deterrence on other parties in determining whether to impose punitive damages, and therefore finds the bankruptcy court was within its discretion not to do so.

HASKELL v. GOLDMAN, SACHS & CO.
(IN RE GENESIS HEALTH VENTURES, INC.) (GENESIS I)
United States Bankruptcy Court for the District of Delaware
324 B.R. 510 (2005), *affirmed in part and vacated in part, remanded*, 340
B.R. 729 (2006)

HONORABLE JUDITH H. WIZMUR. (U.S. Bankruptcy Court, District of New Jersey, Sitting by Designation)

. . . .

Facts

The Genesis Health Ventures, Inc. ("Genesis") and Multicare AMC, Inc. ("Multicare") debtors filed separate Chapter 11 bankruptcy cases on June 22, 2000. The debtors' Joint Plan of Reorganization was filed on July 6, 2001 and confirmation hearings were held on August 28 and 29, 2001. Debtors' plan was confirmed on September 12, 2001. . . .

Two and a half years later, plaintiffs filed this complaint on January 24, 2004 in the Supreme Court for the State of New York. The complaint was removed to the United States District Court for the Southern District of New York, transferred to the United States District Court for the District of Delaware, and then referred to the Delaware bankruptcy court.

The plaintiffs are comprised of 275 investors who, on October 2, 2001, collectively held 55% of all debentures ("Senior Subordinated Notes") issued by Genesis, with a face value in excess of $205 million. The debentures were subordinated to about $1.3 billion in senior debt. Defendant Goldman Sachs & Co. purchased about half of the Genesis senior debt participations shortly before the debtors' bankruptcy filings. Goldman became the largest senior creditor of both Genesis and Multicare, and served as the underwriter for the DIP and exit financing.

Plaintiffs allege that Goldman, Highland Capital Partners, another senior debt participant, and Mellon Bank N.A., the debtors' lead senior lender bank, ("Senior Lenders") "conspired with Genesis management to put the Company into bankruptcy and 'cram down' a reorganization plan that would eliminate junior creditors (including plaintiffs) and existing stockholders, while conveying virtually total ownership of Genesis to the senior creditors." The confirmed plan merged Genesis and Multicare, extinguished the Old Common Stock of both companies, and distributed about 94% of the newly issued stock of the reorganized, combined entities to the Senior Lenders. The junior creditors, including the Genesis Senior Subordinated Note claimants, received an approximate dividend of 7.34%, plus New Warrants.

Plaintiffs allege that the enterprise value of Genesis was misrepresented at confirmation as being about $1.3 billion. The enterprise value was based on a multiple of the Genesis budgeted EBITDA (earnings before interest, taxes, depreciation, and amortization) for 2001, which was projected at $158 million, down from between $205 and $210 million for the fiscal years 1998 and 1999. In August 2001, shortly before the confirmation hearing, the debtor presented its historical LTM EBITDA (last twelve months EBITDA) for the preceding 12 month period, which supported the $158 million projection. Plaintiffs contend that "both the Budgeted EBITDA projections and the LTM EBITDA were 'cooked', to depress EBITDA and thereby depress the valuation of Genesis." Because the LTM EBITDA was presented only six days prior to the confirmation hearing, plaintiffs complain that they were unable to challenge the EBITDA in a timely manner.

Plaintiffs assert causes of action for fraud, conspiracy to commit fraud and gross negligence. More specifically, plaintiffs assert in Count One of their complaint that

> Genesis and Hager [the Chief Financial Officer of Genesis] were directly
> involved in the preparation of all the misleading financial information that

led to the under-valuation of Genesis.

> Goldman, Mellon and Highland controlled this entire process, periodically reviewing in detail the financial information prepared by Genesis management on a monthly basis, to assure that EBITDA data were matching the "target" of about $158 million, and that sufficient adjustments were being made to the budgeted EBITDA to bring about the same result. They offered enormous financial inducements to Genesis management to perpetrate this fraud, and they were the principal beneficiaries of the fraud. Goldman also took all the steps needed to freeze MC's cash and lines of credit so that it could not pay its obligations to Genesis, thus forcing Genesis to draw down almost $200 million from its DIP lending facility.

Complaint at PP184, 185. In support of these allegations, plaintiffs contend that Genesis management improperly decreased the debtors' EBITDA by deducting a host of unsubstantiated and unwarranted items.

In Count Two, plaintiffs allege that

> Goldman, Mellon and Highland were aware that the financial information being released by Genesis, and upon which the reorganization valuation of the Company would be determined, was false and misleading and had been designed to defraud the junior creditors of Genesis, and would be relied upon by the plaintiffs and the Court.

> Goldman, Mellon and Highland conspired with, orchestrated and rewarded Genesis and its management, and in particular defendant George Hager, for perpetrating this fraud.

Complaint at PP191, 192. In Count Three, plaintiffs allege that

> By virtue of their positions as debtor in a bankruptcy proceeding, as the chief financial officer of the debtor, as senior creditors of the debtor, and as proponents of a bankruptcy reorganization plan that would drastically affect the junior creditors, defendants owed the junior creditors of Genesis a duty of care, including the duty to provide fair, accurate and complete information.

> Defendants violated that duty of care by disseminating false and misleading financial information that misled the bankruptcy court and the plaintiffs concerning the true financial condition and prospects of Genesis. Defendants' conduct was such an extreme and severe departure from due care as to constitute gross negligence, and was therefore not released as a result of the Genesis bankruptcy.

Plaintiffs believe that if Genesis had been properly valued, there would have been sufficient value for the subordinated debenture holders to recover the full par value of their debentures. They seek an award of damages in an amount not less than $200 million, plus interest, costs and fees.

Defendants view plaintiffs' complaint as another attempt to alter the distribution to creditors provided for under the debtors' confirmed Chapter 11 plan. Allowing the plaintiffs a recovery against the debtors in this action "would have the direct effect of diluting the value of its common stock distributed to its former senior creditors, and a judgment against the Senior Lenders named in this suit would have the effect of transferring distributions made to them under Plan into the hands of the subordinated debentureholders."

Discussion

. . . .

I. *Plaintiffs' Complaint is Time-Barred Under 11 U.S.C. § 1144*

The Confirmation Order approving the debtors' reorganization plan was entered on September 12, 2001. The plaintiffs' complaint was filed on January 24, 2004.

Section 1144 provides that, "on request of a party in interest at any time before 180 days after the entry of the order of confirmation, and after notice and a hearing, the court may revoke such order if and only if such order was procured by fraud." 11 U.S.C. § 1144. This six month time limitation is strictly construed, and courts have enforced the bar even where fraud is later discovered beyond the deadline. . . . The allegation by the plaintiffs that they had insufficient opportunity to uncover the fraud prior to the confirmation of the debtors' plan, and only discovered the alleged fraud by various means after the expiration of the six month limitation, does not alter the effectiveness of the bar here.

Instead, the threshold question is whether the plaintiffs' quest for money damages from the debtors and the other defendants, based on allegations of pre-confirmation fraud, constitutes a collateral attack on the confirmation order, which would be time-barred, or whether it represents a separate cause of action against the various defendants, which is not proscribed by § 1144.

On its face, the statute pertains only to the revocation of a confirmation order procured by fraud. Some courts have viewed fraud allegations seeking monetary damages, made against the debtor and others associated with a confirmed plan of reorganization, to constitute an impermissible collateral attack on a debtor's reorganization which would "allow [the plaintiffs] to do indirectly what they no longer may do directly because of 11 U.S.C. § 1144." *Hotel Corp. of the South v. Rampart 920, Inc.*, 46 B.R. 758, 770–71 (E.D. La. 1985), *aff'd*, 781 F.2d 901 (5th Cir. 1986).

Other courts adopt a more nuanced approach to the applicability of § 1144, examining whether the case involves an attempt to "'redivide the pie' by a disgruntled participant in the Plan," or whether the relief sought would upset the confirmed plan. *In re Coffee Cupboard. Inc.*, 119 B.R. 14, 19 (E.D.N.Y. 1990) (citing to *In re Emmer Bros. Co.*, 52 B.R. 385, 392 (D. Minn. 1985)). If a judgment awarding the plaintiff money damages would not ultimately affect the plan distributions made to the creditor body, the cause of action premised on fraud may proceed. For example, in *In re Circle K Corp.*, 181 B.R. 457 (Bankr. D. Ariz. 1995), the complaint alleged improper conduct, defective disclosures and erroneous valuation information in connection with the confirmation of the debtor's plan of reorganization. The court determined that although the plaintiffs were clearly "disgruntled creditors,"

Id. at 462, the cause of action may proceed because "the Court can fashion a remedy that does not upset the confirmed plan, i.e., monetary damages." *Id.* The court reflected that the remedies sought are intended "to redress harm and divest alleged tort-feasors of wrongfully obtained property, without affecting innocent parties and creditors." *Id.* at 459. Similarly, in *Emmer*, an independent cause of action against the debtor premised on an undisclosed asset could proceed because an adjudication of the dispute would not upset the confirmed plan. And in *In re Crown-Globe. Inc.*, 107 B.R. 60 (Bankr. E.D. Pa. 1989), causes of action based on conversion, intentional misrepresentation and negligent misrepresentation survived a motion to dismiss based on § 1144, whereas a quest for equitable subordination did not. The equitable subordination count sought to shift the priority of claims as they were paid under debtor's confirmed plan, and therefore represented an untimely attempt to revoke the confirmation of the debtor's Chapter 11 plan. *Id.* at 62. The court concluded that the equitable subordination count was time barred under § 1144.

Applying these concepts to this case, I conclude that the plaintiffs' causes of action asserted against the debtor Genesis Health Ventures, Inc. must be dismissed as time-barred under 11 U.S.C. § 1144. Because money damages, rather than a revocation of the confirmation order, are sought by the plaintiffs against the debtor, it may appear at first blush that section 1144 does not apply. However, the impact of a significant money damages award against the debtor would be to "redivide the pie", to upset the confirmed plan, and to negatively affect innocent parties and creditors who received value in the forms of new equity and new debt in the reorganized debtor. Section 1144 was designed to limit challenge to the viability of the reorganized entity emerging from Chapter 11, to fix the liabilities of the reorganized debtor and to provide certainty and finality to the confirmation process.

> [A] Chapter XI proceeding [is] focused towards rehabilitating a business, which if successful, is to the benefit of all persons who had dealings with the debtor. Such plans are not easily devised, and once accomplished a short time for challenging such plan is necessary to keep alive the potential life of that business. Uncertainty of continued operations, injected by a Sword of Damocles in the form of fraud allegations which can be filed at any time in the future, would render meaningless the whole purpose of a Chapter XI proceeding.

In re Newport Harbor Assocs., 589 F.2d 20, 24 n. 6 (1st Cir. 1978). *See also In re Orange Tree Assocs., Ltd.*, 961 F.2d 1445, 1447–48 (9th Cir. 1992).

I conclude that as to the debtor, the complaint is time-barred by operation of 11 U.S.C. § 1144.

[The court concluded that, with respect to the non-debtor defendants, the complaint was barred under the doctrines of claim and issue preclusion. — Eds.]

On appeal, the District Court affirmed the Bankruptcy Court's dismissal with respect to the debtor, but vacated and remanded with respect to the non-debtor defendants. In the portion of the opinion on remand that follows, the Bankruptcy Court considers whether the claims against the non-debtor defendants were also time-barred by operation of § 1144.

HASKELL v. GOLDMAN, SACHS & CO.
(IN RE GENESIS HEALTH VENTURES, INC.) (GENESIS II)
United States Bankruptcy Court for the District of Delaware
355 B.R. 438 (2006)

PETER J. WALSH, UNITED STATES BANKRUPTCY JUDGE.

Even where a party does not explicitly seek revocation, § 1144's time limitation applies to relief that would "redivide the pie" or otherwise upset a confirmed plan. *In re Coffee Cupboard Inc.*, 119 B.R. 14, 19 (E.D.N.Y. 1990) (citing *In re Emmer Bros. Co.*, 52 B.R. 385, 392 (D. Minn. 1985)). Obviously, Plaintiffs commenced this action more than 180 days after the confirmation order. Therefore, if their action amounts to an attempt to revoke the confirmed Plan, it is time barred. On the other hand, if the action is truly independent, § 1144 is inapplicable. *See S.N. Phelps & Co. v. Circle K Corp. (In re Circle K Corp.)*, 181 B.R. 457, 462 (Bankr. D. Ariz. 1995). Plaintiffs identify a number of authorities that support the conclusion that an action based on the post-confirmation discovery of fraudulent conduct is not subject to § 1144's time restriction. For example, in *Emmer Bros.*, the plaintiff sought money damages for a defendant's failure to disclose certain material facts during the bankruptcy proceedings. *Emmer Bros.*, 52 B.R. at 392. The court held that the time limitation in § 1144 was not applicable to such an "independent cause of action." *Id.* at 391–92.

Likewise, in *Circle K*, the creditor plaintiffs sought to revoke the plan based on misrepresentations and omissions concerning the valuation information used in the plan confirmation proceedings. *Circle K*, 181 B.R. at 459. The court rejected the plaintiffs' request to revoke the plan. However, after the 180-day period had expired, the plaintiffs amended their complaint and sought damages instead of revocation. Though the allegations in the amended complaint were "nearly identical" to the original, the relief sought had changed. *Id.* at 462. As a result, the court held that § 1144 did not bar the plaintiffs from proceeding, because "the Court can fashion a remedy that does not upset the confirmed plan, i.e., monetary damages." *Id.*

Despite the factual similarities between the instant case and *Circle K*, Defendants have chosen to address that case only in passing. In a couple of sentences, Defendants dismiss *Circle K* outright because the action there was brought within 180-days of the confirmation order. That, however, is irrelevant. Section 1144 either applies or not. If the action is tantamount to revoking the plan, it applies; and if § 1144 applies, it imposes an 180-day limitation. On the other hand, if the action is truly independent, it does not apply; and if § 1144 does not apply, then, of course, the 180-day limitation also does not apply. In *Circle K*, the court determined that the "relief sought is not to have the confirmation order revoked. Plaintiffs have ended their attack on the confirmation order and now seek damages or restitution." *Circle K*, 181 B.R. at 462. As such, Defendants have failed to offer any meaningful distinction between *Circle K* and the instant matter.

Further, I find the reasoning of *Circle K* and the cases cited therein persuasive. What if a creditor filed a false or inflated claim and this fact was not discovered prior to plan distributions and was discovered more than 180 days after plan confirmation? The effect would be to unfairly inflate that creditor's distribution while deflating the distributions to other similarly situated creditors. Why deny the adversely affected creditors from pursuing a fraud claim against the wrongdoing creditor, with no impact on the reorganized debtor or the plan? In this Court's view, under the facts alleged here (assuming they are proven at trial), there ought to be a remedy to redress the harms suffered and a mechanism to divest the alleged tortfeasors of their ill-gotten gains, at least where doing so would not affect innocent parties. See *id.*; *see also* 8 Collier on Bankruptcy 1144.04[2][a] (Alan N. Resnick & Henry J. Sommers eds. 15th ed. rev. 2005) ("While the court is without power after expiration of the [180-day] deadline to revoke the confirmation order, there may be other avenues to provide relief to parties affected by fraud during the chapter 11 case. . . . The most likely form the relief will take is to allow a party injured by fraud to maintain an action for damages caused by the fraud.").

. . . .

Defendants argue that for purposes of § 1144 no distinction should be made between a damage action against a debtor and one against its creditors. I disagree for two reasons.

First, as the other bankruptcy judge in this case observed, the impact of a substantial money judgment against the Debtor would "negatively affect innocent parties and creditors who received value in the forms of new equity and new debt in the reorganized debtor." Section 1144's primary concern is protecting innocent third parties who relied on the confirmation order. Thus, a judgment against a debtor that would frustrate the reliance of innocent third parties would be impermissible under § 1144.

In contrast, an independent money judgment against a creditor guilty of fraud would only affect that particular creditor. If Plaintiffs are ultimately successful here, Defendants will have to satisfy the judgment out of their own pockets. Such a payout would only impact Defendants' present property interests and would do so without regard to the Plan distributions that occurred almost five years ago. Also, if Plaintiffs succeed on the merits there would be no adverse impact on the Debtor or any party in interest in the chapter 11 case other than Defendants. . . . Thus, unlike an action against the Debtor, the damage claim here would not "redivide the pie" as between two classes of claims. *See Circle K*, 181 B.R. at 462.

Second, allowing Plaintiffs to proceed against the Debtor in this case would have necessarily upset the confirmed Plan. Such a proceeding would entail revoking the Debtor's discharge. Revocation of the discharge would have the effect of changing the Plan's distribution scheme entirely. All claims would revert back to the status that they had on the date of the petition, and any impairment effected by the Plan would be nullified. Clearly, this would operate to revoke the Plan.

In contrast, Defendants here are non-debtors and are not protected by the discharge. Allowing a proceeding against them does not entail revoking the Plan. As a result, I disagree with Defendants' assertion that it "is no more permissible under § 1144 against Defendants remaining in this case than it was against the Debtor" and "that no real distinction can be drawn between the dismissed claims against the Debtor and the claims against Defendants."

Moreover, I disagree with Defendants' assertion that, if anything, it is more permissible to pursue a debtor than it is to pursue a specific group of wrongdoing creditors. According to Defendants, "[i]f Plaintiffs may not indirectly affect the Plan distribution scheme through a money damages claim against the Debtor, it follows *a fortiori* that they may not directly affect that distribution scheme by compelling the Senior Lenders to pay over $200 million of their distribution to junior, subordinated creditors." This misses the point. The very fact that Plan distribution is routed through the Debtor renders a judgment against the Debtor more significant, not less. A judgment against the Debtor could alter the rights of many different groups of creditors and interest holders. In other words, it could hurt innocent creditors and their subsequent good faith transferees, and it would reallocate these innocent parties' Plan distributions to Plaintiffs. The net effect of this would be to give non-plaintiff parties (regardless of fault) a smaller share of the pie and Plaintiffs a larger slice. This clearly would amount to "redividing the pie."

As Defendants suggest, it is true that if Plaintiffs succeed against them, then Plaintiffs will benefit to the extent of Defendants' detriment. But this is true in all damage actions. Under Defendants' conception, no party could ever sue any creditor who received a distribution without upsetting the confirmed plan. This view is not supported by the language of § 1144, the policies of the Bankruptcy Code, or the case law. Accordingly, the Court concludes that § 1144 does not bar this action.

NOTES AND QUESTIONS

(1) *Absolute Deadline.* Section 1144 states that a request to revoke a confirmation order must be made within 180 days after the date of the entry of that confirmation order. Requests made after that date are untimely and must be dismissed. Bankruptcy Rule 9024 is to the same effect, and Bankruptcy Rule 9006(b)(2) prohibits the court from enlarging this time period, which applies even if the fraud is not discovered until after the 180-day window has closed. The reason for allowing the fraud to "ride through," if it is not detected soon enough, has been explained as follows:

> There is a compelling reason for finality of reorganization plans. A Chapter 11 proceeding is focused towards rehabilitating a business, which if successful, is to the benefit of all persons who had dealings with the debtor. Such plans are not easily devised, and once accomplished a short time for challenging such plan is necessary to keep alive the potential life of that business. Uncertainty of continued operations, injected by a Sword of Damocles in the form of fraud allegations which can be filed at any time in the future, would render meaningless the whole purpose of a Chapter XI proceeding.

> . . . .

> [U]nless a reorganized debtor can assure new creditors as to the amount of his actual liabilities without a contingent addition of the old debts, he will start with a handicap in a race which he has already once lost.

Dale C. Eckert Corp. v. Orange Tree Assoc., Ltd. (In re Orange Tree Assoc., Ltd.), 961 F.2d 1445, 1447–48 (9th Cir. 1992) (citations omitted). Or as another bankruptcy court put it:

> Nor should there be any great mystery as to why § 1144 is so circumspect. Any number of scenarios can and do play out under the terms of a confirmed plan. Credit is extended, assets are sold, corporate entities are created or merged, and so on. Presumably mindful of the intricate chain of events that is often set in motion by the order of confirmation, Congress made the considered choice that only fraud would warrant an attempt to "unscramble the egg," and even then only within the 180-day time frame imposed by § 1144. "Absent fraud, parties must be able to rely on the confirmed plan. [Otherwise,] a confirmed Chapter 11 debtor would be stillborn on the confirmation date. No future creditor would lend money to the Debtor. The creditors would fear that pre-petition security interests could be resurrected."

In re Winom Tool and Die, Inc., 173 B.R. 613, 616 (Bankr. E.D. Mich. 1994) (internal citations omitted).

If, after confirmation, a reorganization plan is modified, the modified plan "becomes the plan," Code § 1127(b), and the 180-day period runs from the date the plan is modified, not from the initial confirmation date. *See, e.g., In re TM Carlton House Partners, Ltd.*, 110 B.R. 185, 188–89 (Bankr. E.D. Pa. 1990).

(2) *Absolute Fraud.* Cause for revocation of a confirmation order has been found where the debtor entered into a secret side agreement to pay two creditors in full, but the plan provided for only partial payment (*Ogden v. Ogden Modulars, Inc.*, 180 B.R. 544 (Bankr. E.D. Mo. 1995)); where the debtor intentionally concealed the existence of assets (*Kelly v. Giguere (In re Giguere)*, 165 B.R. 531 (Bankr. D.R.I. 1994)); where the debtor failed to disclose that its key manager had been indicted on 28 counts of mail fraud and blamed for the failure of another business (*Official Committee of Unsecured Creditors v. Michelson (In re Michelson)*, 141 B.R. 715 (Bankr. E.D. Cal. 1992)); and where the debtor misrepresented the value of property (*U.S. v. Kostoglou (In re Kostoglou)*, 73 B.R. 596 (Bankr. N.D. Ohio 1987)).

§ 10.06 ENFORCEMENT OF PLAN PROVISIONS; POST CONFIRMATION JURISDICTION OF THE BANKRUPTCY COURT

As we've seen, confirmation of a reorganization plan may be the highpoint of a Chapter 11 case, but it is not the end of the case. Many things go on after confirmation, and some things may go wrong between the time a plan is confirmed and the time the case is closed.

Take a simple example. Suppose that in its plan, Amphy proposed to pay unsecured creditors 25% of their claims in cash, on the effective date of the plan, and an additional 50% in five annual installments of 10% on the anniversary of the effective date. Suppose that the reorganized Amphy fails to make the first anniversary payment — or, for that matter, the fifth? What are the creditors' remedies?

A confirmed plan has the status of a binding contract between the debtor and its creditors and equity security holders and is interpreted according to ordinary contract law principles. This concept is embodied in Code § 1141(a), which establishes the general rule that "the provisions of a confirmed plan bind the debtor, any entity issuing securities under the plan, any entity acquiring property under the plan, and any creditor, equity security holder, or general partner in the debtor." *See, e.g., Charter Asset Corp. v. Victory Markets, Inc. (In re Victory Markets, Inc.)*, 221 B.R. 298, 303 (B.A.P. 2d Cir. 1998); *McFarland v. Leyh (In re Texas General Petroleum Corp.)*, 52 F.3d 1330, 1335 (5th Cir. 1995).

A debtor's obligations under a confirmed plan modify and supersede the debtor's prepetition and preconfirmation obligations. If the debtor fails to satisfy a plan obligation, the original obligation is not reinstated. Thus:

> . . . Confirmation fixes the reach of claims that . . . the debtor treats in the plan.
>
> . . . .
>
> Where the debtor effects a composition, he is relieved of his old debts and simply has the burden of achieving the promises made in the composition. The composition thus operates as an absolute settlement, and the failure to pay unpaid obligations created by the plan will not revive the old debts.

In re The Stratton Group, Ltd., 12 B.R. 471, 474 (Bankr. S.D.N.Y. 1981).

The failure of the debtor to perform its obligations under the plan is not grounds for revoking the confirmation order. Code § 1144 provides the sole grounds for revocation. The creditor's remedy is to enforce the obligations embodied in the confirmed plan.

> With confirmation, the automatic stay is generally terminated. Creditors are freed from the restrictions of Section 362(a) and, in the event of a default following confirmation, are entitled to file suit in an appropriate forum based upon the terms of the plan, in order to enforce those terms just as they would any other agreement. This remedy gives creditors the opportunity to enforce their right to receive just what they bargained for in the confirmed plan; there is no right to claim anything more.

In re Jordan Mfg. Co., 138 B.R. 30, 38 (Bankr. C.D. Ill. 1992). *See also In re Curry*, 99 B.R. 409 (Bankr. C.D. Ill. 1989); *In re Depew*, 115 B.R. 965 (Bankr. N.D. Ind. 1989).

What is the appropriate forum in which to enforce a plan obligation? Consider the opinion that follows.

GRAY v. POLAR MOLECULAR CORPORATION
(IN RE POLAR MOLECULAR CORPORATION)

United States Bankruptcy Court for the District of Massachusetts
195 B.R. 548 (1996)

JOAN N. FEENEY, UNITED STATES BANKRUPTCY JUDGE.

. . . .

II. FACTS

On February 2, 1993, Polar filed its petition under Chapter 11 of the United States Bankruptcy Code. On May 14, 1993, the Court, for cause, ordered the appointment of the Trustee, thereby replacing the Debtor's management. On December 20, 1994, the Court confirmed the Plan, which was submitted by Mark L. Nelson and the Ad Hoc Committee to Save Polar Molecular Corporation.

On December 29, 1995, the same day the Trustee filed the instant Complaint, the Debtor filed a Motion For Entry Of Final Decree. The Court denied the Motion For Entry Of Final Decree because of the pendency of the Complaint. At the time the Trustee filed his Complaint, Polar had already made its initial payments to its creditors, as required by the Plan. The Debtor contends that the Plan has been substantially consummated.

. . . .

[T]he Trustee agreed.

Pursuant to the Plan, the Plan proponents established a $300,000 fund which was distributed to holders of allowed general unsecured claims on the Plan's effective date. In addition, the Plan provided for further contingent distributions to be made to these general unsecured claimants from, inter alia, the Debtor's post-confirmation income. These supplemental dividends are based on the Debtor's income through December 31, 1997. Under the Plan, the amount of these future distributions is to be calculated pursuant to a formula based on the Debtor's "Gross Margin."

As a mechanism for ensuring the Debtor's compliance with its post-confirmation Plan obligations, the Plan requires the Debtor to provide the Trustee with annual financial statements, including a calculation of Gross Margin, and copies of annual federal tax returns for the relevant periods. Additionally, the Plan provides for the retention by this Court of jurisdiction of this case. The Plan provides, in relevant part, the following:

> The Bankruptcy Court shall retain jurisdiction of this case pursuant to the provisions of Chapter 11 of the Code and for the following purposes, inter alia. . . .

> (d) To determine all controversies and disputes arising under, or in connection with, the Plan and to interpret or construe the Plan or any order previously entered in this case or, if necessary, to cure any defect in the

Plan or otherwise to modify the Plan pursuant to the provisions of section 1127 of the Code;

(e) To determine all motions, adversary proceedings and litigated matters pending on the Confirmation Date or filed thereafter within any applicable statutory period; . . .

(i) To effectuate payments under, and performance of, the provisions of the Plan; and

(j) To determine such other matters and for such other purposes as may be provided for in the Confirmation Order.

The Order confirming the Plan (the "Confirmation Order") echoes the Plan language with respect to the retention of jurisdiction.

The Trustee's Complaint raises issues regarding the propriety of the calculation of Gross Margin and, therefore, of the sufficiency of the first installment of the post-confirmation dividends. In his Complaint, the Trustee claims that if Polar had properly accounted for its Gross Margin it would have remitted an additional $11,114.09. . . .

III. DISCUSSION

The Debtor's Motion To Dismiss raises the following four issues: (1) whether this Court has subject matter jurisdiction over the issues raised in the Complaint, (2) assuming the Court does have subject matter jurisdiction over the dispute, whether mandatory abstention is appropriate, or (3) whether discretionary abstention is appropriate. . . .

1. Subject Matter Jurisdiction

A. The Positions Of The Parties

i. The Debtor's Position

The Debtor views the dispute as a simple contract dispute and tort claim based solely on state law. The Debtor contends that this is not a case that "arises under" or "arises in" a case under Title 11, because it invokes no substantive right provided by Title 11. As such, Polar argues that this Court has no subject matter jurisdiction under 28 U.S.C. § 1334. . . .

Polar also takes the position that the Plan has been substantially consummated and that no assets of the estate are involved in this dispute. Polar contends that the action has nothing to do with the administration of the estate, but is merely a claim asserted against its post-confirmation assets. . . .

ii. The Trustee's Position

The Trustee views this proceeding as an action pursuant to sections 1141 and 1142 of the Code to compel the Debtor to make the required payments and to otherwise comply with the express terms of the Plan. The Trustee asserts that the action pertains to the Plan itself and that, therefore, the action "arises under" title 11. On this basis, the Trustee argues that Court has the requisite subject matter jurisdiction to determine the issues raised by the Complaint under 28 U.S.C. § 1334.

The Trustee asserts that, under the Plan, the Court expressly retained post-confirmation jurisdiction over actions such as the one at bar. The Trustee further argues that even without a specific retention of jurisdiction in a plan or confirmation order, bankruptcy courts maintain post-confirmation jurisdiction over actions which raise issues concerning the execution, implementation, administration or interpretation of a plan of reorganization and the enforcement of a confirmation order.

. . . .

B. The Statutory Sources Of Jurisdiction

i. 28 U.S.C. § 1334

After confirmation, there is no new statutory source of the bankruptcy court's jurisdiction. Jurisdiction remains governed by 28 U.S.C. § 1334 which provides, in relevant part, the following:

(a) Except as provided in subsection (b) of this section, the district courts shall have original and exclusive jurisdiction of all cases under title 11.

(b) . . . the district courts shall have original but not exclusive jurisdiction of all civil proceedings arising under title 11, or arising in or related to cases under title 11.

. . . .

The jurisdiction of the district court granted under 28 U.S.C. § 1334 is referred to the bankruptcy court for "any or all proceedings arising under title 11 or arising in or related to a case under title 11." 28 U.S.C. § 157.

In order for § 1334 "arising under" jurisdiction to apply, the action at bar must be "created or determined by a statutory provision of title 11." An action seeking "an order requiring the debtor or other necessary party to execute the provisions of a confirmed plan *is a proceeding arising under Title 11." In re Harlow Properties, Inc.,* 56 Bankr. 794, 797 (Bankr. 9th Cir. 1985) (emphasis added). In contrast, "'related to' jurisdiction encompasses only disputes that affect the payments to the bankrupt's other creditors or administration of the bankrupt's estate." *In re Southern Industrial Banking Corp.,* 63 Bankr. 331, 335 (Bankr. E.D. Tenn. 1986).

ii. 11 U.S.C. § 1142

Section 1142(b) of the Code specifically addresses the bankruptcy court's post-confirmation jurisdiction. Section 1142 provides:

> (a) Notwithstanding any otherwise applicable nonbankruptcy law, rule, or regulation relating to financial condition, the debtor and any entity organized or to be organized for the purpose of carrying out the plan shall carry out the plan and shall comply with any orders of the court.

> (b) The court may direct the debtor and any other necessary party to execute or deliver or to join in the execution or delivery of any instrument required to effect a transfer of property dealt with by a confirmed plan, and to perform any other act, including the satisfaction of any lien, that is necessary for the consummation of the plan.

Regarding § 1142(b), the bankruptcy court in *In re Cary Metal Products, Inc.*, 152 Bankr. 927, 931 (Bankr. N.D. Ill. 1993), stated that "the plain text leaves little doubt that post-confirmation jurisdiction exists to the extent necessary to consummate the plan." Other courts agree, finding their post-confirmation jurisdiction grounded in § 1142(b). *See In re Terracor*, 86 Bankr. 671 (D. Utah 1988), where the court stated that "the clear intent of Section 1142(b) is . . . to assure that the terms and provisions of the confirmed Chapter 11 plan are carried out until the plan is completed and a final decree is entered closing the case." Likewise, in *In re Pioneer Inv. Serv. Co.*, 141 Bankr. 635, 641 (Bankr. E.D. Tenn. 1992), the court held that "the bankruptcy court's retention of post-confirmation jurisdiction, while limited, exists to ensure compliance with the provisions of title 11 and to ensure the proper execution and consummation of the debtor's plan."

C. Striking A Balance In The Exercise Of Jurisdiction

Although it is well-settled that the bankruptcy court retains post-confirmation jurisdiction to interpret and enforce a confirmed plan of reorganization, courts have long struggled to define the limits of and judiciously exercise this jurisdiction. In a frequently cited quotation contemplating this issue, the Second Circuit stated:

> We have had occasion before to deplore the tendency of District Courts to keep reorganized concerns in tutelage indefinitely by orders purporting to retain jurisdiction for a variety of purposes, extending from complete supervision of the new business to modifications of detail in the reorganization.

> . . . .

> Since the purpose of reorganization clearly is to rehabilitate the business and start it off on a new and to-be-hoped-for more successful career, it should be the objective of the courts to cast off as quickly as possible all leading strings which may limit it and hamper its activities and throw doubt upon its responsibility. It is not consonant with the purposes of the Act, or feasible as a judicial function, for the courts to assume to supervise a business somewhat indefinitely. Nevertheless the court must retain some jurisdiction after confirmation of a plan to see that it is consummated. We

have, therefore, pointed out the existence of such complementary and auxiliary jurisdiction of the court to protect its original confirmation decree, prevent interference with the execution of the plan and otherwise aid in its operation.

North American Car Corp. v. Peerless W. & V. Mach. Corp., 143 F.2d 938, 940 (2d Cir. 1944) (citations omitted). In another case decided under the Bankruptcy Act, the Tenth Circuit Court of Appeals commented on post-confirmation jurisdiction: "a court may retain jurisdiction, after confirmation, to guarantee that the plan of reorganization is complied with, but it may not keep the corporation in 'perpetual tutelage' by exercising control over all aspects of the corporate conduct or by assuming jurisdiction over controversies between the reorganized corporation and third parties." *Claybrook Drilling Co. v. Divanco, Inc.*, 336 F.2d 697, 701 (10th Cir. 1964).

Courts have given much consideration to what constitutes the proper balance in the exercise of post-confirmation jurisdiction. In *Matter of Leeds Bldg. Prods., Inc.*, 160 Bankr. 689 (Bankr. N.D. Ga. 1993), the court acknowledged that it "does not lose all jurisdiction once a chapter 11 plan has been confirmed," but stated that "its role is limited to matters involving the execution, implementation, or interpretation of the plan's provisions, and to disputes requiring the application of bankruptcy law." The confirmed plan in Leeds required the debtor to enter into a trust indenture in order to make distributions to unsecured creditors over a ten year period. The trust indenture was funded by a note from the debtor. The indenture trustee commenced an adversary proceeding seeking judgment in the sum of the unpaid note, based on the debtor's alleged default under the terms of the trust indenture. The Leeds court found that, by executing the note and the trust indenture, the debtor had implemented the relevant plan provisions and that there was no question as to the plan's interpretation. For this reason, the Leeds court found that the dispute before it did not come "within its limited postconfirmation jurisdiction." *Id.* at 691. Likewise, in *In re J.T. Gerken Trucking, Inc.*, 10 Bankr. 203, 204 (Bankr. N.D. Ohio 1981), the court held that "affirmation of the [collective bargaining] agreement in the plan does not confer jurisdiction upon the court over post confirmation controversies. A confirming court's jurisdiction is limited to matters concerning the operation of the plan."

Taking a broader view of post-confirmation jurisdiction, the court in *In re Joint Eastern & Southern Dist. Asbestos Lit.*, 129 Bankr. 710, 794 (E. & S.D.N.Y. 1991), retained and exercised jurisdiction over class action litigation involving asbestos tort claimants and the trust established for payment of their present and future claims which had been created under the debtor's confirmed plan of reorganization. The court ruled that a "post-confirmation bankruptcy court retains jurisdiction over matters concerning the implementation or execution of a confirmed plan." *Id.*, 129 Bankr. at 794. . . . *See also Harlow Properties, Inc.*, 56 Bankr. 794 (Bankruptcy Appellate Panel of the Ninth Circuit ruled that bankruptcy court properly retained jurisdiction of creditor's motion for order to sell certain real property pursuant to the debtor's confirmed plan); *In re Blue Diamond Coal Co.*, 163 Bankr. 798, 809 (Bankr. E.D. Tenn. 1994) (bankruptcy court exercised post-confirmation jurisdiction over dispute where purchaser of debtor's assets sought order prohibiting U.S. Department of Labor from imposing liability upon it as "successor operator" of coal mine, as court had "the authority to construe the terms of a plan that it confirmed and to ensure that the plan is properly executed and consummated"); *In re Campbell Sixty Six Exp., Inc.*, 147 Bankr. 200 (Bankr. W.D. Mo. 1992) (bankruptcy court retained jurisdiction over adversary proceeding arising from post-confirmation sale of real property under confirmed liquidating Chapter 11 Plan); *In re Baker*, 118 Bankr. 24, 27 (Bankr. S.D.N.Y. 1990) (bankruptcy court retained post-confirmation jurisdiction to interpret terms of lease and purchase option granted post-petition by the debtor).

Similarly, the court in *In re Tri-L Corp.*, 65 Bankr. 774, 779 (Bankr. D. Utah 1986) stated that, while "it is contrary to the purposes of the Code and the judicial function for the bankruptcy court to retain jurisdiction over every aspect of the reorganized debtor, . . . the court must retain some jurisdiction after confirmation to see that the plan is consummated." The *Tri-L* court concluded that "the court may expressly retain jurisdiction over the plan, during its consummation, under a provision of the plan itself or the order of confirmation." *Id.* at 778.

i. Substantial Consummation

Courts that have struggled to find the proper balance in the exercise of post-confirmation jurisdiction have recognized that jurisdiction may be limited following the "substantial consummation" of a plan. *See In re Bankeast Corp.*, 132 Bankr. 665, 667 (Bankr. D. N.H. 1991), and *In re DN Associates*, 165 Bankr. 344, 346 (Bankr. D. Me. 1994). Although the *Bankeast* Court did rule that it would retain jurisdiction "only to the point of substantial consummation of the plan," it implicitly recognized a broader grant of jurisdiction than it chose to exercise. Notwithstanding its recognition that "upon substantial consummation the court's role is further diminished," the DN Associates court rejected the argument that it was divested of jurisdiction to rule upon the post-confirmation fee applications of certain professionals "simply because the confirmed plan was substantially consummated . . . ." The court stated flatly that "this is *not* the law." 165 Bankr. at 346–47 (emphasis added).

Although substantial consummation and the reduction of jurisdiction are concomitant, substantial consummation alone does not divest this Court of jurisdiction. The Code defines substantial consummation in section 1101 as follows:

In this chapter —

    (2) "substantial consummation" means —

        (A) transfer of all or substantially all of the property proposed by the plan to be transferred;

        (B) assumption by the debtor or by the successor to the debtor under the plan of the business or of the management of all or substantially all of the property dealt with by the plan; and

        (C) commencement of distribution under the plan.

"Substantial consummation" is a defined term which relates, inter alia, to one of several grounds for dismissal under § 1112(b) of the Code. The District Court in

Terracor, 86 Bankr. at 676 n. 12, distinguished "consummation" of a plan from "substantial consummation," noting that "consummation of a plan involves many different acts, one of which is the 'substantial consummation' of a plan." The *Terracor* court found that it retained jurisdiction because the plan had not been "*fully* consummated." *Id.* at 676 (emphasis in the original).

As the terms of a plan of reorganization are fulfilled, there are necessarily fewer plan issues which might arise. At the point of substantial consummation, many of a plan's provisions will have been carried out. For this reason, simple logic dictates that at this stage in a reorganization the bankruptcy court's post-confirmation jurisdiction is reduced. *See In re Omega Corp.*, 173 Bankr. 830, 834 (Bankr. D. Conn. 1994) ("the post-confirmation constriction of the bankruptcy court's jurisdiction results not from a change in the statutory basis for jurisdiction over proceedings arising under title 11 or arising in or related to a title 11 case, *see* 28 U.S.C. § 1334(b) (West 1993) — but rather from the fact that the universe of matters related to a case is diminished once confirmation is achieved.") Although upon the substantial consummation of a plan the court's jurisdiction is reduced, the court is not without jurisdiction to enforce the remaining unperformed terms of the confirmed plan. A contrary holding would render the provisions of § 1142 of the Code meaningless.

The Court also notes that such a narrow view of post-confirmation jurisdiction would render meaningless the distinction between § 1112(b)(7) and § 1112(b)(8), and would entirely eviscerate a court's ability to act under § 1112(b)(8) after substantial consummation. Section 1112(b)(7) provides that the "inability to effectuate substantial consummation of a confirmed plan" constitutes cause for which the court may dismiss or convert a case to a case under chapter 7. Section 1112(b)(8) provides that "material default by the debtor with respect to a confirmed plan" also constitutes such cause. If the scope of the bankruptcy court's post-confirmation jurisdiction did not extend beyond the substantial consummation of a case, § 1112(b)(8) would be largely superfluous.

ii. The Retention Of Jurisdiction Under A Confirmed Plan

Other courts that have sought to find the proper balance in the exercise of post-confirmation jurisdiction have considered the effect of plan clauses which set forth the scope of retained jurisdiction. Many courts have found such clauses to be compelling. . . .

Notwithstanding the influence of plan provisions regarding the retention of post-confirmation jurisdiction, it is well settled that a court cannot retain jurisdiction where none exists. In *Tri-L Corp.*, 65 Bankr. at 778, the court stated that "[a] reservation of jurisdiction beyond what is necessary to effectuate the plan of reorganization is beyond the power of the bankruptcy court. . . . The bankruptcy court cannot obtain that power merely by inserting a provision in the plan or order of confirmation reserving jurisdiction."

D. The Scope Of Post-Confirmation Jurisdiction In The Present Case

In light of the factors discussed above, the Court finds that the Trustee states a cause of action to enforce the Plan and that resolution of the issues raised by the Complaint will directly affect the amount of supplemental dividends to be distributed to the unsecured creditors. As such, the Court finds that the issues raised by the Complaint arise under § 1142 of the Code and that they fall well within the jurisdictional grant of § 1334 as a proceeding "arising under" title 11 and "arising in or related to" a case under title 11.

The Court further concludes that, in this case, the proper balance regarding the exercise of post-confirmation jurisdiction will be achieved only if the Court retains jurisdiction and determines the issues raised in the Complaint. The Court finds the facts in the *Leeds* and *J.T. Gerken* cases to be distinguishable from those in the present case. Unlike the dispute between the Trustee and the Debtor, the disputes in *Leeds* and in *J.T. Gerken* both arise from separate and independently enforceable agreements (the indenture trust and the collective bargaining agreements), which were adopted under the respective debtors' plans. In contrast, the Trustee in this case seeks to directly enforce Plan provisions. Furthermore, neither the controversy raised in *Leeds* nor in *J.T. Gerken* pertained to the amount of the distribution to creditors under the respective confirmed plans.

. . . .

2. Mandatory Abstention

Having decided that the Court has subject matter jurisdiction, the Court reaches the question of whether it must abstain from hearing the Complaint. Mandatory abstention is governed by 28 U.S.C. § 1334(c)(2), which provides:

> Upon timely motion of a party in a proceeding based upon a State law claim or State law cause of action, related to a case under title 11 but not arising under title 11 or arising in a case under title 11, with respect to which an action could not have been commenced in a court of the United States absent jurisdiction under this section, the district court shall abstain from hearing such proceeding if an action is commenced, and can be timely adjudicated, in a State forum of appropriate jurisdiction.

The Court has determined that the Trustee's Complaint is grounded on claims "arising under title 11." For this reason, the mandatory abstention provisions of § 1334(c)(2) are inapplicable. Section 1334(c)(2) applies only to proceedings based on a state law claim or state law cause of action related to a case under title 11, not to claims arising under title 11.

3. Discretionary Abstention

Discretionary abstention is governed by 28 U.S.C. § 1334(c)(1), which provides that:

> Nothing in this section prevents a district court in the interest of justice, or in the interest of comity with State courts or respect for State law, from

abstaining from hearing a particular proceeding arising under title 11 or arising in or related to a case under title 11.

The Court finds that the interests of justice and fairness to all parties who negotiated and voted to accept the Plan weigh heavily in favor of this Court retaining jurisdiction over the Complaint. The clauses regarding the retention of jurisdiction set forth in the Plan are significant and were agreed to by the parties. More importantly, the issues at hand go to the heart of consummation of the Plan, involving enforcement of its terms and affecting the amount of future distributions to unsecured creditors. Because there is no related proceeding commenced in state court and because this Court is familiar with the Plan and the parties involved, this Court can most efficiently rule on the matter. For these reasons, the Court shall, in its discretion, decline to abstain from the instant proceeding and exercise its retained jurisdiction over the Complaint.

NOTES AND QUESTIONS

(1) In *Zahn Associates v. Leeds Bldg. Prods., Inc.*, 160 B.R. 689, 691 (Bankr. N.D. Ga. 1993), the court held that an action by creditors to enforce a promissory note executed by the debtor pursuant to a confirmed plan was beyond the scope of its postconfirmation subject matter jurisdiction:

> [T]his adversary proceeding does not concern the execution or implementation of the Plan, or the interpretation of its provisions. Section 4.5 of the Plan required the Debtor to make certain payments to the unsecured creditors. In order to give effect to this requirement, the Debtor executed a promissory note and a trust indenture with Zahn as trustee. In so doing, the Debtor has implemented this provision of the Plan, and there is no question as to its interpretation.

> Furthermore, the matters involved in this proceeding do not involve the application of bankruptcy law in any way. The dispute itself arises out of a contract, and by its own terms the obligations are subject to the laws of the State of Georgia. Specifically, Georgia law applies to decide if a default has occurred, if there was a mutual departure from the original contract terms, and if a proper acceleration of the Note has taken place. In their briefs, the parties have relied almost exclusively upon Georgia law in making their arguments. Therefore, it is clear that this matter does not require the application of bankruptcy law.

Based on the same reasoning, a number of bankruptcy courts have refused to hear actions to enforce plan defaults. *See, e.g., In re T.S.P. Indus., Inc.*, 117 B.R. 375 (Bankr. N.D. Ill. 1990); *In re Depew*, 115 B.R. 965 (Bankr. N.D. Ind. 1989); *In re Curry*, 99 B.R. 409 (Bankr. C.D. Ill. 1989). Do these courts simply have a cramped view of postconfirmation jurisdiction, or are these cases distinguishable from *Polar Molecular?*

(2) Code § 1142(b) authorizes the bankruptcy court to direct the debtor (and any other necessary party) to perform "any act" necessary for the consummation of a plan. Courts have invoked § 1142(b) as a basis for ordering a plan funder to advance the funds he promised, (*Official Unsecured Creditors' Committee of Erie*

Hilton Joint Venture v. Siskind (In re Erie Hilton Joint Venture), 137 B.R. 165 (Bankr. W.D. Pa. 1992)); for authorizing a creditors' committee to retain professionals to search for missing creditors entitled to plan payments (*In re Goldblatt Brothers, Inc.*, 132 B.R. 736 (Bankr. N.D. Ill. 1991)); and to enjoin creditors from continuing actions based on claims that were dealt with in the plan (*In re Johns-Manville Corp.*, 97 B.R. 174 (Bankr. S.D.N.Y. 1989)).

(3)   You will recall that the commencement of a bankruptcy case accelerates the maturation of claims. Code §§ 101(5) and 502(b)(1). What happens if a confirmed plan proposes to pay claims in 10 annual installments and the debtor defaults after making one installment payment? Would a suit to enforce the plan obligation be a suit to recover only the installment payments in default or the total amount owed? In *In re Jordan Mfg. Co.*, 138 B.R. 30, 38 (Bankr. C.D. Ill. 1992), the court held that in the absence of an acceleration clause in the plan, the creditors would be relegated to suing for only the installments due.

> The general non-bankruptcy rule is that where a debtor defaults on an installment obligation which does not contain an acceleration clause, the creditor must pursue each installment without accelerating the total obligation. If the objecting creditors have a problem, it should have been addressed at the confirmation hearing by objecting to the plan and seeking an acceleration provision. Having failed to do so, they are bound by the terms of the new obligations arising out of the confirmed plans, and they must accept whatever procedural problems they might encounter in attempting to enforce those obligations in the appropriate forum.

(4)   In theory, creditors have two other remedies in the event of a postconfirmation default. One is to move in bankruptcy court for dismissal of the case or conversion of the case to Chapter 7 because of the debtor's "inability to effectuate substantial consummation of a confirmed plan," "material default . . . with respect to a confirmed plan," or "termination of a plan by reason of the occurrence of a condition specified in the plan." Code §§ 1112(b)(7), (8), (9). Interestingly, a reorganized debtor does not have an absolute right to convert a case under § 1112(a), because the reorganized debtor is no longer a debtor in possession.

The term "material default" as used in § 1127(a)(8) encompasses a failure by the debtor to make plan payments when they come due. *In re Jankins*, 184 B.R. 488, 494 (Bankr. E.D. Va. 1995). Although a material default is grounds for conversion or dismissal, it does not compel it, and courts have been reluctant to convert or dismiss a case when, for example, other creditors are being paid and the disgruntled creditor has other remedies, *Id.*, or when compliance with the plan, though delayed, still appears possible, *In re 12th & N Joint Venture*, 63 B.R. 36, 38 (Bankr. D.D.C. 1986). An example of the kind of failed "condition" that might justify conversion or dismissal under § 1127(b)(9) is the failure of a debtor to obtain necessary financing or to close a sale of assets as contemplated by the plan.

Whether conversion of the case would actually produce the result — the orderly liquidation of assets — presumably desired by unpaid creditors is less than clear. In *In re T.S.P. Industries, Inc.*, 117 B.R. 375 (Bankr. N.D. Ill. 1990), the debtor confirmed its plan and paid all priority claims in full. Five months later, it made the first installment payment due to unsecured creditors. When the debtor failed to make any subsequent installment payments, the U.S. Trustee moved for conversion or dismissal. The court considered whether conversion or dismissal would be in the best interests of the creditors:

> What is most important here is the effect of confirmation on the property of the estate. Once a plan has been confirmed, "in the absence of any contrary provisions in a plan title to property revests in the debtor along with normal ownership rights," the debtor is then no longer a debtor in possession and the bankruptcy estate ceases to exist unless the plan provides otherwise.

> Another effect of confirmation, although not expressly stated in section 1141, is that the automatic stay is terminated. This is so because, as noted above, (1) the stay that protects property of the estate ends when that property is no longer property of the estate, which occurs when the property vests in the debtor upon confirmation; and (2) the stay that protects the debtor and property of the debtor ends when the debtor is discharged, which also happens upon confirmation under section 1141(d).

> . . . .

> The question before this Court is whether conversion will benefit creditors and the estate. The U.S. Trustee says that it will because a chapter 7 trustee would be able to liquidate assets. But would he?

> A chapter 7 trustee can "collect and reduce to money the property of the estate," § 704(1), but there is nothing that authorizes a trustee to liquidate any other property. There are no provisions in the Bankruptcy Code that provide for the recreation of an estate upon the post-confirmation conversion of a confirmed chapter 11 to a case under chapter 7. Put another way, once property has vested in the Debtor, conversion will not revest that property in the estate.

> Section 348 of the Code provides:

> (a) Conversion of a case from a case under one chapter of this title to a case under another chapter of this title constitutes an order for relief under the chapter to which the case is converted, but, except as provided in subsections (b) and (c) of this section, does not effect a change in the date of the filing of the petition, the commencement of a case, or the order for relief.

> An estate is created at the commencement of a case (section 541) and the date of the commencement (section 301) is not changed by conversion; therefore a new estate is not created at the time of conversion.

> . . . .

> Therefore, the conversion of this case to a case under chapter 7 would not create a new estate or convert property of the Debtor into property of the estate.

> This conclusion is also consistent with the cases holding that confirmed chapter 11 plans do not become ineffective as a result of conversion, and

property distributed under a plan should not be redistributed.

. . . .

Finally, nothing in the Code would reinstate the automatic stay upon conversion. Based upon this reading of the Bankruptcy Code, the "benefit" the U.S. Trustee argues that creditors would get from conversion turns out to be illusory. Since a chapter 7 trustee could sell only property of the estate and sue only on the estate's claims for relief, and since even after conversion there would be no property of the estate, the trustee could not benefit creditors in the way envisioned by the U.S. Trustee. Furthermore, without the protection of the automatic stay, nothing would prevent individual creditors from competing with a rather toothless trustee for whatever property there may be.

The U.S. Trustee may be right that Congress intended that a confirmed chapter 11 plan may be converted, but only if conversion, rather than dismissal, would be in the best interests of the creditors. But that does not render section 1112(b) and section 1141 in conflict. For one thing, section 1141 provides only that the property of the estate vests in the debtor at confirmation except as otherwise provided in the plan or the order confirming the plan. Where the plan provided for conversion and the retention of jurisdiction over the property in the event of default, one court held that conversion was appropriate. *Matter of Iberis Int'l, Inc.*, 72 Bankr. 624, 626 (Bankr. W.D. Wis. 1986).

Post-confirmation conversion of a chapter 11 case also may be in the best interest of the creditors when there is a preference or a fraudulent conveyance that occurred before the commencement of the chapter 11 proceeding and the debtor currently has no significant assets. In that situation the power to avoid the questionable transaction would be lost if the case were dismissed. But if the case were converted, the chapter 7 trustee could exercise his or her powers to recover property that, under . . . § 541(a)(3), would become property of the estate for the benefit of creditors.

117 B.R. at 377–79. *Accord In re K & M Printing, Inc.*, 210 B.R. 583 (Bankr. D. Ariz. 1997); *In re Winom Tool and Die, Inc.*, 173 B.R. 613 (Bankr. E.D. Mich. 1994); *In re Modern Steel Treating Co.*, 130 B.R. 60 (Bankr. N.D. Ill. 1991). *But see In re Calania Corp.*, 188 B.R. 41 (Bankr. M.D. Fla. 1995) (any properties the debtor owned on the date of confirmation would be property of the estate in a superseding Chapter 7 case, but property acquired postconfirmation would not be included); *Bezner v. United Jersey Bank (In re Midway, Inc.)*, 166 B.R. 585 (Bankr. D.N.J. 1994) (property of the estate in converted Chapter 7 case included any property that the debtor owned on the date of conversion).

Question: If conversion of a Chapter 11 case to a Chapter 7 case *does* create a Chapter 7 estate consisting of all the property the debtor owned at the time of confirmation, would that make conversion tantamount to revocation of the order confirming the plan and an end run around the requirements of Code § 1144? *See In re Winom Tool and Die, Inc.*, 173 B.R. 613, 616 (Bankr. E.D. Mich. 1994).

The effect of dismissal is arguably less problematic, because, unlike § 348, which contains no provision for revesting property of the reorganized entity in the estate, § 349(b)(3) does provide that "dismissal of a case . . . revests the property of the estate in the entity in which such property was vested immediately before the commencement of the case." It is only arguably less problematic, because if there is no "property of the estate" at the time of dismissal because the debtor has used or sold its property to meet plan obligations or to operate the business, there is no property to revest in the former debtor. *In re Depew*, 115 B.R. 965 (Bankr. N.D. Ind. 1989).

Some have suggested that the dearth of cases discussing the effect of postconfirmation dismissal may result from the fact that many plans provide for remedies in the event of default. Frank R. Kennedy & Gerald K. Smith, *Postconfirmation Issues: The Effects of Confirmation and Postconfirmation Proceedings*, 44 S.C. L. REV. 621, 728 (1993). The scarcity of cases may also result from the fact that dismissal simply permits creditors to do what they already could have done in the event of a plan default: commence an action against the reorganized debtor to enforce its obligations under the plan.

(5) Bankruptcy Code § 350(a) states that "After an estate is fully administered and the court has discharged the trustee, the court shall close the case." Bankruptcy Rule 3022 is to similar effect. The term "fully administered" is not defined in the Bankruptcy Code. The 1991 Advisory Committee Note to Bankruptcy Rule 3022, states:

> Entry of a final decree closing a chapter 11 case should not be delayed solely because the payments required by the plan have not been completed. Factors that the court should consider in determining whether the estate has been fully administered include (1) whether the order confirming the plan has become final, (2) whether deposits required by the plan have been distributed, (3) whether the property proposed by the plan to be transferred has been transferred, (4) whether the debtor or the successor of the debtor under the plan has assumed the business or the management of the property dealt with by the plan, (5) whether payments under the plan have commenced, and (6) whether all motions, contested matters, and adversary proceedings have been finally resolved.

See In re JMP-Newcor Int'l, Inc., 225 B.R. 462, 464 (Bankr. N.D. Ill. 1998). Bankruptcy Code § 350(b) gives bankruptcy courts discretion to reopen cases "to administer assets, to accord relief to the debtor, and for other cause." In *In re Nylon Net Co.*, 225 B.R. 404, 406 (Bankr. D. Tenn. 1998), the court refused the debtor's request to reopen a case 10 years after confirmation for the purpose of enjoining creditors from suing in state court to enforce the debtor's plan obligations. The court held that in light of the amount of time that had elapsed and the fact that the suits were essentially breach of contract actions, the state court was the most efficient and appropriate forum.

§ 10.07   SERIAL FILINGS: THE CHAPTER 22 PROBLEM

In spite of the requirement in Code § 1129(a)(11) that a plan, if it is to be confirmed, be feasible, it is well known that many reorganized debtors fail. As the National Bankruptcy Review Commission observed, "Even the most carefully crafted plans of reorganization sometimes encounter circumstances that warrant adjustment. Events that might be out of the control of the reorganized debtor can change circumstances sufficiently to put the plan at risk." *Bankruptcy The Next Twenty Years: Report of the National Bankruptcy Review Commission* at 601 (1997). Professor Mark Roe has suggested that many reorganized companies fail because they exit Chapter 11 too heavily encumbered by debt. As a result, future profits go to creditors and the company's shares have little value. Mark J. Roe, *Bankruptcy and Debt: A New Model for Corporate Reorganization*, 83 Colum. L. Rev. 527 (1983). Professors LoPucki and Whitford found that although "Chapter 11 is not a complete failure . . . [p]articularly disturbing is the evidence that many large, publicly held companies emerge from Chapter 11 with too much debt and refile for bankruptcy at a strikingly high rate." Lynn M. LoPucki and William C. Whitford, *Patterns in the Bankruptcy Reorganization of Large, Publicly Held Companies*, 78 Cornell L. Rev. 597, 611 (1993).

May a debtor that defaults on its obligations under a confirmed plan file another Chapter 11 petition?

IN THE MATTER OF JARTRAN, INC.
United States Court of Appeals for the Seventh Circuit
886 F.2d 859 (1989)

Cudahy, Circuit Judge.

In this case we are asked to determine the novel question of the propriety of serial Chapter 11 bankruptcy filings. The debtor originally filed a petition for reorganization under Chapter 11, which was confirmed and substantially consummated. Less than one and a half years later, the debtor filed a second Chapter 11 petition, which had as its goal the liquidation of the reorganized entity. If the second Chapter 11 filing is proper, the original plan for reorganization approved as a result of the first Chapter 11 petition will presumably be superseded by a new plan. One of the creditors under the original plan objects to this potential alteration of its rights and claims. The bankruptcy court, however, ruled that the serial filing was permissible and that the creditor was not automatically entitled to an administrative priority in the second case by virtue of guarantees in the original reorganization plan. *In re Jartran, Inc.*, 71 Bankr. 938 (N.D. Ill. 1987). The district court affirmed, *In re Jartran, Inc.*, [Nos. 87 C 4989 and 86 B 3691] (N.D. Ill. 1988), and we do likewise.

I.

In 1981 Jartran, Inc. ("Jartran"), a company that rented and leased trucks on a nationwide basis, filed a petition in bankruptcy under Chapter 11 (*Jartran I*). Jartran's Fifth Amended Plan of Reorganization was confirmed in its third modified form ("Plan") on September 29, 1984, and was subsequently substantially consummated. On March 4, 1986, the reorganized Jartran filed a second Chapter 11 petition, this time with the aim of liquidating rather than reorganizing the company (*Jartran II*).

Of some potential import to events in this case was ongoing litigation in the Ninth Circuit, which resulted in a (more than likely unanticipated) $40 million judgment against Jartran. This judgment was affirmed by the Court of Appeals in July of 1986, four months after Jartran filed its second Chapter 11 petition. *U-Haul Int'l, Inc. v. Jartran, Inc.*, 793 F.2d 1034 (9th Cir. 1986). For a fuller discussion of the facts, we refer to the bankruptcy court opinion in this case. *In re Jartran, Inc.*, 71 Bankr. 938 (Bankr. N.D. Ill. 1987). Here we summarize only those facts pertinent to the issues on appeal.

Fruehauf Corporation ("Fruehauf"), a creditor under the original Chapter 11 Plan, argues that this second Chapter 11 filing was improper and should be dismissed. Alternatively, Fruehauf argues that it is entitled to an administrative priority in the current proceedings.

. . . .

The central issue is whether a debtor whose original plan of organization has failed may file a new liquidating Chapter 11 rather than converting to Chapter 7 for liquidation. Fruehauf points to a number of provisions of the Code indicating that this method of liquidation was not contemplated either by the drafters of the Code or by the authors of its subsequent amendments. Fruehauf may well be correct. When the Code, its legislative history or the commentators to date discuss what should happen in the event a Chapter 11 reorganization fails, the universe of available options seems to comprise either conversion to Chapter 7 or liquidation within the existing Chapter 11 case. Nonetheless, it is equally clear that the provisions of the Code permit the arrangement at issue here; serial Chapter 11 filings are permissible under the Code if filed in good faith, as are liquidating Chapter 11 plans. That the drafters may not have fully realized the results of these provisions in combination does not mean that they cannot be so used. . . .

First, Fruehauf asserts that the serial filing in this case was improper and should be dismissed or converted to a Chapter 7 under section 1112 of the Code. Fruehauf is relying heavily upon two cases in which serial filings were not permitted. In *In re AT of Maine, Inc.*, the court noted that under the Code, modifications of confirmed plans are not permissible after the plans have been substantially consummated. 56 Bankr. 55, 56–57 (Bankr. D. Me. 1986) (citing 11 U.S.C. §§ 1127(b), 1101(2)). The debtor in that case had filed a second Chapter 11 petition that would have had the effect of modifying its obligations under the previously confirmed plan, thereby enabling the debtor to evade the terms of that plan. The court dismissed the case as a bad faith filing. 56 B.R. at 58. The court in *In re Northampton Corp.*, 39 Bankr. 955 (Bankr. E.D. Pa. 1984), similarly declined to permit a serial Chapter 11 filing where the debtor sought to submit a new reorganization plan. The Northampton court observed the Code's general prohibition against modification of substantially modified plans, noting that in some cases "[the] filing of a chapter 11 petition, with an eye toward curing defaults arising under a previously confirmed chapter 11 plan, is so akin to modifying the previous plan" as to be impermissible. *Id.* at 956. The court refused to allow the debtor in that case to evade its responsibilities through the filing of successive Chapter 11 petitions, concluded that it had "cause" under section 1112(b) for converting the case to Chapter 7 and converted the case.

Section 1112(b) provides that "the court *may* convert a case under this chapter to a case under chapter 7 of this title or may dismiss a case under this chapter, whichever is in the best interest of creditors and the estate, for cause . . . ." 11 U.S.C. § 1112(b) (emphasis supplied). Although section 1112(b) does not explicitly provide that a lack of good faith may constitute cause, section 1129(a)(3) does require that plans be "proposed in good faith"; courts have sensibly considered bad faith to be an acceptable basis for conversion or dismissal. *See In re AT of Maine*, 56 B.R. at 58; *In re Baumgartner*, 57 Bankr. 513 (N.D. Ohio 1986); *In re G-2 Realty Trust*, 6 Bankr. 549 (Bankr. D. Mass. 1980); see also 5 *Collier on Bankruptcy* para. 1112.03 (15th ed. 1989).

The courts in *AT of Maine* and *Northampton* certainly could have concluded that in light of the Code's policy against modification of substantially consummated plans, a serial Chapter 11 filing designed to evade an existing plan was in bad faith. However, the bankruptcy court in the case before us viewed the situation here as quite different; here the debtor has not submitted a new reorganization plan with the aim of evading responsibilities under the old reorganization plan. Rather, the new plan is for liquidation — and the bankruptcy court specifically found that "*Jartran II* is not an attempt to modify the terms of the Plan, but rather is a good faith admission that Jartran was unable to continue operating as a going concern." *In re Jartran*, [No. 86 B 3691, at 9] (Bankr. N.D.Ill. 1987). There is no ground for concluding that this finding of good faith by the bankruptcy court was erroneous, nor for concluding that the bankruptcy court erred in treating the second filing as a separate case from the already confirmed and consummated *Jartran I*. Were we faced with an appeal from a confirmed liquidation plan in which Jartran effectively evaded all responsibility under the previous reorganization plan, we might have grounds for rejecting the bankruptcy court's finding. But there simply is nothing in the record presented to us at this stage that would provide the kind of glaring indication of error required for this court to substitute its judgment for that of the bankruptcy court on this issue. Further, conversion or dismissal under section 1112(b) is in the bankruptcy court's discretion ("the court may convert"), *see In re Sheehan*, 58 Bankr. 296 (Bankr. D. S.D. 1986), and we cannot discern that the court abused that discretion in refusing to convert or dismiss this case.

It is true that a number of Code provisions taken together, along with their legislative history, might contribute to an expectation that when Chapter 11 plans fail, liquidation will proceed either through conversion to Chapter 7 or through liquidation in the same Chapter 11 action.

. . . .

Liquidations within reorganization proceedings had posed difficulties for years before the enactment of the Code, which clearly adopted a policy of permitting substantial liquidations within reorganization proceedings. 11 U.S.C. §§ 1123(a)(5)(B), 1123(b)(4); *see* 3 W. Norton, *Bankruptcy Law and Practice* § 59.10, at 59-9, 59-10 (1981); Anderson and Wright, *Liquidating Plans of Reorganization*, 56 Am. Bankr. L.J. 29 (1982); Hurley, *Chapter 11 Alternative: Section 363 Sale of*

All of the Debtor's Assets Outside a Plan of Reorganization, 58 Am. Bankr. L.J. 233, 233–34 (1984). As one commentator has written, "bringing in new parties and attorneys in the middle or at the end of the reorganization process to begin a liquidation in a chapter 7 proceeding is generally not the most practical, efficient, expeditious, or most effective manner of liquidating estates," Anderson and Wright, *Liquidating Plans of Reorganization*, 56 Am. Bankr. L.J. at 47, and the Code provisions take account of this concern. Although "the purpose and spirit" of Chapter 11 remains reorganization rather than liquidation, *id.* at 50; *see also* Epstein, *Consequences of Converting a Bankruptcy Case*, 60 Am. Bankr. L.J. 339, 339 (1986), the new provision permits a failed reorganization plan to proceed to liquidation without conversion. When this happens, the creditors have the protections owed under the original Chapter 11 plan, including any administrative expense priority to which they are entitled by virtue of their participation in the reorganization. Alternately, section 1112(b) permits conversion to Chapter 7 of Chapter 11 plans that cannot be effectuated. In cases of conversion, creditors may still be entitled to administrative expense priority for preconversion assumed executory contracts or unexpired leases under section 365(g). *See In re Chugiak Boat Works*, 18 B.R. 292 (Bankr. D. Alaska 1982). . . .

This court has not yet determined that creditors are indeed entitled to administrative expense priority for preconversion assumed executory contracts or leases.[11] However, it is certainly an open question in this court (and creditors aware of the decision *In re Chugiak Boat Works* would be cognizant of the possibility) that preconversion assumed contracts or leases might be entitled to administrative expense priority. As the court in *In re Chugiak Boat Works* recognized, this kind of protection would serve the important purpose of encouraging creditors to participate in reorganization plans, for "there would be little chance of attracting potential customers or creditors to deal with a financially troubled debtor if the performance of the debtor's obligations to those entities was not somehow assured." 18 B.R. at 298. The Code's prohibition on modification after substantial performance serves

---

[11] And, as the court in *In re Chugiak Boat Works* noted, the current provisions of the Code are not entirely clear on this point. Before the Code was enacted, the Act unambiguously provided that "when a contract which is entered into or assumed in a superseded proceeding is rejected, the resulting liability shall constitute a cost of administration of the superseded proceeding." 11 U.S.C. § 378(b) (1967) (amended 1978). Now the issue is dealt with by two provisions. Section 365(g) states that

> . . . the rejection of an executory contract or unexpired lease of the debtor constitutes a breach of such contract or lease . . . if such contract or lease has been assumed under this section [or under a confirmed chapter 11 plan] . . . [and] if before such rejection the case has been converted under section 1112
>
> . . . .
>
> (i) immediately before the date of such conversion, if such contract or lease was assumed before such conversion; or
>
> (ii) at the time of such rejection, if such contract or lease was assumed after such conversion.

Section 503(b) provides that "the actual, necessary costs and expenses of preserving the estate" will be treated as administrative expenses. *In re Chugiak Boat Works* views these two sections, taken together, as a strong indication that the Code had embraced the previous policy of the Act, guaranteeing administrative priority for claims based upon subsequently breached assumed contracts. We do not reach the issue in this case; we merely observe the possibility that § 365(g) may provide such protection, a possibility of which creditors who had checked the relevant case law would be aware.

this same goal, as does use of a "good faith" filing requirement to prevent debtors from evading responsibilities under prior plans.

Here, however, the bankruptcy court has determined that no such evasion is intended by the second Chapter 11 petition — and that the second petition, rather than seeking to modify the Master Leases, has a purpose entirely distinct from that of the first petition (liquidation). *See* Lander & Warfield, *A Review and Analysis of Selected Post-Confirmation Activities in Chapter 11 Reorganizations*, 62 Am. Bankr. L.J. 203, 232 ("if a confirmed plan does not itself provide an exclusive remedy upon default and if the second bankruptcy case is intended to effect the liquidation of the reorganized debtor's assets, the courts seem willing to permit successive filings."). Although it is conceivable that subsequent developments could shed doubt upon the validity of the bankruptcy court's findings, there is no reason at this point to suspect that they were erroneous. Fruehauf may well have bargained in the first Chapter 11 action under the assumption that it was guaranteed an administrative priority should the plan fail, whatever the form of the liquidation.[12] But, as we have noted, there is no prohibition of serial good faith Chapter 11 filings in the Code — indeed, there is not even a time limit on successive filings parallel to that imposed on individuals or family farmers. 11 U.S.C. § 109(g). As the district court noted, Congress could easily have included repeat corporate debtors in that section; its failure to do so indicates that corporate debtors are exempt from even the minimal constraints on serial filings imposed on other kinds of debtors. *Cf. NLRB v. Bildisco & Bildisco*, 465 U.S. 513, 522–23, 104 S. Ct. 1188, 79 L. Ed. 2d 482 ("Obviously, Congress knew how to draft an exclusion for collective-bargaining agreements when it wanted to; its failure to do so in this instance indicates that Congress intended that § 365(a) apply to all collective bargaining agreements covered by the NLRA."). Once a bankruptcy plan is effectuated, all indications from the Code would incline us to treat the reorganized entity as we would any other company.

Fruehauf has, of course, argued strenuously that a successive Chapter 11 filing for the purpose of liquidation is unfair to it because it has put large amounts of equipment — essential to the carrying on of Jartran's business — at risk only with

---

[12] This might be understandable, given that experts in the field have apparently described the universe of possible alternatives as encompassed by conversion to Chapter 7 or liquidation within the same Chapter 11 proceeding. *See, e.g.*, the discussion on conversion in *Collier on Bankruptcy*.

> If a chapter 7 liquidation would maximize the amount received by creditors, conversion is proper. This analysis is complicated to a degree by the fact that liquidation is one of the means by which a chapter 11 plan can be effectuated. Thus, the court must compare the costs and benefits of a chapter 7 versus a chapter 11 liquidation.

5 *Collier on Bankruptcy* para. 1112.03(2)(d)(ii) (15th ed. 1989). Here the benefits of conversion (it is assumed that conversion would mean conversion to Chapter 7) are weighed against those of liquidating within the existing Chapter 11 proceeding. Conversion to a distinct Chapter 11 action, or dismissal so that the parties can institute a new Chapter 11 action, are not considered as possibilities. Of course, these discussions all center upon the options available should problems arise *during* a reorganization; here we are confronted with a decision to liquidate reached, arguably, *after* the first Chapter 11 was substantially consummated. That is why we reach the result we do. However, it remains the case that the Code, legislative history and commentators to date simply do not consider the possibility of a situation in which a completely new liquidating Chapter 11 case could be used to deal with problems that arise in the course of consummation of a prior Chapter 11 plan. This is relevant not to our disposition, but to parties' possible expectations.

the assurance of an administrative priority if efforts to salvage Jartran's business failed. Fruehauf contends that permitting a successive filing for purposes of liquidation may discourage creditors from agreeing to Chapter 11 arrangements in the future since this outcome in many cases deprives creditors of protection in the event the arrangements fail. This is an outcome, however, that the Code does not exclude, given good faith. Therefore, despite the persuasive policy arguments made by Fruehauf, it is not for us to invalidate the outcome without some more plausible basis in the statute.

Furthermore, although the framers of the Code were concerned about protecting creditors, they had other policy concerns, including "rationaliz[ing] the various forms of relief available to a failing business, making business reorganization a quicker, more efficient procedure, and providing greater protection for debtors, creditors, and the public interest." House Report at 5. The consolidation of Chapters X and XI of the old Act into Chapter 11 of the new Code, without any limitation as to serial filings, had as its aim a more rational, flexible method for permitting commercial debtors to continue in business while ensuring that similarly situated creditors were treated equitably.

. . . .

The Code clearly by its terms permits serial good faith Chapter 11 filings, even where the effect is to circumvent protections generally afforded creditors under the Code's provisions for failed reorganizations. With that knowledge, creditors may begin to bargain for more protection in reorganizations, or may, as Fruehauf argues, resist participating in reorganizations altogether. All this is mere speculation, however, and further consideration of potential policy problems and their remedies would rest with Congress rather than the courts.

. . . .

Once the second Chapter 11 filing is determined to be both distinct from the first filing and proper, Fruehauf's administrative priority claims are fairly easily dismissed. To receive an administrative priority in *Jartran II*, Fruehauf must demonstrate its claims relative to *Jartran II*; an administrative priority in *Jartran I* does not translate to an administrative priority in *Jartran II*. Fruehauf asserts several bases for its claim of administrative priority in *Jartran II*.

First, Fruehauf claims a priority under section 365(g) of the Bankruptcy Code, which provides:

> Except as provided in subsections (h)(2) and (i)(2) of this section, the rejection of an executory contract or unexpired lease of the debtor constitutes a breach of such contract or lease
>
> . . . .
>
> (2) if such contract or lease has been assumed under this section or under a plan confirmed under chapter 9, 11, 12 or 13 of this title
>
>> (A) if before such rejection the case has not yet been converted under section 1112, 1307, or 1208 of this title, at the time of such rejection; or

(B) if before such rejection the case has been converted under section 1112, 1307, or 1208 of this title

(i) immediately before the date of such conversion, if such contract or lease was assumed before such conversion; or

(ii) at the time of such rejection, if such contract or lease was assumed after such conversion.

11 U.S.C. § 365(g). Fruehauf insists that leases assumed under *Jartran I* fall within the scope of this provision. However, we are now dealing with *Jartran II*, and the leases have not been assumed in this proceeding. Thus section 365(g)(2) is inapplicable on its face.

Second, Fruehauf claims a priority under 11 U.S.C. section 503(b), which permits administrative expense claims for "the actual, necessary costs and expenses of preserving the estate." 11 U.S.C. § 503(b)(1)(A). However, Fruehauf seeks priority for expenses incurred prior to *Jartran II* — namely, the balance due under leases assumed in *Jartran I*, the costs of marshalling and repossessing equipment done prior to *Jartran II*, and the balance due on defaulted payments by Jartran for lost, stolen and destroyed vehicles. None of these expenses were actual or necessary for preserving the estate in *Jartran II*, which was not yet extant.

Finally, Fruehauf claims a section 503 priority for expenses incurred in marshalling and repossessing equipment since the filing of *Jartran II*. In order to qualify as "actual and necessary" administrative expenses, expenditures must benefit the estate as a whole rather than just the creditor claimant.

. . . .

The bankruptcy court in this case ruled that Fruehauf acted in its own interest in repossessing its own equipment, a finding that is well-supported and sensible. Of course, if after the filing of *Jartran II* Fruehauf marshalled equipment not its own, for the benefit of the estate as a whole, then it is entitled to an administrative expense to reimburse it for its efforts in that regard.

. . . .

Because the Bankruptcy Code at no point interdicts good faith serial Chapter 11 filings, the bankruptcy court acted properly in refusing to dismiss the second Chapter 11 petition at issue in this case. Once this second action is deemed a separate and independent Chapter 11 case, Fruehauf may not claim an automatic administrative priority in the second case simply by pointing to the provisions of the original reorganization Plan. Whether the final disposition in the second Chapter 11 case will be adequate as regards Fruehauf we cannot determine at this point, perhaps a good indication of the value of awaiting a final order before seeking an appeal in some cases.

AFFIRMED

IN RE DEED AND NOTE TRADERS, LLC
United States Bankruptcy Appellate Panel for the Ninth Circuit
2012 Bankr. LEXIS 1513 (2012)

Before: PAPPAS, DUNN and JURY, BANKRUPTCY JUDGES.

Appellants appeal the order of the bankruptcy court confirming the chapter 11 plan of reorganization filed in this case by debtor Deed & Note Traders, LLC ("DNT"). We AFFIRM.

Facts

DNT is an Arizona limited liability company that was formed in 1993. Since then, it has engaged in the real estate business in Tucson, Arizona, purchasing, rehabilitating, leasing and selling residential properties. DNT is wholly owned by the Kinas Family Trust, and David Kinas ("Kinas") is the principal manager.

DNT financed the acquisition of its properties using its own operating income and through the many loans it obtained from individual investors. These were generally short-term, high interest loans. It was DNT's business practice to hold a property for about a year, during which time it would rehabilitate the property, and then refinance the loan with traditional lenders at market rates. As property values increased, DNT would also sell property in its inventory at a profit.

In December 2006, the Arizona attorney general investigated the business practices of DNT and, after lengthy negotiations, DNT and the state entered into a Consent Agreement. Under the terms of the agreement, DNT was obliged to sell a number of houses back to their original owners and "agreed to pay a large sum as and for attorney fees incurred by the state." These payments and transactions occurred at the beginning of a declining real estate market and, according to DNT, practically eliminated any operating reserves previously held by DNT. DNT's financial problems were exacerbated in August 2007 when First Magnus Financial Corporation, a large provider of traditional and other residential loan programs in Arizona, shut down and filed for bankruptcy.

DNT's First Bankruptcy Case

The combination of fines, the loss of funding sources for buyers from DNT's inventory, and the corresponding loss of sales revenue caused DNT to file its first petition for protection under chapter 11 on September 7, 2007. On September 20, 2007, DNT filed its schedules in which it listed a total of $40,581,976.00 in real property assets and $29,807,073.00 in secured claims against those properties. The total unsecured debt was $706,208.12, most of which was debt held by insiders and the secured creditors.

DNT filed its plan and disclosure statement on December 26, 2007; the plan was amended on April 24 and May 22, 2008. We refer to the twice-amended plan as the "First Plan." All claims of the appellants in this appeal were classified as Class 4 Secured Claims in the First Plan. These claims were to be treated as follows:

- All claimants would retain their respective security interests on the properties securing their claims.

- The arrears on these claims, together with accrued unpaid interest at the contract rate, were added to the principal balance on the secured debts as of the effective date of the plan. This amount (i.e., the arrears plus the unpaid principal balance) was the new "outstanding balance" on the secured creditors' claims.

- The claimants would receive monthly deferred interest-only payments on the outstanding balance. The interest accruing on the outstanding balance was based on the published 30-year residential mortgage rate for the Tucson area provided on the internet website, bankrate.com, from and after the effective date.

- The claims would be paid in full by DNT, either at the time of sale of the secured property or upon refinancing the obligation, or on or before a stated maturity date. The maturity date for first-priority liens was the seventh anniversary of the effective date; the maturity date for any junior liens was the fifth anniversary.

On September 16, 2008, DNT reported to the bankruptcy court that all objections to the First Plan had been resolved by stipulation. The bankruptcy court entered an order confirming the First Plan on October 23, 2008. The effective date was November 3, 2008.

In the year after the effective date, there were almost a hundred motions for relief from stay, notices of default, or associated pleadings filed by secured creditors alleging DNT's failure to make monthly payments under the First Plan. Many of these motions were granted. However, the record contains no information regarding foreclosures or other actions taken by the Class 4 Secured Creditors.

On March 9, 2009, DNT filed a motion for entry of a Final Decree and Order Closing Case in the bankruptcy case. Three creditors who are not involved in this appeal (the "Cherry Group") filed objections to the entry of final decree, arguing that DNT had failed to make payments under the First Plan and other irregularities. On May 4, 2009, the Cherry Group filed a motion asking the bankruptcy court to revoke the order confirming the First Plan on generally the same grounds as their objections to final decree. The bankruptcy court ordered that the motion to revoke and DNT's motion for a final decree be considered at a hearing on September 2, 2009.

At that hearing, counsel for DNT and the Cherry Group jointly informed the bankruptcy court that the Cherry Group was withdrawing the motion to revoke the confirmation order and the objections to entry of a final decree. DNT represented that it would prepare the order for the final decree.

Before entry of any final decree, appellant Wells Fargo, N.A., moved to convert the bankruptcy case to a chapter 7 case on November 11, 2009. Wells Fargo alleged, inter alia, that there had been mismanagement of estate funds by DNT and diversion of assets to insiders, and that DNT's actions constituted a material default under the First Plan. After multiple continuances, the bankruptcy court held a hearing on the motion to convert on January 5, 2010. Again, at the hearing, counsel for the parties informed the court that the issues had been resolved. A joint stipulation withdrawing the motion to convert was entered on February 5, and approved by the bankruptcy court on February 8, 2010. As all objections and impediments to entry of a final decree had been overcome, on February 8, 2010, the bankruptcy court also entered the final decree and order closing the case.

DNT's Second Bankruptcy Case

Only four days after entry of the final decree and order closing the case in the first bankruptcy case, on February 12, 2010, DNT filed a second chapter 11 petition. DNT's schedules, filed on March 16, 2010, list $19,858,452.00 in real property assets and $27,085,119.94 in secured claims on those properties. Total unsecured debt was $591,935.88.

DNT proposed a plan of reorganization in the second bankruptcy case on April 2, 2010 (the "Second Plan"). The only significant difference between the First and Second Plans, as the parties have acknowledged in this appeal, was DNT's proposal to reduce the Class 4 Secured Creditors' allowed claims to the "market value" of the properties securing those claims as of the effective date of the plan. In other words, the Second Plan proposed to "cramdown" these claims.

The Appellants, each holding loans secured by separate properties, filed ten motions to dismiss the second bankruptcy case on May 21, 2010. These motions argued in identical language that DNT's Second Plan violated § 1127(b), and the principle of finality of orders, and that DNT was attempting to circumvent the prohibition on modification of a confirmed, substantially consummated plan by a subsequent chapter 11 case.

In addition to the dismissal motions, over the next few months, over sixty objections to confirmation of the Second Plan were filed by creditors, including all of the Appellants. These objections to confirmation generally parroted the arguments made by the Appellants in the motions to dismiss.

The bankruptcy court held several hearings on the motions to dismiss and confirmation of the Second Plan, beginning in August, and culminating on December 22, 2010. Before the December 22 hearing, DNT had submitted a unilateral offer to amend the plan so as to not cramdown on six of the ten loans involved in the motions to dismiss, and either to abandon those properties or consent to relief from stay in favor of the secured creditor. As to the remaining four loans and properties pertaining to creditors filing motions, DNT indicated its position that the properties were worth more than the amount of the respective debts secured by them, such that the creditors' rights were thus not impaired under the Second Plan.

At the hearing, after counsel were heard, the bankruptcy court denied the motions to dismiss the bankruptcy case, concluding that, as the result of DNT's amendment, none of the secured creditors were impaired under the Second Plan. The denial of these motions to dismiss was not appealed.

The bankruptcy court then conducted an evidentiary hearing on plan confirmation. The court heard testimony from Kinas regarding his management of DNT, why DNT failed to meet its obligations under the First Plan, and the requirements for confirmation of the Second Plan. Kinas was then cross-examined by attorneys for various creditors. After hearing the testimony and closing arguments of counsel, the bankruptcy court overruled the objections to confirmation and confirmed the Second Plan.

In its oral decision, the bankruptcy court first observed that, in its earlier ruling denying the motions to dismiss, it had not commented on the focus of the secured creditors' argument, that DNT was attempting to violate § 1127(b). The bankruptcy court rejected this argument and found that DNT was not attempting to thwart the First Plan's treatment of over-secured creditors because the Second Plan treated them no differently. Simply put, as to over-secured creditors, the court concluded that they were not significantly impaired under either Plan, and that DNT had not violated § 1127(b) and the principle of finality of confirmation orders regarding those creditors.

As the court then observed, DNT's proposed cramdown of the claims of under-secured creditors was a different matter:

> A more difficult call is for the properties and the creditors secured by those properties who were not crammed down in the first case and are being crammed down in the second case, all of the arguments about 1127 and 1141 clearly the debtor here is seeking a modification of the terms of the first plan. The question is — is it justifiable[?] Is it justifiable? And if it's justifiable, is the treatment being offered to these creditors in good faith? That it seems to me is the crux of the difficult decision here. I look at this under the totality of the circumstances test, I believe, for good faith. So the plan terms are short basically. This is not an extended period of time of a stretch out. The interest rate isn't being modified from the first plan. Those are good things. It's the cramdown itself which is the essence of the problem. But unlike the few cases I've been able to find on this, I'm not sure this is a situation where all of the burden is being shifted to the secured creditors because, in fact, all they were ever going to get is the value of the property because of the nature of the anti-deficiency statute in Arizona. I believe that the debtor has met its burden here, but I would say it's a very, very close call.

The bankruptcy court decided that the Second Plan should be confirmed, and the objections to confirmation overruled. It entered an order confirming the Second Plan on February 10, 2011. Appellants filed a timely appeal on February 24, 2011.

. . . .

Discussion

. . . .

II. The bankruptcy court did not clearly err in determining that extraordinary and unforseen circumstances were present in this case which justified DNT's proposal to cramdown secured claims in the Second Plan.

The Code makes clear that a debtor's right to modify a confirmed chapter 11 plan is subject to conditions. The appellants have maintained, both in the bankruptcy court and on appeal, that § 1127(b) prohibits DNT's confirmation of a chapter 11 plan proposing to change the terms of the treatment of their claims under the substantially consummated First Plan. While case law unquestionably allows debtors to engage in serial filings of chapter 11 cases, what is in dispute here is the sort of justification required before a bankruptcy court should endorse a debtor's second plan proposing to modify the terms of a prior, confirmed and substantially consummated plan.

The only two courts of appeals to examine this question hold that serial chapter 11 filings are not per se impermissible. In *Fruehauf Corp. v. Jartran (In re Jartran)*, the Seventh Circuit observed that,

> there is no prohibition of serial good faith Chapter 11 filings in the Code — indeed, there is not even a time limit on successive filings parallel to that imposed on individuals or family farmers. 11 U.S.C. § 109(g). As the district court noted, Congress could easily have included repeat corporate debtors in that section; its failure to do so indicates that corporate debtors are exempt from even the minimal constraints on serial filings imposed on other kinds of debtors.

886 F.2d 859, 869–70 (7th Cir. 1989). The court addressed another serial chapter 11 case in *In re Official Comm. of Unsecured Creditors*, 943 F.2d 752, 757 (7th Cir. 1991). Although both of these cases painted the authority to file serial chapter 11's with broad brush strokes, neither provided clear guidance on whether, and to what extent, the plan proposed in the second chapter 11 case could modify creditor treatment in the first plan.

Following shortly after the Seventh Circuit decisions, the Fifth Circuit decided *In re Elmwood Dev. Corp.*, 964 F.2d 508, 511 (5th Cir. 1992). As described by the court,

> This case raises for this circuit the de novo issue of the extent to which a serial filing of a Chapter 11 petition evidences a lack of good faith on the part of the debtor. We conclude that the mere fact that a debtor has previously petitioned for bankruptcy relief does not render a subsequent Chapter 11 petition "per se" invalid. This conclusion is consistent with the Supreme Court's recent teaching in *Johnson v. Home State Bank* 501 U.S. 78, 111 S. Ct. 2150, 115 L. Ed. 2d 66 (1991). The *Johnson* Court held that serial Chapter 7 and Chapter 13 petitions are not categorically prohibited. The Court reasoned that because Congress has enumerated certain instances in which serial filings are per se impermissible, there is no absolute prohibition in instances not so enumerated. The Court considered the good faith requirement to be adequate protection from abusive serial filings.

Id. at 511. In providing guidance on when a second plan may modify the terms of the first, the court states: "A second petition would not necessarily contradict the original proceedings because a legitimately varied and previously unknown factual scenario might require a different plan to accomplish the goals of bankruptcy relief." *Elmwood*, 964 F.2d at 511–12. In short, *Elmwood* stands for the proposition that, in proposing yet a second chapter 11 plan, the debtor must demonstrate some sort of genuine need to reorganize as the result of unforeseen changes in circumstance which contribute to the debtor's default under its obligations under the earlier plan. *Id.* Indeed, in *Elmwood*, the court cited the national credit crunch in the early 1990s as an example of changed circumstances in real estate markets that might have justified modification of the debtor's earlier plan. But because the credit crunch and resulting depressed real estate market had existed for several years before substantial consummation of the first plan, the Fifth Circuit ruled that those conditions, under the facts of that case, were sufficiently foreseeable that they would not justify a modification of the first plan. *Id.* at 512.

Arizona bankruptcy courts have recognized that serial chapter 11 filings are permissible if made in good faith. *United States v. Shepherd Oil, Inc. (In re Shepherd Oil, Inc.)*, 118 B.R. 741, 747 (Bankr. D. Ariz. 1990) (citing favorably to *Jartran*). Later case law supports both the principle that serial chapter 11 filings are not per se impermissible, and that a second plan may modify the first plan where there are extraordinary circumstances that are unforeseeable. . . . Even the Appellants appear to agree that "a confirmed plan of reorganization that has been substantially consummated is not subject to modification by filing a second bankruptcy case *unless* the second filing is in good faith and necessitated by unforeseeable circumstances." Appellants' Reply Br. at 8 (emphasis added).

The question presented to the Panel is, did the bankruptcy court clearly err in finding that there were extraordinary, unforeseeable circumstances present that allowed DNT to propose a second chapter 11 plan that modified the secured creditors' rights under the First Plan? The bankruptcy court found that, while it was a "close call," justification for this extraordinary approach to dealing with DNT's finances existed:

> Those cases do talk about the fact that a simple change in economic circumstances isn't enough. . . . This was, at least in this state, a depression. The level at which things fell off the cliff was not foreseeable in my opinion and more importantly what was not foreseeable was the freeze in the credit markets that would have made it impossible for the Debtor to get refinancing. So, I find in the circumstances of this case that what happened to the economy was the equivalent of an airplane flying into a factory. So that's the finding.

Hr'g Tr. 18:24–19:10, December 22, 2010. The bankruptcy court indicated on the record that it had invested time in reviewing real property appraisals connected with this case. It is axiomatic that in a busy bankruptcy court such as Arizona, a bankruptcy judge is frequently exposed to facts and information about how economic conditions in that district affect the parties coming before the court. The bankruptcy judge need not ignore its particular knowledge of such matters; the Supreme Court has endorsed on multiple occasions the principle that a federal judge may take judicial notice of catastrophic economic conditions. *Allied Structural Steel Co. v. Spannaus*, 438 U.S. 234, 249, 98 S. Ct. 2716, 57 L. Ed. 2d 727 (1978) (discussing "the broad and desperate emergency economic conditions of the early 1930's"); *Home Bldg. & Loan Assoc. v. Blaisdell*, 290 U.S. 398, 445, 54 S. Ct. 231, 78 L. Ed. 413 (1934) (recognizing emergency powers of a state in response to severe economic conditions); *Edwards v. Kearzey*, 96 U.S. 595, 602–03, 24 L. Ed. 793 (1877) (discussing economic conditions in several states of the South after the Civil War). In short, the bankruptcy court had a legal and evidentiary foundation for its finding of fact that extraordinary circumstances were present in this bankruptcy case.

The Appellants have not challenged the bankruptcy court's analysis of extraordinary market conditions surrounding DNT's reorganization cases. Rather, they contend that the deteriorating real estate market was foreseeable to DNT, observing that immediately following confirmation of DNT's First Plan, its manager admitted that the Arizona real estate market was in decline. But the Appellants confuse two distinct economic conditions: the real estate market (i.e., the supply and demand for properties) and the state of the credit market (i.e., the availability of loans for property acquisition and financing).

While the real estate market may have been in decline in 2007 prior to confirmation of the First Plan, the extent of the problems to come in the broader credit market, on which DNT would have to rely for funding of its acquisitions, refinancing, and to fund purchasers of its properties, would devolve into what one court described as a "seizure" following the bankruptcy filing of Lehman Brothers in September 2008. As it turned out, there was a "crisis in the subprime market that . . . spread to the rest of the real estate market, collapse of the financial markets generally, [and] market-wide liquidity crisis." *In re Lehman Bros. Sec. & ERISA Litig.*, 799 F. Supp.2d 258, 264 (S.D.N.Y. 2011). It was this unanticipated collapse in the general availability of credit, not the possibly foreseeable decline in the Arizona housing market, that convinced the bankruptcy court in this appeal to find:

> The level at which things fell off the cliff was not foreseeable in my opinion, and more importantly what was not foreseeable was the freeze in the credit markets that would have made it impossible for the debtor to get refinancing.

Hr'g Tr. 19:3–7, December 22, 2010.

The Appellants offered no evidence to the bankruptcy court, nor have they given us a reasoned argument, to show that the credit market freeze in Autumn 2008 would have been foreseeable when DNT submitted its First Plan in December 2007, or its amended plans in early 2008. Instead of advancing any fully-developed argument why the filing of DNT's second bankruptcy case, and the need for its Second Plan, was not under extraordinary and unforseeable circumstances, the Appellants have repeatedly challenged the good faith of DNT in pursuing a second bankruptcy filing. In their briefs, the Appellants suggest that DNT manipulated the bankruptcy system by seeking entry of a final decree, waiting eleven months for entry of that decree without amending its plan, and then filing a second chapter 11 case only four days after entry of the final decree. The facts do not support the Appellants' bad faith argument.

It is true that eleven months elapsed from the time DNT filed its motion and entry of the final decree. But that delay was not solely caused by any lack of diligence on DNT's part. The facts instead establish that DNT submitted the motion for final decree after substantially consummating the First Plan by beginning the distributions to creditors, something the Appellants have not disputed. But three creditors objected to the motion, and in turn moved to revoke confirmation of the

First Plan in May. The bankruptcy court decided that it could not enter a final decree while a motion to revoke was on the table, so it ordered that the motions to revoke and for final decree be heard together. After several continuances, the hearing was held on September 2, 2009, at which DNT and the creditors announced a settlement and withdrawal of the motion to revoke. DNT indicated to the court that it would prepare a final decree order.

Shortly thereafter, Appellant Wells Fargo moved to convert the case to chapter 7 on November 11. Again, entry of the final decree was continued along with the conversion motion. After more continuances, the bankruptcy court held a hearing on the motion to convert on January 5, 2010. Wells Fargo opted to withdraw the motion to convert, and a joint stipulation doing so was filed on February 5, and approved by the bankruptcy court on February 8, 2010. All objections and impediments to entry of final decree being withdrawn, on February 8, 2010, the court then entered the final decree and order closing the case. In short, the eleven-month delay between filing the motion for final decree and entry of the order was not necessarily the result of delay by DNT, and we find no merit in the Appellants' suggestion that the facts demonstrate a lack of good faith in this respect. Like the bankruptcy court, in light of changing financial conditions, we also find it unsurprising that DNT would quickly file a second petition under chapter 11 within four days. Indeed, according to the testimony of Kinas, DNT's worsening cash flow problems and lack of access to credit threatened the existence of the company at the time of filing the second petition.

III. The bankruptcy court did not abuse its discretion in confirming the Second Plan and did not clearly err in ruling that the plan met the good faith standard of § 1129(a)(3).

From the beginning of the second bankruptcy case, the bankruptcy court cautioned the parties that the lynchpin for confirmation of a second plan would center on the requirement that DNT was proceeding in good faith as required in § 1129(a)(3). It is the bankruptcy court's decision on this single confirmation element that forms the basis of the Appellants' appeal.

Section 1129(a)(3) provides that a bankruptcy court shall confirm a plan only if the "plan has been proposed in good faith and not by any means forbidden by law." Section 1129(a)(3) does not define good faith. . . . However, under the decisions interpreting this Code provision, a plan may be found to be proposed in good faith where it achieves a result consistent with the objectives and purposes of the Code. . . . The bankruptcy court's good faith determination must be based on the totality of the circumstances. . . .

In this case, while there are facts supporting the bankruptcy court's view that it was a "very, very close call," the court did not clearly err in determining that the plan was proposed in good faith. The court's analysis on this issue conformed with that dictated by Ninth Circuit case law, in that the bankruptcy court considered the totality of the circumstances. The court found that the interest rate terms proposed for secured creditors' claims were unchanged between the First and Second Plans. The repayment term for secured loans under the Second Plan was relatively short, not an extended "stretch out." As discussed above, the court also determined that § 1127(b) was not a bar to DNT's proposed cramdown in the Second Plan because, the court found, extraordinary, unforseeable circumstances existed as compared to those surrounding confirmation of the First Plan. And finally, the court determined that, under Arizona's anti-deficiency law, the most a creditor with a lien on a house would likely receive in a liquidation or relief from stay scenario would be the foreclosure value of that property ("All the [creditors] were ever going to get is the value of the property because of the nature of the anti-deficiency statute in Arizona." Hr'g Tr. 84:7, December 22, 2010.) Thus, DNT's proposal to pay secured creditors the "market value" was consistent with the value of their state law rights.

. . . .

The bankruptcy court found, under all these circumstances, that DNT had shown it acted in good faith by filing the second bankruptcy petition and in proposing its Second Plan. Opposed to this was the Appellants' continuing argument that DNT made a calculated and tactical decision to wait for the first bankruptcy case to be closed rather than in good faith seeking to amend the First Plan. But the bankruptcy court's finding on good faith rejected this contention, resolving a disputed question of fact. Even if there are facts to support the Appellants' argument, where there are "two permissible views of the evidence, the factfinder's choice between them cannot be clearly erroneous." *Cooter & Gell v. Hartmarx Corp.*, 496 U.S. 384, 400–01, 110 S. Ct. 2447, 110 L. Ed. 2d 359 (1990).

. . . .

CONCLUSION

We AFFIRM the bankruptcy court's order confirming the Second Plan.

NOTES AND QUESTIONS

(1) The National Bankruptcy Review Commission has recommended that Code § 1127(b) be amended to permit modification after confirmation of a plan until the later of (1) substantial consummation, or (2) two years after the date on which the confirmation order is entered. The Commission members explained that "[b]ecause Class voting governs the modification process, the majority of each class of creditors — and not just the debtor or plan proponent — still would decide whether a modification is prudent," but that enlarging the modification window might avert the need for successive filing by giving debtors an opportunity to "de-leverage" or undertake other curative measures outside of bankruptcy. *Bankruptcy the Next Twenty Years: Report of the National Bankruptcy Review Commission* at 602–604 (1997).

(2) In *Jartran*, the court emphasized that the second filing was for the purpose of liquidating the company, rather than for taking a second crack at reorganizing, and from this inferred that the debtor was acting in good faith. Is a debtor who files for the purpose of modifying a confirmed plan necessarily acting in bad faith? The answer, apparently, depends on why the debtor seeks to escape the terms of the confirmed plan. In *In re Casa Loma Assocs.*, 122 B.R. 814 (Bankr. N.D. Ga. 1991), the debtor, which operated an apartment complex, had its plan confirmed on January 8, 1988. In March, 1990, the debtor defaulted on its plan obligations and on

April 6, 1990, filed a second Chapter 11 petition. The debtor asserted that the second filing was necessitated by several changes in circumstance:

(a) The economic marketplace surrounding the Property changed such that rental income remained constant rather than increased, as projected by Debtor in connection with the Casa Loma I plan.

(b) In order to maintain occupancy and cash flow, Debtor has been required to accept tenants of lower socio-economic background, which has resulted in increased vandalism, [eviction] actions and rental concessions, which in turn has resulted in increased operating expenses.

(c) After substantial consummation of the Casa Loma I plan, a federal law was enacted prohibiting discrimination against children as tenants. The Property, previously an all-adult apartment complex, suffered increased vacancies and increased operating expenses as a result of its admission of children.

(d) After substantial consummation of the Casa Loma I plan, Debtor discovered concealed and unanticipated fire damage to the Property which required substantial expenditures to repair.

(e) After substantial consummation of the Casa Loma I plan, Debtor discovered undisclosed and unanticipated structural defects in one of its buildings, which necessitated substantial expenditure to repair and resulted in temporary reduction in income.

122 B.R. at 815. The bankruptcy judge found that for the second filing to be permitted, a two-prong test had to be satisfied. First, the second case had to have been filed in good faith, and second, the filing had to have been necessitated "as a result of unforeseen changed circumstances." *Id.*, at 818. The court found that a showing of "an honest intent and a real need and ability to effectuate a reorganization" would satisfy the good faith requirement, 122 B.R. at 817, but that more than a simple change in circumstances or an error in earnings projections would be required to satisfy the changed circumstances part of the formula. The court explained:

In the instant case, if Debtor relied merely on changed market conditions to support the second Chapter 11 filing . . . Debtor would have failed to show sufficiently changed circumstances to warrant a second filing. Debtor, however, has shown an unanticipated change in federal law and the discovery of fire damage and structural defects, which were unknown at the time of substantial consummation of the plan in *Casa Loma I*, which substantially affected Debtor's ability to perform under the *Casa Loma I* plan. Additionally, other factors which would support dismissal of Debtor's petition as having been filed in bad faith have not been shown. Debtor appears to have a reasonable prospect of successful reorganization. Therefore, dismissal of Debtor's second Chapter 11 petition will be denied.

122 B.R. at 819. Indeed, at least one court has found that a second filing is presumptively a bad faith filing when it is done for the purpose of dealing with events that could have been anticipated by the debtor. In *In re Mableton-Booper*

Associates, 127 B.R. 941 (Bankr. N.D. Ga. 1991), the debtor, which operated an office building, filed its Chapter 11 petition in June 1986 after defaulting on payments to its mortgagee. Its reorganization plan, which provided for the curing of mortgage defaults and reinstatement of the original loan agreement terms, was confirmed on April 17, 1987. Unable to make the plan payments or to get the mortgagee to join in a voluntary restructuring, the debtor filed again. The debtor explained the need for the second filing this way:

> Debtor cites a number of allegedly changed circumstances that necessitated the second filing. First, it claims that Tom Burke, a former property manager, mismanaged the Property due to the use of illegal drugs, accepted poor quality tenants, and did not maintain the Property properly, resulting in a loss of tenants and an increase in expenses.
>
> . . . .
>
> Second, Debtor undertook substantial repairs to the building and infrastructure of the Property, including a new roof and air conditioner within the past year. Third, the principal balance of the debt came due. Finally, the market for office space has softened, causing a more competitive leasing environment.

127 B.R. at 942. The bankruptcy judge found that the second filing reeked of bad faith:

> In this case the changed circumstances were not unanticipated. First, Mr. Burke's drug use was not known to the Court when it confirmed Debtor's first plan, but Mr. Somekh [a general partner of the debtor who, the court pointed out, had "a net worth of over $40 million"] admitted to his knowledge of Mr. Burke's condition prior to the confirmation. The resulting poor management and deterioration of the Property were therefore entirely foreseeable. Second, the evidence does not indicate that the repairs to the roof and air conditioner were the result of some hidden defect; instead, these are also foreseeable expenses that were calculable at the time of the first confirmation. Third, the maturity of Debtor's obligation under the plan in December of 1990 was obviously anticipated by all parties prior to confirmation and indeed prior to Debtor's first filing. Finally, changed market conditions alone are not sufficiently changed circumstances to warrant a second filing. . . . The Court concludes that Debtor did not make a sufficient showing of unanticipated changed circumstances to justify the filing of a new petition, and that the new filing was in bad faith.

127 B.R. at 944. Interestingly, the mortgagee had argued that the default under the plan and the new filing resulted solely from the failure of the debtor's partners to make the cash infusions that had been promised in the plan. Although one might reasonably expect that this assertion, if true, would have affected the tone of the case, nothing in the opinion indicates that it was in any way dispositive.

TABLE OF CASES

[References are to pages]

[References are to pages]

[References are to pages]

D

[References are to pages]

[References are to pages]

In re (see name of party)

In the Matter of (see name of party)

[References are to pages]

[References are to pages]

[References are to pages]

[References are to pages]

[References are to pages]

[References are to pages]

INDEX

[References are to sections.]

[References are to sections.]

[References are to sections.]

[References are to sections.]

[References are to sections.]

I

IMPAIRMENT OF CLAIMS OR INTERESTS
(See CHAPTER 11 PLAN, subhead: Impairment of claims or interests)

INDUBITABLE EQUIVALENT
Adequate protection . . . 3.07[C]
Cramdown . . . 9.10[B][2]

INSIDERS
Confirmation of plan, disclosure of identity of prospective insider requirement for . . . 9.11[H]

INTELLECTUAL PROPERTY LICENSES
Executory contracts rejection of . . . 7.03[F]

INTEREST
Impairment of claims or interests (See CHAPTER 11 PLAN, subhead; Impairment of claims or interests)
Secured claims, allowance of interest on . . . 8.04[C]
Sell free and clear of claims and interests (See PRE-PLAN SALE OF DEBTOR'S BUSINESS, subhead: Sell free and clear of claims and interests)
Unsecured claims and equity interests, dissenting class of (See CRAMDOWN, subhead: Unsecured claims and equity interests, dissenting class of)

J

JURISDICTION OF BANKRUPTCY COURTS
Post-confirmation . . . 10.06

L

LEASES
Debtor-landlord, executory contracts rejection of real property leases by . . . 7.03[D]
Nonresidential real estate leases that have terminated . . . 7.06[D]

LICENSE
Executory contract rejection of intellectual property . . . 7.03[F]

LIENS
Adequate protection, replacement liens effect on . . . 3.07[B]
Existing liens, subordination of . . . 5.03[D]
Sale of collateral with liens . . . 9.10[B][2]
Superpriority claims
    Existing liens, subordination of . . . 5.03[D]
    Non-priming liens, and . . . 5.03[B]

LIQUIDATION
Advising client . . . 1.02[A]
Valuation and . . . 1.09[C]

LOYALTY, DUTY OF (See OPERATION OF BUSINESS, subhead: Duty of loyalty)

M

MANAGEMENT OF BUSINESS (See OPERATION OF BUSINESS)

MEETINGS OF CREDITORS
Procedure . . . 1.05[F]

MOOTNESS
Confirmation of plan, appeal of . . . 10.04

N

NOTICE
Creditors, to . . . 10.02
Future claimants, adequate notice to . . . 6.02[D]

O

OFFICERS, DIRECTORS AND
Operation of business (See OPERATION OF BUSINESS, subhead: Fiduciary duties of officers and directors)
Stockholders right to meet and elect directors when debtor remains in possession . . . 4.05

OPERATION OF BUSINESS
Generally . . . 4.01
Appointment of examiners . . . 4.03
Approaches to . . . 4.04
Authority to operate and manage business . . . 4.06[B]
Business judgment rule
    Chapter 11, in . . . 4.06[D]
    Deepening insolvency . . . 4.06[E][3][d]
Competing interests in chapter 11, living with . . . 4.06[F]
Debtor in possession
    Authority to operate and manage business . . . 4.06[B]
    Directors, stockholders right to meet and elect . . . 4.05
    Duties of . . . 4.06[A][1]
    Loyalty, duty of . . . 4.06[E][2]
    Rights and powers of . . . 4.06[A][2]
    Stockholders right to meet and elect directors . . . 4.05
Directors
    Debtor remains in possession, stockholders right to meet and elect directors when . . . 4.05
    Fiduciary duties of officers and directors (See subhead: Fiduciary duties of officers and directors)
Duty of care . . . 4.06[D]
Duty of loyalty
    Debtor in possession . . . 4.06[E][2]
    Fiduciary duties of officers and directors (See subhead: Fiduciary duties of officers and directors)